INSIDE THE SUPREME COURT: THE INSTITUTION AND ITS PROCEDURES

Second Edition

By

Susan Low Bloch
Professor of Law
Georgetown University Law Center

Vicki C. Jackson
Carmack Waterhouse Professor of Constitutional Law
Georgetown University Law Center

Thomas G. Krattenmaker
Of Counsel, Wilson Sonsini Goodrich & Rosati
Washington, D.C.

AMERICAN CASEBOOK SERIES®

THOMSON
™
WEST

Mat # 18370840

American Casebook Series and West Group are trademarks registered in the U.S. Patent and Trademark Office.

COPYRIGHT © 1994 WEST PUBLISHING CO.
© 2008 Thomson/West
      610 Opperman Drive
      P.O. Box 64526
      St. Paul, MN 55123
      1–800–313–9378

Printed in the United States of America

ISBN: 978–0–314–25834–2

 *TEXT IS PRINTED ON 10% POST CONSUMER RECYCLED PAPER*

*For my husband, Rich, whose love and patience supported me
throughout this process, and our children, Rebecca and
Michael, whose careers as young lawyers inspire me
and make me proud.*

S. L. B.

*For my husband, Bob Taylor, and children, Jacob, Michael
and Sophie, whose love and patience sustained me,
and to my father, Ted Jackson, whose life in
the law is an inspiration.*

V. C. J.

*For Bevra , who inspired me, and for Lily,
whom I hope to inspire.*

T. G. K.

*

Preface to the Second Edition

Our second edition generally follows the structure of the first edition, with a few modifications. We have added a new co-author, Professor Vicki C. Jackson, who has enriched the book significantly. Professors Bloch and Jackson took primary responsibility for updating the research. Tom Krattenmaker continued his involvement with the book, joining Bloch and Jackson in the final organizing and editing stages.

While retaining the basic structure of the first edition, this edition updates it considerably and adds Questions and Comments throughout the chapters. Chapter One now introduces students to two principal cases, *Planned Parenthood v. Casey* (as in the first edition) and *Lawrence v. Texas*. In addition, it has a more extended discussion of the Court's role generally and the role of *stare decisis*. Chapter Two retains its focus on the appointment process; we have updated the materials with excerpts from the nomination and confirmation proceedings of John Roberts and Samuel Alito, with readings on some of the more recent controversies including the role of the American Bar Association, and with discussions of proposals to modify the appointment process. Chapter Three continues to focus on the certiorari process and to provide materials designed to enable students to conduct "mock" conferences on real, pending petitions for certiorari. Its new materials include a detailed historical treatment of the Judges' Bill of 1925, excerpts from the ongoing scholarly discussion of the reasons for the dramatic decline in the number of cases granted cert in recent years, and brief studies of two special circumstances: death penalty litigation and certiorari prior to judgment.

Chapter Four retains the two major case studies of the first edition, the abortion cases (with some updating) and the Nixon Tapes case (followed by a brief Note on *Bush v. Gore*). Chapter Five covers the same topics as in the first edition, but with substantial sections of new material, reflecting a burgeoning scholarship on the role of the Chief Justice, the law clerks, and the advocates, including the Solicitor General and amici curiae. Finally, Chapter Six is no longer concerned with proposals to establish a new national court of appeals; few observers think the Court today is over-worked and such proposals appear to have run their course, at least for now. We continue to explore proposals to expand public access to the Court and its proceedings and we have added two new sections. One addresses recent controversies that some believe threaten the independence of the judiciary, and the other discusses some proposed reforms affecting the appointment and tenure of Supreme Court Justices, including term limits or mandatory retirement ages for the Justices.

We completed most of our research in 2006, noting some developments from 2007. We officially closed the book on updates with the Supreme Court's adoption of new rules on July 17, 2007.

We are enormously indebted to many people. Our Research Assistants over the last few years have been very helpful, so we would like to thank Professor Bloch's RAs—Nicholas Boski, Angela Butcher, Susan Cooke, Charles Eberle, Kelly Falls, William Fanaras, Ariel Goldman, Glenn Laken, Ted Metzler, Andrew Smith, and Roxanne Tingir, and Professor Jackson's RAs—James Caputo, Eric Cochran, Jason Cohen, A. Laura Collier, Alida Dagostino, Nancy Dinsmore, Amber Dolman, Andrew Eberle, Justin Ford, Joseph Gallagher, Soraya Kelly, Maria Kokiasmemos, Rebecca Lee, Kristy Martin, Emily O'Brien, Jeffrey Poulin, and Michael Scherzer. We would also like to thank Ralph Freeman, Terican Gross, Soraya Howard, Roselle Singer and Steven Wagner for their excellent administrative assistance. And, of course, we want to thank the many librarians and staff in Faculty Support who have helped us over the years. In the first edition, we thanked Georgetown Law Center staff including Charles Barnes, Mary Ann DeRosa, Leonard Gavin, Toni Patterson, and Vicki White, as well as a Georgetown student, Antonio Anaya, and we repeat those thanks here, for this work builds on that of the first edition. For this edition, we add a specific note of thanks as well to George Belton, Sylvia Johnson, Toni Patterson (again), Ronnie Rease, and Cathy Strain, who along with many other staff provided us with invaluable aid. Among the many wonderful librarians who have helped us, we want to specifically thank Jennifer Locke Davitt, Catherine Dunn, Barbara Monroe, Thanh Nguyen, Sara Sampson, Mabel Shaw, and Amy Taylor. Finally, we are also very grateful for the continuous support and encouragement from Georgetown Deans Judith C. Areen and T. Alex Aleinikoff, and the Georgetown University Law Center Writer's Grants that facilitated our work.

Our families have provided us much needed support, space (physical and emotional), and sustenance beyond measure throughout this long process. Specifically, we want to thank Rich, Rebecca, and Michael Bloch, Bob, Jacob, Michael, and Sophie Taylor, and Bevra, John, and Caitlin Barile Krattenmaker.

Tributes
(from the First Edition)

Three people planted the seeds of this book in the 1960s. Professor Glendon A. Schubert published *Constitutional Politics* in 1960. Subtitled "The Political Behavior of Supreme Court Justices and the Constitutional Policies That They Make," this book introduced wider audiences to the view that the political and institutional dimensions of the Supreme Court could be studied systematically and that such study could enhance one's appreciation of the quality of U.S. constitutional law. Professor J. Roland Pennock's seminar in Public Law and Jurisprudence at Swarthmore College and Professor Louis Henkin's seminar on The Supreme Court at Columbia Law School made this study come alive and raised many of the questions explored in this book.

Most of our work has consisted of a lot of research, seeking materials that might shed light on the politics of the Supreme Court. For magnificent help in conducting this research, we are indebted to hundreds of Georgetown University Law Center students[1] who have taken our seminar and found ever better materials for subsequent students to study. Most especially, we have been blessed in the past few years with a succession of energetic, dedicated, and talented research assistants who are virtually co-authors of this book. Each deserves a personal paragraph of thanks, but we have to settle for thanking them collectively. Thanks, then, to Mark Adams, Sharon Albright, Patrick Brown, Matthew McCabe, Katherine Miller, and Marc Sorini.

Our colleagues at Georgetown, as well as at several schools throughout the country, for many years have helped us locate materials and track down issues. In this regard, it would be unfair not to single out Professor Vicki Jackson of Georgetown, who has provided aid and comfort at every step of this journey. In addition, Professor Steve Wermiel, of Georgia State helpfully reviewed the entire manuscript and suggested many valuable additions. We are also very grateful for the continuous support and encouragement from Georgetown Dean Judith C. Areen and Georgetown University Law Center Writer's Grants that greatly facilitated our work.

Our families have helped us keep this project going, by pretending to be interested in reading the final product and by making space available, in countless ways, for the time necessary to get it done. Bless you, to

---

[1] At the time we wrote this book, Thomas G. Krattenmaker was Professor of Law at Georgetown University Law Center.

Rich, Rebecca, and Michael Bloch and to Bevra, Ken, and John Krattenmaker.

The debt we owe to all the people mentioned above is incalculable. In the final analysis, however, what really drove us to organize and create this book was the inspiration we received from Justice John M. Harlan and Justice Thurgood Marshall, the finest public servants we have ever known and the best bosses we have ever had. If readers find things of value in this book, as we hope they will, please let that discovery be another testament to the memories of these great Justices.

Note on Editing

As in the first edition, we did not want the materials selected for this book to appear as thirty second sound bites, so we have tried to let our authors have their say. But we have also tried to hold everyone to his or her central points. We have eliminated most citations (including internal references) and footnotes without indicating their omission. Other omissions are generally indicated by ellipses or brackets, as appropriate; textual material that has been added, or slightly modified, is indicated by brackets.

*

Acknowledgments

We would like to thank the following for their permission to reprint their writings:

Henry J. Abraham, *Justices, Presidents, and Senators: A History of the U.S. Supreme Court Appointments from Washington to Clinton,* Fourth Edition (1999). Reprinted with permission of Rowman & Littlefield Publishers, Inc.

Susan Behuniak-Long, *Friendly Fire: Amici Curiae and* Webster v. Reproductive Health Services, 74 Judicature 261 (1991). Copyright © 1991 by Susan Behuniak-Long and the American Judicature Society. Reprinted with permission of Susan Behuniak.

William J. Brennan, Jr., *In Defense of Dissents*, 37 Hastings L.J. 427 (1986). Copyright © by University of California, Hastings College of the Law. Reprinted with permission of the Hastings Law Journal.

William J. Brennan, Jr., *The National Court of Appeals: Another Dissent*, 40 U. Chi. L. Rev. 473 (1973). Copyright © 1973 by the Chicago Law Review. Reprinted with permission of the Chicago Law Review.

Steven G. Calabresi & James Lindgren, *Term Limits for the Supreme Court: Life Tenure Reconsidered*, Harvard Journal of Law & Public Policy, Vol. 29, No. 3 (2006): pp. 769-876. Reprinted with permission of the Harvard Journal of Law & Public Policy.

Lincoln Caplan, *The Tenth Justice: The Solicitor General and the Rule of Law* (1987). Reprinted with permission of Lincoln Caplan.

Erwin Chemerinsky, *Ideology and the Selection of Federal Judges.* This work, copyright 2003 by Erwin Chemerinsky, was originally published in 36 U.C. Davis L. Rev. 619 (2003), copyright 2003 by the Regents of the University of California. Reprinted with permission of the U.C. Davis Law Review and Erwin Chemerinsky.

Erwin Chemerinsky, *Opening Closed Chambers*, 108 Yale L.J. 1087 (1999). Copyright © 1999 by the Yale Law Journal. Reprinted with permission of the Yale Law Journal and Erwin Chemerinsky.

Erwin Chemerinsky & Catherine Fisk, *In Defense of Filibustering Judicial Nominations*, 21 Cardozo L. Rev. 331 (2005). Copyright © 2005 by the Cardozo Law Review. Reprinted with permission of Erwin Chemerinsky, Catherine Fisk, and the Cardozo Law Review.

Stephen Choi & Mitu Gulati, *A Tournament of Judges?*, 92 Cal. L. Rev. 299 (2004). Copyright © 2004 by the California Law Review, Inc. Reprinted from California Law Review, Vol. 92 No. 1, 299-322, by permission of Stephen Choi, Mitu Gulati, and the California Law Review, Inc.

Margaret Meriwether Cordray & Richard Cordray, *The Philosophy of Certiorari: Jurisprudential Considerations in Supreme Court Case Selection*, 82 Wash. U. L. Q. 389 (2004). Copyright © 2004 by the Washington University Law Quarterly. Reprinted with permission of Margaret Meriwether Cordray, Richard Cordray, and the Washington University Law Review.

Margaret Meriwether Cordray & Richard Cordray, *The Supreme Court's Plenary Docket*, 58 Wash. & Lee L. Rev. 737 (2001). Copyright © 2001 by the Washington & Lee Law Review. Reprinted with permission of Margaret Meriwether Cordray, Richard Cordray, and the Washington & Lee Law Review.

Sue Davis, *Power on the Court: Chief Justice Rehnquist's Opinion Assignments*, 74 Judicature 66 (1990). Copyright © 1990 by Sue Davis and the American Judicature Society. Reprinted with permission of Sue Davis.

Drew S. Days, III, *When the President Says "No": A Few Thoughts on Executive Power and the Tradition of Solicitor General Independence*, 3 J. App. Prac. & Process 509 (2001). Copyright © 2001 by the Journal of Appellate Practice and Process. Reprinted with permission of the Journal of Appellate Practice and Process and Drew Days.

Neal Devins, *Explaining* Grutter v. Bollinger, 152 U. Pa. L. Rev. 347 (2003). Copyright © 2003 by the University of Pennsylvania Law Review. Reprinted with permission of Neal Devins, the University of Pennsylvania Law Review, and William S. Hein & Company, Inc.

Bruce Ennis, *Effective Amicus Briefs*, 33 Cath. U. L. Rev. 603 (1984). Copyright © 1984 by Catholic University Law Review. Reprinted with permission of the Catholic University Law Review.

Lee Epstein, *A Better Way to Appoint Justices*, Christian Science Monitor, Mar. 17, 1992 at 19. Copyright © 1992 by Lee Epstein and The Christian Science Monitor. Reprinted with permission of Lee Epstein.

Lee Epstein & Jack Knight, *The Choices Justices Make*. Copyright © 1998 by CQ Press, a division of Congressional Quarterly Inc. Reprinted with permission of CQ Press, Lee Epstein, and Jack Knight.

Ward Farnsworth, *The Case for Life Tenure*, in *Reforming the Court* (Paul Carrington & Roger Cramton, eds.) pp. 251-269. Copyright © 2006 by Carolina Academic Press. Permission granted by Paul Carrington, Roger Cramton, and the Carolina Academic Press, Durham, North Carolina.

Ward Farnsworth, *The Ideological Stakes of Eliminating Life Tenure*, Harvard Journal of Law & Public Policy Vol. 29, No. 3 (2006): pp. 879-890. Reprinted with permission.

Paul A. Freund, *Appointment of Justices: Some Historical Perspectives*, 101 Harv. L. Rev. 1146 (1988). Copyright © 1988 by The Harvard Law Review Association. Reprinted with permission of the Harvard Law Review Association.

David J. Garrow, *The Lowest Form of Animal Life? Supreme Court Clerks and Supreme Court History*, 84 Cornell L . Rev. 855 (1999). Copyright © 1999 by Cornell Law Review. Reprinted with permission of the Cornell Law Review and David Garrow.

Michael J. Gerhardt, *The Constitutionality of the Filibuster*, 21 Const. Comm. 450 (2004). Copyright © 2004 by Constitutional Commentary. Reprinted with permission of Constitutional Commentary and Michael Gerhardt.

Michael J. Gerhardt, *The Federal Appointments Process: A Constitutional and Historical Analysis* (excerpts from pp. 295-97). Copyright © 2000 by Duke University Press. All rights reserved. Reprinted with permission of the publisher and Michael Gerhardt.

Michael J. Gerhardt, *Merit vs. Ideology*, 26 Cardozo L. Rev. 353 (2005). Copyright © 2005 by the Cardozo Law Review. Reprinted with permission of the Cardozo Law Review and Michael Gerhardt.

Michael J. Gerhardt, *Toward a Comprehensive Understanding of the Federal Appointment Process*, Harvard Journal of Law & Public Policy, Vol. 21, No. 2 (1997): 467, 482-495. Copyright © 1997 by The Harvard Journal of Law & Public Policy. Reprinted with permission.

Ruth Bader Ginsburg, *Speaking in a Judicial Voice*, 67 N.Y.U. L. Rev. 1185 (1992). Copyright © 1992 by the New York University Law Review. Reprinted with permission of Justice Ruth Bader Ginsburg and the New York University Law Review.

Linda Greenhouse, *Telling the Court's Story: Justice and Journalism at the Supreme Court*, 105 Yale L. J. 1537 (1996). Copyright © 1996 by the Yale Law Journal. Reprinted with permission of the Yale Law Journal and Linda Greenhouse.

Edward A. Hartnett, *Questioning Certiorari: Some Reflections Seventy-Five Years After the Judges' Bill*, 100 Colum. L. Rev. 1643 (2000). Copyright © 2000 by the Columbia Law Review. Reprinted with permission of the Columbia Law Review.

Arthur D. Hellman, *The Shrunken Docket of the Rehnquist Court*, 1996 Sup. Ct. Rev. 403. Copyright © 1996 by the University of Chicago Press. Reprinted with permission of the University of Chicago Press.

Vicki C. Jackson, *Packages of Judicial Independence: The Selection and Tenure of Article III Judges*, 95 Geo. L.J. 965 (2007). Copyright © 2007 by the Georgetown Law Journal. Reprinted with permission of Vicki Jackson and the Georgetown Law Journal.

Marianne Jennings & Nim Razook, *Duck When a Conflict of Interest Blinds You: Judicial Conflicts of Interest in the Matters of Scalia and Ginsburg*, 39 U.S.F. L. Rev. 873 (2005). Copyright © 2005 by University of San Francisco Law Review. Reprinted with permission of the University of San Francisco Law Review.

Joseph D. Kearny & Thomas W. Merrill, *The Influence of Amicus Curiae Briefs on the Supreme Court*, 148 U. Pa. L. Rev. 743 (2000). Copyright © 2000 by the University of Pennsylvania Law Review. Reprinted with permission of the University of Pennsylvania Law Review and William S. Hein & Company, Inc.

John P. Kelsh, *The Opinion Delivery Practices of the United States Supreme Court 1790-1945*, 77 Wash. U. L. Q. 137 (1999). Copyright © 1999 by the Washington University Law Quarterly. Reprinted with permission of the Washington University Law Review and John P. Kelsh.

Sally Kenney, *Puppeteers or Agents? What Lazarus's Closed Chambers Adds to Our Understanding of Law Clerks at the U.S. Supreme Court*, 25 L. & Soc. Inquiry 185 (2000). Copyright © 2000 by Wiley-Blackwell Publishing Ltd. Reprinted with permission of Sally Kenney and Wiley-Blackwell Publishing Ltd.

James Lindgren & William P. Marshall, *The Supreme Court's Extraordinary Power to Grant Certiorari Before Judgment in the Court of Appeals*, 1986 Sup. Ct. Rev. 259. Copyright © 1986 by the University of Chicago Press. Reprinted with permission of the University of Chicago Press.

Dahlia Lithwick, *A High Court of One: The Role of the "Swing Voter" in the 2002 Term*, in *A Year at the Supreme Court* (Neal Devins and Davison M. Douglas, eds.) pp. 11-31. Copyright © 2004 by the Duke University Press. All rights reserved. Reprinted with permission of the Duke University Press.

Laura E. Little, *The Judicial Appointments Process: The ABA's Role in Prescreening Federal Judicial Candidates: Are We Ready to Give Up on the Lawyers?*, 10 Wm. & Mary Bill Rts. J. 37 (2001). Copyright © 2001 by the William & Mary Bill of Rights Journal. Reprinted with permission of the William & Mary Bill of Rights Journal.

John Anthony Maltese, *The Selling of Supreme Court Nominees*. Copyright © 1995, 1998 by the Johns Hopkins University Press. Reprinted with permission of The Johns Hopkins University Press.

Boyce F. Martin, Jr., *Gee Whiz, The Sky is Falling*, 106 Mich. L. Rev. First Impressions 1 (2007). Copyright © 2007 by The Michigan Law Review Association. Reprinted with permission of the Michigan Law Review and Boyce Martin, Jr.

Alpheus T. Mason, *The Chief Justice of the United States: Primus Inter Pares,* 17 J. Pub. L. 20 (1968). Copyright © 1968 by the Emory Law Journal. Reprinted with the permission of the Emory Law Journal.

Tony Mauro, *The Right Legislation for The Wrong Reasons*, 106 Mich. L. Rev. First Impressions 8 (2007). Copyright © 2007 by The Michigan Law Review Association. Reprinted with permission of the Michigan Law Review and Tony Mauro.

Michael W. McConnell, *The Rule of Law and the Role of the Solicitor General*, 21 Loy. L.A. L. Rev. 1105 (1988). Copyright © 1988 by the Loyola of

Los Angeles Law Review. Reprinted with permission of Michael McConnell and the Loyola of Los Angeles Law Review.

John McGinnis & Michael Rappaport, *Supermajority Rules and the Judicial Confirmation Process*, 26 Cardozo L. Rev. 543 (2005). Copyright © 2005 by the Cardozo Law Review. Reprinted with permission of John McGinnis, Michael Rappaport, and the Cardozo Law Review.

Roy M. Mersky & Tobe Liebert, eds., *The Supreme Court Nominations, 1916-2005,* Vol. 20A, *reprinting* U.S. Senate Judiciary Committee Holds a Hearing on the Nomination of John Roberts To Be Chief Justice of the United States Supreme Court (Transcript, U.S. Senate Judiciary Comm., Exec. Sess., Sept. 22, 2005). Published by William S. Hein & Co., Inc. Reprinted with permission of William S. Hein & Co., Inc.

Roy M. Mersky & Tobe Liebert, eds., *The Supreme Court Nominations, 1916-2006,* Vol. 21B, *reprinting* U.S. Senate Judiciary Committee Meets to Vote on the Nomination of Judge Samuel Alito to the United States Supreme Court (Transcript, U.S. Senate Judiciary Comm., Exec. Sess., Jan. 13, 2006). Published by William S. Hein & Co., Inc. Reprinted with permission of William S. Hein & Co., Inc.

Henry Paul Monaghan, *The Confirmation Process: Law or Politics?*, 101 Harv. L. Rev. 1202 (1988). Copyright © 1988 by The Harvard Law Review Association. Reprinted with permission of the Harvard Law Review Association.

Thomas R. Morris, *States Before the U.S. Supreme Court: State Attorneys General as Amicus Curiae,* 70 Judicature 298 (1987). Copyright © 1987 by Thomas R. Morris and the American Judicature Society. Reprinted with permission of Thomas R. Morris.

Alan B. Morrison & D. Scott Stenhouse, *The Chief Justice of the United States: More than Just the Highest Ranking Justice,* 1 Const. Comm. 57 (1984). Copyright © 1984 by Constitutional Commentary. Reprinted with permission of Alan Morrison, D. Scott Stenhouse, and Constitutional Commentary.

David M. O'Brien, *Join-3 Votes, The Rule of Four, The Cert Pool, and The Supreme Court's Shrinking Plenary Docket,* 13 J. L. & Pol. 779 (1997). Copyright © 1997 by the Journal of Law and Policy. Reprinted with permission of the Journal of Law and Policy.

David M. O'Brien, *Storm Center: The Supreme Court in American Politics*, Sixth Edition. Copyright © 2003, 2000, 1996, 1993, 1990, 1986 by David O'Brien. Used by permission of W.W. Norton & Company, Inc.

H.W. Perry, Jr., *Deciding to Decide: Agenda Setting in the United States Supreme Court*. Reprinted by permission of the publisher from "A Decision Model" in DECIDING TO DECIDE: AGENDA SETTING IN THE UNITED STATES SUPREME COURT by H.W. Perry, Jr., pp. 274-284, Cambridge, Mass.: Harvard University Press, Copyright © 1991 by the President and Fellows of Harvard College.

Cornelia T.L. Pillard, *The Unfulfilled Promise of the Constitution in Executive Hands,* 103 Mich. L. Rev. 676 (2005). Copyright © 2005 by The Michigan Law Review Association. Reprinted with permission of Cornelia Pillard and the Michigan Law Review.

Robert Post, *The Supreme Court Opinion as Institutional Practice: Dissent, Legal Scholarship, and Decisionmaking in the Taft Court,* 85 Minn. L. Rev. 1267 (2001). Copyright © 2001 by Robert Post. Reprinted with permission of Robert Post.

William H. Rehnquist, *The Supreme Court: How It Was, How It Is.* Copyright © 1987 by William H. Rehnquist. Reprinted with permission of Alfred A. Knopf, a division of Random House, Inc.

William H. Rehnquist, *The Supreme Court.* Copyright © 2001 by William H. Rehnquist. Reprinted with permission of Alfred A. Knopf, a division of Random House, Inc.

Judith Resnik, *Judicial Selection and Democratic Theory: Demand, Supply and Life Tenure,* 26 Cardozo L. Rev. 579 (2005). Copyright © 2005 by Judith Resnik. Reprinted with permission of Judith Resnik and the Cardozo Law Review.

Judith Resnik & Lane Dilg, *Responding to a Democratic Deficit,* 154 U. Pa. L. Rev. 1575 (2006). Copyright © 2006 by University of Pennsylvania Law Review. Reprinted with permission of Lane Dilg, Judith Resnik, the University of Pennsylvania Law Review and the William S. Hein & Company, Inc.

John C. Roberts, *Majority Voting in Congress: Further Notes on the Constitutionality of the Senate Cloture Rule,* 20 J. L. & Politics 505 (2004). Copyright © 2004 by the Journal of Law and Politics. Reprinted with permission of the Journal of Law and Politics.

John G. Roberts, Jr., *Oral Advocacy and the Reemergence of a Supreme Court Bar,* 30 Sup. Ct. Hist. 68 (2005). Copyright © 2005 by Wiley-Blackwell Publishing Ltd. Reprinted with permission of Chief Justice John Roberts and Wiley-Blackwell Publishing Ltd.

Ira P. Robbins, *Justice By the Numbers: The Supreme Court and the Rule of Four—Or Is It Five?,* 36 Suffolk U. L. Rev. 1 (2002). Copyright © 2002 by the Suffolk University Law Review. Reprinted with permission of the Suffolk University Law Review.

David M. Rosenzweig, Note, *Confessions of Error in the Supreme Court by the Solicitor General,* 82 Geo. L. J. 2079 (1994). Reprinted with permission of the publisher, Georgetown Law Journal © 1994.

Ronald D. Rotunda, *The Role of Ideology in Confirming Federal Judges,* 15 Geo. J. Legal Ethics 127 (2001). Reprinted with permission of the publisher, Georgetown Journal of Legal Ethics © 2001.

Rebecca Mae Salokar, *The Solicitor General: The Politics of Law.* Material excerpted from "The Solicitor General" by Rebecca Mae Salokar from

The Solicitor General: The Politics of Law by Rebecca Mae Salokar. Used by permission of Temple University Press. © 1992 by Temple University. All Rights Reserved.

Glendon Schubert, *Constitutional Politics*. From SCHUBERT, *CONSTITUTIONAL POLITICS*, 1E. © 1960 Wadsworth, a part of Cengage Learning, Inc. Reproduced with permission of Cengage Learning, Inc. www.cengage.com/permissions.

Bernard Schwartz, *The Ascent of Pragmatism: The Burger Court in Action*. Copyright © 1990 by Bernard Schwartz. Reprinted by permission of Brian Schwartz, son of Bernard Schwartz.

Elliot E. Slotnick, *Media Coverage of Supreme Court Decision Making: Problems and Prospects*, 75 Judicature 128 (1991). Copyright © 1991 by the American Judicature Society and Elliot E. Slotnick. Reprinted with permission of Elliot E. Slotnick.

Lawrence B. Solum, *Empirical Measures of Judicial Performance: A Tournament of Virtue*, 32 Fla. St. U. L. Rev. 1365 (2005). Copyright © 2005 by the Florida State Law Review. Reprinted with permission of the Florida State Law Review.

John Paul Stevens, *The Life Span of a Judge-Made Rule*, 58 N.Y.U. L. Rev. 1 (1983). Copyright © 1983 by the New York University Law Review. Reprinted with permission of the New York University.

David R. Stras, *Book Review Essay: The Supreme Court's Gatekeepers: The Role of Law Clerks in the Certiorari Process*, 85 Tex. L. Rev. 947 (2007). Copyright © 2007 by the Texas Law Review. Reprinted with permission of David Stras and the Texas Law Review.

David Strauss & Cass Sunstein, *The Senate, The Constitution, and The Confirmation Process*, 101 Yale L.J. 1491 (1992). Reprinted by permission of The Yale Law Journal Company and William S. Hein Company from The Yale Law Journal, Vol. 101, pages 1491-1524.

Stuart Taylor, Jr., *Ruing Fixed Opinions*, N.Y. Times, Feb. 22, 1988 at A16. Copyright © 1988 by The New York Times Company. Reprinted with permission of The New York Times.

Jeffrey Tulis, *Constitutional Abdication: The Senate, The President, and Appointments to the Supreme Court*, 47 Case W. Res. L. Rev. 1331 (1997). Copyright © 1997 by Case Western Reserve Law Review. Reprinted with permission of the Case Western Reserve Law Review.

Mark Tushnet, *A Court Divided: The Rehnquist Court And The Future Of Constitutional Law*. Copyright © 2005 by Mark Tushnet. Used by permission of W. W. Norton & Company, Inc.

Mark Tushnet, *Foreword: The New Constitutional Order and the Chastening of Constitutional Aspiration*, 113 Harv. L. Rev. 29 (1999). Copy-

We also thank our colleague, Richard J. Lazarus, for giving us permission to quote from his unpublished paper, *Advocacy Matters: Before and Within the Supreme Court: Transforming the Court by Transforming the Bar* (August 5, 2007), which we understand is forthcoming in the Georgetown Law Journal.

*

Summary of Contents

Table of Contents

Table of Cases

The principal cases are in bold type. Cases cited or discussed in the text are roman type. References are to pages. Cases cited in principal cases and within other quoted materials are not included.

*

Table of Authorities

References are to pages.

Court: 1920–1966" (Ph.D. Dissertation, State University of New York at Buffalo, 1971), **837**

Quinn, Kevin M., Theodore W. Ruger, Pauline T. Kim & Andrew D. Martin, *The Supreme Court Forecasting Project: Legal and Political Science Approaches to Predicting Supreme Court Decisionmaking*, 104 Colum. L. Rev. 1150 (2004), **684**

Rahdert, Mark, *Comparative Constitutional Advocacy*, 56 Am. U. L. Rev. 553 (2007), **1062**

Rappaport, Michael, & John McGinnis, *Supermajority Rules and the Judicial Confirmation Process*, 26 Cardozo L. Rev. 543 (2005), **331**

Rathjen, Gregory James, *Policy Goals, Strategic Choices, and Majority Opinion Assignments in the U.S. Supreme Court: A Replication*, 18 Am. J. Pol. Sci. 713 (1974), **725**

Razook, Nim, & Marianne M. Jennings, *Duck When a Conflict of Interest Blinds You: Judicial Conflicts of Interest in the Matters of Scalia and Ginsburg*, 39 U.S.F. L. Rev. 873 (2005), **1058, 1059, 1061**

Rehnquist, William H., Address to the American Law Institute, 75 A.L.I. Proc. 55 (1998), **755**

_____, *Grand Inquests: The Historic Impeachments of Justice Samuel Chase and President Andrew Johnson* (1992), **1121**

_____, Letter to Senator Joseph Lieberman, June 7, 1993, **1047**

_____, Letter to Senator Patrick Leahy, Jan. 26, 2004, reprinted in *Irrecusable and Unconfirmable*, 7 Green Bag 2d 277 (2004), **1060**

_____, 1991 Year–End Report on the Federal Judiciary, Third Branch, Jan. 1991, at 1, **775**

_____, 1993 Year–End Report on the Federal Judiciary (1993), **755**

_____, *The Supreme Court: How it Was, How it Is* (1987), **496, 808, 809**

_____, *The Supreme Court* (2001), **563, 364, 365, 401, 563, 1054, 1060**

Resnik, Judith, *Judicial Selection and Democratic Theory: Demand, Supply and Life Tenure*, 26 Cardozo L. Rev. 579 (2005), **253, 307, 330**

_____, & Lane Dilg, *Responding to a Democratic Deficit: Limiting the Powers and the Term of the Chief Justice of the United States*, 154 U. Pa. L. Rev. 1575 (2006), **752, 1116**

Revesz, Richard L., *Environmental Regulation, Ideology, and the D.C. Circuit*, 83 Va. L. Rev. 1717 (1997), **277**

Rex. E. Lee Conference on the Office of the Solicitor General, Transcript, 2003 BYU L. Rev. 1, **874**

Reynolds, Glenn Harlan, *Taking Advice Seriously: An Immodest Proposal for Reforming the Confirmation Process*, 65 S. Cal. L. Rev. 1577 (1992), **306**

Robbins, Ira P., *Justice by the Numbers: The Supreme Court and the Rule of Four—Or Is It Five?*, 36 Suffolk U. L. Rev. 1 (2002), **511**

Roberts, Caprice L., *The Fox Guarding the Henhouse? Recusal and the Procedural Void in the Court of Last Resort*, 57 Rutgers L. Rev. 107 (2004), **1061**

Roberts, John C., *Majority Voting in Congress: Further Notes on the Constitutionality of the Senate Cloture Rule*, 20 J. L. & Politics 505 (2004), **341**

Roberts, John G., Jr., Address at Georgetown University Law Center (June 7, 1997), **364**

_____, *Oral Advocacy and the Reemergence of a Supreme Court Bar*, 30 J. Sup. Ct. Hist. 68 (2005), **816**

Rohde, David W., *Policy Goals, Strategic Choice and Majority Opinion Assignments in the U.S. Supreme Court*, 16 Midwest J. of Pol.Sci. 652 (1972), **724**

Rosen, Jeffrey, *Disorder in the Court*, Time, July 10, 2006, at 26, **594, 596**

_____, *Roberts' Rules*, The Atlantic Online, January/February 2007, **739**

Rosenzweig, David M., Note, *Confessions of Error in the Supreme Court by the Solicitor General*, 82 Geo. L.J. 2079 (1994), **919**

Rotunda, Ronald D., *The Role of Ideology in Confirming Federal Judges*, 15 Geo. J. Legal Ethics 127 (2001), **267**

Ruger, Theodore W., *The Chief Justice's Special Authority and the Norms of Judicial Power*, 154 U. Pa. L. Rev. 1551 (2006), **267**

_____, *The Judicial Appointment Power of the Chief Justice* 7 U. Pa. J. Const. L. 341 (2004), **757**

_____, Pauline T. Kim, Andrew D. Martin, & Kevin M. Quinn, *The Supreme Court Forecasting Project: Legal and Political Science Approaches to Predicting Supreme Court Decisionmaking*, 104 Colum. L. Rev. 1150 (2004), **684**

Rutkus, Denis Steven, & Maureen Bearden, Cong. Research Serv., *Supreme Court Appointment Process: Role of the President, Judiciary Committee, and Senate* (Order Code RL 31989, June 25, 2007), **89**

Salokar, Rebecca Mae, *The Solicitor General: The Politics of Law* (1992), **835, 917**

Savage, David, & Richard A. Serrano, *Ginsburg Stands by Involvement with Group; The Supreme Court Justice Says She*

INSIDE THE SUPREME COURT: THE INSTITUTION AND ITS PROCEDURES

Second Edition

*

INTRODUCTION

A. SCOPE AND PURPOSES OF THE BOOK

More than three generations ago, then-professors Frankfurter and Landis, in their classic treatise, *The Business of the Supreme Court,* wrote that "the history of the Supreme Court, as of the Common Law, derives meaning to no small degree from the cumulative details which define the scope of its business, and the forms and methods of performing it—the Court's procedure, in the comprehensive meaning of the term."[1] We take our cue from this observation. Like Frankfurter and Landis, we believe that the Supreme Court's substantive output, as any other organization's, is influenced by the structure of the institution, its personnel and its procedures.

As lawyers, scholars, students, or citizens, we care principally about the end results of the Supreme Court's processes—the three or four volumes of decisions the Court hands down each year. These decisions constitute, in a very practical sense, our constitutional law. If we are to comprehend that law fully, we should know something about the institution that generates it. For those who wonder where all this law comes from, and how it gets made, this book provides some answers.

The Court also decides many other issues, including federal statutory and administrative law, federal common law, federal civil and criminal procedure questions, and issues of treaty law, as well as disputes between two or more states. These decisions, like those of constitutional law, are sometimes quite controversial, and prompt legislative responses. But because the Court's constitutional decisions are more difficult for the political branches to respond to, we focus in this book primarily, though not exclusively, on the Court's decisionmaking in constitutional law cases.

The Constitution itself has very little to say about the Supreme Court of the United States (as it is officially designated). Article III mandates that there shall be one Supreme Court, grants the Justices life tenure and protection against diminution in salary, and defines the outer limits of the Court's jurisdiction.[2] Article II distributes power over the process of appointing Justices,[3] and Article I contemplates that one of the Justices should serve as Chief Justice.[4]

---

1. Felix Frankfurter & James Landis, *The Business of the Supreme Court* vi (1928).

2. U.S. Const. art. III, §§ 1, 2.

3. U.S. Const. art. II, § 2.

4. U.S. Const. art. I, § 3.

The Framers left the other institutional details of the Court and its processes to be worked out over time. Thus, it was left to Congress, the President, the Court, or the habits of history to answer such questions as: What kinds of people get appointed to the Court? How many Justices should be on the Court? What kinds of cases will the Court adjudicate? How do these cases get onto the Court's docket? How might the process of case selection influence the kinds of cases chosen for plenary review? How do the Justices, individually and collectively, reach their decisions and draft their opinions? What roles are played by people or institutions closely connected to the Court, such as the Justices' law clerks, the Solicitor General, amici curiae (literally translated as "friends of the court"), and other advocates? To what extent should the Court conduct its business in public, to what extent behind closed doors?

The readings collected in this book are intended to provide some answers to—or at least some insights about—these questions, and will focus primarily, though not exclusively, on how constitutional law is made. Since the First Edition, there has been an explosion in scholarly work—in law, in history and in the social sciences—about the Court. In response, although we have retained some of the original readings, we have replaced and/or added others. Our goal has been to identify important scholarly work and significant ideas published on these topics, together with critical analytical commentary by thoughtful, experienced students of the Court, and present them in a way that is accessible to students and useful for classroom teachers. In each chapter, we hope that readers will inquire into how and to what extent the Supreme Court's institutional make-up and procedures influence the Court's decisions, including its choice of what cases to hear, the results the opinions reach and the quality and durability of their reasoning. Readers can also ask whether alterations in the institution might change the law the Court announces.

Although this book explores the Court as an institution, we believe that its materials can illuminate and deepen the study of constitutional law. The Court's adjudications—its holdings, doctrines, results, case-law—should remain the principal focus of a study of U.S. constitutional law. But immersing oneself in the process by which that law is forged should be part of that study as well.

B. DIFFERENT MODELS OF JUDICIAL REVIEW

Another way to understand what motivates this book is to recall that the American way of producing judge-made constitutional law is just that, the American way. Many other countries do it differently.[5] This once again raises questions of whether and how the institution and

---

5. Specific illustrations of other countries' practices are drawn from Mauro Cappelletti, *The Judicial Process in Comparative Perspective* (1989) and Vicki C. Jackson & Mark Tushnet, *Comparative Constitutional Law* (2d ed. 2006).

its processes make a difference, in the nature of the law that is produced or in the role of the Court within its own system.

We assume that most of our readers probably have at least a passing familiarity with the American system of judicial review, sometimes called a "decentralized" or "diffuse" system of judicial review. In this system, all courts—state and federal—exercise the power to test laws against the United States Constitution. They generally do so, however, only as an aspect of adjudicating concrete cases that arise in the course of exercising their jurisdiction. Thus, judges in the United States who have authority to issue constitutional interpretations also construe and apply statutes and unwritten law (common law) in the cases they consider. Judicial authority to make constitutional decisions is thus "diffused" to a wide range of courts. Moreover, federal courts in the United States, including the Supreme Court, engage in constitutional interpretations only in the context of resolving a concrete lawsuit, whose nonconstitutional dimensions are also generally within their compass. The Supreme Court thus functions as a "generalist" court. Such a decentralized model of constitutional interpretation has also been employed in Argentina, Australia, Canada, India and Japan.

By contrast, most Western European countries follow a different model. In the European system, a specialized, centralized "constitutional court" is the only tribunal empowered to render binding judicial interpretations of the national constitution or to invalidate laws. Other courts, often controlled by one or more "supreme courts," decide cases involving statutory interpretation, criminal law, civil disputes, or administrative law issues. The specialized constitutional court is often empowered to rule on the constitutionality of proposed or recently adopted legislation before any concrete controversy arises under the statute. Austria, France, Germany, Italy, and some eastern European nations have employed such centralized, specialized "constitutional courts." Some countries use a hybrid system, combining elements of both centralized and decentralized review. See Vicki C. Jackson & Mark Tushnet, Comparative Constitutional Law 466 (2d ed. 2006) (discussing Brewer–Carías' work on Latin America).

The methods and purposes of case selection differ among these systems. The United States Supreme Court has to superintend federal statutory, administrative and common law as well as constitutional law and occasional issues of federal treaty law. Under the European model, the constitutional court has only constitutional law responsibilities (though it may have responsibility for resolving a limited range of other issues, including election disputes). The United States Supreme Court has substantial discretion over which cases within its jurisdiction to hear; other courts may function with more mandatory forms of jurisdiction. Further, constitutional courts may be empowered to hear constitutional complaints brought directly to them by persons claiming constitutional violations. Under the American model, complaints of constitutional violations usually are handled initially by ordinary trial courts. Appellate courts come into the picture only as reviewers of trial court decisions. Although some scholars believe that these two models of review are converging,[6] the existence of these two quite different models of judicial review of constitutional issues suggest the benefits of institutional comparisons, which requires deep knowledge of the respective institutions.

Consider how these two models—the American and European models—generate different issues concerning the make-up and processes of courts. Do judges who deal only with constitutional cases require different skills than those more "generalist" judges of the U.S. system? Should the political requirements for their selection differ? Should their tenure differ? Most constitutional courts in Europe impose nonrenewable term limits on their Constitutional Court judges—for example, the justices of the German Constitutional Court serve 12 year nonrenewable terms, as do those in Spain; constitutional court judges in Italy serve nine year nonrenewable terms. See generally Jackson & Tushnet, at 497–500.

How judicial review of constitutional questions is organized may reflect different institutional and national histories; it may also reflect different understandings of the nature of constitutional law and the role of courts. The United States Supreme Court's institutional design and behavior can be evaluated, in part, by asking about the impact of our own national history on the Court's evolution and about whether the Court's design and institutional processes help the Court perform the particular roles we assign to it. Understanding that other western constitutional democracies with judicial review have made different choices about the institutional structure and process for constitutional adjudication expands the context for evaluating the effects of the particular methods of choosing Supreme Court judges, selecting cases and adjudicating disputes in the United States.

C. ORGANIZATION

Chapter One provides a more detailed, concrete demonstration of the propositions just advanced. There we begin with edited versions of two recent Supreme Court decisions. The first, *Planned Parenthood of Southeastern Pennsylvania v. Casey,* presents a controversial, closely divided set of opinions concerning the constitutional right of abortion, in which the Court was asked to but did not overrule *Roe v. Wade.* Following *Casey,* we present *Lawrence v. Texas,* another controversial

---

6. See, e.g., Victor Ferreres Comella, *The European Model of Constitutional Review of Legislation: Toward Decentralization?*, 2 I·CON 461, 470–82 (2004) (arguing that nominally centralized review systems in Europe are under pressure towards decentralization and noting that ordinary court judges increasingly interpret statutes in light of their constitution or the supranational laws of Europe); Alec Stone Sweet, *Why Europe Rejected American Judicial Re-* *view: And Why It May Not Matter*, 101 Mich. L. Rev. 2744 (2003); see also Jackson & Tushnet, at 466–69, 481–85. As you read the first case excerpted in Chapter One, ask yourself whether the posture in which the Court decided that case differs in any significant respect from that of a European court engaged in "abstract review," at the request of dissenting legislators, of the constitutionality of a law that has just been enacted.

case challenging a state law that outlawed homosexual sodomy. Again the Court was asked to overturn a prior precedent and, this time, the majority did. Both of these cases concern especially controversial issues of constitutional law. While they are not unrepresentative of the range of constitutional decisions the Court is asked to address every Term, readers should be aware that many of the cases the Court decides are not about constitutional law; many, including many constitutional cases, are less controversial than these; and every Term some cases are decided unanimously. The opinions in these two cases are particularly interesting and were chosen, in part, because they offer unusually frank and pointed discussions among the Justices about the Court's role.

The book then proceeds to consider the processes and standards for the appointment of Supreme Court Justices in the United States (Chapter Two), the methods and criteria for case selection or agenda setting (Chapter Three), the manner in which the Justices agree on and produce formal opinions (Chapter Four), the roles played by various key participants in the institution—including the Chief Justice, the Solicitor General, amici curiae, and the law clerks (Chapter Five), and some proposals for modifying the institution or related processes (Chapter Six).

Chapter One

THE COURT IN ACTION

On January 22, 1973, the Supreme Court handed down its decision in *Roe v. Wade,* 410 U.S. 113, announcing for the first time that the Constitution protects a woman's fundamental right to choose an abortion. *Roe,* though decided by a seven-to-two vote on the Court, became an enormously controversial opinion that continues to generate virulent debates through the present time. The decision has affected how virtually everyone—including the public, the Justices, the President, the Solicitor General, and amicus curiae—views the Court and the Constitution. The abortion controversy has also affected public perceptions of the manner in which people outside the Court should play their roles, stimulating debate over such issues as whom the President should appoint to the Court and how much control the White House should exercise over the Solicitor General. For those reasons we have chosen to begin our studies by examining the Court's major reformulation of doctrine in this controversial area, Planned Parenthood of Southeastern Pennsylvania v. Casey, 505 U.S. 833 (1992).

In this section, we provide an edited version of *Casey,* followed by two sets of questions. The first set poses the kinds of inquiries one might expect to pursue in a conventional course on constitutional law. These questions focus on the Justices' reasoning—so that the reader may try to define the holding of *Casey,* to discern the doctrine regarding abortion rights on which that holding rests, and to identify the various values the Justices use in defining and resolving the issues *Casey* presents.

The second set of questions leads the reader through *Casey* as it might appear to one concentrating not on formal legal doctrine but on the Supreme Court as a decision-making institution and the processes it employs to make decisions. For example, we ask about the parties' strategy in seeking Supreme Court review and about the role the presidential nomination and the senatorial confirmation process played in shaping *Casey*'s outcome. If *Roe* had not been decided as it was, would Judge Robert Bork have been confirmed? If *Roe* had been decided as it was and Bork, instead of Kennedy, had been confirmed, what would have been the likely outcome in *Casey*? Do the answers to these questions tell us something about *Roe,* the appointment process, both, or neither? Exploring these and the other questions we raise after *Casey* illustrates the significance that the institution and its processes can have on the substance of constitutional law.

In the next section, we explore a more recent Supreme Court decision on another controversial topic, the constitutional status of laws prohibiting homosexual sodomy. In Bowers v. Hardwick, 478 U.S. 186 (1986), a closely divided Court had upheld application of a Georgia sodomy law to punish two gay men engaged in consensual sexual relations in their home. Justice Powell, who retired soon thereafter, confessed after his retirement that his decision to join the majority in *Bowers* was a mistake. In Lawrence v. Texas, 539 U.S. 558 (2003), excerpted below, the Court reversed that decision, drawing on its own jurisprudence, including *Roe* and *Casey*, to hold unconstitutional criminal prohibitions of homosexual sodomy between consenting adults.

We go on in the final section to ask some additional questions about the Court's institutional processes, this time from a comparative perspective. We focus here on three asserted distinctions between the "American" and the "European" model of constitutional adjudication relating to "case or controversy" limitations on the judicial power, the timing of constitutional adjudication, and *stare decisis*.

A. DECIDING CASES

1. PLANNED PARENTHOOD OF SOUTHEASTERN PENNSYLVANIA v. CASEY, 505 U.S. 833 (1992)

JUSTICE O'CONNOR, JUSTICE KENNEDY, and JUSTICE SOUTER announced the judgment of the Court and delivered the opinion of the Court with respect to Parts I, II, III, V–A, V–C, and VI, an opinion with respect to Part V–E, in which JUSTICE STEVENS joins, and an opinion with respect to Parts IV, V–B, and V–D.

I

Liberty finds no refuge in a jurisprudence of doubt. Yet 19 years after our holding that the Constitution protects a woman's right to terminate her pregnancy in its early stages, Roe v. Wade, 410 U.S. 113 (1973), that definition of liberty is still questioned. Joining the respondents as amicus curiae, the United States, as it has done in five other cases in the last decade, again asks us to overrule *Roe*.

At issue in these cases are five provisions of the Pennsylvania Abortion Control Act of 1982 as amended in 1988 and 1989. The Act requires that a woman seeking an abortion give her informed consent prior to the abortion procedure, and specifies that she be provided with certain information at least 24 hours before the abortion is performed. § 3205. For a minor to obtain an abortion, the Act requires the informed consent of one of her parents, but provides for a judicial bypass option if the minor does not wish to or cannot obtain a parent's consent. § 3206. Another provision of the Act requires that, unless certain exceptions apply, a married woman seeking an abortion must sign a statement indicating that she has notified her husband of her intended abortion. § 3209. The Act exempts compliance with these three requirements in the event of a "medical emergency," which is defined in § 3203 of the Act. In addition to the above provisions regulating the performance of abortions, the Act imposes certain reporting requirements on facilities that provide abortion services. §§ 3207(b), 3214(a), 3214(f).

Before any of these provisions took effect, the petitioners, who are five abortion clinics and one physician representing himself as well as a class of physicians who provide abortion services, brought this suit seeking declaratory and injunctive relief. Each provision was challenged as unconstitutional on its face. The District Court entered a preliminary injunction against the enforcement of the regulations, and, after a 3–day bench trial, held all the provisions at issue here unconstitutional, entering a permanent injunction against Pennsylvania's enforcement of them. 744 F.Supp. 1323 (E.D.Pa.1990). The Court of Appeals for the Third Circuit affirmed in part and reversed in part, upholding all of the regulations except for the husband notification requirement. 947 F.2d 682 (1991). We granted certiorari.

... [A]t oral argument in this Court, the attorney for the parties challenging the statute took the position that none of the enactments can be upheld without overruling *Roe v. Wade*. We disagree with that analysis; but we acknowledge that our decisions after *Roe* cast doubt upon the meaning and reach of its holding. ... [W]e find it imperative to review once more the principles that define the rights of the woman and the legitimate authority of the State respecting the termination of pregnancies by abortion procedures.

After considering the fundamental constitutional questions resolved by *Roe,* principles of institutional integrity, and the rule of stare decisis, we are led to conclude this: the essential holding of *Roe v. Wade* should be retained and once again reaffirmed.

It must be stated at the outset and with clarity that *Roe*'s essential holding, the holding we reaffirm, has three parts. First is a recognition of the right of the woman to choose to have an abortion before viability and to obtain it without undue interference from the State. Before viability, the State's interests are not strong enough to support a prohibition of abortion or the imposition of a substantial obstacle to the woman's effective right to elect the procedure. Second is a confirmation of the State's power to restrict abortions after fetal viability, if the law contains exceptions for pregnancies which endanger the woman's life or health. And third is the principle that the State has legitimate interests from the outset of the pregnancy in protecting the health of the woman and the life of the fetus that may become a child. These principles do not contradict one another; and we adhere to each.

II

Constitutional protection of the woman's decision to terminate her pregnancy derives from the Due Process Clause of the Fourteenth Amendment. It declares that no State shall "deprive any person of life, liberty, or property, without due process of law." The controlling word in the cases before us is "liberty.". . .

. . . It is tempting, as a means of curbing the discretion of federal judges, to suppose that liberty encompasses no more than those rights already guaranteed to the individual against federal interference by the express provisions of the first eight amendments to the Constitution. But of course this Court has never accepted that view.

. . .

It is a promise of the Constitution that there is a realm of personal liberty which the government may not enter. We have vindicated this principle before. Marriage is mentioned nowhere in the Bill of Rights and interracial marriage was illegal in most States in the 19th century, but the Court was no doubt correct in finding it to be an aspect of liberty protected against state interference by the substantive component of the Due Process Clause in Loving v. Virginia, 388 U.S. 1, 12 (1967). . . .

Neither the Bill of Rights nor the specific practices of States at the time of the adoption of the Fourteenth Amendment marks the outer limits of the substantive sphere of liberty which the Fourteenth Amendment protects. See U.S. Const., Amend. 9. . . .

The inescapable fact is that adjudication of substantive due process claims may call upon the Court in interpreting the Constitution to exercise that same capacity which by tradition courts always have exercised: reasoned judgment. Its boundaries are not susceptible of expression as a simple rule. That does not mean we are free to invalidate state policy choices with which we disagree; yet neither does it permit us to shrink from the duties of our office. As Justice Harlan observed:

> "Due process has not been reduced to any formula; its content cannot be determined by reference to any code. The best that can be said is that through the course of this Court's decisions it has represented the balance which our Nation, built upon postulates of respect for the liberty of the individual, has struck between that liberty and the demands of organized society. If the supplying of content to this Constitutional concept has of necessity been a rational process, it certainly has not been one where judges have felt free to roam where unguided speculation might take them. The balance of which I speak is the balance struck by this country, having regard to what history teaches are the traditions from which it developed as well as the traditions from which it broke. That tradition is a living thing. A decision of this Court which radically departs from it could not long survive, while a decision which builds

on what has survived is likely to be sound. No formula could serve as a substitute, in this area, for judgment and restraint." *Poe v. Ullman*, 367 U.S., at 542 (opinion dissenting from dismissal on jurisdictional grounds).

Men and women of good conscience can disagree, and we suppose some always shall disagree, about the profound moral and spiritual implications of terminating a pregnancy, even in its earliest stage. Some of us as individuals find abortion offensive to our most basic principles of morality, but that cannot control our decision. Our obligation is to define the liberty of all, not to mandate our own moral code. The underlying constitutional issue is whether the State can resolve these philosophic questions in such a definitive way that a woman lacks all choice in the matter, except perhaps in those rare circumstances in which the pregnancy is itself a danger to her own life or health, or is the result of rape or incest.

. . .

Our law affords constitutional protection to personal decisions relating to marriage, procreation, contraception, family relationships, child rearing, and education. . . . These matters, involving the most intimate and personal choices a person may make in a lifetime, choices central to personal dignity and autonomy, are central to the liberty protected by the Fourteenth Amendment. At the heart of liberty is the right to define one's own concept of existence, of meaning, of the universe, and of the mystery of human life. Beliefs about these matters could not define the attributes of personhood were they formed under compulsion of the State.

These considerations begin our analysis of the woman's interest in terminating her pregnancy but cannot end it, for this reason: though the abortion decision may originate within the zone of conscience and belief, it is more than a philosophic exercise. Abortion is a unique act. It is an act fraught with consequences for others: for the woman who must live with the implications of her decision; for the persons who perform and assist in the procedure; for the spouse, family, and society which must confront the knowledge that these procedures exist, procedures some deem nothing short of an act of violence against innocent human life; and, depending on one's beliefs, for the life or potential life that is aborted. Though abortion is conduct, it does not follow that the State is entitled to proscribe it in all instances. That is because the liberty of the woman is at stake in a sense unique to the human condition and so unique to the law. The mother who carries a child to full term is subject to anxieties, to physical constraints, to pain that only she must bear. That these sacrifices have from the beginning of the human race been endured by woman with a pride that ennobles her in the eyes of others and gives to the infant a bond of love cannot alone be grounds for the State to insist she make the sacrifice. Her suffering is too intimate and personal for the State to insist, without more, upon its own vision of the woman's role, however dominant that vision has been in the course of our history and our culture. The destiny of the woman must be shaped to a large extent on her own conception of her spiritual imperatives and her place in society.

While we appreciate the weight of the arguments made . . . that *Roe* should be overruled, the reservations any of us may have in reaffirming the central holding of *Roe* are outweighed by the explication of individual liberty we have given combined with the force of stare decisis. We turn now to that doctrine.

III

A

. . .

. . . [W]hen this Court reexamines a prior holding, its judgment is customarily informed by a series of prudential and pragmatic considerations designed to test the consistency of overruling a prior decision with the ideal of the rule of law, and to gauge the respective costs of reaffirming and overruling a prior case. Thus, for example, we may ask whether the rule has proved to be intolerable simply in defying practical workability; whether the rule is subject to a kind of reliance that would lend a special hardship to the consequences of overruling and add inequity to the cost of repudiation; whether related principles of law have so far developed as to have left the old rule no more than a remnant of abandoned doctrine; or whether facts have so changed or come to be seen so differently, as to have robbed the old rule of significant application or justification.

. . .

1

Although *Roe* has engendered opposition, it has in no sense proven "unworkable," representing as it does a simple limitation beyond which a state law is unenforceable. . . .

2

. . .

. . . Abortion is customarily chosen as an unplanned response to the consequence of unplanned activity or to the failure of conventional birth control, and except on the assumption that no intercourse would have occurred but for *Roe*'s holding, such behavior may appear to justify no reliance claim. Even if reliance could be claimed on that unrealistic assumption, the argument might run, any reliance interest would be *de minimis*. This argument would be premised on the hypothesis that reproductive planning could take virtually immediate account of any sudden restoration of state authority to ban abortions.

To eliminate the issue of reliance that easily, however, one would need to limit cognizable reliance to specific instances of sexual activity.

But to do this would be simply to refuse to face the fact that for two decades of economic and social developments, people have organized intimate relationships and made choices that define their views of themselves and their places in society, in reliance on the availability of abortion in the event that contraception should fail. The ability of women to participate equally in the economic and social life of the Nation has been facilitated by their ability to control their reproductive lives. The Constitution serves human values, and while the effect of reliance on *Roe* cannot be exactly measured, neither can the certain cost of overruling *Roe* for people who have ordered their thinking and living around that case be dismissed.

3

No evolution of legal principle has left *Roe*'s doctrinal footings weaker than they were in 1973. No development of constitutional law since the case was decided has implicitly or explicitly left *Roe* behind as a mere survivor of obsolete constitutional thinking.

It will be recognized, of course, that *Roe* stands at an intersection of two lines of decisions.... The *Roe* Court itself placed its holding in the succession of cases most prominently exemplified by *Griswold v. Connecticut*. When it is so seen, *Roe* is clearly in no jeopardy, since subsequent constitutional developments have neither disturbed, nor do they threaten to diminish, the scope of recognized protection accorded to the liberty relating to intimate relationships, the family, and decisions about whether or not to beget or bear a child.

Roe, however, may be seen not only as an exemplar of *Griswold* liberty but as a rule (whether or not mistaken) of personal autonomy and bodily integrity, with doctrinal affinity to cases recognizing limits on governmental power to mandate medical treatment or to bar its rejection. If so, our cases since *Roe* accord with *Roe*'s view that a State's interest in the protection of life falls short of justifying any plenary override of individual liberty claims. Cruzan v. Director, Missouri Dept. of Health, 497 U.S. 261, 278 (1990). ...

Finally, one could classify *Roe* as *sui generis*. If the case is so viewed, then there clearly has been no erosion of its central determination. The original holding resting on the concurrence of seven Members of the Court in 1973 was expressly affirmed by a majority of six in 1983, see Akron v. Akron Center for Reproductive Health, Inc., 462 U.S. 416 (1983) (*Akron I*), and by a majority of five in 1986, see Thornburgh v. American College of Obstetricians and Gynecologists, 476 U.S. 747 (1986). ... More recently, in Webster v. Reproductive Health Services, 492 U.S. 490 (1989), although two of the present authors questioned the trimester framework in a way consistent with our judgment today, see *id.*, at 518 (REHNQUIST, C.J., joined by WHITE, and KENNEDY, JJ.); *id*, at 529 (O'CONNOR, J., concurring in part and concurring in judgment), a majority of the Court either decided to reaffirm or declined to address the constitutional validity of the central holding of *Roe*.

Nor will courts building upon *Roe* be likely to hand down erroneous decisions as a consequence. Even on the assumption that the central holding of *Roe* was in error, that error would go only to the strength of the state interest in fetal protection, not to the recognition afforded by the Constitution to the woman's liberty. . . .

The soundness of this prong of the *Roe* analysis is apparent from a consideration of the alternative. If indeed the woman's interest in deciding whether to bear and beget a child had not been recognized as in *Roe*, the State might as readily restrict a woman's right to choose to carry a pregnancy to term as to terminate it, to further asserted state interests in population control, or eugenics, for example. Yet *Roe* has been sensibly relied upon to counter any such suggestions. E.g., Arnold v. Board of Education of Escambia County, Ala., 880 F.2d 305, 311 (CA11 1989) (relying upon *Roe* and concluding that government officials violate the Constitution by coercing a minor to have an abortion). . . .

4

[T]ime has overtaken some of *Roe*'s factual assumptions: advances in maternal health care allow for abortions safe to the mother later in pregnancy than was true in 1973 and advances in neonatal care have advanced viability to a point somewhat earlier. But these facts go only to the scheme of time limits on the realization of competing interests, and the divergences from the factual premises of 1973 have no bearing on the validity of *Roe*'s central holding, that viability marks the earliest point at which the State's interest in fetal life is constitutionally adequate to justify a legislative ban on nontherapeutic abortions. . . .

5

. . . An entire generation has come of age free to assume *Roe*'s concept of liberty in defining the capacity of women to act in society, and to make reproductive decisions. . . . Within the bounds of normal *stare decisis* analysis, then, and subject to the considerations on which it customarily turns, the stronger argument is for affirming *Roe*'s central holding, with whatever degree of personal reluctance any of us may have, not for overruling it.

B

In a less significant case, *stare decisis* analysis could, and would, stop at the point we have reached. But the sustained and widespread debate *Roe* has provoked calls for some comparison between that case and others of comparable dimension that have responded to national controversies and taken on the impress of the controversies addressed. Only two such decisional lines from the past century present themselves for examination, and in each instance the result reached by the Court accorded with the principles we apply today.

The first example is that line of cases identified with Lochner v. New York, 198 U.S. 45 (1905), which imposed substantive limitations on legislation limiting economic autonomy in favor of health and welfare regulation, adopting, in Justice Holmes' view, the theory of laissez-faire. The *Lochner* decisions were exemplified by Adkins v. Children's Hospital of D.C., 261 U.S. 525 (1923), in which this Court held it to be an infringement of constitutionally protected liberty of contract to require the employers of adult women to satisfy minimum wage standards. Fourteen years later, West Coast Hotel Co. v. Parrish, 300 U.S. 379 (1937), signaled the demise of *Lochner* by overruling *Adkins*. In the meantime, the Depression had come and, with it, the lesson that seemed unmistakable to most people by 1937, that the interpretation of contractual freedom protected in *Adkins* rested on fundamentally false factual assumptions about the capacity of a relatively unregulated market to satisfy minimal levels of human welfare. . . .

The second comparison that 20th century history invites is with the cases employing the separate-but-equal rule for applying the Fourteenth Amendment's equal protection guarantee. They began with Plessy v. Ferguson, 163 U.S. 537 (1896), holding that legislatively mandated racial segregation in public transportation works no denial of equal protection, rejecting the argument that racial separation enforced by the legal machinery of American society treats the black race as inferior. . . . But this understanding of the facts and the rule it was stated to justify were repudiated in Brown v. Board of Education, 347 U.S. 483 (1954). . . .

The Court in *Brown* observ[ed] that whatever may have been the understanding in *Plessy*'s time of the power of segregation to stigmatize those who were segregated with a "badge of inferiority," it was clear by 1954 that legally sanctioned segregation had just such an effect. Society's understanding of the facts upon which a constitutional ruling was sought in 1954 was thus fundamentally different from the basis claimed for the decision in 1896. . . .

West Coast Hotel and *Brown* each rested on facts, or an understanding of facts, changed from those which furnished the claimed justifications for the earlier constitutional resolutions. Each case was comprehensible as the Court's response to facts that the country could understand, or had come to understand already, but which the Court of an earlier day, as its own declarations disclosed, had not been able to perceive. As the decisions were thus comprehensible they were also defensible, not merely as the victories of one doctrinal school over another by dint of numbers (victories though they were), but as applications of constitutional principle to facts as they had not been seen by the Court before. . . .

. . . Because neither the factual underpinnings of *Roe*'s central holding nor our understanding of it has changed (and because no other indication of weakened precedent has been shown) the Court could not pretend to be reexamining the prior law with any justification beyond a present doctrinal disposition to come out differently from the Court of 1973. To overrule prior law for no other reason than that would run counter to the view repeated in our cases, that a decision to overrule should rest on some special reason over and above the belief that a prior case was wrongly decided.

C

... [O]verruling *Roe*'s central holding would not only reach an unjustifiable result under principles of *stare decisis*, but would seriously weaken the Court's capacity to exercise the judicial power and to function as the Supreme Court of a Nation dedicated to the rule of law. . . .

... As Americans of each succeeding generation are rightly told, the Court cannot buy support for its decisions by spending money and, except to a minor degree, it cannot independently coerce obedience to its decrees. The Court's power lies, rather, in its legitimacy, a product of substance and perception that shows itself in the people's acceptance of the Judiciary as fit to determine what the Nation's law means and to declare what it demands.

... The Court must take care to speak and act in ways that allow people to accept its decisions on the terms the Court claims for them, as grounded truly in principle, not as compromises with social and political pressures having, as such, no bearing on the principled choices that the Court is obliged to make. Thus, the Court's legitimacy depends on making legally principled decisions under circumstances in which their principled character is sufficiently plausible to be accepted by the Nation.

The need for principled action to be perceived as such is implicated to some degree whenever this, or any other appellate court, overrules a prior case. This is not to say, of course, that this Court cannot give a perfectly satisfactory explanation in most cases. . . .

In two circumstances, however, the Court would almost certainly fail to receive the benefit of the doubt in overruling prior cases. There is, first, a point beyond which frequent overruling would overtax the country's belief in the Court's good faith. ... If that limit should be exceeded, disturbance of prior rulings would be taken as evidence that justifiable reexamination of principle had given way to drives for particular results in the short term. The legitimacy of the Court would fade with the frequency of its vacillation.

That first circumstance can be described as hypothetical; the second is to the point here and now. Where, in the performance of its judicial duties, the Court decides a case in such a way as to resolve the sort of intensely divisive controversy reflected in *Roe* and those rare, comparable cases, its decision has a dimension that the resolution of the normal case does not carry. It is the dimension present whenever the Court's interpretation of the Constitution calls the contending sides of a national controversy to end their national division by accepting a common mandate rooted in the Constitution.

The Court is not asked to do this very often, having thus addressed the Nation only twice in our lifetime, in the decisions of *Brown* and *Roe*.

But when the Court does act in this way, its decision requires an equally rare precedential force to counter the inevitable efforts to overturn it and to thwart its implementation.... [T]o overrule under fire in the absence of the most compelling reason to reexamine a watershed decision would subvert the Court's legitimacy beyond any serious question.

... Some cost will be paid by anyone who approves or implements a constitutional decision where it is unpopular, or who refuses to work to undermine the decision or to force its reversal. The price may be criticism or ostracism, or it may be violence. An extra price will be paid by those who themselves disapprove of the decision's results when viewed outside of constitutional terms, but who nevertheless struggle to accept it, because they respect the rule of law. To all those who will be so tested by following, the Court implicitly undertakes to remain steadfast, lest in the end a price be paid for nothing. The promise of constancy, once given, binds its maker for as long as the power to stand by the decision survives and the understanding of the issue has not changed so fundamentally as to render the commitment obsolete....

... Like the character of an individual, the legitimacy of the Court must be earned over time. So, indeed, must be the character of a Nation of people who aspire to live according to the rule of law. Their belief in themselves as such a people is not readily separable from their understanding of the Court invested with the authority to decide their constitutional cases and speak before all others for their constitutional ideals. If the Court's legitimacy should be undermined, then, so would the country be in its very ability to see itself through its constitutional ideals....

The Court's duty in the present case is clear. In 1973, it confronted the already-divisive issue of governmental power to limit personal choice to undergo abortion, for which it provided a new resolution based on the due process guaranteed by the Fourteenth Amendment. Whether or not a new social consensus is developing on that issue, its divisiveness is no less today than in 1973, and pressure to overrule the decision, like pressure to retain it, has grown only more intense. A decision to overrule *Roe*'s essential holding under the existing circumstances would address error, if error there was, at the cost of both profound and unnecessary damage to the Court's legitimacy, and to the Nation's commitment to the rule of law. It is therefore imperative to adhere to the essence of *Roe*'s original decision, and we do so today.

IV

. . .

... [M]uch criticism has been directed at *Roe* [for the trimester scheme], a criticism that always inheres when the Court draws a specific rule from what in the Constitution is but a general standard. We conclude, however, that the urgent claims of the woman to retain the ultimate control over her destiny and her body, claims implicit in the meaning of liberty, require us to perform that function. Liberty must not be extinguished for want of a line that is clear. And it falls to us to give some real substance to the woman's liberty to determine whether to carry her pregnancy to full term.

We conclude the line should be drawn at viability, so that before that time the woman has a right to choose to terminate her pregnancy. We adhere to this principle for two reasons. First, as we have said, is the doctrine of *stare decisis....* *Roe* was a reasoned statement, elaborated with great care. We have twice reaffirmed it in the face of great opposition. . . .

The second reason is that the concept of viability, as we noted in *Roe,* is the time at which there is a realistic possibility of maintaining and nourishing a life outside the womb, so that the independent existence of the second life can in reason and all fairness be the object of state protection that now overrides the rights of the woman. . . . [T]here is no line other than viability which is more workable. . . . The viability line also has, as a practical matter, an element of fairness. . . . In some broad sense it might be said that a woman who fails to act before viability has consented to the State's intervention on behalf of the developing child.

The woman's right to terminate her pregnancy before viability is the most central principle of *Roe v. Wade.* It is a rule of law and a component of liberty we cannot renounce.

On the other side of the equation is the interest of the State in the protection of potential life. . . . The weight to be given this state interest, not the strength of the woman's interest, was the difficult question faced in *Roe.* . . .

. . . *Roe v. Wade* speaks with clarity in establishing not only the woman's liberty but also the State's "important and legitimate interest in potential life." That portion of the decision in *Roe* has been given too little acknowledgement and implementation by the Court in its subsequent cases. Those cases decided that any regulation touching upon the abortion decision must survive strict scrutiny, to be sustained only if drawn in narrow terms to further a compelling state interest. Not all of the cases decided under that formulation can be reconciled with the holding in *Roe* itself that the State has legitimate interests in the health of the woman and in protecting the potential life within her. In resolving this tension, we choose to rely upon *Roe,* as against the later cases.

Roe established a trimester framework to govern abortion regulations. Under this elaborate but rigid construct, almost no regulation at all is permitted during the first trimester of pregnancy; regulations designed to protect the woman's health, but not to further the State's interest in potential life, are permitted during the second trimester; and during the third trimester, when the fetus is viable, prohibitions are permitted provided the life or health of the mother is not at stake. Most of our cases since *Roe* have involved the application of rules derived from the trimester framework.

The trimester framework no doubt was erected to ensure that the woman's right to choose not become so subordinate to the State's interest in promoting fetal life that her choice exists in theory but not in fact. We do not agree, however, that the trimester approach is necessary to accomplish this objective. . . .

Though the woman has a right to choose to terminate or continue her pregnancy before viability, it does not at all follow that the State is prohibited from taking steps to ensure that this choice is thoughtful and informed. . . .

We reject the trimester framework, which we do not consider to be part of the essential holding of *Roe*. . . . A logical reading of the central holding in *Roe* itself, and a necessary reconciliation of the liberty of the woman and the interest of the State in promoting prenatal life, require, in our view, that we abandon the trimester framework as a rigid prohibition on all previability regulation aimed at the protection of fetal life. The trimester framework suffers from these basic flaws: in its formulation it misconceives the nature of the pregnant woman's inter- est; and in practice it undervalues the State's interest in potential life, as recognized in *Roe*.

As our jurisprudence relating to all liberties save perhaps abortion has recognized, not every law which makes a right more difficult to exercise is, *ipso facto*, an infringement of that right. . . .

. . . Numerous forms of state regulation might have the incidental effect of increasing the cost or decreasing the availability of medical care, whether for abortion or any other medical procedure. The fact that a law which serves a valid purpose, one not designed to strike at the right itself, has the incidental effect of making it more difficult or more expensive to procure an abortion cannot be enough to invalidate it. Only where state regulation imposes an undue burden on a woman's ability to make this decision does the power of the State reach into the heart of the liberty protected by the Due Process Clause.

. . .

. . . The very notion that the State has a substantial interest in potential life leads to the conclusion that not all regulations must be deemed unwarranted. Not all burdens on the right to decide whether to terminate a pregnancy will be undue. . . .

. . .

A finding of an undue burden is a shorthand for the conclusion that a state regulation has the purpose or effect of placing a substantial obstacle in the path of a woman seeking an abortion of a nonviable fetus. A statute with this purpose is invalid because the means chosen by the State to further the interest in potential life must be calculated to inform the woman's free choice, not hinder it. And a statute which, while furthering the interest in potential life or some other valid state interest, has the effect of placing a substantial obstacle in the path of a woman's choice cannot be considered a permissible means of serving its legitimate ends....

... What is at stake is the woman's right to make the ultimate decision, not a right to be insulated from all others in doing so. Regulations which do no more than create a structural mechanism by which the State, or the parent or guardian of a minor, may express profound respect for the life of the unborn are permitted, if they are not a substantial obstacle to the woman's exercise of the right to choose.... Regulations designed to foster the health of a woman seeking an abortion are valid if they do not constitute an undue burden.

... We give this summary:

(a) To protect the central right recognized by *Roe v. Wade* while at the same time accommodating the State's profound interest in potential life, we will employ the undue burden analysis as explained in this opinion. An undue burden exists, and therefore a provision of law is invalid, if its purpose or effect is to place a substantial obstacle in the path of a woman seeking an abortion before the fetus attains viability.

(b) We reject the rigid trimester framework of *Roe v. Wade*. To promote the State's profound interest in potential life, throughout pregnancy the State may take measures to ensure that the woman's choice is informed, and measures designed to advance this interest will not be invalidated as long as their purpose is to persuade the woman to choose childbirth over abortion. These measures must not be an undue burden on the right.

(c) As with any medical procedure, the State may enact regulations to further the health or safety of a woman seeking an abortion. Unnecessary health regulations that have the purpose or effect of presenting a substantial obstacle to a woman seeking an abortion impose an undue burden on the right.

(d) Our adoption of the undue burden analysis does not disturb the central holding of *Roe v. Wade*, and we reaffirm that holding. Regardless of whether exceptions are made for particular circumstances, a State may not prohibit any woman from making the ultimate decision to terminate her pregnancy before viability.

(e) We also reaffirm *Roe*'s holding that "subsequent to viability, the State in promoting its interest in the potentiality of human life may, if it chooses, regulate, and even proscribe, abortion except where it is necessary, in appropriate medical judgment, for the preservation of the life or health of the mother." *Roe v. Wade*, 410 U.S., at 164–165.

These principles control our assessment of the Pennsylvania statute, and we now turn to the issue of the validity of its challenged provisions.

V

[The Court upheld all but one of the challenged provisions, including requirements for a 24-hour waiting period between initial consultation and performance of the procedure, and requirements that physicians provide specific forms of information to the patient, requirements that the Court had previously invalidated.]

B

. . .

In *Akron I*, 462 U.S. 416 (1983), we invalidated an ordinance which required that a woman seeking an abortion be provided by her physician with specific information "designed to influence the woman's informed choice between abortion or childbirth." As we later described the *Akron I* holding in *Thornburgh v. American College of Obstetricians and Gynecologists*, 476 U.S., at 762, there were two purported flaws in the Akron ordinance: the information was designed to dissuade the woman from having an abortion and the ordinance imposed "a rigid requirement that a specific body of information be given in all cases, irrespective of the particular needs of the patient...."

To the extent *Akron I* and *Thornburgh* find a constitutional violation when the government requires, as it does here, the giving of truthful, nonmisleading information about the nature of the procedure, the attendant health risks and those of childbirth, and the "probable gestational age" of the fetus, those cases go too far, are inconsistent with *Roe*'s acknowledgment of an important interest in potential life, and are overruled.... It cannot be questioned that psychological well-being is a facet of health. Nor can it be doubted that most women considering an abortion would deem the impact on the fetus relevant, if not dispositive, to the decision. In attempting to ensure that a woman apprehend the full consequences of her decision, the State furthers the legitimate purpose of reducing the risk that a woman may elect an abortion, only to discover later, with devastating psychological consequences, that her decision was not fully informed....

We also see no reason why the State may not require doctors to inform a woman seeking an abortion of the availability of materials relating to the consequences to the fetus, even when those consequences have no direct relation to her health. An example illustrates the point. We would think it constitutional for the State to require that in order for there to be informed consent to a kidney transplant operation the recipient must be supplied with information about risks to the donor as well as risks to himself or herself. A requirement that the physician make available information similar to that mandated by the statute here was described in *Thornburgh* as "an outright attempt to wedge the Commonwealth's message discouraging abortion into the privacy of the informed-consent dialogue between the woman and her physician." 476 U.S., at 762. We conclude, however, that informed choice need not be defined in such narrow terms that all considerations of the effect on the fetus are made irrelevant.... This requirement cannot be considered a substantial obstacle to obtaining an abortion, and, it follows, there is no undue burden.

. . .

The Pennsylvania statute also requires us to reconsider the holding in *Akron I* that the State may not require that a physician, as opposed to a qualified assistant, provide information relevant to a woman's informed consent. 462 U.S., at 448. Since there is no evidence on this record that requiring a doctor to give the information as provided by the statute would amount in practical terms to a substantial obstacle to a woman seeking an abortion, we conclude that it is not an undue burden. . . .

Our analysis of Pennsylvania's 24-hour waiting period between the provision of the information deemed necessary to informed consent and the performance of an abortion under the undue burden standard requires us to reconsider the premise behind the decision in *Akron I* invalidating a parallel requirement. We consider that conclusion to be wrong. The idea that important decisions will be more informed and deliberate if they follow some period of reflection does not strike us as unreasonable, particularly where the statute directs that important information become part of the background of the decision. . . .

Whether the mandatory 24-hour waiting period is nonetheless invalid because in practice it is a substantial obstacle to a woman's choice to terminate her pregnancy is a closer question. The findings of fact by the District Court indicate that because of the distances many women must travel to reach an abortion provider, the practical effect will often be a delay of much more than a day because the waiting period requires that a woman seeking an abortion make at least two visits to the doctor. The District Court also found that in many instances this will increase the exposure of women seeking abortions to "the harassment and hostility of anti-abortion protestors demonstrating outside a clinic." 744 F.Supp., at 1351. As a result, the District Court found that for those women who have the fewest financial resources, those who must travel long distances, and those who have difficulty explaining their whereabouts to husbands, employers, or others, the 24-hour waiting period will be "particularly burdensome." *Id.*, at 1352.

These findings are troubling in some respects, but they do not demonstrate that the waiting period constitutes an undue burden. . . . In light of the construction given the statute's definition of medical emergency by the Court of Appeals, and the District Court's findings, we cannot say that the waiting period imposes a real health risk.

We also disagree with the District Court's conclusion that the "particularly burdensome" effects of the waiting period on some women require its invalidation. A particular burden is not of necessity a substantial obstacle. Whether a burden falls on a particular group is a distinct inquiry from whether it is a substantial obstacle even as to the women in that group. And the District Court did not conclude that the waiting period is such an obstacle even for the women who are most burdened by it. Hence, on the record before us, and in the context of this facial challenge, we are not convinced that the 24–hour waiting period constitutes an undue burden.

. . .

C.

Section 3209 of Pennsylvania's abortion law provides, except in cases of medical emergency, that no physician shall perform an abortion on a married woman without receiving a signed statement from the woman that she has notified her spouse that she is about to undergo an abortion. The woman has the option of providing an alternative signed statement certifying that her husband is not the man who impregnated her; that her husband could not be located; that the pregnancy is the result of spousal sexual assault which she has reported; or that the woman believes that notifying her husband will cause him or someone else to inflict bodily injury upon her. A physician who performs an abortion on a married woman without receiving the appropriate signed statement will have his or her license revoked, and is liable to the husband for damages.

The District Court heard the testimony of numerous expert witnesses, and made detailed findings of fact regarding the effect of this statute. These included:

"273.   The vast majority of women consult their husbands prior to deciding to terminate their pregnancy. . . .

"279.   The 'bodily injury' exception could not be invoked by a married woman whose husband, if notified, would, in her reasonable belief, threaten to (a) publicize her intent to have an abortion to family, friends or acquaintances; (b) retaliate against her in future child custody or divorce proceedings; (c) inflict psychological intimidation or emotional harm upon her, her children or other persons; (d) inflict bodily harm on other persons such as children, family members or other loved ones; or (e) use his control over finances to deprive her of necessary monies for herself or her children. . . .

"281.   Studies reveal that family violence occurs in two million families in the United States. This figure, however, is a conservative one that substantially understates (because battering is usually not reported until it reaches life-threatening proportions) the actual number of families affected by domestic violence. In fact, researchers estimate that one of every two women will be battered at some time in their life. . . .

"282.   A wife may not elect to notify her husband of her intention to have an abortion for a variety of reasons, including the husband's illness, concern about her own health, the imminent failure of the marriage, or the husband's absolute opposition to the abortion. . . .

"283.   The required filing of the spousal consent form would require plaintiff-clinics to change their counseling procedures and force women to reveal their most intimate decision-making on pain of criminal sanctions. The confidentiality of these revelations could not be guaranteed, since the woman's records are not immune from subpoena. . . .

"284. Women of all class levels, educational backgrounds, and racial, ethnic and religious groups are battered. . . .

"285. Wife-battering or abuse can take on many physical and psychological forms. The nature and scope of the battering can cover a broad range of actions and be gruesome and torturous. . . .

"286. Married women, victims of battering, have been killed in Pennsylvania and throughout the United States. . . .

"287. Battering can often involve a substantial amount of sexual abuse, including marital rape and sexual mutilation. . . .

"288. In a domestic abuse situation, it is common for the battering husband to also abuse the children in an attempt to coerce the wife. . . .

"289. Mere notification of pregnancy is frequently a flashpoint for battering and violence within the family. The number of battering incidents is high during the pregnancy and often the worst abuse can be associated with pregnancy . . . The battering husband may deny parentage and use the pregnancy as an excuse for abuse. . . .

"290. Secrecy typically shrouds abusive families. Family members are instructed not to tell anyone, especially police or doctors, about the abuse and violence. Battering husbands often threaten their wives or her children with further abuse if she tells an outsider of the violence and tells her that nobody will believe her. A battered woman, therefore, is highly unlikely to disclose the violence against her for fear of retaliation by the abuser. . . .

. . .

"294. A woman in a shelter or a safe house unknown to her husband is not 'reasonably likely' to have bodily harm inflicted upon her by her batterer, however her attempt to notify her husband pursuant to section 3209 could accidentally disclose her whereabouts to her husband. Her fear of future ramifications would be realistic under the circumstances.

"295. Marital rape is rarely discussed with others or reported to law enforcement authorities, and of those reported only few are prosecuted. . . .

"296. It is common for battered women to have sexual intercourse with their husbands to avoid being battered. While this type of coercive sexual activity would be spousal sexual assault as defined by the Act, many women may not consider it to be so and others would fear disbelief. . . .

"297. The marital rape exception to section 3209 cannot be claimed by women who are victims of coercive sexual behavior other than penetration. The 90–day reporting requirement of the spousal sexual assault statute, 18 Pa.Cons.Stat.Ann. § 3218(c), further narrows the class of sexually abused wives who can claim the exception, since many of these women may be psychologically unable to discuss or report the rape for several years after the incident. . . .

"298. Because of the nature of the battering relationship, battered women are unlikely to avail themselves of the exceptions to section 3209 of the Act, regardless of whether the section applies to them." 744 F. Supp., at 1360–1362.

These findings are supported by studies of domestic violence. [The Court then summarized the findings of several studies of spousal abuse.]

. . .

The limited research that has been conducted with respect to notifying one's husband about an abortion, although involving samples too small to be representative, also supports the District Court's findings of fact. The vast majority of women notify their male partners of their decision to obtain an abortion. In many cases in which married women do not notify their husbands, the pregnancy is the result of an extramarital affair. Where the husband is the father, the primary reason women do not notify their husbands is that the husband and wife are experiencing marital difficulties, often accompanied by incidents of violence.

This information and the District Court's findings reinforce what common sense would suggest. In well-functioning marriages, spouses discuss important intimate decisions such as whether to bear a child. But there are millions of women in this country who are the victims of regular physical and psychological abuse at the hands of their husbands. Should these women become pregnant, they may have very good reasons for not wishing to inform their husbands of their decision to obtain an abortion. . . .

The spousal notification requirement is thus likely to prevent a significant number of women from obtaining an abortion. It does not merely make abortions a little more difficult or expensive to obtain; for many women, it will impose a substantial obstacle. We must not blind ourselves to the fact that the significant number of women who fear for their safety and the safety of their children are likely to be deterred from procuring an abortion as surely as if the Commonwealth had outlawed abortion in all cases.

. . .

. . . The unfortunate yet persisting conditions we document above will mean that in a large fraction of the cases in which § 3209 is relevant, it will operate as a substantial obstacle to a woman's choice to undergo an abortion. It is an undue burden, and therefore invalid.

. . .

In keeping with our rejection of the common-law understanding of a woman's role within the family, the Court held in *Danforth* that the Constitution does not permit a State to require a married woman to obtain her husband's consent before undergoing an abortion. 428 U.S., at 69. The principles that guided the Court in *Danforth* should be our guides today. For the great many women who are victims of abuse inflicted by their husbands, or whose children are the victims of such abuse, a spousal notice requirement enables the husband to wield an effective veto over his wife's decision. Whether the prospect of notification itself deters such women from seeking abortions, or whether the husband, through physical force or psychological pressure or economic coercion, prevents his wife from obtaining an abortion until it is too late, the notice requirement will often be tantamount to the veto found unconstitutional in *Danforth*. The women most affected by this law— those who most reasonably fear the consequences of notifying their husbands that they are pregnant—are in the gravest danger.

The husband's interest in the life of the child his wife is carrying does not permit the State to empower him with this troubling degree of authority over his wife. The contrary view leads to consequences reminiscent of the common law. A husband has no enforceable right to require a wife to advise him before she exercises her personal choices.... A State may not give to a man the kind of dominion over his wife that parents exercise over their children.

Section 3209 embodies a view of marriage consonant with the common-law status of married women but repugnant to our present understanding of marriage and of the nature of the rights secured by the Constitution. Women do not lose their constitutionally protected liberty when they marry. The Constitution protects all individuals, male or female, married or unmarried, from the abuse of governmental power, even where that power is employed for the supposed benefit of a member of the individual's family. These considerations confirm our conclusion that § 3209 is invalid.

. . .

VI

Our Constitution is a covenant running from the first generation of Americans to us and then to future generations. It is a coherent succession. Each generation must learn anew that the Constitution's written terms embody ideas and aspirations that must survive more ages than one. We accept our responsibility not to retreat from interpreting the full meaning of the covenant in light of all of our precedents. We invoke it once again to define the freedom guaranteed by the Constitution's own promise, the promise of liberty.

. . .

JUSTICE STEVENS, concurring in part and dissenting in part.

. . .

The Court is unquestionably correct in concluding that the doctrine of *stare decisis* has controlling significance in a case of this kind, notwithstanding an individual Justice's concerns about the merits. The central holding of Roe v. Wade, 410 U.S. 113 (1973), has been a "part of our law" for almost two decades. It was a natural sequel to the protection of individual liberty established in Griswold v. Connecticut, 381 U.S. 479 (1965)....

II

My disagreement with the joint opinion begins with its understanding of the trimester framework established in *Roe*. Contrary to the suggestion of the joint opinion, it is not a "contradiction" to recognize that the State may have a legitimate interest in potential human life and, at the same time, to conclude that that interest does not justify the regulation of abortion before viability (although other interests, such as maternal health, may). The fact that the State's interest is legitimate does not tell us when, if ever, that interest outweighs the pregnant woman's interest in personal liberty. It is appropriate, therefore, to consider more carefully the nature of the interests at stake.

. . .

Weighing the State's interest in potential life and the woman's liberty interest, I agree with the joint opinion that the State may " 'expres[s] a preference for normal childbirth,' " that the State may take steps to ensure that a woman's choice "is thoughtful and informed," and that "States are free to enact laws to provide a reasonable framework for a woman to make a decision that has such profound and lasting meaning." Serious questions arise, however, when a State attempts to "persuade the woman to choose childbirth over abortion." *Ante*, at 878. Decisional autonomy must limit the State's power to inject into a woman's most personal deliberations its own views of what is best. The State may promote its preferences by funding childbirth, by creating and maintaining alternatives to abortion, and by espousing the virtues of family; but it must respect the individual's freedom to make such judgments.

. . .

... Under these principles, §§ 3205(a)(2)(i)–(iii) of the Pennsylvania statute are unconstitutional. Those sections require a physician or counselor to provide the woman with a range of materials clearly designed to persuade her to choose not to undergo the abortion. While the Commonwealth is free, pursuant to § 3208 of the Pennsylvania law, to produce and disseminate such material, the Commonwealth may not inject such information into the woman's deliberations just as she is weighing such an important choice.

Under this same analysis, §§ 3205(a)(1)(i) and (iii) of the Pennsylvania statute are constitutional. Those sections, which require the physician to inform a woman of the nature and risks of the abortion procedure and the medical risks of carrying to term, are neutral requirements comparable to those imposed in other medical procedures. Those sections indicate no effort by the Commonwealth to influence the woman's choice in any way. If anything, such requirements *enhance*, rather than skew, the woman's decisionmaking.

III

The 24-hour waiting period required by §§ 3205(a)(1)–(2) of the Pennsylvania statute raises even more serious concerns....

. . .

... [T]here is no evidence that the mandated delay benefits women or that it is necessary to enable the physician to convey any relevant information to the patient. The mandatory delay thus appears to rest on outmoded and unacceptable assumptions about the decisionmaking capacity of women....

... A woman who has, in the privacy of her thoughts and conscience, weighed the options and made her decision cannot be forced to reconsider all, simply because the State believes she has come to the wrong conclusion.[1]

Part of the constitutional liberty to choose is the equal dignity to which each of us is entitled. A woman who decides to terminate her pregnancy is entitled to the same respect as a woman who decides to carry the fetus to term. The mandatory waiting period denies women that equal respect.

IV

In my opinion, a correct application of the "undue burden" standard leads to the same conclusion concerning the constitutionality of these requirements....

. . .

JUSTICE BLACKMUN, concurring in part, concurring in the judgment in part, and dissenting in part.

I join parts I, II, III, V–A, V–C, and VI of the joint opinion of JUSTICES O'CONNOR, KENNEDY, and SOUTER, *ante.*

Three years ago, in Webster v. Reproductive Health Services, 492 U.S. 490 (1989), four Members of this Court appeared poised to "cas[t] into darkness the hopes and visions of every woman in this country" who had come to believe that the Constitution guaranteed her the right

---

1. [Footnote 5 in original] The joint opinion's reliance on the indirect effects of the regulation of constitutionally protected activity ... is misplaced; what matters is not only the effect of a regulation but also the reason for the regulation....

to reproductive choice.... But now, just when so many expected the darkness to fall, the flame has grown bright.

I do not underestimate the significance of today's joint opinion. Yet I remain steadfast in my belief that the right to reproductive choice is entitled to the full protection afforded by this Court before *Webster*. And I fear for the darkness as four Justices anxiously await the single vote necessary to extinguish the light.

I

Make no mistake, the joint opinion of Justices O'Connor, Kennedy, and Souter is an act of personal courage and constitutional principle. In contrast to previous decisions in which Justices O'Connor and Kennedy postponed reconsideration of Roe v. Wade, 410 U.S. 113 (1973), the authors of the joint opinion today join Justice Stevens and me in concluding that "the essential holding of *Roe v. Wade* should be retained and once again reaffirmed." In brief, five Members of this Court today recognize that "the Constitution protects a woman's right to terminate her pregnancy in its early stages."...

... What has happened today should serve as a model for future Justices and a warning to all who have tried to turn this Court into yet another political branch.

· · ·

... [W]hile I believe that the joint opinion errs in failing to invalidate the other regulations, I am pleased that the joint opinion has not ruled out the possibility that these regulations may be shown to impose an unconstitutional burden. The joint opinion makes clear that its specific holdings are based on the insufficiency of the record before it. I am confident that in the future evidence will be produced to show that "in a large fraction of the cases in which [these regulations are] relevant, [they] will operate as a substantial obstacle to a woman's choice to undergo an abortion." *Ante*, at 895.

II

[Justice Blackmun argued that "the Pennsylvania statute's provisions requiring content-based counseling, a 24–hour delay, informed parental consent, and reporting of abortion-related information must be invalidated."]

A

· · ·

State restrictions on abortion violate a woman's right of privacy in two ways. First, compelled continuation of a pregnancy infringes upon a woman's right to bodily integrity by imposing substantial physical intrusions and significant risks of physical harm. During pregnancy, women experience dramatic physical changes and a wide range of health consequences. Labor and delivery pose additional health risks and physical demands. In short, restrictive abortion laws force women to endure physical invasions far more substantial than those this Court has held to violate the constitutional principle of bodily integrity in other contexts.

Further, when the State restricts a woman's right to terminate her pregnancy, it deprives a woman of the right to make her own decision about reproduction and family planning—critical life choices that this Court long has deemed central to the right to privacy. The decision to terminate or continue a pregnancy has no less an impact on a woman's life than decisions about contraception or marriage. Because motherhood has a dramatic impact on a woman's educational prospects, employment opportunities, and self-determination, restrictive abortion laws deprive her of basic control over her life. . . .

A State's restrictions on a woman's right to terminate her pregnancy also implicate constitutional guarantees of gender equality. By restricting the right to terminate pregnancies, the State conscripts women's bodies into its service, forcing women to continue their pregnancies, suffer the pains of childbirth, and in most instances, provide years of maternal care. The State does not compensate women for their services; instead, it assumes that they owe this duty as a matter of course. This assumption—that women can simply be forced to accept the "natural" status and incidents of motherhood—appears to rest upon a conception of women's role that has triggered the protection of the Equal Protection Clause. See, e.g., Mississippi Univ. for Women v. Hogan, 458 U.S. 718, 724–726 (1982); Craig v. Boren, 429 U.S. 190, 198–199 (1976). . . .

B

. . .

. . . *Roe* identified two relevant State interests: "an interest in preserving and protecting the health of the pregnant woman" and an interest in "protecting the potentiality of human life." 410 U.S., at 162. With respect to the State's interest in the health of the mother, "the compelling point . . . is at approximately the end of the first trimester," because it is at that point that the mortality rate in abortion approaches that in childbirth. *Roe*, 410 U.S., at 163. With respect to the State's interest in potential life, "the 'compelling' point is at viability," because it is at that point that the fetus "presumably has the capability of meaningful life outside the mother's womb." *Ibid*. In order to fulfill the requirement of narrow tailoring, "the State is obligated to make a reasonable effort to limit the effect of its regulations to the period in the trimester during which its health interest will be furthered." *Akron*, 462 U.S., at 434.

In my view, application of this analytical framework is no less warranted than when it was approved by seven Members of this Court in *Roe*. . . .

. . .

The [most telling] criticism of the trimester framework is that it fails to find the State's interest in potential human life compelling throughout pregnancy. No Member of this Court—nor for that matter, the Solicitor General, Tr. of Oral Arg. 42—has ever questioned our holding in *Roe* that an abortion is not "the termination of life entitled to Fourteenth Amendment protection." 410 U.S., at 159. Accordingly, a State's interest in protecting fetal life is not grounded in the Constitution. Nor, consistent with our Establishment Clause, can it be a theological or sectarian interest. It is, instead, a legitimate interest grounded in humanitarian or pragmatic concerns.

... But ... legitimate interests are not enough. To overcome the burden of strict scrutiny, the interests must be compelling.... "The viability line reflects the biological facts and truths of fetal development; it marks that threshold moment prior to which a fetus cannot survive separate from the woman and cannot reasonably and objectively be regarded as a subject of rights or interests distinct from, or paramount to, those of the pregnant woman. At the same time, the viability standard takes account of the undeniable fact that as the fetus evolves into its postnatal form, and as it loses its dependence on the uterine environment, the State's interest in the fetus' potential human life, and in fostering a regard for human life in general, becomes compelling. As a practical matter,... it establishes an easily applicable standard for regulating abortion while providing a pregnant woman ample time to exercise her fundamental right with her responsible physician to terminate her pregnancy." 492 U.S., at 553–554.

· · ·

In sum, *Roe*'s requirement of strict scrutiny as implemented through a trimester framework should not be disturbed....

· · ·

III

... THE CHIEF JUSTICE'S criticism of *Roe* follows from his stunted conception of individual liberty. While recognizing that the Due Process Clause protects more than simple physical liberty, he then goes on to construe this Court's personal-liberty cases as establishing only a laundry list of particular rights, rather than a principled account of how these particular rights are grounded in a more general right of privacy. This constricted view is reinforced by THE CHIEF JUSTICE'S exclusive reliance on tradition as a source of fundamental rights.... Given THE CHIEF JUSTICE'S exclusive reliance on tradition, people using contraceptives seem the next likely candidate for his list of outcasts.

Even more shocking than THE CHIEF JUSTICE'S cramped notion of individual liberty is his complete omission of any discussion of the effects that compelled childbirth and motherhood have on women's lives. ... THE CHIEF JUSTICE'S view of the State's compelling interest in maternal health has less to do with health than it does with compelling women to be maternal.

. . .

Under his standard, States can ban abortion if that ban is rationally related to a legitimate state interest—a standard which the United States calls "deferential, but not toothless." Yet when pressed at oral argument to describe the teeth, the best protection that the Solicitor General could offer to women was that a prohibition, enforced by criminal penalties, *with no exception for the life of the mother*, "could raise very serious questions." Tr. of Oral Arg. 49. . . .

. . .

But, we are reassured, there is always the protection of the democratic process. While there is much to be praised about our democracy, our country since its founding has recognized that there are certain fundamental liberties that are not to be left to the whims of an election. A woman's right to reproductive choice is one of those fundamental liberties. Accordingly, that liberty need not seek refuge at the ballot box.

IV

In one sense, the Court's approach is worlds apart from that of THE CHIEF JUSTICE and JUSTICE SCALIA. And yet, in another sense, the distance between the two approaches is short—the distance is but a single vote.

I am 83 years old. I cannot remain on this Court forever, and when I do step down, the confirmation process for my successor well may focus on the issue before us today. That, I regret, may be exactly where the choice between the two worlds will be made.

CHIEF JUSTICE REHNQUIST, with whom JUSTICE WHITE, JUSTICE SCALIA, and JUSTICE THOMAS join, concurring in the judgment in part and dissenting in part.

The joint opinion, following its newly-minted variation on *stare decisis*, retains the outer shell of Roe v. Wade, 410 U.S. 113 (1973), but beats a wholesale retreat from the substance of that case. We believe that *Roe* was wrongly decided, and that it can and should be overruled consistently with our traditional approach to *stare decisis* in constitutional cases. We would uphold the challenged provisions of the Pennsylvania statute in their entirety.

I

. . . [P]etitioners insist that we reaffirm our decision in *Roe v. Wade, supra,* in which we held unconstitutional a Texas statute making it a crime to procure an abortion except to save the life of the mother.[1a] We

1a. [Footnote 1 in original] Two years after *Roe,* the West German constitutional court, by contrast, struck down a law liberalizing access to abortion on the grounds that life developing within the womb is constitutionally protected. Judgment of February 25, 1975, 39 BVerfGE 1 (translated in Jonas & Gorby, West German Abor-

agree with the Court of Appeals that our decision in *Roe* is not directly implicated by the Pennsylvania statute, which does not prohibit, but simply regulates, abortion. But, as the Court of Appeals found, the state of our post-*Roe* decisional law dealing with the regulation of abortion is confusing and uncertain, indicating that a reexamination of that line of cases is in order....

In *Roe v. Wade*, the Court recognized a "guarantee of personal privacy" which "is broad enough to encompass a woman's decision whether or not to terminate her pregnancy." 410 U.S., at 152–153. We are now of the view that, in terming this right fundamental, the Court in *Roe* read the earlier opinions upon which it based its decision much too broadly. Unlike marriage, procreation and contraception, abortion "involves the purposeful termination of potential life." Harris v. McRae, 448 U.S. 297, 325 (1980).... One cannot ignore the fact that a woman is not isolated in her pregnancy, and that the decision to abort necessarily involves the destruction of a fetus....

Nor do the historical traditions of the American people support the view that the right to terminate one's pregnancy is "fundamental." The common law which we inherited from England made abortion after "quickening" an offense. At the time of the adoption of the Fourteenth Amendment, statutory prohibitions or restrictions on abortion were commonplace.... By the turn of the century virtually every State had a law prohibiting or restricting abortion on its books.

We think, therefore,... that the Court was mistaken in *Roe* when it classified a woman's decision to terminate her pregnancy as a "fundamental right" that could be abridged only in a manner which withstood "strict scrutiny." In so concluding, we repeat the observation made in Bowers v. Hardwick, 478 U.S. 186 (1986): "Nor are we inclined to take a more expansive view of our authority to discover new fundamental rights imbedded in the Due Process Clause. The Court is most vulnerable and comes nearest to illegitimacy when it deals with judge-made constitutional law having little or no cognizable roots in the language or design of the Constitution."

· · ·

II

· · ·

In our view, authentic principles of *stare decisis* do not require that any portion of the reasoning in *Roe* be kept intact.... Erroneous decisions in constitutional cases are uniquely durable, because correction through legislative action, save for constitutional amendment, is impossible. It is therefore our duty to reconsider constitutional interpretations

tion Decision: A Contrast to *Roe v. Wade*, 9 J. Marshall J. Prac. & Proc. 605 (1976)). In 1988, the Canadian Supreme Court followed reasoning similar to that of *Roe* in striking down a law which restricted abortion. Morgentaler v. Queen, 1 S.C.R. 30, 44 D.L.R. 4th 385 (1988).

that "depart from a proper understanding" of the Constitution. *Garcia v. San Antonio Metropolitan Transit Authority*, 469 U.S., at 557....

The joint opinion discusses several *stare decisis* factors which, it asserts, point toward retaining a portion of *Roe*. Two of these factors are that the main "factual underpinning" of *Roe* has remained the same, and that its doctrinal foundation is no weaker now than it was in 1973. Of course, what might be called the basic facts which gave rise to *Roe* have remained the same—women become pregnant, there is a point somewhere, depending on medical technology, where a fetus becomes viable, and women give birth to children. But this is only to say that the same facts which gave rise to *Roe* will continue to give rise to similar cases. It is not a reason, in and of itself, why those cases must be decided in the same incorrect manner as was the first case to deal with the question....

... [A]ny traditional notion of reliance is not applicable here. ....

... The joint opinion thus turns to what can only be described as an unconventional—and unconvincing—notion of reliance, a view based on the surmise that the availability of abortion since *Roe* has led to "two decades of economic and social developments" that would be undercut if the error of *Roe* were recognized.... Surely it is dubious to suggest that women have reached their "places in society" in reliance upon *Roe*, rather than as a result of their determination to obtain higher education and compete with men in the job market, and of society's increasing recognition of their ability to fill positions that were previously thought to be reserved only for men.

In the end, having failed to put forth any evidence to prove any true reliance, the joint opinion's argument is based solely on generalized assertions about the national psyche, on a belief that the people of this country have grown accustomed to the *Roe* decision over the last 19 years and have "ordered their thinking and living around" it. As an initial matter, one might inquire how the joint opinion can view the "central holding" of *Roe* as so deeply rooted in our constitutional culture, when it so casually uproots and disposes of that same decision's trimester framework. Furthermore, at various points in the past, the same could have been said about this Court's erroneous decisions that the Constitution allowed "separate but equal" treatment of minorities, see Plessy v. Ferguson, 163 U.S. 537 (1896), or that "liberty" under the Due Process Clause protected "freedom of contract." See Adkins v. Children's Hospital of D.C., 261 U.S. 525 (1923); Lochner v. New York, 198 U.S. 45 (1905)....

Apparently realizing that conventional *stare decisis* principles do not support its position, the joint opinion advances a belief that retaining a portion of *Roe* is necessary to protect the "legitimacy" of this Court....

[T]he joint opinion goes on to state that when the Court "resolve[s] the sort of intensely divisive controversy reflected in *Roe* and those rare, comparable cases," its decision is exempt from reconsideration under established principles of *stare decisis* in constitutional cases....

... It appears to us very odd indeed that the joint opinion chooses as benchmarks two cases in which the Court chose not to adhere to erroneous constitutional precedent, but instead enhanced its stature by acknowledging and correcting its error, apparently in violation of the joint opinion's "legitimacy" principle. See *West Coast Hotel Co. v. Parrish, supra*; *Brown v. Board of Education, supra*. One might also wonder how it is that the joint opinion puts these, and not others, in the "intensely divisive" category, and how it assumes that these are the only two lines of cases of comparable dimension to *Roe*. There is no reason to think that either *Plessy* or *Lochner* produced the sort of public protest when they were decided that *Roe* did....

Taking the joint opinion on its own terms, we doubt that its distinction between *Roe,* on the one hand, and *Plessy* and *Lochner,* on the other, withstands analysis. The joint opinion acknowledges that the Court improved its stature by overruling *Plessy* in *Brown* on a deeply divisive issue. And our decision in *West Coast Hotel,* which overruled *Adkins v. Children's Hospital, supra*, and *Lochner,* was rendered at a time when Congress was considering President Franklin Roosevelt's proposal to "reorganize" this Court and enable him to name six additional Justices in the event that any member of the Court over the age of 70 did not elect to retire. It is difficult to imagine a situation in which the Court would face more intense opposition to a prior ruling than it did at that time, and, under the general principle proclaimed in the joint opinion, the Court seemingly should have responded to this opposition by stubbornly refusing to reexamine the *Lochner* rationale, lest it lose legitimacy by appearing to "overrule under fire."

· · ·

There is also a suggestion in the joint opinion that the propriety of overruling a "divisive" decision depends in part on whether "most people" would now agree that it should be overruled.... The Judicial Branch derives its legitimacy, not from following public opinion, but from deciding by its best lights whether legislative enactments of the popular branches of Government comport with the Constitution....

... The decision in *Roe* has engendered large demonstrations, including repeated marches on this Court and on Congress, both in opposition to and in support of that opinion. A decision either way on *Roe* can therefore be perceived as favoring one group or the other. But this perceived dilemma arises only if one assumes, as the joint opinion does, that the Court should make its decisions with a view toward speculative public perceptions. If one assumes instead, as the Court surely did in both *Brown* and *West Coast Hotel,* that the Court's legitimacy is enhanced by faithful interpretation of the Constitution irrespective of public opposition, such self-engendered difficulties may be put to one side....

The end result of the joint opinion's paeans of praise for legitimacy is the enunciation of a brand new standard for evaluating state regulation of a woman's right to abortion—the "undue burden" standard. As indicated above, *Roe v. Wade* adopted a "fundamental right" standard under which state regulations could survive only if they met the requirement of "strict scrutiny." While we disagree with that standard, it at least had a recognized basis in constitutional law at the time *Roe* was decided. The same cannot be said for the "undue burden" standard, which is created largely out of whole cloth by the authors of the joint opinion. It is a standard which even today does not command the support of a majority of this Court. And it will not, we believe, result in the sort of "simple limitation," easily applied, which the joint opinion anticipates. In sum, it is a standard which is not built to last.

... Because the undue burden standard is plucked from nowhere, the question of what is a "substantial obstacle" to abortion will undoubtedly engender a variety of conflicting views. For example, in the very matter before us now, the authors of the joint opinion would uphold Pennsylvania's 24–hour waiting period, concluding that a "particular burden" on some women is not a substantial obstacle. But the authors would at the same time strike down Pennsylvania's spousal notice provision, after finding that in a "large fraction" of cases the provision will be a substantial obstacle. And, while the authors conclude that the informed consent provisions do not constitute an "undue burden," JUSTICE STEVENS would hold that they do....

. . .

The sum of the joint opinion's labors in the name of stare decisis and "legitimacy" is this: *Roe v. Wade* stands as a sort of judicial Potemkin Village, which may be pointed out to passers by as a monument to the importance of adhering to precedent. But behind the facade, an entirely new method of analysis, without any roots in constitutional law, is imported to decide the constitutionality of state laws regulating abortion. Neither *stare decisis* nor "legitimacy" are truly served by such an effort.

... [T]he Constitution does not subject state abortion regulations to heightened scrutiny. A woman's interest in having an abortion is a form of liberty protected by the Due Process Clause, but States may regulate abortion procedures in ways rationally related to a legitimate state interest. Williamson v. Lee Optical of Okla., Inc., 348 U.S. 483, 491 (1955); cf. Stanley v. Illinois, 405 U.S. 645, 651–653 (1972). With this rule in mind, we examine each of the challenged provisions [and find each sustainable].

III

. . .

C

Section 3209 of the Act contains the spousal notification provision....

... Such a law requiring only notice to the husband "does not give any third party the legal right to make the [woman's] decision for her, or to prevent her from obtaining an abortion should she choose to have one performed." *Hodgson v. Minnesota, supra,* 497 U.S. at 496 (KENNEDY, J., concurring in judgment in part and dissenting in part).... The District Court found that the notification provision created a risk that some woman who would otherwise have an abortion will be prevented from having one. For example, petitioners argue, many notified husbands will prevent abortions through physical force, psychological coercion, and other types of threats. But Pennsylvania has incorporated exceptions in the notice provision in an attempt to deal with these problems. For instance, a woman need not notify her husband if the pregnancy is the result of a reported sexual assault, or if she has reason to believe that she would suffer bodily injury as a result of the notification. 18 Pa.Cons. Stat. § 3209(b) (1990). Furthermore, because this is a facial challenge to the Act,... it is not enough for petitioners to show that, in some "worst-case" circumstances, the notice provision will operate as a grant of veto power to husbands. *Ohio v. Akron Center for Reproductive Health,* 497 U.S., at 514. Because they are making a facial challenge to the provision, they must "show that no set of circumstances exists under which the [provision] would be valid."... *Ibid.* This they have failed to do.

The question before us is therefore whether the spousal notification requirement rationally furthers any legitimate state interests. We conclude that it does. First, a husband's interests in procreation within marriage and in the potential life of his unborn child are certainly substantial ones.... The State itself has legitimate interests both in protecting these interests of the father and in protecting the potential life of the fetus, and the spousal notification requirement is reasonably related to advancing those state interests. By providing that a husband will usually know of his spouse's intent to have an abortion, the provision makes it more likely that the husband will participate in deciding the fate of his unborn child, a possibility that might otherwise have been denied him. This participation might in some cases result in a decision to proceed with the pregnancy.

... The State also has a legitimate interest in promoting "the integrity of the marital relationship." 18 Pa.Cons.Stat. § 3209(a) (1990).... In our view, the spousal notice requirement is a rational attempt by the State to improve truthful communication between spouses and encourage collaborative decisionmaking, and thereby fosters marital integrity. [I]n our view, it is unrealistic to assume that every husband-wife relationship is either (1) so perfect that this type of truthful and important communication will take place as a matter of course, or (2) so imperfect that, upon notice, the husband will react selfishly, violently, or contrary to the best interests of his wife....

· · ·

JUSTICE SCALIA, with whom THE CHIEF JUSTICE, JUSTICE WHITE, and JUSTICE THOMAS join, concurring in the judgment in part and dissenting in part.

My views on this matter are [that the] permissibility of abortion, and the limitations upon it, are to be resolved like most important questions in our democracy: by citizens trying to persuade one another and then voting.... A State's choice between two positions on which reasonable people can disagree is constitutional even when (as is often the case) it intrudes upon a "liberty" in the absolute sense. Laws against bigamy, for example—which entire societies of reasonable people disagree with—intrude upon men and women's liberty to marry and live with one another. But bigamy happens not to be a liberty specially "protected" by the Constitution.

That is, quite simply, the issue in this case: not whether the power of a woman to abort her unborn child is a "liberty" in the absolute sense; or even whether it is a liberty of great importance to many women. Of course it is both. The issue is whether it is a liberty protected by the Constitution of the United States. I am sure it is not. I reach that conclusion not because of anything so exalted as my views concerning the "concept of existence, of meaning, of the universe, and of the mystery of human life." Rather, I reach it for the same reason I reach the conclusion that bigamy is not constitutionally protected—because of two simple facts: (1) the Constitution says absolutely nothing about it, and (2) the longstanding traditions of American society have permitted it to be legally proscribed.

...The Court's statement that it is "tempting" to acknowledge the authoritativeness of tradition in order to "cur[b] the discretion of federal judges," *ante,* at 847, is of course rhetoric rather than reality; no government official is "tempted" to place restraints upon his own freedom of action, which is why Lord Acton did not say "Power tends to purify." The Court's temptation is in the quite opposite and more natural direction—towards systematically eliminating checks upon its own power; and it succumbs.

... I will not swell the United States Reports with repetition of what I have said before; and applying the rational basis test, I would uphold the Pennsylvania statute in its entirety. I must, however, respond to a few of the more outrageous arguments in today's opinion, which it is beyond human nature to leave unanswered. I shall discuss each of them under a quotation from the Court's opinion to which they pertain.

> **"The inescapable fact is that adjudication of substantive due process claims may call upon the Court in interpreting the Constitution to exercise that same capacity which by tradition courts always have exercised: reasoned judgment."**
> *Ante,* at 849.

Assuming that the question before us is to be resolved at such a level of philosophical abstraction, in such isolation from the traditions of American society, as by simply applying "reasoned judgment," I do not see how that could possibly have produced the answer the Court arrived at in Roe v. Wade, 410 U.S. 113 (1973). Today's opinion describes the methodology of *Roe,* quite accurately, as weighing against the woman's interest the State's " 'important and legitimate interest in protecting the potentiality of human life.' " . . . But "reasoned judgment" does not begin by begging the question, as *Roe* and subsequent cases unquestionably did by assuming that what the State is protecting is the mere "potentiality of human life." . . . The whole argument of abortion opponents is that what the Court calls the fetus and what others call the unborn child is a human life. . . . Thus, whatever answer *Roe* came up with after conducting its "balancing" is bound to be wrong, unless it is correct that the human fetus is in some critical sense merely potentially human. There is of course no way to determine that as a legal matter; it is in fact a value judgment. Some societies have considered newborn children not yet human, or the incompetent elderly no longer so. . . .

The emptiness of the "reasoned judgment" that produced *Roe* is displayed in plain view by the fact that, after more than 19 years of effort by some of the brightest (and most determined) legal minds in the country, after more than 10 cases upholding abortion rights in this Court, and after dozens upon dozens of amicus briefs submitted in this and other cases, the best the Court can do to explain how it is that the word "liberty" *must* be thought to include the right to destroy human fetuses is to rattle off a collection of adjectives that simply decorate a value judgment and conceal a political choice. . . . Those adjectives might be applied, for example, to homosexual sodomy, polygamy, adult incest, and suicide, all of which are equally "intimate" and "deeply personal" decisions involving "personal autonomy and bodily integrity," and all of which can constitutionally be proscribed because it is our unquestionable constitutional tradition that they are proscribable. It is not reasoned judgment that supports the Court's decision; only personal predilection. . . .

"Liberty finds no refuge in a jurisprudence of doubt." *Ante,* at 844.

One might have feared to encounter this august and sonorous phrase in an opinion defending the real *Roe v. Wade,* rather than the revised version fabricated today by the authors of the joint opinion. The shortcomings of *Roe* did not include lack of clarity: Virtually all regulation of abortion before the third trimester was invalid. But to come across this phrase in the joint opinion—which calls upon federal district judges to apply an "undue burden" standard as doubtful in application as it is unprincipled in origin—is really more than one should have to bear.

. . .

The joint opinion explains that a state regulation imposes an "undue burden" if it "has the purpose or effect of placing a substantial obstacle in the path of a woman seeking an abortion of a nonviable fetus." An obstacle is "substantial," we are told, if it is "calculated, [not] to inform the woman's free choice, [but to] hinder it." This latter statement cannot possibly mean what it says. *Any* regulation of abortion that is intended to advance what the joint opinion concedes is the State's "substantial" interest in protecting unborn life will be "calculated [to] hinder" a decision to have an abortion. It thus seems more accurate to say that the joint opinion would uphold abortion regulations only if they do not *unduly* hinder the woman's decision. That, of course, brings us right back to square one: Defining an "undue burden" as an "undue hindrance" (or a "substantial obstacle") hardly "clarifies" the test. Consciously or not, the joint opinion's verbal shell game will conceal raw judicial policy choices concerning what is "appropriate" abortion legislation.

... I agree, indeed I have forcefully urged, that a law of general applicability which places only an incidental burden on a fundamental right does not infringe that right, ... but that principle does not establish the quite different (and quite dangerous) proposition that a law which directly regulates a fundamental right will not be found to violate the Constitution unless it imposes an "undue burden." It is that, of course, which is at issue here: Pennsylvania has consciously and directly regulated conduct that our cases have held is constitutionally protected. The appropriate analogy, therefore, is that of a state law requiring purchasers of religious books to endure a 24–hour waiting period, or to pay a nominal additional tax of 1 cent. The joint opinion cannot possibly be correct in suggesting that we would uphold such legislation on the ground that it does not impose a "substantial obstacle" to the exercise of First Amendment rights. The "undue burden" standard is not at all the generally applicable principle the joint opinion pretends it to be; rather, it is a unique concept created specially for this case, to preserve some judicial foothold in this ill-gotten territory. In claiming otherwise, the three Justices show their willingness to place all constitutional rights at risk in an effort to preserve what they deem the "central holding in *Roe*."

· · ·

To the extent I can discern *any* meaningful content in the "undue burden" standard as applied in the joint opinion, it appears to be that a State may not regulate abortion in such a way as to reduce significantly its incidence. The joint opinion repeatedly emphasizes that an important factor in the "undue burden" analysis is whether the regulation "prevent[s] a significant number of women from obtaining an abortion"; whether a "significant number of women ... are likely to be deterred from procuring an abortion"; and whether the regulation often "deters" women from seeking abortions. We are not told, however, what forms of "deterrence" are impermissible or what degree of success in deterrence is too much to be tolerated.... Thus, despite flowery rhetoric about the State's "substantial" and "profound" interest in "potential human life," and criticism of *Roe* for undervaluing that interest, the joint opinion permits the State to pursue that interest only so long as it is not too successful.... Reason finds no refuge in this jurisprudence of confusion.

"While we appreciate the weight of the arguments ...
**that *Roe* should be overruled, the reservations any of us may
have in reaffirming the central holding of *Roe* are outweighed by the explication of individual liberty we have
given combined with the force of *stare decisis*."** *Ante,* at 853.

The Court's reliance upon *stare decisis* can best be described as
contrived. It insists upon the necessity of adhering not to all of *Roe,* but
only to what it calls the "central holding." It seems to me that *stare
decisis* ought to be applied even to the doctrine of stare decisis, and I
confess never to have heard of this new, keep-what-you-want-and-throw-
away-the-rest version. I wonder whether, as applied to Marbury v.
Madison, 1 Cranch 137 (1803), for example, the new version of *stare
decisis* would be satisfied if we allowed courts to review the constitutionality of only those statutes that (like the one in *Marbury*) pertain to the
jurisdiction of the courts.

I am certainly not in a good position to dispute that the Court *has
saved* the "central holding" of *Roe,* since to do that effectively I would
have to know what the Court has saved, which in turn would require me
to understand (as I do not) what the "undue burden" test means. I must
confess, however, that I have always thought, and I think a lot of other
people have always thought, that the arbitrary trimester framework,
which the Court today discards, was quite as central to *Roe* as the
arbitrary viability test, which the Court today retains. It seems particularly ungrateful to carve the trimester framework out of the core of *Roe,*
since its very rigidity (in sharp contrast to the utter indeterminability of
the "undue burden" test) is probably the only reason the Court is able to
say, in urging *stare decisis*, that *Roe* "has in no sense proven 'unworkable.' " I suppose the Court is entitled to call a "central holding"
whatever it wants to call a "central holding"—which is, come to think of
it, perhaps one of the difficulties with this modified version of *stare
decisis*. I thought I might note, however, that the following portions of
Roe have not been saved:

• Under *Roe,* requiring that a woman seeking an abortion be
provided truthful information about abortion before giving informed
written consent is unconstitutional, if the information is designed to
influence her choice, *Thornburgh,* 476 U.S., at 759–765; *Akron I*, 462
U.S., at 442–445. Under the joint opinion's "undue burden" regime (as
applied today, at least) such a requirement is constitutional.

• Under *Roe,* requiring that information be provided by a doctor,
rather than by nonphysician counselors, is unconstitutional, *Akron I,
supra*, at 446–449. Under the "undue burden" regime (as applied today,
at least) it is not.

• Under *Roe,* requiring a 24–hour waiting period between the time
the woman gives her informed consent and the time of the abortion is
unconstitutional, *Akron I, supra*, at 449–451. Under the "undue burden"
regime (as applied today, at least) it is not.

• Under *Roe,* requiring detailed reports that include demographic data about each woman who seeks an abortion and various information about each abortion is unconstitutional, *Thornburgh, supra,* at 765–768. Under the "undue burden" regime (as applied today, at least) it generally is not.

> **"Where, in the performance of its judicial duties, the Court decides a case in such a way as to resolve the sort of intensely divisive controversy reflected in *Roe* ..., its decision has a dimension that the resolution of the normal case does not carry. It is the dimension present whenever the Court's interpretation of the Constitution calls the contending sides of a national controversy to end their national division by accepting a common mandate rooted in the Constitution."** *Ante,* at 866–67.

The Court's description of the place of *Roe* in the social history of the United States is unrecognizable. Not only did *Roe* not, as the Court suggests, *resolve* the deeply divisive issue of abortion; it did more than anything else to nourish it, by elevating it to the national level where it is infinitely more difficult to resolve....

... *Roe* fanned into life an issue that has inflamed our national politics in general, and has obscured with its smoke the selection of Justices to this Court in particular, ever since. And by keeping us in the abortion-umpiring business, it is the perpetuation of that disruption, rather than of any *pax Roeana,* that the Court's new majority decrees.

> **"[T]o overrule under fire ... would subvert the Court's legitimacy....**
>
> **"... To all those who will be ... tested by following, the Court implicitly undertakes to remain steadfast.... The promise of constancy, once given, binds its maker for as long as the power to stand by the decision survives and ... the commitment [is not] obsolete....**
>
> **"[The American people's] belief in themselves as ... a people [who aspire to live according to the rule of law] is not readily separable from their understanding of the Court invested with the authority to decide their constitutional cases and speak before all others for their constitutional ideals. If the Court's legitimacy should be undermined, then, so would the country be in its very ability to see itself through its constitutional ideals."** *Ante,* at 867–68.

The Imperial Judiciary lives. It is instructive to compare this Nietzschean vision of us unelected, life-tenured judges—leading a Volk who will be "tested by following," and whose very "belief in themselves" is mystically bound up in their "understanding" of a Court that "speaks before all others for their constitutional ideals"—with the somewhat more modest role envisioned for these lawyers by the Founders.

"The judiciary ... has ... no direction either of the strength or of the wealth of the society, and can take no active resolution whatever. It may truly be said to have neither Force nor Will but merely judgment...." The Federalist No. 78, 393–394 (G. Wills ed. 1982).

Or, again, to compare this ecstasy of a Supreme Court in which there is, especially on controversial matters, no shadow of change or hint of alteration ("There is a limit to the amount of error that can plausibly be imputed to prior courts," *ante,* at 866), with the more democratic views of a more humble man:

"[T]he candid citizen must confess that if the policy of the Government upon vital questions affecting the whole people is to be irrevocably fixed by decisions of the Supreme Court, ... the people will have ceased to be their own rulers, having to that extent practically resigned their Government into the hands of that eminent tribunal." A. Lincoln, First Inaugural Address (Mar. 4, 1861).

It is particularly difficult, in the circumstances of the present decision, to sit still for the Court's lengthy lecture upon the virtues of "constancy," of "remaining steadfast," of adhering to "principle." Among the five Justices who purportedly adhere to *Roe,* at most three agree upon the *principle* that constitutes adherence (the joint opinion's "undue burden" standard)—and that principle is inconsistent with *Roe.* To make matters worse, two of the three, in order thus to remain steadfast, had to abandon previously stated positions. It is beyond me how the Court expects these accommodations to be accepted "as grounded truly in principle, not as compromises with social and political pressures having, as such, no bearing on the principled choices that the Court is obliged to make.". . .

. . .

... [T]he notion that the Court must adhere to a decision for as long as the decision faces "great opposition" and the Court is "under fire" acquires a character of almost czarist arrogance. We are offended by these marchers who descend upon us, every year on the anniversary of *Roe,* to protest our saying that the Constitution requires what our society has never thought the Constitution requires. These people who refuse to be "tested by following" must be taught a lesson. We have no Cossacks, but at least we can stubbornly refuse to abandon an erroneous opinion that we might otherwise change—to show how little they intimidate us.. . .

. . .

... [T]he American people love democracy and the American people are not fools. As long as this Court thought (and the people thought) that we Justices were doing essentially lawyers' work up here—reading text and discerning our society's traditional understanding of that text— the public pretty much left us alone. Texts and traditions are facts to study, not convictions to demonstrate about. But if in reality our process of constitutional adjudication consists primarily of making *value judg-*

ments, then a free and intelligent people's attitude towards us can be expected to be (ought to be) quite different. The people know that their value judgments are quite as good as those taught in any law school— maybe better. If, indeed, the "liberties" protected by the Constitution are, as the Court says, undefined and unbounded, then the people should demonstrate, to protest that we do not implement their values instead of ours. Not only that, but confirmation hearings for new Justices should deteriorate into question-and-answer sessions in which Senators go through a list of their constituents' most favored and most disfavored alleged constitutional rights, and seek the nominee's commitment to support or oppose them. Value judgments, after all, should be voted on, not dictated; and if our Constitution has somehow accidently committed them to the Supreme Court, at least we can have a sort of plebiscite each time a new nominee to that body is put forward. . . .

. . .

There comes vividly to mind a portrait by Emanuel Leutze that hangs in the Harvard Law School: Roger Brooke Taney, painted in 1859, the 82d year of his life, the 24th of his Chief Justiceship, the second after his opinion in *Dred Scott*. He is all in black, sitting in a shadowed red armchair, left hand resting upon a pad of paper in his lap, right hand hanging limply, almost lifelessly, beside the inner arm of the chair. He sits facing the viewer, and staring straight out. There seems to be on his face, and in his deep-set eyes, an expression of profound sadness and disillusionment. Perhaps he always looked that way, even when dwelling upon the happiest of thoughts. But those of us who know how the lustre of his great Chief Justiceship came to be eclipsed by *Dred Scott* cannot help believing that he had that case—its already apparent consequences for the Court, and its soon-to-be-played-out consequences for the Nation—burning on his mind. I expect that two years earlier he, too, had thought himself "calling the contending sides of national controversy to end their national division by accepting a common mandate rooted in the Constitution."

. . .

We should get out of this area, where we have no right to be, and where we do neither ourselves nor the country any good by remaining.

———

Questions and Comments

A. Looking at *Casey* as a doctrinal exposition of constitutional law, we might ask questions such as the following:

1. Precisely how (if at all) did *Casey* change the law? For example, consider, after *Casey,* whether and to what extent the practical power of the state to prevent or discourage abortion has changed with respect to (a) a wealthy, educated, adult woman in her first month of pregnancy who has

firmly determined to have an abortion; (b) a destitute, educated, adult woman in her first month of pregnancy who firmly desires to have an abortion but has no funds to pay for one; (c) a median income, poorly educated adult woman in her first month of pregnancy who is unsure whether to have an abortion or to continue the pregnancy to birth.

2.   Although the *Casey* joint opinion says it is rejecting the *Roe* trimester approach, viability generally occurs at the outset of the third trimester and the *Casey* joint opinion appears to continue *Roe's* treatment of post-viability/third trimester abortions. Consequently, the doctrinal changes effected by *Casey* appear to be (a) to collapse the first two trimesters into one pre-viability period and (b) to apply to all pre-viability abortions an "undue burden" standard.[2] What new facts or new theories or new insights required these Justices, assertedly highly attuned to the value of *stare decisis*, to make these changes?

3.   What is an "undue burden"? Why was the husband notification, but not the 24-hour waiting period, an undue burden? Did opponents of the law simply fail to present sufficient evidence of the costs a 24-hour waiting period imposes? Or is the point that, for these purposes, burdens are not measured by economic costs but by physical risks? If Pennsylvania levied a $75 tax on each abortion, would that be an undue burden?

4.   The Joint Opinion seems to rest, in some measure, upon the conclusions that the state has a legitimate interest in potential life and that this interest was undervalued in *Roe* and its progeny. Yet the Joint Opinion also seems to conclude (or assume) that this state interest becomes more potent (or more legitimate) as the pregnancy progresses. Therefore, for example, post-viability abortions may be much more closely regulated for the sole reason that the state's countervailing interest is much higher. Why does the state's interest in potential life become stronger when the life is capable of existence outside the womb? Why isn't the state's interest in potential life at its highest when the life can be sustained only if it remains in the womb?

5.   The Joint Opinion and the opinion of Justice Blackmun seek to describe with greater precision the basis for *Roe's* conclusion that a woman's decision whether or not to seek an abortion is a constitutionally protected right. Do these opinions equally well explain why homosexual acts, between consenting adults, are constitutionally protected? What about bigamy, or polygamy? To what extent do these opinions rest on equality concerns; to what extent on personal liberty? Would the reasoning in Chief Justice Rehnquist's opinion on the derivation of constitutional rights permit the conclusion that the Constitution protects the use of contraceptives? or the migration of persons from state to state?

6.   We don't know of a single case where the Supreme Court said, "The existing interpretation of this aspect of the Constitution is wrong, but, the

2.   It may be helpful to remember that, if the Justices who composed the *Casey* Court were asked whether the constitutional law of abortion rights should include an "undue burden" test, they would probably vote, 6–3, that it should not. (The six would be Rehnquist and the three who joined him, plus Blackmun and Stevens, although for different reasons.) The undue burden test became the controlling doctrine, however, because only if at least some members of the plurality opinion in *Casey* could be convinced that an abortion regulation were an undue burden would the regulation be invalidated.

principle of *stare decisis* nevertheless compels us to adhere to it." Consequently, the Joint Opinion's discussion of *stare decisis*, and its role in defining the Court's legitimacy, is difficult to evaluate. Does the Joint Opinion (which, in the name of *stare decisis*, overrules *Roe*'s trimester framework and several interpretations of *Roe* written by the same Justices who sat on the *Roe* Court) mean to establish a new principle of precedent: that the precedent which *stare decisis* protects is the subsequently discovered "central holding" of the case rather than the precise results the opinion reaches, the rules of law it announces, or the reasoning process it employs?

B.   Looking at *Casey* as the product of an institution, with its own personnel and procedures, we might ask questions such as the following. It is the purpose of the remaining chapters to explore these types of questions.

    1.   Should *Casey* be understood principally as the outcome, not of intellectual or legal debates over the meaning of "liberty" and "due process," but of fierce contests between a Republican Presidency and a majority Democratic Senate over control of the Supreme Court? Is *Casey* the most visible result of the Senate's rejection of President Reagan's nomination of Judge Robert Bork (which led to the nomination of Justice Kennedy)? Is Justice Scalia correct that the Court's adherence to *Roe* legitimizes turning confirmation hearings into plebiscites on value judgments?

    2.   Petitioners filed their certiorari petition far in advance of its due date. What could they seek to gain by this strategy? Respondents filed their response to the petition for certiorari in less than their allotted time, thus further increasing the chance that the Court would hear and decide *Casey* before the 1992 elections. Why would they choose to do this? Can the Court appropriately consider the potential impact on an upcoming election in deciding whether to grant certiorari and when to schedule the case for argument? When all the *Casey* dust has settled, the result is an opinion that, like the Court of Appeals' opinion, applies an "undue burden" test and upholds all but one of the contested laws. Why, then, did the Court decide to hear the case in the first place? Which Justices do you think voted to grant certiorari? Consider the possibility of a strategic miscalculation in such decisions.

    3.   Footnote 11 of Justice Blackmun's opinion (omitted above) changed from its original form in *U.S. Law Week*, which publishes Supreme Court opinions immediately after they are announced. In *Law Week*, Blackmun referred to Chief Justice Rehnquist's opinion as a "plurality opinion." 60 *U.S.L.W.* 4825 n. 11 (June 30, 1992) ("Obviously, I do not share the plurality's views of homosexuality as sexual deviance.") By the time Blackmun's opinion was published in the official reports, he referred to that opinion as "The Chief Justice's." 505 U.S. at 940 n.11 ("Obviously, I do not share The Chief Justice's views of homosexuality as sexual deviance.") What do these facts suggest about the likely evolution of the decision-making process in this case? See the discussions in Chapters Four and Five, below, regarding the cases leading up to *Casey*, particularly Webster v. Reproductive Health Services, 492 U.S. 490 (1989).

    4.   Given what we now know about the various justices' attitudes about the issues posed by *Casey*, what do you think would have been the elements of a truly effective amicus curiae brief (a) in support of the Pennsylvania

statutes, (b) in opposition to those statutes? Would such a brief be concerned principally with arguing law or with presenting facts? In whose name(s) would it be submitted?

5.   The Joint Opinion dwells at some length on the Court's legitimacy in the eyes of the public. Does that discussion contribute to or detract from the Court's legitimacy? To what extent does the Court gain public support because of the procedures it employs? Consider, for example, the role of oral argument, of expressing judgments through written legal opinions, of conducting most of the Court's business in secret, of managing its own docket.

6.   *Roe* not only helped to make abortion services legally available, but it also generated a backlash, giving momentum to the pro-life (anti-abortion) movement. It is now more than 15 years since the *Casey* decision. What effect did the plurality in *Casey* hope their opinion would have on the controversy over *Roe*? What effects (if any) do you think the *Casey* opinions have had on pro-life and pro-choice activists? On public views? On legislators considering abortion laws? After *Casey*, the anti-abortion movement focused on efforts to ban particular types of abortions. See Chapter Four (C) below. Compare Stenberg v. Carhart, 530 U.S. 914 (2000)(invalidating state "partial birth" abortion law for, *inter alia*, failure to include a health exception for the mother) with Gonzales v. Carhart, 127 S.Ct. 1610 (2007) (upholding federal "partial birth" abortion ban, even though it lacked a health exception for the mother). What, if any, effects—on activists, citizens and lawmakers—would you expect *Gonzales v. Carhart* to produce? Is it appropriate, or not, for Justices to consider likely political reactions to their opinions in deciding how to vote, or what to write?

7.   The role of *stare decisis* might be used as a lens to examine one of the recurring questions about Supreme Court decisionmaking: to what extent is it based on "law", to what extent on the Justices' policy views or other factors? Should the Court's decisions be understood within a legal model of decision-making, as the development and application of legal doctrine? Or instead as the product of particular Justices' attitudes, policy preferences, or ideological views—within an "attitudinal model"? For a helpful exploration, see Howard Gillman, *What's Law Got to Do with It? Judicial Behavioralists Test the "Legal Model" of Judicial Decision Making*, 26 Law & Social Inquiry 465, 485–96 (2001) (reviewing, Harold J. Spaeth & Jeffrey A. Segal, *Majority Rule or Minority Will: Adherence to Precedent on the Supreme Court* (1999)). Spaeth and Segal, prominent scholars who are proponents of the attitudinal model as an account of judging, tested the "legal model" by examining whether dissenting Justices in major cases later treat the case as a precedent constraining their decisions.[3] Finding that they did so in only a small percentage (11.9%) of reviewed votes, Spaeth and Segal regard this as further evidence for the "attitudinal" or behavioralist model. Gillman's review raises a number of questions. First, he notes, jurists and scholars may not agree that strict adherence to *stare decisis* in the Supreme Court is legally appropriate, much less a useful criterion for measuring

3. Note that under this methodology, *Casey* could not serve as a full test of the *stare decisis* effects of *Roe* as a constraint because O'Connor, Kennedy, and Souter were not on the Court that decided *Roe*; of the original *Roe* Court, only Justice Blackmun and Chief Justice Rehnquist were still on the Court when *Casey* was decided, and each voted in accord with his original *Roe* vote.

whether judges are judging according to law. *Id.* at 481–82. Second, he argues, there is a distinction between a view of law as an "external constraint" (which may motivate much of the behavioralist and attitudinalist research) and a view of law as a "state of mind within a practice." These distinctions, he suggests, are important to understanding what a legal model of decisionmaking entails, a necessary predicate to testing for it; understanding a legal model based on law "as a state of mind within a practice" might require researchers to focus, for example, on whether judges view themselves as constrained legal interpreters or as more freewheeling politicians. *Id.* at 485-96. A larger point that emerges from Gillman's review is the difficulty, in some cases, of distinguishing between judging according to one's own preferences and judging according to the law. On Gillman's account, would Rehnquist's failure to treat *Roe* as binding precedent, given his original dissent, be evidence of a lack of legal constraint? or of intellectual consistency?

2. LAWRENCE V. TEXAS, 539 U.S. 558 (2003)

[In 1986, a narrowly divided 5–4 Court had upheld the criminal conviction of a gay man for consensual sex with another adult male, in a private home, under the Georgia anti-sodomy statute. Bowers v. Hardwick, 478 U.S. 186 (1986). The Court rejected constitutional arguments that such conduct was constitutionally protected liberty that the state could not impinge on absent compelling interests. One year later, Justice Lewis Powell retired from the Court, and in 1990, acknowledged that he viewed his having joined the majority in *Bowers* as a mistake. See Nat Hentoff, *Infamous Sodomy Law Struck Down: 'What Was the State of Georgia Doing in Hardwick's Bedroom?'*, Village Voice, December 16–22 1998, at 30 (" 'I think I probably made a mistake in the *Hardwick* case,' Powell said. Later, Powell added, 'I do think it was inconsistent in a general way with *Roe*. When I had the opportunity to reread the opinions a few months later, I thought the dissent had the better of the arguments.' "); see also John C. Jeffries, *Justice Lewis F. Powell, Jr.,* 530 (1995). As you will see, *Casey* and the abortion line of decisions play an important role in this distinct area of controversy. After the *Lawrence* decision, we again pose two sets of question: the first designed to explore the structure of the opinions in *Lawrence*, their relationship to *Casey* and their implications for the future; the second designed to probe some institutional differences between the *Lawrence* and the *Casey* decisions.]

JUSTICE KENNEDY delivered the opinion of the Court.

Liberty protects the person from unwarranted government intrusions into a dwelling or other private places. In our tradition the State is not omnipresent in the home. And there are other spheres of our lives and existence, outside the home, where the State should not be a dominant presence. Freedom extends beyond spatial bounds. Liberty presumes an autonomy of self that includes freedom of thought, belief, expression, and certain intimate conduct. The instant case involves liberty of the person both in its spatial and more transcendent dimensions.

I

The question before the Court is the validity of a Texas statute making it a crime for two persons of the same sex to engage in certain intimate sexual conduct.

In Houston, Texas, officers of the Harris County Police Department were dispatched to a private residence in response to a reported weapons disturbance. They entered an apartment where one of the petitioners, John Geddes Lawrence, resided. The right of the police to enter does not seem to have been questioned. The officers observed Lawrence and another man, Tyron Garner, engaging in a sexual act. The two petitioners were arrested, held in custody over night, and charged and convicted before a Justice of the Peace.

... The applicable state law is Tex. Penal Code Ann. § 21.06(a) (2003). It provides: "A person commits an offense if he engages in deviate sexual intercourse with another individual of the same sex." The statute defines "deviate sexual intercourse" [to include anal sex]....

The petitioners ... challenged the statute as a violation of the Equal Protection Clause of the Fourteenth Amendment and of a like provision of the Texas Constitution. Tex. Const., Art. 1, § 3a. Those contentions were rejected. The petitioners, having entered a plea of *nolo contendere*, were each fined $200 and assessed court costs of $141.25.

[After an en banc hearing which considered the petitioners' federal constitutional arguments under both the Equal Protection and Due Process Clauses of the Fourteenth Amendment, the Texas Court of Appeals rejected the constitutional arguments and affirmed the convictions, deeming] our decision in Bowers v. Hardwick, 478 U.S. 186 (1986), to be controlling on the federal due process aspect of the case. *Bowers* then being authoritative, this was proper.

We granted certiorari, 537 U.S. 1044 (2002), to consider three questions:

> 1. Whether petitioners' criminal convictions under the Texas "Homosexual Conduct" law—which criminalizes sexual intimacy by same-sex couples, but not identical behavior by different-sex couples—violate the Fourteenth Amendment guarantee of equal protection of laws?

> 2. Whether petitioners' criminal convictions for adult consensual sexual intimacy in the home violate their vital interests in liberty and privacy protected by the Due Process Clause of the Fourteenth Amendment?

> 3. Whether *Bowers v. Hardwick, supra,* should be overruled?"

The petitioners were adults at the time of the alleged offense. Their conduct was in private and consensual.

II

We conclude the case should be resolved by determining whether the petitioners were free as adults to engage in the private conduct in the exercise of their liberty under the Due Process Clause of the Fourteenth Amendment to the Constitution. For this inquiry we deem it necessary to reconsider the Court's holding in *Bowers*.

There are broad statements of the substantive reach of liberty under the Due Process Clause in earlier cases, including Pierce v. Society of Sisters, 268 U.S. 510 (1925), and Meyer v. Nebraska, 262 U.S. 390 (1923); but the most pertinent beginning point is our decision in Griswold v. Connecticut, 381 U.S. 479 (1965).

In *Griswold* the Court invalidated a state law prohibiting the use of drugs or devices of contraception and counseling or aiding and abetting the use of contraceptives. The Court described the protected interest as a right to privacy and placed emphasis on the marriage relation and the protected space of the marital bedroom.

After *Griswold* it was established that the right to make certain decisions regarding sexual conduct extends beyond the marital relationship. In Eisenstadt v. Baird, 405 U.S. 438 (1972), the Court invalidated a law prohibiting the distribution of contraceptives to unmarried persons. The case was decided under the Equal Protection Clause; but with respect to unmarried persons, the Court went on to state the fundamental proposition that the law impaired the exercise of their personal rights. It quoted from the statement of the Court of Appeals finding the law to be in conflict with fundamental human rights, and it followed with this statement of its own:

> "It is true that in *Griswold* the right of privacy in question inhered in the marital relationship.... If the right of privacy means anything, it is the right of the individual, married or single, to be free from unwarranted governmental intrusion into matters so fundamentally affecting a person as the decision whether to bear or beget a child."

The opinions in *Griswold* and *Eisenstadt* were part of the background for the decision in Roe v. Wade, 410 U.S. 113 (1973). As is well known, the case involved a challenge to the Texas law prohibiting abortions, but the laws of other States were affected as well. Although the Court held the woman's rights were not absolute, her right to elect an abortion did have real and substantial protection as an exercise of her liberty under the Due Process Clause. The Court cited cases that protect spatial freedom and cases that go well beyond it. *Roe* recognized the right of a woman to make certain fundamental decisions affecting her destiny and confirmed once more that the protection of liberty under the Due Process Clause has a substantive dimension of fundamental significance in defining the rights of the person.

In Carey v. Population Services Int'l, 431 U.S. 678 (1977), the Court confronted a New York law forbidding sale or distribution of contraceptive devices to persons under 16 years of age. Although there was no single opinion for the Court, the law was invalidated. Both *Eisenstadt* and *Carey*, as well as the holding and rationale in *Roe*, confirmed that the reasoning of *Griswold* could not be confined to the protection of rights of married adults. This was the state of the law with respect to some of the most relevant cases when the Court considered *Bowers v. Hardwick*.

The facts in *Bowers* had some similarities to the instant case. A police officer, whose right to enter seems not to have been in question, observed Hardwick, in his own bedroom, engaging in intimate sexual conduct with another adult male.... The conduct was in violation of a Georgia statute making it a criminal offense to engage in sodomy. One difference between the two cases is that the Georgia statute prohibited the conduct whether or not the participants were of the same sex, while the Texas statute, as we have seen, applies only to participants of the same sex. Hardwick was not prosecuted, but he brought an action in federal court to declare the state statute invalid. He alleged he was a practicing homosexual and that the criminal prohibition violated rights guaranteed to him by the Constitution. The Court, in an opinion by Justice White, sustained the Georgia law. Chief Justice Burger and Justice Powell joined the opinion of the Court and filed separate, concurring opinions. Four Justices dissented. 478 U.S., at 199 (opinion of Blackmun, J., joined by Brennan, Marshall, and Stevens JJ.); *id.*, at 214 (opinion of Stevens, J., joined by Brennan and Marshall, JJ.).

The Court began its substantive discussion in *Bowers* as follows: "The issue presented is whether the Federal Constitution confers a fundamental right upon homosexuals to engage in sodomy and hence invalidates the laws of the many States that still make such conduct illegal and have done so for a very long time." That statement, we now conclude, discloses the Court's own failure to appreciate the extent of the liberty at stake. To say that the issue in *Bowers* was simply the right to engage in certain sexual conduct demeans the claim the individual put forward, just as it would demean a married couple were it to be said marriage is simply about the right to have sexual intercourse. The laws involved in *Bowers* and here are, to be sure, statutes that purport to do no more than prohibit a particular sexual act. Their penalties and purposes, though, have more far-reaching consequences, touching upon the most private human conduct, sexual behavior, and in the most private of places, the home. The statutes do seek to control a personal relationship that, whether or not entitled to formal recognition in the law, is within the liberty of persons to choose without being punished as criminals.

This, as a general rule, should counsel against attempts by the State, or a court, to define the meaning of the relationship or to set its boundaries absent injury to a person or abuse of an institution the law protects. It suffices for us to acknowledge that adults may choose to enter upon this relationship in the confines of their homes and their own private lives and still retain their dignity as free persons. When sexuality finds overt expression in intimate conduct with another person, the conduct can be but one element in a personal bond that is more enduring. The liberty protected by the Constitution allows homosexual persons the right to make this choice.

Having misapprehended the claim of liberty there presented to it, and thus stating the claim to be whether there is a fundamental right to engage in consensual sodomy, the *Bowers* Court said: "Proscriptions against that conduct have ancient roots." In academic writings, and in many of the scholarly amicus briefs filed to assist the Court in this case, there are fundamental criticisms of the historical premises relied upon by the majority and concurring opinions in Bowers. Brief for Cato Institute as Amicus Curiae 16–17; Brief for American Civil Liberties Union et al. as Amici Curiae 15–21; Brief for Professors of History et al. as Amici Curiae 3–10. We need not enter this debate in the attempt to reach a definitive historical judgment, but the following considerations counsel against adopting the definitive conclusions upon which *Bowers* placed such reliance.

At the outset it should be noted that there is no longstanding history in this country of laws directed at homosexual conduct as a distinct matter. Beginning in colonial times there were prohibitions of sodomy derived from the English criminal laws passed in the first instance by the Reformation Parliament of 1533. The English prohibition was understood to include relations between men and women as well as relations between men and men. See, e.g., King v. Wiseman, 92 Eng. Rep. 774, 775 (K. B. 1718) (interpreting "mankind" in Act of 1533 as including women and girls). Nineteenth-century commentators similarly read American sodomy, buggery, and crime-against-nature statutes as criminalizing certain relations between men and women and between men and men. [Citations omitted.] The absence of legal prohibitions focusing on homosexual conduct may be explained in part by noting that according to some scholars the concept of the homosexual as a distinct category of person did not emerge until the late 19th century. See, e.g., J. Katz, *The Invention of Heterosexuality* 10 (1995); J. D'Emilio & E. Freedman, *Intimate Matters: A History of Sexuality in America* 121 (2d ed. 1997) ("The modern terms *homosexuality* and *heterosexuality* do not apply to an era that had not yet articulated these distinctions"). Thus early American sodomy laws were not directed at homosexuals as such but instead sought to prohibit nonprocreative sexual activity more generally. This does not suggest approval of homosexual conduct. It does tend to show that this particular form of conduct was not thought of as a separate category from like conduct between heterosexual persons.

Laws prohibiting sodomy do not seem to have been enforced against consenting adults acting in private. A substantial number of sodomy prosecutions and convictions for which there are surviving records were for predatory acts against those who could not or did not consent, as in the case of a minor or the victim of an assault. As to these, one purpose for the prohibitions was to ensure there would be no lack of coverage if a predator committed a sexual assault that did not constitute rape as defined by the criminal law. Thus the model sodomy indictments presented in a 19th-century treatise ... addressed the predatory acts of an adult man against a minor girl or minor boy. Instead of targeting relations between consenting adults in private, 19th-century sodomy prosecutions typically involved relations between men and minor girls or minor boys, relations between adults involving force, relations between adults implicating disparity in status, or relations between men and animals.

To the extent that there were any prosecutions for the acts in question, 19th-century evidence rules imposed a burden that would make a conviction more difficult to obtain even taking into account the problems always inherent in prosecuting consensual acts committed in private. Under then-prevailing standards, a man could not be convicted of sodomy based upon testimony of a consenting partner, because the partner was considered an accomplice. A partner's testimony, however, was admissible if he or she had not consented to the act or was a minor, and therefore incapable of consent. [Citations omitted.] The rule may explain in part the infrequency of these prosecutions. In all events that infrequency makes it difficult to say that society approved of a rigorous and systematic punishment of the consensual acts committed in private and by adults. The longstanding criminal prohibition of homosexual sodomy upon which the *Bowers* decision placed such reliance is as consistent with a general condemnation of nonprocreative sex as it is with an established tradition of prosecuting acts because of their homosexual character.

... Despite the absence of prosecutions, there may have been periods in which there was public criticism of homosexuals as such and an insistence that the criminal laws be enforced to discourage their practices. But far from possessing "ancient roots," *Bowers*, 478 U.S., at 192, American laws targeting same-sex couples did not develop until the last third of the 20th century. The reported decisions concerning the prosecution of consensual, homosexual sodomy between adults for the years 1880–1995 are not always clear in the details, but a significant number involved conduct in a public place. See Brief for American Civil Liberties Union et al. as Amici Curiae 14–15, and n. 18.

It was not until the 1970's that any State singled out same-sex relations for criminal prosecution, and only nine States have done so. [Citations omitted.] Post–*Bowers* even some of these States did not adhere to the policy of suppressing homosexual conduct. Over the course of the last decades, States with same-sex prohibitions have moved toward abolishing them. [Citations omitted.]

In summary, the historical grounds relied upon in *Bowers* are more complex than the majority opinion and the concurring opinion by Chief Justice Burger indicate. Their historical premises are not without doubt and, at the very least, are overstated.

It must be acknowledged, of course, that the Court in *Bowers* was making the broader point that for centuries there have been powerful voices to condemn homosexual conduct as immoral. The condemnation has been shaped by religious beliefs, conceptions of right and acceptable behavior, and respect for the traditional family. For many persons these are not trivial concerns but profound and deep convictions accepted as ethical and moral principles to which they aspire and which thus determine the course of their lives. These considerations do not answer the question before us, however. The issue is whether the majority may use the power of the State to enforce these views on the whole society through operation of the criminal law. "Our obligation is to define the liberty of all, not to mandate our own moral code." Planned Parenthood of Southeastern Pa. v. Casey, 505 U.S. 833, 850 (1992).

Chief Justice Burger joined the opinion for the Court in *Bowers* and further explained his views as follows: "Decisions of individuals relating to homosexual conduct have been subject to state intervention throughout the history of Western civilization. Condemnation of those practices is firmly rooted in Judeao–Christian moral and ethical standards." As with Justice White's assumptions about history, scholarship casts some doubt on the sweeping nature of the statement by Chief Justice Burger as it pertains to private homosexual conduct between consenting adults. See, e.g., Eskridge, *Hardwick and Historiography*, 1999 U. Ill. L. Rev. 631, 656. In all events we think that our laws and traditions in the past half century are of most relevance here. These references show an emerging awareness that liberty gives substantial protection to adult persons in deciding how to conduct their private lives in matters pertaining to sex. "History and tradition are the starting point but not in all cases the ending point of the substantive due process inquiry." County of Sacramento v. Lewis, 523 U.S. 833, 857 (1998) (Kennedy, J., concurring).

This emerging recognition should have been apparent when *Bowers* was decided. In 1955 the American Law Institute promulgated the Model Penal Code and made clear that it did not recommend or provide for "criminal penalties for consensual sexual relations conducted in private." ALI, Model Penal Code § 213.2, Comment 2, p. 372 (1980). It justified its decision on three grounds: (1) The prohibitions undermined respect for the law by penalizing conduct many people engaged in; (2) the statutes regulated private conduct not harmful to others; and (3) the laws were arbitrarily enforced and thus invited the danger of blackmail. ALI, Model Penal Code, Commentary 277–280 (Tent. Draft No. 4, 1955). In 1961 Illinois changed its laws to conform to the Model Penal Code. Other States soon followed. Brief for Cato Institute as Amicus Curiae 15–16.

In *Bowers*, the Court referred to the fact that before 1961 all 50 States had outlawed sodomy, and that at the time of the Court's decision 24 States and the District of Columbia had sodomy laws. 478 U.S., at 192–193. Justice Powell pointed out that these prohibitions often were being ignored, however. Georgia, for instance, had not sought to enforce its law for decades. *Id.*, at 197–198, n. 2 ("The history of nonenforcement suggests the moribund character today of laws criminalizing this type of private, consensual conduct").

The sweeping references by Chief Justice Burger to the history of Western civilization and to Judeo–Christian moral and ethical standards did not take account of other authorities pointing in an opposite direction. A committee advising the British Parliament recommended in 1957 repeal of laws punishing homosexual conduct. The Wolfenden Report: Report of the Committee on Homosexual Offenses and Prostitution (1963). Parliament enacted the substance of those recommendations 10 years later. Sexual Offences Act 1967, § 1.

Of even more importance, almost five years before *Bowers* was decided, the European Court of Human Rights considered a case with parallels to *Bowers* and to today's case. An adult male resident in Northern Ireland alleged he was a practicing homosexual who desired to engage in consensual homosexual conduct. The laws of Northern Ireland forbade him that right. He alleged that he had been questioned, his home had been searched, and he feared criminal prosecution. The court held that the laws proscribing the conduct were invalid under the European Convention on Human Rights. Dudgeon v. United Kingdom, 45 Eur. Ct. H. R. (1981) ¶ 52. Authoritative in all countries that are members of the Council of Europe (21 nations then, 45 nations now), the decision is at odds with the premise in *Bowers* that the claim put forward was insubstantial in our Western civilization.

In our own constitutional system the deficiencies in *Bowers* became even more apparent in the years following its announcement. The 25 States with laws prohibiting the relevant conduct referenced in the *Bowers* decision are reduced now to 13, of which 4 enforce their laws only against homosexual conduct. In those States where sodomy is still proscribed, whether for same-sex or heterosexual conduct, there is a pattern of nonenforcement with respect to consenting adults acting in private. The State of Texas admitted in 1994 that as of that date it had not prosecuted anyone under those circumstances. State v. Morales, 869 S.W.2d 941, 943, 37 Tex. Sup. Ct. J. 390.

Two principal cases decided after *Bowers* cast its holding into even more doubt. In Planned Parenthood of Southeastern Pa. v. Casey, 505 U.S. 833 (1992), the Court reaffirmed the substantive force of the liberty protected by the Due Process Clause. The *Casey* decision again confirmed that our laws and tradition afford constitutional protection to personal decisions relating to marriage, procreation, contraception, family relationships, child rearing, and education. In explaining the respect the Constitution demands for the autonomy of the person in making these choices, we stated as follows:

> "These matters, involving the most intimate and personal choices a person may make in a lifetime, choices central to personal dignity and autonomy, are central to the liberty protected by the Fourteenth Amendment. At the heart of liberty is the right to define one's own concept of existence, of meaning, of the universe, and of the mystery of human life. Beliefs about these matters could not define the attributes of personhood were they formed under compulsion of the State."

Persons in a homosexual relationship may seek autonomy for these purposes, just as heterosexual persons do. The decision in would deny them this right.

The second post-*Bowers* case of principal relevance is Romer v. Evans, 517 U.S. 620 (1996). There the Court struck down class-based legislation directed at homosexuals as a violation of the Equal Protection Clause. *Romer* invalidated an amendment to Colorado's constitution which named as a solitary class persons who were homosexuals, lesbians, or bisexual either by "orientation, conduct, practices or relationships," and deprived them of protection under state antidiscrimination laws. We concluded that the provision was "born of animosity toward the class of persons affected" and further that it had no rational relation to a legitimate governmental purpose. *Id.*, at 634.

As an alternative argument in this case, counsel for the petitioners and some amici contend that *Romer* provides the basis for declaring the Texas statute invalid under the Equal Protection Clause. That is a tenable argument, but we conclude the instant case requires us to address whether *Bowers* itself has continuing validity. Were we to hold the statute invalid under the Equal Protection Clause some might question whether a prohibition would be valid if drawn differently, say, to prohibit the conduct both between same-sex and different-sex participants.

Equality of treatment and the due process right to demand respect for conduct protected by the substantive guarantee of liberty are linked in important respects, and a decision on the latter point advances both interests. If protected conduct is made criminal and the law which does so remains unexamined for its substantive validity, its stigma might remain even if it were not enforceable as drawn for equal protection reasons. When homosexual conduct is made criminal by the law of the State, that declaration in and of itself is an invitation to subject homosexual persons to discrimination both in the public and in the private spheres. The central holding of *Bowers* has been brought in question by this case, and it should be addressed. Its continuance as precedent demeans the lives of homosexual persons.

The stigma this criminal statute imposes, moreover, is not trivial. The offense, to be sure, is but a class C misdemeanor.... Still, it remains a criminal offense with all that imports for the dignity of the persons charged.... Just this Term we rejected various challenges to state laws requiring the registration of sex offenders. We are advised that if Texas convicted an adult for private, consensual homosexual conduct under the statute here in question the convicted person would come within the registration laws of a least four States [Idaho, Louisiana, Mississippi, and South Carolina] were he or she to be subject to their jurisdiction.... [T]he Texas criminal conviction carries with it the other collateral consequences always following a conviction....

The foundations of *Bowers* have sustained serious erosion from our recent decisions in *Casey* and *Romer*. When our precedent has been thus weakened, criticism from other sources is of greater significance. In the United States criticism of Bowers has been substantial and continuing, disapproving of its reasoning in all respects, not just as to its historical assumptions. See, e.g., C. Fried, *Order and Law: Arguing the Reagan Revolution—A Firsthand Account* 81–84 (1991); R. Posner, *Sex and Reason* 341–350 (1992). The courts of five different States have declined to follow it in interpreting provisions in their own state constitutions parallel to the Due Process Clause of the Fourteenth Amendment, see Jegley v. Picado, 349 Ark. 600, 80 S. W. 3d 332 (2002); Powell v. State, 270 Ga. 327, 510 S. E. 2d 18, 24 (1998); Gryczan v. State, 283 Mont. 433, 942 P.2d 112 (1997); Campbell v. Sundquist, 926 S.W.2d 250 (Tenn. App. 1996); Commonwealth v. Wasson, 842 S.W.2d 487 (Ky. 1992).

To the extent *Bowers* relied on values we share with a wider civilization, it should be noted that the reasoning and holding in *Bowers* have been rejected elsewhere. The European Court of Human Rights has followed not *Bowers* but its own decision in *Dudgeon v. United Kingdom*. See P. G. & J. H. v. United Kingdom, App. No. 00044787/98, ¶ 56 (Eur. Ct. H. R., Sept. 25, 2001); Modinos v. Cyprus, 259 Eur. Ct. H. R. (1993); Norris v. Ireland, 142 Eur. Ct. H. R. (1988). Other nations, too, have taken action consistent with an affirmation of the protected right of homosexual adults to engage in intimate, consensual conduct. See Brief for Mary Robinson et al. as Amici Curiae 11–12. The right the petitioners seek in this case has been accepted as an integral part of human freedom in many other countries. There has been no showing that in this country the governmental interest in circumscribing personal choice is somehow more legitimate or urgent.

The doctrine of *stare decisis* is essential to the respect accorded to the judgments of the Court and to the stability of the law. It is not, however, an inexorable command. Payne v. Tennessee, 501 U.S. 808, 828 (1991) ("*Stare decisis* is not an inexorable command; rather, it 'is a principle of policy and not a mechanical formula of adherence to the latest decision' "). In *Casey* we noted that when a Court is asked to overrule a precedent recognizing a constitutional liberty interest, individual or societal reliance on the existence of that liberty cautions with particular strength against reversing course. 505 U.S., at 855–856; see also *id.*, at 844 ("Liberty finds no refuge in a jurisprudence of doubt"). The holding in *Bowers*, however, has not induced detrimental reliance comparable to some instances where recognized individual rights are involved. Indeed, there has been no individual or societal reliance on *Bowers* of the sort that could counsel against overturning its holding once there are compelling reasons to do so. *Bowers* itself causes uncertainty, for the precedents before and after its issuance contradict its central holding.

The rationale of *Bowers* does not withstand careful analysis. In his dissenting opinion in *Bowers*, Justice Stevens came to these conclusions:

"Our prior cases make two propositions abundantly clear. First, the fact that the governing majority in a State has traditionally viewed a particular practice as immoral is not a sufficient reason for upholding a law prohibiting the practice; neither history nor tradition could save a law prohibiting miscegenation from constitutional attack. Second, individual decisions by married persons, concerning the intimacies of their physical relationship, even when not intended to produce offspring, are a form of "liberty" protected by the Due Process Clause of the Fourteenth Amendment. Moreover, this protection extends to intimate choices by unmarried as well as married persons." 478 U.S. at 216 (footnotes and citations omitted).

JUSTICE STEVENS' analysis, in our view, should have been controlling in *Bowers* and should control here.

Bowers was not correct when it was decided, and it is not correct today. It ought not to remain binding precedent. *Bowers v. Hardwick* should be and now is overruled.

The present case does not involve minors. It does not involve persons who might be injured or coerced or who are situated in relationships where consent might not easily be refused. It does not involve public conduct or prostitution. It does not involve whether the government must give formal recognition to any relationship that homosexual persons seek to enter. The case does involve two adults who, with full and mutual consent from each other, engaged in sexual practices common to a homosexual lifestyle. The petitioners are entitled to respect for their private lives. The State cannot demean their existence or control their destiny by making their private sexual conduct a crime. Their right to liberty under the Due Process Clause gives them the full right to engage in their conduct without intervention of the government. "It is a promise of the Constitution that there is a realm of personal liberty which the government may not enter." *Casey, supra,* at 847. The Texas statute furthers no legitimate state interest which can justify its intrusion into the personal and private life of the individual.

Had those who drew and ratified the Due Process Clauses of the Fifth Amendment or the Fourteenth Amendment known the components of liberty in its manifold possibilities, they might have been more specific. They did not presume to have this insight. They knew times can blind us to certain truths and later generations can see that laws once thought necessary and proper in fact serve only to oppress. As the Constitution endures, persons in every generation can invoke its principles in their own search for greater freedom.

The judgment of the Court of Appeals for the Texas Fourteenth District is reversed, and the case is remanded for further proceedings not inconsistent with this opinion.

It is so ordered.

JUSTICE O'CONNOR, concurring in the judgment.

The Court today overrules Bowers v. Hardwick, 478 U.S. 186 (1986). I joined *Bowers*, and do not join the Court in overruling it. Nevertheless, I agree with the Court that Texas' statute banning same-sex sodomy is unconstitutional. Rather than relying on the substantive component of the Fourteenth Amendment's Due Process Clause, as the Court does, I base my conclusion on the Fourteenth Amendment's Equal Protection Clause.

The Equal Protection Clause of the Fourteenth Amendment "is essentially a direction that all persons similarly situated should be treated alike." Cleburne v. Cleburne Living Center, Inc., 473 U.S. 432, 439 (1985); see also Plyler v. Doe, 457 U.S. 202, 216 (1982). Under our rational basis standard of review, "legislation is presumed to be valid and will be sustained if the classification drawn by the statute is rationally related to a legitimate state interest." Cleburne v. Cleburne Living Center, supra, at 440 [also citing Romer].

Laws such as economic or tax legislation that are scrutinized under rational basis review normally pass constitutional muster, since "the Constitution presumes that even improvident decisions will eventually be rectified by the democratic processes." Cleburne, supra, at 440; see also ... Williamson v. Lee Optical of Okla., Inc., 348 U.S. 483 (1955). We have consistently held, however, that some objectives, such as "a bare ... desire to harm a politically unpopular group," are not legitimate state interests. Department of Agriculture v. Moreno, supra, at 534. When a law exhibits such a desire to harm a politically unpopular group, we have applied a more searching form of rational basis review to strike down such laws under the Equal Protection Clause.

We have been most likely to apply rational basis review to hold a law unconstitutional under the Equal Protection Clause where, as here, the challenged legislation inhibits personal relationships. In Department of Agriculture v. Moreno, for example, we held that a law preventing those households containing an individual unrelated to any other member of the household from receiving food stamps violated equal protection because the purpose of the law was to " 'discriminate against hippies.' " The asserted governmental interest in preventing food stamp fraud was not deemed sufficient to satisfy rational basis review. In Eisenstadt v. Baird, we refused to sanction a law that discriminated between married and unmarried persons by prohibiting the distribution of contraceptives to single persons. Likewise, in Cleburne we held that it was irrational for a State to require a home for the mentally disabled to obtain a special use permit when other residences—like fraternity houses and apartment buildings—did not have to obtain such a permit. And in Romer v. Evans, we disallowed a state statute that "imposed a broad and undifferentiated disability on a single named group"—specifically, homosexuals....

The statute at issue here makes sodomy a crime only if a person "engages in deviate sexual intercourse with another individual of the same sex." Sodomy between opposite-sex partners, however, is not a crime in Texas. That is, Texas treats the same conduct differently based solely on the participants. Those harmed by this law are people who have a same-sex sexual orientation and thus are more likely to engage in behavior prohibited by § 21.06.

The Texas statute makes homosexuals unequal in the eyes of the law by making particular conduct—and only that conduct—subject to criminal sanction. . . .

[T]he effect of Texas' sodomy law is not just limited to the threat of prosecution or consequence of conviction. Texas' sodomy law brands all homosexuals as criminals, thereby making it more difficult for homosexuals to be treated in the same manner as everyone else. Indeed, Texas itself has previously acknowledged the collateral effects of the law, stipulating in a prior challenge to this action that the law "legally sanctions discrimination against [homosexuals] in a variety of ways unrelated to the criminal law," including in the areas of "employment, family issues, and housing." State v. Morales, 826 S.W.2d 201, 203 (Tex. App. 1992).

Texas attempts to justify its law, and the effects of the law, by arguing that the statute satisfies rational basis review because it furthers the legitimate governmental interest of the promotion of morality. In *Bowers*, we held that a state law criminalizing sodomy as applied to homosexual couples did not violate substantive due process. We rejected the argument that no rational basis existed to justify the law, pointing to the government's interest in promoting morality. 478 U.S. at 196. . . . *Bowers* did not hold that moral disapproval of a group is a rational basis under the Equal Protection Clause to criminalize homosexual sodomy when heterosexual sodomy is not punished.

This case raises a different issue than *Bowers*: whether, under the Equal Protection Clause, moral disapproval is a legitimate state interest to justify by itself a statute that bans homosexual sodomy, but not heterosexual sodomy. It is not. Moral disapproval of this group, like a bare desire to harm the group, is an interest that is insufficient to satisfy rational basis review under the Equal Protection Clause. See, e.g., *Department of Agriculture v. Moreno, supra*, at 534; *Romer v. Evans*, 517 U.S., at 634–635. Indeed, we have never held that moral disapproval, without any other asserted state interest, is a sufficient rationale under the Equal Protection Clause to justify a law that discriminates among groups of persons.

Moral disapproval of a group cannot be a legitimate governmental interest under the Equal Protection Clause because legal classifications must not be "drawn for the purpose of disadvantaging the group burdened by the law." *Id.*, at 633. Texas' invocation of moral disapproval as a legitimate state interest proves nothing more than Texas' desire to criminalize homosexual sodomy. But the Equal Protection Clause prevents a State from creating "a classification of persons undertaken for its own sake." *Id.*, at 635. And because Texas so rarely enforces its sodomy law as applied to private, consensual acts, the law serves more as a statement of dislike and disapproval against homosexuals than as a tool to stop criminal behavior. The Texas sodomy law "raises the inevitable inference that the disadvantage imposed is born of animosity toward the class of persons affected."

Texas argues, however, that the sodomy law does not discriminate against homosexual persons. Instead, the State maintains that the law discriminates only against homosexual conduct. While it is true that the law applies only to conduct, the conduct targeted by this law is conduct that is closely correlated with being homosexual. Under such circumstances, Texas' sodomy law is targeted at more than conduct. It is instead directed toward gay persons as a class. "After all, there can hardly be more palpable discrimination against a class than making the conduct that defines the class criminal." *Id.*, at 641 (SCALIA, J., dissenting) (internal quotation marks omitted). When a State makes homosexual conduct criminal, and not "deviate sexual intercourse" committed by persons of different sexes, "that declaration in and of itself is an invitation to subject homosexual persons to discrimination both in the public and in the private spheres." *Ante*, at 575.

Indeed, Texas law confirms that the sodomy statute is directed toward homosexuals as a class. In Texas, calling a person a homosexual is slander per se because the word "homosexual" "imputes the commission of a crime." Plumley v. Landmark Chevrolet, Inc., 122 F.3d 308, 310 (CA5 1997) (applying Texas law); *see also* Head v. Newton, 596 S.W.2d 209, 210 (Tex. App. 1980). The State has admitted that because of the sodomy law, being homosexual carries the presumption of being a criminal. See *State v. Morales*, 826 S. W. 2d, at 202–203 ("The statute brands lesbians and gay men as criminals and thereby legally sanctions discrimination against them in a variety of ways unrelated to the criminal law"). Texas' sodomy law therefore results in discrimination against homosexuals as a class in an array of areas outside the criminal law. See *ibid.* In *Romer v. Evans*, we refused to sanction a law that singled out homosexuals "for disfavored legal status." 517 U.S. at 633. The same is true here. The Equal Protection Clause " 'neither knows nor tolerates classes among citizens.' " *Id.* at 623 (quoting Plessy v. Ferguson, 163 U.S. 537, 559 (1896) (Harlan, J. dissenting)).

A State can of course assign certain consequences to a violation of its criminal law. But the State cannot single out one identifiable class of citizens for punishment that does not apply to everyone else, with moral disapproval as the only asserted state interest for the law. The Texas sodomy statute subjects homosexuals to "a lifelong penalty and stigma. A legislative classification that threatens the creation of an underclass . . . cannot be reconciled with" the Equal Protection Clause. *Plyler v. Doe*, 457 U.S., at 239 (Powell, J., concurring).

Whether a sodomy law that is neutral both in effect and application, see Yick Wo v. Hopkins, 118 U.S. 356 (1886), would violate the substantive component of the Due Process Clause is an issue that need not be decided today. I am confident, however, that so long as the Equal Protection Clause requires a sodomy law to apply equally to the private consensual conduct of homosexuals and heterosexuals alike, such a law would not long stand in our democratic society. In the words of Justice Jackson:

"The framers of the Constitution knew, and we should not forget today, that there is no more effective practical guaranty against arbitrary and unreasonable government than to require that the principles of law which officials would impose upon a minority be imposed generally. Conversely, nothing opens the door to arbitrary action so effectively as to allow those officials to pick and choose only a few to whom they will apply legislation and thus to escape the political retribution that might be visited upon them if larger numbers were affected."

Railway Express Agency, Inc. v. New York, 336 U.S. 106, 112–113 (1949) (concurring opinion).

That this law as applied to private, consensual conduct is unconstitutional under the Equal Protection Clause does not mean that other laws distinguishing between heterosexuals and homosexuals would similarly fail under rational basis review. Texas cannot assert any legitimate state interest here, such as national security or preserving the traditional institution of marriage. Unlike the moral disapproval of same-sex relations—the asserted state interest in this case—other reasons exist to promote the institution of marriage beyond mere moral disapproval of an excluded group.

A law branding one class of persons as criminal solely based on the State's moral disapproval of that class and the conduct associated with that class runs contrary to the values of the Constitution and the Equal Protection Clause, under any standard of review. I therefore concur in the Court's judgment that Texas' sodomy law banning "deviate sexual intercourse" between consenting adults of the same sex, but not between consenting adults of different sexes, is unconstitutional.

JUSTICE SCALIA, with whom THE CHIEF JUSTICE and JUSTICE THOMAS join, dissenting.

"Liberty finds no refuge in a jurisprudence of doubt." Planned Parenthood of Southeastern Pa. v. Casey, 505 U.S. 833, 844 (1992). That was the Court's sententious response, barely more than a decade ago, to those seeking to overrule Roe v. Wade, 410 U.S. 113 (1973). The Court's response today, to those who have engaged in a 17–year crusade to overrule *Bowers v. Hardwick*, is very different. The need for stability and certainty presents no barrier.

Most of the rest of today's opinion has no relevance to its actual holding—that the Texas statute "furthers no legitimate state interest which can justify" its application to petitioners under rational-basis review. *ante*, at 18 (overruling *Bowers* to the extent it sustained Georgia's anti-sodomy statute under the rational-basis test). Though there is discussion of "fundamental propositions," *ante*, at 4, and "fundamental decisions," *ibid*., nowhere does the Court's opinion declare that homosexual sodomy is a "fundamental right" under the Due Process Clause; nor does it subject the Texas law to the standard of review that would be appropriate (strict scrutiny) if homosexual sodomy were a "fundamental right." Thus, while overruling the *outcome* of *Bowers*, the Court leaves strangely untouched its central legal conclusion: "Respondent would have us announce ... a fundamental right to engage in homosexual sodomy. This we are quite unwilling to do." 478 U.S., at 191. Instead the Court simply describes petitioners' conduct as "an exercise of their liberty"—which it undoubtedly is—and proceeds to apply an unheard-of form of rational-basis review that will have far-reaching implications beyond this case. *Ante*, at 564.

I

I begin with the Court's surprising readiness to reconsider a decision rendered a mere 17 years ago in *Bowers v. Hardwick*. I do not myself believe in rigid adherence to *stare decisis* in constitutional cases; but I do believe that we should be consistent rather than manipulative in invoking the doctrine. Today's opinions in support of reversal do not bother to distinguish—or indeed, even bother to mention—the paean to *stare decisis* coauthored by three Members of today's majority in *Planned Parenthood v. Casey*. There, when *stare decisis* meant preservation of judicially invented abortion rights, the widespread criticism of *Roe* was strong reason to *reaffirm* it:

> "Where, in the performance of its judicial duties, the Court decides a case in such a way as to resolve the sort of intensely divisive controversy reflected in *Roe*[,] ... its decision has a dimension that the resolution of the normal case does not carry.... To overrule under fire in the absence of the most compelling reason ... would subvert the Court's legitimacy beyond any serious question." 505 U.S., at 866–867.

Today, however, the widespread opposition to *Bowers*, a decision resolving an issue as "intensely divisive" as the issue in *Roe*, is offered as a reason in favor of *overruling* it. See *ante*, at 576–77. Gone, too, is any "enquiry" (of the sort conducted in *Casey*) into whether the decision sought to be overruled has "proven 'unworkable,' " *Casey, supra*, at 855.

Today's approach to *stare decisis* invites us to overrule an erroneously decided precedent (including an "intensely divisive" decision) *if*: (1) its foundations have been "eroded" by subsequent decisions, *ante*, at 576–77; (2) it has been subject to "substantial and continuing" criticism, *ibid.*; and (3) it has not induced "individual or societal reliance" that counsels against overturning, *ante*, at 16. The problem is that *Roe* itself—which today's majority surely has no disposition to overrule—satisfies these conditions to at least the same degree as *Bowers*.

(1) ... The Court's claim that *Planned Parenthood v. Casey, supra*, "casts some doubt" upon the holding in *Bowers* (or any other case, for that matter) does not withstand analysis. As far as its holding is concerned, *Casey* provided a *less* expansive right to abortion than did *Roe, which was already on the books when Bowers was decided*. And if the Court is referring not to the holding of *Casey*, but to the dictum of its famed sweet-mystery-of-life passage, *ante*, at 574 (" 'At the heart of liberty is the right to define one's own concept of existence, of meaning,

of the universe, and of the mystery of human life' ") . . . I have never heard of a law that attempted to restrict one's "right to define" certain concepts; and if the passage calls into question the government's power to regulate *actions based on* one's self-defined "concept of existence, etc.," it is the passage that ate the rule of law.

I do not quarrel with the Court's claim that *Romer* "eroded" the "foundations" of *Bowers'* rational-basis holding. But *Roe* and *Casey* have been equally "eroded" by Washington v. Glucksberg, 521 U.S. 702, 721 (1997), which held that *only* fundamental rights which are " 'deeply rooted in this Nation's history and tradition' " qualify for anything other than rational basis scrutiny under the doctrine of "substantive due process." *Roe* and *Casey*, of course, subjected the restriction of abortion to heightened scrutiny without even attempting to establish that the freedom to abort *was* rooted in this Nation's tradition.

(2) *Bowers*, the Court says, has been subject to "substantial and continuing [criticism], disapproving of its reasoning in all respects, not just as to its historical assumptions." *Ante*, at 576. . . . Of course, *Roe* too (and by extension *Casey*) had been (and still is) subject to unrelenting criticism, including criticism from the two commentators cited by the Court today. See Fried, *supra*, at 75 ("*Roe* was a prime example of twisted judging"); Posner, *supra*, at 337 ("[The Court's] opinion in *Roe* . . . fails to measure up to professional expectations regarding judicial opinions"); Posner, *Judicial Opinion Writing*, 62 U. Chi. L. Rev. 1421, 1434 (1995) (describing the opinion in *Roe* as an "embarrassing performance").

(3) That leaves, to distinguish the rock-solid, unamendable disposition of *Roe* from the readily overrulable *Bowers*, only the third factor. "There has been," the Court says, "no individual or societal reliance on *Bowers* of the sort that could counsel against overturning its holding. . . ." *Ante*, at 577. It seems to me that the "societal reliance" on the principles confirmed in *Bowers* and discarded today has been overwhelming. Countless judicial decisions and legislative enactments have relied on the ancient proposition that a governing majority's belief that certain sexual behavior is "immoral and unacceptable" constitutes a rational basis for regulation. See, e.g., Williams v. Pryor, 240 F.3d 944, 949 (CA11 2001) (citing *Bowers* in upholding Alabama's prohibition on the sale of sex toys on the ground that "the crafting and safeguarding of public morality . . . indisputably is a legitimate government interest under rational basis scrutiny"); Milner v. Apfel, 148 F.3d 812, 814 (CA7 1998) (citing *Bowers* for the proposition that "legislatures are permitted to legislate with regard to morality . . . rather than confined to preventing demonstrable harms"); Holmes v. California Army National Guard 124 F.3d 1126, 1136 (CA9 1997) (relying on *Bowers* in upholding the federal statute and regulations banning from military service those who engage in homosexual conduct); Owens v. State, 352 Md. 663, 683, 724 A.2d 43, 53 (1999) (relying on *Bowers* in holding that "a person has no constitutional right to engage in sexual intercourse, at least outside of marriage"); Sherman v. Henry, 928 S.W.2d 464, 469–473 (Tex. 1996) (relying on *Bowers* in

rejecting a claimed constitutional right to commit adultery). We ourselves relied extensively on *Bowers* when we concluded, in Barnes v. Glen Theatre, Inc., 501 U.S. 560, 569 (1991), that Indiana's public indecency statute furthered "a substantial government interest in protecting order and morality," *ibid.*, (plurality opinion); see also *id.*, at 575 (Scalia, J., concurring in judgment). State laws against bigamy, same-sex marriage, adult incest, prostitution, masturbation, adultery, fornication, bestiality, and obscenity are likewise sustainable only in light of *Bowers'* validation of laws based on moral choices. Every single one of these laws is called into question by today's decision; the Court makes no effort to cabin the scope of its decision to exclude them from its holding. See *ante,* at 11 (noting "an emerging awareness that liberty gives substantial protection to adult persons in deciding how to conduct their private lives in matters pertaining to sex" (emphasis added)). The impossibility of distinguishing homosexuality from other traditional "morals" offenses is precisely why *Bowers* rejected the rational-basis challenge. "The law," it said, "is constantly based on notions of morality, and if all laws representing essentially moral choices are to be invalidated under the Due Process Clause, the courts will be very busy indeed." 478 U.S. at 196.[4]

What a massive disruption of the current social order, therefore, the overruling of *Bowers* entails. Not so the overruling of *Roe*, which would simply have restored the regime that existed for centuries before 1973, in which the permissibility of and restrictions upon abortion were determined legislatively State-by-State. *Casey*, however, chose to base its *stare decisis* determination on a different "sort" of reliance. "People," it said, "have organized intimate relationships and made choices that define their views of themselves and their places in society, in reliance on the availability of abortion in the event that contraception should fail." 505 U.S., at 856. This falsely assumes that the consequence of

---

4. [Footnote 2 in original] While the Court does not overrule *Bowers'* holding that homosexual sodomy is not a "fundamental right," it is worth noting that the "societal reliance" upon that aspect of the decision has been substantial as well. See 10 U.S.C. § 654(b)(1) ("A member of the armed forces shall be separated from the armed forces ... if ... the member has engaged in ... a homosexual act or acts"); Marcum v. McWhorter, 308 F.3d 635, 640–642 (CA6 2002) (relying on *Bowers* in rejecting a claimed fundamental right to commit adultery); Mullins v. Oregon, 57 F.3d 789, 793–794 (CA9 1995) (relying on *Bowers* in rejecting a grandparent's claimed "fundamental liberty interest" in the adoption of her grandchildren); Doe v. Wiginton, 21 F.3d 733, 739–740 (CA6 1994) (relying on *Bowers* in rejecting a prisoner's claimed "fundamental right" to on-demand HIV testing); Schowengerdt v. United States, 944 F.2d 483, 490 (CA9 1991) (relying on *Bowers* in upholding a bisexual's discharge from the armed services); Charles v. Baesler, 910 F.2d 1349, 1353 (CA6 1990) (relying on *Bowers* in rejecting fire department captain's claimed "fundamental" interest in a promotion); Henne v. Wright, 904 F.2d 1208, 1214–1215 (CA8 1990) (relying on *Bowers* in rejecting a claim that state law restricting surnames that could be given to children at birth implicates a "fundamental right"); Walls v. Petersburg, 895 F.2d 188, 193 (CA4 1990) (relying on *Bowers* in rejecting substantive-due-process challenge to a police department questionnaire that asked prospective employees about homosexual activity); High Tech Gays v. Defense Industrial Security Clearance Office, 895 F.2d 563, 570–571 (CA9 1988) (relying on *Bowers'* holding that homosexual activity is not a fundamental right in rejecting—on the basis of the rational-basis standard—an equal-protection challenge to the Defense Department's policy of conducting expanded investigations into backgrounds of gay and lesbian applicants for secret and top-secret security clearance).

overruling *Roe* would have been to make abortion unlawful. It would not; it would merely have *permitted* the States to do so. Many States would unquestionably have declined to prohibit abortion, and others would not have prohibited it within six months (after which the most significant reliance interests would have expired). Even for persons in States other than these, the choice would not have been between abortion and childbirth, but between abortion nearby and abortion in a neighboring State.

To tell the truth, it does not surprise me, and should surprise no one, that the Court has chosen today to revise the standards of *stare decisis* set forth in *Casey*. It has thereby exposed *Casey*'s extraordinary deference to precedent for the result-oriented expedient that it is.

II

. . .

Texas Penal Code Ann. § 21.06(a) (2003) undoubtedly imposes constraints on liberty. So do laws prohibiting prostitution, recreational use of heroin, and, for that matter, working more than 60 hours per week in a bakery. But there is no right to "liberty" under the Due Process Clause, though today's opinion repeatedly makes that claim.... The Fourteenth Amendment *expressly allows* States to deprive their citizens of "liberty," *so long as "due process of law" is provided:*

"No state shall ... deprive any person of life, liberty, or property, *without due process of law.*" Amdt. 14 (emphasis added).

Our opinions applying the doctrine known as "substantive due process" hold that the Due Process Clause prohibits States from infringing *fundamental* liberty interests, unless the infringement is narrowly tailored to serve a compelling state interest. *Washington v. Glucksberg*, 521 U.S. at 721. We have held repeatedly, in cases the Court today does not overrule, that *only* fundamental rights qualify for this so-called "heightened scrutiny" protection—that is, rights which are " 'deeply rooted in this Nation's history and tradition,' " *ibid*. See Reno v. Flores, 507 U.S. 292, 303 (1993) (fundamental liberty interests must be "so rooted in the traditions and conscience of our people as to be ranked as fundamental" (internal quotation marks and citations omitted)); United States v. Salerno, 481 U.S. 739, 751 (1987) (same). See also Michael H. v. Gerald D., 491 U.S. 110, 122 (1989) ("We have insisted not merely that the interest denominated as a 'liberty' be 'fundamental' ... but also that it be an interest traditionally protected by our society") ... All other liberty interests may be abridged or abrogated pursuant to a validly enacted state law if that law is rationally related to a legitimate state interest.

Bowers held, first, that criminal prohibitions of homosexual sodomy are not subject to heightened scrutiny because they do not implicate a "fundamental right" under the Due Process Clause, 478 U.S., at 191–194. Noting that "proscriptions against that conduct have ancient roots," *id.*, at 192, that "sodomy was a criminal offense at common law and was forbidden by the laws of the original 13 States when they ratified the Bill of Rights," *ibid.*, and that many States had retained their bans on sodomy, *id.*, at 193, *Bowers* concluded that a right to engage in homosexual sodomy was not " 'deeply rooted in this Nation's history and tradition,' " *id.*, at 192.

The Court today does not overrule this holding. Not once does it describe homosexual sodomy as a "fundamental right" or a "fundamental liberty interest," nor does it subject the Texas statute to strict scrutiny. Instead, having failed to establish that the right to homosexual sodomy is " 'deeply rooted in this Nation's history and tradition,' " the Court concludes that the application of Texas's statute to petitioners' conduct fails the rational-basis test, and overrules *Bowers'* holding to the contrary, see *id.*, at 196. "The Texas statute furthers no legitimate state interest which can justify its intrusion into the personal and private life of the individual." *Ante*, at 578.

.   .   .

III

The Court's description of "the state of the law" at the time of *Bowers* only confirms that *Bowers* was right. *Ante*, at 566. The Court points to Griswold v. Connecticut, 381 U.S. 479, 481–482 (1965). But that case *expressly disclaimed* any reliance on the doctrine of "substantive due process," and grounded the so-called "right to privacy" in penumbras of constitutional provisions *other than* the Due Process Clause. *Eisenstadt v. Baird* likewise had nothing to do with "substantive due process"; it invalidated a Massachusetts law prohibiting the distribution of contraceptives to unmarried persons solely on the basis of the Equal Protection Clause. Of course *Eisenstadt* contains well known dictum relating to the "right to privacy," but this referred to the right recognized in *Griswold*—a right penumbral to the *specific* guarantees in the Bill of Rights, and not a "substantive due process" right.

Roe v. Wade recognized that the right to abort an unborn child was a "fundamental right" protected by the Due Process Clause. The *Roe* Court, however, made no attempt to establish that this right was " 'deeply rooted in this Nation's history and tradition' "; instead, it based its conclusion that "the Fourteenth Amendment's concept of personal liberty . . . is broad enough to encompass a woman's decision whether or not to terminate her pregnancy" on its own normative judgment that anti-abortion laws were undesirable. . . . We have since rejected *Roe's* holding that regulations of abortion must be narrowly tailored to serve a compelling state interest, see *Planned Parenthood v. Casey*, 505 U.S. at 876 (joint opinion of O'CONNOR, KENNEDY AND SOUTER, JJ.); *id.*, at 951–953 (REHNQUIST, C.J., concurring in judgment in part and dissenting in part)—and thus, by logical implication, *Roe's* holding that the right to abort an unborn child is a "fundamental right." See 505 U.S. at 843–912 (joint opinion of O'CONNOR, KENNEDY AND SOUTER, JJ.)

(not once describing abortion as a "fundamental right" or a "fundamental liberty interest").

... It is (as *Bowers* recognized) entirely irrelevant whether the laws in our long national tradition criminalizing homosexual sodomy were "directed at homosexual conduct as a distinct matter." *Ante*, at 7. Whether homosexual sodomy was prohibited by a law targeted at same-sex sexual relations or by a more general law prohibiting both homosexual and heterosexual sodomy, the only relevant point is that it was criminalized—which suffices to establish that homosexual sodomy is not a right "deeply rooted in our Nation's history and tradition." ...

... [T]he Court admits that sodomy laws were enforced against consenting adults (although the Court contends that prosecutions [for private behavior] were "infrequent," *ante*, at 9). I do not know what "acting in private" means; surely consensual sodomy, like heterosexual intercourse, is rarely performed on stage. If all the Court means by "acting in private" is "on private premises, with the doors closed and windows covered," it is entirely unsurprising that evidence of enforcement would be hard to come by. (Imagine the circumstances that would enable a search warrant to be obtained for a residence on the ground that there was probable cause to believe that consensual sodomy was then and there occurring.) Surely that lack of evidence would not sustain the proposition that consensual sodomy on private premises with the doors closed and windows covered was regarded as a "fundamental right," even though all other consensual sodomy was criminalized. There are 203 prosecutions for consensual, adult homosexual sodomy reported in the West Reporting system and official state reporters from the years 1880–1995. See W. Eskridge, *Gaylaw: Challenging the Apartheid of the Closet* 375 (1999) (hereinafter *Gaylaw*). There are also records of 20 sodomy prosecutions and 4 executions during the colonial period. J. Katz, *Gay/Lesbian Almanac* 29, 58, 663 (1983). *Bowers'* conclusion that homosexual sodomy is not a fundamental right "deeply rooted in this Nation's history and tradition" is utterly unassailable.

Realizing that fact, the Court instead says: "[W]e think that our laws and traditions in the past half century are of most relevance here. These references show *an emerging awareness* that liberty gives substantial protection to adult persons in deciding how to conduct their private lives *in matters pertaining to sex*." *Ante*, at 571–572 (emphasis added). Apart from the fact that such an "emerging awareness" does not establish a "fundamental right," the statement is factually false. States continue to prosecute all sorts of crimes by adults "in matters pertaining to sex": prostitution, adult incest, adultery, obscenity, and child pornography. Sodomy laws, too, have been enforced "in the past half century," in which there have been 134 reported cases involving prosecutions for consensual, adult, homosexual sodomy. *Gaylaw* 375. In relying, for evidence of an "emerging recognition," upon the American Law Institute's 1955 recommendation not to criminalize " 'consensual sexual relations conducted in private,' " *ante*, at 11, the Court ignores the fact that this recommendation was "a point of resistance in most of the states that considered adopting the Model Penal Code." *Gaylaw* 159.

In any event, an "emerging awareness" is by definition not "deeply rooted in this Nation's history and traditions," as we have said "fundamental right" status requires. Constitutional entitlements do not spring into existence because some States choose to lessen or eliminate criminal sanctions on certain behavior. Much less do they spring into existence, as the Court seems to believe, because *foreign nations* decriminalize conduct.... *Bowers'* ... holding is ... devoid of any reliance on the views of a "wider civilization," see *id.*, at 196. The Court's discussion of these foreign views (ignoring, of course, the many countries that have retained criminal prohibitions on sodomy) is therefore meaningless dicta. Dangerous dicta, however, since "this Court ... should not impose foreign moods, fads, or fashions on Americans." Foster v. Florida, 537 U.S. 990 n. (2002) (THOMAS, J., concurring in denial of certiorari).

IV

... [T]he Court ... rests its holding [on] the contention that there is no rational basis for the law here under attack. This proposition is so out of accord with our jurisprudence—indeed, with the jurisprudence of *any* society we know—that it requires little discussion.

The Texas statute undeniably seeks to further the belief of its citizens that certain forms of sexual behavior are "immoral and unacceptable," *Bowers, supra*, at 196—the same interest furthered by criminal laws against fornication, bigamy, adultery, adult incest, bestiality, and obscenity. *Bowers* held that this was a legitimate state interest. The Court today reaches the opposite conclusion. The Texas statute, it says, "furthers no *legitimate state interest* which can justify its intrusion into the personal and private life of the individual," *ante*, at 18 (emphasis added). The Court embraces instead JUSTICE STEVENS' declaration in his *Bowers* dissent, that "the fact that the governing majority in a State has traditionally viewed a particular practice as immoral is not a sufficient reason for upholding a law prohibiting the practice," *ante*, at 17. This effectively decrees the end of all morals legislation. If, as the Court asserts, the promotion of majoritarian sexual morality is not even a *legitimate* state interest, none of the above-mentioned laws can survive rational-basis review.

V

Finally, I turn to petitioners' equal-protection challenge. ... On its face § 21.06(a) applies equally to all persons. Men and women, heterosexuals and homosexuals, are all subject to its prohibition of deviate sexual intercourse with someone of the same sex. To be sure, § 21.06 does distinguish between the sexes insofar as concerns the partner with whom the sexual acts are performed: men can violate the law only with other men, and women only with other women. But this cannot itself be a denial of equal protection, since it is precisely the same distinction regarding partner that is drawn in state laws prohibiting marriage with someone of the same sex while permitting marriage with someone of the opposite sex.

The objection is made, however, that the antimiscegenation laws invalidated in Loving v. Virginia, 388 U.S. 1, 8 (1967), similarly were applicable to whites and blacks alike, and only distinguished between the races insofar as the *partner* was concerned. In *Loving*, however, we correctly applied heightened scrutiny, rather than the usual rational-basis review, because the Virginia statute was "designed to maintain White Supremacy." *Id.*, at 6, 11. A racially discriminatory purpose is always sufficient to subject a law to strict scrutiny, even a facially neutral law that makes no mention of race. See Washington v. Davis, 426 U.S. 229, 241–242 (1976). No purpose to discriminate against men or women as a class can be gleaned from the Texas law, so rational-basis review applies. That review is readily satisfied here by the same rational basis that satisfied it in *Bowers*—society's belief that certain forms of sexual behavior are "immoral and unacceptable," 478 U.S., at 196. This is the same justification that supports many other laws regulating sexual behavior that make a distinction based upon the identity of the partner—for example, laws against adultery, fornication, and adult incest, and laws refusing to recognize homosexual marriage.

· · ·

JUSTICE O'CONNOR simply decrees application of "a more searching form of rational basis review" to the Texas statute. *Ante*, at 580. The cases she cites do not recognize such a standard, and reach their conclusions only after finding, as required by conventional rational-basis analysis, that no conceivable legitimate state interest supports the classification at issue. See *Romer v. Evans*, 517 U.S. at 635; Cleburne v. Cleburne Living Center, Inc., 473 U.S. 432, 448–450 (1985); Department of Agriculture v. Moreno, 413 U.S. 528, 534–538 (1973). Nor does JUSTICE O'CONNOR explain precisely what her "more searching form" of rational-basis review consists of. It must at least mean, however, that laws exhibiting " 'a . . . desire to harm a politically unpopular group,' " *ante*, at 2, are invalid even though there may be a conceivable rational basis to support them.

This reasoning leaves on pretty shaky grounds state laws limiting marriage to opposite-sex couples. JUSTICE O'CONNOR seeks to preserve them by the conclusory statement that "preserving the traditional institution of marriage" is a legitimate state interest. *Ante*, at 585. But "preserving the traditional institution of marriage" is just a kinder way of describing the State's *moral disapproval* of same-sex couples. Texas's interest in § 21.06 could be recast in similarly euphemistic terms: "preserving the traditional sexual mores of our society." In the jurisprudence JUSTICE O'CONNOR has seemingly created, judges can validate laws by characterizing them as "preserving the traditions of society" (good); or invalidate them by characterizing them as "expressing moral disapproval" (bad).

* * *

Today's opinion is the product of a Court, which is the product of a law-profession culture, that has largely signed on to the so-called homosexual agenda, by which I mean the agenda promoted by some homosexual activists directed at eliminating the moral opprobrium that has traditionally attached to homosexual conduct. I noted in an earlier opinion the fact that the American Association of Law Schools (to which any reputable law school *must* seek to belong) excludes from membership any school that refuses to ban from its job-interview facilities a law firm (no matter how small) that does not wish to hire as a prospective partner a person who openly engages in homosexual conduct. See *Romer*, *supra*, at 653.

One of the most revealing statements in today's opinion is the Court's grim warning that the criminalization of homosexual conduct is "an invitation to subject homosexual persons to discrimination both in the public and in the private spheres." *Ante*, at 575. It is clear from this that the Court has taken sides in the culture war, departing from its role of assuring, as neutral observer, that the democratic rules of engagement are observed. Many Americans do not want persons who openly engage in homosexual conduct as partners in their business, as scoutmasters for their children, as teachers in their children's schools, or as boarders in their home. They view this as protecting themselves and their families from a lifestyle that they believe to be immoral and destructive. The Court views it as "discrimination" which it is the function of our judgments to deter. So imbued is the Court with the law profession's anti-anti-homosexual culture, that it is seemingly unaware that the attitudes of that culture are not obviously "mainstream"; that in most States what the Court calls "discrimination" against those who engage in homosexual acts is perfectly legal; that proposals to ban such "discrimination" under Title VII have repeatedly been rejected by Congress, see Employment Non–Discrimination Act of 1994, S. 2238, 103d Cong., 2d Sess. (1994); Civil Rights Amendments, H. R. 5452, 94th Cong., 1st Sess. (1975); that in some cases such "discrimination" is mandated by federal statute, see 10 U.S.C. § 654(b)(1) (mandating discharge from the armed forces of any service member who engages in or intends to engage in homosexual acts); and that in some cases such "discrimination" is a constitutional right, see Boy Scouts of America v. Dale, 530 U.S. 640 (2000).

Let me be clear that I have nothing against homosexuals, or any other group, promoting their agenda through normal democratic means. Social perceptions of sexual and other morality change over time, and every group has the right to persuade its fellow citizens that its view of such matters is the best. That homosexuals have achieved some success in that enterprise is attested to by the fact that Texas is one of the few remaining States that criminalize private, consensual homosexual acts. But persuading one's fellow citizens is one thing, and imposing one's views in absence of democratic majority will is something else. I would no more *require* a State to criminalize homosexual acts—or, for that matter, display *any* moral disapprobation of them—than I would *forbid* it to do so … It is indeed true that "later generations can see that laws once thought necessary and proper in fact serve only to oppress," *ante*, at 18; and when that happens, later generations can repeal those laws. But it is the premise of our system that those judgments are to be made by the people, and not imposed by a governing caste that knows best.

One of the benefits of leaving regulation of this matter to the people rather than to the courts is that the people, unlike judges, need not carry things to their logical conclusion. The people may feel that their disapprobation of homosexual conduct is strong enough to disallow homosexual marriage, but not strong enough to criminalize private homosexual acts—and may legislate accordingly. The Court today pretends that it possesses a similar freedom of action, so that we need not fear judicial imposition of homosexual marriage, as has recently occurred in Canada (in a decision that the Canadian Government has chosen not to appeal). See Halpern v. Toronto, 2003 WL 34950 (Ontario Ct. App.); Cohen, Dozens in Canada Follow Gay Couple's Lead, Washington Post, June 12, 2003, p. A25. At the end of its opinion—after having laid waste the foundations of our rational-basis jurisprudence—the Court says that the present case "does not involve whether the government must give formal recognition to any relationship that homosexual persons seek to enter." *Ante*, at 578. Do not believe it. More illuminating than this bald, unreasoned disclaimer is the progression of thought displayed by an earlier passage in the Court's opinion, which notes the constitutional protections afforded to "personal decisions relating to marriage, procreation, contraception, family relationships, child rearing, and education," and then declares that "persons in a homosexual relationship may seek autonomy for these purposes, just as heterosexual persons do." *Ante*, at 574 (emphasis added). Today's opinion dismantles the structure of constitutional law that has permitted a distinction to be made between heterosexual and homosexual unions, insofar as formal recognition in marriage is concerned. If moral disapprobation of homosexual conduct is "no legitimate state interest" for purposes of proscribing that conduct, *ante*, at 578; and if, as the Court coos (casting aside all pretense of neutrality), "when sexuality finds overt expression in intimate conduct with another person, the conduct can be but one element in a personal bond that is more enduring," *ante*, at 567; what justification could there possibly be for denying the benefits of marriage to homosexual couples exercising "the liberty protected by the Constitution," *ibid.*? Surely not the encouragement of procreation, since the sterile and the elderly are allowed to marry. This case "does not involve" the issue of homosexual marriage only if one entertains the belief that principle and logic have nothing to do with the decisions of this Court. Many will hope that, as the Court comfortingly assures us, this is so.

The matters appropriate for this Court's resolution are only three: Texas's prohibition of sodomy neither infringes a "fundamental right" (which the Court does not dispute), nor is unsupported by a rational relation to what the Constitution considers a legitimate state interest, nor denies the equal protection of the laws. I dissent.

JUSTICE THOMAS, dissenting.

I join JUSTICE SCALIA's dissenting opinion. I write separately to note that the law before the Court today "is ... uncommonly silly." Griswold v. Connecticut, 381 U.S. 479, 527 (1965) (Stewart, J., dissenting). If I were a member of the Texas Legislature, I would vote to repeal it. Punishing someone for expressing his sexual preference through non-commercial consensual conduct with another adult does not appear to be a worthy way to expend valuable law enforcement resources.

Notwithstanding this, I recognize that as a member of this Court I am not empowered to help petitioners and others similarly situated. My duty, rather, is to "decide cases 'agreeably to the Constitution and laws of the United States.'" *Id.*, at 530. And, just like Justice Stewart, I "can find [neither in the Bill of Rights nor any other part of the Constitution a] general right of privacy," *ibid.*, or as the Court terms it today, the "liberty of the person both in its spatial and more transcendent dimensions," *ante*, at 562.

––––––––

Questions and Comments

A. Looking at *Lawrence* as a doctrinal exposition, and comparing the structure of the opinions in *Lawrence* and *Casey*, we might ask the following questions:

1. Why does Justice Kennedy, co-author of the plurality opinion in *Casey*, spend so little time discussing *stare decisis* in *Lawrence*? Does his opinion suggest that the distinction from *Casey* is obvious? That *Bowers* was more clearly wrongly decided than *Roe*? (Recall the Court's statement that the "continuance [of *Bowers*] as precedent demeans the lives of homosexual persons.") Why do you think Justice Kennedy did not respond at greater length to Justice Scalia's attack on the asserted inconsistency in the treatment of *stare decisis* in *Casey* and in *Lawrence*?[5]

2. What is the legal standard under which the Court is evaluating the constitutional question? How, if at all, does it relate to the "undue burden" standard in *Casey*?

3. What are the implications of the decision for the constitutionality of laws restricting marriage to the union of a male and a female person? to laws against bigamy? to exclusion of open homosexuals from the U.S. armed services? to prohibition of prostitution between consenting adults? Does the

5. See Ruth Bader Ginsburg, *The Day, Berry and Howard Visiting Scholar: An Open Discussion with Justice Ruth Bader Ginsburg*, 36 Conn. L. Rev. 1033, 1043–44 (2004) ("The Court concluded in the *Lawrence* case that *Bowers v. Hardwick* was a very wrong decision, inconsistent with what we regard as essential to due process and equal protection—the entitlement of all of us to governmental respect for our human dignity. The Court thought *Bowers v. Hardwick* was so wrong, and that no other decisionmaker was likely to correct us, so the Court overturned the precedent. The *Casey* troika certainly did not regard *Roe v. Wade* that way. Recall that at the time *Roe* was decided in 1973 it was hardly controversial. It was a 7–2 judgment, not 5–4 as *Bowers* was.")

Court's rationale allow states any room to regulate matters of intimate morality among adults? How does the majority opinion differ from that of Justice O'Connor's in this respect?

4. Although this was a criminal prosecution in *Lawrence*, the punishment was a nominal fine. Did the particular posture of this case as a criminal enforcement action affect the Court's judgment or reasoning?

5. Why does the Court twice refer to a decision of the European Court of Human Rights? Do you agree with Justice Scalia's dissent that it is irrelevant? Why did Chief Justice Rehnquist cite the German and Canadian abortion decisions in his dissent in *Casey*? Why does Justice Scalia refer to a recent Canadian decision in his dissent in *Lawrence*? How is his usage of foreign law different from or similar to the Court's?

B. Looking at *Lawrence* as the product of an institution, with its own structure and procedures, we might ask these questions:

1. Should the course of the internal deliberations, or the later-expressed disagreement of one member of a 5–4 majority, affect the *stare decisis* value of an opinion? The *Bowers* case had an interesting procedural history in the Court. Initially, the Court had voted internally to deny certiorari (that is, deny review on the merits), but Justice White thought certiorari should be granted and threatened to publish an opinion dissenting from the denial. That threat prompted several vote changes and certiorari was granted. (Chapter Three gives a more detailed account of those events.)

Once the case was argued, the Court met in conference to discuss the case. (The conference is a meeting held shortly after oral argument at which the Justices express their views and opinions are preliminarily assigned.) The initial vote in conference was 5–4 to strike the Georgia statute down. Justices Brennan, Marshall, Blackmun, and Stevens (with misgivings) believed the case "involved the question of 'sexual privacy in the home,' and voted to strike down the law." John C. Jeffries, Jr. *Justice Lewis F. Powell, Jr.* 522 (1995). Chief Justice Burger, Justices White, O'Connor, and Rehnquist found there was no fundamental right to sodomy and voted to uphold the law. Justice Powell was in the middle: "On the one hand, he was not persuaded that Hardwick had any fundamental constitutional right to engage in homosexual sodomy. On the other hand, Powell thought it would violate the Eighth Amendment 'to punish him criminally (*imprisonment*) for conduct based on a natural sexual urge, privately, and with a consenting partner.' Powell's views were finely balanced, but the case had to be decided one way or the other. Since his Eighth Amendment theory barred criminal punishment, he voted against the Georgia law." *Id.*[6] However, upon further reflection, Powell concluded that he should not decide the question of cruel and unusual punishment in this case, since there had been no punishment and no one had raised the issue. "On April 8, Powell wrote his colleagues:

---

6. See also Del Dickson, ed., *The Supreme Court in Conference (1940–85)*, at 824 (2001) (suggesting, based on Justice Brennan's Conference Notes, that Powell said, "We ought to decriminalize this conduct. This statute has not been enforced for fifty years. Robinson v. California [370 U.S. 660 (1962)], invalidating criminal status of drug addiction may be relevant. The case rested on the Eighth Amendment. If we accept the allegation that only acts of sodomy can satisfy this fellow, isn't that pertinent? I would treat it as such, and hold that in the context of the home this conduct is not criminally punishable.")

'At Conference last week, I expressed the view that in some cases it would violate the Eighth Amendment to imprison a person for a private act of homosexual sodomy.' Powell adhered to that view, but 'upon further study as to exactly what is before us,' concluded that his 'bottom line' should be to uphold Georgia's law. Accordingly, he changed his vote.'' Jeffries, *supra*, at 524. (Jeffries' quotations are from Powell's conference notes.)

Powell's change of mind changed the outcome in *Bowers*. Strikingly, as noted earlier, Powell "later admitted that 'he probably made a mistake' in siding with the majority." *Id.* at 530.

Should this history be relevant to the *stare decisis* weight given to *Bowers* by the *Lawrence* Court? Why or why not?

2. With Powell having decided to vote against the petitioner in *Bowers*, Justice White was assigned to draft the opinion for the majority. (For discussion of how opinions are assigned, see Chapter Four, below.) At first, Powell planned not to join White's opinion and, instead, to write his own, concurring only in the judgment. Jeffries, *supra,* at 525. But, one month later, Powell changed his mind and joined White's opinion, thereby giving it five votes and making it an opinion of the Court. Powell wrote his own short concurrence as well, suggesting that the harshness of the penalties under the statute might violate the Eighth Amendment. See 478 U.S. at 197. If Powell had not joined White's opinion, but instead had simply concurred in the judgment (for example, on the ground that the Eighth Amendment issue was not squarely presented), there would not have been an opinion for the Court. Why do you think Powell chose to join the White opinion? His biographer, John Jeffries, suggests that "age and health played their part, as Powell was now seventy-eight years old and still recuperating from a major illness the year before. Infirmity made it more difficult to translate Powell's uncertain views into law." Jeffries, at 526. Note that Powell retired in June 1987, one year after *Bowers*. (In Chapter Six, we discuss the possibility of age and term limits.)

3. The only Justices who were on the Court for both *Bowers* and *Lawrence* were Rehnquist, O'Connor, and Stevens. Note that neither Rehnquist nor Stevens voted differently in *Lawrence* than one might have expected based on their vote in *Bowers*; and Justice O'Connor voted to strike down the Texas law but refused to join the Kennedy opinion overturning *Bowers*. Do you think O'Connor's position in *Bowers* influenced her decision to rely on the Equal Protection Clause, instead of the Due Process Clause, to strike down the Texas law?

4. In *Casey*, the Solicitor General supported the constitutionality of the Pennsylvania statute and urged the Court to overrule *Roe*. No amicus brief on behalf of the United States was filed in *Lawrence*. Was the interest of the United States of a different magnitude in the *Lawrence* case? What factors might account for the differing posture of the United States in these two cases? (See Chapter Five for a discussion of the role of these actors in the litigation process.)

5. What was the relationship between the Court's decision in *Lawrence* and social and political change resulting from the movement for civil rights and equality for gays and lesbians? Does the opinion itself suggest that this movement, reflected in changed social attitudes and changed state laws, had

an impact on the Court's understanding of the constitutional claims? Does the *Lawrence* opinion risk creating a backlash of energized "anti-gay" activism? Energized anti-Court activism? Should either of these possibilities matter to the Justices? Is it possible to have decisions that recognize equality of subordinated groups that do not carry such risks? And what are the risks of *not* recognizing such constitutional claims once social and political movements have changed consciousness and other laws? For thoughtful discussions, see, e.g., William N. Eskridge, Jr, *Body Politics: Lawrence v. Texas and the Constitution of Disgust and Contagion,* 57 Fla. L. Rev. 1011 (2005); William N. Eskridge, Jr., *Channeling: Identity–Based Social Movements and Public Law*, 150 U. Penn. L. Rev. 419 (2001). See also, William N. Eskridge, Jr., *Pluralism and Distrust: How Courts Can Support Democracy By Lowering the Stakes of Politics*, 114 Yale L. J. 1279, 1305–06 (2005) (praising Justice O'Connor's opinion in *Lawrence* for "channeling" discussion away from harmful group stereotypes without signalling "disrespect" for "traditionalists").

B. COMPARATIVE INSTITUTIONAL PERSPECTIVES: JUSTICIABILITY, TIMING, AND *STARE DECISIS*

Several features have been said to distinguish the U.S. system of constitutional adjudication from that followed by other countries. As noted in the Introduction to this book, the U.S. Supreme Court sits to review a wide range of federal questions, not only issues of constitutional law; it is in that sense a "generalist" court. Moreover, it may hear only those concrete disputes that are "cases or controversies" within the meaning of Article III; it does not exercise "advisory" jurisdiction or decide purely abstract disputes. By contrast, in many European countries, a specialized constitutional court sits, somewhat apart from the ordinary courts, to decide only constitutional questions. In these "centralized" systems of judicial review, proceedings may be brought before the constitutional court as soon as a law is passed by the legislature, and without a concrete "case or controversy" within the meaning of U.S. constitutional law. In Germany, for example, a group of dissenting legislators can immediately challenge the constitutionality of a national law before the German Constitutional Court in a form of "abstract" review. In the United States, the Court has held, legislators do not have standing to raise such abstract challenges.[7] In France, the Conseil Constitutionnel may review the constitutionality of national laws only within a very short time window after the law has passed the national legislature but before it is promulgated by the President—review occurs just before the law goes into effect. In the United States, a challenge to a

7. Raines v. Byrd, 521 U.S. 811 (1997)(legislators did not have standing to pursue claim that the Line Item Veto was unconstitutional because the injury complained of, injury to official power, was not concrete or personal to the legislators.) Af-ter President Clinton exercised the veto and the City of New York was aggrieved, it had standing to challenge the veto and the Court struck the veto down. See Clinton v. City of New York, 524 U.S. 417 (1998).

law that had not been signed by the President (or enacted through the veto override process) would be considered unripe.[8] And the doctrine of *stare decisis* is sometimes said to distinguish common law from civil law systems,[9] a distinction that should not be drawn too sharply in the realm of constitutional adjudication, but one that probably accounts for the distinctive tendency of the U.S. Supreme Court to reason primarily from the Court's own precedents in many constitutional cases.

Consider how these concerns—of justiciability, timing of review, and *stare decisis*—were or were not important in *Casey, Lawrence*, and the cases discussed below.

1. BUSH V. GORE—The Court and the 2000 Election

The presidential election of November 7, 2000 led to several decisions by the Supreme Court between election day and December 12, 2000. In this 35 day period, the Court issued an opinion in Bush v. Palm Beach Co. Canvassing Bd., 531 U.S. 70 (December 4, 2000) (per curiam) (*Bush I*), then issued a stay of a recount ordered by the Florida Supreme Court, Bush v. Gore, 531 U.S. 1046 (December 9, 2000) (*Bush II*) and then three days later, on December 12, 2000, issued an opinion that in effect ended the election contest, Bush v. Gore, 531 U.S. 98 (*Bush III*).

Bush I—The Dec. 4 opinion

BUSH V. PALM BEACH CO. CANVASSING BD., 531 U.S. 70 (2000)

PER CURIAM

The Supreme Court of the State of Florida interpreted its elections statutes in proceedings brought to require manual recounts of ballots, and the certification of the recount results, for votes cast in the quadrennial Presidential election held on November 7, 2000. Governor George W. Bush, Republican candidate for the Presidency, filed a petition for certiorari to review the Florida Supreme Court decision. We granted certiorari on two of the questions presented by petitioner: whether the decision of the Florida Supreme Court, by effectively changing the State's elector appointment procedures after election day, violated the Due Process Clause or 3 U.S.C. § 5, and whether the decision of that court changed the manner in which the State's electors are to be

---

8. See, e.g., United Public Workers v. Mitchell, 330 U.S. 75 (refusing to overturn a statute that posed a hypothetical threat to First Amendment rights where the challenging party had not yet been prosecuted under the statute); but cf. New York v. United States, 505 U.S. 144 (1992) (adjudicating challenge to provisions in statute which were not effective until several years later).

9. See, e.g., M. Cappelletti, *The Judicial Process in a Comparative Perspective* (1989); but cf. Gunther Weiss, *The Enchantment of Codification in the Common-Law World*, 25 Yale J. Int'l L. 435 (2000). However, although the formal doctrine of *stare decisis* comes from the common law world, many constitutional courts do give weight to their own prior decisions.

selected, in violation of the legislature's power to designate the manner for selection under Art. II, § 1, cl. 2 of the United States Constitution.

On November 8, 2000, the day following the Presidential election, the Florida Division of Elections reported that Governor Bush had received 2,909,131 votes, and respondent Democrat Vice President Albert Gore, Jr., had received 2,907,351, a margin of 1,784 in Governor Bush's favor. Under Fla. Stat. § 102.141(4) (2000), because the margin of victory was equal to or less than one-half of one percent of the votes cast, an automatic machine recount occurred. The recount resulted in a much smaller margin of victory for Governor Bush. Vice President Gore then exercised his statutory right to submit written requests for manual recounts to the canvassing board of any county. See § 102.166. He requested recounts in four counties: Volusia, Palm Beach, Broward, and Miami–Dade.

[A dispute arose concerning the authority of the canvassing boards, the Secretary of State (hereinafter Secretary), and the Elections Canvassing Commission, which led to state court litigation; the state court concluded that the Secretary of State had discretion to accept late amended returns in the statewide certification of the returns, if they were proffered by November 15. On November 16, the Secretary determined to accept none of the late returns submitted by the four counties. In litigation initiated by the Florida Democratic Party and Vice President Gore arguing that the Secretary had acted improperly, the Florida Supreme Court entered an order enjoining final certification of the results pending further court order.]

. . . As the [Florida Supreme] Court saw the matter, there were two principal questions: whether a discrepancy between an original machine return and a sample manual recount resulting from the way a ballot has been marked or punched is an "error in vote tabulation" justifying a full manual recount; and how to reconcile what it spoke of as two conflicts in Florida's election laws: (a) between the time frame for conducting a manual recount under Fla. Stat. § 102.166 (2000) and the time frame for submitting county returns under §§ 102.111 and 102.112, and (b) between § 102.111, which provides that the Secretary "shall . . . ignore" late election returns, and § 102.112, which provides that she "may . . . ignore" such returns.

With regard to the first issue, the court held that, under the plain text of the statute, a discrepancy between a sample manual recount and machine returns due to the way in which a ballot was punched or marked did constitute an "error in vote tabulation" sufficient to trigger the statutory provisions for a full manual recount.

With regard to the second issue, the court held that the "shall . . . ignore" provision of § 102.111 conflicts with the "may . . . ignore" provision of § 102.112, and that the "may . . . ignore" provision controlled. . . . The court relied in part upon the right to vote set forth in the Declaration of Rights of the Florida Constitution in concluding that late manual recounts could be rejected only under limited circumstances.

The court then stated: "Because of our reluctance to rewrite the Florida Election Code, we conclude that we must invoke the equitable powers of this Court to fashion a remedy...." The court thus imposed a deadline of November 26, at 5 p.m., for a return of ballot counts. The 7–day deadline of § 102.111, assuming it would have applied, was effectively extended by 12 days. The court further directed the Secretary to accept manual counts submitted prior to that deadline.

[The Supreme Court indicated concern over two issues: first, whether the state court's interpretation of state law was inconsistent with the provisions of Article II of the U.S. Constitution, that "Each State shall appoint, in such Manner as the Legislature thereof may direct," the presidential electors, a provision described, in a different context, in McPherson v. Blacker, 146 U.S. 1, 25 (1892), as " 'operating as a limitation upon the State in respect of any attempt to circumscribe the legislative power'."]

There are expressions in the opinion of the Supreme Court of Florida that may be read to indicate that it construed the Florida Election Code without regard to the extent to which the Florida Constitution could, consistent with Art. II, § 1, cl. 2, "circumscribe the legislative power." The opinion states, for example, that "to the extent that the Legislature may enact laws regulating the electoral process, those laws are valid only if they impose no 'unreasonable or unnecessary' restraints on the right of suffrage" guaranteed by the state constitution....

[In addition, the Court noted, the Florida Supreme Court had not fully addressed the impact of 3 U.S.C. § 5, a "safe harbor" provision concerning the effect of the state certifying electors by December 12. Because the grounds for the Florida Supreme Court decision were unclear in these regards, the Court "remanded for further proceedings not inconsistent with this opinion."]

_____

Bush II—The Stay Order of December 9

On remand, on December 8 the Florida Supreme Court ordered, *inter alia*, a by-hand tabulation of 9,000 ballots in Miami Dade County and manual recounts in all Florida counties where "undervotes" (ballots on which no vote had been registered during the machine count) had not been subject to manual tabulation, to begin immediately. Republican candidates Bush and Cheney filed an emergency application before the Supreme Court to stay the Florida Court's mandate. This application was granted on December 9. The Supreme Court's order reads as follows:

The application for stay presented to Justice Kennedy and by him referred to the Court is granted, and it is ordered that the mandate of the Supreme Court of Florida, case No. SC00–2431, is hereby stayed pending further order of the Court. In addition, the application for stay is treated as a petition for a writ of certiorari, and petition for writ of certiorari granted. The briefs of the parties, not to exceed 50 pages, are to be filed with the Clerk and served upon opposing counsel on or before 4 p.m. Sunday, December 10, 2000. Rule 29.2 is suspended in this case. Briefs may be filed in compliance with Rule 33.2 to be replaced as soon as possible with briefs prepared in compliance with Rule 33.1. The case is set for oral argument on Monday, December 11, 2000, at 11 a.m., and a total of 1 1/2 hours is allotted for oral argument.

Bush v. Gore, 531 U.S. 1046 (2000).

Four Justices dissented from this order, in an opinion written by Justice Stevens:

> JUSTICE STEVENS, with whom JUSTICE SOUTER, JUSTICE GINSBURG, and JUSTICE BREYER join, dissenting.
>
> ... [A] stay should not be granted unless an applicant makes a substantial showing of a likelihood of irreparable harm. In this case, applicants have failed to carry that heavy burden. Counting every legally cast vote cannot constitute irreparable harm. On the other hand, there is a danger that a stay may cause irreparable harm to the respondents—and, more importantly, the public at large—because of the risk that "the entry of the stay would be tantamount to a decision on the merits in favor of the applicants." ... Preventing the recount from being completed will inevitably cast a cloud on the legitimacy of the election.
>
> It is certainly not clear that the Florida decision violated federal law. The Florida Code provides elaborate procedures for ensuring that every eligible voter has a full and fair opportunity to cast a ballot and that every ballot so cast is counted. [Citation omitted.] In fact, the statutory provision relating to damaged and defective ballots states that "no vote shall be declared invalid or void if there is a clear indication of the intent of the voter as determined by the canvassing board." [Citation omitted.] In its opinion, the Florida Supreme Court gave weight to that legislative command. Its ruling was consistent with earlier Florida cases that have repeatedly described the interest in correctly ascertaining the will of the voters as paramount. [Citations omitted.] Its ruling also appears to be consistent with the prevailing view in other States. [Citation omitted.] As a more fundamental matter, the Florida court's ruling reflects the basic principle, inherent in our Constitution and our democracy, that every legal vote should be counted. See Reynolds v. Sims, 377 U.S. 533, 544–555 (1964) [Citations omitted].
>
> Accordingly, I respectfully dissent.

531 U.S. at 1047–48.

Justice Scalia responded to this dissent with a concurring opinion:

> JUSTICE SCALIA, concurring.
>
> ... On the question of irreparable harm ... the issue is not, as the dissent puts it, whether "counting every legally cast vote can

constitute irreparable harm." One of the principal issues in the appeal we have accepted is precisely whether the votes that have been ordered to be counted are, under a reasonable interpretation of Florida law, "legally cast votes." The counting of votes that are of questionable legality does in my view threaten irreparable harm to petitioner, and to the country, by casting a cloud upon what he claims to be the legitimacy of his election. Count first, and rule upon legality afterwards, is not a recipe for producing election results that have the public acceptance democratic stability requires. Another issue in the case, moreover, is the propriety, indeed the constitutionality, of letting the standard for determination of voters' intent— dimpled chads, hanging chads, etc.—vary from county to county, as the Florida Supreme Court opinion, as interpreted by the Circuit Court, permits. If petitioners are correct that counting in this fashion is unlawful, permitting the count to proceed on that erroneous basis will prevent an accurate recount from being conducted on a proper basis later, since it is generally agreed that each manual recount produces a degradation of the ballots, which renders a subsequent recount inaccurate."

Id., at 1046–47.

———

Bush III: The Final Decision of December 12

On December 12, 2000, the Court issued its last ruling in this matter. Bush v. Gore, 531 U.S. 98 (2000). In a "per curiam" opinion from which four Justices dissented, the Court found that the order for manual recounts, which the state court had directed be conducted under an "intent of the voter" standard,[10] violated the Equal Protection clause because of the absence of more specific rules to implement this standard, which might result in the same ballot being counted differently by different counters. "We are presented with a situation where a state court with the power to assure uniformity has ordered a statewide recount with minimal procedural safeguards. Where a court orders a statewide remedy there must be at least some assurance that the rudimentary requirements of equal treatment and fundamental fairness are satisfied." *Id.*, at 109. Because the federal statute provided a "safe harbor" for state results certified by December 12 and because the Court concluded that Florida statutes manifested an intent to bring the state within that safe harbor, the Court concluded that a remand would serve no purpose since it would be impossible to conduct a recount that both met the safe harbor of December 12 and complied with Equal Protection standards.

Chief Justice Rehnquist, who joined the per curiam opinion, also wrote separately in a concurrence joined by Justices Scalia and Thomas.

10. See 531 U.S. at 102 ("A 'legal vote,' as determined by the [Florida] Supreme Court, is 'one in which there is a "clear indication of the intent of the voter." ' ").

He argued that under *McPherson v. Blacker*, the state court interpretation of Florida law had so far departed from a correct interpretation that its views could not be treated, for the purpose of Article II, Section 1, clause 2, as representing the decision of the state legislature. Although recognizing that under Erie R. Co. v. Tompkins, 304 U.S. 64 (1938), state courts ordinarily can make definitive pronouncements of state law, the Constitution had devolved power only on the state *legislature* to determine the manner in which electors are chosen. "The text of the election law itself, and not just its interpretation by the courts of the States, takes on independent significance" for federal purposes. *Id.* at 113. The concurrence presented an extended argument that the state court had "departed from the legislative scheme" in its interpretation of state law. *Id.* at 113–18.

There were several dissenting opinions as well. Two of the four dissenters, Justices Souter and Breyer, believed that there was a serious equal protection concern with the state's method of conducting the recount, but all four of the dissenters argued that the Court's remedy of cutting off the recount was unjustified.

Justice Stevens, with whom Justices Ginsburg and Breyer joined, disagreed with Chief Justice Rehnquist on the meaning of Article II, emphasizing that the Constitution refers to the legislature "thereof"— meaning, the legislature of the state, acting constrained by the state constitution which the Florida court had relied on as an aid to interpretation of the state statute. On the equal protection violation found by the per curiam, Justice Stevens argued that while the use of differing standards for determining voter intent in different counties may raise "serious concerns," they are "alleviated—if not eliminated—by the fact that [under the Florida court order] a single impartial magistrate will ultimately adjudicate all objections arising from the recount process." *Id.* at 126. In a notable closing, Justice Stevens wrote:

> What must underlie petitioners' entire federal assault on the Florida election procedures is an unstated lack of confidence in the impartiality and capacity of the state judges who would make the critical decisions if the vote count were to proceed. Otherwise, their position is wholly without merit. The endorsement of that position by a majority of this Court can only lend credence to the most cynical appraisal of the work of judges throughout the land. It is confidence in the men and women who administer the judicial system that is the true backbone of the rule of law. Time will one day heal the wound to that confidence that will be inflicted by today's decision. One thing, however, is certain. Although we may never know with complete certainty the identity of the winner of this year's Presidential election, the identity of the loser is perfectly clear. It is the Nation's confidence in the judge as an impartial guardian of the rule of law.

Id. at 128–29. Justices Ginsburg, Souter, and Breyer also filed separate dissenting opinions.

Questions and Comments

1. Think about the timing of this litigation, and how it may have affected the process—including the lawyers' investigation of the facts, their preparation of the arguments, and the Justices' time for deliberation and writing.

2. In *Casey* and *Bush*, we have seen the use of joint and per curiam opinions, respectively. Why would an opinion issue without a single identified author? Note: The opinion in Cooper v. Aaron, 358 U.S. 1 (1958), rejecting Arkansas' defiance of the *Brown v. Board of Education* decision, was signed by all nine Justices—issued not as a per curiam, but as a joint opinion. Does a joint opinion signify something different from a per curiam?

3. In note 2 of her dissent in *Bush III*, Justice Ginsburg suggested that the Court erred in deciding some or all of the issues before it. She wrote:

> Even in rare cases in which a State's "manner" of making and construing laws might implicate a structural constraint, Congress, not this Court, is likely the proper governmental entity to enforce that constraint. See U.S. Const. Amend 12; 3 U.S.C. Sections 1–15; cf. Ohio *ex rel* Davis v. Hildebrant, 241 U.S. 565 (1916) (treating as a nonjusticiable political question whether use of a referendum to override a congressional districting plan enacted by the state legislature violates Art. I, Section 4); Luther v. Borden, 7 How. 1, 42 (1849).

531 U.S. at 142 n.2. Should the Court have treated *Bush v. Gore* as raising a nonjusticable political question? For discussion, see Rachel Barkow, *More Supreme Than Court*: *The Fall of the Political Question Doctrine and the Rise of Judicial Supremacy*, 102 Colum. L. Rev. 237 (2002).

4. Consider this passage in the last per curiam opinion:

> The recount process, in its features here described, is inconsistent with the minimum procedures necessary to protect the fundamental right of each voter in the special instance of a statewide recount under the authority of a single state judicial officer. Our consideration is limited to the present circumstances, for the problem of equal protection in election processes generally presents many complexities.

Bush III, 531 U.S. at 109. What are the *stare decisis* implications of such a decision? How would the principle of *stare decisis* apply to the use by different counties of different voting machines, some of which had a higher rate of accurately reading ballots than others? To manual counts in some counties as compared to machine counts in others? To confusing ballots in one county as compared to another? Is this passage an appropriate caution about the particular context of the decision? An inappropriate effort to avoid the ordinary requirement for principled development of the law?

5. The per curiam noted that without more detailed statewide standards, citizens in different counties who marked their ballots identically would have their vote counted or not for no reason whatsoever, a result inconsistent with the right to vote and the principle that a state may not, by "arbitrary and disparate treatment, value one person's vote over that of another." *Bush III*, 531 U.S. at 104. The per curiam's equal protection

discussion has been criticized for ignoring the rights of those voters whose ballots were not counted at all but whose intent was reasonably discernible as compared to those voters whose ballots were counted. On the merits and demerits of the various arguments, an extensive law review literature has been generated, much of it quite critical of the Court's reasoning. For a sampler, see *The Vote: Bush, Gore, and the Supreme Court* (Cass R. Sunstein & Richard A. Epstein, eds., 2001).

2. DICKERSON V. UNITED STATES—Congress, the Court and *Stare Decisis*

In Miranda v. Arizona, 384 U.S. 436 (1966), the Court held that the Constitution requires the police to warn persons held in custody, as suspects of a crime, of their rights to remain silent and to consult with an attorney. Three years later, Congress enacted 18 U.S.C. § 3501, attempting to return to the "totality of the circumstances" test that had been used prior to *Miranda* to analyze Fifth Amendment challenges to the admission of statements—i.e., under "the totality of the circumstances" were the statements made voluntarily? The U.S. Justice Department, however, determined that it would not rely on the statute, in light of its questionable constitutionality, and the statute lay unused for decades. Paul Cassell, *The Statute That Time Forgot:18 U.S.C. § 3501 and the Overhauling of Miranda*, The Independent Institute, Working Paper #11 (1999).

However, in 1999, the Fourth Circuit, as urged by an amicus curiae and not by either the government or the defendant, relied on the statute to reverse a district court decision excluding evidence. United States v. Dickerson, 166 F.3d 667 (4th Cir. 1999). The Supreme Court granted certiorari, and the issue of the statute's constitutionality before the Court turned, in important part, on whether *Miranda* warnings were required by the Constitution. In a decision for a 7–2 Court, Chief Justice Rehnquist argued both that *Miranda* was a constitutional decision and that *stare decisis* required adherence to it as a constitutional decision. Therefore the statute was found to be unconstitutional. Dickerson v. United States, 530 U.S. 428 (2000).

Compare the plurality opinion in *Casey* with the following statements from the *Dickerson* opinion:

> Whether or not we would agree with *Miranda's* reasoning and its resulting rule, were we addressing the issue in the first instance, the principles of *stare decisis* heavily weigh against overruling it now. While "stare decisis is not an inexorable command," particularly when we are interpreting the Constitution, "even in constitutional cases the doctrine carries such persuasive force that we have always required a departure from precedent to be supported by some 'special justification'."

> We do not think there is such justification for overruling *Miranda*. *Miranda* has become embedded in routine police practice to the point where the warnings have become part of our national

culture. While we have overruled our precedents when subsequent cases have undermined their doctrinal underpinnings, we do not believe this has happened to the *Miranda* decision. If anything, our subsequent cases have reduced the impact of *Miranda* on legitimate law enforcement while reinforcing the decision's core ruling that unwarned statements may not be used as evidence in the prosecution's case in chief.

The disadvantage of the *Miranda* rule is that statements which may by no means be involuntarily made by a defendant who is aware of his "rights" may nonetheless be excluded and a guilty defendant go free as a result. But experience suggests that the totality of the circumstances test which Section 3402 seeks to revive is more difficult than *Miranda* for law enforcement officers to conform to and for courts to apply in a consistent manner. The requirement that *Miranda* warnings be given does not of course dispense with the voluntariness inquiry. But . . . cases in which a defendant can make a colorable argument that a self incriminating statement was compelled despite the fact that the law enforcement authorities adhered to the dictates of *Miranda* are rare.

In sum, we conclude that *Miranda* announced a constitutional rule that Congress may not supersede legislatively. Following the rule of *stare decisis* we decline to overrule *Miranda* ourselves."
530 U.S. at 444.

In some contrast with *Dickerson*, consider Payne v. Tennessee, 501 U.S. 808 (1991). In *Payne*, the Court *sua sponte* directed the parties to brief the question, not raised in the petition, whether to overrule recent decisions in Booth v. Maryland, 482 U.S. 496 (1987) and South Carolina v. Gathers, 490 U.S. 805 (1989), prohibiting use of victim impact statements before capital sentencing juries. In an opinion for a 6–3 Court, Chief Justice Rehnquist made these comments on *stare decisis*:

> *Stare decisis* is the preferred course because it promotes the evenhanded, predictable and consistent development of legal principles, fosters reliance on judicial decisions, and contributes to the actual and perceived integrity of the judicial proces0s. . . . Nevertheless, when governing decisions are unworkable or badly reasoned, "this Court has never felt constrained to follow precedent." *Stare decisis* is not an inexorable command; rather it "is a principle of policy and not a mechanical formula of adherence to the latest decision." . . . This is particularly true in constitutional cases, because in such cases "correction through legislative action is practically impossible." . . . Considerations in favor of *stare decisis* are at their acme in cases involving property and contract rights, where reliance interests are involved. . . . the opposite is true in cases such as the present one involving procedural and evidentiary rules.

> Applying these general principles, the Court has during the past 20 Terms overruled in whole or in part 33 of its previous constitutional decisions. [Footnote omitted.] *Booth* and *Gathers* were decided

by the narrowest of margins, over spirited dissents challenging the basic underpinnings of those decisions. They have been questioned by Members of the Court in later decisions, and have defied consistent application in the lower courts.... Reconsidering these decisions now, we conclude ... that they were wrongly decided and should be, and now are, overruled....

501 U.S. at 827–830.

In his last dissent before retiring, Justice Thurgood Marshall sharply criticized the *Payne* majority:

Power, not reason, is the new currency of the Court's decision-making. Four terms ago, a five-Justice majority of this Court held that 'victim impact' evidence of the type at issue in this case could not constitutionally be introduced during the penalty phase of a capital trial.... By another 5–4 vote, a majority of this Court rebuffed an attack upon this ruling just two Terms ago. [Citation omitted.] Nevertheless, having expressly invited respondent to renew the attack, today's majority overrules *Booth* and *Gathers* and credits the dissenting views expressed in those cases. Neither the law nor the facts supporting *Booth* and *Gathers* underwent any change in the last four years. Only the personnel of this Court did.

... [T]he majority declares itself free to discard any principle of constitutional liberty which was recognized or reaffirmed over the dissenting votes of four justices with which five or more justices *now* disagree.

... [T]he continued vitality of literally scores of decisions must be understood to depend on nothing more than the proclivities of the individuals who *now* comprise a majority of this Court....

... [T]his impoverished conception of *stare decisis* cannot possibly be reconciled with the values that inform the proper judicial function. ... [S]*tare decisis* is important not merely because individuals rely on precedent to structure their commercial activity but because fidelity to precedent is part and parcel of a conception of "the judiciary as a source of impersonal and reasoned judgments," ... [a function] more critical in adjudication involving constitutional liberties than in adjudication involving commercial entitlements.... [T]he "strong presumption of validity" to which "recently decided cases" are entitled is "an essential thread in the mantle of protection that the law affords the individual.... It is the unpopular or beleaguered individual—not the man in power—who has the greatest stake in the integrity of the law.".....

... [T]he majority's debilitated conception of *stare decisis* would destroy the Court's very capacity to resolve authoritatively the abiding conflicts between those with power and those without. If this Court shows so little respect for its own precedents, it can hardly expect them to be treated more respectfully by the state actors whom those decisions are supposed to bind.

Id., at 844, 851, 852–853 (Marshall, J., dissenting).

Questions and Comments

1.   Consider whether Justice Marshall's dissent finds echoes in the plurality opinion in *Casey*? In the dissents in *Lawrence*? Consider whether it enhances the legitimacy of law to adhere to a constitutional ruling a majority of the current Justices believes is wrongly decided? Should the Court ever write an opinion that states, "Even though decision X was wrongly decided, for reasons of *stare decisis* we adhere to it."? Should it matter whether a prior 5–4 decision is overturned by a 5–4 vote? A 6–3 vote (as was the case in *Payne*)?

2.   It has been said that the "decentralized" system of judicial review in the United States, permitting constitutional issues to "percolate" in the lower courts, together with its insistence on standing and justiciability rules, allows the Court time to provide a "sober second thought" about the constitutionality of legislation. Alexander M. Bickel, *The Least Dangerous Branch* 26 (2d ed. 1986), borrowing the phrase from Harlan Fiske Stone, *The Common Law in the United States,* 50 Harv. L. Rev. 4, 25 (1936). According to this view, by awaiting concrete applications of a statute and litigation up through the lower courts, not only does time pass (and passions cool), but the concrete manifestations of particular disputes may demonstrate constitutional questions not fully contemplated at the time of enactment. As noted above, in European systems, it is often true that "abstract" judicial review of national laws is available at the time of enactment or promulgation. Was *Casey*, however, in effect a case of "abstract review"? *Lawrence* appears as a very traditional "case"—did its posture as review of a criminal conviction notably affect the Court's analysis? What about *Bush v. Gore* and *Dickerson v. United States*—to what extent do they meet traditional Article III requirements of justiciability? Note that in *Dickerson*, the issue before the Court— whether a federal statute in effect "overruling" *Miranda* in federal prosecutions in favor of a totality of the circumstance test was constitutional and should be applied to defeat Dickerson's Fifth Amendment challenge—was not argued or defended by the Justice Department nor by the defendant, but was a point raised only by an amicus curiae.[11]

3.   How did timing affect the Court's process of adjudication in *Casey*? In *Lawrence*? In *Bush v. Gore*? In *Dickerson*? Who controlled the time when the issue was adjudicated? Was the Court providing a "sober second look"?

---

11.   The Fourth Circuit, on reviewing an interlocutory appeal by the government from the district court decision suppressing a confession, *sua sponte* relied on 18 U.S.C. 3501. "[We are not bound by the fact that] the Department of Justice, elevating politics over law, prohibited the U.S. Attorney's Office from arguing that Dickerson's confession is admissible under the mandate of § 3501. Fortunately, we are a court of law and not politics. Thus, the Department of Justice cannot prevent us from deciding this case under the governing law simply by refusing to argue it." 166 F.3d 667, 672 (4th Cir. 1999). In the Supreme Court, an attorney was appointed to argue for the constitutionality of the statute: "Because no party to the underlying litigation argued in favor of § 3501's constitutionality in this Court, we invited Professor Paul Cassell to assist our deliberations by arguing in support of the judgment below." 530 U.S. 428, 442 n.7 (2000).

4. The role of *stare decisis* has come to play a major role in the confirmation hearings of Supreme Court Justices. See Chapter Two below (discussing Senator Specter's views on "super-duper precedents".)

5. The early Terms of the Roberts Court have already generated critiques for asserted failures to give *stare decisis* effects to past decisions, including *Roe* and *Casey*. See Linda Greenhouse, *Precedents Begin to Fall for Roberts Court*, N.Y. Times, June 21, 2007, at A21.[12] Consider in light of the Court's evolution as of the time when you are studying these materials whether that evolution provides support for generalizing from Justice Marshall's argument in *Payne* that the continuing power of *stare decisis* is subject to the shifting sensibilities of the Court's membership.

12. Greenhouse states that "experienced listeners have learned to take ... professions of devotion to precedent '*cum grano salis*,' Latin for 'with a grain of salt.' " *Id.*, at A21. She points to two decisions in the 2006 Term to support this assertion: Gonzales v. Carhart, 127 S. Ct. 1610 (2007) (upholding the federal Partial–Birth Abortion Act of 2003, barring women from obtaining a "partial birth" abortion except where necessary to save the woman's life, but not to protect her health), which, she points out, many say "overruled 'by stealth' " Stenberg v. Carhart, 530 U.S. 914 (2000) (ruling unconstitutional a Nebraska act which barred women from obtaining a "partial birth" abortion except where necessary to save the woman's life); and Bowles v. Russell, 127 S. Ct. 2360 (2007) (ruling that the Court does not recognize the "unique circumstances" exception to excuse the untimely filing of a notice of appeal), which explicitly overturned Thompson v. INS, 375 U.S. 384 (1964) (allowing the unique circumstances exception for an untimely filing of a notice of appeal).

Chapter Two

APPOINTING SUPREME COURT JUSTICES

Supreme Court Justices have substantial discretion over what cases they hear; moreover, they do their own work aided only by a very small staff. Consequently, the character and ability of the individual Justices importantly affect the quality and nature of the Supreme Court's work. This is an institution where the identity of its personnel clearly matters.

Article II, Section 2 of the United States Constitution provides that the President "shall nominate, and by and with the Advice and Consent of the Senate, shall appoint . . . Judges of the supreme Court." From the first Supreme Court appointments by President Washington until the most recent appointments, the process of selecting Supreme Court Justices has been the subject of intense discussion and debate.

The materials begin in Part A by providing background on the debate over the Constitution's appointment provisions, followed by an historical overview of the confirmation process, including a discussion of how the Chief Justice is chosen. The materials consider the roles of the President, the Senate, and outside groups, including the American Bar Association which, over the decades, has had a special role in the evaluative process. Part B provides what we call Case Studies, excerpts from a number of relatively recent confirmation hearings. Finally, Part C evaluates the appointment process and asks how it might be improved.

A. THE HISTORY OF THE JUDICIAL APPOINT-MENT PROCESS

Since the founding of our government in 1789, we have had 110 Justices; Samuel Alito's appointment on January 31, 2006 made him the 110th. To fill those positions, we have had 158 nominations, 122 of which were confirmed, 36 were not.[1] While each rejected nomination is a

---

1. The 158 nominations consisted of 139 persons; 19 of the 158 nominations were of people nominated more than once. (The dif-ference between the 122 confirmations and the 110 Justices who served reflects the fact that some confirmed nominees declined the

story unto itself, the 23% failure rate of nominations is a significant feature of the process. According to one 1972 study, an important relationship exists between presidential weakness and Senate rejection of nominees. See Thomas Halper, *Senate Rejection of Supreme Court Nominees*, 22 Drake L. Rev. 102 (1972) (proposing and offering empirical verification of a "jackal theory" that the Senate is most likely to oppose the President on a Supreme Court nominee when the President is "especially weak," as when the President is a lame duck who cannot be reelected or is unusually unpopular).[2]

Supreme Court Justices do not have a fixed term; under Article III of the Constitution they "hold their Offices during good Behaviour," and vacancies therefore arise irregularly. Nonetheless, all but three of the 43 Presidents made at least one nomination; the three Presidents who had no such opportunity were William Henry Harrison, Zachary Taylor, and Jimmy Carter. Harrison and Taylor died shortly after taking office; and Carter's years simply saw no vacancy.[3]

While the Constitution does not require that a Supreme Court Justice (or any federal judge) be a lawyer, all Justices have, in fact, been trained in the law.[4] Some, but certainly not all, have had prior judicial experience. Among the 110 people who have served on the Court as of 2007,[5] only 30 had ten or more years of experience on any judicial tribunal before being appointed to the Court and 41 had no judicial experience at all.[6] Indeed, five of the seventeen Chief Justices had no

appointment and that five persons served as both Associate and Chief Justice.) For a listing of all nominations to the Court and their outcomes, see Denis Steven Rutkus & Maureen Bearden, Cong., Research Serv., *Supreme Court Nominations, 1789–2005: Actions by the Senate, the Judiciary Committee, and the President* 19 (Order Code RL 33225, Jan. 5, 2006). See also Denis Steven Rutkus, Cong. Research Serv., *Supreme Court Appointment Process: Role of the President, Judiciary Committee, and Senate* 61 (Order Code RL 31989, June 25, 2007) (list of Supreme Court nominations not confirmed by the Senate). Of the 36 unsuccessful nominations, 11 were rejected by the Senate roll-call votes, 11 were withdrawn by the President, and 14 lapsed at the end of a congressional session without a Senate vote. *Id.* at 59.

2. Halper also found that when the Court itself was particularly unpopular, there was a higher rate of Senate rejection of nominees. *Id.* at Table 4.

3. See Rutkus & Bearden, *supra*, at 19. One other President, Andrew Johnson, made no appointments to the Supreme Court, but it was not for lack of a vacancy. After the Civil War and the assassination of President Lincoln, Johnson was too unpopular to get his one nominee, Henry Standbury, confirmed. And in the Judiciary Act of

1866, Congress reduced the number of Justices from ten to seven prospectively, providing that no Justice would be replaced until the number of Justices on the Court was down to six and the next nominee would be the seventh appointment. Judiciary Act of 1866, ch 10, 14 Stat. 209. Two seats went unfilled until this law was repealed after Johnson left office; the 1869 statute restored the Court to nine members, as it has been since. See Act of April 10, 1869, ch. 22, § 1, 16 Stat. 44.

4. Only 63 of the 110 attended law school, and, of those, only 46 graduated. Henry Abraham, *Justices, Presidents and Senators* 45 (1999).

5. Of these 110, five served as both Associate Justices and as Chief Justice, bringing the total number of positions filled to 115. For a history of the number of Justices on the Court, see Peter G. Fish, "Justices, Number of," *The Oxford Companion to the Supreme Court of the United States* (Kermit L. Hall, ed., 2005).

6. For a list of all the Justices with no prior judicial experience, see *Supreme Court Justices Without Prior Judicial Experience Before Becoming Justices*, Findlaw Constitutional Center, http://Supreme.lp.findlaw.com/supreme_court/justices/nopriorexp.

judicial experience before becoming Chief Justice: John Marshall, Roger Taney, Morrison R. Waite, Melville W. Fuller, and Earl Warren. And Associate Justices appointed with no prior judicial experience included Joseph Story, Charles Evans Hughes, Louis D. Brandeis, Harlan Fiske Stone, Felix Frankfurter, Robert H. Jackson, Lewis F. Powell, Jr. and William H. Rehnquist.

The demographics of those appointed to the Court have been the subject of considerable attention. According to leading scholars, appointees historically have been white, male, Protestant, Anglo–Saxon, of upper-middle to high social status with many years in public service, and from populous states. See, e.g., Henry Abraham, *Justices, Presidents and Senators* 44–45 (1999); Thomas Halper, *Supreme Court Appointments: Criteria and Consequences*, 21 N.Y.L. Forum 563 (1976). The current Court has more demographic diversity than this historic norm. As of 2007, of the 110 persons to serve on the Court, there have been two women, two African–Americans, 11 Catholics, and 7 Jewish appointees. Lee Epstein et al., *The Supreme Court Compendium: Data, Decisions & Developments* 280–89 (4th ed. 2007).

In this chapter, we examine the who and the why behind all these numbers: who gets nominated and ultimately appointed. In the first excerpt below, Professors Strauss and Sunstein describe the history of the Constitutional Convention's adoption of the appointment process as we now know it. This history addresses the decision to give the nomination power to the President and the advice and consent powers to the Senate. Thereafter, excerpts from Professor Henry Abraham's book describe the range of empirical considerations employed in nominating and confirming a candidate. He concludes that there are a variety of reasons to account for the Senate's failure to confirm a nominee, including, among others, the popularity of the President. The section ends with excerpts from Professors Paul Freund and Henry Monaghan, each of whom offers empirical accounts and normative perspectives from within the legal academy on the changing roles of the President and Senate.

In Section 2, we excerpt several readings that both continue and supplement the historical narrative of the nomination process, focusing more on the twentieth century. Professor Michael Gerhardt locates Supreme Court nominations within the larger political relationships of the President and Congress, while Professor John Anthony Maltese outlines changes in the structure of Senate confirmation hearings, focusing on the increased presence of the nominee and the direct questioning of him or her during the confirmation process. David Yalof's excerpt focuses on changes in the President's process of selecting nominees since the Reagan Administration.

html. For the judicial experience of the other Justices, see Lee Epstein et al., *The Supreme Court Compendium: Data, Deci-* *sions & Developments* 280–89 (4th ed. 2007).

Sections 3 and 4 more briefly note two special features of the appointment process: nominating and confirming a Chief Justice, and the American Bar Association's role in the appointment process.

While these materials serve principally as background for subsequent analysis, they also raise several questions on their own. Given that Article III of the Constitution includes no explicit qualifications for federal judges, including Supreme Court Justices, why has every nominee to the Court been a lawyer? Prior political involvement and previous judicial experience are frequently traits of successful nominees; do these facts reflect important qualifications for the job or do they serve as surrogates for other values (such as predictability or centrism) that Presidents and Senators may seek?

1. Constitutional Design and the History of the Confirmation Process

David Strauss & Cass Sunstein,[7] *The Senate, the Constitution, and the Confirmation Process*, 101 Yale L.J. 1491, 1494–1502 (1992)

I. THE CONSTITUTION

The Constitution fully contemplates an independent role for the Senate in the selection of Supreme Court Justices. Article II, Section 2 provides that the President "shall nominate, and by and with the Advice and Consent of the Senate, shall appoint ... Judges of the supreme Court." These words assign two distinct roles to the Senate—an advisory role before the nomination has occurred and a reviewing function after the fact. The consent requirement, if the Senate takes it seriously, places pressure on the President to give weight to senatorial advice as well. At the same time, the advisory function makes consent more likely. The clause thus envisions a genuinely consultative relationship between the Senate and the President. It assumes a deliberative process, jointly conducted, concerning the composition of the Court.

History supports this view of the text. The most explicit and elaborate contemporaneous exposition was given by George Mason in 1792. Mason wrote:

> I am decidedly of opinion, that the Words of the Constitution ... give the Senate the Power of interfering in every part of the Subject, except the Right of nominating. ... The Word "*Advice*" here clearly relates in the Judgment of the Senate on the Expediency or Inexpediency of the Measure, or Appointment; and the Word "*Consent*" to their Approbation or Disapprobation of the Person nominated; oth-

---

7.   Strauss is the Harry N. Wyatt Professor of Law, University of Chicago Law School and served as Special Counsel to the United States Senate Committee on the Judiciary in connection with the appointment of David H. Souter to the Supreme Court; Sunstein is the Karl N. Llewellyn Professor of Jurisprudence, University of Chicago Law School and Department of Political Science and was a law clerk for Thurgood Marshall.

erwise the word *Advice* has no Meaning at all—and it is a well known Rule of Construction, that no Clause or Expression shall be deemed superfluous, or nugatory, which is capable of a fair and rational Meaning. The Nomination, of Course, brings the Subject fully under the Consideration of the Senate; who have then a Right to decide upon its Propriety or Impropriety. The peculiar Character or Predicament of the Senate in the Constitution of the General Government, is a strong Confirmation of this Construction.

As the records of the Constitutional Convention demonstrate, the Constitution's drafters widely shared Mason's view. The Convention had four basic options of where to vest the appointment power: it could have placed the power (1) in the President alone, (2) in Congress alone, (3) in the President with congressional advice and consent, or (4) in Congress with Presidential advice and consent. Some version of each of these options received serious consideration.

The ultimate decision to vest the appointment power in the President stemmed from a belief that he was uniquely capable of providing the requisite "responsibility." A single person would be distinctly accountable for his acts. At the same time, however, the Framers greatly feared a Presidential monopoly of the process. They worried that such a monopoly might lead to a lack of qualified and "diffused" appointees, and to patronage and corruption. The Framers also feared insufficient attentiveness to the interests of different groups affected by the Court.

An important feature of the debates was the Framers' effort to design the appointments process in a way that would protect the interests of the small states. In thinking about the appointment of Supreme Court Justices, the Framers thus focused on the likelihood that nominees would be attentive to the various interests affected by the Court. Conflicts between large and small states, a principal political question of the founding period, present a much less important issue today. But there are now other conflicting interests that are profoundly affected by the composition of the Supreme Court. The Framers contemplated a senatorial role precisely to protect such interests, and to assure a degree of political oversight of the likely votes of Supreme Court nominees. The central importance of this political concern to the selection process, as that process was originally designed, strongly argues against a Presidential monopoly today.

The compromise that finally emerged—the system of advice and consent—was designed to counteract all of these various fears. Throughout the Convention, representatives of the smaller states were especially skeptical of a large Presidential role and insistent on the need for the safeguards that the Senate could provide. Representatives of the larger states, concerned with congressional partiality and lack of responsibility, sought to constrain the Senate. The requirement of senatorial advice and consent simultaneously responded to both sets of concerns.

A. The Early Agreement on Congressional Appointment

It is important to understand that during almost all of the Convention, the Framers agreed that the Senate alone or the legislature as a whole would appoint the judges. The current institutional arrangement emerged in the last days of the process. On June 5, 1787, the standing provision required "that the national Judiciary be [chosen] by the National Legislature." James Wilson spoke against this provision and in favor of Presidential appointment. He claimed that "intrigue, partiality, and concealment" would result from legislative appointment, and that the President was uniquely "responsible." John Rutledge responded that he "was by no means disposed to grant so great a power to any single person. The people will think we are leaning too much towards Monarchy."

James Madison agreed with Wilson's concerns about legislative "intrigue and partiality," but he "was not satisfied with referring the appointment to the Executive." Instead, he proposed to place the power of appointment in the Senate, "as numerous eno' to be confided in—as not so numerous as to be governed by the motives of the other branch; and as being sufficiently stable and independent to follow their deliberative judgments." Thus, on June 5, by a vote of nine to two, the Convention accepted the vesting of the appointment power in the Senate.

On June 13, Charles Cotesworth Pinckney and Roger Sherman tried to restore the original provision for appointment of the Supreme Court by the entire Congress. Madison renewed his argument and the motion was withdrawn.

The issue reemerged on July 18. Nathaniel Ghorum claimed that even the Senate was "too numerous, and too little personally responsible, to ensure a good choice." He suggested, for the first time, that the President should appoint the Justices, with the advice and consent of the Senate—following the model set by Massachusetts. Wilson responded that the President should be able to make appointments on his own, but that the Ghorum proposals were an acceptable second best. Alexander Martin and Sherman endorsed appointments by the Senate, arguing that the Senate would have greater information and—a point of special relevance here—that "the Judges ought to be diffused," something that "would be more likely to be attended to by the 2d. branch, than by the Executive." Edmund Randolph echoed this view.

In the end, Wilson's proposal that the President alone make appointments was rejected by a vote of six to two. At that point, Ghorum moved, as an alternative, that the President should nominate and appoint judges with the advice and consent of the Senate. On this the vote was evenly divided, four to four.

Madison then proposed Presidential nomination with an opportunity for Senate rejection, by a two-thirds vote, within a specified number of days. Changing his earlier position, Madison urged that the executive would be more likely "to select fit characters," and that "in case of any flagrant partiality or error, in the nomination, it might be fairly presumed that ⅔ of the 2d. branch would join in putting a negative on it." Pinckney spoke against this proposal, as did George Mason, who argued: "[A]ppointment by the Executive [is] a dangerous prerogative. It might even give him an influence over the Judiciary department itself."

The motion was defeated by six to three. By the same vote, the earlier Madison proposal, in which the Senate would appoint the Justices, was accepted.

The issue next arose on August 23. Robert Morris argued against the appointment of officers by the Senate, considering "the body as too numerous for the purpose; as subject to cabal; and as devoid of responsibility." But it was not until September 4 that the provision appeared in its current form. Morris made the only recorded pronouncements on the new arrangement and seemed to speak for the entire, now unanimous assembly. Morris said, "[A]s the President was to nominate, there would be responsibility, and as the Senate was to concur, there would be security." Great weight should be given to the remarks made by Morris because of their timing. The Convention accepted the provision with this understanding.

B. The Meaning of the Shift to Presidential Appointment With Advice and Consent by the Senate

This picture leaves something of a puzzle. For almost all of the Convention, the appointment power was vested in the Senate. At the last moment, it was shifted to the President, with the advice and consent of the Senate. What accounts for the shift?

We speculate that two developments played an important role. First, on July 16, 1787, the Convention approved the Great Compromise, allowing equal representation for the states within the Senate despite their differences in population. This additional security for the small states may have provided those states with a degree of reassurance that made a Presidential initiative in the appointments process significantly less threatening. That reassurance, going to the structure of the document, may have made it less necessary to insist on limiting the President's role in appointments.

Second, the assessment of Presidential powers appears to have changed in a major way when the Founders devised the Electoral College, thereby allowing a degree of representation of states *qua* states in the selection of the President. As we have seen, much of the resistance to Presidential power came from the small states, which feared that the President would be inattentive to their interests. Once it was decided that the President would be selected through the new, protective route, the small states had a new degree of security against the obvious risks, from their point of view, of pure majoritarianism. They therefore would have found it less threatening to vest the power of appointment in the President in the first instance. The Framers could accomplish the central goal of ensuring "responsibility" without undue risk to state interests.

But there is no evidence of a general agreement that the President should have plenary power over the appointments process. On the contrary, the ultimate design mandated a role for the Senate in the form of the advice and consent function. In this way, it carried forward the major themes of the debates. With respect to the need for a Presidential role, the new system ensured "responsibility" and guarded against the risk of partiality in the Senate. With respect to resistance to absolute Presidential prerogative, the principal concerns included (1) a fear of "monarchy" in the form of exclusive Presidential appointment; (2) a concern for "deliberative judgments;" (3) a belief that "the Judges ought to be diffused," that is, diverse in terms of their basic commitments and alliances; (4) a fear of executive "influence over the Judiciary department itself;" and (5) a desire for the "security" that a senatorial role would provide.

As Mason's comments suggest, the Senate's role was to be a major one, allowing the Senate to be as intrusive as it chose. Even Hamilton, perhaps the strongest defender of Presidential power, emphasized that the President "was bound to submit the propriety of his choice to the discussion and determination of a different and independent body." Of course, the President retained the power to continue to offer nominees of his selection, even after an initial rejection. He could continue to name people at his discretion. Crucially, however, the Senate was granted the authority to continue to refuse to confirm. It also received the authority to "advise."

These simultaneous powers would bring about a healthy form of checks and balances, permitting each branch to counter the other. That system was part and parcel of general deliberation about Supreme Court membership. The Convention debates afford no basis for the view that the Senate's role was designed to be meager. On the contrary, they suggest a fully shared authority over the composition of the Court. That shared authority was to include all matters that the Senate deemed relevant, including the nominee's point of view.

As we have noted, this argument derives particular force from the centrality of the question of states' interests to the debate over the appointments process. The split between the large and small states was among the most important political issues of the period. Some delegates were fearful that all judicial nominees would come from large states. More generally, state rivalry, dominating the debates over the appointments clause, was the functional equivalent of the most sharply disputed of current legal and political debates. There can be no question that the "advice and consent" role was intended to provide, in Morris' terms, "security." And there can be no question that a central aspect of "security" was the power to refuse to confirm nominees insensitive to the interests of a majority of the states. In this sense, political commitments were understood to be a properly central ingredient in senatorial deliberations.

C.   The Early Practice

The practice of the Senate in the early days of the republic and thereafter attests to the same conclusion. George Washington's nomination of John Rutledge, then Chief Justice of South Carolina, as Chief Justice of the United States is the most revealing case in point. Rutledge's challenge to the Jay Treaty, negotiated by Washington with Great Britain, played a pivotal role in the confirmation process. The Jay Treaty was challenged by the Republicans as a concession to Britain but approved by the Federalists as a way of keeping the peace. Rutledge attacked the treaty in a prominent speech in Charleston. The Federalists sought to block the Rutledge appointment on straightforwardly political grounds. Hamilton, a leader of the support for the Jay Treaty, led the opposition to Rutledge. The Senate ultimately rejected Rutledge for political reasons, by a vote of fourteen to ten.

Nor was the Rutledge rejection unique. In 1811, the Senate rejected Madison's appointment of Alexander Wolcott, partly on the basis of political considerations. In 1826, President Adams' appointment of Robert Trimble was nearly rejected on political grounds. The 1828 nomination of John Crittenden, a Whig, was ultimately prevented through postponement, and squarely on ideological grounds. Similar episodes occurred in the first half of the nineteenth century. In fact, during the nineteenth century, the Senate blocked one of every four nominees for the Court, frequently on political grounds.

The Senate has at times insisted on the "advice" segment of its constitutional mandate. In 1869, President Grant nominated Edwin Stanton after receiving a petition to that effect signed by a majority of the Senate and the House. In 1932, the Chair of the Judiciary Committee, George W. Norris, insisted on the appointment of a liberal Justice to replace Oliver Wendell Holmes. Greatly influenced by a meeting with Senator William Borah, President Hoover eventually appointed Benjamin Cardozo to the Court. The Senator persuaded President Hoover to move Cardozo, then at the bottom of the President's list of preferred nominees, to the top.

D.   The Constitutional Structure

We have established that the constitutional text and history support an independent role for the Senate in the confirmation process. In the particular context of judicial appointments, there is an additional and highly compelling concern, one that stems from constitutional structure. It may be granted that the Senate ought generally to be deferential to Presidential nominations involving the operation of the executive branch. For the most part, executive branch nominees must work closely with or under the President. The President is entitled to insist that those nominees are people with whom he is comfortable, both personally and in terms of basic commitments and values.

The case is quite different, however, when the President is appointing members of a third branch. The judiciary is supposed to be independent of the President, not allied with him. It hardly needs emphasis that the judiciary is not intended to work under the President. This point is of special importance in light of the fact that many of the Court's decisions resolve conflicts between Congress and the President. A Presidential monopoly on the appointment of Supreme Court Justices thus threatens to unsettle the constitutional plan of checks and balances.

Constitutional text, history, and structure strongly suggest that the Senate is entitled to assume a far more substantial role than it has in the recent past. There are analogies to proposed legislation and treaties, and to the Presidential veto. No one thinks that the Senate must accept whatever bill or treaty the President suggests simply because it is a "competent" proposal; it would be odd indeed to claim that the President must sign every bill before looking closely at the merits. Under the Constitution, the role of the Senate in the confirmation process should be approached similarly.

Henry Abraham, *Justices, Presidents, and Senators* (1999)

Introductory Reflections—Of Criteria, Evaluations, and Judgments

It may be helpful to identify what history demonstrates as the ascertainable decisional reasons or motivations for the presidential selections of members of the Supreme Court. A quartet of steadily occurring criteria would appear to emerge quite clearly, notwithstanding specific assertions or analyses to the contrary. In no particular order of avowal or significance, that quartet embraces: first, objective merit, second, personal friendship, third, balancing "representation" or "representativeness" of the Court; and fourth, "real" political and ideological compatibility. Obviously, more than one of these factors—and, indeed, sundry others—were present in most nominations to the Court, and in some cases all four were. Yet it is entirely possible to point to one as the overriding one. Thus, a classic and well-known illustration of presidential selection based purely on the first category, objective merit qua merit, is that of Democrat Benjamin Nathan Cardozo by Republican Herbert Hoover to succeed Justice Holmes early in 1932. That public opinion and senatorial insistence practically had to put the president on a rack to prompt him to choose Cardozo is beside the point. He did—and he would ultimately be credited for it as "the finest act of his career as President."

Examples that point to the second category, that is, personal and political friendship as the overriding causation for presidential choice, abound. Among the several illustrations that come to mind quickly, yet were nonetheless unquestionably characterized by merit, is President Andrew Jackson's selection—or more accurately, selections—of Roger Brooke Taney for associate justice (unsuccessful) and chief justice (successful). Taney had been Jackson's longtime close friend, loyal adviser, and confidant. President Truman's four appointments (Harold H. Burton, Fred M. Vinson, Tom C. Clark, and Sherman Minton) fall into this category, as do, to cite three other chief executives: those by William Howard Taft of Horace H. Lurton, by John F. Kennedy of Byron R. White, and by Lyndon B. Johnson of Abe Fortas.

The third category, the "representation" or "representativeness" of a putative selectee, has become increasingly prevalent. Thus, such "representative" or "equitable" factors as race, gender, religion, and geography, lately especially the first two, are frequently advanced as a major consideration, sometimes as the controlling one. Among a host of illustrations are the obvious selections of Thurgood Marshall (race) and Sandra Day O'Connor (gender) by Presidents Lyndon B. Johnson and Ronald W. Reagan, respectively; President Lincoln's fruitful search for an outstanding trans-Mississippi lawyer (he found him in Samuel F. Miller); President Cleveland's insistence on geographic appropriateness in the person of his new chief justice, Melville W. Fuller of Illinois (to date 31 of the 50 states have been "represented".) . . .

The fourth, political and ideological compatibility, has arguably been the controlling factor. It has been that demonstrably in a large majority of instances, and understandably so. The legion of examples includes, for one, President Harding's Chief Justice Taft-inspired selection of ex-U.S. Senator and ex-U.S. Congressman George Sutherland from Utah (one of the very few of foreign birth—England—to reach the Court). An experienced lawyer as well as legislator, Sutherland allied himself with Harding when the two served together in the U.S. Senate, the association culminating in the role of brain truster to the president. He could have had any position in the latter's administration; but he preferred to accept spot troubleshooting assignments at home and abroad—in the frank anticipation of a Court vacancy.

Perhaps one ought to recognize a fifth factor: speaking to a capacity audience at the annual dinner of the American Law Institute on May 19, 1983, Justice O'Connor chose as her topic the process of selection of Supreme Court justices. . . . Her conclusion was:

> [W]hile there are many supposed criteria for the selection of a Justice, when the eventual decision is made as to who the nominee will be, that decision from the nominee's viewpoint is probably a classic example of being the right person in the right spot at the right time. Stated simply, you must be lucky.

· · ·

How They Get There

That the Senate takes its confirmation role seriously is documented by its refusal to confirm [more than 20%] of the Supreme Court nominees forwarded to it in the more than two centuries of our history as a nation. . . . Just why were [these nominees not confirmed]? Among the more prominent reasons have been: (1) opposition to the nominating president, not necessarily the nominee; (2) the nominee's involvement with one or more contentious issues of public policy or, simply, opposition to the nominee's perceived jurisprudential or sociopolitical philosophy (i.e., politics); (3) opposition to the record of the incumbent Court, which, rightly or wrongly, the nominee presumably supported; (4) senatorial courtesy (closely linked to the consultative nominating process); (5) a nominee's perceived political unreliability on the part of the party in power; (6) the evident lack of qualification or limited ability of the nominee; (7) concerted, sustained opposition by interest or pressure groups; and (8) fear that the nominee would dramatically alter the Court's jurisprudential lineup. Usually several of these reasons—not one alone—figure in the rejection of a nominee, to which poor timing and poor presidential management of a nomination—e.g., Reagan in Bork's case—could readily be added. The purpose of this list is merely to suggest some applicable prototypes.

Paul A. Freund,[8] *Appointment of Justices: Some Historical Perspectives*, 101 Harv. L. Rev. 1146, 1146–62 (1988)

The recent proceedings on three successive nominations to the Supreme Court raise anew recurring questions about the role and process of senatorial advice and consent. The questions, which are intertwined, relate to the standards and criteria to be applied and to the means whereby the Senate should inform itself in order to fulfill its role. This brief essay will address the two issues in order. The recent episodes will emerge as a convergence of two twentieth-century currents: toward a broader conception of a nominee's essential qualifications, and toward a wider participation, within and without the Senate, in the process of judging those qualifications. Though focus on the nominee's character remains paramount, the other dominant factors have shifted from sectional and party affiliations to social and judicial philosophy, and the normal procedure has changed from secret Senate hearings and debates to an intensive public inquiry into those broadened criteria.

. . .

To appreciate the appointing process in its first century one must keep in mind both the nature of the Court's business in that period and the corresponding nature of the political system. Whereas the Framers contemplated "one Supreme Court" and a governmental structure safeguarded against partisan factions, events very early overcame these assumptions. The bulk of the Justices' business consisted of individual circuit duties, and the rise of organized parties produced intense demands, in Congress and in the press, for partisan loyalty. The identification of a seat with a particular circuit led to a controlling influence of the senators from that region in the confirmation process. Thus parochialism combined with partisanship to shape appointments to the Court.

---

8. Carl M. Loeb University Professor, Emeritus, Harvard University.

The system, however flawed, did produce, however fortuitously, some outstanding Justices. The appointment of Joseph Story is illustrative. On the death in 1810 of Justice William Cushing of Massachusetts, President Madison looked to New England for a successor. Two of his nominees, Levi Lincoln and John Quincy Adams, both of Massachusetts, declined after being confirmed. Alexander Wolcott, of Connecticut, was rejected, although Madison's party controlled the Senate, because the New England Federalists were offended by Wolcott's strict enforcement, as United States Attorney, of the highly unpopular Embargo and Non–Intercourse Acts, and because even Madison's party was unenthusiastic about the nomination. Story, the fourth nominee, aged thirty-two, nominally of Madison's Democratic–Republican party in Massachusetts, was nominated and confirmed despite Thomas Jefferson's warning, abundantly vindicated during a long and powerful tenure, that he was at heart a Federalist, a "pseudo-Republican." . . .

Factional divisions of another kind, this time intraparty divisions, bedeviled President Tyler's repeated attempts in 1843 and 1844 to fill two vacancies on the Court, those left by the deaths of Justices Smith Thompson of New York and Henry Baldwin of Pennsylvania. To fill the Thompson vacancy Tyler looked to New York and, in December 1843, nominated John C. Spencer, a scholarly lawyer who had served as Secretary of War and then as Secretary of the Treasury. It was a time when a charismatic party leader could wield great power; unfortunately for Spencer he encountered both the opposition of the New York Whigs and the enmity of Henry Clay, who clearly dominated the party against a politically weak President. After the Senate's rejection of Spencer, Tyler nominated Chancellor Reuben Walworth of New York, who also ran afoul of the state political machine, and whose nomination was withdrawn after the Senate postponed action on it. A third effort succeeded. Following the defeat of the Whigs in the election of 1844, Tyler submitted the name of his third choice, Samuel Nelson, chief justice of the New York Supreme Court, who was promptly confirmed.

Meanwhile the Baldwin vacancy had arisen, and Tyler looked to Pennsylvania. His weakness within his own Whig party proved insurmountable. Two successive nominations failed: that of Edward King, a judge in Philadelphia, was tabled until the election and then withdrawn; on that of John M. Read of Philadelphia, a former United States Attorney, no action was taken. Not until twenty-eight months after Baldwin's death, and after a new election, was the vacancy filled, when President Polk's nomination of Robert M. Grier of the Pittsburgh area was speedily confirmed.

In the absence of open hearings and debates in the Senate on nominations, appraisals of nominees were furnished by a politically polarized press and by intimate correspondence among influential figures in legal and political circles. The range and worth of the latter can be epitomized by two assessments of John Read. Richard Peters, the former Reporter of the Supreme Court and a faithful Whig, wrote to Justice McLean that Read was "as suited for a Judge as I am for an admiral." James Buchanan, welcoming the ascendancy of the Democrats, wrote that there were few, if any, lawyers in Philadelphia superior to Read, and that "[h]e holds a ready and powerful political pen and is a gentleman of the strictest honour and integrity."

The appointment of a Chief Justice, though less constrained by local politics, could nevertheless conform to what Justice Frankfurter called "that odd lottery by which men get picked for the Supreme Court." In the case of President Grant's multiple efforts to fill the vacancy caused by the death in 1873 of Chief Justice Salmon P. Chase, parochialism was replaced by ineptitude. After Roscoe Conkling of New York, seemingly intent on still higher office, declined the nomination, Grant nominated his Attorney General, George H. Williams of Oregon. The nomination drew fire from several sides on the basis of incompetence and lack of character. Williams was linked to the abrupt removal of a United States Attorney in Oregon who was investigating political frauds in that state. The final stroke was the discovery that Williams had purchased with public funds a landaulet, complete with a footman, and two horses for the use of himself and his wife (herself a focus of disapproval in Washington)—perquisites not enjoyed by senators. Facing rejection, the nominee asked that his name be withdrawn.

Grant's next choice was an eccentric one. He nominated Caleb Cushing of Massachusetts, seventy-four years old, an able lawyer with a history of shifting political allegiances. It appears that the nomination was based on a strange sense of protocol. In England, Sir Roundell Palmer, chief British counsel in the *Alabama* claims arbitration at Geneva, had recently been created Lord Chancellor Selborne. Symmetry suggested that Cushing, who was the senior American counsel at Geneva, be similarly honored, if only for a short tenure. The Judiciary Committee reported the nomination favorably, though without enthusiasm. A revelation from the Civil War files of the War Department, however, brought the appointment to a sudden halt. In 1861 Cushing had written a letter, in a friendly vein, to President Jefferson Davis of the Confederacy, recommending a former clerk in the Attorney General's office for a suitable position, citing the young man's allegiance to the Confederate cause. Grant was appalled when the letter was shown to him and promptly recalled the nomination, removing an injunction of secrecy applicable to the letter.

The fixation on international symmetry, however, was not removed. Morrison R. Waite, a practicing lawyer in Cleveland, had been the third in rank of our counsel at Geneva, serving with Cushing and William M. Evarts, and he became Grant's third nominee for the center seat on the Court. Although Waite was little known outside Ohio, the Senate, with a sense of relief, readily confirmed him. Judge Ebenezer Rockwood Hoar remarked that Waite was the luckiest individual known to the law, an innocent third party without notice. As it turned out, the lucky ones were the Court and the country.

The circuit-riding duties of the Justices, which had been ameliorated, were finally eliminated by the Circuit Court of Appeals Act of 1891. That legislation did not abruptly end the tendency to make an appointment from the state or circuit of the retiring judge. The most pronounced example of this practice was the so-called New England seat on the Court, a succession broken only in 1932 with the justly acclaimed appointment by President Hoover of Chief Judge Benjamin N. Cardozo of New York to succeed Justice Holmes. . . .

From 1894 to 1930 there were no further rejections, but the focus of concern in the Senate underwent a marked shift, coincident with the Court's increased activity in judging the merits of social and economic legislation under the due process clauses of the fifth, and especially the fourteenth, amendments. The turning point was President Wilson's nomination, in late January, 1916, of Louis D. Brandeis of Boston. He was one of the very few nominees to the Court who had held no public office, but he was a nationally-known public figure because of his challenges to such established practices and institutions as bankers' control of big business, interlocking corporate directorships, the New Haven railroad management, abuses in industrial life insurance, and inefficient corporate consolidations. In courts, in print, and in legislative hearings, he had championed savings bank life insurance, cooperatives, minimum-wage and maximum-hour laws, collective bargaining, and the responsibility of labor unions. He regarded himself as a conservative, in the sense of Macaulay's dictum that to reform is to preserve, but he was perceived in the upper reaches of Boston's financial and business community as a dangerous radical.

The opposition couched its attack in terms of questionable character and lack of judicial temperament, and occasionally anti-Semitism became overt, but essentially the campaign against the nominee rested on the repugnance of his social and economic views. Writing in *The New Republic*, Walter Lippmann put it concisely: Brandeis was deemed untrustworthy only by "the powerful but limited community which dominated the business and social life of Boston. He was untrustworthy because he was troublesome." Lippmann was responding to a petition opposing the nomination circulated by President A. Lawrence Lowell of Harvard, signed by fifty-five prominent Bostonians. Notably missing among the signatures was that of President Emeritus Charles W. Eliot, Boston's (and perhaps the nation's) first citizen, who wrote a deeply-felt, appreciative letter highly praising the nomination. On a lower level, of the eleven Harvard Law School professors, nine signed an endorsement, with one dissenting and one not voting. Labor unions signified their support. Opposed was the president of the American Bar Association, Elihu Root, joined by six of the sixteen living ex-presidents of the association, including William Howard Taft.

Four agitated months elapsed between the nomination and ultimate confirmation. Both sides mounted organized campaigns. During this period Brandeis himself made no public statement, but he was energetic in fortifying his lieutenants with suggestions and detailed documentation for their use. His law partner, Edward F. McClennen, took up residence in Washington, where he kept in touch with Attorney General Thomas Gregory, and was assisted at a distance, and through occasional conferences, by George W. Anderson, United States Attorney in Boston, Professor Felix Frankfurter, Norman Hapgood, editor of *Harper's Weekly*, and others. Briefs and counter-briefs, petitions, memoranda, and letters poured forth from both sides to the Judiciary Committee, the President, and the weekly and daily press. The hearings before a subcommittee, which were open to the public at the behest of Attorney General Gregory, produced two thousand printed pages.

The outcome was anticlimactic. The full committee voted favorably on strict party lines, ten to eight, and the Senate confirmed on June 1, 1916, by a vote of forty-seven to twenty-two, with only one Democrat breaking ranks. The successful outcome owed much to President Wilson, whose resolute support rested on close personal association with Brandeis, an unofficial adviser in the early years of the administration. "I can never live up to my Brandeis appointment," the President later remarked to Hapgood. Anticlimactic though the final result may have been, the whole episode was indeed a watershed; in the nature of the nominee, in the underlying conflict of forces, in the organized campaigning, and in the breadth of participation at the confirmation stage, it foreshadowed the shape of future appointment battles.

Economic interests, close to the surface in the controversy over Brandeis, emerged undisguised when President Hoover nominated Charles Evans Hughes to succeed Chief Justice Taft in 1930. This time roles were reversed. The opposition was led by Progressives and some Democrats, who, viewing the nominee's representation of utilities and other major corporations, perceived him as a menacing reactionary. The critics identified the arguments advanced on behalf of private clients as the judicial philosophy of the counsel, giving too little weight to Hughes' record as an Associate Justice from 1910 to 1916. To paraphrase Professor Zechariah Chafee, it is better to judge a nominee by the books in his library at home than by a list of clients in his office. At least it proved so in the case of Hughes. Confirmed by a vote of fifty-two to twenty-six, on the Court he found occasion to reject many of the controverted positions he had taken at the bar.

. . .

One vacant seat remained to be filed by President Hoover, owing to the death of Justice Edward T. Sanford of Tennessee. Within a few weeks of Hughes' confirmation the President submitted the name of Judge John J. Parker of North Carolina, a member of the Fourth Circuit Court of Appeals. In the Senate, the Progressives and liberal Democrats, sensing the strength they had displayed in the contest over Hughes, determined to wage an intensive attack on what they perceived to be the Republicans' "southern strategy."

The aftershock of the Hughes debates proved to be more severe than those earlier tremors. Although the immediate reaction to the nomination among labor spokesmen and blacks in North Carolina was favorable, national leaders of those groups soon mounted an assault. The principal witnesses in the opposition were William Green, president of the American Federation of Labor, and Walter White, acting executive secretary of the National Association for the Advancement of Colored People. Labor opposed Parker because of an opinion he wrote upholding a "yellow dog" contract as the basis for enjoining a strike for union recognition; the latter group found offensive a political speech by Parker in his unsuccessful gubernatorial bid in 1920—a speech in which, to rebut charges that he was a Negro sympathizer, he asserted that Negroes did not want the suffrage and Republicans did not want them to vote. After extensive debate the Senate rejected the nomination, forty-one to thirty-nine, with the opposition composed of an odd coalition of Progressives, liberal Democrats, and southern Democrats representing states with a substantial black voting population. The vacancy thus left was filled by the nomination of Owen J. Roberts of Philadelphia and his unanimous immediate approval by the Senate. In one of the ironies of history, Judge Parker later showed himself to be more supportive of New Deal measures than was Justice Roberts. In response to a remark suggesting this comparison, Justice Black observed that "John Parker was a better judge after the hearing than before it."

A third vacancy in the Hoover administration arose with the retirement of Justice Holmes in January 1932, but the process of filling it was substantially less political than that for the first two vacancies. Despite his misgivings about placing a third New Yorker on the Court (to join Hughes and Stone), the President was persuaded to nominate Judge Cardozo, who was unanimously approved. It was probably the most popular act of the administration (though this may be faint praise), and it suggests that one of the most politically advantageous decisions that a weakened President can take is to appoint to the Supreme Court a universally respected jurist.

The next significant confirmation battles occurred in the 1960's. President Johnson's attempt in the summer of 1968 to elevate Justice Fortas to the Chief Justiceship failed through a combination of circumstances, political and personal. The President's own power was ebbing as an election approached; there was a growing sentiment that the course of the Court under Chief Justice Warren should be altered; there was uneasiness about Fortas' advisory relationship with the President, which included support of his military policy in Vietnam; and there was disquiet about the Justice's acceptance of funds furnished by former clients. Finally, some members of the Senate were offended when, after the conclusion of four days of questioning by the Judiciary Committee, Fortas declined an invitation to testify further about outside activities. Although the committee approved the nomination by a vote of eleven to six, senators mounted a filibuster and a motion for cloture failed to gain the necessary two-thirds vote; Fortas eventually requested withdrawal of the nomination. Shortly thereafter he resigned as Associate Justice.

A backlash from the Fortas episode appeared to be responsible for the rejection of Judge Clement Haynsworth, Jr., of the Fourth Circuit Court of Appeals, President Nixon's nominee in 1969 to succeed Justice Fortas. The Judiciary Committee hearings revealed that Haynsworth had ruled on cases involving corporations in which he had a minor shareholder's interest. Although the conflict of interest might otherwise have seemed inconsequential, and although the American Bar Association committee endorsed Haynsworth, the situation aroused a sauce-for-the-goose sentiment, and the nomination was defeated, fifty-five to forty-five.

President Nixon's second nominee, Judge G. Harrold Carswell of the Fifth Circuit Court of Appeals, drew a torrent of opposition. Although he also received approval from the American Bar Association committee, Carswell met with vehement and widespread disapproval, not least in the academic community, because of the nominee's apparent racial bias and, more generally, his want of professional stature. The nomination was defeated fifty-one to forty-five.

The vacancy on the Supreme Court was finally filled by the appointment of Judge Harry Blackmun of the Eighth Circuit Court of Appeals, whose nomination was promptly and unanimously approved by the Judiciary Committee and the Senate. Any geographic imperative was clearly laid to rest as Justice Blackmun joined his fellow Minnesotan, Chief Justice Burger, on the Court. Any inference that a conservative Southerner could not be confirmed was subsequently negated in 1971 by President Nixon's acclaimed appointment of Lewis F. Powell, Jr., of Virginia, whose enlightened position on civil rights had been quietly effective, and who was warmly and unanimously approved by the Judiciary Committee and confirmed by the Senate with only one negative vote.

As a cautionary note in appraising the appointment process, it should be pointed out that significant issues may be unforeseen. While, for example, issues of economic due process and federal-state powers dominated the confirmation debates on Hughes, his replacement of Taft in fact ushered in a period of marked invigoration of the guarantees of civil liberties and civil rights, providing a foundation for future advances in these areas. Moreover, even if the issues remain constant, a nominee's subsequent views may on occasion turn an appointment into a presidential disappointment, as when Justice Holmes failed to support President Theodore Roosevelt's antitrust program, when Justice Stone, formerly President Coolidge's Attorney General, became an ally of Justices Holmes and Brandeis, or when Justice Clark joined in overturning President Truman's takeover of the steel mills during the Korean War. Contingency, which has had a conspicuous role in the process of appointment, is not eliminated once an appointment is made.

II.

The history of unsuccessful nominations has suggested that, although politics in the partisan sense has never ceased to be a factor, it has been increasingly outweighed by politics in the larger, Aristotelian sense—a perception that an individual's identity is conditioned by his or her associations, inclinations, and sympathies, concomitant with a heightened awareness of the Supreme Court's role in the social, economic, and political life of the nation. This broadened conception of the appropriate standards for appointment to the Supreme Court has been accompanied, as was said at the outset, by more openness and wider participation in the appointment process itself. Every schoolchild knows that the Senate met in closed session through the years 1789–93. What is less familiar is the fact that thereafter, when the Senate met to act upon nominations of all types, it normally sat in closed executive session until 1929, and that the practice of calling on a nominee for the Supreme Court to appear before the Judiciary Committee did not begin until 1939.

Until 1929 the practice was to consider all nominations in closed executive session unless the Senate, by a two-thirds vote taken in closed session, ordered the debate to be open. Objections to closed sessions were repeatedly raised by Senators, but to no avail, save that in isolated instances, as in the nomination of Brandeis in 1916 and that of Stone in 1925, the shield of secrecy was removed by a vote of the requisite majority.

.   .   .

A separate and troublesome question arises over calling the nominee before the Judiciary Committee or a subcommittee. It was not until the nomination of Felix Frankfurter in 1939 that the practice began of questioning a nominee to the Court. The bitterly contested nominations of Brandeis, Hughes, and Parker were all debated and resolved without an appearance by the nominee. Brandeis, to be sure, did meet with two doubtful Senators at an informal dinner in Washington at the home of Norman Hapgood. Judge Parker replied to charges against him by letters and telegrams after an adverse report by the Judiciary Committee, but the Committee had rejected a motion to permit him to make an appearance.

Professor Frankfurter was urged by Steve Early, presidential assistant at the White House, to appear before the Committee, and a few days before the hearings he received a telegram from Senator Neely of West Virginia, chairman of the subcommittee, inviting him to "be present, at your pleasure, either in person or by counsel." Frankfurter told Early that his teaching duties had priority, and replied to Neely that he had "no wish to make any statement in support of my own nomination," adding that he had asked Dean Acheson "to put himself at the disposal of your Committee." When these responses were made public, Frankfurter received a telegram from his sagacious old friend C.C. Burlingham of the New York bar, advising with characteristic pungency that the declination should rest on the availability of the nominee's public record and that the reference to law school duties was "feeble." Acheson did attend the first day of hearings to "hold a watching brief." That day produced a series of adverse witnesses close to the outer edge of reality.

When the hearings resumed two days later Frankfurter himself was present, accompanied by Acheson. He read the following opening statement:

> I am very glad to accede to this committee's desire to have me appear before it. I, of course, do not wish to testify in support of my own nomination. Except only in one instance, involving a charge against a nominee concerning his official act as Attorney General, the entire history of this committee and of the Court does not disclose that a nominee to the Supreme Court has appeared and testified before the Judiciary Committee. While I believe that a nominee's record should be thoroughly scrutinized by this committee, I hope you will not think it presumptuous on my part to suggest that neither such examination nor the best interests of the Supreme Court will be helped by the personal participation of the nominee himself. I should think it improper for a nominee no less than for a member of the Court to express his personal views on controversial political issues affecting the Court. My attitude and outlook on relevant matters have been fully expressed over a period of years and are easily accessible. I should think it not only bad taste but inconsistent with the duties of the office for which I have been nominated for me to attempt to supplement my past record by present declarations.
>
> That is all I have to say.

Questioning followed, some of it manifestly hostile, revolving around charges, most of which had been aired by witnesses on the first day, that sought to link Frankfurter to the Communist Party through the Sacco–Vanzetti case, his friendship with Professor Harold Laski, the British Labor Party publicist, and especially his membership on a national committee of the American Civil Liberties Union.... Pressed continually to state his own views on Communism, Frankfurter gave a ringing statement of his profound attachment to the principles of the American Constitution, which were antithetical to the tenets of Communism as he understood them. This passionate expression met with prolonged applause from the spectators. The nomination was unanimously approved by the Committee and the Senate. Subsequently Frankfurter recalled the experience: "I thought that it would be just a little room where we'd sit around. I found that this was Madison Square Garden." He then added, ... "In fact, I took charge. It was the only thing to do."

. . .

Ten years after Frankfurter's precedent-breaking appearance, his misgivings were echoed by Judge Sherman Minton of the Seventh Circuit Court of Appeals, nominated to the Court by President Truman in 1949, who respectfully declined the Judiciary Committee's invitation to appear for questioning. His letter referred to Frankfurter's statement, spoke of "serious questions of propriety," and pointed to his public record as a senator and judge. His prior service as a senator from Indiana brought into play senatorial courtesy, which may have averted a more disruptive conflict over his position. As it was, several Republicans, unhappy over President Truman's fourth appointment of a Democrat to the Court, voiced strong criticism of Minton's stand and of the too-relaxed questioning of previous nominees. Minton's nomination, acceptable to the two Republican members from his state, was endorsed by a nine-to-two vote of the Judiciary Committee; a motion to recommit lost, forty-five to twenty-one. Finally the nomination was confirmed by the Senate, forty-eight to sixteen.

Thus there was a sea-change in the practice of the Senate in less than twenty years after the nomination of Judge Parker in 1930. Parker desired to testify and was refused; Minton was asked to testify and only reluctantly was his refusal accepted. Subsequently, the questioning of nominees, with varying degrees of intensity and relevance, has been treated as traditional. . . .

Henry Paul Monaghan,[9] *The Confirmation Process: Law or Politics?*, 101 Harv. L. Rev. 1202 (1988)

In testimony before the Senate Judiciary Committee, I argued (and still believe) that Judge Robert Bork possessed surpassing qualifications for an appointment to the Supreme Court. Subsequently, I became persuaded that my submission was incomplete. Additional argument was necessary to establish that my testimony, if accepted, imposed a constitutional duty on senators to vote for confirmation. To my surprise, further reflection convinces me that no such argument is possible.

From the beginning, presidential nominations to the Supreme Court have been embroiled in public controversy. President Washington's nomination in 1795 of John Rutledge to succeed Chief Justice Jay was a harbinger of things to come. Judge Rutledge had been a member of the constitutional convention, an Associate Justice of the Supreme Court between 1789 and 1791, chief justice of the Supreme Court of South Carolina, and Chief Justice of the Supreme Court for four months under a recess appointment. Nonetheless, the Federalist-dominated Senate rejected the nomination, largely because of Judge Rutledge's public opposition to the Jay Treaty. During the following century, the Senate rejected or tabled Supreme Court nominations for virtually every conceivable reason, including the nominee's political views, political opposition to the incumbent President, a desire to hold the vacancy for the next President, senatorial courtesy, interest group pressure, and on occasion even the nominee's failure to meet minimum professional standards. Indeed, in the first 105 years of American constitutional history, almost one-fourth of the nominees (20 out of 81) failed to win confirmation; others were confirmed only after intense controversy.

9. Harlan Fiske Stone Professor of Constitutional Law, Columbia University   School of Law.

However, during the past century, the Senate's actual role in the appointment process has diminished. In the twentieth century, presidential ascendancy has so increased that public controversy seldom has resulted in unfavorable Senate action.

The intense and highly publicized controversy accompanying the Senate's rejection of Judge Robert Bork and the withdrawal of Judge Douglas Ginsburg nine days later are occasions for taking stock. Do these incidents portend important and lasting shifts in the existing structure of the appointment process? Do they signify that the Senate now can and should reclaim the early constitutional pattern by adopting a more aggressive role in the appointment of Supreme Court judges?

In this commentary, I want to submit two claims—one normative, the other empirical—and to raise one question. The normative claim is that the Senate's role in the appointment of Supreme Court judges is properly viewed as largely "political" in the broadest sense of the term: no significant affirmative constitutional compulsion exists to confirm any presidential nominee. So viewed, the Senate can serve as an important political check on the President's power to appoint. Moreover, the political nature of the Senate's role, like that of the President, helps ameliorate the "countermajoritarian difficulty": by increasing the likelihood that Supreme Court judges will hold views not too different from those of the people's representatives, the Senate can reduce the tension between the institution of judicial review and democratic government.

The empirical claim is that, at least for the foreseeable future, the overriding political power of the modern Presidency will continue to confine the Senate's actual role in the appointment process to its current dimensions. The Senate is incapable of systematically assuming any role greater than that of providing a check against the appointment of nominees perceived to be morally unworthy or too radical. In this respect, the unanimous confirmations of Judges Kennedy and Scalia reveal far more than does the rejection of Judge Bork.

·   ·   ·

I.

We take for granted that the President will nominate a person whose general constitutional philosophy the President endorses. "There is," as Chief Justice Rehnquist recently stated, "no reason why a President should not do this." For the President, the confirmation process itself is entirely political in the ordinary sense of the term. He has selected an appointee satisfactory to him—a judgment that may include the nominee's philosophy, as well as a wide range of factors not associated with merit in a narrow sense, such as the appointee's contribution to the diversity of the Court. The President then seeks the Senate's consent, not its advice, and usually he can count on ordinary politics to obtain that consent. But nothing in the language of the appointments clause, in its origins, or in the actual history of the appointment process supports a constitutionally based presidential "right" to mold an independent branch of government for a period extending long beyond his electoral mandate. Rather (and to my surprise), all the relevant historical and textual sources support the Senate's power when and if it sees fit to assert its vision of the public good against that of the President.

At the time of the constitutional convention, the American governmental structure reflected pronounced popular distrust of executive power. The power of governors to appoint was everywhere sharply restricted and, not surprisingly, several delegates to the constitutional convention (including John Rutledge) urged a restricted presidential appointment power. Although the Virginia plan contemplated that appointments to all national offices would be made entirely by the legislature, the desirability of a significant presidential role gained early recognition, and presidential authority to appoint all officers "not otherwise provided for" was quickly and firmly established. However, the appointment of federal judges remained controversial throughout the entire convention. On Madison's motion, the power to appoint Supreme Court judges was vested in the Senate, where it remained until nearly the end of the convention. After certain delegates objected that the Senate was too large to discharge this function effectively, the existing constitutional provisions finally emerged as a compromise.

The Constitution is silent on what criteria the Senate should use in giving "Advice and Consent," but the goal of the provision was clearly to help secure meritorious appointees. In this endeavor, both the constitutional text and its historical origins indicate that "Advice" was intended to be more than a redundant synonym for "Consent." President Washington actually sought and received advice on appointments, as he did on foreign affairs and treaties. However, the Constitution failed to provide any regular institutional mechanism for securing meaningful Senate "Advice"—as distinguished from the Senate's "Consent," which could be rendered simply with a vote. This omission allowed the authors of *The Federalist* to accept the goal of meritorious appointments, but to discount the Senate's affirmative role in that regard. *The Federalist* assumed that the power to appoint was an inherently executive function and insisted that the President's power to nominate was virtually equivalent to the power to appoint. The constitutional scheme described in *The Federalist* limited the Senate to the role of "an excellent check" against presidential corruption and incompetence. Envisioning the Senate's role thus constrained, *The Federalist* opined that "[i]t is ... not very probable that the President's nomination would often be overruled." Interestingly, *Federalist* No. 78 assumes that the mode of appointing Supreme Court judges raises no issue distinct from that of "appointing officers of the union in general."

Nonetheless, once the new government began to operate, the actual process of appointment took on a shape different from that envisaged by either the Framers or the authors of *The Federalist*. Patronage became important, and the senators quickly established a powerful role in the nomination of federal officials who functioned within their states. More importantly, Supreme Court nominations moved along their own track, one in which the Senate viewed the nominee's judicial ideology—to say nothing of overtly partisan political considerations—as relevant. The latter development was perhaps inevitable. Concepts such as "merit" and "the public interest" might have seemed relatively uncontroversial to the Framers, but they became far more problematic as social divisions first generated and then legitimated political parties. The line between notions like public interest and merit on the one hand and simple party advantage on the other blurred in practice, partly because it was unclear in principle.

The relevant constitutional law is minimal, and largely negative in character. In theory, the President alone can nominate; beyond that, both the President and the Senate share a common responsibility for the appointment of morally and professionally fit persons to the Court. The Senate has the duty to reject any nominee whose appointment it believes will not advance the public good as the Senate understands it. But the polycentric nature of the common good and the actual history of the appointments clause persuades me to go one step further: generally stated, no affirmative constitutional compulsion to confirm exists.

The entire appointment process is best understood as largely beyond the operation of norms of legal right or wrong; instead it involves mainly questions of prudence, judgment, and politics. We are better off recognizing a virtually unlimited political license in the Senate not to confirm nominees. Most current assessments of the Senate's role reject this, either explicitly or implicitly. For example, many insist that Presidents have a "right" to appoint any "qualified" nominee. Moreover, in both the Bork and Kennedy confirmation hearings, the senators rejected any open-ended view of their authority. They seemed to assume that they were under a duty to confirm unless Judge Bork fell outside the mainstream of legal thinking. If I am right, however, that the Senate's role in the appointment process should be political in nature, then a nominee may be rejected on the basis of statesmanship, prudence, common sense, and politics, rather than constitutional right and duty. Therefore, a nominee may be rejected without the Senate having to establish humiliating propositions, such as that the nominee is a dangerous radical. More generally, a political view of the appointment process of Supreme Court judges "affords the Senate an opportunity to carry on in another context its persistent struggle with the executive branch to shape the contours of public policy." In addition, the entire appointment process—nomination and confirmation—can be seen as an additional way to moderate the countermajoritarian difficulty. Chief Justice Rehnquist recently wrote: "When a vacancy occurs on the Court, it is entirely appropriate that that vacancy be filled by the President, responsible to a national constituency, as advised by the Senate, whose members are responsible to regional constituencies. Thus, public opinion has some say in who shall become judges of the Supreme Court." I would add only that when the Senate musters enough votes to reject a nomination, its "regional" constituencies are likely to be the equivalent of a "national" constituency.

II.

The Senate's actual role in the conformation process depended upon the shifting balance of political power between Congress and the President. The Senate's significant nineteenth-century role reflected the general congressional dominance of that era. Scarcely one hundred years ago, Woodrow Wilson argued that national government was congressional government—more precisely, "government by the chairmen of the Standing Committees of Congress." Wilson put aside the President with the dismissive observation that his "business ... occasionally great, is usually not much above routine." Although some such model of congressional government could be defended as late as the beginning of the New Deal, modern government is presidential government, at least in its most important aspects. Presidential ascendancy in the appointment process reflects this fact.

The modern Presidency, even a lame-duck Presidency facing a Senate controlled by the opposite party, has enormous resources for mobilizing support and for disciplining those senators who refuse to go along. Such resources—party discipline, ideology, and various carrots and sticks—can be concentrated on any issue of significant importance to the President. One could speculate extensively about why those resources failed in the case of Judge Bork. For us it suffices that the Bork proceedings themselves arose in a special context, one in which the administration's hard-line attitude on judicial nominations had left a bitter residue. Many parties were spoiling for a fight, and Judge Bork, who was perceived as far outside the mainstream of legal thinking, was the perfect catalyst to provoke one. Such a configuration is unlikely to be repeated frequently, suggesting Judge Bork's rejection portends no important institutional changes in the President's ability to win confirmation of nominees.

The institutionally important point is that it takes enormous energy for senators to unite in order to resist the President. Once undertaken, such conduct cannot easily be sustained, as evidenced by the relief with which the Senate greeted Judge Kennedy's nomination. The senators made every effort to see him as different from Judge Bork, regardless of whether he actually was. Commenting on Judge Kennedy's "smooth sailing" on his initial Senate visit, Senator John McCain, a conservative Republican from Arizona, put the point well: the Senate was simply "weary" of fighting. "Nobody wants to go through that again. There's just too much blood on the floor." At most, Judge Bork's hearings may have established a tradition of more probing Senate interrogation of a nominee, but the political background in which the entire confirmation process functions remains one with a powerful Presidency. To be sure, the rejection reminds us that periodically the American people seem to need a battle over a Supreme Court appointment. But symbolism aside, the hard fact is that the President's vision of what is proper judicial philosophy ultimately will prevail, as Judge Kennedy's confirmation demonstrates.

Nonetheless, some believe that Judge Bork's rejection shows that the Senate's role is less marginal than I have argued. The Senate's failure to confirm Judge Bork is said to reflect popular rejection of original understanding theory and popular acceptance of a general constitutional right to privacy. Although these contentions initially appear plausible, when carefully analyzed their flaws become apparent. In fact, Judge Bork did not avow original understanding as the sole basis for legitimate judicial decisionmaking. Moreover, the abortion cases, the most frequently cited illustration of Judge Bork's rejection of a constitutional right to privacy, actually involve autonomy or freedom from regulation, not privacy. Furthermore, the claim that, at least in exceptional circumstances, the Senate acts as a court of popular opinion endorsing or rejecting certain constitutional views is unpersuasive. Confirmation proceedings cannot be construed as referenda of any sort on judicial philosophies—except perhaps at the far margins—because the Senate is simply not equipped to proffer or register constitutional judgments of such magnitude. This is particularly true when, as in the case of Judge Bork, commentators seek to extract such judgments from a bitter, wideranging, and complex nomination proceeding that focused upon a multitude of issues involving the Reagan Presidency and a number of Supreme Court decisions.

. . .

Questions and Comments

1.   Based on the historical materials you have thus far read, would you agree with Professor Monaghan that the Senate is under no duty to presume in favor of confirming a President's nominee? Why or why not?

2.   Of the eight reasons given by Professor Abraham describing circumstances that have led the Senate to refuse to confirm a nomination to the Supreme Court, which are the most important—from a normative perspective and from an empirical perspective? Consider here also the claim by Professor Halper that a President's weakness or unpopularity is correlated with an increased rate of rejection.

2.   Political Perspectives on the Modern Appointment Process

The next readings focus greater attention on the political setting of appointments in the post-World War II period. As you will see, Professor Gerhardt suggests that the dynamic at work in judicial nominations should be understood within the broader context of all presidential nominations requiring advice and consent, and more generally, within the context of President–Congress interactions. Professor Maltese focuses on the role of interest groups and their effects on Presidents, nominees and the process as a whole. And Professor Yalof argues that the procedures and criteria used within the Executive Branch to select Supreme Court nominees have changed in ways that may adversely affect the process, by providing the President with too much information presented in advocacy mode. As you read, consider which of the changes described in these readings is of greatest significance and what is its effect, if any, on who is nominated and confirmed to the Court.

Michael Gerhardt,[10] *Toward a Comprehensive Understanding of the Federal Appointments Process,* 21 Harv. J. L. & Pub. Pol'y 467 (1997)

HISTORICAL CHANGES AND PATTERNS

Post-ratification history—that is, the actual practice of presidents and senators with regard to the nomination process, occurring after the ratification of the Constitution—is another major component of a comprehensive theory of the federal appointments process. Two aspects of this history shed light on the operations and dynamics of the federal appointments process: (1) the social and historical developments affecting federal appointments; and (2) the patterns or past practices within the federal appointments process. This Part examines the significance and implications of each of these aspects of history in order to complete a descriptive analysis of the federal appointments process.

A. Historical Developments

Several significant post-ratification developments have helped to clarify and shape the allocation of power among, the relationships between, and the internal organizations of the principal actors routinely involved in appointments matters. These developments are: the rise and partial decline of political parties; the increase in the size and influence of the national government; the evolution of Senate procedures and committee structures; the growth of organized interest groups; and the expanding media coverage of the federal appointments process. Each of these developments has affected the way in which the president and the Senate have constructed their internal organizations for making administrative and other kinds of decisions; each has also affected president-Senate interaction on federal appointments matters.

1. The Decline of Political Parties

Political parties began to take shape during the second term of George Washington's presidency, and party differences culminated in an

---

10. Professor, Case Western Reserve University School of Law (formerly) and presently the Arthur B. Hanson Professor of Law at the William & Mary School of Law.

intensely partisan campaign for the presidency in 1796. Washington's successor, John Adams, used fierce loyalty to the Federalist party as a criterion for awarding federal appointments.

Two main reasons explain the early and rather persistent dominance of party membership in the federal appointments process. First, appointments make excellent rewards for repayment of a president's or senator's loyal supporters. Second, a nominee's allegiance to a political party often proves to be a useful proxy for his or her political philosophy. One early example of a politician attempting to take advantage of this phenomenon was President John Adams's attempt to stack the federal judiciary with more than fifty loyal Federalists on the eve of the inauguration of his Democratic–Republican rival, Thomas Jefferson.

In the Nineteenth Century, political parties functioned principally as an organizational framework for Senate action. In the current century, however, their influence has declined in this area. Several factors explain this diminishing influence, including the establishment of a large federal bureaucracy; the electorate's increasing concern with personality and issues and decreasing tendency to identify with a single political party; split ticket voting; the Supreme Court's striking down on First Amendment grounds of most forms of patronage based on party loyalty; the rise of interest groups; major shifts in the composition and agendas of the national parties; and a shift in the source of presidential authority from personality, parties, and interest groups to independent political apparatuses and mass communications technologies enabling direct appeals to the people. This shift has meant that the presidential nominations in this century face some different challenges than those posed in previous eras.

In the Nineteenth Century, stronger party organization meant that sustained opposition to presidential nominees was easier. The most dramatic illustration of this phenomenon occurred in the waning days of John Tyler's presidency, when the Senate rejected five of the six nominees whom President Tyler had proposed to fill two Supreme Court vacancies. President Tyler's nominees were generally considered by people at the time—including the Whig leadership—to be well-qualified. But several Senate factions, each of which included presidential aspirants, despised Tyler and wanted to save the vacancies for whomever was chosen to succeed him in the upcoming presidential election.…

In this century, the Senate has been unable to sustain opposition to a president's Supreme Court nominations to the same degree, although it has come close during two short periods. In the early 1970s, the Senate rejected two of President Nixon's Supreme Court nominations before approving a third. In 1987, the Senate rejected President Reagan's nomination of Judge Robert Bork to the Court and then helped to force the withdrawal of the next nominee, Douglas Ginsburg, before it approved the third nominee, Anthony Kennedy.

The decline of political parties has coincided with the infusion into the political process of a much broader range of potential influences—

personal and otherwise—and factional interests. Consequently, as political parties have declined, partisanship has not. Indeed, partisanship, by which I mean loyalty to some factional interest, still remains a major factor in the appointments process. For instance, in making federal appointments, presidents have increasingly looked to additional indicia of a prospective nominee's political philosophies. Particularly, presidents make judgments based on the amount of support the prospective nominee possesses from interest groups, the nominee's patrons, and the president's own trusted advisers.

Even in decline, though, political parties have remained among the most powerful factions contending for control of the federal appointments process. After close personal association with the president or one of the president's closest friends, significant stature in the president's political party has consistently been an important qualification for many federal appointments. In this century, at least eighty-two percent of presidential appointees, either to judicial or nonjudicial offices, legitimately have been able to claim the president's political party as their own.

2.   The Growth of the National Government

The expansion of the size of the national government and of the scope of presidential authority is another important historical development shedding light on the meaning of the appointments power. . . . [T]wo related facts are clear. First, it is plain that the United States presently has a presidential rather than a congressional government. Second, the Appointments Clause has provided an opportunity for shifts in authority to occur. As the amount of responsibility assumed by the national government has grown, Congress has created more offices requiring presidential nomination and Senate confirmation. Further, as these offices have become more numerous, the president's supervisory and administrative authority has also grown. Under the Appointments Clause, the president has primary responsibility both for choosing the people occupying these new offices and for overseeing their actions. Thus, the president now has responsibility for a much larger segment of the government than do the Congress and the Judiciary.

. . . As a practical matter, as more offices are created by Congress, senators have more chances to consult with the president on federal appointments and related legislative matters. Senators also possess more bargaining chips to use in these consultations. Therefore, the potential number of contestable nominations has expanded considerably.

Although the Senate has not in fact rejected or otherwise blocked Supreme Court nominations to the same degree in this century as it did in the last, it has had available more presidential nominations that could potentially be blocked. Further, a trend is emerging in which the Senate has interfered increasingly with presidential nominations. The interference, particularly over the past two decades, has taken the form of increased opposition to (rather than the outright rejection of) more presidential nominations. The opposition has occurred with particular frequency with respect to judicial nominations and nominations in the areas of national security, the environment, economics, and civil rights. Moreover, the potential to keep presidential appointees in check exists regardless of whether these appointees have been subject to the Senate's constitutional confirmation authority. Particularly important among Congress's means of interfering have been Congress's oversight and appropriations authorities, which have been extended to cover virtually every aspect of the executive branch.

Although this trend of increased opposition might seem to indicate that the Congress is gaining power in the appointments arena, the president has retained an upper hand in the federal appointments process. This is because, although the number of confirmable posts has increased multifold, the Senate's capacity to defeat some portion of the nominees for these posts, during a given legislative session, has remained relatively static. Although the supposition of presidential ascendancy could be challenged on the ground that senators do not need many chances to thwart or embarrass the president on appointments matters in order to hurt the presidency or help themselves politically, it is clear at least with respect to appointments (if not the separation of powers generally) that the executive, and not the legislature, has become potentially the most dangerous branch. This is true because the president has unparalleled ability to energize, direct, and shape the national government's performance and agenda through his formal powers, not the least of which is his nominating authority. This danger is tempered, however, by the fact that the presidency is also the most accountable branch. The president, as a single figure, is watched more closely by the public and by the media than any other government official or institution.

3. Evolution of the Senate

A third historical development shedding light on the Appointments Clause is the structural changes that have occurred regarding the election of senators and the operations of the Senate. For example, the Seventeenth Amendment, passed in 1913, provided for popular election of senators, as opposed to election by state legislatures. This Amendment was the product of the Progressive Era, in which the Senate was widely condemned for being out of touch with the electorate. Thus, the Amendment was widely viewed at the time as an endorsement of the importance of the popular will in lawmaking.

One obvious effect of the Seventeenth Amendment was to make the Senate's constitutionally imposed duties, such as the confirmation of presidential nominees, subject to popular review, comment, and reprisal. Although there is no hard evidence establishing precisely how much the Seventeenth Amendment has influenced the kinds of people elected to the Senate or the nature of the Senate's proceedings or activities, this change has surely had at least some effect. . . .

Beyond the reforms instituted by the Seventeenth Amendment, the Senate has made several important changes in its internal operations and procedures in response to its growing agenda, the television age, and the expansion of presidential power. Provoked by the decline in power of political parties, the rise of interest groups and factions, and the expansion of media coverage of the Senate since the 1960s, these changes have caused the evolution of the Senate from a collegial body into one dominated by individuals with separate agendas, and from a body deliberating as a whole into one in which delegations of substantial authority regarding agenda setting and scheduling are made by the whole body of the Senate to smaller units within it. These Senate committees, led by their powerful chairpersons, often have a disproportionate influence on debates. Chroniclers of the rise in presidential power have glossed over these developments. Yet, an understanding of these events is crucial to appreciating the nature and operations of the appointments process.

Only since 1929 has the Senate operated under the rule that its sessions are open to the public unless ordered closed by a majority vote. By contrast, from 1789 until 1929, the Senate with very few exceptions considered all nominations in closed executive session. The move to public hearings was prompted partly by uncontrollable press leaks about Senate business (mostly by the senators interested in applying public and other pressure to open them) and the desire of many senators to conduct Senate business in public so that the public would be more aware of its actions. Public hearings have raised the stakes for all concerned in confirmation hearings.

Requiring a nominee to appear personally to testify before the appropriate Senate committee or subcommittee is another major procedural change. The first instance of this practice occurred in 1925. Harlan Fiske Stone, President Calvin Coolidge's attorney general, appeared on his own initiative to answer specific questions posed by Senator Thomas Walsh, a member of the Senate Judiciary Committee, about then-Attorney General Stone's refusal to dismiss an indictment against another senator. The Senate easily confirmed Justice Stone after he distinguished himself with the reasonableness, candor, and professionalism of his answers. For the next thirty years, nominees appeared intermittently. One of the most important such appearances during this period was made in 1939 by Felix Frankfurter, who became the first nominee to a high governmental post to answer a Senate Committee's questions fully and in person.

The pattern of Supreme Court and other nominees appearing to answer Senate committee questions firmly took hold, however, in the 1950s. This trend was triggered by the Warren Court's decision in *Brown v. Board of Education*, striking down segregation of the races in public schools. Southern segregationist senators who dominated the Judiciary Committee demanded that the very next nominee—John Harlan in 1955—appear before the Committee to express his views on desegregation or risk rejection. He agreed, and the pattern was set. All subsequent Supreme Court nominees have appeared before the Senate Judiciary Committee and have been questioned about their jurisprudence or opinions about "the hot constitutional issues of the moment."

The aggrandizement of Senate committees has made it easier for smaller blocs of senators, committee chairpersons, or even individual senators to thwart nominations. Moreover, numerous procedural mechanisms and Senate rules have been developed that committees and their chairs have frequently manipulated to impede nominations. The first signs of opposition to a nomination usually have surfaced in the Senate Judiciary Committee, which is responsible for conducting preliminary confirmation hearings. Its members have often tried, with mixed success, to project the image of being more independent and less partisan than their colleagues on other committees, and achievement of this appearance has frequently worked to their political advantage. This nonpartisan stance, when it has been achieved, has been important to the status of the Judiciary Committee and is encouraged and bolstered by the popular conception of an independent federal judiciary.

4.   The Advent of Interest Groups

The proliferation, especially in the past three or four decades, of organized interest groups is yet another important development. . . . [11]

. . .

No case better illustrates the impact of interest groups on a nomination's fate than that of President Reagan's nomination of Judge Robert Bork to be an associate Supreme Court justice in 1987. The Bork nomination faced early, united, and vociferous opposition from the alliance of labor and civil-rights interest groups traditionally tied to the Democratic party. Feminist and pro-choice groups also joined this alliance, although until the battle over Judge Bork's confirmation, these groups had functioned largely as single-issue interest groups, cutting across party lines. They became potent supporters of the Democratic cause in an effort to prevent Judge Bork from tipping the ideological orientation of the Court too far to the right. The participation of these groups signaled to Democrats that the Bork nomination was an occasion for attacking the Republican party for having corrupted the Court. They also persuaded moderate Republicans from marginal constituencies who had feared the potency of this important single issue to oppose Bork's nomination. In the aftermath of Judge Bork's defeat, many conservatives have moved to form their own organizations to counteract the influence of liberal interest groups closely aligned with the Democratic party.

5.   The Media's Expansion

In the Twentieth Century, the development of new media outlets, including radio, network television, and cable, has expanded news coverage about federal appointments, subjecting the process to increasing public scrutiny. This increased coverage has had several consequences. It raises the stakes for the nominee and the other political actors involved in the process by making it much harder to downplay missteps; by pressuring a president to name a nominee quickly in the hopes of avoiding leaks and putting the opposition off guard; by inducing a

---

11.   [Editors' Note: See the Maltese excerpt below for further discussion.]

president to be overly cautious before naming a nominee in order to ensure his or her confirmability; and by facilitating mobilization for or against a nomination through the greater dissemination of information that supporters or opponents might need. The expansion of new information technologies has helped to strengthen the media's control of the news and consequently the public's perception of circumstances surrounding appointments matters.

B.   Confirmation Patterns

Despite the influence exerted by history on the operations of the appointments process, the reasons for presidential nominations and senatorial support or opposition to those nominations have remained remarkably constant over time. Presidents and senators have made appointments decisions based on their respective calculations regarding various long-term and short-term considerations. The long-term factors have entailed a nominee's philosophy about the role of the national government in American society and the relationship between the different branches of the federal government. Short-term factors have included a nominee's political party, chances for confirmation, domicile, age, and benefactors or supporters. Both long and short-term concerns have been influenced by political circumstances, the state of presidential-Senate relations, and presidents' and senators' other priorities and ambitions for the federal office being filled. For instance, the relevant political philosophy for nonjudicial nominees invariably has been their viewpoints on the appropriate functions or duties of the offices to which they have been nominated and on the office's significance to the president's agenda, whereas for judicial nominees, the relevant ideology relates to their basic attitudes about constitutional interpretation generally and sometimes about specific areas such as property, economics, federalism, race, privacy, or gender.

Presidents and senators have differed in the ways in which they have combined these factors and the sequence in which they have taken them into account. For example, in deciding on a broad pool of suitable candidates for a confirmable post, presidents have been influenced by grander political concerns, such as commitment to a particular constitutional philosophy or the long-term relations between the federal and state governments or between federal institutions. In making a choice from within this set, however, presidents have been guided by pragmatic concerns, such as party loyalty, ease of confirmation, and the potential ramifications of confirmation on presidential popularity.

Compare, for example, the criteria President Clinton used to narrow the pool of candidates for replacement of Justice Blackmun down to Interior Secretary Bruce Babbitt and Judges Richard Arnold and Stephen Breyer with the standards that guided his choice among these three individuals. President Clinton instructed his staff to assemble a list of prospective candidates for the Court based on capacity for taking a leadership role on the Court and possession of a "progressive" judicial ideology, including a commitment to constitutional stability, an energetic national government, and a sensitive reading of the individual-rights provisions of the Constitution. The President chose from among the names assembled, however, on the grounds of their appeal to certain constituencies, age and health, and likelihood for confirmation.

The converse is true once a nomination reaches the Senate. In the Senate, opposition to a nomination initially develops for partisan or even personal reasons; the opposition generally succeeds, however, only if it can be framed in terms of grander political factors, including the preservation of constitutional ideals such as federalism or the preservation of individual liberties.

Consider, for example, senators' reactions to the nominations of Robert Bork and Zoe Baird.[12] Initially, the opposition to Judge Bork followed partisan lines. By the time of his nomination, Democratic senators were eager to block additional Republican nominees to the Supreme Court. They could not block Judge Bork's confirmation, however, unless they found a way to frame their opposition in nonpartisan terms that would resonate with a majority of the Senate, including some moderate Republican senators. In the aftermath of Judge Bork's defeat, Republican senators eagerly sought a chance to get even with Democrats; President Clinton's election gave them their first meaningful opportunity. Their challenge was to find a nominee whom it would be appropriate to oppose. They chose Zoe Baird, successfully grounding their opposition on nonpartisan bases. They argued that her failure to pay Social Security taxes for domestic servants deprived her of the moral authority she would need as attorney general to oversee enforcement of the law.

. . .

C. The Role of the Media in the Appointments Process

The popularity of personalizing the appointments process is attributable in large part to the media's widespread use of this technique in covering appointments matters. The predominance of this practice is understandable for several reasons. First, describing appointments matters in personal terms makes intuitive sense, given that the rise or fall of a particular individual—the nominee—plays a central role, and that other persons, including presidents and senators, have serious stakes in the outcomes. Second, this practice provides a convenient hook for grabbing a substantial audience because people will be more interested in stories that cater to their emotions. In addition, describing appointments matters in personal terms is relatively easy for reporters because the approach does not require any special training.

The media's predominant practice of personalizing the appointments process has been both a blessing and a curse. It has been a blessing to the extent that the media has helped to shed light on a process that for

---

12. [Editors' note: Zoe Baird was nomi-   General.]
nated by President Clinton to be Attorney

much of American history occurred behind closed doors. Before the Senate made its proceedings public, the press had to rely on leaks from participants for information about such proceedings. Today's more wide-spread coverage has helped to educate the public about the interaction between the president and the Senate in this area and about the backgrounds and qualifications of some of the nation's most powerful leaders.

The media's coverage of the appointments process has also posed two serious problems. First, the press often gets carried away. It has frequently been involved as much in making the news as it has in reporting it. Perhaps no incident better illustrates this tendency than the reports made about Judge Bork's video rentals in the later stages of his confirmation hearings. Judge Bork's substantial public and academic record should have provided more than enough fodder for meaningful Senate debate about the propriety of his nomination to the Supreme Court. Second, the media's relentless quest for drama within the appointments process often has come at the expense of coverage of the significant legal issues surrounding confirmation contests. For example, the media helped to fuel the controversy over President Clinton's nomination of Lani Guinier to head the Justice Department's Civil Rights Division by spending considerably more time reporting the opposing side's representations about her academic writings than independently assessing the accuracy of those representations.

. . . The media has rarely attempted to put into broader context a president's method of choosing a nominee or the confirmation contests between presidents and senators. For example, a great deal of attention during President Clinton's first search for a Supreme Court nominee was placed on his indecision and his reluctance to provoke controversy and weaken his sagging popularity. The media paid almost no attention to his need to appoint a justice who fit his criteria and also preserve the necessary political coinage to get health-care reform and other portions of his then pending legislative agenda through Congress. Media discussion of such pragmatic concerns would have helped to increase the public's appreciation of the institutional ramifications of such confrontations. . . .

John Anthony Maltese,[13] *The Selling of Supreme Court Nominees* (1995)

The Senate confirmation process . . . changed considerably over the years between John Parker's nomination in 1930 and Clement Haynsworth's in 1969. Most of those changes are related to the increasingly public nature of the process. This chapter looks at these changes and examines how three participants in the Supreme Court selection pro-

13. Albert Berry Saye Professor, University of Georgia.

cess—organized interests, the nominees themselves, and the presidents who choose them—have responded to the opening of the Senate confirmation process.

As we shall see, interest groups and nominees have increasingly used public testimony and other types of public appeal to influence senators and to mobilize broader public support for their cause. Since the 1980s, presidents have also made it a routine practice to make public appeals on behalf of their nominees. In short, all three participants pay much more attention to the mobilization of public opinion than participants ever did in the nineteenth century.

. . .

Public confirmation hearings were virtually nonexistent prior to the 1916 Brandeis nomination. Even after that, it took many years for the Senate Judiciary Committee to routinely hold full-fledged public hearings on nominations. Instead, committee proceedings were usually pro forma affairs that were closed to the public. A few witnesses testified when Warren Harding nominated Pierce Butler in 1922, and reporters were present when Harlan Fiske Stone testified before the committee in 1925, but the first full-scale public hearings after Brandeis did not come until the Parker nomination in 1930. The Parker hearings [in 1930] were the first Supreme Court nomination hearings to have testimony by representatives of organized interest groups. Moreover, Parker was the first nominee kept off of the bench by interest group pressure. (Organized interests played a role in blocking Rutherford Hayes's nomination of Stanley Matthews in 1881, but they were unable to block Matthews' confirmation when James Garfield renominated him that same year.) Thus, the Parker proceedings were the first to take on many of the characteristics of "modern" confirmation proceedings.

Still, the Parker proceedings were quite different from today's norm. By today's standards, the Parker hearings were perfunctory. A subcommittee, rather than the full Judiciary Committee, held them. The hearings took place on one day and lasted less than three hours. Only two organized interests testified. The nominee himself did not appear, nor did President Hoover make any public statements on behalf of his beleaguered nominee. The published record of the committee's proceedings totaled only eighty-three pages.

In comparison, the full Judiciary Committee held hearings on Haynsworth. They took place over a period of eight days. Representatives from twelve organized interests testified, and several others submitted written material for the public record. Haynsworth testified before the committee, and President Nixon spoke on his behalf at a press conference designed to rally support for the nomination. The length of the published record of the committee's proceedings was 762 pages.

In terms of the length of the hearings, the array of interests testifying, the nominee's testimony, and the White House efforts to bolster public support for its nominee, the Haynsworth proceeding may be characterized as the first truly modern one. The proceedings for Lyndon Johnson's nominations of Thurgood Marshall in 1967 and of Abe Fortas to be chief justice in 1968 also contend for that distinction, but the array of interest group testimony was limited in both cases (one group testified at the Marshall hearings and four testified at the Fortas hearings), and by today's standards the White House engaged in only paltry efforts to build public support for its nominees.

Comparisons with more recent confirmation proceedings are useful. Hearings for Robert Bork lasted twelve days. Representatives from over twenty groups testified (with written material submitted for the record by over a hundred other groups). Bork himself testified for five days. The published record of the committee proceedings filled 6,511 pages. President Ronald Reagan made over thirty public statements on Bork's behalf, and the White House waged a major (though largely unsuccessful) public relations offensive to build support for its nominee. Even the relatively uncontroversial nomination of David Souter in 1990 resulted in five days of committee hearings, testimony by representatives from twenty-six interest groups, three days of testimony by Souter, 1,119 pages of proceedings, and ten public statements by President George Bush on behalf of his nominee.

Public opinion is a key ingredient in modern Supreme Court confirmation battles. Through testimony before the Judiciary Committee and a variety of other public appeals, a wide range of actors attempt to mold public opinion in hopes of influencing the outcome.

The Emergence of Public Hearings

Our knowledge of pre–1929 Supreme Court confirmation proceedings is far from complete. It is especially difficult to delineate the role of the Senate Judiciary Committee in the first forty or so years of its existence. Although the Senate created the Judiciary Committee in 1816 (along with eleven other standing committees), surviving records of committee proceedings relating to Supreme Court nominees date back only as far as the mid–1800s. Even in the years since then, there are substantial gaps in the committee's records. . . .

The first public hearings for a Supreme Court nominee appear to have been for Brandeis in 1916, although the Senate Judiciary Committee held closed hearings (complete with testimony from witnesses) as early as 1873, when President Ulysses S. Grant nominated his attorney general, George H. Williams, to succeed Salmon P. Chase as chief justice. Prior to the Williams nomination, the committee had often met and offered its recommendation on nominees to the full Senate, but there is no evidence that the committee had previously called witnesses or otherwise engaged in thorough investigative hearings on nominees.

After the Brandeis hearings in 1916, the Senate Judiciary Committee did not hold another round of full-fledged public hearings for a Supreme Court nominee until Parker in 1930 (although subcommittee questioning of nominee Harlan Fiske Stone was open to reporters in 1925). A subcommittee of the Judiciary Committee conducted the Brandeis and Parker hearings, and the practice of a subcommittee holding public hearings continued until 1941. No published records of committee proceedings exist for the Rutledge (1943), Burton (1945), or Vinson (1946) nominations. ... Since 1949, the full Judiciary Committee has held public hearings on all Supreme Court nominees; before that year, public hearings were almost always perfunctory affairs. For instance, public hearings on Franklin Roosevelt's nomination of William O. Douglas in 1939 lasted five minutes. Even the Parker hearings in 1930 lasted less than three hours. Only the Brandeis hearings in 1916 rivaled today's public hearings in terms of length. But no organized interests testified at the Brandeis hearings. Instead, the committee summoned individuals who had business dealings with Brandeis. Through such testimony, the committee attempted to determine Brandeis's "judicial temperament."

Speaking Out: Interest Groups

... It is only since Nixon's nominations of William Rehnquist and Lewis Powell in 1971 that organized interests have testified at public hearings for every Supreme Court nominee. ...

Prior to Haynsworth in 1969, only a smattering of interests testified about Supreme Court nominees. Although Harry Truman's nomination of Tom Clark in 1949 attracted testimony from representatives of ten groups, few hearings attracted more than one or two, and several did not attract any. Of the twenty-nine nominations from Hughes through Burger (1930–69), representatives for an average of only 1.2 groups testified per nominee. Haynsworth's hearings in 1969 attracted testimony from representatives of 11 groups. The fifteen public hearings for Supreme Court nominees from Haynsworth through Breyer have elicited testimony from an average of 13.1 groups. With regard to the array of groups testifying, Haynsworth's nomination was a turning point.

With the emergence of televised proceedings in 1981, public testimony became a way for interest groups to obtain free exposure to a mass audience. But testimony before the Judiciary Committee is now only one of the ways that interest groups make public their stand on Supreme Court nominees. They use public opinion polls to help target their appeals and focus group sessions to help fashion their messages. For instance, groups opposing the nomination of Robert Bork in 1987 formed a Media Task Force to plan and coordinate public appeals against Bork. Using polling data, the task force pinpointed the salient issues in different parts of the country. It then targeted different anti-Bork messages at different parts of the country based on those polls. Thus, anti-Bork activists stressed his threat to environmental protection in the West but in the South stressed that Bork would "turn back the clock" on civil rights. Senators from southern and border states who were dependent upon black votes for reelection were particularly sensitive to the civil rights issue. Thus, southern Democrats who had previously voted for the "strict constructionist" nominees of Republican presidents did not vote for Bork. In fact, only one southern Democrat, Ernest Hollings of South Carolina, voted for Bork.

Groups opposed to Bork took the then unusual approach of running television, radio, and print advertisements against Bork. The most famous was a television spot narrated by actor Gregory Peck. The camera focused on a traditional four-person nuclear family standing on the steps of the Supreme Court, the father pointing to the words Equal Justice Under Law while his two children looked on. Over this picture, Peck narrated: "There's a special feeling of awe people get when they visit the Supreme Court of the United States, the ultimate guardian of our liberties." But, Peck continued, Robert Bork "defended poll taxes and literacy tests, which kept many Americans from voting. He opposed the civil rights law that ended Whites Only signs at lunch counters. He doesn't believe the Constitution protects your right to privacy. And he thinks freedom of speech does not apply to literature and art and music." The camera showed the family in profile, looking in awe at the Supreme Court, then moved to the face of the youngest child. "Robert Bork could have the last word on your rights as citizens, but the Senate has the last word on him," Peck concluded. "Please urge your senators to vote against the Bork nomination, because if Robert Bork wins a seat on the Supreme Court, it will be for life—his life and yours."

The anti-Bork coalition also set up press briefings, arranged interviews, and mailed information packets to reporters covering the "Bork beat." Its database could print out mailing labels for some two thousand journalists and an additional seventeen hundred editorial writers. It also made prepackaged radio stories ("actualities") available to local radio stations around the country for use on their news programs.

Radio actualities are the audio equivalent of a written press release. They contain a sound bite (a brief spoken statement by a prominent individual) surrounded by a voice wrap (a narrative that sounds like a news report that sets up the sound bite). Radio stations could then broadcast the actuality in its entirety, leaving the impression that it was an independently produced news story. Or they could edit it and use just the sound bite as part of their own reporter's story. Actualities containing anti-Bork sound bites of the Reverend Jesse Jackson and NAACP director Benjamin Hooks were targeted at black radio stations in the South. Actualities with sound bites from Sierra Club officials were targeted at radio stations in the West, while those with sound bites of Antonia Hernandez of the Mexican–American Legal Defense and Education Fund were targeted at the Southwest.

Since the Bork nomination, interest groups have routinely coordinated public campaigns for and against Supreme Court nominees. Speaking out through testimony at Senate Judiciary Committee hearings is an important part of that process.

Speaking Out: Nominees

For three days in October 1991, millions of Americans sat riveted to their television screens by the emotional testimony of Anita Hill and Clarence Thomas before the Senate Judiciary Committee. Hill, a professor of law at the University of Oklahoma, charged that Thomas, George

Bush's nominee to replace Justice Thurgood Marshall on the United States Supreme Court, had sexually harassed her when she worked for him in the Department of Education's Office of Civil Rights and, later, when she served as his personal assistant when he became chairman of the Equal Opportunity Employment Commission (EEOC). The EEOC is a government organization that deals with sexual harassment claims. As its chairman, Thomas effectively served as the nation's chief enforcement official on sexual harassment.

No congressional hearings since Watergate so captured the interest of the American people. Clarence Thomas's testimony on Friday night, October 11, captured higher ratings than baseball's American League playoff game between Toronto and Minneapolis for the World Series.... Such public fascination with the Senate Judiciary Committee proceedings was unprecedented. Even the hearings for Robert Bork paled by comparison. In fact, the ratings for the Bork hearings were so low that ABC, CBS, and NBC stopped televising them after the first day.

In the wake of the Thomas–Hill hearings some felt that the process had become *too* public. For instance, President George Bush, complained that the sexually explicit testimony of Hill and Thomas should have been heard behind closed doors.

. . .

[The first Justice Harlan (the first southerner nominated after the Civil War) responded by letter to suspicions that had been raised about his Republican and Unionist bona fides. But more typically, nominees in the late nineteenth century remained silent. For example,] Melville W. Fuller, nominated for chief justice in 1888 by President Grover Cleveland, refused to respond to charges even when explicitly asked to do so by Chairman Edmunds of the Judiciary Committee. Edmunds submitted his request to Fuller in a letter of June 11, 1888. Fuller wired back: "While assuring the Committee that I intend no disrespect to them I cannot consent to reply to anonymous aspersions of the character referred to in yours of the eleventh."

Typically, nominees also refused to speak to the press. When Benjamin Harrison nominated George Shiras, Jr. to the Court in 1892, reporters tracked down Shiras in his hometown of Pittsburgh. But Shiras declined to comment, saying simply: "The United States Senate has not acted as yet upon my appointment and it would be indelicate of me to say anything." Similarly, when reporters questioned Louis Brandeis in Washington after Woodrow Wilson nominated him to the Court in 1916, Brandeis refused to comment. "I have nothing whatever to say," he told reporters. "I have not said anything and will not." Throughout his tumultuous confirmation battle, Brandeis remained publicly silent. When pressed for a comment by the rabidly Republican New York *Sun*, Brandeis responded: "I have nothing to say about anything, and that goes for all time and to all newspapers, including both the *Sun* and the moon."

Public silence by the nominees did not mean that they were above indirect (and at times even direct) lobbying of senators. For instance, Shiras and Brandeis countenanced the use of surrogates to make their case for them. Among those acting on behalf of Shiras were several of his former classmates from Yale University. One of them, Albert W. Bishop, wrote Shiras on July 22, 1892: "The Committee on the Judiciary [will] meet again this morning. Last evening I dined with [Senator Randall Lee] Gibson. He will take care of the Democratic members."

Brandeis and his advisers decided that it would be unwise for him to testify on his own behalf at the Judiciary Committee hearings, even though many witnesses were testifying against him. To do so would give the appearance that Brandeis was on trial. His advisers even convinced him to leave Washington while the Senate considered his nomination. They then arranged for George Anderson, a federal district attorney, to serve as a staff member of the committee. There he would act as the nominee's chief advocate, although he did so under the guise of being a mere "fact finder" for the committee. Despite Anderson's claim at the hearings that he did "not appear for Mr. Brandeis or for the friends of Mr. Brandeis," that was precisely his function. He was in constant contact with Brandeis and his supporters and was even allowed to cross-examine witnesses who appeared before the committee.

Brandeis also received strong support from one of his law partners, Edward McClennen, who set up shop in Washington and served as a liaison between Brandeis and his supporters. As witnesses appeared before the committee, Brandeis and another of his law partners, George R. Nutter, sent McClennen a steady stream of explanatory letters and memoranda. McClennen, himself, testified at length during the committee hearings, with Anderson leading off the questioning. Brandeis also held frequent conferences with Anderson.

After a solid month of committee hearings, Brandeis was frustrated. Critics had distorted his record and questioned his character. Some were motivated by anti-Semitism (Brandeis would be the first Jew to sit on the Supreme Court). Thus, Brandeis suggested in a letter to McClennen that perhaps he should appear before the committee after all. "I have accepted the opinion that it would be unwise for me to go down to Washington and appear [before the committee]," he wrote, "but if the proceedings continue on the lines which have been taken ... I think I would rather go down and testify." McClennen shot back that that was a bad idea. "What you could say has been said by the papers and the witnesses," he wrote. "You would dignify the adverse claims by coming here. And your presence would surely be misconstrued to mean that you were seeking the position."

For two more months, Brandeis stayed in Boston. But by early May, just over three months after leaving Washington, Brandeis briefly returned. He did not testify before the committee, but he did meet informally with two influential Democratic committee members who were likely to vote against him, James A. Reed of Missouri and Hoke

Smith of Georgia. The meeting took place on May 14, 1916, at a carefully planned social gathering at the apartment of Norman Hapgood, the editor of Harper's Weekly and a strong supporter of Brandeis. Brandeis won over both senators and promptly returned to Boston. When the Judiciary Committee voted on the nomination on May 24, both Reed and Smith supported Brandeis; the final committee vote was 10 to 8 in favor of confirming Brandeis. The full Senate voted 47 to 22 to confirm Brandeis on June 1.

The Brandeis battle was a precursor of the confirmation battles we now take for granted, complete with dramatic public hearings and full-blown press coverage. What was distinctly traditional was Brandeis's public silence, but even that tradition soon changed. On January 28, 1925, Attorney General Harlan Fiske Stone came to Capitol Hill, where the Senate Judiciary Committee questioned him for over four hours. Nominated by Calvin Coolidge to fill the vacancy left by the resignation of Associate Justice Joseph McKenna, Stone became the first Supreme Court nominee ever to testify before the committee. Stone did not discuss his judicial philosophy. Instead, he responded to charges leveled against him concerning his conduct as U.S. attorney general.

The press and the bar had greeted the Stone nomination enthusiastically.... But the Senate was raring for a fight. Cleavages between the progressive and conservative wings split the Republican party....

The Stone nomination quickly became part of the fight between progressives and conservatives. Stone's predecessor as attorney general, Harry M. Daugherty, had launched an investigation into Senator Wheeler that resulted in an indictment by a Montana grand jury in April 1924. The grand jury charged that Wheeler had taken $10,000 for appearing before the General Land Office of the Interior Department on behalf of oil claims made by his client, Gordon Campbell. Wheeler represented Campbell after having been elected to the Senate but before he actually took office. Although the payment was for Wheeler's legal services, Daugherty claimed that it violated a U.S. statute that prohibited members of Congress from receiving compensation in return for using their influence with U.S. departments.

Wheeler claimed that the indictment was politically motivated. No doubt he was correct. President Warren Harding had chosen Daugherty as attorney general because he was a close personal friend, and in his new post, Daugherty became a model of corruption. As Alpheus Thomas Mason writes, "Lurid tales of his exploits had long concerned even the shabby politicians of Harding's administration." Such exploits included "all night poker-and-liquor parties" that served as the meeting place for "shady barons of industry" and "captains of bootleg and highjack"; "lucrative traffic in Department of Justice liquor permits, [with] the 'deals' [being] handled by Jess Smith, Daugherty's valet, charge d'affaires, and buffer"; the " 'shadowing' of congressmen who dared expose, or had exposed, the Harding scandals; stock market speculation by the Attorney General himself under an assumed name, and so on." At the time that Daugherty brought the indictment against Wheeler, Wheeler was the chairman of a Senate committee investigating Daugherty and the Justice Department. The Senate's own investigation of the charges against Wheeler exonerated him and suggested that the indictment was part of an effort by Daugherty to discredit the senator.

The same month that the Montana grand jury brought the indictment against Wheeler, Daugherty resigned as attorney general and was replaced by Harlan Fiske Stone. Stone fully recognized the political motivation of Daugherty's indictment of Wheeler, but he was not convinced that meant Wheeler was innocent. Therefore, he ordered a new investigation. The results of that investigation convinced Stone that Wheeler was, in fact, part of a broader land fraud scheme. In early December 1924, Stone ordered that the new charges be submitted to a District of Columbia grand jury.

On January 5, 1925, President Coolidge nominated Stone to sit on the Supreme Court. One of the members of the Judiciary Committee was Senator Thomas J. Walsh (D–Mont.), who had served as Wheeler's counsel. Stone informed Walsh on January 16 that he was submitting the new evidence against Wheeler to a grand jury. Walsh evidently believed that this marked the beginning of the end of the matter. Walsh assumed that Stone would drop the Montana indictment and apparently felt that the District of Columbia grand jury would not indict. Three days later, he voted for Stone along with the rest of the Judiciary Committee. Stone, however, quickly made it clear that he had absolutely no intention of dropping the Montana indictment. Walsh met with Stone at the Department of Justice on January 22 to try to convince him otherwise, but the attorney general refused to give in. On Friday, January 24, Walsh stood up, on the Senate floor and demanded that Stone's Supreme Court nomination be sent back to the Judiciary Committee.

Shaken, Republican leaders went straight to the White House, where they met with Stone and the president. Stone suggested that the facts were such that the Senate could not reject him if they were properly aired. He therefore suggested that he appear before the Judiciary Committee. Everyone agreed. President Coolidge also let it be known to the press that he would not withdraw the nomination and that he had no objection to the nomination being sent back to the Judiciary Committee.

On Monday, the Senate unanimously approved the motion to recommit the nomination, and two days later Stone appeared before the committee to testify. His appearance was a resounding success. Most of the questions dealt with the Wheeler case. Unable to hurt Stone on that score, Senator Walsh implied that Stone was part and parcel of a corrupt department. An expert cross-examiner, Walsh methodically ran through a list of officials in the Justice Department that Daugherty had hired and that Stone had retained. In so doing, he implied that Stone had perpetuated the corruption of his predecessor. The tactic had little effect. Stone was unflappable. Despite questioning designed to bait him into "some indiscreet action or statement," Stone remained "forthright, courteous, and cooperative." His supporters were ecstatic and the press raved about his performance. On February 2, the Judiciary Committee again approved the nomination. Three days later, the full Senate voted to confirm by a vote 71 to 6. Walsh and Wheeler abstained.

For a time, Stone's testimony before the Judiciary Committee appeared to be an anomaly. Charles Evans Hughes did not appear before the committee when President Hoover nominated him to be chief justice in 1930, nor did John J. Parker, Owen Roberts, Benjamin Cardozo, Hugo Black, or Stanley Reed, although Parker wanted to and Reed showed up at the hearings in case the committee had any questions (which it did not). But, even though he did not testify, Hugo Black did go to the public in an extraordinary fashion shortly after his confirmation. Rumors that Black, a senator from Alabama, may have once belonged to the Ku Klux Klan emerged in August 1937 during Senate consideration of his nomination to be a Supreme Court justice. The Senate voted against investigating the charge by a vote of 66 to 15 on August 17 and confirmed him by a vote of 63 to 16 the same day.

Then, on September 13, Ray Sprigle published the first in a series of stories in the *Pittsburgh Post–Gazette* showing not only that Black had been a member of the Klan but also that he appeared to still be a member. Klan records showed that Black joined the Klan on September 11, 1923, and resigned on July 19, 1925, when he began his campaign for the U.S. Senate. But after winning the Democratic nomination (tantamount to Senate election in Alabama at that time), Black attended a statewide Klan meeting on September 2, 1926, at the great hall of the Invisible Empire in Birmingham. . . . There, "under the beaming smile of Imperial Wizard of the Invisible Realm Hiram Wesley Evans," Black and Graves were given the golden Grand Passport of the Alabama Klan, which accorded them life membership in the KKK.

Black then addressed the Klansmen . . . accepted the Grand Passport and thanked those assembled for their support. "I realize that I was elected by men who believe in the principles that I have sought to advocate and which are the principles of this organization," he said. "It is indeed pleasing to me to be present on this occasion. . . . I thank the Grand Dragon. He has stood by me like a pillar of strength . . . I thank you, friends, from the bottom of my heart."

In the 1920s, the Klan enjoyed its peak popularity in Alabama, with up to ninety thousand members. Arguably, no politician could hope to win public office without its support. But the implication that Black might still be a member was devastating. Black, on vacation in Paris with his wife, refused comment. Reports began circulating that White House aides felt Black should resign from the court, and columnists talked of impeachment. President Roosevelt refused comment until Black returned to the United States. Black set sail for the United States on September 25 and scheduled an unprecedented radio address to the

American people on October 1. All three national radio systems carried the speech, canceling their normal commercial programs. The speech gave Black the opportunity to present his case directly to an audience of some fifty million radio listeners. Shortwave radio carried the address around the world. Black said that he wanted the opportunity of a radio speech to ensure that his remarks would not be misquoted or otherwise distorted.

In his half-hour speech, Black said that "no ordinary maneuver executed for political advantage" would justify a public response by a Supreme Court justice. But because the charges against him threatened "the existing peace and harmony between religious and racial groups in our country," Black felt compelled to reply. Black insisted that the insinuations that he was prejudiced against "people of the Jewish and Catholic faiths, and against members of the Negro race" were false. "I believe that my record as a Senator refutes every implication of racial or religious intolerance," he said. "It shows that I was of that group of liberal Senators who have consistently fought for the civil, economic and religious rights of all Americans, without regard to race or creed."

Black told the American people that the insinuations of racial and religious intolerance were based on the fact that he had once joined the Ku Klux Klan. "I did join the Klan," he said. "I later resigned. I never re-joined.... I never have considered and I do not now consider the unsolicited card given to me shortly after my nomination to the Senate as a membership of any kind in the Ku Klux Klan. I never used it. I did not even keep it. Before becoming a Senator I dropped the Klan. I have had nothing whatever to do with it since that time. I abandoned it. I completely discontinued any association with the organization."

Black insisted that he had never preached intolerance at any meeting of any organization. Even the transcript of his 1926 speech to the Klan bears this statement out, although Black did not refer to it during his radio address. Speaking to the Klansmen, Black had stressed that "the real Anglo–Saxon sentiment" was embodied in the "heaven-born principles of liberty which were written in the Constitution of this country." "I shall endeavor with all my heart and mind and conscience to be fair to every man and every woman and every boy and every girl and every child," he told the Klan. What he liked about the Klan, he told them in 1926, was "not the burning of crosses. It is not attempting to regulate anybody." Instead, "I see a bigger vision. I see a vision of America honored by the nations of the world. Not only honored by the nations, but with a smile of the great God of the universe, beaming down upon it as it remains true to the principles of human liberty."

Black stressed his tolerance in his 1937 radio address: "I number among my friends many members of the colored race. ... Some of my best and most intimate friends are Catholics and Jews. Shortly after I moved to Birmingham, more than a quarter of a century ago, I formed one of the most valued friendships of my life with a son of Jewish faith.... He stood so nearly in the place of a father to me that while in the Army in 1918 I designated this trusted Jewish friend as sole executor of my will."

Black ended his speech by saying that he would have nothing further to say on the subject. "I believe the character and conduct of every public servant, great and small, should be subject to the constant scrutiny of the people. . . . It is in this spirit that I now bid those who have been listening to me goodnight."

Editorial reaction was mixed, but the speech appears to have been very successful in influencing public opinion. Surveys taken by the Institute of Public Opinion before and after the speech showed "one of the sharpest changes ever measured in an Institute poll." Before the speech, a nation-wide poll conducted by the institute showed that 59 percent of those polled thought Black should resign. After the speech, only 44 percent thought he should resign. In some regions of the country, Black's support had increased as much as twenty-five percentage points. . . . When asked after the speech if Congress should remove Black, 75 percent of the Democrats polled and 55 percent of the Republicans said no. The speech even affected those groups most likely to be offended by Klan membership, like blacks, Catholics, and Jews. The institute concluded that their survey showed "how quickly the debate has subsided."

Black joined the Court when its 1937 term began on October 11. The Court quickly rejected a challenge to Black's right to sit and turned to other business. Black's long tenure on the Court confirmed his commitment to civil liberties.

In 1939, Felix Frankfurter became the first nominee since Stone to testify. His nomination by Franklin D. Roosevelt on January 5, 1939, was greeted with great enthusiasm in most quarters. Peers held him in high regard, and a Gallup Poll showed strong public support as well. Like Brandeis before him, however, Frankfurter faced opposition from anti-Semites, who were quick to point out that Brandeis already filled the Court's "Jewish seat." "If we put another Jew on the Court, then the Jew element in the Court will represent 29 million of the population," one angry lawyer wrote to the Judiciary Committee—and that, he pointed out, was far more than the Jewish population in the United States. Then he demanded to know: "Would you put two Negroes on the Court, or two Chinese on the Court, or two Japanese?"

Although the committee received many anti-Semitic letters concerning Frankfurter, much of the opposition was couched in terms of Frankfurter's foreign birth and his perceived "radicalism." Some even pointed to his membership in the American Civil Liberties Union as proof of his radical tendencies. A subcommittee held public hearings on the nomination on January 11 and 12. Elizabeth Dilling, (author of *The Red Network*), insisted that Frankfurter was a communist. . . . [S]he added, "I don't want the kind of colleges that Justice Brandeis was connected with, where they teach communism and have free love and nudist colonies." Taken aback, Senator Norris asked, "You have some feeling against Harvard Law School?" "Yes," Mrs. Dilling emphatically replied.

Frankfurter wanted to keep his distance from the hearings, and especially from the "crackpots" (as he later termed them) who were testifying. Therefore, he sent Dean Acheson, then a lawyer engaged in private practice, to represent him at the hearings. In executive session, however, subcommittee members informed Acheson that they wanted Frankfurter himself to appear. Reluctantly, Frankfurter did so the next day. Newspaper coverage of the first day of hearings stressed the inconsistencies in the testimony. The *New York Times* noted that witnesses "opposed the nominee because he was a Jew, because he was born abroad, because he was 'the fixer' for an alien conspiracy, because he was an 'incompetent lawyer,' because he was a 'brilliant lawyer' but un-American," and so forth. . . .

By the time Frankfurter appeared, the hearings had become something of a media circus. As he entered the room, a mob of reporters and onlookers greeted him. Acheson later wrote that the large Caucus Room where the hearing was held was "jam-packed"—"so packed that police had to precede us like icebreakers to open a path to the witness table." Frankfurter opened with a brief statement. . . .

. . . The toughest questioning came from Senator Pat McCarran (D–Nev.), a self-proclaimed anticommunist crusader, but the assembled crowd was clearly on the side of Frankfurter. When McCarran asked Frankfurter if he believed in the doctrine of Karl Marx, Frankfurter replied that he did not believe that McCarran himself could be "more attached to the theories and practices of Americanism" than was he. According to the *New York Times*, that response elicited an ovation from the audience that lasted over two minutes.

Still, supporters of Frankfurter on the committee were concerned that Frankfurter was not refuting McCarran's charges directly enough. At one point during the questioning, Senator Matthew M. Neely (D–W.Va.) conferred privately with Dean Acheson. Neely told Acheson that Chairman Henry F. Ashurst (D–Ariz.) believed that Frankfurter should respond point-blank to the question of whether he was or ever had been a communist. A negative response, they believed, would effectively halt McCarran. Acheson agreed and relayed the message to Frankfurter. He also "urged him to be sensible and not reply by asking the Chairman what he meant by 'Communist.' " Thus, when the rest of the committee had finished its questions, Senator Neely asked the question for Chairman Ashurst:

> *Senator Neely*: . . . The chairman, with great reluctance, propounds one inquiry that he thinks ought to be answered as a matter of justice to you. Some of those who have testified before the committee have, in a very hazy, indefinite way, attempted to create the impression that you are a Communist. Therefore, the Chair asks you the direct question: Are you a Communist or have you ever been one?

Dr. Frankfurter: I have never been and I am not now.

Senator McCarran: By that you mean that you have never been enrolled as a member of the Communist Party?

Dr. Frankfurter: I mean much more than that. I mean that I have never been enrolled, and have never been qualified to be enrolled because that does not represent my view of life, nor my view of government.

With that, Acheson recalls, a "great roar came from the crowded room. People shouted, cheered, stood on chairs, and waved. The Chairman, banging his gavel, was inaudible." Finally he quieted the room long enough to adjourn the proceedings. . . .

Despite the dramatic media coverage of Frankfurter's testimony, the relative unimportance of nominees' testimony continued to be assumed for some years after the Frankfurter hearings. . . . When Dwight D. Eisenhower nominated Earl Warren to be chief justice in [1953], the Judiciary Committee chose not even to ask Warren to testify.

During the Warren hearings, Deputy Attorney General William P. Rogers reminded the Senate Judiciary Committee Subcommittee in executive session that the Senate had never asked a nominee for chief justice to testify. . . . Besides, Warren was a recess appointee and was already sitting on the Court when his confirmation hearings took place. As Rogers reminded the subcommittee: "I doubt very much if you could elicit much information which you do not have already, unless you in some way conflicted with matters now pending before the Court."

Nonetheless, William J. Brennan and Potter Stewart, both of whom were also Eisenhower recess appointees, did testify before the Judiciary Committee. Brennan had already been sitting on the Court for four months when he finally testified on February 26 and 27, 1957. He made it clear that "having taken an oath of office" as a sitting Supreme Court justice, it was his "obligation" not to discuss any matters pending before the Court. He did, however, answer general questions about the proper scope of constitutional interpretation. As a Catholic, he was also asked which was greater, his allegiance to the pope or his allegiance to the Constitution. But the most remarkable aspect of Brennan's appearance was questioning by Senator Joseph McCarthy (R–Wisc.).

Like Senator McCarran before him, McCarthy was a hard-line anti-communist crusader. McCarthy was concerned because Brennan had, in various speeches, criticized the highly emotional communist investigations of that era. Brennan said in a 1954 speech that "some practices in the contemporary scene" were "reminiscent of the Salem witch hunts," that those practices "engender[ed] hate and fear by one citizen of another," thereby bringing the country "perilously close to destroying liberty in liberty's name," and that some of the procedures used at anticommunist hearings smacked of "barbarism." In a 1990 interview with Nat Hentoff, Brennan said that he had made speeches all around Monmouth County, New Jersey, calling McCarthy "all sorts of names."

"Hell," he added, "when I made those speeches I had no idea I would ever get to sit on the Supreme Court.... So when Eisenhower announced he was going to appoint me, McCarthy issued a statement saying that I was supremely unfit for the Supreme Court."

McCarthy did not sit on the Judiciary Committee, but he wanted to question Brennan anyway. "At first, there was resistance to McCarthy's sitting in on the committee," Brennan told Hentoff. "He was in decline. He had already been censured, and he died not long after my hearings." But, Brennan added, "I thought those who were against his sitting with the committee were wrong. There's absolutely nothing in the Constitution which limits the advice and consent function of the Senate. Nothing. And, because each senator has to cast his own vote on the matter, he should be able to interrogate the nominee if he wants to." According to Brennan, McCarthy asked him about "the craziest things" and that those who heard the exchanges at the hearings "did not think it was one of Senator McCarthy's finest hours."

Even fellow senators were embarrassed by McCarthy's questioning. The end of the first day of Brennan's testimony culminated in an explosion from Senator McCarthy: "I have been reading in every left-wing paper, the same type of gobbledegook that I find in your speeches [where you talk] about the barbarism of committees [and] Salem witch hunts. I just wonder if a Supreme Court Justice can hide behind his robes and conduct a guerilla warfare against investigating committees." ... Later, the Judiciary Committee voted 11 to 0 to recommend that Brennan be confirmed, which the full Senate did by voice vote.

Every Supreme Court nominee since John Marshall Harlan in 1955 has testified before the Judiciary Committee. Increasingly, senators have tried to pin down a nominee's judicial philosophy. On occasion, they even ask how a nominee would vote in particular cases. This trend began in the mid–1950s, prompted largely by the Supreme Court's desegregation decision in *Brown v. Board of Education*. Conservative southern Democrats argued that *Brown* was an "activist" ruling, in which the Court changed the meaning of the Civil War Amendments to the constitution. Thus, when Dwight D. Eisenhower nominated Potter Stewart in 1959, southern Democrats on the Committee bombarded him with questions about *Brown* and his judicial philosophy.

Senator Olin Johnston from South Carolina asked: "Do you consider yourself what is termed a 'creative judge' or do you consider yourself a judge that follows precedent?" "I don't really consider myself a 'creative' or 'non-creative' judge," Stewart replied. "I like to try to be a good one." Johnston then pressed him on the Civil War Amendments. Should they be applied according to their understanding when they were ratified or according to contemporary understanding? Stewart evaded the question. Johnston tried to pin Stewart down on *Brown*. How had the Court changed the constitution through the *Brown* decision? Again Stewart hedged. Then Senator John McClellan from Arkansas picked up the questioning. "Do you agree with the view, the reasoning the logic applied

... and the philosophy expressed by the Supreme Court in arriving in its decision in the case of *Brown v. Board of Education* on May 17, 1954?" Stewart tried to get at the issue indirectly: "I am an Ohioan. I live in a state where as a matter of state law, since the 19th century, it has been illegal to discriminate or segregate among school children on the basis of race. That is the law. And so ... the basic decision [in *Brown*] did not shock me or appear wrong to me."

But McClellan was not satisfied. He repeated his question, Did Stewart agree with the reasoning, logic, and philosophy of *Brown*? To which Stewart finally replied: "Senator, if I may, basically the answer is 'yes.'" Senator Thomas Hennings (D–Mo.) then interrupted with a point of order: "I do not think it proper to inquire of a nominee for this court or any other his opinion as to any of the decisions or the reasoning upon decisions which have heretofore been handed down by that court." After considerable debate, in which several senators argued that they could ask whatever they wanted and Stewart was free not to respond, Senator Hennings withdrew his point of order.

In fact, most nominees have refused to discuss cases with members of the Judiciary Committee. During his 1986 confirmation hearings, Antonin Scalia went so far as to refuse comment on *Marbury v. Madison*, the 1803 case involving the Court's power of judicial review. But Robert Bork—with an extensive public record of law review articles, speeches, and other public remarks—took the unusual approach in his 1987 hearings of talking at length about his judicial philosophy and about specific cases that the Court had decided. His was the longest and most detailed public testimony of any Supreme Court nominee. In addition, he actively courted the press, starting with an hour-long interview with *New York Times* reporter Stuart Taylor Jr. some two months before his confirmation hearings began. "It was our way of humanizing him and showing that he didn't have horns," according to White House lobbyist Tom Korologos. But some critics accused Bork of undergoing a "confirmation conversion" and using his public testimony to moderate his controversial stands on issues such as free speech and the right to privacy.

In terms of the specificity of his testimony, Bork remains an anomaly. In the wake of Bork's Senate rejection, presidents nominated individuals with little in the way of a public record that interest groups and other opponents could use against them, individuals whom the press labeled "stealth nominees." Given the emotional debate over abortion rights, President Bush particularly sought nominees who had not taken a public stand on abortion. During his confirmation hearings in 1991, senators asked Clarence Thomas where he stood on the abortion issue over seventy times during his three days of testimony. Thomas went so far as to say, in response to questioning from Senator Patrick Leahy (D–Vt.), that he had never discussed *Roe v. Wade*, the 1973 Supreme Court case that extended the constitutional right of privacy to protect a woman's right to have an abortion. Even as a student at Yale Law School at the time the Supreme Court handed down the decision, Thomas claimed never to have discussed it.[14]

Leahy was incredulous. "Have you ever had a discussion of *Roe v. Wade*, other than in this room?" he asked, provoking laughter from those assembled in the committee room. Nervously, Thomas answered: "If you are asking me whether or not I have debated the contents of it, the answer to that is no, Senator," "Let me ask you this," Leahy continued. "Have you made any decision in your own mind whether you feel *Roe v. Wade* was properly decided, without stating what that decision is?" Thomas replied: "I have not made, Senator, a decision one way or the other with respect to that important decision."

A year earlier, David Souter had avoided the question with more aplomb when Senator Howard Metzenbaum (D–Ohio) pushed him on the question. Metzenbaum, in an obvious attempt to put Souter on the defensive, lectured Souter about testimony he had heard from women who had illegal abortions prior to *Roe*. "They were women about your age," Metzenbaum told Souter. "They told horrible stories." One woman, "who was poor and alone, self-aborted," he continued. "It is a horrible story, just a horrible story, with knitting needles and a bucket." "My real question to you is not how you would rule on *Roe v. Wade* or any other particular case coming before the Court," Metzenbaum concluded. "But what does a woman face when she has an unwanted pregnancy . . .? I would just like to get your view and your own thoughts of that woman's position under those circumstances."

Souter gave a masterful reply. It was an intimate narrative that deflected Metzenbaum's question, underscored Souter's sensitivity to the issue, and effectively silenced the senator. It also reinforced efforts by President Bush and other members of his administration to portray Souter as fair—a "kinder, gentler" Supreme Court nominee than Bork, who was defeated largely because of the perception that he was unfair. Yet Souter's reply achieved all that without giving any indication whatsoever of how he would vote on abortion cases.

Souter responded to Metzenbaum's question by recalling an incident that happened when he was in law school, serving as a freshman dormitory adviser at Harvard College. One afternoon, Souter recalled, a freshman came to him "in pretty rough shape." The boy told Souter that his girlfriend was pregnant and that she was going to try to have a self-abortion but that she didn't know how to do it. She was afraid to tell her parents and afraid to go to the health clinic, and the boy asked Souter to talk with her. "I will not try to say what I told her," Souter told Metzenbaum, "but I spent two hours in a small dormitory bedroom that afternoon . . . listening to her and trying to counsel her . . . and your question has brought that back to me." Souter looked Metzenbaum

14. [Editors' note: See Case Studies in Section B.]

straight in the eye and said with conviction: "I know what you were trying to tell me, because I remember that afternoon."

The emotional impact of that reply helped to deflect questions about Souter's stand on abortion.... Although he refused to comment on abortion cases, Souter did state in his testimony that he believed in a constitutional right to privacy, even though it is not explicitly enumerated in the Constitution. "I believe that the due process clause of the 14th amendment does recognize and does protect an unenumerated right of privacy," he said. But so, too, did Clarence Thomas. Simply stating a belief in a constitutional right to privacy says nothing about how one would rule on the abortion question, which pits the right to privacy of the mother against the potential right to life of the fetus. In fact, Thomas voted to overrule *Roe v. Wade* in 1992, while Souter co-authored a majority opinion reaffirming (though modifying) *Roe*.

Today, Supreme Court nominees are carefully coached for their televised testimony before the Judiciary Committee. Mock question-and-answer sessions, known as "murder boards," are a routine preparation for their appearances. For a nominee to refuse to appear before the committee in this day and age would be unthinkable.

Speaking Out: Presidents

Just as Supreme Court nominees used to maintain absolute public silence during Senate consideration of their nomination, presidents used to refrain from public comment on their nominees. Presidents felt that to make public comments would be to stoop to "politics" in a process that was supposed to be (but of course never was) untainted by political considerations. Besides, presidents generally refrained from overt public appeals in the nineteenth and early twentieth centuries. Scholars of the presidency, such as Jeffrey Tulis, remind us that during that period presidents avoided the practice of public appeals because they thought it would "manifest demagoguery, impede deliberation, and subvert the routines of republican government." The avoidance of public appeals reflected the founders' fear of "pure" or "direct" democracy. Although the founders felt that public consent was a requirement of republican government, they nonetheless felt that the processes of government should be insulated from the whims of public opinion. In short, presidents shunned the now commonplace practice of direct public appeals because it went against the existing interpretation of the constitutional order.

That interpretation of the constitutional order changed in the twentieth century. Increasingly, public appeals became an important strategic device used by presidents to win support of their policies and influence other policymakers. Today, public support does not just elect presidents, it is a president's most visible source of ongoing political power. More than ever before, presidents and their surrogates take messages directly to the people in an attempt to mold mandates for policy initiatives. A strategy of presidential power based on such appeals is known as "going public." . . .

Even after going public became more commonplace, presidents were unwilling use the tactic overtly to promote Supreme Court nominees. Thus, Woodrow Wilson did not speak publicly on behalf of Louis Brandeis, and Herbert Hoover, although he drafted several versions of a public statement decrying the Senate's defeat of Parker, decided against issuing any of them. . . .

Before Reagan, Supreme Court nominees were lucky if the president *ever* publicly uttered their name after nominating them. Even the nomination announcement was often left to the White House press secretary or a Justice Department spokesperson. When presidents did make the announcement, it was usually done in the relative obscurity of an intimate news conference. For instance, President Harry Truman's announcement of his nomination of Senator Harold H. Burton (R–Ohio) was the last of six brief announcements that he made during a news conference in his office on September 18, 1945. Truman chose Burton to replace Owen Roberts, one of just two Republicans left on the Court. . . . When Truman announced his intention to nominate Burton, the reporters reacted with "subdued laughter and a surprised low whistle," but they did not ask the president any questions about the nomination. The Democrat-controlled Senate asked no questions either. It dispensed with Judiciary Committee hearings and simply approved the nomination of their colleague by voice vote the next day.

Now presidents announce their Supreme Court nominees with great fanfare, and they follow up on the announcement with public statements aimed at eliciting popular support for the nominee. . . .

With his nomination of Robert Bork in 1987, Reagan broke all records. From July 1 through October 23, 1987, he waged a full-scale public campaign on behalf of Bork, making a total of thirty-three public statements on behalf of his nominee (including his initial announcement of the nomination). Evening newscasts of the three major television networks covered twenty of those statements; two were carried "live" in their entirety on prime-time television. . . .

Subsequent nominees have all drawn public statements of support from the president who nominated them. . . .

[P]residents [today] use institutionalized staff units in the White House to mobilize public appeals by a wide range of individuals on behalf of their Supreme Court nominees. In fact, this is only one of several ways that modern presidents have responded to changes in the confirmation process and have attempted to increase their influence on the final Senate vote. The confirmation process is now a distinctly public affair, with all of its participants grappling with each other for public support.

David Alistair Yalof,[15] *Pursuit of Justices: Presidential Politics and the Selection of Supreme Court Nominees* **168–87, 206–07 (1999)**

. . . [M]any social scientists have been drawn to study heated confirmation battles as a means of gaining broad new insights into the nature of Supreme Court recruitment. By contrast, this study offers a quite different perspective from which to analyze Supreme Court recruitment: it focuses instead on the building of consensus and the resolution of conflicts during the initial nominating stage of the appointment process. Such an alternative way of viewing the process in way discounts the influence that a looming confirmation battle may have an initial deliberations over prospective candidates. . . .

Consider the political tightrope modern presidents must walk as they attempt to choose nominees in this highly charged political atmosphere. Organized interests on all sides of the political spectrum may try to influence their choice of a candidate at the outset. Senators, attuned to these changes in the political environment, may assume more aggressive postures against a rumored nominee even before the president has formally designated him or her for a Supreme Court seat. Increased media attention may scare some potential nominees away, further constraining presidential discretion. Fortunately, modern presidents do possess the means to respond to heightened expectations in this context. The steady growth and expansion of executive branch resources has afforded chief executives the ability to invest considerable manpower into the selection of candidates. Officials now enjoy access to sophisticated computer research technology for finding information about prospective nominees. Additionally, the growth in size and influence of the federal judiciary has expanded the pool of qualified candidates available to the president when filling any one vacancy.

I have attempted to document the nominee selection process as it unfolded during seven separate administrations between 1945 and 1987. . . .

. . . .

[One] modern trend in Supreme Court recruitment [is] federal circuit court judges have become the "darlings" of the selection process in modern times. Eisenhower was arguably the first president to aggressively pursue such a strategy. His public commitment to choose justices with prior judicial experience led him to name federal circuit judges to three of the five vacancies that arose during his administration. Almost a decade later Nixon picked up where Eisenhower left off: four of Nixon's six high court nominees were federal appeals judges, including his choice for chief justice, Warren Burger. Gerald Ford chose John Paul Stevens of the U.S. Court of Appeals for the Seventh Circuit to fill a vacancy on the Court in 1975. A decade later President Reagan confirmed his preference

---

15. Assistant Professor of Political Science, University of Connecticut.

for federal circuit court judges by nominating four consecutive federal appeals judges to associate justice vacancies beginning in 1986. While only a third of the fifteen individuals nominated between 1945 and 1968 were federal appeals judges; sixteen of nineteen nominees since then have emerged from this elite pool of candidates.

. . .

Several factors have contributed to this heightened interest in federal appeals judges. Although hardly dispositive, federal appellate opinions offer perhaps the best gauge available for predicting an individual's future voting behavior on the Supreme Court. Thus an administration committed to a particular ideological blueprint may gravitate towards federal circuit judges who have addressed many of these same issues before. During the Reagan administration, several academics with Supreme Court aspirations (Bork, Scalia, Ralph Winter, and Richard Posner, to name just a few) accepted prestigious judgeships on the circuit courts, allowing administration officials to watch as their judicial philosophies matured. Federal appeals judges also make for less controversial nominees before the U.S. Senate. Most escape the public's attention during their tenures on the courts of appeals. Opposition groups may be forced to expend considerable resources trying to turn a federal appeals judge into a political lightning rod during the confirmation process. Admittedly, candidates for circuit court judgeships undergo a far less rigorous path to Senate confirmation than candidates for the Supreme Court, but they may benefit from having already survived the scrutiny of a complete FBI investigation and ABA review. Nearly all have already testified at least once before the Senate Judiciary Committee. Even more crucial are the ties many federal appeals judges enjoy to political patrons in the Senate. A senator from that judge's home state was probably responsible for his or her being offered that federal judgeship in the first place. Such connections with senators may later prove critically important when that judge is named to the U.S. Supreme Court.

Finally, most circuit court judges chart a course of moderation on policy issues, carefully avoiding the polarizing viewpoints that later make for a troublesome paper trail. By contrast, law professors, congressmen, executive branch officials and others often achieve success in those positions precisely because they are willing to confront society's most heated public controversies. The active recruitment of federal circuit judges for the Supreme Court may thus represent a de facto move by presidential administrations to steer away from candidates whose legal philosophies fit into simple "black" or "white" categories, and towards more moderate candidates whose positions are difficult to categorize.... Even Robert Bork, noted for his controversial views on abortion, free speech, and other constitutional issues as a law professor, exercised uncharacteristic restraint and caution during his five years on the bench. Opponents of Bork's nomination were eventually forced to seek most of their ammunition from his earlier writings as a law professor. Even the ABA—which later split on the issue of Bork's fitness for the high court—regarded Bork's circuit court opinions as both "balanced in judgment" and "fair in treatment of the arguments of losing parties and dissenters."

The patterns depicted above are indeed striking. Yet perhaps the most significant development of all has been the overall shift in the locus of candidate winnowing and vetting from the president himself to subordinates in the White House, the Justice Department, and elsewhere. In effect, the president has yielded what was traditionally a quite "personal" decision to various executive branch officials under his command. Criteria-driven frameworks for decisionmaking have facilitated this development: presidents may feel more comfortable transferring discretion to subordinates when that discretion is cabined within clearly defined guidelines. As was the case during the Eisenhower administration, those criteria may later prove so restrictive as to hinder a comprehensive search for candidates. The criteria may also prove too broad to effectively assist subordinates charged with weeding through lists of prospective candidates. In the latter case, a fierce battle among presidential advisors with competing viewpoints is likely to ensue. In either event, the president's overall goals and interests may not be maximized. . . .

[Yalof describes the use of three different decisional frameworks used to select nominees: a "single candidate" selection process where the President has in mind the particular person he wished to nominate (as was the case when Eisenhower nominated Warren); a completely "open" process (as when President Ford asked Attorney General Levi to conduct the search that ended up with Justice John Paul Stevens); and] a "criteria-driven" framework for decisionmaking. Fully half of the twenty-eight nominees addressed in [Yalof's] book emerged out of this type of selection framework, including eleven of thirteen nominations since 1969. . . .

A president may prefer the criteria-driven selection framework for several reasons. He may perceive the need to strategize in advance about future vacancies. Perhaps the president wants to reassure vital constituencies of his commitment to their particular causes or interests. He may also view the appointment of Supreme Court justices as a high policy priority of his administration, worthy of advance consideration. . . .

. . .

. . . [U]nlike in the "single-candidate" framework . . . , [in a criteria-driven framework] political leaders and prospective candidates themselves may influence the president's choice within these restrictions. Presidents Eisenhower, Nixon, and Reagan each relied heavily on top advisors to manage the selection process once a vacancy occurred, canvassing the available pool of candidates for likely nominees who might satisfy the administration's prescribed criteria. Eisenhower directed Attorney General Brownell in 1956 to find a state judge who was Catholic, a Democrat, and below the age of sixty. William Brennan was one of few judges in the country able to satisfy each of those stringent conditions. For his final two nominations, Eisenhower insisted on Republican judges from the U.S. Court of Appeals between the ages of fifty and sixty; he gave in on the minimum age requirement in 1958 only after Attorney General William Rogers persuaded him of forty-three-year-old Potter Stewart's merits. Within those boundaries there was room to maneuver.... Richard Nixon was determined to name as associate justice a southerner with a conservative record, preferably under the age of sixty. He viewed experience as a federal judge preferable, though not a hard and fast requirement. Clement Haynsworth and G. Harrold Carswell fit the president's criteria precisely, although each of their two candidacies met with disastrous consequences in the Senate. Harry Blackmun received a nomination only after a reluctant President Nixon introduced a new filter in the final hour: Blackmun was a Minnesota native, and thus fit the president's sudden need for a federal appeals judge from the North. In late 1971 Nixon nominated Lewis Powell, a sixty-four-year-old Democrat from Virginia with no previous judicial experience: with the appointment of a confirmable southerner now the president's top priority, Nixon was forced to abandon other criteria (Powell violated his age criterion) that had limited the pool substantially up to that point.

As Ronald Reagan's priorities for the Court shifted during his two terms in office, so did his administration's criteria for selecting Supreme Court nominees. In 1981 Reagan sought to fulfill an earlier campaign promise to name the first woman to the Supreme Court. During the second term his administration placed considerably greater weight on ideological criteria, sifting through opinions written by prospective justices for evidence of conservative leanings. By the time Warren Burger announced his retirement as chief justice in May 1986, the Justice Department had already effectively narrowed the list of potential Supreme Court candidates to six federal appeals judges. By doing its homework well in advance, the administration was able to streamline the selection process once an actual vacancy arose. The Justice Department's list stayed virtually intact even after Burger made his retirement plans known. President Reagan did not unduly limit the subsequent selection process, however: the pool of young, conservative, federal appeals judges considered by his administration was still large enough to allow the flexible pursuit of administration interests. Accordingly, his administration was able to choose between more controversial conservative candidates (Ginsburg, Bork, and Scalia) favored by Meese's Justice Department, or those who were considered more readily confirmable (i.e., Anthony Kennedy).

UNDERMINING PRESIDENTIAL INTERESTS?
MULTIPLE ADVISORS, OVERLAPPING RESPONSIBILITIES

One of the defining characteristics of the modern presidency has been its heavy reliance on White House and executive branch bureaucracies for assistance in decisionmaking. In this spirit, recent presidents have increasingly turned to trusted advisors and subordinates to aid them in their Supreme Court recruitment efforts. Frustrated by an increasingly hostile atmosphere for appointments, President Nixon enlisted multiple officials both inside and outside the White House to aid him in the process of screening potential nominees. Similarly, during his two terms in office President Reagan unabashedly relied on a troika of high-level advisors (the attorney general, the White House chief of staff, and the White House Counsel) to help him identify and select Supreme Court candidates. In turn, each of those officials aggressively deployed their own departmental resources to size up the field of potential candidates. Yet despite such an impressive show of executive branch manpower, both of those two administrations suffered embarrassing nomination mishaps and squandered precious political capital in the process. Did the delegation of decisionmaking authority to so many different offices and advisors actually undermine presidential interests in this context?

. . .

At least one school of organizational theory posits that if one part of an organization simply duplicates a function being performed by another, negative consequences will be caused to the organization as a whole. From an economic perspective this makes perfect sense: duplicative functions cause an unnecessary drain on the organization's resources. Even more troubling, however, is the negative impact such overlapping responsibilities may have on the quality of information produced by the separate departments. Specifically, the quality of information and advice received by the organization's head (in this case the president) from department heads suffers when the latter are thrust into a competition of sorts, with each trying to inject their own interests into the political equation.

. . .

... Because each official's success as an advocate determines his subgroup's general prestige and status within the administration, subgroup members' respect and willingness to work for that official "will be greatly affected by the degree to which he is able to influence his own superiors through vigorous advocacy." Officials at all levels understand that "a bureau headed by a 'tiger' who 'fights for his men'—that is, who advocates their specialized functions against others—tends to have a higher esprit de corps than a bureau headed by an impartial official who sympathizes equally with other bureaus." These cultural expectations in turn only encourage department heads to further behave like advocates; after all, others may interpret an attitude of compromise by him or her as a sign of weakness or apathy.

The negative effects that such behavior may have on actual nomination decisions should not be underestimated. When a bureau (whether it is the Justice Department, the White House Counsel's Office, or the Office of the White House Chief of Staff) reaches its own conclusions on the merits of any given issue, it normally prepares some type of communication or memorandum in support of its findings. However, in a competitive environment, that message "necessarily leaves out or drastically simplifies many of the inputs that went into the actual choice process. . . . [O]fficials in other parts of the bureau thus see only the rather simplified final result." "Outcome optimism" also pervades this process [in which the positive consequences of the argued for result are overestimated.] . . .

Clearly a president may not be acting on the best information available to him under these conditions; rather, he is forced to choose among competing versions of the alleged truth, each crafted to counter the others. Presidential decisionmaking surely suffers as a consequence. . . .

. . .

Before 1969, most presidents were able to minimize internal conflict within their administrations in this context of Supreme Court recruitment. Presidents Truman and Johnson pursued deeply personal goals in recruiting Supreme Court nominees, and their so-called advisors on this matter played little (if any) role in the selection process. Presidents Eisenhower and Kennedy shared little in common except for their strict attention to partisan goals and their respective commitments to grant broad and exclusive selection authority to their attorneys general. Indeed, Eisenhower insisted that all other officials in his administration (including Special Counsel Bernard Shanley) go through the attorney general with any suggestions or recommendations for Supreme Court vacancies. Because Brownell was the only authoritative figure in the process aside from the president himself the risk of corrupt information was reduced considerably. In fact, in early 1957 Brownell dutifully recommended Charles Whittaker, the candidate who best fit the president's carefully defined criteria (a Midwestern federal appeals court judge, Republican, under sixty) even though he personally lacked enthusiasm for Whittaker's candidacy. . . .

By contrast, examples abound of internal competition interfering with, and in some cases corrupting, recruitment efforts during the Nixon and Reagan administrations. Declining to consider any personal goals in selecting his Supreme Court nominees, Nixon relied on the expertise of subordinates to help him fulfill policy goals (the creation of a more conservative court) and partisan goals (shoring up southern support for his administration). Those objectives were quickly undermined, however, by two critical handicaps the administration was laboring under: his attorney general's lack of political effectiveness and the unduly restrictive filters Nixon insisted on applying to each Supreme Court vacancy. Following back-to-back Senate rejections of Haynsworth and Carswell, Nixon refused to replace Mitchell with a more qualified selection authority; instead the president invited numerous other officials into the decisionmaking process to possibly spar with Mitchell—Pat Buchanan, John D. Ehrlichman, Bud Krogh, David Young, and Richard Moore. Even with this bevy of advisors, the administration continued to suffer under the weight of its own distorted information channels. In 1971,

Richard Poff's expected nomination came undone publicly because Pat Buchanan (Poff's chief supporter in the White House) conveniently overlooked the negative effects of his favorite candidate's support for the Southern Manifesto. . . .

The Reagan administration breathed life once again into Nixon's multiple-advisor scheme, instituting it as formal administration policy. Attorney General William French Smith may have master-minded the selection of Sandra Day O'Connor in 1981, but her nomination also required the approval of White House Counsel Fred Fielding, whose office generated its own list of candidates to recommend to the president. Fielding, looking out for the president's policy interests, might have had misgivings about any candidate whose position on abortion rights was open to question. But the more moderate attorney general was more concerned with the president's partisan goals (appointment of a female, smooth confirmation), and so he redoubled his efforts on O'Connor's behalf. During his second term, Reagan relied on aides from three different offices to provide critical input concerning Supreme Court candidates. When political circumstances were favorable for the administration—as they were in 1986—Attorney General Edwin Meese was able to pursue the administration's policy goals without regard to partisan concerns: Antonin Scalia's nomination was a victory for partisan and policy goals; indeed it was a home run on both counts.

By contrast, Meese's insistence the following year on the pursuit of policy goals at all costs ultimately dealt a serious blow to the administration's partisan interests. Despite warnings of a possible confirmation fight, Meese and his assistants argued forcefully on behalf of Bork, pressing for an announcement mere days after Powell's retirement. The quick rush to judgment benefitted Meese's aggressive pursuit of policy goals, as potentially competing points of view in the White House Counsel's Office were denied the necessary time to mobilize. This competition among advisors may have exaggerated Meese's perceived costs of losing; after all, Bork's replacement might now be some other official's first choice, rather than Meese's own second choice. The competition thus indirectly encouraged this rush to judgment and discouraged more reasoned contemplation about Bork's candidacy. . . .

. . .

[The author recommends that] one eminently qualified presidential advisor (either the attorney general or the White House Counsel) must be entrusted with the bulk of recruitment responsibilities; ideally, that individual should combine political savvy with formidable legal expertise. Although it may be preferable to establish some guidelines for judicial recruitment, overly restrictive criteria may unduly hamper the selection process, undercutting even the most diligent advisors' best efforts to choose a qualified Supreme Court nominee. It may also force the quality of selection outcomes down to its lowest common denominator. A president should rarely involve more than one executive branch office or agency in this decisionmaking process early on—by encouraging numerous officials to assume overlapping responsibilities, the president risks reducing the quality of the information he receives. The lesson is clear: modern presidents have *too much* information about prospective candidates at their disposal. Judicial selection mechanisms should thus be designed with an eye towards filtering information for the president in as unbiased a fashion as possible.

. . .

EPILOGUE
THE SELECTION PRACTICES OF BUSH AND CLINTON . . .

. . . [N]either of these two presidents took the lessons of past chief executives enough to heart. Bush's selection process was a creature of rigid and unyielding criteria: only federal appeals judges ever garnered serious consideration from his administration, with state judges, trial judges, and others all but ignored. Additionally, Bush seized upon the same "three-person committee" format that had led to internal strife and factionalism during the latter part of the Reagan administration. While Souter and Thomas were the favorite candidates of Sununu [White House Chief of Staff] and Gray [White House Counsel], respectively, it is unclear whether their appointments actually maximized Bush's overall best interests. Regardless, only a limited set of alternatives was ever presented to him. At the opposite extreme, Clinton was barely willing to delegate any significant decisionmaking power to subordinates, like Truman and Johnson before him. Without a manager entrusted with sufficient authority over the selection process, a myriad of candidacies fell in and out of favor in accordance with the president's shifting sense of moods. Both presidents clearly suffered from a case of "confirmability myopia": Bush and Clinton desperately wanted to avoid the embarrassment and humiliation of an ugly confirmation defeat. For better or worse, the ill-fated 1987 nomination of Robert Bork had continued to cast its long and influential shadow over all high court nominations in its wake.

---

3. The Role of the ABA in the Appointment Process

From the 1950s until 2001, the Standing Committee on the Judiciary of the American Bar Association played an unusually significant role in screening and evaluating federal judicial nominees, including Supreme Court nominees. In the following excerpt, Professor Laura Little describes the Committee's history and role in the judicial selection process, including differences between lower court and Supreme Court nominations. Following this excerpt, we reprint the letter of March 22, 2001, by which the George W. Bush Administration announced its decision to abandon the ABA's special role in pre-screening candidates.

Laura E. Little,[16] *The ABA's Role in Prescreening Federal Judicial Candidates: Are We Ready to Give Up on the Lawyers?*, 10 Wm. & Mary Bill Rts. J. 37 (2002)

. . .

In 1952, the attorney general for President Eisenhower concluded that the administration needed an independent review body to examine the qualifications of potential judicial nominees so that the administration could more ably resist pressure to repay political debts by appointing individuals of questionable talents and abilities to the federal bench. The Eisenhower Administration thereafter sought the views of the American Bar Association on potential federal judicial nominees. The ABA's role quickly became institutionalized as an adjunct to the executive's constitutional role of nominating federal judges.

According to public accounts, United States presidents in the modern era have used a judicial selection committee staffed by senior White House and Department of Justice officials to develop a list of federal judicial nominees. As part of this committee, the Justice Department has confidentially provided the names of potential judicial nominees to the ABA Standing Committee on the Federal Judiciary to obtain that Committee's evaluation of judicial candidates.

The ABA Committee has fifteen members—two from the Ninth Circuit, one from the other twelve judicial circuits, and one member-at-large. The president of the ABA appoints the members for staggered three-year terms, and no member serves more than two terms. The ABA Committee's "sole function" is to evaluate prospective nominees to the Supreme Court of the United States, United States Circuit Courts of Appeals, United States District Courts, and the Court of International Trade. The Committee only evaluates candidates referred by the attorney general or the White House and formally omits from its evaluation "a prospective nominee's philosophy or ideology." Instead, the Committee seeks to confine its inquiry "to issues bearing on a prospective nominee's professional qualifications."

The procedures for ABA evaluation differed for prospective Supreme Court nominees and nominees to lower courts. Before the Bush Administration eliminated early ABA input [in 2001], potential lower court nominees commenced the evaluation process by completing an ABA-designed questionnaire and submitting it to White House officials and the ABA Committee. Using the questionnaire answers, an ABA Committee member examined the candidate's legal writings and interviewed a cross-section of lawyers, judges, and legal educators in the candidate's community, as well as members of professional organizations and other groups interested in the nomination process. The candidate also met with the ABA Committee. A committee member then prepared a written

16. Professor of Law and James E.   Beasley School of Law.
Beasley Chair in Law, Temple University

report that summarized the interviews, evaluated the candidate's qualifications, and tentatively rated the candidate using three categories: "well qualified," "qualified," and "not qualified." This informal evaluation served as a "prediction as [to] what the ABA's formal inquiry [would] find."

The ABA Committee then communicated this informal rating of lower court nominees to the Justice Department on a confidential basis. If the Justice Department so requested, the ABA Committee then prepared a formal report, which included a rating polled from the entire Committee. The chair of the ABA Committee thereafter communicated this rating to the Justice Department, occasionally sharing the reasons behind the rating. The ABA Committee generally did not, however, reveal committee sources or the internal, informal reports of individual Committee members. Finally, the attorney general evaluated the rating in light of other information and communicated the rating to the president along with a recommendation whether to nominate the candidate.

The presidents, of course, retained their discretion over whether to nominate, varying in their decisions whether or not to nominate persons rated "unqualified." When the president approved the candidate, the nomination and the complete dossier were sent to the Senate Judiciary Committee, which already should have received its own appraisal report from the ABA Committee directly. In the rare event that a president proceeded with the nomination of an individual rated "[n]ot [q]ualified," the ABA Committee opposed "the nomination in such ways as may be appropriate under the circumstances."

For prospective Supreme Court nominees, all Committee members participated in the investigation and teams of law school professors and practicing lawyers examined the legal writings of the nominee. While the same factors were considered for lower court nominations, "the Committee's investigation [was] based on the premise that the Supreme Court requires a person with exceptional professional qualifications." The Committee provided its ratings of prospective nominees confidentially to the attorney general "and, after nomination, reported [the ratings] to the Senate Judiciary Committee." A Committee representative may explain the reasons for the rating at the Senate's confirmation hearing, while seeking to preserve source confidentiality.

Although presidents have not consistently followed the same procedures for Supreme Court nominations, they roughly followed the procedures outlined above for lower court nominations from 1952 through the Clinton years. Nevertheless, presidents have varied in their esteem for the ABA and the weight they accorded to ABA ratings. A high water mark appeared in 1969 when Deputy Attorney General Richard Kleindienst told the ABA Convention that the Nixon Administration had accorded the ABA's Federal Judiciary Committee absolute veto power over all federal judicial candidates it considered unqualified. Nixon, however, later changed his mind, and a long period of reduced deference has followed.

Before George W. Bush's decision to oust the ABA from early participation, another particularly low point of ABA esteem occurred during the Reagan Administration. Reagan, like Carter, kept the ABA Standing Committee on the Federal Judiciary at arm's length. Yet unlike earlier administrations, the Reagan Administration did not always wait for the ABA's formal report before the attorney general sent over official nominating documents—and sometimes acted before receiving an informal report from the ABA. Although liberals apparently were unhappy with the ABA during this time, Republican displeasure was resounding and unanimous—particularly in reaction to the ABA Committee's failure to recommend unanimously Robert Bork as "well qualified" for the Supreme Court (four Committee members apparently found Bork unqualified for lack of a judicial temperament).

Retribution initially came in the form of scrutiny: first, the Senate convened a hearing devoted to the ABA Committee and its role in the confirmation process; next, suit was filed against the Justice Department and the ABA for violating the federal open meeting law by keeping judicial evaluation records confidential. The Supreme Court decided this suit in favor of the ABA.[17] The most recent retribution for the Bork nomination, some say, came to reduce the ABA vetting role. Whatever the precise causal relationship for the "bad blood," one cannot deny that the ABA's most aggressive enemies have, in recent years, been powerful Republicans.

Letter From the President's White House Counsel, Alberto Gonzales, to ABA President, Ms. Martha W. Barnett

March 22, 2001

Dear Ms. Barnett:

Thank you for taking the time to meet with Attorney General Ashcroft and me on March 19. We very much appreciated the opportunity to visit with you and benefited from your perspective on the judicial selection process. In addition to hearing from you, we have carefully studied and considered the history and practice of American Bar Association involvement in judicial selection. Although the President welcomes the ABA's suggestions concerning judicial nominees, the Administration will not notify the ABA of the identity of a nominee before the nomination is submitted to the Senate and announced to the public.

---

17. [Footnote 39 in original] See Pub. Citizen v. United States Dep't of Justice, 491 U.S. 440, 467 (1989) (holding that the Federal Advisory Committee Act does not apply to the Justice Department's solicitation of the ABA Committee views on prospective judicial nominees). For analysis of the legal issues in this suit, see, for example, R. Townsend Davis, Jr., *Note, The American Bar Association and Judicial Nominees: Advice Without Consent?*, 89 Colum. L. Rev. 550 (1989).

There is a long tradition by which Members of Congress, interest groups, and individual citizens provide suggestions to the President about potential judges. We will continue to welcome such suggestions from all sources, including the ABA. The issue at hand, however, is quite different: whether the ABA alone—out of the literally dozens of groups and many individuals who have a strong interest in the composition of the federal courts—should receive advance notice of the identities of potential nominees in order to render pre-nomination opinions on their fitness for judicial service. In our view, granting any single group such a preferential, quasi-official role in the nomination process would be unfair to the other groups that also have strong interests in judicial selection. As Senator Biden asked in 1994, "Why the ABA and not the National Bar Association?" The same question could be asked with respect to numerous other groups.

The question, in sum, is not whether the ABA's voice should be heard in the judicial selection process. Rather, the question is whether the ABA should play a unique, quasi-official role and thereby have its voice heard before and above all others. We do not think that kind of preferential arrangement is either appropriate or fair.

It would be particularly inappropriate, in our view, to grant a preferential, quasi-official role to a group, such as the ABA, that takes public positions on divisive political, legal, and social issues that come before the courts. This is not to suggest that the ABA should not adopt policy positions or express its views. But considerations of sound constitutional government suggest that the President not grant a preferential, quasi-official role in the judicial selection process to a politically active group.

Our decision to treat the ABA in the same manner as all other interested parties mirrors the approach taken in recent decades by Presidents of both parties with respect to Supreme Court nominees, as well as the approach taken by the Senate Judiciary Committee in 1997 when it ended the ABA's quasi-official role in the Senate confirmation process. As Chairman Hatch explained at that time, "[p]ermitting a political interest group to be elevated to an officially sanctioned role in the confirmation process not only debases that process, but, in my view, ultimately detracts from the moral authority of the courts themselves."

Finally, let me reiterate that the Administration fully welcomes the ABA, like other interested parties, to provide suggestions regarding potential judges. Similarly, once the President submits a nomination to the Senate, the ABA like every other interested party is free to evaluate and express its views concerning the President's nominee.

Thank you again for your time and your views, as well as for your service to the ABA and the profession. The Administration looks forward to working with you in the months ahead on issues of concern to the legal profession.

Sincerely yours,

Alberto R. Gonzales
Counsel to the President

For further discussion of the role of the ABA in Supreme Court nominations, see Section C, below.

4. Special Considerations in the Appointment of the Chief Justice

The Constitution contemplates that there will be a Chief Justice but does not provide any special way he or she is to be chosen. From the beginning, the Chief has been chosen in the same manner as any other Justice—nomination by the President and confirmation by the Senate. When the President decides whom to nominate, he or she may choose someone already on the Court or someone from outside. Either way, that nominee will have to be confirmed by the Senate, even if the person has already been confirmed as an Associate Justice. Of the seventeen Chief Justices we have had in this country (see Appendix A), only five had previously served as Associate Justices on the Court, namely: John Rutledge, Edward D. White, Charles E. Hughes, Harlan F. Stone, and William H. Rehnquist. Of these, only three (White, Stone, and Rehnquist) were sitting as Associate Justices at the time they were nominated and confirmed to be Chief Justice. Note that when a President nominates someone already on the Court to be the Chief, he will then also have to nominate someone to replace him or her. Thus, there will have to be two confirmation hearings instead of just one for a Chief coming from outside the Court. For a discussion of factors to be considered in appointing a Chief Justice, see the Case Study of the appointment of John Roberts in Section B of this chapter and the discussion of the role of the Chief Justice in Chapter Five, Section A, below.

Questions and Comments

1. Consider again the question asked previously, whether Senators should accord a presumption in favor of confirmation to a President's Supreme Court nominee? Why or why not?

2. Based on your readings thus far, what do you think is the most important change in the procedures used to select and confirm nominees to the Court? Some possible candidates:

> (1) increased information about candidates available through better technology;

> (2) more focus on courts of appeals judges as the pool from which to draw nominees;

> (3) an increase in what Professor Yalof calls "criteria driven" presidential searches;

(4) perhaps relatedly, an increase in what Professor Sheldon Goldman has referred to as "policy agenda" nominations, that is, those driven by the President's substantive goals for the Court as a decisionmaker;

(5) a change in how the President's search for candidates is conducted;

(6) the shift from closed to open Senate hearings and the expectation, developed in the 1950s, that nominees would themselves testify at their hearings;

(7) the presence of cameras at these open hearings and enhanced media reporting on confirmation and nomination processes;

(8) an increase in the role of interest groups.

3.   Mark Silverstein is a political scientist who, along with David Yalof, has argued that the confirmation process significantly changed in the late 1960s, in response to changing perceptions of the Court's role in substantive policy issues. See Mark Silverstein, *Judicious Choices: The New Politics of Supreme Court Confirmations* 6 (1994) (arguing that the confirmation process is now a more "thoroughly democratic process," as a "consequence of profound changes in American politics and institutions," the most important of which is "the heightened activism of the modern federal judiciary"). Silverstein says that "the current process is disorderly, contentious, and unpredictable," precisely because it is a democratic one. Writing in 1994, he predicted that when the two political parties are closely balanced in Congress, more moderate, technically competent nominees will be selected. "That a politicized system of selecting and confirming our judges may mean that people of stature, a Brandeis and a Holmes, a Marshall and a Warren, do not find their way to the Court is a consequence that must be measured against a paramount commitment to self-rule." *Id.*, at 165. More generally, because the political dynamics of confirmations will reflect those of other issues, he argues, when interest group politics dominate in the policy sphere they will dominate in the confirmation process as well. Do events since the publication of his book confirm or disprove his claims?

B. THE NOMINATION AND CONFIRMATION OF SUPREME COURT JUSTICES—CASE STUDIES

This section presents several case studies of the Senate Committee process on specific nominations, successful and unsuccessful. Although readers may gain a good understanding of the confirmation process from the secondary materials presented and some professors may want to skip assigning any of the materials in this section, we include these case studies because of the value to students of being exposed to the original records and materials, hearing transcripts and committee reports. Reading one or more of these case studies offers a more contextualized understanding of what goes on and also provides a basis for a more critical perspective on others' evaluations of the confirmation hearing process. Readers will, of course, remember, that the nomination process begins in the Executive Branch—but the more visible and public aspects of the process are those that occur in the Senate, as illustrated below.

We start with brief excerpts from two confirmation hearings—Thurgood Marshall's and Antonin Scalia's—involving persistent questioning designed to reveal their opinions of specific cases. A longer excerpt from the Senate Judiciary Committee Report on the unsuccessful nomination of Judge Robert Bork follows. His nomination is regarded by many as a turning point in the nature of the confirmation process; reading the Senate Judiciary Committee Report is one of the best ways to get a sense of the tenor and tone of the debate at that time.

After the Bork nomination failed, there was much speculation over the effects: would Presidents nominate "stealth" candidates, without written records? Would they avoid controversial candidates, or those clearly identified with particular ideological approaches? We thus include excerpts of the confirmation process for several, though, for reasons of length, not all, successful nominations that illustrate the process as it developed after the defeat of Bork's nomination in 1987. Specifically, we have included excerpts from the Senate processes for David Souter, Clarence Thomas, Ruth Ginsburg, John Roberts and Samuel Alito. We include the Senate Committee Report on the nomination of Souter, both because his views on many constitutional topics were largely unknown to the public at the time of the nomination, generating much speculation and talk of a "stealth" candidacy, and because his discussion of *stare decisis* in the confirmation hearing raises interesting resonances with the Joint Opinion in *Casey* (discussed in Chapter One above). The Thomas nomination involved a high level of controversy even before contested allegations of personal misconduct arose, which led to additional hearings and, in turn, to changes in later confirmation procedures in the Senate. Ginsburg's appointment, involving as it did a successful nomination of a well-known women's rights advocate, challenges the idea that Presidents would nominate only those candidates whose views on important matters were largely unknown. Finally, we include materials on the two most recent nominations at the time of this edition, made after an eleven year period without change on the Court—those of Chief Justice Roberts and Justice Alito. Although no Committee Report exists with respect to these last two nominations, portions of their confirmation hearings are excerpted below.

In reading these materials, ask whether the Senators applied the proper standards of evaluation, whether the level of questioning by the Senators was appropriate, whether the answers given were adequate, and whether you would have voted to confirm each of these nominees.

1. Before Bork: Thurgood Marshall and Antonin Scalia

In 1986, Judge Antonin Scalia of the U.S. Court of Appeals for the D.C. Circuit, a former law professor, was nominated and confirmed to the Supreme Court. You may find it interesting to compare the responses of later nominees to questions about specific cases with those of Judge Scalia in 1986. Strom Thurmond, then-Chair of the Senate Judiciary Committee, asked Judge Scalia the following question:

> The Supreme Court's decision in *Marbury v. Madison* is viewed as the basis of the Supreme Court's authority to interpret the Constitution and issue decisions which are binding on both the executive and legislative branches. Do you agree that *Marbury* requires the President and the Congress to always adhere to the Court's interpretation of the Constitution?

Judge Scalia responded:

> *Marbury v. Madison* is one of the pillars of the Constitution. To the extent that you think a nominee would be so foolish, or so extreme as to kick over one of the pillars of the Constitution, I suppose you should not confirm him. But I do not think I should answer questions regarding any specific Supreme Court opinion, even one as fundamental as *Marbury v. Madison*.

> If you could conclude from anything I have written, or anything I have said, that I would ignore *Marbury v. Madison*, I would too be in trouble, without your asking me specifically my views on *Marbury*.[18]

Judge Scalia was confirmed 98–0 on September 17, 1986. 132 Cong. Rec. 23, 813 (1986).

Compare also the questioning of Judge Thurgood Marshall of the U.S. Court of Appeals for the Second Circuit in his 1967 confirmation hearing. Senator John L. McClellan from Arkansas was one of several senators who hoped to obtain Marshall's commitment to overturn *Miranda v. Arizona*, 384 U.S. 436 (1966), the decision requiring police officers to inform suspects of their rights before beginning any custodial interrogation. Marshall, as Solicitor General, had argued for its overturning, but at his confirmation hearings he refused to say whether he would, if the case arose again and he were on the Court, vote in accordance with the position he had espoused as Solicitor General. The following colloquy ensued.[19]

> SENATOR McCLENNAN: . . . Do you subscribe to the philosophy expressed in the majority of the *Miranda* opinion . . . ?

> JUDGE MARSHALL: I would say again, I respectfully state to you, Senator, that this is certainly a case that is on its way to the Supreme Court right now.

> SENATOR McCLELLAN: But it is already ruled on. This is the ruling of the Court.

18. Nomination of Judge Antonin Scalia: Hearings before the Committee on the Judiciary, United States Senate, 99th Cong. 2nd Sess. 33 (1986).

19. Nomination of Thurgood Marshall to be an Associate Justice of the Supreme Court of the United States: Hearings Before the Committee on the Judiciary, United States Senate, 90th Cong. 1st Sess. 10 (1967).

JUDGE MARSHALL: But there are other cases. The *Miranda* case is not the end. The case itself says in three or four places in the opinion that they do not know what Congress intends to do, they do not know—

SENATOR McCLELLAN: I am not talking about legislation. I am asking you now about the Constitution. Do you think that the Constitution requires that that evidence be excluded?

JUDGE MARSHALL: I cannot comment on what is coming up to the Court.

SENATOR McCLELLAN: But this has already been there.

JUDGE MARSHALL: But there are hundreds of other ones on the way that are variations on this.

SENATOR McCLELLAN: Of course there are, but this is specific and has been done.

JUDGE MARSHALL: Well, Senator, I respectfully say that it would be improper for me to tell you and the committee or anybody else how I intend to vote.

SENATOR McCLELLAN: It is not improper, may I say, for me to weigh your reluctance to answer.

JUDGE MARSHALL: It certainly is not. . . .

Senator McClellan pursued the colloquy for several more exchanges, with no more success. Senator McClellan was a member of the Senate Judiciary Committee and voted against the confirmation of Thurgood Marshall. (McClellan did not vote on the Senate floor). Marshall was ultimately confirmed by a vote of 62 to 11, with 20 Senators not voting. 113 Cong. Rec. 24, 656 (1967).

2. The Nomination of Robert Bork

As the following report indicates, Judge Bork was not at all reticent; he willingly answered virtually all the Senators' questions. Despite (or perhaps because of) this, he was rejected. The Senate Judiciary Committee voted 9–5 to recommend that his nomination be rejected.[20] Judge Bork refused to withdraw his name and President Reagan, sympathetic to Judge Bork's desire to obtain a vote of the full Senate, did not retract the nomination. On October 23, 1987, the Senate voted 58–42 not to confirm Robert Bork, the largest margin of defeat ever for a Supreme Court nominee.[21]

Why was Judge Scalia confirmed unanimously in 1986, while a year later Judge Bork endured this defeat, even though many believe that

20. Voting to report the nomination with a negative recommendation were Senators Biden, Kennedy, Byrd, Metzenbaum, DeConcini, Leahy, Heflin, Simon, and Spector. Voting against the negative recommen-dation were Senators Thurmond, Hatch, Simpson, Grassley, and Humphrey.

21. David Savage, *Turning Right: The Making of the Rehnquist Supreme Court* 146 (1992).

Judge Scalia was as conservative as Judge Bork? Some possibilities: First, the President's party (the Republicans) had control over the Senate in 1986, when Justice Scalia was confirmed, but not in 1987, when Judge Bork's nomination came up. Perhaps relatedly, President Reagan's standing in 1987 had suffered considerably due to the unfolding Iran–Contra scandal. Third, Scalia was replacing a conservative (Warren Burger), while Bork was nominated to replace Justice Powell, at the time viewed as being at the center of the Court. While all of these factors may have played a role, readers should also note that on the same day that Justice Scalia was confirmed, William H. Rehnquist was confirmed as Chief Justice by a vote of 65–33, so a quiescent Senate in 1986 cannot fully account for Scalia's unanimous vote. Thus, some conjecture that the Senate was more focused on the controversies surrounding the elevation of Rehnquist to be Chief. A fourth possibility that must be considered is the nature of the responses given by the nominee.

As you read through the following materials, consider whether a new model of nominee responses—somewhere between Justice Scalia's hesitation to say much about *Marbury* and Judge Bork's eagerness to detail his views on a range of subjects—has now emerged.

Nomination of Robert H. Bork To Be an Associate Justice of the United States Supreme Court, S. Exec. Rep. No. 100–7, 100th Cong., 1st Sess. (1987)

Mr. Biden, from the Committee on the Judiciary, submitted the following REPORT together with ADDITIONAL, MINORITY, AND SUPPLEMENTAL VIEWS

The Committee on the Judiciary, to which was referred the nomination of Judge Robert H. Bork to be an Associate Justice of the United States Supreme Court, having considered the same reports unfavorably thereon, a quorum being present, by a vote of nine yeas and five nays, with the recommendation that the nomination be rejected.

CONTENTS[22]

22. [Editors' Note: Although we produce only brief excerpts, we include the table of contents of the report so the reader can see its full breadth.]

23. [Editors' Note: The ABA rating was "well qualified," with the following vote:
ten "well qualified," one "not opposed," four "not qualified." Lee Epstein, et al., *The Supreme Court Compendium: Data, Decisions & Developments,* p. 390 (Table 4–16: American Bar Association Rating of Supreme Court Nominees, 1956–2006) (2007)(hereinafter Epstein, *Compendium,*

ABA Ratings). See discussion in Little excerpt in Section A, *supra.*]

II. THE NOMINEE

Judge Bork was born on March 1, 1927, in Pittsburgh. He attended the University of Pittsburgh for a short time and then enlisted in the United States Marine Corps in 1945. He served until 1946, when he was honorably discharged. . . . He received his law degree from the University of Chicago Law School in 1953. From 1953–1954, he was a research associate with the University of Chicago Law School's Law and Economics Project. From 1954–1962, the nominee engaged in the private practice of law. . . . From 1962–1973, the nominee was a member of the faculty of the Yale Law School. . . . From 1973–1977, Judge Bork served as Solicitor General of the United States. In this capacity, he argued a number of cases before the Supreme Court. Judge Bork briefly served as Acting Attorney General from 1973–1974. In 1977, Judge Bork returned to the faculty of the Yale Law School. . . . In 1981, Judge Bork returned to private practice as a partner in Kirkland & Ellis, working out of the Washington office. From 1982 to the present, Judge Bork has served as a judge on the U.S. Court of Appeals for the District of Columbia Circuit.

. . .

PART TWO: THE CONSTITUTION'S UNENUMERATED RIGHTS

I. JUDGE BORK'S VIEW OF THE CONSTITUTION DISREGARDS THIS COUNTRY'S TRADITION OF HUMAN DIGNITY, LIBERTY AND UNENUMERATED RIGHTS

. . .

The hearings reaffirmed what many understand to be a core principle upon which this nation was founded: Our Constitution recognizes inalienable rights and is not simply a grant of rights by the majority. Chairman Biden's opening statement identified these fundamental principles:

> I believe all Americans are born with certain inalienable rights. As a child of God, I believe my rights are not derived from the Constitution. My rights are not derived from any government. My rights are not derived from any majority. My rights are because I exist. They were given to me and each of my fellow citizens by our Creator, and they represent the essence of human dignity. (Comm. Print Draft, Vol. 1, at 68.)

This image of human dignity has been associated throughout our history with the idea that the Constitution recognizes "unenumerated rights." These are rights beyond those specifically mentioned in the Constitution itself, rights that are affirmed by the grand open-ended phrases of the document: "liberty," "due process," "equal protection of the laws" and others. The sober responsibility of preserving the meaning and content of these rights has fallen to the judiciary, and especially to the Supreme Court.

Against this understanding of the Constitution, and of human dignity, Judge Bork offers an alternative vision—that Americans have no rights against government, except those specifically enumerated in the Constitution. The contrast was stated cogently by Professor Philip Kurland:

> I think it makes all the difference in the world whether you start with the notion that the people have all the liberties except those that are specifically taken away from them, or you start with the notion, as I think Judge Bork now has, that they have no liberties except those which are granted to them. (Comm. Print Draft, Vol. 3, at 1391.)

. . .

A.   *Judge Bork's Judicial Philosophy Does Not Recognize the Concept of Unenumerated Rights and Liberties*

1.   Judge Bork's Core Theory

Judge Bork has consistently described his constitutional theory as "intentionalist," meaning that he considers it the function of a judge to determine the intentions of the body that wrote the laws and to apply those intentions to the case brought before the court. Interpreting law is thus a matter of discerning the original intent of those responsible for making it. . . . [Judge Bork] reaffirmed this view in his opening statement . . . :

> The judge's authority derives entirely from the fact that he is applying the law and not his own personal values. . . . How should a judge go about finding the law? The only legitimate way is by attempting to discern what those who made the law intended. . . . [(Comm. Print Draft, Vol. 1, at 78–79.)]

. . .

2.   Judge Bork's Judicial Philosophy Leads Him to Conclude that the Constitution "Specified Certain Liberties and Allocates All Else to Democratic Processes"

The implications of Judge Bork's theory of original intent are quite clear from his writings, speeches and testimony. The most dramatic consequence of his theory is the rejection of the concept of unenumerated rights and liberties. He has consistently held to the view . . . that the Constitution should not be read as recognizing an individual right unless that right can be specifically found in a particular provision of the document.

In particular, Judge Bork has repeatedly rejected the well-established line of Supreme Court decisions holding that the liberty clauses of the Fifth and Fourteenth Amendments protect against governmental invasion of a person's substantive personal liberty and privacy. He has said, for example, that:

> [T]he choice of "fundamental values" by the Court cannot be justified. Where constitutional materials do not clearly specify the value to be preferred, there is no principled way to prefer any claimed human value to any other. The judge must stick close to the text and the history, and their fair implications, and not construct new rights. ("Neutral Principles and Some First Amendment Problems," 47 *Indiana Law Journal* 1, 8 (1971).)

Judge Bork has also disregarded the text of the Ninth Amendment, which provides that "[t]he enumeration in the Constitution of certain rights, shall not be construed to deny or disparage other retained by the people." . . .

. . . [His] suggested disregard for the Amendment is consistent with Judge Bork's general recommendation about a judge's role "when his studies leave him unpersuaded that he understands the core of what the Framers intended" with respect to a particular constitutional provision:

> [The judge] must treat [the provision] as nonexistent, since, in terms of expression of the framers' will, it is nonexistent. . . . When the meaning of a provision . . . is unknown, the judge has in effect nothing more than a water blot on the document before him. . . .

According to Judge Bork, "[t]he Constitution specified certain liberties and allocates all else to democratic processes." ("Judicial Review and Democracy," *Society,* Nov./Dec. 1986 at 7; emphasis added.) Thus, under Judge Bork's view, the court interferes with the "democratic process" whenever it recognizes a right that is not specified in the Constitution. As he said in a 1985 speech and reaffirmed at the hearings, the Constitution is essentially a zero-sum system, in which rights for some necessarily come only at the expense of others:

> SENATOR SIMON. One point, at a speech at Berkeley in 1985, you say . . . "[When] a court adds to one person's constitutional rights it subtracts from the rights of others." Do you believe that is always true?
>
> JUDGE BORK. Yes, Senator. I think it's a matter of plain arithmetic. . . .
>
> SENATOR SIMON. I have long thought it is kind of fundamental in our society, that when you expand the liberty of any of us, you expand the liberty of all of us.
>
> JUDGE BORK. I think, Senator, that is not correct. (Comm. Print Draft, Vol. 1, at 289, 421; emphasis added.)

B. This Nation Was Conceived with the Recognition of Pre-existing Inalienable Rights that the Constitution Does Not Specifically Enumerate But Nonetheless Acknowledges and Protects

The founding documents of American constitutionalism—the Declaration of Independence, the Constitution and the Bill of Rights—were accepted not because they exhausted the protection of basic rights but because they expressly protected unenumerated rights as well. . . .

. . .

[T]he history surrounding the drafting and ratification of the Bill of Rights indicates that there had to be an express guarantee that unenumerated rights would be fully protected. The Ninth Amendment is at the core of both the Constitution and the ratification debates. The concept of unenumerated rights illustrates the depth of the tradition that the Founders meant to protect by the Ninth Amendment.

C. Judge Bork's Approach to Liberty and Unenumerated Rights Is Outside the Tradition of Supreme Court Jurisprudence

Judge Bork's approach to liberty and unenumerated rights sets him apart from every other Supreme Court Justice. Indeed, not one of the 105 past and present Justices of the Supreme Court has ever taken a view of liberty as narrow as that of Judge Bork. As Professor Tribe testified:

> If [Judge Bork] is confirmed as the 106th Justice, [he] would be the first to read liberty as though it were exhausted by the rights . . . the majority expressly conceded individuals in the Bill of Rights. . . . (Tribe statement, Comm. Print Draft, Vol. 2, at 7.)

In particular, Judge Bork's philosophy is outside the mainstream of such great judicial conservatives as Justices Harlan, Frankfurter and Black, as well as such recent conservatives as Justices Stewart, Powell, O'Connor and Chief Justice Burger. Each of these members of the Court accepted and applied some concept of liberty, substantive due process and unenumerated rights.

. . .

II. The Theory of Precedent or "Settled Law" Held by Judge Bork Cannot Transform His Judicial Philosophy Into an Acceptable One for the Supreme Court

A. While Judge Bork's Theory of Precedent Appears to Lessen the Friction Between His Philosophy of Original Intent and Accepted Supreme Court Decisions, It Leaves Many Uncertainties and Concerns

Judge Bork has applied his theory of the Constitution to attack a large number of Supreme Court decisions, including many landmark cases. Reconsidering these cases would reopen debate on many significant issues. Perhaps this is why Judge Bork said in response to a question by Senator Thurmond, "anybody with a philosophy of original intent requires a theory of precedent." (Comm. Print Draft, Vol. 1, at 101.) While a theory of precedent appears to lessen the friction between Judge Bork's philosophy and accepted Supreme Court decisions, it creates in the end many uncertainties and concerns of its own.

Under questioning by Senator Thurmond, . . . Judge Bork said:

What would I look at [before overruling a prior decision]? Well, I think I would look and be absolutely sure that the prior decision was incorrectly decided. That is necessary. And if it is wrongly decided— and you have to give respect to your predecessors' judgment on these matters—the presumption against overruling remains, because it may be that there are private expectations built up on the basis of the prior decision. It may be that governmental and private institutions have grown up around that prior decision. There is a need for stability and continuity in the law. There is a need for predictability in legal doctrine. (Comm. Print Draft, Vol. 1, at 101.)

Later, in response to a question from Senator Heflin, Judge Bork added countervailing considerations—considerations that argued in favor of overruling a precedent:

Now, of course, against [upholding a precedent] is—if it is wrong, and secondly, whether it is a dynamic force so that it continues to produce wrong and unfortunate decisions. I think that was one of the reasons the court in Erie Railroad against Tompkins overruled Swift against Tyson, a degenerative force, but I think what Brandeis or somebody can maybe call dynamic potential. (Comm. Print Draft, Vol. 1, at 268.)

. . .

Finally, Judge Bork concluded his testimony by emphasizing his respect for precedent:

... [W]hen I say [the result in a case is required by] "the law," I regard precedent as an important component of the law. As I have described many times here, there are a number of important precedents that are today so woven into the fabric of our system that to change or alter them would be, in my view, unthinkable. (Comm. Print Draft, Vol. 1, at 721–22.)

B. Judge Bork's Combination of Original Intent and Settled Law Creates an Irresolvable Tension Between His Oft–Repeated Desire to Reformulate Constitutional Law and His Willingness to Follow a Decision He Believes To Be Profoundly Wrong

1. Judge Bork Has Often Announced His Firm Conviction that Many Supreme Court Decisions Are Flatly Wrong and Ought To Be Overruled

. . .

During the hearings, Senator Kennedy played an audio tape of the question and answer period following a 1985 speech in which Judge Bork made perhaps his clearest declaration to that effect:

I don't think that in the field of constitutional law precedent is all that important. I say that for two reasons. One is historical and traditional. The court has never thought constitutional precedent was all that important. The reason being that if you construe a statute incorrectly, the Congress can pass a law and correct it. If you construe the Constitution incorrectly Congress is helpless. Everybody is helpless. If you become convinced that a prior court has misread the Constitution I think it's your duty to go back and correct it. Moreover, you will from time to time get willful courts who take an area of law and create precedents that have nothing to do with the name of the Constitution. And if a new court comes in and says, "Well, I respect precedent," what you have is a ratchet effect, with the Constitution getting further and further away from its original meaning, because some judges feel free to make up new constitutional law and other judges in the name of judicial restraint follow precedent. I don't think precedent is all that important. I think the importance is what the Framers were driving at, and to go back to that. (*Canisius College Speech,* October 8, 1985, *quoted in* Comm. Print Draft, Vol. 1, at 523–24, emphasis added.)

Following the playing of this tape, the following exchange took place:

> SENATOR KENNEDY. Those statements speak for themselves. Your own words cast strong doubt upon your adherence to precedent that you think is wrong.

> JUDGE BORK. Senator, you and I both know that it is possible, in a give and take question and answer period, not to give a full and measured response. You and I both know that when I have given a full and measured response, I have repeatedly said there are some things that are too settled to be overturned.

> *C.* . . .

Judge Bork has said that "the Court's treatment of the Bill of Rights is theoretically the easiest to reform." (*Attorney General's Conference Speech,* Jan. 24–26, 1986, at 9.) Decisions involving the Bill of Rights largely involve the expansion of individual rights. As such, complex social institutions and economic structures do not usually build up around them. They are thus typically different from cases like those expanding the power of Congress to regulate commerce or the power of the U.S. government to issue paper money as legal tender. These latter cases have become, in Judge Bork's words, "the basis for a large array of social and economic institutions, [therefore] overruling them would be disastrous." (Comm. Print Draft, Vol. 1, at 102.) . . .

During the committee hearings, Judge Bork for the first time made some specific references to individual rights decisions that were, in his view, "settled." They were *Brandenburg, Shelley v. Kraemer* and *Bolling v. Sharpe,* and some of the freedom of the press cases. Each is, to varying degrees, difficult to square with Judge Bork's announced criteria for refusing to overrule a decision. Even putting that aside, however, there still is a tremendous area—in which the Court has given content to unenumerated rights and liberties—where his prior stated positions are not in the least constrained by his statements before the committee concerning settled law.

D. . . .

The Supreme Court's prior decisions, whether settled or not, cannot cover all new situations, under even the broadest reading of those cases. It is in the context of these new cases that Judge Bork's theory of original intent would stand without any of the constraining influence of precedent. . . .

. . .

III. THE EQUAL PROTECTION CLAUSE AND GENDER DISCRIMINATION

. . . One of the more troubling aspects of Judge Bork's philosophy of equality under the Constitution is his application of the general language of the [Equal Protection] Clause to discrimination on the basis of gender.

. . .

Prior to the hearings, Judge Bork engaged in a sustained critique of applying the Equal Protection Clause to women. He argued that to extend the Clause to women departs from the original intent of the Fourteenth Amendment, produces unprincipled and subjective decision-making and involves the courts in "enormously sensitive" and "highly political" matters.

In 1971, for example, then-Professor Bork said that "cases of race discrimination aside, it is always a mistake for the court to try to construct substantive individual rights under the . . . equal protection clause . . ." ("Neutral Principles" at 17, 11.)

Judge Bork reiterated that position more than 10 years later, after ascending to the bench . . .

. . .

As recently as June 10, 1987, less than a month before his nomination, Judge Bork reiterated his view:

> I do think the Equal Protection Clause probably should have been kept to things like race and ethnicity. . . . (*Worldnet Interview,* June 10, 1987, at 12; emphasis added.)

B. Judge Bork's Testimony at the Hearings Was His First Publicly Expressed Approval of Including Women Within the Scope of the Equal Protection Clause

During his testimony, Judge Bork publicly stated for the first time that he now believes that the Equal Protection Clause should be extended beyond race and ethnicity, and should apply to classifications based on gender. According to Judge Bork, "[e]verybody is covered—men, women, everybody." (Comm. Print Draft, Vol. 1, at 230.) Judge Bork explained that all forms of governmental classifications were unconstitutional unless they had a "reasonable basis." (*See, e.g.,* Comm. Print Draft, Vol. 1, at 135, 230, 231, 306, 309.) He also said that he would reach the same results that the Supreme Court had reached in virtually all of its recent sex discrimination cases. (*See e.g.*, Comm. Print Draft, Vol. 1, at 306; 309.) . . .

Judge Bork's rationale for his change in position was that the Equal Protection Clause should be interpreted according to evolving standards and social mores about the role of women:

> As the culture changes and as the position of women in society changes, those distinctions which seemed reasonable now seem outmoded stereotypes and they seem unreasonable and they get struck down. That is the way a reasonable basis test should be applied. (Comm. Print Draft, Vol. 1, at 135.)

C. . . .

. . . Judge Bork's . . . position that the Equal Protection Clause covers women does not go to the heart of the debate over the Court's role in reducing gender discrimination. The central debate concerns the standard of equal protection that should apply in such cases. . . . The pertinent question is thus whether Judge Bork's currently expressed position would adequately protect women from [gender-based] discrimination. For several reasons, the committee believes that it would not.

1. The "Reasonable Basis" Test Has Previously Been Used to Uphold Discriminatory Legislative Classifications

Prior to the 1970s, the Supreme Court used a "reasonableness" concept to uphold a variety of legislative classifications based on gender. . . .

. . .

4. Judge Bork's "Reasonable Basis" Test Cannot Be Explained in Terms That Are Consistent With His Original Intent Framework and Is Contrary to His Own Guidelines for Judicial Decision–Making

The standard articulated by Judge Bork during his testimony seems unmoored from his basic methodology. . . . [A]s Professor Gewirtz asks rhetorically: "How can an 'originalist' who believes that the 14th Amendment was not intended to embody a principle concerning sex equality find a warrant to displace a legislature's use of sex classifications?" (Gewirtz statement, Comm. Print Draft, Vol. 2, at 1195.)

Furthermore, Judge Bork's "reasonable basis" test seems to be at odds with his own decision-making framework, which seeks to minimize a judge's subjective preferences and values. "It is hard to imagine a more vague and unpredictable standard than asking whether there is a 'reasonable basis' for a law." (Gewirtz statement, Comm. Print Draft, Vol. 2. at 1195.) . . .

. . .

[A]s Professor Williams, focusing on Judge Bork's standard of review, concluded:

> Judge Bork's view on women's equality under the Constitution makes his nomination for a position on the highest court in the

land a matter of deep uneasiness for persons concerned with the equality of the sexes. (Williams testimony, Comm. Print Draft, Vol. 2, at 956.)

. . .

X. JUDGE BORK'S SO-CALLED "CONFIRMATION CONVERSION:" THE WEIGHT THE SENATE MUST GIVE TO NEWLY ANNOUNCED POSITIONS

. . .

In the committee's view, the issue is not whether Judge Bork was candid in those aspects of his sworn testimony that seem to contradict many of his previously announced positions.... Rather, "the real issue is what weight the Senate should give to these newly expressed views," (Leahy Statement at 6), in light of Judge Bork's "judicial disposition in applying principles of law which he has so long decried." (Specter statement, Cong. Rec., S 13319.)

The Committee has concluded that Judge Bork's newly announced positions are not likely fully to outweigh his deeply considered and longheld views. The novelist William Styron cut to the heart of this matter when he said that the Senate must decide whether Judge Bork's new positions reflect "a matter not of passing opinion but of conviction and faith." (Comm. Print Draft, Vol. 2, at 585.) "Measured against this standard, Judge Bork's testimony ... mitigates some of his previous statements, but does not erase them from the record which the Senate must consider." (Leahy statement, Cong. Rec. at S 13129.) Underscoring this conclusion is, in Senator Heflin's words, "the absence of writings or prepared speeches which recite a change in his earlier views and the reasons for such change." (Heflin Closing Statement at 4.) In the end, the Committee is concerned that Judge Bork will bring to the "constitutional controversies of the 21st century" the conviction and faith of his long-held judicial philosophy and not that of his newly announced positions.

There were three principal changes in positions that Judge Bork announced for the first time, at least publicly, at the hearings. These related to: (1) the Equal Protection Clause of the Fourteenth Amendment and gender discrimination, (2) dissident political speech under the First Amendment, and (3) First Amendment protection for artistic expression.

. . .

... On the related questions of liberty, unenumerated rights and the right to privacy, Judge Bork's views have not changed in any substantial degree. He still challenges the role of the Supreme Court in defining liberty; he still challenges the legitimacy of *Griswold* and its progeny; and he still maintains that the people of the nation have only those rights that are specified in the text of the Constitution.

The hearing record is ... quite clear. In some areas, Judge Bork has come to rest at a point near the consensus that was reached by the Supreme Court and by most legal scholars almost a quarter-century ago. In other areas, Judge Bork's views have not changed at all, and place him at odds with every Supreme Court Justice, past or present. Once again, Senator Leahy's words reflect the conclusion of the Committee:

> This ... shows that Judge Bork's views are now different from some of the more isolated positions he previously sought to defend. But it also shows that, at this point in his long career, he still does not demonstrate a passion for vindicating the individual rights of Americans that matches his passion for a rigorous and coherent legal theory of the Constitution. (Leahy statement, Cong. Rec. at S 13129.)

And in the words of Senator Heflin:

> A life-time position on the Supreme Court is too important a risk to a person who has continued to exhibit—and may still possess—a proclivity for extremism in spite of confirmation protestations. (Heflin closing statement at 6.)

. . .

MINORITY VIEWS

Introduction

The hearings on Judge Bork were some of the most far-ranging, probing, and exhaustive ever undertaken by the Committee. The nominee was the most open and forthright to appear before the Committee. The hearings focused on several basic areas: the qualifications of the nominee; the nominee's view of the Constitution; the nominee's view of the role of the judiciary; the nominee's views on specific issues such as civil rights, the right of privacy; First Amendment rights, antitrust issues, and criminal law issues; his view of precedents; and his role in dismissing Watergate special prosecutor Archibald Cox. In each instance, Judge Bork's record and thoughtful responses place him well within the conservative mainstream of American jurisprudence.

As for qualifications, no one seriously questions that Judge Bork is eminently qualified by virtue of his ability, integrity and experience. Therefore, opponents attacked Judge Bork in other areas, such as his view of the judiciary's role in our democracy. However, Judge Bork's belief that judges should merely interpret, and not make, law is clearly the accepted view of most Americans. Additionally, Judge Bork's understanding of Constitutional principles of limited federal power is both intellectually honest and comports with historical and contemporary analysis of this great document.

The major criticisms leveled at Judge Bork are the result of misunderstandings by his critics: First, a misunderstanding of the difference between the role of a professor and that of a judge, and second, a misunderstanding of Judge Bork's position on substantive issues. Despite sloganeering and misrepresentations to the contrary, Judge Bork is well within the judicial mainstream on such issues as individual liberties, civil rights, the First Amendment, criminal law issues, antitrust matters, and the value of precedent.

Along with a vast number of judges and legal scholars, Judge Bork disapproves of a Court-created generalized "right of privacy." What this means is that Judge Bork does not believe that judges are free, at their whims, to create new "rights." His view that Constitutional rights must have a basis in the Constitution is being portrayed by some as extremism, as an unpredictable philosophy. In reality, Judge Bork's comprehensive theory of jurisprudence is firmly based in our judicial history, and is at least as predictable as any other judicial philosophy, and certainly more so than one which strains to "create" new rights.

· · ·

A. QUALIFICATIONS

Judge Robert Heron Bork is among the most qualified nominees to the Supreme Court in recent history. Former Chief Justice Warren Burger said Judge Bork is one of the best qualified candidates for the Supreme Court in 50 years. . . .

Even members of the Committee who are opposed to Judge Bork's confirmation acknowledged Judge Bork's fitness for the Supreme Court. . . .

· · ·

Those who support this nomination are even stronger in their praise for Judge Bork. Those who testified on his behalf include former President Ford and former Chief Justice Burger. Seven former Attorneys General supported his nomination. . . . In addition, Justice John Paul Stevens took this unusual step of publicly endorsing Judge Bork's elevation to the Supreme Court. . . .

· · ·

Judge Griffin Bell, former Attorney General during the Carter administration was among a number of prominent Democrats voicing support for Judge Bork, declaring that "if [he] were in the Senate [he] would vote for" Judge Bork. He said, "I like to see a man go to the Court who is going to be his own judge, be his own man, and I think that is the way it is going to turn out." Former White House Counsel Lloyd Cutler testified on behalf of Judge Bork's nomination and gave his view that:

> On the whole, I think he would come much closer as a sitting Justice if he is confirmed to a Justice like Justice Powell and Justice Stevens—and I remind you that that is precisely what Justice Stevens himself said, that "you will find in Judge Bork's opinions a philosophy similar to that you will see in the opinions of Justice

Stewart, Justice Powell, and some of the things that I ... have written."

. . .

Judge Bork, continuing in the long tradition of eminent jurists from John Marshall to Hugo Black to the two most recent appointees to the Supreme Court, believes that judges may override the policy choices made by democratic bodies only if that choice conflicts with a right that can fairly be discerned from the text, history and structure of the Constitution. Where the Constitution is silent—and it is deliberately silent on some of the most fundamental issues—those choices are to be made by the political process. Judges cannot impose their own version of "goodness" on legislatures....

. . .

To be sure, the Judiciary must be "activist" in that it zealously protects and furthers values that can actually be found in the Constitution and applies those values to conditions that the framers did not foresee. So there is nothing to the charge that faithfulness to the original meaning of the framers would somehow lead to diminution of constitutional values or exclude from constitutional protection such modern developments as electronic surveillance or the broadcast media. Again, Judge Bork himself has made this point quite eloquently when he wrote:

> The important thing, the ultimate consideration, is the constitutional freedom that is given into our keeping. The judge who refuses to see new threats to an established constitutional value, and hence provides a crabbed interpretation that robs the provision of a sole, fair and reasonable meaning fails in his judicial duty. That duty, I repeat, is to ensure that the powers and freedom the framers specified are made effective in today's circumstances.... In a case like this, it is the task of the judge in this generation to discern how the framers' values, defined in the context of the world they knew, apply to the world we know. The world changes in which unchanging values find their application. *Ollman v. Evans,* 750 F.2d at 995–96 (Bork, J., concurring).

However, the fact that a judge should give full scope to *constitutional* values in light of new threats to that value, cannot and does not mean that a judge is thereby free to somehow invent and impose *new* values wholly divorced from anything in the Constitution because he believes that these values are more "in tune" with the values shared by contemporary society. In the first place, it borders on the absurd to suggest that nine (or five) unelected, life-tenured judges are better able to discern and implement "consensus" values of a diverse, pluralistic society than are the elected, fixed-term representatives who have adopted the law being invalidated.

Most fundamentally, however, to engage in such judicial activism is to deprive others of perhaps the most fundamental right secured to them in the Constitution: the right to self-government. Every time a court invents a new right, it correspondingly diminishes the area of democratic choice. While some may applaud this shrinking of democracy, because they are unable to convince others of the wisdom of their policies, this result can only be attained at the expense of democracy and the freedom of the American people.

The current judicial controversy over the constitutionality of the death penalty illustrates this distinction, as well as the wisdom of Judge Bork's judicial philosophy. Some justices believe that convicted murderers have a constitutional "right" not to be subjected to capital punishment. Of course, the source of this "right" is not the Constitution. To the contrary, the Constitution expressly acknowledges the availability of capital punishment in at least four different places. . . .

Consequently, some Justices look *beyond* the Constitution to create such a right, asserting that the death penalty is inconsistent with "evolving standards of decency that mark the progress of a maturing society." *Gregg v. Georgia,* 428 U.S. 153, 227 (1976) (Brennan, J., dissenting). This, of course, is the "enlightened" judicial philosophy to which Judge Bork's opponents insists he must subscribe. The capital punishment controversy perfectly illustrates why such a philosophy is illegitimate in a society dedicated to Government by the people and the accuracy of Judge Bork's observation that "a judge who looks outside the Constitution looks inside himself—and nowhere else." *A Conference on Judicial Reform,* June 14, 1982, at 5.

As with all invented rights, a right to be free of capital punishment is not derived from any evolving moral standard of *society,* but only the judge's personal moral code. As with all invented rights, it does not enhance freedom but redistributes it. Inventing rights for murderers denies rights to victims and, more important, the right of society to fix appropriate punishment for violent crime.

Of course, inventing rights can be used to serve "conservative" as well as "liberal" political ends. For example, in the early part of this century, the Supreme Court used the vague language of the due process clause of the 14th Amendment to strike down a host of economic and social legislation, typified by Justice Peckham's conclusion in *Lochner v. New York,* 198 U.S. 45 (1905), that "[t]he general right [of an employer] to make a contract in relation to his business is part of the liberty of the individual protected by [the due process clause] of the 14th Amendment of the Federal Constitution." . . .

. . .

Judge Bork has indicated that the adoption of any extraconstitutional values through the due process clause is an illegitimate judicial usurpation of legislative authority. See Bork, *The Constitution, Original Intent, and Economic Rights,* 23 San Diego L. Rev. 823 (1986). Judge Bork has therefore clearly indicated that he will apply the Constitution neutrally. He will not put his views ahead of the law by prohibiting States from adopting progressive social reform legislation that interferes with free market. By the same token, he will not put the views of certain groups ahead of the law and recast the Constitution to accommodate their agenda. He will apply the Constitution and laws of the United States neutrally, without regard to the results. It is therefore most difficult to discern a *principled* or *consistent* basis for opposing Judge Bork's confirmation as Supreme Court Justice. Accordingly, it must be that Judge Bork's opponents deem fit only those judges who invent rights with which they agree. If the radical agenda consequently becomes a litmus test for confirmation to be a Federal judge, this irretrievably politicizes the judiciary, threatens its basic independence, and makes an end run around the democratic process to produce results that the people do not want and that are deeply rooted only in the conscience of the special interest groups and of a majority of the life-tenured, unelected Justices of the Supreme Court before whom these groups argue.

. . .

H.   Judge Bork and Justice Scalia

The fact that Judge Bork is firmly situated within the constitutional mainstream is closely related to another, perhaps more interesting question that has already been raised. Last year, 98 Senators voted to confirm Judge Antonin Scalia to be an Associate Justice of the United States Supreme Court, and not one opposed the nomination. As discussed above, Justice Scalia, like Judge Bork plainly believes that the Constitution is to be interpreted as law, and not as a warrant for the imposition of the judge's moral predilections on society. If anything, Justice Scalia adheres to a more stringent view of the ability of judges to evolve constitutional guarantees to take account of modern circumstances than does Judge Bork. Compare *Ollman v. Evans,* 750 F.2d 970, 993 (D.C.Cir.1984) (Bork, J., concurring), with *id.* at 1036 (Scalia, J., dissenting).

Judge Bork and Judge Scalia served together for 4 years on the D.C. Circuit. In 86 cases on which they sat together, they agreed 84 times. That is 98 percent agreement. And the only significant case on which they disagreed was *Ollman,* in which Judge Bork was to Judge Scalia's left. Many of the cases that became most controversial at Judge Bork's hearings, moreover, were cases joined by Judge Scalia on the D.C. Circuit. [Citations omitted.] . . .

. . .

RIGHT TO PRIVACY

Another area Judge Bork discussed was the Constitution's protection of individual liberty. As Judge Bork's testimony before, and subsequent letters to the Committee indicated, the Constitution protects numerous and important aspects of liberty. For instance, the First Amendment protects freedom of speech, press, and religion; the Fourth Amendment protects "[t]he right of the people to be secure in their persons, houses, papers, and effects, against unreasonable searches and seizures;" and the Sixth and Seventh amendments protect the right to trial by jury. All of these freedoms and more are fundamental. Judge Bork has made it quite plain that, in his view, a judge who fails to give these freedoms their full and fair effect fails in his judicial duty. But Judge Bork has also stated that merely because a judge must be tireless to protect the liberties guaranteed by the Constitution does not mean that judges should make up a right to liberty or personal autonomy not found in the Constitution. Once a judge moves beyond the constitutional text, history, and the structure the Constitution creates, he has only his own sense of what is important or fundamental to guide his decision-making. . . .

[W]here the constitutional materials do not specify a value to be protected and have thus left implementation of that value to the democratic process, an unelected judge has no legitimate basis for imposing that value over the contrary preferences of elected representatives. When a court does so, it lessens the area for democratic choice and works a significant shift of power from the legislative to the judicial branch. While the temptation to do so is strong with respect to a law as "nutty" and obnoxious as that at issue in *Griswold v. Connecticut,* 381 U.S. 479 (1965), the invention of rights to correct such a wholly misguided public policy inevitably involves the judiciary in much more difficult policy questions about which reasonable people disagree, such as abortion or homosexual rights.

. . .

. . . It is difficult to understand why abortion is a constitutionally protected liberty but homosexual sodomy is not. Neither activity is mentioned in the Constitution, both involve activity between consenting adults, and "[p]roscriptions against [both activities] have ancient roots."

Judge Bork said it this way at the hearings:

[L]et me repeat about this created, generalized, and undefined right to privacy in *Griswold.* Aside from the fact that the right was not derived by Justice Douglas in any traditional mode of constitutional analysis, . . . we do not know what it is. We do not know what it covers. It can strike at random. *For example the Supreme Court has not applied the right of privacy consistently and I think it is safe to predict that the Supreme Court will not.* For example, if it really is a right of sexual freedom in private, as some have suggested, then *Bowers v. Hardwick,* which upheld a statute against sodomy as applied to homosexuals, is wrongly decided. Privacy to do what, Senators? You know, privacy to use cocaine in private? Privacy for businessmen to fix prices in a hotel room? We just do not know what it is. (Emphasis added.)

Some have said that the principle may be that individuals have a constitutional right to use their bodies as they wish. Not only is this principle to be found nowhere in the Constitution, but also its application would invalidate laws against prostitution, consensual incest among adults, bestiality, drug use, and suicide, not to mention draft laws and countless safety measures such as laws requiring the use of seat belts and motorcycle helmets. This principle is thus far too general to support a particular decision without sweeping in these other cases. Unless the American people decide that judges should be given far more authority and responsibility for running our society, the Constitution requires that they follow the law.

. . .

But those who now urge reliance on the Ninth Amendment see a different set of natural rights emanating from the Ninth Amendment. For example, Professor Tribe filed a brief with the Supreme Court in *Bowers v. Hardwick* suggesting that one of the rights "retained by the people" under the Ninth Amendment is the right to engage in homosexual sodomy. Equally plausible are claims that the Ninth Amendment protects drug use, mountain climbing, and consensual incest among adults. Certainly the text of the amendment makes no distinction among any of these "rights." Therefore, unless the Ninth Amendment is to be read to invalidate all laws that limit individual freedoms, judges who invoke the clause selectively will be doing nothing more than imposing their subjective morality on society. The Constitution nowhere authorizes them to do so.

Although Justice Goldberg's concurrence in *Griswold* invoked the Ninth Amendment, Judge Bork has explained that the problems just discussed are probably the reason why the Supreme Court has *never* rested a decision on the Ninth Amendment. . . . Unless someone can find a way both to read the Ninth Amendment to apply against the States and to discover which additional rights are retained by the people, there is no principled way for a judge to rely on the clause to invalidate State laws.

. . .

CONCLUSION

As these views indicate, Judge Robert Bork is eminently qualified by ability, integrity, and experience to serve as Associate Justice of the Supreme Court. The failure of the Senate to confirm him will be a failure larger than simply denying one qualified nominee a place on the Court. It will be a disservice to the process by rewarding those who have turned the nominating process into a negative campaign of distortions; it will be a disservice to the judiciary of this country who should not be forced to endure such a politicized process; and most importantly, it will be a disservice to the American people, who not only will be denied the service of this intellect on the Court, but will also see the judiciary have its independence threatened by activist special interest groups.

3. The Nomination of David Souter

On July 20, 1990, Justice Brennan announced his resignation from the Court. With surprising swiftness, President Bush nominated David Souter to be his replacement. Few had heard of him and he quickly became known as the "stealth candidate." The ABA unanimously rated him "well qualified."[24] After three days of hearings, the Judiciary Committee approved his nomination by a vote of 13–1.[25] On October 2, 1990, the Senate, voting 90–9, confirmed Souter as the 105th Justice.

In reading the Senate Judiciary Report, consider whether the President was well-advised to select someone so unknown and so inexperienced in the federal sector. Or was selecting someone relatively unknown and whose primary experiences came in state government a logical and predictable reaction to the Bork hearings? Note that Justice O'Connor, when nominated, had held no federal office—not even the brief period on a federal appeals court that Souter had.

——————

Nomination of David H. Souter To Be an Associate Justice of the United States Supreme Court, S. Exec. Rep. No. 101–32, 101st Cong., 2d Sess. (1990)

Mr. Biden, from the Committee on
the Judiciary, submitted the following
REPORT together with ADDITIONAL
AND MINORITY VIEWS

The Committee on the Judiciary, to which was referred the nomination of Judge David H. Souter to be an Associate Justice of the United States Supreme Court, having considering the same, reports favorably thereon, a quorum being present, by a vote of 13 yeas and 1 nay, with the recommendation that the nomination be approved.

III. The Nominee

Judge Souter was born on September 17, 1939, in Melrose, Massachusetts. He received his Bachelor of Arts degree from Harvard College in 1961. Judge Souter was a Rhodes Scholar, and attended Magdalen College, Oxford, between 1961 and 1963. He received his legal education at Harvard Law School, which he attended from 1963 to 1966. From 1966 to 1968, the nominee engaged in the private practice of law with the Concord, New Hampshire law firm of Orr and Reno.

The nominee served for 10 years in the office of Attorney General for the State of New Hampshire. ... From 1971 to 1976, the nominee was Deputy Attorney General. And from 1976 to 1978, he was Attorney

24. Epstein, *Compendium, ABA Ratings, supra,* at 390.

25. Only Senator Kennedy voted against the motion to report the nomination with a favorable recommendation.

General. From 1978 to 1983, the nominee served as Associate Justice of the Superior Court of New Hampshire. From 1983 to 1990, the nominee served as Associate Justice of the Supreme Court of New Hampshire.

In 1990, President Bush appointed Judge Souter to the U.S. Court of Appeals for the First Circuit, a position he held for five months before his nomination to the Supreme Court. ... [After noting that the ABA had unanimously found Judge Souter to be "well qualified," the ABA's highest rating, the Committee Report concluded:]

V.   COMMITTEE RECOMMENDATION

A majority of the committee has voted to favorably report to the Senate the nomination of Judge David Hackett Souter to be an Associate Justice of the United States Supreme Court. Consequently, we hereby recommend that the Senate, pursuant to Article II of the Constitution, offer its consent to the President's nomination.

ADDITIONAL VIEWS OF CHAIRMAN BIDEN

INTRODUCTION

... No nominee in a quarter-century had come to this committee with less known about his constitutional philosophy than David Souter. And no nomination—at any time since the 1930s—had come before the Senate at a moment of such importance, in terms of setting the future direction of the Supreme Court.

At this critical moment, this committee had an obligation to learn all that it could about Judge Souter's constitutional philosophy.... I believe that the burden of proof rested on the nominee to demonstrate that he is the person whom the Senate should confirm to sit on the nation's highest court.

In my view, Judge Souter met his burden of proof with respect to some matters, and failed to do so with respect to others....

In several areas, there were reassuring signs [describing his testimony in the areas of freedom of speech and religion.] ...

. . .

In the area of *stare decisis*, Judge Souter detailed a philosophy that shows a proper respect for precedent. And quite hearteningly, Judge Souter particularly emphasized that—before the Supreme Court reverses a prior ruling—it should take into account "whether private citizens ... have relied upon the precedent in their own planning to such a degree that ... it would be a great hardship in overruling it now." (Transcript, Sept. 13, at 137.) This distinguishes Judge Souter from other nominees, who said that they would look only to whether governmental structures and social institutions have been built up around a particular decision— Judge Souter's view is, quite obviously, more reassuring than this more limited approach.

And, finally, for this side of the ledger—and most importantly—Judge Souter categorically rejected the archconservative judicial philosophy of "original intent:" the view that the meaning of constitutional provisions should be limited to the specific intentions of their framers.

This doctrine—as Judge Souter himself acknowledged—would undermine many of the most important decisions the Supreme Court has given us through the years: *Brown v. Board of Education,* 347 U.S. 483 (1954); the one person, one vote rulings; and the Court's rulings that outlaw discrimination against women.

. . .

In all of these critical respects, Judge Souter clearly proved to the committee that his judicial philosophy was sound—and even highly commendable. In all of these critical respects, Judge Souter met his burden of proof—and then some.

As these Additional Views indicate, in four other areas, though, Judge Souter left the committee with a more mixed record.

First, there is the area of establishment of religion. Here, Judge Souter criticized the prevailing Supreme Court rule of *Lemon v. Kurtzman,* 403 U.S. 602 (1971) . . . [but] we were left with a very unclear picture of how Judge Souter approaches this important issue. . . .

Second, there is the area of race discrimination. Here, too, some things Judge Souter said were quite hopeful: He called the struggle for racial equality the "most tragic" problem confronting the nation, and he suggested that . . . at least some types of affirmative action programs are permissible.

Yet aspects of Judge Souter's record as Attorney General of New Hampshire and of his testimony before the committee were troubling. Again, the record is a mixed one.

Third, there is the area of gender discrimination. Judge Souter criticized the Supreme Court's current middle-tier scrutiny for laws that discriminate on the basis of gender, and even implied that the basis for his criticism was that the Court's existing standard fails to provide adequate protection for women's rights.

Yet I found disappointing Judge Souter's failure to indicate clearly whether his standard in this area would, in fact, be more rigorous—or, inappropriately, less rigorous—than current law. . . .

Finally, there is the area of privacy and reproductive choice. Here, Judge Souter did say some encouraging things. He agreed that there is a marital right to privacy, and that the right of married couples to make choices about procreation is "at the core" of that fundamental right. (Transcript, Sept. 13, at 116.) He agreed that the Constitution protects unenumerated rights, and more specifically, that there is substantive content in the Due Process Clauses of the Fifth and Fourteenth Amendments, and the Ninth Amendment. . . .

And perhaps most importantly, he flatly rejected the methodology being advanced by Chief Justice Rehnquist and Justice Scalia for determining when, in the future, privacy rights will be recognized by the Court. Judge Souter said that he "could not accept [their] view" (Transcript, Sept. 14, at 160)—and I find that very, very encouraging.

... [H]owever, I found most troubling Judge Souter's declaration that the issue of whether unmarried persons have any fundamental right of privacy is "an open question." (Transcript, Sept. 17, at 230.) I firmly believe that this is not an "open question:" Individuals do have a right to privacy, that right is fundamental, and the Supreme Court—in 26 opinions, written by 10 different justices over the past 17 years—has recognized this fundamental right.

Between the privacy issues on which Judge Souter met his burden of proof—and the issue on which Judge Souter failed—is one vital privacy issue that Judge Souter declined to speak to altogether: whether a woman's fundamental right not to be pregnant continues after her birth control fails.

... I feel that Judge Souter could have told us far more about his views in this area without compromising his judicial independence, or indicating how he would vote on a request to overrule *Roe v. Wade,* 410 U.S. 113 (1973). Judge Souter's refusal to talk at all about his philosophy in this area frustrated the committee's exercise of its constitutional responsibilities....

In sum, then, we have before us a nominee that satisfied his burden of proof with respect to some issues, straddled the line on others, failed on some, and left us with a question mark on still other matters.... [A]fter weighing the evidence closely, and studying the record intensely, I decided to vote to confirm David Souter as Associate Justice of the Supreme Court.

Taking Judge Souter at his word, I believe that he clearly demonstrated himself not to be a doctrinaire legal conservative. He clearly distinguished himself from a quite broad school of legal conservatism—including some conservative positions now being taken by members of the current Court:

> He rejected Justice Scalia's cramped formula for determining when fundamental, unenumerated rights should be acknowledged;

> He rejected two shibboleths of the rigid interpretivists by saying that the Due Process Clause does protect substantive liberties—and that the meaning of constitutional provisions cannot be limited to the "original intent" of their framers;

> He rejected the Court's recent majority opinion in the *Smith* case, on religious freedom; and

> He rejected the conservative view that courts must stay out of the realm of addressing "profound social problems"—indeed, Judge Souter insisted that the court must intervene in these areas when a "vacuum of responsibility" exists. (Transcript, Sept. 14, at 14.)

This repeated rejection of the precepts of modern arch-conservative legal thought—of rigid interpretivism—proved to me what Judge Souter was not: Namely, he is not the sort of man who, if confirmed, would run roughshod over the important precedents handed down by the Supreme Court over the past three decades.

. . . Beyond proving what he is not, Judge Souter also proved to me, affirmatively, that much about his philosophy—about his approach to dealing with the issues of the future—merits my consent to his confirmation.

Weighing most heavily in this respect were Judge Souter's statements that he believes that judges must vindicate rights not explicit in the Constitution; that the Due Process Clause protects unenumerated liberties; that a fundamental right to privacy exists; that he would use a broader, and not a narrow, methodology in deciding when the Court should recognize such rights; and the judges must use the Bill of Rights to protect the rights of minorities.

These statements, of course, give me no clear sense of how Judge Souter is going to rule on any one particular case. That is how it should be: I believe that searches should not be made for case-specific commitments from the nominee. But what these statements—and many others—do indicate is that Judge Souter has an approach on most issues that—though far more conservative than I would hope for the Court—is nonetheless an acceptable one.

I believe that this was true for "most issues." Unfortunately, Judge Souter's refusal to discuss reproductive choice leaves me with no indication at all of where he will come out on this issue . . . [or] how he thinks about this constitutional question.

What Judge Souter did tell the committee, however, was this: "I have not made up my mind and I do not go on the court saying I must go one way or I must go another way." (Transcript, Sept. 14, at 128.) This statement goes a step beyond refusing to tell us his view on reproductive freedom, and tells us—if Judge Souter is to be believed, and I do believe him—that his mind is an open one.

. . . I strongly believe that a woman's right to choose is fundamental, and protected by our Constitution. And I believe that any attempts to read that right out of the Constitution are misdirected, and reflect a mistaken understanding of the true majesty of the Liberty Clause of the Fourteenth Amendment to our Constitution.

I also know, however, that the President of the United States has the diametrically opposed view. The President has pledged to see *Roe* overruled, and believes it to be wrong. He obviously has no intention of submitting, and will never submit, a nominee who adheres to my view on this matter. I know that—we all know that.

It is one thing to reject a nominee who would come to the Court opposed to reproductive freedom; if the President attempted to send up such a nominee—one who shared the President's view on the choice question—he or she would find a serious fight in the Senate. But if this committee were to go a step further, and also reject a nominee who genuinely seems to be open-minded on this question—neither committed to the President's view or the opposing viewpoint—if we make that a litmus test for confirmation—we will have an eight-member Court for a long time to come.

Under the circumstances of sharp diversion between the White House and the Senate, I believe that the best we can hope for is a judge who has an expansive methodology for interpreting privacy rights generally, and a genuinely—and I emphasize genuinely—open-minded view of a woman's privacy right after conception occurs. Judge Souter is not the sort of judge I would nominate if I were president, but I think that he is about the best we can expect in the divided-government situation we now face.

Of course, this does not mean that I can be confident that Judge Souter will vindicate a woman's right to choose. . . . It does mean, in my view, that he is about the best we are going to do on this score from this Administration.

With this realistic lens as my perspective, I supported Judge Souter's confirmation. I do not do so enthusiastically, and . . . I do not do so without reservation.

. . .

PART EIGHT: JUDGE SOUTER'S VIEWS ON *STARE DECISIS*

The doctrine of *stare decisis*—"to stand by things decided"—protects and promotes the stability, efficiency and legitimacy of the legal system. Judge Souter's record on the New Hampshire Supreme Court, as well as his testimony before the committee, suggest that the nominee has a healthy respect for precedent, and that he would exercise caution and prudence when asked to reverse existing doctrine.

A.   While a Member of the New Hampshire Supreme Court, Judge Souter Showed Great Deference to Precedent

. . .

For example, in two cases, he joined a majority opinion because he thought the issue was controlled by existing precedent, even though he disagreed with that precedent. . . .

. . .

B.   Judge Souter's Testimony Also Evinces a Strong Respect for Precedent

Under questioning by Senator Thurmond, Judge Souter articulated his theory of *stare decisis* and the "series of considerations which courts should bear in mind in deciding whether a prior precedent should be followed or should not be." (Transcript, September 13, at 135.)

The first question to be addressed, Judge Souter testified, is whether the court concludes that the precedent was correct when originally decided. He stated that if a determination is made that the case was not correctly decided, several factors must then be evaluated.

The first factor listed by Judge Souter was the "degree and the kind of reliance that has been placed upon" the precedent. Elaborating on this "reliance," Judge Souter said:

> We ask in some context[s] *whether private citizens in their lives have relied upon [the precedent] in their own planning to such a degree that, in fact, it would be a great hardship in overruling it now.* (Transcript, Sept. 13, at 137 (emphasis added).)

In response to questioning by Senator Specter about the kinds of cases to which this factor would be relevant, Judge Souter made clear that "I can certainly tell you that the issue of reliance is not an issue which is limited to commercial cases." (Transcript, Sept. 17, at 247.) While Judge Souter did not elaborate on the non-commercial cases to which this factor would apply, it is encouraging that he explicitly rejected limiting this factor to the commercial context.

The second factor identified by Judge Souter is "whether legislatures have relied upon [the precedent], in legislation which assumes the correctness of that precedent." (Transcript, Sept. 13, at 137.)

The third factor he identified is "whether the court in question or other courts have relied upon it, in developing a body of doctrine." Elaborating on this factor, Judge Souter said:

> If a precedent, in fact, is consistent with a line of development which extends from its date to the present time, then the cost of overruling that precedent is, of course, going to be enormously greater and enormously different from what will be the case in instances in which the prior case either has not been followed or the prior case has simply been eroded, chipped away at, as we say, by later determinations. (Transcript, Sept. 13, at 137–38.)

Finally, Judge Souter noted the well-recognized distinction between the application of *stare decisis* in statutory cases and its application in constitutional cases. He suggested looking to "other means of overruling the precedent"—that is, legislation enacted by Congress—in the context of statutory cases. (Transcript, Sept. 13, at 138.)

These factors constitute a thoughtful and reasoned approach to stare decisis. Importantly, when discussing the question of reliance, Judge Souter emphasized the degree to which private citizens have relied on the case—as opposed to the reliance of governmental and private institutions, which can limit the applicability of this factor to commercial and administrative law decisions. By focusing on the degree of reliance by private citizens and by explicitly extending this factor beyond simply commercial law cases, Judge Souter appears to recognize the precedential value of decisions in the areas of civil rights and civil liberties. While I am concerned about the degree to which he would consider the fact that a prior decision had been "chipped away at," on balance I have concluded that the factors identified by Judge Souter are appropriate.

Judge Souter's approach to *stare decisis* is important not only because of the factors he listed, but also because of the factors he did not list. Some justices have noted, for example, that because they are oath-bound to the Constitution, they owe little or no deference to prior decisions interpreting the Constitution. Justice Scalia has argued, for example, that it would violate his oath to uphold the Constitution were he to adhere to a prior decision that he considers to be "a plainly unjustified intrusion upon the democratic process in order that the Court might save face." (*South Carolina v. Gathers,* 109 S.Ct. 2207, 2218 (1989) (Scalia, J., dissenting) . . .) . . . Judge Souter made no reference at all to this argument and in no way suggested that his oath might lessen the need to pay appropriate deference to prior constitutional decisions.

. . .

CONCLUSION

In supporting the confirmation of David Hackett Souter, I am not saying that I am giving this nominee, or any other nominee, the "benefit of the doubt." Nor am I saying that a nominee need only prove himself or herself not to be extremist to win this committee's approval.

The burden of proof is on the nominee—and it is a burden that this nominee, in my view, just barely met. Any future nominee who fails to meet that burden—and again, I emphasize how close this nominee came to that line—will be vigorously opposed by me.

The Administration should be careful not to learn the wrong lesson from the committee's lop-sided vote in Judge Souter's favor. Our approval is not a sign that the Senate intends to be lax about exercising its advice and consent power, or intends to use that power only to screen out extremist nominees. Rather, it is a sign that we take this power seriously, and that we intend to exercise it responsibly—and in doing so, Judge Souter falls within the sphere of candidates acceptable to this committee.

Other nominees, if more conservative than this one, could well fall outside of that sphere:

> For example, a nominee who criticizes the notion of unenumerated rights, or the right to privacy, would, in my view, be unacceptable.

> A nominee whose view of the Fourteenth Amendment's Equal Protection Clause has led him or her to have a cramped vision of the Court's role in creating a more just society would, in my view, be unacceptable.

> And a nominee whose vision of the First Amendment's guarantees of freedom of speech and religion would constrain those provisions' historic scope would, in my view, be unacceptable.

But Judge Souter is not such a nominee. *His vision of the Constitution is not mine—but it is clearly not that of the Court's hard-line conservatives, either. He is not a man whom I would nominate to the Court—but he is not a man whose nomination I will oppose....*

ADDITIONAL VIEWS OF SENATOR HATCH

Judge Souter's excellent educational and legal background and his demonstrated knowledge of the law at the hearing all attest to his competence and ability. I believe he will join the Supreme Court with an independent mind, willing to consider different points of view on the cases which will come before him.

I also believe that he will seek to interpret and apply the law according to its original meaning. I do not believe that he will impose his own policy preferences on the American people in the guise of judging. The role of the judicial branch is to enforce the provisions of the Constitution and the laws we enact in Congress as their meaning was originally intended by their framers. That meaning must then be applied to the facts and circumstances before the judge—facts and circumstances perhaps never contemplated by the framers of the legal provision being applied. But the meaning—the underlying principle of the provision—does not change.

· · ·

Some urge us to reject Judge Souter because he did not commit himself to uphold *Roe v. Wade.* But what would happen if different senators impose litmus tests on a variety of issues—could any nominee ever be confirmed?

MINORITY VIEWS OF SENATOR EDWARD M. KENNEDY

I oppose the confirmation of Judge David H. Souter to the Supreme Court.

· · ·

In the past half century, the Supreme Court has played a central role in the effort to make America a better and fairer land. The Court outlawed school segregation in the 1950's, removed barriers to the right to vote in the 1960's, and established a far-reaching right to privacy, including the right to abortion in the 1970's. In other ways as well, the Supreme Court strengthened the basic rights of minorities and took steps to end the second-class status of women in our society. But in the decade of the 1980's, ... the Court has seemed to pause in carrying out this important role, and in many cases has actually turned back the clock. On many of these issues, the current Court seems to be divided 4–4, so that the Senate's decision on this nomination is likely to tip the balance in one direction or the other.

In considering a Supreme Court nomination, the Senate must make two inquiries. The first is the threshold issue: Does the nominee have the intelligence, integrity, and temperament to meet the responsibilities of a Supreme Court Justice?

But that is only the beginning, not the end, of the inquiry. The Senate also must determine whether the nominee possesses a clear commitment to the fundamental values at the core of our constitutional democracy.

In this second inquiry, the burden of proof rests with the nominee. Our constitutional freedoms are the historic legacy of every American. They are too important, and the past sacrifices made to protect those freedoms have been too great, to be entrusted to judges who lack this clear commitment. If a Senator is left with substantial doubts about a nominee's dedication to these core values, our own constitutional responsibility requires us to oppose the nomination.

This is not to suggest any single-issue litmus test. Nominees should be judged on their overall approach to the Constitution. I have frequently supported nominees whose views on particular constitutional issues are very different from my own. But the Senate should not confirm a Supreme Court nomination unless we are persuaded that the nominee is committed to upholding the essential values at the heart of our constitutional tradition.

.   .   .

Judge Souter has a distinguished intellectual background. He has spent the great majority of his legal career in public service. But aspects of his record on the bench and while serving in the New Hampshire Attorney General's Office have raised troubling questions about the depth of his commitment to the indispensable role of the Supreme Court in protecting individual rights and liberties under the Constitution.

Far from dispelling these concerns, Judge Souter's testimony before this committee reinforced them. In particular, my concerns center on the fundamental constitutional issues of civil rights, the right to privacy, and the power of Congress and the courts to protect these basic rights....

———

4. The Nomination of Clarence Thomas

On June 27, 1991, Justice Thurgood Marshall announced his retirement. Although he had always hoped "to serve out his term," that is, to serve for his entire life, he explained his unexpected decision in typically colorful language; he decided to retire because, he said: "I am getting old and coming apart."[26] Once again, President Bush named his nominee

26. Linda Campbell, *Health May be Fading, But Marshall's Wit Still Sharp,* Chicago Tribune, June 29, 1991, at C1. When asked whether he thought President Bush should replace him with an African- American, Marshall observed: "... there's no difference between a black snake and a white snake; they'll both bite." Bob Dart, *Marshall's Choice for Successor?,* The At-

very quickly. On July 1, 1991, four days after Marshall's announcement, Bush nominated Clarence Thomas, an African–American judge on the U.S. Court of Appeals for the D.C. Circuit who had previously been chairman of the Equal Employment Opportunity Commission. In explaining his selection, President Bush stated that Judge Thomas' race had not been a factor in the nomination. The ABA rated Thomas "qualified," with 12 committee members voting "qualified," 2 "not qualified," and 1 recusal.[27]

The following section has two parts. The first contains excerpts from the Report of the Senate Judiciary Committee. On September 27, 1991, the Committee split evenly, 7–7, in its decision whether or not to report favorably on the nomination,[28] and voted to report the nomination, without any recommendation, to the full Senate so that it could vote. The accompanying report, excerpted herein, explains why the Committee was divided. Reading the excerpts from the Committee Report, consider whether Thomas' race mattered in the hearings. Should it have? Consider, also, whether Thomas' responses raised the so-called "confirmation conversion" issue that played so large a role in the Bork report and if so, whether it was treated similarly. Note that the Report was written before the occurrence of the events described in the next paragraph below.

Just one day before the full Senate was scheduled to vote on the nomination, on October 6, 1991, the media published leaked allegations that Clarence Thomas had sexually harassed Anita Hill ten years earlier. (Anita Hill had worked with Thomas at the Department of Education and then had become his assistant when he was named Chairman of the EEOC. At the time of the Thomas nomination, Hill was a tenured professor of law at the University of Oklahoma.) Confronted with an overwhelming outcry from women's groups against proceeding with the vote in the face of this allegation, the Senate unanimously decided to delay the vote for one week and to reopen the hearings to allow Thomas and Hill to testify.[29] (Under Senate procedures, a unanimous vote was required to delay the scheduled vote.) The resulting three days of hearings were widely viewed, garnering better ratings than the competing championship games in major league baseball.[30] At the end of these hearings, on October 15, 1991 the Senate, by a vote of 52–48, confirmed Clarence Thomas, who thereby survived the closest confirmation vote in the twentieth century.[31]

lanta Journal and Constitution, June 29, 1991, at A10.

27. Epstein, *Compendium, ABA Ratings, supra* at 390.

28. Voting against the motion to report the recommendation favorably were Senators Biden, Kennedy, Metzenbaum, Simon, Kohl, Heflin, and Leahy (all Democrats). Voting in favor of the motion were Senators Thurmond, Brown, Hatch, Simpson, Grass-

ley, Spector, and DeConcini (the only Democrat on this side).

29. 137 Cong. Rec. S14,565–66 (daily ed. October 8, 1991).

30. John Carmody, *The TV Column,* The Washington Post, October 15, 1991, at E4.

31. David G. Savage, *Turning Right,* 449 (1992).

The second set of excerpts, after the Judiciary Committee Report, are floor statements by two Senators concerning these unusual proceedings and the process by which each Senator finally decided how to cast his ultimate vote. In reading the statements of Senators Byrd and DeConcini, consider the following questions: Was the confirmation process for the Thomas nomination an adequate and appropriate forum in which to address accusations of personal misconduct such as sexual harassment? Should such conduct, if established, be treated as a disqualification? Who should bear the burden of proof in such proceedings? What position(s) did Senators Byrd and DeConcini take on these issues?

Nomination of Clarence Thomas To Be an Associate Justice of the United States Supreme Court, S. Exec. Rep. No. 102–15, 102d Cong., 1st Sess. (1991)

Mr. Biden, from the Committee on the Judiciary, submitted the following REPORT together with ADDITIONAL AND SUPPLEMENTAL VIEWS

The Committee on the Judiciary, to which was referred the nomination of Judge Clarence Thomas to be an Associate Justice of the U.S. Supreme Court, having considered the same, reports the nomination, a quorum being present, without recommendation, by a vote of 13 yeas and 1 nay, having failed to report favorably thereon, by a vote of 7 yeas and 7 nays.

. . .

III. The Nominee

Judge Thomas was born on June 23, 1948, in Savannah, GA. He received his bachelor of arts degree from Holy Cross College in 1971. Judge Thomas pursued his legal education at Yale Law School, receiving his juris doctor in 1974. From 1974 to 1977, the nominee served as an assistant attorney general for the State of Missouri. From 1977 to 1979, Judge Thomas worked as an attorney for the Monsanto Co., located in St. Louis, MO. From 1979 to 1981, the nominee was a legislative assistant for U.S. Senator John C. Danforth, of Missouri. In 1981, the nominee served for 2 months as a consultant to the Office of Civil Rights, U.S. Department of Education. He then served for 10 months as Assistant Secretary for Civil Rights, U.S. Department of Education. From 1982 to 1990, the nominee was Chairman of the Equal Employment Opportunity Commission. In 1990, President Bush appointed Judge Thomas to the United States Court of Appeals, a position he held for 17 months before his nomination to the Supreme Court.

. . .

ADDITIONAL VIEWS OF CHAIRMAN BIDEN

The decision to oppose the confirmation of a nominee to the U.S. Supreme Court is a solemn one. And with respect to this nominee, Judge Clarence Thomas, I have no doubt about his character, credentials, competence, or credibility. Instead, the basis for my opposition to the confirmation of Judge Thomas concerns his judicial philosophy—the approach he would use in deciding how to interpret the enabling phrases of our Constitution.

INTRODUCTION

. . . Over the course of his professional life, [Judge Thomas] had expressed views that aligned him with the ultraconservatives seeking to fundamentally alter our society. The constitutional philosophy set forth in Judge Thomas' articles and speeches would result in radical, and in my opinion undesirable, changes in the relationship between government and individuals.

First, Judge Thomas seemed to advocate a change in the degree to which society could protect the environment, the workplace, and the public health and safety. . . . [approving] the notion of an activist Court that would greatly increase the constitutional protection given to economic and property rights, striking down laws that regulated businesses and corporations.

Second, Judge Thomas appeared to seek a change in the degree to which government could interfere in the personal lives of individuals. Judge Thomas had praised or associated himself with arguments for greater government control over matters of family and personal life . . . and the most private realm of decisions concerning procreation and other intimate matters.

Third, Judge Thomas had endorsed an extreme view of separation of powers which, if taken to the conclusion endorsed by its advocates, would radically redefine the balance of power between the branches of the Federal Government. . . . Judge Thomas seemed to advocate a major shift in power away from the legislative branch and toward the executive branch.

In short, Judge Thomas' writings and speeches sketch a judicial philosophy that, if realized, would reverse the balance this country has struck between the rights of individuals, the obligations of businesses and corporations, and the power of government. The question concerning me as the hearings began was whether this was an accurate picture of Judge Thomas' judicial philosophy.

During the hearings, Judge Thomas sought to explain his views. I accept the sincerity of his testimony, and some of his explanations satisfied my concerns. On balance, however, my concerns remain. First of all, I was troubled by Judge Thomas' repeated resistance to discussing his own views when asked about decisions of the Supreme Court. Perhaps the best way to gain insight into a nominee's judicial philosophy is to use the Supreme Court's existing constitutional and statutory decisions to frame the dialogue.

Judge Thomas' reluctance even to comment on already decided cases, apparently for fear of revealing his own views, was pronounced. I discussed this with him in the final hours of his testimony, after hearing yet another of his refusals to discuss a legal principle:

> The CHAIRMAN. ... Judge, you are going to be ... a judge who is not bound by *stare decisis*, ... and so I am a little ... edgy when you give an answer and you say, "well, that's the policy," as if you are still going to be a Circuit Court of Appeals judge....
>
> JUDGE THOMAS. Well, I understand that, Mr. Chairman, but what I have attempted to do is to not agree or disagree with existing cases.
>
> The CHAIRMAN. You are doing very well at that.
>
> JUDGE THOMAS. The point that I am making or I have tried to make is that I do not approach these cases with any desire to change them, and I have tried to indicate that, to the extent that individuals feel, well, I am foreclosed from a—
>
> The CHAIRMAN. If you had a desire to change it, would you tell us?
>
> JUDGE THOMAS. I don't think so.... (Transcript, Sept. 16, at 172–73.)

Judge Thomas' last comment appears to have been said in jest, but in the end, he had declined comment or provided only vague remarks on the many constitutional issues—great and small, contentious and settled—about which he was asked. Perhaps Judge Thomas was advised that this approach was a sound political strategy designed to ensure confirmation. If that is the case, it is not a strategy I am prepared to accept.

. . .

Judge Thomas may ultimately turn out to be a Justice who will strike a balance between the individual, government, and businesses and corporations in a way that is acceptable. But, based on the record before me, I am not certain he would. Given what is at stake with this nomination—and given where the Court stands now—I cannot take the chance.

. . .

PART TWO: JUDGE THOMAS' VIEWS ON PRIVACY, REPRODUCTIVE FREEDOM, AND UNENUMERATED RIGHTS

In supporting the nomination of Justice Souter to the Court last year, I emphasized that a nominee bears the burden of proving that he or she falls within the sphere of candidates acceptable to this committee, and ... that a nominee who rejected the notion that our Constitution protects unenumerated rights, including the right to privacy, would, in my view, be unacceptable. . . . [because] such a nominee would put at risk not only those rights the Court has already acknowledged, . . . [and would lack] an expansive view of our Constitution that would guide us safely into the future.

. . .

Prior to the hearings, Judge Thomas' record on the right of privacy, reproductive freedom, and unenumerated rights generally—while not definitive—was troubling. To the extent he had expressed views, they were hostile to these concepts. While Judge Thomas had [not] addressed the issue of abortion, . . . [m]y concern was his apparently much broader criticism of an unenumerated right of privacy—of the very idea that there is a realm of intimate matters into which the Government may not intrude.

During the hearings, Judge Thomas conceded that the Constitution, and in particular the 14th amendment, protects some sort of privacy right, at least for married couples. But Judge Thomas declined to provide full answers to most of the questions he was asked on this subject.

He declined to describe in detail his overall methodology for approaching privacy claims. He did not reveal a decisive view on whether individuals had a right of privacy protected by the liberty clause of the 14th amendment. Nor did he say whether, in his view, the scope of the right of privacy—for married or single people—extended in any circumstances to decisions about procreation. His reticence to answer these questions, in light of his prior record, is profoundly troubling. He has failed to convince me that he endorses a broad and expanding conception of the Constitution's protection of the right of privacy.

A. *Judge Thomas Has Criticized Judicial Recognition of an Unenumerated Right of Privacy*

In a series of speeches and articles, Judge Thomas implied his disagreement with those who believe the Constitution grants broad protection to the right of each individual to make intimate decisions without government intrusion. . . .

At the hearing, Judge Thomas seemed first to concede that every individual, whether single or married, had a right of privacy with respect to matters of procreation:

> The CHAIRMAN. . . . Now, you said that the privacy right of married couples is fundamental, and as I understand it now, you told me—correct me if I am wrong—that the privacy right of an individual on procreation is fundamental. Is that right?

> JUDGE THOMAS. I think that is consistent with what I said and I think consistent with what the Court held in *Eisenstadt v. Baird* [405 U.S. 438 (1972)]. (Transcript, Sept. 12, at 50.)

Shortly thereafter, however, he spoke only of a marital right to privacy in responding to a question asked by Senator Kennedy:

JUDGE THOMAS. Senator, ... I think I have indicated here today and yesterday that there is a privacy interest in the Constitution, in the liberty component of the Due Process Clause, and that marital privacy is a fundamental right, and marital privacy then can only be impinged on or only be regulated if there is a compelling State interest.... (Transcript, Sept. 12, at 82.)

As a result, I asked Judge Thomas again about his belief in an individual's right to privacy:

The CHAIRMAN. Judge, very simply, if you can, yes or no: Do you believe that the Liberty Clause of the Fourteenth Amendment of the Constitution provides a fundamental right to privacy for individuals in the area of procreation, including contraception?

JUDGE THOMAS. Senator, I think I answered earlier yes, based upon the precedent of *Eisenstadt v. Baird.*

The CHAIRMAN. Well, you know, ... *Eisenstadt v. Baird* was an equal protection case. ...That is not the question I am asking you. Let me make sure and say it one more time. Do you believe the Liberty Clause of the Fourteenth Amendment of the Constitution provides a fundamental right of privacy for individuals in the area of procreation, including contraception?

JUDGE THOMAS. I think I have answered that, Senator.

The CHAIRMAN. Yes or no?

JUDGE THOMAS. Yes, and—

. . .

I have expressed on what I base that, and I would leave it at that. (Transcript, Sept. 12, at 119–20.)

In an attempt to more clearly understand his views, I submitted to Judge Thomas, after the hearings, a written question on the right of privacy.... Judge Thomas' answer to this question, in its entirely, was as follows:

As I sought to make clear in my testimony, I believe that *Eisenstadt* was correct on both the privacy and equal protection grounds.

. . .

The result of Judge Thomas' reticence to discuss his views is that, ... even after my repeated attempts to engage him in a dialogue on this issue, I am left without any clear idea of what Judge Thomas means when he says the 14th amendment protects a right of privacy. What is the scope and nature of that right? Where does it come from? Who enjoys this right? These questions remain unanswered.

. . .

    B. Judge Thomas Refused to Discuss His Views on Reproductive Freedom

. . .

    I was disappointed by Judge Thomas' reticence to discuss the issue of reproductive freedom even at the most general level.... I am not referring to the specific question of whether the result in *Roe v. Wade* was correct—a question I did not ask Judge Thomas. But Judge Thomas would not even discuss, for example, whether a woman has any protected liberty interest at stake in matters of procreation, or whether the Court should apply strict scrutiny in reviewing such an asserted interest. Answering these questions would not have revealed whether Judge Thomas agreed with *Roe,* because even if Judge Thomas had acknowledged that women have a fundamental right to choose whether to continue a pregnancy, he could still disagree with the result in *Roe.*

    My concern is that in refusing to discuss the broader question of whether we, as individuals, have a right to make intimate decisions free from Government intrusion, I can not begin to understand how Judge Thomas would approach any number of cases in which the Court will determine the future relationship of individuals and Government in our society.... I am not comfortable that Judge Thomas would strike an appropriate balance between the right of individuals and the Government as we move into the next century.

    C. Judge Thomas Did Not Explain How He Would Use History and Tradition to Determine Whether an Asserted Liberty Interest Is Constitutionally Protected

    Judge Thomas was similarly reluctant to expound the general methodology he would use to determine whether an asserted liberty interest is protected by the Constitution. Judge Thomas told the committee that the meaning of the Constitution's broad phrases—like "liberty"—are not "self-defining" and must be interpreted based on the Framers' intent and our history and traditions. (Transcript, Sept. 12, at 27.) ... All the Justices now on the Court look to history and tradition ..., but they do so in different ways, with radically different results. The key question is whether the Court will protect only those interests supported by a specific and longstanding tradition, or whether a less constricted view of liberty will govern.

    This debate was most clearly framed in the case of *Michael H. v. Gerald D.,* 491 U.S. 110 (1989), involving the asserted liberty interest of a biological father to see his child. There, Justice Scalia, in a footnote joined only by Chief Justice Rehnquist, argued that the Constitution protects an interest only if it has been recognized at "the most specific level at which a relevant tradition can be identified." (*Id.* at 127 n. 6.) Thus, Justice Scalia looked at whether the asserted interest fit within a tradition of protecting what he called the "marital family"; he expressly rejected the idea that the interest be more broadly defined in terms of "parenthood" or "personal relationships." (*Id.*)

Justices O'Connor and Kennedy rejected this portion of Justice Scalia's opinion, expressly because they found this methodology overly constricting:

> [Justice Scalia] sketches a mode of historical analysis to be used when identifying liberty interests protected by the Due Process Clause of the Fourteenth Amendment that may be somewhat inconsistent with our past decisions in this area. [Citing *Griswold v. Connecticut* and *Eisenstadt v. Baird*.] On occasion the Court has characterized relevant traditions protecting asserted rights at levels of generality that might not be "the most specific level" available. *I would not foreclose the unanticipated by the prior imposition of a single mode of historical analysis.* (*Id.* at 132, O'Connor, J., concurring, (citations omitted) (emphasis added).)

Referencing this case, I asked Judge Thomas how he would define the interest at stake or use history and traditions to help give meaning to the broad phrases of the Constitution:

> The CHAIRMAN. . . . Do you concur with the rationale offered by Justice Scalia [in *Michael H. v. Gerald D.*] as to how one is to determine whether or not an interest asserted by a person before the Court? . . .
>
> JUDGE THOMAS. Senator, again, that is a very recent case and I am in the position of not wanting to comment on that specifically, but I am very skeptical—
>
>   · · ·
>
> I am skeptical, when one looks at tradition and history, to narrow the focus to the most specific tradition. I think that the effort should be to determine the appropriate tradition or the tradition that is most relevant to our inquiry, and to not take a cramped approach or narrow approach that could actually limit fundamental rights.
>
>   · · ·
>
> The CHAIRMAN. . . . as I understand it, you are not taken with the Scalia approach.
>
> JUDGE THOMAS. Skeptical.
>
>   · · ·

Judge Thomas' failure to expressly reject Justice Scalia's methodology—stopping at expressing his "skepticism"—is unfortunate. I note that Justice Souter, when asked this same question last year, stated emphatically that he "would not accept" Justice Scalia's approach, and he explained how he would instead seek out the most "reliable evidence" including evidence of "great generality." . . .

PART THREE: JUDGE THOMAS' VIEWS ON THE CONSTITUTIONAL PROTECTION OF ECONOMIC AND PROPERTY RIGHTS

. . .

In my view, Judge Thomas' testimony put to rest suspicions that he would begin his service on the Court with a conscious agenda to change the current law as it pertains to economic due process.

. . .

His testimony with respect to the takings clause is somewhat more ambiguous ... [I]n these exchanges he reverted etc. to more equivocal statements, such as "I have no quarrel with," perhaps suggesting more willingness to change the law in these areas than in the due process area.

. . .

In an exchange with Senator Brown, Judge Thomas discussed the current law respecting economic and property rights.

> SENATOR BROWN. I guess I would like an indication from you as to whether or not you think property rights deserve a lesser protection in the Constitution, greater protection under the Constitution than other rights, or whether it is a balancing between rights when these questions arise. Would you share with us your view on that?

> JUDGE THOMAS. Senator, my point has been that property rights, of course, deserve some protection, and I think they are, as are our other rights, important rights. The Court in looking at the economic regulations of our economy and our society has attempted to move away from certainly the *Lochner* era cases and not act as a super-legislature. And I indicated that that is appropriate. . . .

> I think that . . . there is some developing in the taking area, and perhaps if I am fortunate enough to be confirmed to the Court, perhaps I would be called upon to rule on those issues. But I would be concerned about the diminishment or the diminishing, diminution of any rights in our society. But that is not to say in any way that I disagree with the standards that the Court applies to protecting those rights today (Transcript, Sept. 11, at 154–155.)

Senator Brown returned to this line of questioning later in the hearings.

> SENATOR BROWN. Do you find laid out in our Constitution language that calls for a second-class level of protection for property rights?

> JUDGE THOMAS. Senator, I think that we have certainly—as we have discussed in these hearings, I have said in my own writings that there should be a recognition of property rights—economic rights, and I was talking in that case more about my grandfather and his ability to, as you say, earn his living, not be denied that.

But I think what the courts have done in the regulation of the social and economic affairs of our country has been—and I think appropriately so. As I have noted, I have no quarrel with the equal protection analysis that the Court uses. The Court has tried to defer to the decision of the legislature. In other words, the balances should be struck by this body or by the political branches and not second-guessed by the courts. I have no reason to quarrel with that approach. It recognizes that the considerations are very complex and involve any number of factors that are best left to the legislative branch.

This exchange led me to return once more to the takings clause issue, because it was unclear whether Judge Thomas meant to say that he had no quarrel with the Court's current equal protection analysis, as it applies to economic regulation, or whether he meant to include the takings clause analysis, too.

THE CHAIRMAN.

... [Y]ou said you have no quarrel with what the Court does, how the Court deals now with regard to regulations of property.

. . .

So my question is this: Do you agree with the state of the law as it is now with regard to property ... ? Or do you agree with Senator Brown who said it is wrong the way we are doing it now; property and the test applied to the taking of property should be elevated to the same level as other constitutional rights—i.e., the case he cited, the right to privacy in Moore?

What is your position?

JUDGE THOMAS. Senator, I think that I indicated ... that the current manner of equal protection analysis I have no quarrel with.... With respect to the area of the current law, in the area of taking, I have no basis to quarrel with that either. (Transcript, Sept. 13, at 120–125.)

On the basis of this testimony, it amounts to mere guesswork to try to determine whether Judge Thomas rejects the ultra-conservative approach to the takings clause being promoted by Professor Epstein and others, or whether he is being abundantly cautious because he is aware that takings clause cases come to the Court with some regularity....

. . .

PART FIVE: JUDGE THOMAS' VIEWS ON CIVIL RIGHTS

. . .

In a 1988 article in the Lincoln Review, Thomas implied that women should not be able to take advantage of anti-discrimination laws. In discussing a recent book by Thomas Sowell, who argues that the absence of women in certain jobs is due to their choice rather than to discrimination, then head of EEOC Thomas wrote:

> [Sowell's book] has a useful, concise discussion of discrimination faced by women.... [B]y analyzing all the statistics and examining the role of marriage on wage earning for both men and women, Sowell presents a much-needed antidote to cliches about women's earnings and professional status. In any event, women cannot be understood as though they were a racial minority group, or any kind of minority at all. ("Thomas Sowell and the Heritage of Lincoln: Ethnicity and Individual Freedom," Lincoln Review (Winter 1988).)

. . .

At the hearings, Judge Thomas was asked specifically about the statement just quoted:

> SENATOR DECONCINI. Sowell also explained pay inequities between the genders by claiming that "Women are typically not educated as often in such highly paid fields of mathematics, science, and engineering, nor attracted to physically taxing and well-paid fields such as construction work, lumber-jacking, coal mining and the like."

> What are your thoughts about that conclusion?

> JUDGE THOMAS. Well, I can't say whether or not women are attracted or not attracted to those areas. I think that is a normative comment there.

. . .

> Again, my point in saying that his argument could be an antidote to the debate is because he attempts to disaggregate and to not simply say all of the reasons. It is not to say that I adopted ... all of his conclusions and his assertions. I simply don't and did not at that time. (Transcript, Sept. 11, at 64–65.)

When asked specifically about the standard of review for claims of gender discrimination, Judge Thomas said: "Senator, I have no reason and had no reason to question or to disagree with the three-tier approach." (Transcript, Sept. 11, at 59.)

These answers once again express Judge Thomas' recurring theme: He has no reason to question, or disagree with, or quarrel with current constitutional interpretation. Yet this is not particularly reassuring given his strongly expressed views before the hearings began....

. . .

As Chairman of the EEOC, Judge Thomas was a strong supporter of stiff penalties for individuals who had been found guilty of discrimination, as well as for remedies that would make whole individuals who could prove that they themselves had been victims of discrimination. However, ... in a 1988 book, Thomas characterized congressional at-

tempts to remedy discrimination as ignoring constitutional mandates.
. . .

Judge Thomas also specifically criticized the Supreme Court's decisions acknowledging the constitutionality of appropriately drawn affirmative action programs.

. . .

In part, Judge Thomas responded to questions about his prior views by emphasizing that they were policy positions, not the products of judicial reasoning. Even so, it was evident that . . . he does have some considered views, and . . . they diverge from those of important Supreme Court decisions. For example:

> SENATOR BROWN. Judge, in the past you have expressed some concerns about racial quotas. If I understand your position as it has been articulated at this hearing, it has been an interest or an advocacy of affirmative action, but an opposition to racial quotas as a method of achieving those advances. I wonder if you could articulate the differences you see and the reasons for them.

> JUDGE THOMAS. As I indicated earlier, Senator, throughout my adult life, I have advocated the inclusion of those who have been excluded.

> . . .

> The difficulty comes with how far do you go without being unfair to others who have not discriminated or unfair to the person who is excluded, and at that range I thought—and, again, this was the policy position that I advocated—that it was appropriate to draw the line at preferences and goals and timetables and quotas. (Transcript, Sept. 11, at 164–65.)

Asked further about the issue, Judge Thomas had the following exchange:

> SENATOR SPECTER. . . . In a context where blacks have been egregiously discriminated against, it is clear that that is going to happen in the future under the same circumstances, and the way to prevent future victims is to set the goal, and my question to you is, isn't that a reasonable course which the Federal courts followed and the Supreme Court upheld, and, of course, which you disagreed with?

> JUDGE THOMAS. It is certainly the course that the Supreme Court has upheld, and I disagree with that as certainly a policy-maker. (Transcript, Sept. 13, at 27.)

. . .

CONCLUSION

A year ago, during the Senate's consideration of Justice Souter's nomination, I made it clear that, with respect to judicial philosophy, the "burden of proof" was on the nominee to demonstrate his or her suitability for the Court and clearly lay out for us his or her methodology for interpreting the Constitution.

. . .

In my view, Judge Thomas has not met this burden. It is not that I know for certain that he will take the Court in troubling new directions; rather, it is that I have too many doubts about his judicial philosophy to be confident that he will not. . . .

. . .

ADDITIONAL VIEWS OF SENATOR METZENBAUM

. . .

A. RECORD AT THE EEOC

Clarence Thomas was chairman of the Equal Employment Opportunity Commission from 1982 to 1990. He was the chief law enforcement official responsible for protecting women, minorities, and the elderly from discrimination. But as Chairman of the EEOC, Judge Thomas pursued policies which undermined legal protections for minorities, women, and the elderly—the very people who are most in need of protection by the Supreme Court.

Judge Thomas' record with respect to age discrimination is particularly troubling. During his tenure as EEOC Chairman, thousands of older workers who believed that they were victims of age discrimination lost their right to bring age bias suits in Federal court because of the negligence of his agency. Despite assurance from Clarence Thomas that he would correct the problem, Congress found it necessary on two separate occasions—in 1988 and again in 1990—to pass legislation to restore the rights of these older workers to file age discrimination suits in Federal court.

Judge Thomas' record with respect to sex discrimination in employment is also particularly troubling. . . .

Judge Thomas' unrelenting hostility toward effective civil rights enforcement tools such as class action suits and affirmative action remedies hurt women and minorities. . . .

Judge Thomas' supporters suggest that his childhood experiences of surmounting poverty and segregation demonstrate that, if confirmed, he would show sensitivity and concern regarding civil rights cases that come before the Court. But Judge Thomas does not appear to have brought that experience to bear during his 8 years as the Nation's top civil rights law enforcement official. While Judge Thomas' background and life-story are both impressive and inspiring, his track record at the EEOC is the single best indicator of his approach to civil rights issues should he be confirmed for the Court.

. . .

B.   JUDGE THOMAS' LEGAL CREDENTIALS

Judge Clarence Thomas simply does not have the exceptional and distinguished legal credentials which one expects to find in a Supreme Court nominee. He practiced law for only 5 years, stopping at age 31. In his questionnaire, he did not identify a single case which he had argued in Federal court. By his own admission, he did not play a significant role in drafting any briefs filed by the EEOC during his tenure there. In addition, he does not have an extensive record of scholarship or expertise in an area of law, and he has served as a judge for a mere 17 months.

Julius Chambers, the director of the NAACP Legal Defense and Educational Fund, testified that Judge Thomas "does not meet the standards for elevation to the United States Supreme Court." The Legal Defense Fund reviewed the legal and related law and government experience of Judge Thomas and compared his credentials with those of the other 48 Justices who were appointed to the Court in this century. The NAACP Legal Defense Fund found that virtually every Supreme Court Justice appointed in the 20th century possessed at least two of seven basic qualifications for the Court.[32] The Legal Defense Fund found that, at this stage of his career, Judge Thomas has not yet shown any of these fundamental qualifications. The review noted that all but 8 of the 48 Justices in this century had at least 10 years experience practicing law. . . .

Judge Thomas' supporters recognize that his legal and judicial record are not strong reasons to vote in his favor. Accordingly, they stress his capacity for growth. I do not believe that Justices who need to grow into the job should be put on the Supreme Court. . . .

ADDITIONAL VIEWS OF SENATOR PATRICK J. LEAHY

. . .

THE SENATE SHOULD NOT CONSENT TO JUDGE THOMAS' NOMINATION.

After considering Judge Thomas' record and his testimony before this committee, I cannot consent to his nomination to be an Associate Justice of the Supreme Court. . . . After reviewing his past record and listening to his testimony, I am left with too many doubts to vote in favor of Judge Thomas' confirmation. I have doubts about his legal ability, which . . . is largely untested. I have doubts raised by his refusal

---

32. [Editors' Note: A footnote in the original report states that the Legal Defense Fund "identified the following seven basic qualifications: (1) a substantial law practice either in the private or public sector, generally covering more than 10 years, (2) extensive legal scholarship or teaching, (3) significant experience as a judge, generally for five or more years, (4) the highest level of expertise in a particular area of the law, (5) superior intellect, (6) ability to persuade and lead, and (7) generally outstanding achievement over the course of their career."]

to answer questions and his repeated disavowals of his earlier speeches and writings.

Furthermore, I have doubts about how Judge Thomas views the fundamental constitutional right to privacy, including a woman's right to choose. The most astonishing statement in these hearings was Judge Thomas' claim that he has never discussed the merits of *Roe v. Wade,* 410 U.S. 113 (1973), the most controversial Supreme Court case of the last quarter-century. Transcript of the Confirmation Hearings of Judge Clarence Thomas To Be an Associate Justice of the Supreme Court of the United States, hereinafter "Transcript," Sept. 11, 1991 at 102–05.

In the face of these doubts, the fact that Clarence Thomas is a fine person who has overcome what for many have been insurmountable obstacles is not a sufficient justification for a lifetime appointment to the Supreme Court.

. . .

. . . Judge Thomas' embrace of Lewis Lehrman's article—"The Declaration of Independence and the Right to Life"—was of particular concern to me. The consequence of Lehrman's thesis that a fetus has an inalienable right to life beginning at conception is that any termination of a pregnancy would constitute murder. . . .

Despite repeated questions from me and other members of the Committee, Judge Thomas did not categorically state that he disagreed with the Lehrman article. Instead, he explained that he invoked the article in his speech to a conservative audience to find "unifying principles in the area of civil rights" [Transcript, Sept. 11, 1991 at 96] and that he does "not endorse" Lehrman's conclusion. Transcript, September 13, 1991 at 21. . . .

. . . At the time Judge Thomas embraced the Lehrman article, did he understand its implications? Was he not sufficiently concerned about its conclusion to think twice about calling it a "splendid example" regardless of the audience he was trying to sway? . . .

[N]othing disturbed me more than Judge Thomas' statement that he has never discussed the merits of *Roe v. Wade* with anyone:

> SENATOR LEAHY. Judge, you were in law school at the time *Roe v. Wade* was decided. . . . You would accept, would you not, that in the last generation *Roe v. Wade* is certainly one of the more important cases to be decided by the U.S. Supreme Court.
>
> JUDGE THOMAS. I would accept that it has certainly been one of the more important, as well as one that has been one of the more highly publicized and debated cases.
>
> SENATOR LEAHY. So, . . . it would be safe to assume that when that came down, you were in law school [where] recent case law is oft[en] discussed, [and] that *Roe v. Wade* would have been discussed in the law school while you were there?

JUDGE THOMAS. The case that I remember being discussed most during my early part of law school was I believe ... *Griswold* ... and we may have touched on *Roe v. Wade* at some point and debated that, but let me add one point to that. Because I was a married student and I worked, I did not spend a lot of time around the law school doing what the other students enjoyed so much, and that is debating all the current cases and all of the slip opinions. My schedule was such that I went to classes and generally went to work and went home.

SENATOR LEAHY. Judge Thomas, I was a married law student who also worked, but I also found at least between classes that we did discuss some of the law, and I am sure you are not suggesting that there wasn't any discussion at any time of *Roe v. Wade?*

JUDGE THOMAS. Senator, I cannot remember personally engaging in those discussions.

SENATOR LEAHY. Have you ever had discussion of *Roe v. Wade,* other than in this room, in the 17 or 18 years it has been there?

JUDGE THOMAS. Only, I guess, Senator ... in the most general sense that other individuals express concerns one way or the other, and you listen and you try to be thoughtful. If you are asking me whether or not I have ever debated the contents of it, [the] answer to that is no, Senator.

SENATOR LEAHY. Have you ever, [in] private gatherings or otherwise, stated whether you felt that it was properly decided or not?

JUDGE THOMAS. Senator, in trying to recall and reflect on that, I don't recollect commenting one way or the other. There were, again, debates about it in various places, but I generally did not participate. I don't remember or recall participating, Senator.

SENATOR LEAHY. So you don't ever recall stating whether you thought it was properly decided or not?

JUDGE THOMAS. I can't recall saying one way or the other, Senator.

Transcript, September 11, 1991 at 102–05.

I have given a lot of thought to this exchange. It is deeply troubling. It is hard to believe that there is a thoughtful lawyer in this country— much less a federal judge or a nominee to the Supreme Court—who has not discussed or expressed his view on *Roe v. Wade.* ...

CONCLUSION

... I am left with too many doubts to vote in favor of Judge Thomas' confirmation. I am concerned that he lacks the legal wisdom and judicial experience necessary ... I am concerned about the differences between his hearing testimony and his prior speeches and writings. I am concerned by his refusal to answer significant and legitimate questions. Finally, . . . I am concerned that Judge Thomas will be a less than vigilant guardian of the fundamental right to privacy. . . .

ADDITIONAL VIEWS OF MESSRS. THURMOND, HATCH, SIMPSON, GRASSLEY AND BROWN

We strongly support Judge Clarence Thomas' nomination. . . .

JUDGE THOMAS' BACKGROUND AND QUALIFICATIONS

Judge Clarence Thomas was born June 23, 1948, in Pin Point, GA, a rural community near Savannah. His father left the family when Judge Thomas was still a small child. For the first years of his life Judge Thomas lived in a house with no indoor plumbing, moving at one point to a cramped tenement in Savannah. At the age of 7, he went to live with his maternal grandparents, Myers and Christine Anderson.

His grandfather, though barely literate, owned and managed an ice and fuel oil delivery business for which Judge Thomas worked after school. Mr. Anderson was also active in the local chapter of the NAACP. Judge Thomas learned many important lessons such as hard work and discipline from his grandparents and he has applied these lessons throughout his life.

The Andersons sent Judge Thomas to schools in Savannah, where he was taught by Franciscan nuns. The nuns underscored his grandparents' teaching about the importance of education.

In 1964, Judge Thomas transferred to St. John Vianney Minor Seminary near Savannah, where for most of the succeeding three years he was the only black student in his class. At this point in his life, Judge Thomas intended to become a priest. However, after spending several months at Immaculate Conception Seminary in Missouri, he changed his mind and transferred to Holy Cross College in Massachusetts. He supported his education through a combination of scholarships, loans, and jobs. He worked in the free breakfast program and tutored in the local community. He graduated with honors in 1971.

Judge Thomas then went to Yale Law School. While a law student, he worked summers for New Haven legal assistance and for a small civil rights law firm in Savannah. He graduated from law school in 1974.

Throughout his life, Judge Thomas has seized the opportunities that the American system offers to all. As Judge Thomas said on being nominated by President Bush, "only in America could this have been possible," for someone born in poverty and segregation to be nominated to the Supreme Court. In the President's words, Judge Thomas exemplifies "the endless possibilities of the American dream."

Judge Thomas' legal career is a long record of accomplishment. Most of his life he has been dedicated to public service. In 1974, John C. Danforth, then the attorney general of Missouri, hired him as an assistant attorney general. Judge Thomas practiced in both the trial and appellate courts, and argued several cases before the Missouri Supreme

Court. In 1977, he joined the legal staff of the Monsanto Co. where he was involved in matters relating to contracts, antitrust law, environmental regulation and products liability. In 1979, he became a legislative assistant to Senator Danforth.

In 1981, Judge Thomas was appointed by President Reagan to be the Assistant Secretary for Civil Rights at the United States Department of Education. One year later, he was again nominated by President Reagan to be the Chairman of the Equal Employment Opportunity Commission; he was reappointed to that position in 1986. The EEOC, an agency that employs more than 3100 persons and has an annual budget of $180 million, enforces title VII of the Civil Rights Act of 1964, which prohibits discrimination based on race, color, religion, sex, or national origin. The EEOC also enforces laws against discrimination based on age or disability. During Judge Thomas' tenure at the EEOC, he performed a management miracle, transforming an inefficient and dispirited agency into an effective and dynamic enforcer of the civil rights laws. Judge Thomas emphasized the need to provide specific relief for individual victims of discrimination. Judge Thomas' tenure as Chairman was the longest in the history of the Commission. A strong indication of the success of his tenure and the respect that he engendered among his coworkers is that the employees of the EEOC have named the Commission's new headquarters building after him.

On March 12, 1990, Judge Thomas assumed his present position on the United States Court of Appeals for the District of Columbia Circuit, to which he was appointed by President Bush. During his time on the bench, he has written opinions in such areas as criminal law, antitrust law and trade regulation, constitutional law, and administrative law. He has participated in more than 140 decisions of the court. His opinions have been lucid and scholarly. None of his decisions has been reversed, either by the District of Columbia Circuit en banc or by the Supreme Court.

Throughout his confirmation hearing, we believe that Judge Thomas demonstrated the qualifications of character necessary for an Associate Justice of the Supreme Court of the United States. As well, he is highly qualified professionally. Simply said, he is intelligent, decent, honest, openminded, and fair. He brings to his judicial office a willingness to listen, to consider, and to analyze carefully.

In addition to Judge Thomas being highly qualified, we believe that he will bring a unique perspective of life that has required him, as he stated, to "touch on virtually every aspect, every level of our country, from people who couldn't read and write to people who were extremely literate, from people who had no money to people who were very wealthy." (Tr., 9/12/91, at 59.) Members of this committee, from both sides of the aisle, have called the story of Judge Thomas' life "impressive and truly inspiring" (Tr. 9/10/91, at 44, remarks of Sen. Simpson); "admirable" (*id.*, at 18, remarks of Sen. Thurmond); and "an uplifting tale of a youth determined to surmount the barriers of poverty, segregation and discrimination" (*id.* at 53–54, remarks of Sen. Metzenbaum).

When Judge Thomas was before the Judiciary Committee regarding his nomination to be a judge of the U.S. Court of Appeals, he explained why he pursued the law as a profession:

> [T]he reason I became a lawyer was to make sure that minorities, individuals who did not have access to this society gained access. Now, I may differ with others as to how best to do that, but the objective has always been to include those who have been excluded.

. . .

No sitting Senator or other member of the Supreme Court has a background that is even remotely similar. Judge Thomas, as he has promised, would "bring to th[e] Court ... an understanding and the ability to stand in the shoes of other people across a broad spectrum of this country." (Tr., 9/12/91, at 59–60.) The Court—and the country—will benefit from that understanding.

PRESUMPTION IN FAVOR OF THE NOMINEE

We believe that the President's nominee to the Supreme Court comes before the Judiciary Committee and the Senate with a presumption in his or her favor.

... Presidential primacy in making judicial appointments is reflected in the structure of the Constitution itself: the appointment power is assigned in Article II's enumeration of executive powers, not in the legislative powers of article I. The advice and consent function was never intended to permit substitution of the Senate's judgment for the President's in determining who should be selected from among the qualified and fit. Performance of the Senate's duty in accordance with the Constitution requires that the Senate as a whole respect the President's preeminent role in this process by according the President's nominee a presumption of qualification, and fitness.

Of course, this presumption of fitness may be overcome in individual cases if a nominee's character is found to be seriously flawed, that a nominee lacks integrity or judicial temperament, or that a nominee is deficient in professional qualifications. In historical context, the Senate's role is properly viewed as a vigorous check against any "spirit of favoritism" and the appointment of "unfit characters." "The Federalist" No. 76 (J. Cooke ed. 1961), at 513. Short of such potentially disabling infirmities, the burden rests on those who would challenge the President's nominee to expose disqualifications to that nominee's confirmation.

As well, a nominee should not be rejected for any alleged failure to assure this committee about his or her positions on specific, controversial issues. Those who would have Judge Thomas demonstrate his fitness by meeting certain specific, substantive litmus tests misunderstand the role of the Senate in the advise and consent process. The failure to meet substantive standards would disqualify countless otherwise intelligent, fair, and capable individuals from serving on the Supreme Court.

These "burdens of proof," whether general or specific, represent an "unwarranted, and in our view inappropriate, attempt to redefine the roles of the President and the Senate as they are now defined in the Constitution." S. Exec. Rep. No. 32 at 75. We believe the imposition of such burdens threatens the integrity of the confirmation process, denigrates the dignity of the Supreme Court as an institution, and impugns the integrity of nominees to that Court as individuals.

. . .

JUDGE THOMAS WAS APPROPRIATELY RESPONSIVE TO THE COMMITTEE'S QUESTIONS

We believe that Judge Thomas responded openly, thoughtfully, and responsibly to the wide range of questions propounded to him during the hearings. Judge Thomas properly declined to express an opinion or position on particular issues that he could be required to resolve as a member of the Court or in his present role as a circuit judge. In this regard, he adhered to a long-standing tradition that is absolutely essential to the maintenance of an independent judiciary.

Judge Thomas was questioned extensively by some Committee members regarding his views on the various abortion-related issues raised by *Roe v. Wade* and its progeny. In all, Judge Thomas was asked more than ninety questions on the abortion issue. In response, Judge Thomas repeatedly explained the well-established principles that make such testimony improper. For example, in response to a question from Senator Leahy, Judge Thomas explained:

> [F]or me to respond to what my views are on those particular issues would really undermine my ability to be impartial in those cases. I have attempted to respond as candidly and openly as I possibly can, without in any way undermining or compromising my ability to rule on . . . these cases. (Tr., 9/11/91, at 99.)

If Supreme Court nominees could be forced to stake out their positions on the crucial legal issues of the day under the pressure of the confirmation process, the principle of judicial independence would be irreparably compromised. As former Chief Justice Burger explained the problem in a 1990 article:

> To expect a nominee to make commitments, or even to engage in substantive discussion of a case yet unseen, borders on the preposterous. . . . To call on a nominee for advance views as to questions that may come before the Court is really not unlike asking a potential juror how he or she will decide a particular case that the jury has not yet heard. A trial judge would reprimand a lawyer for such conduct. (Burger, "How Far Should the Questions Go?," Parade Magazine, Sept. 16, 1990, at 10, 14.)

Senator Hatch stressed Judge Thomas' current status as a sitting Federal judge when he raised his deep concerns on the subject of case-specific questioning:

> So, you are a sitting judge on one of the Nation's highest courts, and whatever the outcome of these hearings may be, you are still going to be a judge for the rest of your life, for the rest of your professional life, if you so choose to be.

> You simply do not have the freedom to answer every question as a sitting judge, every question that every Senator might have on this panel or might wish to be answered, and that goes for questions from both sides of the aisle, not just the other side of the aisle. (Tr. 9/12/91, at 87.)

These principles are fully consistent with the standard of responsiveness traditionally adopted by previous Supreme Court nominees. For example, Justice Thurgood Marshall was reticent in questioning during his confirmation hearing. Whereas today some believe the most controversial constitutional issues are the abortion issues raised by *Roe v. Wade*, at the time of Justice Marshall's confirmation hearings in 1967 the burning issue concerned the Supreme Court's decision in *Miranda v. Arizona* and related rulings expanding the rights of criminal suspects and defendants. Some Judiciary Committee members were just as anxious to extract Thurgood Marshall's views on *Miranda* in 1967 as some current committee Members are to learn Clarence Thomas' views on *Roe* today.

The exchanges on the *Miranda* decision between Thurgood Marshall and various Senators bear a remarkable resemblance to the questioning of Clarence Thomas with respect to *Roe v. Wade* and the abortion issue. In both instances, Senators pressed the nominee to disclose his views and opinions on a prominent holding that was certain to be revisited in future cases; in both instances the nominee steadfastly refused to compromise his capacity to participate impartially in such future cases by signalling his approach to such cases as a condition of confirmation; and in both cases the nominee was legally and ethically correct in resisting the pressure to telegraph his views.

Supreme Court nominees such as, Abe Fortas, Sandra Day O'Connor, Antonin Scalia, and David Souter consistently refused to answer questions on specific issues likely to come before the Court in future cases. In particular, nominees appearing before the Judiciary Committee in the "post-*Roe*" era have properly declined to respond to relentless efforts to elicit their views on the evolving and unsettled legal questions raised by the abortion controversy. . . .

———

The following statements by Senators Byrd and DeConcini were made on the floor of the Senate during a special three day Judiciary Committee hearing held to explore Professor Anita Hill's allegations of sexual harassment. Senator DeConcini's statement appears first because it summarizes the basic dispute in the beginning.

————

Statement of Senator DeConcini, 137 Cong. Rec. S14951–14953 (daily ed. Oct. 22, 1991)

THE NOMINATION OF JUDGE CLARENCE THOMAS

.   .   .

The Judiciary Committee has been highly criticized for its [failure to investigate and take] action on these allegations before the Judiciary Committee vote on September 27. Let me just say that many have lost sight of the condition of confidentiality that Professor Hill demanded of Chairman Biden. Ultimately, the decision of her confidentiality was taken from Professor Hill when her confidential statement to the chairman was leaked to the press. Unfortunately, the process that ensued has, I fear, scarred Judge Thomas and Professor Hill for life—they have both been through a dreadful ordeal.

.   .   .

The allegations of Professor Hill are extremely serious: That Judge Thomas sexually harassed her—that he used vile, demeaning, and disgusting language with her in conjunction with his quest to date her while she was employed by him.

Unfortunately, despite the extensive investigation and exhaustive hearings—amounting to 32 hours and 23 witnesses, the results are inconclusive.

Claims of sexual harassment are difficult to prove because there are often no witnesses. However, by the same token, those accused of sexual harassment have virtually no defense because they cannot prove a negative. The claims of Professor Hill are egregious but so too is the injustice perpetrated when we attempt to adjudicate a 10–year-old claim through a political process that deprives an accused of the most basic safeguards of due process and fairness.

For this Senator, the burden of proof was on the accuser, Professor Hill. In this country, it is a basic right of our legal system that the benefit of the doubt rests with the accused. These are very serious allegations of personal conduct. This is not a question of ideology or judicial philosophy. It is for that reason that these charges must meet the burden of proof that we afford every defendant in our legal system.

Granted, this was not a court of law with the rules of evidence and the usual protection for a defendant. But that does not lessen the need to require these allegations to overcome the presumption that Judge Thomas is not guilty of these allegations. And those who suggest that the burden of proof is not on Professor Hill would have to deny that Judge

Thomas was on trial this past week. Clearly Judge Thomas' integrity and reputation were on trial.

The evidence supporting the allegations of Professor Hill do not meet any reasonable burden of proof that they must overcome. The allegations cannot stand by themselves and what little supporting evidence that has been provided is inadequate.

. . .

I have not been convinced that Professor Hill's allegations occurred. And for that reason I cannot withdraw my support for the nomination of Judge Thomas to the U.S. Supreme Court. To do otherwise would open up the nominations process to all sorts of unsubstantiated allegations.

Professor Hill alleges that Clarence Thomas' sexual harassment commenced at the Office of Civil Rights for the Department of Education during the winter of 1981. In 1983, Clarence Thomas became the Chairman of the Equal Employment Opportunity Commission [EEOC]. Shortly thereafter, Anita Hill followed him to the EEOC. Professor Hill testified that after being subjected to his verbal assaults at the Office of Civil Rights she never sought alternative employment. Moreover, she asserted that when he left the Department of Education to become the Chairman of the EEOC that she would not have a job. Therefore, she had no recourse but to follow him to his new place of employment.

However, Ms. Berry, a personnel specialist at the Office of Civil Rights testified that as a "schedule A" employee Anita Hill had job security and was informed of her employment rights when she assumed the position. In addition, Mr. Singleton, Clarence Thomas' successor as the Assistant Secretary for the Office of Civil Rights, submitted an affidavit that stated that not only would Anita Hill continue to have a position she would have been able to maintain the same position that she occupied at the time of Clarence Thomas' departure. . . .

One victim of sexual harassment testified that it is not unusual for a victim of sexual harassment to follow her harasser. However, another victim of sexual harassment, Ms. Brown, moved me very deeply when she testified most passionately:

> Let me assure you that the last thing I would ever have done is follow the man who did this to a new job, call him on the phone or voluntarily share the same air space ever again.

The claims of Professor Hill portrayed a very dark side of Clarence Thomas, a side that had not previously surfaced through five FBI background investigations and heated confirmation hearings for Government positions. If this dark side of Clarence Thomas existed, surely someone other than Anita Hill would have seen it. . . .

Due to Clarence Thomas' conservative ideology, his previous confirmations have been highly contested—this is not a man who has eluded scrutiny but rather has been in the public eye for quite some time. Why is Professor Hill the only one who witnessed his cruelty and abuse?

Opponents of Clarence Thomas would say that Professor Hill is not alone; Angela Wright has also come forward, within the last week, and made allegations of sexual behavior in the office.

However, Angela Wright was fired by Clarence Thomas. By her own admission she was fired because she didn't accomplish the job that Clarence Thomas directed. Regarding her dismissal, Judge Thomas testified that he was dissatisfied with her job performance and he finally decided to fire her when she called someone a faggot, a slur that was unacceptable in the workplace. Moreover, after she came forward and requested to testify against Clarence Thomas she withdrew this request at the last minute. In my judgment, this places her credibility in serious doubt.

. . .

I know that many women believe that we in the Senate, and men in general just don't get it—we don't understand. I for one agree that few men can truly understand the quiet desperation experienced by victims of sexual harassment. However, I believe that we do get it. My mother was a victim of sexual harassment and was fired for rejecting her boss' sexual overtures. Believe me, as a son knowing what happened to his mother, I get it. The use of power in the workplace over women in order to extract sexual gratification is despicable and must not be tolerated. The victimization of women at work, at home, and in the streets, is something that must be stopped.

. . .

I believe that Judge Thomas and Professor Hill have been pawns in a calculated game staged by interest groups that believe that the ends justify the means. If these groups are successful in their objective of defeating Judge Thomas, then these groups are the only winners—and the price for them was cheap because Professor Hill, Judge Thomas, and the American public are picking up the tab. . . .

———

Statement of Senator Byrd, 137 Cong. Rec. S14630–14634 (daily ed. Oct. 15, 1991)

. . .

I have not previously spoken on this subject. I have indicated from the very beginning to the President and to one or two Senators—Senator Dole in particular—that it was my inclination to vote for the confirmation of Judge Thomas. And my inclination was based on my support of conservative nominees to the courts.

I believe that if there is to be a liberal body it should be the legislative body. I believe that the courts should be conservative. . . . I was impressed to hear Judge Thomas say . . . that he believed his role as a judge to be that of interpreting the Constitution and the laws of the United States, not that of rewriting or remaking the laws. I did not like the Warren court, and have so stated many times on this floor, because, in my view, it sought to fulfill the functions of the legislature instead.

I prepared a statement in support of the confirmation of Judge Thomas. And when I left the Hill on last Thursday evening, . . . I left my speech in support of Judge Thomas on my desk, prepared to state today that I was going to vote for Judge Thomas to be an Associate Justice on the U.S. Supreme Court.

. . .

I taped the testimony of Anita Hill, and I taped the testimony of Judge Thomas. I taped their appearances and I have replayed them.

. . .

Mr. President, I have concluded that I shall vote against the nomination of Judge Thomas.

. . .

. . . I believe Anita Hill. I believe what she said. I watched her on that screen intensely and I replayed, as I have already said, her appearance and her statement. I did not see on that face the knotted brow of satanic revenge. I did not see a face that was contorted with hate. I did not hear a voice that was tremulous with passion. I saw the face of a woman, 1 of 13 in a family of southern blacks who grew up on a farm and who early in her life belonged to the church, who belongs to the church today, and who was evidently reared by religious parents. We all saw her family as they came into the hearing room—the aging father, the kind mother, hugging their daughter, giving her solace and comfort in her hour of trial.

. . .

She was a reluctant witness. There are those who ask why did she not come forward in the previous confirmation hearings? She simply was not contacted in the previous hearings. They ask, why did she wait 10 years? . . . . She explained that she was reluctant to come forward, she explained that she did not want to go forward. She explained that she did not even want to be there in that large chamber in the Russell Building that day and at that time. She explained that she had spoken to other individuals very early on—1981, 1982, 1983, 1987—and those same persons came forward later in the hearings and corroborated the fact that she had, indeed, talked about this several years ago.

. . .

This woman was not fantasizing. As one who has lived a long life and who has had the opportunity to see many people in my life, in all walks of life, I think I have some ability to form an opinion of another person when I listen to that person, when I look into his eyes, to determine in my own view whether he may be fantasizing, whether he is out of his mind, whether he is some kind of nut, whether he is a psychopath. It comes through. None of that came through to me in Anita Hill's statements.

. . .

. . . To those who wish to think of a confirmation hearing as a court case, as having the surroundings and carrying the environment of trial, one may see things perhaps differently. This is not a court case. This is a confirmation hearing. . . .

Mr. President, what are my other reasons, aside from believing Anita Hill? I was offended by Judge Thomas' stonewalling the committee. He said he wanted to come back before the committee and clear his name. . . . Well, he was given the opportunity to clear his name, but he did not even listen to the principal witness, the only witness against him. He said he did not listen to her. He was "tired of lies."

What kind of judicial temperament does that demonstrate? He did not even listen to her. What Senator can imagine that, if he were the object of scrutiny in such a situation, he would not have listened to the witness so that he would know how best to respond, how to defend himself, how to clear his name? But, instead, Judge Thomas came back and said he did not even listen. He set up a wall when he did that, because it made it extremely difficult for members of the committee to ask him what he thought about this or that which she said?

. . .

I have substantial doubts after this episode about the judicial temperament of Judge Thomas, doubts that I did not have prior to last weekend's hearings. How can we have confidence if he is confirmed that he will be an objective judge, willing to decide cases based on the evidence presented if, in the one case that will matter most to him in his lifetime, he shut his eyes and closed his ears and closed his mind, and did not even bother to watch the sworn testimony of Anita Hill?

. . .

Another reason why I shall vote against Judge Thomas: He not only effectively stonewalled the committee; . . . he managed his own defense by charging that the committee proceeded to "high-tech lynchings of uppity blacks."

Mr. President, in my judgment, that was an attempt to shift ground. That was an attempt to fire the prejudices of race hatred, and shift the debate to a matter involving race.

I frankly was offended by his injection of racism into the hearings. This was a diversionary tactic intended to divert both the committee's and the American public's attention away from the issue at hand, the issue being, which one is telling the truth? . . .

So instead of focusing on the charges and attempting to be helpful to the committee in clearing his name, he invoked racism. Of course, he was embittered by the leak, and he was justified to so state. But, instead, he indicted the whole committee, he indicted the Senate, and he indicted the process. Not everybody in the Senate is guilty of leaking material. . . .

. . . I think it was blatant intimidation, and, I am sorry to say, I think it worked. I sat there and I wondered: Who is going to ask him some tough questions? Are they afraid of him?

He said to Senator Metzenbaum, "God is my judge; you are not my judge, Senator." Well of course, God is also my judge. I am not God. But I do have a vote. And I have a responsibility to make a determination as to how I shall vote. That kind of talk, that kind of arrogance will never get my vote.

. . .

[Sen. Byrd condemned leaks as "deplorable" and "reprehensible" and stated that he would vote to expel a Senator if the Senator leaked and would fire a staffer who did so.] But, [he noted,] there will always be leaks—always. But the unfortunate way in which this information has come to light should not be enough to cause us to disregard the possible relevancy . . . and the possible accuracy of a charge which so pertains to the character and the temperament of an individual being considered for this august and powerful position.

. . .

. . . Instead of making an effort to clear his name . . ., he shifted the blame to the process and to race prejudice.

I think it is preposterous. A black American woman was making the charge against a black American male. Where is the racism? Nonsense; nonsense!

. . .

Mr. President, this question of giving the benefit of the doubt, I have heard it said, well, if you have a doubt against this . . . then you should give the benefit of the doubt to Judge Thomas. He is the nominee.

Mr. President, of all the excuses for voting for Judge Thomas, I think that is the weakest one that I have heard. When are Senators going to learn that this proceeding is not being made in a court of law? This is not a civil case; it is not a criminal case wherein there are various standards of doubt, beyond a reasonable doubt, so on and so on; if you have a doubt, it should be given to Thomas.

Why? This is a confirmation process, not a court case. We are talking about someone who was nominated for one of the most powerful positions in this country. Some say, he will only be one of nine men. But suppose it is a divided Court, four to four in a given case. That one man will make the difference. Suppose it is a divided Court and he does not show up for some reason, he does not vote on a matter. A tie is in essence a decision in some cases.

. . .

Such an honor of sitting on the Supreme Court of the United States should be reserved for only those who are most qualified and those whose temperament and character best reflect judicial and personal commitments to excellence.

. . .

[H]e will be on that Court 30 years, if he lives out the psalmist's span of life. He will affect the lives of millions. He will make decisions which will impact on their ability to own a car or even to eat a Big Mac. Their liberty, their lives, their property, will be in his hands.

I realize it is possible that in the process a man could have been wronged. If it were a criminal trial, it would be different. That is what it is not.

. . .

... Let us not get all confused about what we are doing. This is a confirmation process. And if there is a doubt, I say resolve it in the interest of our country and its future, and in the interest of the Court. Let us not have a cloud of doubt for someone who is going to go on that court and be there for many years.

Perhaps we need to clean up the process if we can. But the "process" is a constitutional process, and it has done us well for over two centuries. And as far as I am concerned the benefit of the doubt will go to the Court and to my children and to my grandchildren and to my country.

5. The Nomination of Ruth Bader Ginsburg

On March 19, 1993, Justice Byron White announced that he would be resigning at the end of the 1992 Term. By making his announcement several months before the end of the term, Justice White gave the newly-elected President the luxury of several months of deliberation. When resignations are announced at the end of the Term, Presidents frequently feel pressure to nominate someone quickly so that there is enough time to have the confirmation hearings and seat the new appointee before the start of the next term on the first Monday of October.[33]

33. Occasionally, Justices give the President advance, confidential notice several months before they publicly announce their retirement at the end of the term. Justice Potter Stewart, for example, told President Reagan on April 21, 1981 that he intended to retire at the end of the term; the public was not informed until June 18 of that year. Ed Magnuson, *The Brethren's First Sister: A Supreme Court Nominee and A*

President Clinton took advantage of the time given him by White's early announcement and on June 14, 1993 nominated Judge Ruth Bader Ginsburg, Circuit Judge on the U.S. Court of Appeals for the D.C. Circuit (the same court from which Justices Scalia and Thomas had come). The ABA unanimously rated her "well qualified."[34]

After a relatively short period, the Senate began its confirmation hearings on July 20, 1993. Judge Ginsburg, in her opening statement, gave her view of the function of the public hearing.

_____

Nomination of Ruth Bader Ginsburg To Be Associate Justice of the Supreme Court of the United States: Hearings Before the S. Comm. on the Judiciary, 103d Cong. 55 (1993) (Prepared Statement of Judge Ginsburg)

. . .

You have been supplied, in the five weeks since the President announced my nomination, with hundreds of pages about me, and thousands of pages I have penned—my writings as a law teacher, mainly about procedure; ten years of briefs filed when I was a courtroom advocate of the equal stature of men and women before the law; numerous speeches and articles on that same theme; thirteen years of opinions—well over 700 of them—decisions I made as a member of the U.S. Court of Appeals for the District of Columbia Circuit; several comments on the roles of judges and lawyers in our legal system. That body of material, I know, has been examined by the Committee with care. It is the most tangible, reliable indicator of my attitude, outlook, approach, and style. I hope you will judge my qualifications principally on that written record spanning thirty-four years, and that you will find in it assurance that I am prepared to do the hard work, and to exercise the informed, independent judgment that Supreme Court decisionmaking entails.

I think of these proceedings much as I do of the division between the written record and briefs, on the one hand, and oral argument on the other hand, in appellate tribunals. The written record is by far the more important component in an appellate court's decisionmaking, but the oral argument often elicits helpful clarifications and concentrates the judges' minds on the character of the decision they are called upon to make.

There is, of course, this critical difference. You are well aware that I come to this proceeding to be judged as a judge, not as an advocate. Because I am and hope to continue to be a judge, it would be wrong for me to say or preview in this legislative chamber how I would cast my vote on questions the Supreme Court may be called upon to decide. Were

Triumph for Common Sense, Time Magazine, July 20, 1981, at 8.

34. Epstein, _Compendium, ABA Ratings, supra_ at 390.

I to rehearse here what I would say and how I would reason on such questions, I would act injudiciously.

Judges in our system are bound to decide concrete cases, not abstract issues; each case is based on particular facts and its decision should turn on those facts and the governing law, stated and explained in light of the particular arguments the parties or their representatives choose to present. A judge sworn to decide impartially can offer no forecasts, no hints, for that would show not only disregard for the specifics of the particular case, it would display disdain for the entire judicial process.

Similarly, because you are considering my capacity for independent judging, my personal views on how I would vote on a publicly debated issue were I in your shoes—were I a legislator—are not what you will be closely examining. As Justice Oliver Wendell Holmes counseled: "[O]ne of the most sacred duties of a judge is not to read [her] convictions into [the C]onstitution[]." I have tried, and I will continue to try, to follow the model Justice Holmes set in holding that duty sacred. . . .

———

After three days of hearing, appropriately described as a "love-fest," the Senate Judiciary Committee voted unanimously to recommend the confirmation of Judge Ginsburg. As one of the members of the Senate Judiciary Committee, Senator Howell Heflin, noted: "Back-slapping ha[d] replaced back-stabbing." Even Senator Strom Thurmond, who had voted against Ruth Ginsburg's confirmation to the U.S. Court of Appeals thirteen years earlier, agreed to this nomination. One week after the committee's vote, Judge Ginsburg was confirmed by the whole Senate by a vote of 96–3, joining Sandra Day O'Connor to become the second woman to serve on the Supreme Court.

In reading the following excerpts from the Report of the Judiciary Committee, examine Judge Ginsburg's method of dealing with the difficult question of how someone with a substantial track record who has written numerous controversial academic articles, legal briefs, and judicial opinions can answer substantive questions without impairing her ability to make independent judgments once on the high court. In particular, compare her answers regarding the death penalty with those regarding abortion.

Does Judge Ginsburg's successful confirmation process belie the predictions made after the hearings of Judge Bork and Judge Souter that henceforth only "stealth candidates" with little or no paper trails can be successfully confirmed? Or was this "love-fest" simply the result of a Democratic President facing a Democratic Senate? Or did it come about because, before nominating Judge Ginsburg, President Clinton consulted with Senator Hatch, the ranking Republican on the Senate Judiciary

Committee? Are there lessons that future Presidents and Senators can and should draw from this experience?

———

Nomination of Ruth Bader Ginsburg To Be an Associate Justice of the United States Supreme Court, S. Exec. Rep. No. 103–6, 103d Cong., 1st Sess. (1993)

Mr. BIDEN, from the Committee on the Judiciary,
submitted the following
REPORT
together with
ADDITIONAL VIEWS

The Committee on the Judiciary, to which was referred the nomination of Judge Ruth Bader Ginsburg to be an Associate Justice of the U.S. Supreme Court, having considered the same, reports favorably thereon, a quorum being present, by a vote of 18 yeas and 0 nays, with the recommendation that the nomination be approved. . . .

INTRODUCTION

The Senate Judiciary Committee unanimously recommends the confirmation of Judge Ruth Bader Ginsburg to be an Associate Justice of the U.S. Supreme Court. This unanimity results from two facts: First, Judge Ginsburg's qualifications and judicial temperament are indisputable. Second, and most important, Judge Ginsburg's extensive judicial record and style mark her as a true consensus candidate.

Judge Ginsburg is a nominee who holds a rich vision of what our Constitution's promises of liberty and equality mean, balanced by a measured approach to the job of judging. She accepts the Constitution as an evolving charter of government and liberty—as a limited grant of power *from* the people *to* the government—not a narrow list of enumerated rights. At the same time, she speaks and practices judicial restraint, understanding that a judge must work within our constitutional system—respecting history, precedent, and the respective roles of the other two branches.

The balance that Ruth Bader Ginsburg achieves—between her vision of what our society can and should become, and the limits on a judge's ability to hurry that evolution along—will serve her well on the Supreme Court.

· · ·

II. THE NOMINEE

Judge Ginsburg was born on March 15, 1933, in Brooklyn, NY. She received her bachelor of arts degree from Cornell University in 1954. Judge Ginsburg pursued her legal education, first at Harvard Law School and then at Columbia Law School, receiving her juris doctor in

1959. From 1959 to 1961, the nominee served as law clerk to Judge Edmund L. Palmieri, U.S. district court judge for the Southern District of New York. ... From 1966 to 1969 she was an associate professor and from 1969 to 1972, the nominee was a full professor at Rutgers. From 1972 to 1980, the nominee was a professor at Columbia University School of Law. From 1973 to 1974, she was a consultant to the U.S. Commission on Civil Rights. From 1972 to 1973, Judge Ginsburg was the director of the Women's Rights Project at the American Civil Liberties Union; from 1973 to 1980, she served as a general counsel....

In 1980, President Carter nominated Judge Ginsburg to the U.S. Court of Appeals for the District of Columbia. She has served on that court from 1980 to the present. President Clinton nominated her to the Supreme Court on June 14, 1993.

. . .

PART 2: JUDGE GINSBURG'S JUDICIAL PHILOSOPHY AND CONSTITUTIONAL METHODOLOGY

I. JUDGE GINSBURG BELIEVES THE CONSTITUTION IS AN EVOLVING DOCUMENT

Judge Ginsburg's written record and testimony before the committee amply demonstrate that she believes the Constitution is a living document that adjusts to modern notions of ordered society to retain its vitality. She rejects any formulation of original intent that would freeze the Constitution in time, limiting its broad clauses to situations specifically contemplated by the framers. For example, in a speech given to the Eighth Circuit Judicial Conference, she said:

> [A] too strict "jurisprudence of the framers' original intent seems to me unworkable, and not what Madison or Hamilton would espouse were they with us today. It cannot be, for example, that although the founding fathers never dreamed of the likes of Dolly Madison or even the redoubtable Abigail Adams ever serving on a jury, we would today say it is therefore necessary or proper to keep women off juries."

> We still have, cherish, and live under our eighteenth century Constitution because, through a combination of three factors or forces— change in society's practices, constitutional amendment, and judicial interpretation—a broadened system of participatory democracy has evolved, one in which we take just pride. (Ruth Bader Ginsburg, Remarks on Women Becoming Part of the Constitution, Address Before the Eighth Circuit Judicial Conference (July 17, 1987), in 6 Law & Ineq. J. 17, 17 (1988) [hereinafter cited as "Remarks"]).

Judge Ginsburg recognizes that our Constitution has grown from a document with a cramped view of "We, the People" to one increasingly inclusive of traditionally excluded social groups, including women and racial minorities. In her view, this evolution toward a more inclusive understanding of our Constitution's meaning is consistent with the broad intent of the framers. She believes that judges do their jobs properly when they act in accordance with the framers' "original understanding," but she does not find that "understanding" confining.

The nominee believes the framers understood that the Constitution would not remain static, constrained by the specific notions of the framers themselves. She believes they intended the Constitution to be subject to a careful process of extension—either through amendment, interpretation, or social practice. . . . Through the [historical] process . . . she describes, . . . the Constitution grew—ultimately abolishing slavery and giving women the right to vote through amendment, recognizing women's equality through interpretation, and eliminating most voting qualifications other than age and citizenship through a combination of amendment, legislation, and social convention.

The nominee further articulated her view of the framers' original understanding in testimony before the committee. Judge Ginsburg testified in response to a question from the Chairman:

> [T]he immediate implementation in the days of the Founding Fathers in many respects was limited. "We the People" was not then what it is today. The most eloquent speaker on that subject was Justice Thurgood Marshall when, during the series of Bicentennials when songs of praise of the Constitution were sung, he reminded us that the Constitution's immediate implementation, even its text, had certain limitations, blind spots, blots on our record. But he said that the beauty of this Constitution is that, through a combination of interpretation, constitutional amendment, laws passed by Congress, "We the People" has grown ever larger. So now it includes people who were once held in bondage. It includes women who were left out of the political community at the start.
>
> So I hope that begins to answer your question. The view of the Framers, their large view, I think was expansive. Their immediate view was tied to the circumstances in which they lived. (Transcript, July 20, at 112.)

When Senator Hatch asked the nominee whether she agreed with the statement, "the only legitimate way for a judge to go about defining the law is by attempting to discern what those who made the law intended," the nominee replied:

> I think all people could agree with that, but as I tried to say in response to the Chairman . . ., trying to divine what the Framers long ago intended, at least I have to look at that two ways. One is what they might have intended immediately for their day, and one is their larger expectation that the Constitution was meant to govern, not for the passing hour, but for the expanding future. And I know no better illustration of that than to take the great man who wrote the Declaration of Independence, who also said, for our state, a pure democracy, there would still be excluded from our deliberations women who, to prevent depravation of morals or ambiguity of issues, should not mix promiscuously in gatherings of men.

Now I do believe that Thomas Jefferson, were he alive today, would say that women are equal citizens. ... So I see an immediate intent about how an ideal is going to be recognized at a given time and place, but a larger aspiration as our society improves. I think the Framers were intending to create a more perfect union that would become ever more perfect over time. (Transcript, July 20, at 131–32).

In short, Judge Ginsburg believes that the effort to divine the framers' specific original intent is an appropriate starting point in constitutional review, but she rejects the notion that the inquiry ends where it begins.

II.   JUDGE GINSBURG ADVOCATES JUDICIAL RESTRAINT

One theme that emerged from the committee's extensive review of Judge Ginsburg's written record, as well as her testimony, is her belief in a judicial branch that moves incrementally. A careful adherent to a case-by-case method of gradual evolution in the law, Judge Ginsburg believes the Court should move in "measured motions." This view is exemplified by the following testimony from her opening statement:

My approach [to judging], I believe, is neither liberal nor conservative. Rather, it is rooted in the place of the judiciary, of judges, in our democratic society. The Constitution's preamble speaks first of "We, the People," and then of their elected representatives. The judiciary is third in line and it is placed apart from the political fray so that its members can judge fairly, impartially, in accordance with the law, and without fear about the animosity of any pressure group.

In Alexander Hamilton's words, the mission of judges is "to secure a steady, upright, and impartial administration of the laws." I would add that the judge should carry out that function without fanfare. She should decide the case before her without reaching out to cover cases not yet seen. She should be ever mindful, as Judge and then Justice Benjamin Nathan Cardozo said, "Justice is not to be taken by storm. She is to be wooed by slow advances." (Transcript, July 20 at 91–92.)

Judge Ginsburg has written extensively about how the judicial branch should take incremental steps, allowing legislatures and society to address and respond to court-ordered changes. In her Madison Lecture, ... [she] wrote, "[W]ithout taking giant strides and thereby risking a backlash too forceful to contain, the Court, through constitutional adjudication, can reinforce or signal a green light for a social change." (Madison Lecture at 36–37.)

As an example of this process at work, the nominee cited the gender equality cases of the 1970's, from *Reed v. Reed,* 404 U.S. 71 (1971), through *Craig v. Boren,* 429 U.S. 190 (1976). Prior to *Reed,* the Supreme Court had never found gender discrimination unconstitutional under the 14th amendment. In this line of cases, however, the Court developed a new theory of gender equality under the Constitution—ultimately concluding in *Craig* that gender classifications would be subjected to an intermediate standard of equal protection scrutiny.... The nominee wrote of this development:

> For the most part, the Court was neither out in front of, nor did it hold back, social change. Instead, what occurred was what engineers might call a "positive feedback" process, with the Court functioning as an amplifier—sensitively responding to, and perhaps moderately accelerating, the pace of change, change toward shared participation by members of both sexes in our nation's economic and social life. (Remarks at 24.)

· · ·

At least in part, Judge Ginsburg's prescription for cautious judicial advances reflects a recognition of the limitations under which the Court operates. The judiciary lacks a "sword" with which to enforce its pronouncements [as she has written about]....

III.   JUDGE GINSBURG ACKNOWLEDGES THAT COURTS MUST ACT BOLDLY WHERE THE POLITICAL PROCESS WILL NOT ADMIT CONSTITUTIONALLY NECESSARY CHANGE

In her Madison Lecture, Judge Ginsburg wrote:

> I do not suggest that the Court should never step ahead of the political branches in pursuit of a constitutional precept. *Brown v. Board of Education* [347 U.S. 483], the 1954 decision declaring racial segregation in public schools offensive to the equal protection principle, is the case that best fits the bill. Past the midpoint of the twentieth century, apartheid remained the law enforcement system in several states, shielded by a constitutional interpretation the Court itself advanced at the turn of the century—the 'separate but equal' doctrine. (Madison Lecture at 33–34 (footnotes omitted).)

She wrote that "prospects in 1954 for dismantling racially segregated schools were bleak." (Madison Lecture at 34.) To paraphrase her argument: political actors were unlikely to be moved to desegregate the schools because a national consensus to support such bold legislative initiatives was lacking.

... Judge Ginsburg suggests that judges walk a fine line. In the context of discussing her litigation attacking laws that discriminated based on gender, she wrote, "Challenges to [gender-based] laws put the courts in the sticky marshland between constitutional *interpretation* in our system, a proper judicial task, and constitutional *amendment,* a job reserved to the people's elected representatives." (Ginsburg, The Meaning and Purpose of the Equal Rights Amendment, Address Before the Colloquim on Legislation for Women's Rights, Oosterbeek, Netherlands 10 (September 27, 1979) [hereinafter, Meaning and Purpose].)

· · ·

During the hearing, the chairman asked the nominee to reconcile her position that courts must move incrementally with her support for a case like *Brown* where the Court took a bold step. In response, the nominee first reconciled her approval of *Brown* with her view of judicial restraint by pointing out that *Brown* "wasn't born in a day," even though it produced change "perhaps a generation before state legislators in our southern states would have budged on the issue." (Meaning and Purpose at 2.) Judge Ginsburg testified:

> Thurgood Marshall came to the Court showing it wasn't equal, in case after case, in four cases, at least, before he wanted to put that before the Court, *Sweatt v. Painter,* [339 U.S. 629 (1950)], *McLaurin* [*v. Oklahoma State Regents,* 339 U.S. 637 (1950)], *Gaines* [*v. Canada,* 305 U.S. 337 (1938)]. He set the building blocks, until it was obvious to everyone that separate couldn't be equal.
>
> . . .
>
> But *Brown* itself . . . didn't say racial segregation . . . is going to be ended [root and] branch by one decision. *Brown* was in 1954, and it wasn't until *Loving v. Virginia* [388 U.S. 1] in 1967 that the job was over, even at the Supreme Court level, even at the declaration level. (Transcript, July 20, at 123–124.)
>
> . . .

Senator DeConcini pursued this issue in an effort to discern the methodology she would employ to recognize a case in which it is appropriate for the Court to lead society. The nominee stated, "[W]hen political avenues become dead-end streets judicial intervention in the politics of the people may be essential in order to have effective politics." (Transcript, July 21, at 13.) She gave as an example the legislative reapportionment case of *Baker v. Carr,* 369 U.S. 186 (1962), in which the Court established the principle of one person, one vote. . . .

IV.   JUDGE GINSBURG'S THEORY OF *STARE DECISIS*

The committee is satisfied that Judge Ginsburg holds an appropriate respect for the principle of *stare decisis* and abiding understanding of the value of precedent. At the same time, she recognizes the importance of achieving the correct result in matters of constitutional interpretation, where the Court is the final arbiter. She distinguishes the somewhat diminished importance of *stare decisis* in the constitutional context from statutory interpretation, when stability becomes more important and errors by courts can be corrected by legislatures. . . .

Judge Ginsburg rejects the view of some theorists that the doctrine of *stare decisis* is of less importance in areas such as criminal law. These theorists believe *stare decisis* applies with the most force with respect to contract or property rights, where, according to the theory, stability is more important because of the public's reliance on settled law.

. . .

Judge Ginsburg's testimony in other contexts exemplified her respect for precedent and inclination to adhere to the principle of *stare decisis.* She agreed with Senator Hatch's assertion that the abortion funding cases of *Maher v. Roe,* 432 U.S. 464 (1997), and *Harris v. McRae,* 448 U.S. 297 (1980), were the Supreme Court's precedent. She stated that she had no "agenda to displace them." (Transcript, July 22, at 28.) Likewise, in response to Senator Grassley, she expressed the view that the Supreme Court's decision in *Planned Parenthood v. Casey,* 112 S.Ct. 2791 (1992), reflected the importance of precedent. . . .

PART 3: JUDGE GINSBURG'S VIEWS ON UNENUMERATED RIGHTS, PRIVACY, AND REPRODUCTIVE FREEDOM

. . .

Judge Ginsburg's testimony and writings on unenumerated rights, the right of privacy, and reproductive freedom set her apart from all other recent nominees to the Supreme Court. Judge Ginsburg enthusiastically embraced the concept of unenumerated rights and the right of privacy. She also forthrightly supported a woman's right to reproductive freedom, under either a privacy or an equal protection analysis.

I. JUDGE GINSBURG EMBRACED THE CONCEPT OF UNENUMERATED RIGHTS, INCLUDING A RIGHT OF PRIVACY

. . .

In clear and unequivocal terms, Judge Ginsburg expressed support for and appreciation of the concept of unenumerated rights—the view that each American citizen has rights independent of and apart from those specifically listed in the Constitution. She stated, in response to the very first question of the hearings, by Chairman Biden:

> I think the Framers are shortchanged if we view them as having a limited view of rights, because they wrote, Thomas Jefferson wrote, 'We hold these truths to be self-evident, that all men are created equal, that they are endowed by their Creator with certain inalienable rights, that among these'—among these—'are life, liberty, and the pursuit of happiness,' and that Government is formed to protect and secure those rights.

> Now when the Constitution was written, as you know, there was much concern over a Bill of Rights. There were some who thought a Bill of Rights dangerous because one couldn't enumerate all the rights of the people; one couldn't compose a complete catalogue. . . .

> But there was a sufficient call for a Bill of Rights, and so the Framers put down what was in the front of their minds in the Bill of Rights.

> . . . And then . . . the Framers were fearful that this limited catalogue might be understood, even though it is written as a restriction on Government rather than a conferring of rights of people, that it might be understood as skimpy, as not stating everything that is.

And so we do have the Ninth Amendment stating that the Constitution shall not be construed to deny or disparage other rights. So the Constitution ... the whole thrust of it is people have rights, and Government must be kept from trampling on them. (Transcript, July 20, at 110–11.)

Judge Ginsburg here compared the American Constitution to the French Declaration of the Rights of Man, which confers rights, rather than restricting government, and thus (unlike the Constitution) presupposes a world in which citizens have no rights other than those specifically given. (Transcript, July 20, at 111.)

· · ·

Judge Ginsburg testified that in determining whether an asserted unenumerated right is protected by the Constitution—in particular, by the broadly worded Due Process Clause of the 14th Amendment—she would follow the approach articulated by Justice Harlan in *Poe v. Ullman,* 367 U.S. 497 (1961), and by Justice Powell in *Moore v. City of East Cleveland,* 431 U.S. 494 (1977).

Justice Harlan wrote in *Poe,* in arguing for a flexible conception of due process, not limited by the specific rights granted elsewhere in the Constitution:

> Due process has not been reduced to any formula; its content cannot be determined by reference to any code. The best that can be said is that through the course of this Court's decisions it has represented the balance which our Nation, built upon the postulates of respect for the liberty of the individual, has struck between that liberty and the demands of organized society. If the supplying of content to this Constitutional concept has of necessity been a rational process, it has certainly not been one where judges have felt free to roam where unguided speculation might take them. The balance of which I speak is the balance struck by this country, having regard to what history teaches are the traditions from which it developed as well as the traditions from which it broke. That tradition is a living thing. A decision of this Court which radically departs from it could not long survive, while a decision which builds on what has survived is likely to be sound. No formula could serve as a substitute, in this area, for judgment and restraint. (367 U.S. at 542 (Harlan, J., dissenting).)

Judge Ginsburg testified that "I associate myself with *Poe v. Ullman* and the method that is revealed most completely by Justice Harlan in that opinion." (Transcript, July 22, at 62.)

· · ·

Significantly, Judge Ginsburg rejected the method adopted by Justice Scalia to identify interests protected by the Due Process Clause. . . . in ... *Michael H. v. Gerald D.,* 491 U.S. 110, 127, n. 6 (1989)[.] ... In response to a question from Chairman Biden, Judge Ginsburg associated herself with the views of Justices O'Connor and Kennedy on this subject, as opposed to those of Justice Scalia.

. . .

In adopting Justice Harlan's approach, and rejecting Justice Scalia's, Judge Ginsburg has selected a method for identifying unenumerated rights in keeping with the Constitution's majestic and capacious language. As Justices O'Connor and Kennedy recognized in *Michael H.,* "requiring specific approval from history before protecting anything in the name of liberty" effectively "squashes . . . freedom." 491 U.S. at 132. It is Justice Harlan's approach—an approach of measured change and rooted evolution—that comports with both the intent and the draftsmanship of the Constitution. Judge Ginsburg's embrace of this approach provides excellent reason to support her.

. . .

Judge Ginsburg's testimony left no doubt that she supports the Supreme Court's recognition of a general, unenumerated right to privacy. Her views were evident in an exchange with Senator Leahy:

SENATOR LEAHY. Is there a constitutional right to privacy?

JUDGE GINSBURG. There is a constitutional right to privacy which consists I think of at least two distinguishable parts. One is the privacy expressed most vividly in the Fourth Amendment, that is the government shall not break into my home or my office, without a warrant, based on probable cause; the government shall leave me alone.

The other is the notion of personal autonomy; the government shall not make my decisions for me; I shall make, as an individual, uninhibited, uncontrolled by my government, the decisions that affect my life's course. Yes, I think that whether it has been lumped under the label, privacy is a constitutional right, and it has those two elements, the right to be let alone and the right to make basic decisions about one's life course. (Transcript, July 21, at 54–55.)

. . .

. . . In response to a question of the chairman, Judge Ginsburg stated:

The line of cases that you just outlined, the right to marry, the right to procreate or not, the right to raise one's children, the degree of justification that the State has to have to interfere with that is very considerable. (Transcript, July 22, at 53.)

Judge Ginsburg thus indicated that the right to privacy protected by the Constitution is a right of real meaning and consequence.

Judge Ginsburg's willing acknowledgment of the right to privacy, her characterization of the strength of that right, and most of all, her understanding of the values underlying that right—all of these set Judge Ginsburg apart from most recent nominees to the Supreme Court. . . .

II. JUDGE GINSBURG SUPPORTS THE RIGHT OF
WOMEN TO REPRODUCTIVE FREEDOM

. . .

The premise of [Judge Ginsburg's] Madison Lecture is that the Constitution protects in some measure the right of women to choose for themselves whether or not to terminate a pregnancy. Judge Ginsburg thus wrote that the Court should have struck down the extreme anti-abortion law under review in *Roe v. Wade*—a law she characterized as "intolerably shackl[ing] a woman's autonomy." (Madison Lecture at 23.)

Similarly, in her testimony, Judge Ginsburg left no doubt of her conviction that the Constitution protects the right to choose. In her most strikingly articulated of many statements on the issue, Judge Ginsburg told Senator Brown:

This is something central to a woman's life, to her dignity. It is a decision that she must make for herself. And when government controls that decision for her, she is being treated as less than a fully adult human responsible for her own choices. (Transcript, July 21, at 106.)

In response to another question of Senator Brown, exploring whether fathers may have rights relating to the decision to terminate a pregnancy, Judge Ginsburg added that "in the end it's [a woman's] body, her life. . . . [I]t is essential . . . that she be the decision maker, that her choice be controlling." (Transcript, July 21, at 108.)

In the Madison Lecture, Judge Ginsburg seemed to argue that the right to terminate a pregnancy arose from the equal protection guarantee, rather than from the right to privacy. . . .

In her testimony, Judge Ginsburg repeatedly stated that her emphasis on the equality aspect of reproductive freedoms was meant to supplement, rather than supplant, the traditional privacy rationale for the right to terminate a pregnancy. This point emerges clearly in the following exchange between Judge Ginsburg and Senator Feinstein:

SENATOR FEINSTEIN. If I understand what you are saying you are saying that *Roe* could have been decided on equal protection grounds rather than the fundamental right to privacy. . . .

JUDGE GINSBURG. Yes, Senator, except in one respect. I never made it either/or. . . . I have always said both, that the equal protection strand should join together with the autonomy of decision making strand; so that it wasn't a question of equal protection or personal autonomy, it was a question of both.

. . .

So I would have added another underpinning, one that I thought was at least as strong, perhaps stronger. But it was never equal protection rather than personal autonomy. It was both. (Transcript, July 21, at 193–94.)

. . .

Judge Ginsburg's effort to highlight the equality dimension of reproductive freedoms thus serves to enhance, rather than diminish, these important rights. Judge Ginsburg's analysis focuses on an aspect of reproductive rights the Court recently hinted at in *Casey v. Planned Parenthood*—the effect of these rights on the status of women in our society. In Judge Ginsburg's view, this analysis need not result in a weaker level of constitutional scrutiny than that demanded by the Court in *Roe.* It is true that gender discrimination currently receives only intermediate scrutiny, whereas the recognition of a fundamental right of privacy, as occurred in *Roe,* provokes strict scrutiny. But Judge Ginsburg made clear that equality is but one aspect of reproductive freedom; and she further noted on several occasions that the Court may yet hold sex distinctions to demand strict scrutiny.

In another aspect of her Madison Lecture, as well as in an earlier article, Judge Ginsburg suggested that the Court in *Roe* went too far too fast—that it should have struck down only the extreme anti-abortion law before it, leaving for another day the question of the constitutionality of other, more moderate abortion restrictions. Such an approach, Judge Ginsburg posited in the Madison Lecture, "might have served to reduce, rather than to fuel controversy." (Madison Lecture at 23.) According to Ginsburg, quoting *Roe* itself, "there was a marked trend in state legislatures 'toward liberalization of abortion statutes.'" (*Id.* at 32 (footnote omitted).) If *Roe* had limited its ruling—if it had, in Judge Ginsburg's words, "invited ... dialogue with legislators"—that trend might well have continued. (*Id.*) By issuing its decision in *Roe,* Ginsburg argued, the Court halted this process, provoked popular backlash, and "prolonged divisiveness." (*Id.* at 37.)

Senator Metzenbaum and Judge Ginsburg engaged in an exchange on this subject:

> Senator Metzenbaum. Would you not have had some concern, or do you not have some concern, that had the gradualism been the reality, that many more women would have been denied an abortion or would have been forced into an illegal abortion and possibly an unsafe abortion?
>
> Judge Ginsburg. Senator, we can't see what the past might have been like. I wrote an article that was engaging in what if. I expressed the view that if the Court had simply done what courts usually do, stuck to the very case before it and gone no further, then there might have been a change, gradual changes.

. . .

There was the one thing that one can say for sure: There was a massive attack on *Roe v. Wade.* It was a single target to hit at. I think two things happened. One is that a movement that had been very vigorous became relaxed. . . .

So one side seemed to relax its energy, while the other side had a single target around which to rally, but that is my 'what if,' and I could be wrong about that. My view was that the people would have accepted, would have expressed themselves in an enduring way on this question. And as I said this is a matter of speculation, this is my view of what if. Other people can have a different view. (Transcript, July 20, at 183–84.)

. . .

Questions remain open as to the approach Judge Ginsburg would follow, if confirmed, in cases soon to come before the Court involving abortion regulations. Judge Ginsburg, in responding to questions posed by Senator Metzenbaum, would not comment on whether the right to choose remains a fundamental right after *Casey;* neither would she comment on the level of scrutiny that should be applied to abortion regulations or on the permissibility of any particular regulations. (Transcript, July 20, at 184–85; July 21 at 196.) These questions are of obvious importance with respect to the future scope of reproductive freedoms.

But the committee knows far more about Judge Ginsburg's views on reproductive rights than it has known about any previous nominee's. Judge Ginsburg's record and testimony suggest both a broad commitment to reproductive freedoms and a deep appreciation of the equality and autonomy values underlying them.

PART 4: JUDGE GINSBURG'S VIEWS ON EQUAL PROTECTION AND CIVIL RIGHTS

. . . As a lawyer, [Judge Ginsburg] led the effort to bring women within the coverage of the equal rights clause of the 14th amendment. Her continued work in the field, as a scholar and a judge, and her testimony before the committee evidences Judge Ginsburg's deep and principled commitment to the ideal of equal protection of the laws.

I.   Judge Ginsburg's Career Marks Her as a Leading Scholar
and Advocate in the Area of Equal Protection

A.   *Judge Ginsburg's record as an advocate*

Before her appointment to the circuit court, Judge Ginsburg worked as an advocate to provide women with equal protection of the laws. Her work is justly renowned. As much as any other advocate, Judge Ginsburg is responsible for the celebrated Supreme Court decisions of the 1970's guaranteeing women's rights—decisions which still comprise the mass of governing constitutional law in this area. . . .

B.   *Sex discrimination* . . .

In [her scholarship and advocacy], Judge Ginsburg has made the case for treating women as full and equal citizens under the laws and Constitution. She describes the injury to *both* sexes from unequal treatment based on gender stereotypes. As an advocate, Judge Ginsburg often selected cases in which the gender differential most obviously penalized men, as a way of awakening an all-male bench to the reality of harm. Tradition portrayed these sex-based classifications as shelters for women, but Judge Ginsburg insisted that this portrayal was flawed. She explained how stereotypical thinking tends to become self-fulfilling, as when a law offers women fewer employment opportunities in the name of protection, but in reality serves to bar women from economic equality and independence.

.   .   .

A recent criticism of Judge Ginsburg's approach asserts that formal equality under the laws will not serve to achieve real equality for women. This criticism contends that Judge Ginsburg and others of her generation have not appreciated that sex-based laws can benefit women, whose different situation—both biological and social—demands not identical but different treatment.

Senator Specter spelled out this scholarly criticism and asked Judge Ginsburg for her reaction to it. Judge Ginsburg said that "[w]hat you discuss, Senator Specter, I think reflects largely a generation[al] difference." (Transcript, July 21, at 70.) She stated that she continues to bring "a certain skepticism" to supposed legislative protection of women. Judge Ginsburg observed, for example, that in the hearing room "most of the faces that I see are not women's faces." (*Id.*) Judge Ginsburg explained that she would moderate her skepticism about special legislative protection for women "if the legislature were just filled with women and maybe one or two men." (*Id.* at 70–71.)

In her testimony, Judge Ginsburg repeatedly mentioned the possibility of applying a "strict scrutiny" standard of review to gender-based distinctions, rather than the current intermediate standard. Use of a strict scrutiny standard would represent a significant doctrinal shift, making almost all sex-based distinctions unlawful.... Judge Ginsburg did not specifically advocate this change. But her remarks suggest her openness to its consideration.

Judge Ginsburg told the committee that the Court had not settled the question of whether strict scrutiny should apply to gender-based distinctions:

> [H]eightened scrutiny, as I said before, for sex classifications is not necessarily the stopping point, as O'Connor made clear in the *Mississippi University For Women* case. [*Mississippi University For Women v. Hogan*, 458 U.S. 718 (1982).] Sex as a suspect classification remains open.... [T]he Court has left that question open, and it may get there. (Transcript, July 21, at 195; see also Transcript, July 20, at 123; Transcript, July 22, at 185–91.)

Here, Judge Ginsburg refers to a suggestive footnote in *Mississippi University For Women* (1982), in which the Court concluded: "We need not decide whether classifications based upon gender are inherently suspect." 458 U.S. at 724 n. 9.

Most observers ... have instead accepted the view that the Supreme Court in the 1976 case of *Craig v. Boren* decided that a middle-tier standard is appropriate for gender cases. *See* 429 U.S. at 190. This conclusion seems particularly valid in light of the Supreme Court's reiteration of the *Craig* standard in *Heckler v. Mathews,* 465 U.S. 728 (1984)—2 years *after* its 1982 footnote in *Mississippi University For Women.* 458 U.S. at 724 n. 9. The Supreme Court then described the middle tier standard as "firmly established." . . . .

Judge Ginsburg's testimony, highlighting the *Mississippi University for Women* footnote, thus seems to indicate her openness to continue doctrinal change—in particular, heightening the scrutiny for gender-based distinctions. . . . Still, Judge Ginsburg declined to commit herself definitively when Senator DeConcini pressed her about whether "strict scrutiny should be the beginning point on any gender issue brought before the Court." (*Id.*).

C. Race discrimination and affirmative action

Judge Ginsburg's record and testimony demonstrate an awareness of the lingering effects of our national history of racism and racial discrimination. She also accepts the continued need to remedy the effects of racial discrimination in appropriate cases. She offered no hints of how she would rule in specific cases, but her testimony expressed support for continued efforts to root out discrimination. . . .

. . .

Under questioning by Senator Simon during the confirmation hearing, Judge Ginsburg ... cited approvingly Justice Powell's opinion in the landmark case of *University of California Bd. of Regents v. Bakke,* 438 U.S. 265 (1978) in which the Court affirmed the right of governmental entities to take race into account for certain purposes in a way consistent with the equal protection clause ... [which had held] that a governmental actor might well offer a sufficient rationale for an affirmative action program ... not specifically tied to past discrimination. Asked by Senator Simon whether she had any philosophical objection to the use of set-asides, the nominee stated:

> [I]n many of these cases, there really is underlying discrimination, but it's not easy to prove, and sometimes it would be better for society if we didn't push people to the wall and make them say, yes, I was a discriminator, that the kind of settlement that is encouraged in these plans is a better, healthier thing for society than to make everything fiercely adversarial, so that it becomes very costly and bitter.
>
> [R]ather than make it a knockdown-drag-out fight, it would be better for there to be this voluntary action, always taking into account that there is an interest, as there was in the *O'Donnell* case, of the people who say but why me, why should I be the one made to

pay, I didn't engage in past discrimination, and that's why these things must be approached with understanding and care. (Transcript, July 21, at 133–34.)

Under questioning by Senator Feinstein, the nominee expressed a preference for goals and timetables, rather than rigid quotas.... Her record and testimony document Judge Ginsburg's recognition of the continued reality of race and sex discrimination, both overt and subtle. She has demonstrated an open-minded approach to finding solutions for this ongoing national problem.

D. Discrimination based on sexual orientation

The nominee did not indicate in any way how she might rule on the assertion that discrimination based on sexual orientation violates the Constitution. She refused to comment on the issue in response to Senators Thurmond, Brown, and Cohen on the grounds that the question would undoubtedly come before the Court. (See Transcript, July 20, at 177; Transcript, July 22, at 191–92; Transcript, July 22, at 146.)

In her testimony, the nominee spoke broadly about our country's abhorrence of discrimination of any sort, including discrimination based on sexual orientation. In response to a question by Senator Kennedy, she said, "I think rank discrimination against anyone is against the tradition of the United States and is to be deplored. Rank discrimination is not part of our nation's culture. Tolerance is, and a generous respect for differences based on—this country is great because of its accommodation of diversity." (Transcript, July 22, at 10–11; see also *id.* at 146 (questioning by Senator Cohen).)

.   .   .

PART 10: JUDGE GINSBURG'S VIEWS ON CRIMINAL LAW AND PROCEDURE

.   .   .

Judge Ginsburg has never ruled on death penalty questions and, like Justice Kennedy before her, declined to take a firm position on these questions during the hearing. (See Hearings on nomination of Anthony Kennedy, Tr. 12/15/87, at 208, where then Judge Kennedy refused to discuss the constitutionality of the death penalty on the ground that the issue involved a "constitutional debate of ongoing dimension.") Judge Ginsburg stated in response to questioning by Senator Hatch:

At least since 1976, the Supreme Court, by large majorities, has rejected the position that the death penalty under any and all circumstances is unconstitutional. I recognize that there is no judge on the Court that takes the position that the death penalty is unconstitutional under any and all circumstances....

There are many questions left unresolved. They are coming constantly before that Court.... I can tell you that I do not have a closed mind on this subject. I don't want to commit—I don't think it would be consistent with the line I have tried to hold to tell you that I will definitely accept or definitely reject any position. I can tell you that I am well aware of the precedent, and I have already expressed my views on the value of precedent. (Transcript, July 22, at 16.)

. . .

Conclusion

... The record amply demonstrates that Ruth Bader Ginsburg merits the support of the committee and the entire Senate.

Some members of the committee have expressed concern that Judge Ginsburg answered fewer questions during the hearings than they would have liked. But a careful comparison of Judge Ginsburg's answers with those of other recent nominees reveals that Judge Ginsburg supplies as much—or more—information about her views as anyone who has appeared before the committee in the last 5 years. During the course of her testimony, Judge Ginsburg in fact told the committee a great deal. . . .

Judge Ginsburg's refusal to answer all the committee's questions also should be viewed in light of her substantial judicial record. In this respect, Judge Ginsburg's nomination might be contrasted to that of David Souter. Almost nothing was known about Justice Souter's constitutional philosophy or his approach to judging at the time of his nomination. By contrast, each member of the committee had ample means, prior to Judge Ginsburg's hearing, to discover much pertinent information—indeed, the most pertinent information—about Judge Ginsburg's judicial approach and method. In more than 300 signed appellate opinions, and more than three score articles, Judge Ginsburg told the Senate and the American people an enormous amount about herself even before the hearings opened.

None of this is to say that the committee is fully satisfied with the responsiveness of Judge Ginsburg's answers. But we have not been fully satisfied for many years, and perhaps will not be for as many longer. Given Judge Ginsburg's extensive written record and her willingness to answer questions at least as fully as other recent nominees, the committee sees no reason for this issue to bar her appointment.

Judge Ginsburg is open-minded, nondoctrinaire, fair, and independent. She respects and loves the law. She honors the concept of individual rights. She brings to constitutional interpretation an understanding that the Constitution is an evolving document, together with an appreciation that the most secure evolution is also the most rooted. She will be a fine Associate Justice of the United States Supreme Court.

. . .

ADDITIONAL VIEWS OF SENATOR COHEN

Members of this committee have expressed the hope that soon-to-be Justice Ginsburg will exercise restraint on the Court. Other members pray that her past activism as an advocate will be revived on the Court.

Both groups are likely to be disappointed. Nothing that has been said during the committee's deliberations and nothing that will be said on the Senate floor during the debate on the nomination will have a scintilla of influence upon her performance as a Justice on the Supreme Court. She is going to follow her own inner guides without regard to any of our importuning.

. . .

As the committee's unanimous vote on the nomination indicated, we all believe Judge Ginsburg meets the highest standards of professional competence and integrity, that she has a highly disciplined mind and a distinguished record as a jurist and an advocate, and should be confirmed overwhelmingly.

The hearings on the Ginsburg nomination, however, have highlighted concerns about the role of the Judiciary Committee in the "advice and consent" process and the expectations of the public about that role. Editorial writers in major newspapers characterized the committee as a band of Lilliputians who tried vainly to tie up a legal giant with trivial and petty pursuits. Others have suggested that Judge Ginsburg is "a methodical, passionless technician," and that what is really required on the Court is a "radical maverick" to cancel the radicalism of conservative justices.

Whatever one's characterization of Judge Ginsburg, only a single view of the committee emerged from the hearings and it was not a complimentary one. Members were accused of asking the wrong questions, failing to ask tough questions, or crossing the line between exploring judicial philosophy and that of social and legal policy.

Judge Ginsburg declared in her opening statement that she was setting the guidelines for the scope of her testimony. She indicated that any subject on which a nominee had written, lectured or taught was, in her view, open to inquiry but that other areas were not, particularly if they involved issues that might come before the Court at some future (however remote) time.

To allow a nominee to decide what he or she will testify to during the course of a hearing puts the members of the committee in the position of either having to accept the nominee's terms as dictated or vote against the nomination. I believe it is incumbent upon the committee to work on a bipartisan basis to establish responsible guidelines for what will be expected of future nominees. Nominees can, of course, decide whether they will abide by those rules and the committee members can then decide what action to take in response.

____

6. The Nominations of John G. Roberts, Jr. and of Samuel A. Alito, Jr.

From the appointment of Justice Breyer in 1994 until 2005, the

Court experienced no vacancies and thus no new appointments.[37] Then, on July 1, 2005, Justice O'Connor announced her retirement, to become effective upon her replacement. President George W. Bush promptly nominated John G. Roberts, Jr., then Circuit Judge on the United States Court of Appeals for the D.C. Circuit, as her replacement. As Judge Roberts was preparing for his confirmation hearings, suddenly, on September 3, Chief Justice Rehnquist died; Rehnquist had been ill but had said he was not going to retire. President Bush promptly decided to nominate Judge Roberts to be the new Chief Justice. The ABA unanimously rated him "well-qualified."[38] After four days of hearings from September 12 to 15, the Judiciary Committee, on September 20, 2005, voted 13–5 to recommend the confirmation of John Roberts to be Chief Justice, with all the Republicans and 3 Democrats voting for him. Sheryl G. Stolberg, *Panel Approves Roberts, 13–5, as 3 of 8 Democrats Back Him,* New York Times, Sept. 23, 2005, at A1 (the 3 Democrats were Leahy, Kohl, and Feingold). On September 29, 2005, by a vote of 78–22, John Roberts became the seventeenth Chief Justice of the United States, taking the seat of the Justice for whom he had clerked in the 1980 Term. 151 Cong. Rec. S10650–S10651 (daily ed. Sept. 29, 2005) (roll call vote no. 245). President Bush had his Chief Justice, but now had to choose a new nominee for the O'Connor seat.

Bush's White House Counsel, Harriet Miers, had been conducting the search for Supreme Court nominees. There was considerable pressure on Bush to name a woman to replace O'Connor and the compiled list included a number of female judges. Bush's prior choice of Roberts for Justice O'Connor's seat had raised some concern among those who did not want Ruth Ginsburg to be the only woman. So few were surprised when, on the second go round, he nominated a woman to fill O'Connor's seat, but many were very surprised to learn that the woman he was nominating was his Counsel, Harriet Miers. But Miers had difficulty preparing for the Senate hearings. She had not had much experience in constitutional law and found that her "practice sessions were going poorly and her meetings with senators—even Senate Republicans—were going no better." Jan Crawford Greenberg, *Supreme Conflict* 280 (2007). Thus, on October 26, after Bush and his chief of staff realized that she would probably not fare well in the upcoming hearings, Harriet Miers withdrew her name.

Shortly thereafter, President Bush nominated Samuel A. Alito, Jr., a judge on the U.S. Court of Appeals for the Third Circuit, to take the seat of Sandra Day O'Connor. The ABA unanimously rated him "well qualified," with one recusal.[39] His confirmation process was more partisan and less celebratory than that of John Roberts, as the final votes illustrate. After five days of hearings, January 9–13, 2006, the Commit-

---

37. That long stretch of continuity was itself remarkable; the longest prior stretch was from 1812 to 1823. Such continuity can have an effect on the Justices' work-product, allowing them to anticipate their colleagues' views on a variety of issues.

38. Epstein, *Compendium, ABA Ratings, supra* at 390.

39. Epstein, *Compendium, ABA Ratings, supra* at 390.

tee voted on January 24, 2006, strictly along party lines, 10–8, to recommend Alito's nomination. The full Senate scheduled debate for January 26, 2006. After several days of debate, the Senate voted, 72–25, to invoke cloture, end debate, and vote. On January 31, 2006, the Senate voted to confirm by a vote 58–42.[40] He was sworn in immediately and became the 110th Justice of the Supreme Court.

For some reason, the Senate Judiciary Committee did not prepare formal reports on either the Roberts or Alito confirmation hearings. Thus, we present here our best effort to convey the important aspects of the Committee hearings through the views of the members of the Committee found in the available transcripts and records. (For the Roberts and Alito hearings, see *Confirmation Hearing on the Nomination of John G. Roberts, Jr. To Be Chief Justice of the United States: Hearing Before the S. Comm. on the Judiciary*, 109th Cong. (Sept. 12–15, 2005); *Confirmation Hearing on the Nomination of Samuel A. Alito, Jr. To Be An Associate Justice of the Supreme Court of the United States: Hearing Before the S. Comm. on the Judiciary*, 109th Cong. (Jan. 9–13, 2006); see also *The Supreme Court of the United States Nominations, 1916–2005* (Roberts), Vols. 20–20C (eds. Roy M. Mersky & Tobe Liebert, 2006); *The Supreme Court of the United States Nominations, 1916–2006* (Alito), Vols. 21–21D (eds. Roy M. Mersky & Tobe Liebert, 2007).)

a. John G. Roberts, Jr.

The following is a summary of the September 22 discussion of the Judiciary Committee which took place before its 13–5 vote to recommend confirmation: we generally follow the order in which the Senators spoke—alternating between Republicans and Democrats, according to seniority.[41]

Senator Arlen Specter (R–PA), the Chair, opened the session by noting that he believed that Roberts had "acquitted himself well. I have long believed that nominees answer about as many questions as they think they have to in order to be confirmed. I believe that Judge Roberts answered questions a few more; only a few more, but a few more. Some nominees have refused to comment about cases, even those decided a long time ago in the realm of clear, unchallengeable law. Judge Roberts answered questions if he thought that the case was not likely to come before the court." Transcript, Senate Judiciary Comm., Sept. 22, 2005, p. 2. Specter was "pleased to hear [Roberts'] flexibility, in his comment that the framers were crafting a document that they intended to apply in a meaningful way down through the ages. So it's not a static document; it's not a matter of original intent." While noting that Roberts did not

40. 152 Cong. Rec. S 385 (Jan. 31, 2006).

41. The following summary is based on, and all quotations herein are from, *U.S. Senate Judiciary Committee Holds A Hearing on The Nomination of John Roberts To Be Chief Justice of the United States Supreme Court* (Transcript, U.S. Senate, Judiciary Comm. Exec. Sess., Sept. 22, 2005), *reprinted in* Mersky & Liebert, eds., *The Supreme Court of the United States Nominations, 1916–2005, supra*, Vol. 20A, Document 24.

adopt the phrase "living constitution," Specter pointed out that Roberts did say that "the clauses of liberty and due process were expansive and could be applied in a very broad context." *Id.*

With respect to *stare decisis*, Specter concluded that Roberts "showed a very real respect for precedent. [Roberts] talked about the factors of reliance and how long the case had been in effect; whether it had been reaffirmed; talked about the potential of *Roe* and *Casey v. Planned Parenthood* being a super-precedent." *Id.* In Specter's words, "having survived 38 efforts to overturn it," *Roe v. Wade* could now be called "a super-duper-precedent," a term Specter admitted was "just Judiciary [Committee] talk," not Supreme Court terminology. *Id.* Whatever the term, Specter concluded Roberts showed sufficient respect to convince him, a pro-choice Republican, to vote for Roberts.

Senator Orrin Hatch (R–UT), the past chair of the committee, pointed out that he had participated in this process for the past 29 years, with all but one of the current Supreme Court Justices. Noting that he was voting yes, Hatch called Roberts "the best [nominee he'd] ever seen, and that's really saying something because some of the others have been absolutely tremendous as well." *Id.* at 7.

Senator Patrick Leahy (D–VT), having been in the Senate for 30 years and on the Judiciary Committee for most of those years, complained about the administration's "lack of cooperation with the Senate on this nomination." *id.* at 9, both initially for the O'Connor seat and later for the position of Chief Justice. He also complained about the administration's failure to produce the requested memos from the time Roberts served as principal deputy to Solicitor General Kenneth Starr, noting that the "precedent from Chief Justice Rehnquist's hearing and others go just the other way." *Id.* Notwithstanding these objections, Leahy decided that he would vote "yes," taking Roberts "at his word that he does not have an ideological agenda." *Id.* at 11.

Senator Diane Feinstein (D–CA) voted no.[42] She expressed disappointment in Roberts' answers, particularly his use of the answer "I have no quarrel with" in response to questions about cases involving the areas of adoption rights, the right to privacy as applied to a single person, Title IX and its remedies, the Americans with Disabilities Act and its adoption by the states, and denial of free education to illegal alien children. *Id.* at 6. She noted that Thomas used the phrase eight times on eight different topics and "yet when faced with these topics on the court, he took a position indicating that he did, in fact, have a quarrel with [these issues: abortion, church and state separation, precedent, commerce clause.] He took a clear position that contradicted his use of the words, 'I have no quarrel with.' So I came to believe that 'I have no quarrel with' is a kind of term of art of equivocation." *Id.* She concluded: "I basically believe that once someone has earned a right, they should not lose that right. And the rights coming before the court this upcoming

42. Senator Feinstein spoke out of order because, as Senator Leahy explained, she had to leave to manage a major appropriations bill on the floor of the Senate.

session and other sessions ... are really critical rights. And I am the only woman on this committee. And when I started, I said that was going to be my bar. And he didn't cross my bar." *Id.* at 7.

Senator Charles Grassley (R–IA) expressed his strong support for Roberts, noting that he hoped he would not find 10 years hence, that he was wrong about him "like I was about Souter." He noted that he was disappointed with how Souter turned out, but then observed: "So in the end you have to trust our judgment, and sometimes that judgment's going to be wrong. But that's what the confirmation process is about. ...[I]t basically gets you back to where Alexander Hamilton said we were meant to be: that is to make sure that the confirmation process protects us against political hacks getting on the Supreme Court or people who are totally incompetent." *Id.* at 12.

Senator Edward Kennedy (D–MA) was also skeptical. He observed: "John Roberts is a highly intelligent nominee. He has argued 39 cases before the Supreme Court, and won more than half of them. He is adept at turning questions on their head while giving seemingly appropriate answers. These skills served him well as a Supreme Court advocate ... [but] did not contribute to a productive confirmation process. At the end of the fours days of hearings, we still know very little more than we knew when we started." *Id.* at 15. Although Roberts said he would decide cases "according to the rule of law," Kennedy observed, "the rule of law does not exist in a vacuum. Constitutional values and ideals inform all legal decisions, but John Roberts never shared with us his own constitutional values and ideals. [Roberts] said that a judge should be like an umpire, calling the balls and strikes but not making the rules. But we all know that with any umpire, the call may depend on your own point of view. An instant replay from another angle can show a very different result. Umpires follow the rules of the game. But in critical cases, it may well depend on where they are standing when they make the call. The same is true of judges." *Id.*

Kennedy concluded that "there is insufficient evidence ... that Judge Roberts' view of the rule of law would include as paramount the protection of basic rights. The values and perspectives displayed over and over again in his record cast doubt on his view of voting rights, women's rights, civil rights, and disability rights. ...[I]n the four days of hearings, there is precious little in the record to suggest that Chief Justice John Roberts would espouse anything less than the narrow and cramped view that Staff Attorney John Roberts [in the Solicitor General's office] so strongly advocated in the 1980s ... In my 43 years in the United States Senate, I have supported more nominees for the Supreme Court by Republican presidents than by Democratic presidents. But there is clear and convincing evidence that John Roberts is the wrong choice for chief justice. I oppose the nomination." *Id.* at 16–18.

Senator Jon Kyl (R–AZ) said he "disagreed strongly with" Kennedy's characterization of Roberts' testimony. *Id.* at 18–19. He noted that "it's not appropriate here to try to respond to ... every comment made," but said that "it's important . . . to note that there appear to be two very different views as to what Judge Roberts actually testified to. . . . I'm just going to refer to three newspaper editorials, not because I think these papers or the editorials are the last word on the subject, but because they are well-known relatively liberal organs in our country and, obviously, start from a basis of some skepticism with respect to nominations of President Bush and in particular the Roberts nomination." First, he reported the *Chicago Tribune* said: " 'Americans can see for themselves why Roberts richly deserves to be confirmed. He has the mind, the manner, and the modesty to be a fine chief justice. He came across as intellectual but not calculating, collegial but not unctuous, deferential but not phony. His evident devotion to the law and to the Constitution ought to humble those partisans who want Supreme Court justices instead to evangelize for political causes.' " *Id.* at 19. Next, Kyl pointed to the *Los Angeles Times*, which said " 'It would be a damning indictment of petty partisanship in Washington if an overwhelming majority of the Senate does not vote to confirm . . . Roberts to be the next chief justice of the United States. . . . Roberts is an exceptionally well qualified nominee well within the mainstream of American legal thought who deserves broad bipartisan support.' " *Id.* Finally, Kyl quoted the *Washington Post* which said: " 'John G. Roberts should be confirmed. . . . He is overwhelmingly well-qualified, possesses an unusually keen legal mind and practices a collegiality of the type an effective chief justice must be. . . .' " *Id.* Kyl concluded simply that he agreed with all those assessments and "will happily support" Roberts' confirmation. *Id.* at 20.

Senator Joseph Biden (D–DE), former chair of the Judiciary Committee, put his questioning in historical perspective: "For the past 25 years since the Scalia nomination in 1986, I have focused . . . very intently on each nominee's commitment to defending fundamental rights recognized as being protected by the Constitution and . . . fully embraced by the American. . . . [T]he line used by several of our justices is the right to be let alone and the right to make basic decisions about one's life's course. To me, that is the central, most fundamental consequential decision and decisions that any person in the court will make for their entire tenure. . . . [T]he crux of the intellectual debate [is] whether we will have an increasing protection for human liberty and dignity or whether those protections will be diminished. . . ." *Id.* at 20. Stating that it was "a very close call," Biden announced that he would vote "no." *Id.*

Biden commented more generally on the hearings, comparing them to a Kabuki dance, "a stylized dance that goes on. We all sit down and we reread everything that the person has ever said. They sit down in the White House or wherever and they look at films of all of the hearings that went before. Everybody figures out it's kind of an 'I gotcha' game, . . . when, in fact it shouldn't be that at all." *Id.* at 20–21. Biden noted parenthetically: "Maybe we should go back to the pre–1925 rule and just look at what they wrote and said and make our judgments based on that. Because it's very, very difficult. I understand why nominees don't want to let us know what they think, even though the American people, in my view, are entitled to know what they think...." *Id.* at 21.

Biden explained his "no" vote because he had: "serious doubts that Judge Roberts will fall into the category of the justices from Chief Justice Marshall to Souter, Kennedy, Ginsburg, O'Connor, who look at the Constitution, quoting Marshall, 'as a Constitution intended to endure for the ages to come and consequently to be adapted to the various crises of human affairs.' That [it is] an expanding document.... For the past 20 years, where I've been convinced that a nominee would protect fundamental constitutional rights, I voted to confirm them, including O'Connor, Kennedy and Souter. Democratic nominees as well, Ginsburg and Breyer." *Id.* However, where he had doubts about the nominees' commitments to fundamental constitutional rights, "I voted against their confirmation, including Rehnquist and Thomas." With Justice Scalia, Biden said he had made an exception, one that he now regrets: "[Scalia's] rulings on the court to restrict or repeal fundamental rights ... convinced me that all future nominees would have to answer those questions about their judicial philosophy concerning these rights before I voted." *Id.* Rejecting the idea of a presumption to confirm, Biden asserted that "a nominee, because he has been nominated or she has been nominated, is not entitled to the job," and that the Senate had to act "as representatives of the American people" in deciding whether to confirm. *Id.* at 21–22.

Finally, Biden concluded:

[A]s I said during the Ginsburg hearing, if a nominee, although it is their right, does not answer questions that go not to what they would decide but how they would decide, I will vote against that nominee regardless of who it is. I've closely reviewed Judge Roberts' past writings ... and his testimony before this committee. Though I and other committee members gave Judge Roberts ample opportunity, in my view he did not provide to the American people any assurances that he embraced fully the Constitution's enduring values when it comes to fundamental constitutional rights. During the confirmation hearing [of] Justice Kennedy, ... [in response to] the question ... about what factors he would use in considering the scope of the right to privacy, Justice Kennedy stated ... "The essentials of the right to human dignity, the injury to the person, the harm to the person, the anguish to the person, the inability of a person to manifest his or her personality, the inability of a person to obtain his or her own self's fulfillment, the inability of a person to reach his or her potential"—that's the scope of the right to privacy he saw.

[I]n contrast, Justice Roberts declined to associate himself with anything approaching the broad sweep of Justice Kennedy's vision.... Not only would Judge Roberts not tell this committee how broadly the right to privacy extends, he declined even to endorse the general right to privacy. In response to Senator Schumer['s statement:] 'I assume that you disagree with Justice Thomas' views that there is no general right to privacy?' ... [Roberts] said, 'Well, I think that question depends, obviously, on the modifier and what you mean by 'general.' ... Most disturbing, he repeatedly said he believed in the right to privacy as does, quote, 'every member of the court to some extent or another.' He's right, I want to know to what extent. Because if it's the extent to which Thomas and Scalia believe in the right to privacy I cannot support, in good conscience, this man. (*Id*. at 22.)

Senator Russell Feingold (D–WI) noted that the "scrutiny" he applies to a Supreme Court nominee is "the highest of any nomination. And that the scrutiny to be applied to the position of chief justice must, of course, be the highest." *Id*. at 29. "Because the Supreme Court ... has the power to revisit and reverse its precedents, I believe that anyone who sits on that court must not have a preset agenda to reverse precedents with which he or she disagrees, and must recognize and appreciate the awesome power and responsibility of the court to do justice when other branches of government infringe on or ignore the freedoms and rights of all citizens." *Id*. Accordingly, one of Feingold's key concerns was to ascertain Roberts' view of precedent and *stare decisis*, noting that "many important precedents seem to be hanging by a thread." *Id*. Applying that standard, Senator Feingold decided to vote "yes:"

> In both our private meeting and in his hearing, Judge Roberts demonstrated a great respect for precedent and for the importance of stability and settled expectations. His themes of modesty and humility showed appropriate respect for the work of the justices who have come before him. He convinced me that he will take these issues very seriously with respect to both the constitutional right to privacy and many other issues of settled law.

> ... Judge Roberts did not expressly say how he would rule if asked to overturn *Roe v. Wade*. But if Judge Roberts abides by what he said about how he would approach the question of *stare decisis*, I think he should vote to uphold *Roe*.

> He certainly left some wiggle room ... But it will be difficult to overrule *Roe* or any other important precedents while remaining true to his testimony about stability and settled law, including his statement that he agrees with the outcome in *Griswold v. Connecticut*.

> I know that the American people will be watching him very closely on that question, and I personally will consider it a reversal of huge proportions and a grave disappointment if he ultimately does attempt to go down that road.

> I was also impressed that Judge Roberts does not seem inclined to unduly rein in Congress' power under the commerce clause. He repeatedly called attention to the court's decision in *Gonzales v. Raich* as indicating that the court is not headed inexorably in the

direction it turned in the *Lopez* and *Morrison* cases limiting Congress' power.... (*Id.* at 29–30.)

But Senator Feingold noted that, even though he was voting "yes," he did have some serious reservations. He was troubled that Roberts refused to answer "many of our reasonable questions." He was also concerned that Roberts did not "acknowledge that many of the positions he took as a member of the Reagan administration ... were misguided or in some cases were even flat-out wrong." *Id.* at 31. Like others, Feingold objected to the Administration's refusal to turn over documents from when Roberts was in the Solicitor General's office, noting that, in the future, he might not overlook such a refusal. Finally, he expressed disappointment that Roberts' failure to recuse himself in the *Hamdan* case in the D.C. Circuit, once it became clear he was being considered by the president for a Supreme Court appointment. Notwithstanding these concerns, Feingold concluded that "Roberts has the legal skills, the intellect, and the character to be a good chief justice," and therefore, voted to confirm him. *Id.* at 34.

Senator Richard Durbin (D–IL) agreed that the standard should be very high: "Next to the vote on whether America goes to war, the most important votes we cast as senators are for justices on the Supreme Court.... The decisions made by those nine justices can change the face of democracy in America and the lives of American people far more than any law that we pass in Congress. And the vote for a chief justice is even more significant." *Id.* at 48. "Pray[ing] that John Roberts will prove, as chief justice of the Supreme Court of the United States, that he has not only a great legal mind but also an understanding heart," Durbin voted "no"—since he wasn't sure about the "heart." *Id.*

Senators Lindsay Graham (R–SC), John Cornyn (R–TX), and Chuck Schumer (D–NY) focused on the reality that much of what the Senators were saying was addressed, not to the Roberts' confirmation, but rather to who the next nominee would be—the nomination not having yet been made. As Senator Graham observed, Judges Scalia, Ginsburg, and Breyer were reported out of the Senate Judiciary Committee with unanimous votes, yet Roberts, with equally impressive credentials, was going to get a split vote. Similar results were to be expected in the full Senate. What was the difference, he asked. In his view, there were two different conceptions of the role of the Senate. In Graham's view, the president was owed deference in his choice of nominee. In the view of others, Graham said, the nominee's view on particular issues was crucial. Graham saw this as "a fundamental shift" from "what the standard ha[d] been in the past to what it will be the future and noted that he had "a lot of concern" with that shift:

> We all have different value systems and we all have different hot-button items. And if we start judging the nominee on, 'Will you show allegiance to what I think is most important in the country?' then we're going to politicize the process to the point that I think the role of the president has been dramatically changed and under-

mined. And woe be on to those judges who have to figure out how to navigate our value systems, our beliefs and show allegiance to our heart. (*Id.* at 36.)

Graham, after commending the President for his "good service to this nation" in choosing Roberts, concluded with advice to the President on the O'Connor vacancy: "You have another choice awaiting you. Listen to our Democratic colleagues. Listen to what we have to say. But at the end of the day, [I] ask you to do one thing for the good of your presidency and all to follow: Fulfill your campaign promise of selecting a strict constructionist, well-qualified person who loves the law more than they love politics." *Id.* at 38.

Senator Cornyn was also worried about the next appointment. Quoting from the various newspaper editorials that lauded Roberts, Cornyn concluded: "I simply don't recall an instance where a president has nominated a more accomplished individual to the United States Supreme Court." and questioned how there could be any votes against him. *Id.* at 44–45. He wondered if Democrats on the Committee would not vote for Roberts, then who will they vote for? Answering his own question, Cornyn predicted: "I don't believe some [Democrats] would ever vote to confirm any nominee of this president." *Id.*

Senator Chuck Schumer answered Senator's Graham's question as to the difference between previous nominations—Ginsburg, Scalia, Breyer—and this one:

> In my judgment, some years ago, a number of extreme groups and individuals decided that they could not abide the direction that America was going in. They tried to change America through the presidency.... They tried to change it through Congress, but they could not because those are elected branches of government and electoral politics fundamentally decides things in the middle. So they decided to try and change America through the courts, the one non-elected branch of government.... In 2000, they helped elect a president who embraced their vision.... that America could and should be changed through the courts. And he signaled his agreement by repeating ... that he'd appoint judges in the mold of Antonin Scalia and Clarence Thomas.
>
> That meant that the president subscribed to their viewpoint that America should be radically changed through the courts and that the clock should be rolled back using legal theories like originalism and strict constructionism.... (*Id.* at 38.)

Expressing concern that any nominee of President Bush would presumably embrace these views, Schumer commented that his presumption along those lines could "be rebutted ... through answering of questions and the production of documents. And here, regrettably, there was too much lacking." Although Robert was "a good witness.... everyone seemed to emerge from the hearing with a different view of what he actually said." Voting "yes," Schumer feared, "might indicate acceptance not only of a nominee's strategic decision to avoid answering important and proper questions about decided cases, but also an administration's decision to refuse to let the American people have important information about nominee in the form of important documents." He expressed hope that "the next nominee will be more forthcoming ... about his or her legal views, and that all relevant documents will be provided." *Id.* at 39–40.

Like Senator Feinstein, Senator Schumer was struck by parallels between the testimony of Roberts and Thomas:

> To me, particularly troubling are the eerie parallels between Judge Roberts' testimony and Judge Thomas', especially given President Bush's declaration that he'd nominate justices in the mold of Justice Thomas. The echoes of then-Judge Thomas' empty reassurances that he was a mainstream jurist are ringing in the ears of every senator who listened to many nearly identical statements from Judge Roberts last week.

> I was particularly troubled by his answers in two areas, the constitutional right to privacy and the Congress' commerce clause power to protect the rights and improve the lives of American people. At this hearing, for example, Judge Roberts said he believes, quote, "There is a right to privacy, protected as part of the liberty guarantee in the due process clause," unquote.

> At this hearing, then-Judge Thomas made the almost identical statement. He said, quote, "I, with respect to the privacy interest, would continue to say that the liberty component of the due process clause is the repository of that interest."

> We all know as a Supreme Court justice, however, Justice Thomas has repeatedly urged the most narrow interpretation of privacy interests possible, in *Casey* and *Lawrence* and every other opportunity.

> At this hearing, ... Judge Roberts repeatedly assured the committee he had no quarrel with various Supreme Court decisions on privacy, women's rights, civil rights, education and other important issues.

> The same assurance was made by Justice Thomas at his hearings. But when given the opportunity to consider those cases with which he had, quote, "no quarrel," from the bench, he voted to overrule. He had no quarrel with *Eisenstat*, and made his ruling in *Lawrence*. He had no quarrel with the *Lemon* test, and then ridiculed it in the *Lamb's Chapel* case.

> . . .

> .... [A]fter Judge Roberts seemingly answered a question about his belief in a constitutional right of privacy, I asked him if he agreed or disagreed with Justice Thomas' view that there's no general right to privacy in the Constitution. He refused to give his view.... In fact, I

asked him if he could name a single opinion written by Justice Thomas with which he disagreed. He refused. (*Id.* at 40–41.)

Senator Schumer then answered John Cornyn's question: "If we can't vote for this nominee, who could we vote for?" Schumer answered:

> Someone who answers questions fully and who makes his or her record fully available; someone who gives us the significant level of assurance with some answers in a record that he or she is not an ideologue.

> Judge Roberts is clearly brilliant. His demeanor suggests he well might not be an ideologue. But he did not make the case strongly enough to bet the whole house. There's a good chance, perhaps even a majority chance, that Judge Roberts will be like Justice Rehnquist on the bench. . . . That's why I struggled with this decision so long and so hard. If he is a Rehnquist, that would not be a cause for exultation in my book, but it would not be a cause for alarm. The court's balance will not be altered.

> But there is a reasonable danger that he will be like Justice Thomas, the most radical justice on the Supreme Court . . . . . [T]he risk that he might be a Thomas and the lack of any reassurance that he won't, particularly in light of this president's professed desire to nominate people in that mold, is just not good enough. . . .

> Because of that risk and its enormous consequences for generations of Americans, I cannot vote yes. I must reluctantly cast my vote against confirmation. (*Id.* at 41–42.)

Thereafter, the Committee voted 13–5 to recommend the confirmation and the Senate voted 78–22 to confirm John Roberts as the 17th Chief Justice of the United States. He was sworn in on September 29, 2005. 151 Cong. Rec. S 10650 (daily ed. Sept. 29, 2005).

---

b.   Samuel A. Alito, Jr.

The Senate Judiciary Committee held hearings on the Alito nomination on January 9–13, 2006, before voting on January 24, 2006.[43] The following is a description of the debate among the Judiciary Senate Committee members before they voted 10–8 to recommended confirmation.[44]

There was no dispute that Samuel Alito was highly qualified. A graduate of Princeton University and Yale Law School, Alito had spent

43.   Except as otherwise noted, the following summary is based on, and all quotations herein are from, *U.S. Senate Judiciary Committee Meets to Vote on The Nomination of Judge Samuel Alito to the U.S. Supreme Court* (Transcript, U.S. Senate Judiciary Comm. Exec. Sess., Jan. 24, 2006), *reprinted in* Mersky & Liebert, eds.,

The Supreme Court of the United States Nominations, 1916-2006, supra, Vol. 21B, Document 34.

44.   The order of presentation generally follows the order in which the comments were made, but with some reorganization to present topics in a more organized way.

virtually his entire professional life in public service. After clerking for Circuit Judge Leonard I. Garth on the Third Circuit from 1976–77, Alito served as Assistant U.S. Attorney in New Jersey, Assistant to the Solicitor General, Deputy Assistant Attorney General, and U.S. Attorney for the District of New Jersey. In 1990, he was appointed to the United States Court of Appeals for the Third Circuit, the position he held when President George W. Bush nominated him to the Supreme Court in 2005.[45]

As Senator Jon Kyl (R–AR) observed, "Samuel Alito is one of the most qualified men or women ever to come before the Senate. He has more federal judicial experience than any nominee since the Taft administration... [and] brings more appellate qualification to the table than any other sitting Supreme Court justice when nominated." Transcript, Senate Judiciary Comm., Jan. 24, 2006, p.20.

Senator Specter (R–PA) said he was voting yes because Alito is "qualified." Specter found "his personal background ... exemplary. His professional qualifications are outstanding. His educational achievements are of the highest order. And I believe that ... he has answered questions as far as he could go. He did not decline to answer questions based on the fact that cases might come before him, but instead, on the issues, discussed the considerations that would guide him in coming to his decisions. He did not say what his ultimate decision would be, as he should not, because no nominee ought to be asked to decide in advance how he is going to rule on any specific case. On the issue of a woman's right to choose, it is my judgment that he went as far as he could go. He emphasized the factor of *stare decisis* and precedents, and the reliance factor, which was paramount in the *Casey* decision. He agreed with Justice Harlan's dissent in *Ullman v. Poe* about the Constitution being a living document. Agreed with Cardozo in *Palko* about representing the values of our society. And agreed with Chief Justice Rehnquist, who changed his views on *Miranda* over three decades, when police practices had become embedded in the culture of a society. And it is my view that a woman's right to choose has been embedded in the culture of our society. But our function is to vote on nominees; and justices must decide the ultimate question." *Id*. at 4-5.

Specter continued: "[Alito's] statements about *Roe* as settled law were very, very similar to what Chief Justice Roberts had to say. Chief Justice Roberts said *Roe* was settled in beyond, but he left room for *stare decisis* and precedents to be changed, and so did Judge Alito, as I think any nominee must in terms of not making an ultimate decision." *Id*. at 5.

Finally, Specter noted: "We have seen ... that there is no rule as to how nominees will act when they're on the court. When Justice Souter was up, the National Organization of Women flooded Capitol Hill with a

45. See The Supreme Court Historical Society, *History of the Court, The Current Court, Samuel Anthony Alito, Jr.*, available at, http://www.supremecourthistory.org/02_history/subs_current/images_b/010.html.

rally: 'Stop Souter or women will die.' And there was a similar pamphlet distributed as to Judge Alito. Justice Kennedy and Justice O'Connor spoke in very, very strong terms against abortion rights before they came to the court, and we know that Souter and Kennedy and O'Connor wrote the joint opinion in *Casey* . . . and have been staunchly in favor of a woman's right to choose." *Id.*

The Republicans were particularly impressed by the personal testimonials, especially by those judges who had sat with Alito on the Third Circuit. As Senator Mike DeWine (R–OH) said: "We can judge a man by his record. We can judge him by his judicial philosophy. But, really, there is no better judge of a man than those who really know him best." *Id.* at 25. In the words of Senator Jeff Sessions (R–AL): "His fellow judges . . . could not have been more complimentary. It was almost stunning the respect they had, the genuine admiration and affection that they had for Judge Alito. I don't think I've ever seen a panel . . . more impressive. . . ." *Id.* at 30–31. Indeed, the panel of seven current and former Third Circuit colleagues was noteworthy. While judges, including sitting federal judges, have testified previously in the confirmation hearings, having a whole panel of fellow judges testifying for a colleague is most unusual.[46]

Senator Hatch (R–UT) lamented that Alito was going to get a partisan vote in contrast to the strongly bipartisan support Ginsburg and Breyer had gotten only a decade earlier: "[T]he Senate overwhelmingly confirmed [them] because we acknowledged their obvious qualifications and judicial temperament. And we gave the president . . . the deference required by the separation of powers. By that traditional standard, Judge Alito should receive at least as much support as they did. Judge Alito is exceptionally well-qualified. . . . [T]he American Bar Association unanimously . . . gave Judge Alito its highest, well-qualified rating. . . . Under the standards that we used not that long ago, this would have been more than enough to confirm Judge Alito in short order." *Id.* at 10.

In Hatch's view: "The reason why so many senators and the political interests to which they cater will not support Judge Alito is that they cannot support the kind of limited judiciary that he represents. . . . The debate over judicial appointments in general and over this nomination in particular, is about whether the American people and those they

---

46. For example, in the 1971 hearing for William Rehnquist as Associate Justice, sitting judge Walter Craig testified as a fellow Arizona Bar Association member and former ABA president; in the hearing for Robert Bork, retired Chief Justice Burger testified; in the confirmation hearing for Clarence Thomas, Senior Judge Jack Tanner of the Western District of Washington testified; and, in the hearing for John Roberts, retired Judge Nathaniel Jones of the Sixth Circuit testified. See generally *Supreme Court of the United States: Hearings and Reports on Successful and Unsuccessful Nominations of Supreme Court Justices*, compiled by Roy Mersky & J. Myron Jacobstein (2006). But there is no record of a panel of judges, sitting or retired, colleagues or not, testifying at all. According to Professor Mary Clark (American University Law School), who is engaged in ongoing scholarly research on this topic, it is highly unusual for sitting judges to testify in a confirmation hearing, and, until the Alito hearing, unheard of for a panel of judges, including sitting colleagues, to testify at all.

elect still have the power to make the law and define the culture, or whether judges, unelected judges, should do it for us instead. Like America's founders, Judge Alito clearly believes in self-government, that the people not judges, should make the law, and that judges have an important role, but must know and stay in their proper place. That is why his critics oppose him, and that is why he must be confirmed." *Id.* at 11.

The Democrats did not question Alito's credentials; their comments were principally concerned with the manner in which Judge Alito did—and did not—answer the questions, the answers he gave to some of the controversial issues, and his view of *stare decisis*, especially with respect to what Senator Specter had, in the committee meetings, termed "super-duper-precedent."

Senator Schumer gave three reasons for voting against Judge Alito, reasons that were repeated by most of the other Democratic Senators. First, Alito was not "forthcoming about his own constitutional views on too many issues, despite in many instances having a prior written record on those views." Second, his record on the bench was "very far out of the mainstream on these issues." And finally, "the only mitigating factor Judge Alito offer[ed] is not a rejection of those views, but rather a pledge to respect *stare decisis*," a pledge that, Schumer explained, did not give him much comfort. *Id.* at 41–45.

The Democrats widely complained of assertedly evasive answers. Senator Russell Feingold (D–WI) called Alito's answers "practiced and opaque." *Id.* at 35. Senator Schumer labeled them "artful evasions and pleasant banalities. . . . Time and time again, Judge Alito took cover in platitudes about the law with which no nominee [who] has ever come before this committee could have disagreed, [noting that Alito said eight times that he would keep an open mind and six times that no one is above the law.]" Schumer observed that Judge Alito "sought to give the impression that he . . . simply did what the law requires. But there is much that this facile formulation ignores. . . . [V]ery often, what the law requires means different things to different people of good faith. So these statements tell us absolutely nothing about his views and can hardly be reassuring to anyone. The American people were entitled to honest answers, not practiced platitudes. . . . [A]s these hearings evolve and as witnesses perfect the artful dodge, the only people being disserviced are the American people. Even a supporter of Judge Alito, Stuart Taylor of the National Journal, described the nominee's performance in these terms: 'Again and again Alito ducked and dodged. The questions seemed fair. The answers seemed lame, evasive, even infuriating, to those of us who want straight answers.' " *Id.* at 41–42.

Democrats also lamented the President's failure to consult with the Senate before he nominated Alito. In the words of Senator Leahy (D–VT): "I reminded [the president] of his biggest campaign promise . . . to be a uniter and not a divider when it came to a Supreme Court nomination. . . . There are many, many, many people in this country who would have had from 90 to 100 votes in the Senate. Democrats and Republicans would have joined eagerly to support them. We have nine members of the Supreme Court today. Seven of those nine members were nominated by Republican presidents; two by a Democrat. I voted for eight of those nine members. I try very hard not to have partisan votes on Supreme Court nominees. . . ." Leahy voted no because, he said: "The president is in the midst of a radical realignment of the powers of the government and its intrusiveness into the private lives of Americans. And I believe this nomination is part of that plan. I am concerned that if we confirm this nominee we will . . . tip the balance in the Supreme Court radically away from the constitutional checks and balances and the protection of Americans' fundamental rights." *Id.* at 5. Senator Kennedy (D–MA) similarly commented: "The nomination of Judge Alito is particularly significant because it comes at a time of new challenges for the nation and for the court. Suddenly in this new century, we face unprecedented claims by the White House for sweeping expansions of presidential power that are grave threats to the rule of law." *Id.* at 12.

Democrats raised concern about Alito's record on the Fourth Amendment and the death penalty. Senator Feingold observed: "In almost every Fourth Amendment case in which Judge Alito wrote an opinion, he either found no constitutional violation or argued that the violation should not prevent the illegally obtained evidence from being used. In more than a dozen dissents in criminal or Fourth Amendment cases, not once did Judge Alito argue for greater protection of individual rights than the majority." Feingold was also concerned about Alito's approach to the death penalty. "Judge Alito participated in five death penalty cases that resulted in split panels, and in every single one of those he voted against a death row inmate. . . . I found Judge Alito's answers to my questions about the death penalty to be chilling. He focused almost entirely on procedures and deference to state courts and didn't appear to recognize the extremely weighty constitutional and legal rights involved in any case where a person's life is at stake. I was particularly troubled by his refusal to say, in response to my question, that an individual who went through a procedurally perfect trial but was later proven innocent had a constitutional right not to be executed."

The Democrats were also worried about *Roe v. Wade* and the right to privacy, in light of Alito's testimony before the Senate as well as some of his prior statements, such as a 1985 job application to the Solicitor General. Senator Kohl (D–WI) noted that Alito "had expressed a legal view that there was no [woman's right to choose] and worked hard to craft a legal strategy that would chip away at and ultimately eliminate that right from the Constitution." *Id.* at 23. Senator Kennedy feared that "[w]e have every reason to believe he'll do exactly that if confirmed to the Supreme Court." *Id.* at 14–15. Senator Kohl noted that "even today, he is unwilling to declare that *Roe v. Wade* is settled law, a pronouncement that Chief Justice Roberts made with ease. Judge Alito felt free to confirm that one person, one vote, integrated schools, and some privacy rights were settled, but not a woman's right to choose." *Id.* at 23.

The Democrats were also concerned with Alito's apparent deference to the executive. They were particularly upset with Alito's comment in his job application to the Justice Department in 1985 that he believed "very strongly in the supremacy of the elected branches of government." *Id.* at 13 (Kennedy). While, in the hearings, Alito called this comment "inapt," the Democrats were troubled by the fact that he would ever have thought that. As Senator Feingold noted: "Judge Alito's record and his testimony have led me to conclude that his impulse to defer to the executive branch would make him a dangerous addition to the Supreme Court at a time when cases involving executive overreaching in the name of fighting terrorism are likely to be such an important part of the court's work." *Id.* at 35.

In addition, there was discussion of Alito's narrow view of congressional power generally and the reach of anti-discrimination laws in particular. Senator Kohl observed: "He raised the bar to unreachable heights in employment discrimination cases, to the point where the majority of his court [the third circuit] concluded that he was attempting to eviscerate the laws entirely." *Id.* at 23.

In sum, the Democrats said that they voted "no" because they believed Alito was "out of the mainstream," *id.* at 41 (Schumer), the criticism that doomed the Bork nomination. The Republicans disagreed. As Senator Coburn asked "what is mainstream? There certainly would be a debate between a constituent from Oklahoma and New York or California on what mainstream is." *Id.* at 55. At the end of five days of hearings, the Committee vote divided along party lines. That was noticeably different from the Committee's vote in the Roberts confirmation, when three Democrats had voted with the Republicans.

The Republicans questioned the difference and also asked why the Democratic response to Alito was so different from the Republican response to Clinton's nomination of Judges Ginsburg and Breyer. As Senator Graham noted, the Senate had voted strongly in favor of Judge Ginsburg even though she was clearly "pro-choice" and was, in fact, taking the seat of Justice White, one of the two dissenters in *Roe*. Graham observed that some said the difference between the vote for Ginsburg and that for Alito was that Senator Hatch had been consulted by President Clinton before the nomination and Hatch had suggested Ginsburg. But Graham dismissed that fact. He said "I really do worry that we're going to take the Supreme Court nominating process and boil it down to abortion. And that won't be good for the country." Graham warned: "We're no longer advising and consenting. We're jockeying for the next election. And over time we will erode the quality of the judiciary." *Id.* 39-41. Hatch, too, argued that under "a reasonable, objective, or traditional standard, the Senate would overwhelmingly confirm this exceptional nominee. Only about a dozen years ... ago, the Senate applied such a standard and overwhelmingly confirmed two nominees of President Clinton. They were at least as liberal as Judge Alito is said to be conservative.... We knew that [both were social liberals,] and yet we voted for them because they were qualified and they were put forward by a constitutionally elected president of the United States who had the right to do so."[47] *Id.* at 9.

Senator Feinstein (D-CA) tried to explain the difference between Clinton's appointments and Bush's. In her view, the nation and the Court were much more polarized than previously; in addition, she noted that President Bush had expressed his desire "to take the court even further to the right than it has been in the last 10 years." That, she said, was a "consequential movement," indicating "a very different day and time than when Justice Ginsburg and Justice Breyer were before" the Committee. Senator Feinstein concluded: "I believe that decisions in this court are not mathematical computation of legal points.... [T]he fact of the matter is that legal philosophy and personal views do play a role on the Supreme Court. ...It is my conclusion that Judge Alito would most likely join Justices Thomas and Scalia in the originalist and strict constructionist interpretations of the Constitution." Senator Feinstein also stated: "[T]he fundamental right to liberty is at question in this nominee.... [T]his is a hard vote. But it's a vote that is made with the belief that legal thinking and personal views at time of crisis, at time of conflict and at times of controversy do mean something. And those of us who don't agree with the view have to stand up and vote no. So I am one of those." *Id.* at 26–30. Senator Kohl agreed: "Judge Alito does have the right to see, read, and interpret the Constitution narrowly. But we have theobligation to decide whether or not his views have a place on the Supreme Court." *Id.* at 24.

Finally, many Senators were concerned about the effects on nominee's families of aggressive questioning by their colleagues. Senator John Cornyn (R–TX), like Biden, questioned whether the whole hearing process should be reconsidered. Saying that the current process "treats Supreme Court nominees more like piñatas than human beings," Cornyn said that such treatment should not be tolerated, though on balance, the hearings had served a useful purpose. *Id.* at 46–47. Senator Tom Coburn (R–OK) sounded a similar note of alarm about the hearings: "[T]he points that have been made about the conduct of the hearings and the future course of judicial nominations ... should not go unheeded. We will not have people come forward to serve this nation if we continue the process that was held this time." *Id.* at 55.

———

Questions and Comments

1. What do the confirmation hearings accomplish? Do recent confirmation hearings suggest that the process is working well or should it be

47. Ginsburg was confirmed 96–3; Breyer 87–9.

modified? If so, how? In Justice Ginsburg's hearing, Senator Cohen suggested that the committee should "work on a bipartisan basis to establish responsible guidelines for what will be expected of future nominees." What might such guidelines look like? Would they be useful? Constitutional?

2. Are the hearings, in the words of Senator Biden, just a stylized "kabuki dance" used by the Senators to get television coverage ("face time") and to show off their knowledge? Even if they are, do they nonetheless educate the public about the role of the Supreme Court? Are these proceedings valuable "teaching moments?" If so, what is being taught?

3. What conceptions of the Court are expressed in the various Senators' questions?

4. Senator Biden referred to Justice Anthony Kennedy's answers from his 1987 confirmation to explain his dissatisfaction with Chief Justice Roberts' discussion of liberty. What effects—on Presidents, nominees, and Senators—does the availability of this 'precedential' record have? Consider also the comparisons some Senators made between Justice Roberts' and Justice Thomas' "no quarrel with" answers; and compare Justice Ginsburg's "no agenda to replace" answers to the questions on the abortion funding cases.

5. Proposals to return to past procedures, under which nominees rarely if ever appeared in person, surface periodically. Consider the reasons for and against such a proposal. If you think it is a good idea to change this practice, would it be politically possible to do so?

6. Compare Justice Souter's remarks on *stare decisis* at his confirmation hearings with the Joint Opinion in *Casey* (see Chapter One, above). Is the Joint Opinion consistent with his earlier comments about *stare decisis*? If so, should this be viewed as a predictable result of the principles he set forth or as raising a concern that a Justice might feel too constrained by his prior testimony? If not, does that raise other kinds of concerns?

7. The Judiciary Committee Report on the Bork nomination referred to the views of author William Styron. Was this appropriate? May a political process of confirmation consider a wider range of sources, and a wider range of factors, than other kinds of job selection processes? than the sources considered by adjudicators?

8. Could the sequence of decisionmaking in the Senate on the Thomas nomination have affected the outcome? By the time Anita Hill's allegations surfaced, many Senators had announced their decision or made up their minds. Would the outcome have been different had Hill's allegations been publicly considered by the Senate Judiciary Committee in the first place, before its divided 7–7 report issued?

9. Consider the following argument:

The altered relation of President and Congress in the appointment of justices of the Supreme Court represents a remarkable institutional rupture in American political development. In the nineteenth century, nominations to the Supreme Court were the frequent occasion for conflict between the executive and the legislature over the composition of the Court, the power of competing partisan objectives, and the character of the constitutional order. Since the administration of William McKinley, the Senate has tended to defer to the President's choices, serving in most cases as a political rubber stamp for his nominations, his understanding of the Constitution, and his partisan objectives. Although every individual instance of institutional cooperation is not necessarily an example of irresponsibility, the century-long pattern of senatorial deference to the President is a remarkable illustration of constitutional abdication.

Jeffrey K. Tulis, *Constitutional Abdication: The Senate, The President, and Appointments to the Supreme Court*, 47 Case W. Res. 1331 (1997). In earlier times, he argues, the political culture permitted the constitutional separation of powers to serve its intended function:

> In the nineteenth century, Senators appealed to the full array of arguments and considerations available to presidents. They also took advantage of, or created, a large menu of political devices to effect their will. Nominees were formally confirmed, formally rejected, rejected through postponement, rejected through forced withdrawal, and precluded through control over the structure of the judicial body itself. In addition, one Senate (joined by colleagues in the House) successfully petitioned Abraham Lincoln to nominate Samuel Freeman Miller. Although well known to lawyers and doctors (he had both law and medical degrees) and very well regarded by people Lincoln trusted, Lincoln did not know Miller himself. He followed the wishes of the legislature and Miller was confirmed within thirty minutes after the nomination was formally considered.

Id. at 1353.

Bork's defeat, Tulis argues, was the "exception that proves the rule" that today we live in "an era of deference:"

> [A]t the very time when the political order appeared to work as designed, most consider it to have failed. This is the meaning of institutional conflict in an era of deference. To be sure, the conduct of Senators did not meet the standard of conduct of the ablest nineteenth century leaders, such as Webster, Clay, or Calhoun, but that too is a symptom of the same problem. Senators were hesitant in many of their questions, follow-ups were not ... probing ..., considerable effort was devoted to securing the testimony of dozens of experts, generally law school professors, on the merits and demerits of Bork's views because Senators were not capable of unassisted inquiry. These features of the contemporary scene, like the revulsion for politics that the process induced, are the product of a kind of political amnesia. Senators, like citizens, are out of practice. Their counterparts in the nineteenth century knew what they were doing.

Id. at 1356–57. Tulis plainly regrets this aspect of today's political culture. Consider his critique as you read the next section on proposals to modify the process.

C. REFORMING THE APPOINTMENT PROCESS

The constitutional design of the appointment process has not changed since it was first adopted in 1789. But there have been various times in our history when the process has come under serious criticism and been the target of numerous proposals to modify aspects of the process and/or the constitutional design.

In response to the emotionally-charged, politically divisive confirmation battles over the Bork and Thomas nominations, commentators offered a variety of reform proposals—including heightened voting rules for confirmation, greater consultation between the President and the Senate during the nomination stage, avoiding questioning nominees about legal issues, improved techniques for confidential investigation of allegations of personal improprieties, limiting public hearings or even abandoning nominee appearances at those hearings.

More recently, critical attention has focused on the tenure of Supreme Court Justices. The membership on the Court had remained constant for more than a decade: from the time of Stephen Breyer's appointment in 1994 until John Roberts took the seat of Chief Justice Rehnquist in 2005, an unusually long period of continuity. Recent proposals for term limits, mandatory retirement, financial incentives to encourage retirement, or even changes in the nature of the duties of Supreme Court Justices, are in part a response to a perception that average tenures of Supreme Court Justices are increasing. Proposals for change in the tenure of Supreme Court Justices are noted here but discussed in more detail in Chapter Six. Most of the readings in this chapter focus on the nomination and confirmation process itself.

In the first excerpt below, Professor Judith Resnik argues that the judicial selection process must be understood within the context of a broader set of concerns. She identifies two reforms she favors (involving super majority voting in the Senate and shortening the time served by the Justices), which are explored in further readings, but the broader concerns she raises of democratic accountability and judicial independence bear on many of the issues discussed in this subsection.

_____

Judith Resnik,[48] *Judicial Selection and Democratic Theory: Demand, Supply and Life Tenure*, 26 Cardozo L. Rev. 579 (2005)

. . .

The immediate problem prompting this Symposium [on the appointment of federal judges] is the conflict about federal judicial appointments that occurred between 2002 and 2004, when Republicans held the Presidency and by a slim margin also controlled the Senate. The President nominated a series of individuals whom the Democrats opposed for lower court judgeships. (That problem has survived the election of 2004, as the Republicans kept the Presidency and gained some Senate seats

48. Arthur Liman Professor of Law, Yale Law School.

but not the sixty now required to end filibusters.) The saliency of the conflict has been heightened by three facts: a keen appreciation of the amount of interpretative power held by judges, the opportunities to fill a relatively small number of life-tenured federal judgeships (particularly at the appellate level with Supreme Court nominations in the offing), and the long standing role that the federal judiciary has played in American policymaking.

But the underlying issues go beyond the conflict in the United States. Countries around the world are considering the relationship between the idea of democratic government and judicial selection. Who should select judges? How much public scrutiny ought to accompany the selection of judges? With what form of information provided to whom? What do calls for "transparency" and "accountability" mean in relationship to judicial selection? These questions are not unique to the United States, as is evident from contemporary proposals in Canada and in the United Kingdom to change selection methods for their judiciaries....

... [S]ome of the critics of current processes make claims that "democratic values" require change.... As I explain, the fact that a country is a democracy tells one a good deal about rights to justice and equality but less than might be expected about how to select judges. Unless one is of the view that all officials in a democracy ought to be elected, it is difficult to derive one specific process for judicial selection from the fact that a country is a democracy. One may, however, be able to rule out certain criteria or kinds of procedures for judicial selection— such as by inheritance or by excluding persons based on their identity as members of certain groups.

. . .

[T]he form that the life-tenured judgeship has taken in the United States is anomalous when compared with those created by other democracies which, like the United States, are committed to judicial independence. Most countries provide mandatory ages for retirement or for fixed, non-renewable terms of office. In contrast, in the United States, those who do have life-tenured positions serve relatively long terms— often of more than twenty years. Not only do such persons hold the power of judgment for long periods of time, they also control the timing of their resignations, enabling them to give political benefits to a particular party.

I argue that both features are problematic for a democracy but are remediable. Given the flexibility with which the Supreme Court has approached Article III in the last decades and found constitutional the devolution of judicial power to non-life-tenured judgeships, Article III could also be reread to permit fixed times for retirement. Further, Congress could create incentives such as pension benefits or penalties to encourage judges to step aside after a set number of years.

. . .

[Furthermore] an analysis of the process of appointments in the United States . . . suggest[s] that a less apologetic stance towards conflict is appropriate. The political scrutiny of individuals nominated to hold life-tenured judgeships is an understandable response to the particular shape, history, and place of national judgeships in this federation. Given that Article III judges are at the top of a large judicial hierarchy and hold a rare form of power for an unusually long period of time, and given that the Constitution mandates that such judges must be selected through the political decisions of both the President and the Senate, such judgeships ought to be doled out sparingly.

That attention is appropriately paid does not mean that the form taken by the current controversies is optimal. My concern is that the Senate often does too little rather than too much. Despite all the hoopla, most persons nominated to be Article III judges are confirmed by large majorities. Further, much of the political manoeuvering occurs pre-nomination in an eclectic fashion with less rationality across candidates than might be hoped. I suggest that, as a means of expressing how unique life-tenured jobs are in democracies and how deep the political consensus about the propriety of appointing persons to such positions ought to be, the Senate should rely on a practice of requiring sixty votes for approval. Knowing that most confirmation votes currently exceed that number, I do not imagine that this form of structural intervention would have a great impact on the number of judges confirmed but rather that it would underscore the normative peculiarity of life tenure and help to reduce the sense of entitlement that presidents have about the selection power.

Of course, other proposals aspiring to reduce the judgeships battles have appeal, as is illustrated by the many calls for bi-partisan selection processes as well as by the use of merit selection commissions in other countries. But underappreciated in current discussions of federal appointments is that controversy about individuals to serve as jurists is both a longstanding feature of American politics and reflective of the role that law itself plays in American politics. From the nomination of John Rutledge in 1795 to the nomination of Melvin Fuller in 1888 to the nomination of Robert Bork in 1987 to the debates during the last four years, partisans have used individual nominations to make political arguments about what they hope United States law will be.

Contestation is not a recent artifact of televised Senate hearings or the conflicts over Robert Bork and Clarence Thomas. . . . Moreover, debates about individuals seeking confirmation have been repeatedly used as a means of articulating legal norms. From the legality of the Jay Treaty in the eighteenth century to the role of railroads and unions in the nineteenth century to the rights of women in the twentieth century and gay marriage in the twenty-first, conflict over nominations has helped to identify certain issues as powerfully divisive and others as so settled as to be seen as nonpolitical.

What has changed in the United States is that, with the growth in the number of life-tenured judgeships at the lower ranks and with the innovations in information technology, parties in power have gained the ability to fill many seats with individuals identified with certain approaches to American law. Life-tenured appointments were always an opportunity for patronage.... [T]he creation of new judgeships is of political moment, as can be seen from the fact that Congress is more likely to do so when it is dominated by the same party that holds the Presidency. And, with the swelling ranks and information technologies making visible both the attitudes of nominees and voting patterns of appointees, politicians have come to see seats on the federal judiciary as an opportunity for what Professors Jack Balkin and Sanford Levinson call "partisan entrenchment," by which they mean that a particular party can use its power of judicial selection to extend temporally that party's authority to change the governing legal regime.

Such efforts to capture judiciaries stem not only from elected politicians but also now from "repeat players," such as the Chamber of Commerce, the Federalist Society, the American Trial Lawyers' Association, and the Alliance for Justice, all eager to influence the selection processes on the state and federal level. Technology has also facilitated new means of doing combat about judgeships and has increased the funds needed to wage effective battles over nominations. Although state judicial elections have drawn much of the fire on the issue of financing campaigns, federal judicial appointments are also expensive processes, with partisans investing significant sums to promote or to block particular individuals.

In light of the function and history of life-tenured judgeships in the United States, the intensification of politics around judicial selection in this country is understandable. Whatever the drafters of the Constitution intended from their decision to allocate the power of appointment between the two other branches, the shape of the contemporary conflict is an artifact of changes over two centuries in the structure of Senate committees and staff, in the bureaucratization of the Presidency, in the expansion of federal law, in the kinds and numbers of federal judges, and in the technology of information.

Further, while a shift to a less contentious process with bi-partisan selection commissions has a great deal of appeal, such a change requires bi-partisan commitment to a very different idea of the import of a federal judgeship. Attitudes in the United States towards judging assume the political dimensions of legal decisions and that professional "legal" judgments are not insulated and discrete from their "political" consequences. Who the life-tenured judges are is a matter of great political moment for this nation, and to alter the level of conflict would require a change in the underlying political dynamics of which nomination fights are expressive.

But identifying that decisions on judgeships [are] events of political moment does not result in a conclusion that current processes produce a particularly useful form of political exchange. Thus, I outline a few changes that could be made, including trying to increase senatorial involvement by reliance on supermajority approval rules. Revisiting the format of judicial office-holding is also necessary because of democratic commitments to constrained and diffused power, with norm production generated through dialogic processes. No one person (judges included) ought to hold too much power for too long. To reduce the power now held by the life-tenured, one could cushion the impact of each individual selected, either by adding many more life-tenured judgeships and/or by shortening the terms of service. To alter the import of life tenure, Congress could create incentives for judges to shorten their length of service and the Court could reread the meaning of "good behavior" to sanction a term limit.

. . . The U.S. federal system has developed a very public politicized system with input from a range of constituencies. In some Commonwealth countries, commentators decry the lack of popular input into judicial selection. But when democracies have other techniques for making appointments, or better specification of the judicial role, or legal pre-commitments to certain kinds of judicial selection processes and other means of debating legal norms, one would be hard pressed to advocate that they adopt practices like those for the life-tenured judiciary in the United States. Turning individuals—who have not yet taken their seats nor faced the particular legal and factual questions as they emerge through litigation—into vehicles for debating the shape of social values is not the only nor necessarily a good way to have such debates. Both the people and the ideas become caricatures, and the peculiar decisionmaking processes of adjudication, with its fact-full specificity, become lost.

. . .

Generic calls for "transparency" and "accountability" sound appealing but the application of those values in the context of judicial appointments is cumbersome and often in tension with the very charter to be a judge. Demands for "accountability" can result in worrisome incursions on the aspirations for adjudication—that judges form decisions based on a particular and peculiar process focused on specific problems and influenced by a specific intersection of law, fact, and context.

Indeed, the point of judicial independence is to render judges immune from certain forms of political accountability. Moreover, given that judges are insulated deliberately and often have charters longer than the terms of office for most elected positions, the electorate has a challenging task of holding the appointing politicians "accountable." At best, politicians seeking reelection can be challenged for appointing jurists who are themselves unlikely to suffer any direct consequences. Even if the issue of a politician's vote on a particular judge has sufficient saliency to result in defeating that politician, the jurist often remains in office. And, in those jurisdictions that do require judges to stand for reelection or be subject to a reappointment process that entails popular input, those processes are criticized precisely because they permit popular retaliation against judges. . . .

---

1. What Should Be the Standards for Nominating and Confirming a Justice?

This section explores historical practice and current debates over the role of different criteria for appointing Justices—a candidate's background and personal characteristics, her ideology, her judicial temperament and professional qualifications, her prior experience, or her performance against quantitative measures of productivity, influence in citations, and independent opinion-writing. In the first excerpt, Professor Vicki Jackson provides some constitutional and historical background about the selection of federal Article III judges, including Supreme Court Justices. In the next two excerpts, Professors Erwin Chemerinsky and Ronald Rotunda disagree over the history and propriety of Presidents and Senators considering a Supreme Court nominee's ideology as a factor in the selection process.

In the readings that follow, Professors Stephen Choi and Mitu Gilati propose a "tournament of judges" in which judges on the lower courts would be rated based on various "objective" criteria (largely relating to production and citation of opinions) in order to provide the President, Senate, and the general public with an "objective" measure of their qualifications for the Supreme Court. This controversial proposal has been subjected to considerable criticism and generated a lively discussion, which is why it is included here. In the other excerpts that follow, Professor Michael Gerhardt applauds the focus on merit, but explores the difficulty in separating "merit" from "ideology," and discusses alternative criteria to be considered. Finally, Professor Lawrence Solum disagrees with the tournament idea, suggesting that it may reward what he believes are "bad" characteristics in judges and fails to capture the "virtues" that are desirable in high court judges.

Vicki C. Jackson,[49] *Packages of Judicial Independence: The Selection and Tenure of Article III Judges,* 95 Geo. L. J. 965 (2007)

. . .

SELECTION CRITERIA: IDEOLOGY, PARTISANSHIP, AND EXCELLENCE

The Constitution specifies no qualifications for appointment as an Article III judge, though surrounding historical materials suggest an

---

49. Carmack Waterhouse Professor of Constitutional Law, Georgetown University Law Center.

expectation that only highly competent lawyers should be appointed. But, competence is not inconsistent with partisan affiliation or particular ideologies, considerations which have long played a role both in the selection of nominees by Presidents and in the Senate's willingness to confirm. Ideological rejections—that is, rejections motivated by disagreement with the nominee's or the administration's policies or legal views—go back to the first administration of President Washington and the Senate's rejection of his choice for Chief Justice (John Rutledge). In 1835, soon-to-be Chief Justice Taney's nomination to the Court was initially blocked because of partisan, ideological disputes of the Jacksonian period; Judge John Parker's nomination in 1930 failed because of opposition from civil rights and labor groups; and the nomination of Abe Fortas as Chief Justice in 1968 failed, in part, because of political opposition to the decisions of the Warren Court—all well before the Bork nomination.

Over time, the relative roles of merit, ideology, political patronage, geography, other demographic factors, or friendship ties have varied, as has the influence of Senators in the selection process. Nominees have tended to be of the same political party as the President who nominates them, though a small percentage are not. Presidential administrations have varied in the rigor with which they have pursued "policy agendas" in appointments, especially on the lower courts; some scholarship suggests that a necessary prerequisite for doing so effectively has been a powerful coordinating role from the White House Counsel's office. For many years the ABA had been given names of possible nominees before they were announced for professional evaluation, but this practice was ended in 2001.[50] In the last two decades, in a larger political setting in which several politically polarizing issues are linked to court decisions, confirmation battles informed by ideological divides have seemed more intense, accompanied by contentious resort to senatorial prerogatives in challenging presidential agendas. The role (or apparent role) of ideology may have been enhanced by interest groups (some of which use judicial nominations as rallying tools) and by media coverage that tends to focus on conflict and thus on political or ideological differences in the nomination process.[51]

· · ·

There is widespread agreement about the non-ideological qualities that nominees for Article III courts should have (though not about how to measure them): personal integrity; high intelligence; good professional training and experience; the capacity to think and write clearly about legal issues; and "judicial temperament," consisting of a willingness to

50. [Editors' Note: See discussion in Section A, above.]

51. [Editors' Note: See discussion in Section A, above.]

bring an impartial mind to bear and a more ephemeral quality lawyers call "good judgment." In addition, there is agreement that the bench should be open to qualified nominees regardless of race, ethnicity, religion, or gender. There is considerable disagreement, however, over how much of a role ideological perspectives should play. Some argue for a focus only on "character" and the non-ideological components described above; others argue that it is appropriate for Presidents to pursue their ideological agendas through judicial appointments that pay close attention to judicial ideology, or for Senators to contest appointments on those grounds. Still others argue that, while there is a role for ideology, it is important for the federal bench as a whole to have a balance among a diversity of perspectives; and for some, the President may consider ideology within moderate limits, and the Senate may decide to block nominees on the same grounds if the ideological choice is "too extreme."

In recent years, the national party platforms have included statements about judicial appointments (generally framed in public-regarding terms), and national political controversy has frequently revolved around issues before the courts (today including abortion, gay marriage, takings of property, rights of detainees and criminal defendants, the death penalty, and presidential authority to act against terrorism). Ideology and partisanship are thus likely, as a practical matter, to continue to play roles in the selection, and confirmation, of federal judges. To think that ideological predisposition is irrelevant in deciding cases that involve hotly contested constitutional or statutory questions is to ignore what we know about judicial decisionmaking;[52] to think that judging is only about a judge's political or policy attitudes is to miss the constraining force of law and of the judicial role.[53]

The justifications for considering ideological predispositions may be strongest at the Supreme Court. The Court is the final judicial decision-maker on contested issues of constitutional law, as well as on a wide range of statutory, procedural, federal common law, and international law issues. Due to changes in its jurisdictional statutes over the twentieth century, the Court now has almost complete discretion over which appellate cases to decide.[54] Given this discretion, nominees' views of the Court's role and what kind of cases it should hear would be relevant.

---

52. [Footnote 63 in original] The "attitudinal model" of judging predicts that judges will seek to advance their own policy preferences or "attitudes" in deciding cases. See [Tracey George, *Court Fixing*, 43 Ariz. L. Rev. 9, 33 (2001)]. See generally [Jeffrey A. Segal & Harold J. Spaeth, *The Supreme Court and the Attitudinal Model* (1993)], at 64–72, 208–25. Many studies in this model support the relevance of the party affiliation of the appointing President or party affiliation of the judge (as proxies for the judge's underlying "attitude") to voting patterns in decided cases. See [George, *Court Fixing*,] at 33–36 & nn. 88, 89 (summarizing and citing the literature

on the influence of ideology on judicial decisions).

53. [Footnote 64 in original] See generally [Barry Friedman, *The Politics of Judicial Review*, 84 Tex. L. Rev. 257, 270–305 (2005)]; see also George, *supra*, at 35 (noting that the magnitude of difference in views between judges of different political affiliations is "not as strong as it is between voters or congressional representatives" of different affiliations—a finding consistent with some constraint associated with judging).

54. [Editors' Note: See discussion in Chapter Three, below.]

Because of the Court's discretion over its docket, a higher percentage of the argued cases are controversial and fall between established lines of authority and legal argument. These are the cases in which the judges' legal predispositions may play a greater role in the decision—not necessarily because of a general absence of law, as distinct from politics, in constitutional interpretation but because judges' experience and viewpoints matter in interpreting law in open areas.[55] On either account, one would expect greater scrutiny of Supreme Court nominees' predispositions than of lower court judges. But it is also important to note that the U.S. Supreme Court remains a "generalist" court.[56] Unlike more "specialized" constitutional courts in Europe, the U.S. Court sits to decide not only constitutional issues but also a broad range of cases. The need for its Justices to be able to handle that range emphasizes the need for excellent legal capacity and may moderate the role of ideology.[57]

· · ·

————

Erwin Chemerinsky,[58] *Ideology and the Selection of Federal Judges*, 36 U.C. Davis L. Rev. 619 (2003)

· · ·

In this essay, I want to make two points, one descriptive and the other normative. Descriptively, I will argue that Presidents and Senates always have considered ideology in the judicial selection process. I also will offer some thoughts as to why the fights over judicial selection seem to have increased in recent years. Normatively, I will argue that the consideration of ideology, by Presidents and Senates, is desirable.

55. [Footnote 68 in original] ... cf. [Barry Friedman, *The Politics of Judicial Review,* 84 Tex. L. Rev. 257, 333–34 (2005)] (concluding that while judicial review "is embedded in politics," it "is not quite of it. Politics and law are not separate, they are symbiotic."). But see Richard Posner, *The Supreme Court, 2004 Term—Foreword: A Political Court,* 119 Harv. L. Rev. 31, 40 (2005) (arguing that in "open" constitutional cases, decision is political, not legal, in character).

56. [Footnote 69 in original] For example, a quick review of U.S. Law Week's recent summary of the Court's forty-nine "civil cases" in the Term ending June 2006 found that well over half involved primarily statutory or procedural problems, such as whether certain joint ventures are per se violations of the Sherman Antitrust Act, the effect of a failure to move for judgment as a matter of law on review of sufficiency of the evidence, or the scope of Title VII's protection from employer retaliation

against those who complain of discrimination. See Supreme Court Term in Review, 2005–06: Civil Cases, 75 U.S.L.W. 3057 et seq. (Aug. 8, 2006).

57. [Footnote 70 in original] Cf. Carsten Smith, *Judicial Review of Parliamentary Legislation: Norway as a European Pioneer,* 2000 Pub. L. 595, 605 (having "judicial review ... implemented by judges whose main duties are ordinary application of the law, ensur[es] to a large degree that they apply recognized judicial methodology"). This observation, if correct, might support the arguments of those who favor some diminution in the discretion the Supreme Court has over what cases it takes, to assure an appropriate mix of nonconstitutional as well as constitutional questions.

58. Alston & Bird Professor of Law and Professor of Political Science, Duke University School of Law.

Throughout this paper, I am defining "ideology" as the views of a judicial candidate that influence his or her likely decisions as a judge. This includes, for example, the individual's philosophy of judging and constitutional interpretation, such as whether the person would be an originalist or a non-originalist in interpreting the Constitution. Ideology also includes the individual's views on disputed legal questions, such as current controversies over the right to abortion, affirmative action, the death penalty, and separation of church and state.

. . .

I. Competing Visions for How to Evaluate Judicial Candidates

Underlying the debate over the appropriate role of ideology in judicial selection is the question of how judges should be evaluated. Three different models have been advanced as to how judicial candidates should be selected and evaluated. Each has its strong supporters. One might be termed the professional qualifications model. Under this approach, candidates for judicial office—state or federal—should be evaluated only on the basis of their credentials: their education, the nature of their practice, their prior judicial experience, and any other indicia of their competence and ability to serve as a judge. The professional qualifications model expressly excludes consideration of an individual's ideology or likely voting in particular cases.

The criteria, which the American Bar Association (ABA) uses in evaluating nominees, reflects this model. The ABA's rating of a judicial candidate is based on the individual's "integrity, professional competence and judicial temperament;" evaluation is not supposed to include consideration of the individual's views or ideology. Likewise, a report of the Twentieth Century Fund's Task Force on Judicial Selection declared that "choosing candidates for anything other than their legal qualifications damages the public's perception of the institutional prestige of the judiciary and calls into question the high ideals of judicial independence."

After Robert Bork was rejected for a seat on the United States Supreme Court, Professor Bruce Ackerman lamented this as a "tragedy" on the grounds that Bork was "among the best qualified candidates for the Supreme Court of this or any other era. Few nominees in our history compare with him in the range of their professional accomplishments." Obviously, Ackerman was using this professional qualifications model in defending Bork.

A second model can be termed the judging skills model. Under this approach, in addition to professional qualifications, it is permissible for the evaluator—be it the voter in a judicial election, the Executive, or the Senate—to examine the candidate's skills as a judge, assuming that the candidate has served in a prior judicial position. Supporters of this approach look to factors such as the judicial candidate's use of precedent, the quality of his or her written opinions, and his or her temperament on the bench. As with the professional qualifications approach, the judging skills model expressly excludes consideration of an individual's ideology in evaluating potential judges.

For example, ... Professor Judith Resnik in her Senate testimony against Robert Bork focused on his judging skills and not on his ideology. She criticized the breadth of Bork's opinions and his resolution of questions not raised in the specific cases before him.

A third approach can be termed the ideological orientation model. Although this model certainly includes evaluation of professional qualifications and judging skills, it differs from the first two approaches because it expressly permits consideration of an individual's ideology in the selection process. Specifically, the evaluator is allowed to examine a judicial candidate's views on important issues in deciding whether to approve or reject the individual. For example, Chief Justice Rose Bird [of the California Supreme Court] was opposed for retention because of her opposition to capital punishment and also for her liberal rulings protecting employees and consumers. Judge Robert Bork was opposed because of his writings criticizing Supreme Court decisions protecting the right of privacy, applying the equal protection clause to gender discrimination, and using the First Amendment to protect speech not concerned with the political process.

Admittedly, these three models are oversimplifications.... Within each there are many specific questions that must be answered, including: how to appropriately measure professional qualifications; how to evaluate judicial behavior; what are the permissible ways for determining ideology? Also, it is not always possible, in practice, to neatly separate the models. Professional qualifications are looked to, in large part, as a way of predicting judging skills.

I want to emphasize that there is no relationship between these models and political viewpoints....

... During the Clinton years, the Republican Senate used ideology to delay and deny confirmation to those it regarded as too liberal. In the current Bush presidency, the Democratic Senate has rejected Charles Pickering and Priscilla Owens [for lower court appointments] largely because of their conservative ideology. My point is simply that both sides of the ideological spectrum use each of these models when it serves their purpose.

II. Ideology Always Has Mattered in Judicial Selection

The debate over whether ideology should matter in the judicial selection process has been about whether it is appropriate for the United States Senate to consider the views of the prospective judge during the confirmation process. No one seems to deny that it is completely appropriate for the President to consider ideology in making appointments. Presidents, of course, always have done so. Every President has appointed primarily, if not almost exclusively, individuals from the President's political party....

Senates always have done the same, using ideology as a basis for evaluating presidential nominees for the federal bench. Early in American history, ... [t]he Senate rejected [President Washington's nominee, John] Rutledge for the position as Chief Justice because of its disagreement with Rutledge's views on the United States treaty with Great Britain.

[Chemerinsky goes on to review other Senate rejections of Supreme Court nominees in the 19th and 20th centuries.] ...

In 1987, the Senate rejected Robert Bork, even though he had impeccable professional qualifications and unquestioned ability. Bork was rejected because of his unduly restrictive views of constitutional law, including rejecting constitutional protection of a right to privacy, limiting freedom of speech to political expression, and denying protection for women under equal protection. The defeat of Robert Bork was in line with a tradition as old as the republic itself.

Those who contend that ideology should play no role in judicial selection are arguing for a radical change from how the process has worked from the earliest days of the nation. Never has the selection or confirmation process focused solely on whether the candidate has sufficient professional credentials.

There is a widespread sense that the focus on ideology has increased in recent years.... There are several explanations for why there is intense focus on ideology at this point in American history. First, the demise in a belief in formalism by the general public encourages a focus on ideology. People increasingly have come to recognize that law is not mechanical, that judges often have great discretion in deciding cases. People realize that how judges rule on questions like abortion and affirmative action and the death penalty and countless other issues is a reflection of the individual jurist's views. *Bush v. Gore* simply reinforced the widespread belief that the political views of judges often determine how they vote in important cases. Thus, Democratic voters want Democratic Senators to block conservative nominees and Republican voters want Republican Senators to block liberal nominees. This creates a political incentive for Senators to do so, and means that they certainly do not risk alienating their core constituency by using ideology in evaluating nominees.

Second, the lack of "party government" in recent years explains the increased focus on ideology.... [C]onfirmation fights are usually a product of the Senate and the President being from different political parties.

Finally, confirmation fights occur when there is the perception of deep ideological divisions over issues likely to be decided by the courts.... Interest groups on both sides of the ideological divide have strong reasons for making judicial confirmation a high priority because they know what is at stake in who occupies the federal bench.

III. Ideology Should Be Considered in the Judicial Selection and Confirmation Process

Of course, the above description is not a normative defense of the desirability of considering ideology in evaluating judicial nominees. Normatively, there are many reasons why ideology should be considered in the judicial selection process.

First, . . . ideology should be considered because ideology matters. Judges are not fungible; a person's ideology influences how he or she will vote on important issues. It is appropriate for an evaluator—the President, the Senate, the voters in states with judicial elections—to pay careful attention to the likely consequences of an individual's presence on the court.

This seems so obvious as to hardly require elaboration. Imagine that the President appoints someone who turns out to be an active member of the Ku Klux Klan or the American Nazi Party and repeatedly has expressed racist or anti-semitic views. Assume that the individual has impeccable professional qualifications: a degree from a prestigious university, years of experience in high level law practice, and a strong record of bar service. I would think that virtually everyone would agree that the nominee should be rejected. If I am correct in this assumption, then everyone agrees that ideology should matter and the only issue is what views should be a basis for excluding a person from holding judicial office.

On the Supreme Court, the decisions in a large proportion of cases are a product of the judges' views. The federalism decisions of recent years—limiting the scope of Congress' powers under the commerce clause and section five of the Fourteenth Amendment, reviving the Tenth Amendment as a limit on federal power, and the expansion of sovereign immunity—almost all have been 5–4 rulings that reflect the ideology of the Justices. . . . Criminal procedure cases often require balancing the government's interests in law enforcement against the rights of individuals; this balancing will reflect the individual Justice's views. . . .

Second, the Senate should use ideology precisely because the President uses it. . . . Under the Constitution, the Senate should not be a rubber-stamp and should not treat judicial selection as a presidential prerogative. The Senate owes no duty of deference to the president and, as explained above, never has shown such deference through American history.

Finally, ideology should be considered because the judicial selection process is the key majoritarian check on an anti-majoritarian institution. Once confirmed, federal judges have life tenure. A crucial democratic check is the process of determining who will hold these appointments. A great deal of constitutional scholarship in the last quarter of a century has focused on what Professor Alexander Bickel termed the "counter-majoritarian difficulty"—the exercise of substantial power by unelected judges who can invalidate the decisions of elected officials. The most significant majoritarian check is at the nomination and confirmation stage. Selection by the President and confirmation by the Senate properly exists to have majoritarian control over the composition of the federal courts.

.   .   .

Unless one believes in truly mechanistic judging, it is clear that judges possess discretion and that the exercise of discretion is strongly influenced by an individual's preexisting ideological beliefs. In cases involving questions of constitutional or statutory interpretation, the language of the document and the intent of the drafters often will be unclear. Judges have to decide the meaning, and this often will be a product of their views. Many cases, especially in constitutional law, require a balancing of interests. The relative weight assigned to the respective claims often turns on the judge's values. Given the reality of judicial decision making, it is impossible to claim that a judge's ideology will not impact his or her decisions.

Opposition to considering ideology must be based on the [idea], that even though ideology matters, it is undesirable to consider it. One argument is that having the Senate consider ideology will undermine judicial independence. Professor Stephen Carter makes this argument:

> [I]f a nominee's ideas fall within the very broad range of judicial views that are not radical in any nontrivial sense—and Robert Bork has as much right to that middle ground as any other nominee in recent decades—the Senate enacts a terrible threat to the independence of the judiciary if a substantive review of the nominee's legal theories brings about a rejection.

But Professor Carter never explains why judicial independence requires blindness to ideology during the confirmation or selection of a federal judge. Judicial independence means that a judge should feel free to decide cases according to his or her view of the law and not in response to popular pressure. As such, Article III's assurance of life tenure and its protection against a reduction in salaries, provide independence. Judges are free to decide each case according to their conscience and best judgment; they need not worry that their rulings will cause them to be ousted from office. Professor Carter never justifies why this is insufficient to protect judicial independence. He subtly shifts the definition of independence from autonomy while in office to autonomy from scrutiny before taking office. But he does not explain why the latter, freedom from evaluation before ascending to the bench, is a prerequisite for judicial independence in the former, far more meaningful sense.

Another argument against considering ideology is that it will deadlock the selection process—liberals will block conservatives and vice versa. The reality is that this is a risk only when the Senate and the President are from different political parties. . . . There have been times when a number of nominations have been rejected, such as the Senate defeating [several] pick[s] for the Supreme Court by President Tyler and rejecting two nominations in a row by President Nixon. But in over 200 years of history, deadlocks have been rare.

Most importantly, ... when the Senate and the President are controlled by different parties, the solution to deadlocks is in the President's hands: nominate individuals who will be acceptable to the Senate. Presidents will have to select more moderate individuals than if the Senate was controlled by their political party. President Clinton undoubtedly was forced to select less liberal, more moderate judges, because the Senate was Republican-controlled for the last six years of his presidency. ...

Finally, some suggest that using ideology is undesirable because it will encourage judges to base their rulings on ideology. The argument is that ideology has to be hidden from the process to limit the likelihood that once on the bench judges will base their decisions on ideology. ... Long ago, the Legal Realists exploded the myth of formalistic value-neutral judging. Having the judicial confirmation process recognize the demise of formalism won't change a thing in how judges behave on the bench.

In summary, the argument for considering ideology in judicial selection is simple: people should care about the decisions likely to come from a court on important issues; the ideological composition of the court will determine those decisions; and the appropriate place for majoritarian influences in the judicial process is at the selection stage.

· · ·

Ronald D. Rotunda,[59] *The Role of Ideology in Confirming Federal Court Judges*, 15 Geo. J. Legal Ethics 127 (2001)

... [I]in the summer and fall of 2001, the United States Senate Subcommittee on Administrative Oversight and the Courts of the Committee on the Judiciary, chaired by Democratic Senator Charles E. Schumer of New York, conducted a series of hearings ... on the role of the Senate in confirming federal judges, ranging from district judges all the way to the U.S. Supreme Court. In hearings before this Subcommittee, and in the popular press, some academics and commentators have argued that any judicial nominee should assume the burden of proof to justify his or her nomination, even though the Senate considers the nominee only after the judicial candidate has already crossed several hurdles, such as a Presidential nomination, an extensive FBI background check and an evaluation and rating of each nominee by the ABA Committee on Judicial Selection. Moreover, these commentators argue that the Senate should frankly and openly consider legal views of the judicial nominee, and vote against one who, in the view of the particular

59. University Professor and Professor of Law, George Mason U. School of Law.

Senator, might not vote the right way on disputed legal issues. Commentators candidly urged Senators to apply a "litmus-test" to nominees and make sure that the Senators have "nailed down their [the nominees'] view" on the topics that the Senators feel are important. Some Senators may be persuaded.

Senator Charles Schumer of New York, for example, has said that he would specifically ask the nominee how he would vote on particular legal issues—campaign finance, gun control, and privacy—that are likely to come before an Article III Court:

> For instance, I'd ask the nominee "What's your views on the First Amendment? How broad, how narrow?" And then I'd say, "Well, how does that stack up in terms of campaign finance reform? Would you vote to knock out much of campaign finance reform?" That's a great debate on the court. I'd ask: "What are your views of the Second Amendment? Do you believe that, for instance, it pertains just to militias or to the average person?" That's a great debate. And then I'd ask: "Would your views on the Second Amendment have you rule that any kind of licensing or registration of hand guns wouldn't be allowed? What's your views on privacy? Do you believe there's a constitutional right to privacy? And do you believe that right to privacy would allow the court to make a decision on a woman's right to choose, to guarantee that right?"

Senators have not normally asked such questions of judicial nominees.... When nominees started testifying and appearing at the hearing, the Judiciary Committee would not insist on answers as to how they might rule on legal questions nor would it punish a nominee for refusing to answer.

For example, Justice Ruth Bader Ginsburg described what did *not* happen during her confirmation hearing to the D.C. Circuit, in June of 1980. An organization called the United Families of America proposed that the Senate Committee ask judicial nominees a series of questions to test the nominee's "balance:" "Can the Congress limit the jurisdiction of the federal courts in, say, school busing cases? Do parents have any rights with respect to abortions performed on their minor children? Present law and practice of the armed forces of the United States bar women from combat positions. Could that exemption withstand a constitutional challenge? What principles ought federal judges to follow in deciding social policy cases?" Senator Howard Metzenbaum, the chair, refused to ask the questions and said so in no uncertain terms: "You don't mean that every nominee up for confirmation ought to have his or her views explored ... on all of the controversial issues ... ?" Later, then-Judge Ginsburg wrote that she found the questions a "frightful prospect."

The tradition has been for the Senate not to require nominees to explain how they would vote on particular legal questions.... Senator Schumer of New York has argued that some Senators really have considered ideology, though they do it under the table: "The not-so-dirty little secret of the Senate is that we do consider ideology, but privately." We may assume that he is correct and that some Senators, at times, may consider such issues. However, to recognize that some Senators may have considered a nominee's political affiliation or ideology does not lead to the conclusion that Senators should consider such factors, anymore than recognizing that sin exists means that we should aspire to it.

That is the topic of this essay: Should Senators ask judicial nominees how they would vote on particular legal questions? More precisely, should nominees answer such questions? If a Senator asks a judicial nominee whether his or her views of the Second Amendment indicate that the nominee would "rule that any kind of licensing or registration of hand guns wouldn't be allowed," what should the nominee say?

Obviously, if Senators may properly ask such questions, it would not do for the nominee to respond, "I haven't thought much about the Second Amendment and I would like to see the facts of the particular case." In that instance, we would expect the Senator to reply, "Please think about it and come back in a month and give me your answer. And, if the facts of the case matter, tell me under which set of facts would you invalidate a federal law." Indeed, if Senators have a right to secure answers to legal questions, we might expect Senators to ask the nominee to submit written answers to a host of legal issues.

We are not surprised if Senators ask the Secretary of State designate, or a Attorney General designate his or her views on questions of policy, because political appointees are supposed to make policy based on political judgments. Politicians are supposed to make promises as to how they would vote. But judges are supposed to apply the law based on legal principles. Granted, there may be judges who, at times, may rule a particular way because of their view of politics. But, like sin, to recognize that it exists is not to aspire to it.

My conclusion on this issue is simple enough: the rules of judicial ethics, our traditions, and our history all counsel that neither the President nor the Senators should ask judicial nominees how they expect to decide legal questions. The Senators should ask nominees if they have made any promises to the President or his aides, other than the faithful performance of their judicial duties. The Senate should reject any nominee who has made such promises. We want fair courts—not liberal courts, not conservative courts, not moderate courts, but fair courts, and by "fair," I mean we want judges who will call them as they see them, without regard to politics, even if their decisions (*e.g.*, the desegregation decisions) will not be popular.

A.   . . .

The old saw, "if it ain't broke don't fix it," applies to the present proposals to change the role of the Senate. While proponents of change are no doubt acting in good faith when they urge the Senate to "change the ground rules" for confirming judicial nominees, they should first assume the burden of proving a need for a change. We have today—and we have had for the entire twentieth century—the most powerful and respected judiciary in the world.

Foreign lawyers in the newly emerging democracies in Eastern Europe, South America, and the Far East admire our legal system. Even if they do not fully understand our system ... they know that ours is the system that they would like to emulate.... Lawyers and judges throughout the world all say that they want their judicial systems to be like our federal system. They want their judges to be like our Federal judges....

... Given the fact that the Senate has been confirming federal judges for years, and the product is admired around the world, one wonders why we should think of changing the way the Senate confirms. There is no reason to change presumptions or change the way the confirmation process works when the present system has produced—over a period that spans several lifetimes—the best judiciary in the world.

. . .

B. JUDICIAL NOMINEES MAY NOT PROMISE—OR APPEAR TO PROMISE—TO VOTE PARTICULAR WAYS ON LEGAL ISSUES

It has long been a basic principle of judicial ethics that any person who is a candidate for appointment or election to a judicial office "shall not make pledges or promises of conduct in office other than the faithful and impartial performance of the duties of the office."

It is wrong for a nominee to promise to vote a certain way, to promise (or appear to promise) to vote to overrule or to not overrule a particular precedent, or promise to approach a legal problem with a particular mind set.

The Senate should not confirm anyone who would make such promises. I cannot believe that former Presidents Bush or Clinton or their aides would have asked such questions, nor that such questions would be asked in the vetting process under President George W. Bush.

It is permissible for Senators to ask nominees if they have made any promises—other than "the faithful and impartial performance of the duties of the office"—to the President or to any Senator. If the nominee has made other promises, then the Senate should know what they are. But neither the Senate nor the President should seek such promises. Consequently, the Senate should not confirm someone who has made such promises and who treats the judicial office as an elected office....

. . .

C. JUDGES SHOULD NOT RULE AS POLITICIANS ONCE THEY ARE ON THE BENCH

The argument that the Senators should vote on judicial nominees based on the Senators' views on how the nominees will vote on legal issues assumes that judges vote based on who appointed them to the court. The judges are human, to be sure. They put on their robes, two legs at a time, and sometimes they make mistakes, which is why we have courts of appeal. But they act in good faith in coming to their conclusions. The Constitution gives Article III judges lifetime tenure and salary protection so that their rulings will not be based on the election returns. They know that their ultimate judge is history, not the politics of the moment, so one should not expect judges to rule as Republicans or Democrats once they are on the bench.

. . .

D. OUR HISTORICAL EXPERIENCE SHOWS THAT PRESIDENTS, SENATORS AND OTHERS ARE UNABLE TO PREDICT HOW JUDICIAL NOMINEES WILL ACT ONCE THEY HAVE LIFETIME TENURE

Commentators, Presidents, and Senators may think that they can predict how a nominee will vote once that person is confirmed, but our historical experience should teach us to be more humble. We do not know what the major legal issues will be ten, fifteen, or even five years from now, much less what might be the "liberal" or "conservative" answer to them. We cannot predict with any accuracy how nominees will act once they become judges. History has repeatedly taught us that lesson. It is easy to assert that one can foretell how the candidate will vote, but Professor Alexander Bickel, a distinguished legal historian, advised years ago: "You shoot an arrow into a far-distant future when you appoint a Justice. And not the man himself can tell you what he will think about some of the problems that he will face."

It is easy to find examples to support Bickel's thesis. The National Organization for Women recently rallied in Washington, D.C., demonstrating because of its concern that Justice O'Connor might retire soon and NOW feared her replacement. However, when President Reagan appointed her, NOW was substantially less enthused. . . .

. . .

Presidential batting averages are as poor as those of NOW or other groups. President Roosevelt appointed both Felix Frankfurter and William O. Douglas, two Justices who were both thought liberal before they were appointed. Although the same President appointed them, once they were on the bench, they were as alike as oil and vinegar.

Nixon appointed both Burger and Blackmun, and the press promptly dubbed them the Minnesota twins. After a while, it was clear that these twins did not really share the same parentage. Some Court watchers believe that they can prophesy what a nominee will do by looking at his record. This belief may be a factor encouraging presidents to look primarily at lower-court judges when choosing appointees to the High Court. Both Burger and Blackmun were lower court judges before being elevated to the Supreme Court. Yet, they taught us that, like generals who are always fighting the last war, past practices do not control the future. We can look to history not for prophecy, but for conjecture.

In our early history, Presidents were no more prescient. Consider President James Madison's appointment of Joseph Story in 1811. Madison was a member of the Democratic–Republic party. His mentor, Thomas Jefferson, had defeated the last Federalist to hold the presidency, John Adams. Story, like his father before him, and like Madison, was also a Democratic–Republican. President Madison expected that the strong-willed Story would serve as an intellectual counterweight to the views of Federalist Chief Justice John Marshall. Yet, once on the Court, Story often supported and expanded Marshall's views. Some contemporaries concluded that he even out-Marshalled Marshall.

Even short-term predictions are wrong. President Theodore Roosevelt appointed Oliver Wendell Holmes to the Court because he thought Holmes would strengthen federal power over interstate commerce. In one of the first major opinions after Holmes was appointed, the Court upheld federal power but Holmes dissented. T.R. then announced that he "could carve out of a banana a judge with more backbone than that."

The difficulty in predicting a nominee's performance is also well illustrated in more modern times by FDR's appointment of Alabama Senator Hugo Black. Black, generally viewed as a Roosevelt crony, had enthusiastically supported Roosevelt's ill-fated efforts to pack the Court. He had even once been a member of the Ku Klux Klan. . . . But Black surprised his critics. If the Senators had tried to predict how Black would rule on racial and free speech issues, they most certainly would have guessed wrong, and we would have been deprived of one of the greatest Justices in our nation's history.

. . .

Recall that Professor Alexander Bickel said that not even "the man himself can tell you what he will think about some of the problems that he will face." This simple fact is illustrated by no less a judicial titan than Judge Henry Friendly, a great judge and prolific author. In one case, when one of the parties cited to him one of his own articles indicating how an issue should be decided, Judge Friendly decided that he disagreed with what he himself had earlier written; the genius of the common law system, he recognized, is that judges must make the decisions in the context of concrete cases, not in the context of law review articles. Judge Friendly dissented, while the majority relied on Friendly's law review article.

Judge Friendly did not know how he would rule on the legal issue until he had to decide the legal issue, even though he had thought about the problem and had written an article about it coming to a firm conclusion, a conclusion that he later rejected.

. . .

If we treat federal courts as an investment and not as a speculation, then the President and the Senators and the media as well should worry less about how a judicial nominee might vote on any particular issue, a prediction that is typically incorrect, than about what they think of the nominee's personal integrity, good faith, and intellectual ability. The alternative, trying to predict how a justice will act on particular legal issues years from now is difficult, if not impossible, because we do not know what those issues are. Even less do we know what the liberal or conservative answers to those questions might be.

————

Questions and Comments

1.   Consider in light of the readings whether the President's responsibility in identifying a candidate to nominate differs from the responsibility of the Senate in deciding whether to confirm? Should the Senate simply try to assure that the nominee is honest and competent or should it try to ascertain and evaluate the nominee's legal philosophy? What is entailed in pursuing any of these questions? How can the Senate determine "honesty," "competence," or "legal philosophy?" Should the President and/or the Senate consider whom the nominee is replacing and how the nominee is likely to affect the balance on the Court? or the demographics?

2.   A question that affects every confirmation hearing is whether the Senate should seek to ascertain the nominee's views on certain issues. If Presidents are likely choose their nominees, at least in part, on the basis of predictions as to how they will vote, is it logical and proper for Senators to also try to satisfy themselves about the nominee's views? Professor Jackson, in another passage in the article excerpted above, wrote that:

> [T]oday Senators ask questions designed to probe the nominee's views, about legal interpretation and about particular substantive areas, in a public exploration which some applaud and others would abandon in favor of prior practice. From the vantage of judicial independence, the concern is that judges who indicate how they would rule with respect to pressing legal issues of the day will be unable to maintain the appearance or actuality of impartiality and open-mindedness to argument that is expected of judges. Nominees from both parties tend to draw some line between general questions, which they will answer, and questions that may come before them as judges, which they will not—perhaps reflecting a pragmatic consensus that differences in approach to interpretation matter, but can be probed only to a limited extent through direct questioning without compromising other important values.

Do you agree? Or is this a completely unsatisfactory compromise? Should a nominee be chosen by the President and evaluated by the Senate without regard to likely future rulings but only on measures of professional competence and personal integrity? Or should a full and fair exploration of the nominee's views—including views with respect to issues that may come before the Court—be the order of the day?

3.   Even if ideology may be considered, is it appropriate for the President to ask a nominee how she or he would vote on an issue? For a Senator to do so? Is there a difference—is it more permissible for Senators to question in a public setting than for the President to do so in a private

setting? Or is questioning a nominee about his or her views in either setting, with the idea of either not nominating or voting against the candidate if the President or Senator, respectively, disagrees, inconsistent with the belief that independent judicial review should restrain government power?

Stephen Choi & Mitu Gulati,[60] *A Tournament of Judges?*, 92 Cal. L. Rev. 299 (2004)

... We argue that the benefits from introducing more (and objective) competition among judges are potentially significant and the likely damage to judicial independence negligible. Among the criteria that could be used [in a competitive 'tournament' to choose Supreme Court justices from among court of appeals judges] are opinion publication rates, citations of opinions by other courts, citations by the Supreme Court, citations by academics, dissent rates, and speed of disposition of cases. Where political motivations drive the selection of an alternative candidate, our proposed system of objective criteria will make it more likely that such motivations are made transparent to the public. Just as important, a judicial tournament for selection to the Supreme Court will serve not only to select effective justices, but also to provide incentives to existing judges to exert effort.

I. Background, Impetus, and the Basic Idea

... We propose a "Tournament of Judges" where the reward to the winner is elevation to the Supreme Court.... The question of who will be selected to replace [Chief Justice Rehnquist, and Justices O'Connor and Stevens, all at this time rumored to be thinking of stepping down,] has thus been the subject of debate in many newspapers. And the discussion has been almost entirely political (focusing on litmus tests such as a candidate's likely position on abortion). Occasionally, a nominee's intellectual ability is mentioned, but this topic has time and time again been placed to the side in favor of a discussion of the nominee's political beliefs.

We believe that the present Supreme Court selection system is so abysmal that even choice by lottery might be more productive. We also believe that politics is primarily to blame. The present level of partisan bickering has ... undermined the public's confidence in the objectivity of those justices that are ultimately selected.

. . .

The norm today appears to be that a candidate for the Supreme Court must first sit on a federal circuit court of appeals before she may be considered for a seat on the Court.... That such a norm appears to exist currently is convenient for our idea of a rank-order tournament

60. Choi is Murray and Kathleen Bring Professor of Law, New York University School of Law; Gulati is Professor of Law, Duke University School of Law.

because the circuit judges can be ranked on the basis of their performances under roughly identical conditions. Among the criteria used would be opinion publication rates, citations of opinions by other courts, citations by the Supreme Court, citations by academics, dissent rates, and speed of disposition of cases. . . .

The selection of future Supreme Court justices on the basis of such objective criteria would make clear (and thereby reduce) the role that politics plays in both the initial process of selecting a candidate and the often highly political Senate confirmation proceedings. . . .

An initial objection to our plan might be that the mere existence of easily obtainable numerical measures does not necessarily mean that these measures will effectively predict who will make a skilled justice. Our response is to point out how badly the present selection system works without such measures. No matter how weak our objective bright-line predictors are, we contend that our system would outperform the current one. . . .

We also believe that a judicial tournament would provide appellate judges with the otherwise absent external incentive to exert greater effort than they currently do . . . (for example, publishing more opinions or hearing oral argument in more cases). . . .

. . .

II. FORMULATING OBJECTIVE TOURNAMENT CRITERIA

. . . We suggest only a preliminary set of objective criteria with the hope that others will improve upon them.

a. Quality of the Judicial Product: We focus first on the most easily measurable aspect of the judicial task: opinion writing. Circuit court judges write lots of opinions (roughly between five and ten times the number of majority opinions that Supreme Court justices do). These opinions are then used by other judges to decide subsequent cases. Opinions are thus the judicially created "products" that form the raw materials for the construction of other similar products. For judges and academics, the products are free. . . .

Whether a judge's opinion is used as a product is determined by market forces. Judges use opinions written by other judges as the tools required to write their own opinions. Presumably, the best opinions will be cited more often than others. They may even be cited by the Supreme Court.

. . . Some will be the subject of academic analysis, some will be included in casebooks (although the quality argument is more attenuated here—casebook authors being fond of not only the better opinions, but also the ones that are more controversial and lend themselves to debate). The point is that there is a market test available for assessing the quality of opinions. We can look at the frequency with which a judge's opinion is used by a variety of consumers (including, for example, citation counts). Because circuit court judges write lots of opinions, the market test allows us to rank them in terms of the quality of those opinions.

. . .

... [T]he market for judicial opinions is relatively free of ... imperfections. For one, judicial opinions may be obtained at no cost by judges and, in many areas of the law, are abundant. There are also a large number of producers (over 160 circuit judges), and they all have identical resources (the same income, the same number of law clerks, the same perks). Finally, the customers, often the judges themselves, are sophisticated about the products from which they are choosing. We expect therefore that in this market the opinions used the most are likely to be the ones that judges find the most useful for their own production of opinions.

Indeed, the particular nature of the products (that they are free) means not only that competition is likely to occur effectively, but that we should be able to see clear and outright winners of the tournament. All judges will cite the best opinions. And to the extent certain "superstar" judges tend to write the best opinions, other judges will repeatedly look to these judges for guidance in the future....

More refined methods of measuring citation counts are also possible. Those compiling citation rankings could assign a judge a positive score for favorable citations and a negative score for unfavorable citations (thereby curbing the incentive to take extreme positions in their opinions). Supreme Court and en banc reversals could also be counted against the judge.

Focusing on Supreme Court reversals, however, may unfairly penalize judges with different political views from those on the Court. To control for this possibility, the tournament could take into consideration both the political affiliation of the court of appeals judge and that of the reversing majority....

Variables outside of a particular judge's control may also affect the number of times she is cited. Judges with a longer tenure on the bench are likely to have a longer citation list. As controls, rankings could focus on the number of citations per year or per opinion....

A more complicated issue arises if one views an opinion as a team product. Circuit court decisions are generally rendered in groups of three.... Our tournament gives only the writing judge credit for an opinion.

The "team product" problem may ultimately prove unsolvable. It would be difficult for an outside evaluator to know much more than the fact that the writing judge did significantly more work on the opinion than the other two. That said, giving all the credit to the writing judge is a reasonable approximation, since in a large number of three-judge panels those judges most inclined to write high citation opinions tend to outperform their colleagues.

. . .

b.   Caseload Performance: ... It is arguably in the public interest for the justice to exert maximal effort. This would mean that she would use her clerks minimally, dissent as often as would be warranted, and vote to grant certiorari in as many cases as is possible. The selection of a Supreme Court justice, therefore, should involve a prediction about the effort that a circuit judge is going to exert if elevated. Objective factors could focus on the effort that she exerted while she was a circuit judge. We could look at how many opinions (versus short form dispositions) the judge published, how many concurring and dissenting opinions she wrote, how many opinions she wrote in which she took on primary responsibilities (as opposed to delegating to clerks), and the overall number of cases which she played a role in deciding during a given period of time.

c.   Independence: Another part of the judicial mission is to decide cases impartially. One measure of impartiality is the willingness of a judge to decide cases independent of political ideology.

Evidence suggests that judges fall short of this mark.[61] This willingness is measurable. For each circuit court judge, for example, the frequency with which the judge is in opposition to another judge selected by the same president (or a president from the same political party) serves as one measure of the willingness of a judge to take an independent approach. Judges who are systematically more willing to disagree with politically like-minded judges are, we speculate, more unbiased in their approach to individual cases.

... Focusing on the number of times a judge is cited, her performance in disposing of cases, and whether she resolves disputes independently, does not produce a perfect test for promotion. The best soldiers are not always the best leaders. The best law students are not necessarily the best legal academics. Likewise, judges with low citation counts as circuit court judges could well move on to write high quality opinions as Supreme Court justices.... Bright-line rules are necessarily both over- and under-inclusive in their reach.

... Determining the proper weights [for each factor] is not easy....

Nonetheless, we believe that judges who score high on any one of our objective criteria are likely to score high on the majority of the other criteria. A judge who has an impact through her opinion-writing in the judicial community is likely also to have an impact among casebook

---

61. [Footnote 28 in original]. For example, in an empirical study of cases related to environmental law, Richard Revesz demonstrated that judicial decisions in the D.C. Circuit are significantly correlated with the political party of the president who nominated particular judges. See Richard L. Re-vesz, *Environmental Regulation, Ideology, and the D.C. Circuit,* 83 Va. L. Rev. 1717 (1997). [Editors' Note: For work that has disagreed with Revesz, see, e.g., Harry T. Edwards, *The Effects of Collegiality on Judicial Decisionmaking,* 151 U. Pa. L. Rev. 1639 (2003).]

authors. Likewise, judges who work harder on their opinions are correspondingly less likely to adhere blindly to one particular political viewpoint or another.

Opponents may contend that the objective factors on which we focus may still fail to promote the most effective form of competition. Competition based primarily on citation count, for example, may lead judges to focus too much attention on formulating and drafting opinions.... Even more troublesome, judges seeking citations may search out novel viewpoints, no matter how outrageous and untenable.... Judges may also only cite their friends (or similar-minded colleagues) who will agree to reciprocate in order to enhance their joint chances of advancing to the Court....

Solutions to these problems are nonetheless possible. Focusing on multiple criteria is one. Rating judges not only on the number of opinions they produce but also on the citation count per opinion (or per given time period) in addition to the number of cases which they dispose of in any particular time period forces ambitious judges to seek balance. Judges seeking to boost the number of opinions they write at the expense of the quality of such opinions, for example, may find that their citation count per opinion will drop. Likewise, judges who focus too much effort on writing long, detailed opinions may find that their overall number of cases handled drops. Once the more egregious abuses are reduced (if not eliminated) through a balanced set of objective criteria, we believe that encouraging judges to increase their objective rankings would be good for the justice system as a whole. Focusing on objective criteria may give judges an incentive to increase their levels of effort and output.

... [T]he question is whether objective criteria work better than the selection process we have today. Given how politicized the selection of Supreme Court justices currently is, the use of any objective factors will lead to a marked improvement.

· · ·

By focusing first on objective criteria, our proposal forces into the open more subjective criteria used in the selection of a judge. Let politics play a role but only in a transparent manner....

III. THE EFFECT OF THE TOURNAMENT ON CIRCUIT COURT JUDGE BEHAVIOR

The possibility exists that judges may simply ignore competition. After all, with life tenure why care about competition? Moreover, if the only fruit of competition is a seat on the Supreme Court, most judges may consider the likelihood too remote for it to be worthwhile to compete. Two responses come to mind. First, judges may in fact care about goals other than elevation to the Court. Judges in particular may care about their reputational standing among other judges....

· · ·

One group of outsiders the judges might care about is the set of potential law clerks.... [I]f individual-judge rankings are made available, law students will pay attention to them, especially if those rankings translate into different post-clerkship job prospects. And if the law clerks begin to use the rankings, that will cause at least some judges to care about them.

Second, ... [i]f the magnitude of the benefit of a position on the Court is high enough, even a low likelihood will induce judges to compete....

. . .

To the extent that the possibility of promotion to the Supreme Court can provide the 160–plus active circuit judges with the incentive to work harder, that itself would yield significant social dividends. The circuit courts decide upwards of 27,000 cases a year on the merits.... If the introduction of a tournament for promotion to the Court is able to increase effort levels even a small amount on every case the circuit courts hear, the overall effects will be dramatic.

IV. POSSIBLE OBJECTIONS . . .

a. ABA and Other Rankings: A number of groups, including the ABA, already evaluate and rank candidates for the Supreme Court.... Thus, a critic might ask whether our proposal adds anything new. Our response is that the rankings that the ABA and other groups use are different from a tournament system. They do not focus on the current judicial performance of all potential nominees. Instead, they evaluate only a handful of potential candidates.... The analysis of the candidates is also largely qualitative and subjective, and, as discussed, allows for significant political bias.... Additionally, under the ABA's system, all of the candidates could end up with a rating of "well qualified." Such a system is anything but a tournament.

. . .

b. Judges Prefer Not to Compete: ... Judges, viewing themselves as professional elites, may feel that they do not need external competitive inducements to do their jobs well. The prospect of competition may even be received with contempt by judges striving to exist "above the fray." ... [E]ven if a large number of judges choose to avoid competition, a tournament system should help reduce the appearance of political bias that exists today....

c. Promotions For Women and Minorities Will Be Hurt: A related criticism of our proposal might be that focusing exclusively on objective criteria may disproportionately harm the interests of women and minorities. To the extent that the numbers of women and minority judges are small and such judges are relatively inexperienced, criteria based on standing among peer judges (such as citation counts) may create an exclusionary barrier. We are not hostile to the notion of providing some degree of preference for the selection of women and minority judges....

[L]ike politically motivated appointments, any move to favor a judge for gender or racial reasons should be made transparent. . . .

d.   The Problematic Norm of Requiring Prior Judicial Experience: Our proposal takes, as its starting point, the norm of picking justices with prior circuit court experience. . . . [S]uch a norm . . . restricts the pool of possible candidates. Giants like Brandeis and Cardozo would not have made it onto the Court had such a norm been rigidly adhered to during their times. Second, it creates homogeneity in terms of prior experience. . . . [H]omogeneity in prior experience is likely to produce homogeneity in decisions. One answer to these objections is that the norm is not one of our choosing. The norm already exists. . . .

The value of a norm of prior circuit court experience is that it creates an apprenticeship period . . . [which] serves to produce data on how the candidates performed in a job that is close in nature to the job they are seeking. . . . These types of apprenticeship periods are crucial in promotion tournaments used by law firms, investment banks, and academic institutions. . . . [T]he norm in most law firms of choosing partners from the associate ranks is not generally a rigid one. In exceptional circumstances, firms are willing to hire laterals. Since information on these laterals is . . . harder to interpret (and therefore future performance harder to predict), the bar for them is generally set higher. . . . By analogy, even assuming that data as a circuit court judge is the best predictor of future performance as a justice, we may have circumstances where a candidate demonstrates such extraordinary performance on some other job (such as a district court judge, legislator, state supreme court justice, lawyer, or legal academic) that one can predict that the person will make a better justice than any of the other candidates with circuit court experience.

We have no problem with modifying the tournament in such a manner. . . .

e.   Politics Redux: . . . Whatever other objections exist, the one that we do not see room for is the argument that the tournament would hurt judicial independence. If anything, the pressures that appellate judges may currently feel to attract political sponsors by making decisions that please those sponsors would be eliminated. Indeed, if there is an objection to our system at all, it is that judges will be made too independent under it. The tournament will thus have eliminated one of the few popular checks on an otherwise independent judiciary. Whether this would be desirable is a topic for another paper.

. . .

——————

Michael J. Gerhardt,[62] *Merit vs. Ideology*, 26 Cardozo L. Rev. 353 (2005)

. . .

. . . Choi and Gulati's project . . . does at least three things absent from the vast majority of legal commentaries on judicial selection. First,

62.   Arthur B. Hanson Professor of Law at the Wm. & Mary School of Law.

Choi and Gulati are willing to discuss merit. They do not just focus on what has gone wrong with a particular nomination or with the confirmation process. Their focus is not on what is ailing in the process but on what we might be able to find positive within it. Second, they eschew labels. They refuse to play the popular game of pigeon-holing judges based on their supposed ideology, or pre-commitments, to certain outcomes or ways of thinking about constitutional issues, regardless of the facts of particular cases. They refuse to characterize candidates in extreme terms. Their concern is with merit, plain and simple.... Third, they dare to employ empirical analysis in assessing the quality of a particular judge's performance on the bench.... Empirical analysis is common to the fields of corporate law, securities, and law and economics; however, it is uncommon in legal scholarship assessing either judicial performance or the federal judicial selection process.

In this essay, I will use each of three different factors that I believe distinguish Choi and Gulati's project as lenses through which to discuss the apparent tension between merit and ideology in the federal judicial selection process, including the curious reluctance of many public officials and legal scholars to find an objective, or at least consensus-building, measure of merit to guide critical assessment of judicial nominations....

· · ·

I. MERIT

It is rare in symposia or other studies on judicial selection to talk at length about merit. This reticence is surprising because it elides a basic question that presumably is of great interest to everyone concerned about the quality of judging: how do we measure fitness for office and particularly how do we determine who is best qualified for appointment to the United States Supreme Court? ...

B. Imagining the Ideal Nominee

Imagine, for a moment, you have been asked by the President to draft a list of qualifications for a nominee to the Supreme Court. Imagine further that you do not know which particular president has made this request. You are behind the Rawlsean veil of ignorance as to knowing anything particular about the President's party or the composition of the Senate. Is it possible to draft such a list, and if so, what would be on it?

It is not hard to imagine that some criteria are bound to make the list, though reaching consensus on the activities that would satisfy them may be difficult. First, we expect a nominee to have a high degree of legal acumen. We expect the nominee to be highly intelligent, perhaps to have performed quite well in law school, maybe even to have attended an elite law school. At the very least, we would want to make sure that the nominee has very sound legal skills; asks intelligent, probing questions; thinks clearly if not imaginatively about legal problems; identifies legal issues in a wide range of problems; is trained at problem-solving; and understands the special duties that she will be called upon to discharge.

Second, we expect a nominee to have an excellent judicial temperament. The ideal temperament for a justice is presumably to have the capacity to make decisions even-handedly, to be open-minded in listening to and considering the arguments in the cases that come before him, and to be respectful to litigants and other justices with differing opinions. A judicial temperament requires, of course, a disposition to follow, rather than to rewrite, the law. The nominee also needs to be able to handle the intense pressures that come with the responsibilities of a Supreme Court Justice.

Collegiality is a third criterion for an ideal nominee to the Court. Collegiality requires getting along with the other justices. It also entails being able to build coalitions and to maintain cordial relations with other justices, regardless of the extent to which one may agree or disagree with their views in particular cases. Maintaining cordial relations is no easy feat on a Court once described by Justice Holmes as "nine scorpions in a bottle." Not all people who must work together in relatively close quarters successfully maintain respect and civility over long periods of time, but the ideal nominee must have some such capability.

The fourth criterion for the ideal nominee is excellent writing ability. The ideal nominee should be able to write clear, coherent opinions. It is especially important that the ideal nominee have the ability to craft opinions that reflect and can maintain the support of a majority of the justices in a given case. Moreover, it is important for the nominee to be able to compose opinions relatively quickly given the time pressures under which justices operate.

Fifth, significant and meaningful professional experience is indispensable to an ideal nominee to the Court. This experience need not all have been in the public sector, but the more experience a nominee has first-hand with the legal system from top to bottom the better. Meaningful experience might include serving in a significant public office, which might enrich the nominee's understanding of the system from which the laws appealed to her Court will come. Rich professional experience is bound to sharpen a nominee's judgments, and provide a solid foundation from which to approach the significant legal questions that come routinely before the Supreme Court.

Sixth, integrity is essential to the ideal nominee. A nominee's integrity must be beyond question in order for her to be able to exercise the moral authority of a Supreme Court justice. Justices embody the law, and they need to comply with the very laws they expect all others to follow.

Closely related to nominees' integrity is their character. Stephen Carter and Larry Solum are just two of the many scholars who insist that a justice ought to have a strong, moral character. At the very least, having a strong, moral character means having the courage of one's convictions and the strength not to alter one's opinions, or decide cases, for the sake of currying peer or public esteem.

There are other qualifications that ideal nominees might arguably need to satisfy. Besides the factors already mentioned, presidents might also be interested in a nominee's religion, ethnicity, gender, and health. These other factors might be important in diversifying the Court's composition or satisfying under-represented segments of society. Moreover, the age of a nominee has been very important to presidents who wanted to ensure that their appointee could serve on the Court long after they had left office.

Of course, the criteria that are relevant for determining ideal nominees are one thing, while the things which presidents or their advisers might consider in order to measure them are another. The values of those charged with selecting a nominee will inevitably influence what they choose to look at and how they will perceive it. Moreover, it might simply be unrealistic—or dangerous—to ignore factors such as timing, the president's party, the composition of the Senate, the nominee's political or party affiliation, or the composition of the Court. For instance, the composition of the Senate might be quite pertinent to a nominee's chances for confirmation. Indeed, a president might be inclined to choose different people, depending on whether his party controls the Senate or whether the minority has enough members to filibuster a contested nomination. Certain factors are bound to complicate the nominating process. For instance, the proximity of the next presidential election cannot be ignored, because the opposing party has successfully rejected or delayed more than a few Supreme Court nominees in the hopes of preserving the vacancies for presidents from their parties. And we have not yet mentioned a nominee's likely ideology or how well a potential candidate interviews for the job as possible complicating factors.

The large number of potential considerations helps to explain why some presidents, or their advisers, might prefer to break the nominating process into first-and second-order selection criteria. The first might allow for a relatively sizeable list of potential candidates, while the second might be used to cut the list down to size, if not down to one. Interviews might be used to cut a narrowed list even further, at which point a great deal depends on the interviewer, the questions asked, and the nominees' responses.

... A Supreme Court nominee usually enters the confirmation phase with at least a presumption, or likelihood, that he or she will be confirmed. It thus usually takes something rather significant—not just some deviation from an ideal—to put a nomination in trouble. Nevertheless, the stronger a nominee's credentials, or the more closely he or she approximates an ideal, the tougher it may be to undermine the nomination. Thus, a look at another way in which to determine ideal credentials might be fruitful for providing at least one significant measure for evaluating the relative strengths of particular nominations.

C.   Determining Merit in Reverse

... This section considers ... whether it is possible to infer from the justices we might generally agree were "great" or "excellent" what they might have had in common prior to their appointments. The question is whether the signs of at least potential "greatness" or "excellence" were evident at the times of the appointments of those who later proved themselves to be first-rate justices.

I will use two examples to illustrate this tack. The first is the man for whom this Law Review takes its name: Justice Benjamin Cardozo. Justice Cardozo makes many, if not all, the lists of great justices, so the question naturally arises as to whether, or in what ways, this greatness was evident at the time of his nomination. Throughout his career—first as a lawyer specializing in appellate briefs, then as a judge and later Chief Judge of the New York Court of Appeals—Cardozo, nominally a Democrat, had enjoyed the confidence of all political factions.... He was also the author of several highly regarded books, and had received honorary degrees from many universities, including Yale, Columbia (his alma mater), and Harvard. Many of his decisions in such areas as torts and contracts had influenced judges and courts throughout the nation. Thus, he evidently had, by the time of his appointment, compiled ample judicial experience, shown considerable legal acumen, and demonstrated excellent judicial temperament, collegiality, and leadership on a prominent court. His integrity and character were beyond reproach.

My second example involves another New Yorker, Charles Evans Hughes, whom many believe was a first-rate jurist (not once but twice!). When Hughes was first nominated and confirmed to the Supreme Court in 1910, he already had outstanding credentials. He had been an active practitioner with one of the leading law firms in the country and a leader of the New York and national bars, and had devoted himself to substantial public service. At the time President Taft appointed Hughes as an Associate Justice, Hughes was serving with distinction as the Governor of New York. As an Associate Justice, Hughes authored a number of significant opinions and demonstrated respect for his colleagues and opposing arguments and had an even-handed temperament. After leaving the Court six years later to run unsuccessfully for President of the United States, he served as President of the American Bar Association, argued several cases successfully before the Supreme Court, performed significant pro bono work, served for four years as secretary of state under Presidents Harding and Coolidge, and served on the Permanent Court of International Justice. Few nominees to the Court have matched his record of public service prior to the Court, and fewer have had records of public service respected by the leaders of both parties, though this did not save him from having a significant minority of senators vote against his nomination as Chief Justice for fear of his allegiance to big business. Hughes brought statesmanship to the task of judging.

My point is not to suggest that either Cardozo or Hughes ought to be viewed as the model appointee to the Court. Rather, my point is that if we are sincerely interested in measuring merit we might be able to infer from their records, as of the respective times of these two widely respected jurists' appointments, appropriate criteria for meritorious appointments to the Court. It is, however, not clear that we can ever discuss merit without some reference to ideology.... Consequently, we need to consider the implications of the linkage of merit to ideology in the federal judicial selection process.

II. THE BATTLE OVER THE MAINSTREAM IN CONSTITUTIONAL LAW

. . .

Perhaps the most intense conflict that Republicans and Democrats have had over the past two decades in the selection process has been over who occupies the mainstream in constitutional law. Each side claims that its nominees are within the mainstream and the contested nominees of the other are not, as evidenced by the struggle over the Supreme Court nomination of Robert Bork. More recently, Democrats have supported six filibusters against judicial nominees whose views on constitutional issues are, in their judgment, outside of the mainstream. The defenders argue that just the opposite is true.

The contest to define the mainstream has not been merely rhetorical. A good deal is at stake. Each side desperately wants its nominees to be viewed as occupying the middle, rather than the extreme end of the spectrum in constitutional law. The middle is the safest, strongest ground. Moreover, opposing nominees because they are outside the mainstream puts the other side on the defensive. More importantly, each side appreciates the enormous stakes involved, for with each victory each side advances one step further in building a foundation for an enduring constitutional vision....

Although it is not hard to understand why political leaders care intensely about securing the mainstream—or the middle—in constitutional law, it is harder for someone outside of, or not invested in, the process to determine what counts as the middle. I consider in the next section some of the difficulties with determining the mainstream in constitutional law and propose some ways in which to figure out what is the mainstream, or middle.

A. Problems with Defining the Middle in Constitutional Law

There are several major problems with identifying the mid-ground in contemporary constitutional law. First, empirical analysis cannot easily capture what counts as the middle because the choices of what to emphasize or count are value-laden. Anyone looking to define the middle, or the mainstream (the two are not necessarily the same) in constitutional law must make judgments about relevance: are all cases relevant? Should we only look at the judgments or outcomes in particular cases, or should we also look at the reasoning ...? Where, for instance, do seemingly obvious cases like *Roe v. Wade*, *Lawrence v. Texas*, and *Lee v. Weisman* fit? Some might argue that they are clearly on the "left" in constitutional law, but some others might argue they are consistent with a libertarian perspective on the right....

Second, an even bigger problem for defining the middle or the mainstream in constitutional law is that the categories we deploy in assessing judicial performance as well as the nominees' views are not necessarily fixed. Because of the phenomenon of ideological drift, categories are not static; particular perspectives on constitutional law associated with particular political factions may over time be appropriated by or become associated with different political factions ....

A third problem with fixing the middle ground in constitutional law is that justices sometimes shift their attitudes about constitutional law either generally or in particular cases. Justice Harry Blackmun is often described as evolving, or growing, over time into a more "liberal" justice. Others might move in the other direction....

A related problem with using the categories of "liberal" and "conservative" to describe judicial performance is that judicial nominees may not have fixed attitudes about constitutional law. Some people seem to assume that at least some nominees have ideological commitments at the times of their nominations that are impervious to change, but it seems virtually impossible to prove that this is true especially when the nominees themselves disclaim holding any such commitments.

Fifth, legal academics have done little to illuminate what may fall inside or outside the mainstream of constitutional law. Most legal scholars appear interested less in finding common ground than in delivering the knock-out punch against opposing points of view....

Sixth, the media hinders sophisticated discussions of judicial performance. The media has begun to shirk its traditional role in educating the public.... The media prefers drama and conflict, because it gets people's attention. The media thus prefers to stick with the simple labels of "liberal" and "conservative." ...

B.   Sketching the Middle

Assessing ideologies is difficult without having some yardstick with which to measure them.... [T]he question is how accurately can we describe a middle course or the contours of the mainstream in constitutional law?

... First, we can identify the middle ground as what each of the contending sides in confirmation contests seeks to occupy. We can thus define it at least as an aspiration....

A second possibility is to define the mainstream as the pool of people who have made it successfully through the confirmation process. . . . The problem with this understanding of the mainstream is that it fails to take into account the facts that many people make it through the process without close scrutiny and that presidents and senators have not agreed with everything decided by the judges whom they have approved.

Moreover, defining the mainstream as those whom the Senate has confirmed merely gives each side an incentive to push the envelope. With each victory in the confirmation process, each party has expanded the possibilities for its nominees.

. . .

Third, the mainstream could be understood as simply consisting of the views of those at the center of the Court. Today that would presumably mean Justice O'Connor, because she almost never dissented in the October 2003 Term. The problem is that she did not decide these cases alone, and it is unclear why those with whom she joined in majority opinions ought to be excluded from the mainstream. Moreover, the center can shift, and there is no guarantee that she will be there as often next year. . . .

The fourth and final possibility is to define the mainstream as something more dynamic and broader than a specific Court or specific Justice at a particular moment in time. For one thing, the Court is not alone in making constitutional law. Our political leaders make a great deal of constitutional law, much of which eludes judicial review. Moreover, the Court approves the vast majority of the constitutional decisions that it does review. It would also be wrong to assume that every Court decision reflects mainstream constitutional values. Sometimes the Court gets it wrong, as it did in *Chisholm v. Georgia*, *Dred Scott v. Sanford*, and *Korematsu v. United States*. The constitutional views of presidents and senators are relevant to the makeup of the mainstream, because they have the power to try to move the Court in different directions or perhaps keep it on course by virtue of their respective authority in the appointments process. They also have the power to shape enduring policies. Consequently, it is possible to define the mainstream as the dominant doctrine, outlook, and thinking on constitutional law over time. The Supreme Court provides the doctrine, the courts and national political leaders shape the outlook of an era, and all of these along with constitutional commentators in a wide variety of fora inform the thinking on constitutional law. This perspective on the mainstream has the virtue of encapsulating the constitutional activities of a given era. The main problem with this perspective is that there is no method on which all people could agree for determining the relevant doctrine, outlook, and thinking of a particular era. . . . It is a challenge, to say the least, for someone to step outside of his or own time to develop a credible perspective on it.

III.   PROVING IDEOLOGY MATTERS

Proving what many people suppose—that ideology matters more than anything else to most presidents in nominating judges and most senators in voting on their confirmation—is no small feat. . . .

B.   How to Show Ideology Matters

. . . Once one sets out to demonstrate the particular significance of a single factor, such as ideology, the task becomes somewhat more complicated. . . . Thus, we need to determine, even before we can prove the hypothesis or theory underlying much of the discussion in this symposium—that ideology matters significantly in the confirmation process—what proxies stand for ideology and what other variables are potentially relevant to outcomes in the confirmation process.

One cannot prove that ideology matters without initially determining how ideology manifests itself. . . . The most obvious possibilities are statements and actions of nominees that accord with, or explicitly embrace, particular ideologies. If the nominees have been judges, then their opinions might reflect ideologies or perhaps the absence of them. In addition, they might have given speeches, written articles or books, or made statements that reflect ideological commitments or their absence. If the nominees have not been judges, then their activities in the public or private sectors might reflect their commitments to certain ideologies, though these can be disavowed as merely doing the bidding of superiors or clients. . . . Also relevant may be the testimony and the support of those claiming to know the nominees best. Put slightly differently, one might ask which groups support nominees and why or on what bases. But people who are not judges, even if they are academics, can credibly claim that their public musings do not reflect what they would do as judges because their duties as judges require them to do things, such as following precedent, that they are not required to accept as scholars or commentators.

It is easier to settle on the independent variables other than ideology. The first is Senate composition. Presidents often take the composition of the Senate into account in deciding on whom to nominate and when. The strength of a president's party's representation in the Senate is obviously important, because it determines which parties control the Judiciary Committee, the agenda on the floor of the Senate, and the length of debate. If the minority party controls at least forty seats in the Senate, it can then block some judicial nominations by filibustering them. . . .

A second factor is timing. Election years tend not to be good times for presidents to make judicial nominations, particularly to the Supreme Court. In the nineteenth century, the Senate did not act on at least nine Supreme Court nominations, supposedly because the majority party was trying to keep the vacancies open until after the next presidential election. In President Clinton's final year in office, the Senate did not act on more than sixty of his judicial nominations. Similarly, the Democratically-led Senate did not act on dozens of the first President Bush's judicial nominations in his final year in office, presumably because of a desire to keep as many judicial vacancies for the next President.

. . .

Third, sponsoring senators may make a difference to the fate of at least some judicial nominations. The more powerful the senator, the more likely it is that nominees he has supported will be confirmed. For instance, the Senate has confirmed a number of nominees who worked for Senator Hatch....

Fourth, a president's popularity might have an effect on a nomination's fate. The President's political strength, as reflected in his approval ratings with the public, might show the risks involved in a fight with the President. The more closely a nomination is identified with the President or the more it means to him or his policies, the more likely that the popularity of the president or his policies will be an important factor....

A related factor may be party cohesion or fidelity. The extent to which senators from the same party are willing to stand together on judicial nominations makes a big difference as to whether they can successfully filibuster or defeat nominations in Committee or on the Senate floor....

The sixth factor is whether the blue-slip process is in place at time of a nomination. The blue-slip process allows a senator to block a nomination made to an office in that senator's home state. This process is usually available to senators from both parties, but sometimes presidents or Senate leaders have restricted it to senators only from the president's party. If this process is in place in whatever form, it expands senators' opportunities to block nominations. It particularly reinforces the strength of the majority party in the Senate....

Seventh, the number of witnesses called for and against nominations is likely to be pertinent to their chances to succeed in the confirmation process. The number of people testifying, particularly against a nomination, is likely to signal some problem with the nomination.... Some people may be opposed because of their supposed ideological commitments, but one must go behind these numbers in order to determine this information.

Eighth, the American Bar Association's ratings on nominees may affect the fate of nominations. Positive ratings do not guarantee confirmation, but negative or largely unfavorable ratings are bound to lower considerably a nominee's chances for confirmation. Even split ratings can be problematic, though not necessarily fatal. The American Bar Association comes as close as any group to providing a "neutral" assessment of a nominee's qualifications, and its ratings may be used by either side in a confirmation contest depending on the extent to which they are favorable or unfavorable.

These are just eight factors, besides ideology, that are likely to affect the fate of judicial nominations. The odds are that nominations will not falter simply because of one of these factors. Moreover, it is possible, if not likely, that the stated grounds of opposition to judicial nominations might not be entirely credible; they might reflect, at least to some extent, a pretext to oppose a nomination. For instance, the Judiciary Committee never acted on President Clinton's nomination of Elena Kagan to the U.S. Court of Appeals for the District of Columbia in 2000. She never got a hearing, much less a vote, on her nomination, in spite of her strong credentials. Indeed, she is now the Dean of Harvard Law School. No one expressed opposition to her because of her ideology. Instead, opposition . . . focused more on whether the appellate court to which she had been nominated had a caseload to justify filling all of the seats to which the President had nominated people. Some people might view this opposition as merely a pretext to preclude the confirmation of someone whom the opposition party feared might be a liberal activist or who would then occupy a seat that it would have preferred for one of its own to occupy. After President Bush took office, Republican leaders changed position and acknowledged the court's caseload justified filling all its seats. And President Bush then nominated Miguel Estrada to one of them. It is possible that at least some opposition to the Estrada nomination derived in part from a desire for payback, though the grounds cited by opponents related to Estrada's temperament and imputed judicial ideology. Although payback is another possible factor that needs to be monitored in the confirmation process, it is hard to verify, because senators rarely acknowledge that it is the basis for their opposition.

In the final analysis, proving that ideology significantly affects the fate of nominations is not easy. Proving it may be so difficult that many people simply opt for anecdotal evidence or merely analyzing the appeal of a particular nominee's ideology. . . . The higher, or more powerful, the court to which someone has been nominated, the more likely senators will be concerned about the person's likely judicial ideology. In any event, as long as senators do not fear the President, senators remain relatively free to pick and choose which nominees to oppose and on what bases.

CONCLUSION

I close with a challenge. I challenge others to talk more openly about merit in judicial selection and particularly whether merit can be defined separately from ideology. If it can, then we have to wonder why more scholars, presidents, and senators do not separately define these concepts. If not, then we need to explain why we should not simply join forces with the many social scientists who believe that judges are simply policymakers who wear robes.

———

Lawrence B. Solum,[63] *Empirical Measures of Judicial Performance: A Tournament of Virtue,* **32 Fla. St. U. L. Rev. 1365 (2005)**

I. Introduction: The Measure of Merit

How ought we to select judges? One possibility is that each of us should campaign for the selection of judges who will transform our own values and interests into law. An alternative is to select judges for their excellence—that is, for the possession of the judicial virtues: intelligence, wisdom, incorruptibility, sobriety, and justice. In an influential and provocative series of articles, Stephen Choi and Mitu Gulati reject both these options and argue instead for a tournament of judges—the selection of judges on the basis of measurable, objective criteria, which they claim point toward merit and away from patronage and politics. Choi and Gulati have gotten something exactly right: judges should be selected on the basis of merit-we want judges who are excellent. But Choi and Gulati have gotten something crucial terribly wrong: they have mistaken measurability for merit. A tournament of judges would be won by judges who possess arbitrary luck and the vices of originality and mindless productivity; the contest would be lost by those who possess the virtues of justice and wisdom. The judicial selection process should not be transformed into a game.

. . . Choi and Gulati's idea is a rare and valuable thing—an idea that is both completely wrong and wonderfully illuminating . . .

II. What Is Judicial Excellence?

. . . What makes one judge better than another? Choi and Gulati largely beg this fundamental question—focusing instead on particular metrics of judicial performance. . . .

. . .

. . . Choi and Gulati begin with the question, What aspects of judicial performance can we easily measure? Only after the measurability question is answered do they then ask, What qualities of good judging are the readily available metrics likely to measure? Of course, as a way of getting started, this method has much to commend itself. If one wants to conduct a tournament of judges, one must work with the data that is available. But getting started is one thing, and serious analysis is another. For us to take Choi and Gulati seriously, their analysis needs to be supplemented by . . . the specification of the actual criteria for judicial excellence.

Why is specification of the criteria for judicial excellence necessary? In order to determine whether a tournament of judges will improve judicial selection or make it worse, we need to know how the easily measurable aspects of judicial excellence relate to those that are difficult

---

63. John E. Cribbet Professor of Law & Professor of Philosophy, University of Illi- nois College of Law.

to measure. That relationship is crucial, because there is no a priori reason for ruling out the possibility that focusing on the measurable might have the unintended consequence of favoring judges with serious defects....

B.   The (Mostly) Uncontested Judicial Virtues (and Vices) ...

... Whereas Choi and Gulati work backwards, from measurability to virtue, we shall work forwards, starting with the notion of judicial virtue. By "virtue" I mean a dispositional quality of mind or character that is constitutive of human excellence, and the "judicial virtues" include both the human virtues that are relevant to judging and any particular virtues that are associated with the social role of judges. We begin with an account of those judicial virtues upon which we can mostly agree—which I shall call the [mostly] "uncontested judicial virtues"....
"Uncontested" in this context reflects the notion that these virtues are based on noncontroversial assumptions about what counts as good judging and on widely accepted beliefs about human nature and social reality; the qualifier "mostly" reflects the fact that even an account of judicial excellence based on widely shared assumptions will be contested by some.

... While there is a good deal of argument about which judges are the best, there is actually an astonishing amount of consensus about two related questions, Who are the very worst judges? and What are the worst judicial vices? No one thinks that the best judges are corrupt, drunk, cowardly, foolish, or stupid. This consensus suggests a strategy for articulating a theory of the uncontested judicial virtues. Let us begin with the worst judicial vices and identify the characteristics that are necessary to correct those defects. These characteristics will constitute the uncontested judicial virtues.

1.   Judicial Incorruptibility and Judicial Sobriety

One judicial vice on which there is likely to be near universal agreement is "corruption." Judges who sell their votes undermine the substantive goals of the law, because corrupt decisions are at least as likely to be wrong as they are to be substantively correct. Moreover, corrupt decisions undermine the rule-of-law values of productivity and uniformity of legal decisions and likewise undermine public respect for the law and public acceptance of the law as legitimate.

. . .

There is another vice that is closely related to corruption but distinct from greed. Judges can become corrupted because their desires are not in order—because they crave pleasure or the status conferred by the possession of fine things. Judges, like the rest of us, can be corrupted by a taste for designer shoes, fast cars, loose companions, or intoxicating substances....

... One might argue that intemperance is a purely private vice ....
But a disposition to disproportionate desires for such pleasures can lead

to more than corruption. Most obviously, a judge who is intoxicated (or high) on the bench is likely to be prone to error. . . .

. . . Of course, an intemperate judge can get lucky and "get away with it," either appearing to do well or even actually doing well despite disordered desires. But in such cases "getting away with it" is a matter of luck; an intemperate judge is simply not reliable. A really damaging misstep is always just one cosmopolitan away.

The virtue that corresponds to the vice of intemperance could be called temperance . . . [b]ut I propose that we . . . name this virtue "judicial sobriety."

2.　Judicial Courage

Fear is one of the most powerful and familiar of the emotions. The disposition to feel too much fear makes us cowardly; the disposition to insufficient fear makes us rash. Courage represents a mean between cowardice and rashness. Let's call the judicial form of this virtue "judicial courage."

We might usefully subdivide the virtue of courage into two parts—which I shall call "physical courage" and "civic courage." That judges need physical courage in order to be excellent as judges is a lamentable fact in many societies. We have recently been reminded of this fact by the tragic experiences of federal district judge Joan Lefkow, who was threatened by one defendant and whose husband and mother were murdered by a party to another case. A judge who could be intimidated by threats of physical violence could not reliably do justice. . . .

Judicial courage has a second dimension. . . . [I]n addition to physical danger, judges may fear consequences of their actions that threaten status and social approval. This fear is dangerous because the law may require judges to make unpopular decisions. A judge who ordered school integration in the South might be shunned socially. In societies where the judicial branch wields significant power in cases involving hot-button issues (abortion, end-of-life disputes, and so forth), there will be occasions where doing what the law requires may be profoundly unpopular. For this reason, judges need the virtue of civic courage—the disposition to put the regard of one's fellows in its proper place and to take it into account in the right way, on the right occasions, and for the right reasons. A judge with this virtue will not be tempted to sacrifice justice on the altar of public opinion. . . .

3.　Judicial Temperament and Impartiality

Like fear, anger is an emotion both familiar and powerful. Judges, like the rest of us, may be hot-tempered or cool and collected. And, like the rest of us, judges are likely to find themselves in situations where a hot temper could produce intemperate actions. This is especially true of trial judges. . . . Some lawyers may deliberately attempt to provoke the judge in order to elicit legal mistakes or "on the record" behavior that displays animus toward a party, which may serve as the basis for an appeal.... Intemperate judicial behavior may lead the judge to misapply the law or to distort the applicable legal standards in "the heat of anger." Moreover, a hotheaded judge may become partial—pulling against the party who is the object of anger and displaying favoritism to that party's opponent.

Aristotle identified ... "good temper" as the corrective virtue for the vice of bad temper. In the judicial context, this virtue is so important that we have a phrase that expresses the virtue as a distinctively judicial form of excellence—"judicial temperament." This phrase reflects our sense that the virtue of "good temper" is essential for good judging.

Is judicial temperament also required for judges who do not supervise trials? ... [G]ood temper is essential for excellence in appellate judging. Appellate judges hear cases in panels or en banc—which create opportunities for friction among the judges themselves. Hot tempers can destroy collegiality and, with it, the opportunity for compromise and mutual understanding. Moreover, even a brief can elicit anger, and if anger becomes rage, it can have a blinding effect, depriving the judge of the ability to recognize the merits of an argument or a weakness in the judge's own conception of the legal issues in a case.

... [W]hen a party flouts the law or disrespects the participants in a legal proceeding, anger may be appropriate.... But judges with the virtue of judicial temperament will not display their anger by ruling against an offending party on issues that are close or by exercising discretion on incidental matters so as to disfavor the anger-provoking party.

One reason that anger is an especially dangerous vice for judges is that anger can produce bias. For this reason, the virtue of judicial temperament is closely related to another judicial virtue, "judicial impartiality." This virtue is a familiar feature of our conception of good judging. We want judges to be neutral arbitrators. A judge should be open to the law and evidence and not be biased in favor of one side or another. Such impartiality should extend not just to the parties but should also encompass the causes, movements, special interests, and ideologies that may be associated with those parties. When a judge takes the bench or lifts her pen to write an opinion, she should put aside her allegiance to left or right, liberal or conservative, religiosity or secularism.

It is a mistake, however, to view impartiality as synonymous with disinterest. The virtue of impartiality is not cold-blooded. This is because the role of judge requires insight and understanding into the human condition. A good judge perceives the law and facts from a human perspective. Some facts are hot-charged with emotional salience. Some legal rules are morally charged—engaging our sense of indignation when juxtaposed with violative behavior. So the impartial judge is not cold-blooded; she is not indifferent to the parties that come before her. Rather, the judge with the virtue of judicial impartiality has evenhanded sympathy for all the parties to a dispute....

4. Diligence and Carefulness

Judging is hard work, involving its share of drudgery. Some trials are long and boring. Some opinions require long hours of research and even longer hours of careful drafting. The temptation to shirk this work is accentuated by the fact that judges are not (and should not be) closely supervised. And the lack of supervision is compounded in jurisdictions that grant judges life tenure or long terms in office. . . .

What is the virtue that corresponds to the vice of sloth? We might call it diligence. The diligent judge has the right attitude toward judicial work, finding judicial tasks engaging and rewarding. But more than a good attitude is required. An excellent judge must have an appropriate "energy level"—a product of both physical and mental health. The combination of these traits should translate into a judge who is capable of hard work when hard work is required. . . .

Carefulness is closely related to diligence. No one can sensibly doubt that judicial carelessness is a vice. Careless decisions, careless drafting, careless research—any of these can lead to substantive injustice. Carefulness is especially important in the context of judging, because excellent judging frequently requires meticulous attention to details. . . . An excellent judge has an eye for detail and a devotion to precision.

5. Judicial Intelligence and Learnedness

Can anyone doubt that stupidity is a judicial vice? All humans need intelligence to function well—but some tasks require more intelligence on more occasions. Judging is the kind of task that almost always requires smartness and sometimes requires extraordinary intelligence. Both law and facts can be complex. Only a judge with intelligence will be able to sort out the complexities of the rule against perpetuities or penetrate the mysteries of a complex statute. But more than intelligence is required. A truly excellent judge must also be learned in the law, because one cannot start from scratch in each and every case and because there is at least some truth to the notion that the law is a seamless web. . . .

The need for judicial intelligence and learnedness is accentuated rather than diminished in an adversary system . . . [in which] successful advocates will try to make a bad case appear better by deploying sophistry and rhetoric. Intelligent and learned judges can "see through" the obfuscation.

6. Craft and Skill

So far, our investigation has focused on what Aristotle called the moral and intellectual virtues. These are dispositions of character and mind that make for human excellence. Good judging requires more than good character and intellectual ability. That is because judging includes elements of craft, and therefore a good judge must possess a skill set—the particular learned abilities that are to good judging what good bowing technique is to archery or good draftsmanship is to architecture.

A full account of judicial craft is far beyond the scope of this Essay, but one particular aspect of judicial craft and skill demands attention. Excellence in judging (especially good appellate judging) requires particular skill in the use of language. Good judges must be good communicators.... Written communication skills are especially important for appellate judges in a common law system, because of the doctrine of stare decisis. Because appellate opinions set precedent, a badly written opinion can misstate the law or state the law in a misleading way. A really well-drafted opinion, on the other hand, can clarify the obscure and illuminate the meaning of murky legal texts.

· · ·

C.   The (Mostly) Contestable Judicial Virtues

One advantage of a theory of judicial excellence is that it reveals a large zone of agreement. For all practical purposes, we can agree that judges should be incorruptible, courageous, good-tempered, diligent, skilled, and smart. But these (mostly uncontested) virtues do not tell the whole story about judicial excellence....

· · ·

[Professor Solum argues that there are two conceptions of the "virtues of justice"—the first, "justice as fairness," which he criticizes as essentially result-oriented; the second, "justice as lawfulness," which he argues is the correct "virtue of justice," based on distinctions between first and second order judgments and between public and private judgments.]

2.   Competing Conceptions of Equity and Practical Wisdom

But the virtue of justice may not be exhausted by the lawfulness conception. Even if we concede that in ordinary cases justice requires adherence to the law, the question remains whether there are extraordinary cases—cases in which excellent judges would depart from the law (or, to put it differently, decide that the law does not really apply)....

... [T]he positive law is cast in the form of abstract and general rules; such rules may lead to results that are unfair in those particular cases that do not fit the pattern contemplated by the formulation of the rule. If lawfulness were the whole story about the virtue of justice, then an excellent judge would apply the rule "come hell and high water," even if the rule led to consequences that were absurd or manifestly unjust. But this implication of the lawfulness conception seems odd and unsatisfactory. Another way of conceptualizing this concern is to distinguish between two styles of rule application, which I shall call "mechanical" and "sensitive."

Does the excellent judge apply the rules in a rigid and mechanical way? Or does a virtuous judge correct the rigidity of the lawfulness conception with equity? ... As Roger Shiner puts it,

Equity is the virtue shown by one particular kind of agent—a judge—when making practical judgments in the face of the limitations of one particular kind of practical rule—those hardened customs and written laws that constitute for some society that institutionalized system of norms that is its legal system.

But there is a problem with supplementing the lawfulness conception of the virtue of justice with the notion of equity. . . . [T]he virtue of equity seems to require the exercise of first-order private judgments of fairness. . . . Without constraint, private judgment threatens to swallow public judgment, and then we are on a slippery slope that threatens to transform the lawfulness conception into the fairness conception.

The trick is to constrain equity while preserving its corrective role. . . . An Aristotelian account of the virtue of equity gives us three points of traction. The first point of traction is . . . [that] [e]quity is not doing what the judge believes is fair when that belief conflicts with the law; rather, equity is doing what the spirit of the law requires when the expression of the rule fails to capture its point or purpose in a particular factual context. The second point of traction is provided by the virtue of justice itself. A judge [with the virtue of justice as lawfulness] is not tempted to use equity to avoid the constraining force of the law. [Such a judge] has internalized the normative force of the law; such a judge wants to do as the law requires.

The third point of traction is provided by Aristotle's understanding of the intellectual virtue of practical wisdom, or . . . the quality that we describe as "good judgment" or "common sense." A judge with the virtue of practical wisdom, a phronimos, has the ability to perceive the salient features of particular situations. In the context of judging, we can use Llewellyn's phrase, "situation sense," or by way of analogy to the phrase "moral vision," we can say that a sense of justice requires "legal vision," the ability to size up a case and discern which aspects are legally important. . . .

This account of equity can be contrasted with two rival accounts. On the one hand, we can imagine a conception of judging as pure equity—the idea that the judge would simply do the right thing in each particular fact situation. This conception of equity is simply a version of the fairness conception of the virtue of justice. On the other hand, we can imagine a conception of judging that limits equity to the vanishing point—perhaps to those cases where the application of the rule is truly absurd. Neither of these two alternatives offers a fully satisfactory account of the virtue of equity. . . .

III. DISCERNING EXCELLENCE

Excellent judges possess the judicial virtues. They are incorruptible and sober, courageous, good-tempered, impartial, diligent, careful, smart, learned, skilled, just, and wise. . . .

A. Screening for Judicial Vice

The first step in discerning excellence is the simplest. The initial screen for judicial excellence eliminates candidates who are incontrovertibly vicious—corrupt, ill-tempered, cowardly, unintelligent, or foolish....

If we want to effectively screen for vice, we want to select judges (and especially Supreme Court Justices) from candidates who have a track record that is likely to expose these vices. This suggests that Supreme Court Justices ought to be selected from judges or lawyers who have extensive experience in public life. Serious moral and intellectual defects may not be apparent at age thirty, but they are likely to have been exposed after two decades in public life....

B. Detecting the Phronimos [those with practical wisdom]

... Our ordinary lives involve interactions with friends and colleagues whom we recognize as having good practical judgment; we ask them for advice and emulate their choices. Practical wisdom is harder to theorize than it is to recognize....

... Given the separation of powers and the code of judicial ethics, judges may become cloistered—isolated from everyone but their friends and family, judicial colleagues, and law clerks. Opinions give evidence of craft and the intellectual virtues but provide an imperfect window on the judge's practical wisdom. For this reason, it is especially important that judges—at least those who would be willing to serve on the Supreme Court—engage in practical activities that expose them to public life. Civic or charitable activities and service on judicial commissions are two obvious opportunities for judicial immersion in a public life of practical activity. Supreme Court Justices should be selected from among those who have demonstrated their possession of practical wisdom, both from the bench and in wider public life.

C. Recognizing the Nomimos

If judicial opinions are an imperfect window on the virtue of practical wisdom, they are well suited for the task of recognizing which judges are lawful and which are results-oriented. Although disregard for the rule of law can be masked by clever opinion writing, a persistent pattern of lawlessness is truly difficult to conceal. By way of contrast, a judge who is nomimos will strive to stay within the letter and spirit of existing law. Judges who believe in the rule of law attempt to give statutory or constitutional language its full due, eschewing interpretations that create unnecessary or artificial vagueness or ambiguity. Judges who believe in the rule of law will strive to follow precedent rather than evade it.

... Judges with the vice of results-orientation are likely to wear it on their sleeve rather than conceal it underneath their robes.

... In sum, we have good reason to believe that we can screen for vice, discern the possession of practical wisdom, and recognize true dedication to the rule of law. The fact that we have the capacity to recognize judicial virtue, however, does not entail that we can quantify it. A tournament of virtue, on the other hand, promises something that might appear to be a very great good. ... The hard question is whether the variables that can be quantified are good proxies for true judicial virtues.

IV.   THE MISMEASUREMENT OF VIRTUE

... Can we quantify judicial virtue? I will argue that the most reasonable answer to this question is "no." Before I do, however, we should examine the case for quantification, as stated by Choi and Gulati.

A.   The Case for Quantification

Choi and Gulati make the case for measurement by introducing the distinction between absolute and relative measurement of judicial excellence:

> ... [J]ust as it is impossible to articulate what special factor makes Lance Armstrong the best cyclist in the world, it is impossible to reduce Justice Benjamin Cardozo's greatness as a judge to numbers. But one can look at how many times Armstrong has won the Tour de France and compare his numbers to those of his peers. Similarly, one can look at Justice Cardozo's opinions and see how often they were cited by other judges, how often they were discussed in law reviews, and how often they made their way into casebooks. Justice Cardozo's numbers can then be compared to those of his peers ...

In other words, they argue that we can develop an ordinal scale for judicial excellence, even if we cannot develop a cardinal scale.

Before we go any further, however, we ought to observe that the analogy ... between bicycle racing and judging is a rather tenuous one. In the case of bicycle racing, there is an objective and quantifiable measure of performance. The first to finish is the winner; participants in the race are ranked (both cardinally and ordinally) by time. In racing, the output of the contestants is ultimately the time it takes each racer to finish, which can easily be compared across racers. In judging, there are many outputs: rulings, opinions, jury instructions, and so forth. These outputs cannot easily be compared across cases and judges. There is no scale that permits objective comparisons to be made.

B.   Measuring the Wrong Qualities

Choi and Gulati's ... measures ... for example, citation rates and productivity not only fail to capture the essence of judicial excellence, they may, at least in some circumstances, measure judicial vice. Choi and Gulati assume that judges who write lots of opinions that are cited a lot are better judges than those who write fewer opinions and get fewer citations. But are these assumptions correct?

1. Citation and the Rule of Law

Choi and Gulati seem to assume that citation rate correlates with judicial excellence. Their argument for this conclusion is actually somewhat obscure. It begins with the idea that there is a "market" for judicial opinions.... [They argue that:]

> Unlike many other markets, however, the market for judicial opinions is relatively free of ... imperfections. For one, judicial opinions may be obtained at no cost by judges and, in many areas of the law, are abundant.

"No cost" is ambiguous. Choi and Gulati are right if they simply mean that judges do not personally pay a monetary price for access to law libraries and electronic legal databases. But this does not mean that the production of citations to other judges' opinions is cost-free. Citing is an expensive business, but the price is paid in terms of time. Finding opinions takes time. Reading them takes time. Citing them properly takes time ....

The price that judges pay in terms of time is an opportunity cost. Whether judges research, read, and cite on their own or have their clerks do this work, the time devoted to this activity is not available for other activities. Moreover, the time resource is finite. A judge's own time is finite.... Clerk time is also finite; judges are limited in the number of clerks they can employ....

The fact that citations are costly has important implications for answering the question whether citation rates measure the quality of judicial opinions....

> ... If Judge B's opinion turns up early in Judge A's search for authority, then it will be more likely to be cited. As we all know, there are many basic propositions of law for which many possible opinions could be cited. In each federal circuit, for example, there are opinions on basic procedural matters (standards of appellate review, standards for summary judgment, and so forth) where hundreds or thousands of prior opinions will state the proposition of law.

> A rational judge will not read all of these opinions and cite the opinion that does the best job of stating the law. Rather, the rational judge will read enough authority to be reasonably sure of the correct statement of the rule. When it comes to citations, we would expect judges to "satisfice" and not "optimize." The opinions that are cited are likely to be the opinions the judge encounters first, and as a practical matter, this means that they are likely to be the opinions that result from traditional research methods.... [J]udges are highly likely to cite authority that is already widely cited.... And the more judges that cite the authority, the greater the likelihood that it will garner further citations.

. . .

Choi and Gulati's claim—that all judges will cite the best opinions—is clearly false once we look at citation through the lens of networking theory. In the language of network economics, we can call this a process of "preferential attachment." Opinions that are well situated in the network of citations will be cited many times; opinions that are more obscurely situated in the network will be cited rarely or not at all. The result is the so-called " 'rich get richer' phenomenon." Opinions that are initially cited for a proposition will be cited over and over for that same proposition.

In other words, the citation rate of a given opinion (and hence of the author judge) will depend in large part on the position of the opinion in the ecology of the network of authority. The first opinion to state a given proposition will be likely to generate many citations. . . . Occupying a very favorable node (or position in the ecology of the citations network) can result in an extraordinary number of citations; occupation of an unfavorable node can result in no citations at all. The important thing is that these differences can occur even though the proposition stated is exactly the same. For this reason, citation rates do not necessarily track quality. But this understates the problem with citation rates as a proxy for judicial excellence. . . . [I]t seems quite likely that frequency of citation will be a function of originality. The first case to state a proposition is, all else being equal, highly likely to become an important node in the citation network. . . . But it is hardly clear that novelty makes for good law or that originality is a judicial virtue. This is not to say that originality is never appropriate, but a truly virtuous judge will only be original when the law itself requires originality.

Indeed, I have argued that the opposite is true under normal conditions. The excellent judge is [one] who follows the law rather than makes it. . . . The very best judges are experts at avoiding originality. And the very worst judges may be the most original. Very bad judges may use the cases that come before them as vehicles for changing the law, transforming the rules laid down into the rules that they prefer. This kind of results-oriented . . . judging may produce many original propositions of law and hence a high citation rate, but this is a measure of judicial vice and not judicial virtue.

This is not to say that a high citation rate is necessarily an indicator of judicial vice. . . . Some judges may have high citation rates because the luck of the draw has handed them a disproportionate share of cases with truly new legal questions. But even if this is so, it does not follow that these are the best judges. Luck is not virtue.

2. Productivity and Carefulness . . .

[A]re the judges who write the most or longest opinions the best judges? Choi and Gulati have argued that short opinions are actually an indicator of judicial excellence, because shortness is a proxy for judges writing their own opinions as opposed to delegating that task to clerks. If total number of pages is not a good proxy for diligence, then what about the number of opinions written? It is certainly possible that the number of opinions written per time period is a proxy for judicial excellence, but this is not necessarily the case. The number of opinions written is surely a function of the number of opinions assigned. Assigning judges may attempt to equalize workloads; this might result in a judge who is given a difficult writing assignment being assigned fewer opinions.... The question whether there is a relationship between number of opinions written and judicial excellence seems to depend on a variety of empirical questions....

3.   Fame Versus Excellence

There is a more general problem with Choi and Gulati's approach to measuring judicial excellence. The judges who are cited most and who write the most opinions may well be the judges who want to be famous.... Fame and glory (or external recognition) are powerful motivators, but it is not clear that a desire for fame is a virtue for judges. Indeed, the claim that excellent judges seek fame and glory seems somewhat counterintuitive.

There is nothing wrong with a desire for external recognition; humans as social creatures may naturally desire recognition by their fellows. But an excessive desire for fame is likely to be inconsistent with judicial virtue. The virtue of justice—the central component of judicial excellence—requires that judges aim at giving litigants what they are due, that to which they are entitled by the rules laid down. To the extent that judges decide cases on the basis of a desire for the fame and glory that come with winning a tournament of judges, they risk departing from the actions required by the virtue of justice; to put it more bluntly, a tournament of judges may create incentives to do injustice in order to win....

C.   Gaming the Tournament of Judges

If there were a tournament of judges that influenced the selection of Supreme Court Justices, we may confidently predict that some judges would play to win....

1.   Gaming the Productivity Measure

Choi and Gulati propose that we measure the number of opinions and dissents as well as the number of cases in which judges participate. How could this measure be gamed? Tournament leaders will wish to maximize the number of opinions and dissents. If not assigned an opinion, a judge will have a strong incentive to dissent. If two politically aligned judges sit on the same panel and one of the two is a tournament leader while the other is not, there will be a strong incentive to hand the opinion to the leader. ...

2.   Gaming the Citation Frequency Measure

The opportunities for gaming this measure are obvious. Academics will now have an incentive to cite their favorites to influence tournament results. Likewise with both lower court judges and Supreme Court Justices. A set of second-order tactics will be likely to emerge. The composition of law school faculties can be influenced by state legislatures and by the wealthy alumni of private universities. The lower federal court benches are selected by the President and the Senate. Moreover, judges themselves can change their opinion writing so as to maximize the opportunities for both citing other judges (allies in the tournament) and for being cited. Opinions will become longer and long string cites will become the rule. Basic and uncontroversial issues will be discussed in depth. . . .

3. Gaming the Judicial Independence Measure

Choi and Gulati propose that we measure independence by voting records. Judges would score points for voting against a judge appointed by a President of the same party as appointed that judge. There are several ways to game this measure. The most obvious way is to dissent when a same-party judge is in the majority and the decision would otherwise be unanimous. . . . [I]f you are a tournament leader and the case is not on a hot-button issue about which you care deeply, it may well be in your interest to score some independence points by deciding the case in a way you believe is wrong. . . .

D. The Costs of a Gamed Tournament

. . .

1. Damage to the Rule of Law

One thing that is very difficult to measure objectively is whether a judge has decided in accord with the law—rather than on the basis of either ideology or to gain an advantage in the tournament. The virtue of justice is not rewarded in the tournament. No points are assigned for getting the law right. Moreover, too high a regard for justice is likely to be punished. Judges who vote based on the merits will lose opportunities to write opinions and dissents. Judges who agonize about getting it right will be diverting precious time from the opportunity to score points by getting it long, that is, producing lots of long and citable opinions. And judges who get it right are unlikely to produce opinions with lots of novel propositions of law—and hence lots of citations.

2. The Exclusion of Soft Variables

Practical wisdom . . . is a key component of judicial excellence, but the tournament of judges does not award points to judges who have common sense, which is the ability to size up a situation and penetrate to the issues that are truly important. Indeed, the judges who possess this virtue are likely to be rather weak performers in the tournament of judges. They are likely to perceive that scoring points at the expense of doing justice is a rather poor excuse for judging. They are likely to lag behind their more canny and competitive colleagues.

3. Decreased Transparency

Choi and Gulati claim transparency as an advantage for the tournament of judges, but the opposite may be the result of their proposal. The tournament is likely to create an illusion of objectivity. Behind the scenes, however, there would be manipulation of opinion counts, citation counts, and independent decision counts. This will especially be true if one party controlled the Presidency, the Senate, the Supreme Court, and a majority of court of appeals slots at the beginning of the tournament. That party would have enormous strategic advantages in gaming the tournament, but the political nature of the selection process would effectively be masked by the apparently neutral and objective basis that the tournament results would provide for the selection of Supreme Court Justices.

4. A Crisis

... [I]magine a court populated by judges who had won Choi and Gulati's tournament. These judges would be without the virtues of integrity, wisdom, or justice. They would have been selected for the ability to manipulate the tournament results. In order to do this, the winning judges would be those who are willing to elevate self-interest over the interests of the public and the parties who appear before them. And these clever but vicious judges would be entrusted with the ultimate constitutional authority.

V. Conclusion: The Redemption of Spectacular Failure

If viewed as a serious proposal for reform of the judicial selection process, Choi and Gulati have a spectacularly bad idea—a real stinker. This can be true even if the retroactive application of Choi and Gulati's selection criteria identifies excellent judges. The reason for this is obvious. No one had an incentive to game Choi and Gulati's hypothetical tournament. The participants could not predict that the tournament would exist....

Sometimes, however, bad ideas spark good debates.... As a thought experiment, the tournament of judges is a marvel, precisely because it invites rigorous analysis of the judicial selection process. In the end, Choi and Gulati's tournament of judges invites us to ask two questions: What constitutes judicial excellence? and How can we select judges who possess them? Those questions are worth answering.

————

Questions and Comments

1. Although most scholars would reject the idea of a tournament, in which consideration was limited to the objective factors discussed by Choi and Gulati, do Choi and Gulati make a good case for considering, as at least one factor for elevating a lower court judge to the Supreme Court, the kind

of influence and output that can be counted numerically? Or do those factors not reach the qualities one is trying to measure?[64]

2.   Consider how much overlap there is between Professors Gerhardt's and Solum's accounts of uncontroversial measures of judicial excellence. Would Gerhardt disagree with any of Solum's "mostly uncontested" virtues?

3.   Would Solum's distinction between the virtue of justice as fairness and the virtue of justice as lawfulness require inquiry into ideology? Does your answer suggest some difficulties in defining what we mean by ideology?

4.   By what means would a candidate's "practical wisdom" and "open-mindedness" be discerned? Or is it incapable of assessment? Until 2001, the ABA Standing Committee on the Judiciary was able to conduct interviews—before a nomination was announced—with colleagues, opposing counsel and others who had practiced with possible nominees over a long period in order to obtain candid assessments of their qualities. Consider whether the loss of this opportunity will interfere with obtaining such "soft" information. Are there other alternatives for gathering this information?

5.   Is the trend toward appointing court of appeals judges to the Supreme Court a good one? Why has it been growing? What are the benefits? What are the costs? As Professor Jackson has observed, looking to the lower courts for nominees to the Supreme Court has the advantage of "providing opportunity to evaluate judicial temperament and craftsmanship." Vicki C. Jackson, *Packages of Judicial Independence: The Selection and Tenure of Article III Judges*, 95 Geo. L. J. 965, 983 (2007). In addition, existing judges have survived at least one Senate confirmation hearing. But, as Jackson also points out, nominating judges may "create undesirable incentives for [judicial] decisions made with an eye to advancement through necessarily political confirmation processes." *Id.* at 983–84. Moreover, looking only or mainly to that pool may limit the diversity of the bench and unnecessarily overlook potential nominees with valuable other experiences, such as Presidents (Taft), governors (Warren), and legislators (Senator Black). *Id.*; see also, Lee Epstein, Jack Knight, & Andrew D. Martin, *The Norm of Prior Judicial Experience and Its Consequences for Career Diversity on the U.S. Supreme Court,* 91 Cal. L. Rev. 903, 908–917 (2003).

6.   How likely is it that today's hot button issues will remain important 10 to 15 years from now? How good are we at predicting what are likely to be the hot button issues of tomorrow? What, if any, implications does your answer to these questions have for how nominees are chosen and confirmed? If the issues are likely to differ, does this lend support to those who urge a focus on characteristics like practical wisdom and open-mindedness? Alternatively, does it make it more important to probe the nominee's views on a wide range of issues?

2.   Invigorating the Senate's Role to "Advise"?

The Constitution provides that the Senate is to give "Advice and Consent" in the appointment process. We have some idea of what

---

64.   In addition to Gerhardt and Solum, consider Steven Goldberg, *Federal Judges and the Heisman Trophy*, 32 Fla. St. U. L. Rev. 1237 (2005) (suggesting that the meas-ures of an excellent lower court judge may not predict greatness as a Supreme Court Justice).

"consent" means, although as the foregoing discussion reveals, there is controversy over the standards to be used. But what does the "advice" part mean? Some Presidents have consulted with the Senate, or more likely, with individual Senators, before making their nomination. One famous anecdote tells of President Hoover's sending the Senate a list of those he was thinking of nominating for a vacancy on the Supreme Court. The list was ranked in order of preference with Cardozo at the bottom. Senator William Borah, then head of the Foreign Relations Committee, reportedly returned it to Hoover, commenting, "Your list is all right, but you handed it to me upside down." A consensus among law school faculties, bar leaders, and the strong views of some sitting members of the Court no doubt also helped to persuade President Hoover, who was initially reluctant to nominate a second Jew and another New Yorker to sit on the Court, to choose Cardozo. Henry Abraham, *Justices, Presidents, and Senators* 153–54 (1999). More recently, President Clinton is said to have consulted with Senator Hatch (R–UT), then Chair of the Senate Judiciary Committee, before he nominated Ginsburg and Breyer.

But such examples are relatively unusual. While Senators have historically exercised considerable influence on the nomination—as well as the confirmation—of judges to the federal district courts and courts of appeals, Presidents have been much less inclined to defer in the selection of Supreme Court Justices. Should that practice be changed? Should the Senate have more of a role in advising the President at the nomination stage? If so, what might that role be and how might it be implemented? The article by Sunstein and Strauss, excerpted above in Section A, suggests that the Senate should be more assertive in exercising its constitutional authority to give "advice" to the President. Does the Constitution contemplate such a role or only authorize the President to voluntarily seek such advice?

Professor Glenn Reynolds has suggested ways for the Senate to be more engaged at the "advice" stage, proposing that the Senate draft a list of nominees for each Supreme Court vacancy. See Glenn Harlan Reynolds, *Taking Advice Seriously: An Immodest Proposal for Reforming the Confirmation Process*, 65 S. Cal. L. Rev. 1577 (1992). According to Professor Reynolds' proposal, if the President selects from the Senate's list, the nominee would receive what he calls a "fast-track" confirmation. If the President does not select from that list, the nominee would face the rigors of the traditional confirmation process. (In fact, it can be argued that, to some extent, President Clinton, in effect, used a variation of this idea when he discussed potential nominees with Senator Hatch before nominating Ginsburg and Breyer.) Reynolds argues that his proposal would implement the requirement of the appointments clause that the Senate as a whole give both advice and consent, and is consistent with the implication of the word "advice" that the Senate's advice not bind the President in any way.

Questions and Comments

1. Are there differences in the capacities of Presidents, as heads of the Executive Branch, and Senators, as legislators, to take the initiative to engage in the kind of vetting and investigation that these days typically accompanies selection of a Supreme Court nominee? Are these differences of constitutional significance? Of political significance? Why hasn't the Senate developed a practice, along the lines Professor Reynolds has proposed, of developing its own list?

2. Should the role of the Senate vary with the different types of appointments it confirms? Note that Article II, Section 2 of the Constitution prescribes the appointment process for Justices of the Supreme Court, as well as for Ambassadors and Cabinet officials. The language used for all these situations is the same: The President "shall nominate, and by and with the Advice and Consent of the Senate, shall appoint...." Should the role of the Senate be the same in all these appointments? Or should there be more deference to the President in the case of Cabinet officials and less with respect to life-tenured judges?

3. Other western democracies have moved to make the process by which persons are appointed to the highest constitutional court more consultative and transparent. For example, consider the Constitution Act of 2005 in the United Kingdom, creating a Supreme Court whose members (after the present Law Lords cease their service) would be selected on the recommendation of a Commission, including members of the judiciary and others.[65] Would use of advisory nominating commissions be helpful to U.S. Presidents? Would they improve the process? Even if they would improve the process for the appointment of lower court judges, would they necessarily improve appointments to the Supreme Court? If so, how should the nominating commissions be constructed? Are there constitutional issues to be considered?'

4. Consider Professor Resnik's cautionary comment on the use of independent nominating commissions:

> [M]any states use forms of merit selection. Further, regulations governing the selection of federal magistrate judges require that screening panels, composed of a variety of kinds of persons, play a role in vetting nominees. In the spring of 2003, Senator Charles Schumer, a Democrat from New York, made such a proposal. He suggested that the Senate and President create nominating commissions for each state and each federal circuit, to be composed of an equal number of members chosen by the President and by the opposition party's Senate leader. The nominating commissions would have the power to propose a single candidate for each vacancy that the President was obliged to nominate

65. President Carter used advisory nominating commissions to recommend names of proposed candidates for federal courts of appeals positions during his presidency, an effort that helped him expand the pool of women and minorities to consider; President Reagan, however, abandoned the use of commissions. Some states, as well as the District of Columbia, use nominating commissions to recommend persons for judicial office and to constrain the authority of elected officials in their selection.

absent "evidence" that a candidate was "unfit for judicial service." The White House objected that such a process would "transfer the nomination power of the President and the confirmation power of the Senate to a group of unelected and unaccountable private citizens."

As this exchange suggests, independent commissions have appeal precisely because they devolve powers of appointment that are held directly by political branches to another level. To do so—as some states have in their "merit selection" mechanisms—requires placing faith either in experts or in group-based processes to generate a search for qualities in prospective judges that may make them wise judges but not necessarily attractive to more politically-engaged appointing bodies. The very devolution, however, also can be criticized for producing a selection process less "democratic" than is the appointment of judges by elected officials. Moreover, what power is in fact delegated turns on the details of particular nomination commissions, which vary in their compositions and their ability to constrain the range of options of the elected branches. Yet another dimension is the degree of publicity surrounding nominations, as the lobbyists now attuned to the President and Senate could aim their persuasive efforts in other directions or attempt to affect the reputations of individuals under consideration.

Resnik, *Judicial Selection and Democratic Theory, supra,* at 638–39.

Would it be fair to say that the U.S. Constitution contemplates a political appointment and confirmation process? Would it be fair to say that if enough Senators want to be more active in the "advice" stage, there would be nothing to stop them except their political judgment as to the consequences?

3.   Should There Be a Special Role for the ABA?

As noted earlier, until 2001 the ABA had a special role in evaluating potential nominees before the President finalized the nomination. In March 2001, the President announced that the ABA would no longer have that special role and would be given no advance look at potential nominees. See Gonzales' letter in Section A, above. The first excerpt from Daniel Troy, a private practitioner critical of the ABA, gives some understanding of the background for the White House's decision, reflecting some of the criticisms made of the ABA's special role. In the next excerpt, Professor Laura Little evaluates the history of the ABA's participation, criticizes the White House's decision to terminate that special role, and recommends that, with some changes, the ABA should be allowed to resume its prior advisory function.

———

The Role of the American Bar Association in the Judicial Selection Process: Hearing Before the S. Comm. on the Judiciary, 104th Cong., 2d Sess., 87–88 (1996) (prepared testimony of Daniel E. Troy)[66]

... [M]y position is that there is considerable value in a neutral, balanced evaluation of the credentials of judicial nominees. Beginning in the 1950s and until the mid-late 1970s, to the best of my knowledge, the ABA fulfilled such a function. During the past 20 years, though, the ABA's evaluations have become overtly political. Either the ABA must purge politics from its process, or its special, quasi-official role should be reconsidered, and its views treated like those of any other group.

In my testimony today, I wish to make the following points. First, the ABA's House of Delegates, its policy-making body, consistently adopts resolutions favoring liberal causes. Part of the reason the House takes such position is because of the over-representation of special interest groups, and because of the lack of expertise of the Delegates on many of the issues on which they are voting. Those resolutions form the basis for the ABA's lobbying agenda, which the ABA seeks to implement with the help of a large Washington office staffed with a number lobbyists.

Second, the members of the ABA's Standing Committee on the Federal Judiciary, who perform the ABA's judicial evaluations, tend to be Democrats. Although members of that Committee must agree to give up activities on behalf of political parties or federal candidates while on the Committee, as well as political contributions, many continue to be active in the formulation of ABA policies and in lobbying on its behalf.

Third, despite protestations to the contrary, the ABA's Standing committee on the Federal Judiciary does indeed take the political views of nominees into, account, and does tend to regard less favorably nominees whose views are not consonant with the ABA's liberal philosophy.

Before proceeding, I wish to add the following caveats. First, the ABA's right to evaluate judicial nominees and to opine on their competence is not at issue here. The right to speak out on judicial nominees— indeed, on any of the public policy issues that the ABA addresses—is protected by the First Amendment. The sole issue to which I direct my remarks is whether the ABA should continue to enjoy a special, quasi-official role in the process....

Second, the ABA can and does make important contributions to the formulation of governmental policy. My primary quarrel with the ABA is

---

66. Partner at Wiley, Rein and Fielding, Washington, D.C. Mr. Troy's testimony indicated that at this time, "I specialize in communications law and complex civil appellate litigation, with a special emphasis on constitutional issues.... I have served on the ABA's Working Group on Regulatory Reform, and been the co-chair of the Judicial Review Committee (1994–95).... From 1987 to 1990, I worked in the Department of Justice's Office of Legal Counsel. Before that, I clerked for Judge Robert H. Bork when he was on the D.C. Circuit...."

that it spends too much time and effort on divisive and often secondary issues. . . .

. . . I am [not] alone in my sentiments that the ABA's liberal tilt deserves the organization and its members. The ABA has lost approximately 40,000 member since 1992, when it first began supporting abortion rights. In my judgment, many of these individuals are among those whom Justice Lewis Powell, a former ABA President, warned would be "lost, fractionated or embittered by [the ABA's] involvement in political controversy."

I. The ABA's Liberal Positions

A. The House of Delegates' Resolutions

It is not hard to prove that today's ABA reflects the views of a dominant, liberal elite. To give but a few illustrations, in the past few years, the ABA has:[67]

[On "Cultural Issues," the ABA "endorsed affirmative action," "opposed laws protecting unborn children," "endorsed [unrestricted] funding for the National Endowment for the Arts," "opposed the denial of welfare benefits to a mother who has an additional child while on welfare," "essentially opposed Proposition 187" concerning denial of benefits to illegal immigrants, "opposed a constitutional amendment on school prayer," and "supported 'motor voter' registration." On "International Issues", it has "favored ratification of the Start II Treaty with the USSR," "urged the U.S. to rejoin UNESCO" and to remain in the International Labor Organization, "urged reestablishment of rule of law in Guatemala," "opposed proliferation" of weapons of mass destruction. On "Economic Issues," it has favored "single payer" health care plans and in 1994, "supported universal access to health care;" "opposed federal medical professional liability tort law changes generally, and federal products liability reform." On "Criminal Law issues," it has supported bans on assault weapons, opposed amendments to the Federal Rules of Evidence concerning the defendants' past similar acts in cases involving sexual assault, "opposed abolishing the exclusionary rule," "opposed mandatory minimum sentences," "opposed efforts to limit prisoner access to federal courts in capital and noncapital habeas corpus reforms" while maintaining that it favors streamlining of habeas corpus, and approved "creation of programs that allow criminals and their victims" to meet under monitored circumstances to address various issues.]

Not all of these positions are bad, although some are utterly outside of the realm of the ABA's expertise. Some others, though, are arguably within the ABA's "core" role, which most acknowledge as legitimate, to promote the administration of justice. All of these positions, however,

---

67. [Editors' Note: In the editors' summary that follows, we use Mr. Troy's words   in quotations.]

are unquestionably more associated with the left rather than the right side of the political spectrum (other than perhaps the international law issues). As one left-wing critic of the ABA remarked to me in private conversation, "the ABA is the establishment, and to the extent the establishment is liberal, so is the ABA."

B.   The Make-up of the House of Delegates

One of the reasons for these outcomes is the composition of the House of Delegates, which is by no means democratic. The House of Delegates consists of 542 delegates, who represent state and local bar associations, ABA sections, and affiliate organizations. There is a ratio of one delegate for about 700 members, but there is no one-person-one-vote principle in the ABA. To illustrate, the national Lesbian and Gay Law Association (NLGLA) has affiliate status, and thus gets to send a representative to the House of Delegates. When that status was granted in 1992, the NLGLA had 473 members, only 160 of whom were ABA members. By contrast, the approximately 40,000 Florida Bar Association had only 8 delegates, or one for each 5,000 members.

Other small groups with affiliate status—and House of Delegates representation—include the National Bar Association, the National Association of Women Judges, the National Association of Women Lawyers, the National Asian–Pacific American Bar Association, and the Hispanic National Bar Association. By contrast, the entire Bar of the City of New York gets only two House of Delegates seats. Special interest groups are therefore dramatically over-represented in the House of Delegates.

Moreover, as former Assistant Attorney General for the Office of Legal Counsel Theodore B. Olson, has pointed out, "the ABA has no legitimate process for collecting or reflecting the views of its members on social issues." He wonders:

> Is it reasonable or rational to have Antitrust Section delegates voting on abortion policies? Were they selected for that purpose? Do they have any expertise on that subject? Have they polled the members of their section or are they representing only their individual views? Why does a delegate who is a patent lawyer have a vote equivalent to [700] ABA members on the issue of the death penalty? Why does the Asian Bar Association have a vote on the Independent Counsel statute [which the ABA supported]? . . . And if one Florida lawyer gets [one five-thousandths] of a delegate vote on an issu[e] involving AIDS or immigration, why should a member of the National Lesbian and Gay Law Association get one one-hundred-sixtieth of a vote?

Thus, the structure of the House of Delegates contributes to the pervasively liberal bias that permeates many of the ABA's activities.

. . .

II. The Composition of the Standing Committee on the Federal Judiciary

As noted, ABA Policy requires that members of the Standing Committee promise not to engage in party politics while on the committee. This includes a moratorium on contributions to candidates for national political office. It is not hard, however, to find out a committee member's political preferences by examining the beneficiaries of their campaign contributions before (and after) their tenure on the Committee.

The majority of the current committee are Democrats, as has been the case in the past. Using Federal Election Committee data, there are currently nine Democrats on the Committee, including the Chair, and five Republicans. (One individual gave money to candidates from both parties, and is not counted.) Two of these individuals have a history of giving relatively sizable amounts of money—in excess of $10,000 to Democrats. None of the Republicans have contributed more than $2500. According to FEC reports, individuals who have been members of the Standing Committee since 1992 have contributed $60,500 to Democrats and $11,683 to Republicans.

. . .

III. The Standing Committee's Biased Track Record

Despite the ABA's vigorous denials, it cannot be seriously doubted in 1996 that the ABA's Standing Committee on the Federal Judiciary has, for at least the last twenty years or so, taken ideology into account in evaluating judicial nominees. The most prominently cited example is the treatment of Judge Robert H. Bork, by the Standing Committee. But an examination of that Committee's treatment of nominees with comparable records but divergent political views further illustrates its bias....

[Troy reviews the ABA's ratings of several Democratic and Republican nominees to federal courts of appeals who he claims are comparable but received different ratings, and concludes as follows:]

It is not credible ... that these judgments were made without regard to the ideology of these nominees and of the administrations that proposed them. Incidentally, the Committee does not publicly announce the basis for its ratings.

That being said, there would be value in a more comprehensive and systematic analysis of the ABA's ratings of judicial nominees in different administrations. A regression analysis could more conclusively detect whether the ABA was assigning the same weight to similar credentials, without regard to the views of the nominee. Until such an analysis is performed, though, I must conclude that the anecdotal evidence supports the conclusion that the ideology of the nominees and of the Administration that proposed them influences the Standing Committee's ratings.

We need not limit our inquiry to the ABA's actions, however; the ABA's own words indicate the prevalence of ideology in the process as well. The ABA has a pamphlet describing this Committee (which, as noted, is staffed by one of the ABA's top lobbyists). That document, which was revised in 1991, essentially admits to any fair reader that the Standing Committee takes political views into account. The pamphlet says on the first page that "[t]he Committee does not consider a prospective nominee's philosophy or ideology." But the description later proclaims that "[i]n investigating judicial temperament, the Committee considers the prospective nominee's compassion, decisiveness, open-mindedness, sensitivity . . . freedom from bias and commitment to equal justice." Here's what Judge Silberman has to say about the addition of what he calls the "codewords compassion and sensitivity."

> Now, compassion is a desired trait in human beings generally, but it is susceptible to misuse as a criterion for judicial temperament. It seems to me that it suggests that a putative nominee will permit emotion to overrule reason. Or it may mean the prospective judge will consistently violate his or her oath to dispense equal justice to the rich and the poor—presumably by favoring the poor. In other words, there may be tension between fairness and compassion.

. . .

It seems to me impossible to deny that, whether overtly or covertly, consciously or unconsciously, philosophy and ideology play a significant role in the ABA's evaluation of nominees to the federal bench. Even the Washington Post, which is not normally considered a bastion of conservativism, agrees with this critique—or at least it did in 1989. In that year, the Washington Post published the following editorial:

> Dissatisfaction with the ABA's exercise of its unaccountable power has been growing since the Bork nomination. Five members of the screening committee refused to support the candidate, not for objective reasons such as his legal ability or reputation for integrity, but because, according to the association's president, they disagreed with his views respecting constitutional principles or their application, particularly within the ambit of the Fourteenth Amendment. Controversy flared when it was learned that the ABA committee was sharing information on potential nominees with liberal groups such as the People for the American Way and the Alliance for Justice while freezing out conservative organizations. . . .

> There is value in having a nominee's professional peers evaluate his competence and professional ethics. It is also useful to have the testimony of colleagues who disagree with a nominee's legal philosophy or political positions. But these are separate functions, and they appear to have been confused in some recent cases. If the bar association wishes to retain its special position as objective advisor on professional qualifications, it will have to do so under tighter rules.

Res ipsa loquitur.

CONCLUSION

I wish to emphasize that there may have been—and there may in the future be a role for the ABA to play in evaluating the professional competence of judicial nominees without regard to a nominee's politics. Certainly the White House and the Department of Justice would not provide an "independent assessment" of a nominee's credentials and experience, nor could such an assessment by the Senate Judiciary committee be free of politics. In fact, when the ABA was first brought into the process by Attorney General Herbert Brownell, its role was limited to such an objective evaluation.

Even so vocal a critic of the ABA's current role in the evaluation of judicial nominations as Judge Lawrence H. Silberman has acknowledged that, when he was Deputy Attorney General during the Nixon administration, "the Standing Committee performed a salutary function.... I could not imagine how I could have performed my job without the ABA's running interference, blocking the efforts of some Senators to place unqualified persons on the bench." But, regrettably, the Standing Committee has strayed far from the task and has injected ideology into the process.

What should be done? First, members of the Standing Committee should not simultaneously hold any other leadership position within the ABA.... Second, the ABA might be required to spell out the justifications for its ratings. This will enable us to test against bias. Third, there is no need for the ABA to play its quasi-official role in connection with Supreme Court nominees. Such individuals receive adequate scrutiny from the press, the public, this Committee, the Administration, and other special interest groups.

But all of these reforms presuppose that the ABA has purged politics from its process. Unless the ABA can demonstrate that it has done so, however its role in evaluation of judicial candidates should be the same as any other pressure group. Many groups, from the National Rifle Association to the National Abortion Rights Action League, submit reports about judicial nominees. And Senators can do what they will with those reports. The question for this Committee is, however, whether a private, politicized organization, that represents fewer than one-half of the Nation's lawyers, should be given a formal role in judicial selection that often amounts to a veto on otherwise objectively qualified judicial nominees, simply because the ABA does not agree with the nominee's ideology.

Laura E. Little,[68] *The ABA's Role in Prescreening Federal Judicial Candidates: Are We Ready to Give Up on the Lawyers?* 10 Wm. & Mary Bill Rts. J. 37 (2002)

[In a portion of this article excerpted above in Section A, Professor Little provided historical background up to the March 2001 Gonzales letter announcing that the ABA's special role in pre-screening possible judicial nominees was ending.]

Perhaps most notable about the Bush Administration's letter is its suggestion that integrating a national bar association's opinions on judicial selection "detracts from the moral authority of courts." Not only is this statement symptomatic of the declining dignity and prestige of lawyers generally, but it also illustrates the costs of the ABA's decision to take positions on controversial social issues. While the ABA's decision to speak out prompts concern, the suggestion that the decision should disqualify the organization from its judicial vetting role appears based on oversimplistic thinking. The resolve to express public positions is not only supported by our society's ideal of lawyers as opinion leaders, but is also consistent with nuanced understanding of impartiality in the courts.

The [Administration's] statement's implicit contempt for lawyers and the American Bar Association should not, however, go unheeded. The ABA's explicitly controversial positions have surely contributed to its public relations problems and have magnified suspicions that the ABA uses judicial evaluations to implement policy objectives under the whitewash of "judicial fitness." Whether or not the ABA is guilty of this subterfuge, the broadly held suspicion of the organization's lack of candor is not helpful to the ABA, the federal government, or the public. The solution, however, is not to ax the lawyers from the early judicial evaluation, but to improve their contributions through refined procedures.

· · ·

II.   THE ABA AS AN INTEREST GROUP AND THE APPOINTMENT PROCESS

The George W. Bush Administration and other critics of the ABA suggest that the organization enjoys the status of just another interest group possessing a political or ideological orientation on who should staff the federal judiciary. This view of the bar association ignores the association's unique expertise. . . .

A.   Lawyers' Expertise

. . . [D]ebate over whether lawyers should participate intimately in the appointment of federal judges is not new to our country. In fact, Benjamin Franklin quipped during the constitutional debates that the delegates should consider the method for judicial appointments used in

68. Professor of Law and the James E.   School of Law.
Beasley Chair in Law at Temple University

Scotland, "in which the nomination proceeded from the Lawyers." Lawyers enjoyed a particular benefit, Franklin wryly suggested, because they were in a position to chose strategically those appointees with law practices the remaining lawyers could lucratively divide among themselves.

Apparent jest aside, Franklin's implication that lawyers may be in a unique position to know the details of nominees' careers and law practices merits attention. In evaluating judicial candidates, lawyers not only have relationships with the right people to answer questions about candidates, but—knowing the temptations and soft spots in legal doctrine and procedure—lawyers are also able to ask the right questions. This access is aided by the structure of the ABA, with its local and national organization giving ABA interviewers the resources to access individuals with personal knowledge of potential nominees.

Given the range of executive appointments necessary for our federal government to function, our constitutional structure clearly envisions that the president and Senate will look to others to assist in appointments.... [W]hen the appointment involves officials who will staff the adjudicative process of developing and applying legal principles, those who possess special knowledge of that process—lawyers—are the most natural agents to assist with appointment decisions. Knowledge of law, legal method, and governmental institutions combine with rhetorical skills to make lawyers particularly well-suited to evaluate who, in the sea of hopeful legal practitioners, should sit as a judge.

Militating against this reasoning is the identity of those whom the lawyers are advising: professional politicians who themselves may be lawyers.... Moreover, ... the president and senators have plenty of lawyers on their staffs to assist them in evaluating judicial candidates. On the other hand, those staff members are likely to have networks duplicative of their bosses and have a primary duty to the senator's or president's public policy agendas.... [T]he ABA can tap its members' legal expertise in an independent setting, bringing a fresh perspective to the question of judicial fitness and using criteria and procedures that can remain consistent across changing presidential administrations.

B.   Has the ABA Disqualified Itself by Becoming Too Politicized?

Some say the ABA's historical clout comes in part from its ability to make an impartial judgment about the fitness of judicial candidates free from political or ideological bias. The Bush Administration and others suggest that the ABA lost credibility in its neutrality claim by taking positions on controversial issues.... A balanced, well-developed understanding of our constitutional judicial appointments process, impartiality principles, and the social role of lawyers all support a contrary conclusion....

1.   Political Battles are an Inevitable Part of the Appointment Process

... The Constitution leaves the president, the attorney general, and anyone else in the executive branch free to seek advice from whatever sources she desires and to weigh the advice in whatever way she chooses. The Bush Administration's argument instead seems to derive from concern that the judiciary's independence suffers where a "quasi-official" participant such as the ABA has known public policy preference— particularly on issues that a potential nominee may later encounter as a judge. Because of these expressed views, the March letter reasons, an agent such as the ABA "debases" the confirmation process and "detracts from the moral authority of courts."

Our Constitution's appointment process is not sufficiently pristine to afford much weight to this reasoning. Whether or not the Framers so intended, the process is already so politicized, and judicial candidates so exposed to influence during nomination and confirmation, that the ABA's public policy announcements in contexts removed from judicial evaluation are unlikely to change the process's character, much less erode the "moral authority of the courts."

. . .

. . . [M]ost scholars agree that the Constitution's Appointments Clause represents the judgment to employ a power struggle—in the form of a separation of powers apparatus—for appointing judicial officers in a manner that ensures balance, accountability, and energetic evaluation of candidates.

The Framers' debates reflect a struggle between those who feared executive power, with its tendency toward monarchical abuse, and those who feared irresponsibility of the legislature. The Framers resolved the tension with a compromise, seeking balance through the input of actors with varying inclinations, strengths, and interests. As Hamilton explained, the division of power between the president and the Senate provided "an excellent check upon a spirit of favoritism in the [p]resident, and would tend greatly to prevent the appointment of unfit characters [nominated as a result of] State prejudice, from family connection, from personal attachment, or from a view of popularity."

The process established by the Framers is by definition sometimes rancorous. After all, the Constitution suggests that the president "may have to pay a price if he ignores the Senate's advice;" that is, the Senate may withhold its constitutional power of consent over a given nominee. At least in Hamilton's estimation, politics would play an important role in ensuring that the president and the Senate experience political ramifications for abuse of their powers during the process.

. . .

. . . [T]he possibility exists that the ABA, although identified with certain policy perspectives, may ultimately reduce furor in the process. From the time of the Constitution's ratification, most presidents apparently navigated the appointments process by pursuing an informal give and take with the Senate, even before formally nominating candidates. Within the last 40 years, presidents found it expedient to consult with the ABA at an early juncture, a practice consistent with the presidential approach of informally evaluating candidates' capabilities and preferences in light of political practicalities. As an expert—albeit outside voice—the ABA is often able to anticipate problems with potential nominations. Its input can assure that controversy is avoided and consensus is achieved, a state of affairs presumably part of what the Bush Administration was concerned about "debasing."

. . .

2.   Impartiality and Public Perception of Impartiality in the Courts

Particularly in a time of divided government—which has haunted us in the recent past and may well continue for the foreseeable future—the work of a third party (even a third party sometimes viewed as allied with one political party or another) can help to avoid stalemates, disingenuous presidential assurances about avoiding litmus tests and inquiries into nominees' ideology, and other possible shams. Not only is this extra voice consistent with the Constitution's confirmation structure, but it also reinforces public confidence in impartiality in our courts. Balanced, unbiased justice more likely emerges through a checks and balances process, with actors possessing competing perspectives. In such a system, the public more readily believes that good things happen to people (such as receiving a federal judicial nomination) because they have successfully navigated the scrutiny of diverse . . . actors, rather than simply because some insider wired them for the job.

. . . [T]he ABA can check favoritism, acting as a thorn in the side of the executive, by "saying 'no' to the political muscleboys" and by "taking flak for the Senators." Second, and perhaps even more importantly, the ABA contributes to impartiality and public confidence in the confirmation process by simply expressing a separate voice, with incentives independent of those motivating the Executive and the Senate and with an informed opinion on judicial qualification.

In the present era—where dominant legal thought no longer views law as a set of neutral principles existing in a state of nature and awaiting discovery in the hands of competent judges—the concept of impartiality is elusive and complex. . . . Prevailing thought now allows judges many preconceptions and personal perspectives, not as evidence of bias, but as simply part of an individual decisionmaker's point of view.

Because true impartiality is now deemed illusory and perhaps not even desirable, one can argue that the best-designed governmental system allows diffused impartiality to emerge from the confluence of diverse perspectives and opinions. . . . According to this line of thinking (which is frequently offered to promote the American jury system), any bias or preconception on the part of the American Bar Association is not disqualifying, but acts instead to balance other biases or preconceptions already present in the system.

Given that the ABA Committee is not burdened with the same political baggage as the president and Senate, and enjoys different skills and resources, its point of view likely stands as a contrast and a complement to the official government agents. This model of a process with diffuse interests competing to arrive at the best results is reflected throughout the constitutional debates, in which delegates repeatedly condemned partiality and favoritism in the appointment process. For example, ... Roger Sherman argued that, unlike the Executive, the Senate would bring to "their deliberations a more diffuse knowledge of characters." Sherman added, "[i]t would be less easy for candidates to intrigue with them." ... [The ABA's] assistance is certainly a logical and appropriate complement of the Framers' design.

3. The Advantage of Consistency and Stability

The appointment system's integrity, as well as public esteem for its products, are also enhanced by consistent and stable procedures, tested and followed across significant periods of time.... In addition to standardizing qualification guidelines and evaluation procedures themselves, ABA participation at a crucial stage in nomination can bring greater credibility to the process and, thus, greater respect for the appointees.

4. The Role of Lawyers in Society

As noted above, a significant aspect of the Bush Administration decision to eliminate the ABA's prescreening function is the administration's implicit contempt for the legal profession today. Suggested in the March 2001 letter ... is the notion that—because the legal profession has stooped so low as to use its flagship organization to endorse public policy positions—lawyers no longer deserve a special voice in judges' selection. Legal and academic literature currently maintains that the legal profession has lost its claim to dignity and exclusivity because "lawyers have become less independent and objective." Thus, the argument goes, the public no longer benefits from preserving influential or special avenues for lawyers to express opinions.

While perhaps appropriately sensitive to the divisive effect of ABA positions on controversial subjects, this reasoning misconceives lawyers' role in society....

... [T]he crisis in the legal profession and the decline in public esteem for lawyers is well documented. Much concern exists that lawyers "have lost [their] moral bearings." The result, some maintain, is a "[l]oss of self restraint and dignity that ... has transformed all too many lawyers into the kind of hustlers that the bar once strongly condemned."

But we might not be ready to give up on lawyers' special contributions to judicial selection. We might not be ready to diminish them to the status of other political interest groups with no expertise other than commitment to their members' ideological beliefs. After all, lawyers still remain the group most familiar with judicial processes. Moreover, commitment to social justice and reasoned development of opinions on the issues most troubling society is entirely consistent with the traditional model of lawyering, a model bemoaned as atrophied by those tempted to oust lawyers from influential roles in society. In other words, the paradigmatic lawyer-statesman is valued by society as an opinion leader. Mere articulation of controversial opinions should not therefore automatically damn lawyers to allegations of unprofessionalism.

Spiteful rejection of lawyers and their guidance can negatively affect the public. For example, lawyers' loss of dignity can "undermine the public's respect for the fairness of the judicial process and eventually its willingness to accept the outcomes of that process." Moreover, the quality of the legal profession may further erode, ... discouraging individuals with excellent skills and broad intellectual interests from entering the law and thereby protecting the public from unchecked client self-interest.

. . .

5. Crisis in the ABA's Public Relations

The Bush decision to eliminate the ABA from its special vetting role is ... symptomatic of a public relations problem for the American Bar Association itself. The precise source of animosity is complex. On one hand, the administration points to ABA public positions on controversial issues as the cause of the ABA ouster. Underlying this explicit explanation may be more specific complaints about the ABA's votes in the Bork nomination and other ABA interactions with the Ronald Reagan and George H. W. Bush Administrations. In addition, the animosity may derive from more diffuse sources, such as concern with lawyers engaged in power mongering and the generalized impression that lawyers create rules for the primary purpose of benefitting only themselves, whether the rules concern multidisciplinary practice, professional ethics, judicial selection, or other matters.... Nevertheless, the specific concerns flowing from partisanship perceptions and public policy positions deserve close attention by those concerned with the ABA's role in judicial selection.

a. Perceptions of Partisanship

The perception of ABA partisanship is difficult to cure because most ABA decisions on judicial nominees are likely to displease one side of the political spectrum or another. Indeed, Republicans have not always been the party that felt undermined by ABA judicial ratings. Moreover, although beliefs in ABA partisanship are deeply held, the allegations are sometimes hyperbolic or unsubstantiated.

After the Bush Administration's March 2001 ouster of the ABA, the organization used statistics to rebut the suggestion of partisanship. In particular, the ABA trumpeted that, of the almost 2000 judicial candidates formally nominated by the last nine administrations, the Committee found twenty-six nominees to be unqualified, twenty-three of those individuals being nominees of Democratic presidents and three being nominees of Republicans. From this point, the ABA pressed the inference that recent history does not support a Democratic bias.

But this statistic does not tell the whole story. Lacking, for example, are figures on how many potential nominees the ABA tentatively rated as unqualified. For it is this tentative rating, made before the candidate becomes a formal nominee, that President Bush has eliminated from the process. The tentative rating is the one that is so crucial to potential nominees' fates and that the ABA argues so persuasively is key to the organization's ability to help make "the federal judiciary the envy of the world." In official literature, the ABA does not include figures on how many potential candidates have been tentatively rated as unqualified, saying instead that "no one knows" how many "potential candidates were never nominated because of the Committee's evaluation" because "the information is never revealed by the respective administration."

Statistics available from non-ABA sources are more ambiguous on the partisanship issue. A recent study of confirmed court of appeals judges found that for the individuals of this group who possessed no prior judicial experience, the ABA granted a "well-qualified" rating to substantially more of President Clinton's nominees than nominees of President George H. W. Bush. Specifically, the study asserts that when the Bush and Clinton court of appeals nominees are viewed together, "being nominated by Bill Clinton was a stronger positive variable than any other credential or than all other credentials put together." Statistics from other sources could also arguably be read as suggesting a Democratic bias, but might be more fairly interpreted as inconclusive on the partisanship issue, or as representing a trivial difference between nominees by the two political parties. While the criticisms may not be balanced, one alleged practice from recent years has contributed prominently to the partisanship perception. According to critics, the ABA Standing Committee on Federal Judiciary improperly chose to cooperate more with "liberal" groups, both in soliciting information about potential nominees and in selecting with whom to share information. The ABA has discontinued the practice of furnishing lists of prospective nominees to organizations, explaining that "[i]n reexamining its operating procedures, the Standing Committee has concluded that a practice of furnishing lists of prospective nominees to organized groups is inconsistent with its concerns for confidentiality and obligations to the President." The negative fallout from this type of partisanship allegation has been exacerbated by criticism that the ABA is not an organization for all lawyers, and that entire segments of the legal profession are insufficiently represented in ABA membership and leadership.

b.   Public Position on Controversial Issues

[T]raditional models of lawyers in society value the contributions of lawyers as opinion leaders. Articulation of positions on difficult social issues should not be branded as evidence of partiality that disqualifies lawyers or bar associations from participating in the government processes, such as judicial selection. To so argue would unduly discourage lawyers from sharing with other citizens the deliberative powers developed in legal training and the practice of law. Taking stances on controversial issues and developing reasoned positions based on formal legal concepts and competing moral principles is the essence of good lawyering.

Yet the judgment so valued in lawyers may also counsel against taking positions in such a way and under such circumstances as to cause unnecessary furor and acrimony. The positive contribution of communicating positions on controversial social issues begins to wane if opinions are developed and communicated in a dogmatic, insensitive or overaggressive way. Moreover, a fine line exists between lawyers as champions of social justice and lawyers stridently reinforcing existing schisms in society and self-interestedly pursuing their own policy perspectives. The backlash from ABA policy positions suggests that the ABA may not always have navigated this line successfully.

Sometimes problems may have emerged simply as a result of timing. As Professor Michael Gerhardt observed with regard to the ABA's reproductive choice stance, the ABA's reputation for impartiality in the context of judicial selection suffered because the ABA vote on the reproductive choice issue "coincided with the increased intensity with which the Senate Judiciary Committee questioned judicial nominees about their views on abortion rights," thus giving "the appearance that the ABA was taking sides in a public debate."

The ABA may have also unrealistically believed itself capable of developing a unified position from a membership that is in fact pluralistic and divided.... [W]hether it be a fault of the ABA or an artifact of circumstances beyond the organization's control[,] the ABA's position-taking has created an unfortunate, broadly held conception of the organization as strident, imprudent, and incapable of balanced deliberation. The ABA is advised to evaluate the toll resulting from its policy positions and to inquire whether it can take positions on divisive issues while continuing as an institution meriting respect from official quarters and representing all lawyers, irrespective of ideological or political preferences.

c. Subterfuge

... [E]ven more damaging ... is the perception that the ABA uses judicial evaluations as subterfuge.... The insinuation that the ABA suffers from lack of candor, abuse of power, and deceptive techniques makes it even more important that the organization—and its Standing Committee on the Federal Judiciary—seek out ways to improve their reputations. To this end, I sketch below preliminary suggestions for changes in Standing Committee procedure.

III. ANTIDOTES TO PROBLEMS OF PARTIALITY AND PERCEPTION

A. Existing Protection

... Perhaps the biggest restraint on the Standing Committee is its reactive (rather than proactive) orientation. That is, the Committee does not actually generate names of potential nominees, but "evaluates the qualifications of actual and putative nominees" proposed by the president. Although the ABA may have originally wished that the Standing Committee take a more proactive role in nominations, the organization seems ultimately to have concluded that taking on the reputation as "judge-maker" would diminish the prestige and effectiveness of the Committee.

The other major category of protections in place are designed to separate the functions of opinion leader and judicial evaluator within the ABA organization. Steps already taken to reinforce the integrity of the Committee's work include requirements that the Committee keep its work separate from the remainder of the ABA organization and preventing the ABA's Board of Governors, House of Delegates and Officers from becoming "involved in any way in the evaluations of candidates." Governing Principles of the Committee provide that each member must agree: (1) while on the Committee and for one year thereafter, not to seek or accept a federal judgeship; and (2) while on the Committee "not to participate in or contribute to any federal election campaign or engage in partisan political activity." Governing principles also require each member to do her committee work personally and independently.

In service of its desire to maintain impartiality, the ABA has expressly disavowed evaluation of nominees' jurisprudential views. Critics are quick to point out, however, that this policy was a long time coming, developed only after negative public relations and a series of modifications and negotiations.

B.   Possible Changes in Procedure ...

1.   Size and Composition of the Committee

In 1996, a bipartisan group prepared a study released by the University of Virginia's White Burkett Miller Center of Public Affairs. Commenting on the ABA Standing Committee, the Miller study ultimately concluded that although the ABA Committee "has been criticized, alternatively by liberals and conservatives, the committee is useful in evaluating the professional qualifications of judicial nominees." ...

The Miller Report .. [advocated] that the ABA expand the size of the Standing Committee. This suggestion is a sound response to complaints about bias and lack of balanced representation in the Standing Committee. The ABA has been dogged by complaints that its membership is narrow and unrepresentative of the legal profession. This criticism replicates itself within the context of the Standing Committee, especially where it remains a small, clubby subset of the ABA elite.

It is true that the ABA represents only a portion of the nation's lawyers, and its membership is also not precisely representative of the profession as a whole. This representation problem was exacerbated in the past by the tendency of the Standing Committee on Federal Judiciary to be dominated by white men. Traditionally, the ABA Committee is said to have been composed of "largely ... older, well-to-do, Republican, business-oriented corporation attorneys." Consequently, suspicion arose that the Committee viewed "being wealthy and conservative as positive traits and being liberal and outspoken as uncharacteristic of 'a sound judicial temperament.' " Now that the ABA is associated with policy positions deviating from conservative dogma, this perception may be changing.

The ABA has taken significant strides in expanding representation in its general membership and leadership, as well as in the composition of its Standing Committee on Federal Judiciary. Yet to avoid the claim that it has simply replaced a conservative bias on the Standing Committee with a liberal one, the ABA may find that expanding the size of the Committee to include a broader cross-section of the organization would be an easily executed and well-received innovation. Expanding the Committee's size would also respond to those critics who argue that, because the Standing Committee is dominated by trial lawyers, the Committee's recommendations too heavily emphasize trial experience as necessary for judicial qualification.

A more complicated question is whether, in expanding the Committee, ABA leadership should pursue an explicit policy of demographic and political diversity of its members. In defense of its efforts to ensure the Committee's impartiality, ABA leadership has stated that an aspect of Committee members' backgrounds that remains an unknown during the process of selecting members is political affiliation. One wonders whether, under a theory of diffuse impartiality, the ABA leadership may better serve the country and better rebuff allegations of partisanship and ideological subterfuge if it adopted a policy of selecting members for the Standing Committee drawn from a balanced cross-section of political parties and/or demographic groups.

2. Enforcement of Committee Policies

As noted above, the ABA has worked hard to implement many protections designed to ensure that the Standing Committee's work is independent of the ABA's policy-making efforts.... Further efforts by the ABA either to enhance its enforcement mechanisms, or at least to improve the public perception that the mechanism works, would serve the Standing Committee's credibility and esteem.

3. Confidentiality

The Miller Study's more problematic suggestion would require the Standing Committee to provide the administration and the Senate Judiciary Committee with a brief, but official, statement of reasons behind its judicial evaluations. Although many have echoed this recommendation, complications arise because of the Standing Committee's unqualified confidentiality policy.

The ABA maintains that it cannot render accurate evaluations without confidentiality—a position possessing both force and common sense. After all, confidentiality not only loosens the tongues of informants, but saves embarrassment of individuals found to lack the requisite qualifications before their names appear in public sources. Standard social science technique encourages confidentiality as a handservant for accuracy. Within the context of judicial selection, added elements of power and intrigue make confidentiality an even more valuable tool for ensuring that the forces of political favoritism do not motivate nominations. In fact, the United States Supreme Court has even suggested that confidentiality of Justice Department consultations with the ABA Committee may be constitutionally mandated, as necessary to ensure the effectiveness of the president's Article II power to nominate federal judges.[69]

Intimately tied to confidentiality is timing. Once a potential candidate has been nominated, the nominee takes on the power of a near-judge, with the potential to affect the fortunes of those whose opinions are most often sought in the evaluation process. Thus, lawyers who may practice in front of the judge are less likely to share negative information, prudently aware that their statements may eventually make their way to the judge's ears. Likewise, judges may be wary of disparaging the character or legal abilities of a near colleague in whom the judge may rely for a vote on an appellate panel, a workplace favor, or camaraderie in a sometimes very isolated job.

Perhaps for these reasons, the early history of ABA participation in federal judicial selection (1958–1963) suggests that the Standing Committee's potence and effectiveness in helping to sort through candidates and to identify subtle but important differences among them is diminished considerably if the ABA is relegated to a later point in the process. ABA input before the name gets submitted to the Senate is crucial, in large measure because of the possibility for confidentiality at that stage. The controversy surrounding the ABA prescreening function actually demonstrates this point: the prescreening role must have considerable influence, or those opposed to the ABA would not likely fight so hard to eliminate it.

Confidentiality, however, does not mean that the ABA Standing Committee should be absolved of all responsibility for explaining its actions. Moreover, persuasive reasons weigh heavily against confidentiality. As Professor William Ross argues, the ABA's judicial ratings would be far more useful to the Senate Judiciary Committee—which enters the picture later in the time line—if detailed reports, with explanations for the ratings, are provided. In addition, as the Miller Study explains, the ABA Committee may avoid some charges of partisanship or ideological motivation by providing reasons for its evaluation. The Standing Committee's insistence on confidentiality has contributed to the negative impression that it smugly believes itself above any obligation to explain its decisions. Third, the process of articulating reasons may assist

69. [Footnote 155 in original] Pub. Citizen v. United States Dep't of Justice, 491 U.S. 440, 466 (1989) (noting that lower court made this constitutional holding and stating that requiring disclosure of Justice Department consultations with the ABA Committee "would present formidable constitutional difficulties").

committee members in thoughtful consideration of the qualities that bear on quality judging ... [and] may even help committee members sort ideological or partisan bias unwittingly coloring their evaluation. Finally, explaining its views to the public reinforces the ABA's public service role of educating the public on law and government.

One possible compromise between these competing concerns may come from parsimoniously controlling what is disclosed. For example, the arguments outlined above suggest that confidentiality is particularly important at the early stages of investigation. With this in mind, the ABA may be able to accommodate, at least partially, Senator Grassley's suggestion that the Standing Committee should at least provide a written report on "not qualified" ratings. At the same time, this suggestion implicates a new set of competing concerns of fairness to potential nominees. As Professor William Ross points out, the ABA needs to be particularly sensitive to claims of unfairness by persons who are not nominated because of a negative rating. Moreover, giving the candidate and executive branch the dignity of explanations behind a negative rating may foster a more informed inquiry as to the accuracy of the ABA's assessment. On the other hand, publication of reports explaining unqualified ratings may embarrass persons under consideration and harm their professional standing. Moreover, disclosure may have a deleterious effect on the accuracy of the information obtained because of the possibility that sources could be identified even if not named in the report.

Although a close call, the arguments in favor of confidentiality are weightier than those arguing against secrecy. I reach this decision by discounting some of the fairness concerns weighing in favor of disclosing reasons for unfavorable ratings. ... I am persuaded by the observations of Professor Ross that a judgeship is not itself a "right" for all successful lawyers, and that those who have had their hopes for a judgeship dashed are likely to continue with the level of professional success that originally made them eligible for the judgeship. I also note that although making an exception to confidentiality may cause accuracy to suffer considerably, the other side of the balance is not equally weighty: the quality of judgeship candidates is unlikely to diminish if no exception to confidentiality is made and the policy stays as is. In so reasoning, I assume that the pool of qualified judicial candidates will continue to be larger than the amount of available positions. Despite my conclusion that unqualified confidentiality should presently remain the policy, I urge further thought on the issue, recognizing the possibility of a future compromise that more adequately satisfies the competing concerns.

CONCLUSION ...

It behooves us to continue to consider innovations, given that the issue is not resolved and is likely to reemerge. At present, I ultimately settle on a continued, prominent role for the ABA in prescreening judicial candidates with a concomitant change in ABA orientation and attitude. This orientation and attitude change should include frank discussion of past problems and a willingness to consider and to implement further procedural changes, including searching for ways to explain ratings, increasing the size and representation on the Standing Committee, reinforcing the wall of separation between the Committee and the ABA policy-making branches, and taking other actions to facilitate good relations with the public and to eliminate the perception of inappropriate bias and partisanship.

———

Questions and Comments

1. Review the Gonzales letter in Section A, above. To what extent does its rationale respond to the concerns expressed by Mr. Troy in his 1996 Senate Judiciary Testimony?

2. Professor Little identifies a concern over the ability of the ABA to obtain candid assessments of proposed nominees. Others have raised a specific concern that once a nominee is announced, colleagues—assuming the likelihood of confirmation—will be far less willing to share candid but negative assessments. Are interviews with colleagues, opposing counsel and others with whom a nominee has interacted professionally over a career relevant to any of the appropriate criteria for selecting good judges? Are there other ways to evaluate them?

4. Should the Senate's Voting Rules or Other Procedures Be Modified?

Frustrated with the bitterly divided, unpleasant confirmation process that has become all too common, observers have proposed a number of possible reforms aimed at changing the voting procedures followed by the Senate in an effort to influence both who is nominated by the President and the nature of the ensuing confirmation process.

a. Require a Supermajority to Confirm?

A number of scholars have suggested that requiring a heightened majority vote in the Senate would improve the nomination and confirmation process, as indicated in the first three excerpts below. In 1992, after the very closely divided vote on the nomination of Clarence Thomas, Professor Lee Epstein suggested that, in order to combat partisan confirmation proceedings and the possible appointment of partisan judges, the Constitution should be amended to require a two-thirds vote to confirm a Supreme Court nominee. In her view, this would lead to more cooperation between the president and the Senate, and the nomination of Justices based more on merit and less on ideology. The more recent excerpt by Professor Judith Resnik argues for a supermajority vote (three-fifths is her suggestion) for all federal judges, not so much to avoid discussion of ideology, but to encourage the selection of candidates with broader appeal. Professors John McGinnis and Michael Rappaport discuss the advantages of adopting a supermajority voting requirement for confirmation of Supreme Court Justices, but not for lower court judges. See also Bruce Ackerman, 2 *We The People: Transformations* 407 (1998) (requiring a supermajority to confirm would prevent "an ideological President with a weak mandate [from using] a slim Senatorial majority to ram through a constitutional revolution.... Super-majority requirements have proved their value in modern European systems; we should take these lessons seriously as we reflect on our [system.])"

Professor Michael Gerhardt disagrees with these suggestions. In an excerpt from *The Federal Appointments Process*, Gerhardt argues that requiring a supermajority would significantly muddle the confirmation process, without assuring that it would have the desired effects. Indeed, Gerhardt suggests that a change in the confirmation vote may actually have the opposite of the intended effect by eliminating qualified candidates with "paper trails" that may indicate their ideological leanings.

————

Lee Epstein,[70] *A Better Way to Appoint Justices*, Christian Science Monitor, March 17, 1992, at 19

We need to take a radical step to alter the entire nomination and confirmation process—and thus the political calculus of the president and the Senate: Let's amend the Constitution and require two-thirds of the Senate to confirm Supreme Court justices. This is a drastic proposal. No one likes to tinker with the Constitution. The framers erected an intricate system of government in which manipulation of one part inevitably affects the way another functions.

But the framers had little idea of the role the Supreme Court would come to play in United States politics. Nor did they envision the role politics would play in the court's decisions. Rather they imagined, as Alexander Hamilton wrote, a court full of principled justices who would "declare the sense of the law" through "inflexible and uniform adherence to the rights of the Constitution and of individuals."

That is why the framers developed the unique system of nomination, confirmation, and life tenure: to keep justices above partisan politics. Had they foreseen courts of recent eras, courts composed largely of legal activists eager to see their values etched into law, they would have devised a different scheme.

From the beginning, presidents have tried to pack the court with partisan or ideological soulmates. After his party lost the election of 1800, President John Adams and lame-duck Federalist senators hastily

---

70. Associate Professor of Political Science at Washington University at the time of this article; now Beatrice Kuhn Professor of Law at Northwestern University.

appointed a host of like-minded federal judges before the Jeffersonians came into power.

Although neither the confirmation process nor the court itself has ever measured up to the Constitution's lofty expectations, at no time in the past were they simultaneously so out of control. Requiring a two-thirds confirmation vote for justices would start to realize the framers' vision.

— A two-thirds vote would change, for the better, the political calculations of the president. Presidents—be they Democrats or Republicans—would have to rethink whom they nominated to the court. To gain approval of their nominees, they would need true bipartisan support, not just a few crossover votes. That would require them to place far more stock in candidates' legal credentials. It also would compel presidents to seek the advice of senators of both parties before making nominations.

— A two-thirds vote would also change, for the better, thinking in the Senate. If presidents gave senators a greater role at the "advice" stage, it would help to eliminate the sort of proceedings we have experienced in recent years—unacceptable candidates would never make it that far. Confirmation hearings would serve as forums to discern nominees' legal qualifications to sit on the Supreme Court, rather than as showcases for senators on the Judiciary Committee.

— A two-thirds vote is required for the approval of treaties (by the Senate) and the proposal of constitutional amendments (both Houses); who sits on the Supreme Court is today of similar importance. The framers required two-thirds votes for matters of great national importance. What has become more important—at least on domestic matters—than decisions of the US Supreme Court? Courts of the last three decades have enunciated public policy on reapportionment, affirmative action, and abortion.

— A two-thirds vote would not eliminate qualified candidates. Since the emergence of the modern Supreme Court (a date scholars fix at around 1937), only one successful nominee to be an associate justice might have failed to gain 67 Senate votes—Mr. Thomas. William Rehnquist might still have attained confirmation as an associate justice (he had 68 votes in 1971), but he might not have been able to ascend to the chief justiceship (he received only 65 votes in 1986).

I stress the word "might," because a change in the rules would significantly alter the calculus of both the president and the Senate. With a two-thirds requirement, Ronald Reagan might not have sought to elevate Mr. Rehnquist (or pursued the confirmation of Robert Bork), nor might President Bush have nominated Thomas. Alternatively, Rehnquist might have received more votes from the Senate if it was operating under the constraints of a two-thirds rule.

My point is not to second-guess past votes; it is to suggest that a two-thirds requirement would not restrict the pool of serious candidates. It may, though, reduce it just enough to eliminate those who have no business sitting on the most important judicial body in our nation.

———

Judith Resnik,[71] *Judicial Selection and Democratic Theory: Demand, Supply, and Life Tenure,* **26 Cardozo L. Rev. 579, 637–38 (2005)**

. . .

I [have] proposed that the Senate turn to a supermajority rule, requiring sixty votes as a threshold for a nomination to be confirmed. . . . [W]hile the Constitution does not impose that requirement, the Senate could do so in an effort to mark the import of a life-tenured position—at all levels of the federal judicial system.

. . . [S]uch a rule would not (were other factors constant) have produced radically different results in the last decade. During the two terms of President Clinton and up until June of 2003 of the first term of President Bush, six persons—three Clinton and three Bush nominees— were seated on the lower federal courts by votes of fewer than sixty.[72] More recently, in several instances, opponents of a few nominees have used a filibuster, but two of those judges were then seated as recess appointments. While these vivid conflicts have dominated the press in recent years, more than ninety percent of those nominated in the last decade for the lower courts have been confirmed with the support of ninety or more senators. Hence, my concern is that the Senate has been too accommodating, approving too many candidates, too quickly.

A supermajority rule of sixty could nonetheless have some use. Such a requirement could create incentives for the President to put forth individuals about whom a broad consensus of approval exists. The rule would have its most powerful impact at the Supreme Court level, where the stakes are the highest. Further, this relatively modest "supermajority" would not over-empower a senatorial "fringe" (as forty senators represent a significant part of American political opinion) but would likely generate movement towards a middle ground. Also, a supermajority rule would underscore senatorial commitment to the constitutional role of "Advice and Consent."

———

71. Arthur Liman Professor of Law, Yale Law School.

72. [Editors' Note: According to Chart 5 on page 636 of this article, a total of 548 Article III lower court judges were con-firmed during the time period studied; thus, the 6 judges who were confirmed with votes of less than 60 constituted about 1% of the total.]

John McGinnis & Michael Rappaport,[73] *Supermajority Rules and the Judicial Confirmation Process*, 26 Cardozo L. Rev. 543 (2005)

Introduction

In this essay we consider the policy wisdom of two possible uses of supermajority rules to improve the confirmation process and the quality of judges appointed through that process. We first look at an express Senate rule that would require a supermajority (of perhaps 60 percent) for confirmation of judicial nominees. As we discuss below, an implicit Senate supermajority rule for judicial confirmations may in fact already be emerging through the use of the filibuster.

We provide the first comprehensive calculus to assess the costs and benefits of an express Senate supermajority rule for confirmations, using a formula for evaluating supermajority rules that we have advanced elsewhere. In our previous work, we have argued that supermajority rules can improve political governance in certain situations and we have advocated supermajority rules in a variety of contexts.

Assessing the benefits of a confirmation supermajority rule involves many subtle considerations and depends on both assumptions about the nature of jurisprudence and the level of judges (Supreme Court or lower federal court) to whom it would be applied. On the realist assumption that judges essentially vote their preferences on constitutional issues, we believe that an express Senate supermajority rule for confirmations of Supreme Court justices would probably be beneficial in the long term, but only if the rule itself was adopted by a bipartisan consensus and applied prospectively to future presidents. In contrast, if one believes that the goal of appointing justices who will adhere as closely as possible to the original understanding of the Constitution is desirable and possible, a supermajority rule would probably not be beneficial in current circumstances because supermajority rules encourage appointments with bipartisan support and one party is generally opposed to originalism.

On realist assumptions about judging, the best argument for an express Senate supermajority rule for Supreme Court confirmations is that it tempers the countermajoritarian difficulty that has grown more acute as justices have generated a large body of precedent that has departed from the original understanding of the Constitution. A supermajority rule would require that justices empowered to entrench new principles through judicial amendments of the Constitution must enjoy a substantial consensus of support before they could take office. Because of this consensus, the decisions of such judges would enjoy greater legitimacy and would be less likely to systematically subvert majoritarian values.

73. McGinnis is Class of 1940 Research Professor, Northwestern University Law School; Rappaport is University Professor, University of San Diego School of Law.

It may seem paradoxical that a supermajority rule can help protect majoritarian values. But we believe that supermajority rules can have this beneficial effect when some particular circumstance prevents majority rule from reflecting majority sentiment. In this case, the problem for majority rule is that votes on judicial nominees elicit a high degree of party solidarity. Therefore, confirmation votes under majority rule are likely to reflect the median sentiment in one party rather than the Senate as a whole. The advantage of supermajority rules is that by requiring more bipartisan consensus they move the locus of confirmation power toward the median senator.

On the other hand, supermajority rules may also impose costs by leading to holdouts and substantial delays in the Supreme Court nomination process. The delays could result in nominations being held up during elections, thereby creating referenda on particular nominees and unduly politicizing the selection process. To help reduce these holdout costs, the adoption of a confirmation supermajority rule should occur by a consensus of the parties and be applied prospectively to a President whose identity was not known when the rule was adopted. If one party initiates a new supermajority rule through a unilateral decision to filibuster nominees of the President of the opposing party, the holdout costs are likely to be very high. This transition to a supermajority confirmation rule would generate high holdouts costs because the first presidents operating under a novel and contested rule would be unlikely to compromise on their selections for nominations, which would be necessary to secure confirmation under the emerging supermajority rule. Thus, a supermajority rule applied without a consensus would provoke bitter fights and lengthy delays.

While we believe that a supermajority rule might be desirable for Supreme Court appointments, we reject imposing an express supermajority rule to the confirmation of lower federal court judges. The countermajoritarian difficulty is less acute with lower court judges because their countermajoritarian power is limited by Supreme Court precedent. Moreover, because there are more judges appointed to the lower courts, as a whole they are more likely to be representative of the broad spectrum of jurisprudential opinion than are the justices of the Supreme Court, where a few appointments can make dramatic and sometimes aberrational shifts in jurisprudence. Indeed, the jurisprudential diversity potentially offered by the lower court judges confirmed under majority rule can itself be a mechanism of judicial restraint and development of the law, as a few outlying judges can provide both discipline and insight though dissents. A supermajority confirmation rule would unduly narrow the jurisprudential diversity that can be obtained among the thousand lower court federal judges.

. . .

Most of the attention on supermajority rules and the confirmation process has understandably focused on the rise of the filibuster as an implicit supermajority rule. The filibuster itself has a substantial defect as a supermajority rule. Its ostensible purpose of encouraging more deliberation is usually a cover for outright opposition to the measure or nominee proposed. It thus makes it harder for the public, which is rationally ignorant of politics, to understand the positions of their senators.

On realist assumptions about judging, an express supermajority confirmation rule for Supreme Court judges might well be beneficial, but only if it were adopted by a bipartisan consensus and applied to a President not yet elected. A supermajority confirmation rule for lower court judges, however, would probably not be beneficial under any circumstances, because it would decrease the diversity of the bench without the benefit of disciplining unreviewable entrenchments....

Michael J. Gerhardt,[74] *The Federal Appointments Process: A Constitutional and Historical Analysis* (rev. ed. 2003)

... A Supermajority Requirement for Supreme Court Confirmations

One provocative proposal is to adopt a constitutional amendment requiring a supermajority Senate vote for the confirmation of Supreme Court justices. Bruce Ackerman ... argues that the proposal is designed to make the selection of Supreme Court justices more democratic by changing the dynamics of Court appointments. In his view, the proposal would ensure that appointments are likely to come from presidents who are extremely popular or command considerable public support. Moreover, the requirement would prevent "an ideological President with a weak mandate [from using] a slim Senatorial majority to ram through a constitutional revolution." In addition, the proposal would force presidents "to consult with the political opposition and select distinguished professionals who would adopt an evolutionary approach to constitutional interpretation." Other scholars support the proposal because they believe it would force presidents not so much to find justices who would adopt any particular approach to constitutional interpretation but rather who would be consensus candidates, that is, Court nominees with impeccable credentials who could easily win confirmation and avoid contentious hearings.

The proposal would undoubtedly change the dynamics of Supreme Court confirmation proceedings because each senator would know that his or her vote would have added weight under the new system. The alteration in dynamics would, however, make the future of Supreme Court confirmation proceedings quite unpredictable. First, a supermajority requirement is not needed to encourage presidents to pick consensus candidates, as reflected most recently in President Clinton's nominations of Ruth Bader Ginsburg and Stephen Breyer, both of whom were easily confirmed. Second, a supermajority vote would not necessarily result in

---

74. Arthur B. Hanson Professor of Law at the William & Mary School of Law.

the appointment of superior justices. Conceivably it could have kept a number of eminently qualified people off the Court in spite of their strong records. Third, it is not clear that the supermajority vote would democratize (i.e., enhance or impede popular sovereignty) in the appointments of Supreme Court justices. It is quite possible that a popular president could still fail to win confirmation of his or her well-qualified nominee because of some hostile faction in the Senate.

Moreover, it is not clear why the supermajority requirement necessarily would lead to the appointment of justices who would follow Ackerman's preferred "evolutionary approach to constitutional interpretation." Ackerman fails to show why the proposed requirement necessarily would result in the appointment of justices with some (but not other) kinds of viewpoints regarding constitutional interpretation. Nor has Ackerman shown how the appointment of justices who adhere to an evolutionary approach would represent a vindication of popular sovereignty, for he has not shown that the American people favor this or any other particular approach to constitutional interpretation. In addition, Ackerman assumes the supermajority requirement would dissuade a president from nominating "constitutional visionaries," but a president disposed to find such a visionary might still find that person in the guise of a nominee who lacks a paper trail reflecting how he or she would perform on the Court once confirmed. The fact that a nominee lacks a paper train of an ideology does not mean the person lacks certain ideological viewpoints.

Indeed, it is conceivable that the dynamic brought about by the proposal would be more likely to frustrate rather than facilitate the making of meritorious appointments (though, as we have seen, there has historically been considerable disagreement over what constitutes merit). The more accomplished a Supreme Court nominee, the more likely the nominee has done or said something in his or professional life to stir the opposition of some faction. And the two-thirds requirement empowers a small fraction—at least one-third of the Senate—to wield a veto power over Supreme Court nominations. Rather than fulfill Ackerman's (and others') desire to ensure that confirmation of Supreme Court nominee will occur only with overwhelming public support, this proposal would make it easier for a nominee's opponents to block a nomination because they would have to persuade fewer people than they do at present.

The final problem with the supermajority requirement is that it is hard to reconcile with the Founder's reasons for requiring such a vote for removals and treaty ratifications but not for confirmations. The Founders reserved a two-thirds supermajority voting requirement to shift the presumption against certain matters they expected not to arise routinely in order to ensure greater deliberation on them, decrease the chances for political or partisan reprisals on removals and treaty ratifications, and protect an unpopular minority from being abused in Senate votes on these questions. The framers required a simple majority for confirmations to balance the demands of relatively efficient staffing of the government with the need to check abusive exercises of the president's discretion (as well as the composition or direction of the federal judiciary).

―――――

Questions and Comments

1. Are proposals for supermajority voting designed to eliminate or diminish the role of ideology in the confirmation process? Or are they rather intended to eliminate from consideration those with more "extreme" positions, to encourage Presidents to nominate people from the "mainstream?"

2. To the extent their goal is to diminish the role of ideology, are they likely to be effective? For those who believe it is healthy to consider ideology in the nomination and confirmation process, would this still be possible under a supermajority voting rule?

3. Would adoption of a supermajority rule make it more likely that Presidents will nominate "stealth" candidates with little or no written track record on the most controversial issues?

b.   Modify or Eliminate the Senate Judicial Filibuster?

The prior section considered proposals to require a supermajority vote to confirm Supreme Court Justices. The filibuster rule permits debate on a subject to continue until it is cut off by a "cloture" vote of at least 60 members.[75] Both the filibuster and the cloture vote to cut off debate, which are in some respects analogous to supermajority requirements for legislative action, are procedural departures from ordinary business, and controversy has recently surrounded their use in the context of judicial nominations.

This debate came to a head in the early 2000s when the Democrats used the filibuster to delay and/or defeat a number of George W. Bush's nominations to the lower courts. The Republicans claimed the use of the filibuster in the context of judicial nominations, what they termed "judicial filibusters," was unprecedented. Democrats responded that the use of filibusters against judicial nominations was not new and had, in fact, been used successfully against the nomination of Abe Fortas to be Chief Justice in 1968.[76] This debate was, by any measure, heated; and

75. Senate Rules place no general limits on how long consideration of a nominee (or most other matters) may last. As a recent Congressional Research Service Report explains: "Owing to this lack of general time limits, opponents of a nomination may be able to use extended debate ... to prevent a final vote from occurring. Although a voting majority may be prepared to vote for a nominee, the nomination cannot be confirmed as long as other Senators ... are able to prevent the vote from occurring.... The motion for cloture is the only procedure by which the Senate can vote to place time limits on its consideration of a matter. It is, therefore, the Senate's most usual

means of attempting to overcome a filibuster. When the Senate adopts a cloture motion (by a 3/5 vote) on a matter, known as 'invoking cloture,' further consideration of the matter is limited to 30 hours [during which no Senator, other than the floor leaders and managers of the debate, may occupy more than one hour in debate.]" Richard S. Beth & Betsy Palmer, Cong. Research Serv., *Cloture Attempts on Nominations* 1 (Order Code RL 32878, Apr. 22, 2005) (referencing Senate rule XXII).

76. For a helpful chart, Nominations Subjected to Cloture Attempts, 1968–2004, see Beth and Palmer, *supra,* at 7 (Table 4).

the Republicans suggested eliminating the "judicial filibuster" by what was termed the "nuclear option," essentially, eliminating a super-majority voting rule by a majority vote. As Professors Fisk and Chemerinsky explain:

> Under Senate Rule XXII of the Standing Rules of the Senate, three-fifths of the Senate (sixty Senators) may end debate by an affirmative vote. Rule XXII also provides that if the measure being debated is to amend the Senate Rules, the necessary affirmative vote shall be two-thirds of the Senators present and voting. Finally, because the Senate considers itself a continuing body and, unlike the House, does not adopt new Rules at the beginning of each Congress, the Standing Rules continue in effect and there is no opportunity to change a rule by majority vote.

Catherine Fisk & Erwin Chemerinsky, *In Defense of Filibustering Judicial Nominations*, 26 Cardozo L. Rev. 331, 334 (2005). The proposed "nuclear option" was a device by which a simple majority of the Senate could change a rule, specifically Rule XXII, instead of requiring the supermajority normally required to change Senate Rules. See Fisk & Chemerinsky, *supra*, for the details of this device.

The "nuclear option" was so named because most Senators and observers believed that its actual use or implementation would fundamentally alter the workings of the Senate, not only with respect to judicial appointments but with respect to potentially all Senate business.[77] So for many in the Senate it was a welcome relief when on May 25, 2005, fourteen Senators (7 Republicans and 7 Democrats) announced an agreement to avert the use of the "nuclear option." Charles Babington & Shailagh Murray, *A Last–Minute Deal on Judicial Nominees; Senators Agree on Votes for 3; 2 Could Still Face Filibusters*, Wash. Post, May 24, 2005, at A1; Carl Hulse, *Compromise in the Senate: The Overview*, N.Y. Times, May 24, 2005, at A1. Under the agreement, the fourteen agreed to vote on three of the controversial Bush nominees while reserving the right to filibuster others in "extraordinary circumstances." *Id.* The agreement saved the filibuster; the seven Republicans' promise not to get rid of the filibuster deprived the Senate of the majority it needed to kill the filibuster. According to the *Washington Post*, "[l]eaders of both parties said the pact's greatest implications will surface when Bush fills a Supreme Court vacancy.... Democrats, who [were holding] 44 of the Senate's seats, were eager to retain filibuster powers in hopes of dissuading Bush from nominating a staunch conservative." Babington & Murray, *supra*.[78]

---

77. Filibusters have a long tradition in the Senate and their proposed elimination generated considerable controversy. See, e.g., David S. Law & Lawrence B. Solum, *Judicial Selection, Appointments Gridlock, and the Nuclear Option*, 15 J. Contemp. Legal Issues 51, 58–63 (2006).

78. As discussed in Section B, above, the nominations of John Roberts and Samuel Alito came shortly after this agreement. We leave it to the reader to decide whether the agreement "dissuaded" President Bush from nominating "a staunch conservative."

Thus, while the potential to use a filibuster to stall or thwart a judicial appointment still exists, there is, at least as of mid-2007, a disinclination either to use it or to abolish it. But, if past is prologue, the question of the appropriateness of the judicial filibuster may recur and could arise, as it has before, in the context of a Supreme Court nomination.[79]

Questions and Comments

1.   How does reliance on a filibuster compare with a formal rule change (by Senate rule or by constitutional amendment) to require supermajority votes for Supreme Court Justices? Professor Jackson has argued: "The filibuster is a device available in unusual cases (because political restraints prevent its use more generally) to require supermajority voting to end debate. The filibuster differs significantly from a general rule requiring a supermajority vote for judicial nominees: the latter suggests that a high degree of consensus should ordinarily be required for judicial appointments, while reliance on the filibuster suggests that supermajority voting rules need special justification and are a departure from the norm." Jackson, *Packages of Independence, supra,* at 999. Does this view place too much weight on form over substance?

2.   Are the arguments for and against the filibuster different in settings involving legislation than in settings involving confirmation? In settings involving confirmation of Cabinet level appointees and those involving Article III life-tenured federal judges? In settings involving Supreme Court Justices and other life-tenured federal judges? In addition to the readings you have already done, consider these views:

i) Defending the filibuster, Professors Fisk and Chemerinsky argue that a filibuster is not necessarily countermajoritarian, since a majority of Senators may, in fact, represent a minority of the population.[80] But even where a

79.   See, e.g., Betsy Palmer, Cong. Research Serv., *Evolution of the Senate's Role in the Nomination and Confirmation Process: A Brief History* 12 (Order Code RL 31948, March 29, 2005) ("The first clear-cut example of a successful use of a filibuster against a nomination, including taking a cloture vote, occurred in 1968 over President Lyndon Johnson's decision to elevate Associate . . . Justice Abe Fortas to be Chief Justice."). Although the CRS Report notes some debate on this point, it defends its view that Fortas was, in fact, subject to a successful filibuster. See *id.* at 12, n.50 (noting that "debate on the motion to proceed to the Fortas nomination consumed more than 25 hours over five days" and that "the leader of the fight against Fortas . . . said his group was prepared to 'keep the debate going indefinitely.' "). See also *Hatch Lambasts Petty, Partisan Filibuster Against Alito,* 2006 States News Service, Jan. 30, 2006 (noting attempted short fili-

buster against Alito, followed by Senate vote to invoke cloture).

80.   See Fisk & Chemerinsky, *supra,* at 336. As they suggest, with two Senators from each state, whether a filibuster is "majoritarian" or "countermajoritarian"— with respect to the population represented—depends entirely on which Senators support the filibuster. If the six Senators from the large population states of California, New York and Texas (with a combined population of about 79 million persons) oppose a proposed action, they along with 35 other Senators could easily represent a majority of the population. See U.S. Census Bureau, United States—States; and Puerto Rico, GCT-TI-R (Population Estimates) (geographies ranked by estimate) (data set for 2006), available at, http://factfinder.census. gov (showing a total U.S. population of just under 300 million, with the 21 largest states by population including over 220 million persons). Under current rules, more

filibuster is used to oppose action favored by Senators representing a majority of the population, they argue that it is a historically legitimate check on the power of the executive and should be preserved.

... Normatively, there are good reasons for having non-majoritarian features of American government, including the filibuster. The Constitution and a number of government processes that it ordains are designed to protect minorities of various kinds, including political, social, and racial minorities. The religion clauses of the First Amendment are designed to protect religious minorities. The post-Civil War amendments are designed to protect racial minorities. The Constitution cannot be changed by a majority of the population. The constitutional limits on legislative action, including of course the Bill of Rights, thwart the will of the majority of the state and federal government and executives. The filibuster, to the extent that it blocks or delays legislative action, is one among many restraints on a legislative majority.

A check is especially important when it comes to federal judges. Of all the branches of government, the federal judiciary is obviously the least majoritarian. A President elected by a minority of the voters, as President Bush was during his first term, can pick federal judges and have them confirmed by Senators representing a minority of the population. The federal judges then hold their positions for life, subject only to the extremely unlikely possibility of impeachment. It is therefore misguided to criticize filibustering judicial nominations as anti-majoritarian, when the entire nature of the federal judiciary is anti-majoritarian. The filibuster is just another check that exists within an overall process that is filled with checks and balances.

... The real effect of the filibuster is to push nominees for the federal judicial bench more to the middle.... The filibuster thus has a moderating effect on the composition of the federal bench in two ways: the Senate blocks the most extreme nominees from being confirmed and the President is given a strong incentive to pick more from the middle....

At a time when the country is deeply ideologically divided, as it is today, choosing judges more from the middle is a good thing. It means that judges' views align with the views of a larger number of people....

. . .

Some ... argue that there is less justification for filibustering judges than for filibustering legislation because, as Professor Calabresi put it, "if a mistake is made with a judicial confirmation ... impeachment is always available to rectify the error. There is no similarly easy remedy if Congress passes a bad law." On the contrary: it is far easier to repeal a law than to impeach a judge. Impeachment requires a vote of two-thirds of the Senate after action by the House. Only a few judges

than 40 Senators may be needed to defeat a motion for cloture, thus sustaining a filibuster. Forty-one Senators might represent more than two-thirds of the population—or they might represent only a minority of the population: the population represented by the 42 Senators from the smallest population states, according to the same Census Bureau source, is just over 32 million.

have been impeached, while thousands and thousands of bills have been passed and repealed. Professor Calabresi's argument points in exactly the opposite direction of his conclusion: it explains why the filibuster for judges is particularly important.

Fisk & Chemerinsky, *In Defense of Filibustering Judicial Nominations*, *supra,* at 337–44.

ii) Michael J. Gerhardt, *The Constitutionality of the Filibuster*, 21 Const. Comment. 445 (2004) argues that the filibuster is authorized by the Constitution's provisions giving each House of Congress the authority to make their own rules, and supported by historic practice. Indeed, he notes:

> Throughout the long history of its deployment in the Senate, the filibuster has not been restricted to delaying floor votes on legislation. It has been often used to thwart presidential nominations. The first recorded instance in which it was clearly and unambiguously employed to defeat a judicial nomination occurred in 1881. At the time, Republicans held a majority of the seats in the Senate but were unable to end a filibuster employed near the end of the legislative session to preclude a floor vote on President Rutherford B. Hayes's nomination of Stanley Matthews to the Supreme Court. Though Matthews eventually served as an Associate Justice, it was only because Hayes's Republican successor, President James Garfield, renominated Matthews in the next legislative session. (There were fourteen occasions in the nineteenth century when the Senate held no floor votes on Supreme Court nominations.) A recent Congressional Research Service study shows that from 1949 through 2002, senators have employed the filibuster against 35 presidential nominations, on 21 of which senators sought and invoked cloture ... Seventeen of the 35 nominations filibustered were to Article III courts.... Four of the 35 filibustered nominations failed altogether—then-Associate Justice Abe Fortas to be Chief Justice and Judge Homer Thornberry to be an Associate Justice in 1968, Sam Brown to be Ambassador in 1994, and Dr. Henry Foster to be Surgeon General in 1995. Other nominations have failed without having been formally filibustered; for example, Senator Jesse Helms's threat of a filibuster nullified President Clinton's intention to nominate then-Assistant Attorney General Walter Dellinger as Solicitor General. Another dramatic use of the filibuster occurred when Republican senators filibustered five of President Clinton's nominations to the State Department in order to gain leverage in a dispute over whether the State Department adequately investigated allegations that a former Clinton campaign worker had improperly searched the records of 160 former political appointees and publicly disclosed the contents of two of the files. As John McGinnis and Michael Rappaport concluded in their extended study of the Constitution's supermajority voting requirements, "the continuous use of filibusters since the early Republic provides compelling support for their constitutionality."[81]

81. Fisk & Chemerinsky, also comment on historical arguments, noting that "Professor Kmiec [in congressional testimony] suggested that a filibuster that prevented Rutherford B. Hayes from filling vacancies in the 46th Congress seemed permissible because the vacancies should 'more properly [be] filled by the newly elected James A.

Professor Gerhardt goes on to identify and respond to the leading arguments against filibuster. His summary follows:

> First, the filibuster is arguably illegitimate, because it is not included among the supermajority voting requirements explicitly set forth in the Constitution. The second claim is that the filibuster allows a minority within the Senate to impede a president's nominating authority. The argument is that filibusters affect nominations and legislation differently. A nomination has no constituent parts, while a bill does. Thus, a filibuster can effectively nullify a nomination in its entirety, whereas filibustering legislation might affect only a portion of it. The third argument is that the filibuster can preclude the Senate from fulfilling its institutional obligations, including providing "Advice and Consent" on presidential nominations. The filibuster arguably impedes the entitlement of a majority of the Senate to render final votes on any matter it likes. The final argument against the filibuster is that Rule XXII, which requires at least two-thirds of the Senate to agree to end a filibuster against a motion to amend Rule XXII, is unconstitutional because it violates the basic principle that a current legislature may not tie the hands of a future one.
>
> Each of these arguments is unpersuasive. First, these arguments are circular. They each assume rather than establish the conclusion that majority rule is a fixed, constitutional principle within the Senate. Second, they cannot be reconciled with the constitutional structure as it was designed or has evolved. Third, Article I contains no explicit or implicit antientrenchment principle that would preclude the Senate from adopting procedural rules that carry over from one session to the next and may only be altered with supermajority approval.

Gerhardt points out institutional safeguards against abuse of the filibuster. "If the majority's will were frustrated, the Constitution provides two remedies. The first is to provide a president with the power to make recess appointments and thereby circumvent the obstruction of a substantial minority of senators. The second is to allow the President and those who have supported his contested nominations to exact revenge through the political process or to seek common ground to resolve their differences with a substantial minority of their colleagues. Whichever path they follow is constitutional, just as constitutional as the filibuster itself." *Id.* at 484. He thus concludes:

> [T]he filibuster is best understood as a classic example of a nonreviewable, legislative constitutional judgment. It has the same claim to constitutionality as many other countermajoritarian practices within the Senate, including the committee structure and unanimous consent requirements. The Constitution permits all of these practices, though it does not mandate any of them. These practices define the Senate's

Garfield.' While there may be some superficial appeal to the idea that a lame-duck President ought not to be choosing judges whose tenure will long outlast his, the same argument could be used to argue that a President should never nominate judges because almost invariably a federal judge remains on the bench long after any particular President, and his party, have left the White House. Filibusters are more likely to succeed at the end of a legislative session, but they are neither more nor less legitimate then than at any other time." Fisk & Chemerinsky, *supra*, at 345.

uniqueness as a political institution, particularly its historic commitments to various objectives—respecting the equality of its membership and to minority viewpoints; encouraging compromise on especially divisive matters; and facilitating stability, order, and collegiality in the long run. The principal checks on these practices, including the filibuster, are political. They include the Senate Rules, the need to maintain collegiality within the institution, and the political accountability of senators for their support of, or opposition to, specific filibusters. *Id.* at 449–50.

3. If the filibuster rule were to be changed, there is some disagreement over whether it can lawfully be changed by simple majority vote (the so-called nuclear option) or whether a change in the rule would itself require a supermajority vote. Professors Fisk and Chemerinsky, who oppose any change in the present cloture rule (which requires 60 votes to terminate debate), also argue that as a matter of policy, if any change is to be made to the cloture rule, the change should be made through the normal Senate procedures which require a two-thirds vote to change the rules, and not through the divisive approach of the "nuclear option." In an earlier article, however, these authors had argued that while the filibuster itself is constitutional, the entrenchment of the filibuster rule (by Senate rules requiring a two-thirds vote to change it) is not constitutional. See Catherine Fisk & Erwin Chemerinsky, *The Filibuster*, 49 Stan. L. Rev. 181 (1997). But cf. Virginia Seitz & Joseph R. Guerra, *A Constitutional Defense of "Entrenched" Senate Rules Governing Debate*, 20 J.L. & Politics 1 (2004) (responding to the 1997 Fisk–Chemerinsky article and arguing that "Senate Rules that require a supermajority to end debate on an amendment to the Senate Rules are constitutionally permissible" based on history and practice).

On the other hand, Professor John C. Roberts, Professor of Law and Dean Emeritus of DePaul University Law School, suggests that:

> ... [T]he Cloture Rule, and therefore the filibuster itself, are in fact subject to the will of a simple majority of the Senate at any time. I argue that this is true both as a matter of Senate practice and of constitutional principle.... [If] the Cloture Rule were binding in some legal sense on a simple majority of senators, it would be unconstitutional. I base my constitutional conclusion on the Constitution's inherent majority voting rule for the enactment process, on the Rulemaking Clause in Article I, Section 5, and on the anti-entrenchment principle (which I see as required by the Constitution)....

John C. Roberts, *Majority Voting in Congress: Further Notes on the Constitutionality of the Senate Cloture Rule*, 20 J.L. & Politics 505 (2004).[82] He concludes:

---

82. Roberts further explains why he believes the Constitution requires that the Senate remain free to change its own rules by simple majority vote:

[B]inding supermajority rules like the Cloture Rule would be invalid ... [under] the long-established principle that one legislature cannot bind a future one. This idea, often referred to as the anti-entrenchment principle, expresses a basic

norm of republican government, that each group of elected representatives, who may have very different social, economic and political views from the preceding one, should be able to work its will. While the anti-entrenchment principle does not appear as such in the Constitution, it can be readily grasped... [as] an earlier and more general expression of the second element of the Constitution's

> The perennial dispute about the filibuster and the validity of the Senate Cloture Rule is not in the final analysis a legal or a constitutional one. It is about power, politics, tradition and stability. Senators have already demonstrated that they can modify the Cloture Rule both directly and indirectly through majority vote. As Lyndon Johnson and Robert Byrd well knew, the philosophical, jurisprudential and constitutional arguments were really just window dressing. Both the filibuster and the Cloture Rule exist because the Senate wants them to exist.

Id. at 547.

4. If you were a member of the Senate, would you favor retaining or eliminating the filibuster? In general? For judicial nominees? For Supreme Court nominees? Are these questions related? If the filibuster rule for Supreme Court nominees were repealed, what effects might this have—not only on Supreme Court nominations but on, for example, possible efforts to change the size of the Court? The terms of the Justices? See Chapter Six, below, for further discussion of proposals for term limits for Supreme Court Justices.

c.   Limit the Nature of the Hearings?

A different set of approaches focuses, not on the voting rules, but on the way the confirmation hearings are conducted, including the nominee's involvement and the role of the press. As noted earlier, the custom of having the nominee testify before the Senate is relatively recent and that of televising the procedures even more recent. Should these trends be reconsidered? Should television be taken out of the Senate hearing room?

After the Thomas confirmation, the Senate Judiciary Committee, in effect, did so for the initial examination of allegations of personal wrongdoing. Following the extraordinary public exploration of Anita Hill's accusations against Clarence Thomas during his confirmation hearings, several observers suggested more refined methods of investigating such charges.

For example, Lloyd Cutler (who had been White House Counsel for Presidents Carter and Clinton), argued that having the committee sit in executive session was a "better way to deal with charges of personal misbehavior for nominees for high government office." Lloyd Cutler, *Why Not Executive Sessions?*, Wash. Post, Oct. 17, 1991, at A 23. The Senate's constitutional power to ratify treaties reflected the Framers' view that as a smaller body, the Senate "could be entrusted to keep

Rulemaking Clause. They embody exactly the same idea of continuous legislative autonomy, preserving the full freedom of action in each body of legislators over time....

... Keep in mind that advocates of entrenchment must accept not only the relatively mild form represented by a sixty percent supermajority requirement, but also the more extreme forms such as a ninety percent required majority or a complete prohibition on repeal or amendment.... [I]t is easy to see how such requirements encroach on the power of succeeding legislatures to determine their own rules of proceeding, and in effect modify the Rulemaking Clause for subsequent legislatures without going through the procedures mandated by Article V.... *Id.* at 520, 543.

secrets and could hear the most delicate aspects of the reasons for and against a treaty without making them public." *Id.* Cutler argued that the Senate's Intelligence and Armed Services committee had a good record of being "leakproof," even in sensitive matters, and that the Senate as a whole had met in executive session without damaging leaks. He thus proposed that if a "charge of personal misconduct" arose, the Senate committee should first decide if the charge was "substantial enough to require an evidentiary hearing." If so, he suggested, the committee should then conduct any hearing in a non-public executive session, taking other precautions as well; "following the practice of the Senate Intelligence Committee," the committee should keep only a single copy of the transcript and secure it "under lock and key for senators only to examine in the committee's office." He further suggested that the committee then file a report to the Senate, with discretion whether to keep it secret (presenting it "to the full Senate in executive session") or make it public. Although Cutler acknowledged that leaks could still occur, he argued that even if they did, the situation would be an improvement because (1) there would be no videotape, but only a report; (2) "the hearing itself would be . . . shorter and to the point;" and (3) both the nominee and any accuser would suffer less invasion of their privacy.

As indicated below, two years later, Senator Biden, as Chair of the Judiciary Committee, announced a change in the Committee's procedures responsive to some of these concerns.

———

Remarks by Senator Joseph Biden on the Confirmation Process for Ruth Bader Ginsburg, 139 Cong. Rec. 15747, 15749 (July 15, 1993)

. . .

[A] critical step toward restoring the integrity of the hearings relates to the manner in which the Committee handles investigative matters.

. . .

So we have changed . . . certain policies concerning Supreme Court nominees as it relates to the investigative side. . . .

First, as in the past, the committee will review all, and fully, FBI reports on the nominee. Staff, and only staffers with security clearance predesignated, will review that file and other investigative materials on a confidential and bipartisan basis. An important change in procedure that I am going to implement . . . has been adopted to ensure that the Judiciary Committee will not again be placed in the difficult position of possessing information about a Supreme Court nominee from a source unwilling to share that information with all other Senators.

. . . I want everyone to understand. . . . [A]ny individual who comes to the Judiciary Committee with allegations against the Supreme Court nominee is now notified that all that information will be placed in the nominee's confidential file and shared, on a confidential basis, with all U.S. Senators, not just those on the committee, before the Senate votes on that nomination.

Second, because ultimately the questio[n] with respect to investigations of Supreme Court nominees is the credibility and character of the nominee, the committee will conduct a closed session with all future nominees starting with Judge Ginsburg. No issues of policy or jurisprudence will be discussed in this closed portion of the hearing. The purpose of the session will be to ask the nominee face to face on the record under oath about any investigative issues that have been raised. The hearing will be conducted in accordance with Senate Rule XXVI, which permits the committee to go into closed session to protect the privacy of the nominee in considering confidential information. And any Senator under the Senate rules who violates the confidentiality of that hearing is subject to expulsion from the U.S. Senate. A closed hearing will be conducted for each and every nominee whether or not there has been any investigative matter raised. It will be routine.... And every single nominee, as long as I am chairman, will be part of that closed process I described.

The transcript of that session will be made part of the confidential record of the nomination and made available to all Senators under penalty of expulsion if they divulge the information....

Third, to ensure that all Senators are aware of any charges in the committee's possession, the committee will hold a closed, confidential briefing session for Senators on all Supreme Court nominations; Senators only, no staff. So every Senator should be put on notice.... [A]ny Senator, just like with the CIA material, will be able to come over himself or herself and sit down on a day designated with the investigative staff sitting there and ask any question about anything that has been raised and made available to them—all that has been raised.

At this briefing, all Senators will be invited, under rigorous restrictions to protect confidentiality, to inspect the documents and reports we will have compiled. The briefing will be offered following the completion of the committee action and before the nomination goes to the floor. I intend these three steps to help restore the confidence in our investigative procedures and to reassure the public about the seriousness with which we take such matters as part of the confirmation process and, equally important, to protect the integrity and privacy and the rights of the nominee.

I also hope that the whole of the nomination and confirmation process will contribute to ... the confidence of the American people in the women and men who will serve on the Supreme Court....

Questions and Comments

1. The Judiciary Committee has continued to follow the practice of meeting in closed session with every Supreme Court nominee to examine the required FBI Report and investigate any "other investigative issues." See *Nomination of Stephen G. Breyer to be an Associate Justice of the Supreme Court of the United States: Hearings Before the S. Comm. on the Judiciary*, 103d Cong. 239 (Statement of Chair, Senator Biden: "It is now standard operating procedure that there is a closed session that every [Supreme Court] nominee . . . will participate in, where we go over . . . those matters that we are not able to discuss in public, that is, the FBI report."); *Confirmation Hearing on the Nomination of John G. Roberts, Jr. To Be Chief Justice of the United States: Hearing Before the S. Comm. on the Judiciary*, 109th Cong. 450 (2005) (Statement of Chair, Senator Arlen Specter: "During Senator Biden's tenure as chairman, the practice was initiated of conducting closed sessions with each nominee for the Supreme Court, to ask the nominee on the record, under oath, about all investigative charges against the person, if there were any. These hearings are routinely conducted for every Supreme Court nominee, even where there are no investigative issues to be resolved. In doing so, those outside the committee cannot infer that the committee has received adverse, confidential information about a nominee."); *Confirmation Hearing on the Nomination of Samuel A. Alito, Jr. To Be an Associate Justice of the Supreme Court of the United States: Hearings Before the S. Comm. on the Judiciary*, 109th Cong. 640 (2006) (Statement of Chair, Senator Arlen Specter: "After our morning session, the committee met in executive session and reviewed confidential date on the background of Judge Alito. And it was found to be in order."). These confidential hearings are in addition to the public hearings with nominees and others testifying that have been routine since the 1950s.

2. In arguing for closed executive sessions on allegations of personal wrongdoing, Lloyd Cutler suggested that without the television cameras and nation-wide audience, "senators would waste much less time in irrelevant discourses . . . and could concentrate on developing the facts." Cutler, *supra*. Would this argument apply as well to questions addressed to the nominees about subjects likely to come before the Court? Are there other ways of reducing "irrelevant discourses," but doing so without interfering with the transparency and accountability generally associated with the Senate's role in the confirmation process?

3. Should the Senate consider curtailing or eliminating the testimony of nominees to the Court? Remember that practice only became the norm in the 1950s. As Professor Gerhardt notes in *Toward a Comprehensive Understanding of the Federal Appointments Process*, 21 Harv. J. L. & Pub. Pol'y 467, 533 (1998):

> This change would arguably put additional pressure on presidents to nominate, and on the Senate to confirm, only those candidates whose accomplishments and records could speak sufficiently for themselves. This proposal also arguably would protect judicial independence from being threatened in the confirmation process by overly aggressive sena-

torial questioning about nominees' likely voting patterns or judicial ideologies.

See also *Judicial Roulette: Report of the Twentieth Century Fund Task Force on Judicial Selection* 8–11 (1988) (suggesting that, except where a question of personal wrongdoing arises, the Senate should re-institute prior practice so that "Supreme Court nominees should no longer be expected to appear as witnesses during the Senate Judiciary Committee's hearings on their confirmation"). However, Gerhardt concludes this proposal is "ill-considered for at least two reasons:"

> First, as a practical matter, the tradition of having judicial nominees testify before the Senate is already too well-established to be abandoned. Although restricting the personal testimony of judicial nominees would probably be welcome news to the nominees themselves, presidents would hesitate to support such a proposal because they might be criticized for hiding their nominees from public scrutiny; and senators would similarly be inclined not to support such a reform because they might be criticized for deferring too much to the president and not exercising their constitutional authority to advise and consent more energetically. Second, nominee testimony provides, in many cases, the only chance for most of the public to learn about the nominees. Testimony is often the last, if not only, forum in which a nominee can be held accountable for his or her professional record, which is directly reflective of his or her qualifications.

Gerhardt, *Toward a Comprehensive Understanding*, at 553. Do you agree?

5. Changing the Justices' Terms—Modifying Life Tenure?

Some critics believe that it is life tenure, coupled with increased longevity and the unpredictability of the occurrence of judicial vacancies, that has made the appointment process so contentious. Life tenure, some argue, can no longer be justified, given longer life spans, the attraction of being a Supreme Court Justice, and contemporary commitments to democracy and accountability.

In 1988, after the Bork defeat was followed by the unsuccessful nomination of Douglas Ginsburg at the relatively young age of 41, Professor Henry Monaghan observed that, if Ginsburg had been confirmed, he might have served four decades. Reflecting on this possibility, Professor Monaghan proposed:

> [C]onsideration of two kinds of limitations on judicial tenure. The first is an age limit. I think it quite astounding that a majority of Supreme Court judges bordered on eighty years of age before Chief Justice Burger and Justice Powell retired. The Court's workload is very heavy, and it is doubtful that many octogenarians would be able to devote the energy necessary to the task. As Aristotle said, "that judges of important causes should hold office for life is a disputable thing, for the mind grows old as well as the body." The

graying of the Court can only work to ensure even greater delegation of responsibility to law clerks.

My second suggestion is premised on a distrust of relatively unaccountable powerholders. The suggestion is that no one be permitted to serve for more than some fixed and unrenewable term, such as fifteen or twenty years. Governor Winthrop once described judges as "gods upon earth," and that surely is true of the Supreme Court judges. It seems dubious policy to leave such power in any person's hands for too long. In light of these concerns, and of the defects in the original justifications for life tenure, the burden should be on those who favor the continuation of the present arrangement to come forth with their argument. Or is the short response to both of my suggestions, "If it ain't broke, don't fix it."?

Henry Paul Monaghan, *The Confirmation Process: Law or Politics?*, 101 Harv. L. Rev. 1202, 1211 (1988).

A decade and a half later, motivated in part by the unusually long period of continuity with no new appointments between the 1994 arrival of Breyer and the 2005 appointment of Roberts, a number of other scholars have developed proposals for term limits or age limits for Supreme Court Justices. In Chapter Six, we examine these and other reform proposals in more detail.

Chapter Three

SETTING THE COURT'S AGENDA

Each year, parties in thousands of cases pending in the state and lower federal courts seek the attention of the Supreme Court. The Court has almost complete discretion to pick and choose, from the cases presented to it, which to review and adjudicate on the merits. The Court, in effect, sets its own agenda as it decides which cases it will hear.

From an advocate's viewpoint, then, the first job is to convince the Court to hear the case, not necessarily to persuade the Court to a particular view of it. To the student of the Court, its discretion over its agenda means that the law the Court makes through its published opinions must be influenced, in some substantial manner, by the standards the Court employs at the screening stage—deciding which petitions for a writ of certiorari to grant. As it selects only a comparative handful from the thousands of cases offered for review each year, the Court sends strong signals about the kinds of cases, types of issues, and categories of litigants it favors.[1] For these reasons, a study of the Supreme Court's case selection process should be a central feature of an analysis of the institutional processes of constitutional lawmaking.

In a petition for a writ of certiorari—the Latin term meaning "to be more fully informed"—the litigants are asking the Court to become informed about their case by requesting the lower court to send up the record. The Court has complete discretion to determine whether to grant this request. As discussed below, in exercising its discretion the Court operates under a "Rule of Four"—if four Justices want to grant the petition, it will be granted. One of the principal aims of this chapter is to explore what factors influence the decision whether to grant certiorari.

A central question is the extent to which the Court's agenda-setting function is dictated by institutional concerns, on the one hand, or by the various Justices' views about shaping the law, on the other. In recent years, the Court has received between roughly 6,000 and 8,000 petitions each year but has granted review to between roughly 80 and 110 cases a

---

1. These observations are forcefully voiced by Justice Brennan in William J. Brennan, *The National Court of Appeals:* *Another Dissent*, 40 U. Chi. L. Rev. 473, 482–85 (1973) (excerpted in Section B of this chapter, below).

year (on the lower end in more recent years), well down from earlier periods when it would hear argument on 150 or more cases each year . . . The principal function of the process is to weed out the vast majority of cases and deny them further review. Thus, most petitions must be denied without regard to the ideology or status of the petitioning party. In this sense, the certiorari process certainly is governed by institutional concerns.

With respect to those cases that are granted, or are seriously considered as potentially "certworthy," however, the Court (or, perhaps more accurately, any particular Justice who votes on the matter) may be motivated by either of two distinct goals. First, the decision whether to grant certiorari in close cases might be governed principally by a desire to further institutional goals not closely connected to particular ideological views about constitutional law. Thus, for example, the Court or the Justice might be searching for cases that reflect conflicts among the lower courts that cannot be resolved except at the Supreme Court level; the institutional motivation is for the Court to help assure a uniform interpretation of federal law. Alternatively, however, the Court or the justice might be seeking primarily to further a set of ideological views about the shape of the law. For example, the Court or the Justice might be interested in cases that would be good vehicles for expanding the First Amendment's protection of freedom of religion or the Fourth Amendment's protection against unreasonable searches and seizures, or alternatively, for cutting back in these or other areas. Obviously, in some cases, these institutional and ideological factors coincide. But, in the cases where these issues do not coincide, the question of how large a role different Justices' view of the law plays in voting on certiorari petitions remains an interesting question.

The Court has not always had so much *discretionary* jurisdiction over its docket; most of its jurisdiction until the early 20th century was *obligatory*. In the Judiciary Act of 1925, often called the Judges' Bill, Congress expanded the Court's certiorari jurisdiction, giving the Justices considerable (though not complete control) over the number of cases they would hear and decide on the merits. But they had no control over the number of cases seeking review and that number continued to escalate. By the 1950s, scholars began to worry about the effects of the rising docket on the Justices' capacities to give appropriate deliberative time to their work. See Henry M. Hart, Jr., *The Supreme Court, 1958 Term—Foreword: The Time Chart of the Justices*, 73 Harv. L. Rev. 84 (1959) (expressing concern over the effects of the Court having about 1300 petitions for certiorari and 1700 total cases per Term during the prior years). Because of this escalation, many Court watchers in the 1970s and 1980s suggested new ways for the Court to deal with so many petitions, including creation of a new national court of appeals or "cert-court." By the early 1980s, the Court was receiving 4000 requests for review each year, and the number of petitions for certiorari continued to grow, reaching more than 8,000 annually in the 2000s. However, starting in the late 1980s and early 1990s, the number of cases in which review was granted began to drop, going from as many as 170–80 cases per term in the mid–1970s and early 1980s to as few as 74 to 80 cases per term in recent years.[2] That self-generated decline in the number of cases granted review has reduced the pressure for statutory changes to reduce the Justices' workload and has, instead, spawned a new literature concerned with how few cases the Court is deciding.

These statistics, reflecting the Court's recent change in cert-granting practice, give new urgency to the questions of this Chapter: First, whatever the final number of petitions granted—whether it is 80 or 150—how does the Court decide which of the thousands of petitions filed should become one of those relatively few heard on the merits? Second, why has the number of petitions granted declined so markedly since the 1990s? The materials that follow are divided into four sections.

Section A provides a more detailed description of the different ways cases may come to be heard in the Court, and reproduces some of the jurisdictional statutes and Supreme Court rules governing the certiorari process.

Section B describes the history of the certiorari jurisdiction and the process by which the Court receives, considers, and votes on petitions for writs of certiorari. We begin with Professor Edward Hartnett's article, describing the genesis of the Judges' Bill of 1925, and the expansion of the Supreme Court's control of its discretionary docket. We then give several inside views—from Justices on the Court—of the certiorari process. Thereafter, we provide some views from outside the Court— from both law professors and political scientists.

Section C focuses on the recent decline in the number of petitions for certiorari that are granted each term. While the total number of petitions filed has not decreased significantly, the number of cases heard on the merits has declined markedly since the early 1990s. From the 1960s through the late 1980s, the number of cases granted review remained within a range of about 130 to 170 cases per year. But as noted earlier, in the 1990s, the number of petitions granted began to drop and now averages about 80 cases per term.[3] This section tries to assess the reasons for this decreasing docket and to consider what responses, if any,

---

2. See David R. Stras, *The Supreme Court's Gatekeepers: The Role of Law Clerks in the Certiorari Process*, 85 Texas L. Rev. 947, 965 (2007)("[T]he reduction in the Court's plenary docket began in 1986, when William Rehnquist became Chief Justice and Antonin Scalia was appointed to the Court. In October Term 1986, the Court issued 153 signed and orally argued per curiam opinions, but by October Term 1989, that number had declined to 131. The decline then accelerated, with only eighty-six such opinions released during October Term 1993. Since then, the Court's plenary docket has oscillated between seventy-four and ninety-two signed and orally argued per

curiam opinions, with most of the recent Terms on the low side of that range.")

3. There are two categories of certiorari petitions: "paid" and "in forma pauperis" or "IFPs." (The difference is explained further below at p. 353.) While the number of "paid" petitions has decreased since 2000, the number of "IFP" petitions has grown. Thus the total number of petitions filed has remained about the same, somewhere between 7200 and 8000 per term. See *The Supreme Court Compendium: Data, Decisions, and Developments* 74–75 (Lee Epstein et al. eds., 4th ed. 2007) [hereinafter *The Supreme Court Compendium*].

are appropriate. Reform proposals range from the extreme of abolishing the Court's discretion to set its agenda to simply trying to modify the Court's calendar to deal with its shrinking docket.[4]

Section D considers two sets of special circumstances: those surrounding petitions for certiorari, habeas petitions and motions for stays in challenges to the death penalty and those cases involving certiorari prior to judgment. In both categories, the Court may be asked to act with more than its usual speed—by death-sentenced prisoners seeking stays, by prosecutors seeking to proceed with executions pursuant to state court judgments, and by parties in federal cases seeking Supreme Court review without benefit of a court of appeals decision.

Finally, Section E provides three perspectives on the Supreme Court's role in society, as expressed in part through the certiorari process. These scholars offer very different assessments, ranging from Professor Hartnett's concern that the Court is too empowered to set its own agenda, to Professor Arthur Hellman's view that the Court is too "Olympian," pronouncing law from on-high, and detached from the work of the lower courts, to Professor Mark Tushnet, who sees a Court with more "chastened" aspirations.

In addition to the materials presented in the chapter, readers will learn even more, we have discovered, if they also engage themselves in the actual process. Those with access to the Supreme Court can study certiorari (or "cert") petitions pending before the Court and try to predict their outcome or join with others to conduct a mock "cert conference." Alternatively, one can read lower court opinions in cases for which cert petitions are pending, try to construct the arguments for and against granting certiorari, and then try to predict the outcome or conduct a mock conference.

A. JURISDICTION, GOVERNING STATUTES AND RULES

Although the vast majority of requests for review in the Court are made by petitions for certiorari, there are a number of other bases for jurisdiction. A few cases invoke the Court's original jurisdiction and typically involve boundary disputes between States.[5] One of the more

---

4. The Court has modified its argument schedule to accommodate the reduced load. Instead of hearing four arguments per day on each scheduled day of argument (2 cases from 10 am to noon and 2 cases from 1 to 3 pm), the Court has generally been hearing only two cases per day (from 10 am to 12 noon).

5. Article III grants the Supreme Court original jurisdiction over a small class of cases. See U.S. Constitution Art. III, § 2 ("In all Cases affecting Ambassadors, other public Ministers and Consuls, and those in

which a State shall be Party, the Supreme Court shall have original Jurisdiction."). Most cases that fall within the scope of this grant may also be (and usually are) filed originally in federal district courts. See 28 U.S.C. § 1251 (giving federal district courts concurrent jurisdiction over many cases falling within the Supreme Court's original jurisdiction.) For discussion of the Supreme Court's use of special masters in original jurisdiction cases, see Anne–Marie C. Carstens, *Lurking in the Shadows of Judicial Process: Special Masters in the Supreme*

recent was a dispute between New York and New Jersey over the ownership of certain portions of Ellis Island.[6]

Most parties seeking the Supreme Court's attention want the Court to review a judgment of a lower court—either state or federal. There are three routes, depending on the nature of the dispute, by which to invoke the Supreme Court's appellate jurisdiction: (1) appeal as a matter of right, (2) certification, and (3) petition for a writ of certiorari.

The first category, appeal as a matter of right (sometimes called "mandatory appeals"), is for those cases that Congress has decided are so important that the Supreme Court *must* decide them. Although at one time the Court's mandatory appellate jurisdiction included, for example, all cases in which a state court found an Act of Congress unconstitutional, or in which a federal court found a state statute unconstitutional, these cases are now generally heard only by writ of certiorari.[7] Today, mandatory appeals to the Supreme Court are available only in a small number of cases, mostly from decisions of three-judge federal district courts. Although more rare than in the past, they do still exist.[8] Although the Court need not hold oral argument to decide an appeal but may act summarily, a summary affirmance has precedential effect, see Hicks v. Miranda, 422 U.S. 332 (1975), in contrast to a denial of certiorari, which has no precedential effect.[9]

Certification occurs when a lower federal appellate court "certifies" a question to the Supreme Court, asking the Justices to clarify a question of federal law. The Justices have discretion to decide whether or not to answer such a question. 28 U.S.C. § 1254(a); Supreme Court Rule 19.3. Commonly invoked in the early part of the twentieth century, the certification process has become quite rare in recent years.[10]

Court's Original Jurisdiction Cases, 86 Minn. L. Rev. 625 (2002).

6. New Jersey v. New York, 526 U.S. 589 (1999).

7. See Robert L. Stern et al., *Supreme Court Practice* § 2.7, at 82–84 (8th ed. 2002) (hereinafter Stern & Gressman, *Supreme Court Practice*).

8. For example, challenges under the Voting Rights Act of 1965, 42 U.S.C. § 1973 (2004) must be heard by a three-judge district court. See, e.g., Vieth v. Jubelirer, 541 U.S. 267 (2004) (direct appeal from district court as provided by Voting Rights Act of 1965). In addition, Congress will occasionally direct that a new statute likely to generate constitutional challenges must have those challenges adjudicated in the first instance by a three-judge court and then by appeal as of right to the Supreme Court. See, e.g., United States v. Eichman, 496 U.S. 310 (1990) (direct appeal from district court as provided by Flag Protection Act of 1989); McConnell v. FEC, 540 U.S. 93 (2003) (direct appeal from district court as

provided by Bipartisan Reform Act of 2002), 2 U.S.C. § 431 (2004) (the "McCain–Feingold" Campaign Finance Law).

9. With appeals, the Court must schedule argument, summarily affirm or reverse, or "dismiss for want of a substantial federal question;" there is no discretion to refuse to rule on an appeal, assuming it is jurisdictionally proper. Especially under some older jurisdictional statutes since repealed, an issue could arise whether a request properly fell into the Court's appellate jurisdiction or should have been filed as a petition for certiorari.

10. See 17 Charles Alan Wright et al., *Federal Practice and Procedure* § 4038, at 107 (3d ed. 2007) (describing as the Court's view that "the course of wisdom is to accept certified questions only in circumstances that would warrant certiorari before judgment"). One of the most recent requests for review of a certified question came from the Second Circuit, sitting en banc, asking the Court to rule on the constitutionality of the Sentencing Guidelines, shortly after the

The route of certiorari is the most common avenue to the Supreme Court.[11] And therefore most of the rest of this chapter focuses on certiorari petitions ("cert" petitions, in the jargon.) Readers should be aware that there are two categories of these petitions: paid petitions, in which the petitioner is required to pay a filing fee and to supply numerous copies of the petition to the Court, and *"in forma pauperis"* or "IFP" petitions, where the filing fee is waived (for indigent persons, often prisoners).[12] Today, there are far more IFP petitions filed than paid, but the rate of granting paid petitions has always greatly outnumbered exceeded the rate at which IFPs are granted.[13]

Court's closely contested decision in Blakely v. Washington, 542 U.S. 296 (2004). The Second Circuit's request asserted:

> [W]e believe this is one of those "rare instances" when "the proper administration and expedition of judicial business" warrants certification of a question to the Supreme Court. *Blakely* not only casts a pall of uncertainty on more than 220,000 federal sentences imposed since *Apprendi* was decided, but it also raises the prospect that many thousands of future sentences may be invalidated or, alternatively, that district courts simply will halt sentencing altogether pending a definitive ruling by the Supreme Court. We are convinced that a prompt and authoritative answer to our inquiry is needed avoid a major disruption in the administration of criminal justice in the federal courts–disruption that would be unfair to defendants, to crime victims, to the public, and to the judges who must follow applicable constitutional requirements.

United States v. Penaranda, 375 F.3d 238 (2d Cir., 2004). The Supreme Court refused to certify the question but only after it had addressed the same question in another case brought by the United States.

On August 2, 2004, the Supreme Court granted the Solicitor General's ("SG") request to grant certiorari in two other cases that the SG said offered better vehicles to decide the constitutionality of the Federal Sentencing Guidelines. United States v. Booker, 542 U.S. 956 (2004); United States v. Fanfan, 542 U.S. 956 (2004). One of the reasons given by the SG for preferring the *Booker* case over *Penaranda* was that it offers the Court

> the benefit of a concrete judgment examining the applicability of *Blakely;* in *Penaranda,* no court has rendered a decision resolving the *Blakely* issues. [*Booker*] also has the benefit of questions presented that were formulated by the petitioning party, in accordance with the customary practice of this Court. The adversary

system contemplates that the parties will normally frame the questions for courts to review. While Congress has retained certification by a court of appeals as a mode of Supreme Court review, it has rarely been employed in recent years. ... Adherence to the normal adversary mode of review has the advantage of settled and well-understood procedures.

Petition for a Writ of Certiorari at 26–27, *Booker*, 542 U.S. 955 (No. 04–104). The SG noted that "[a]fter deciding [*Booker*] and *Fanfan*, the Court could dispose of *Penaranda* as appropriate." *Id.* at 27, n.12. The Court heard expedited arguments in *Booker* and *Fanfan* in September, 2004 and decided them on January 12, 2005. United States v. Booker, 543 U.S. 220 (2005). On January 24, 2005, the Court dismissed the Second Circuit's certified question. United States v. Penaranda, 543 U.S. 1117 (2005).

11. See Charles Alan Wright et al., *Federal Practice and Procedure* § 4004, at 22 (3d ed. 2007); see also, Daniel R. Coquillette, *The Anglo–American Legal Heritage* 248 (1999) (noting that while the writ of certiorari is today used "as a general vehicle of discretionary appeal," in English history the writ had a more narrow function, for example, to review criminal indictments and local administrative orders).

12. See Supreme Court Rule 12, reproduced below.

13. According to *The Supreme Court Compendium*, in recent years the number of paid petitions filed with the Court has ranged from 2749 in 1980 (2935 in 1981) to a low of 2041 in 2004, the last year for which *The Compendium* reports data. See, *The Supreme Court Compendium supra*, at 74–75. The number of IFP petitions filed has grown from 2371 in 1980 to 6543 in 2004 (with as many as 7209 filed in 2002). *Id*. During that same period, the percentage of paid petitions granted ranged between 5–7% in the 1980s, and dropped to a range of 3–4% in the 2000s. *Id*. The percentage of IFPs granted ranged between 2% and 0.3%

In the materials below, we set out the formal rules—the more significant provisions of the U.S. Code governing Supreme Court jurisdiction and the central portions of the Supreme Court's own rules, particularly Supreme Court Rule 10, concerning petitions for review. As will be seen, the jurisdictional statutes mandate some minimal criteria that must be met before the Supreme Court can hear a case:

- Cases coming from the state courts must be controlled by an issue of federal law.

- The case must come from the highest lower court from which review can be had;[14] one cannot, for example, appeal a ruling from a state trial court directly to the U.S. Supreme Court without seeking whatever appellate review the state courts offer.

- Generally, the controversy must have been finally adjudicated in the courts below; one cannot, for example, halt a trial in mid-course in order to ask the Supreme Court to review a ruling on the admissibility of evidence.

- Finally, the certiorari petition must be filed within the established time limits and in proper form.

28 U.S.C. §§ 1251–1259 contain the principal federal statutes defining the Supreme Court's jurisdiction. We excerpt portions of them below. In addition, this section reproduces some of the Supreme Court Rules that pertain to certiorari.

1. Jurisdictional Statutes, 28 U.S. Code §§ 1251–1257

§ 1251. Original jurisdiction

(a) The Supreme Court shall have original and exclusive jurisdiction of all controversies between two or more States.

(b) The Supreme Court shall have original but not exclusive jurisdiction of:

in the 1980s (though in most years of this decade the grant rate was between 1% and 2%) and between 0.1% and 0.2% in the 2000s.

The number of IFP filings has not always exceeded paid filings. For example, in 1950 there were 640 paid requests for review (14% of which were granted), but only 415 IFP requests (of which 4% were granted). By 1960, there were 789 paid requests for review (with a grant rate of 11%), and 1085 IFP requests (with a grant rate of 2%); and in 1970, 1903 paid requests for review were filed (11% of which were granted), and 2289 IFPs, of which 2% were granted. *The Supreme Court Compendium* at 72–73. The Harvard Law Review also provides statistics each Term on the number of requests for review filed and granted. See footnotes 67, 82 below in this chapter. While the methods of counting appear to vary from those used in *The Supreme Court Compendium* both data sets indicate similar trends in the relative ratios of paid petitions to IFPs filed, and in the grant rates for the two categories.

14. The Supreme Court is empowered to grant certiorari in federal cases before the relevant circuit court has ruled on the matter (i.e., issue "certiorari before judgment"), see 28 U.S.C. § 1254; Supreme Court Rule 11, and has done so in some cases of great public interest, including United States v. Fanfan, 543 U.S. 220 (2005), discussed above. See generally, discussion in Section D, below.

(1) All actions or proceedings to which ambassadors, other public ministers, consuls, or vice consuls of foreign states are parties;

(2) All controversies between the United States and a State;

(3) All actions or proceedings by a State against the citizens of another State or against aliens.

. . .

§ 1253. Direct appeals from decisions of three-judge courts

Except as otherwise provided by law, any party may appeal to the Supreme Court from an order granting or denying, after notice and hearing, an interlocutory or permanent injunction in any civil action, suit or proceeding required by any Act of Congress to be heard and determined by a district court of three judges. . . .

. . .

§ 1254. Courts of appeals; certiorari; certified questions

Cases in the courts of appeals may be reviewed by the Supreme Court by the following methods:

(1) By writ of certiorari granted upon the petition of any party to any civil or criminal case, before or after rendition of judgment or decree;

(2) By certification at any time by a court of appeals of any question of law in any civil or criminal case as to which instructions are desired, and upon such certification the Supreme Court may give binding instructions or require the entire record to be sent up for decision of the entire matter in controversy.

. . .

§ 1257. State courts; certiorari

(a) Final judgments or decrees rendered by the highest court of a State in which a decision could be had, may be reviewed by the Supreme Court by writ of certiorari where the validity of a treaty or statute of the United States is drawn in question or where the validity of a statute of any State is drawn in question on the ground of its being repugnant to the Constitution, treaties, or laws of the United States, or where any title, right, privilege, or immunity is specially set up or claimed under the Constitution or the treaties or statutes of, or any commission held or authority exercised under, the United States.

(b) For the purposes of this section, the term "highest court of a State" includes the District of Columbia Court of Appeals.[15]

. . .

15. Review by writ of certiorari of decisions of the Supreme Court of the Common- wealth of Puerto Rico is authorized, in roughly comparable terms, by 28 U.S.C.

2.   Supreme Court Rules

Supreme Court Rules 10–16 govern the procedures for filing petitions for certiorari and they are excerpted below. Of particular interest is
Rule 10, which contains the Court's statement of the criteria employed
in ruling on certiorari petitions. (A word of caution: practitioners need to
have a much wider knowledge of all the rules before filing any petition
or other pleading with the Court.)[16] These rules were last modified on
July 17, 2007, to become effective on October 1, 2007.[17]

Rule 10. Consideration Governing Review on Writ of Certiorari

1.   Review on a writ of certiorari is not a matter of right, but of
judicial discretion. A petition for a writ of certiorari will be granted only
for compelling reasons. The following, although neither controlling nor
fully measuring the Court's discretion, indicate the character of reasons
the Court considers:

>   (a) a United States court of appeals has entered a decision in
> conflict with the decision of another United States court of appeals
> on the same important matter; has decided an important federal
> question in a way that conflicts with a state court of last resort; or
> has so far departed from the accepted and usual course of judicial
> proceedings, or sanctioned such a departure by a lower court, as to
> call for an exercise of this Court's supervisory power;

>   (b) a state court of last resort has decided an important federal
> question in a way that conflicts with the decision of another state
> court of last resort or of a United States court of appeals;

>   (c) a state court or a United States court of appeals has decided
> an important question of federal law that has not been, but should
> be, settled by this Court, or has decided an important federal
> question in a way that conflicts with relevant decisions of this Court.

A petition for a writ of certiorari is rarely granted when the asserted
error consists of erroneous factual findings or the misapplication of a
properly stated rule of law.

Rule 11. Certiorari to a United States Court of Appeals Before Judgment

A petition for a writ of certiorari to review a case pending in a
United States court of appeals, before judgment is entered in that court,
will be granted only upon a showing that the case is of such imperative

---

§ 1258. Another provision authorizes re-
view by certiorari of certain decisions of the
U.S. Court of Appeals for the Armed
Forces. See 28 U.S.C. § 1259.

16. For example, other parts of the
rules address how documents are to be prepared. In addition, the rule concerning amicus briefs was recently amended to require
persons intending to file amicus briefs at
the jurisdictional stage to provide notice to
counsel of record. See Supreme Court Rule
37.

17. The most up-to-date version of the
Supreme Court Rules, including notes on
recent changes, is on the Supreme Court's
website, at http://www.supremecourtus.gov/
ctrules/2007rulesofthecourt.pdf.

public importance as to justify deviation from normal appellate practice and to require immediate determination in this Court. See 28 U.S.C. § 2101(e).

Rule 12. Review on Certiorari; How Sought; Parties

1. Except as provided in paragraph 2 of this Rule, the petitioner shall file 40 copies of a petition for a writ of certiorari, prepared as required by Rule 33.1, and shall pay the Rule 38(a) docket fee.

2. A petitioner proceeding *in forma pauperis* under Rule 39 shall file an original and 10 copies of a petition for a writ of certiorari prepared as required by Rule 33.2, together with an original and 10 copies of the motion for leave to proceed *in forma pauperis....* An inmate confined in an institution, if proceeding *in forma pauperis* and not represented by counsel, need file only an original petition and motion.

3. Whether prepared under Rule 33.1 or Rule 33.2, the petition shall comply in all respects with Rule 14 and shall be submitted with proof of service as required by Rule 29. The case then will be placed on the docket. It is the petitioner's duty to notify all respondents promptly, on a form supplied by the Clerk, of the date of filing, the date the case was placed on the docket, and the docket number of the case....

4. Parties interested jointly, severally, or otherwise in a judgment may petition separately for a writ of certiorari; or any two or more may join in a petition. A party not shown on the petition as joined therein at the time the petition is filed may not later join in that petition. When two or more judgments are sought to be reviewed on a writ of certiorari to the same court and involve identical or closely related questions, a single petition for a writ of certiorari covering all the judgments suffices. A petition for a writ of certiorari may not be joined with any other pleading, except that any motion for leave to proceed *in forma pauperis* shall be attached.

5. [Detailed provisions for a conditional cross-petition, that is, a cross-petition that otherwise would be untimely, are omitted.]

6. All parties to the proceeding in the court whose judgment is sought to be reviewed are deemed parties entitled to file documents in this Court, unless the petitioner notifies the Clerk of this Court in writing of the petitioner's belief that one or more of the parties below have no interest in the outcome of the petition. A copy of such notice shall be served as required by Rule 29 on all parties to the proceeding below.... All parties other than the petitioner are considered respondents, but any respondent who supports the position of a petitioner shall meet the petitioner's time schedule for filing documents, except that a response supporting the petition shall be filed within 20 days after the case is placed on the docket, and that time will not be extended. Parties who file no document will not qualify for any relief from this Court.

7. The clerk of the court having possession of the record shall keep it until notified by the Clerk of this Court to certify and transmit it. In

any document filed with this Court, a party may cite or quote from the record, even if it has not been transmitted to this Court. . . .

Rule 13. Review on Certiorari: Time for Petitioning

1. Unless otherwise provided by law, a petition for a writ of certiorari to review a judgment in any case, civil or criminal, entered by a state court of last resort or a United States court of appeals (including the United States Court of Appeals for the Armed Forces) is timely when it is filed with the Clerk of this Court within 90 days after the entry of the judgment. A petition for a writ of certiorari seeking review of a judgment of a lower state court that is subject to discretionary review by the state court of last resort is timely when it is filed with the Clerk within 90 days after the entry of the order denying discretionary review.

2. The Clerk will not file any petition for a writ of certiorari that is jurisdictionally out of time. See, e.g., 28 U.S.C. § 2101(c).

3. The time to file a petition for a writ of certiorari runs from the date of entry of the judgment or order sought to be reviewed, and not from the issuance date of the mandate (or its equivalent under local practice). But if a petition for rehearing is timely filed in the lower court by any party, or if the lower court appropriately entertains an untimely petition for rehearing or sua sponte considers rehearing, the time to file the petition for a writ of certiorari for all parties (whether or not they requested rehearing or joined in the petition for rehearing) runs from the date of the denial of the petition for rehearing or, if the petition for rehearing is granted, the subsequent entry of judgment.

4. A cross-petition for a writ of certiorari is timely when it is filed with the Clerk as provided in paragraphs 1, 3, and 5 of this Rule, or in Rule 12.5. . . .

5. For good cause, a Justice may extend the time to file a petition for a writ of certiorari for a period not exceeding 60 days. An application to extend the time to file shall set out the basis for jurisdiction in this Court, identify the judgment sought to be reviewed, include a copy of the opinion and any order respecting rehearing, and set out specific reasons why an extension of time is justified. . . . An application to extend the time to file a petition for a writ of certiorari is not favored.

Rule 14. Content of a Petition for a Writ of Certiorari

1. A petition for a writ of certiorari shall contain, in the order indicated:

    (a) The questions presented for review, expressed concisely in relation to the circumstances of the case, without unnecessary detail. The questions should be short and should not be argumentative or repetitive. If the petitioner or respondent is under a death sentence that may be affected by the disposition of the petition, the notation "capital case" shall precede the questions presented. The questions shall be set out on the first page following the cover, and no other information may appear on that page. The statement of any question presented is deemed to comprise every subsidiary question fairly included therein. Only the questions set out in the petition, or fairly included therein, will be considered by the Court.

(b) A list of all parties to the proceeding in the court whose judgment is sought to be reviewed (unless the caption) of the case contains the names of all the parties, and a corporate disclosure statement as required by Rule 29.6.

(c) If the petition exceeds five pages or 1,500 words, a table of contents and a table of cited authorities. The table of contents shall include the items contained in the appendix.

(d) Citations of the official and unofficial reports of the opinions and orders entered in the case by courts or administrative agencies.

(e) A concise statement of the basis for jurisdiction in this Court, showing:

> (i) the date the judgment or order sought to be reviewed was entered (and, if applicable, a statement that the petition is filed under this Court's Rule 11);

> (ii) the date of any order respecting rehearing, and the date and terms of any order granting an extension of time to file the petition for a writ of certiorari;

> (iii) express reliance on Rule 12.5, when a cross-petition for a writ of certiorari is filed under that Rule, and the date of docketing of the petition for a writ of certiorari in connection with which the cross-petition is filed;

> (iv) the statutory provision believed to confer on this Court jurisdiction to review on a writ of certiorari the judgment or order in question; and

> (v) if applicable, a statement that the notifications required by Rule 29.4(b) or (c) have been made.

(f) The constitutional provisions, treaties, statutes, ordinances, and regulations involved in the case, set out verbatim with appropriate citation. If the provisions involved are lengthy, their citation alone suffices at this point, and their pertinent text shall be set out in the appendix referred to in subparagraph 1(i).

(g) A concise statement of the case setting out the facts material to consideration of the questions presented, and also containing the following:

> (i) If review of a state-court judgment is sought, specification of the stage in the proceedings, both in the court of first instance and in the appellate courts, when the federal questions sought to be reviewed were raised; the method or manner of raising them and the way in which they were passed on by those courts; and pertinent quotations of specific portions of the record or summary thereof, with specific reference to the places in the record where the matter appears ..., so as to show that

the federal question was timely and properly raised and that this Court has jurisdiction to review the judgment on a writ of certiorari . . .

(ii) If review of a judgment of a United States court of appeals is sought, the basis for federal jurisdiction in the court of first instance.

(h) A direct and concise argument amplifying the reasons relied on for allowance of the writ. See Rule 10.

(i) An appendix containing, in the order indicated:

(i) the opinions, orders, findings of fact, and conclusions of law, whether written or orally given and transcribed, entered in conjunction with the judgment sought to be reviewed;

(ii) any other relevant opinions, orders, findings of fact, and conclusions of law entered in the case by courts or administrative agencies, and . . .;

. . .

(vi) any other material the petitioner believes essential to understand the petition.

If the material required by this subparagraph is voluminous, it may be presented in a separate volume or volumes with appropriate covers.

2. All contentions in support of a petition for a writ of certiorari shall be set out in the body of the petition, as provided in subparagraph 1(h) of this Rule. No separate brief in support of a petition for a writ of certiorari may be filed, and the Clerk will not file any petition for a writ of certiorari to which any supporting brief is annexed or appended.

3. A petition for a writ of certiorari should be stated briefly and in plain terms and may not exceed the word or page limitations specified in Rule 33.

4. The failure of a petitioner to present with accuracy, brevity, and clarity whatever is essential to ready and adequate understanding of the points requiring consideration is sufficient reason for the Court to deny a petition.

5. If the Clerk determines that a petition submitted timely and in good faith is in a form that does not comply with this Rule or with rule 33 or Rule 34, the Clerk will return it with a letter indicating the deficiency. A corrected petition submitted in accordance with Rule 29.2 no more than 60 days after the date of the Clerk's letter will be deemed timely.

Rule 15. Briefs in Opposition; Reply Briefs; Supplemental Briefs

1. A brief in opposition to a petition for a writ of certiorari may be filed by the respondent in any case, but is not mandatory except in a capital case, see Rule 14.1(a), or when ordered by the Court.

2. A brief in opposition should be stated briefly and in plain terms and may not exceed the word or page limitations specified in Rule 33. In addition to presenting other arguments for denying the petition, the brief in opposition should address any perceived misstatement of fact or law in the petition that bears on what issues properly would be before the Court if certiorari were granted. Counsel are admonished that they have an obligation to the Court to point out in the brief in opposition, and not later, any perceived misstatement made in the petition. Any objection to consideration of a question presented based on what occurred in the proceedings below, if the objection does not go to jurisdiction, may be deemed waived unless called to the Court's attention in the brief in opposition.

3. Any brief in opposition shall be filed within 30 days after the case is placed on the docket, unless the time is extended by the Court or a Justice, or by the Clerk under Rule 30.4. Forty copies shall be filed, except that a respondent proceeding *in forma pauperis*, under Rule 39, including an inmate of an institution, shall file the number of copies required for a petition by such a person under Rule 12.2, together with a motion for leave to proceed *in forma pauperis*, a copy of which shall precede and be attached to each copy of the brief in opposition. If the petitioner is proceeding *in forma pauperis,* the respondent shall prepare its brief in opposition, if any, as required by Rule 33.2, and shall file an original and 10 copies of the brief. . . .

4. No motion by a respondent to dismiss a petition for a writ of certiorari may be filed. Any objections to the jurisdiction of the Court to grant a petition for a writ of certiorari shall be included in the brief in opposition.

5. The Clerk will distribute the petition to the Court for its consideration upon receiving an express waiver of the right to file a brief in opposition, or, if no waiver or brief in opposition is filed, upon the expiration of the time allowed for filing. If a brief in opposition is timely filed, the Clerk will distribute the petition, brief in opposition, and any reply brief to the Court for its consideration no less than 10 days after the brief in opposition is filed.

6. Any petitioner may file a reply brief addressed to new points raised in the brief in opposition, but distribution and consideration by the Court under paragraph 5 of this Rule will not be deferred pending its receipt. . . .

7. If a cross-petition for a writ of certiorari has been docketed, distribution of both petitions will be deferred until the cross-petition is due for distribution under this Rule.

8. Any party may file a supplemental brief at any time while a petition for a writ of certiorari is pending, calling attention to new cases, new legislation, or other intervening matter not available at the time of the party's last filing. A supplemental brief shall be restricted to new matter and shall follow, insofar as applicable, the form for a brief in opposition prescribed by this Rule. . . .

Rule 16. Disposition of a Petition for a Writ of Certiorari

1. After considering the documents distributed under Rule 15, the Court will enter an appropriate order. The order may be a summary disposition on the merits.

2. Whenever the Court grants a petition for a writ of certiorari, the Clerk will prepare, sign, and enter an order to that effect and will notify forthwith counsel of record and the court whose judgment is to be reviewed. The case then will be scheduled for briefing and oral argument. If the record has not previously been filed in this Court, the Clerk will request the clerk of the court having possession of the record to certify and transmit it. A formal writ will not issue unless specially directed.

3. Whenever the Court denies a petition for a writ of certiorari, the Clerk will prepare, sign and enter an order to that effect and will notify forthwith counsel of record and the court whose judgment was sought to be reviewed. The order of denial will not be suspended pending disposition of a petition for rehearing except by order of the Court or a Justice.

B. THE CERTIORARI PROCESS IN ACTION

1. A Quick Overview

So how does the Court process these thousands of petitions and decide which will be the lucky few cases to get its full attention? First, the mechanics. Petitions for writs of certiorari ("cert petitions") and oppositions to the granting of such writs ("opp certs"), along with any amicus briefs in support of or in opposition to granting certiorari, are filed with the Clerk of the Supreme Court.[18] Once a week, the Clerk's Office distributes to each Justice's chambers copies of those cert petitions for which opp certs have been received or for which the time to file an opp cert has expired.[19] In addition, any appeals that have been filed are also distributed.

---

18. The Clerk of the Court is not be confused with the Justices' law clerks. The former is a senior, permanent administrator, with a large staff, who manages the Court's litigation docket.

19. As noted, those who cannot afford the filing fee and copying costs (principally incarcerated prisoners seeking direct or collateral review of their convictions) may file petitions "in forma pauperis" (IFP). Prisoners need supply only one copy of their petitions; others filing IFP must provide additional copies. See Supreme Court Rule 12.2. Before the introduction of the mass photocopying machine, "IFP" petitions (often handwritten) were sent only to the Chief Justice's chambers, where the Chief's law clerks prepared summaries and circulated only the summaries to the other chambers. Today, the Clerk of the Court provides each Justice with a photocopy of each IFP petition, duplicating them for the petitioner, instead of requiring that the petitioner supply multiple copies for the Court. Occasionally, the Court has found that a prisoner has utilized this "free ride" to excess. See, e.g., *In re* McDonald, 489 U.S. 180 (1989) (refusing, over four dissents, to permit Jessie McDonald to file IFP and directing the Clerk not to receive any further IFP filings from him, finding that his 73 IFP filings from 1971 to 1989 constituted an abuse of the process). The Prison Litigation Reform Act of 2000 now contains a "three strikes" provision that, inter alia, bars IFP actions by prisoners who have previously filed three frivolous claims, "unless the prisoner is un-

Parties who prevail below are generally not required to file oppositions. Sometimes the prevailing party will believe that the cert petition is so evidently frivolous that it needs no response. While the Court retains the power to grant a petition in the absence of a response, it prefers to hear from the opposition before granting a petition. Therefore, if the time for a response has expired and the Court is considering granting the petition, the Court typically will "Call For a Response," or more colloquially "CFR," before it acts on the petition.

Occasionally, the prevailing party will acquiesce in the granting of certiorari. While private parties rarely do this, the Solicitor General (SG) does, on occasion, conclude that its (the Government's) victory below was, in fact, erroneous, and will "confess error," urging the Court to grant the petition and overturn the judgment. And, on occasion, the SG will support certiorari without confessing error in order to obtain Supreme Court resolution of an important issue.[20] The Court, of course, remains free to deny the petition, notwithstanding the government's acquiescence or confession of error, or to grant the petition and schedule the case for argument, notwithstanding the government's attempt to surrender.

Each Justice follows his or her own practice for determining how he or she will vote on a cert petition. Until about the 1920s, each Justice studied by himself each petition for review. (At that time, these were usually mandatory appeals and the issue was simply whether to grant a hearing or decide the case on the papers.) After the Judges' Bill of 1925 converted much of the Court's jurisdiction to the discretionary certiorari jurisdiction, the Justices developed a new practice in which each Justice had his law clerks provide one or two page summaries of the cert petitions and opp certs, and made his judgment largely on the basis of these clerks' memos.

Cert Pool: That practice persisted until the mid-1970s when, largely at the urging of Justice Powell, several Justices formed a "cert pool." Initially, only a few Justices—those most recently appointed to the Court—joined the pool. Others, like Justices Brennan, Douglas, Marshall, Stevens, and Stewart, believed it was dangerous for all the chambers to be working from the same memo and refused to join the pool. Nevertheless, as more senior Justices have retired, each of the successors joined the pool. Most recently, Chief Justice Roberts and Justice Samuel Alito joined the pool,[21] notwithstanding some misgivings Roberts had

der imminent danger of serious physical injury." 28 U.S.C. § 1915(g) (2000).

Copies of IFP petitions are not supplied to the Court's depository libraries around the country. Consequently, most retrospective academic research on the Court's cert practice has been limited to the study of paid petitions, which are permanently stored in public libraries.

20. For example, on May 20, 2005 Acting Solicitor General Paul D. Clement filed

a brief in support of certiorari in Rodriguez v. United States (docket 04–1148), asking the Court to resolve an issue of how lower courts are to implement the Justices' ruling on federal Sentencing Guidelines in United States v. Booker, 543 U.S. 220 (2005). The Court denied the petition on June 27, 2005. 545 U.S. 1127 (2005).

21. See Tony Mauro, *Courtside*, Legal Times, September 18, 2006, at 10 (indicating that Roberts and Alito plan to partici-

expressed several years earlier, before he was nominated.[22] Today, all but Justice Stevens belong to the pool.[23] If past is prologue, when Justice Stevens leaves the Court, his successor will also be likely to join the pool. For an interesting discussion of how the certiorari practice was described to Congress in the hearings in 1924 when the Court was seeking this increased discretion and how the current practice has deviated from that description, see the article by Hartnett below in this Section. For a discussion of the role the cert pool plays in a Justice's decision to grant cert, see Section C, below.

Under the cert pool system, a week's petitions are divided evenly among all the law clerks whose Justices belong to the pool. The clerks prepare memos on the cases assigned to them, and all Justices who participate in the pool receive the "pool memos." The Justices then base their individual votes on the pool memo (with or without supplementation from their own clerks). As its name suggests, the pool is designed to reduce the number of cert petitions that each pool clerk must review, thus freeing up law clerk time for other tasks, including more in-depth review of their assigned cert petitions. From discussions with former clerks, it is clear that the pool memo, with or without supplementation from the chamber's law clerks, is usually the most important document on which those justices in the pool base their judgment. The Justices rarely go behind the memo to examine the petitions themselves. However, as Justice Ginsburg has noted, when a Justice is in doubt, he or she will "check the petitions and responses, and do whatever other homework is required to determine whether a case is certworthy."[24] Justices who are not in the pool (at this time only Justice Stevens) have had their own clerks prepare cert memos, either on every case or on selected cases. According to Professor O'Brien, Justice Stevens has his law clerks prepare memos only on those petitions he deems important. Stevens "reviews those and reads the lower-court opinions on all cases to be discussed at conference. For Stevens, the preliminary screening of cases consumes about a day and a half per week." David O'Brien, *Storm Center: The Supreme Court in American Politics* 142 (6th ed. 2003).

Conferences on Petitions: Petitions filed during the summer recess are accumulated and considered in a September conference devoted

pate in the pool, "at least for the current term").

22. John Roberts, while still in private practice, had indicated, in a 1997 talk at Georgetown University Law Center, that the "cert pool's power 'is a little disquieting,' because it makes the law clerks 'a bit too significant' in the certiorari process." Tony Mauro, *Roberts May Look to Stay Out of the Pool,* Legal Times, August 15, 2005, at 8. Roberts noted that when he was a law clerk to then-Associate Justice Rehnquist, only five of the nine Justices were in the pool. That "effectively guaranteed that errors in how a case was summarized would

be caught by other clerks in other chambers. With only one Justice outside the pool, Roberts said, that check was diminished. One possible remedy, Roberts said, might be to create 'two parallel pools' that would in effect check each other and limit the influence of any one clerk over the handling of a case." *Id.*

23. See Chief Justice William Rehnquist, *The Supreme Court* 232–33 (2001).

24. Justice Ruth Ginsburg, *Remarks for American Law Institute Annual Dinner* (May 19, 1994), 38 St. Louis U. L. J. 881, 883 (1994).

solely to cert petitions. Such conferences generally go on for several days and typically dispose of over one-quarter of all cases presented to the Court in a calendar year.[25] Once the Term starts—on the first Monday in October—the cert petitions, and their oppositions, and any appeals, distributed to chambers during one week are put on a list to be disposed of at the next week's conference. Those conferences, unlike the September conference, are likely to include discussion of and voting on argued cases as well as on the cert petitions.

As will be discussed in the excerpt below by Chief Justice Rehnquist, prior to 1930, it was customary for the Justices to vote, in conference, on each petition. Chief Justice Hughes, however, initiated the "dead list," a list of cert petitions that he deemed not worthy of discussion, which he circulated to the entire Court before the conference. Such petitions were to be denied without conference discussion absent objection from any other chamber. Today, the "dead list" has evolved into a "discuss list." The Chief Justice circulates before the conference a list of those petitions that he believes do merit discussion and voting. Each of the Associate Justices may then add other cases to the discuss list. Once the discuss list is compiled in this fashion, all other petitions set for that week's conference, i.e., those not on the discuss list, will be automatically denied at the conclusion of the conference. Usually, fewer than 30 percent of the petitions scheduled for disposition at a conference appear on the discuss list. See Justice Stevens' essay in Section B, below.

The conference takes place in a room next to the Chief Justice's office. During these conferences, no one other than the Justices is permitted to be present.[26] Justice Brandeis reportedly once said the reason the Court is so respected is that "we do our own work." To get a message into the Justices while the Court is in conference, one must knock on the door and wait for the most junior Justice to answer. This led Justice Rehnquist, when he occupied that position, to describe himself as "the highest paid messenger in town."[27] Justice Stephen Breyer who, after ten years on the Court, was, in 2004, still the most junior justice and the longest serving junior Justice in recent memory, described himself as the "the oldest, youngest Justice."[28] He noted that he had become very adept at answering the door and receiving the coffee.

Based on scholarly work and reportage on the Court under Chief Justices Burger and Rehnquist, the Court's consideration of petitions would typically proceed along the following lines:[29] For each case on the discuss list, the Chief Justice would state the case summarily and

---

25. Recently, as the Court's calendar has shrunk and it has become necessary to fill the calendar and provide the parties sufficient time for briefing their cases, the Court has announced the cert grants shortly after the conference, instead of waiting to announce on opening day, the First Monday of October.

26. For more discussion of the conference, *see* Chapter Four, below.

27. Rehnquist, *supra*, at 234.

28. Stephen Breyer, Speech at the American Constitution Society Conference in Washington, D.C. (June 18, 2004).

29. There is no reason to think that the pattern has changed under Chief Justice Roberts, but it is too early to know that for sure.

announce his vote. Discussion and voting would then proceed by seniori-ty, from most senior to least senior. (Seniority is calculated by the number of years served on the Supreme Court, except that the Chief Justice is always regarded, for purposes of ordering discussion and voting, as most senior regardless of when he or she joined the Court.) Discussions at this stage are usually quite brief; most Justices, when their turn comes, simply announce their vote.

Pre-conference communication among the Justices on whether or not to grant cert in particular cases is quite rare. Attempts at persua-sion, apart from conference discussions, usually take the form of opin-ions dissenting from the denial of cert. (A Justice planning to write such a dissent would announce those intentions at the conference so that the Chief would know to postpone any public announcements.) These dis-sents are circulated among the Justices before a final vote is announced and occasionally lead the Justices to change their minds and agree to grant cert. As noted earlier in Chapter One and described in more detail below at p. 429, the decision to grant cert in *Bowers v. Hardwick* in 1986 was influenced by Justice White's threatened dissent from a denial of cert. See Dennis Hutchinson, *The Man Who Once Was Whizzer White* 451–52 (1998).

Disposition of Petitions: The usual choice is between granting and denying cert. Many years ago, the Court adopted the so-called Rule of Four.[30] That is, if four Justices vote to grant cert, cert is granted—even if a majority votes to deny. For those conscious of strategic options, the Rule of Four presents both opportunities and risks. A Justice who wants to advance the law in a certain direction may be able to get an issue on the Court's agenda by persuading only three others of its importance. As Justice Stevens noted, the Rule of Four "gives each member of the Court a stronger voice in determining the makeup of the Court's docket [and] increases the likelihood that an unpopular litigant, or an unpopular issue, will be heard in the country's court of last resort."[31] On the other hand, if four Justices join to grant cert in order to seek a particular outcome in a particular case, they may wind up losing a five to four vote

---

30. This practice is usually traced to 1925, when Congress expanded the Su-preme Court's discretionary (certiorari) ju-risdiction in place of its mandatory (appeal) jurisdiction. In congressional testimony, the Justices told Congress that the Court fol-lowed a rule of four, an assertion often said to be a reason why Congress agreed to give the Court more control over its own agenda. There is some evidence, however, that the Court during the 1930s followed a practice in which cert might be granted if only two or three justices strongly urged that course. See David M. O'Brien, *Storm Center: The Supreme Court in American Politics* 247 (3d ed. 1993). For at least the past 25 years, however, four votes to grant have been re-quired. See David M. O'Brien, *Join–3 Votes,*

The Rule of Four, the Cert Pool, and the Supreme Court's Shrinking Plenary Docket, 13 J. L. & Pol. 779, 784–88 (1997), excerpt-ed below. For a discussion of whether four is *always* sufficient, see Section D, below (discussing the Court's practice in granting stays in death penalty cases).

31. Justice John Paul Stevens, *The Life Span of a Judge–Made Rule,* 58 N.Y.U. L. Rev. 1 (1983). Writing at a time when the docket seemed to be mushrooming out of control, Justice Stevens suggested that the rule could, and should, be changed in order to reduce the number of petitions granted. As noted, the concern with a mushrooming docket has diminished considerably.

on the merits, thus enshrining in the U.S. Reports a precedent they do not favor and might have been able to avoid by voting to deny cert.

"Grant" and "deny" are not the only options available. Several other dispositions are available and occasionally appropriate:

(1) A Justice may cast a "Join 3" vote. This means that the Justice will provide a fourth vote if three others vote to grant, but is otherwise to be considered as voting to deny.

(2) If a petition raises an issue that is likely to be resolved by, or substantially affected by, a pending case in which cert has already been granted, the Court will generally vote to "hold" the petition. When the Court votes to hold a petition, no further action is taken at that time. No public announcement is made. Rather, the petition will be relisted for a conference decision after the case for which it is being held is decided.[32] Sophisticated litigants, such as the Solicitor General, who are aware of this option will often suggest it themselves in appropriate cases.

(3) The Court will occasionally decide to adjudicate a case summarily, on the merits, without further briefing or oral argument. It then grants cert and reverses (or affirms) simultaneously. This route is usually taken only when a substantial majority of the Court confidently believes the case was wrongly (or rightly) decided below and does not warrant full briefing and oral argument. See, e.g., City of San Diego v. Roe, 543 U.S. 77 (2004) (unanimous summary reversal of Ninth Circuit holding that a police officer fired for selling sexually explicit videos online was protected by a First Amendment right to comment on matters of public concern). But see Leis v. Flynt, 439 U.S. 438 (1979) in which the Supreme Court summarily reversed a judgment by a vote of 5–4, hardly a substantial majority.[33]

(4) The Court can ask for further assistance or input. If some Justices think the petition should be granted, but no "opp cert" has been filed, the Court is likely to vote first to request such a filing, by calling for a response ("CFR"). If the case involves a significant issue of federal law, but the federal government is not a party to the lawsuit and has not yet offered its view, the Court may "invite" the Solicitor General to file an amicus brief expressing the views of the United States. (As noted in Chapter Five, the Solicitor General finds these "invitations" virtually impossible to refuse.) And, a Justice can ask that a case be "relisted" for consideration at a later conference if more time is needed for research within chambers.

---

32. Usually, the Justice who writes the majority opinion in the case for which the petition is being "held" will be asked to make a recommendation to the conference as to how to dispose of the "held" petitions in light of the new precedent. As noted below, a "grant, vacate, and remand to reconsider in light of . . ." is the most common disposition for "held" petitions.

33. One of the dissenters thought the case should be heard; three of them thought the judgment below was correct. As the dissenter noted: "This surely is not a case that should be decided before respondents have been given an opportunity to address the merits. Summary reversal 'should be reserved for palpably clear cases of . . . error.' Such reversals are egregiously improvident when the Court is facing a 'novel constitutional question.'" 439 U.S. at 457 (Stevens, J., dissenting).

(5) If the Court believes that some new development, relevant to the disposition of the case has intervened between the decision below and the consideration of the cert petition, it may grant cert, vacate the decision below, and remand to the lower court with instructions to reconsider its judgment in light of that intervening development. This action is known as a "GVR"—for "grant, vacate, and remand." The GVR is the most common response to those cert petitions held for a pending case. In *Lawrence v. Chater*, 516 U.S. 163 (1996) and *Stutson v. United States,* 516 U.S. 193 (1996), the Court spoke to the criteria for issuing GVRs and hinted at a willingness to increase their use. First, the Court must find that "intervening developments, or recent developments that [it has] reason to believe the court below did not fully consider, reveal a reasonable probability that the decision below rests upon a premise that the lower court would reject if given the opportunity for further consideration." Second, it must be apparent "that such a redetermination may determine the ultimate outcome of the litigation." Third, the Court will consider the equities of the case: "If it appears that the intervening development, such as a confession of error in some but not all aspects of the decision below, is part of an unfair or manipulative litigation strategy or if the delay and further cost entailed in a remand are not justified by the potential benefits of further consideration by the lower court, a GVR order is inappropriate." Applying these standards, the Court GVR'd both cases, in each of which the Solicitor General announced at the cert stage that it had changed its position from that argued below.[34]

What Makes a Case Certworthy? Supreme Court Rule 10 lays out the factors that generally guide the Justices in deciding whether or not a case is "certworthy."[35] Generally the most important factors are whether, with respect to an important question of federal law, the decision below conflicts with prior Supreme Court precedent or with decisions by other courts. The assumption behind this Rule is that the Supreme Court is not there simply to correct errors. Absent major changes in the Court's schedule for disposing of adjudicated cases, the Court cannot conceivably adjudicate on the merits more than approximately two to three percent of the cases for which cert petitions are filed. Consequently, every Justice has to approach virtually every single cert petition with a strong presumption that it will be denied. The impact of this is

34. Justices Scalia and Thomas disagreed with the issuance of GVRs in these two cases, accusing the Court of utilizing such dispositions too easily and suggesting that vacating without finding error in the judgment below was inconsistent with Article III. According to Justice Scalia, the Court's GVR power should be limited to three distinct categories of cases: "(1) [W]here an intervening factor has arisen that has a legal bearing upon the decision, (2) where ... clarification of the opinion below is needed to assure our jurisdiction, and (3) ... where the respondent or appel-lee confesses error in the judgment below." *Stutson*, 516 U.S. at 191 (Scalia, J., dissenting). For a good discussion of this debate, see Theodore B. Olson & John Bush, *Two Recent High Court Cases List GVR Criteria*, National Law Journal, July 29, 1996, at B10 (suggesting that litigants be alert for any development that might be grounds for a GVR and to focus the cert petition on that development).

35. For the text of Rule 10, see Section A, above.

mitigated by the fact that virtually every case that comes to the Supreme Court has already received at least one level of appellate review.

Admittedly, it is possible that another look by another court might lead to a more "correct" or a more "just" result. But that possibility alone is not considered a sufficient reason for the Supreme Court to hear a case. In the familiar words of Justice Jackson: "[R]eversal by a higher court is not proof that justice is thereby better done. There is no doubt that if there were a super-Supreme Court, a substantial proportion of [the Supreme Court's] reversals of [lower] courts would also be reversed."[36] Thus, as Chief Justice Hughes said, litigants who have argued unsuccessfully in the federal courts of appeals or state appellate courts "have had their day in court. If further review is to be had by the Supreme Court it must be because of the public interest in the questions involved."[37]

No Precedential Effect of Cert Denials: Considerations such as these explain why the Justices are usually careful to assert that the denial of certiorari should not be taken as an indication of the Court's views on the merits of a case. Legally, the denial of a cert petition has no precedential consequence, as we have noted already. While a grant of certiorari, statistically speaking, should be cause for concern for the respondent,[38] it is much more difficult to draw any inference about the Justices' views of the merits of a case from the denial of cert. Given the vast numbers of cases in which cert is denied, the very limited amount of time the Justices can spend on each petition, and the institutional reasons for cert denials, the reasons for such a no-precedent rule are clear.

Petitions for Rehearing: Supreme Court Rule 44.2 provides that the petitioner can seek rehearing within 25 days of the denial of a petition for certiorari. This rehearing petition cannot simply repeat the arguments made in the original petition; "its grounds shall be limited to intervening circumstances of a substantial or controlling effect or to other substantial grounds not previously presented." Supreme Court Rule 44.2. Moreover, the Rule of Four does not apply to a grant of a rehearing; there must be five votes to grant a petition after an initial denial. Stern & Gressman, *Supreme Court Practice, supra,* at 732. Thus, granting a petition after an initial denial is almost unheard of—but not quite. In *Boumediene v. Bush,* a case questioning the constitutionality of the Military Commissions Act of 2006, the Court, after initially denying

---

36. Brown v. Allen, 344 U.S. 443, 540 (1953) (concurring opinion). Justice Jackson was referring to Supreme Court review of state court decisions, but the point is applicable to federal courts as well.

37. Letter from Chief Justice Hughes to Senator Wheeler (March 21, 1937), *reprinted in* S. Rep. No. 711, 75th Cong., 1st Sess. 38, 39 (1937).

38. According to Segal and Spaeth, the reversal rates for cases granted cert in the 1995–2000 terms ranged from 51.6% to 65%. Segal & Spaeth, *The Supreme Court and the Attitudinal Model Revisited* 264 (2002). See also *The Supreme Court, 2004 Term: The Statistics,* 119 Harv. L. Rev. 415, 426 (2005) (Table 2(D)) (showing that of the cert granted cases decided with a full opinion, more than 70% were reversed or vacated and only 28% were affirmed).

cert on April 2, 2007, 127 S. Ct. 1478, invited a response to the petition for rehearing on June 4, 2007, 127 S. Ct. 1725, and then granted the petition for rehearing, vacated the earlier denial of cert, and granted certiorari on June 29, 2007, 127 S. Ct. 3078. For further discussion, see Chapter Six, Section B, below.

Dismissals as Improvidently Granted: Occasionally, the Court becomes convinced, after reading the briefs and hearing the oral argument in a case, that it was a mistake to have granted cert and would be a further mistake to proceed to adjudicate the case. When this occurs, it is usually because the Court discovers on plenary review that the case does not squarely or clearly present the issue that was assumed to be present when cert was granted. The usual procedure in such cases is to Dismiss as Improvidently Granted ("DIG") the writ of certiorari and thus be rid of the case. For a helpful review of the literature and an empirical study of all cases that were "DIGed" in the period 1954–2004, see Michael E. Solimine & Rafael Gely, *The Supreme Court and the DIG: An Empirical and Institutional Analysis*, 2005 Wis. L. Rev. 1421.[39] DIGing a case represents a waste of time and resources, both on the part of the litigants and the Court, and is therefore to be avoided. Obviously, the

39. Solimine and Gely describe the debate within the Court over whether, in light of the Rule of Four, a case should be "DIGed" with fewer than six votes. See *id.* at 1441–49. They find that in the great majority of cases, decisions to DIG received at least six votes in the period under study. *Id.* at 1448 (also finding that in over 53% of the decisions to DIG, the Court was unanimous). However, it is not unheard of for the Court to DIG a case over dissent; in the Solimine & Gely study, in 9% of the "DIGed" cases, the vote was five to four. For a recent DIG over four dissents, see Medellin v. Dretke, 544 U.S. 660 (2005) (DIGing the case where, after cert had been granted to a judgment in the federal court of appeals, a presidential memo issued indicating that petitioner's claim should be considered in the state courts). The Court was deeply divided on the disposition of the case, issuing four separate opinions totaling forty pages, including a lengthy dissent by Justice O'Connor. Joined by three other Justices, she argued that the Court should not have dismissed the writ (thereby leaving in place the lower federal court's judgment) but should have vacated that judgment and remanded to the federal court of appeals for reconsideration in light of the President's determination. Justice O'Connor wrote:

> The Court dismisses the writ (and terminates federal proceedings) on the basis of speculation: Medellin *might* obtain relief in new state court proceedings—because of the President's recent memorandum

about whose constitutionality the Court remains rightfully agnostic, or he *might* be unable to secure ultimate relief in federal court—because of questions about whose resolution the Court is likewise, rightfully, undecided. These tentative predictions are not, in my view, reason enough to avoid questions that are as compelling now as they were when we granted a writ of certiorari, and that remain properly before this court. It seems to me unsound to avoid questions of national important when they are bound to recur.

Id. at 673. Justice O'Connor's concerns were well-founded. Texas' highest criminal court refused to comply with the President's memo. See Ex parte Medellin, 223 S.W.3d 315 (Tex. Crim. App. 2006). Medellin's lawyers again sought Supreme Court review and the Court granted cert in April, 2007. See Medellin v. Texas, 127 S. Ct. 2129 (2007).

In 2006, the Court dismissed a cert grant by a 5–3 vote, with Chief Justice Roberts not participating. *See* Laboratory Corporation of America Holdings, dba LABCORP v. Metabolite Laboratories, 126 S. Ct. 2921 (2006). The case had been granted when Justice O'Connor was still on the Court, but dismissed after Justice Alito took her seat, leading some observers to conjecture that O'Connor had been the fourth vote to grant, but that in her absence, there were no longer four who wanted to hear and decide the case.

best way to avoid it is to do careful screening at the cert stage. In fact, it was the desire to avoid these mistaken grants that provided a significant impetus behind the Justices' decision to "pool" their law clerks' efforts.

2. History of the Expansion of the Certiorari Jurisdiction

Edward A. Hartnett,[40] *Questioning Certiorari: Some Reflections Seventy–Five Years After the Judges' Bill*, 100 Colum. L. Rev. 1643 (2000)

INTRODUCTION

Seventy-five years ago, the modern Supreme Court was born. In February of 1925, in the closing days of a lame duck session of Congress, Congress agreed to give the Justices of the Supreme Court what Chief Justice William Howard Taft had aggressively sought from the moment he took his seat on the Supreme Court: a far-ranging power to pick and choose which cases to decide. Shortly thereafter, the Court began the process of incorporating the Bill of Rights against the states, starting with the First Amendment's free speech clause, and then physically removed itself from the Senate's shadows and into its own marble palace.

Congress was remarkably willing to delegate to the Court the case selection power sought by Taft, even as it resisted for another decade delegating to the Court the power to promulgate rules of civil procedure. Senator Thomas Walsh, a progressive Democrat from Montana whose determined opposition blocked the Rules Enabling Act until his death, attempted a lonely fight against the bill sought by the Court. He described that bill–widely dubbed the Judges' Bill—as exemplifying "that truism, half legal and half political, that a good court always seeks to extend its jurisdiction, and that other maxim, wholly political, so often asserted by Jefferson, that the appetite for power grows as it is gratified." Yet even Senator Walsh ultimately relented, noting "I have been accused of standing in the way of a good many of these proposed statutes that are asked for by the Supreme Court of the United States, and I do not feel like standing alone on the matter."

In the seventy-five years that have followed, we have grown accustomed to the idea that the Supreme Court sets its own agenda, and tend to take it for granted. Congress has expanded the Court's discretionary power still further, and entire books are devoted to the agenda-setting process of the Court.

In the process, we also seem to have simply forgotten that in the years before the Judges' Bill, the Court decided far more cases than the one hundred fifty that we have somehow convinced ourselves is the most

40. Richard J. Hughes Professor for Constitutional and Public Law and Service, Seton Hall University School of Law.

that the modern Supreme Court—aided by multiple law clerks and computers—can possibly be expected to decide. Although the decline in recent years to under one hundred decided cases has attracted some attention, most readers are likely surprised that in the hearings concerning the Judges' Bill, the Solicitor General estimated that the number of cases of public gravity that the Court could decide on the merits was between four hundred and five hundred.

In addition, current certiorari practice differs substantially from the practice described to Congress in convincing it to adopt the Judges' Bill. As detailed below, the Justices explained to Congress that they read and discussed every petition, granted certiorari not only whenever four (or sometimes three) thought appropriate, but also as a matter of course whenever there was a conflict in the circuit courts of appeals. Moreover, they stated that certiorari in constitutional cases would only be denied when the decision for which review was sought was clearly correct, expressing confidence that no constitutional question of any real merit or doubt would be denied review. Although the Justices assured Congress that they intended to continue these methods and not relax their vigilance as the number of petitions increased, only one of these methods—the rule of four—has survived.

At this juncture, seventy-five years after the passage of the Judges' Bill, it is appropriate not only to trace the development of certiorari in the Supreme Court, but also to raise questions about the consistency of current certiorari practice with classic conceptions of judicial review, judicial power, and the rule of law.

. . .

I. The Modest Birth of the Supreme Court's Discretionary Jurisdiction:
A Reassuring Fallback Provision upon Creation
of the Circuit Courts of Appeals

For over one hundred years, the Supreme Court had no power to pick and choose which cases to decide. Instead, just as Congress decided which cases and controversies from the list contained in Article III, Section 2, would be decided by the lower federal courts, so too it decided which of those cases and controversies would be decided by the Supreme Court. As a formal matter, of course, the Constitution itself grants the Supreme Court jurisdiction over all cases and controversies listed in Article II, Section 2, and allocates those cases and controversies between original and appellate jurisdiction. . . . [But] so long as Congress did not attempt to expand the Supreme Court's jurisdiction to cases and controversies not listed in Article III or to add to its original jurisdiction, the Supreme Court was required to decide those cases within its congressionally-defined jurisdiction and was prohibited from deciding cases outside its congressionally-defined jurisdiction.

. . .

... [T]he number of cases that the Court was obligated to decide grew dramatically after the Civil War. The result was both a growing number of cases decided each term and a growing backlog of delayed cases. In 1860, the Court had 310 cases on its docket and decided 91; in 1870, the Court had 636 cases on its docket and decided 280; in 1880, the Court had 1,202 cases on its docket and decided 365; and in 1886, the Court had 1,396 cases on its docket and decided 451. By 1888, the Court was more than three years behind in its work, and when the 1890 Term opened, the Court had "reached the absurd total of 1800" cases on its appellate docket and was obligated to decide them all.

Congress responded in 1891 by creating the circuit courts of appeals, giving the Supreme Court mandatory appellate jurisdiction over many of their decisions, but declaring others "final." For those cases in which the decision of the circuit court of appeals was declared "final," however, the Supreme Court nevertheless was granted appellate jurisdiction if the circuit court of appeals certified to the Supreme Court a question of law or if the Supreme Court granted a writ of certiorari to bring the judgment before it for review....

. . .

Certiorari made its first appearance in the Senate substitute for the House bill. At the time, however, other differences between the House and Senate bills were viewed as far more important. The House bill would have transformed the old circuit courts into purely appellate courts, transferred the original jurisdiction of those courts to the district courts, created two new circuit judgeships per circuit, and required virtually all cases decided in the district court to be appealed to the circuit courts before any review in the Supreme Court. The House bill encountered serious opposition in the Senate, perhaps most significantly because Republican President Benjamin Harrison would get to appoint the eighteen new circuit judges....

The Senate substitute, by contrast, preserved the already existing circuit courts, created new circuit courts of appeals, and routed some appeals to the new circuit courts of appeals while routing others directly to the Supreme Court.... Significantly, it called for only one new circuit judge per circuit, rather than the two provided for in the House bill.... A bare majority of the Senate Judiciary Committee favored this proposal, and no one on that committee favored the House bill. Instead, the alternative favored by the minority of the Senate Judiciary Committee (including its Chairman, Senator Edmunds) would avoid the appointment of any new judges by authorizing the Supreme Court to sit in panels of three to hear and decide cases that did not present constitutional questions.

In support of the proposal to permit the Supreme Court to sit in panels of three, Senator Vest pointed to similar arrangements in Rhode Island and California and argued that "the real question that ought to have our attention is as to the manner of business and not as to the jurisdiction of the Supreme Court." He added:

The Senator from New York [Senator Evarts], with his long political experience, ... declared here as one of the principal arguments for this bill that it was much preferable to the legislation of the House of Representatives, because we had under this bill only nine new judges instead of eighteen. If it is better to have but nine, it is better not to increase the number at all.

... Senators debated whether the proposal for panels was consistent with the constitutional mandate of one Supreme Court.... Senator Evarts did not retreat from his earlier position that the panel proposal was constitutional, arguing instead that his proposal had far broader support and therefore a far better chance of actually being enacted. Others noted that some of the Justices doubted the constitutionality of the panel plan and that most were "terribly opposed" to it.... But there was no debate about certiorari.

Instead, Senator Evarts explained the certification provision in the bill proposed by the majority of the Senate Judiciary Committee and then added:

[A]nother guard against the occurring diversity of judgments or of there being a careless or inadvertent disposition of important litigation by these courts ... is that the Supreme Court shall have a right, in any of these cases that are thus made final, by certiorari to take up to itself for final determination this or that case, and in that way the scheme of the committee does firmly and peremptorily make a finalty on such subjects as we think in their nature admit of finalty, and at the same time leaves flexibility, elasticity, and openness for supervision by the Supreme Court.

Thus it seems certiorari was envisioned as a sort of fallback provision should the circuit courts of appeals prove, on occasion, to be surprisingly careless in deciding cases or issuing certificates. Moore and Vestal state that Evarts viewed certification and certiorari as "parallel provisions." Indeed, in the first two years after the Evarts Act, only two petitions for certiorari were granted.

The Senate adopted the Evarts proposal, and in the closing days of the lame duck session of the 51st Congress [in 1891], the House acceded to the Senate. Thus was born the "then revolutionary, but now familiar, principle of discretionary review of federal judgments on writ of certiorari."[41]

II.   THE UNCERTAIN EXPANSION OF DISCRETION REGARDING REVIEW OF STATE COURT JUDGMENTS

The revolution did not spread to review of state court judgments until 1914, nearly twenty-five years later. From 1789 until 1914, Supreme Court review of state court judgments was governed by one central principle: The Supreme Court was obligated to review a final

41. [Footnote 58 in original] Richard H. Fallon et al., *Hart & Wechsler's The Feder-* *al Courts and the Federal System* 37 (4th ed. 1996) ...

judgement rendered by a state court system that denied a federal claim or defense, but had no jurisdiction to review a state court judgment that upheld a federal claim or defense. In 1914, the Supreme Court was empowered for the first time to review a state court judgment upholding a federal claim or defense. This new category of cases opened to Supreme Court review—in principle, doubling the number of state court judgments subject to review—was made reviewable by the discretionary writ of certiorari. . . .

The year 1916 marks the first congressional authorization for the Supreme Court to decline to review a state court judgment denying a federal claim or defense. The 1916 statute was sufficiently ambiguous, however, that it was quite difficult to tell just how large the shift from mandatory to discretionary jurisdiction actually was. . . .

To the extent that Congress focused at all on this aspect of the bill—a bill whose primary announced purpose was to change the date on which the Supreme Court's annual term began from the second Monday in October to the first—it appears to have largely focused on relieving the Court from the obligation to decide run-of-the-mill tort cases brought under the Federal Employers' Liability Act (FELA). . . .

Nevertheless, the Court interpreted the 1916 Act to eliminate from its mandatory jurisdiction not only FELA cases or other federal statutory cases, but also cases raising constitutional objections to state executive action. It held that the "mere objection to an exercise of authority under a statute, whose validity is not attacked, cannot be made the basis of a writ of error."[42] As a result of this "judicial emasculation of 'authority',", a litigant who raised federal constitutional objections to a particular exercise of an authority under a statute, but did not challenge the validity of the statute, no longer had a right to Supreme Court review and had to content himself with petitioning for certiorari. In this way, the Supreme Court produced a fundamental change in the relationship between itself and state courts in constitutional cases—a change far larger than Congress evidently anticipated. As we shall see, this was not the last time that the Court expanded its discretionary control over its caseload beyond that contemplated by Congress.

III. WILLIAM HOWARD TAFT AND THE QUEST FOR "ABSOLUTE AND ARBITRARY" DISCRETION

Enter William Howard Taft, who repeatedly sought to use procedural reform to bolster judicial power and the rights of property. In 1914, having lost his 1912 campaign for reelection as President, Taft had called for the Supreme Court's mandatory appellate jurisdiction to be limited to "questions of constitutional construction." In all other cases, argued Taft, litigants should be given an "opportunity" to "apply for a writ of certiorari to bring any case from a lower to the Supreme Court,

---

42. [Footnote 70 in original] Jett Bros. Distilling Co. v. City of Carrolton, 252 U.S. 1, 6 (1920). . . .

so that it may exercise absolute and arbitrary discretion with respect to all business but constitutional business." When he fulfilled his lifelong ambition in 1921 and became Chief Justice of the United States, he began to work toward increasing the Court's "absolute and arbitrary discretion."

[The success of] Taft's quest ... depended in no small measure on his willingness to depart from tradition and marshal the Court to actively promote legislation.... Taft relied heavily on the support of the American Bar Association (ABA). The ABA's strategy, in turn, was to convince Congress that the Court's proposal was too complicated for anyone else to understand, and to warn Members of Congress not to make fools of themselves by trying. The strategy worked: In both the Senate and the House, in both the Judiciary Committee and on the floor, virtually everyone simply deferred to the Court rather than engage in serious discussion or debate. Indeed, after the Judges' Bill was passed by both houses, a Congressman told Taft that he "never knew of a case in which such an important bill went through so smoothly and in such a short time," and attributed this to its origin with the Court....

A. *Initial Resistance to Taft's Proposal*

... As soon as the Justices gathered in Washington for the October 1921 term, Taft appointed Justices Day, Van Devanter, and McReynolds to a committee charged with drafting a bill to reform the Supreme Court's jurisdiction.

. . .

... When the Court's proposal was ready, Taft sent it to Senator Cummins and Representative Joseph Walsh of Massachusetts (not to be confused with Senator Thomas Walsh) for introduction in Congress and gave a speech to the New York County Lawyer's Association "extolling the merits of the plan."

. . .

In trying to convince Congress to expand certiorari, Taft was "anxious" to refute as without "the slightest foundation" the suggestion that the then-existing certiorari practice permitted each Justice a certain number of certiorari per term as a personal privilege. He explained that "each member of the court ... examines both briefs and the record so far as the briefs may suggest the necessity of doing so."

Taft also presented his view of "the proper basis for determining the class of cases which should be reviewed by the Supreme Court."

No litigant is entitled to more than two chances, namely, to the original trial and to a review, and the intermediate courts of review are provided for that purpose. When a case goes beyond that, it is not primarily to preserve the rights of the litigants. The Supreme Court's function is for the purpose of expounding and stabilizing principles of law for the benefit of the people of the country, passing upon constitutional questions and other important questions of law for the public benefit. It is to preserve uniformity of decision among the intermediate courts of appeal.

He noted that "whenever a petition for certiorari presents a question on which one circuit court of appeals differs from another, then we let the case come into our court as a matter of course."

Taft then turned to other methods of limiting the jurisdiction of the Supreme Court. He rejected the idea of dividing the court into parts, imposing high costs on litigants, or relying on amount-in-controversy requirements. He acknowledged that another method "has been carefully to define the character of cases which shall come before the court," but objected that "it is a very difficult thing to include all the important cases, and it is a very difficult thing to exclude the unimportant cases." Rather than attempt this difficult task, Taft proposed letting the Supreme Court decide what was important and what was unimportant.

· · ·

Under Taft's 1922 proposal, no litigant would be entitled to Supreme Court review of a judgment of a circuit court of appeals. Taft did point out, however, that the Supreme Court would not be alone in deciding what was important. He noted that in any case in which the Supreme Court could grant certiorari to a circuit court, the circuit court could itself certify the question to the Supreme Court, thus "plac[ing] the question of review also in the discretion of the Circuit Court of Appeals."

Taft addressed review of state court judgments only briefly ... [suggesting a change so that] " ... the case in which an authority under a State or under the United States is drawn in question is put in the certiorari class."

· · ·

Several weeks after Taft's appearance before the House Judiciary Committee, Judge Benjamin I. Salinger of Iowa testified passionately before that committee against eliminating mandatory review of state court judgments denying federal constitutional claims. In his view, "the great function of the Supreme Court is to protect rights given by treaty, the Constitution, or other Federal law." ... He observed that the Court does not hear argument on certiorari, and does not issue opinions when denying certiorari. As a result, "no standard is set," and Salinger claimed that the clerk of the Court had told him that "there was no standard." He promised to raise the matter with the American Bar Association.

[T]he most recent suggestion from the ABA was from its Committee on Jurisprudence and Law Reform, a committee chaired by Everett Wheeler that included Henry Waters Taft. On June 1, 1921—before William Howard Taft was nominated Chief Justice—the Committee noted that the burden on the Supreme Court could be relieved either by "materially limiting" the right to appeal to the Supreme Court or by

increasing the number of the Justices to twelve, six to constitute a quorum, and "the concurrence of five ... necessary to render a decision." Although the committee did not seek an ABA resolution on this subject, it clearly favored the latter proposal, explaining that it "would enable the court to be in session almost continuously, and thus to dispose of a much greater amount of business without impairing uniformity of decision," and that a "similar provision has for many years been in effect in the State of New York and has worked to advantage there."
. . .

In April of 1922, Henry Taft wrote to his brother describing the prior year's ABA Committee report, noting that he was on the committee, and inquiring, "what do you think of this suggestion and how will it fit in with your general scheme?" Chief Justice Taft responded immediately that the Justices "are all of them very much opposed to increasing the number of the Court," and expressing his hope that "nothing will be done to give us a town meeting." A handwritten note adds, "Consider the danger of setting a precedent to a Demagouge [sic] Democratic Administration."

Although Solicitor General James Beck originally favored the proposal suggested by the ABA committee, Chief Justice Taft successfully lobbied him to support the Court's proposal instead. Beck testified in favor of the bill and, like Taft, sought to dispel misconceptions about how petitions for certiorari were handled:

> Let me correct ... the impression very prevalent among the bar, that writs of certiorari are treated in a perfunctory way, namely, that they are divided up among the nine justices and in that way the burden of passing upon them is not as great as the figures would indicate. The fact of the matter is quite the contrary, that the nine justices, every one of them, are responsible on their consciences for a careful study of each application for a certiorari; that they then vote in consultation, and, as I understand it, if four of the nine justices favor the granting of the application, even though they be not a majority, yet on the ground of resolving doubts in favor of the appeal, the appeal is allowed, so that four justices can grant, but all nine justices must pass upon the application.

He urged that the Court should be spared "trivial cases that go there as a matter of right" so that it could devote more time to substantial and important litigation, noting that caseload pressures had led the Court to reduce the time for argument from two hours per side to one hour per side. . . .

Beck asserted that "somebody must determine ... what are the cases of public importance" and that "the court can do that far better than any hard and fast law describing what cases shall be heard and what cases shall not be heard." Beck was remarkably candid about his underlying view of the role of the Supreme Court. He called the Court a "quasi-constitutional convention" whereby the "whole form of government is being slowly evolved, the superstructure slowly erected, brick on brick, pillar upon base, and capital upon pillar. . . ."

In April, Taft visited the House personally to lobby several legislators. . . . Despite these efforts, the bill was not even reported from committee. . . .

A few weeks later, in a speech before the Virginia Bar Association, Senator Thomas Walsh—whose persistence had broken open the Teapot Dome scandal—vehemently criticized the Court's proposal. . . . Walsh criticized the 1916 Act as making "an unfortunate innovation in limiting the cases in which a review of the decisions of the State courts might be had as of right," and urged that the Taft proposal to further limit such review "ought not to command the support of the bar. . . ." He suggested that " 'importance' is a highly elastic term," and that certiorari practice left the Court with "unrestrained discretion." He predicted that a court with such discretion would not be inclined to hear intricate cases involving law with which the judges were not already familiar.

· · ·

B.   Taft Pursues a Strategy to Gain Political Support

Faced with little evident interest in the House, and outright hostility in the Senate, Taft turned to the ABA. In August of 1922, he spoke to the ABA's annual meeting in support of the bill . . . Not surprisingly, as the former President of the ABA (among other things), Taft was more successful with the ABA than with Congress.

[Although the previous year] the ABA's Committee on Jurisprudence and Law Reform had proposed to increase the size of the Court to twelve, with six to constitute a quorum and five necessary to concur in a decision, . . . the committee's report [in 1922] . . . was presented by none other than Henry W. Taft. He devoted only one paragraph of his five pages of remarks to the "subject of reducing the business of the Supreme Court." . . . [H]e stated that the committee's "consideration of the subject has led it to make recommendations in line with those which were explained by the Chief Justice this morning, in his address." The ABA adopted the report, and its committee worked for the passage of the Judges' Bill.

C.   The Senate Hearings

The ABA's support was not enough, and in December 1923, Taft . . . convinced [President] Coolidge to let him draft a portion of Coolidge's first State of the Union message—a passage noting that the "Supreme Court needs legislation revising and simplifying the laws governing review by that court, and enlarging the classes of cases of too little public importance to be subject to review."

A subcommittee of the Senate Judiciary Committee scheduled hearings for February of 1924, and Senator Cummins—upon whom Taft was relying to get the bill through—chatted with Taft about who should testify. They agreed that it would be best if Taft did not testify himself, lest it provoke some of his old enemies. In his stead appeared Van Devanter, McReynolds, and Sutherland. Why these three? As Taft explained in a letter to Thomas Shelton of the ABA, "McReynolds is a Democrat and knows many of the Senators. Sutherland has been a Senator, and Van Devanter is one of the most forcible of our Court and most learned on questions of jurisdiction." . . .

. . .

Before the hearings, Taft spoke with Cummins and, on the basis of that conversation, made suggestions to his colleagues about what they should say at the hearings. The two major arguments presented for the bill mirrored Taft's own: "the need for codification of the scattered statutes and the even greater need for the Court to be able to reject the piddling claims which were so frequently brought before it as a matter of right."

. . .

Justice Van Devanter began by acknowledging that the bill had "received the consideration of several members of the Supreme Court," but immediately denied that the Justices would "wish to step into the legislative field" or "presume to suggest a course of legislation." He explained that they only took the matter up because they were asked to do so by "some members" of the Senate and House Judiciary Committees. . . .

. . .

Van Devanter . . . explained the process by which the Court decides petitions for certiorari, noting that "each member of the court makes his own examination" of "the petition, record, and briefs." He noted that a vote is taken on each petition in conference "in the same way that we vote in other cases" and that "if there be occasion for discussion," then "discussion is had as in other matters." He then added, "Not only that, but whenever the vote is relatively close the conference makes it a practice to grant the petition." At this juncture, evidently intending to highlight the point, Justice Sutherland interjected with a question: "Even though a majority be against it?" Van Devanter answered:

> Yes. For instance, if there were five votes against granting the petition and four in favor of granting it, it would be granted, because we proceed upon the theory that when as many as four members of the court, and even three in some instances, are impressed with the propriety of our taking the case the petition should be granted.

Senator Cummins, apparently to meet a possible criticism that expanded certiorari might make the Court a court for the rich, asked whether the Court gives "greater heed to the amount involved or to the character of the questions involved." After both Justices Van Devanter and McReynolds said that the character of the question was decidedly more important, Justice Van Devanter took the opportunity to explain more fully how the Court proceeded:

The inquiry is, first, whether or not the case is one in which a petition for certiorari will lie at all; next, whether the questions presented in the case are of wide or public importance or concern only the parties to the particular case; next, whether there is any conflict between the decision that is complained of and decisions on the same question in other circuit courts of appeal or in the Supreme Court; and next, if any of the questions determined by the circuit court of appeals be questions of State law, whether or not there is a conflict between the decision of that court thereon and the decisions of the court of last resort in the State on the same questions. Whenever we find such a conflict that, without more, leads to the granting of the petition. . . .

Senator Spencer then asked,

What would be your judgment as to the advisability of placing any legislative limitation upon the discretionary power to grant the writ, as, for example, when the decision of the circuit court of appeal is different from that of the district court, or when in the judgment of two or three of the justices of the Supreme Court, the writ ought to be granted?

Justice Van Devanter opposed any such limitation, . . . [and] noted,

When I speak of a discretionary jurisdiction on certiorari, I do not mean, of course, that the Supreme Court merely exercises a choice or will in granting or refusing the writ, but that it exercises a sound judicial discretion, gives careful thought to the matter in the light of the supporting and opposing briefs, and resolves it according to recognized principles.

To justify the proposed increase in the Court's discretion to refuse review of state court judgments that deny federal claims, Justice Van Devanter noted that in the 1922 Term only 20 of the 111 cases brought on writ of error from state court resulted in reversals. He observed that a writ of error "often is sought and used for mere purpose of delay," which "operates to the disadvantage of the party who prevailed in the State court." He acknowledged, of course, that the party who was victorious in state court could move to affirm if the federal question had obviously been rightly decided. Why was this not a sufficient protection? Van Devanter stated that lawyers tended not to make such motions but instead to "merely await the time when the case will be reached in the regular order." That might be a year or more, while petitions for certiorari are acted upon at once. . . .

[T]his description makes it appear that denying certiorari would be simply a speedy way to resolve easy cases on the merits.

· · ·

Justice McReynolds spoke briefly, declaring that he "heartily favored the bill." . . . While the 1916 amendment "afforded material relief . . . it is far from perfect and does not go far enough."

Justice Sutherland, too, commented briefly on the Judges' Bill. . . .

. . . "I can say this much about it, from my observation thus far, that a very large proportion of the cases that come to that court . . . ought never to be there at all."

. . .

The Senate Judiciary Committee reported the bill favorably. . . . [Its] report expressed confidence that

> the right of the circuit courts to certify questions to the Supreme Court and the right to file a petition for certiorari will furnish ample opportunity for all cases to go from the circuit court of appeals to the Supreme Court which ought to be heard by the latter tribunal.

The report also emphasized that "a large number of cases which fall within the obligatory jurisdiction of the court are taken there simply for delay."

After the Senate Judiciary Committee Report, but before the House Judiciary Committee considered the Judges' Bill, the First Session of the 68th Congress adjourned, with the Second Session to begin after the November election.

D.   The 1924 Election

Federal judicial power was one of the major issues in the presidential election of 1924. Robert La Follette, unable to convince the Republican Party to adopt his progressive platform—including proposals to authorize Congress to re-enact statutes the Supreme Court had invalidated and to elect federal judges for ten-year terms—ran as a Progressive against the incumbent Republican Calvin Coolidge and the Democrat John W. Davis. . . .

. . .

Coolidge won 382 electoral votes to Davis's 136 and La Follette's 13. Although "party loyalty and prosperity would probably have ensured Coolidge's victory" anyway, the "Republicans' assiduous exploitation of the Court issue may have lured many voters into the Coolidge camp." In any event, "the landslide victory of a ticket that had made opposition to Court reform the premier issue of its campaign chilled all movements to curb the powers of the Supreme Court." . . .

E.   The House Hearings

Shortly after the election, in November of 1924, Taft renewed his push for the Judges' Bill with members of the lame duck Congress . . . [and] again persuaded President Coolidge to support the bill in his State of the Union message to Congress. Coolidge noted that the Judiciary Committee of the Senate had favorably reported the bill and called for its "immediate favorable consideration" by Congress.

As Taft prepared for House Judiciary Committee hearings scheduled for December of 1924, Brandeis worried about what Taft might say and noted privately his "grave doubt" about the bill. But Brandeis—widely known as one of the "Great Dissenters"—agreed to suppress his dissent, reasoning that "in relation to proposed legislation directly affecting the Court, the Chief Justice, when supported by a clear majority, should be permitted to speak for it as a unit; and differences of view among its members should not be made a matter of public discussion." He authorized Taft to say that "the Court approves the bill—without stating whether or not individual members approve it."

[In the hearings,] Justice Van Devanter ... reiterated that discretionary jurisdiction "does not mean that the court is authorized merely to exercise a will in the matter but rather that the petition is to be granted or denied according to a sound judicial discretion." This discretion enables the Court "to deny a review unless it appears that the questions presented are of public importance or of wide general interest, or that in the interest of uniformity that court should consider and decide them." He also explained in some detail the consideration that each member of the Court gives to each petition, the discussion in conference of any disagreement, and the practice of "always granting the petition when as many as four think that it should be granted, and sometimes when as many as three think that way."

. . .

... Justice Van Devanter ... [also noted] that some state cases—the number "can not be accurately estimated, but I should say there may be a good many of them"—were being shifted from obligatory to discretionary jurisdiction. Linking this proposed change in review of state court judgments to his justification of discretionary jurisdiction as an efficient way to handle frivolous appeals, he posited an example of a state court decision that was clearly correct under a recent Supreme Court precedent, and argued that a certiorari petition in such a case should obviously be denied....

Congressman Andrew Montague asked, "Although you ask for discretionary power, you propose to exercise it in the method you have heretofore exercised it?" Justice Van Devanter replied, "Certainly."

. . .

As Justice Sutherland began his remarks, Congressman Montague interrupted to ask, "I do not know whether this should go on the record, but if it is proper for me to ask, do you wish to appear as the authors of this [bill]?" Justice Van Devanter jumped in to answer:

> The matter in some way came to the attention of the Judiciary Committee of the Senate. The chairman of that committee communicated with the Chief Justice and requested that the court, members of the court out of their experience, should prepare a bill which would meet the situation. The court hesitated at first, but as a result of further conferences between the Chief Justice and the chairman of the Judiciary Committee of the Senate, the court appointed a committee which drafted the bill....

Chairman Graham added that he was glad that the question was asked "because it has made clear that the Supreme Court has not prepared the bill, thrusting it upon our attention as to what should be done, but that it has been prepared at the request of the Judiciary Committee of the Senate."

Unfortunately, it is difficult to credit Justice Van Devanter's explanation. . . .

. . .

Chief Justice Taft spoke last. He described the existing jurisdictional scheme as "a trap in which counsel and litigants too often are caught." He emphasized the care with which each certiorari petition is handled, noting:

> I write out every case that comes up for certiorari and I read it to the court. . . . And then having stated the case I go around and ask each member of the court, who has his memorandum, as to what view he takes. Then having discussed the case we vote on it.

Congressman Montague, in turn, emphasized that "when you ask for this large discretionary power you do not intend to relax close scrutiny on these cases," to which Taft responded, "No; we do not."

Taft went on to explain, with Van Devanter's help, that it was "easy" to decide rather quickly whether the questions involved are "debatable," or "of such importance as to warrant an investigation," or are ones as to which "the circuit courts of appeals have differed." He closed with the following:

> I only want to emphasize another feature. Often in the legislature there is resounding eloquence on the subject that every poor man should have the opportunity to carry his case to the last court. There is no statement that is so unfounded as that. The truth is that it is in the interest of the poor litigant that litigation should be ended, and my dear friends, there is nothing that offers such an opportunity for delay as a suggestion that a profound constitutional question is involved in sustaining a verdict in favor of the poor litigant when the rich litigant has a long purse with which to continue the litigation.
>
> It is a mistake to suppose that the mere suggestion of a constitutional question is something that should require the case going right through. . . . [The Court] ought to have a prompt opportunity, to clear away by saying, "This case, although it purports to involve a constitutional question, really does not, and we cut it off."

. . .

A few weeks later, on January 6, 1925, the Judiciary Committee issued a report recommending the bill. . . .

The report quoted at length from Justice Van Devanter's statement of how the petitions for certiorari are handled, beginning with his assertion that the Court does not "merely ... exercise a will in the matter" but rather a "sound judicial discretion," and concluding with his description of the rule of four.... Nowhere did the report attempt to describe how the bill would change the Court's jurisdiction over state court judgments.

F.   The Senate Debate ...

G.   The House "Debate" ...

Congressman McKeown described the bill as "one of the most important bills that has been before the House this Congress,".... When he offered an amendment regarding Indian titles, however, he was told that he should not be offering a floor amendment to a bill prepared by Justices of the Supreme Court. Congressman Graham was "unable to disclose at [the] moment" the effect of the proposed McKeown Amendment, and "for that reason" urged the House to "pass the bill as the court officials have recommended it." The McKeown amendment was rejected, leading Congressman Blanton to then protest, "How on earth may we expect to frame sane legislation under the present surroundings? This is a most important bill, ... and yet I dare say there are not five men here who have heard the bill read or have heard any discussion of the amendment offered." Nevertheless, after a question about its effect on appeals from the Canal Zone, the Judges' Bill was passed without a roll call.

As Frankfurter and Landis aptly put it, the "questions raised from the floor were slight and singularly unenlightened," and the "House behaved like an uninformed and indifferent ratifying body, manifesting no awareness that it was passing a bill involving really great changes in the disposition of federal litigation."

This was precisely what [the ABA President] had sought. His strategy was to convince the members of the House "that this bill was of such a highly technical order that the Bar Association did not feel itself prepared or qualified to act," and warned them "against exposing a tremendous lot of ignorance." ...

H.   Taft Compromises with Copeland and Walsh

[Senator Copeland's concerns over] the bill's disparity in treatment between state courts, whose judgment would, in some instances be subject to mandatory review, and the circuit courts, whose judgments would not [required some amendment to be worked out.]

... Rather than provide for obligatory jurisdiction of circuit court judgments upholding state statutes or invalidating federal statutes, the amendment provided for obligatory jurisdiction to review circuit court judgments invalidating state statutes.

Although Senator Copeland thought that the amendment corrected the problem "to some extent," he remained concerned that when "lawyers should discover that the circuit court of appeals had become courts of last resort on constitutional questions there would be considerable surprise and dissatisfaction." Senator Walsh, who supported this amendment, explained that it placed the state courts and circuit courts "on a perfect parity, allowing a writ of error from the circuit court of appeals under conditions exactly the same, except reversed." . . . [T]he amendment was approved [and the bill adopted].

. . .

Only Senator Heflin of Alabama spoke in opposition [to approval of the final bill], arguing that judges "who may be looking for the least work possible and for longer periods of leisure" should not be empowered to deny humble citizens' right to appeal. . . .

. . .

Preoccupied with more pressing matters and willing to leave the responsibility to others, Senators "deferred to the prestige of the Supreme Court and its Chief Justice, whose energetic espousal largely helped to realize the Court's proposal."

The next day, when the bill returned to the House, Congressman Graham moved to concur in the Senate amendment. . . .

When Congressman Graham was asked to explain the Senate amendment, he conceded that he could do little explaining "as I have not the bill before me." He continued, "It does not involve any organic change or even an important change. It was inserted to satisfy the objection of Senator Walsh." With that, the House agreed to the Senate amendment by a voice vote.

Taft was pleased with his success. . . .

His decade long quest to increase the Court's "absolute and arbitrary discretion" reached fruition on February 13, 1925, when the Judges' Bill was signed into law by President Coolidge. "Bereft of a clogged docket, freed from its obligatory jurisdiction over 'minor' litigation, the Court would be in a stronger position to perform its 'higher function'—constitutional interpretation in general, the defense of property in particular."

IV.   Give 'Em an Inch . . .

"It is clear that Congress in passing the Judiciary Act of 1925 relied heavily on judicial explanation of the need for the power and the manner in which it would be used." Apart from Senator Walsh, Congress did not critically evaluate the Justices' arguments—indeed, it cooperated in the charade that the idea for the bill originated outside the Court and did not press for details upon learning that the facade of unanimity was only a facade. Yet seventy-five years of experience under the Judges' Bill demonstrates the continuing truth of Walsh's critique: "it exemplifies that truism, half legal and half political, that a good court always seeks to extend its jurisdiction, and that other maxim, wholly political, so often asserted by Jefferson, that the appetite for power grows as it is gratified."

In advocating their bill, the Justices frequently argued that they needed the discretionary power to refuse to decide cases in order to avoid frivolous appeals. But they never adequately explained why the power of summary affirmance was not sufficient for this purpose.... To the extent that the court was concerned about hearing oral argument in frivolous cases, a much less radical solution was possible: Read the briefs before deciding whether to hear oral argument.

Of course, the Justices also pointed to "unimportant" cases clogging the docket. But while Taft originally spoke of giving the Court arbitrary discretion and letting it decide what was important, Van Devanter took a different tack. He told the Congress that the Court did not exercise choice or will, but instead decided petitions for certiorari "according to recognized principles." But although the Justices assured Congress that certiorari is always granted when there is a conflict between courts of appeals and would always be granted when there was an arguable constitutional claim, they never explained what the supposedly recognized principles were. Instead, Van Devanter changed the subject and provided detail about the care with which petitions are considered. But careful consideration is no substitute for governing principles to apply. Effectively, then, the Court had achieved absolute and arbitrary discretion over the bulk of its docket.

With this achievement under its belt, the Court (as Walsh's maxim predicted) sought to extend that discretion by (among other things) claiming the power to issue limited writs of certiorari, by subjecting ostensibly mandatory appeals to discretionary review, and by practically eliminating the certification power of courts of appeals.

A. Limited Grants of Certiorari

Soon after the Judges' Bill became law, the Court claimed the authority to issue limited grants of certiorari, that is, to decide to decide only a particular issue in a case, ignoring the other issues. It asserted this power even though certiorari under the Evarts Act brought up the whole case, and even though one of Taft's arguments for the Judges' Bill was that there was a "greater need" for discretion as to cases from the circuit courts of appeals than from state courts, because in the former the "power of review extends to the whole case and every question presented in it" rather than only to the federal questions.

Indeed, in the famous *Olmstead* case in 1928 involving the admissibility of wiretap evidence, Chief Justice Taft's opinion for the Court asserted the authority to limit review to constitutional questions, thereby ignoring possible nonconstitutional grounds of decision. Taft even chided Justices Brandeis, Holmes, and Stone for addressing nonconstitutional grounds for their conclusion that the evidence was inadmissible. Taft offered no answer to Stone's objection that, under the law enacted by Congress, "this Court determines a case here on certiorari with the same power and authority, and with like effect, as if the cause had been brought [here] by unrestricted writ of error or appeal." Nor did Taft explain why it was appropriate to decide whether the constitution permitted the admission of the evidence without first deciding whether the law of evidence permitted its admission.

This practice of limited grants of certiorari has become so uncritically accepted that, under current Supreme Court rules, no writ of certiorari brings before the Court all questions presented by the record, as such writs did under the Judiciary Act of 1891. Instead, "[o]nly the questions set out in the petition, or fairly included therein, will be considered by the Court." . . . As the Court has explained, this rule not only serves the respondent's interest in not having to respond to issues not raised by her adversary, but also serves the Court's interest in "forc[ing] the parties to focus on the questions the Court has viewed as particularly important."
. . .

Put slightly differently, the Supreme Court does not so much grant certiorari to particular cases, but rather to particular questions. Especially in light of its expressed lack of interest in simple error correction, the result can well be the affirmance of judgments that, while correct as to the controversial issue on which certiorari is granted, are nevertheless erroneous because based on a simpler error that the Supreme Court declines to consider.

B.   The Expansion of Discretion from Certiorari to Ostensibly Mandatory Appeals

The same year that the Court decided the *Olmstead* case and claimed the power to issue limited writs of certiorari, it also laid the groundwork for extending its discretion to cases within its mandatory jurisdiction. . . . It promulgated a new rule, Rule 12, requiring the filing of a jurisdictional statement within thirty days of docketing an appeal. In the 1929 Term, this rule was used to dismiss some thirty-six appeals.

Significantly, [under Rule 12] . . counsel were obliged to demonstrate that the federal question involved was substantial and (at least) "persuade the Court that the record presents an issue that is not frivolous and is not settled by prior decisions." Frankfurter and Landis predicted:

> Plainly, the criterion of substantiality is neither rigid nor narrow. The play of discretion is inevitable, and wherever discretion is operative in the work of the Court the pressure of its docket is bound to sway its exercise. To the extent that there are reasonable differences of opinion as to the solidity of a question presented for decision or the conclusiveness of prior rulings, the administration of Rule 12 operates to subject the obligatory jurisdiction of the Court to discretionary considerations not unlike those governing certiorari.

Their prediction was accurate. . . . Eventually it became commonplace to conclude that "[t]he discretionary-mandatory distinction between certiorari and appeal has been largely eroded" and that [t]he jurisdiction that is obligatory in form is discretionary in fact. This, of course, further increased judicial power.

... Congress, rather than objecting to the Court's non-compliance with the statute, instead amended the statute to conform to the Court's practice.

C. The Practical Elimination of Certification

In the hearings on the Judges' Bill, it was repeatedly noted that the Supreme Court would not alone control its jurisdiction, but that the courts of appeals, by use of certification, would share in that control. Yet just as the Court increased its power to set its own agenda by tending to treat appeals more like petitions for certiorari, so too it largely deprived the lower courts of their promised role in controlling the Supreme Court's docket. ...

Frankfurter and Landis acknowledged in 1930 that "[p]etitions for certiorari the Court can deny, but questions certified must be answered." Yet they already detected the Court's "hostility" to the certification process. That hostility continued, leading the courts of appeals to be quite reluctant to issue certificates. In the decade from 1927 to 1936, courts of appeals issued seventy-two certificates, while in the decade from 1937 to 1946, that number dropped to twenty. Writing in 1949, Moore and Vestal explained that one reason for the Court's hostility was that the Court "apparently felt that a broad use of certification would frustrate the Court's proper functioning as a policy-determining body by greatly restricting the time available for the discretionary side of its docket." ...

In 1957, the Court went so far as to conclude that certification should not be used to handle conflicts between different three-judge panels of the same court of appeals, noting that it "is primarily the task of a Court of Appeals to reconcile its internal difficulties," such as by sitting en banc. Ironically, the Supreme Court chastised the court of appeals, observing that it "is also the task of a Court of Appeals to decide all properly presented cases coming before it." In the period from 1946 until 1985, the Court accepted only four certificates. At this point, certification is practically a dead letter....

. . .

In short: At every turn, the Court has acted to maximize its institutional independence from Congress, litigants, and other courts. The earliest indication of the Court's interest in providing itself the widest possible scope for setting its own agenda was the energetic campaign of the Taft period justices for the 1925 Judiciary Act. Subsequently, the Court has whittled away at the small remaining portion of its jurisdiction that was intended to be obligatory. The Court has now worked itself into the position that it is no longer expected to decide any case as a matter of course....

Questions and Comments

1.   Recall the description given in the overview above of the "cert pool" and of the "discuss list." Consider to what extent each of these developments is consistent with or diverges from the practice as represented to Congress in connection with the passage of the Judges' Bill of 1925.

2.   As you have read, there were a number of proposals in the 1920s for other kinds of changes affecting the Court, from Robert LaFollette's proposal that Supreme Court Justices be elected for ten year terms, to the ABA Committee's initial proposal to remedy workload growth by increasing the size of the Court to 12 and sitting in panels of 6. Would either or both of these proposals, or any part thereof, have required a constitutional amendment? Was the expansion of the Court's discretionary jurisdiction a better solution? Why or why not?

3.   For developments in the Court's mandatory and discretionary appellate jurisdiction since 1925, see Richard H. Fallon, Jr., et al., *Hart & Wechsler's The Federal Courts and The Federal System* 1554–56 (5th ed. 2003). Among the more significant changes were the elimination of direct appeals in certain federal criminal cases in 1970, a 1976 change repealing certain requirements for three-judge courts, thus eliminating as well the prospect of direct review under the Court's obligatory jurisdiction, and the 1988 legislation, noted earlier, that eliminated "virtually all of the Supreme Court's mandatory jurisdiction over appeals from the lower federal courts." *Id.* at 1555. Does this record suggest that Congress was unhappy with how the Court dealt with its certiorari jurisdiction?

4.   Chief Justice Taft took a very active role in obtaining revision of the jurisdictional stages. How would such activity by the Chief Justice be regarded today? Note that both Chief Justices Rehnquist and Roberts have called for congressional attention to the need for judicial salary increases. On the many roles of the Chief Justice, see Chapter Five, Part A, below.

3.   Views From the Inside: The Justices

The criteria listed in Rule 10 give only a cursory insight into the mind of a Justice voting to grant or deny a petition for certiorari. What do the Justices have to say? In a remarkably candid work, Justice Brennan describes the importance of the agenda-setting function of certiorari, and explains which cases were most readily and quickly denied. In the next article, Justice Stevens describes the use of the Rule of Four and questions whether a majority vote might instead be preferable; and, in his response to a dissent from a denial of certiorari, he objects to publication of such dissents, describing their potentially skewing influence on external perceptions of the Court's review process. And finally, Chief Justice Rehnquist shares his perspective on the history and role of certiorari, responding to various criticisms of the process.

William J. Brennan, Jr.,[43] *The National Court of Appeals: Another Dissent*, 40 U. Chi. L. Rev. 473, 477–483 (1973)

. . .

The method of screening the cases differs among the individual Justices, and thus I will confine myself to my own practice. That practice reflects my view that the screening function is second to none in importance—a point I shall touch upon more fully a little later. I try not to delegate any of the screening function to my law clerks and to do the complete task myself. I make exceptions during the summer recess when their initial screening of petitions is invaluable training for next Term's new law clerks. And I also must make some few exceptions during the Term on occasions when opinion work must take precedence. When law clerks do screening, they prepare a memorandum of not more than a page or two in each case, noting whether the case is properly before the Court, what federal issues are presented, how they were decided by the courts below, and summarizing the positions of the parties pro and con the grant of the case.

For my own part, I find that I don't need a great amount of time to perform the screening function—certainly not an amount of time that compromises my ability to attend to decisions of argued cases. In a substantial percentage of cases I find that I need read only the "Questions Presented" to decide how I will dispose of the case. This is certainly true in at least two types of cases—those presenting clearly frivolous questions and those that must be held for disposition of pending cases. Because of my familiarity with the issues of pending cases, the cases to be held are, for me, easily recognizable. For example, we heard argument early this Term in eight obscenity cases because we decided to undertake a general re-examination of that subject. Every agenda since then has included several cases of conviction or injunction under state obscenity laws and I simply mark those cases "hold." Similarly, with other cases I can conclude from a mere reading of the question presented that for me at least the question is clearly frivolous for review purposes. For example, during recent weeks, I thought wholly frivolous for review purposes questions such as: "Are Negroes in fact Indians and therefore entitled to Indians' exemptions from federal income taxes?" "Are the federal income tax laws unconstitutional insofar as they do not provide a deduction for depletion of the human body?" "Is the 16th Amendment unconstitutional as violative of the 14th Amendment?" and only last week, "Does a ban on drivers turning right on a red light constitute an unreasonable burden on interstate commerce?"

43. Associate Justice, Supreme Court of the United States. This article was written in the 1970s to respond to the then-pending proposals to deal with the seemingly-ever expanding cert-load. The reduction in the Court's caseload since the 1990s has removed this issue from the concerns of most Court-watchers today. We include the article here for its still-current insights into the cert process.

Nor is an unduly extended or time-consuming examination required of many of the cases that present clearly nonfrivolous questions. For very often even nonfrivolous questions are simply not of sufficient national importance to warrant Supreme Court review. And after a few years of experience, it is fair to say that a Justice develops a "feel" for such cases.

. . .

I should emphasize here that the longer one works at the screening function, the less onerous and time-consuming it becomes. I can state categorically that I spend no more time screening the 3,643 cases of the 1971 Term than I did screening half as many in my first Term in 1956. Unquestionably, the equalizer is experience, and for experience there can be no substitute. . . . I subscribe completely to the observation of the late Mr. Justice Harlan that "Frequently the question whether a case is 'certworthy' is more a matter of 'feel' than of precisely ascertainable rules." . . .

[A]pproximately 30 percent of all cases docketed annually (that means in this Term, 1,100 cases) are placed on the "Discuss List" each Term. Under this system, a single Justice may set a case for discussion at conference and, in many instances, that Justice succeeds in persuading three or more of his colleagues that the case is worthy of plenary review. Thus, the existing system provides a forum in which the particular interests or sensitivities of individual Justices may be expressed, and therefore assures a flexibility that is essential to the effective functioning not only of the screening process but also of the decisional process of which it is an inseparable part.

. . .

. . . [D]issents from denial of review frequently have had [an important impact] upon the development of the law. Such dissents often herald the appearance on the horizon of a possible reexamination of what may seem . . . to be an established and unimpeachable principle. Indeed, a series of dissents from denials of review played a crucial role in the Court's reevaluation of the reapportionment question and the question of the application of the Fourth Amendment to electronic searches. Actually, every Justice has strong feelings about some constitutional view that may not yet command the support of a majority of the Court. For example, I thought that the Court was quite wrong in adopting "same evidence" rather than "same transaction" as the test of "same offense" for the purposes of double jeopardy. The question has recurred in case after case since the Court made that choice a few years ago. In each instance I and two of my colleagues have recorded our continued adherence to my minority view. Another example is the view shared by Mr. Justice Douglas with the late Mr. Justice Black in obscenity cases. They dissented in 1957 from the holding that obscenity does not enjoy First Amendment protection, and in every obscenity case since then Mr. Justice Douglas and, until his death, Mr. Justice Black, recorded their dissent from applications of the holding that obscenity is not protected speech. Only a brave man would say that their view could never prevail in the Court. The history of their dissents that have become law in cases involving reapportionment, the right to counsel, and the application of the Bill of Rights to the States are too fresh in mind to ignore....

For the more statistically oriented, the subjective nature of the decision whether a particular case is of sufficient "importance" to merit plenary consideration is amply demonstrated by the voting pattern of the Justices in the screening process. Under our rules, a case may be granted review only if at least four of the nine Justices agree that such review is appropriate. It is noteworthy that, of the cases granted review this Term, approximately 60 percent received the votes of only four or five of the Justices. In only 9 percent of the granted cases were the Justices unanimous in the view that plenary consideration was warranted. Thus, insofar as the key determinant is the "substantiality" of the question presented, there can be no doubt that the appraisal is necessarily a subjective one.

Finally, it should be noted that the recommendation that the breadth of the Court's screening function be curtailed rests in part upon what I consider to be the mistaken assumption that the screening function plays only a minor and separable part in the exercise of the Court's fundamental responsibilities. In my view, the screening function is inextricably linked to the fulfillment of the Court's essential duties and is vital to the effective performance of the Court's unique mission "to define the rights guaranteed by the Constitution, to assure the uniformity of federal law, and to maintain the constitutional distribution of powers in our federal union."

The choice of issues for decision largely determines the image that the American people have of their Supreme Court. The Court's calendar mirrors the ever changing concerns of this society with ever more powerful and smothering government. The calendar is therefore the indispensable source for keeping the Court abreast of these concerns. Our Constitution is a living document and the Court often becomes aware of the necessity for reconsideration of its interpretation only because filed cases reveal the need for new and previously unanticipated applications of constitutional principles.

For example, the Due Process Clauses provide that no person shall "be deprived of life, liberty or property without due process of law." The interest of the defaulting conditional sales purchaser in the refrigerator or kitchen stove or bedroom furniture that he bought on time clearly does not constitute "property" in the traditional sense of the word. Similarly, welfare benefits, automobile driver's licenses, retail liquor licenses, and the like were traditionally viewed as "statutory entitlements," rather than as "property." Vast societal changes over the past few decades, however, have substantially altered the function and importance to the individual of these previously unprotected interests. A long series of seemingly unimportant cases filed in the Court over a period of years gradually generated an awareness of these societal changes and of the consequent need for constitutional reinterpretation. As a result, recent construction of the Due Process Clause requires government to afford notice and hearing before terminating "statutory entitlements" or repossessing goods. Another example may be seen in the area of criminal procedure. The Sixth Amendment's guarantee of the "Assistance of Counsel for his defense" is in terms applicable "in all criminal prosecutions." Are police interrogations or preliminary hearings part of the "criminal prosecution" for the purposes of this guarantee? The Court has held that they are in light of the serious abuses revealed in cases that reached our docket.

·   ·   ·

The point is that the evolution of constitutional doctrine is not merely a matter of hearing arguments and writing opinions in cases granted plenary review. The screening function is an inseparable part of the whole responsibility.

John Paul Stevens,[44] *The Life Span of a Judge–Made Rule,* 58 N.Y.U. L. Rev. 1 (1983)

·   ·   ·

Whenever four justices of the United States Supreme Court vote to grant a petition for a writ of certiorari, the petition is granted even though a majority of the Court votes to deny.... Since 1925, most of the cases brought to the Supreme Court have been by way of a petition for a writ of certiorari ... rather than by a writ of error or an appeal requiring the Court to decide the merits.

In their testimony in support of the Judges' Bill [of 1925], members of the Court explained that they had exercised discretionary jurisdiction in a limited number of federal cases since 1891 ... and also in a limited number of cases arising in the state courts since 1914. They described ... [their] procedures ... in processing their discretionary docket and made it clear that they intended to continue to follow those practices in managing the enlarged certiorari jurisdiction ... [to] be created by the enactment of the Judges' Bill.

Several features of the Court's practice were emphasized in order to demonstrate that the discretionary docket was being processed in a responsible, nonarbitrary way. These four are particularly worthy of note: (1) copies of the printed record, as well as the briefs, were distributed to every justice; (2) every justice personally examined the papers and prepared a memorandum or note indicating his view of what should be done; (3) each petition was discussed by each justice at conference; and (4) a vote was taken, and if four, or sometimes just

44. Associate Justice, Supreme Court of the United States.

three, justices thought the case should be heard on its merits, the petition was granted. From Justice Van Devanter's testimony about the small numbers of petitions (under 400 a term), it is fair to infer that the practice of making an individual review and having a full conference discussion of every petition was not particularly burdensome. Indeed, ... the number was so small that the Court was then contemplating the possibility of granting an oral hearing on every petition for certiorari. Times have changed and so have the Court's practices.

In the 1947 Term, when I served as a law clerk to Justice Rutledge, the practice of discussing every certiorari petition at conference had been discontinued. It was then the practice for the Chief Justice to circulate a so-called "dead list" identifying the cases deemed unworthy of conference discussion. Any member of the Court could remove a case from the dead list, but unless such action was taken, the petition would be denied without even being mentioned at conference.

In the 1975 Term, when I joined the Court, I found that other significant procedural changes had occurred. The "dead list" had been replaced by a "discuss list"; now the Chief Justice circulates a list of cases that he deems worthy of discussion and each of the other members of the Court may add cases to that list. In a sense, the discuss list practice is the functional equivalent of the dead list practice, but there is a symbolic difference. In 1925, every case was discussed; in 1947 every case was discussed unless it was on the dead list; today, no case is discussed unless it is placed on a special list.

Other changes have also occurred. It is no longer true that the record in the court below is routinely filed with the certiorari petition. It is no longer true that every justice personally examines the original papers in every case. Published dissents from denials of certiorari were unknown in 1925 but are now a regular occurrence. Today law clerks prepare so-called "pool memos" that are used by several justices in evaluating certiorari petitions. The pool memo practice may be an entirely proper response to an increase in the volume of certiorari petitions from seven or eight per week when the Judges' Bill was passed in 1925 to approximately 100 per week at the present time. It is nevertheless noteworthy that it is a significant departure from the practice that was explained to the Congress in 1924.

The rule that four affirmative votes are sufficient to grant certiorari has, however, survived without change. Indeed, its wisdom has seldom, if ever, been questioned. Perhaps it is time to do so.

The doctrine of *stare decisis* teaches us to respect well-settled rules. A proponent of change confronts a strong presumption against stirring up sleeping animals, for the consequences of change are never completely predictable. I am neither persuaded myself nor prepared to shoulder the burden of persuading my colleagues, that the Rule of Four should be abandoned—either temporarily or permanently. I am, however, prepared to demonstrate that it would be entirely legitimate to reexamine the rule, that some of the arguments for preserving the rule are unsound, and that there are valid reasons for making a careful study before more drastic solutions to the Court's workload problems are adopted.

First, I would put to one side any suggestion that the representations made to Congress when the 1925 Judges' Bill was enacted created some sort of estoppel that would make it dishonorable for the Court to change the Rule of Four. The Justices' testimony in 1924 contained a complete and candid explanation of the practices then being followed and a plain expression of an intent to continue to follow essentially the same practices in the future. The purposes of the testimony were to demonstrate that the selection of cases for review would be based on neutral and relevant considerations, rather than the arbitrary choice of particular justices, and that the Court would continue to hear an adequate number of cases. The testimony, however contained no representation or even suggestion that the Court might not make various procedural changes in response to changes in the condition of its docket. I have found nothing in the legislative history of the 1925 Act that limits the Court's power to modify its internal rules governing the processing of its certiorari docket.

But even if I have misread that history, ample precedent—and therefore the doctrine of *stare decisis*—supports the proposition that the Court has the authority to modify the certiorari procedures that were being followed in the 1920's. The Court has already eliminated the record filing requirement; it has abandoned the practice of individual discussion of every petition at conference; there have been substantial changes in the way each individual justice evaluates each certiorari petition. In my judgment, each of those procedural modifications was an entirely legitimate response to a dramatic change in the character of the docket. They are precedents that establish the legitimacy of making such other internal procedural changes—specifically including a possible modification of the Rule of Four—as may be appropriate to cope with a problem whose present dimensions were not foreseen in 1925.

During most of the period in which the Rule of Four was developed, the Court had more capacity than it needed to dispose of its argument docket. The existence of the rule in 1924 provided a persuasive response to the concern—expressed before the Judges' Bill was enacted—that the Court might not accept enough cases for review if its discretionary docket were enlarged. In my judgment, it is the opposite concern that is now dominant. For I think it is clear that the Court now takes far too many cases. Indeed, I am persuaded that since the enactment of the Judges' Bill in 1925, any mismanagement of the Court's docket has been in the direction of taking too many, rather than too few, cases.

In his talk on *Stare decisis* in 1944, Justice Jackson noted that the substitution of discretionary for mandatory jurisdiction had failed to cure the problem of overloading because judges found it so difficult to resist the temptation to correct perceived error or to take on an interesting question despite its lack of general importance. In a letter written to Senator Wheeler in 1937 describing the workload of the Supreme Court,

Chief Justice Hughes, after noting that less than twenty percent of the certiorari petitions raised substantial questions, stated: "I think that it is the view of the members of the Court that if any error is made in dealing with these applications it is on the side of liberality." In a recent letter Paul Freund, who served as Justice Brandeis' law clerk in 1932, advised me that the Justice "believed the Court was granting review in too many cases—not only because of their relative unimportance for the development or clarification of the law but because they deprived the Court of time to pursue the really significant cases with adequate reflection and in sufficient depth."

It can be demonstrated that the Rule of Four has had a significant impact on the number of cases that the Court has reviewed on their merits. A study of Justice Burton's docket book for the 1946 and 1947 Terms reveals that, in each of those Terms, the decision to grant certiorari was supported by no more than four votes in over twenty-five percent of the granted cases. It is, of course, possible that in some of those cases a justice who voted to deny might have voted otherwise under a Rule of Five, but it does seem fair to infer that the Rule of Four had a significant impact on the aggregate number of cases granted.

A review of my own docket sheets for the 1979, 1980, and 1981 Terms confirms this conclusion. No more than four affirmative votes resulted in granting over twenty-three percent of the petitions granted in the 1979 Term, over thirty percent of those granted in the 1980 Term, and about twenty-nine percent of those granted in the 1981 Term. In my judgment, these are significant percentages. If all—or even most—of those petitions had been denied, the number of cases scheduled for argument on the merits this Term would be well within the range that all justices consider acceptable.

Mere numbers, however, provide an inadequate measure of the significance of the cases that were heard because of the rule. For I am sure that some Court opinions in cases that were granted by only four votes have made a valuable contribution to the development of our jurisprudence. My experience has persuaded me, however, that such cases are exceptionally rare. I am convinced that a careful study of all of the cases that have been granted on the basis of only four votes would indicate that in a surprisingly large number the law would have fared just as well if the decision of the court of appeals or the state court had been allowed to stand. To enable interested scholars to consider the validity of this judgment, I have prepared footnotes listing twenty-five cases granted certiorari by a mere four votes in the 1946 Term and thirty-six such cases granted certiorari in the 1979 Term.[45]

The Rule of Four is sometimes justified by the suggestion that if four justices of the Supreme Court consider a case important enough to warrant full briefing and argument on the merits, that should be

45. [Editors' Note: The number of Justices voting in favor of certiorari is generally not made public. Such information is usually available only if and when a Justice's papers become public, usually after the Justice's death.]

sufficient evidence of the significance of the question presented. But a countervailing argument has at least equal force. Every case that is granted on the basis of four votes is a case that five members of the Court thought should not be granted. For the most significant work of the Court, it is assumed that the collective judgment of its majority is more reliable than the views of the minority. Arguably, therefore, deference to the minority's desire to add additional cases to the argument docket may rest on an assumption that whether the Court hears a few more or a few less cases in any term is not a matter of first importance.

History and logic both support the conclusion that the Rule of Four must inevitably enlarge the size of the Court's argument docket and cause it to hear a substantial number of cases that a majority of the Court deems unworthy of review. . . .

. . . [But the] Court has a greater capacity to solve its own problems than is often assumed. We might, for example, simply abandon the Rule of Four, or perhaps refuse to follow it whenever our backlog reaches a predetermined point. But there are reasons to beware of such a procedural change. For even if the Rule of Four had nothing more than a distinguished parentage, an unblemished reputation, and a venerable age to commend itself to posterity, it would be entitled to the presumptive protection provided by the rule of *stare decisis*. Moreover, the Rule of Four has additional redeeming virtues. It gives each member of the Court a stronger voice in determining the makeup of the Court's docket. It increases the likelihood that an unpopular litigant, or an unpopular issue, will be heard in the country's court of last resort. Like the danger of awakening a sleeping dog, the costs of change are not entirely predictable. Surely those costs should not be incurred if less drastic solutions to the Court's problems are available.

At least two such solutions are quite obvious. If Congress were concerned about our plight, it could provide us with significant help by promptly removing the remainder of our mandatory jurisdiction. Second, . . . in the processing of our certiorari docket we are often guilty of ignoring the teachings of the doctrine of judicial restraint; if we simply acted with greater restraint during the case selection process, we might be able to manage the docket effectively under the Rule of Four. But if neither of these remedies materializes or is effective, we may find it necessary to acknowledge that the Rule of Four is a luxury we can no longer afford. . . .

Singleton v. Commissioner, 439 U.S. 940, 942–46 (1978)

Opinion of MR. JUSTICE STEVENS respecting the denial of the petition for writ of certiorari.

[JUSTICE STEVENS is responding to a dissent from a denial of certiorari published by JUSTICE BLACKMUN, joined by JUSTICES MARSHALL and POWELL.]

What is the significance of this Court's denial of certiorari?....
Almost 30 years ago Mr. Justice Frankfurter provided us with an answer
to that question that should be read again and again:

> This Court now declines to review the decision of the Maryland
> Court of Appeals. The sole significance of such denial of a petition
> for writ of certiorari need not be elucidated to those versed in the
> Court's procedures. It simply means that fewer than four members
> of the Court deemed it desirable to review a decision of the lower
> court as a matter "of sound judicial discretion." Rule 38, paragraph
> 5. A variety of considerations underlie denials of the writ, and as to
> the same petition different reasons may lead different Justices to the
> same result. This is especially true of petitions for review on writ of
> certiorari to a State court. Narrowly technical reasons may lead to
> denials. Review may be sought too late; the judgment of the lower
> court may not be final; it may not be the judgment of a State court
> of last resort; the decision may be supportable as a matter of State
> law, not subject to review by this Court, even though the State court
> also passed on issues of federal law. A decision may satisfy all these
> technical requirements and yet may commend itself for review to
> fewer than four members of the Court. Pertinent considerations of
> judicial policy here come into play. A case may raise an important
> question but the record may be cloudy. It may be desirable to have
> different aspects of an issue further illumined by the lower courts.
> Wise adjudication has its own time for ripening. Since there are
> these conflicting and, to the uninformed, even confusing reasons for
> denying petitions for certiorari, it has been suggested from time to
> time that the Court indicate its reasons for denial. Practical consid-
> erations preclude. In order that the Court may be enabled to
> discharge its indispensable duties. Congress has placed the control of
> the Court's business, in effect, within the Court's discretion. During
> the last three terms the Court disposed of 260, 217, 224 cases,
> respectively, on their merits. For the same three terms the Court
> denied, respectively, 1,260, 1,105, 1,189 petitions calling for discre-
> tionary review. If the Court is to do its work it would not be feasible
> to give reasons, however brief, for refusing to take these cases. The
> time that would be required is prohibitive, apart from the fact as
> already indicated that different reasons not infrequently move dif-
> ferent members of the Court in concluding that a particular case at
> a particular time makes review undesirable. It becomes relevant
> here to note that failure to record a dissent from a denial of a
> petition for writ of certiorari in no ways implies that only the
> member of the Court who notes his dissent thought the petition
> should be granted.

Inasmuch, therefore, as all that a denial of a petition for a writ of
certiorari means is that fewer than four members of the Court
thought it should be granted, this Court has rigorously insisted that
such a denial carries with it no implication whatever regarding the
Court's views on the merits of a case which it has declined to review.

The Court has said this again and again; again and again the admonition has to be repeated.

Opinion respecting the denial of the petition for writ of certiorari in Maryland v. Baltimore Radio Show, 338 U.S. 912, 917–919 (1950).

When those words were written, Mr. Justice Frankfurter and his colleagues were too busy to spend their scarce time writing dissents from denials of certiorari. Such opinions were almost nonexistent. It was then obvious that if there were no need to explain the Court's action in denying the writ, there was even less reason for individual expressions of opinion about why certiorari should have been granted in particular cases.

There were none in 1945 or 1946, and I have been able to find only one in the 1947 Term. See dissent in Chase National Bank v. Cheston, and companion cases, 332 U.S. 792 . . .

Times have changed. Although the workload of the Court has dramatically increased since Mr. Justice Frankfurter's day, most present Members of the Court frequently file written dissents from certiorari denials. It is appropriate to ask whether the new practice serves any important goals or contributes to the strength of the institution.

One characteristic of all opinions dissenting from the denial of certiorari is manifest. They are totally unnecessary. They are examples of the purest form of dicta, since they have even less legal significance than the orders of the entire Court which, as Mr. Justice Frankfurter reiterated again and again, have no precedential significance at all.

Another attribute of these opinions is that they are potentially misleading. Since the Court provides no explanation of the reasons for denying certiorari, the dissenters' arguments in favor of a grant are not answered and therefore typically appear to be more persuasive than most other opinions. Moreover, since they often omit any reference to valid reasons for denying certiorari, they tend to imply that the Court has been unfaithful to its responsibilities or has implicitly reached a decision on the merits when, in fact, there is no basis for such an inference.

In this case, for example, the dissenting opinion suggests that the Court may have refused to grant certiorari because the case is "devoid of glamour and emotion." I am puzzled by this suggestion because I have never witnessed any indication that any of my colleagues has ever considered "glamour and emotion" as a relevant consideration in the exercise of his discretion or in his analysis of the law. With respect to the Court's action in this case, the absence of any conflict among the Circuits is plainly a sufficient reason for denying certiorari. Moreover, in allocating the Court's scarce resources, I consider it entirely appropriate to disfavor complicated cases which turn largely on unique facts. A series of decisions by the courts of appeals may well provide more meaningful guidance to the bar than an isolated or premature opinion of this Court.

As Mr. Justice Frankfurter reminded us, "wise adjudication has its own time for ripening."

Admittedly these dissenting opinions may have some beneficial effects. Occasionally a written statement of reasons for granting certiorari is more persuasive than the Justice's oral contribution to the Conference. For that reason the written document sometimes persuades other Justices to change their votes and a case is granted that would otherwise have been denied. That effect, however, merely justifies the writing and circulating of these memoranda within the Court; it does not explain why a dissent which has not accomplished its primary mission should be published.

It can be argued that publishing these dissents enhances the public's understanding of the work of the Court. But because they are so seldom answered, these opinions may also give rise to misunderstanding or incorrect impressions about how the Court actually works. Moreover, the selected bits of information which they reveal tend to compromise the otherwise secret deliberations in our Conferences. There are those who believe that these Conferences should be conducted entirely in public or, at the very least, that the votes on all Conference matters should be publicly recorded. The traditional view, which I happen to share, is that confidentiality makes a valuable contribution to the full and frank exchange of views during the decisional process; such confidentiality is especially valuable in the exercise of the kind of discretion that must be employed in processing the thousands of certiorari petitions that are reviewed each year. In my judgment, the importance of preserving the tradition of confidentiality outweighs the minimal educational value of these opinions.

In all events, these are the reasons why I have thus far resisted the temptation to publish opinions dissenting from denials of certiorari.

———————————

William H. Rehnquist,[46] *The Supreme Court* 232–38(2001)

[A] petition for certiorari is, stripping away the legal verbiage, a request to the Supreme Court to hear and decide a case that the petitioner has lost either in a federal court of appeals or in a state supreme court. The Supreme Court rules tell a lawyer what a petition for certiorari should contain: a copy of the lower-court opinion that the lawyer wishes to have reviewed, a statement of the legal question or questions that the case presents, and a statement of the reasons why the lawyer thinks the Supreme Court should review his case. A small fraction of the cases we review come to us in ways other than by petition for certiorari, but the difference is not important for the purpose of giving a general sketch of how the Supreme Court operates.

46. Chief Justice of the United States.

Eight members of the Court—all except Justice Stevens—have pooled their law clerks in order to facilitate the consideration of the petitions for certiorari. During the first term in which I served on the Court, there was no "cert pool," and each chambers did all of its own certiorari work as well as its other work. I could not help but notice that my clerks were frequently pressed for time, scrambling between having memos describing the certiorari petitions ready when they should be, and drafts or revisions of Court opinions or dissents ready when they should have been. Lewis Powell, who had come on the Court at the same time I had, was also bothered by this phenomenon, and suggested that all the law clerks be pooled for purposes of writing memos describing the facts and contentions in each petition for certiorari. As it turned out, only five members of the Court as it then stood decided to join the pool, but when Sandra O'Connor was appointed in 1981 she became the sixth member of the pool, and every succeeding appointee has joined.

Each of the thirty-odd law clerks in the pool divide among themselves the task of writing memos outlining the facts and contentions of each of the some four thousand petitions for certiorari that are filed each term, and these memos are then circulated to the chambers whose clerks comprise the pool. When the memos come into my chambers, I ask my clerks to divide them up three ways, and that each law clerk read the memo and, if necessary, go back to the petition and response in order to make a recommendation to me as to whether the petition should be granted or denied.

Although our Court otherwise operates by majority rule, as would be expected, the granting of certiorari has historically required only the votes of four of nine justices. . . .

When I get the annotated certiorari memos from my law clerks, I review the memos and indicate on them the way I intend to vote at conference. I don't necessarily always vote the way I had planned to vote, however; something said at conference may persuade me either to shift from a "deny" to a "grant" or vice versa.

I would guess that several thousand of the petitions for certiorari filed with the Court each year are patently without merit; even with the wide philosophical differences among the various members of our Court, no one of the nine would have the least interest in granting them. As soon as I am confident that my new law clerks are reliable, I take their word and that of the pool memo writer as to the underlying facts and contentions of the parties in the various petitions, and with a large majority of the petitions it is not necessary to go any further than the pool memo. In cases that seem from the memo perhaps to warrant a vote to grant certiorari, I may ask my clerk to further check out one of the issues, and may review the lower court opinion, the petition, and the response myself.

During the time I am away from my chambers in the summer, when there are no conferences, the certiorari memos are mailed to me and I review them there and return them to my chambers. Over the summer the petitions for certiorari simply accumulate, and by the time we have our annual September conference, . . . nearly two thousand petitions for certiorari will be waiting. These are disposed of at the September conference in the same manner that petitions are disposed of at our regular conferences.

Shortly before each such conference, the Chief Justice sends out a list of the petitions he wishes to have discussed. After the Chief's "discuss list" has come around, each of the associate justices may ask to have additional cases put on this list. If at a particular conference there are one hundred petitions for certiorari on the conference list, the number discussed at conference will range from fifteen to thirty. The petitions for certiorari that are not discussed at conference are denied without any recorded vote.

Whether or not to vote to grant certiorari strikes me as a rather subjective decision, made up in part of intuition and in part of legal judgment. One factor that plays a large part with every member of the Court is whether the case sought to be reviewed has been decided differently from a very similar case coming from another lower court: If it has, its chances for being reviewed are much greater than if it hasn't. Another important factor is the perception of one or more justices that the lower-court decision may well be either an incorrect application of Supreme Court precedent or of general importance beyond its effect on these particular litigants, or both.

I have on occasion described the certiorari process to groups interested in the work of the Court, and find occasional raised eyebrows at one or more of its aspects. I have been asked whether or not the use of the law clerks in a cert pool didn't represent the abandonment of the justices' responsibilities to a sort of internal bureaucracy. I certainly do not think so. The individual justices are quite free to disregard whatever recommendation the writer of the pool memo may have made, as well as the recommendation of his own law clerks, but this is not a complete answer to the criticism. It is one thing to do the work yourself, and it is another thing to simply approve the recommendation of another person who has done the work. But the decision whether to grant certiorari is a much more "channeled" decision than the decision as to how a case should be decided on the merits; there are really only two or three factors involved in the certiorari decision—conflict with other courts, general importance, and perception that the decision is wrong in the light of Supreme Court precedent. Each of these factors is one that a well-trained law clerk is capable of evaluating, and the justices, of course, having been in the certiorari-granting business term after term, are quite familiar with many of the issues that come up. I would feel entirely different about a system that assigned the preparation of "bench memos"—memoranda that summarize the contention of the parties and recommend a particular result in an argued case—to one law clerk in a large pool of clerks.

Another criticism I have heard voiced is that the great majority of petitions for certiorari are never even discussed at conference and are simply denied without being taken up by the justices as a group. I do not think this is a valid criticism. For the sixty years since the enactment of the Certiorari Act of 1925, there have been significant ideological divisions on the Court, such that one group of justices might be inclined to review one kind of case, and another group inclined to review another kind of case. When one realizes that any of nine justices, differing among themselves as they usually do about which cases are important and how cases should be decided, may ask that a petition for certiorari be discussed, the fate of a case that is "dead listed" ("dead listing" a case is the converse of putting a case on the "discuss list") is a fate well deserved. It simply means that none of the nine justices thought the case was worth discussing at conference with a view to trying to persuade four members of the Court to grant certiorari. It would be a totally sterile exercise to discuss such a case at conference, since no justice would be a proponent of granting it and it would end up being denied in less time than it takes to write this paragraph.

Examination of the certiorari process naturally brings up the question of the precise role of the Supreme Court in our country's legal system. Many would intuitively say that the task of the "highest court in the land" is to make sure that justice is done to every litigant, or some similarly general and appealing description. The Supreme Court once played a role in the federal system corresponding fairly closely to that description, but the days when it could do so are long gone.

The first Congress in 1789 established the Supreme Court of the United States and lower federal courts, which were essentially trial courts. In the lower courts witnesses testified, documents were received in evidence, and at the close of the trial the judge or the jury ruled in favor of one of the parties and against the other. Congress provided that appeals from these decisions should lie to the Supreme Court of the United States, and the task of the latter Court in these early days was to do what any other appellate court traditionally does: make sure that the trial was fairly conducted, that the judge correctly applied the law, and that the evidence supported the result reached by the lower court. In its earlier days, . . . the Court did not have a great deal to do as an appellate court—for several decades it sat in Washington for only a few weeks a year, hearing appeals from the lower federal courts and from state supreme courts. Indeed, the justices spent far more of their time circuit riding as trial judges in the geographic circuits to which they were assigned than they did as appellate judges in Washington.

But this rather easygoing picture changed before the Civil War, when the Justices had to spend more of their time sitting as appellate judges and still found themselves falling behind in their docket. After the Civil War, court congestion increased. Congress expanded the jurisdiction of the lower federal courts so that they could hear types of cases they had previously been denied the authority to hear. Congress began to enact regulatory legislation, which created new kinds of lawsuits that could be brought in the federal courts. Finally, both the commercial activity and the population of the United States continued to increase dramatically, and both of these kinds of growth naturally caused more litigation. By 1890 it took three and a half years between the time a case was first docketed in the Supreme Court and the time it was orally argued before the justices. Court congestion is not often a major concern of Congress, but these extreme delays caused the legal profession to rise up in righteous indignation, and in 1891 Congress responded by creating the federal circuit courts of appeals.

The federal circuit courts of appeals were regional appellate courts. Congress provided that in cases where the federal trial courts had jurisdiction, not because of a federal question involved in the case but only because one of the parties was a citizen of one state and the other a citizen of another, appeal from the decision of the trial court would lie not to the Supreme Court of the United States but to the federal court of appeals in the geographic region in which the trial courts lay. Review of the decision of the court of appeals could not be had automatically in the Supreme Court, but only if the Supreme Court agreed to review the decision.

Other acts of Congress in the early part of this century, culminating in the Certiorari Act of 1925, further limited the access of parties to Supreme Court review. After 1925, review not only of diversity cases but of most federal-question cases decided by the federal trial courts was to be had as a matter of right not in the Supreme Court but in the federal courts of appeals. Further review by the Supreme Court was made to depend on the discretionary decision of that court to hear the case. Chief Justice William Howard Taft was one of the architects of the Certiorari Act of 1925, and his biographer, Henry F. Pringle, summarizes his view of the role of the Supreme Court in these words:

> It was vital, he said in opening the drive for the Judges' Bill, that cases before the Court be reduced without limiting the function of pronouncing "the last word on every important issue under the Constitution and the statutes of the United States." A supreme court, on the other hand, should not be a tribunal obligated to weigh justice among contesting parties. "They have had all they have a right to claim," Taft said, "when they have had two courts in which to have adjudicated their controversy." [Pringle, 1965, II: 997–98]

There are thousands of state court judges in this country at the present time and hundreds of federal judges. Each of these has sworn to uphold the Constitution and laws of the United States, and the overwhelming majority of these judges are capable of applying settled law to the facts of the cases before them, and are eager to do so. Occasionally, trial judges make mistakes, but the courts of appeals sit to correct these mistakes within the federal system, and state appellate courts sit to do the same in every state. It would be a useless duplication of these functions if the Supreme Court of the United States were to serve simply as an even higher court for the correction of errors in cases involving no generally important principle of law. The Supreme Court, quite correctly in my opinion, instead seeks to pick from the several thousand cases it is annually asked to review, those cases involving unsettled questions of federal constitutional or statutory law of general interest.

The number of cases that we decide on the merits has varied considerably since I came to the Court. For the first fifteen years of my tenure, we would decide an average of about a hundred and fifty cases each term. Then the number began to drop sharply, and in each of the last few terms of the twentieth century we have decided less than a hundred. This difference is due in part to Congress allowing us more discretion in granting certiorari, and in part to our becoming more selective in the cases we take. Even with less than a hundred cases, we are quite well occupied in doing what we ought to do—in the words of Chief Justice Taft, pronouncing "the last word on every important issue under the Constitution and the statutes of the United States"—without trying to reach out and correct errors in cases where the lower courts may have reached an incorrect result, but where the result is not apt to have any influence beyond its effects on the parties to the case.

Questions and Comments

1.   None of these Justices suggests that the Court should return to the methods described in the 1920s for processing cert petitions. After reading these excerpts, has your evaluation of the effects of the "cert pool" memo changed? Is it likely that Justices with experience will be able to decide to deny the vast majority of cases based on the Question Presented, and in the remaining cases could use their own law clerks and their own knowledge to make decisions, as in the days before the cert-pool?

2.   Why does Justice Stevens oppose publication of dissents from denials of certiorari? Could his objections be cured by having concurring Justices explain why they voted to deny certiorari? Would that "cure" be worse, from his point of view, than the "disease" of the published dissents? Why?

---

4.   Views From the Outside: The Academy

This section examines some of the empirical studies that attempt to discern how the Justices apply Rule 10 and decide whether or not to grant cert. In an important study of the Court's docket from 1953 to 1983, Professor Arthur Hellman was able to identify four categories of cases that make up the majority of the Court's grants. Arthur D. Hellman, *Case Selection in the Burger Court: A Preliminary Inquiry*, 60 Notre Dame L. Rev. 947 (1985). His key findings, many supported by other research, were:

• First, cases which presented an intercircuit conflict made up about one-third of the docket in the average term.

• Second, cases which involved a compelling government interest were more likely to be granted. The Court was likely to find a compelling interest when a lower court held a federal statute unconstitutional and the U.S. government was the party seeking review.[47]

• Third, the Court was more likely to hear a case that raises a difficult question that is repeatedly litigated, even if there is no circuit conflict. Hellman uses as an example the case of *Metropolitan Edison Co. v. NLRB* (1982), which questioned whether an employer commits an unfair labor practice by disciplining union officials more severely than other union employees for taking part in an unlawful work stoppage. A series of appellate opinions over the prior five years had generated considerable confusion as to what considerations were relevant and how much weight they should be given. Though there was no square circuit conflict, the question was a doubtful and recurring issue that the Court sought to resolve.

• Finally, Hellman observed that federal/state conflicts made up a distinct subgroup of those remaining cases granted. In particular, cases in which a state court rejects a federal or constitutional claim or a federal court invalidates official state action were likely to be granted review by the Supreme Court.

These factors, identified by Professor Hellman, continue to be significant today, though the mix of cases involving these factors may differ. Other indicators are also relevant. Thus, for example, if a case has been heard by a circuit court *en banc*, a grant is more likely. See Tracey George & Michael Solimine, *Supreme Court Monitoring of the United States Court of Appeals En Banc*, 9 S. Ct. Econ. Rev. 171 (2001). In addition, a judge's dissent from a denial of rehearing en banc may attract the Supreme Court's attention. As Patricia Wald, former Chief Judge of the United States Court of Appeals for the D.C. Circuit, suggested, such dissents are often "thinly disguised invitations to certiorari."[48] Patricia M. Wald, *The D.C. Circuit: Here and Now*, 55 Geo. Wash. L. Rev. 719, 719 (1987).

But to what extent are the Justices influenced by their own policy views and to what extent do the Justices behave strategically so as to try to achieve outcomes that match their policy views? Scholars differ in

47. See also, e.g., Lawrence Baum, *The Supreme Court* 199–200 (5th ed. 1995) (noting that for the 1992 Term, the Court granted 71% of the petitions filed by the Solicitor General and only 1 percent of all others); Gregory A. Caldeira & John R. Wright, *Organized Interests and Agenda Setting in the U.S. Supreme Court*, 82 Am. Pol. Sci. Rev. 1109–1127 (1988) (suggesting that amicus filing by the Solicitor General may indicate presence of a compelling government interest).

48. For a possible example of an "invitation to certiorari" that was not accepted, see Southern Oregon Barter Fair v. Jackson County, Oregon, 401 F.3d 1124 (9th Cir. 2005) (seven judges dissenting to the denial of rehearing en banc on the ground that the panel misinterpreted Thomas v. Chicago Park District, 534 U.S. 316 (2002)), *cert. denied sub nomine* Southern Oregon Barter Fair v. Oregon, 546 U.S. 826 (2005).

their views on the impact of institutional concerns, political attitudes, legal constraints, and strategic factors on many aspects of the Court's decisionmaking, including the certiorari decision. An important model in political science is the so-called "attitudinal" model, which views judges' own attitudes as a primary determinant of their judicial behavior. The classic work is Jeffrey A. Segal & Harold J. Spaeth, *The Supreme Court and the Attitudinal Model* (1993). Lawyers, however, tend to see the Court's decisionmaking in terms of the law, or institutional concerns. For helpful discussion of the more general relationship between legal, political, and institutional factors in the Court's decisionmaking, see, e.g., Barry Friedman, *The Politics of Judicial Review*, 84 Tex. L. Rev. 257 (2005); H.W. Perry, Jr., *Deciding to Decide: Agenda Setting in the United States Supreme Court* (1991).

The discretionary character of the certiorari process allows room for many factors to influence decisions, as this section explores. In the first reading below, Professors Margaret and Richard Cordray argue that Justices are primarily influenced by jurisprudential considerations in determining which cases merit review. Specifically, whether a Justice subscribes to what the Cordrays call a "rule-articulating," "standard-setting," or "incrementalist" approach to decisionmaking affects that Justice's willingness to grant a high volume of cases. Additionally, a Justice's views on the necessity of resolving circuit splits will also influence cert grants, along with a Justice's sense of the proper role of the Court in bringing about social change.

Next in this section, two political scientists, Professors Lee Epstein and Jack Knight, offer a more strategic account of the Justices' decisions on cert petitions. They state their basic premise in the first chapter. "On our account, a major goal of all justices is to see the law reflect their preferred policy position, and they will take actions to advance this objective." Lee Epstein & Jack Knight, *The Choices Justices Make* 11 (1998). Having said that, they acknowledge that "institutional legitimacy" is also an important goal and constraint. *Id.* Nonetheless, they note: "legitimacy, like most goals scholars ascribe to justices, is a means to an end, and that end is the substantive content of the law. This claim," they assert, "is not ... particularly controversial. Justices may have goals other than policy, but no serious scholar of the Court would claim that policy is not prime among them." *Id.* at 12. Epstein and Knight examine both "aggressive grants" and "defensive denials" of cert petitions. They also explore the use of dissents from denials of cert to try to get other Justices to change their mind and turn a denial into a grant.[49]

Finally, we provide brief excerpts from a study conducted by Professor H.W. Perry, Jr., who concludes that some political scientists' emphasis on strategic decision-making is overstated. H.W. Perry, Jr., *Deciding*

49. Epstein and Knight contrast their approach with the so-called "attitudinal model" in which Justices' votes are a function of the values and the facts of the case and which does not contemplate strategic interaction over votes. Epstein & Knight, *supra*, at 57, n. a, citing Jeffrey A. Segal & Harold J. Spaeth, *The Supreme Court and the Attitudinal Model*, (1993).

to Decide: Agenda Setting in the United States Supreme Court 14–15 (1991). On Perry's account, each Justice employs two different approaches to voting on cert petitions—a "strategic" or outcome "mode", where the justice cares strongly about the outcome, and a "legalistic" or "jurisprudential" mode on other issues. He concludes that "the strategic behavior in case selection [as opposed to the jurisprudential behavior] is the exception, even among the justices we would consider the most 'political'." *Id.* at 275 n.5.

Margaret Meriwether Cordray & Richard Cordray,[50] *The Philosophy of Certiorari: Jurisprudential Considerations in Supreme Court Case Selection,* **82 Wash. U. L. Q. 389 (2004)**

. . . [T]he Court's muscular authority over case selection in the modern era now gives it the unchallenged prerogative in almost every instance to choose whether to resolve or to bypass important controversies that are brought before it in particular cases. . . .

. . .

The importance of this work is all the more striking in view of the unusual manner in which it is performed. In sharp contrast to traditional judicial decisionmaking, the Justices typically make decisions about whether to grant certiorari according to vague guidelines that afford them maximum discretion, based on very little collegial deliberation, with virtually no public disclosure or explanation of their actions and subject to no precedential constraints.

The secrecy of the Court's deliberations and actions at the threshold stage makes analysis of the nature of the Court's agenda-setting work difficult, since the Court typically does not publish its certiorari votes and rarely explains them in any detail. Nonetheless, a number of political scientists have mined the docket books of retired Justices in order to develop a better grasp of this critical function. Their analysis of the data has done much to clarify the extent to which the criteria articulated in the Court's rule on certiorari (such as the presence of a conflict among the lower courts) and strategic considerations about the likelihood of prevailing on the merits actually motivate the Justices' decisionmaking.

In this Article, we offer a fuller jurisprudential analysis of the gatekeeping choices that the Justices make as they set the direction in which the Court will proceed. Using more recent data ... from the docket books of Justices Brennan and Marshall, we show that rule-based

50. Margaret Cordray is Professor of Law, Capital Law School; Richard Cordray is Adjunct Professor, Ohio State University College of Law, and clerked for Justices White and Kennedy.

and strategic factors, while undeniably important, cannot adequately account for the Justices' voting behavior at the certiorari stage. Although the Justices consider the very same cases and materials, in light of the same criteria set out in the Court's rule, they come to quite different conclusions about which cases merit plenary review. Even Justices closely aligned in decisions on the merits often have dramatically different voting records on certiorari.

We suggest that other, more jurisprudential considerations also affect the individual Justices' judgments about the quantity and content of the Court's proper workload. In particular, we contend that a Justice's views about what role the Supreme Court should play in the judicial system and American life—including his or her views on the nature of precedent, the importance of uniformity in federal law, and the Court's appropriate role in effectuating social change—play a central role in shaping his or her decisions about case selection.

I.   THE IMPORTANCE AND UNIQUENESS OF THE CERTIORARI PROCESS

A.   *The Importance of the Certiorari Process*

. . .

. . . Through their decisions on which cases to hear, the Justices set the Court's priorities. The Court's agenda might, for example, be weighted in favor of achieving the maximum degree of national uniformity in the application of federal law by emphasizing cases presenting conflicts in the lower courts. Alternatively, its docket might be focused on particular social issues to enable the Court to serve as an aggressive force for societal change. Further, the types of cases that the Justices choose can affect the manner in which they supervise and guide the lower courts. There is a spectrum of views about how this supervisory function is most effectively performed, ranging from a preference for issuing decisions with broad rules of general applicability to a preference for use of incremental, step-by-step decisions in the common law tradition. Ultimately the guidance given—whether in broad or narrow form—is in the majority's opinion on the merits. But the Court's decisions about which cases to place on its plenary docket may affect its ability to pursue its preferred approach. Thus, for example, if the Court prefers to use a more incremental approach to create a body of decisions to guide the lower courts, it must have clusters of cases in discrete areas available for plenary review and decision.

. . . [T]he Court's case-selection decisions . . . [thus] mak[e] a crucial contribution to the lasting body of national law that the Supreme Court eventually compiles.

B.   *The Peculiarly "Unjudicial" Nature of Certiorari Decisionmaking*

. . .

. . . The most striking feature of the [certiorari] process is that it lacks most of the trappings of traditional judicial decisionmaking—

collegial deliberation, constraining criteria, majority rule, and public accountability. Indeed, the unique system that the Justices use in deciding which cases to grant for full consideration on the merits provides the Justices with virtually unfettered discretion in shaping the content of the Court's docket.

Each week, hundreds of petitions are circulated to the individual chambers where the Justices and their law clerks review them. At this stage, the Justices act almost entirely on their own in deciding which cases are worthy of review. This isolation is driven in part by tradition and in part by necessity; as a practical matter, the sheer volume of petitions virtually eliminates the possibility of oral argument or any more collegial deliberation. Following this initial review, most petitions are readily found to be unworthy, and the Court simply denies them unless a Justice circulates a request to put a case on the "discuss" list prior to conference.

Those cases placed on the discuss list do receive some form of collective consideration and then a vote in conference. Because of the crush of work, though, this discussion is almost invariably brief ... [and] there is no opportunity for the collegial deliberation in a more public setting that often occurs among the Justices at the oral argument of cases heard on the merits. The certiorari process is thus "relatively atomistic with decisions being made within chambers and the outcome on cert. being primarily the sum of nine individual decision processes." Put differently, "the extent to which the nine Justices operate as 'nine little law firms' is maximized here."

In making these highly individualized decisions, the Justices operate under virtually no formal constraints. The Court's own Rule 10 sets out the considerations governing review on certiorari. . . .

These criteria, laden as they are with malleable terms such as "important," "usual," "should," and "conflict" do not serve to exert much meaningful restraint on the decisionmaking process. Even so, the Court takes further steps to forestall any constraint by noting that review "is not a matter of right, but of judicial discretion," and cautioning that the criteria articulated in Rule 10 are "neither controlling nor fully measuring [of] the Court's discretion."

· · ·

The unconstrained nature of the Court's case selection criteria is facilitated by the intense privacy and secrecy of the Court's approach to disposing of petitions: no record of the Court's vote is ever published (regardless of whether the case is granted or denied), and typically no opinion or explanation is ever rendered for the Court's action. The relatively rare breaches of this unspoken norm over the years are the exceptions that prove the rule [noting Justice Douglas' publishing his "grant" votes in his later years and the regular dissents from cert denials by Justices Brennan and Marshall in death penalty cases.] ... [T]he result of this private decisionmaking process is to divorce the case selection process from precedential constraints, thus minimizing any obligation of consistency from case to case.

There are two main justifications for this secrecy. The first is limited resources: the crush of work in processing thousands of petitions each term simply does not permit any more elaborate procedures. In explaining why the Court does not provide the reasons for its case selection decisions, Justice Rehnquist was explicit: "there is simply not the time available to formulate statements of reasons why review is denied or appeals are affirmed or dismissed without argument."

The other main justification is greater flexibility: The Court wants and believes that it needs the ability to wait for the "right" case, to allow an appropriate amount of "percolation" of issues in the lower courts, and to control the size of its docket. This rationale is more telling because it is an explicit acknowledgment that the Court prefers to minimize the judicial character of its certiorari decisionmaking in order to achieve other administrative objectives—including its ability to achieve specific goals through the case selection process itself.... [N]ot only [would] it ... be burdensome to justify its certiorari decisions to the public, but perhaps also ... it would be somewhat difficult ... [or] undesirable to have to do so.

But the price of the streamlined procedures and uninhibited flexibility is the absence of accountability.... [T]he votes cast on certiorari seem almost legislative or prerogative in character. Although presumably the Justices faithfully strive to apply the general substantive criteria set forth in Rule 10, each Justice maintains enormous latitude to vote to grant or deny a particular case for "any reason the Court sees fit." Moreover, the decision that a Justice makes in any given case at the certiorari stage imposes no precedential constraint on his or her judgment about even the very same issue if (or, more likely, when) it arises in another case.

Despite the lack of formal constraints and accountability, the Justices share some understanding of what they are trying to accomplish at this threshold stage and hence what kinds of issues are important enough to warrant full review. As Provine concluded from her study of the Vinson Court, the Justices' shared "conception of their role ... prevents them from using their votes simply to achieve policy preferences." Yet even Provine is dubious about the Justices' degree of self-restraint: "self-imposed limits of rule conceptions, it is important to note, are essentially the only limits upon judicial discretion in case selection. Case selection approximates and even exceeds plenary decision making in the scope it provides for the exercise of unfettered judicial judgment."[51]

The contrast between the processes that the Court has devised for case selection and for plenary decisionmaking is thus quite stark. At the threshold stage, decisions are made atomistically, with little collegial

51. [Editors' note: The authors are quoting from Doris Marie Provine, *Case* *Selection in the United States Supreme Court* 174–75 (1980)]

deliberation, and are based on a very brief review of the documentation.... At the merits stage, decisions are made after extensive study .. and are based on a more explicit and intensive presentation ... and collective exchange that occurs both in public—at oral argument—and in the Justices' private conference. At the threshold stage, decisions can be ... made with a mere plurality vote; whereas a precedential decision at the merits stage requires majority support. At the threshold stage, decisions are made based on criteria that are designed to preserve immense discretion; at the merits stage, there are elaborate procedural and interpretive norms that often influence and channel the Justices' decisionmaking. Finally, at the threshold stage votes typically are kept secret.... At the merits stage, the Justices publish both their individual votes and the reasons for the Court's holding.... [A]t the merits stage the accepted principle of *stare decisis* exerts further pressure on each Justice to justify his or her position in light of the Court's prior precedents....

This striking disparity between the Court's decisionmaking process at the certiorari stage and its more familiar process at the merits stage reinforces one Justice's comment that "it is really hard to know what makes up this broth of the cert. process." In the next section, we examine what is known about the kinds of considerations that influence the Supreme Court's decisionmaking on certiorari.

II.   RULE-BASED AND STRATEGIC FACTORS AFFECTING CERTIORARI DECISIONS

. . .

Not surprisingly [in light of Rule 10], researchers have found that the existence of an actual conflict between the lower courts or between the lower court and a Supreme Court precedent is a potent determinant. There is strong evidence that the presence of genuine conflict between the circuit courts of appeals, between state supreme courts, between federal courts and state courts, or between the lower court and Supreme Court precedent dramatically increases the probability that the Court will grant a case. Indeed, even allegations of a conflict between lower court decisions, where actual conflict is absent, increase the likelihood that the Court will grant certiorari.

In determining whether the case presents an important federal question, the second key criterion in Rule 10, the Court looks to a variety of indicators. Among these, a consistent standout is the presence of the United States as a petitioner in the case. When the Solicitor General seeks review on behalf of the United States, the Court is far more likely to grant certiorari.... The Solicitor General's success is attributable in part to the rigorous screening that he performs to cull out cases appropriate for review, as well as the general expertise and quality of the lawyers in his office. But perhaps most significantly, the key "importance" criterion for review is almost necessarily met when the federal government seeks review asserting that the government is directly and substantially affected by a lower court decision or that decisional conflicts are requiring it to operate differently in various parts of the country.

Amicus curiae briefs filed in support of (or even in opposition to) the petition for certiorari also serve to flag importance. In an innovative study, Gregory Caldeira and John Wright hypothesized that, because it is expensive to prepare amicus briefs, the Court can and does use amicus activity as an indicator of the importance or practical significance of a case. Specifically, they proposed that "amicus curiae participation by organized interests provides information, or signals—otherwise largely unavailable—about the political, social, and economic significance of cases on the paid docket and that justices make inferences about the potential impact of their decisions by observing the extent of amicus activity."[52]

The results of the authors' statistical analysis of the petitions for certiorari filed in the 1982 Term bore out this proposition. Caldeira and Wright found that when a case involves an actual conflict or when the United States is the petitioner, the filing of just one amicus brief in support of the petition increases the likelihood that the Court will grant certiorari by forty to fifty percent, and the filing of two or three amicus briefs increases the likelihood ever more. Tellingly, they also found that amicus briefs filed in opposition to certiorari increased the likelihood of a grant, presumably because these too signal the importance of the issue.[53]

Researchers have also suggested that a case is more likely to be granted if the court immediately below reversed the lower court, or if a judge dissented from the decision. There has also been some attempt to correlate the likelihood of a grant with substantive areas—for example, it has been suggested that the court is more inclined to grant cases involving civil liberties than economic issues—but recent analysis raises questions about the extent to which the Court may favor certain issue areas over others. In any event, these factors appears to exert far less influence on the Court's decision to grant certiorari than the three major determinants of genuine conflict, the United States as petitioner, and the presence of amicus briefs.

B.   *Ideological and Strategic Considerations on Certiorari*

Researchers have also identified other, more political, influences on the Court's decisionmaking at the certiorari stage. . . . [I]t is useful to distinguish between the various ways in which a Justice could give play to ideological preferences in his or her certiorari votes.

First, Justices might vote to grant or deny certiorari not merely because of the national importance of the issue or the existence of conflicting decisions in the lower courts, but also based on their own

---

52. [Editors' Note: The authors are referring to Gregory A. Caldeira & John R. Wright, *The Discuss List: Agenda Building in the Supreme Court*, 24 Law & Soc'y Rev. 807, 816 (1990).]

53. [Editors' Note: See also, Joseph Kearney & Thomas Merrill, *The Influence of Amicus Curiae Briefs on the Supreme Court*, 148 U. Pa. L. Rev. 743 (2000) excerpted in Chapter Five, below.]

ideological predilections. Thus, a Justice would be more likely to vote to grant a case where he or she was uncomfortable with the ... result below and would be inclined to vote to reverse on the merits. Second, Justices might vote to grant or deny certiorari in a somewhat more sophisticated manner that takes into account the likely position of their colleagues, with a view to the ultimate outcome on the merits. Engaging in this kind of strategic voting, a Justice might vote to deny certiorari even if he or she disagreed with the result below if the Justice believed that the unappealing result would likely be affirmed in any decision on the merits. And third, in pursuing these objectives, it is also possible that the Justices ... could consciously form explicit coalitions that would work as power blocs in setting the Court's plenary agenda.

Numerous scholars have contended that the Justices' agenda-setting decisions are motivated, at least in part, by their own ideological inclinations; in other words a Justice is more likely to vote ideological preferences. Indeed, Chief Justice Rehnquist seems to have recognized as much: "There is an ideological division on the Court, and each of us have some cases we would like to see granted, and on the contrary some of the other members ... would not like to see them granted." ...

[A] growing body of scholarship indicates that the Justices do engage in strategic voting at the certiorari stage.... The Supreme Court's two-stage voting process (deciding to grant certiorari and then deciding the case on the merits) is ripe for strategic manipulation since the decisionmaking at the first (certiorari) stage occurs in the secrecy of the Justices' private conference, with no justification provided publicly, and the Justices have sufficient familiarity with the preferences of their colleagues to predict with some confidence how they will cast their votes at the later (merits) stage.[54] ...

In 1959, Glendon Schubert initiated the debate over the existence and extent of strategic voting in certiorari decisions.[55] Using game theory and votes on the merits in Federal Employers' Liability Act cases during the 1942–1948 Terms, Schubert speculated that four liberal Justices were engaging in bloc voting on certiorari to shape the law in that area. This proposition was eye-catching because it not only raised the possibility that the Justices acted strategically in their decisionmaking, but also that they deliberately formed power alliances to attain their goals.

When the docket books of Justice Burton became available to the public, researchers were able to test Schubert's hypothesis against the actual votes cast by the Justices at the certiorari stage. After examining the voting patterns on the Vinson Court, Marie Provine found that the votes of putative bloc members did not conform to the power-oriented

---

54. [Editors' Note: Readers should note that this article was written in 2004, in the tenth year of an unusually long period with no new appointees to the Court. Between September 2005 and January 2006, the Court's membership was changed by two new appointments.]

55. [Editors' Note: The authors cite Glendon Schubert, *The Certiorari Game*, in *Quantitative Analysis of Judicial Behavior* 210–67 (Glendon Schubert ed., 1959).]

pattern that Schubert had predicted. She concluded that, despite the ease and effectiveness with which power-bloc voting could be accomplished, "a shared conception of the proper role of a judge prevents the justices from exploiting the possibilities for power-oriented voting in case selection." This conclusion is strongly supported in the work of H.W. Perry, who conducted extensive interviews of five Justices and sixty-four former law clerks. Perry found that at the certiorari stage the Justices' decisionmaking is highly independent, with only rare attempts at persuasion or accommodation and with no vote trading at all.

But the absence of evidence of bloc voting at that juncture in the Court's history does not eliminate the possibility that it occurred at other times. Moreover, it does not preclude the possibility that Justices engage individually in strategic voting. Despite the intuitive appeal of this possibility, some scholars have contended that the Justices do not cast their votes on certiorari with a view to how the Court is likely to decide the case on the merits. Using certiorari data from Justice Burton's papers, for example, Provine argued that the Justices were not result-oriented in their case selection decisions, at least as a general matter. Rather, she contended that case selection decisions were primarily driven by a Justice's own evaluation of the merits of the case and his or her "beliefs about the proper work and workload of the Supreme Court."

The weight of the evidence, however, now favors the view that the Justices do act strategically in their decisionmaking at the certiorari stage. In a recent study, Gregory Caldeira, John Wright, and Christopher Zorn provided strong empirical evidence that strategic voting not only occurs but is routine and has a substantial impact on the content of the Court's plenary docket.[56] Using data from the 1982 Term, they had two key findings: (1) there was a substantial correlation between a Justice's own ideological position and his or her vote on certiorari; and (2) there was strong evidence that the Justices consider the likely result on the merits in deciding how to vote. Further, they estimated that the strategic use of "defensive denials"—that is, a vote to deny certiorari to fend off an undesirable result on the merits, despite the Justice's own preference to grant the case—accounted for at least eighteen omissions from the Court's plenary docket in the 1982 Term.

Although they might take issue with claims about the extent of its use, several Justices have acknowledged the existence of the defensive denial. In Perry's interviews with five Justices, all of them recognized, with varying degrees of approval, that Justices use this strategic device. Indeed, one Justice responded to Perry's inquiry about defensive denials by saying: "Certainly, it's a standard of the way we behave, and it's a perfectly honorable standard. I think anyone who suggests that this is an objective institution is just wrong; the notion that we are objective is just

---

56. [Editors' Note: The authors cite Gregory A Caldeira, et al., *Sophisticated Voting and Gate–Keeping in the Supreme* *Court*, 15 J. L. Econ. & Org. 549, 553–71 (1999).]

fallacious." The clerks likewise agreed that they and at least some of the Justices took such strategic considerations into account, though not all realized that their own Justice did too.

Through his interviews, Perry also identified several other strategic tools that the Justices use. These include employing "aggressive grants," where the Justices reach out to take cases for strategic reasons; looking for cases that are "good vehicles" because they have a fact situation that might pull in a swing Justice or allow the Justice to move doctrine in a desired direction; and sending signals in merits opinions to encourage litigants to bring certain types of cases.

In the end, the question seems to be less whether the Justices engage in strategic voting than how extensively they do so. . . .

III.   THE INFLUENCE OF THE INDIVIDUAL JUSTICES' VIEWS ON THE PROPER ROLE OF THE SUPREME COURT

The set of rule-based and strategic factors discussed above does much to explain the Court's agenda-setting decisions. But . . . the rule-based and strategic factors fail to account for important phenomena. . . . [The Justices] reach dramatically different conclusions about which cases merit plenary review. In the 1982 Term, for example, Justices White and Rehnquist examined the thousands of applications and each voted to grant review in over 230 cases. Yet in the same term, based on the same sample of cases, Justice Powell and Chief Justice Burger each voted to grant review in more than 100 fewer cases. In the 1990 Term, to take another example, Justice White again voted to grant review in more than 200 cases, whereas Justice Scalia, Kennedy, and Stevens voted to grant review only half as often. Earlier studies of the Vinson Court show that the same kinds of disparities have persisted for decades, even with different personnel and different universes of legal issues.

Equally paradoxical is the fact that even though some Justices routinely win on the merits, they vote infrequently to grant review. Justice Kennedy, for example, dissented in only fourteen cases during the 1990 Term. Yet he voted to grant only 101 cases that term, the second fewest on the Court, and considerably fewer than Justice O'Connor, who was the only Justice to dissent less often on the merits. By contrast, Justice Blackmun was one of the more frequent dissenters during the 1990 Term and yet he voted to grant 142 cases that Term, more than anyone except Justice White. Similarly paradoxical examples from an earlier period [exist.] . . .

To understand these various phenomena, analysis of the agenda-setting function requires greater emphasis on each Justice's distinctive views and voting record, as opposed to focusing on the court's aggregate decisionmaking. . . . As the Justices apply the key criterion of Rule 10— that the case present an "important question" that is either unsettled or is the source of a conflict in the lower courts—each Justice's sense of what is "important" is shaped by his or her philosophy about the court's proper role in the judicial system and in society. These jurisprudential considerations thus exert a subtle but important influence on a Justice's views about the appropriate number and mix of cases on the Court's merits docket.

A.   The Complex and Uniquely Impressionistic Nature of Decisionmaking on Certiorari

Because decisionmaking at the certiorari stage is completely unfettered, the voting behavior of each Justice is constrained only by his or her own individual sense of what kinds of cases merit the Court's attention. Over the years, Justices across the ideological spectrum have acknowledged the uniquely impressionistic nature of the task.... [Quotations from Rehnquist, Brennan and Douglas omitted.] Justice Harlan likewise stated that "frequently the question whether a case is 'certworthy' is more a matter of 'feel' than of precisely ascertainable rules."

Interestingly, this "feel" for which cases are most appropriate for plenary review seems to remain fairly stable for each Justice over time.... This consistency is likely attributable to the lack of collegial deliberation at the certiorari stage, as the isolated nature of the decisionmaking process prevents the kind of peer influence that might cause an individual Justice's approach to case selection to evolve....

[W]hat elements combine to create this "feel"? ...

On the more practical side, for some Justices (and perhaps for all Justices to some degree).... [the] capacity of the Court's docket—that is, how many cases it is manageable for the Court to resolve in a given term—can become an important constraint on their willingness to vote to grant a case. For example, during the Burger Court, which routinely decided approximately 150 cases per term, Justice Brennan argued that the Court could not do more, stating: "There is a limit to human endurance, and with the ever increasing complexity of many of the cases that the Court is reviewing in this modern day, the number 150 taxes that endurance to its limits.... At the same time, however, Justice White consistently opined that the Court was wrongly abdicating one of its core duties by failing to grant review in many cases to protect the uniformity of federal law."

... For purposes of this discussion, however, we focus on more theoretical elements in decisionmaking at the certiorari stage, which might be called "jurisprudential" concerns. These factors encompass each Justice's view on the role that the Court should play within the judicial system itself and within the national government....

B.   The Significance of Jurisprudential Approach for Decisionmaking on Certiorari

1.   View on How Precedent Guides and Superintends the Lower Courts

There is extensive discussion in the legal literature about the different approaches that the Justices take in resolving cases on the merits....

Under a rule-articulating approach, the Court sets out broad and clear rules that not only control the outcome in the particular case on its specific set of facts, but are also consciously intended to govern many other situations where the facts are somewhat different but the same principles are nonetheless operative. Advocates of this approach contend, in essence, that the Court should generate opinions that cast a substantial precedential shadow covering a meaningful amount of legal terrain. The chief virtues of this approach are that rules enhance fairness by requiring decisionmakers to act consistently, and they increase the predictability of results.

Under a standard-setting approach, the Court applies the background principle or policy to the fact situation, taking into account all relevant factors. This approach is epitomized by reliance on the "balancing test," through which the Court identifies multiple factors as the relevant criteria for decisionmaking in a particular area, and then instructs the lower courts to apply a prescribed formula that leaves them with discretion to weigh those factors in deciding future cases. The primary advantages of a standard-setting approach are that standards promote fairness by enabling decisionmakers to consider all factors relevant to the individual case, and standards are sufficiently flexible to permit decisionmakers to adapt to changing circumstances.

Under an incrementalist approach, the Court seeks only to resolve the dispute before it, allowing the law to develop "not through the pronouncement of general principles, but case-by-case, deliberately, incrementally, one-step-at-a-time." The core of this approach is the notion that judges do not pronounce the law … (either by articulating broader rules or by formulating balancing tests), but rather they shape the law by resolving disputes and … creating a pattern of judgments through deciding a sufficient number of discrete cases in an area…. The incrementalist approach … differs from a standard-setting approach in one key aspect: a Justice employing a standard-setting approach seeks to lay down a formula that identifies the most relevant factors to guide further judicial decisionmaking in the area, whereas a Justice employing an incrementalist approach consciously seeks to decide cases as narrowly as possible…. The main benefits of an incrementalist approach are that it reduces the risk and cost of errors in judicial decisionmaking and leaves maximum room for further deliberation and action by the other political branches.

Our purpose is not to join the debate on the relative merits of these approaches, but rather to suggest that a Justice's view of the proper mode of decisionmaking can influence his or her decisions about case selection…. [E]ach Justice's sense of how the Supreme Court most effectively creates precedent to guide and supervise the lower courts can provide important context for his or her decisions about which cases merit plenary review.

Justice Scalia, for example, has championed the rule-articulating approach. He has argued strongly that, wherever it is possible to do so, opinions should be written expansively to explain the rules of general application that control the result in the particular case because "the establishment of broadly applicable general principles is an essential component of the judicial process." Justice Scalia has justified this view, in part, based on a functional understanding of how the Supreme Court should fulfill its supervisory role at the apex of the judicial system. He has noted, in particular, that a "common-law, discretion-conferring approach is ill suited . . . to a legal system in which the Supreme Court can review only an insignificant proportion of the decided cases." . . .

[The authors argue that an implication from Justice Scalia's rule-articulating approach is this:] All other things being equal, it would seem that he would be disinclined, on average, to vote to grant certiorari as often as a Justice with a narrower view of precedent. Justice Scalia has candidly stated that little is to be gained from granting certain kinds of cases, or cases in certain areas of the law, where the Court has already developed the governing rules to the maximum degree of productiveness. . . . [E]xamples of such unhelpful cases [are] those raising issues under the Commerce Clause and disputes about whether a given search or seizure was reasonable. In these and other cases where the Court either decides outcomes based explicitly on the unique circumstances or employs balancing tests involving an evaluation of multiple factors to arrive at results, Justice Scalia contends that it unproductively "begins to resemble a finder of fact more than a determiner of law."

. . . At bottom, the main consequences of his jurisprudential approach on the merits appear to be twofold: altering the mix of cases to favor areas that are more susceptible to articulation of clear legal rules, and necessitating fewer total precedents since the Court can effectively guide the lower courts with a more selective group of opinions that provide general rules with broad applicability.

[T]he information available about Justice Scalia's voting record is consistent with this expectation. In his first four full terms after joining the Court, he voted to grant review in fewer cases than any other Justice—averaging almost ten fewer grant votes per term than Justice Stevens, who as next in rank. One would not predict this stingy-record based on Justice Scalia's votes on the merits during those same terms, since he was regularly winning at that stage. . . . [I]t was not that Justice Scalia was voting "strategically" based on a calculation that he would not prevail on the merits. Instead, his different approach to the case selection process seems to derive from his distinct conception of the appropriate mode of decisionmaking and hence his views on how many precedents are required to fulfill the Court's central responsibilities.

Sanford Levinson has suggested that Justice Scalia's voting behavior on certiorari is out of step with his "unrelenting [advocacy] for the notion of the judge as positivistic enforcer of formalistic rules." Noting that Justice Scalia did not vote to grant many of the cases presenting conflicts among the circuits . . . Levinson questions how Justice Scalia can "fit his own behavior" within the commitment to rules that he has so insistently proclaimed. Viewed through a merits prism, Justice Scalia's willingness to bypass many cases involving conflicts—which Rule 10 states is one of the principal bases for granting certiorari—does appear paradoxical.

But Justice Scalia undoubtedly sees case selection through a different prism.... [I]t seems that Justice Scalia sees the task of case selection as distinct from the task of deciding cases on the merits because the goals at each stage are so fundamentally different. Whereas equal treatment and predictability are essential values at the merits stage, the key focus at the certiorari stage is to build a docket that will best enable the Court to carry out its crucial supervisory responsibilities at the head of the judicial system. This leads Justice Scalia to be willing to "tolerate a fair degree of diversity" in lower court decisions in order to reserve space on the Court's docket for cases in which it can best accomplish the more compelling work of crafting and issuing opinions that lay down clear rules of broad applicability.

At the opposite pole from the rule-articulating approach, Justice White epitomized the incrementalist approach. "The function of a judge, as White often reiterated, is to decide cases, not to write essays or to expound theories." In implementing this view, he "remained an incrementalist, self-effacing." Although Justice White was respectful of the principle of stare decisis, he tended to regard the decision reached in each case as the specific judgment rendered on a particular set of facts. When the constellation of facts differed in a later case, he was not reluctant to conclude that statements and observations made in the opinion from the earlier case would not control the Court's judgment.... "For White, the focus on the discrete case imposed a discipline that deterred loose or expansive exercise of the judicial power."

· · ·

In order for the incrementalist approach to be effective, the Court must take a sufficient number of cases in each distinct area to be able to create the body of judgments that are necessary to guide the lower courts. The Court might thus need several decisions to supply the guidance that Justice Scalia would prefer to provide through ... [a] general rule in a single case. But under the incrementalist approach, the Court does not need to formulate a rule that will produce acceptable results in a broad run of cases; rather the Court focuses on resolving only the dispute at hand, which eases the burdens of deciding each case. The main consequence of this jurisprudential approach on the merits is thus to require more precedents in each area but with each precedent expected to carry a lighter load in terms of illuminating the law.

Justices White's voting record on certiorari is consistent with this hypothesis. On both the Burger and the Rehnquist Courts, he invariably cast the most votes each term to grant review on the merits. Moreover, in cases that were granted on a bare four votes during that period, Justice White provided the essential fourth vote for review more often than any other Justice....

The Justices who incline more generally to a "standard-setting" or "balancing" approach present yet another perspective on case selection. One would expect that adherents to this view of precedent, all else being equal, would not tend to be extreme in their decisions on certiorari— neither seeking to confine the Court to a smaller number of opinions written with an eye to settling broad principles nor demanding a large number of judgments to create the pattern necessary to set a direction for the lower courts. In recent decades, Justice Powell has been the most devoted proponent of a balancing approach in many areas of the law and, to a lesser extent, Justice O'Connor has as well. With respect to both, the expected moderation is found in the voting data. During the last four terms of the Burger Court, Justice O'Connor ranked fourth in the number of grant votes per term, lagging far behind Justices White and Rehnquist but running well ahead of Justice Stevens at the low end. Justice Powell likewise came in near the middle, though he voted to grant somewhat fewer cases than Justice O'Connor. During the first five terms of the Rehnquist Court, after Justice Powell's retirement, Justice O'Connor remained at exactly the same ordinal—comfortably in the middle of the Court.

. . .

In the end, we do not wish to suggest that the jurisprudential hypotheses we have posited in this section are determinative of Justices' voting behavior on certiorari. As discussed further below, the blend of influences that affect each Justice's decisionmaking is far more complex than these artificially-tidy pigeonholes might indicate. Yet among the considerations constituting the subjective "feel" for the importance of an issue that each Justice brings to bear on case selection is undoubtedly his or her own understanding of what the Court is trying to accomplish when it decides cases on the merits. . . .

2. *Views on the Importance of Ensuring Uniformity* . . .

Another consideration for each Justice is the degree to which he or she is willing to tolerate disagreements among the lower courts. . . .

All of the Justices no doubt agree, on some level, that resolving conflicts among the lower courts is an essential task of the Supreme Court. . . . But there appears to be a surprisingly large variance in the importance that individual Justices attach to achieving uniformity in the application of federal law.

Justice White, of course, was at the far end of the spectrum; he fiercely advocated that a principal task of the Court is "to provide some degree of coherence and uniformity in federal law throughout the land." Indeed, departing from the general practice of maintaining the secrecy of certiorari votes, he frequently published dissents from denial of certiorari criticizing the Court for failing in its "special obligation to intercede and provide some definitive resolution of the issues." As an Associate Justice, Justice Rehnquist also was a staunch advocate of the need for national uniformity. . . .

This special emphasis on resolving conflicts is founded on several points. First, the strong policy in favor of uniformity is reflected in the Constitution itself, which vests the "one Supreme Court" with the judicial power to uphold and interpret federal law as "the supreme Law of the Land." Second, some view the Judges' Bill of 1925, which gave the Justices the authority to exercise control over most of their plenary docket, as designed to help achieve uniformity; indeed, some believe that the legislation was based on an explicit commitment that the Justices made to Congress to protect the uniformity of federal law in return for Congress' ceding the Court so much control over case selection. Third, conflicts create undesirable incentives for litigants to engage in forum shopping and for repeat players to continue litigating issues that they have lost in some jurisdictions in the hope of attaining a better outcome elsewhere. And finally, it is widely regarded as unfair and unseemly for litigants to receive different treatment based merely on the geographic accident of where their cases were filed.

Nonetheless, many of the Justices have indicated a far greater tolerance for conflicts, especially in their endorsement of the concept of "percolation," whereby the Court consciously allows conflicts to persist until the lower courts have offered more extensive guidance about the differing views on the legal issue presented. Then-Justice Rehnquist scoffed at the notion that percolation was valuable:

> And to go further and suggest that it is actually desirable to allow important questions of federal law to "percolate" in the lower courts for a few years before the Supreme Court takes them on seems to me a very strange suggestion; at best it is making a virtue of necessity.

But other Justices have strongly defended its use. Justice Stevens, for example, has noted:

> Although one of the Court's roles is to ensure the uniformity of federal law, we do not think that the Court must act to eradicate disuniformity as soon as it appears. . . . Disagreement in the lower courts facilitates percolation—the independent evaluation of a legal issue by different courts. The process of percolation allows a period of exploratory consideration and experimentation by lower courts before the Supreme Court ends the process with a nationally binding rule. The Supreme Court, when it decides a fully percolated issue, has the benefit of the experience of those lower courts. Irrespective of docket capacity, the Court should not be compelled to intervene to eradicate disuniformity when further percolation or experimentation is desirable.

Justice Ginsburg, too, has lauded the benefits of percolation: "We have in many instances recognized that when frontier legal problems are presented, periods of 'percolation' in, and diverse opinions from, state and federal appellate courts may yield a better informed and more enduring final pronouncement by this Court."

Embracing the concept of percolation demonstrates a willingness to tolerate disuniformity for a time—the period needed for multiple lower courts to address an issue and flesh out the relevant considerations—but not necessarily forever. Some Justices, however, have less concern about the existence of conflicts in general. Justice Stevens is of this view: "I would like to suggest, first, that the existence of differing rules of law in different sections of our great country is not always an intolerable evil and, second, that there are decisionmakers other than judges who could perform the task of resolving conflicts on questions of statutory construction."

The implications for case selection are straightforward. All else being equal, the higher the priority a Justice places on resolving conflicts, the more frequently he or she is likely to vote to grant review....

The voting data seems to bear out this prediction. Justice Stevens, who not only sees percolation as beneficial, but also has a higher tolerance for allowing conflicts to exist, has a relatively low grant rate. In the last four terms of the Burger Court, for example, he voted to grant review less often than any other Justice. In the first five terms of the Rehnquist Court, he remained in the lower end of the spectrum, outdone in his parsimony only by the extremely low totals compiled by Justices Scalia and Kennedy. In contrast, Justice White, who advocated tirelessly for the resolution of conflicts, made that a priority in his case selection decisions by regularly voting to grant review in cases involving conflicts. Moreover, he usually had the highest grant rate throughout both periods and, by the time he retired, he was regularly voting to grant over fifty percent more cases than any other Justice.

.   .   .

Chief Justice Rehnquist is an interesting case.... [W]hile an Associate Justice, he championed the need for uniformity and deprecated percolation. Indeed, as recently as the mid–1980s, when the Court was still hearing approximately 150 cases per term, he found the tiny percentage of cases that the Court was able to review "intolerable," stating that it was "simply not enough to assure that the views of the Supreme Court in various areas of the law shall, over the long run, prevail." ... In addition, his voting behavior on certiorari was consistent with these views. In the 1982 and 1983 Terms, he outpaced even Justice White to lead the Court in voting to grant cases. In the 1984 and 1985 Terms, however, the number of cases in which he supported review began to decline, and this slide continued after he was appointed as Chief Justice in 1986. A change in his views about how important it is to resolve conflicts may account for this abrupt shift in his approach—since he has not reiterated his criticism of percolation or disuniformity in recent years, instead stating that he "no longer votes to take a case just because it is 'interesting.' " His ascent to the Chief Justiceship, with its distinct responsibilities, likely also played a prominent role in altering his behavior on certiorari.

.   .   .

3. *Special Interest in Certain Legal Issues and in Effectuating Social Change*

Another element in the "feel" that individual Justices have for which cases are sufficiently important to deserve plenary review is their special concern for . . . certain areas of the law. . . . Justice Brennan, for example, observed that an essential feature of the certiorari process is that it "provides a forum in which the particular interests or sensitivities of individual justices may be expressed."

. . . [I]n areas where a Justice has a strong personal interest, strategic considerations play an unusually heavy role. . . . Indeed, Perry argued that in areas where they have a special interest, Justices employ a different and far more strategic decisional calculus:

> The justice usually knows how he wants doctrine to develop in the area, and he therefore acts strategically at the cert. decision. That is, a case is seen as certworthy if it is one where the justice thinks he will win on the merits, and if it allows him to move doctrine in the way he wishes.

While particular interest in specific areas affects the decision processes of all Justices in varying degrees, some Justices take matters even further by consciously pressing to shape the direction of American law and society by means of the Court's agenda. . . .

The paradigmatic example of a Justice with this approach is Justice Brennan. He believed that the "federal courts have been delegated a special responsibility for the definition and enforcement of the guarantees of the Bill of Rights and the Fourteenth Amendment" and that these vital guarantees "are ineffectual when the will and power to enforce them is lacking." By the 1961 Term, Justice Brennan was thus "taking an active leadership role in trying to find cases that would promote his reforms." And he was very successful: "In the years between 1961 and 1969, the Supreme Court interpreted the Fourteenth Amendment to nationalize civil rights, making the great guarantees of life, liberty, and property binding on all governments throughout the nation. In so doing, the Court fundamentally reshaped the law of this land." As the Court's prevailing ideology became more conservative with the shift from Chief Justice Warren to Chief Justice Burger in 1969, Justice Brennan continued to push the Court's agenda, though he moved to social issues on which he was more likely to win. He was consistently joined in these efforts by Justice Marshall, who had developed similar views on the Court's appropriate role from his many years of crusading as a lawyer for school desegregation.

While Justices Brennan and Marshall promoted a liberal agenda, this broader conception of the role of the Court—as an instrument of social change—is not viewpoint specific. A conservative Justice might also hold a similarly broad conception of the Court's role and thus seek to build an agenda that would enable it to steer the course of social change in a conservative direction. When Chief Justice Burger joined the Court in 1969, for example, he actively sought to undo the "adventurous egalitarianism" of the Warren Court and reinforce the forces of social order by strengthening the position of law enforcement. He was soon joined by Justice Rehnquist, who candidly stated that he and the Chief Justice sought "a halt to . . . the sweeping rules made in the days of the Warren Court." Although Chief Justice Burger's quest was ultimately less successful than expected, his efforts to shape the Court's agenda to achieve this broader goal had distinct implications for decisionmaking at the case selection stage.

Other Justices, in contrast, believe that the Court should maintain a lower profile and not consciously seek to be an engine of social change. Justice White, for example, "saw no major role for the Court in directing the course of the nation's social change" and "when asked what was his greatest case, declined to identify any particular case, observing that he did not perceive that it was his job to decide great cases but simply to decide cases." Many other Justices have shared this traditional preference, viewing the Court's proper role as responsive rather than proactive. . . .

These different conceptions of the Court's proper role in American society have ramifications for the Justices' decisions on case selection. . . . A Justice who prefers that the Court maintain a more reactive posture will presumably not reach out aggressively for cases that will effectuate social change. Moreover, such a Justice may actively avoid cases that raise socially divisive issues or questions that, in the Justice's view, properly belong to the other branches of government.

. . . [A] Justice who . . . actively seeks to drive certain doctrines in a particular direction will likely skew his or her votes in favor of cases that can advance those doctrines—as long as the Justice believes that he or she will prevail on the merits. Indeed, if such a Justice is pessimistic about prevailing on the merits then he or she might well engage in a "defensive denial" to avoid a decision that would potentially undermine the preferred direction of judicial doctrine. . . . All other things being equal, when such a Justice is confident of routinely winning he or she would likely vote to grant cases more aggressively; conversely, when the Justice regularly expects to lose he or she would likely vote to grant fewer cases, perhaps as a general matter but at least in those areas of greatest interest and concern.

With regard to quantity, the voting data on Justices Brennan and Marshall is consistent with this expectation. During the 1960s, when they were confident of delivering a majority vote in most important cases, their grant rates were relatively high. Yet by the last few terms before they retired, fraught with concern that the Court was "involved in a new curtailment of the Fourteenth Amendment's scope," their grant rates had dropped dramatically. And though their overall totals remained at or near the Court's declining median in voting to grant review, this fact masked a shift in the composition of their grant votes. From the "paid" list of ordinary cases, they were casting far fewer grant votes than the median and were rivaling Justice Stevens' figures at the low end of the spectrum; however, from the list of "in forma pauperis" cases filed by indigents and prisoners, which consisted mainly of criminal procedural issues and alleged civil rights violations, they supported review far more often than any of the other Justices.

This continued emphasis on criminal justice and civil rights issues at first seems somewhat surprising given the strong conservative trend of the Court. But the Court's results in such cases were far from uniform, leaving open the possibility that Justices Brennan and Marshall could win if they found sufficiently compelling cases. Moreover, their interest in criminal justice and civil rights issues remained intense, especially in capital cases. Indeed, in capital cases, they cared deeply not only about shaping the doctrine, but also about voiding death sentences in individual cases.

In sum, Justices who have a special interest in certain kinds of issues, especially the kinds of issues that involve the Court in shaping the direction of broader social change, are likely to be much more sensitive to strategic considerations in those areas. . . .

C. *Further Consideration of the Factors Affecting Decisionmaking on Certiorari*

. . . [O]ur central point is that each Justice's particular conception of what role the Supreme Court should play in the judicial system and in American life inevitably informs his or her views about what makes an issue "important" enough to address and resolve on the merits.

These perspectives somehow blend together with rule-based and strategic considerations to form the contours of each Justice's voting behavior on certiorari. . . .

. . .

. . . Our discussion of three "jurisprudential" variables—views on the nature of precedent, the importance of uniformity in federal law, and the Court's proper role in shaping the law and effectuating social change—represents only a sampling of the kinds of influences that can affect the Justices' decisional calculus. External influences, such as the enactment of new legislation, realignment among the lower courts, economic developments, and changes in the public's social and political interests, also can exert unpredictable influences on the Justices' views about which issues are sufficiently "important" to justify the Court's granting of plenary review at any given point in time. So do more idiosyncratic factors. . . .

The complexity of decisionmaking at the certiorari stage is exacerbated by the varying weights that the different factors may carry with regard to each individual case, which makes quantification of the importance of each factor virtually impossible. Justice Douglas captured this fact in his vivid description of the certiorari process: "The electronics industry—resourceful as it is—will never produce a machine to handle these problems. They require at times the economist's understanding, the poet's insight, the executive's experience, the political scientist's understanding, the historian's perspective." Nonetheless, it is worthwhile to explore the various considerations that may underlie the Justices' case selection decisions so as to facilitate a better understanding of that critical function by those who observe the Court, those who participate before it as litigants, and those who serve on it. Although, ultimately, it is hard to imagine that the case selection process could or should be confined by purely objective factors, a greater appreciation of the considerations that can and do shape the Justices' certiorari decisions may prove to be valuable in allowing a more conscious consideration of the appropriate content of the key "importance" criterion. . . .

Lee Epstein & Jack Knight,[57] *The Choices Justices Make* (1998)

. . .

Bargaining

. . .

. . . [T]he cert decision contains all the makings of a classic bargaining problem. First, justices want to reach an agreement over whether to hear a case; if they are consistently unable to reach such agreements, they will fail to attain their main goal of issuing policy proclamations. Second, justices often disagree over which agreement—to grant or deny—is better. Available data suggest that at least one justice votes to grant certiorari in nearly 50 percent of the cases the Court discusses and denies, and at least one votes to deny cert in 98 percent that the Court grants. Finally, justices have various tools at their disposal to enable them to bargain with their colleagues, with a potentially powerful one being the threat to issue an opinion dissenting from a denial of certiorari. . . .

We look at these circulated dissents as bargaining tools because their primary purpose is to force justices to change their votes from denies to grants. Justice Stevens said as much in a rather odd opinion in which he complained about the practice [quoting from his opinion in *Singleton* excerpted above]. . . .

Other justices and their clerks concur: "After [the cert] conference . . . there were certainly attempts at persuasion. . . . The major vehicle for this was a dissent from denial; I mean, those were addressed to the Court as much as they are to the public. . . ." Another simply said that dissents from denials "are often attempts to persuade other justices—at least threats of denials [sic] are."

57. Epstein is now Beatrice Kuhn Professor of Law and Professor of Political Science, Northwestern University; Knight is Professor of Political Science, Washington University in St. Louis.

The justices have also supplied reasons for the effectiveness of this form of bargaining. Most important is that these dissents represent threats to the institutional integrity of the Court. . . .

Rather than see a dissent go unanswered or a private vote published, justices may succumb to the threat and join the dissenter. That may be what happened in *Bowers v. Hardwick*, in which the Court considered the constitutionality of a Georgia law outlawing sodomy. When an insufficient number of his colleagues voted to hear the case, Justice White circulated a rather pointed dissenting opinion. His major claim was that the circuit court's decision, which held that the Georgia law infringed on Hardwick's constitutional rights, conflicted with decisions in other circuits especially a case out of the District of Columbia holding that no constitutional right to engage in homosexual activity exists. "Given this lack of consistency among the Circuits on this important constitutional question," White wrote, "I would grant the petition." . . .

White's threat of going public with the dissent worked. Within a week of its circulation, White had picked up a sufficient number of votes to grant cert. The Brennan, Marshall, and Powell files were difficult to interpret, but the following events seem to have transpired. After White filed his dissent, Rehnquist and Brennan joined it. Rehnquist felt so strongly about hearing the case that he told White he "anticipate[d] writing a little something" himself. At the next day's conference, White picked up a fourth vote, Marshall's, but six days later Brennan changed his vote to a deny. Chief Justice Burger saved White's cause by agreeing to a grant. Later, White garnered enough votes to write a landmark majority opinion reversing the lower court's decision.[58]

Is *Bowers* an anomaly? Or do justices attempt to bargain this way on a regular basis? On the one hand, we would not expect to find justices filing dissents in every case in which they disagree with the Court's decision to deny the cert petition. It may be that another justice has already written such an opinion, which they can join. Or they may not wish to spend precious time writing a dissent if they think they will ultimately fail to pick up four votes. We should also keep in mind the risk justices take in circulating dissents. If they do not convert a sufficient number of justices, they face the choice . . . of retracting their writing or publishing it. On occasion, they must publish so that their future threats will be credible. But therein lies the risk. For the reasons provided by Stevens, justices may be less than keen to make public their private disagreements. On the other hand, because a dissent from a cert denial is one of the few bargaining mechanisms available to the justices during this stage, we should find some evidence of its use—and, *occasionally*, of its successful uses. This follows from the fact that the primary reason justices file such dissents is to change votes; they would have no reason to circulate them if they thought they would never have such an effect.

58. [Editors' note: What these authors call a "landmark" opinion was overturned 17 years later in *Lawrence v. Texas*, as discussed in Chapter One, above.]

With these expectations noted, let us turn to the data. We ... consult[ed] the case files of several justices and the publicly available records for two terms of the Burger Court, 1982 and 1983. We could obtain data on "successes"—those instances in which dissents pick up three or more votes—only from the private files because, if a justice converts a deny to a grant via a dissenting opinion, that dissent is never made public. To gather information on failures, we relied on Harold J. Spaeth's U.S. Supreme Court Judicial Database, which contains information on published dissenting opinions. We also consulted the private records of Justices Brennan and Marshall, where we found unpublished dissents—those that were retracted by writers when they did not succeed in converting a sufficient number of votes.

Table 3–1 displays the results yielded by these procedures. As indicated, the justices invoked this particular bargaining tool with some selectivity. In only 19 percent of the cases in which they desired to see cert granted, but the Court denied, did they circulate a written dissent. For the reasons we have discussed, this finding is not unexpected. What is interesting, however, is that some justices use this tool far more frequently than others: Rehnquist circulated fourteen dissents, only five fewer than the number of majority opinions he wrote during the 1983 term, and White and Marshall issued them in more than a third of the cases in which they disagreed with the Court's denial.

TABLE 3-1
Dissents from Denials of Certiorari

Justice	N of Conference Votes Cast to Grant Cert when the Court Initially Denies	N of Opinions* Dissenting from Denial of Cert that Did Not Get Fourth Vote	N of Opinions Dissenting from Denial of Cert that Got Fourth Vote
Burger	20	4	0
Brennan	22	2	0
White	50	14	6
Marshall	14	11	0
Blackmun	36	0	0
Powell	23	1	1
Rehnquist	80	10	4
Stevens	17	1	1
O'Connor	23	0	0
Total	285	43	12

Data Sources: We thank Gregory A. Caldeira for supplying the vote data in column 1. Data on published and unpublished dissents are from the U.S. Supreme Court Judicial Database and the case and administrative files of Justices William J. Brennan Jr. and Thurgood Marshall, Library of Congress; and Lewis F. Powell Jr., Washington and Lee University School of Law.

*Published and unpublished.

Note: Data on conference votes and the number of published opinions are from the 1982 term; all other data are from the 1983 term. The rationale for the difference in years is that almost all 1982 term dissenting opinions that succeeded in picking up a fourth vote were eventually decided on their merits in the 1983 term.

Data Note: Column 1 includes only cases in which a vote was taken; column 2 includes only dissenting opinions (not votes) and excludes stock dissents, such as those Brennan and Marshall issued in all death penalty cases that the Court refused to hear. For an explanation, including the data and more detailed coding rules, navigate to: *http://www.artsci.wustl.edu/~polisci/epstein/choices/*.

Equally intriguing is that this form of bargaining occasionally has the desired results: about 23 percent of the fifty-five dissents succeeded in picking up four votes. To put it another way, of the 150 or so cases decided with an opinion during the 1983 term, 9 started as denials of cert. These included two significant cases, New York v. Quarles[59] and Bose Corp. v. Consumers Union of the United States.[60]

Quarles began in 1980 with a woman reporting to two New York police officers that she had been raped by a tall black man who was armed. When the officers drove to the site they spotted the alleged assailant, Benjamin Quarles, ordered him to stop, and asked him where his weapon was. Quarles responded, "The gun is over there." At this

59. [End note 12 in original] 467 U.S. 649 (1984).

60. [End note 12 in original] 466 U.S. 485 (1984).

point the officers placed Quarles under arrest and read him his *Miranda* rights. But a trial court judge excluded Quarles's statement concerning the gun because he had spoken before hearing his rights.

The case made its way to the Supreme Court, but on April 14, 1983, the justices voted to deny cert. In response, Burger filed a short statement saying that he dissented from the denial and would prefer to reverse summarily the decision of the court below. About a month later, Rehnquist circulated a dissenting opinion in which he not only urged his colleagues to hear the case but offered his view on *how* the Court should decide it. Rehnquist believed that the state's argument, namely that the justices should adopt a public safety exception to the *Miranda* rule, was entitled to "careful consideration. If there are ever to be 'exigent circumstances' this case would seem to be as likely a candidate as any."

On May 23, the Court took another vote on cert, which resulted in a success for Rehnquist: he picked up a sufficient number of votes (Burger, Powell, and O'Connor) for a grant. About a year later, the Court followed the course of action Rehnquist had suggested in his dissent and carved out a public safety exception to *Miranda*; in fact, Rehnquist wrote the majority opinion.

Bose Corporation v. Consumers Union followed a similar path, at least initially. This suit involved a maker of stereo speakers, the Bose Corporation, which believed that *Consumer Reports* magazine had reviewed one of its products with "reckless disregard" for the truth. In mid-April 1983, when the Court voted on whether to hear the case, only Rehnquist and White cast clear votes to grant. O'Connor voted to reverse summarily or to deny; the Chief Justice [Burger] voted to "Join 3," meaning—in all likelihood—that he would go along with a grant if three others voted for it, and the rest voted to deny. His colleagues' votes prompted White to file a dissent a week later, which Rehnquist, Brennan, and O'Connor joined. In the dissent, White like Rehnquist in *Quarles* freely offered his opinion on how the case should come out on the merits. He believed that the court of appeals had applied the wrong standard of review and would have vacated its judgment. Unlike Rehnquist in *Quarles*, however, White failed to prevail on the merits. The Court went on to affirm the decision of the lower court, resulting in a victory for the Consumers Union.

From these cases and the data displayed in Table 3–1, what do we learn about bargaining at the cert stage? The first and most obvious lesson is that the decision over cert does indeed present the justices with opportunities for bargaining. Granting cert is an inherently strategic decision, and Court members seem well aware of their mutual dependencies. Second, justices take advantage of at least one tool—dissent from a denial of cert—that enables them to bargain with their colleagues. Although they circulate them selectively, just as we expected, they do circulate them, and with a modicum of success. Finally, because bargaining is a form of interdependent interaction, we can begin to understand the importance of such strategic behavior for the course of the law. One has only to consider *Bowers, Quarles, Bose,* and many other cases that the Court never would have decided had it not been for the threat of going public with an opinion dissenting from the denial of cert.

.   .   .

FORWARD THINKING

The overall contention of this chapter is that we cannot understand the choices justices make—from the decision on certiorari through the choice of policy in the majority opinion—without taking into account the strategic nature of the decision-making context. Justices, we argue, do not make their choices in isolation; they must and do pay some heed to the preferences of others and the actions they expect others to take.

Important support for our argument, we believe, would come from evidence demonstrating that justices are "forward-thinking" actors, meaning that they make a particular choice based on what they think will happen in the future. Consider the decision to grant cert. If justices think prospectively, we would expect them to vote to deny or grant review based on what they think will happen at the merits stage. . . . After all, why would a policy-oriented justice vote to review a case if she did not think her side could muster the support of at least four others at the merits stage?

In fact, data suggest that justices do . . . think prospectively before they agree to hear a case. By way of evidence, [earlier] we discussed reversal rates, providing support for the proposition that justices grant cert to cases that they want to *reverse* in accordance with their policy preferences. One could argue, therefore, that reversal rates provide clear evidence of strategic calculations: a justice would vote to hear only those cases she thinks the majority will reverse. But one could just as easily argue that such rates are the product of pure preference-driven behavior: a justice votes to hear cases she wants to reverse, regardless of how she thinks the Court will vote.

To overcome this problem of behavioral equivalence, let us turn to two kinds of conduct that would be difficult to explain if justices did not think prospectively at the cert stage: aggressive grants and defensive denials. A grant of certiorari is described as *aggressive* when the justices take a case that may not warrant review "because they have calculated that it has certain characteristics that would make it particularly good for developing a doctrine in a certain way, and the characteristics make it likely to win on their merits." Typically, scholars have suggested that such grants occur when a justice *agrees* with a lower court ruling and believes that the majority of the Court will go along. By this logic, she votes to grant cert because she hopes to give the ruling the weight of a Supreme Court affirmance to make it the policy of the nation. When justices deny cert to cases that they would like to hear because they believe that they will not prevail at the merits stage, they are issuing a *defensive denial*. Many analysts interpret this action as a clear form of sophisticated behavior. On this account, a defensive denial is most likely to occur when a justice votes against cert, even though she disliked the lower court decision, because she believes that the Court will probably affirm the decision.

Do justices regularly engage in these forms of strategic behavior? They say they do. As one put it, "I might think that the Nebraska Supreme Court made a horrible decision, but I wouldn't want to take the case, for if we take the case and affirm it, then it would become precedent." The classic logic of a defensive denial. By the same token, the justices' clerks—who are charged with making recommendations on cert to the justices—occasionally couch their memoranda in strategic terms. Consider the advice Marshall's clerk offered to his boss in *Wiegand v. United States*. In this case the U.S. Court of Appeals for the Ninth Circuit had upheld a search warrant that agents had used to seize child pornography from a man's house, a decision contrary to Marshall's preferences:

> Petitioner argues that the terms of the warrant are so broad that they permit the seizure of materials protected by the First Amendment.... The First Circuit seemed to be troubled by a similar argument ... noting that "the question of whether a warrant authorizing seizures of films depicting sexual activity by children under 18 violates the particularity requirement of Fourth Amendment is a significant one of current interest." Thus, there is an incipient split [among] the Circuits here on an important question. Nonetheless I would not vote to grant on this issue, because I think that this Court will not find any First Amendment problem with such a warrant. Seems to me that a defensive denial is in order.

More systematic evidence comes from a recent investigation of cert voting during the Court's 1982 term. Unlike many other research efforts in this area, this study went to great lengths to include variables to account for the ideological preferences of the individual justices *along with* those of their colleagues. The results are clear. While the authors find strong evidence of policy voting, defined as voting to grant or deny based on ideological preferences, they show that there is equally strong support for strategic behavior, defined as voting to grant or deny inconsistently with one's ideal policy point. They also find that such strategic behavior takes the form of both aggressive grants and defensive denials.[61]

Consideration of the Preferences and Expected Behavior of External Actors

Most claims about the existence (or lack thereof) of forward thinking at the cert stage assess the extent to which justices base their decision to deny or grant cert on what they think will happen at the merits stage. On our account, strategic justices do more than consider the preferences

---

61. [End Note 3 in original] The study is Caldeira, Wright, and Zorn, "Strategic Voting and Gatekeeping in the Supreme Court," (paper presented at the 1996 annual meeting of the American Political Science Association, San Francisco).

and expected actions of their colleagues; they also take into account the likely reactions of other relevant actors, such as Congress and the president. The logic here ... is straightforward: if the objective of justices is to see their favored policies become the ultimate law of the land, then they must take into account the preferences of other major actors and the actions they expect them to take. If they do not, they risk seeing massive noncompliance with their rulings, meaning that their policy fails to take on the force of law; or having Congress replace their most preferred position with their least; or other forms of retaliation, such as removing the Court's jurisdiction to hear cases, keeping judicial salaries constant, and impeaching justices.

Translating this claim to the cert stage, we would expect a strategically oriented justice to engage in two kinds of behavior: (1) declining to hear a case if she believed a merits decision favorable to her preferred policy position would anger relevant external actors and (2) agreeing to hear a case that relevant actors wanted the Court to resolve, even if she would be unable to place policy on her ideal point.

DECLINING TO DECIDE CASES. The first expectation—refusing to decide certain disputes—flows directly from our claims about the importance of the policy goals and the existence of strategic interaction on the Court: justices would be loath to take cases, even if they believed they could obtain the necessary support for their position inside the Court, if they simultaneously believed that political actors would move policy far from their ideal points.

Anecdotal support for this "dispute-avoidance" proposition abounds. There are, for example, many salient and, seemingly, certworthy petitions that the Court has denied over the years at least in part because it wanted to avoid collision with Congress and the president. The justices never resolved the question of the constitutionality of the Vietnam War, despite its obvious importance and many requests to do so. In addition, Supreme Court clerks occasionally point out the political consequences of accepting petitions. Sociolegal scholar Doris Provine provides a nice example. After the Court issued its highly controversial decision in *Brown v. Board of Education* in 1954, it was asked the very next year to resolve a challenge to a miscegenation law (*Naim v. Naim*). Justice Harold Burton's clerk made the following recommendation to his boss:

> In view of the difficulties engendered by the segregation cases it would be wise judicial policy to duck this question for the time being ... [but] I don't think we can be honest and say that the claim is unsubstantial.... It is with some hesitation ... that I recommend that we NPJ ["note probable jurisdiction," the functional equivalent of granting review]. This hesitation springs from the feeling that we ought to give the present fire a chance to burn down.

Burton declined to take his clerk's advice .... [62]

. . .

62. [Editors' Note: The Court at first issued a per curiam order stating, inter alia, that the record was inadequate to make clear the relationship that the couple (who

... We supply further evidence from more recent data on cases involving equal employment practices.... [D]uring the 1978 term, when the Republican Court was more conservative than the Democratic Congress and president, the justices rejected nearly 90 percent of these petitions, although many presented important issues. Why? On our account, the Republican majority on the Court, while believing it could prevail on the merits, thought that the Democratic president and Congress would override the Court's decision. Rather than see its holdings reversed, it avoided the dispute. When the political landscape changed in the early 1980s with the election of Ronald Reagan and a Republican Senate, the Court also moved in a more conservative direction. During the 1982 term, it agreed to hear 28 percent of the employment cases—nearly 15 percent more than it did in 1978 and more than four times its average acceptance rate (6 percent) for that term.

. . .

AGREEING TO DECIDE CASES. Just as justices are loath to take cases that may ultimately lead to the creation of "unfavorable" policy or collisions with Congress, we suspect that they are equally reluctant to ignore disputes that the government wants them to resolve—even if they believe that they would be unable to set policy on their ideal points. Avoiding such cases might generate a backlash just as great as deciding cases against the interests of other government actors.

This proposition follows from the fact that perceptions that the Court is dodging its responsibilities may generate attacks on its institutional authority.... [W]e have only to recall that during the mid–1930s, when the Court was under siege from Congress and the president, one of the charges against it was that it "was using its discretionary jurisdiction to duck important cases." The justices responded to this allegation by assuring Congress that they follow the nonmajority Rule of Four precisely because they prefer "to be at fault in taking jurisdiction rather than to be at fault in rejecting it."

The justices' reply quelled this particular congressional concern, and it may have helped to stave off dramatic plans to change the fundamental nature of the Court. Still, this historical episode and several others indicate that the justices occasionally open themselves up to criticism by ducking cases, even if the critics are using the dispute-avoidance charge

had married in North Carolina) had to the State of Virginia, thus preventing the constitutional issue from being presented in " 'clean cut and concrete form, unclouded by such problems.' " The Court vacated the judgment and "remanded to the Supreme Court of Appeals [of Virginia] in order that the case may be returned to the Circuit Court of the City of Ports-mouth for action not inconsistent with this opinion." Naim v. Naim, 350 U.S. 891 (1955). Five months later, the Supreme Court denied a motion to recall the mandate and set the case for oral argument, stating—again by unsigned per curiam order, and without any explanation—that the Virginia court's decision (on remand from the Supreme Court's prior order) adhering to its earlier decision and refusing to send the case back to the trial court "leaves the case devoid of a properly presented federal question." Naim v. Naim, 350 U.S. 985 (1956). The decision was widely criticized at the time as unprincipled.]

as a ruse to accomplish other objectives. More systematic data suggest that the justices may be responding to these criticisms or, at the very least, hoping to deter them by taking cases the government wants them to decide, even if that is not their desire. For example, of the five employment cases ... that the Republican 1978 Court agreed to decide, the Democratic federal government played a role in all but one. More general analyses demonstrating the phenomenal success of the United States at the cert stage also shore up the point.... Caldeira and Wright's research, which took into account a range of explanations for the cert decision including whether the United States was a petitioner, reaches a similar conclusion: even if a government petition presents no evidence of real conflict and no amici file in its support, the likelihood of Court review is a staggering 37 percent, compared with an average review rate of 8 percent for the term Caldeira and Wright examined.

There are many possible explanations for these findings. Provine writes, "Because of their quality, the clerks and justices probably read [U.S.] petitions with special care." Caldeira and Wright focus on the solicitor general, who represents the United States in Court. They suggest that the "solicitor general's expertise is evidently highly respected by the justices.' " But neither these reasons nor others that scholars have offered [But none] preclude the possibility that a fear of retaliation plays some role in explaining the Court's unusual willingness to resolve government disputes ...

... When deciding whether to hear cases, not only do Court members take into account the preferences of their colleagues and the actions they expect them to take at the merits stage, but also they consider the likely reactions of other political actors, most notably members of Congress. Such calculation, as we have argued, occasionally leads them to avoid taking disputes that they may want to resolve and, at times, to take cases that they may not want to decide.

· · ·

The Rule of Four

· · ·

... The Rule of Four ... has two important characteristics ... : the justices share knowledge of it, and they have informed external communities of its existence and maintenance.

Moreover, like all institutions, the Rule of Four provides information to assist the justices in making choices. Most obvious is that a justice knows that she *generally* must attract at least three other votes to hear a case. If she does not, she will need to bargain with her colleagues, perhaps by circulating a dissent from a certiorari denial, to attain the requisite number.

As the emphasis on the word "generally" indicates, exceptions occur. Consider, for example, the course of events in New York v.

Uplinger,[63] in which a lower court struck down a state law that prohibited loitering "in a public place for the purpose of engaging, or soliciting another person to engage, in deviate sexual intercourse or other sexual behavior of a deviate nature." Four justices had voted to hear the case, but Brennan voted to deny cert, no doubt fearing that his colleagues would reverse the lower court's decision. During the conference on the merits, Brennan led a charge to have the Court dismiss certiorari as improvidently granted (a "DIG"). He took this step, we suspect, because he thought it would produce the best possible outcome, given his distaste for the law. A DIG, while establishing no Supreme Court precedent, would at least allow the lower court ruling to stand. As it turned out, Brennan was able to secure a majority of five for the DIG by circulating an unsigned written (per curiam) opinion. But the opinion elicited a harshly worded dissent from Rehnquist, who had voted to grant certiorari and against Brennan's DIG:

> Today the Court dismisses the writ of certiorari in this case as improvidently granted.... In so doing the Court leaves untouched a decision invalidating *in toto* a statute designed to protect individual citizens and residential neighborhoods from lewd conduct that affronts peoples' sensibilities in the most intimate of matters and that made people apprehensive about walking neighborhood streets. Four members voted to grant certiorari in this case, yet the majority advances no convincing reason for side-stepping the "Rule of Four" and dismissing the case now.

With these words, Rehnquist was doing more than informing Brennan that he well understood his motives for the DIG. He was making a public proclamation that Brennan's opinion conflicted with the Rule of Four (because four justices wanted to decide the case) and diminished the rule's importance. Justice Stevens also expressed concern. In a private memorandum to Brennan, dated March 1, 1984, he wrote, "If you can get five votes on your per curiam, I will happily make a sixth; alternatively I can make a fifth if one of the original votes to grant will join you. I am most reluctant, however, to join this kind of disposition over the dissent of four Members of the Court, who voted to grant the case, even though, as you know, I think this was a particularly unwise grant."

What concerned Rehnquist and Stevens was that in any case in which only four justices supported certiorari, a subset of deniers could turn around and try a DIG, as Brennan had done. If this behavior occurred on a regular basis, justices would be unable to develop reliable expectations about the course of cases that attain a minimum winning certiorari vote, and, in the long term, it would undermine the rule as a norm structuring the internal dynamics of the Court.

Rehnquist eventually withdrew his dissenting opinion in *Uplinger*, but he may have won the larger battle. During the rest of the Burger Court years, the Court voted to DIG only one case, and it was by a

63. [End note 7 in original] 467 U.S. 246 (1984).

conference vote of 6–3. But we would not want to conclude that DIGs (above the objections of four justices) will never occur again. Indeed, this deviation and others from the Rule of Four would not be unexpected from a Court full of policy-oriented justices. Rather, what the *Uplinger* story suggests is that systematic departures from the Rule of Four remain rare because they may generate informal sanctions such as a Rehnquist-type dissent, which would make public otherwise private information about the certiorari vote. Accordingly, the rule assures the justices that, in the main, cases obtaining four or more votes will receive consideration on their merits.

Uplinger suggests another way the Rule of Four figures into the justices strategic calculations: it helps them anticipate what their colleagues will do at the plenary stage. Brennan's knowledge of the justices' votes on certiorari, coupled with his beliefs about their preferences, must have propelled him to try the DIG. He felt certain that the majority would reject his preferred position and that a DIG was the best he could do. More generally, . . . the Rule of Four invites forward thinking. Policy-oriented justices know that if they are to attain their goals they must take those cases that they believe will lead to their preferred outcomes and request those that will not. But if they fail at the review phase, as Brennan did in *Uplinger*, then they can use their knowledge of certiorari votes to bargain at the later stages. Seen in this way, the Rule of Four assists justices in making their strategic calculations throughout the decision-making process.

But—and this is crucial—just because justices know of the existence of the Rule of Four and realize that it induces prospective thinking does not mean that they will be able to gauge *with certainty* their colleagues' future actions. The rule only helps them to formulate guesses that they must supplement with other information, such as knowledge of their colleagues' prior policy preferences. There are two reasons. In *Uplinger* we saw evidence of the first—the existence of multiple strategies for making choices at the cert stage. The second is the ability of justices to cast ambiguous cert votes.

We begin with the strategy problem, namely, that forward thinking does not always lead justices to adopt one particular strategy over others. As we discussed . . . , the reversal strategy—voting to *grant* certiorari and then voting to *reverse* on the merits—may be the most common, and the DIG, the least. But in between are others, including the aggressive grant approach, in which justices take cases to *affirm* a lower court outcome that they favor. The existence of multiple strategies makes it difficult for justices to formulate expectations about their colleagues' likely actions unless they take into account other factors.

To see this, recall the reaction to White's dissent from the Court's denial of certiorari in *Bowers v. Hardwick*. Apparently believing that White was pursuing an *aggressive grant* strategy, Brennan and Marshall expressed their support for White's dissent. But, when Rehnquist (Brennan's ideological opposite) also joined the dissent, Brennan changed his vote, presumably because Rehnquist's "join" made him aware that White was actually pursuing a reversal strategy. By the same token, justices will be unable to formulate reliable expectations about their colleagues' future actions if they base those expectations solely on the assumption that they will follow a *reversal strategy* . . . .

Equally confounding to justices attempting to formulate expectations about their colleagues' likely behavior at the merits stage is the ambiguous certiorari vote. Typically, such a vote takes the form on a "Join 3" or a "pass." Because justices cast these votes for many different reasons—as one justice put it, "All nine of us use the term 'Join 3.' But I think we each have our own meaning"—they may be even less useful in formulating expectations about outcomes at the merits stage than an outright grant or deny. . . .

. . .

In short, ambiguous votes and multiple strategies complicate the task justices face in using the information they obtain from the certiorari vote to formulate expectations. The Rule of Four—a norm of no small consequence—certainly assists them in making these calculations, but they must supplement that information with other evidence concerning their colleagues' preferences. Only by doing so are they likely to feel confident in the beliefs they formulate.

H.W. Perry, Jr.[64], *Deciding to Decide: Agenda Setting in the United States Supreme Court* 274–84 (1991)

[After interviewing five Justices, sixty-four law clerks, seven judges on the federal courts of appeal, four lawyers from the Solicitor General's office, and one person from the Supreme Court Clerk's Office, Perry concludes that, while strategic decision-making does take place, it is not the dominant factor. Perry argues that there are two different sets of decisional processes used by Justices in deciding whether to grant cert.]

. . . [T]he decisional steps for one case may look very different from those used by the same justice to evaluate another case. Likewise, the same case may be treated differently by different justices. I call these channels "decision modes." This conceptualization offers a synthesis and a more helpful way of addressing the question of whether or not the justices act "politically" or "legally," "ideologically" or "judge-like."

I have named the two modes of decision making the "outcome mode" and the "jurisprudential mode." . . . Briefly, if a justice cares strongly about the outcome of a case on the merits at the time of the cert. decision, then he will enter the outcome mode to decide whether or not to take the case. If, however, the justice does not feel particularly strongly about the outcome of a case on the merits, he enters the

64. Associate Professor of Law and Government, University of Texas.

jurisprudential mode with all its attendant steps. The steps differ in the two modes. Oversimplifying at this point, when in the jurisprudential mode, the justice makes his decision based on legalistic, jurisprudential types of considerations such as whether or not there is a split in the federal circuit courts of appeals. In the outcome mode, while the justice does not ignore jurisprudential concerns, they do not dominate his decision process. Rather, it is dominated by strategic considerations related to the outcome of the case on the merits. Jurisprudential concerns play a rather different role in the calculus.

To suggest that sometimes justices feel constrained by jurisprudential factors, while at other times they act on their own predispositions in a strategic manner, is nothing new. What this model adds is a bit of precision in defining when and how the "political" and "legal" natures of the justices interact—at least in the agenda-setting process.[65] There are several things to notice about this model. First, the model is one of individual, not collective, decision making. Second, it is not the case that some justices are "jurisprudes" and others "outcomers." Each of them uses each mode, though they may use them with differing frequencies. Third, as stated, the names of these modes were well-considered. One should not assume that cases that trigger the outcome mode are necessarily those of great social import, ideologically laden, or with great public policy implications. Likewise, cases triggering the jurisprudential mode are not necessarily the ones that present only technical "legal" questions. *What triggers one mode or the other is simply the degree of concern about the outcome on the merits.* Fourth, the two different modes do not suggest that a justice is a Dr. Jekyll and Mr. Hyde.

It became clear early on in the interviewing that the decision process was one of decisional winnowing steps. Informant after informant described the process as one whereby "first you look for X, if X is not present then you can throw out the case. If X is present, then you look for Y. . . ." The notion that there were two fairly distinguishable modes of decision making came somewhat later. A couple of things basically led to this conclusion. First was the fact that an informant would say something and mean one thing; later in the interview, he would use virtually the same words but mean something different. I noticed this first with the different meanings people ascribed to "good vehicle." In fact, when I asked one justice whether it meant a good fact situation or something that would help him win on the merits, he answered, "both." Follow-up, however, suggested that it meant different things at different times. Also, justices and clerks would be giving jurisprudential descriptions suggesting that the process was objective and then would proceed to describe situations where strategy was clearly the driving force. The discussion of defensive denials provides a good example.

---

65. [Footnote 5 in original] I agree with Doris Marie Provine, *Case Selection in the United States Supreme Court* (Chicago: University of Chicago Press, 1980), except that I think she has the impetus backward. She sees justices acting strategically but tempered by their perception of a judge's role. I would argue that the strategic behavior in case selection is the exception, even among the justices we would consider the most "political."

Perry: There is one thing I want to clarify. Does a defensive denial come only on issues that particularly concern a justice?

Justice: I was just going to say that you need to use this idea of defensive denials with an awful lot of caveats. Defensive denials are the rarity, I've just given you an example; when you feel strongly about the Fourth Amendment as I do, I would use it. I just think that whether or not something is done in good faith is irrelevant to the Fourth Amendment issue.

Perry: Would this suggest that on some cases you might well know what the vote on the merits will be, at least you think you know, but you really wouldn't care that much about cert., where on others you'd be more strategic?

Justice: Yes . . .

It was clear that strategic considerations tended to be the exception rather than the rule for all of the justices, though some justices were clearly strategic more often than others.

Second, I started hearing things that challenged some of my preconceptions about the different justices. For example, I assumed that some justices would be very strategic in the cert. process, whereas other justices would exhibit "legalistic" behavior. I was quite surprised to find out that, at times, the latter justices could and did act as strategically in cert. decisions as the former. Conversely, at times, the former were driven by jurisprudential-type concerns when I would have expected less ideological behavior.

Witness the remarks of clerks from several different chambers where one would expect the justice to be less ideological and more "judge-like":

Justice_____ was more judge-like than many of the others, although he does have a particular interest in [an area of law].

. . . He might vote because he wants to develop the law in those areas. But on other areas his cert. vote was more neutral

Or this clerk:

Justice _____ I think more than others would vote more on if an issue needed to be decided, although from time to time he did think in terms of an outcome determination.

From the same chamber:

I mean he believes so strongly in _____ [an opinion he wrote] that when a case [in that area] would come up he would look right at the merits to see if it was an attempt to undercut [his opinion.]

And finally, one said about his justice:

Certain buttons could be pushed. There were a narrow category of cases that he had very strong views on and he would come to a quick decision ... One was a technical/legal area. The other was an area of public policy.

So in other words, for the cert. process, it does not make sense to characterize some justices as "ideologues" and others as "judge-like," or as "activists" vs. "restraintists," "jurisprudes" vs. "outcomers." Rather, they all exhibit at one time or another an outcome orientation or a jurisprudential one; therefore, the interesting thing was to determine how the two orientations differed and what triggered them.

. . .

Clearly, the first thing that the justices consider, and this determination is really made by the clerks, is whether or not a petition is frivolous. The next critical juncture in the model is the extent to which a justice cares strongly about the outcome on the merits. I shall skip the discussion of this decision mode for now and move down the jurisprudential channel.

Jurisprudential Mode

If the justice does not care strongly about the outcome of a case on the merits, the next question asked is whether or not there is a split in the circuits. Recall that most informants said that the first thing or main thing they looked for, after frivolity, was a split in the circuits. Much of the clerk's time is spent at this stage trying to determine if there is actually a split. Frequently, it is obvious that no such split exists, or at least the case being petitioned is sufficiently distinguishable so that one can claim that an actual split has not developed. The determination of no legitimate conflict usually leads to denial. If there is not a legitimate conflict, in rare cases the Court agrees to resolve an issue or a particular case if there is a strong need to do so. Almost invariably, these are cases where the solicitor general pleads the need for immediate action because delay would cost the federal government vast amounts of money, or the extant decision might put current governmental operating procedures in chaos. The Court would prefer to have the benefit of the consideration of as many circuits as possible, certainly more than one, before it renders an opinion, but in such cases that is not possible. It must be emphasized that such situations are rare, and the solicitor general carefully guards his reputation for an accurate assessment of a situation. . . . [I]t is not in his interest to lead the Court astray.

The existence of a legitimate split does not assure that a case will be granted, however. The justice then asks whether or not the split is over an important issue. Recall ... that importance may mean several things, and different things to different justices in different situations.

. . .

If there is a legitimate conflict, and it involves an important issue, the next question that a justice considers is the need or desire for more "percolation." Though he desires more percolation, if there is a compelling reason to take the case at this time, he will usually vote to grant.

But reasons are usually "compelling" only when the solicitor general says a decision is crucial. If no such argument is made, the case will be denied, to allow more percolation.

Even though there is a legitimate circuit split with several circuits having ruled, and there is no desire or need for additional percolation, the justice still asks if this particular case is a "good vehicle." In the jurisprudential mode, being a good vehicle is determined by such things as: is the issue clear and "squarely presented"? Is the record below clear? Is the fact situation nonambiguous? Can the primary issue be reached, or will some confounding issue have to be decided first, which would preclude a decision on the major issue? Are there potential problems such as standing or mootness? In other words, a justice considers procedural jurisprudential concerns to determine if the case is a good vehicle.

The jurisprudential mode is a series of fundamentally jurisprudential considerations. They are the types of things that one learns in law school. And as difficult as it is for us political scientists to accept at times, Supreme Court justices are very much lawyers who are trained and socialized in this vein, and they very much believe in the necessity and desirability of judges acting along such lines. Justices, too, have the idealized notion of what it means to be a dispassionate jurist, and they often try to act accordingly.

Outcome Mode

When a justice cares a lot about the outcome of a case on the merits, he seems to exhibit different behavior—behavior that is much more strategic and is more in line with the decision making portrayed by political scientists. Even though most of what my informants said was definitely in a jurisprudential mode, they would frequently say things like, "of course there are exceptions." This would usually be in response to a question I asked on whether or not a vote on cert. could be seen as a preliminary vote on the merits. The answer would usually be "no," except that they were more predisposed to take cases that they perceived to be wrongly decided than ones correctly decided. On many cases, they had no predisposition, but even if they did, they did not calculate in any strategic sense what the outcome on the merits would be. To be sure, once the case was taken, there was an effort to win. But the decision to grant cert. was not made on a strategic calculation of the outcome.

There are cases, however, where after frivolity, outcome is the driving force behind behavior on the cert. decision. Now this is not to say that the justice has completely decided himself how all aspects of the opinion should look. But if the area is that important to him, he probably has a fairly well-developed idea of how doctrine should proceed; therefore, he has a good idea of how he will vote on the merits, and he probably has a good idea of how his colleagues will vote. As might be expected, those cases about which a justice would care strongly are often ones of great importance. All the justices have very strong feelings about issues such as affirmative action, obscenity, and the exclusionary rule.

But such intense concern about outcome is not confined to cases of great societal importance. Indeed, the fervor may be about a technical issue. Each justice seems to have certain areas, large and small, where he feels strongly about how doctrine should proceed or, for some reason, cares strongly about the outcome of a particular case. It may well be something about which the rest of the brethren are dispassionate. The "big issues" may not always lead to the outcome mode. A justice might see an issue as one of great public importance at one time, but later find that it has become a more jurisprudential question for him. In other words, once a controversial area of law has become fairly well settled, the justice may become a jurisprude on the issue; *stare decisis* becomes more important. Nevertheless, important issues usually continue to engender outcome-oriented responses—even from the justices we think of as being least ideological.

When entering the outcome decision mode, the first thing that the justice does is try to make an assessment of whether or not he will win on the merits. If he thinks he will not, he will vote to deny the case. The one mitigating situation in this outcome-driven behavior would be if it would be institutionally irresponsible not to take the case; for example, if the SG convinces him that refusal to decide the issue now would be disastrous, or if it is a decision where the Supreme Court simply must act. An example of the latter might be something like the Nixon tapes case. It is also possible that declining to decide a major circuit split would at some point come to be seen as irresponsible. But in the outcome mode a justice, like everyone else, is very good at selective perception and is far more likely to avoid taking the case if he can do so in good conscience. He will at least try to wait for a better case. With the caveat of institutional irresponsibility, if the justice perceives that he will lose on the merits, the vote will be to deny. My informants frequently and openly referred to these cases as "defensive denials."

Much of the political science literature suggests a justice's decision process stops here—"If I can win, grant." A potential win on the merits is not enough to vote to grant, however. The next question that a justice asks is whether or not the case is a good vehicle. Here "good vehicle" means something different from what it did in the other mode. Good facts here might mean ones that would be most likely to pull a swing justice. Or good facts would be those that would allow the justice to move doctrine in the particular way he wanted. It might be quite possible to win the case, but it might not be the best way to get to one's ultimate goal. To be sure, jurisprudential factors are not irrelevant. For example, a messy fact situation might not serve one's cause. Even if the present case could be won, given the messy facts it might allow the next case to be distinguished on the facts in such a way that would make things worse. One might win the battle and lose the war. That said, messy facts or other jurisprudential problems certainly do not stop justices when they want to reach an issue. Every Court observer has seen the Court reach out to make a ruling, running roughshod over things such as standing, ripeness, or the policy of not reaching the Constitutional question if non-Constitutional issues are dispositive. And yet the same justice who does this—and they all do it [at] one time or the other—will decry such behavior when his brethren do it, claiming that they are simply trying to reach a certain result. I suspect that the presence of a good vehicle is often just too good to pass up in a strategic sense, and this may help explain why we often see such cases being adjudicated despite their jurisprudential problems.

If a justice cares strongly about the outcome of a particular case, his calculations as to why a case is a good or bad vehicle may be complex and highly strategic. The particular fact situation might appeal to a swing vote; say, for example, it is a case of child abuse that so outrages another justice that it might pull his vote on the merits whereas a different fact situation might not. Even more strategically, if the case enables one justice to make his arguments for cert. in jurisprudential terms, though his motive is outcome, he may be better able to persuade another justice who happens to be a jurisprude on this issue. Undoubtedly, most arguments at conference to grant cert. are made in jurisprudential terms, likewise to deny. To the extent that this can be done persuasively, it may allow one to avoid the appearance of being simply result oriented, and it may disarm an opponent. The factors, then, of what constitutes a "good vehicle" in the outcome mode are not wholly different from those in the jurisprudential mode, but they are more complex and are largely driven by strategic considerations.

If the present case is not a good vehicle, the question that remains is, is a better case likely? If yes, vote to deny; if no, vote to grant and hope for extraordinarily persuasive capabilities after the case has been submitted for decision. One of the problems with some of the political science literature is that it seems to suggest that if a justice can win on the merits, he will want to take the case. Ironically, such an assumption does not allow the justices to be political and strategic enough.

Living with Inconsistency

Would intelligent, diligent, honest justices allow themselves to have a double standard for decision making? Before one answers that, it should be pointed out that a double standard is not necessarily a bad thing. It may well suggest flexibility. Should a justice always be a "jurisprude"? Socialization in the law seems to suggest that being a jurisprude is admirable, whereas being an outcomer is somehow a necessary evil, which is, of course, poppycock. Being "political" or strategic should not connote anything unseemly. Moreover, having different methods of behavior is not bad *prima facie*. The justices are not being disingenuous or schizophrenic, nor are they engaging in self-delusion when they trumpet the virtues of jurisprudential considerations and principled decision making while at the same time thinking about things like defensive denials.

Witness the President. Every beginning student of the presidency learns that the President wears different hats. At times we expect the President to be politically astute, and if he is not, he is often labeled a failure. Other times, we expect him to be above politics, and if he is not, he incurs our wrath. The point is not that the public is fickle; rather, in order to do a good job, the President must often make decisions in different ways appropriate to the problem at hand. The justices, too, must wear different hats—or should we say different robes? An institution such as the Supreme Court is an enigma to a democratic system, and the justices have always had to deal with tensions in this regard. The Supreme Court is the highest court in the land and as such must direct the legal system. To have a credible legal system where there is the rule of law rather than men suggests an adjudicative body that is "above politics" in some sense. At times the Court is called on to settle a rule of evidence, a technical tax statute. Other times, however, it has to step in and act as a relief pitcher for democracy and decide that separate cannot be equal. Given such different tasks, one should not only expect that the justices would make decisions in different ways, one should probably hope that they would.

Professor Judith Shklar has dealt with conflicting conceptions of the law brilliantly in her book *Legalism*. Though the context was different, her comments go straight to the heart of what I am arguing:

> Yet the quest for the holy grail of perfect, nonpolitical, aloof neutral law and legal decisions persists and remains a test for acceptability. It is also still often said that a politically oriented legal system spells the end of judicial legitimacy. In fact, although it is philosophically deeply annoying, human institutions survive because most of us can live comfortably with wholly contradictory beliefs. Most thoughtful citizens know that the courts act decisively in creating rules that promote political ends—to name only civil rights—of which they may approve. They also insist that the impartiality of judges and of the process as a whole requires a dispassionate, literal pursuit of rules carved in spiritual marble. Changes in these rules are to be made by legislative agencies, but never by the judiciary. All criticism and praise of judicial performances is couched in phrases drawn from this belief, which may seem ridiculous but is not at all socially or psychologically indefensible. Indeed, if we value flexibility and accept a degree of contradiction, this paradox may even seem highly functional and appropriate.

By allowing the justices to act both as outcomers and jurisprudes, but not at the same time, the model provides a better understanding of the certiorari process in the United States Supreme Court....

Questions and Comments

1. The Cordrays contrast the absence of precedential effect of certiorari decisions with the constraints imposed by *stare decisis* on merits decisions. What are the advantages, and disadvantages of maintaining the certiorari process as entirely discretionary? Of treating denials of certiorari as lacking precedential value?

2. One issue on which the Justices themselves diverge is whether the Court has a responsibility to grant cert when presented with questions of law that have been subject to divergent understandings within the federal system. Kenneth Starr asserts that the Court should use its discretion to add "considerably greater clarity to the interpretive process. . . ." Kenneth Starr, *The Supreme Court and its Shrinking Docket: The Ghost of William Howard Taft*, 90 Minn. L. Rev. 1363, 1383 (2006). According to Starr, the Court acts in derogation of its duties when it fails to address points of law that leave litigants unsure of their rights and responsibilities (particularly in commercial contexts). Do you agree with Starr that this is an important responsibility? Or with those Justices who argue for "percolation"?

3. Starr also suggests that the Court "should avoid governing the polity by forcing a cultural agenda." According to Starr, granting cert to hear cases like *Lawrence v. Texas*, 539 U.S. 558 (2003) (holding that anti-sodomy laws violate the Due Process Clause of the Fourteenth Amendment), is a poor use of the Court's limited resources. Recall that Justice White argued for granting certiorari in *Bowers* because there was a conflict in the lower courts. Would Starr have agreed, or disagreed, with the grant of certiorari in *Bowers*? Recall how close *Bowers* came to being decided the other way. Is Starr's real objection to the grant of certiorari in *Lawrence* or to the outcome? Is there an argument to be made that the Court's legitimacy may require its docket to focus less on the most socially controversial areas, so as to use its institutional capital sparingly? What would have happened if the Court had adopted that philosophy in *Brown v. Board of Education* in the 1950s?

4. Do you agree with Knight and Epstein's characterization of the certiorari process as one of "bargaining"? In particular, do you agree with their treatment of the cases in which the circulation of proposed dissents from denial from certiorari resulted in a grant of certiorari as "bargaining" rather than "persuasion"? Can one test whether votes to grant cert result from (1) being persuaded on the merits that the case is certworthy, (2) believing that the case is a good strategic vehicle for the justice's substantive interests, or (3) deciding it would be better for the dissent from denial of cert not to be published?

5. Should the Court continue to have so much discretion over its docket? What are the principal reasons for or against this approach? What are the advantages and disadvantages of mandatory jurisdiction? Would it be practicable, today, to restore significant parts of the Court's mandatory jurisdiction? (Recall the data noted above on the growth in the number of requests for Supreme Court review.) Is there a category of cases today over which the Court should exercise mandatory jurisdiction?

6. Comparative scholars have observed the development of screening mechanisms among high courts in the world, even those that have nominally mandatory jurisdiction. For discussion, see, e.g., Donald Kommers, *Constitutional Jurisprudence of the Federal Republic of Germany* 16–27 (1997) (describing how cases in which the law is clearly settled may be resolved by unanimous decision of three-judge panels). Is there an expected historic progression under which "successful" courts attract more cases than can be given plenary consideration, leading to formal or informal methods of

discretionary screening? Is there an important difference between discretion as to how much consideration on the merits to give and whether to consider a case on the merits at all?

C.   THE INCREDIBLE SHRINKING CASELOAD

As noted above, in the late 1980s and early 1990s the Court began to grant cert in dramatically fewer cases, even though the total number of petitions seeking cert did not significantly decline. While the Court never explained the decline in grants, scholars of the Court have tried to account for this development.

In the first reading below, David M. O'Brien, writing in 1997, notes a number of possible explanations for the shrinking docket: the impact of external forces, as suggested by Justice Souter; the growth of the cert pool; and personnel changes. Based on his examination of Justice Marshall's papers and other materials, O'Brien concludes that the composition of the bench and voting practices have influenced the docket more than the cert pool or external forces (e.g., absence of major new legislation). In particular, O'Brien asserts that a decline in the use of "Join–3" votes may have contributed to the decline in caseload.

Margaret Meriwether Cordray and Richard Cordray, in the next reading, suggest that a comparison to prior periods in history when the Court dramatically reduced its own caseload is illuminating in ascertaining the causes of the decline. They consider a variety of possible influences, including the elimination of the Court's mandatory jurisdiction, fewer filings in particular subject areas, fewer petitions by the government, greater homogeneity among the lower courts, the cert pool and, especially, changes in personnel on the Court. The authors conclude that changes in the Court's personnel have played the most significant role in the reduction, complemented by a more " 'statist' judicial realignment" in the lower courts which has resulted in the Solicitor General's seeking review less often than in the past.

Finally, Professor David Stras' 2006 article analyzes the effects of the cert pool on the cert process. In contrast to the Cordrays and O'Brien, he concludes that the cert pool does influence the Justices' voting and may account for some of the decline in the number of cases granted cert. He suggests that, because a recommendation to grant that turns out to be mistaken is more visible, and thus potentially more embarrassing, than a recommendation to deny, the law clerks writing for the pool are more likely to be conservative in recommending whether or not to grant. That, he suggests, would result in more recommendations to deny.[65]

---

65. See also Kenneth W. Starr, *The Supreme Court and Its Shrinking Docket: The* *Ghost of William Howard Taft,* 90 Minn. L. Rev. 1363, 1376–1377 (2006).

David M. O'Brien,[66] *Join–3 Votes, the Rule of Four, the Cert. Pool, and the Supreme Court's Shrinking Plenary Docket,* 13 J. L. & Pol. 779 (1997)

The "incredibly shrinking" plenary docket of the Supreme Court has drawn considerable attention. In the 1995–1996 Term, the Court heard only 75 hours of oral arguments and decided just 90 cases by written opinions. That is half of the number of a decade ago. Moreover, the total docket has grown rather steadily, reaching over 8,000 cases in the 1994 Term before falling slightly to 7,565 cases in the 1995 Term. Yet, since Justice William H. Rehnquist assumed the chief justiceship in 1986, fewer and fewer cases have been granted annually. Barely one percent of the cases on the docket receive plenary consideration.

. . .

FIGURE 1
Percent of Docket Granted Review, 1968—1995

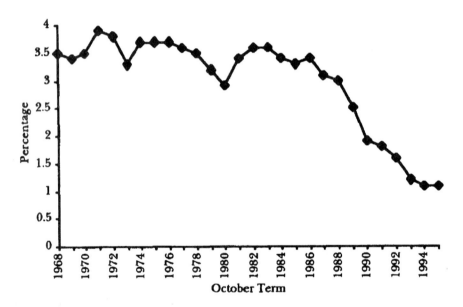

Even some justices are "amazed" by the trend. Prior to arriving at the Court at the start of the 1990 Term, Justice David H. Souter noticed the number had "come down significantly from the historical highs," which reached 184 decisions in the 1981 and 1983 Terms.[67] On the high

66. Leone Reeves and George W. Spicer Professor of Government and Foreign Affairs, University of Virginia.

67. [Editors' Note: Readers will notice some variations in the figures given by different experts for "decisions," "full opinions," "cases decided," and similar terms.

Compare, e.g., *The Supreme Court, 1981 Term, The Statistics,* 96 Harv. L. Rev. 304, 308 (1982) (identifying 167 "written opinions" in 216 cases and 126 "Per Curiam or Memorandum" decisions). Variations arise from a number of factors, including that multiple cases may be consolidated for pur-

bench, he found there had not been a conscious decision to reduce the number. "It had in fact just happened," in his words, "nobody set a quota; nobody sits at the conference table and says, 'We've taken too much. We must pull back.' . . . It simply has happened."

Justice Souter considered a number of possible explanations for the declining plenary docket. All were factors external to the Court. Presidential vetoes of legislation by Ronald Reagan and George Bush may have resulted in "a diminishing supply of new statutes . . . that cried out for some immediate and speedy" interpretation. Under those two Republican administrations, there was neither "much antitrust work" coming from the Department of Justice, nor a great deal of civil rights litigation, except for voting rights cases. As for the rights of the accused, Justice Souter observed that the Fourth Amendment has "been pretty much raked over . . . The basic law, the basic standards . . . are products of the 60s and the 70s and the 80s. There hasn't been an awful lot for us to take." Finally, he agreed with some Court-watchers that, after twelve years of Republican judicial appointments, the Rehnquist Court finds less disagreement with the lower federal courts. Reagan and Bush's lower court appointees may have resulted, in Justice Souter's words, in "a diminished level of philosophical division within the federal courts from which so much of the conflicting opinions tend to arise."

Other external factors may also have played a part. Notably, the Court's discretionary jurisdiction was expanded with the Judicial Improvements and Access to Justice Act of 1988. Virtually all non-discretionary appellate jurisdiction was eliminated, except for appeals in reapportionment cases and suits under Civil Rights and Voting Rights acts, antitrust laws, and the Presidential Election Campaign Fund Act. The Court's "managerial capacity" for controlling the plenary docket by denying cert to more cases thus increased. And afterwards the plenary docket indeed declined, as indicated in Figure 2. But, as the figure shows, the plenary docket started diminishing prior to that jurisdictional change.

poses of Supreme Court review and that there may be questions of judgment whether to treat a per curiam opinion as a full written opinion. By any measure, however, there has been a marked decline in the number of cases granted oral argument and decided by full written opinions in recent years.]

FIGURE 2
Number of Cases Granted Plenary Review, 1968—1995

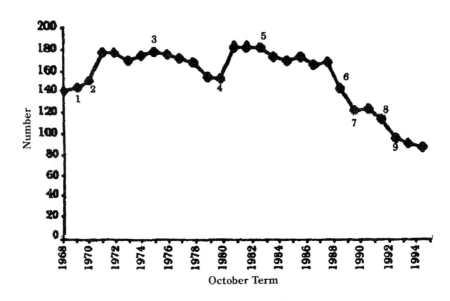

October Term

1. Chief Justice Burger joins the Court.
2. Oral Argument Calendar changed to accommodate more cases.
3. Justice Stevens' first full Term.
4. Justice O'Connor joins the Court.
5. Chief Justice Rehnquist's first Term.
6. Justice Brennan's last Term.
7. Justice Marshall's last Term.
8. Justice White's last Term.
9. Justice Blackmun's last Term.

Factors internal to the Court undoubtedly contributed as well. . . .
As Figure 2 shows, the plenary docket jumped in the 1971 Term to over
170 cases and remained in that range for the rest of the decade. . . .
Following the retirements of Chief Justice Burger at the end of the 1985
Term and Justice Lewis F. Powell, Jr. at the end of the 1986 Term,
however, the plenary docket gradually declined and, then, fell sharply in
the early 1990s.

The increase in the number of cases granted plenary consideration
in the 1970s appears directly related to changes in the Court's operation
made early in Chief Justice Burger's tenure. He had a keen interest in
judicial administration but also constantly lamented the Court's "caseload crisis." One important change he persuaded the others to make was
in the oral argument calendar. Prior to 1970, attorneys in cases granted
oral argument were each given one hour to present their arguments. In
1970, the time allotted each side was reduced to thirty minutes, which in
turn permitted hearing more cases. Instead of hearing 12 cases during a
two week oral argument session, the Burger Court went to hearing 12
cases in three days. Not surprisingly, the number of orally-argued cases
rose from 144 to 151 to 177 during the 1969, 1970, and 1971 Terms.

Besides increasing the space on the oral argument calendar came another change—a change in the justices' voting practice in granting cases. In the early 1970s Chief Justice Burger and some other justices began casting "Join–3" votes, rather than simply voting to grant or deny petitions for certiorari. Because earlier in this century the Court adopted the so-called informal "Rule of Four"—namely, that at least four justices must agree that a case merits review—a Join–3 vote is a vote to provide a fourth vote if others vote to grant review, but is otherwise considered as voting to deny. The introduction of Join–3 votes, arguably, contributed to the Court's taking more cases by lowering the threshold for granting review established by the Rule of Four.

THE RULE OF FOUR AND JOIN–3 VOTES

. . .

By Earl Warren's chief justiceship (1953–1969), the Rule of Four was firmly in place. Cases deemed important by two or three justices were carried over to another conference because other justices might vote to grant review. Such a course was rare and remained governed by the Rule of Four. Moreover, the docket books of Chief Justice Warren and Justice Thurgood Marshall do not record any Join–3 votes. On occasion, three justices voted to grant cases that were denied due to the absence of a fourth vote.

The Rule of Four, to be sure, operates in only a fraction of the cases on the total docket. Yet, the percentage of cases granted on that basis is not insignificant. In 1982, Justice John Paul Stevens concluded that between 20 to 30 percent of the plenary docket was typically granted on only four votes and that those "are significant percentages." . . . A review of Justice Marshall's docket book for the 1990 Term reveals, likewise, that 22 percent of the granted cases had only four votes.

Justice Stevens . . . proposed abandoning the Rule of Four and adopting a "Rule of Five." He did so as an alternative to Chief Justice Burger's proposal for the creation of a national appellate tribunal as a solution to the Court's workload problems. . . .

Justice Stevens' proposal met with opposition within the Court, however. In particular, Justice Marshall contended that the Rule of Four could not be abandoned without consulting Congress, since Justice Van Devanter and others promised to abide by it when pressing for the Judiciary Act of 1925. . . . Although Justice Stevens' proposal was not adopted, several of the justices apparently found it somewhat attractive. During the 1981 Term, Justice Powell had cast a "Join–4" vote. In the 1982 Term, Justices Rehnquist and Sandra Day O'Connor did the same in one case, and Justice Marshall cast three such votes in the 1983 and 1984 Terms. In any event, once support for Chief Justice Burger's proposal faded and the plenary docket began declining, even Justice Stevens reconsidered abandoning the Rule of Four. . . .

. . .

In retrospect, Justice Stevens' diagnosis of the Court's workload problem was right on the mark: some justices simply voted to grant too many cases. . . .

When proposing a Rule of Five, Justice Stevens did not mention that other justices cast Join–3 votes. Still, he had clearly identified the main cause of the Court's workload problem: the Rule of Four no longer imposed the kind of self-restraint it previously had. The introduction of and propensity of some justices to cast Join–3 votes lowered the threshold imposed by the Rule of Four for granting cases, thereby inflating [the] plenary docket. . . .

Although the origin of Join–3 votes remains unclear, such votes were not recorded prior to Burger's chief justiceship, as earlier noted. . . .

Whatever their origin, Join–3 votes were established by the time Justice Stevens joined the Court in 1975. One possible explanation is that in leading conferences, Chief Justice Burger began voting to join three and other justices did the same. Within a few years, Join–3 votes became almost routine, though still relatively infrequent. . . .

Two other factors may bear on the casting of Join–3 votes. First, in the early 1970s, the Court's composition was in flux. Following Justice Blackmun's appointment, Justices Powell and Rehnquist joined the Court in 1971. They came aboard with no prior judicial experience. . . . The increasing size of the total docket and the declining percentage of cases given plenary review caused concerns about the Court's diminishing supervisory capacity and, therefore, may have predisposed some justices to vote to grant review. Second, in response to the "caseload crisis" in 1972, at Justice Powell's suggestion, a majority of the justices agreed to pool their law clerks and have them write memos on incoming petitions for certiorari and appeals. . . . Basically, the cert pool accomplished internally what Freund's Study Group would propose as an external solution to the Court's workload problem, namely, the creation of a national appellate court to screen appeals and refer about 400 appeals to the justices. Freund's Study Group took the "moral stance" that a separate appellate court was preferable to having law clerks do the screening, since such a court would be more professional, visible, and institutionally accountable. However, retired Chief Justice Warren, Justice Douglas, and Justice Brennan denounced the plan as unconstitutional, since the Constitution provides for only "one Supreme Court." The latter two justices also claimed they were underworked, not overworked.

During the 1972 Term, as senior associate, Justice Douglas began systematically noting in the U.S. Reports his vote to grant petitions and dissents from denial of review. . . .

Dissents from the denial of certiorari were once rare but became widespread in the 1970s and early 1980s. . . . In the 1950–1952 Terms, for example, in 106 out of the 2,756 cases denied review at least one dissent was noted (for 3.8 percent of the denials). By contrast, in the 1972 and 1973 Terms, at least one dissent was filed in 926 out of the

6,203 cases denied review (or 14 percent), whereas after Douglas retired, dissents in the 1976–1980 Terms were noted in 818 of the 18,355 cases denied (or 4.4 percent).

In the 1970s, some justices followed Justice Douglas' practice. In 1973, Justice Byron White began noting his votes to grant cases and dissents from denials.... Justice White ... wrote longer dissents from the denial of cases in which he identified a conflict among federal circuit courts or between state supreme court rulings that he deemed demanded the Court's resolution. Moreover, in response to the shrinking plenary docket, his notations increased significantly in the late 1980s and early 1990s.

. . .

The practice of noting votes to grant and dissents from denials is strategic, particularly when joined by other justices. In this way, especially by circulating drafts of proposed dissents, justices may persuade others to reconsider votes to grant cases otherwise denied....

. . .

... [T]he practice of noting votes to grant and dissenting from the denial of cert may have reinforced the introduction of Join–3 votes. That practice, especially when joined by other justices, might have inclined Chief Justice Burger and some others to cast Join–3 votes in anticipation of such notations and dissents from the denial of review.

Regardless of the exact origin of Join–3 votes, the practice of casting such votes was accepted in the 1970s and 1980s. Furthermore, some justices cast an extraordinary share of such votes, whereas other rarely do, if ever. Justice Blackmun led in Join–3 votes. By comparison, Justice Stevens never casts such votes. On and off the bench, he repeatedly warned colleagues not to take cases pointlessly. His view of voting grant was undoubtedly influenced by clerking for Justice Wiley Rutledge in 1947–1948, at a time when the Rule of Four was respected. Other justices Join–3 votes fall somewhere between these two extremes, as illustrated in Table 1.

TABLE 1
Number of Join–3 Votes in Cases Granted With Less Than Four Votes, 1979–90

October Term of

Justice	1979	1980	1981	1982	1983	1984	1985
Blackmun	7	8	7	6	11	13	10
O'Connor			1	1	9	4	8
Burger	4	1	2		7	2	4
White	2	1			1	1	6
Rehnquist	2			1	2	1	1
Powell	5	1		3	1	2	1
Marshall	2	1	2		1	1	
Brennan	2				1		2
Stewart	2	2	2				
Kennedy							
Scalia							
Stevens							

October Term of

Justice	1986	1987	1988	1989	1990	Total (%)
Blackmun	14	3	8	14	6	107 (55)
O'Connor	6	1	5	3	4	42 (21.8)
Burger	4					24 (12.5)
White	4		5	1	1	22 (11.4)
Rehnquist	1	1	1	5	2	17 (8.8)
Powell	3	1				17 (8.8)
Marshall	3	1	1	1		13 (6.7)
Brennan		1	1	1		8 (4.1)
Stewart						6 (3.0)
Kennedy					3	3 (1.5)
Scalia			2			2 (1.0)
Stevens						0 (0.0)

FIGURE 4
Justices Casting Join–3 Votes, 1979–90

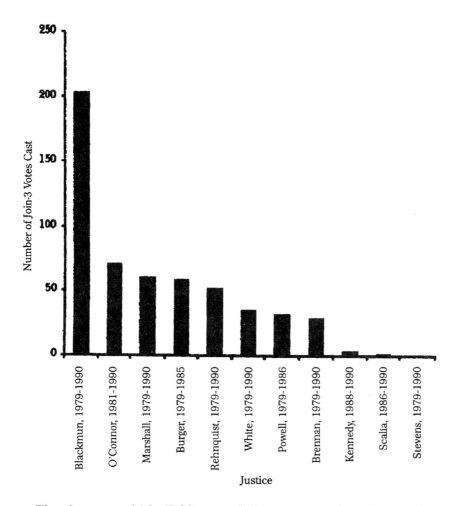

The data on which Table 1 and Figure 4 are based come from Justice Marshall's Bench Memos recording justices' votes on cases granted during the 1979 to 1990 Terms. There are 1,556 memos on cases in which oral arguments were heard during those Terms. Of those, Join–3 votes were cast in 408 (26 percent). More significantly, 192 cases (12 percent) were placed on the plenary docket on the basis of less than four votes to grant plus one or more Join–3 votes. And some cases were granted on the basis of only two votes to grant and two or more Join–3 votes.

Join–3 votes clearly lowered the threshold for granting cases and contributed to the inflation of the plenary docket. Moreover, certain justices frequently cast such votes, as shown by Table 1.... [H]ad these justices not cast Join–3 votes, fewer cases would have been granted. Put differently, had the Rule of Four held, the Burger Court could have reduced its plenary docket by at least 12 percent, and, possibly, by as much as 26 percent.

The key to the Court's "incredibly shrinking" docket in the 1990s, therefore, may be found in the Burger Court's responses to its "workload problem" and inflated plenary dockets in the 1970s and early 1980s. Besides enlarging the plenary docket by changing the oral argument calendar, the Burger Court no longer strictly adhered to the Rule of Four, thereby sacrificing some control over what and how much to decide. As Figure 2 indicates, after an initial increase in 1971, the number of cases annually decided rose again following the 1981 appointment of Justice O'Connor, who cast a fair number of Join–3 votes, less than Justice Blackmun but more than the others. With several justices casting Join–3 votes, by the early 1980s, the numbers granted reached their "historical highs." Following the retirements of Chief Justice Burger and Justice Powell, the plenary docket shrank slowly. Neither Justice Antonin Scalia nor Justice Anthony Kennedy is as inclined as those two or most other former members of the Burger Court to vote to Join–3. The decline continued after the retirements of Justices Brennan and Marshall at the end of the 1989 and 1990 Terms, respectively, and then fell further after the retirements of Justices White and Blackmun at the end of the 1992 and 1993 Terms. In sum, the inflation and contraction in the plenary docket basically registered changes in the Court's composition and case selection process, specifically the predisposition of certain justices to cast Join–3 votes and to grant review.

LAW CLERKS AND THE CERT POOL

However, the cert pool remains, arguably, an independent variable in explaining the shrinking plenary docket. It is still controversial with some Court-watchers that continue to echo Justice Douglas' criticisms. Others who have been converted to opposition include one former clerk for Chief Justice Burger, former-solicitor general and federal appellate judge, Kenneth W. Starr. He complained publicly in 1993 about the cert pool exerting too much influence in the screening process and urged the Court to "disband the cert pool."

The concern about the cert pool has grown because, with the exception of Justice Stevens, every justice appointed during the last two decades joined the pool.... Important cases, according to Starr, are passed over which might have been granted if more justices independently reviewed cert petitions, and the cert pool thereby contributes to the diminishing plenary docket.

Within the Court, even some justices grew concerned about the number belonging to the cert pool and its influence on their agenda-setting. [The author describes an unsuccessful proposal by Justice Kennedy in 1991 to have one justice in the pool on each cert petition not receive the cert pool memo and have a separate memo prepared]

. . .

... [I]t is unclear that the cert pool either determines the amount of scrutiny given petitions or was the underlying factor in the increasing and subsequent decreasing in the size of the plenary docket. . . .

Although not a satisfactory gauge of justices' scrutiny of petitions because, as discussed earlier, some justices oppose the practice of publicizing such votes, notations of votes to grant and dissents from denial provide a measure for the theory that the changes in the plenary docket dovetail with those in the Court's composition and voting practice. As indicated in Figure 5, the number of notations of votes to grant and dissents from denial of review tracks the decline in the plenary docket. . . . The contrasting numbers are striking. In the 1981 Term, when the plenary docket reached its zenith, there were 255 notations of votes to grant additional cases and dissents from denial of review. Five Terms later, in 1986, Rehnquist's first as chief justice, the number fell to 129. By the 1994 and 1995 Terms, there were less than 10 in those combined Terms. As with the diminishing plenary docket, the number of notations of votes to grant and dissents from denial declined in three stages: first, following Chief Justice Burger's retirement and Rehnquist's elevation to the center chair; second, after Justices Brennan and Marshall retired; and, third, following the successive retirements of Justices White and Blackmun.

· · ·

The data ... underscores that members of the Burger Court were far more disposed to grant cases than those composing the Rehnquist Court in the mid–1990s. Certain justices were especially inclined to grant review, and they tried to persuade others to vote to grant review by casting Join–3 votes as well as by circulating and even publishing notations of votes to grant review and dissents from denial. One measure of the justices' pro-review predispositions is their notations to grant and dissents from denial. . . .

· · ·

[There is] considerable variation among the justices on the Burger and Rehnquist Courts. Justice White filed more solo notations of votes to grant and dissents from denial than any other justice. By contrast, perhaps not surprisingly, Justice Blackmun, who held the record for Join–3 votes, more frequently joined other justices in noting votes to grant and dissents from denials than he did in filing his own. Justices Brennan and Marshall sided together most often, especially in death penalty cases, but Justice Brennan was much more likely to join with other justices than to go solo.

It is also worth noting that Rehnquist's behavior changed after his elevation from associate to chief justice. In the early 1980s, he noted votes to grant and dissented from denials in anywhere from 10 to 29 cases per Term, but after becoming chief justice, he rarely published more than three per Term. However, he more than doubled his Join–3 votes after becoming chief justice; during the 1979 to 1985 Terms, he cast an average of three Join–3 votes each Term, whereas in his first five years as chief justice, he averaged more than six per Term.

Although an imperfect measure, [this data] further confirm the theory that the inflation in the plenary docket during the Burger Court years, and its contraction during the Rehnquist Court years, reflects changes in the composition of the bench and the justices' voting practices. . . .

THE IRONIES OF HISTORY

It is, perhaps, unremarkable to conclude that the inflation and contraction of the Court's plenary docket registers changes in the composition of the high bench and the justices' practices in voting on case selection. For the justices, not their law clerks or external forces, ultimately decide what and how much to decide. Nonetheless, the analysis here offers confirmation for the observations of both Justices Souter and Stevens. The "incredibly shrinking" plenary docket, as Justice Souter put it, "in fact just happened," due to changes in the Court's composition. And as Justice Stevens pointed out, the Burger Court's "workload problems" and inflated plenary dockets arose precisely because the justices failed to exercise "great restraint during the case selection process."

We are left, then, with two ironies of history. First, although recognized for his interest in judicial administration, Chief Justice Burger failed to fully appreciate that . . . his Court's "workload problem" was one of its own making. Second, in the 1980s, Justices Rehnquist sided with Chief Justice Burger in lamenting the workload of the Court's expanded plenary docket. As he and other justices repeatedly observed, "For better or for worse—and I happen to think it is better—I think the Supreme Court is committed to hearing and deciding somewhere in the neighborhood of 150 cases each Term." Yet, as chief justice, he has presided for a decade over a Court with a sharply diminishing plenary docket, "one of the most striking developments of the Rehnquist years."

Margaret Meriwether Cordray & Richard Cordray,[68] *The Supreme Court's Plenary Docket*, 58 Wash. & Lee L. Rev. 737 (2001)

. . . [The decline in cert grants] surprised and puzzled both participants and observers. At his confirmation hearings [to become Chief Justice] in 1986, then-Justice Rehnquist said, "I think the 150 cases that we have turned out quite regularly over a period of 10 or 15 years is just about where we should be at." Indeed, in response to questioning about

68. Margaret Cordray is Professor of Law, Capital Law School; Richard Cordray is Adjunct Professor, Ohio State University College of Law, and clerked for Justices White and Kennedy.

whether the size of that caseload might be too great for effective administration, he stated more pointedly, "[m]y own feeling is that all the courts are so much busier today than they have been in the past, that there would be something almost unseemly about the Supreme Court saying, you know, everybody else is deciding twice as many cases as they ever have before, but we are going to go back two-thirds as many as we did before." Justice Souter, who arrived at the Court in the midst of this dramatic decline, said he has been "amazed" at the trend. . . .

. . .

C.   Historical Perspective on the Plenary Docket

. . . [T]he current trend is not unprecedented. Counting forward from the 1926 Term—the first in which the Supreme Court enjoyed substantial control over its own docket—the trajectory of the Court's plenary docket divides into five fairly distinct periods.

The immediate effect of the 1925 legislation . . . was to reduce the number of the Court's signed opinions dramatically, from199 in the 1926 Term to 129 in the 1928 Term. Almost immediately, however, these numbers spiked up again, remaining relatively constant at an average of about 150 plenary decisions per Term for the next 15 years. At that point, the numbers fell precipitously, from 150 in the 1946 Term, to 124 and 132 in the 1947 and 1948 Terms, to 101 in the 1949 Term. For the next seven years, the Court issued an average of slightly more than 100 plenary decisions per Term. Beginning in the 1956 Term, the docket again showed a measurable increase, rising from 100 to 123 plenary decisions. For the next 15 years, the Court issued an average of about 120 plenary decisions per Term. In the 1971 Term, the docket jumped once more, and for almost two decades thereafter the Court again issued about 150 plenary decisions per Term. The most recent sharp decline commenced in the late 1980s.

Of particular interest, the current decline in the Supreme Court's plenary docket has [an] analog in the era just after World War II, when Chief Justice Vinson was appointed to preside over the Court. Then, as now, the Court had experienced a prolonged period of relatively full dockets, issuing an average of about 150 plenary decisions per Term. Suddenly, in just three Terms, the numbers fell to around 100 decisions per Term, where they remained for almost a decade. The most recent decline is comparable, and has now proved even more durable. The reasons for this earlier decline may thus offer clues that will help to explain the current decline.

It is assuredly difficult to isolate the reasons that underlie changes effected within an institution as complex and secretive as the Supreme Court. In that era, as in this one, many external factors conceivably could have contributed to the decline in the plenary docket. The volume of litigation may well have diminished during the years in which the United States was engaged in World War II, which would have meant a subsequent decline in cases wending their way to the Supreme Court.

The flood of legislative activity on the domestic front during the Great Depression diminished during the next decade, which might also have reduced the number of decisional conflicts among the lower courts. This era also encompassed the waning years of a period of prolonged single-party control of the Presidency, which generally imposes some degree of realignment on the lower courts; the resulting harmony in judicial philosophy would be expected to minimize conflicts among the courts that would justify plenary review. Finally, the Supreme Court itself had recently announced its withdrawal from two areas of prior contention by overruling its activist precedents on economic due process issues and by abandoning virtually all adjudication of common law claims.

It is doubtful, however, whether any of these explanations—taken alone or together—goes very far to explain the trimming of the docket by the Vinson Court. The pace of litigation was sluggish during the 1930s, perhaps depressed by economic conditions, and though the number of cases filed in the Supreme Court had changed little during that time, it gradually increased during the 1940s by about 25 percent. The extent of congressional action on the domestic front was probably less influential for our purposes than the cumulative growth of federal laws and agency actions, augmented by new legal problems created by wartime conditions. The prospect of judicial realignment may be more to the point, though Presidents often find it surprisingly hard to impose a comprehensive judicial philosophy upon even the Supreme Court itself, let alone upon the judicial system throughout the entire country. Finally, though the Court did pull back on economic due process and state common law cases, these changes had occurred almost a decade earlier. Moreover, they were probably offset by a profusion of new procedural issues and by the Court's growing assertiveness in exercising the power of judicial review to determine the constitutional rights of individual citizens.

... [S]tudies now published on the workings of the Vinson Court ... point to one overriding factor—changes in personnel—that seems to explain its reduced docket. Upon his appointment to the Court, Chief Justice Vinson viewed it as an important part of his mission to reduce the "conspicuous fractiousness" among its members. One of his strategies was "to cut down the caseload to more manageable proportions, perhaps in order to reduce opportunities for division." He thus came to the Court consciously determined to exert his influence to reduce the size of the docket, which he could do in part by casting his own vote less frequently in favor of plenary review, and in part by attempting to persuade his colleagues to do the same.

Fortunately, the availability of Justice Burton's docket books (and those of certain other Justices) has permitted scholars to assemble figures on the voting patterns of each Justice on the Vinson Court. The data confirms that Chief Justice Vinson accomplished at least the first part of his task, voting to grant certiorari review in fewer cases during his first three Terms than anyone other than Justice Jackson, and voting least frequently to note probable jurisdiction in cases on appeal. Although it is not clear that the Chief Justice managed to exert any significant influence on the votes cast by his colleagues, the withholding of his own vote sufficed to cause at least a modest decline in the docket over this period.

At that juncture, fate took a hand. On July 19, 1949, Justice Murphy died. Less than two months later, on September 10, 1949, Justice Rutledge also died unexpectedly. President Truman thus made two new appointments to the Court between the 1948 and 1949 Terms. The nominees were Tom C. Clark and Sherman Minton, and the Senate promptly confirmed both. . . .

On the Court, both men immediately proved to be even less inclined to grant plenary review than the Chief Justice, who still ranked below the rest of the Justices in this regard. Justice Minton, in particular, voted to grant plenary review in far fewer cases than any other member of the Court—210 times on certiorari and 69 times on appeal over the next four Terms, as compared with 641 and 137 for Justice Black, who topped the list. Even more important, however, was the fact that the two Justices they replaced had been among the most willing to grant plenary review during the three previous Terms. . . . To put the consequences in starker perspective, the average number of votes for plenary review cast per Term by the two former Justices was 340 (159 by Rutledge, 181 by Murphy), but for the two new Justices, this same figure sank to only 174 (70 by Minton, 104 by Clark). It is a telling demonstration of the independent significance of these two changes in personnel that over the same period, the average rate at which every one of the holdover Justices (including Chief Justice Vinson) voted to grant plenary review actually increased.

The effect on the Court's docket was dramatic. The slight decline initiated by Chief Justice Vinson now took on the aura of a full-scale retreat, as the number of plenary decisions immediately collapsed to 101 cases in the 1949 Term. It would not climb back above 114 cases until the 1956 Term, after both Vinson and Minton left the Court, even though the Court was bombarded with academic criticism excoriating the Justices for evading their responsibilities by declining to review and decide major cases.

. . . This data shows that though it is possible that external factors may have contributed modestly to the decline in the plenary docket, the most obvious and compelling explanation is simply that changes in personnel created a Supreme Court that, as a collective body, was much less inclined to grant review. This state of affairs lasted until the personnel changed again; after Earl Warren replaced Vinson as Chief Justice and established himself, and after William Brennan replaced Justice Minton, the plenary docket expanded once again as a consequence of their greater willingness to vote in favor of granting review. . . .

II.   POSSIBLE EXPLANATIONS FOR THE RECENT DECLINE

Lawyers, commentators, and even the Justices themselves have hypothesized a variety of causes for the drop in the Supreme Court's plenary docket over the past decade. For the most part, however, these theories have remained mostly speculative and have not been satisfactorily evaluated in light of numerical data that would allow them to be either verified or falsified.[69] This problem occurs because the close secrecy of the Court's internal deliberations makes it difficult to quantify the Justices' voting behavior in conference....

A. *Elimination of the Court's Mandatory Jurisdiction*

In seeking explanations for the recent decline in the Court's plenary docket, one obvious (but ultimately unpersuasive) candidate is the almost wholesale repeal of the Court's mandatory jurisdiction. Prior to 1988, the Supreme Court enjoyed discretion to determine whether to review most of the cases coming before it, but several important statutes gave litigants a right of appeal to the Supreme Court. In 1988, at the Court's urging, Congress eliminated virtually all of these mandatory appeal provisions, substituting instead discretionary review on certiorari.

. . .

[Before 1988,] ... the Court did, at least on occasion, grant full review to an appeal that it would not otherwise have taken on certiorari. Some commentators, however, opined that the Court was already applying the functional equivalent of its standards for granting certiorari in deciding whether to accord plenary treatment to cases on appeal. The Justices accomplished this by disposing of unmeritorious appeals by dismissing them "for want of a substantial federal question," which had been a regular practice for decades. If this view were correct, repeal of the mandatory jurisdiction statutes would still have the beneficial effect of eliminating the need for summary dispositions and the time-consuming task of resolving technical jurisdictional issues, but it would have no appreciable effect on the size of the plenary docket.

... Did the virtual elimination of the Supreme Court's mandatory jurisdiction meaningfully contribute to the decline in its docket? As Chief Justice Rehnquist has noted, "there is no way of knowing how many of the appeals would have been granted as petitions for certiorari." However, we can develop a close proxy for the answer by comparing: (i) the number of appeals accorded plenary review in the four Terms prior to the 1988 legislation; with (ii) the number of cases granted review on certiorari in which the parties previously would have had a right of appeal, in the four Terms after the legislation had become fully effective.

In order to make the first part of this comparison, we counted the number of appeals on the plenary docket for each Term from 1984–1987.

---

69. [Footnote 74 in original] The one notable exception in this regard is Professor Hellman, whose work attempts to group the Court's caseload into different substantive categories and to draw conclusions from the rate of change in the number of cases on the plenary docket in each category. See Hellman, *supra* ... Indeed, as will be noted, our data tends to confirm some of his conclusions. See *infra* Part II.B (examining number of actions filed in particular subject areas). Yet because his work makes no use of the data available on conference votes from the docket books of various retired Justices, it is necessarily limited....

During that period, the Court gave full consideration to a total of 108 appeals.

In order to make the second part of the comparison, we reviewed every plenary decision that the Court issued during each of the Terms from 1990–1993. In doing so, we applied the appeal criteria that were in place during the 1984–1987 Terms to determine which cases would have been before the Court on appeal, had the now-repealed statutes still been in force. We also assumed that any litigant who would have been entitled to file an appeal would have taken advantage of that route rather than petitioning for certiorari, because the Court granted plenary review more often in cases on appeal and was obliged to provide at least some form of review on the merits in such cases. Within these parameters, we determined that during the four Terms from 1990–1993, the Court granted plenary review in 70 such cases.

A straight comparison of the raw numbers suggests that there was a noticeable decline in appeal-type cases: 108 appeals in the four-year period prior to the 1988 legislation versus 70 "would-have-been" appeals in the four-year period immediately following the legislation, an average of almost 10 fewer cases per year. However, as a percentage of the entire plenary docket during the designated periods, the decline was insignificant. In the 1984–1987 period, the Court issued 609 plenary decisions. The 108 appeals constituted 17.7% of the docket. In the 1990–1993 period, the Court issued 427 plenary decisions. The 70 imputed "appeals" constituted 16.4% of the docket.... [Editors' Note: That is, the authors suggest, the ratio of appeals to certs did not change significantly in the two periods; both the number of imputed appeals on which cert was granted and the number of straightforward cert grants declined in the period from 1990–93.]

Because the decline in the number of appeal-type cases virtually mirrored the decline in the number of traditional certiorari cases, there are two possible ways to explain how curbing the Court's mandatory jurisdiction affected the docket. One possibility is that the Court did exercise its new discretion to cut back significantly on "appeal" cases that were not worthy of certiorari review (at the rate of ten or more per Term), but otherwise continued to take such cases at the same rate that it had in the mid–1980s. At the same time, however, some independent variable was driving down the number of traditional certiorari cases granted plenary review, without affecting the "appeal" cases.

Although this first explanation cannot be ruled out entirely, it is implausible. Far more likely is the possibility that some variable (or variables) independent of the legislative amendments was simultaneously depressing the number of cases granted plenary review in both the traditional certiorari and "appeal" categories, to approximately the same degree. This strongly suggests that in the mid–1980s the Court was not giving plenary consideration to appeals that did not warrant certiorari review, except in perhaps one or two cases per Term, because it had already implemented internal procedures that led it to evaluate appeals and petitions for certiorari in similar fashion when deciding whether to grant review on the merits. . . .

B.   Fewer Actions Filed in Particular Subject Areas

Justice Souter has suggested that the declining docket may be partly attributable to fewer cases being filed in particular subject areas that are highly susceptible to Supreme Court review, such as antitrust and civil rights. Yet a careful examination of the actual case filings reveals that this theory cannot account for the decline.

. . .

Comparison of the 1983–1985 Terms to the 1993–1995 Terms indicates that the number of plenary decisions in almost all of the major substantive areas declined. . . . The categories that declined the most, in terms of total plenary decisions, were civil rights cases, administrative appeals, and search-and-seizure challenges. . . . Over this period, the only major area that bucked the trend and held its firm grip on the docket was freedom of speech.

These figures are troublesome for the hypothesis: they suggest that if fewer cases filed in particular subject areas is the explanation for the shrinking docket, then this has happened on a grand scale, across diverse subjects on the criminal side as well as the civil side of the Court's docket. . . .

. . . [T]he number of applications for plenary review filed in federal criminal cases nearly tripled over this period, and it is implausible that this increase was offset by any corresponding decline in state criminal cases. [T]he suggested hypothesis simply has no traction in these categories.[70]

Although many of the criminal cases were in forma pauperis filings, and the Court grants these at a much lower rate, the in forma pauperis cases were largely exempt from the overall decline in the plenary docket: the Court granted 47 such cases in the 1983–1985 Terms, and 44 such cases in the 1993–1995 Terms. . . .

It is possible, however, that fewer cases were filed in the remaining subject areas on the civil side and thus this factor may play some part in the docket's decline. The only way to evaluate this possibility is to categorize and count the individual [cert] filings. We have done so by counting the cases filed on the appellate docket in each of these categories—civil rights, civil procedure, antitrust, and federal tax—for the 1983–1985 Terms and for the 1993–1995 Terms.

The resulting figures show that this theory does little to explain the contraction in the plenary docket. . . . In civil rights cases, which made up the largest group of filings, the number of paid filings actually

---

70. [Editors' Note: Readers will recall that Justice Souter offered a different explanation with respect to Fourth Amendment cases—not that the case filings were down but rather that the field had been pretty well "raked over" and the Court no longer needed to hear as many of them as in prior decades. See O'Brien, *supra* at 451.]

increases over this period. In the areas of federal tax, civil procedure, and antitrust, there was some decline in the number of cases filed, but nowhere near the decline that occurred in the number of cases that were granted. These figures thus suggest that the evolving interests of the Justices themselves caused more changes in the substantive mix of cases on the plenary docket than the availability of various cases for review.

It remains possible, of course, that petitioners filed fewer meritorious applications for review in recent years. . . . [Yet] the number of cases in which amici filed . . . briefs [in support of certiorari] has increased in recent years, [which] tends to cut against the notion that fewer important cases are now making their way to the Court than in previous years.

. . .

C. Federal Government Seeking Review Less Frequently

A factor that is contributing to the declining docket is the smaller number of cases in which the Solicitor General has been seeking plenary review on behalf of the United States. The Solicitor General is by far the most frequent Supreme Court litigant and the most successful applicant in obtaining plenary review. Indeed, the proportion of the Solicitor General's petitions for certiorari that the Court grants is consistently over fifty percent, whereas paid petitions filed by other parties are granted at a rate of only about three percent.

. . .

Statistics from the Office of the Solicitor General demonstrate that the United States has been seeking plenary review in fewer cases in recent years. During the four Terms from 1984–1987, for example, the Solicitor General sought review in 213 cases by filing either a petition for certiorari or a jurisdictional statement—an average of more than 53 cases per Term. In the next four Terms, however that number slipped to 137 cases—an average of only about 34 per Term. In the next four Terms, the number has remained at this lower level, falling further to 31 cases per Term from 1995–1998. The figures suggest that the decline in requests by the Solicitor General has led to a decline in plenary decisions, since the rate at which these requests are granted remains much higher than for all other parties seeking review. . . .

The Solicitor General's pullback in seeking review accounts for a drop of approximately 15 cases per Term in the Court's plenary docket. In addition, the Solicitor General's less active involvement as amicus at the certiorari stage explain the loss of about 10 more cases per Term because the federal government is just about as successful in supporting another party's application for review as it is in seeking review in its own right. These figures indicate that the drop in filings by the Solicitor General, which occurred over essentially the same period as the decline in the plenary docket, is an independent factor that made a substantial contribution to the decline.

But this fact prompts an even more interesting question: What has caused this decline in the Solicitor General's activity? . . .

There is no indication that the Justice Department has changed its internal petitioning policies or criteria in the last decade. . . . [T]he decline in requests for Supreme Court review has occurred during a period that spans administrations of both political parties and the tenures of multiple occupants in the top departmental positions.[71] . . .

In addition to the decreasing amount of civil litigation involving the federal government, a further factor contributing to the decline in the number of the Solicitor General's applications for review may be that the federal government is winning more of its civil cases in the lower courts. No numbers are kept on the federal government's "winning percentage". . . . Yet one sound indicator is the number of cases in which the opposing party seeks review from the Supreme Court. . . . If this figure is taken as a general proxy for the number of circuit court cases that the federal government won, and "recommendations received" is taken as a general proxy for the number of circuit court cases that the federal government lost, then comparing the two figures over time will shed light on how the federal government is faring in such cases. The results of this comparison do indicate that the federal government is winning more of its civil cases than it was ten years ago. Another indication that it is winning more of its cases is that during a period in which the total amount of the federal government's civil litigation was decreasing, the number of applications for review filed against the federal government in the Supreme Court more than doubled.

This seems plausible enough. Over the course of the last two decades, there is no doubt that the ranks of the federal judiciary have become more conservative and thus probably, on the whole, more "pro-government." Civil libertarians have recognized this development—which itself is an independent factor that discourages certain kinds of lawsuits against government officials and government entities. . . . Even in nonconstitutional cases, new judicial doctrines that explicitly favor the federal government's legal positions have been adopted and established as precedent. In this climate, it is to be expected that the federal government would begin to prevail more often in the lower courts and, as a consequence, the Solicitor General would have fewer occasions to seek plenary review. This, in turn, would cause the Supreme Court to accept fewer cases, as the federal government's high success rate in seeking plenary review would be replaced by the much lower success rate of all other parties. There is no doubt that this explanation is responsible for as much as one-third of the total decline in the Supreme Court's plenary docket.

71. [Footnote 153 in original] . . . Professor Hellman mentions that some Senators had questioned the zeal of Solicitor General Drew Days in criminal cases. . . . As shown below, however, both the number and rate of cases filed by the Solicitor General in criminal cases has remained stable over the past decade. . . .

D. Greater Homogeneity Among the Courts

Another suggested explanation, which we credit in part, is greater homogeneity among the lower courts. According to this theory, a broad judicial realignment resulting from the steady appointment of like-minded federal judges has contributed to the declining docket. Justice Souter describes this homogeneity as one legacy of "the Reagan–Bush era," and he speculates that it is a "rare" phenomenon that probably will be short-lived.

Advocates of this view focus on the possibility that changes within the lower courts have led them to agree more frequently with one another, which we call a "philosophical realignment." . . .

There are two empirical reasons to doubt the extent to which a philosophical realignment can explain the shrinking plenary docket. The first concerns timing. On the surface, the recent changes in the docket seem consistent with this possibility, for the decline commenced in the later stages of prolonged one-party control of the Presidency, from 1981–1993, after the Republicans had made extensive appointments to the district courts and the circuit courts. Yet if philosophical realignment per se tended to explain the falling caseload, then one would expect the numbers to increase again after several years of a Democratic President, and surely they would have done so by 2000, after eight years of Democratic judicial appointments to the lower courts. In fact, however, this has not happened.

Second, a large number of decisional conflicts remain available for the Supreme Court to review. In particular, the "Circuit Split Round-up," a publication that describes those decisional conflicts which can be identified by examining the face of individual lower court opinion, identifies approximately 400 such acknowledged conflicts per year. There appears to be no definitive way to measure whether there are fewer decisional conflicts today than in past years, or whether they may be of lesser significance than in the past. It is certainly clear, however, that even if greater homogeneity among the lower courts has created some form of a philosophical realignment, . . . lower courts continue to create many more decisional conflicts each year than are being reconciled by the Supreme Court.

Nonetheless, the discussion in Part C suggests that one particular form of judicial realignment may have had a tangible effect on the Supreme Court's docket. That is, an apparent realignment in the lower federal courts toward more "pro-government" results—i.e., a "statist realignment"—has led the Solicitor General to seek review less often in civil cases, with a corresponding decline in such cases granted. . . .

A similar development is manifest in federal litigation that involves state and local governments. . . . [T]he number of plenary decisions in federal civil cases involving state and local governments has fallen even more steeply than in cases involving the federal government: from an average of 35 cases per Term from 1983–1985 to fewer than 11 cases per Term from 1993–1995. And it is interesting that the same pattern does not hold for civil litigation involving state and local governments from the state courts: the average number of plenary decisions in such cases per Term was 7 from 1983–1985 and was still 7 from 1993–1995. Although it is conceivable that the state courts (which are not immune to the same political forces felt in the federal courts) could have moved in the same pro-government direction as the lower federal courts, these numbers at least suggest that the state courts did not experience a statist realignment to nearly the same degree.[72]

Outside the arena of government litigation, however, any theory of realignment confronts mixed results. The decline in the number of plenary decisions in private civil litigation has been much less pronounced. . . . [O]ne might surmise that uniformity is harder to achieve in private civil cases, in which the issues involved are more diverse and thus do not fall into clear and consistent patterns. . . .

This statist realignment therefore does reflect an increased commonality of approach among the judges on the lower federal courts in certain types of cases. It is harder to pin down whether this result flows more from a shared outlook of the Reagan–Bush nominees or from the lower courts' conformance to a pro-government philosophy that the Supreme Court has imposed on them. . . .

It should be noted, however, that a statist realignment in the lower federal courts will cause fewer cases to come to the Supreme Court for review, and thus fewer to be granted review, only if the Court itself is comfortable with these pro-government results. . . . For three decades, the Court has been gravitating in favor of government litigants, and the lower courts have surely gotten the message by now.[73] This discussion of

72. [Footnote 197 in original] Professor Hellman analyzes the issue of greater "conservatism in the lower courts" by focusing almost exclusively on state criminal cases and habeas cases, which leads him to suggest that realignment in the lower federal courts has had little to do with the shrinking docket. See Hellman, *supra*. . . . As we have seen, however, a larger portion of the decline is attributable to changes that have occurred in federal civil cases, which is part of the reason why we reach a contrary conclusion.

73. [Footnote 201 in original] See, e.g., . . . David G. Savage, *Turning Right: The Making of the Rehnquist Supreme Court* 453 (1992) (concluding that "change in membership" has eliminated support for "the old agenda"). In the criminal area, with its control now presumably reestablished, the Court's preoccupation with correcting lower court rulings has abated, as the number of plenary decisions in criminal cases from the state courts fell sharply from an average of 20 per Term in 1985–1990 to 6 per Term in 1991–1999. . . . Habeas cases also dropped, though less significantly—

from 10 per Term to 7 per term over the same period. *Id.* The substantial decline in state criminal cases tends to suggest that the statist realignment is explained more by a control realignment than by a homogeneity brought about by a uniform course of judicial appointments to the lower federal bench. See Hellman, *supra* . . . (suggesting control realignment theory). One should note, however, that part of the explanation here may also be that the state courts are learning to interpret and apply the jurisdictional rules laid down in Michigan v. Long, 463 U.S. 1032 (1983), which permit them to insulate more "liberal" criminal decisions from Supreme Court review by placing such rulings on adequate and independent state constitutional grounds. See generally Earl M. Maltz, *The Dark Side of State Court Activism*, 63 Tex. L. Rev. 995 (1985) (discussing this interaction between state courts and Supreme Court). By contrast, the number of plenary decisions in federal criminal cases actually increased over the same period, from 10 per Term to 12 per Term, . . . though this was undoubtedly due to the steep increase that has occurred in federal criminal litigation. . . .

judicial realignment thus points to the need to consider how changes in the Supreme Court itself likely affected the size and shape of its plenary docket.

E.   Changes in Personnel on the Supreme Court

One of the most compelling explanations for the recent decline in the Supreme Court's plenary docket stems directly from changes in personnel. Recall that when a similar decline occurred fifty years ago, the primary cause was the retirement of Justices who had voted aggressively to review cases and their replacement by new Justices who were far less inclined to do so. . . .

Around the period of the most recent decline there were six retirements: Chief Justice Burger in 1986, Justice Powell in 1987, Justice Brennan in 1990, Justice Marshall in 1991, Justice White in 1993, and Justice Blackmun in 1994. The question posed here is whether these changes in personnel, taken singly or together, caused any systematic change in the frequency with which the Court decides to grant review.

Two previous studies provide indirect support for the view that such changes may have played an important role in the decline. In a 1996 article, Professor Hellman analyzed five potential external causes of the shrinking docket. He concluded that they did little to explain the phenomenon, and went on to speculate from comments made by individual Justices that, following the recent retirements, the Court had become more comfortable with using fewer precedents to supervise the lower courts. Professor O'Brien reached a similar conclusion after examining some of the internal procedures that the Court employs in exercising its discretionary power to grant plenary review. [See O'Brien article above.]

. . .

. . . Professor O'Brien's research demonstrates that Justices White, Marshall, and Brennan noted votes to grant review and dissented from denial of review far more frequently than the Justices who replaced them, which he took as suggesting that these newer Justices are less inclined to grant review in general.

These signs must be read with caution, however, because there is no necessary correlation between a willingness to vote for plenary review and a willingness to register that vote publicly. . . . [A]s our data on the Justices' conference votes shows, Justices Brennan and Marshall frequently were public dissenters from denial of review on the Burger and Rehnquist Courts, yet it turns out that they voted relatively infrequently to grant review during this same period.

Professor O'Brien also pierced the judicial veil to a limited extent by using The Thurgood Marshall Papers to shed light on the Justices' voting behavior at conference, though he evaluated only how often individual Justices cast Join–3 votes in those cases where the Court granted plenary review. . . . He found that, during the 1979 to 1990 Terms, the Justices placed at least twelve percent of the cases on the plenary docket with fewer than four outright votes to grant plus one or more Join–3 votes. He then noted that several of the Justices most inclined to use the Join–3 vote retired in the early 1990s. . . .

.   .   .

It bears emphasis, however, that the usefulness of this data on Join–3 votes turns on the meaning of such votes. If Justices casting a Join–3 vote would have cast a vote to grant review had Join–3 not been an option, then the data reveals little about the Justices' overall inclination to grant cases. If, on the other hand, a Join–3 vote is cast in lieu of a vote to deny, then it does suggest a willingness to erode the Rule of Four. . . .

A better way to measure an individual Justice's willingness to grant review would be, of course, to look directly at the number of such votes that he or she cast in conference. . . .

.   .   .

The availability of the private papers of some of the recently retired Justices, which include the conference votes recorded in their docket books, offers new opportunities to compile grant rates at least for those Justices who served on the Court before Justice Marshall's retirement at the end of the 1990 Term. . . . [W]e have been able to determine the rate at which each Justice voted to grant plenary review (of appeals and petitions for certiorari) during the Burger Court era. . . .

The cumulative data suggests that the grant rates of individual Justices, relative to one another, tend to remain fairly constant over time, reflecting a general outlook that does not vary appreciably from one Term to the next. . . . [T]he two clear exceptions to the general rule occurred with the transition from the Warren Court to the Burger Court, when the sharp change in the direction of the Court appears to have correlated with a decline in the number of votes cast for review by Justice Brennan and an increase in the number cast by Justice White.

To some extent, this relative consistency of each Justice's voting behavior compared to that of his or her colleagues is not surprising. . . .

The data on conference votes demonstrates that changes in the Court's personnel have had a dramatic effect on the recent decline in the plenary docket. In the last decade of the Burger Court, the two Justices who consistently voted most frequently to grant plenary review were Justices White and Rehnquist, sometimes by a wide margin over their colleagues. Justices Blackmun, O'Connor, and Powell (usually in that order) were in the middle of the Court, followed by Chief Justice Burger; throughout this period, Justices Brennan, Marshall, and Stevens uniformly voted least often to grant review. . . .

In 1986, Chief Justice Burger retired and Justice Scalia replaced him on the Court. The nomination and confirmation process was an unusual tandem arrangement, because at the same time President Reagan filled the vacancy on the Court, he elevated Justice Rehnquist to the position of Chief Justice. The next year, Justice Powell retired and was replaced by Justice Kennedy, after months of delays caused by confirmation battles in the Senate. The numbers reveal that each of these three changes on the Court played a discernible part in shrinking the docket. Over the course of the next several Terms, both Justice Scalia and Justice Kennedy settled into abnegating roles in the discretionary review process, voting to grant review less often than any other Justice.... Two Justices from the middle tier of the Court were thus replaced by two Justices who voted much less frequently to grant review. At the same time, the voting behavior of now-Chief Justice Rehnquist underwent a dramatic change; from keeping pace with Justice White in an aggressively pro-review first tier on the Court, his total votes for plenary review gradually slipped to where he eventually relinquished the second place to Justice Blackmun. This sudden and marked change in an individual Justice's voting behavior stands as one further exception to the rule of general consistency, though it seems to be directly linked to Justice Rehnquist's perception of his new and distinct role as the Chief Justice.

The consequent shift in the Court's direction was quite significant.... In effect, the aggregate result of these changes in personnel was roughly as if the Rule of Four were now being made to operate on a court composed of slightly more than seven of its former members, rather than nine. The Court's docket bears out this observation, as the number of plenary decisions fell from 156 in the 1985 Term to 132 in the 1989 Term.

. . .

... [T]wo more retirements occurred: Justice Souter replaced Justice Brennan after the 1989 Term, and Justice Thomas replaced Justice Marshall after the 1990 Term. The erosion of the Court's docket had continued even before these events occurred, as approximately half of the argument calendar for the 1990 Term was already set before Justice Brennan's retirement, and the number of plenary decisions declined again to 116 in that Term. Although there has been some speculation that the retirements of these two most liberal Justices caused or accelerated the docket's decline, in retrospect the evidence for this view appears scant. To begin with, for many years both Justice Brennan and Justice Marshall had established themselves at the low end of the spectrum in voting to grant review. And figures from Justice Souter's partial participation in conference votes for the 1990 Term suggest that he may support plenary review about as often as Justice Brennan did. Even if Justice Thomas's voting behavior on discretionary review were similar to that of Justices Scalia and Kennedy, which seems plausible but not inevitable, it is hard to envision how these two changes in personnel, taken together, would have caused any appreciable decline in the Court's docket.

The numbers again seem to bear this out, as the number of plenary decisions briefly stabilized at 116 in the 1990 Term, 110 in the 1991 Term, and 111 in the 1992 Term. Of course, it is quite plausible that

Justices Brennan and Marshall may have cast different kinds of votes on discretionary review, and hence their departure from the Court might have depressed the numbers in certain categories of cases that were set for plenary review. The records for their conference votes show, for example that these two Justices voted more frequently than any other Justice to grant review of criminal cases filed in forma pauperis. . . . Yet there was not significant decline in the number of in forma pauperis cases: the Court granted 74 such cases in the 1986–1989 Terms, and 62 such cases in the 1991–1994 Terms–a drop of only three cases per Term. Even from this perspective, it thus seems that these retirements had only a limited effect on the continuing decline in the docket.

The final round of retirements came in 1993, when Justice Ginsburg replaced Justice White, and in 1994, when Justice Breyer replaced Justice Blackmun. Although no data is available yet to enable us to calculate individual grant rates for these new Justices, it is clear that these two changes had a profound influence on the shrinking of the docket. . . .

The retirement of these two Justices caused an immediate further decline in the number of plenary decisions, to levels never before seen in the Court's modern era. The Court issued 90 plenary decisions in the 1993 Terms, 85 in the 1994 Term, and only 78 in the 1995 Term. The numbers have remained at this level as the composition of the Court has remained unchanged, eventually reaching a new low of 76 plenary decisions in the 1999 Term. In light of the conference data now available, these unprecedented results are understandable. Justice White's voting behavior was so extraordinary that replacing him by someone with even an average grant rate would be tantamount to eliminating the votes caused by a typical Justice for plenary review in a given Term. . . .

. . . Quite apart from issues about who was winning and losing in the lower courts, and what parties were seeking review in which cases from one Term to the next, it is now evident that the Court's personnel changes over this decade were a substantial independent cause of the remarkable decline in its docket . . .

F. Growth of the "Cert Pool"

The foregoing analysis also helps dispel another explanation that has been offered for the declining docket—the allegedly excessive influence of law clerks in screening out cases through operation of the "cert pool.". . .

The mechanism of the cert pool was controversial from its inception, and it remained so for years. . . . [V]arious commentators have . . . voiced concerns that it delegates too much authority to law clerks and has the undesirable effect of largely homogenizing the Court's consideration of applications for review.

It seems unlikely, however, that the cert pool has had much systematic influence on the votes cast by individual Justices to grant or deny plenary review, at least when compared to the dominant factor of the

Justices' own predispositions. All of the Justices had individualized screening mechanisms in place prior to the cert pool, which made varying use of the law clerks. Such supplemental procedures also remained after the pool was in place, and it appears that the varying levels of scrutiny that individual Justices give to the applications does not correlate with their participation in the pool. Moreover, the actual voting behavior of the Justices in the pool has been far from uniform. For example, Justice White belonged to the pool for his last two decades on the Court, yet he consistently supported plenary review in many more cases than the other pool members. Justice Blackmun, though less extreme in this regard, also compiled a high grant rate relative to the other pool members. At the same time, from outside the pool Justice Stevens has had an index that is regularly below that of the average pool member. The supposed boundary between those Justices who do and do not belong to the cert pool is further blurred by frequent consultations among their law clerks.

Indeed, for the first fifteen years after the cert pool made its debut, the number of cases granted plenary review remained in the range of 150 cases per Term. The single period of decline during this period occurred after Justice Stevens replaced Justice Douglas in 1975. Neither belonged to the pool, however, and the drop in the caseload is traceable instead to their very different views of the Court's optimal capacity to hear and decide cases. Notably, after Justice O'Connor arrived at the Court in 1981—and joined the cert pool, unlike her predecessor, Justice Stewart—the plenary docket rose again to about 150 cases per Term, and remained there for the next eight Terms. This pattern defies explanation if the excessive influence of a larger cert pool is an important factor in depressing the Court's docket. It is more likely that the clerks' initial screening simply helps in weeding out the great mass of cases that are universally viewed as marginal and in focusing attention on the remainder.

The only evidence that has been cited to the contrary is that when Justices Brennan and Marshall left the Court in 1990 and 1991, the number of Justices in the cert pool rose from six to eight, with only Justice Stevens remaining out. Because this change occurred during the period of general decline, it has been speculated that this factor may have played a significant role in the changing docket. Yet the steep decline actually was well underway by this time. . . . Even more decisive, however, is the simple fact that Justices Brennan and Marshall themselves were voting to grant fewer cases than most of their colleagues on the Rehnquist Court, though neither belonged to the cert pool. . . . It thus seems virtually certain that the number of Justices in the cert pool has had little or nothing to do with the Court's declining docket.

III.   CONCLUSIONS ABOUT THE CHANGING DOCKET

. . .

Given these explanations for the declining docket, it is likely that the current situation will endure for some time to come, unless or until significant changes occur from new appointments to the Court. . . . At the same time, the confirmed pattern of government attorneys bringing fewer cases to the Court is likely to persist, for though they can anticipate paddling into rougher waters again at some point in the future, there is no apparent reason to believe that this will happen any time soon. For the time being, therefore, the Supreme Court's plenary docket has stabilized at levels that are unprecedented in the modern era.

————————

David R. Stras,[74] *Book Review Essay:*[75] *The Supreme Court's Gatekeepers: The Role of Law Clerks in the Certiorari Process*, 85 Tex. L. Rev. 947 (2007)

. . .

III. Law Clerks and the Supreme Court's Plenary Docket

. . .

A. *The Declining Plenary Docket*

The recent decline in the Court's plenary docket is extraordinary. From a contemporary high of 155 signed opinions in October Terms 1982 and 1983, the Court has retreated to about half of that number in recent Terms. . . . Even more startling is that the reduction in the plenary docket comes at a time when Justices are, more than ever, relying on their law clerks for screening cases and drafting opinions. . . .

The Supreme Court's workload can be measured in a variety of ways, but one reliable and well-accepted technique is the number of cases that the Court disposes of by signed opinion. That statistic is valuable because it measures the number of cases over which the Court gives full, plenary consideration, including oral argument. Starting with the 1800 Term and ending with the 2004 Term, Figure 1 graphically displays the number of signed opinions issued by the Court.

---

74. Associate Professor of Law, University of Minnesota.

75. The essay reviews Todd C. Peppers, *Courtiers of the Marble Palace: The Rise and Influence of the Supreme Court Law Clerk* (2006) and Artemus Ward & David L. Weiden, *Sorcerers' Apprentices: 100 Years of Law Clerks at the United States Supreme Court* (2006).

FIGURE 1
Total Number of Signed Opinions Per Term

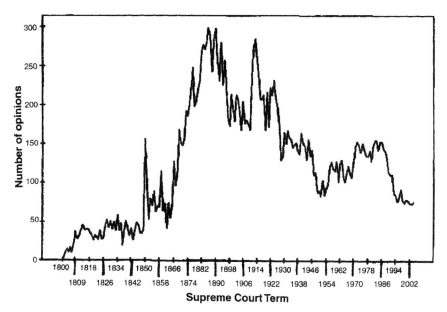

As Figure 1 demonstrates, the reduction in the Court's plenary docket began in 1986, when William Rehnquist became Chief Justice and Antonin Scalia was appointed to the Court. In October Term 1986, the Court issued 153 signed and orally argued per curiam opinions, but by October Term 1989, that number had declined to 131. The decline then accelerated, with only eighty-six such opinions released during October Term 1993. Since then, the Court's plenary docket has oscillated between seventy-four and ninety-two signed and orally argued per curiam opinions, with most of the recent Terms on the low side of that range.

One of the most striking aspects of the declining plenary docket is that it coincides with an unprecedented expansion in the dockets of the lower courts, particularly the United States Courts of Appeals. While the Supreme Court's plenary docket is approximately half as large in 2004 as it was in 1986, the dockets of the federal circuit courts have increased by 82.4% during that same period . . . .

. . . At a time when the lower courts are confronting unprecedented numbers of cases and disposing of more cases summarily, the Supreme Court is deciding, on a relative basis, nearly four times fewer federal cases than it did in 1986, which is a staggering change in less than twenty years . . . .

Perhaps it is unfair to judge the workload of the Supreme Court and its commitment to the supervision of the lower federal courts in light of the total number of cases terminated in the Courts of Appeals because many lower court cases are meritless and fewer than 15% result in petitions for certiorari. But even measuring the Court's production in terms of the total number of petitions for certiorari and jurisdictional statements demonstrates that there has been a fundamental change over the past twenty years. Since October Term 1999, the Court has granted plenary review in less than 1% of the cases in which a petition for certiorari or jurisdictional statement has been filed, which is in stark contrast to the more than 3% of cases that were granted plenary review from October Terms 1981 to 1985. Figure 3 visually presents the Supreme Court's increasing selectivity in all cases in recent years.

FIGURE 3
Percentage of Cases Granted by The Supreme Court

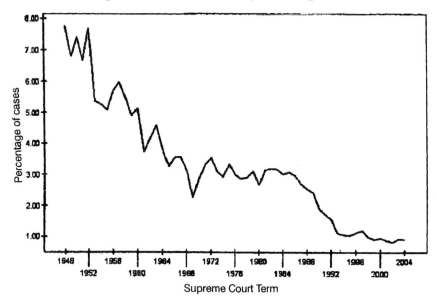

B.   *The Impact of Law Clerks on the Plenary Docket*

. . .

... Kenneth Starr recently wrote that law clerks serve as "mighty 'barriers to entry' to the [plenary] docket." Even Justice Stevens, the lone current holdout from the cert pool, believes that "with more justices sharing the clerks' pool memos, ... the clerks have become increasingly cautious in recommending that the court take up a particular case."

Other scholars and commentators view the matter differently, discounting the link between the plenary docket and the cert pool. For instance, in an anecdotal account of his experiences as a law clerk for Justice Blackmun, Edward Lazarus wrote in *Closed Chambers* that he "doubt[ed] the Court granted any cert. petitions because of something clerks did and, if some clerks did manage to bury a few cases along the way, the same issues, assuming they were worth the Court's time, were sure to resurface."

Similarly, in the most exhaustive study of the Court's plenary docket to date, Margaret and Richard Cordray find it unlikely "that the cert pool has had much systematic influence on the votes cast by individual Justices to grant or deny plenary review, at least when compared to the dominant factor of the Justices' own predisposition." They based that conclusion on their review of the mechanics of the cert pool, and the voting behavior of the Justices.

First, the Cordrays recognized that the Justices who belong to the pool do not rely solely on the pool memo recommendations in casting their votes. To the contrary, most Justices continue to employ individualized screening mechanisms for petitions for certiorari, including the annotation of pool memos and the drafting of supplementary memoranda by their law clerks.

Second, the Cordrays point to the varying voting behavior by Justices within the pool as evidence of the pool's meager influence. In particular, Justices White and Blackmun voted to grant certiorari in far more cases than their other colleagues in the pool, most notably Justices Kennedy and Scalia. In contrast, Justice Stevens, who has never joined the pool, has voted to grant certiorari at a rate lower than all other Justices except Kennedy and Scalia, at least during the 1989 and 1990 Terms.

Third, the Cordrays attempt to refute the argument that an increase in the membership of the pool, from six Justices to eight Justices, has contributed to the shrunken plenary docket. They essentially conclude that the declining docket and the rising influence of the cert pool are nothing more than historical coincidences, linked in time but lacking any causal nexus. For support, they point out that the decline only accelerated after the retirements of Justices Blackmun and White, both of whom were members of the cert pool. Even more decisive, according to the Cordrays, is the fact that three Justices who did not participate in the cert pool, Justices Stevens, Marshall, and Brennan, voted to grant certiorari at a rate well below the average of their colleagues. Accordingly, the Cordrays are "virtually certain that the number of Justices in the cert pool has had little or nothing to do with the Court's declining docket."

While the Cordrays have mounted the most comprehensive attack against the influence of the cert pool on the declining plenary docket, their study still suffers from a lack of completeness.... While the diverse voting behavior of the Justices within (and outside) the pool is informative, it does not *directly* account for the influence of the pool on either the Justices themselves or the Court as a whole....

... [I]t is difficult to know precisely how much impact the pool memoranda have on the decisions of the Justices, because the Court does not usually tell us why a particular petition for certiorari was granted or denied. It is possible that the pool just serves as an initial screening device for the Justices, without much substantive impact on their votes, but it is also possible that the Justices take the recommendations of the law clerks in the pool seriously. The starting point, therefore, of a study of the impact of the cert pool is an assessment of the pool memoranda, the instruments that the law clerks use to communicate with the

Justices. To my knowledge, however, no scholar has engaged in a systematic study of every petition for certiorari from even a single Term of the Supreme Court, and thus there is an analytical hole in the study of the influence of the cert pool.

In this section, I will begin with an analysis of the mechanics of the cert pool, including a critical examination of the theoretical underpinnings for the argument that the pool has influenced the declining docket.... I will then turn to the results of my examination of every pool memorandum from several Terms of the Court. My pilot study reveals at a high level of confidence that the cert pool is considerably more stingy in making grant recommendations than is the Court in its decisions to grant plenary review. Although it is difficult to say exactly how much influence the pool recommendations have on the ultimate decision of whether to grant certiorari, it is safe to say after this study that the pool is not a factor in encouraging the Court to expand its plenary docket and may well be contributing to the decline.

1.   *The Institutional Predisposition Against Granting Certiorari*

. . .

The mechanics of the cert pool have led to a homogenization of the process by which petitions for certiorari are reviewed. Before the creation of the pool, each Justice had his own procedure for screening cases, from Justice Brennan's individual review of each petition (except during summer recess) to the more common delegatory model of Justices such as Stewart and Marshall, who required their law clerks to draft memoranda on the petitions. The process within each chambers was highly individualized, with each Justice using his law clerks in any manner that he wished. A benefit of these divergent approaches was that law clerks who worked on screening cases could tailor their memoranda and recommendations, resulting in greater candor about the cases that would interest their Justice....

In contrast, the cert pool requires the law clerks to follow a standardized format in drafting their memoranda. For instance, a review of pool memoranda in the papers of Justice Blackmun reveals that, at least from 1984 to 1993, each memo contains the following five standardized sections: Summary, Facts and Decisions Below, Contentions (of the parties), Discussion, and Recommendation. More importantly, although law clerks could spend more time on each petition they were assigned, they were no longer able to tailor the pool memoranda to their individual Justices, writing instead for an audience of anywhere from five to eight Justices. The cert pool has thus led to a greater homogenization of the memoranda produced by the law clerks.

Recall, however, that the Cordrays argued that the cert pool did not eliminate the Justices' individualized screening mechanisms. Professor David O'Brien takes the Cordrays' argument one step further by contending that the Justices "in the cert pool might actually give more attention to case selection" based on the ongoing individualized screening mechanisms of each Justice. Professor H.W. Perry cites additional evidence that law clerks for most Justices provide an important check on the cert pool by reviewing and annotating pool memos and highlighting areas of particular interest for their Justices. But his interviews with former law clerks also suggest that, because recommendations to deny a case are the norm, law clerks pay far less attention to those recommendations than to recommendations to grant during the annotation process, increasing the likelihood that an issue of importance will be overlooked. Indeed, Justice Brennan did not join the cert pool in part because "[h]e said that he would find three to four cases a year that the clerks had missed." Therefore, the annotation process is potentially more effective for the less than 1% of cases that earn a grant recommendation from a law clerk in the pool, than it is for the far more common deny recommendation.

Moreover, the current incarnation of the cert pool—with eight of the nine Justices participating—has led to further homogenization. As stated above, when the cert pool was created, four Justices declined to participate. In addition to the check provided by the clerks for the Justices participating in the pool, the four nonparticipating Justices independently reviewed the petitions for certiorari, increasing the likelihood that an important issue warranting the Court's attention would not be overlooked. Justice Stevens has staunchly resisted membership in the pool because he has recognized that having all nine Justices in the pool could result in a greater number of "potential mistakes." Now, instead of four separate chambers providing a balance against the cert pool, the process has become more homogenized, with only Justice Stevens's chambers in a position to independently ensure that certworthy cases are not overlooked. The obvious implication is that, with fewer checks on the cert pool, more certworthy cases could be falling through the cracks.

In addition to homogenization, norms have developed within the cert pool that its creators, the Justices of the 1972 Court, might find surprising. Justice Blackmun initially thought that participation in the cert pool would make law clerks more likely to recommend granting certiorari in the cases that they reviewed. But according to *Sorcerers' Apprentices*, the pressure of writing for five or more Justices has made law clerks more cautious in their recommendations, creating what has become a "hydraulic pressure to say no." As Kenneth Starr has explained, when a clerk is unsure about a recommendation, the "prevailing ethos is that no harm can flow from 'just saying no.'" First, it is less risky to recommend a denial because, as stated above, that recommendation tends to be subject to far less scrutiny than a recommendation to grant a case. Second, a recommendation of deny permits pool authors to avoid the dreaded dismissal of a case as improvidently granted, otherwise referred to as a DIG. The desire to maintain credibility within the pool by avoiding a DIG weighs in favor of recommending a denial when there is the possibility of a vehicle problem or the case just presents a close call. Third, the behavior of law clerks is partly a product of the prevailing norms of the institution to which they belong, and the Court's declining docket surely sends a signal that the fewer grants the better. Borrowing Professor Peppers's framework, the law clerks are an unlikely "agent" of institutional change, especially in light of the short one-year tenure that they currently enjoy with the Court.

A related reason for the hesitancy of law clerks to recommend granting a case may be due to relative inexperience. Incoming law clerks, often fresh off of a clerkship with a judge on the United States Court of Appeals, have little training and even less experience screening the petitions for certiorari. . . . [M]uch of the screening work is done during the summer months, when the Justices are not regularly inside the building. . . .

In the absence of objective factors such as a conflict among the lower courts, the decision about whether to recommend a grant or a denial of certiorari is largely based on subjective factors that law clerks, at least early in their clerkships, may be ill-equipped to evaluate. The natural consequence is that law clerks will focus on objective factors to guide their inquiry, most notably the presence or absence of a split among the lower courts on an issue of federal law. Other possible certworthy cases lacking objectively identifiable characteristics, therefore, might slip through the cracks. . . .

2.   *The Empirical Evidence on the Cert Pool*

. . . In this Section, I begin with a readily falsifiable hypothesis about the cert pool advanced by several scholars: that the cert pool is stingy with its recommendations to grant petitions for certiorari as compared to the certiorari decisions of the Court as a whole. I then turn to a related matter—whether the cert pool and the Justices unduly focus on the presence of a conflict among the lower courts in making decisions about whether to grant certiorari in a case. Finally, instead of examining the level of influence of the cert pool, an inquiry fraught with difficulty due to the absence of compelling data, I look at the correlation and level of agreement between the recommendations of the cert pool and the decisions of the Court, which may provide some clue as to the role and importance of the cert pool in the screening process.

a.   *The Stingy Cert Pool*

A number of scholars and commentators have noted that the presumption in the cert pool is to recommend the denial of certiorari. . . .

In order to evaluate the characteristics of the cert pool, every pool memorandum from October Terms 1984, 1985, 1991, and 1992, was examined to determine whether the pool writer recommended that the Court grant, deny, or take some other action with respect to a petition for certiorari or a jurisdictional statement. The recommendation was then coded, and the total numbers per Term were tallied for each category. The examination demonstrates that, compared to the certiorari decisions of the Court as a whole, the cert pool is stingy in dispensing grant recommendations, and the clerks as a group are remarkably consistent in their stinginess from Term to Term.

Table 1 compares the number of grant recommendations by the cert pool with the number of Opinions of the Court and oral arguments for each of the four Terms studied. Both statistics—the number of Opinions of the Court and number of oral arguments—serve as proxies for the number of cases over which the Court grants full, plenary review. The results are consistent with the hypothesis that the cert pool is operating under a strong presumption that each petition for certiorari be denied. The data from the 1991 Term, for example, show that the Court decided 116 cases, while the pool memo recommended that certiorari be granted in only eighty-six cases. Likewise, for the 1984 Term, the Court decided 151 cases, but the pool recommended that the Court grant plenary review in only 107 cases. For every Term that was studied, the cert pool dispensed grant recommendations considerably less often than the Court granted certiorari.

TABLE 1
Comparison of the Number of Grant Recommendations by the Cert Pool With the Total Number of Opinions of the Court and Oral Argument Sessions, October Terms 1984, 1985, 1991, and 1992[76]

	Supreme Court Term			
	1984	1985	1991	1992
Number of grants suggested by the cert pool	107	111	86	83
Number of opinions of the Court	151	159	116	114
Number of oral argument sessions	175	171	127	116
Total number of cert petitions	4,269	4,289	5,825	6,336

Table 2 compares data over time by displaying the ratio or percentage of grant recommendations by the cert pool to the total number of Opinions of the Court and oral argument sessions. Despite the presence

76. [Footnote 190 in original] The data for the number of opinions and petitions for certiorari were taken from the annual *Harvard Law Review* statistics, while the number of oral arguments sessions per Term was obtained from the Supreme Court Public Information Office. Meanwhile, the number of recommended grants from the cert pool was obtained from a review of every pool memo in the papers of Justice Blackmun from October Terms 1984, 1985, 1991, and 1992. [Editors' Note: The author reviewed pool memos in both paid and IFP cases. See *id*. at 989 n. 224.]

of nearly 100% law clerk turnover on an annual basis and figures from two separate decades, the data show a surprisingly consistent grant-to-plenary decision ratio of between 70% and 75%. The data also permit the rejection, at a .001 confidence level or greater, of the null hypothesis that the Court and the cert pool are equally parsimonious in their views on whether to grant certiorari. In other words, there is less than a 1 in 1,000 chance that the Court itself is as stingy as the cert pool based on the data collected for the four Terms examined in Tables 1 and 2.... Accordingly, the data are strongly supportive of the hypothesis advanced by scholars that the cert pool is stingy in its screening of cases for the Court.

TABLE 2
Number of Grant Recommendations Made by the Cert Pool as a Percentage of the Number of Opinions of the Court and Oral Arguments, October Terms 1984, 1985, 1991, and 1992

	Supreme Court Term			
	1984	1985	1991	1992
Grant recommendations as a percentage of opinions of the Court	70.86	69.81	74.14	72.81
Grant recommendations as a percentage of oral argument sessions	61.14	64.91	67.72	71.55

b. Objective Criteria in Certiorari Review

... The most objective indicia of certworthiness, at least as far as the Rules of the Supreme Court are concerned, are whether "a United States court of appeals has entered a decision in conflict with the decision of another United States court of appeals on the same important matter" and whether "a state court of last resort has decided an important federal question in a way that conflicts with the decision of another state court of last resort or of a United States court of appeals." Ascertaining the presence of a lower court conflict requires less subjectivity from law clerks than determining, for example, whether "a state court or a United States court of appeals has decided an important question of federal law that has not been, but should be, settled by this Court."

Dating at least as far back as the passage of the Judge's Bill in 1925, the Court has placed particular emphasis on the presence of lower court conflict in making the decision about whether to grant certiorari or hear an appeal....

In recent years, lower court conflict has become an increasingly important factor guiding the certiorari decisions of the Court.... [The author's] study of all cases decided by the Supreme Court during the last three Terms ... includes Chief Justice Rehnquist's last two years and the first year for Chief Justice Roberts on the Court. Evaluating petitions for certiorari, lower court opinions, and the Court's opinion to determine whether a case involved a lower court conflict, the study determined that nearly 70% of the cases reviewed by the Court involved a split among the lower courts. The percentage of plenary cases involving a conflict ranged from 58.4% in 2003 to 78.9% in 2004 .....

· · ·

Those numbers contrast starkly with the composition of the Court's plenary docket in the early 1980's. In his important 1996 article in the *Supreme Court Review*,[77] Professor Arthur Hellman presented data on the number of cases involving a circuit conflict on the Court's plenary docket during the 1983–1985 and 1993–1995 Terms. He used the following criteria in determining whether a case involved a "conflict grant":

The Supreme Court stated that it granted review to resolve an intercircuit conflict.

The Court's opinion, although not specifying conflict as the reason for granting review, pointed clearly to the existence of an intercircuit disagreement.

The conflict was explicitly acknowledged by one or more courts of appeals in a case that was brought to the Court's attention before review was granted.

... Hellman's figures on United States Courts of Appeals cases that received plenary review by the Supreme Court during the 1983–1985 and 1993–1995 Terms, ... [show that the] composition of the docket changed considerably from the 1983–1985 period to the 1993–1995 period, with the number of cases involving a conflict rising from 45% during the earlier period to approximately 69% by a decade later. The number of conflict grants has since dropped to 60% during the most recent period, 2003–2005, but the recent decline is not nearly as sizeable as the remarkable increase in conflict cases as a percentage of the total plenary docket in the early 1990s.

· · ·

... [This data] provide only a baseline by which to evaluate the recommendations of the cert pool. Table 5, in contrast, considers directly the question of whether law clerks rely on the presence of conflict among the lower courts in making their recommendations on petitions for certiorari. In conducting the analysis, every plenary case from October Terms 1984 and 1985 reviewing a decision of a United States Court of Appeals was analyzed. Each case, after being categorized as a conflict or nonconflict case ... was then cross-referenced against the corresponding

77. [Editors' Note: Arthur Hellman, *The Shrunken Docket of the Rehnquist Court*, 1996 Sup. Ct. Rev. 403.]

pool memo for that case. The pool memo was then classified as belonging to one of five categories: grant, deny, take some other action, no recommendation, or missing a pool memo. The results of the study are compiled and displayed in Table 5.

TABLE 5
Cert Pool Treatment of Conflict and Non–Conflict Federal Court of Appeals Cases on the Plenary Docket, October Terms 1984 and 1985

| | Supreme Court Term | | | |
| | 1984 | | 1985 | |
	Conflict	No conflict	Conflict	No conflict
Cert pool recommended grant	35	25	25	23
Cert pool recommended deny	6	17	11	18
Cert pool recommended some other action	8	16	11	14
No recommendation	0	2	0	3
Missing pool memo	1	3	1	1
Total number of cert petitions	50	63	48	59

During the 1984 and 1985 Terms, the number of nonconflict grants outnumbered conflict grants by twenty-four cases. Despite the larger universe of nonconflict grants during those two Terms, the cert pool still recommended that the Court grant certiorari in twelve more conflict (60) cases than nonconflict cases (48).

Because the study examines cases that were eventually granted plenary review by the Court, it is not surprising that the Court agreed more often with the recommendation of the cert pool in cases involving a circuit split. In 61.22% of conflict grants, the cert pool agreed that the Court should grant certiorari. Meanwhile, the Court disagreed with the cert pool more frequently in nonconflict cases, with only 39.34% of the pool memoranda within that category recommending a grant. As a consequence, therefore, both in absolute numbers and percentage terms, the cert pool appears to be less comfortable recommending that the Court grant certiorari in a case lacking in objective indicia of certworthiness than it does in a case presenting a square conflict on an issue of law.

c. Correlation and Agreement Between the Cert Pool and the Court

As Professor Robert O'Neil stated in the foreword to *Courtiers*, "remarkably little is reliably known" about the role of Supreme Court law clerks in the judicial process. . . . As Professor Barbara Palmer has noted, Justice Powell's papers contain only the pool memos in granted cases, yet until recently that was the best source of data about the cert pool. However, with the 2004 public release of the papers of Justice Blackmun—who meticulously retained all of his records and correspondence in every case—a quantitative study of the impact of the cert pool is now possible.

The rest of this Review Essay will be dedicated to empirically assessing what role the cert pool recommendations have on the Justices and the Court. As before, in conducting this pilot study, every pool memo from October Terms 1984, 1985, 1991, and 1992 was examined and the recommendation was recorded. The study required an examination of more than 20,000 pool memos and then review of the United States Reports to determine the cases in which the Court ultimately granted review. The total raw numbers for the study are reported in Table 7.

TABLE 7
Recommendations of Pool Memos, by Term
October Terms 1984, 1985, 1991, 1992[78]

Supreme Court Term	1984	1985	1991	1992
Number of grant recommendations	107	111	86	83
Approximate number of deny recommendations	3,864	3,815	5,412	5,882
Number of "some other action" recommendations	298	363	327	371
Total approximate number of pool memos	4,269	4,289	5,825	6,336
Number of opinions of the Court	151	159	116	114

The data reveal a surprisingly strong relationship between the number of plenary decisions by the Court, as expressed by the number of opinions of the Court, and the number of grant recommendations made by the cert pool. The Pearson correlation coefficient between those two variables is a remarkably high .998 at a statistical significance level greater than .01. Although the robustness of this statistic is weakened somewhat by the small sample size (four Terms) and the nonrandomness of the Terms selected, the high correlation coefficient and statistical significance demonstrate, to a reasonable degree of confidence, that there is a relationship between the two variables....

The question raised by the high correlation coefficient is whether the law clerks are driving the size of the plenary docket, or whether other factors account for the strong relationship. One possible explanation is that the decrease in the number of cases on the plenary docket and the number of grant recommendations made by the cert pool both reflect a declining number of certworthy petitions on the Court's docket.

This explanation, while plausible, seems unlikely. Although it is true that the number of paid petitions—or those in which the petitioner is able to pay the filing fee—has actually decreased by about 450 cases since 1984, the total number of petitions has nearly doubled since then. And even ignoring the fact that the in forma pauperis portion of the docket has almost tripled since 1984, the 50% drop in the plenary docket far exceeds the approximately 20% decline in paid cases on the certiorari

78. [Footnote 209 in original] The category labeled "Approximate Number of Deny Recommendations" is an approximation based on the total number of disposed petitions reported each year in the *Harvard Law Review*. This category includes all cases where the cert pool recommended that the Court deny the petition, the cert pool made no recommendation, or the pool memo was missing from the Blackmun papers.

docket.[79] Moreover, at the time of greatest decline in the plenary docket, between 1986 and 1993, there was very little change in the number of paid petitions on the certiorari docket.

It is also possible that the quality of petitions has declined substantially since 1984.... [But] it is hard to believe that a doubling of the number of petitions for certiorari could produce half as many certworthy cases. ...In fact, ... the Court may be failing to review 200 or more circuit splits each year, meaning that it is unlikely that a fundamental decline in the quality of petitions is the driving force behind the massive drop in the plenary docket.

Another possibility is that changes in personnel on the Court are driving the reduction in the plenary docket. At least three other scholars have found merit to this explanation and it has substantial empirical support. But it fails to explain the strong correlation between the number of plenary decisions by the Court and grant recommendations by the cert pool each Term, unless the Justices are instructing law clerks to limit the number of grant recommendations each Term or to otherwise be cautious in dispensing grant recommendations. Neither *Sorcerers' Apprentices* nor *Courtiers* finds any evidence of such a declaration from the Chief Justice or the Court, and, of course, any such declaration would suffer from nearly insurmountable collective action problems. It would require the clerks from each of the chambers participating in the cert pool to work together, either explicitly or implicitly, to reach a target number of grant recommendations....

A more subtle variation of this explanation is that the culture of "just saying no" has become more pronounced in recent years, which is perhaps just a reflection of the philosophies of the members of the Court. Ward and Weiden suggest as much when they state that "[a]s the number of justices and clerks joining the pool and reviewing pool memos increased, clerks became more cautious." The data in this study provide some support for that explanation. Despite the strong correlation between the number of grant recommendations by the cert pool and the number of plenary decisions by the Court, the Justices and the cert pool still disagree on the disposition of a considerable number of cases each Term, ranging from just forty-seven cases in 1992 to seventy-five cases in 1985. It is possible, therefore, that the Justices are exercising independent judgment during the certiorari process and that the law clerks are simply following the leadership and cues of the Justices, who in recent years have granted certiorari in fewer cases than ever before. Although this explanation cannot be discounted, without collective action by all the clerks in the pool, it still fails to explain the remarkably high correlation between the number of grant recommendations by the cert pool and number of plenary decisions by the Court.

A third explanation is that the recommendations of the cert pool are driving the number of cases heard on the merits each year by the Court. This explanation has considerable facial plausibility as some Justices, including the late Chief Justice Rehnquist, have admitted that they do not look at every petition for certiorari that is filed with the Court.

79. [Editors' Note: Recall that a much higher percentage of cases on the paid dock- et, than on the IFP docket, are granted. See Section A, footnote 13, above.]

Moreover, during the 1984 and 1985 Terms, the cert pool recommended that the Court grant certiorari in slightly more than 2.5% of the cases on the certiorari docket. By the 1991 and 1992 Terms, that ratio had dropped to slightly less than 1.4%. Accordingly, the pool is not only stingy compared to the total number of cases in which the Court granted certiorari, but its stinginess has increased over time.

On the other hand, ... [n]either *Sorcerers' Apprentices* nor *Courtiers* suggests that law clerks possess that much power. To the contrary, the Justices still discuss the potentially meritorious petitions for certiorari in conference. Moreover, although there is a high correlation between grant recommendations and plenary decisions, the law clerks and the Justices do not always agree on the appropriate disposition of petitions for certiorari. Accordingly, further study is necessary to determine the robustness of the correlation coefficient as well as to determine which of the foregoing explanations, if any, account for it.

One potential weakness of the correlation coefficient calculated above is that is does not directly measure the agreement between the cert pool and the Court. Instead, it aggregates all the grant recommendations of the cert pool, in both granted and denied cases, and compares that figure to the total number of cases decided by the Court. The Blackmun papers, because they include pool memos from all cases granted and denied during Justice Blackmun's tenure, permit researchers to calculate and analyze for the first time the level of agreement between the cert pool and the Court both within and across Terms.

In conducting the analysis, I separated the cases into five categories: (1) cases in which the pool memo and the Court both agreed on a grant; (2) cases in which the pool memo and the Court both agreed on a denial; (3) cases in which the pool memo suggested a grant, but the Court denied; (4) cases in which the pool memo suggested a denial, but the Court granted; and (5) cases in which the cert pool recommended that some other action be taken by the Court. Table 8 displays the number (and percentage) of cases falling into each of these categories for October Terms 1984, 1985, 1991, and 1992.

TABLE 8

Agreement Between Pool Memo and the Court on Disposition of Petitions for Certiorari, October Terms 1984, 1985, 1991 and 1992[80]

	Supreme Court Term			
	1984	1985	1991	1992
Pool memo suggests grant, and Court grants	1.83% (78)	1.70% (73)	0.93% (54)	1.03% (65)
Pool memo suggests deny, and Court denies	89.88% (3,837)	88.09% (3,778)	92.46% (5,386)	92.38% (5,853)
Pool memo suggests grant, but Court denies	0.68% (29)	0.89% (38)	0.55% (32)	0.28% (18)
Pool memo suggests deny, but Court grants	0.63% (27)	0.86% (37)	0.45% (26)	0.46% (29)
Some other action suggested by pool memo[80]	6.98% (298)	8.46% (363)	5.61% (327)	5.86% (371)
Total number of cert petitions	4,269	4,289	5,825	6,336

. . .

... Using the number of grant recommendations and recommendations to take some other action as proxies for cases that the cert pool found worthy of further consideration by the Court, the percentage of those cases dropped from 10.3% of the certiorari docket in 1984 and 1985 to 7.1% in 1991 and 1992. These figures provide further support for the hypothesis that the cert pool has become increasingly stingy over time.

The level of agreement between the cert pool and the Court has also increased over time, at least as a percentage of the total number of cases on the certiorari docket. For October Terms 1984 and 1985, the total number of cases involving a disagreement between the cert pool and the Court was 1.46%, while that same statistic was just .86% for October Terms 1991 and 1992.

These statistics lend support to the hypothesis that greater homogenization of the cert pool—from six Justices during 1984 and 1985 to eight Justices in 1991 and 1992—has had some impact on the level of agreement between the cert pool and the Court.... During October

---

80. [Footnote 228 in original] It bears noting that this category includes a number of cases in which the cert pool recommended that some other action be taken, but the Court decided to grant certiorari anyway. The separate categorization of these cases accounts for most of the disparity between the number of cases listed as grants ... in Table 8 and the total number of opinions ... in Tables 1 and 7.

Terms 1984 and 1985, six Justices participated in the pool, while three other Justices provided an independent "check" on it. By the 1991 and 1992 Terms, in contrast, only Justice Stevens's chambers independently reviewed petitions for certiorari. As the number of Justices participating in the pool increases, the homogenization theory would predict that the agreement between the Court and the pool would also increase. While the ratio of grant recommendations to cases decided by the Court has remained remarkably consistent over time, the level of agreement between the Court and the cert pool has predictably *increased* as more Justices have joined the cert pool.

While the numbers suggest greater agreement between the cert pool and the Court in more recent Terms, Table 8 does suffer from at least one prominent flaw. Many of the cases on the certiorari docket are frivolous, including a large percentage of those cases in which the cert pool and the Court both agree that a petition should be denied. Thus, it can be argued that Table 8 grossly overestimates the level of agreement between the cert pool and the Court by including all petitions without separately accounting for the level of consensus in which the Court granted certiorari. After removing all cases in which the cert pool recommended that some other action be taken, Table 9 responds to that criticism by bifurcating the data into two groups. First, the Table displays the level of agreement between the cert pool and the Court in all cases in which the Court *either* granted or denied certiorari. It then separately presents the level of agreement in only those cases in which the Court eventually granted certiorari.

TABLE 9
Agreement Between Pool Memo and the Court on
Disposition of Petitions for Certiorari (By Percentage),
October Terms 1984, 1985, 1991 and 1992

	Supreme Court Term			
	1984	1985	1991	1992
Agreement (all cases)	98.59% (3,915)	98.09% (3,851)	98.95% (5,440)	99.21% (5,918)
Disagreement (all cases)	1.41% (56)	1.91% (75)	1.05% (58)	0.79% (47)
Agreement (grants only)	74.29% (78)	66.36% (73)	67.50% (54)	69.15% (65)
Disagreement (grants only)	25.71% (27)	33.64% (37)	32.50% (26)	30.85% (29)

The trend of greater agreement between the cert pool and the Court begins to break down only when the closer and more difficult granted cases are examined. During October Terms 1984 and 1985, the Court and the cert pool agreed on the disposition of 70.2% of the cases in which certiorari was granted, while that same statistic for 1991 and 1992 was a slightly lower 68.4%. The data suggest that the level of agreement between the Court and the cert pool has not been impacted by a change in the number of Justices participating in the pool, casting some doubt on the viability of the homogeneity theory. However, unlike the data for both granted and denied cases, the data for only the granted cases originate from a much smaller sample size.... While the percentage differences from Term to Term look comparably large when only granted cases are considered, the differential amounts to only about three to five cases per Term in one direction or another, hardly enough to make any sweeping conclusions about the cert pool. Further testing of the validity of the homogeneity theory should include data from additional Terms.

It is unsurprising that the level of disagreement between the cert pool and the Court is higher with respect to the granted cases. In contrast to the denied petitions, many of which are frivolous, the cases in which the Court grants certiorari are often very close and are "more a matter of 'feel' than of precisely ascertainable rules." Agreement between the cert pool and the Court about 70% of the time in granted cases does not show that the cert pool lacks influence over the Court's selection of plenary cases, as Professor Palmer claimed in her 2001 study. To be sure, a 30% disagreement rate in that category does demonstrate that the Justices exercise some independent judgment in making their decisions about whether to grant certiorari. However, the approximately 99% agreement in all cases and the nearly 70% agreement in granted cases also reveal that the recommendations of the cert pool are indeed related to the final decisions of the Justices on petitions for certiorari. Without further study, the extent of that relationship is unclear....

A new study by Professors Todd Peppers [the author of *Courtiers*] and Christopher Zorn provides indirect support for the influence of law clerks on the certiorari process.[81] In their study, Peppers and Zorn measure the influence of law clerk ideology (based in part on the law clerks' responses to a survey designed to elicit their membership in the Republican or Democratic parties) on the ultimate decision on the merits in a case.... They ultimately conclude ... that "over and above the influence of the [J]ustices' own policy preferences, those of their clerks have an independent effect on their votes."

· · ·

... [B]y finding clerk influence on those decisions, an area where the deck is stacked "against finding evidence of clerk influence," the study conducted by Peppers and Zorn greatly suggests a finding of clerk influence in the certiorari process as well.

IV. CONCLUSION

· · ·

... [T]he establishment of the cert pool has greatly increased the role of law clerks in the certiorari process. An examination of the pool memoranda from four Terms empirically uncovers three characteristics

---

81. [Editors' Note: The author is referring to Todd C. Peppers & Christopher Zorn, *Law Clerk Influence on Supreme* *Court Decision Making* (Aug. 17, 2006) (unpublished manuscript), available at http://ssrn.com/abstract=925705.]

of the cert pool for the first time: (1) it is stingy with respect to making grant recommendations; (2) it emphasizes objective criteria of certworthiness in making its recommendations, such as the presence of lower court conflict; and (3) there is mounting evidence that the recommendations of the cert pool are correlated with the eventual decisions of the Court on petitions for certiorari.... [T]he empirical evidence further demonstrates that many scholars have too quickly dismissed the impact of the cert pool on the Court's declining plenary docket....

Questions and Comments

1. Consider the importance of the research and statistical methodology on the findings in all three readings above. The divergent conclusions reached by the authors in this section emphasize the need for students of the Court (and other legal institutions) to be able critically to probe the underlying methodologies. As noted above, while the total number of requests for review has grown, that growth has come primarily in the IFPs; paid petitions—which have always had a significantly higher grant rate than the IFPs—have actually decreased in recent years, as the data in footnote below reflect. But, at the same time, the rate at which the Court has granted review to the paid petitions has also declined, though not nearly as steeply as the decline in the grants for IFP cases.[82] Is the decline in the number of paid petitions—at a time when the caseload of the Courts of Appeals has grown substantially, as Stras notes—related to the decline in grant rates? How could this be studied? See also Chapter Five, Section C, below (noting argument by Richard Lazarus that changing characteristics of the Supreme Court Bar may contribute to the decline in grant rate).

2. In a work discussed by Stras, Arthur Hellman, *The Shrunken Docket of the Rehnquist Court*, 1996 Sup. Ct. Rev. 403, Professor Hellman explores five hypotheses for the decrease: the elimination of mandatory jurisdiction,

---

82. The chart below is constructed from data provided in the annual Harvard Law Review Supreme Court Statistics Section. Readers should recall that before 1988, there were more mandatory appellate jurisdiction cases, which had to be entertained if they were jurisdictionally proper; both mandatory appeals and cert petitions are included in the data. We present the Harvard Law Review data from the Terms analyzed by Stras (1984, 1985 and 1991, 1992) as well as for the two most recent Terms for which data from the Harvard Law Review are available. Although the precise numbers may vary from those used by scholars cited elsewhere in this chapter, and may depend on whether, e.g., summary action, such as affirmances without oral argument (especially for years prior to 1988), and GVRs, are included in the "grants", the trend lines are of interest.

TERM	PAID	% GRANT	IFP	% GRANT
OT 1984	2179	11.1%	2082	1.1%
OT 1985	2107	11.2%	2180	1.3%
OT 1991	2069	5.0%	3755	0.5%
OT1992	2087	4.0%	4248	0.3%
OT 2004	1727	4.0%	5815	0.2%
OT 2005	1703	3.7%	6533	0.2%

Compare, *The Supreme Court Compendium, supra*, at 74–75 (Table 2–6), discussed above, Section A, footnote 13. Some data differ, perhaps in part because *The Supreme Court Compendium* does not include summary actions on appeals. See *id.* at 75 note a. But these two sources reveal similar trends. According to the *Compendium*, grant rates in paid cases fell from 7% in OT 1984 and 1985 to a grant rate of 3% for paid cases in OT 2004 (the last Term included in the *Compendium*); while grant rates in IFP cases fell from 1% in OT 1984 and 1985 to a grant rate of 0.2% in 2004. *Id.*

the retirements of liberal Justices, the homogeneity of the courts of appeals, the federal government's losing fewer cases, and the courts of appeals' being more in line with the Supreme Court. Professor Hellman concludes that these hypotheses do not fully or adequately explain the decrease in certs granted. Instead, he concludes that the Justices' view of the Court's role in our political system seems to have shifted due to changes on the Supreme Court bench. A small excerpt of this article appears below in Part E.

3.   H.W. Perry, Jr. suggests another possible reason behind the shrinking caseload: Chief Justice Rehnquist's policy of relisting cases that garnered only four votes to grant. Instead of granting a petition that received only four votes (as had been done in the past), Chief Justice Rehnquist would relist it for a later conference so that the Justices could reconsider whether the case really warranted a grant. Perry, *Deciding to Decide, supra,* at 50–51 ("Once in a while a vote will fall away," quoting a Justice). How large an effect do you think this procedural change might have on the size of the Court's docket?

4.   It seems reasonably clear that changes in personnel between 1986 and 1994 contributed to the decline in the number of cases granted cert. As Professor Richard J. Lazarus points out: "The best evidence that Chief Justice Rehnquist favored a trimming of the docket and did not embrace the view that circuit conflicts presumptively presented legal issues worthy of the Court's attention is the sheer coincidence of the decline of the docket with his ascension to the Chief Justice slot." Richard J. Lazarus, *Advocacy Matters Before and Within the Supreme Court: Transforming the Court by Transforming the Bar*, 96 Geo. L. J. (forthcoming 2008) (manuscript of Aug. 5, 2007, at 26 n.84). Lazarus also notes that Professor Tom Merrill "makes a strong case that Justice Antonin Scalia, who joined the Court at the same time [that Rehnquist became Chief Justice], may in fact be the true agent of change within the Court. *See* Thomas Merrill, *The Making of the Second Rehnquist Court: A Preliminary Analysis,* 47 St. Louis L. J. 569, 643–644 (2003)." Lazarus goes on to point out that the departure of Justice White, who believed passionately that the Court should resolve circuit splits, had an impact; "no one since White has advanced a similar view." Lazarus, *supra.* And finally, as O'Brien noted in the excerpt above, the departures of Brennan, Marshall, Powell, and Blackmun, who frequently voted to "Join–3" meant that, without them, the Rule of Four really meant four.

5.   Should the Court reconsider the criteria it employs in exercising its discretion? Tom Goldstein, an active litigator in the Court, believes the Court gives too much weight to the existence of a circuit split, without focusing sufficient attention on whether the issue merits the Supreme Court's using its scarce resources to resolve the split. He suggests that Congress should act swiftly to resolve statutory ambiguities that engender litigation and "thereby leave the justices free to select cases with an eye to their broader importance," Tom Goldstein, *One Plugged, Thousands to Go,* Legal Times, Nov. 18, 2002, at 68.

6.   Others have suggested that petitioners who allege a circuit conflict should be required to demonstrate that the conflict was considered by the lower court. Thus, Professors Sam Estreicher and John Sexton suggest:

The petitioner should be required to bring the conflict to the attention of the court of appeals. If the appeals panel does not acknowledge the existence of the alleged conflict in its opinion, the petitioner must again raise the issue in the petition for rehearing or suggestion for rehearing *en banc*. In the rare case in which a conflict arises after the petition for rehearing is filed, but before the last date for filing in the Supreme Court, the petitioner should be permitted—indeed, encouraged—to return to the court of appeals for reconsideration based on the allegedly conflicting decision.

Samuel Estreicher & John Sexton, *Improving the Process: Case Selection by the Supreme Court*, 70 Judicature 41 (1986).

7. Should the Court consider modifying the use of the cert pool? Some commentators have suggested the Court should use two or even three pools. See Kenneth Starr, *Rule of Supreme Court Needs a Management Revolt*, Wall Street Journal, Oct. 13, 1993, at A23. Recall as well, John Roberts' comments in 1997, before he was a judge, when he noted that the pool's power is "a little disquieting" because it makes the clerks "a bit too significant" in the cert process; a possible remedy, he said, could be found in the creation of "two parallel pools." See p. 364, note 22 above. After Roberts joined the Court and the cert pool, Mauro observed: "If Roberts plans to implement such a change, he must be biding his time," Tony Mauro, *Roberts Takes His Time in Reshaping the Court*, New York Law Journal, (Dec. 27, 2006, at 1, col.3.) Some years earlier, Justice Kennedy, also worrying about the possibility that one pool memo could influence so many of the Justices' cert votes, suggested that "we alter the system so that in each case one pool member [would] not receive the pool memo but instead [would] perform an independent review of the petition by whatever in-chamber system he or she selects. To insure review isolated from the memo, perhaps the exclusion rotation should be designed so a clerk for the excluded judge has not prepared the memo for that case. This suggestion would impose a slight additional burden, but the benefit of an alternative form of review within the pool system may justify the extra effort." Artemus Ward & David L. Weiden, *Sorcerers' Apprentices: 100 Years of Law Clerks at the United States Supreme Court* 148, (2006) (quoting Anthony Kennedy to William H. Rehnquist, August 6, 1991, Blackmun Papers, Box 1374). The Justices discussed this suggestion two months later, but, according to Blackmun's papers, Justice Kennedy had "retreat[ed]" from his suggestion. *Id.* Recall Justice Rehnquist's comment that "As soon as I am confident that my new law clerks are reliable, I take their word and that of the pool memo writer as to the underlying facts and contentions of the parties in the various petitions, and with a large majority of the petitions it is not necessary to go any further than the pool memo." William H. Rehnquist, *The Supreme Court: How It Was, How It Is* 264 (1987). Could Congress mandate the use of more than one pool or would that be an inappropriate, or even unconstitutional, intervention into internal Court matters?

8. In light of the currently reduced number of cases that the Court is considering on the merits, some have suggested modifying the Court's calendar. To some extent the Court has done so already by scheduling its fall conference a week or two before the first Monday in October, to make sure that there will be enough cases fully briefed and ready to be argued through

December or January. The Court has at times directed expedited briefing, in cases granted only shortly before argument sessions; expedited briefing schedules put lawyers for the parties under intense time pressure. See Margaret Cordray & Richard Cordray, *The Calendar of the Justices: How the Supreme Court's Timing Affects Its Decisionmaking,* 36 Ariz. St. L. J. 183, 221–25 & nn. 198, 199, 200, 203 (2004). The Cordrays have suggested that the Court should make a number of other changes in its calendar, including granting cases during the summer. See *id.* at 226–29 (noting that the Court grants a lower percentage of cases in the first large conference in the fall than it grants at other times during the year, presumably because of the accumulation that builds up over the summer).

9.   Should the Rule of Four be modified? Consider the views of Justice Stevens in Section B above, suggesting the possibility of requiring five instead of four votes for a grant. Note that Stevens made this suggestion in 1983, at a time when the Court was hearing oral argument in 150 or more cases each Term.

10.   Finally, consider these words of Professor Henry M. Hart, Jr., who asked in 1958:

> Does a nation of 165 million realize any significant gain merely because its highest tribunal succeeds in deciding 127 cases by full opinion instead of 117? 137 cases? 147 cases? Or even 157 cases? The hard fact must be faced that the Justices of the Supreme Court of the United States can at best put their full minds to no more than a tiny handful of the troubling cases which year by year are tossed up to them out of the great sea of millions and even billions of concrete situations to which their opinions relate. When this fact is fully apprehended, it will be seen that the question whether this handful includes or excludes a dozen or so more cases is unimportant. It will be seen that what matters about Supreme Court opinions is not their quantity but their quality.

Henry M. Hart, Jr., *Foreword: The Time Chart of the Justices,* 73 Harv. L. Rev. 84 (1958). Do Hart's comments apply with equal force to a halving of the average number of plenary cases decided? Does a decline in the number of cases decided necessarily imply a diminished role for the Supreme Court?

———————

D.   SPECIAL CIRCUMSTANCES: THE DEATH PENALTY AND CERTIORARI BEFORE JUDGMENT

1.   Death Penalty Litigation in the Court

Supreme Court Rule 23, reprinted below, permits parties to petition a Justice to stay the enforcement of a judgment, including a stay of a judgment imposing the death penalty. Generally, such applications are addressed to the Circuit Justice assigned to the circuit from which the case is coming.[83] The Rule does not specify the number of Justices necessary to grant the stay or the criteria considered in determining when a stay is warranted. Generally, to obtain a stay, the applicant must demonstrate that at least four members of the Court are likely to find the cert petition "cert-worthy;" that the petitioner is likely to prevail on the merits; that irreparable harm will occur if the stay is not granted; and that the equities balance in favor of granting the stay. Stern & Gressman, *Supreme Court Practice, supra* at 636–645, 671–704. However, to stay an execution, the Court requires the votes of five Justices. This creates a potential conflict with the Rule of Four, which requires only four votes to grant review in a case. If four Justices agree to review a case but cannot convince a fifth Justice to join them in voting for a stay, the case may be granted and later mooted by the execution of the petitioner. How does the Court reconcile this potential conflict? The answer has been neither simple nor consistent.

Following Rule 23, an article by Professor Mark Tushnet examines some of the difficult issues raised by efforts to seek Supreme Court review in cases in which the death penalty is imminent, discussing in particular Congress's effort in the Anti–Terrorism and Effective Death Penalty Act of 1996 to deal with some of these complexities. Consider how effective Congress's efforts have been and what further actions might be appropriate. Professor Tushnet's conclusion that the AEDPA may have accomplished very little depends on how powerful the original habeas corpus petition to the Supreme Court is as a form of review.[84] Professor Ira Robbins, writing some years later, suggests that original petitions for habeas corpus may, like stays, now require a vote of five, not four, to be heard, thereby undermining its force. Robbins also argues that the "Rule of Five" should not be applied to extraordinary writs for a stay or for the Court to hear an original habeas corpus petition, at least in death penalty cases, but rather that a "Rule of Four" should control so that the Court can have a full decision on the merits.

---

83. See 28 U.S.C. § 42. At the beginning of each term, the Court assigns one or more federal judicial circuits to each Justice. The Chief Justice is traditionally assigned to the District of Columbia Circuit, the Fourth Circuit and the Federal Circuit. Associate Justices are assigned, whenever feasible, to a circuit where they once lived or have some other connection.

84. "Original" petitions for habeas corpus may be brought to the Court within its appellate jurisdiction, to review the "legality of a commitment by order of" a lower court. Richard H. Fallon, Jr., et al, *Hart & Wechsler's The Federal Courts and the Federal System* 1286 (5th ed. 2003); see Ex parte Bollman, 8 U.S. (4 Cranch) 75 (1807); see also Ex parte Yerger, 75 U.S. 85 (1869). According to Supreme Court Rule 20.4, pe-

titions for an extraordinary writ, including a writ of habeas corpus, must show "that exceptional circumstances warrant the exercise of the Court's discretionary powers, and that adequate relief cannot be obtained in any other form or from any other court. This writ is rarely granted." In Felker v. Turpin, 518 U.S. 651 (1996), discussed in Professor Tushnet's article below, the Supreme Court upheld a new statutory provision banning appeals or certiorari review of certain courts of appeals decisions involving successive habeas petitions. *Felker* interpreted the statute not to preclude "original" petitions for habeas corpus and thus avoided a possible constitutional questions under the Exceptions Clause of Article III.

Supreme Court Rule 23. Stays

1. A stay may be granted by a Justice as permitted by law.

2. A party to a judgment sought to be reviewed may present to a Justice an application to stay the enforcement of that judgment. See 28 U.S.C. § 2101 (f).

3. An application for a stay shall set out with particularity why the relief sought is not available from any other court or judge. Except in the most extraordinary circumstances, an application for a stay will not be entertained unless the relief requested was first sought in the appropriate court or courts below or from a judge or judges thereof. . . .

4. A judge, court, or Justice granting an application for a stay pending review by this Court may condition the stay on the filing of a supersedeas bond having an approved surety or sureties. . . .

Mark Tushnet,[85] *"The King of France with Forty Thousand Men:"* Felker v. Turpin *and the Supreme Court's Deliberative Processes,* 1996 Sup. Ct. Rev. 163

I. INTRODUCTION

When the Supreme Court granted certiorari in Felker v. Turpin[86] on May 3, 1996, and ordered an expedited briefing and argument schedule, it seemed that a major constitutional decision might be in prospect. On April 24, the President had signed the Anti–Terrorism and Effective Death Penalty Act of 1996, amending the federal habeas corpus statute. One section of the Act dealt with successive habeas corpus petitions. According to the Act, a habeas petitioner filing a second or successive petition must satisfy certain requirements dealing with the nature of the claim. Initial habeas petitions can be filed directly in the district court. Under the Act, however, second or successive petitions may not. Instead, the court of appeals acts, as the Court put it, as a "gatekeeper" for such petitions: The prospective habeas petitioner must apply to the court of appeals for leave to file the petition in the district court. The court of appeals may grant leave to file only if the petitioner "makes a prima facie showing that the application satisfies" the statute's requirements regarding the nature of the claim. The statute also provides that the court of appeal's "grant or denial" of leave to file "shall not be appealable and shall not be the subject of a petition for rehearing or for a writ of certiorari."

Felker was convicted of murder and sentenced to death. After exhausting his appeals and filing a first unsuccessful habeas petition, he

---

85. Carmack Waterhouse Professor of Constitutional Law, Georgetown University Law Center; currently the William Nelson Cromwell Professor of Law, Harvard Law School.

86. [Footnote 1 in original] 116 S.Ct. 1588 (1996).

filed a motion for leave to file a second petition, in which he would assert a colorable claim of innocence, based on new forensic evidence that the victim had died while Felker was under police surveillance, and a claim that the trial court had given an unconstitutional instruction defining the term "beyond a reasonable doubt." The court of appeals denied leave to file, and Felker applied to the Supreme Court for a writ of certiorari and for an original writ of habeas corpus. The Court directed counsel to submit briefs limited to three questions, one of which was whether the preclusion of review was "an unconstitutional restriction" of the Supreme Court's jurisdiction. The question of the scope of Congress's power to restrict the Court's jurisdiction is one of the most difficult in the law of the federal courts. To Justice Stevens, expediting review was "unnecessary and profoundly unwise," for the Court should consider such questions "with the utmost deliberation, rather than unseemly haste."

And the haste was indeed great. The Court gave the parties two weeks to prepare and file their briefs, and set oral argument for two weeks after that. In 1990 the Court accelerated its consideration of a challenge to the constitutionality of the federal Flag Protection Act of 1989. The statute itself specified that appeals should be expedited, and even so the Court gave the lawyers three weeks to write, and another three weeks to prepare for argument. In 1974 when the Court chose to decide whether President Richard Nixon had to turn over audiotapes from his office, it also gave the lawyers three weeks to write and three more weeks to prepare.

Some expedition might have been appropriate. Had the case been put on a normal briefing and argument schedule, it would not have been heard by the Court until October or November 1996. A decision might not have been rendered before June 1997. Every well-advised person on death row with a nonfrivolous successive claim who did not welcome execution would of course file an application in the court of appeals for leave to file a successive petition in the district court. After leave was denied, as it ordinarily would be, the prospective habeas applicant would then file a petition for review in the Supreme Court raising the constitutional questions pending in *Felker*. And, under the Court's sensible practice, it would hold all those applications until it decided *Felker*.... Executions would be effectively suspended until the Court decided *Felker*.

Although Congress did not expressly direct the Court to expedite review, as it had in the Flag Protection Act, its aim in enacting the Anti–Terrorism and Effective Death Penalty Act was clear enough: to reduce what Congress and the President regarded as excessive delays in carrying out lawful executions. It would have been deeply ironic had a statute designed to expedite executions had the effect of imposing a year-long moratorium on them instead.

... From 1981 to 1991, the Court experienced a fair amount of internal turmoil over the application of the Court's rules in death penalty cases. Those who believed the death penalty to be generally constitutional came to believe that their opponents were manipulating the Court's internal rules simply to delay executions. The Court's experience from 1981 to 1991 sheds additional light on its decision to order an expedited hearing in *Felker*.

II. THE DEATH PENALTY AND THE COURT'S INTERNAL RULES

A. *The Background*

When the Supreme Court upheld the constitutionality of modern death penalty statutes in 1976, capital punishment's supporters might have believed that executions would resume after a relatively brief shakedown period. They were wrong. To adopt a military analogy, death penalty abolitionists continued to fight even as they were forced to retreat. They fought in two ways: relatively large-scale fixed battles over whether the death penalty was administered in a racially discriminatory manner, whether those who were mentally retarded or juveniles at the time they murdered others could be executed, and the like; and guerilla campaigns against the execution of almost anyone sentenced to death, on the ground that particular problems in the defendant's trial invalidated either the conviction or the death sentence.

The big stories about the death penalty were the fixed battles, which death penalty abolitionists regularly lost. Inside the Court, however, the guerilla actions proved to be more irritating, in part because the justices who found the death penalty constitutional in principle sometimes fractured over these individual challenges. . . .

The slow pace of execution may have accurately reflected divisions in the country. Some observers suggested that a large majority of Americans approved of the death penalty in the abstract but were much more divided over how frequently it should be administered, and in which cases. Personal relations became strained when that ambivalence was reflected inside the Court. Two justices, Marshall and Brennan, always voted against capital punishment. In nearly every case, the Court's rules made it possible for them to delay executions if they found one or two allies. The Court's conservatives only gradually discovered that the rules contributed to the guerilla war against capital punishment.

The conservatives' problems arose from the "rule of four." . . .

[S]cheduling argument and drafting opinions can put off the announcement of a judgment for almost a year. But the "rule of four" had other consequences. Suppose a capital defendant applies for review after the state has set a date for his execution. Four justices can get the Court to grant review. But the execution date might fall before briefs were due, before argument is scheduled, or before a Court decision could be expected. Ordinarily the state could go ahead with the execution. Letting a state execute someone whose case was being considered by the Supreme Court struck many justices as peculiarly unfair. They had a procedural device to prevent that. The state would have to wait if the Supreme Court itself issued stay of execution. But, under the Court's rules, it took *five* justices to issue a stay.

The position taken by Marshall and Brennan made the question of when to issue stays of execution particularly difficult for justices who did not think capital punishment was unconstitutional. Perhaps two other justices thought a capital defendant presented a serious claim about his individual case, whose merits the Court should consider, but, the conservatives thought, Marshall and Brennan voted to grant review because they opposed capital punishment completely. Often, then, the four votes to grant review on the merits of a particular challenge seemed almost insincere. Should a justice in the majority join the four others to issue a stay of execution?

There was an even more arcane issue that caused problems. In many areas, not limited to death penalty cases, several cases arrive at the Court presenting similar though not quite identical issues. Sometimes the Court decides to hear a group of related cases. Sometimes, however, it decides to "hold" the related cases until it decides the lead case. Then the justices take a look at the cases they have held in light of the decision they have made. . . .

How many votes should it take to hold a case pending a decision in the related one? For most of [Thurgood] Marshall's tenure, the Court's rules said that a case would be held if three justices thought it related to one in which the Court was hearing argument. The argument for that rule was simple: No one could tell whether the decision in the primary case would affect the related ones until the justices wrote opinions in the primary case. If three justices thought a case was related to the primary one, they might be able to persuade a fourth to grant review in light of the decision, once it was handed down. . . .

Holding cases was not a real problem when the primary case raised a broad-based challenge to the death penalty. If the Court was considering whether the Constitution allowed states to execute people who were minors when they committed their crimes, the Court would hold all cases involving such minors. Once those broad-based challenges were disposed of, the question of which cases to hold became more difficult inside the Court. For, by that time, Marshall and Brennan had been joined by Justices Blackmun and Stevens as reasonably consistent opponents of capital punishment. Too frequently, the conservatives thought, either Blackmun or Stevens became the third vote to hold a case as related when it really had little to do with the primary case.

The problem was exacerbated after the justices heard argument and voted on the principal case. They knew, although the public did not, what the result was going to be. But the justices felt they had to follow what Marshall once called "the fiction that a case is not 'decided' until it is officially announced." If the Court was going to uphold the death penalty in the principal case, the conservatives found it particularly galling that three justices could nonetheless delay executions in cases only tangentially implicating an issue that they knew was about to be rejected.

B. The First Stirrings of Difficulty

In the long run, the conservatives believed themselves most disadvantaged by what they saw as the liberals' manipulation of the Court's rules. But the conservatives themselves took the first steps that divided the Court.

In 1981, five years after the Court again authorized capital punishment, Justice Rehnquist became impatient. He used two cases involving murders committed in 1973 and 1976 as vehicles for a proposal he believed would break the "stalemate" he saw in administering the death penalty. The Court, Rehnquist proposed, should grant review in *every* capital case, even if the claims presented would not ordinarily be treated as worth the Court's time....

Stevens called Rehnquist's bluff. With Marshall and Brennan voting to grant review, Rehnquist's vote in ... two cases left the petitioners only one vote short of getting Supreme Court review. Stevens looked at the cases and chose to vote to grant review—satisfying the rule of four—in the case where the defendant made the stronger constitutional claim. Rehnquist was now faced with the prospect of having the Court hear a case showing that careful examination of constitutional claims in death penalty cases was desirable. To avoid that, he withdrew his vote to grant review in that case. He did publish a dissent from the denial of review in the other case. Stevens responded with an opinion explaining that Rehnquist's proposal was "an improper allocation of the Court's limited resources" because hearing all death penalty cases "would consume over half of [the] Court's argument calendar" on issues of no national significance. He tweaked Rehnquist in observing that death penalty issues "have not been difficult for three Members of the Court"— Marshall and Brennan, of course, but also Rehnquist: Stevens wrote, "[I]f my memory serves me correctly, Justice Rehnquist has invariably voted to uphold the death penalty."

Three years later, tensions within the Court increased as the possibility of more executions grew. The problems seemed minor at first. Early in 1984, Justice Powell noted that defendants' efforts to stay their executions disrupted the Court. He pointed out that the Court's staff had to stay in the building through the night because they could not be sure whether a stay would be sought. Soon after that, the Court accepted Powell's suggestion that it establish procedures to keep the justices informed of the status of death penalty cases.

The justices were notified when a court of appeals was considering a stay of execution, then after it decided whether to issue or deny the stay, then about counsel's plans to seek review and a stay from the Supreme Court. Sometimes, of course, the cases never reached the Court—a lower court, sometimes a state court, would delay the execution. The overall effect was to increase the flow of paper inside the Court, and to heighten the justices' awareness of the details of death penalty cases. The justices became almost micro-managers in death penalty cases. . . .

Again, the conservatives made an already difficult situation worse. In May 1984, James Adams faced execution in Florida. On May 8 he persuaded the federal court of appeals to stay his execution, arguing that his federal habeas corpus petition presented issues that the appeals court was already considering in two other cases. Florida's attorney general immediately went to the Supreme Court, arguing that Adams was barred from presenting his claim at such a late date because he failed to present it in an earlier federal proceeding. On May 9, the justices agreed, voting 5 to 4 to vacate the stay. Marshall was outraged. In a memo to his files he noted that the discussion of the case had taken only 18 minutes, and that his motion to be given 24 hours to write a dissent had been denied. In a published dissent, Marshall chastised the majority for its "indecent desire to rush to judgment in capital cases," which was "especially egregious" when the Court overrode a lower court's decision to issue a stay: "Caution has been thrown to the winds with an impetuousness that is truly astonishing." The Court "appears to have . . . forgotten here . . . that we are not dealing with mere legal semantics; we are dealing with a man's life." Adams was executed on May 10.

C. Tension Escalates: The Problem of Stays of Execution

The next year, Willie Darden's case produced "real bitterness." Darden was convicted of murdering the owner of a furniture store.

Darden's main claim was that his trial was unfair because the prosecutor engaged in serious misconduct. As Powell wrote, the prosecutor's closing argument to the jury "deserves the condemnation it has received from every court to review it." Violating well-established standards, the prosecutor called Darden's "an animal," said that he should not "be out of his cell unless he has a leash on him," said "I wish that I could see him sitting here with no face," criticized the prison authorities for giving Darden a furlough, and stated his personal belief that Darden was guilty. Darden claimed he was innocent; as his lawyer put it, "They took a coincidence and magnified that into a capital case."

The Supreme Court considered Darden's claims serious enough to justify review. In its first consideration of the case in 1977, however, the Court decided it had made a mistake in attempting to review what was so clearly a fact-bound decision with few implications for national law, and dismissed the case "as improvidently granted." After eight years of habeas corpus proceedings, in which the appeals court was severely divided, the case came back to the Supreme Court.

Darden's lawyers had to stay his execution if they were to get the Supreme Court to consider his claims. On September 3, 1985, the Court received an application for a stay. The Court voted to deny the application by a 5–4 vote, and notified the lawyers. Around 9 P.M., the Court received a letter from Darden's lawyers asking that the application for a stay be treated as a request for review of the lower courts' decision that

Darden's trial has not been unfair. Without further discussion, the four justices who voted to grant the stay—Brennan, Marshall, Blackmun, and Stevens—voted to grant review. Powell then joined them to stay Darden's execution, despite his evident belief that Darden's case did not deserve any further consideration. Burger was so upset at what happened that he published an unprecedented dissent from a grant of review. Noting that Darden's claims "have been passed upon no fewer than 95 times by federal and state court judges," Burger said that the Court was wrong to "accept meritless petitions presenting claims that we rejected only hours ago."

The justices discussed what to do over the next few weeks. Powell wrote that the "experience" with granting review in Darden "disturbs me." He called what Brennan and the other justices in the minority had done "more than a little unusual," and was "not at all sure it was done in accordance either with our Rules or precedent." As he saw it, they had "exploited" the rule of four.

. . .

The Court considered changing its rules at the end of September. It had one suggestion—Powell's, to require five votes to grant review—and one formal proposal—Brennan's, to allow a stay with four votes. Brennan wrote a long memo supporting his proposal. Because the "use of capital punishment by the states is only beginning to hit full stride," the Court could expect "the difficulties we experienced" in Darden "to recur." And, because "the law in this area continues to develop and as the views of each of us continue to evolve,"—perhaps here alluding to the positions Blackmun and Stevens were taking—"we must expect more close cases in which at least four Justices are not prepared to make a final decision based only on the papers accompanying a stay application under the staggering time pressures we have experienced." As Brennan saw it, the issue was whether the Court or the states determined when the Court decided to hear cases. He agreed with Blackmun "that this Court should refuse to be pushed into premature review . . . by the states' scheduling of execution dates."

Brennan was clearly concerned that Powell's memorandum expressed a troubling attitude about divisions within the Court. He tried to allay concern that some justices were using the rule of four "in bad faith" by noting that four justices might vote to grant review if "forced to make a last minute decision under great time pressure," but that "with a little more time, there might have been fewer votes." He rejected Powell's claim that anyone had " 'exploit[ed]' anything," saying that "four members of the Court honestly felt that an issue warranting plenary review was presented, and they voted accordingly." After that, Brennan believed, the law and even more strongly the Court's traditions meant that a stay should "automatically" be granted, to avoid the "unpalatable" result that the state could moot the case by executing the defendant.

Brennan continued to defend his proposal, but nothing came of it. Indeed, it seems likely that he offered his proposal at least as much to forestall action on Powell's suggestion—to show that changing the rules would divide the Court once again—as to accomplish a change in the rules. . . .

Procedural irritants continued to disturb relations among the justices. Aubrey Adams was convicted of murdering an eight-year-old girl in 1978. Florida scheduled his execution for early March 1986. By that time death penalty litigators had managed to persuade some courts that it was unconstitutional to try defendants with "death-qualified" juries, whose members said they had no objections in principle to imposing a death sentence. Other courts disagreed, and the Supreme Court had already agreed to decide the question when Adams's application for a stay of his execution arrived at the Court. It had also already voted to reject the challenge, but the decision had not been announced.

Four justices voted to hold the case until the "death-qualification" decision was announced. A majority thought, however, that Adams's case was different, because no potential juror had actually been removed from the jury in the process of death qualification. What should be done about Adams's application for a stay of execution? Powell made it a practice "solely for institutional reasons" to provide the fifth vote for a stay when four justices voted to grant review. Burger occasionally did so as well.

Powell was confused about the state of the votes in Adams's case. At first he thought that four justices had voted to grant review, and therefore he voted for the stay even though he believed that "Adams and his counsel are 'playing games with us.' " When he realized that the four justices had voted only to hold the case until the death-qualification decision was announced, he told his colleagues that he felt "differently about votes to hold," and now voted to deny the stay.

Marshall told his colleagues that the issues needed a full discussion "because these unresolved disputes invite confusion, changes of mind, and strategic behavior when a person's life is at stake." He believed that "whether the vote is a grant or a hold, the power given to four or three by our rules is nugatory if an execution is permitted to moot the case." He said that "the power to issue a stay under these circumstances simply should not depend on an ad hoc act of generosity by some fifth Justice." As Marshall saw it, "the fate of each prisoner . . . seems to depend primarily upon whim and accident." Marshall called the Court's own "contribution to the arbitrariness of the death penalty" itself "alarming."

Brennan may have illustrated the problem of strategic behavior when he responded to Powell's vote change by asserting that his first choice was to grant review, and that his alternative vote was to hold the case. This meant that there might be four votes to grant review, which would trigger Powell's policy. Although Powell continued to believe that the Court was "simply being exploited," he grudgingly voted to grant the stay. But, he wrote, "the effect of the Court's action will not be misunderstood" by anti-death penalty litigators. Pointing to the fact that Adams's lawyers had filed three petitions for review and four applications for stays of execution within the prior week, Powell told his colleagues that "there has been a gross abuse of the processes of our Court." He would not "criticize counsel for taking advantage of us if we permit it," but he thought that the Court should change its rules to avoid "indefinite delay in enforcing the law of the law."

Burger backed Powell up.... Marshall replied to Burger's concerns about death-penalty lawyers by saying that if "lawyers are routinely able to hoodwink three Justices into voting to hold a case that is actually unrelated" to a pending case, "the Court's problems ... far exceed" the procedural matters the justices were considering. As he saw it, "when this Court has chosen to give some number of Justices less than a majority certain powers," such as to grant review or hold a case, "the majority may not take action to void the exercise of such powers," as denying stays of execution would.

In the end, Adams could not get four votes to grant review. Brennan drafted a dissent from the denial of review describing the Court's processes, including a statement that the justices "internally agreed" that once four justices voted to grant review, a fifth would join them to stay an execution. That statement set Burger off. That decision, he said, "must have taken place when I was in Moscow or Peking." He and Powell gave "a 'comity' vote twice," but that did not "establish an 'agreement.'" He also criticized Brennan for proposing to publicize internal discussions....

Brennan took out the draft's statement about an "agreement" to provide a fifth vote for a stay, but he continued to describe the Court's practices as a "rule that the five [voting against review] will give the four an opportunity to change at least one mind." One justice who voted against review "will nonetheless vote to stay." Burger replied that he had "never heard of such a 'rule.' ...." He again mentioned his "practice," but, he wrote, "If that 'practice' does not make an 'agreement,' it certainly does not make a 'rule.'" ... After further delays, Adams was executed on May 4, 1989....

By the late 1980s, the majority's impatience led to occasional sloppiness. Once in 1987 the conservatives voted to grant a state's petition for review of a state court decision vacating a death sentence before the prisoner's response was even due. Marshall drafted what Blackmun called a "devastating dissent" criticizing the Court's action. Referring to comments of some of his colleagues that they would vote to review the case "even though the opposition material had not yet been seen," Blackmun observed, "the Spring rush to judgment is really bad this year." Marshall's dissent led the Court to wait, and in the fall the Court denied the state's application for review. In a 1986 case, the Court was prepared to deny review, but a proposed dissent led the justices to hold the case until another one was decided. After that decision was handed down, the Court vacated the death sentence without hearing argument.

D. Practices Change

Cases like these were too rare to overcome the conservatives' view that the Court was interfering with the fair administration of justice. Under Chief Justice Rehnquist, they adopted the practice of scheduling arguments in capital cases as soon as possible "where it appears that there will be a fair number of 'holds' for the case, because of the desirability of getting the 'lead' case decided and disposing of the 'holds.'" Marshall objected in vain, saying that he saw "no reason to rush in death cases unless it is to save a life."

The practice of granting stays when four justices wanted to grant review eroded as well....

After Brennan retired, the conservatives had the votes not only to deal with cases on the merits but to change the Court's rules. On May 23, 1991, a month before Marshall himself retired, the justices voted to require four votes to hold cases. It was a fitting conclusion to the Court's internal battles, an unpublicized change in procedures designed to restore what Rehnquist had almost a decade earlier called "reasonable peace and harmony." For Marshall, however, it was purchased at the cost of the decent consideration that people sentenced to death ought to receive from the nation's highest court.

With this in the background, it is not surprising that the Court decided to expedite its hearing in *Felker*, nor that there were four dissenters. The Court's experience created an atmosphere in which pursuing the normal course had come to take on a mild smell of manipulation....

III. THE COSTS OF EXPEDITION

In the end, the decision to expedite the hearing in *Felker* did not matter. The Court unanimously held that the statute barred review by writ of certiorari but did not cut off the possibility of review by a writ of original habeas corpus in the Supreme Court. Congress's attempt to speed up executions was rendered almost entirely toothless: Every prospective habeas applicant denied leave to file a second or successive petition by a court of appeals now can file an application for leave to file an original writ in the Supreme Court, instead of filing a petition for certiorari. At least until the Court changes its internal rules, those applications are handled on the same schedule inside the Court as petitions for certiorari. The preclusion of review did nothing to expedite executions.

Did the decision to expedite briefing and argument in *Felker* affect the quality of the Court's opinion? The tight schedule meant that all parties had to file their briefs simultaneously. They had to guess what their opponents would say. Perhaps that led everyone to be quite cautious in their claims about the statute's scope. Notably, there was essentially unanimous agreement in the briefs that the statute did not bar the Court from hearing original habeas petitions. . . .

For the Chief Justice, *Yerger*[87] resolved the question of preclusion of review in *Felker*. Like the 1868 statute, the 1996 one does not "mention[] our authority to entertain original habeas petitions." Because the Court retained the power to hear habeas cases, "there can be no plausible argument that the Act has deprived this Court of appellate jurisdiction" in violation of the Constitution.

. . . [T]he Court's interpretation of the Act makes one wonder what exactly the Act did. The 1868 repeal had some effect even after *Yerger*: It barred Supreme Court review of appeals court decisions in cases involving those seeking habeas with respect to detentions under state authority. What, however, does the 1996 Act do?

A. *Changing the Standard for Supreme Court Review*

. . . The Court's interpretation might mean that the 1996 Act directed the Court to substitute the Act's requirements for the unstructured discretionary decision the Court would make in considering either a certiorari petition or an application for an original writ of habeas corpus. For example, a prospective habeas petitioner denied leave to file a successive writ might seek review on the ground that the court of appeals had misinterpreted the Act's requirement that "the factual predicate for the [new] claim could not have been discovered previously through the exercise of due diligence," in conflict with some other circuit's interpretation of that requirement. In addition to asking whether the Court's usual discretionary standards were satisfied, the Act might direct the Court to ask as well whether "the facts underlying the claim, if proven and viewed in light of the evidence as a whole, would be sufficient to establish by clear and convincing evidence that, but for constitutional error, no reasonable fact-finder would have found the applicant guilty of the underlying offense."

Chief Justice Rehnquist's summary of the Court's holding asserts that "the Act does impose new conditions on our authority to grant relief," but the supporting analysis, if it can be called that, is terse to the point of obscurity. The Act's new requirements, the opinion says, "inform our authority to grant relief." "Inform" does not mean "dictate" or "constrain," as the opinion made clear in its next paragraph: "Whether

---

87. [Editors' note relocating author's text:] After the Civil War, Congress expanded the scope of habeas corpus and simultaneously authorized appeals from circuit court habeas decisions to the Supreme Court. Concerned that a pending case would produce a Court holding that congressional reconstruction was unconstitutional, Congress repealed the provision authorizing appeals in 1868. *Ex parte* McCardle, 74 U.S. 506 (1868), upheld the repeal against a constitutional challenge, the Court carefully noting that the repeal did not affect the jurisdiction the Court had previously had to issue writs of habeas corpus in cases involving those held pursuant to federal authority. When presented with such a case in *Ex parte* Yerger, 75 U.S. 85 (1868), the Court held that the 1868 repeal did not affect the Court's power to issue an original writ of habeas corpus. The 1868 Act did not refer to the Court's own jurisdiction, and, the Court said, repeals by implication were not favored.

or not we are bound by these restrictions, they certainly inform our consideration of original habeas petitions."

Why so cagey? Perhaps out of concern that interesting separation of powers questions would arise if Congress purported to dictate the Court's standards for exercising jurisdiction conferred on it by statute. The "rule of four," for example, is an internal Court rule, not enacted into law in part because of such concerns. Could Congress require that all decisions invalidating state statutes be supported by seven justices? By five . . .? Or, as Justice Souter wondered, could Congress require the Court to write long opinions?

The 1996 Act could properly "inform" the Court's exercise of discretionary authority, however. Recent decades saw the Court itself refashioning the writ of habeas corpus in part on the ground that the courts ought to elaborate statutory details in light of contemporary circumstances. So too with the original writ of habeas corpus: Contemporary circumstances, evidenced by congressional action, bear on the appropriate structure of the writ even if Congress did not—and perhaps cannot—dictate that structure to the Court

B. Changing the Issues the Court Considers

A second way to make the 1996 Act meaningful would be to hold that shifting review from certiorari to the original writ changes the issues the Court will consider. On certiorari the Court would consider whether the court of appeals properly applied the statutory standards for granting leave to file a successive petition. Perhaps on original habeas the Court would consider only the merits of the underlying petition. So, in Felker's case, the Court would consider not whether the federal court of appeals properly denied leave to file but whether the state trial court gave unconstitutional jury instructions.

Felker said nothing about this question, but the two concurring opinions did. Justice Stevens asserted that review of "gatekeeping" decisions remained available through the All Writs Act, and that in the course of exercising original habeas jurisdiction, the Supreme Court could "consider earlier gatekeeping orders entered by the court of appeals to inform our judgment and provide the parties with the functional equivalent of direct review." Justice Souter was a bit more circumspect saying only that Felker had not sought anything other than certiorari or original habeas, but that "if it should later turn out that statutory avenues other than certiorari for reviewing a gatekeeping determination were closed, the question of whether the statute exceeded Congress's . . . powers would be open."

As Justice Souter suggested, the question of the issues open to Supreme Court review would be important "if the court of appeals adopted divergent interpretations of the gatekeeper standard." . . .

Yet interpreting the 1996 Act to leave open review of gatekeeper decisions would increase the puzzle about what the preclusion of review provisions in the Act actually accomplished. Not only would it have failed to expedite the capital punishment process; it would have failed as well to direct attention away from technicalities and toward the merits of the capital defendant's constitutional claims.

C. Avoiding Constitutional Questions

A standard explanation for some interpretations that render statutes meaningless is that such interpretations are necessary to avoid deciding difficult constitutional questions. Would preclusion of review of court of appeals' gatekeeper decisions raise such a question? Notably, Chief Justice Rehnquist's opinion says not a word about construing statutes to avoid constitutional questions, although he invoked that canon in another case involving congressional restrictions on the jurisdiction of the federal courts.

Justice Souter noted the argument that denying Supreme Court review might be inconsistent with the constitutional provision that courts of appeals must be "inferior" to the Supreme Court: the "lower" courts are inferior to no one with respect to questions as to which there is no possibility of Supreme Court review. I think that argument, while ingenious, is a bit too precious. I would think that a court generally subject to Supreme Court review was inferior to the Supreme Court in the constitutional sense even if some of its decisions were not reviewable. . . .

I have suggested that it is not easy to know whether preclusion of Supreme Court review is itself a difficult constitutional question. The path *Felker* took is hard to justify unless there is a "metaprinciple" of statutory interpretation directing the courts to interpret statutes to avoid deciding whether a statute, if interpreted in a particular way, would raise a difficult constitutional question.

. . .

Ira P. Robbins,[88] *Justice by the Numbers: The Supreme Court and the Rule of Four—Or Is It Five?,* **36 Suffolk U. L. Rev. 1 (2002)**

. . . In the early hours of April 14, 2000, Robert Lee Tarver died in Alabama's electric chair, even though four Justices of the United States Supreme Court had voted to review the merits of his case. This situation is not unique. . . . [T]he Supreme Court operates under two sets of rules—those that are published and those that are not. The former specify some Court procedure and purport to guide lawyers and litigants seeking review and relief from the Court. The unpublished set of rules guide the internal decision-making processes of the Court. The Court

---

88. Professor of Law and Justice, Bernard T. Welsh Scholar, American University.

uses these rules to determine which cases to accept and to manage its docket. Unfortunately, however, the Court closely guards information concerning these rules. Indeed, the very existence of internal rules.... can be inferred only from an examination of dissenting opinions and from published statistics on how Justices voted in particular cases....

A recent kernel of information on unpublished Supreme Court rules emerged in February 2000, in a case that concerned the gray area between the Court's Rule of Four and its Rule of Five. Robert Lee Tarver's bizarre trip through the Supreme Court's procedural maze left attorneys and Court watchers unsure of how many votes the Court requires to grant an original writ of habeas corpus....

Four Justices noted that they would have set the case for oral argument, yet the Court denied review. This outcome suggests that the more rigorous Rule of Five threshold may apply to petitions for an original writ of habeas corpus from the Supreme Court, and perhaps for extraordinary writs in general. However, because the Court has not granted original habeas corpus review since 1925, it is difficult to comprehend the Court's action in *Tarver*.... Regardless of the actual meaning of *Tarver*, its multiple interpretations epitomize the problems that the presence of unpublished procedures pose to the Supreme Court's litigants and observers alike. Using *Tarver* as a springboard, this Article discusses the ... Supreme Court's unpublished internal rules; examines how ambiguity and inconsistent application of these rules leave attorneys, petitioners, and observers confounded; and recommends an end to the era of procedural postulating. For too long, the Supreme Court has followed rules that either are not stipulated by Congress or are not clarified by the Court. Moreover, the Court has adhered to these written but unpublished rules with varying levels of commitment....

II. *In re Tarver*:[89] Internal Rules Lead to External Questions

On April 14, 2000, Robert Lee Tarver was executed in Alabama's electric chair. He had been on death row in Alabama since 1986, when he was found guilty of murdering a shopkeeper. Although Alabama has had nearly 200 prisoners on death row in recent years, most of the cases have gone relatively unnoticed by the media. Tarver's case, too, would have received little or no special attention, but for his attempt to have the merits of his case heard directly by the United States Supreme Court on a writ of habeas corpus.

Tarver petitioned the Court for both a writ of certiorari and a writ of habeas corpus. On February 3, 2000, he succeeded in winning a stay only hours before his scheduled execution. Several weeks later, on February 22, the Court lifted the stay and denied certiorari review of Tarver's claim relating to unconstitutional jury composition. In a separate order issued the same day, the Court denied Tarver's original habeas petition, in which he claimed that the method Alabama used to execute its death-row prisoners, electrocution, violated the Eighth

89. [Footnote 9 in original] 528 U.S. 1152 (2000).

Amendment's ban against cruel and unusual punishments. The State of Alabama executed Tarver by electrocution on April 14.

What made this case unusual was not the fact that the Court had issued and then lifted a stay of execution and denied relief, but rather the manner in which this process unfolded. In its order denying Tarver's habeas corpus petition, the Court wrote: "Justice Stevens, Justice Souter, Justice Ginsburg, and Justice Breyer would set the case for oral argument." In other words, even though the application process that Tarver had used to petition the Supreme Court for relief had honored the known, published rules of the Court, the Court's unpublished rules played a vital role in the outcome of his case. While the Supreme Court Rules do state that direct habeas corpus relief from the Supreme Court "is rarely granted," there is nothing in the Court's rules, or anywhere else, indicating that more than four votes were required to entertain Tarver's petition. The Rule of Five ... trumped the Rule of Four....

III. THE WRITS OF CERTIORARI AND HABEAS CORPUS

. . .

Although the internal rules that apply to petitions for certiorari are reasonably well understood, the manner in which the Court disposes of extraordinary writs is much more murky. These extraordinary writs are so deemed because they tend to be used only in cases with unusual issues that have not been resolved within normal appellate procedure. On occasion, the Court receives petitions requesting mandamus, prohibition, or habeas corpus relief. The Supreme Court can issue extraordinary writs only in its appellate capacity, and seldom exercises its authority to grant these writs. Consequently, as the conflicting reports from Supreme Court correspondents demonstrated, when Robert Lee Tarver petitioned the Court for a writ of habeas corpus, even observers well-versed in Supreme Court procedure were unsure what rules governed disposition of the petition....

IV. THE RULE OF FOUR

... While the Rule of Four is a fixed aspect of Supreme Court procedure, its application in certain types of cases has been a source of discussion and disagreement among writers and Supreme Court Justices alike. The Justices use the Rule of Four with certiorari petitions when deciding whether to grant review and set a case for oral argument. By allowing four Justices to control which cases to accept, the Court recognizes the value of the judgment of a substantial minority of its members and gives them the opportunity to impress upon the others the ultimate worth of the case. When the Court uses the Rule of Four, however, is not always clear in situations other than those the Court chooses to reveal.

In addition to deciding whether to grant certiorari, the Court uses a Rule of Four to hold a case pending the outcome of another case in which the Court has granted certiorari. If four Justices vote to hold one or more cases pending the resolution of an issue or issues raised in another case, then those cases will not be dismissed. Rather, the Court will postpone a decision on whether to grant full review. The decision to hold, therefore, is not a decision on the merits of the case, but instead on whether the issues are worthy of further consideration by the Court. . . .

V. THE RULE OF FIVE

A. *Application of the Rule of Five*

Like the Rule of Four, the Rule of Five has played a prominent role in the Supreme Court's decision-making process. It operates when deciding certiorari cases on their merits, as well as when the Court votes to issue a stay of execution. It is also used when the Court grants a petition for a writ of certiorari and simultaneously vacates the decision below and remands the case to the lower court. Further, the Rule of Five is employed in decisions on rehearings, as well as for further motions to the Court.

The Rule of Five makes sense in many situations that the Supreme Court encounters. Adjudication on the merits when five Justices agree allows the case to be concluded in a democratic manner through simple majority rule. The Court is composed of an uneven number of Justices because clear majority decisions allow the appearance of the fairest outcome in particular cases. . . . The Rule of Five thus makes good sense when applied to adjudication on the merits of a case, as well as in situations in which the Court makes a dispositive ruling.

The Rule of Five, however, is not ideal for every decision the Supreme Court must make. As long ago as 1925, . . . [d]uring the congressional hearings on the Judges' Bill, the Justices made it clear that they chose to grant certiorari when a substantial minority of their number so voted. But a vote to grant certiorari is not a vote on the merits of the case. . . . In situations in which a vote must be taken on a matter that is not outcome determinative, use of the Rule of Four is often optimal.

As important as the Rule of Four is, the Rule of Five is still used by the Court to make the vast majority of its decisions. . . . [F]or dispositive rulings, the Rule of Five is more appropriate. But there are some situations in which the Rule of Five is warranted, even absent a truly dispositive ruling. It is appropriately used, for example, to grant certiorari and immediately vacate the lower court's decision and remand the case for further proceedings. This decision to grant, vacate, and remand (sometimes referred to as GVR), which is not necessarily a decision on the merits of the case, nevertheless removes the case from the Supreme Court's docket and vests responsibility for determining the ultimate outcome on the lower court.

The Rule of Five is also used when the Court votes on whether to rehear a case. In this situation, the Justices vote only on the rehearing, and do not decide the final outcome of the case. The Rule of Five is vital in such cases to avoid creating a revolving door through which a case is decided on the merits by a majority of five Justices and subsequently a minority of four Justices votes to rehear the already determined case. . . .

B. *Stays of Execution: . . . The Rule of Five at Its Worst*

Stays in proceedings are periodically necessary to allow the Court to review a case before the state court or lower federal court takes further action. The importance of stays is most critical in death penalty cases in which the Court finds the case compelling enough for review through a writ of certiorari. In this situation, the Rule of Four is applicable to the certiorari petition. While four Justices may vote to review the case, however, those four alone cannot successfully issue a stay of execution because the Supreme Court will issue a stay only if at least five Justices agree. Thus, if four Justices vote to grant certiorari and four vote to stay the execution, the prisoner may well be executed, thus rendering moot the certiorari petition and the issues contained therein. There is a striking injustice between a rule that grants four Justices the power to review a case, yet requires five Justices to keep the inmate alive pending that review. Either a fifth Justice must vote to issue the stay—this vote is sometimes referred to as a "courtesy fifth"—or the Rule of Four is rendered worthless in the given case.

The two best examples of this point are Herrera v. Collins[90] and Hamilton v. Texas.[91] In *Herrera*, the Supreme Court granted certiorari on February 19, 1992—the date of Leonel Torres Herrera's scheduled execution—to address the question of whether it was unconstitutional to execute an innocent person who raised no independent constitutional claim. The same day it granted certiorari, however, the Court denied Herrera a stay of execution. Four Justices—Blackmun, Stevens, O'Connor, and Souter—voted to grant the stay, but they could not secure a courtesy fifth.

Fortunately for Herrera, the Texas Court of Criminal Appeals, also on February 19, vacated the scheduled execution date. On March 9, the Texas trial court set an execution date of April 15. Two days before the scheduled execution, the Texas Court of Criminal Appeals granted a second stay. The majority wrote:

> This Court finds itself in the unenviable position of having a Texas death row inmate scheduled to be put to death while his case is pending review by the highest court in the land, the Supreme Court of the United States of America. Because of the "rule of five," that Court, which agreed to hear the case on the vote of four justices, but refused to stay the execution, once again creates the ultimate dilemma regarding a Texas death row inmate. Once again a death row inmate needlessly has a carrot dangled before him.

90. [Footnote 89 in original] 507 U.S. 1001 (1993).

91. [Footnote 90 in original] 498 U.S. 908 (1993).

The State and the dissenters on this Court apparently believe that this issue should be decided as a matter of "turf war" i.e., protecting one's jurisdiction.

If the Supreme Court had a simple rule that required the same number to agree to hear as to agree to stay, all problems would be solved. They do not and as a result a Texas death row inmate is in the position of having to ask the highest court in Texas for criminal matters to delay his date with death until they decide his case.

Accordingly, we find under the present circumstances that it would be improper for this Court to allow applicant's execution to be carried out before his petition for writ of certiorari is fully reviewed by the Supreme Court.

Therefore, applicant is granted a stay of execution pending further orders by this Court.

While the Supreme Court in *Herrera* did not have to confront the ultimate issue of an execution mooting the grant of certiorari, that precise issue was before the Court several years before, in Hamilton v. Texas.[92] On June 26, 1990, the Court voted to deny a stay of execution to James Edward Smith, whose mother had submitted a next-friend application on his behalf. Justice Brennan, joined in dissent by Justice Marshall, wrote:

> I would grant the petitions for certiorari and the corresponding applications for stay of execution. Indeed, four Members of this Court have voted to grant certiorari in this case, but because a stay cannot be entered without five votes, the execution cannot be halted. For the first time in recent memory, a man will be executed after the Court has decided to hear his claim.

The State of Texas executed Smith that same day. Nearly four months later, on October 9, 1990, the Supreme Court dismissed the certiorari petition as moot. Justice Marshall, joined by Justice Blackmun concurring in the denial of certiorari, wrote: "It is already a matter of public record that four Members of this Court voted to grant certiorari before petitioner was executed. According to established practice, this fact should have triggered a fifth vote to grant petitioner's application for a stay of execution."

This injustice of requiring five votes for a stay of execution is especially clear when one considers the reasons for using the Rule of Four in the first place. As discussed above, the Rule of Four affords a substantial minority of the Justices the opportunity to persuade one other Justice of the wisdom of their view. The value of the Rule of Four was explained at the hearings on the Judges' Bill in 1925, and the Court has used the Rule of Four ever since. In effect, if the Rule of Five for stays trumps the Rule of Four for grants of certiorari, then the goal of the Rule of Four is not fulfilled; the death of the petitioner prevents the full Court from hearing the views of the four, as well as from hearing a

92. [Footnote 97 in original, relocated]
497 U.S. 1016 (1990).

presentation of the merits of the case after briefing and argument from counsel. This problem with stays in death penalty cases is well-known to the Court.... Nonetheless, nothing has yet been done to cure this injustice.

[The author considers the possibility that five justices felt the issue was not important enough for full consideration, because only three states used the challenged method of execution, and argues that, if this were so, it would be inappropriate in light of habeas corpus's historic concern for protecting individual liberty.]

VI. RECOMMENDATIONS, CONCLUSIONS ...

A. *Publish or Perish*

Whether in given circumstances the Supreme Court employs a Rule of Four or a Rule of Five, the rule should be published, ... [K]nowing in advance how many votes are needed with regard to a particular filing helps litigants to understand the Court and its processes....

[A] clearer understanding of Court processes by potential habeas corpus petitioners might reduce the number of frivolous petitions....

. . .

... [C]larity in and notice of the Supreme Court's internal rules would aid Court commentators and others in their attempts to understand the Court's decisions.

B. *A New Rule of Application*

The Rule of Four is methodically applied to certiorari petitions and should be applied to original writs of habeas corpus as well. If the Supreme Court were to apply the Rule of Four to all writ petitions— extraordinary writs as well as petitions for certiorari—then whenever at least four Justices voted to grant the writ, the writ would issue. The case typically would then proceed to oral argument and decision on the merits. Alternatively, if the standard is the more difficult Rule of Five, requiring the vote of a majority of the Justices simply to grant the writ, then necessarily fewer petitions will be granted and the theory upon which the Rule of Four rests—vesting power in a substantial minority that believes an issue merits further consideration—will be weakened.

The fact that writs of habeas corpus are extraordinary writs should not affect the process used to determine whether they should be heard. A petition should either merit further attention from the Court or lack important attributes that would cause the Court to spend time on it.... To employ the Rule of Five for these petitions ... presumes that the view of four Justices in habeas corpus petitions is less important than the view of four Justices in certiorari petitions.

... The grant of a writ of certiorari is not an adjudication of the merits of a case; so, too, with a grant of a habeas writ. The same Rule of Four should apply to both. Indeed, this was the assumption of many Supreme Court reporters and observers—until the *Tarver* case.

Since the Supreme Court's decision in *Tarver*, petitioners and others have been left to guess about the Court's internal rules in original habeas corpus cases. Indeed, the Court's ruling prompted several respected Supreme Court commentators to announce that a new rule had been applied. It may well be that, in the *Tarver* case, the Court heralded a new standard for processing applications for habeas petitions. It is also possible, however, that the rule for Supreme Court review of habeas petitions has always been a Rule of Five, and that the lack of published information about the Court's rules had merely led observers to assume that the Rule of Four applied not only to certiorari petitions, but also to petitions for the extraordinary writs. We simply do not know.

The byzantine rules that the Supreme Court uses to dispose of the thousands of cases it receives annually have gone largely unquestioned for many years.... Habeas corpus doctrines are difficult enough to comprehend, particularly for pro se prisoners. They, and others, should not have to guess about what should be the simplest of matters: how many votes it takes to grant review.... It is time for the Supreme Court to rethink some of its internal rules and, equally importantly, to publish them for all to see.

2. Certiorari Before Judgment in the Federal Courts of Appeals

In addition to the Court's ability to expedite its consideration of cases after the courts of appeals have made their decision (as we saw in *Felker v. Turpin*), the Court can also expedite its consideration of cases still pending in the federal courts. While the Court generally waits for final decisions from the highest court from which a judgment can be had, 28 U.S.C. § 1254 (1) permits the Court to grant cert *before* a federal court of appeals has decided the case. (There is no analogous provision with respect to state court decisions.) Supreme Court Rule 11 provides guidance as to the use of this procedure and is reproduced below.

Rule 11. Certiorari to a United States Court of Appeals Before Judgment

A petition for a writ of certiorari to review a case pending in a United States court of appeals, before judgment is entered in that court, will be granted only upon a showing that the case is of such imperative public importance as to justify deviation from normal appellate practice and to require immediate determination in this Court. See 28 U. S. C. § 2101(e).

The Court has relied on "cert before judgment" in a number of important cases. For an interesting account by Professor Boris Bittker of his experience rushing to get the Supreme Court to grant cert prior to the Court of Appeals judgment in *Ex Parte Quirin*, 317 U.S. 1 (1942), involving the authority of military tribunals to try, convict and sentence to death accused German saboteurs who landed in the United States during World War II, see Boris I. Bittker, *The World War II German Saboteurs' Case and the Writs of Certiorari Before Judgment by the Court of Appeals: A Tale of Nunc Pro Tunc Jurisdiction*, 14 Const. Comm. 431 (1997). Other important cases in which certiorari prior to judgment was issued include several of the most important separation of powers cases in the twentieth century: the Steel Seizure Case, Youngstown Sheet & Tube Co. v. Sawyer, 343 U.S. 579 (1952) (President Truman's seizure of the steel industry to resolve a labor dispute during the Korean War); the Nixon Tapes case, United States v. Nixon, 418 U.S. 683 (1974) (concluding sitting President Nixon was required to turn over to the district court certain tape records made in the White House of conversations reflecting potentially illegal activity subject to related criminal indictments); and the Iran Hostage case, Dames & Moore v. Regan, 453 U.S. 654 (1981) (upholding the executive agreement by which President Carter had ended the hostage crisis with Iran by requiring that claims pending in U.S. courts against Iran be suspended).

Some scholars have been critical of the Court's certiorari before judgment practice, arguing that it has been used unwisely and in haste. These critics assert that clearer criteria are required for the exercise of the Court's discretion than are provided by the standard of "public importance." In the following excerpt, Professors James Lindgren and William Marshall provide such a critique. Although the relevant rule has been modified since their critique (and moved from Rule 18 to Rule 11), the modified rule does not address their principal concerns, and thus their discussion remains helpful in evaluating the present Rule.

James Lindgren & William P. Marshall,[93] *The Supreme Court's Extraordinary Power to Grant Certiorari Before Judgment in the Court of Appeals*, 1986 Sup. Ct. Rev. 259

In June, 1942, eight German agents left their submarines and stepped onto the beaches of Long Island and Florida, thus beginning the events that culminated in *Ex Parte Quirin,* The Nazi Saboteurs Case. Some were arrested shortly after landing, others were apprehended later. On July 2, 1942, President Roosevelt ordered a military commission to try them, instead of the civil courts. Undoubtedly, Roosevelt's purpose in part was to make possible the death penalty, a punishment

---

93. Lindgren was Visiting Professor of Law, University of Virginia; Marshall was Associate Professor of Law, Case–Western Reserve School of Law at the time of this article.

that would have been unavailable in the civil courts. Seven days after the order setting up the commission, the trial began. The defendants, at least one of whom was an American citizen, sought to challenge the jurisdiction of the military tribunal by asking the Supreme Court for an original writ of habeas corpus. On July 29, the Court returned from its summer recess for a special session to hear the case. The Court heard oral arguments, deliberated, wrote a short per curiam opinion, and announced its decision—all within three days.

At oral arguments, the Assistant Attorney General threatened that if the Court held the military commission illegal, the President might defy its order. Also, Justice Frankfurter—ever the law professor—questioned the Court's power to issue an original writ of habeas corpus. The defendants' attorneys were made aware that they should instead ask for a writ of certiorari before a judgment of the court of appeals. Before doing this, the defendants had to go back to the lower courts to perfect an appeal from the district court to the court of appeals, which they did. Just before noon on July 31, the third day of the Court's special session, the defendants' attorneys filed with the Supreme Court a petition for certiorari before judgment. Within a few minutes, the Court not only granted certiorari but issued a brief per curiam opinion on the merits, an opinion obviously written before the Justices had received the petition for certiorari. They upheld the legality of the military tribunal. The Court brushed aside the classic 1867 precedent of Ex parte Milligan,[94] which had held that Milligan, an Indiana lawyer, should not have been tried by a military tribunal during the Civil War. Milligan was not a soldier, Indiana was not a battlefield, and the civilian courts were functioning normally in Indiana at that time. The Nazi saboteurs did not fare as well, because, as the Court later explained, the defendants were belligerents not civilians.

The military trial ended quickly. Two defendants were given long prison sentences. And less than two weeks after the Supreme Court announced its decision, the other six defendants were executed.

Three decades later, the Court was faced with another challenge to Presidential authority. President Nixon was withholding sixty-four tape recordings that had been subpoenaed by Special Prosecutor Leon Jaworski for use in the criminal trial of six of Nixon's former aides. District Judge John Sirica ordered Nixon to produce the tapes. Nixon's attorneys appealed this decision to the circuit court of appeals. But before the case could be heard by the Court of Appeals, Jaworski, who had prevailed below, petitioned the Supreme Court for certiorari before judgment. The Supreme Court granted certiorari, expedited the briefing schedule, and extended the normal term of the Court until the decision was announced.[95]

---

94. [Footnote 13 in original] 4 Wall. 2 (1866).

95. [Editors Note: For discussion of the *Nixon Tapes* case, see Chapter Four, Section C, below.]

In the wake of the Court's unanimous decision on July 24, 1974, Nixon's dilatory strategy dissolved. The decision resulted in the release of the "smoking gun" tape of a conversation showing that Nixon had tried to use the CIA to interfere with the FBI's Watergate investigation. After hearing the tape, Nixon's staff decided that resignation was the only option. The Judiciary Committee of the House of Representatives voted three articles of impeachment in the week following the Supreme Court decision, the tapes were released on August 5, and Nixon himself was finally convinced to resign by the public reaction to the tape. Gerald Ford took the oath of office as President on August 9, 1974, sixteen days after the Court's decision. . . .

. . .

The use of certiorari before judgment has been criticized for unduly rushing the Court's deliberations or for foreshortening efforts at political resolution. In the *Steel Seizure* case, a secret deal settling the strike had been almost worked out under pressure from President Truman, but the deal fell apart when prejudgment certiorari was granted. Justices Burton and Frankfurter broke a long-standing tradition by filing a dissent from a grant of certiorari. Paul Freund was also skeptical of the Court's action. And in the *Nixon* case, the early certiorari prompted criticism by three prominent Supreme Court scholars—Alexander Bickel, Gerald Gunther, and Philip Kurland. . . .

These and other debates over individual grants or denials are brief and impoverished because there are no general principles against which to evaluate any particular grant. Moreover, much of what has been written about the writ is misleading or just plain wrong, . . . describ[ing] the standards so broadly that a litigant is encouraged to think that his case really qualifies for early review.

Supreme Court Rule 18, the rule [then] governing certiorari before judgment, is of little help. The standard it describes, a case of "imperative public importance," is only one of the four classes of cases where the Court has granted the writ. The others are: (1) cases raising issues similar or identical to those in a case already before the court, (2) cases coming back to the Court second time, and (3) cases where the litigants have erroneously taken a direct appeal.[96]

. . .

II. CERTIORARI BEFORE JUDGMENT—GENERAL CONSIDERATIONS

Certiorari before judgment is designed to permit the Court to accomplish two overlapping objectives: increasing the speed of the litigation and bypassing the court of appeals. Ironically, these advantages may at the same time be major disadvantages for promoting good decision making. . . .

96. [Editors' Note: Current Rule 11 is similarly terse, again using only the phrase   "imperative public importance."]

A. Docket Reduction ...

... [E]ven if a case may be considered likely for Supreme Court review, this does not mean that it will continue to be so after a decision in the court of appeals. A clear ruling by the court of appeals or by the Supreme Court in another case may lessen the import of the legal issues presented. Or the applicable statutory law may change. Or the parties may settle or otherwise change their circumstances.

Here the Court's experience in stay petitions is telling. As with early certiorari, a stay is appropriate only if it is likely that the Court will later undertake to decide the case. Yet even a cursory examination of stays reveals that many cases where stays are granted never reach the Supreme Court on the merits. . . .

... The Court must also use resources in denying petitions for certiorari. A rule that invites litigants to file more petitions necessarily increases the Supreme Court's workload, even if on occasion granting the writ would promote the overall efficiency of the federal judicial system.

B. Increasing the Speed of Litigation

1. *Haste.* In rare cases granting certiorari before judgment is a useful tool, a device to shorten litigation when time is particularly crucial. But haste has its inherent problems. Rushed deliberations may cause the Supreme Court to reach a wrong result or to write a poorly reasoned opinion. . . .

An excellent example of where haste was later admitted by the Court as leading to incorrect results was in the civilian court-martial cases, Kinsella v. Krueger[97] and Reid v. Covert.[98] Both cases were presented to the Court without the benefit of an intermediate court decision. Reid was before the Court on direct appeal under 28 U.S.C. § 1252. *Kinsella* was before the Court on certiorari before judgment because it presented issues similar to those in *Reid*. *Reid* and *Kinsella* involved the power of a military court-martial to try the wife of an American serviceman overseas for murdering her husband. The two cases were originally argued on May 3, 1956, in the waning days of the October 1955 Term of the Court. On June 11, 1956, the Court ruled for the first of two times in the case, holding that the courts-martial indeed could try these wives of servicemen.

In both cases, Justices Warren, Black, and Douglas joined in a brief dissent, arguing that more time was needed "than is available in these closing days of the Term in which to write our dissenting views." They promised to file their dissents at the next term. Justice Frankfurter went further, reserving his judgment for a later date:

> Time is required not only for the primary task of analyzing in detail the materials on which the Court relies. It is equally required for adequate reflection upon the meaning of these materials and their

---

97. [Editors' Note: 351 U.S. 470 (1956).]   **98.** [Editors' Note: 352 U.S. 813 (1956).]

bearing on the issues now before the Court. Reflection is a slow process. Wisdom, like good wine, requires maturing.

Frankfurter went on to point out that the "judgments of this Court presuppose full consideration and reconsideration by all [Justices] of the reasoned views of each." Frankfurter argued that in *Kinsella* and *Reid* this interchange of ideas was lacking.

When the Supreme Court reconvened in the fall of 1956, things looked different. It granted petitions for rehearing in both *Reid* and *Kinsella*, held rearguments, and reversed itself by a six to two margin. Justice Harlan, whose changed views contributed to turning a minority into a majority, explained that rehearing "afforded an opportunity for a greater degree of reflection" than was possible in the closing days of the previous term. Thus, not only did the Court reverse itself in a certiorari before judgment case, but undue haste was blamed.

2. *Expedited hearing, stays, and other ways to control the speed of appellate litigation* ... [T]he benefits of certiorari before judgment in shortening litigation may be overstated. In the *Pentagon Papers* case, for example, the parties through the mechanism of expedited appeal were able to obtain Supreme Court review without significant delay. The entire process from filing in the district court through decision in the court of appeals to final judgment in the Supreme Court took less than three weeks. Arguably, then, the time-saving benefits of certiorari before judgment may be gained without losing an intermediate court decision.

Expedited appeal, however, raises problems of its own. A rushed schedule in two appellate courts may not produce a more considered opinion than a somewhat longer deliberation in one court. . . .

. . .

Why might a stay or injunction be better than certiorari before judgment? First, a stay or injunction can avoid the problems inherent in a rushed deliberation. Second, such provisional relief will secure the advantage of an intermediate review—and the possibility that the court of appeals will resolve the case before the Supreme Court hears it.

One line of authorities suggests that a stay rather than certiorari before judgment is the favored procedure. In cases involving ballot access and election law ... the Court has [on occasion] ordered stays or affirmative injunctions. . . .

It might seem that early certiorari should be restricted to cases where a stay or injunction would be inadequate. Whatever the merits of such a proposal, it is not the way the Supreme Court does business. . . . [T]he Court has never made a litigant show the inadequacy of provisional relief as a prerequisite to obtaining early certiorari. . . .

. . .

C. *Bypassing the Court of Appeals*

... Although originally designed to reduce the Supreme Court's docket, the court of appeals has become an increasingly important aid to

Supreme Court decision making. Justice Burton explained this role in his dissent from the grant of certiorari before judgment in the *Steel Seizure* case:

> The Constitutional issue which is the subject of the appeal deserves for its solution all of the wisdom that our judicial process makes available. The need for soundness in the result outweighs the need for speed in reaching it. The Nation is entitled to the substantial value inherent in an intermediate consideration of the issue by the Court of Appeals. Little time will be lost and none will be wasted in seeking it. The time taken will be available also for constructive consideration by the parties of their own positions and responsibilities. Accordingly, I would deny the petitions for certiorari and thus allow the case to be heard by the Court of Appeals.[99]

Burton's thesis implies two separate justifications. First, an intermediate appeal allows the litigants to sharpen their own positions. Second, a decision of the court of appeals filters the issues and gives the Court important legal insights into the case. . . . [T]he court of appeals is much like the Supreme Court—a federal appellate court, detached, nonpartisan, and staffed by the judges with backgrounds similar to the Supreme Court's. Thus it should be the single most useful aid in deciding cases.

. . . The Court has adopted a rule that, absent extraordinary circumstances, it will refuse to consider issues not decided by the court of appeals—even when the case itself is properly before the Court. Indeed, the policy is so strong that the Court has criticized those jurisdictional statutes where Congress has provided a direct appeal from the district court, since they "deprive [the Court] of the valuable assistance of the Court of Appeals."

One reason for avoiding the court of appeals is to protect the intermediate court's authority. In some circumstances, there may be a legitimate concern that a court of appeals decision will be ignored by a party who asserts that a lower court decision is not authoritative. This, for example, is what the White House announced in *United States v. Nixon*. Similarly, in the *Nazi Saboteurs* case, the lawyer for the government warned that President Roosevelt might defy the Supreme Court. Here an intermediate court opinion would have carried little weight. In such circumstances, it may be better to save the court of appeals from the embarrassment of issuing ultimately unenforceable decisions.

In Ex Parte Peru,[100] the Supreme Court may have recognized another situation where a hearing before the court of appeals could be considered harmful. At issue in *Peru* was whether the Court should issue a mandamus to prevent the lower federal courts from continuing to litigate a libel against a Peruvian ship. The Court held that mandamus was appropriate, resting its decision mainly on foreign policy concerns.

99. [Editors' Note: Youngstown Sheet & Tube Co. v. Sawyer, 343 U.S. 937, 938 (1952).]

100. [Footnote 154 in original] 318 U.S. 578 (1943).

The Court also suggested that the "dignity" of the foreign sovereign might suffer if forced to pursue litigation in the lower courts.

Similar concerns must have also been present in Wilson v. Girard.[101] Here President Eisenhower had promised to turn over to Japanese authorities a soldier accused of murdering a Japanese woman. When the soldier tried to block this move by resorting to the federal courts, the Supreme Court granted certiorari before judgment. It was probably hesitant to subject Japan to protracted lower court proceedings after the President had already spoken. Preserving the dignity of particularly important defendants may also in part explain the *Nixon* and *Steel Seizure* cases. There is a legitimate interest in protecting presidents and foreign sovereigns from lengthy litigation in the lower courts.

[Although the authors criticize the idea that related cases should be consolidated before the Court through certs before judgment, in some cases they believe this is appropriate.] The second type of case appropriate for consolidation is illustrated by Bolling v. Sharpe.[102] There, certiorari before judgment was used less to aid the litigants than to aid the Court. *Bolling*, a companion case to *Brown v. Board of Education*, held that the desegregation requirements applicable to the states under the Fourteenth Amendment also applied to the District of Columbia under the Fifth Amendment.

Bolling is notable in several respects. First, the Court took judicial notice of the case and took the unprecedented step of inviting the litigants to petition for early certiorari. Second, unlike the usual consolidation case, resolving the major issue in the pending case would not have direct precedential effect on the *Bolling* litigation. A holding that the Fourteenth Amendment required the states to integrate their schools did not necessarily imply that the Fifth Amendment imposed similar obligations on the United States. Third, although it involved an obvious question of public importance, *Bolling* is not properly understood as a public importance case. If *Brown* had not been before the Court, certiorari before judgment in *Bolling* would not have been granted. It was the pendency of *Brown* that made an early resolution of *Bolling* critical. Had the cases not been consolidated an embarrassing anomaly could have resulted.

If the Court had decided *Brown* without *Bolling*, it would have opened itself up to a serious political attack, forcing the states to integrate while leaving the District of Columbia alone. By hearing the cases together, the Court both protected itself and helped legitimize its decision in *Brown*.... *Brown* has few if any parallels.

Consolidation cases comprise the largest class of certiorari before judgment cases.... Perhaps enunciating a more limited rule for consolidation would reduce the petitions requesting the writ. Even if the Court continues to grant certiorari before judgment on more expansive grounds than suggested here, it should openly state what it is doing and why.

---

101. [Footnote 157 in original] 354 U.S. 524 (1957).

102. [Footnote 229 in original] 347 U.S. 497 (1954).

Such a clarification would at least make it easier for litigants to argue sensibly.

. . . . [T]he grant [of certiorari before judgment] may be appropriate when it is necessary to assist the court in effectively implementing its own decisions [for example, in the face of defiance by or in the lower courts]. Indeed, this . . . circumstance is among the Court's most important uses of the writ.

IV. CONCLUSION

The Supreme Court Rules, like most court rules, are designed to inform litigants about Court procedures and standards and to guide the Court itself in its discretion. Rule 18 [now Rule 11] does neither. It is obsolete and in fact was grossly inaccurate even when it was first promulgated in 1954. It should be rewritten to reflect the four situations in which the writ is available and the major criteria under each situation along the lines delineated in this article. . . .

Questions and Comments

1. Professors Robbins, Lindgren and Marshall argue that the Court's rules provide insufficient information, and insufficient constraint on the Court's discretion, with respect to the number of votes required for certain action by the Court or the criteria by which the Court will exercise its discretion. Earlier readings about the certiorari process also discussed the role of discretion in the Court's exercise of its certiorari jurisdiction. Do you agree that the rules should constrain the Court's discretion more? Provide more information to the litigants about the circumstances in which discretion will be exercised? Or is there a benefit to the Court's retaining the degree of discretion it does in these areas?

2. Note that certiorari before judgment remains an infrequently used method of review. Consider the difficulty of crafting ex ante rules to constrain discretion based on relatively infrequent past occurrences and the uncertainty of future developments.

3. As noted above in Part B, in the 1950s the Supreme Court was sharply criticized for its failure to hear on the merits a case involving the legality of Virginia's anti-miscegenation laws. In Naim v. Naim, 350 U.S. 985 (1956), the appeal from Virginia's highest court involved the issue of the constitutionality of state laws prohibiting interracial marriages. Because the constitutionality of a state statute had been challenged and upheld by the state's highest court, the Supreme Court's jurisdiction was mandatory. Nonetheless, the Supreme Court, in essence, dismissed the case for want of a substantial federal question. Many scholars considered this an unprincipled refusal to exercise a mandatory jurisdiction conferred by Congress. Others, however, regarded the Court's refusal to schedule oral argument as a prudential effort to avoid further backlash against the *Brown v. Board of Education* decision.

Some years later, Alexander Bickel famously wrote, in praise of what he called the Court's "passive virtues," that the Court's capacity to control the timing of when it addressed an issue was essential to its ability to have the legitimacy needed to issue countermajoritarian decisions when necessary. Alexander M. Bickel, *The Supreme Court, 1960 Term–Foreword: The Passive Virtues*, 75 Harv. L. Rev. 40 (1961). Does Bickel suggest that there may be a benefit to not seeking in advance to constrain the Court's discretion to issue extraordinary relief too narrowly? Or is there a difference between discretion to delay or deny decision, on the one hand, and discretion to expedite review or to grant, or not grant a stay or other extraordinary writ, on the other?

4. Is it inconsistent with the rationale for the rule of four votes required to grant cert to require five votes to grant a stay? In all cases? In no cases? Only in death penalty cases?

E. CERTIORARI AND THE ROLE OF THE COURT IN SOCIETY

Is it possible to evaluate the certiorari process without, at the same time, developing a normative framework to evaluate the Court's overall role in our society? In the readings that follow, different frameworks for normative evaluation of the Court's use of its certiorari discretion are suggested. Professor Hartnett asks, in a continuation of the article included in Section A, above, if the Court's exercise of discretion over certiorari is consistent with the Court's classic justifications for judicial review, while Professor Hellman suggests that the Court has grown too "Olympian." Finally, Professor Tushnet's article might be read to suggest that the Court's declining use of the certiorari jurisdiction is part of a much larger story of "chastened" constitutional aspiration.

Edward A. Hartnett,[103] *Questioning Certiorari: Some Reflections Seventy–Five Years After the Judges' Bill*, **100 Colum. L. Rev. 1643 (2000)**

. . .

V. QUESTIONING CERTIORARI

Although the Supreme Court has achieved the ability to select what cases (and what issues in cases) it wants to decide, there remain important questions to be asked: How can this power be reconciled with the classic justification for judicial review? How can a court with such power claim to be exercising judgment rather than will, and is such a

103. Richard J. Hughes Professor for Constitutional and Public Law and Service, Seton Hall University School of Law.

power consistent with the rule of law? Can this power be justified as a form of administrative rather than judicial power?

A. *Judicial Review*

As Alexander Bickel recognized almost four decades ago, there is a deep tension between certiorari and the classic justification for judicial review. Pursuant to that classic justification, judicial review is the byproduct of a court's obligation to decide a case. In *Marbury v. Madison,* Chief Justice Marshall did more than simply assert that it is "province and duty of the judicial department to say what the law is"— in the next two sentences he immediately explained why: "Those who apply the rule to particular cases, must of necessity expound and interpret that rule. If two laws conflict with each other, the courts must decide on the operation of each."

Because a court lacks the luxury of simply avoiding decision, it must sometimes choose between following a statute and following the Constitution. This justification of judicial review, then, is the point of Marshall's famous passage from Cohens v. Virginia:[104]

> It is most true that this Court will not take jurisdiction if it should not: but it is equally true, that it must take jurisdiction if it should. The judiciary cannot, as the legislature may, avoid a measure because it approaches the confines of the constitution. We cannot pass it by because it is doubtful. With whatever doubts, with whatever difficulties, a case may be attended, we must decide it, if it be brought before us. We have no more right to decline the exercise of jurisdiction which is given, than to usurp that which is not given. The one or the other would be treason to the constitution. Questions may occur which we would gladly avoid; but we cannot avoid them. All we can do is, to exercise our best judgment, and conscientiously to perform our duty.

Alexis de Tocqueville and Abraham Lincoln both made the same point. Tocqueville observed, "But the American judge is dragged in spite of himself onto the political field. He only pronounces on the law because he has to judge a case, and he cannot refuse to decide the case." Lincoln, despite his refusal to accept the authoritativeness of the Supreme Court's interpretation of the Constitution in the *Dred Scott* opinion, noted that he was not making "any assault upon the court, or the judges. It is a duty, from which they may not shrink, to decide cases properly brought before them. . . . "

The Supreme Court's certiorari practice, however, completely undercuts this rationale.

Strikingly, in advocating the Judges' Bill, the Justices never attempted to explain its application in cases presenting even arguable constitutional questions. Instead, (as far as their statements to Congress revealed) the only use envisioned in constitutional cases was as a way of

---

104. [Editors' Note: 19 U.S. 264 (1821).]

quickly dealing with claims that were either frivolous or plainly governed by precedent—that is, in cases where the lower court was obviously correct and summary affirmance would be appropriate. Taft expressed confidence that in no case "would a constitutional question of any real merit or doubt escape our review by the method of certiorari," explaining that the restrictions were merely "to keep out constitutional questions that have really no weight or have been fully decided in previous cases and that have only been projected into the case for the purpose of securing delay or a reconsideration of questions the decision of which has already become settled law." In this way, the Justices never had to deal with reconciling certiorari and judicial review. Indeed, perhaps the tension between certiorari and the classic justification for judicial review helps to explain why it was not until 1953 that the Court would definitively hold that a denial of certiorari was not a ruling on the merits of a constitutional challenge.

Alexander Bickel did not attempt a reconciliation either, but instead used certiorari as a lever to argue against the classic conception of judicial review. In contrast to the classic conception, Bickel instead justified judicial review by idolizing the Supreme Court as the institutional representative of "decency and reason," and by asserting that its "constitutional function" is "defin[ing] values and proclaim[ing] principles." Some variant of this view is commonplace (either explicitly or implicitly) among constitutional scholars today, but as John Harrison has correctly observed, "[t]he power to interpret the Constitution ... comes from the case-deciding power. To suggest that the power to interpret is primary and the case deciding power secondary, is to misinterpret the Constitution and to confuse cause and effect." Such a view unhinges the Supreme Court from other courts—all of which exercise the power of judicial review, both within the classic model and in fact. While there is an enormous literature responding to Bickel's "counter-majoritarian difficulty" and "passive virtues," I am not aware of any work that takes up his challenge to reconcile certiorari with the classic conception of judicial review.

A court that can simply refuse to hear a case can no longer credibly say that it had to decide it. If asked, "Why did you exercise the awesome power to declare an Act of Congress unconstitutional?" the Justices of the Supreme Court can no longer say, "Because we had to." Instead, they must say, "Because we chose to." It is true that lower courts can continue to answer, "Because we had to." Perhaps oddly, then, certiorari calls into question the exercise of judicial review by the Supreme Court, but not by lower courts.

This difficulty is particularly acute when we consider limited grants of certiorari, bearing in mind that, under current practice, all grants of certiorari are limited. The Supreme Court not only chooses which cases to decide, but also chooses which questions to answer. Its Justices can no longer say they had to decide the case; even within a case, they cannot even say they had to decide any particular question. To the contrary, they can grant certiorari as to a particular question in a case, ignoring the presence of other legal errors, even if this means that the Court affirms a judgment that is, by hypothesis, erroneous.

B. *Law or Will?*

The inability of the Supreme Court to credibly claim that it has to decide a case highlights another profound tension between certiorari and classic conceptions of judicial power, a tension that extends beyond cases involving constitutional adjudication. The judiciary, as Hamilton explained, is the least dangerous branch because it possesses only judgment, not force or will. But although this description continues to be widely repeated, it is hardly an accurate description of a court that has the power to set its own agenda. While the judiciary still lacks its own military force, the Judges' Bill gave the Supreme Court an important tool with which to exercise will: The ability to set one's own agenda is at the heart of exercising will.

Political scientists are quite blunt about the impact of the Judges' Bill. "In short, because of its broad discretion to set its own agenda, the Court is no longer the passive institution 'with neither force nor will but merely judgment' described by Hamilton...." Indeed, "[m]uch of the Court's power rests on its ability to select some issues for adjudication while avoiding others...." [with the Court emerging] "as an active participant in making policy."

> The power to decide what to decide ... enables the Court to set its own agenda.... The Court now functions like a roving commission, or legislative body, in responding to social forces.[105]

As Provine puts it:

> The Supreme Court's nearly unfettered discretion to set its own agenda.... is part of the foundation of its institutional strength. Court-controlled case selection permits the Court to sidestep or postpone politically damaging disputes....

Perry writes:

> [M]y assumption, of course, is that the Court does in fact set its own agenda and that the only question is how.... [I]f a case does not arise naturally, the justices often invite cases via their written opinions and by various other means.

Of course, many political scientists make similar assumptions about judicial decisions on the merits, seeming to take for granted that the "justices of the Supreme Court are policy entrepreneurs, who seek to fulfill their policy goals through [not only] their case selection policies [but also] their decisions on the merits of the issues." Some legal scholars seem to share this view, and few are so naive as to completely reject the point. Nevertheless, many legal scholars tend to believe that the rule of law is not chimerical and that it requires judges to be meaningfully constrained through (some variant or combination of) the

---

105. [Footnote 433 in original, citing to David M. O'Brien, *Storm Center: The Su-* *preme Court in American Politics* 191 (4th ed. 1996)]....

original understanding of a controlling text, the existence of rules to guide decisionmaking, the obligation to elaborate reasons for decision, and basic requirements of substantive justice.

In the land of certiorari, however, law provides precious little constraint on judicial action. While Justice Van Devanter assured Congress in the hearings regarding the Judges' Bill that petitions were determined by recognized principles, he changed the subject rather than elaborate what those principles were. . . .

[E]xcept for specifying certain types of conflicts [in Rule 10,], the Court has "essentially defined certworthiness tautologically; that is, that which makes a case important enough to be certworthy is a case that we consider to be important enough to be certworthy." Although people might well be able to agree that a case presents an important issue of federal law without agreeing on how that issue should be resolved, it is "difficult indeed to read the Court's own Rule 10 as anything other than an invitation . . . to the making of 'political choice(s)' about what is 'important' enough to demand the overt, highly visible intervention of the United States Supreme Court." Certiorari, then, is difficult to reconcile with the formalist conception of the rule of law.

Such an unconstraining rule imposes some costs on the Court, particularly by encouraging large numbers of petitions. Yet if the Court wanted to reduce the number of petitions filed, it could.

The most effective method of reducing the number of cases filed with the Court that is wholly within the Court's power to effectuate would be the formulation and publication of detailed guidelines regarding the criteria for granting and denying review.

But from Taft on down, the Justices have steadfastly refused to promulgate rules that might constrain their discretion. "One can be assured that the ambiguity of Rule 10 is not some unfortunate oversight by the justices. They have intentionally enunciated murky criteria."

The lack of a constraining text might not be important if there were a body of constraining case law. But there is none. [I]n a sustained defense of judicial discretion in matters of jurisdiction, David Shapiro emphasizes that what he defends is not an ad hoc exercise of will (or even Bickelian "prudence"), but instead "principled discretion." Such principled discretion requires "that criteria drawn from the relevant statutory or constitutional grant of jurisdiction or from the tradition within which the grant arose guide the choices to be made in the course of defining and exercising that jurisdiction." Moreover, it requires that these criteria be "capable of being articulated and openly applied by the courts, evaluated by critics of the courts' work, and reviewed by the legislative branch."

Shapiro argues that such principled discretion is compatible with "the power of judicial review upheld in *Marbury*" because it "carries with it an obligation of reasoned and articulated decision, and can therefore exist within a regime of law." Significantly, Shapiro never links these requirements with certiorari, which, he notes, is an example of "virtually absolute" discretion.

Although commentators early on called for the Court to explain briefly its reasons for denying certiorari, the Court has not obliged. While this refusal to explain "gives the justices greater flexibility in agenda setting," it makes certiorari difficult to reconcile with the legal process conception of the rule of law. Indeed, Alexander Bickel pointed to certiorari as the clearest example of techniques that "cannot themselves be principled in the sense in which we have a right to expect adjudications on the merits to be principled."

It has also been suggested that if "all petitions [were] channeled through experienced Supreme Court lawyers, the inadequacies of [the rule] would be less apparent. Assuming the Court is fairly consistent in its choices, much of what the rule lacks in specificity would be compensated for by the experience of the Supreme Court bar." But the Court has not acted to impose any meaningful limits on membership in its bar. . . . The reason is simple:

> [T]he Court profits by having a large pool of cases from which to make its selections. Were the bar sufficiently organized and capable of limiting itself to the presentation of the few hundred cases each term which are given serious consideration by the Court, the Justices themselves would soon lose the essence of the discretionary power they now possess.[106]

Perhaps the most graphic illustration of how certiorari frequently operates in the area of will and not law is the common practice of defensive denials. . . . Remarkably, "[m]ost justices view defensive denials as an acceptable strategy."

C. Certiorari as Administrative Power

One possible response that defenders of current certiorari practice might make is that the only issue being decided on a certiorari petition is which court will have the last word in a case. . . . So understood, the Supreme Court's power to choose which cases to decide and which to leave for final adjudication by other courts is better viewed as a species of administrative power rather than adjudicative power. The Judges' Bill does share kinship with the Rules Enabling Act, and was born in an era of considerable faith in the notion of neutral expertise in general and neutral expertise regarding the establishment of judicial procedure in particular.

This approach is best represented by two former Supreme Court clerks, Samuel Estreicher and John Sexton, who conducted a detailed legal study of the workings of the certiorari process and advocated treating the Supreme Court as the "manager of a system of courts."[107]

---

106. [Footnote 464 in original, citing Eugene Gressman, *Much Ado About Certiorari*, 52 Geo. L. J. 742, 765 (1964)].

107. [Footnote 469 in original] Samuel Estreicher & John Sexton, *A Managerial Theory of the Supreme Court's Responsibili-*

They urged viewing the Court as a "wise manager" that should "delegate[ ] responsibilities to subordinates and, absent an indication that something is awry, accord[ ] their decisions a presumption of validity." They acknowledged that the Court's rule governing certiorari is "hopelessly indeterminate and unilluminating," and suggested detailed alternative criteria that could supplant "the ever-present tendency of the Justices to conceive of the case selection process in political terms." Making the analogy to administrative law quite explicit, they even suggested that the Court might emulate "the Administrative Procedure Act's rulemaking procedures [by] disseminat[ing its criteria] throughout the legal community."

. . . Faith in such apolitical management by experts has been deeply shaken, not only in administrative law generally, but in procedural law in particular. Debates over the Federal Rules of Civil Procedure reflect this loss of faith, with the rulemaking process seen less and less as something to be left in the hands of neutral experts in the "just, speedy, and inexpensive" decision of cases, but rather an arena for battle over the substantive results of cases. It is hardly surprising in this environment that the Supreme Court has not heeded Estreicher and Sexton's call for clearer and more detailed standards governing certiorari: Not only would any such standards tend to reduce the Court's agenda-setting power, but also the debate over the content of those standards would itself likely be highly political. In any event, it has become far more difficult to justify judicial control over the judicial agenda on the basis of such neutral administrative expertise.

There is a final reason the Court might be reluctant to heed Estreicher and Sexton's advice—a reason that Estreicher and Sexton themselves note:

> One possible criticism is that our managerial conception of the Court's responsibilities is fundamentally at odds with the view that courts are obligatory decision makers who do not "manage" dockets but render justice in all cases properly before them, so that open avowal of the Court's managerial discretion is likely to exacerbate doubts about the legitimacy of its judicial review function.

Estreicher and Sexton reject this criticism and think it "misguided," noting that the Supreme Court "ceased long ago to be a court of mandatory jurisdiction." Their observation is true, but it simply sidesteps the conceptual tension between certiorari practice and judicial review.

. . . *Marbury* . . . rest[ed] the legitimacy of judicial review on a court's obligation to decide a case properly before it. Estreicher and Sexton fail to wrestle with that genuine *Marbury v. Madison* model. . . . The Supreme Court, in contrast, apparently prefers to leave the classic *Marbury* model in place despite its tension with certiorari practice.

ties: The Empirical Study, 59 N.Y.U. L.
Rev. 681, 717 (1984). . . .

VI. THE IMPORTANCE OF CERTIORARI

In questioning certiorari, I do not doubt its importance. Indeed, the power to select cases—like other doctrinal devices that reduce the impact of particular decisions, such as non-retroactivity and qualified immunity—makes it easier for the Supreme Court to change its interpretation of the Constitution. The power to refuse to hear cases enables the Court to bide its time and "to escape, at least temporarily, from the logical implications of an initial unpopular on-the-merits decision." It also enables the Court to intervene selectively, without committing itself to policing a new area it brings under its supervision. As a result, then, the procedural license given by certiorari has had a profound role in shaping our substantive constitutional law.

Consider, for example, the incorporation doctrine. The Supreme Court launched the idea that some of the protections of the Bill of Rights were "incorporated" in the Fourteenth Amendment's due process clause in 1925, four months after the Judges' Bill. Perhaps that was purely coincidental. Perhaps the First Amendment right to freedom of speech would have been applied to the states regardless of whether Congress gave the Court discretionary control over the bulk of its docket.

But would the Supreme Court have incorporated the Fourth, Fifth, Sixth, and Eighth Amendments if it were obliged to review every state judgment that upheld a criminal conviction or sentence over a defendant's objection based on one of these Amendments? And if it did, is it remotely possible that it would have spun out such elaborate doctrinal requirements if it were required to apply and enforce them in every such case? . . .

More generally, the Court's unbridled discretion to control its own docket, choosing not only which cases to decide, but also which "questions presented" to decide, appears to have contributed to a mindset that thinks of the Supreme Court more as sitting to resolve controversial questions than to decide cases. Cases tend to be thought of as "vehicles" for deciding controversial questions, and some distinguished commentators suggest that the role of the Supreme Court is to authoritatively pronounce the law, with the limitation of the judicial power to "cases and controversies" simply a way to limit the occasions for those pronouncements.

Perhaps surprisingly, one of the clearest judicial statements that the Supreme Court should be concerned with deciding controversial issues rather than live cases comes from Chief Justice Rehnquist. In Honig v. Doe,[108] he argued that the Supreme Court should simply exempt itself from the mootness doctrine once it has granted certiorari. The majority of the Court has never explicitly adopted Rehnquist's view, but it has come pretty close. . . .

What is not surprising is that those who believe that the Supreme Court should be the nation's moral leader and view the Court as "a

108. [Editors' Note: 484 U.S. 305 (1988).]

primary instrument of constitutional amendment" applaud its agenda-setting power. This applause was perhaps most audible in the reaction to the 1972 Freund Commission Report calling for a National Court of Appeals. For example, in a remark more in keeping with Taft's original description of his goal than with Van Devanter's more politic argument to the Senate, Eugene Gressman claimed that "informed arbitrariness is at the very heart of the certiorari jurisdiction. The justices are supposed to be motivated to grant or deny review solely by their individual subjective notions of what is important or appropriate for review by the Court." Under the Freund proposal, former Chief Justice Warren asserted, "Inevitably the capacity of the Supreme Court to maintain the Constitution as a living document . . . would be jeopardized."

As Warren saw it, the purpose of the Judges' Bill was "to permit the Court not only to achieve control of its docket but also to establish our national priorities in constitutional and legal matters." "Those standards cannot be captured in any rule or guideline that would be meaningful to an outside group of judges," because what matters are "the concerns and interests and philosophies of the Supreme Court justices." The requisite "broad overlook and an innovative approach to the law and the Constitution . . . are acquired only by those who serve on the Supreme Court." Rotating lower court judges (as proposed by the Freund Commission) would tend "to deny review of those decisions that fall into the traditional molds and that seem correctly decided in terms of precedent and settled law." This would cut off the Supreme Court from cases in which "no one could anticipate that the justices would perceive in those cases the chance to advance the meaning and the application of some aspect of the Bill of Rights."

While it is understandable that those who treat Justices of the Supreme Court as the nation's moral leaders would endorse judicial review coupled with broad agenda-setting power, it is past time to frankly acknowledge that such views are nothing more than a call for mixed government, with one branch—the judiciary—representing the interests and views of the "better" class of society.

CONCLUSION

Justice Brennan once stated that choosing cases is "second to none in importance." Indeed, the Supreme Court's power to set its agenda may be more important than what the Court decides on the merits. Recent scholarship has called into serious doubt the notion that the Supreme Court has been or can be the counter-majoritarian hero of some lawyers' dreams, suggesting instead that the Court lacks both the power and the inclination to deviate very far from prevailing elite opinion. Yet, when one considers the impact of cases such as Prigg v. Pennsylvania,[109] Dred Scott v. Sandford,[110] Brown v. Board of Education[111], Miranda v.

---

109. [Footnote 522 in original] 41 U.S. (16 Pet.) 539 (1842).

110. [Footnote 523 in original] 60 U.S. 393 (1856).

111. [Footnote 524 in original] 347 U.S. 483 (1954).

Arizona,[112] Furman v. Georgia,[113] Roe v. Wade,[114] Bowers v. Hardwick,[115] and Cruzan v. Missouri,[116] it may be that the most significant impact of Supreme Court decisions is to increase the political salience of the issues decided—regardless of which way the Court decides the issues.

Arthur D. Hellman,[117] *The Shrunken Docket of the Rehnquist Court,* **1996 Sup. Ct. Rev. 403**

[As explained above, Professor Hellman explores five hypotheses for the decrease in certiorari grants: the elimination of mandatory jurisdiction, the retirements of liberal justices, the homogeneity of the courts of appeals, the federal government's losing fewer cases, and the courts of appeals' being more in line with the Supreme Court. He concluded that these hypotheses did not fully or adequately explain the decrease in certs granted. Instead, he concludes, the Justices' view of the Court's role in our political system seems to have shifted due to changes on the Supreme Court bench. This is not simply because Justice White, who was most inclined to grant cert to resolve circuit splits, was replaced in 1993 by Justice Ruth Ginsburg who emphasizes that role less. It is also because, says Hellman, the Court in the 1990s believed that it need only issue a few nationally binding decisions rather than strictly monitoring the lower courts, becoming, in Hellman's words "an Olympian Court."]

VIII.   A NEW COURT AND A NEW PHILOSOPHY

What explains the [decline in the number of petitions granted]? One obvious possibility is that the Court of [1996] is not the Court of 10 years ago. Six of the Justices who sat on the Court in the 1983–85 period have retired, and one of the remaining three serves as Chief Justice rather than as an Associate Justice.

I have already considered the theory that the shrinkage of the docket can be attributed to the departure of the Court's most liberal members. The data do not support that hypothesis, at least if we assume that those Justices would have concentrated their efforts on securing review of cases that rejected civil liberties claims. But there is good reason to believe that other personnel changes had substantially greater effect on the case selection process.

During the 1970s and the first half of the 1980s, Warren E. Burger served as Chief Justice of the United States. Burger's public statements leave no doubt that he zealously supported Supreme Court review of

---

112. [Footnote 525 in original] 384 U.S. 436 (1966).

113. [Footnote 526 in original] 408 U.S. 238 (1972).

114. [Footnote 527 in original] 410 U.S. 113 (1973).

115. [Footnote 528 in original] 478 U.S. 186 (1986).

116. [Footnote 529 in original] 497 U.S. 261 (1990).

117. Sally Ann Semenko Endowed Chair and Professor, University of Pittsburgh School of Law.

activist decisions by lower courts, especially those that favored the constitutional claims of criminal defendants. When the late Chief Justice retired at the end of the 1985 Term, counteractivist petitioners lost what was probably their most reliable vote for certiorari.

Justice Byron R. White, although not particularly ideological in his approach to case selection, took an expansive view of the Court's role in providing doctrinal guidance to the lower courts. Justice White retired at the close of the 1992 Term and was succeeded by Ruth Bader Ginsburg. Justice Ginsburg has expressed little sympathy for the idea that every doubtful issue of federal law should be resolved by a national court. Almost certainly, she votes to grant certiorari far less often than did her predecessor.

As an Associate Justice, William H. Rehnquist articulated a view of the Court's role that appears close to that of Chief Justice Burger and Justice White. Since he became Chief Justice, he has moved away from that interventionist approach. He is now willing to deny review in cases whose outcomes or reasoning he disagrees with, but which present no issues of precedential importance.

Finally, Justice Antonin Scalia, who was appointed to Justice Rehnquist's seat when Chief Justice Burger retired, has provided the most detailed jurisprudential justification for a stripped-down plenary docket. Justice Scalia explicitly disavowed the common-law approach of "gradually closing in on a fully articulated rule of law by deciding one discrete fact situation after another until ... the truly operative facts become apparent." Rather, he would extend "the law of rules ... as far as the nature of the question allows," then leave the rest to the lower courts, even if this means "tolerating a fair degree of diversity" in the rules' application.

In short, the Justices who have joined in the Court in the last 10 years take a substantially different view of the Court's role in the American legal system than the Justices of the 1980s. They are less concerned about rectifying isolated errors in the lower courts (except when a state-court decision threatens the supremacy of federal law), and they believe that a relatively small number of nationally binding precedents is sufficient to provide doctrinal guidance for the resolution of recurring issues.

The influence of this philosophy can be seen most readily in the statutory segment of the docket. In the three Terms 1993 through 1995, the Court decided 110 cases involving statutory issues. In 88 of these, the need for precedential guidance was signaled in the clearest possible way: by an intercircuit conflict. Of the remaining 22 cases, nine were brought to the Court by the Federal Government, and five were filed by private parties with the support of the Government. Thus, in this segment of the docket, the Court relies almost entirely on two strong indicia of the need for a national binding decision: the presence of an intercircuit conflict or an assertion of importance backed by the unique credibility of the Solicitor General.

[Professor Hellman offers a similar analysis of what he calls the "governmental powers" segment of the docket, indicating that] the Court's criteria are somewhat more flexible, but, outside the realm of the Supremacy Clause, the emphasis remains on articulating rules rather than on filling in the interstices of existing doctrines....

. . .

... [T]he patterns I have described demonstrate a substantial narrowing of the criteria that the Court applied during the 1980s. In the 1983–85 Terms, the number of statutory cases that received plenary consideration in the absence of either a conflict or the support of the Solicitor General was not eight but 41. The number of residual grants involving governmental powers was not 39 but 84—and that is only the certiorari cases. If appeals are included, the current figure represents a shrinkage of almost two-thirds from that of the earlier period.

The new philosophy is also reflected in the 1995 revision of the Supreme Court's rules. For example, in describing the criteria for a grant of certiorari, the rules now tell petitioners that the existence of an intercourt conflict, without more, is not sufficient; the conflict must involve a question of importance. In addition, for the first time, the rules explicitly state that a petition "is rarely granted when the asserted error consists of ... the misapplication of a properly stated rule of law."

IX. ... An Olympian Court?

From Taft and Hughes onward, the Justices of the Supreme Court have emphasized that the Court's function is not to correct errors in the lower courts, but to "secur[e] harmony of decision and the appropriate settlement of questions of general importance." Under Chief Justice Rehnquist, the Court has moved closer than at any time in its history to acting upon that vision. It resolves direct conflicts between circuits; it responds to pleas by the Solicitor General that vital interests of the Federal Government are at stake; and it guards the supremacy of federal law against apparent violations by state courts. The Court also addresses issues of obvious importance in the realm of governmental powers. Beyond that, with only occasional exceptions, the Court stays its hand.

Many judges and lawyers will see this as a positive development. They share the concern of Justice Ginsburg that centralization of judicial authority tends to carry the " 'imperial' judiciary to its logical limits." In this view, the Court can best serve the needs of the national law by laying down broad principles, leaving their application and elaboration largely to the federal courts of appeals and the state appellate courts. Nor is there any need for the Supreme Court to iron out every wrinkle of statutory interpretation, even some that give rise to apparent intercircuit conflicts. From this perspective, the shrunken docket of the Supreme Court can be seen as the judicial counterpart to the devolution that is taking place in the political branches of the national government.

But there is also a less benign way of viewing this development. The Court, if not imperial, has now become Olympian. The Justices seldom engage in the process of developing the law through a succession of cases in the common-law tradition. Rather, Court decisions tend to be singular events, largely unconnected to other cases on the docket and even more detached from the work of lower courts.

This approach may pose a threat to the effective performance of the Court's functions that is no less serious than that created by an "imperial judiciary." At the simplest level, the Court runs the risk that the paucity of decisions will leave wide gaps in the doctrines governing important areas of law. Consider, for example, the recurring question of the preemptive effect of section 301 of the Labor–Management Relations Act on state-law claims by individual employees. The Court's jurisprudence on the subject consists primarily of two unanimous decisions handed down three years apart. One decision found preemption; the other did not. The Court itself has said, with some understatement, that "the Courts of Appeals have not been entirely uniform in their understanding and application of the principles set down in the two decisions." But the Court has passed up several opportunities to clarify those principles in cases presenting the issue in conventional settings. Instead, the Court accepted review of a complex case in which section 301 was invoked only peripherally and "nonpreemption under 301 was clear beyond peradventure." Variations on this pattern can be seen in the Court's jurisprudence on the discretionary function exception to the Federal Tort Claims Act, the government contractor defense, and personal jurisdiction over nondomiciliaries.

Some will see these gaps as symptomatic of a larger problem in the legal system: an insufficient number of nationally binding precedents. Others will argue that when it comes to expounding the national law, more is not necessarily better. Certainly it is not difficult to find areas and issues that have received sustained attention from the Court, but which continue to generate confusion and conflict.

In any event, the Court's Olympian stance raises concerns that go beyond the adequacy of the doctrinal guidance that the decisions provide. Quite apart from any gaps in precedent, paring the docket may impair the quality of the Court's work in the cases that it does take. When the Court addresses a particular statute or doctrine only in isolated cases at long intervals, the Justices may not fully appreciate how the particular issue fits into its larger setting. They may lose sight of the practical aspects of adjudication that emerge only when judges actually apply their rules to resolve disputes in a variety of factual contexts. The cases that attract the Court's attention may well be ones that involve extreme facts or idiosyncratic lower-court rulings. The resulting decisions, if not tempered by precedents deriving from more routine controversies, may skew the law in a way that would be avoided if the Court regularly adjudicated cases in that area.

Detachment from the work of lower courts gives rise to concerns of a different kind. A prime illustration of the phenomenon is the decision last Term in Whren v. United States.[118] The Court held that a traffic stop supported by probable cause does not violate the Fourth Amendment even if the police officer stopped the vehicle as a "pretext" to investigate more serious crimes "as to which no probable cause or even articulable suspicion existed ." No Justice dissented, and no Justice wrote separately. Nothing in the Court's opinion even hinted that any court or judge had ever viewed the issue differently. A reader might wonder why the Court had granted review in a case whose resolution was so self-evident. In fact, the issue had generated a conflict of long standing among the lower courts, with strongly worded opinions rejecting the position that is now the law of the land.

The Supreme Court need not acknowledge the work of lower courts in every one of its decisions, or even most of them. Nor need the Court attempt to replicate the common-law method in all of the many areas of its jurisprudence. But if the Court recurrently ignores the efforts of lower-court judges to address the issues on its docket, while remaining aloof from the day-to-day operation of the rules it lays down, two consequences can be anticipated. Lower-court judges will no longer feel the spirit of goodwill and cooperation that comes from participation in a shared enterprise. Without that spirit, it is hard to see how a hierarchical judiciary can function effectively. What is worse, the Justices themselves, engaged in work that is increasingly distinct from that of other courts, will have ever greater difficulty in adhering to the line that separates the judicial role from the legislative. The result, ironically, may be a Court that is even more "imperial."

The Court has already moved in that direction. During the same period that the Justices have reduced their role as a source of precedential guidance for lower courts, they have cut a wide swath through controversial issues of public policy, enhancing judicial power and setting at naught the resolutions reached through majoritarian processes. It is a telling fact that although the 1995 Term brought fewer plenary decisions than any previous Term in this century, four of those decisions held Acts of Congress unconstitutional. Four other Acts of Congress were struck down in the 1994 Term. One must go back 60 years to find two consecutive Terms in which eight discrete federal statutes met their doom at the hands of the Court.

Plainly, the Court is not going to withdraw from the arena of public policy; however, the era of shrinkage in the plenary docket may be ending. As the 1996 Term began, the number of cases the Court had accepted for review was substantially higher than it was a year earlier, though still well below the levels of the 1980s. Perhaps the Justices have begun to sense that the Court cannot entirely escape its common-law roots, and that a docket devoted solely to making law may not make law in the most effective way.

---

118. 517 U.S. 806 (1996).

Mark Tushnet,[119] *Foreword: The New Constitutional Order and the Chastening of Constitutional Aspiration*, 113 Harv. L. Rev. 29 (1999)

The decade of the 1990s saw a wave of constitutional transformations around the world. The most dramatic constitutional changes have involved the overthrow of totalitarian governments. No less important have been transformations that have helped turn modern welfare states from a focus on command-and-control regulation to market-oriented regulation as the ambitions of social democracy waned. Throughout the world, national governments increasingly devolve power to subnational governments.

Historically, global waves of constitutional change have prompted change in the United States as well. The framing of the Constitution in 1787–1789, for example, was part of a worldwide movement that historian Robert Palmer called "The Age of Democratic Revolution." Similarly, the Reconstruction era in the United States, and the democratic impulse driving it, were perhaps a late expression of the democratic impulse associated with the "generation of 1848" in Europe. Like those European constitutional efforts, the democratic aspirations of Reconstruction ended in short-run failure. Finally, the world-wide economic depression in the 1920s and 1930s that prompted constitutional transformations such as the end of the Weimar Republic in Germany also occasioned innovations in Australia, Canada, and the United States aimed at developing public responses to the economic crisis.

Perhaps the United States is once again participating in a worldwide movement of constitutional change. It has been clear for more than a decade that the New Deal/Great Society political system is no longer in place, and it is a "now-familiar truth" that "[t]he Warren Court is dead." It has been less clear, however, that the New Deal system has been replaced with a coherent new political and constitutional system. . . ., rather than with a random collection of institutions and decisions lacking any unifying theme. I suggest here that a new constitutional order is indeed in place. . . .

By regime or constitutional order, I mean both the set of institutions through which a nation makes its fundamental decisions over a sustained period, and the principles that guide those decisions. Historically, regime shifts in the United States have occurred through a process of partisan realignments resulting from critical elections that produce large-scale and seemingly permanent shifts in party affiliation, The new constitutional order, however, came about differently. Many political observers in the early 1980s thought that the 1980 election would prove to have been a critical realigning election, one that would lead traditional Democrats to convert permanently to Reagan Republicanism. It did not. Instead, the 1980 election proved to be part of a longer term process of

119. Carmack Waterhouse Professor of Constitutional Law, Georgetown University Law Center; currently the William Nelson Cromwell Professor of Law, Harvard Law School.

partisan dealignment, in which voters reduced their attachment to any party.

An accurate description of the new constitutional order improves our understanding of constitutional developments in several ways. First, it directs attention to the important role that interactions among our constitutional institutions play in shaping the overall system that is our government. For example, we cannot understand the Supreme Court's work as a whole without understanding the interaction between the president and Congress in staffing the Court. Second, an accurate description may improve our ability to anticipate constitutional developments, including future Court decisions. If the new order rejects the constitutional premises on which the New Deal/Great Society regime rested, we should not be surprised to find the Court making decisions that are consistent with that rejection. Similarly, an accurate description may foster a useful reconsideration of which precedents are worth taking seriously. Just as it would have been unwise for constitutional scholars in 1939 to spend much time addressing the substantive due process and Commerce Clause decisions of the pre-New Deal 1920s, so too would it be unwise for us today to spend too much time dealing with those Warren Court decisions that are inextricably part of the New Deal/Great Society constitutional order.

. . . In the most general terms, the new constitutional order is one in which the aspiration of achieving justice directly through law has been substantially chastened. Instead, justice is to be achieved not by national legislation identifying and seeking to promote it, but by individual responsibility and market processes.

Part II describes the Supreme Court's role in the new constitutional order and argues that the Court has reduced, relative to the Warren Court, its own aspirations of achieving justice directly through law. . . .

. . .

Most of my effort is devoted to describing the new constitutional order's characteristics. I must note at the outset, however, that I am deeply skeptical about the normative claims that this new order makes— or refrains from making—on us and our government.

I.   THE EXECUTIVE AND LEGISLATURE IN THE NEW CONSTITUTIONAL ORDER

The United States has experienced a succession of constitutional regimes within the framework of a Constitution whose text has been amended only occasionally. Regimes are constitutional in the sense that they organize all of a society's fundamental political institutions. They encompass the entire range of political actors, from Supreme Court Justices to elected legislators. And, precisely because of their scope, constitutional regimes are constructed not in a single dramatic election but over a period of time during which presidents are elected, Supreme Court Justices are chosen, and the membership of Congress shifts as the regime consolidates its hold.

For my purposes, the relevant regimes are the regime of the New Deal and the Great Society, running from the late 1930s through the early 1970s, and the present regime, which made its first solid institutional gain with the election of Ronald Reagan in 1980 and which, I argue, has been consolidated since the 1994 elections produced a Republican majority in both houses of Congress. The New Deal/Great Society order was characterized by bargaining among pluralist interest groups, many of which gained footholds in the national government's bureaucracies. Its guiding principle was egalitarian liberalism, though of course there was substantial disagreement among the regime's adherents over the best way to ensure equality among all Americans. The new regime, in contrast, proceeds from a handful of well-known, moderately conservative principles; these principles include commitments to scaling back the welfare state while preserving a loose social safety net, and to phasing out command-and-control forms of economic regulation while preserving some public responsibility for ensuring that markets operate safely and without artificial obstructions ....

·   ·   ·

A.   *The Institutions of the New Constitutional Order*

·   ·   ·

... I argue that the interaction between the president and Congress in the new regime produces a government of chastened constitutional aspiration....

1.   *The Possibilities and Limits of Presidential Power in the New Constitutional Order.*—Franklin D. Roosevelt's State of the Union message in 1944 defined the guiding principles of the New Deal/Great Society constitutional order. Roosevelt called for an ambitious "Second Bill of Rights" that included "[t]he right to earn enough to provide adequate food and clothing and recreation" and the rights to "adequate medical care," "a decent home," a "good education," and "adequate protection from the economic fears of old age, sickness, accident and unemployment." Bill Clinton's State of the Union Address in 1996 defined the guiding principle of the new constitutional order: "The era of big government is over." ... [T]he implication was not that the national government would have nothing left to do. Rather, the initiatives of the new constitutional order would simply become small-scale. In other words, the expansive aspirations expressed by Roosevelt, and in the New Deal/Great Society constitutional order as a whole, have become chastened in the new order.

·   ·   ·

2.   *A Polarized Congress in a Divided Government.* ... [T]he new order is characterized by a public that does not participate in politics. Over the last century, voter turnout in national elections has declined by twenty-five percent.... [T]he consequences of the decline are reasonably clear: relatively small groups of voters, rather than party organizations,

now dominate national politics. . . . [D]ivided government, with one party controlling the presidency and a different party controlling at least one house of Congress, is the norm in the new constitutional order.

In opting for divided government, the electorate has reduced the importance of parties as institutions. Many voters no longer identify themselves as Democrats or Republicans. . . . In an era of voter dealignment and the associated decline in voter turnout . . ., political elites have attempted to reconstitute the parties at the elite level. This process of reconstitution has clarified the parties' competing ideological positions. During Ronald Reagan's presidency, for example, the fact that a congressional candidate ran as a Democrat in the North conveyed some clear information about her political commitments. Similarly, the Contract with America provided congressional Republicans with the equivalent of an opposition platform to signal the positions they would take. Voters were able to see what a unified government would offer them, and appeared to reject the options offered by both parties. The voters decided in 1994 to divide the government by turning over Congress to the Republican party, and to continue with divided government by reelecting Clinton in 1996.

Changes within Congress have . . . reinforced the polarization phenomenon. . . . The increased power of party leaders also helps reinforce partisan polarization.

In sum, the new constitutional order consists of a public that does not participate in politics, and weak parties but highly partisan institutions in a divided government. The politics of this new constitutional order operate at elite levels. The combined effect of these developments has been to reduce the scope of what the government seems able to accomplish, and thus the government's apparent relevance. In this new regime, the nation's constitutional aspirations have been reduced to the point that the public appears to regard elite maneuverings in Washington as a soap opera with some modest entertainment value but without much effect on daily life.

B.   Some Implications of the New Constitutional Order

Different constitutional orders produce different outcomes. This section discusses some predictable effects of the new constitutional order's institutional arrangements. After examining the likely legislative output in the new regime, I discuss judicial nominations and presidential impeachment. These two issues have of course received a great deal of attention recently, but little of the analysis has attempted to connect recent events to more basic institutional changes. The section concludes with a brief discussion of the rather limited inferences that can be drawn about the way in which the new regime treats questions of individual rights. . . .

1.   *The Scope of National Policymaking.*—Partisan polarization and divided government have two obvious but important implications for the lawmaking process: only initiatives that have bipartisan support are

likely to be enacted, and polarization makes it difficult to assemble a bipartisan majority for major policy initiatives.... [Although] David Mayhew's study of divided government found that major legislation was enacted at roughly the same rate during periods of divided and unified government[, later] research has qualified Mayhew's conclusions ... by pointing out that divided government takes several forms, and that the forms of party division characterizing the periods of divided government that Mayhew examined allowed for significant cooperation across party lines. Because the new constitutional order is structured to produce more substantial partisan divisions, cooperation across party lines has become increasingly difficult. As Fiorina suggests, perhaps voters "choose [] split control of government so as to frustrate both parties."

In addition, changes in legislative norms have increased the ability of the most partisan members of Congress to obstruct bipartisan cooperation.... [O]nce rarely invoked, the filibuster and other supermajority processes now play a large role in structuring legislation....

In [Barbara] Sinclair's words, the rise of filibustering and other obstructionist tactics have made obstructionism a "[s]tandard [o]perating [p]rocedure." Other political scientists describe the rise of filibustering as "a parliamentary arms race" and suggest that "[o]nce parliamentary strategies such as these have been unleashed, they—like the atom bomb—cannot be uninvented." Routine filibusters thus characterize the new regime.... With each proposed piece of legislation, these attempts to manipulate the process come into play: the opposing party's leadership can use its assets to discipline and reward members to keep them in line, and individual members can "use[] obstructionist tactics ... to undermine ... [major] policy initiatives." The overall effect of these rules and norms has been to impose what is effectively a requirement that legislation (other than budget reconciliation bills) have the support of sixty senators in order to pass.... Any bill that can attract sixty votes is likely to attract a much larger number, and once the threshold of bipartisanship has been crossed, large majorities from both parties will probably sign on.

Partisan polarization and obstructionism do not mean that Congress is inactive in the new constitutional order. After all, members come to Congress with some ambition, either to enact new initiatives or to scale back old ones. But the thickening of governmental institutions and the residual power of interest groups make it difficult to accomplish substantial programmatic change. As Fiorina points out, "the struggle for political credit sometimes makes both parties as likely to compromise behind some legislation as to allow the process to stalemate." The legislative product is therefore likely to be policy initiatives that, while sometimes interesting and experimental, are rather small in scope.

In the end, therefore, bipartisan agreement can be reached, but usually only in the context of some kind of chastened ambition. Bipartisan agreement may be reached on smaller programs, as described above, consistent with the reduced scope of national government in the new constitutional order. Sometimes agreement may be reached on legislation that has largely symbolic meaning. Sometimes bipartisan agreement can be reached on more ambitious programs, such as the 1996 welfare reform and the budget policies that have produced a budget surplus by constraining federal expenditures in an era of substantial economic growth. It is significant, however, that the agreements reached on these more important policies have themselves taken the form of reductions in the national government's scope.

The policies produced by the national government in the new constitutional order, then, are consistent with the idea that our constitutional aspirations have been reduced.

2. *Judicial Nominations.*—The most direct connection between the nation's political institutions and its courts is the nomination and confirmation process. As part of a constitutional order, the nomination and confirmation process has typically been hard to distinguish from other policy-making processes: when interest-group bargaining characterizes general policy-making, it characterizes the nomination and confirmation process as well.

What sorts of judges are likely to be appointed to the federal courts in the new constitutional order of divided government and a highly partisan and polarized Congress? The run of Supreme Court nominations from Robert Bork through Stephen Breyer suggests the answer. A high-profile nomination is likely to be politically costly, at least when one party controls the Senate and the other controls the presidency.... As Mark Silverstein puts it, "[t]he current reality is that the confirmation process now demands a calculation of political variables so complex that even the most experienced and electorally secure senators are often unable to predict the course and outcome of the proceedings." Any reasonably risk-averse president or senator will therefore attempt to avert potential fallout by preferring bland nominees. "The constellation of political and legal forces at work in the nation virtually guarantees a potentially powerful opposition in response to any nomination, and thus the modern president is compelled to seek out nominees who present characteristics certain to forestall, or at least minimize, this opposition." Because "prominence facilitates the mobilization of opposition," the so-called "stealth" nominee, who lacks a substantial record for opponents to attack, should be the characteristic nominee in the new constitutional order. Silverstein summarizes the most likely outcome. "Experienced, competent, noncontroversial jurists with a restrained understanding of the role of the federal judiciary may be the best the modern system can offer." The reduced constitutional ambitions of the types of jurists likely to be nominated to the Supreme Court, in turn, contribute to the overall chastening of constitutional aspirations in the new regime.

Much the same can be said about lower court nominations....

The effect has been to make the mainstream in the new constitutional order more conservative than it was as recently as two decades ago, when Nixon appointees dominated; the liberal judges are not as committed to strong liberal positions as the older conservative judges are to strongly conservative positions. A study of the positions taken by district and court of appeals judges appointed by President Clinton on criminal justice and civil liberties issues shows that Clinton appointees have been more conservative than President Jimmy Carter's appointees, although (unsurprisingly) less conservative than judges appointed by Presidents Reagan and Bush.... In effect, a large number of appointments by a Democratic president have had the effect of institutionalizing the restrained approach to adjudication, and to substantive constitutional principles, that characterizes the new constitutional order.

Although the new constitutional order reduces a president's incentives to nominate high-profile judges, presidents may sometimes calculate that the benefits of making a controversial nomination (to satisfy an important constituency, for example), exceed the costs of attracting opposition. Under the right circumstances, a Republican president supported by a Republican Senate might be able to push through some strikingly conservative nominees to the federal courts, and even to the Supreme Court. The political costs may be high, but sometimes worth bearing. The structures in the new regime, however, suggest that presidents will make such nominations only rarely.... No Democratic president is likely to appoint a judge in the mold of William J. Brennan; nor is such a president likely to want to do so anyway.

4. *Individual Rights*—The nation needed a Second Bill of Rights, according to the constitutional vision of the New Deal/Great Society regime, because combining background rules of property rights with the first Bill of Rights and the Reconstruction amendments failed adequately to promote human flourishing. Racial segregation had to be overcome by aggressive policies of national support for the aspirations of African–Americans; economic inequality had to be addressed through a War on Poverty; the travails of old age had to be reduced by providing health care to the elderly through the Medicare program.

The chastened aspirations of the new constitutional order derive from a somewhat different view of the prerequisites of liberty and flourishing. To some extent this view is more libertarian than that of the New Deal/Great Society order. Background rules of property rights require only minor adjustments to guarantee liberty and human flourishing. Accordingly, small-scale programs with modest aims characterize the new constitutional order: any deficiencies in the provision of health care or in income security after retirement are to be dealt with by market-based adjustments rather than ambitious redistributive initiatives. Similarly, poverty is to be alleviated by ensuring that the poor obtain education and training to allow them to participate actively in the labor market, rather than by providing generous public assistance payments. The new constitutional order thus continues to accept the older view that background rules of property are not enough, while altering the way it supplements them....

Taken together, these features suggest that the new order may back into a form of moderate libertarianism without making libertarianism one of the regime's organizing principles. Moderate libertarianism prevails because the government in the new order simply cannot do very much, and so leaves people alone.

C. Some Qualifications

I must qualify my argument by noting that one part of the analysis is inextricably linked to preferences: the apparent public preference for divided government. This aspect of the new constitutional order may indeed be the most vulnerable to frustration, at least in the short run. It is not difficult to end up with a unified government "by accident." ...

Perhaps the most important qualification I want to make is a clarification of the sense in which the New Deal order has fallen. The New Deal is gone, but only in the sense that the aspirations of government have been chastened; they have not been eliminated. The new constitutional order remains committed to preserving a baseline of New Deal/Great Society protections for some quality-of-life programs ... and a fair amount of pluralistic tolerance. The guiding principle of the new regime is not that government cannot solve problems, but that it cannot solve any more problems.

II. THE SUPREME COURT IN THE NEW CONSTITUTIONAL ORDER

As institutions, courts are parts of constitutional regimes. Courts will conform, at least over time, to the regime's principles. So, for example, the Warren Court participated in the New Deal/Great Society order by acting jointly with Congress and the president to extend the reach of the new order's programmatic liberalism. The image of the Warren Court as an activist Court arose because the New Deal's core constituencies had achieved some degree of success in the political arena but needed assistance in extending their gains. In contrast, the core constituencies of the new constitutional order, and of the present Court, are already well-positioned to succeed in the political arena. They need less help from the Court than did the prior regime's constituencies. The end of big government means the end of a big Court, too.

Put more generally, national policy-making in the new constitutional order preserves much of what has been enacted during the New Deal regime, generates new policies only if they have bipartisan support, and as a result produces new policies with a rather restricted scope. Like the New Deal/Great Society regime, the Warren Court is dead in the sense that the current Court will undertake no dramatic initiatives, but its aspirations—chastened as they are—mean that there will be few dramatic retrenchments on established doctrine either. We can see the degree to which the current Supreme Court confirms this expectation by comparing the current Court with the Court of the New Deal/Great Society constitutional order.

Political scientists often describe the Court as having constituencies because political scientists treat courts, and the Supreme Court in particular, as part of the overall political system. From this point of view, constituencies are important because they can provide support for or opposition to the Court's actions. . . .

. . . I would prefer to identify particular structures that aggregate individual preferences, beliefs, and values to produce outcomes. I believe the relevant structure in this context is the staffing system itself: irregular timing of Supreme Court appointments coupled with life tenure. The irregular timing produces Justices whose preferences, beliefs, and values are likely to be roughly (but only roughly) consistent with those of the president who nominated them and the Senate that confirmed them; life tenure gives these Justices the opportunity to pursue their preferences, beliefs, and values even after the nominating president has left the political scene; and aggregating these irregularly timed appointments may produce the kind of constituency-seeking behavior I have described.

The best description of the modern Court is that it acts in ways that satisfy a rather well-to-do constituency. Some of the modern Court's decisions revived the possibility that large businesses could use the Constitution to protect their interests. In the economic arena, for example, the Court revitalized the Takings Clause and innovatively held that some punitive damage awards violated the Due Process Clause. The Court has similarly expanded the reach of the First Amendment to protect commercial speech, so that regulations of commercial speech are nearly as difficult to sustain as regulations of political speech.

Overall, the modern Court's course can probably be described best by the phrase "country club Republicanism," an ideology that joins protection of the interests of the relatively well-to-do with a modest sense of noblesse oblige with respect to those disadvantaged by the economic system. The Court's abortion jurisprudence is exemplary here. The Court has made abortions readily available to women who can finance their own abortions and have no difficulty traveling to a location where abortions are more immediately available; but the Court has allowed states to restrict the availability of abortions in ways that disproportionately burden women with less money and personal mobility. In other circumstances, the Court has acted upon its sense of noblesse oblige—for example, the Court gave some protection to the disadvantaged when it prohibited states from reducing welfare benefits to families that had recently arrived from another state. Ultimately, the real-world line drawn by the Court's jurisprudence is class-related.

The Court in the new constitutional order seems likely to continue on this path. . . . As we have seen, the encrustation of interest groups around the national government has not disappeared. Those groups continue to be the source of potential support and opposition to the Court, which—understood as a political actor—must therefore continue to be responsive to their concerns. The shift of the political spectrum to the right makes a modest conservatism the judicial position least likely to generate real opposition. Although this conservatism can generate some support for the Court, the Court's actions are likely to be insufficiently forceful in any particular direction to generate any passionate support.

One consequence of the new order for the Court may be a reduction in the Court's role in political life. The new regime's new constituencies have already achieved substantial success in the political arena, leaving to the Court only some modest judicial moves on the margins of the issues that concern those groups. For example, it seems noteworthy that—with only one exception—the bulk of the Court's recent contribution to the law of gender discrimination has been through statutory interpretation, not through constitutional adjudication. The Court's recently articulated restraints on punitive damages are similarly modest, especially in comparison to recent statutory revisions of tort law. Today even the Court's constituencies achieve more of what they seek by securing legislation than by obtaining favorable rulings from the Court.

A.   Administrative Downsizing

When we consider the Court as an institution or bureaucracy, its most notable characteristic in recent years has been the sharp reduction in the scale of its operation. At its peak, the Court heard argument in about 170 cases per Term, whereas during the past five years it has heard argument in fewer than one hundred cases each year. In this section, I explain how this administrative downsizing is consistent with the characteristics of the new constitutional order.

The sheer number of cases decided by the Warren and Burger Courts is a convenient symbol for the role of the Supreme Court in the New Deal/Great Society constitutional order. That order was a regime of big government, in which the Court eventually came to see itself as a participant. An activist government necessarily included an activist Court collaborating with the other branches of the national government to implement the regime's principles. But if the era of big government is over, so too must be the era of big courts. The administrative downsizing of the Court may therefore merely reflect the general reduction in the scope of government in the new constitutional order.

B.   Constitutional Doctrine for a Chastened Government

. . . [D]ownsizing has been substantive as well as well as administrative.

1.   *Minimizing the Scope of the Court's Recent Work.*—The Court's federalism decisions are the most obvious examples of substantive downsizing. The decisions are familiar: United States v. Lopez,[120] which struck down the Gun–Free School Zones Act as beyond the power given Congress in the Commerce Clause; Printz v. United States,[121] which

---

120. [Footnote 187 in original] 514 U.S. 549 (1995).

121. [Footnote 189 in original] 521 U.S. 898 (1997).

invalidated the Brady Handgun Control Act because it forced state executive officials to implement a national program; City of Boerne v. Flores,[122] which invalidated the Religious Freedom Restoration Act for exceeding the scope of Congress's power to remedy court-identified violations of the Free Exercise Clause; and a series of decisions restricting Congress's ability to impose retroactive monetary liability on states because such remedies violated the Eleventh Amendment....

. . .

The cumulative effects of these doctrines can best be understood in light of the institutional characteristics of the new constitutional order. The Court's decisions increase the cost of implementing the national programs that Congress has already enacted, without stating new constitutional principles that would invalidate them. Because the political process is encrusted by the network that links interest groups to the administrative bureaucracy, it is difficult for either the president or Congress to carry out a comprehensive program that would destroy (and then reconstruct) the programs adopted during the New Deal/Great Society regime. A concerted attack on those programs would carry a high political cost as the interest groups rally behind them. Divided government makes such radical revisions nearly impossible.... Existing programs are thus likely to persist, undergoing modest revisions and gradual transformation.

The Court's federalism decisions are, again, compatible with the persistence of, but modest revision in, existing New Deal and Great Society programs.... The Eleventh Amendment decisions, for example, make it more difficult to enforce national law, particularly to the extent that they leave it to the national government—itself committed to a less interventionist stance—to enforce federal law on its own. But they do not either in principle or in practice make it impossible to do so....

The Court's doctrinal revisions and innovations do, however, increase the cost of enacting new programs. Each new judicial decision in this area introduces litigation uncertainty into the legislative process by allowing opponents of new programs to argue credibly that the proposed programs might be held unconstitutional. Opponents can use the ... the Court's federalism decisions in support of arguments that proposed legislation would unconstitutionally exceed the powers given Congress; and the Court's takings decisions in support of arguments that proposed regulation (and even deregulation) would deprive property owners of their property without providing the compensation that the Constitution requires. In addition, as Justice Breyer argued in *College Savings Bank*,[123] the Court's new interest in federalism may discourage the national government from adopting innovative regulatory schemes that call on state enforcement machinery, even schemes that do so in a

122. [Footnote 191 in original] 521 U.S. 507 (1997).

123. [Footnote 210 in original] Florida Prepaid Postsecondary Education Expense Board v. College Savings Bank, 527 U.S. 627 (1999).

manner less intrusive than commandeering and more respectful of state dignity than preemption or command-and-control regulation.

Whether or not constitutional objections to innovative regulatory proposals ultimately prevail in the legislature, even the prospect of constitutional challenges diminishes the incentive to go forward with the proposals. . . .

[And] alternatives to direct regulation [such as reliance on the spending power] may reduce the litigation uncertainty, but with a simultaneous reduction in effectiveness. Thus, although one can describe legislative responses to the Court's decisions that would allow the national government to enforce national law effectively, such legislative responses are unlikely to be forthcoming from the Congress of the new order. In this way, the Court contributes to a reduction in effective national lawmaking activity even though it may not hold many statutes unconstitutional.

Taken together, then, the Court's doctrines limit but do not invalidate the statutory legacy of the New Deal and the Great Society. This conclusion too is consistent with the principle of downsizing. A Court that set out aggressively to transform national policy—from either this or the previous regime—would be the kind of big Court associated with the prior constitutional regime and incompatible with this one.

Whichever story is correct—the one that minimizes the Court's recent decisions or the one that sees those decisions as foreshadowing a larger doctrinal transformation—the central point is this: assumptions about the foundations of constitutional doctrine that seemed settled during the New Deal/Great Society regime are now open to question.

C. A Chastened Judicial Role

The preceding section argued that constitutional doctrine in the new regime will support, and may even encourage, a scaling-back of national legislation. I next argue that the Supreme Court may develop a new self-conception in the new regime. This section examines how recent decisions may be evidence of this new self-conception. I suggest that the present Court displays little anxiety over exercising its power of judicial review because the Justices have taken it to be sufficient that they approach the task of overturning legislation with the appropriate seriousness. The disappearance of anxiety over judicial review and the rhetoric of seriousness have given the Court's work a distinctive character, well-described by Professor Cass Sunstein's term minimalism. Yet . . . [t]he replacement of anxiety by seriousness might encourage the Justices to exercise their power to invalidate statutes more frequently and with greater assertiveness, paradoxically turning the Court into a central actor in the new constitutional regime.

1. *The Disappearance of Anxiety About Judicial Review.*—During the early years of the New Deal constitutional regime, the Court divided over the question of its proper role. At least as New–Deal-era constitutional theorists came to understand the matter, the prior order had

relied on a theoretically indefensible legal formalism to justify the exercise of the power of judicial review. So, for example, New–Deal-era theorists derided Justice Owen Roberts's wooden formulation in United States v. Butler[124] that the Court's "only ... duty" was "to lay the article of the Constitution which is invoked beside the statute which is challenged and to decide whether the latter squares with the former" New–Deal-era theorists similarly rejected Justice George Sutherland's originalist insistence that "[a] provision of the Constitution ... does not mean one thing at one time and an entirely different thing at another time."

With formalism and originalism rejected, however, the justification for judicial review was called into question. As Martin Shapiro put it, the New Deal Justices had vanquished the previous constitutional regime and had taken over the fortress that had defended it. These Justices then faced a divisive choice: they could dismantle the weapons that had impeded them, or they could turn those weapons to their own advantage.

To the extent that he had a coherent constitutional theory, Justice Felix Frankfurter urged the first course. He proposed a generalized theory of judicial deference to decisions taken by democratic majorities. Justice Harlan Fiske Stone's famous "footnote four" provided the theoretical basis for the alternative course. The "footnote four" jurisprudence was the Court's first effort to fit judicial review into the New Deal constitutional order. This jurisprudence simultaneously authorized judicial review and limited the occasions for its exercise. Equally important, this jurisprudence had the advantage of allowing the Court to deploy judicial review primarily on behalf of the political constituencies important in the New Deal constitutional order.

... By the mid–1960s, when the Warren Court had consolidated its position, the "footnote 4" jurisprudence no longer provided sufficient authority for the Court's programmatic liberalism. Instead the Court began to move in the direction of taking the regime's programmatic liberalism as a constitutional mandate. The Equal Protection Clause was the primary vehicle for this movement. Several cases suggested that differential distribution of the goods and services provided by the activist welfare state would violate the Constitution. These cases seemed to imply a new constitutional doctrine: distribution of goods based on market criteria might be unconstitutional unless there was a strong justification for the differential distribution, where those goods were fundamental in some non-constitutional sense....

The Supreme Court, however, never fully signed on to this new doctrine, and the 1996 welfare reform legislation definitively demonstrated that the new constitutional order has rejected programmatic liberalism. Perhaps more interestingly, however, the Justices in the new constitutional order in fact do not seem to have the same anxiety about justifying judicial review that characterized the early years of the New Deal constitutional order, and which continued to dominate scholarly

---

124. [Footnote 254 in original] 297 U.S. 1 (1936).

554 SETTING THE COURT'S AGENDA Ch. 3

concern through the Warren Court years. The Justices have invalidated congressional legislation without seriously mentioning, much less agonizing over, the fact that they were displacing decisions made by a presumptively democratic legislature. For example, last Term's Eleventh Amendment decisions said nothing about the gravity of invalidating democratically adopted legislation. In *City of Boerne v. Flores*, the Court referred to Congress's "right" and "duty to make its own informed judgment on the meaning and force of the Constitution," but only "[w]hen Congress acts within its sphere of power and responsibilities." The Court did not give any weight to the fact that Congress appeared to have decided that it was acting within that sphere.

Because the new constitutional order was established without dramatic confrontations between the Court and the political branches, the Justices had no need to rethink or explain the Court's proper role. They could simply continue to take their role as it had been defined in the prior regime.... Instead of acting aggressively to promote the new regime's principles, as the Warren Court did for its regime, today's Justices appear to have scaled back their aspirations. Relieved of the anxiety of providing elaborate justifications for the exercise of judicial review, they present themselves not as ambitious theorists of constitutional law but as serious-minded adjudicators.

2. *The Role of Constitutional Seriousness.*—The Court's recent substantive due process cases, and in particular the reactions they have prompted from Justice Scalia, provide the best illustrations of the current Court's self-presentation. Justice Scalia's concerns mirror the concerns that were central in controversies over the role of the Court in the New Deal/Great Society constitutional order. Deeply skeptical of the idea of substantive due process, he has attempted to provide an analytic structure that would discipline the Court's decisions in this area. In his most sustained effort, Justice Scalia argued in Michael H. v. Gerald D.[125] that substantive due process decisions could rest only on the judgment that a statute was inconsistent with the traditions of the American people, described at an appropriately concrete level of generality.... As Justice Scalia saw it, the sort of structure he proposed, which the Court seemed to be endorsing, would solve the problem of justifying judicial review in substantive due process cases, in the same terms set by discussions during the New Deal/Great Society constitutional order: it would authorize but constrain judicial review.

As it has turned out, the current Court is not committed to Justice Scalia's approach, because, I believe, the Court does not take the problem of justification to be central in the way it was in the prior regime....

Justice Scalia was disturbed by what he saw as the majority's backsliding. But he was even more upset by the joint opinion of Justices O'Connor, Kennedy, and Souter in *Planned Parenthood of Southeastern Pennsylvania v. Casey*. The joint opinion relied on Justice Harlan's

125. [Footnote 272 in original] 491 U.S. 110 (1989).

dissent in *Poe v. Ullman*, itself a predecessor of *Griswold v. Connecticut*, which was one of the Warren Court's central programmatic cases. According to the joint opinion in *Casey*, "adjudication of substantive due process claims may call upon the Court in interpreting the Constitution to exercise that same capacity which by tradition courts always have exercised: reasoned judgment." The opinion noted that while the "boundaries [of reasoned judgment] are not susceptible of expression as a simple rule," its indeterminacy did not authorize the Court to overturn legislative enactments simply out of disagreement with the legislature's policy choices. The Justices concluded that in *Casey*, however, invalidating the disputed statute was appropriate: there, reasoned judgment supported the proposition that the Constitution barred state legislatures from adopting laws that placed undue burdens on a woman's decision to obtain an abortion. . . .

Perhaps concern for doctrinal emptiness and constraint characterizes only the New Deal constitutional order. Formulations that refer to careful description and reasoned judgment may, despite their doctrinal appearance, be expressing an attitude consonant with the new order's principles. Consider the rhetorical force of these terms: given the choice between reasoned and unreasoned judgment, or between careful and careless description, who would choose the latter? The very terminology of these doctrinal formulations conspicuously announces a certain seriousness about the task at hand, even if they do not provide rules or formulas that constrain the exercise of judgment or determine the outcome of the definitional process.

Perhaps we can say rather tentatively, then, that the new constitutional order has replaced the New Deal regime's concern that judicial review be authorized and constrained, with a concern that judicial review be exercised with an appropriate degree of seriousness. In the new regime, seriousness is a necessary and sufficient condition for exercising the power of judicial review. Justices in the new regime seek to show that they are technically competent lawyers who do small things very well.

Why might seriousness matter? Seriousness may serve a strategic purpose in preserving the Court's position as it awaits the consolidation of a new constitutional order. But seriousness may matter for other reasons. If Justice Scalia serves as the foil for characterizing the new order's judicial project, he may be the foil as well for understanding the importance of seriousness. His widely noted verbal cleverness attracts attention, and he is routinely described as the author with the best writing style on the Supreme Court. He is, in short, an entertaining Justice. And entertainment does characterize one dimension of the new constitutional regime. . . . If Justice Scalia is the Fox Network of the judicial system, the rest of the Court may see itself as National Public Radio, committed to a thoroughly serious self-presentation. Seriousness itself, that is, is one mode of entertainment.

Seriousness may matter, finally, because it might be enough to justify judicial review. Professor Philip Bobbitt has argued, for example, that the practice of judicial review, understood as the dispositive choice among options made available by our modes of constitutional discourse, is justified because it makes possible the exercise of moral choice by a set of our public officials. Seriousness, understood as a virtue in the exercise of this moral choice, therefore helps justify the practice of judicial review. And Professor Frank Michelman has suggested that courts might attempt to obtain agreement on controversial results not by invoking any substantive criteria, but by reverting to what Professor Fried, harkening back to an older era, calls the "artificial reason of the law." Under this formulation, judges might be able to secure assent merely by demonstrating their seriousness as lawyers.

Alexander Bickel once criticized a certain type of enthusiasm for particular Supreme Court decisions as resting solely on "the moral approval of the lines." That was insufficient in the New Deal order. Perhaps what we seek in the new constitutional order is "the moral approval of the justices," both in the sense that we seek to approve of them morally and in the sense that we hope to obtain their moral approval.

3. *A Jurisprudence of Constitutional Minimalism.*—Professor Cass Sunstein has usefully described the Court's current approach to constitutional adjudication as "minimalist." Minimalism can be described as the form that characterizes doctrinal downsizing. Big courts issue big—maximalist—opinions, but a Court that participates in smaller government issues smaller—minimalist—ones.

. . . The very term minimalism resonates with the idea of a chastened constitutional order. Consistent with this idea, [various] minimalist invalidations enforced a reduction in the scope of national power.

At the same time, however, minimalism itself enhances judicial power, as demonstrated by debates in the 1950s and 1960s over the proper form of constitutional adjudication. Proponents of ad hoc balancing took one side of the debate, arguing that courts should take into account every relevant detail of a case, carefully identify the precise interests that compete for vindication, and finally balance those interests. Critics of this view, led by Justices Black and Douglas, argued that ad hoc balancing gave judges too much power, in part because the metaphor of balancing concealed the necessary elements of judgment that go into constitutional adjudication, and in part because opinions justifying outcomes as the result of ad hoc balancing give too little guidance to other lawmakers.

As Sunstein suggests, minimalism is subject to the same criticism. One of Justice Thurgood Marshall's law clerks offered perhaps the most pithy critique of minimalism, in a memorandum explaining why it was hard to tell whether a lower court had followed the Court's affirmative action holding in Wygant v. Jackson Board of Education:[126] "nobody knows what that opinion stands for now that Justice Powell has retired." In other words, to know what a minimalist opinion means, one must go to the source. In a world where minimalist opinions are the general rule, we can never be confident that a statute is constitutional until we ask the Supreme Court. Minimalist opinions thus make the Court the focal point with respect to every statute, hardly the position that a Court aiming to reduce its role in public life would seek.

Minimalism thus cannot be the only path possible for a Court that self-consciously understands its role to be limited. I argued earlier that the Court's new doctrines could foreshadow either further incremental changes in constitutional law or a more dramatic transformation. Minimalism has an analogous but more paradoxical character. Minimalism guarantees no particular results, but it enhances the Court's role in the constitutional system. The most interesting thing about minimalism, then, may be the way the word itself helps to legitimate the doctrine. It is precisely the word one would choose to describe the practices of courts in a constitutional order whose aspirations have diminished. . . .

. . .

III. CONCLUSION: THE SOURCES OF THE NEW CONSTITUTIONAL ORDER

I have offered a number of arguments suggesting that the United States is now immersed in a new constitutional order. At the heart of this new order is a scaling-back of the national government's aspiration to secure justice. Divided government, strongly polarized parties, and reduced citizen participation in politics characterize the structures and incentives of the new regime, with the implication that the national government will undertake few ambitious initiatives. In the courts, a cautious minimalism is consistent with the personal characteristics of the people likely to become federal judges and with the general reduction in the government's aspirations.

. . . [T]he role of constitutional law relative to other institutions is diminishing. Because the new constitutional order is characterized by difficulties in undertaking significant regulatory initiatives, industry and state governments find that they have more room in which to move.

At this point it seems possible to connect my account of the chastening of constitutional aspiration to broader economic trends. Commentators have observed that sovereignty appears to be flowing away from the nation-state. Some sovereignty is flowing upward, to supranational government institutions. Some is flowing downward, to subnational governments. And some, to use political economist Susan Strange's term, is simply evaporating: disappearing as transnational corporations absorb some of the functions classically associated with sovereignty. . . .

A nation-state whose sovereignty has diminished must have chastened constitutional aspirations, and properly so. After all, the nation-

126. [Footnote 323 in original] 476 U.S. 267 (1986).

state will be unable to accomplish much anyway because its initiatives will be subject to discipline by supranational government and non-government organizations.... Perhaps recapturing and realizing an expansive vision of constitutional possibility will require some confrontation with sovereignty's transformation. That, however, is surely likely to take quite a long time, and when (or if) it occurs, we will find ourselves in yet another constitutional regime. For now, a constitutional order with chastened aspirations is what we have, and probably the best we can do.

Questions and Comments

1. Professor Tushnet argues that a new constitutional order is in place in the United States, one that emphasizes achieving justice through individual responsibility and market processes rather than national legislation or constitutional law. As the role of the national government has diminished, says Tushnet, so too has the role of the Supreme Court. The Justices, as members of this new order, may have reduced their caseload to reflect their view that government should play a smaller role in achieving justice. Although Professor Tushnet treats the diminished caseload as a symptom of this more diminished role, would this chastened vision necessarily cause the Court to take a smaller number of cases? Might we not expect more aggressive grants of certiorari in order to invalidate older laws reflecting a different conception of the government's role?

2. *Bush v. Gore* was decided a year after the Tushnet *Foreword*. (It is discussed briefly in Chapter One, above.) Does it confirm or challenge his claims—as to "chastened aspirations" and a "chastened judicial role"? as to a shift away from anxiety over justifying the Court's role in judicial review to a concern for "seriousness" in the exercise of the power of judicial review?

3. If the decline in certiorari were related to a "chastened" set of aspirations, would the mix of cases in which certiorari is granted accord with the substantive values of that "chastened" idea of constitutionalism? What might that mix look like?

4. While many commentators have focused on the decline in the number of cases decided by the Court, Professor Frederick Schauer focuses more on the "salience" of the issues decided. In his Foreword to Harvard Law Review's discussion of the Supreme Court's 2005 Term, Schauer asserts that the Court, over most of its history, has issued far more "low salience" than "high salience" decisions, and that this pattern helps sustain the Court's public acceptance. Agreeing that the Court decides some very important high salience issues, such as "abortion, same-sex marriage, affirmative action, the right to die, and the role of religion in public institutions," Schauer argues that most of the Court's docket is comprised of low salience cases and, in fact, does not deal with many of the most prominent issues on the nation's public agenda, such as the war in Iraq, escalating fuel prices, healthcare, immigration reform, Social Security, the nuclear capability of Iran and North Korea, the estate tax, bird flu, and the minimum wage. See

Frederick Schauer, *Foreword, The Court's Agenda—And the Nation's,* 120 Harv. L. Rev. 4 (2006).

6. Finally, as you begin the next Chapter on the Court's decisionmaking in fully argued cases, consider whether and how the theses you have read—of Hartnett's overly empowered Court, Hellman's Olympian Court, or Tushnet's Court with "chastened" constitutional aspirations—would affect the substance of decisionmaking on merits cases.

Chapter Four

COLLEGIAL DECISION MAKING

Once a cert petition is granted and the case fully briefed, the Court is ready to consider the case on the merits. The materials in this chapter describe how the Court works its way from deciding that a case should be heard to publishing an opinion disposing of the matter.

In the first set of readings, Chief Justice Rehnquist describes how the Court functions, first in hearing oral argument, then in deliberating on these argued cases, and finally in assigning, drafting, circulating and responding to opinions resolving them. Next, a brief Note recounts Justice Scalia's frustration with the brevity of the Court's conferences shortly after he joined the Court. An excerpt from Professor O'Brien's book, *Storm Center: The Supreme Court in American Politics* (6th ed. 2003), gives specific illustrations, drawn from the Justices' own papers, of the opinion writing process. He provides many concrete examples of the types of give and take that occur in the course of fashioning opinions.

Following these overviews, Part B offers several perspectives on opinion writing and deliberative negotiation. It begins with some observations by Supreme Court Justices on the value of dissents. Justice Brennan provides a classic definition and defense of the function of dissenting opinions in constitutional adjudication. Justice Ginsburg (Judge Ginsburg, when she wrote this piece) tempers the Brennan article with some observations on the appropriate limits of style in concurring and dissenting opinions. Her remarks are followed by brief discussions of Justice Scalia's views on separate opinions, Chief Justice Roberts' views on the benefits of consensus, and the first two Terms of the Roberts Court.

Both the Court's practice and the Justices' views about the value and propriety of separate opinions have changed markedly over the years. As David O'Brien notes, compared to the nineteenth and first half of the twentieth century, the number of separate opinions has increased significantly. See O'Brien, *Storm Center, supra* at 296–312. The next two readings attempt to explain this significant increase. John Kelsh, a former law clerk to Chief Justice Rehnquist, argues that 1941 marked a dramatic turning point in the propensity of the Justices to publish separate opinions, one made possible by a slow shift in institutional norms about the legitimacy of and reasons for dissent. Professor Robert Post, analyzing the Taft Court, argues that changes in approach to separate opinions are connected to changing understandings of law and of the Court's role in saying what the law is.

In Section C, we offer excerpts that provide detailed descriptions of the internal deliberations of the Court in two landmark cases, Roe v. Wade, 410 U.S. 113 (1973), and United States v. Nixon, 418 U.S. 683 (1974). These are supplemented by discussion of more recent works on the *Webster* and *Casey* decisions. Together, these readings illustrate the very wide range of methods available to the Justices to try to shape opinions of the Court. By explaining how the Court proceeded from argument to opinion in these dramatic cases, the readings reveal the significance of factors the public usually cannot witness in the development of constitutional law.

These materials present an internal view of the decisional process, trying to illuminate, from the Justices' points of view, how decisions on the merits are made and opinions produced. In evaluating these accounts, readers may want to consider what Professors Kearney and Merrill describe as three different models for understanding how the justices make their decisions:

(1) The legal model, which suggests the Justices resolve cases in accordance with their understanding of the requirements of the authoritative sources of law relevant to the question presented;

(2) The attitudinal model, developed primarily by political scientists, which, as noted above in Chapter Three, assumes the Justices decide cases—either in the short-run, or acting strategically, over the long-run—in accordance with their "fixed ideological preferences;" and

(3) The interest group model, which posits that the Justices seek to resolve cases in accordance with the desires of organized groups that have an interest in the controversy.

See Joseph D. Kearney & Thomas W. Merrill, *The Influence of Amicus Curiae Briefs on the Supreme Court,* 148 U. Pa. L. Rev. 743 (2000), excerpted in Chapter Five, Section D, below. Recall Professor Perry's conclusion, in Chapter Three, that all the Justices used at least two different decisional processes in deciding whether to grant cert, which he referred to as the "jurisprudential mode" and the "outcome mode." As you read the materials below, consider whether multiple models are helpful in describing the decisional processes of the different Justices in deciding the merits over a range of cases.

Whatever approach to deliberation is taken by the individual Justices, decision-making in the Court is necessarily a collegial process. Yet the materials in this chapter suggest that, at least for the average case, the Justices spend relatively little time deliberating on its outcome in each other's presence. Oral argument sometimes serves as a forum for exchanging views among the Justices, but that does not appear to be its principal purpose or focus. Under Chief Justice Rehnquist, during argument weeks the Court held conferences on Wednesdays to discuss the cases argued on Monday, and again on Fridays to discuss the Tuesday and Wednesday arguments. These conferences, attended only by the Justices, are in theory a forum for the sharing of views, but, during the period of the Rehnquist Court, they often entailed little more than announcing votes and tallying who won and who lost. This brevity is in marked contrast to the early days of the Court, when arguments extended over many days and the Justices would often discuss cases over several days or more. And, as the readings below indicate, how the conference is used has varied substantially even among twentieth-century Chief Justices. For a helpful history and description of the conference, see Del Dickson, ed., *The Supreme Court in Conference* (1940–85) 3–126, 875–91 (2001).[1]

Justice Scalia lamented in the 1980s that the Justices did not engage in more substantive exchanges in conference. (Chief Justice Rehnquist similarly commented that when he joined the Court in the 1970s, he also was "surprised and disappointed" at the relative absence of discussion.) What might account for the fact that conference discussions became so abbreviated? Suppose the Justices' conference discussions on argued cases were longer and more intensive. Would that be likely to change results? Or opinions? Would it alter the actual or perceived influence of law clerks? Justice Scalia's lament over abbreviated conferences predated the dramatic decline in the average cases heard per Term. With fewer cases being heard, would you anticipate that the nature of discussion in conference would change?

Note that after the re-argument in *Brown v. Board of Education*, the new Chief Justice, Earl Warren, postponed seeking a vote during the first conference after re-argument.[2] Consider whether there are advantages to not having a collective discussion about the decision of a case come too early in the deliberative process.

Short conferences put pressure on the opinion writing process because the author has less information regarding the individual Jus-

---

1. According to Dickson, the Justices did not meet in conference under the first three Chief Justices. Not until John Marshall became Chief Justice did conferencing on the cases begin, as he instituted a "collective decision-making style [that] encouraged compromise and consensus." Dickson, *The Supreme Court in Conference, supra*, at 875.

2. *Brown* was first argued in the fall of 1952. The Court, which was not unanimous after the first argument, requested re-argument, including briefing of the original meaning of the Fourteenth Amendment. See Bernard Schwartz, *Super Chief: Earl Warren and His Supreme Court* 72–82 (1983); see also Richard Kluger, *Simple*

Justice 683 (1976). While the case was pending re-argument, Chief Justice Vinson passed away, and Earl Warren was appointed in his stead. Many scholars believe that the presence of Warren as Chief Justice made a substantial difference to the Court's ability to announce a unanimous decision. See, e.g., Mark Tushnet & Katya Lezin, *What Really Happened in* Brown v. Board of Education, 91 Colum. L. Rev. 1867, 1876–78 (1991). According to Schwartz, Justice Frankfurter was reported to have said to his law clerks that Vinson's sudden death shortly before the reargument in *Brown* was "the first indication that I have ever had that there is a God." See Schwartz, *Super Chief, supra*, at 72.

tices' particular concerns. The materials as a whole explain the variety of options, or strategies, available to Justices in the opinion writing process. The key point seems to be that it is in this period that greater deliberative interaction takes place as opinions are drafted, circulated, studied and revised, adopted or rejected. Deliberation and negotiation do take place, then, but largely through written, arm's length exchanges rather than through face-to-face oral communications.[3] (The *Nixon Tapes Case*, discussed in Section C, below, may be something of an exception.)

How does this form of largely written interaction affect the Court's process of collegial decision making? During these exchanges of drafts, is too little emphasis placed on shaping an opinion that many Justices are likely to join (and too much on writing concurrences and dissents)? In those cases where, at the end of the process, a solid majority is massed behind a single opinion, what is the point of publishing a dissent or concurrence? On the other hand, one might ask whether, by sweeping all prior negotiations and exchanges of drafts behind one set of published opinions, the process unduly obscures the factors that shape case outcomes?

It is instructive to ponder these questions while reading the materials. Better yet, select a case pending before the Court. With a group, conduct a mock conference on the case and then assign, write and circulate opinions. Such a "mock" experience, which we have observed many times, will be remarkably similar to that described in these readings.

A. INTRODUCTION TO THE COURT'S WORK OF DECIDING CASES

William H. Rehnquist,[4] *The Supreme Court* 252–66 (2001)

How the Court Does its Work: Deciding the Cases

Potter Stewart, with whom it was my privilege to sit as a member of the Court for nearly ten years, passed on to me more than one bit of

3. When we were law clerks, we observed the peculiar phenomenon that a Justice, who wished to join an opinion authored by another Justice, would write a note to the author saying, "Please join me." Grammatically, that seemed backward, but the style was employed universally. Recently, Justice Stevens observed that this habit of expression, which he recalled from his days as a law clerk to Justice Rutledge in 1947, traced back to the time when a single copy of a proposed opinion was circulated. When a Justice received such a proposed opinion, and agreed with it, he would write "Please join me" on the back of the opinion and send it back to the author for circula-

tion to the next chamber. Current practice is to send proposed opinions to all chambers simultaneously. Justice Stevens reported that, although he and Justices senior to him observe this custom of expression even under the changed circumstances, more recently arrived Justices—beginning with Justice O'Connor—now employ more precise instructions, such as "I am pleased to join your opinion." As Justice Stevens commented, on this matter of style "the textualists have taken over from the traditionalists." See Tony Mauro, *Please Join Me,* Legal Times, June 7, 1993, at 10.

4. Chief Justice of the United States.

sound advice in the years. I remember his saying that he thought he would never know more about a case than when he left the bench after hearing it orally argued, and I have found that his statement also holds true for me. When one thinks of the important ramifications that some of the constitutional decisions of the Supreme Court have, it seems that one could never know as much as he ought to know about how to cast his vote in a case. But true as this is, each member must cast votes in each case decided on the merits each year, and there must come a time when pondering one's own views must cease, and deliberation with one's colleagues and voting must begin.

That time is each Wednesday afternoon after we get off the bench for those cases argued on Monday, and Friday for those cases argued on Tuesday and Wednesday.... A buzzer sounds—or, to put it more accurately, is supposed to sound—in each of the nine chambers five minutes before the time for conference, and the nine members of the Court then congregate in the Court's conference room next to the chambers of the Chief Justice. We all shake hands with one another when we come in, and our vote sheets and whatever other material we wish to have are at our places at the conference table. Seating is strictly by seniority: the Chief Justice sits at one end of the table, and the senior associate justice sits at the other end. Unlike those ranged along the sides of the table, we have unrestricted elbow room. But even along the sides, the seating remains by seniority: The three associate justices next in seniority sit on one side, and the four associates having the least seniority are on the opposite side.

To anyone familiar with the decision-making process in other governmental institutions, the most striking thing about our Court's conference is that only the nine justices are present. There are no law clerks, no secretaries, no staff assistants, no outside personnel of any kind.[5] If a messenger from the Marshal's Office—the agency responsible for guarding the door of the conference—knocks on the door to indicate that there is a message for one of the justices, the junior Justice opens the door and delivers it. The junior Justice is also responsible for dictating to the staff of the clerk's office at the close of the conference the text of the orders that will appear on the Court's order list issued on the Monday following the conference.

I think that the tradition of having only the justices themselves present at the Court's conference is a salutary one for more than one reason. Its principal effect is to implement the observation of Justice Brandeis ... that the Supreme Court is respected because "we do our own work." If a justice is to participate meaningfully in the conference, the justice must himself know the issues to be discussed and the

5. [Editors' Note: According to Professor Dickson, much earlier in the Court's history employees were present in the conference to serve the Justices drinks. This practice ended in 1910 when the employees were suspected of leaking word of a decision in a business case that caused a severe reaction on Wall Street. Although the two employees were later found not to be at fault, since that event outsiders are not permitted in the conference room and the most junior Justice answers knocks or goes to the door if contact with the outside is required. Dickson, *supra*, at 14–15.]

arguments he wishes to make. Some cases may be sufficiently complicated as to require written notes to remind one of various points, but any extended reading of one's position to a group of only eight colleagues is bound to lessen the effect of what one says. . . .

In discussions of cases that have been argued, the Chief Justice begins by reviewing the facts and the decision of the lower court, outlining his understanding of the applicable case law, and indicating either that he votes to affirm the decision of the lower court or to reverse it. The discussion then proceeds to the senior associate down to the most junior. For many years there has circulated a tale that although the discussion in conference proceeds in order from the Chief Justice to the junior Justice, the voting actually begins with the junior Justice and proceeds back to the Chief Justice in order of seniority. But, at least during my thirty years on the Court, this tale is very much of a myth; I don't believe I have ever seen it happen at any of the conferences that I have attended.

The time taken in discussion of a particular case by each justice will naturally vary with the complexity of the case and the nature of the discussion which has preceded his. The Chief Justice, going first, takes more time than any one associate in a typical case, because he feels called upon to go into greater detail as to the facts and the lower-court holding than do those who come after him. The truth is that there simply are not nine different points of view in even the most complex and difficult case, and all of us feel impelled to a greater or lesser degree to try to reach some consensus that can be embodied in a written opinion that will command the support of at least a majority of the members of the Court. The lack of anything that is both previously unsaid, relevant, and sensible is apt to be frustrating to those far down the line of discussion, but this is one of the prices exacted by the seniority system. With rare exceptions, each justice begins and ends his part of the discussion without interruption from his colleagues, and in the great majority of cases by the time the junior Justice is finished with his discussion, it will be evident that a majority of the Court has agreed upon a basis for either affirming or reversing the decision of the lower court in the case under discussion.

When I first went on the Court, I was both surprised and disappointed at how little interplay there was between the various justices during the process of conferring on a case. Each would state his views, and a junior justice could express agreement or disagreement with views expressed by a justice senior to him earlier in the discussion, but the converse did not apply; a junior justice's views were seldom commented upon, because votes had been already cast up the line. Probably most junior justices before me must have felt as I did, that they had some very significant contributions to make, and were disappointed that they hardly ever seemed to influence anyone because people didn't change their votes in response to their, the junior justices', contrary ideas. I felt then it would be desirable to have more of a round-table discussion of the matter after each of us had expressed our views. Having now sat in conferences for nearly three decades, and risen from ninth to seventh to first in seniority, I realize—with newfound clarity—that while my idea, while fine in the abstract, probably would not contribute much in practice, and at any rate was doomed by the seniority system to which the senior justices naturally adhere.

Each member of the Court has done such work as he deems necessary to arrive at his own views before coming into conference; it is not a bull session in which off-the-cuff reactions are traded, but instead a discussion in which very considered views are stated. . . .

I have heard both Felix Frankfurter and William O. Douglas describe the conferences presided over by Chief Justice Charles Evans Hughes in which they sat, and I have heard Douglas describe the conferences presided over by Chief Justice Harlan F. Stone. Their styles were apparently very different. Hughes has rightly been described as Jovian in appearance, and, according to Frankfurter, he "radiated authority." He was totally prepared in each case, lucidly expressed his views, and said no more than was necessary. In the words of Frankfurter, you did not speak up in that conference unless you were very certain that you knew what you were talking about. Discipline and restraint were the order of the day.

Understandably, some of the justices appointed by President Roosevelt in the last part of Hughes's tenure resented his tight rein—imposed albeit only by example. Stone was one of those who had disliked the taut atmosphere of the Hughes conference, and when he became Chief Justice [in 1941], he opened up the floor to more discussion. But, according to Douglas, Stone was unable to shake his role as a law-school professor, and as a result he would lead off the discussion with a full statement of his own views, then turn the floor over to the senior Associate Justice; but at the conclusion of the latter's presentation Stone would take the floor once more to critique the analysis of the senior Associate. The conference totally lost the tautness it had under Hughes, and on some occasions went on interminably.

The conferences under Warren Burger were somewhere in between those presided over by Hughes and those by Stone. Since I have become Chief Justice, I have tried to make my opening presentation of a case somewhat shorter than Burger made his. I do not believe that conference discussion changes many votes, and I do not think that the impact of the Chief Justice's presentation is necessarily proportional to its length. I don't mean to give the impression that the discussion in every case is stated in terms of nine inflexible positions; on occasion one or more of those who have stated their views toward the beginning of the discussion, upon seeing that those views as stated are not in agreement with those of the majority, may indicate a willingness to alter those views along the lines of the thinking of the majority. But there is virtually no institutional pressure to do this; dissent from the views of the majority is in no way discouraged, and one only need read the opinions of the Court to see that it is practiced by all of us.

I quite strongly prefer the Hughes style over the Stone style insofar as interruptions of conference discussion are concerned. I think it is very desirable that all members of the Court have an opportunity to state their views before there is any cross-questioning or interruption, and I try to convey this sentiment to my colleagues. But the chief justice is not like the Speaker of the House of Representatives; it would be unheard of to declare anyone out of order, and the chief justice is pretty much limited to leading by example. On rare occasions questioning of a justice who is speaking by one who has already spoken may throw added light on a particular issue, but this practice carries with it the potential for disrupting the orderly participation of each member of the Court in the discussion. At the end of the discussion, I announce how I am recording the vote in the case, so that others may have the opportunity to disagree with my count if they believe I am mistaken.

The upshot of the conference discussion of a case will, of course, vary in its precision and detail. If a case is a relatively simple one, with only one real legal issue in it, it will generally be very clear where each member of the Court stands on that issue. But many of the cases that we decide are complex ones, with several interrelated issues, and it is simply not possible in the format of the conference to have nine people answering either yes or no to a series of difficult questions about constitutional law. One justice may quite logically believe that a negative answer to the very first of several questions makes it unnecessary to decide the subsequent ones, and having answered the first one in the negative will say no more. But if a majority answers the first question in the affirmative, then the Court's opinion will have to go on and discuss the other questions. Whether or not the first justice agrees with the majority on these other issues may not be clear from the conference discussion. The comment is frequently heard during the course of a discussion that "some things will have to be worked out in the writing" and this is very true in a number of cases. Oral discussion of a complex case will usually give the broad outlines of each justice's position, but it is simply not adequate to fine-tune the various positions in the way that the written opinion for the majority of the Court, and the dissenting opinions, eventually will. The broad outlines emerge from the conference discussion, but often not the refinements.

So long as we rely entirely on oral discussion for the exposition of views at conference, I do not see how it could do more than it now does in refining the various views on particular issues. I understand that judges of other courts rely on written presentations circulated by each judge to his colleagues before the conference discussion; this practice may well flesh out more views on the details of a case, but the need to reconcile the differences in the views expressed still remains. There is also a very human tendency to become more firmly committed to a view that is put in writing than one that is simply expressed orally, and therefore the possibility of adjustment and adaptation might be lessened by this approach. At any rate, we do not use it, and I know of no one currently on our Court who believes we should try it.

Our conference is a relatively fragile instrument which works well for the purpose to which we put it, but which also has very significant limitations. As I have said, probably every new justice, and very likely some justices who have been there for a while, wish that on occasion the floor could be opened up to a free-swinging exchange of views rather than a structured statement of nine positions. I don't doubt that courts traditionally consisting of three judges, such as the federal courts of appeals, can be much more relaxed and informal in their discussion of a case they have heard argued. But the very fact that we are nine, and not three, or five, or seven, sets limits on our procedure. We meet with one another week after week, year after year, to discuss and deliberate over some of the most important legal questions in the United States. Each of us soon comes to know the general outlook of his eight colleagues, and on occasion I am sure that each of us feels, listening to the eight others, that he has "heard it all before." If there were a real prospect that extended discussion would bring about crucial changes in position on the part of one or more members of the Court, that would be a strong argument for having that sort of discussion even with its attendant consumption of time. But my years on the Court have convinced me that the true purpose of the conference discussion of argued cases is not to persuade one's colleagues through impassioned advocacy to alter their views, but instead by hearing each justice express his own views to determine therefrom the view of the majority of the Court. This is not to say that minds are never changed in conference; they certainly are. But it is very much the exception, and not the rule, and if one gives some thought to the matter, this should come as no surprise.

The justices sitting in conference are not, after all, like a group of decision-makers who are hearing arguments pro and con about the matter for the first time. They have presumably read the briefs, they have heard the oral arguments of the lawyers who generally know far more about the particular case than the justices do, and they have had an opportunity to discuss the case with one or more of their law clerks.... All in all, I think our conference does about all that it can be expected to do in moving the Court to a final decision of a case by means of a written opinion.

During a given two-week session of oral argument, we will usually hear twelve cases. By Friday of the second week we will have conferred about all of them. Now the time comes for assigning the task of preparing written opinions to support the result reached by the majority.

In every case in which the chief justice votes with the majority, he assigns the case; where he has been in the minority, the senior associate justice in the majority is the assigner. Although one would not know it from reading the press coverage of the Court's work, the Court is unanimous in a good number of its opinions, and these of course are assigned by the chief justice. Since the odds of his being in a minority of one or two are mathematically small, he assigns the great majority of cases in which there is disagreement within the Court but which are not decided by a close vote. When the conference vote produces three or even four dissents from the majority view, the odds of course increase that the chief justice will be one of the dissenters. During my tenure as an associate justice, I received assignments not only from the Chief Justice, but from Justices Douglas, Brennan, White, and Marshall. Sometimes the assignments come around during the weekend after the second week of oral argument, but they can also be delayed until early the following week. Since there are nine candidates to write twelve opinions, the law of averages again suggests that each chambers will ordinarily receive only one assignment.

I know from the time during which I was an associate justice how important the assignment of the cases is to each member of the Court. The signed opinions to a very large extent are the only visible record of a justice's work on the Court, and the office offers no greater reward than the opportunity to author an opinion on an important point of constitutional law. As an Associate Justice I eagerly awaited the assignments, and I think that my law clerks awaited them more than I did. Clerks serve for only one year, and if I was assigned seventeen or eighteen opinions during the course of the year, each of the law clerks would have an opportunity to work on five or six opinions. My clerks were always in high hopes that one of the cases on which they had worked or in which they were really interested and regarded as very important would be assigned to me. Unfortunately, they were frequently disappointed in this respect, because not every case argued during a two-week term is both interesting and important.

As Chief Justice, of course, I have the responsibility for assigning the writing of opinions for the Court in cases where I have voted with the majority. This is an important responsibility, and it is desirable that it be discharged carefully and fairly. The chief justice is expected to retain for himself some opinions that he regards as of great significance, but he is also expected to pass around to his colleagues some of this kind of opinion. I think it also pleases the other members of the Court if the chief justice occasionally takes for himself a rather routine and uninteresting case, just as they are expected to do as a result of the assignment process. At the start of each October term, I try to be as evenhanded as possible as far as numbers of cases assigned to each justice, but as the term goes on I take into consideration the extent to which the various justices are current in writing and circulating opinions that have previously been assigned.

When I assign a case to myself, I sit down with the clerk who is responsible for the case, and go over my conference notes with him . . . . [T]he combination of the notes and my recollection of what was said at conference generally proves an adequate basis for discussion between me and the clerk of the views expressed by the majority at conference, and of the way in which an opinion supporting the result reached by the majority can be drafted. After this discussion, I ask the clerk to prepare a first draft of a Court opinion and to have it for me in ten days or two weeks.

I know that this sort of deadline seems onerous to the new crop of law clerks when, after the October oral argument session, they undertake the first drafting of an opinion for me. I am sure that every law clerk coming to work for a justice of the Supreme Court fancies that the opinion he is about to draft will make an important contribution to jurisprudence, and in the rare case he may be right. But with this goal in mind the law clerk is all too apt to first ponder endlessly, and then write and rewrite, and then polish to a fare-thee-well. This might be entirely appropriate if his draft were a paper to be presented in an academic seminar, or an entry in a poetry contest. But it is neither of these things; it is a rough draft of an opinion embodying the views of a majority of the Court expressed at conference, a rough draft that I may very well substantially rewrite. It is far more useful to me to get something in fairly rough form in two weeks than to receive after four or five weeks a highly polished draft that I feel obligated nonetheless to substantially revise. It is easy in October, when the work of the Court is really just starting up for the term, to imagine that there is an infinite amount of time in which to explore every nuance of a question and to perfect the style of every paragraph of the opinion. But, as I learned long ago, and as the clerks soon find out, there is not an infinite amount of time. By the last week in October, we are already busy preparing for the November oral-argument session, at the end of which we will be assigned more cases in which to prepare opinions for the Court. I feel strongly that I want to keep as current as I possibly can with my work on the Court, in order not to build up that sort of backlog of unfinished work that hangs over one like an incubus throughout the remainder of the term.

When I receive a rough draft of a Court opinion from a law clerk, I read it over, and to the extent necessary go back and again read the opinion of the lower court and selected parts of the parties' briefs. The drafts I get during the first part of the term from the law clerks require more revision and editing than the ones later in the term, after the law clerks are more used to my views and my approach to writing. I go through the draft with a view to shortening it, simplifying it, and clarifying it. A good law clerk will include in the draft things that he might feel could be left out, simply to give me the option of making that decision. Law clerks also have been exposed to so much "legal writing" on law reviews and elsewhere that their prose tends to stress accuracy at the expense of brevity and clarity. Frank Wozencraft, who was my predecessor as assistant attorney general for the Office of Legal Counsel in the Justice Department, imparted to me a rule of thumb that he used in drafting opinions, which I have used since: If a sentence takes up more than six lines of type on an ordinary page, it is probably too long. This rule is truly stark in its simplicity, but every draft I review is subjected to it. Occasionally, but not often, a draft submitted by a law clerk will seem to me to have simply missed a major point I think necessary to support the conclusion reached by the majority at conference; I will of course rewrite the draft to include that point.

. . .

I hope it is clear from my explanation of the way that opinions are drafted in my chambers that the law clerk is not simply turned loose on an important legal question to draft an opinion embodying the reasoning and the result favored by the law clerk. Quite the contrary is the case. The clerk is given, as best I can, a summary of the conference discussion, a description of the result reached by the majority in that discussion, and my views as to how a written opinion can best be prepared embodying that reasoning. The law clerk is not off on a frolic of his own, but is instead engaged in a highly structured task that has been largely mapped out for him by the conference discussion and my suggestions to him.

This is not to say that the clerk who prepares a first draft does not have a very considerable responsibility in the matter. The discussion in conference has been entirely oral, and as I have previously indicated, nine statements of position suffice to convey the broad outlines of the views of the justices; but these statements do not invariably settle exactly how the opinion will be reasoned through. Something that sounded very sensible to a majority of the Court at conference may, when an effort is made to justify it in writing, not seem so sensible, and it is the law clerk who undertakes the draft of the opinion who will first discover this difficulty. The clerk confronting such a situation generally comes back to me and explains the problem, and we discuss possible ways of solving it. It may turn out that I do not share the clerk's dissatisfaction with the reasoning of the conference, and I simply tell him to go ahead. If I agree with the objection or difficulty he sees, we then undertake an exploration for alternative means of writing the same passage in the draft. Similarly, the conference discussion may have passed over a subsidiary point without even treating it; it is not until the attempt is made to draft a written opinion that the necessity of deciding the subsidiary question becomes apparent. Here again, we do the best we can, recognizing that the proof of the pudding will be the reaction of those who voted with the majority at conference when they see the draft Court opinion.

After I have finished my revisions of the draft opinion, I return it to the law clerk who then refines and on occasion may suggest additional revisions. We then print the finished product with the correct formal heading for the opinion.

When the Supreme Court first began to hand down written opinions in the last decade of the eighteenth century, the author of the opinion was designated, for example, "Cushing, Justice." This style was followed until the February 1820 term of the Court when it was replaced by the form, for example, "Mr. Justice Johnson." This style endured for more than one hundred and fifty years, indeed until a year or two before Justice O'Connor was appointed to the Court in 1981. In 1980 Justice White, with great prescience, suggested to the conference that since in the very near future a woman was bound to be appointed, we ought to avoid the embarrassment of having to change the style of designating the author of the opinion at that time by making the change before the event. The conference was in entire agreement, and very shortly thereafter, without any explanation, the manner of designating the author of the opinion became simply, for example, "Justice Brennan." Our desire to avoid later embarrassment was only partially successful, however; the very first day on which opinions in the new style were handed down, the *New York Times* carried a story devoted to the change of style under the by-line of its astute Supreme Court correspondent, Linda Greenhouse.

I have always felt that opinions in printed form are vastly improved over the final draft, even though not a word in the draft has been changed. There is something about seeing a legal opinion in print that makes it far more convincing than it was in typescript. I have the feeling that if we circulated our drafts to the other justices in typescript, we might get many more criticisms than we do with the printed product.

At any rate, circulate them to the other chambers we do, and we wait anxiously to see what the reaction of the other justices will be, especially those justices who voted with the majority at conference. If a justice agrees with the draft and has no criticisms or suggestions, he will simply send a letter saying something such as "Please join me in your opinion in this case." If a justice agrees with the general import of the draft, but wishes changes to be made in it before joining, a letter to that effect will be sent, and the writer of the opinion will, if possible, accommodate the suggestions. The willingness to accommodate on the part of the author of the opinion is often directly proportional to the number of votes supporting the majority result at conference; if there were only five justices at conference voting to affirm the decision of the lower court, and one of those five wishes significant changes to be made in the draft, the opinion writer is under considerable pressure to work out something that will satisfy the critic, in order to obtain five votes for the opinion. Chief Justice Hughes once said that he tried to write his opinions clearly and logically, but if he needed the fifth vote of a colleague who insisted on putting in a paragraph that did not "belong," in it went, and he let the law reviews figure out what it meant.

But if the result at conference was reached by a unanimous or a lopsided vote, a critic who wishes substantial changes in the opinion has less leverage. I willingly accept relatively minor suggestions for change in emphasis or deletion of language that I do not regard as critical, but resist where possible substantial changes with which I don't agree. Often much effort is expended in negotiating these changes, and it is usually effort well spent in a desire to agree upon a single opinion that will command the assent of a majority of the justices.

The senior justice among those who disagreed with the result reached by the majority at conference usually undertakes to assign the preparation of the dissenting opinion in the case, if there is to be one. In the past it was a common practice for justices who disagreed with the opinion of the Court simply to note their dissent without more ado, but this practice is rare today. The justice who will write the dissent notifies the author of the opinion and the other justices of his intention, and will circulate that opinion in due course. Perhaps it would be a more rational system if, in a case where a dissent is being prepared, all of those, except the opinion writer, who voted with the majority at conference, as well as those who dissented, would await the circulation of the dissent, but in most cases this practice is not followed. One reason for the current practice is probably that dissents are usually sent around weeks, and often months, after the majority opinion is circulated. A justice who is doubtful as to his vote at conference, or who has reservations about the draft of the Court opinion, may tell the author that he intends to await the dissent before deciding which opinion to join. But this is the exception, not the rule; ordinarily those justices who voted with the majority at conference, if they are satisfied with the proposed Court opinion, will join it without waiting for the circulation of the dissent.

At our Friday conferences, the first order of business is to decide what opinions are ready to be handed down. The Chief Justice goes in order, beginning with the junior justice, and will ask him if any of his opinions are ready to be handed down. If all of the votes have been received in a case where he has authored the draft of the Court's opinion, he will so advise the conference, and unless there is some objection, his opinion will be handed down at one of the sittings the following week. On that day, at 10:00 a.m., the Clerk's Office will have available copies of his opinion in that particular case for anyone who wishes it. Meanwhile, the first order of business after the Court goes on the bench will be the announcement by that justice of his opinion from the bench. He will describe the case, summarize the reasoning of the Court, announce the result, and announce whatever separate or dissenting opinions have been filed. The decision-making process has now run full circle: A case in which certiorari was granted somewhere from six months to a year ago has been briefed, orally argued, and now finally decided by the Supreme Court of the United States.

Note on Justice Scalia's Views

Consider Justice Scalia's views about the conference, as expressed in this news article written only two years after he joined the Court.

> Justice Antonin Scalia says one thing has disappointed him since he joined the Supreme Court in 1986: the absence of give and take among the Court's members when they meet in conference to discuss and vote in cases they have heard. . . .

> These conferences are the only occasions when the Justices all meet together without clerks or aides, and the confidentiality of what is said is closely guarded.

> "Not very much conferencing goes on" at the conferences, Justice Scalia said at a question-and-answer session after delivering a speech at George Washington University's National Law Center on Tuesday. By

"conferencing," he explained, he meant efforts to persuade others to change their views by debating points of disagreement.

"In fact," he said, "to call our discussion of a case a conference is really something of a misnomer. It's much more a statement of the views of each of the nine Justices, after which the totals are added and the case is assigned."

"I don't like that. Maybe it's just because I'm new. Maybe it's because I'm an ex-academic. Maybe it's because I'm right." In response to another question, Justice Scalia said the Court might improve the quality of its deliberations if it reduced the number of cases it hears to allow more time for each case.[6]

Stuart Taylor, Jr., *Ruing Fixed Opinions*, N.Y. Times, February 22, 1988, at A16.

Note that in Justice Rehnquist's early years he, too, was disappointed by the brevity of conference, though he came to have a different view later. Are there reasons why junior Justices might be particularly unhappy with how conferences in the recent past have been held? Recall that by tradition, the Justices speak in the order of seniority and therefore the junior Justice expresses his or her views last.

Might there be advantages to conferences in which less rather than more is said? Might the weight given to written, as opposed to oral, exchanges improve the quality of the Court's decisions? Is there something about having to write down one's reasoning that enhances the level of thinking? On occasion, as you will read, a Justice assigned an opinion will find it simply does not "write," and circulates an opinion taking an entirely different view.

B. DELIBERATION, NEGOTIATION, DISSENT, AND SEPARATE OPINIONS

1. Overview

David M. O'Brien,[7] *Storm Center: The Supreme Court in American Politics*, 267–69, 277–88 (6th ed. 2003)

OPINION-WRITING PROCESS

Opinions justify or explain votes at conference. The opinion for the Court is the most important and most difficult to write because it represents a collective judgment. Writing the Court's opinion, as Holmes put it, requires that a "judge can dance the sword dance; that is, he can justify an obvious result without stepping on either blade of opposing fallacies." Holmes in his good-natured way often complained about the

---

6. [Editors' Note: Remember that at the time of this comment, the Court was still hearing far more cases than it now hears. See discussion in Part C of Chapter Three, above.]

7. Leona Reaves and George W. Spicer Professor, Woodrow Wilson Department of Politics, University of Virginia.

compromises he had to make when writing an opinion for the Court. "I am sorry that my moderation," he wrote Chief Justice Edward White, "did not soften your inexorable heart—But I stand like St. Sebastian ready for your arrows."

Before he retired from the Court, Justice Blackmun agreed that opinions must often be revised "because other justices say, if you put this kind of a paragraph or say this, I'll join your opinion. So you put it in. And many times the final result is a compromise ... the final result is not what the author would originally have liked to have. But five votes are the answer. . . . So you swallow your pride and go along with it if you can."

. . .

WRITING AND CIRCULATING OPINIONS

. . .

. . . On the Rehnquist Court, only Justice Stevens still regularly does the first draft of opinions; he does them, he says, "for self-discipline." For opinions in cases that they deem important, Justice Scalia and Souter also tend to undertake their own first drafts; the latter does so in a hand-written draft since he is the only justice who does not use a word processor in his chambers. The first drafts of all the other justices' opinions are usually prepared by their clerks. Still, only after a justice is satisfied with an initial draft does the opinion go to the other justices for their reactions.

. . . The practice of circulating draft opinions began around the turn of the [twentieth] century and soon became pivotal in the Court's decision-making process. The circulation of opinions provides more opportunities for the shifting of votes and further coalition building or fragmentation within the Court. Chief Justice Marshall, with his insistence on unanimity and nightly conferences after dinner, achieved unsurpassed unanimity. Unanimity, however, was based on the reading of opinions at conferences. No drafts circulated for other justices' scrutiny. Throughout much of the nineteenth century, when the Court's sessions were shorter and the justices had no law clerks, opinions were drafted in about two weeks and then read at conference. If at least a majority agreed with the main points, the opinion was approved.

In the twentieth century, the practice became that of circulating draft opinions, initially carbon copies, later two photocopies, and now electronically for each justice's examination and comments. Because they gave more attention to each opinion, the justices found more to debate. The importance of circulating drafts and negotiating language in an opinion was underscored when Jackson announced from the bench, "I myself have changed my opinion after reading the opinions of the members of the Court. And I am as stubborn as most. But I sometimes wind up not voting the way I voted in conference because the reasons of the majority didn't satisfy me." Similarly, Brennan noted, "I converted more than one proposed majority into a dissent before the final decision was announced. I have also, however, had the more satisfying experience of rewriting a dissent as a majority opinion for the Court." In one case, Brennan added, he "circulated 10 printed drafts before one was approved as the Court's opinion."

· · ·

How long does opinion writing take? In the average case, Tom Clark observed, about three weeks' work by a justice and his clerks is required before an opinion circulates. "Then the fur begins to fly." The time spent preparing an opinion depends on how fast a justice works, what his style is, how much use of law clerks he makes, and how controversial the assigned case is. Holmes and Benjamin Cardozo wrote opinions within days after being assigned, with little assistance from law clerks. Even into his eighties, Holmes "thirsted" for opinions. Chief Justice Hughes held back assignments from Cardozo because the justice's law clerk, Melvin Segal, complained that Cardozo would spend his weekends writing his opinions and thus he had little to do during the week. Cardozo later gave his clerk responsibility for checking citations and proofreading drafts. But Cardozo still overworked himself, and Hughes continued to hold back assignments for fear that the bachelor's health would fail. By comparison, Frankfurter relied a great deal on his clerks and was still notoriously slow. As he once said, in apologizing to his brethren for the delay in circulating a proposed opinion, "The elephant's period of gestation is, I believe, eighteen months, but a poor little hot dog has no such excuse."

A number of factors affect how long it takes a justice to complete opinion assignments for the Court. Some justices work quickly, as already noted, while others are notoriously slow. In a study of the Vinson Court (1946–1952), Jan Palmer and Saul Brenner found further confirmation for Black's and Douglas's reputation as expeditious opinion writers, and that Frankfurter consistently took more time than his colleagues to complete his opinions. They also found that over the years Chief Justice Vinson, while striving to equalize his opinion assignments, tended to favor "speedy" writers like Black and Douglas, despite his ideological disagreements with them. Among other factors associated with prolonging the time taken to produce an opinion for the Court are (1) the importance and divisiveness of a case, (2) the size of the voting majority at conference, (3) whether the initial vote was to affirm rather than reverse a lower court, (4) whether one or more of the justices later switched their votes, and (5) whether a case had to be reassigned or carried over for another term.

The interplay of professional and psychological pressures on a justice writing the Court's opinion is a complex but crucial part of the Court's decision making. When the practice, in the 1920s and 1930s, was to return comments within twenty-four hours after receipt of a draft, the pressures were especially great. There are no time limits now, but the pressures persist, especially during the last two months of a term, when the justices concentrate on opinion writing.

Whether drafting or commenting on a proposed opinion, justices differ when trying to influence each other. They look for emotional appeals, sometimes personal threats. Justice Clark thought that Warren was the greatest chief justice in the history of the Court and sought his approval of a revised opinion. But he received this disturbing response: "Tom: Nuts. E.W." Shortly after coming to the Court, Brennan wrote Black, "I welcome, as always, every and any comment you will be good enough to make on anything I ever write—whether we vote together at the time or not." By contrast, Justice Marshall had a tendency to simply scribble "B.S." on drafts circulated by Rehnquist.

Douglas could be a real charmer—if he wanted to be—when appealing for modifications in proposed opinions. "I would stand on my head to join with you in your opinion," he told James Byrnes, though continuing, "I finally concluded, however, that I cannot." . . .

By contrast, the style of McReynolds was abrupt—sometimes rude—and usually left little room for negotiation. "This statement makes me sick," he once observed. Frankfurter's approach also could be irritating. He was not above making personal attacks. To threaten his ideological foe Hugo Black, Frankfurter circulated but did not publish the following concurring opinion:

> I greatly sympathize with the essential purpose of my brother (former Senator) Black's dissent. His roundabout and turgid legal phraseology is a *cris de coeur*. "Would I were back in the Senate," he seems to say, "so that I could put on the statute books what really ought to be there. But here I am, cast by Fate into a den of judges devoid of the habits of legislators, simple fellows who have a crippling feeling that they must enforce the laws as Congress wrote them and not as they ought to have been written."

Frankfurter nonetheless usually tempered his criticisms by making fun of his own academic proclivities: "What does trouble me is that you do not disclose what you are really doing." He wrote Douglas, "As you know, I am no poker player and naturally, therefore, I do not believe in poker playing in the disposition of cases. Or has professing for twenty-five years disabled me from understanding the need for these involutions?"

More typically when commenting on circulated drafts, justices appeal to professionalism and jurisprudential concerns. Even McReynolds, perhaps at the prompting of Taft, once appealed to Stone's basic conservatism: "All of us get into a fog now and then, as I know so well from my own experience. Won't you 'Stop, Look, and Listen'?" Such appeals may carry subtly or explicitly the threat of a concurring or dissenting opinion. Stone, in one instance, candidly told Frankfurter, "If you wish to write [the opinion] placing the case on the ground which I think tenable and desirable, I shall cheerfully join you. If not, I will add a few observations for myself."

Justices may suggest minor editorial or major substantive changes. Before joining one of Arthur Goldberg's opinions, Harlan requested that the word "desegregation" be substituted for "integration" throughout the opinion. As he explained, " 'Integration' brings blood to Southerners' eyes for they think that 'desegregation' means just that—'integration.' I do not think that we ought to use the word in our opinions." Likewise, Stewart strongly objected to some of the language in Abe Fortas's proposed opinion in *Tinker v. Des Moines School District* (1969), which upheld the right of students to wear black armbands in protest of the government's involvement in Vietnam. "At the risk of appearing eccentric," Stewart wrote, "I shall not join any opinion that speaks of what is going on in Vietnam as a 'war' [since Congress never formally declared a war in Vietnam]." . . .

Editorial suggestions may also be directed at a justice's use of precedents and basic conceptualization. Douglas, for instance, sent Brennan a letter outlining fourteen changes he thought necessary in the proposed opinion for the watershed reapportionment decision in *Baker v. Carr* (1962). Likewise, Brennan sent a twenty-one-page list of revisions on Earl Warren's initial draft of *Miranda v. Arizona* (1966), which upheld the right of criminal suspects to remain silent at the time of police questioning. At the outset, Brennan expressed his feeling of guilt "about the extent of the suggestions." But he emphasized the importance of careful drafting. Brennan explained, "[T]his will be one of the most important opinions of our time and I know that you will want the fullest expression of my views."

Occasionally, proposed changes lead to a recasting of the entire opinion. Douglas was assigned the Court's opinion in *Griswold v. Connecticut* (1965), in which he announced the creation of a constitutional right of privacy based on the "penumbras" of various guarantees of the Bill of Rights. His initial draft, however, did not develop this theory. Rather, Douglas sought to justify the decision on the basis of earlier cases recognizing a First Amendment right of associational privacy. The analogy and precedents, he admitted, "do not decide this case." "Marriage does not fit precisely any of the categories of First Amendment rights. But it is a form of association as vital in the life of a man or a woman as any other, and perhaps more so." Both Black and Brennan strongly objected to Douglas's extravagant reliance on First Amendment precedents. In a three-page letter, Brennan detailed an alternative approach, as the following excerpt indicates:

> I have read your draft opinion in *Griswold v. Connecticut,* and, while I agree with a great deal of it, I should like to suggest a substantial change in emphasis for your consideration. It goes without saying, of course, that your rejection of any approach based on *Lochner v. New York* is absolutely right. [In *Lochner* (1905), a majority read into the Fourteenth Amendment a "liberty of contract" in order to strike down economic legislation. Although the Court later abandoned the doctrine of a "liberty of contract," *Lochner* continues to symbolize the original sin of constitutional

interpretation—that is, the Court's creation and enforcement of unenumerated rights.] [brackets in original] And I agree that the association of husband and wife is not mentioned in the Bill of Rights, and that that is the obstacle we must hurdle to effect a reversal in this case.

> But I hesitate to bring the husband-wife relationship within the right to association we have constructed in the First Amendment context.... In the First Amendment context, in situations like *NAACP v. Alabama* [1964], privacy is necessary to protect the capacity of an association for fruitful advocacy. In the present context, it seems to me that we are really interested in the privacy of married couples quite apart from any interest in advocacy.... Instead of expanding the First Amendment right of association to include marriage, why not say that what has been done for the First Amendment can also be done for some of the other fundamental guarantees of the Bill of Rights? In other words, where fundamentals are concerned, the Bill of Rights guarantees are but expressions or examples of those rights, and do not preclude applications or extensions of those rights to situations unanticipated by the Framers.

The restriction on the dissemination and use of contraceptives, Brennan explained,

> would, on this reasoning, run afoul of a right to privacy created out of the Fourth Amendment and the self-incrimination clause of the Fifth, together with the Third, in much the same way as the right of association has been created out of the First. Taken together, those amendments indicate a fundamental concern with the sanctity of the home and the right of the individual to be alone.

"With this change of emphasis," Brennan concluded, the opinion "would be most attractive to me because it would require less departure from the specific guarantees and because I think there is a better chance it will command a Court." Douglas subsequently revised his opinion and based the right of privacy on the penumbras of the First, Third, Fourth, Fifth, and Ninth Amendments. But Brennan, nonetheless, joined Justice Goldberg's concurring opinion in *Griswold*.

In order to accommodate the views of others, the author of an opinion for the Court must negotiate language and bargain over substance. "The ground you recommend was not the one on which I voted 'no'—But I think that, as a matter of policy, you are clearly right; and I am engaged in redrafting the opinion on that line," Brandeis wrote to the respected craftsman Van Devanter, adding, "May I trouble you to formulate the rule of law, which you think should be established?"

At times, justices may not feel that a case is worth fighting over. "Probably bad—but only a small baby. Let it go," Sutherland noted on the back of one of Stone's drafts.... Similarly, Pierce Butler agreed to go along with one of Stone's opinions, though noting, "I voted to reverse. While this sustains your conclusion to affirm, I still think reversal would be better. But I shall in silence acquiesce. Dissents seldom aid in the right development or statement of the law. They often do harm. For myself I say: 'Lead us not into temptation.' "

. . .

More than a willingness to negotiate is sometimes required. Judicial temperament and diplomacy are also crucial, as is illustrated by the deliberations behind the landmark decision inaugurating the reapportionment revolution. *Baker v. Carr* (1962) raised two central issues: first, whether the malapportionment of a state legislature is a "political question" for which courts have no remedy; second, the merits of the claim that individuals have a right to equal votes and equal representation. With potentially broad political consequences, the case was divisive, being carried over and reargued for a term. The extreme positions within the Court remained firm, but the center tended to be soft. Allies on judicial self-restraint, Frankfurter and Harlan were committed to their view, expressed in *Colegrove v. Green* (1946), that the "Court ought not to enter this political thicket." At conference, Tom Clark and Charles Whittaker supported their view that the case presented a nonjusticiable political question. By contrast, Warren, Black, Douglas and Brennan thought that the issue was justiciable. They were prepared to address the merits of the case. The pivotal and youngest justice, Potter Stewart, considered the issue justiciable. But he adamantly refused to address the merits of the case. He would vote to reverse the lower-court ruling that the issue was a political question only if the decision was limited to holding that the lower court had jurisdiction to decide the dispute. Stewart did not want the Court to decide the merits of he case.

Assigned the task of drafting the opinion, Brennan had to hold on to Stewart's vote and dissuade Black and Douglas from writing opinions on the merits that would threaten the loss of the crucial fifth vote. After circulating his draft and incorporating the suggested changes, he optimistically wrote Black, "Potter Stewart was satisfied with all of the changes. The Chief is also agreed. It, therefore, looks as though we have a court agreed upon this as circulated." It appeared that the decision would come down on the original five-to-four vote.

Clark, however, had been pondering the fact that in this case the population ratio for the urban and rural districts in the state was more than nineteen to one. As he put it, "city slickers" had been "too long deprive[d] of a constitutional form of government." Clark concluded that citizens denied equal voting power had no political recourse; their only recourse was to the federal judiciary. Clark wrote an opinion abandoning Frankfurter and going beyond the majority to address the merits of the claim.

Brennan faced the dilemma of how to bring Clark in without losing Stewart, and thereby enlarge the consensus. Further negotiations were necessary but limited. Brennan wrote his brethren:

The changes represent the maximum to which Potter will subscribe. We discussed much more elaborate changes which would have taken over a substantial part of Tom Clark's opinion. Potter felt that if they were made it would be necessary for him to dissent from that much of the revised opinion. I therefore decided it was best not to press for the changes but to hope that Tom would be willing to join the Court opinion but say he would go further as per his separate opinion.

Even though there were five votes for deciding the merits, the final opinion in *Baker v. Carr* was limited to the jurisdictional question. Douglas refrained from addressing the merits in his concurring opinion. Stewart joined with an opinion emphasizing the limited nature of the ruling. Clark filed an opinion explaining his view of the merits. Whittaker withdrew from the case, retiring from the Court two weeks later because of poor health. Only Frankfurter and Harlan were left dissenting.

———

Questions and Comments

1. In a later edition of his book, Professor O'Brien offers another example of the internal editing process in Shaw v. Reno, 509 U.S. 630 (1993), which addressed the constitutional limitations on the states' authority to create "majority-minority" districts. See David M. O'Brien, *Storm Center: The Supreme Court in American Politics* 274–75 (7th ed. 2005). Quoting from material in the Blackmun papers, he describes how Chief Justice Rehnquist asked Justice O'Connor to change her draft in light of what he characterized as "two non-substantive concerns:"

> First, on page 7 you say that the Civil War was fought in part to secure the elective franchise to black Americans. One can certainly say that the Civil War was fought to end slavery, but I don't think it is an accurate statement to say that it was fought to secure the elective franchise for blacks. This view gained majority support only during the period of Reconstruction after the Civil War was over.

> Second, on page 23, you say that the Fourteenth Amendment embodies "the goal of a fully integrated society." The Fourteenth Amendment prohibits discrimination; it does not require integration, and I think it is a mistake to intimate that it does even as a "goal."

Id. at 275 (quoting Letter from Chief Justice William H. Rehnquist, June 7, 1993, Blackmun papers, Box 624, Library of Congress). In the published version of *Shaw v. Reno*, Justice O'Connor omits these references, writing for example:

> "The right to vote freely for the candidate of one's choice is of the essence of a democratic society. . . ." Reynolds v. Sims, 377 U.S. at 555. For much of our Nation's history, that right sadly has been denied to many because of race. The Fifteenth Amendment, ratified in 1870 after

a bloody Civil War, promised unequivocally that "the right of citizens of the United States to vote" no longer would be "denied or abridged ... by any State on account of race, color, or previous condition of servitude." U.S. Const., Amdt. 15, § 1.

509 U.S. at 639. Justice O'Connor was writing for a slim 5–4 majority. Is this an example of Justices deliberating within a "legal" model? an "interest group" model? an "attitudinal" model? Or is this an example of what Epstein and Wright would call a "strategic" model in which Justices seek to advance their preferences in a situation of bargaining with other Justices? See Chapter Three, *above*. Might this also be described within an "institutional" model in which the Court is seen as an institution of government whose task—to make decisions—necessarily requires compromise in order to achieve a judgment?

2. Sometimes Justices simply change their minds, upon further reflection after the conference. In Garcia v. San Antonio Metropolitan Transit Authority, 469 U.S. 528 (1985), Justice Blackmun had been assigned, based on his conference vote, to write an opinion for a narrow majority that would have struck down application of the federal minimum wage statute to the city transit authority under National League of Cities v. Usery, 426 U.S. 833 (1976). See David M. O'Brien, *Storm Center* (6th ed. 2003), excerpted below, Chapter Five, Section A. However, Justice Blackmun came to question the Court's prior "attempt to draw a line between 'traditional' and 'nontraditional' state activities in limiting congressional power," and he prepared a draft going the other way. *Id.* As Professor O'Brien notes in a later edition of his book,

> [Blackmun's] draft in *Garcia* was in line with the view of the four dissenters in *Usery*, though it stopped short of overruling that earlier decision. Because he did not circulate the draft until two weeks before the end of the term and reached a result contrary to the conference vote, a majority decided to carry *Garcia* over to the next term and hear rearguments.... The rearguments strengthened Blackmun's resolve and he revised his draft in *Garcia* to expressly overturn *Usery*.

David M. O'Brien, *Storm Center* 263 (7th ed. 2005). The published opinion of the Court explains in some detail why Justice Blackmun was now rejecting the approach of *National League of Cities*, an opinion he had joined nine years earlier. See 469 U.S. at 538–47.[8] Four dissenters (who at conference had been part of a majority including Blackmun) vigorously objected. Into what kind of decisionmaking model does Blackmun's change of mind fall?[9]

---

8. Even at the time he joined the opinion in *National League of Cities*, Justice Blackmun had expressed some reservations. See *National League of Cities*, 426 U.S. at 856 (Blackmun, J., concurring) (stating that he was "not untroubled by certain possible implications of the Court's opinion" and was joining the opinion on the understanding that it would not outlaw federal environmental statutes).

9. For another example of a Justice changing his mind after being assigned to write for the Court, because the draft he wrote "looked quite wrong,", see O'Brien, *Storm Center* (2005), at 264 (describing and quoting from Justice Kennedy's explanation of his change of views in *Lee v. Weisman* (1992)).

2.   The Role of Dissents: Views from the Court

William J. Brennan, Jr.,[10] *In Defense of Dissents*, 37 Hastings L. J. 427, 428–438 (1986)

· · ·

Why do judges dissent? Not many years ago, the writer Joan Didion . . . wrote an elegant essay for the New York Times. The question she addressed, and the title of her essay, was "Why I Write." She said:

> Of course I stole the title . . . from George Orwell. One reason I stole it was that I like the sound of the words: *Why I Write*. There you have three short unambiguous words that share a sound, and the sound they share is this:
>
> I
>
> I
>
> I
>
> In many ways writing is the act of saying I, of imposing oneself upon other people, of saying *listen to me, see it my way, change your mind*.[11]

No doubt, there are those who believe that judges—and particularly dissenting judges—write to hear themselves say, as it were, I I I. And no doubt, there are also those who believe that judges are, like Joan Didion, primarily engaged in the writing of fiction. I cannot agree with either of those propositions.

Of course, we know why judges write *opinions*. It is through the written word that decisions are communicated, that mandates issue. But why *dissent*? . . . After all, the law is the law, and in our system, whether in the legislature or the judiciary, it is made by those who command the majority. As the distinguished legal philosopher H.L.A. Hart declared, "A supreme tribunal has the last word in saying what the law is and, when it has said it, the statement that the court was 'wrong' has no consequences within the system: no one's rights or duties are thereby altered." In view of this reality, some contend that the dissent is an exercise in futility, or, worse still, a "cloud" on the majority decision that detracts from the legitimacy that the law requires and from the prestige of the institution that issues the law. Learned Hand complained that a dissenting opinion "cancels the impact of monolithic solidarity on which the authority of a bench of judges so largely depends." Even Justice Holmes, the Great Dissenter himself, remarked in his first dissent on the Court that dissents are generally "useless" and "undesirable." And more recently, Justice Potter Stewart has labeled dissents "subversive literature." Why, then, does a judge hold out?

---

10. Associate Justice, Supreme Court of the United States.

11. [Footnote 6 in original] N.Y. Times, Dec. 5, 1976, § 7 (Book Review), at 2 (emphasis in original).

Very real tensions sometimes emerge when one confronts a colleague with a dissent. After all, collegiality *is* important; unanimity *does* have value; feelings *must* be respected. . . .

It seems that to explain why a dissenter holds out, we should examine some of the many different functions of dissents. Not only are all dissents not created equal, but they are not intended to be so. In other words, to answer "why write," one must first define precisely what it is that is being written. I do not have an exhaustive list, but let me at least suggest some diverse roles that may be served by a dissent. . . .

In its most straightforward incarnation, the dissent demonstrates flaws the author perceives in the majority's legal analysis. It is offered as a corrective—in the hope that the Court will mend the error of its ways in a later case. Oliver Cromwell captured the thrust of that type of dissent when he pleaded to the General Assembly of the Church of Scotland in 1650, "Brethren, by the bowels of Christ I beseech you, bethink you that you may be mistaken." But the dissent is often more than just a plea; it safeguards the integrity of the judicial decision-making process by keeping the majority accountable for the rationale and consequences of its decision. Karl Llewellyn, who was critical of the frequency with which Supreme Court Justices, of all courts, dissented, grudgingly acknowledged the importance of that role, characterizing it as "rid[ing] herd on the majority." At the heart of that function is the critical recognition that vigorous debate improves the final product by forcing the prevailing side to deal with the hardest questions urged by the losing side. In this sense, this function reflects the conviction that the best way to find the truth is to go looking for it in the marketplace of ideas. It is as if the opinions of the Court—both for majority and dissent—were the product of a judicial town meeting.

The dissent is also commonly used to emphasize the limits of a majority decision that sweeps, so far as the dissenters are concerned, unnecessarily broadly—a sort of "damage control" mechanism. Along the same lines, a dissent sometimes is designed to furnish litigants and lower courts with practical guidance—such as ways of distinguishing subsequent cases. It may also hint that the litigant might more fruitfully seek relief in a different forum—such as the state courts. I have done that on occasion. Moreover, in this present era of expanding state court protection of individual liberties, in my view, probably the most important development in constitutional jurisprudence today, dissents from federal courts may increasingly offer state courts legal theories that may be relevant to the interpretation of their own state constitutions.

The most enduring dissents, however, are the ones in which the authors speak, as the writer Alan Barth expressed it, as "Prophets with Honor." These are the dissents that often reveal the perceived congruence between the Constitution and the "evolving standards of decency that mark the progress of a maturing society," and that seek to sow seeds for future harvest. These are the dissents that soar with passion and ring with rhetoric. These are the dissents that, at their best, straddle the worlds of literature and law.

While it is relatively easy to describe the principal functions of dissents, it is often difficult to classify individual dissents, particularly the great ones, as belonging to one category or another; rather, they operate on several levels simultaneously. For example, the first Justice Harlan's remarkable dissent in Plessy v. Ferguson[12] is at once prophetic and expressive of the Justice's constitutional vision, and, at the same time, a careful and methodical refutation on the majority's legal analysis in that case.

In this masterful dissent, the Justice said that "in view of the Constitution, in the eye of the law, there is in this country no superior, dominant, ruling class of citizens. There is no caste here. Our Constitution is color-blind...." Justice Harlan also foretold, with unfortunate accuracy, the consequences of the majority's position. Said he, the *Plessy* decision would:

> not only stimulate aggressions, more or less brutal and irritating, upon the admitted rights of colored citizens, but will encourage the belief that it is possible, by means of state enactments, to defeat the beneficent purposes which the people of the United States had in view when they adopted the recent amendments of the Constitution....

He addressed, and dismissed as erroneous, the majority's reliance on precedents. "Those decisions," he declared:

> cannot be guides in the era introduced by the recent amendments of the supreme law, which established universal civil freedom, gave citizenship to all born or naturalized in the United States and residing here, obliterated the race line from our systems of governments ... and placed our free institutions upon the broad and sure foundation of the equality of all men before the law.

Justice Harlan, in that dissent, is the quintessential voice crying in the wilderness. In rejecting the Court's view that so-called separate but equal facilities did not violate the Constitution, Justice Harlan stood alone; not a single other justice joined him. In his appeal to the future, Justice Harlan transcended, without slighting, mechanical legal analysis; he sought to announce fundamental constitutional truths as well. He spoke not only to his peers, but to his society, and, more important, across time to later generations. He was, in this sense, a secular prophet, and we continue, long after *Plessy* and long even after Brown v. Board of Education,[13] to benefit from his wisdom and courage.

From what source did Justice Harlan derive the right to stand against the collective judgment of his brethren in *Plessy*? We may ask the same question of Justice Holmes in *Abrams;*[14] of Justice Brandeis in

12. [Footnote 15 in original] 163 U.S. 537, 552 (1896) (Harlan, J., dissenting).

13. [Footnote 19 in original] 347 U.S. 483 (1954).

14. [Footnote 20 in original] Abrams v. United States, 250 U.S. 616, 624 (1919) (Holmes, J., dissenting).

Olmstead;[15] of Justice Stone in *Gobitis;*[16] of Justice Jackson in *Korematsu;*[17] of Justice Black in *Adamson;*[18] or of the second Justice Harlan in Poe v. Ullman; [19] to name but a few of the most famous and powerful dissents of this century. And surely, you may ask the same question of me. How do I justify adhering to my essentially immutable positions on obscenity, the death penalty, the proper test for double jeopardy, and on the eleventh amendment? For me, the answer resides in the nature of the Supreme Court's role.

The Court is something of a paradox—it is at once the whole and its constituent parts. The very words "the Court" mean simultaneously the entity and its members. Generally, critics of dissent advocate the primacy of the unit over its members and argue that the Court is most "legitimate," most true to its intended role, when it speaks with a single voice. Individual justices are urged to yield their views to the paramount need for unity. It is true that unanimity underscores the gravity of a constitutional imperative—witness Brown v. Board of Education[20] and Cooper v. Aaron.[21] But, unanimity is not in itself a judicial virtue.

Indeed, history shows that nearly absolute unanimity enjoyed only a brief period of preeminence in the Supreme Court. Until John Marshall became Chief Justice, the Court followed the custom of the King's Bench and announced its decisions through the seriatim opinions of its members. Chief Justice Marshall broke with the English tradition and adopted the practice of announcing judgments of the Court in a single opinion. At first, these opinions were always delivered by Chief Justice Marshall himself, and were virtually always unanimous. Unanimity was consciously pursued and disagreements were deliberately kept private. Indeed, Marshall delivered a number of opinions which, not only did he not write, but which were contrary to his own judgment and vote at conference.

This new practice, however, was of great symbolic and practical significance at the time. Remember the context of the times when the practice was introduced. As one commentator has observed, when Marshall delivered the opinion of the Court, "[h]e did not propose to announce only the views of John Marshall, Federalist of Virginia." Rather, "he intended that the words he wrote should bear the imprimatur of the Supreme Court of the United States. For the first time, the Court as a judicial unit had been committed to an opinion—a ratio decidendi—in support of its judgments." This change in custom at the

15. [Footnote 21 in original] Olmstead v. United States, 277 U.S. 438, 471 (1928) (Brandeis, J., dissenting).

16. [Footnote 22 in original] Minersville School Dist. v. Gobitis, 310 U.S. 586, 601 (1940) (Stone, J., dissenting).

17. [Footnote 23 in original] Korematsu v. United States, 323 U.S. 214, 242 (1944) (Jackson, J., dissenting).

18. [Footnote 24 in original] Adamson v. California, 332 U.S. 46, 68 (1947) (Black, J., dissenting).

19. [Footnote 25 in original] 367 U.S. 497, 522 (1961) (Harlan, J., dissenting).

20. [Footnote 26 in original] 347 U.S. 483 (1954).

21. [Footnote 27 in original] 358 U.S. 1 (1958).

time consolidated the authority of the Court and aided in the general recognition of the Third Branch as co-equal partner with the other branches. Not surprisingly, not everyone was pleased with the new practice. Thomas Jefferson, who also was a lawyer, was, of course, conversant with the English custom, and was angrily trenchant in his criticism. He wrote that "[a]n opinion is huddled up in conclave, perhaps by a majority of one, delivered as if unanimous, and with the silent acquiescence of lazy or timid associates, by a crafty chief judge, who sophisticates the law to his own mind, by the turn of his own reasoning." In other words, Marshall had shut down the marketplace of ideas.

Of course, Jefferson was overstating matters a bit. In fact, unanimity remained the rule only for the first four years of Marshall's Chief Justiceship, and during that period only one, one-sentence concurrence was delivered, and that by Justice Chase. But, in 1804, Justice William Johnson arrived on the Court from the state appellate court of South Carolina. He tried to perpetuate the seriatim practice of his state court and issued a substantial concurrence in one of the first cases in which he participated. And his colleagues were stunned. Johnson later described their reaction in a letter to Jefferson. "Some Case soon occurred," he wrote:

> in which I differed from my Brethren, and I felt it a thing of Course to deliver my Opinion. But, during the rest of the Session I heard nothing but lectures on the Indecency of Judges cutting at each other, and the Loss of Reputation which the Virginia appellate Court had sustained by pursuing such a Course.

Nonetheless, the short-lived tradition of unanimity had been broken, and, in 1806, Justice Patterson delivered the first true dissent from a judgment and opinion of the Court in Simms v. Slacum.[22] As one historian has observed, considerably understating the case, since that time "dissents were never again a rarity." Even Chief Justice Marshall filed nine dissents from the opinions of the Court during his closing years on the Bench.

What, then, should we make of modern critics of dissents? Charles Evans Hughes answered that question sixty years ago and I think what he said then is as true today. He said:

> When unanimity can be obtained without sacrifice of conviction, it strongly commends the decision to public confidence. But unanimity which is merely formal, which is recorded at the expense of strong, conflicting views, is not desirable in a court of last resort, whatever may be the effect upon public opinion at the time [the case is announced]. This is so because what must ultimately sustain the court in public confidence is the character and independence of the judges. They are not there simply to decide cases, but to decide them as they think they should be decided, and while it may be regretta-

22. [Footnote 35 in original] 7 U.S. (3 Cranch) 300, 309 (1806) (Paterson, J., dissenting).

ble that they cannot always agree, it is better that their independence should be maintained and recognized than that unanimity should be secured through its sacrifice.

In Chief Justice Hughes' view, and in my own, justices do have an obligation to bring their individual intellects to bear on the issues that come before the Court. This does not mean that a justice has an absolute duty to publish trivial disagreements with the majority. Dissent for its own sake has no value, and can threaten the collegiality of the bench. However, where significant and deeply held disagreement exists, members of the Court have a responsibility to articulate it. This is why, when I dissent, I always say why I am doing so. Simply to say, "I dissent," I will not do.

I elevate this responsibility to an obligation because in our legal system judges have no power to *declare* law. That is to say, a court may not simply announce, without more, that it has adopted a rule to which all must adhere. That, of course, is the province of the legislature. Courts *derive* legal principles, and have a duty to explain *why* and *how* a given rule has come to be. This requirement serves a function within the judicial process similar to that served by the electoral process with regard to the political branches of government. It restrains judges and keeps them accountable to the law and to the principles that are the source of judicial authority. The integrity of the process through which a rule is forged and fashioned is as important as the result itself; if it were not, the legitimacy of the rule would be doubtful. Dissents contribute to the integrity of the process, not only by directing attention to perceived difficulties with the majority's opinion, but, to turn one more time to metaphor, also by contributing to the marketplace of competing ideas.

. . . A dissent challenges the reasoning of the majority, tests its authority and establishes a benchmark against which the majority's reasoning can continue to be evaluated, and perhaps, in time, superseded. This supersession may take only three years, as it did when the Court overruled *Gobitis*[23] in *Barnette;*[24] it may take twenty years, as it did when the Court overruled Hammer v. Dagenhart[25] in *Darby;*[26] it may take sixty years as it did when we overruled *Plessy* in *Brown*. The time periods in which dissents ripen into majority opinions depend on societal developments and the foresight of individual justices, and thus vary. Most dissents never "ripen" and do not deserve to. But it is not the hope of eventual adoption by a majority that alone justifies dissent. For simply by infusing different ideas and methods of analysis into judicial decision-making, dissents prevent that process from becoming rigid or stale. And,

23. [Footnote 42 in original] Minersville School Dist. v. Gobitis, 310 U.S. 586 (1940), *overruled,* West Virginia State Bd. of Educ. v. Barnette, 319 U.S. 624 (1943).

24. [Footnote 43 in original] West Virginia State Bd. of Educ. v. Barnette, 319 U.S. 624 (1943).

25. [Footnote 44 in original] 247 U.S. 251 (1918), *overruled,* United States v. Darby, 312 U.S. 100 (1941).

26. [Footnote 45 in original] United States v. Darby, 312 U.S. 100 (1941).

each time the Court revisits an issue, the justices are forced by a dissent to reconsider the fundamental questions and to rethink the result.

I must add a word about a special kind of dissent: the repeated dissent in which a justice refuses to yield to the views of the majority although persistently rebuffed by them. For example, Justice Holmes adhered through the years to his views about the evils of substantive due process, as did Justices Black and Douglas to their views regarding the absolute command of the first amendment.... I adhere to positions on the issues of capital punishment, the eleventh amendment, and obscenity, which I developed over many years and after much troubling thought. On the death penalty, for example, as I interpret the eighth amendment, its prohibition against cruel and unusual punishments embodies to a unique degree moral principles that substantively restrain the punishments governments of our civilized society may impose on those convicted of capital offenses.... For me ... the fatal constitutional infirmity of capital punishment is that it treats members of the human race as nonhumans, as objects to be toyed with and discarded....

This is an interpretation to which a majority of my fellow justices—not to mention, it would seem, a majority of my fellow countrymen—do not subscribe. Perhaps you find my adherence to it, and my recurrent publication of it, simply contrary, tiresome, or quixotic. Or perhaps you see in it a refusal to abide by the judicial principle of stare decisis, obedience to precedent.... Yet, in my judgment, when a justice perceives an interpretation of the text to have departed so far from its essential meaning, that justice is bound, by a larger constitutional duty to the community, to expose the departure and point toward a different path.

This kind of dissent, in which a judge persists in articulating a minority view of the law in case after case presenting the same issue, seeks to do more than simply offer an alternative analysis—that could be done in a single dissent and does not require repetition. Rather, this type of dissent constitutes a statement by the judge as an individual: "Here I draw the line." Of course, as a member of a court, one's general duty is to acquiesce in the rulings of that court and to take up the battle behind the court's new barricades. But it would be a great mistake to confuse this unquestioned duty to obey and respect the law with an imagined obligation to subsume entirely one's own views of constitutional imperatives to the views of the majority. None of us, lawyer or layman, teacher or student in our society must ever feel that to express a conviction, honestly and sincerely maintained, is to violate some unwritten law of manners or decorum. We are a free and vital people because we not only allow, we encourage debate, and because we do not shut down communication as soon as a decision is reached. As law-abiders, we accept the conclusions of our decision-making bodies as binding, but we also know that our right to continue to challenge the wisdom of that result must be accepted by those who disagree with us. So we debate and discuss and contend and always we argue. If we are right, we generally prevail. The process enriches all of us, and it is available to, and employed by, individuals and groups representing all viewpoints and perspectives.

I hope that what I have said does not sound like too individualistic a justification of the dissent. No one has any duty simply to make noise. Rather, the obligation that all of us, as American citizens have, and that judges, as adjudicators, particularly feel, is to speak up when we are convinced that the fundamental law of our Constitution requires a given result. I cannot believe that this is a controversial statement. The right to dissent is one of the great and cherished freedoms that we enjoy by reason of the excellent accident of our American births.

Through dynamic interaction among members of the present Court and through dialogue across time with the future Court, we ensure the continuing contemporary relevance and hence vitality of the principles of our fundamental charter. Each justice must be an active participant, and, when necessary, must write separately to record his or her thinking. Writing, then, is not an egoistic act—it is duty. Saying, "listen to me, see it my way, change your mind," is not self-indulgence—it is very hard work that we cannot shirk.

———

Ruth Bader Ginsburg,[27] *Speaking in a Judicial Voice*, 67 N.Y.U. L. Rev. 1185 (1992)

INTRODUCTION

. . .

James Madison's forecast still brightens the spirit of federal judges. In his June 1789 speech introducing to Congress the amendments that led to the Bill of Rights, Madison urged:

> If [a Bill of Rights is] incorporated into the Constitution, independent tribunals of justice will consider themselves in a peculiar manner the guardians of those rights; they will be an impenetrable bulwark . . . naturally led to resist every encroachment upon rights . . . stipulated for in the Constitution by the declaration of rights.

Today's independent tribunals of justice are faithful to that "original understanding" when they adhere to traditional ways courts have realized the expectation Madison expressed.

In *The Federalist* No. 78, Alexander Hamilton said that federal judges, in order to preserve the people's rights and privileges, must have authority to check legislation and acts of the executive for constitutionality. But he qualified his recognition of that awesome authority. The judiciary, Hamilton wrote, from the very nature of its functions, will always be "the least dangerous" branch of government, for judges hold

---

27. Associate Justice, United States Supreme Court. This Article is based on the James Madison Lecture, given March 9, 1993, when the author was a Judge on the United States Court of Appeals for the District of Columbia Circuit.

neither the sword nor the purse of the community; ultimately, they must depend upon the political branches to effectuate their judgments. Mindful of that reality, the effective judge, I believe and will explain why in these remarks, strives to persuade, and not to pontificate. She speaks in "a moderate and restrained" voice, engaging in a dialogue with, not a diatribe against, co-equal departments of government, state authorities, and even her own colleagues.

.   .   .

COLLEGIALITY IN APPELLATE DECISIONMAKING

I turn now to the first of the two topics this lecture addresses—the style of judging appropriate for appellate judges whose mission it is, in Hamilton's words, "to secure a steady, upright, and impartial administration of the laws." Integrity, knowledge and, most essentially, judgment are the qualities Hamilton ascribed to the judiciary. How is that essential quality, judgment, conveyed in the opinions appellate judges write? What role should moderation, restraint, and collegiality play in the formulation of judicial decisions? As background, I will describe three distinct patterns of appellate opinion-casting: individual, institutional, and in-between.

The individual judging pattern has been characteristic of the Law Lords, who serve as Great Britain's Supreme Court. The Lords sit in panels of five and, traditionally, have delivered opinions seriatim, each panel member, in turn, announcing his individual judgment and the reasons for it.

In contrast to the British tradition of opinions separately rendered by each judge as an individual, the continental or civil law traditions typified and spread abroad by France and Germany call for collective, corporate judgments. In dispositions of that genre, disagreement is not disclosed. Neither dissent nor separate concurrence is published. Cases are decided with a single, per curiam opinion generally following a uniform, anonymous style.

Our Supreme Court, when John Marshall became Chief Justice, made a start in the institutional opinion direction. Marshall is credited with establishing the practice of announcing judgments in a single opinion for the Court. The Marshall Court, and certainly its leader, had a strong sense of institutional mission, a mission well served by unanimity. Marshall was criticized, in those early days, for suppressing dissent. Thomas Jefferson complained: "An opinion is huddled up in conclave, perhaps by a majority of one, delivered as if unanimous, and with the silent acquiescence of lazy or timid associates, by a crafty chief judge, who sophisticates the law to his own mind, by the turn of his own reasoning."

But even Marshall, during his long tenure as Chief Justice, ultimately dissented on several occasions and once concurred with a separate opinion. We continue in that middle way today. Our appellate courts generally produce a judgment or opinion for the court. In that respect, we bear some resemblance to the highly institution-minded civil law judges, although our judges individually claim authorship of most of the opinions they publish. In tune with the British or common law tradition, however, we place no formal limit on the prerogative of each judge to speak out separately.

To point up the difference between individual and institutional modes of judging, I have drawn upon a 1989 letter from a civilian jurist. The letter came from a member of the Conseil d'Etat, the illustrious body created by Napoleon that still serves, among other functions, as Supreme Administrative Court for France. The conseiller who wrote to me had observed, together with several of his colleagues, an appellate argument in the District of Columbia Circuit. The appeal was from a criminal conviction; the prime issue concerned the Fifth Amendment's double jeopardy ban. When the case was decided, I sent our French visitors copies of the slip sheet. It contained the panel's judgment, and three opinions, one per judge. I paraphrase the conseiller's reaction:

> The way the decision is given is surprising for us according to our standards. The discussion of theory and of the meaning of precedents is remarkable. But the divided opinions seem to me very far from the way a judgment should issue, particularly in a criminal case. The judgment of a court should be precise and concise, not a discourse among professors, but the order of people charged to speak in the name of the law, and therefore written with simplicity and clarity, presenting short explanations. A judgment that is too long indicates uncertainty.
>
> At the same time, it is very impressive for me to see members of a court give to the litigants and to the readers the content of their hesitations and doubts, without diminishing the credibility of justice, in which the American is so confident.

The conseiller seems at first distressed, even appalled, at our readiness to admit that legal judgments (including constitutional rulings) are not always clear and certain. In his second thought, however, the conseiller appears impressed, touched with envy or admiration, that our system of justice is so secure, we can tolerate open displays of disagreement among judges about what the law is.

But overindulgence in separate opinion writing may undermine both the reputation of the judiciary for judgment and the respect accorded court dispositions. Rule of law virtues of consistency, predictability, clarity, and stability may be slighted when a court routinely fails to act as a collegial body. Dangers to the system are posed by two tendencies: too frequent resort to separate opinions and the immoderate tone of statements diverging from the position of the court's majority.

Regarding the first danger, recall that "the Great Dissenter," Justice Oliver Wendell Holmes, in fact dissented less often than most of his colleagues. Chief Justice Harlan F. Stone once wrote to Karl Llewellyn (both gentlemen were public defenders of the right to dissent): "You know, if I should write in every case where I do not agree with some of the views expressed in the opinions, you and all my other friends would stop reading [my separate opinions]." In matters of statutory interpretation, Justice Louis D. Brandeis repeatedly cautioned: "[I]t is more important that the applicable rule of law be settled than that it be settled right." "This is commonly true," Brandeis continued, "even where the error is a matter of serious concern, provided correction can be had by legislation." Revered constitutional scholar Paul A. Freund, who clerked for Justice Brandeis, recalled Justice Cardozo's readiness to suppress his dissent in common law cases (the Supreme Court had more of those in pre-*Erie* days), so that an opinion would come down unanimous.

Separate concurrences and dissents characterize Supreme Court decisions to a much greater extent than they do court of appeals three-judge panel decisions. In the District of Columbia Circuit, for example, for the statistical year ending June 1992, the court rendered 405 judgments in cases not disposed of summarily; over 86% of those decisions were unanimous. During that same period, the Supreme Court decided 114 cases with full opinions; only 21.9% of the decisions were unanimous. A reality not highlighted by a press fond of separating Carter from Reagan/Bush appointees accounts in considerable measure for this difference: the character of cases heard by courts of appeals combines with our modus operandi to tug us strongly toward the middle, toward moderation and away from notably creative or excessively rigid positions. . . .

Concerning the character of federal cases, unlike the Supreme Court, courts of appeals deal far less frequently with grand constitutional questions than with less cosmic questions of statutory interpretation or the rationality of agency or district court decisions. In most matters of that variety, as Justice Brandeis indicated, it is best that the matter be definitively settled, preferably with one opinion. Furthermore, lower court judges are bound more tightly by Supreme Court precedent than is the High Court itself.

. . .

On the few occasions each year when we sit en banc—in the District of Columbia Circuit, all twelve of us when we are full strength—I can appreciate why unanimity is so much harder to achieve in Supreme Court judgments. Not only do the Justices deal much more often with constitutional questions, where, in many cases, only overruling or constitutional amendment can correct a mistake. In addition, one becomes weary after going round the table on a first ballot. It is ever so much easier to have a conversation—and an exchange of views on opinion drafts—among three than among nine or twelve.

In writing for the court, one must be sensitive to the sensibilities and mindsets of one's colleagues, which may mean avoiding certain arguments and authorities, even certain words. Should institutional concerns affect the tone of separate opinions, when a judge finds it necessary to write one?

I emphasize first that dissents and separate concurrences are not consummations devoutly to be avoided. As Justice William J. Brennan said in thoughtful defense of dissents: "None of us, lawyer or layman, teacher or student in our society must ever feel that to express a conviction, honestly and sincerely maintained, is to violate some unwritten law of manners or decorum." I question, however, resort to expressions in separate opinions that generate more heat than light. Consider this sample from an April 1991 District of Columbia Circuit decision. The dissenter led off: "Running headlong from the questions briefed and argued before us, my colleagues seek refuge in a theory as novel as it is questionable. Unsupported by precedent, undeveloped by the court, and unresponsive to the facts of this case, the . . . theory announced today has an inauspicious birth." That spicy statement, by the way, opposed an en banc opinion in which all of the judges concurred, except the lone dissenter.

It is "not good for public respect for courts and law and the administration of justice," Roscoe Pound decades ago observed, for an appellate judge to burden an opinion with "intemperate denunciation of [the writer's] colleagues, violent invective, attributi[on]s of bad motives to the majority of the court, and insinuations of incompetence, negligence, prejudice, or obtuseness of [other judges]." Yet one has only to thumb through the pages of current volumes of United States Reports and Federal Reporter Second to come upon condemnations by the score of a court or colleague's opinion or assertion as, for example, "folly," "ludicrous," "outrageous," one that "cannot be taken seriously," "inexplicable," "the quintessence of inequity," a "blow against the People," "naked analytical bootstrapping," "reminiscent . . . of Sherman's march through Georgia," and "Orwellian."

. . .

The most effective dissent, I am convinced, "stand[s] on its own legal footing"; it spells out differences without jeopardizing collegiality or public respect for and confidence in the judiciary. I try to write my few separate opinions each year as I once did briefs for appellees—as affirmative statements of my reasons, drafted before receiving the court's opinion, and later adjusted, as needed, to meet the majority's presentation. Among pathmarking models, one can look to Justice Curtis's classic dissent in the *Dred Scott* case, and, closer to our time, separate opinions by the second Justice John Marshall Harlan.

. . .

_____

Note on Justice Scalia's View of Separate Opinions

For a vigorous argument, echoing some of Justice Brennan's points, in favor of dissenting or concurring opinions that "disagree with the Court's *reasoning*," see Antonin Scalia, *The Dissenting Opinion*, 1994 J.

Sup. Ct. Hist. 33 (arguing that "[a]n opinion that gets the *reasons* wrong gets *everything* wrong which it is the function of an opinion to produce"). For Justice Scalia, "it is worth a dissent" if the majority's reasons are wrong, and at this stage in the Court's development, "announced dissents augment rather than diminish its prestige." Justice Scalia also wrote that:

> When I have been assigned the opinion for the Court in a divided case, nothing gives me as much assurance that I have written it well as the fact that I am able to respond satisfactorily (in my judgment) to all the onslaughts of the dissents or separate concurrences. The dissent or concurrence puts my opinion to the test, providing a direct confrontation of the best arguments on both sides of the disputed points. It is a sure cure for laziness, compelling me to make the most of my case. Ironic as it may seem, I think a higher percentage of the worst opinions of my Court—not in result but in reasoning—are unanimous ones.

Id. at 41.

Questions and Comments

1. Are careful, unanimous opinions possible? Might they be the product of prior (published or unpublished) dissents?

2. Consider the range of arguments offered by Justice Brennan for dissents, and by Justice Scalia for separate opinions (concurring or dissenting). Which ones are most persuasive? Now, consider the arguments offered by Justice Ginsburg: She argues both for temperance in tone and for moderation in issuing separate opinions. Are you persuaded by her on either? on both? on neither?

3. The twentieth century saw a dramatic increase in the numbers of separate opinions being written per argued case. "One scholar has calculated that up until 1928 dissents and concurrences combined were filed in only about fifteen percent of all Supreme Court cases. Between 1930 and 1957 dissents alone were filed in about forty-two percent of all Supreme Court cases. [In the 1992] term, a dissent or separate concurrence was filed in seventy-one percent of all cases." Scalia, *supra*, at 35. After a brief note on the Roberts Court, the next section explores the history of separate opinions, from institutional and jurisprudential perspectives.

Note on Chief Justice Roberts' Views and the "Roberts Court"

On September 29, 2005, John Roberts was confirmed as Chief Justice, following the death on September 3, 2005, of William H. Rehnquist, who had served as Chief Justice for the prior 19 years. In a commencement address given at the Georgetown University Law Center in May, 2006, at the end of his first Term as Chief Justice, Roberts signaled a distinctive approach to the Court's role, placing greater weight than defenders of dissents and separate opinions have on the value of consensus as a tool for judicial minimalism:

> "There are clear benefits to a greater degree of consensus on the court. Unanimity or near-unanimity promote clarity and guidance for the

lawyers and for the lower courts trying to figure out what the Supreme Court meant," Roberts said. "The broader the agreement among the justices, the more likely it is that the decision is on the narrowest possible ground."

Robert Heberle, *Roberts Calls for Consensus on Court*, The Hoya.com (May 21, 2006), available at http://www.thehoya.com/note/5400. Although it is early for scholarly work on the internal workings of the Roberts Court, Jeffrey Rosen commented on its first Term, noting that "[it] began with a surprising number of unanimous decisions, but by the time it adjourned for the summer . . . the usual decorous costume drama that is a Supreme Court term had morphed into something much closer—in vitriol, tension and drama—to a soap opera (OK, a PBS soap opera)." Jeffrey Rosen, *Disorder in the Court*, Time, July 10, 2006, at 26. He described the Justices as "clearly rejuvenated by two new colleagues, Roberts and Samuel Alito," and emphasized that "alliances on the Roberts court are still fluid." Rosen also noted that the Court appeared "less fractured" than the Rehnquist Court, with almost half its decisions unanimous and seven fewer narrowly divided (five to four) decisions than in the recent Rehnquist Court. Rosen credited Roberts' "personality and leadership skills" together with his emphasis on achieving more unanimity on the Court through relatively narrow decisions that would provide more "clarity and guidance." *Id.* (referring to Roberts' 2006 Commencement address at Georgetown University Law Center).

The second Term of the Roberts Court, which ended just before this book went to press, was something of a contrast to the first. In the first Term, 37% of the cases were decided unanimously; in the second Term, only 24% of the argued cases were decided unanimously. Georgetown University Law Center, Supreme Court Institute, *Supreme Court of the United States, October Term 2006 Overview* (June 29, 2007), at 12 (Table 5). In the first Term, 23% of the cases were decided 5–4; in the second Term, 34% of the cases were 5–4 decisions. *Id.* According to the Georgetown Supreme Court Institute, the Roberts Court does not appear to be any "less divided when it addresses the legal issues that have divided the Justices" during recent years. Describing the effect of the two new members, the Institute concludes that "the deepening of a conservative majority on the Court has led to a series of closely divided votes favoring the more conservative position and a corresponding increase in the apparent frustration with the Court's rulings by liberal Justices relegated to oral and written dissents." *Supreme Court of the United States, October Term 2006 Overview*, at 1. This report noted that Justice Kennedy was in the majority on all of the 5–4 decisions of the 2006 Term, emphasizing his centrist position in this Court.

3. Institutional and Jurisprudential Perspectives on Changing Practices

In the very early years of the Court, opinions might issue without being circulated to the entire Court, based only on the Justices' conference discussions. See G. Edward White, *The Internal Powers of the Chief Justice: The Nineteenth–Century Legacy*, 154 U. Pa. L. Rev. 1463, 1471, 1479 (2006) (describing the "practice [in both the Marshall and Taney Courts] of one Justice preparing an opinion of the Court, not circulating it before delivery, and then dispatching it to the Court's reporter for eventual publication"). Professor White concluded that "[t]he legal justifications advanced in Marshall Court opinions were thus typically the product of only one Justice," although it appears that in the early years of the Court the Justices would discuss cases, particularly difficult cases, over a period of days. It was not until the late nineteenth or early twentieth centuries that drafts routinely circulated to the other Justices before being delivered.[28] The contemporary practice is, of course, quite different; not only are draft opinions for the Court circulated but so, too, are potential dissents or separate opinions.[29]

In a dissent in Metromedia, Inc. v. City of San Diego, 453 U.S. 490, 569–70 (1981), then Justice Rehnquist wrote:

> In a case where city planning commissions and zoning boards must regularly confront constitutional claims of this sort, it is a genuine misfortune to have the Court's treatment of the subject be a virtual Tower of Babel, from which no definitive principles can be clearly drawn; and ... I regret even more keenly my contribution to this judicial clangor, but find that none of the views expressed in the other opinions written in the case come close enough to mine to warrant the necessary compromise to obtain a Court opinion.

This passage suggests the difficulties for parties that arise from multiple opinions; it also implicitly raises questions about the possible relationship between fragmented opinions and the Court's legitimacy and efficacy in the constitutional system. But the passage may also shed light on why there has been such growth in the filing of separate opinions, a subject explored more systematically in the next two readings.

———

John P. Kelsh,[30] *The Opinion Delivery Practices of the United States Supreme Court 1790–1945,* **77 Wash. U. L. Q. 137 (1999)**

. . .

I. Introduction

. . .

28. See White, at 1471–72, 1476, 1504–05; see also David M. O'Brien, *Storm Center* 114, 115 (6th ed. 2003).

29. According to Professor White, it was not until 1947 that the U.S. Reports identified the votes of all the Justices participating in a case. See White, *supra*, at 1503–04. Until then, the Reports identified only the writer of the "opinion of the Court," and those Justices who wrote separately or specifically identified themselves as joining in an opinion. This practice of the Reporters facilitated "silent acquiescence," even by Justices whose views were in dissent.

30. The author is now a partner at Sidley Austin, LLP, Chicago, Illinois. He served as a law clerk to the Honorable William H. Rehnquist, Supreme Court of the United States, 1997–1998; and law clerk to the Honorable David B. Sentelle, United States Court of Appeals for the District of Columbia, 1996–1997.

... Prior to John Marshall's appointment as Chief Justice, the Court used no set form to deliver opinions. During his tenure, three important practices were established. First, an overwhelming majority of opinions were delivered by a particular Justice speaking for the Court. Second, other Justices were able to express their views separately from the view of the Court. Third, a great majority of cases were decided unanimously. These practices had great staying power. It wasn't until 1941 that any major external change took place. In that year the nonunanimity rate, which had been low ever since the Marshall Court, exploded. The rate more than doubled between 1940 and 1941 and by 1948 rose to the approximate level it occupies today.

... Early Justices believed that separate opinions were appropriate only in important cases, importance being defined by the presence of a constitutional issue or public interest. This attitude changed gradually over the years. During the Taney period, Justices began to express the belief that dissent was acceptable to protect their own records. This was part of a larger shift toward a view of the Court as atomized rather than unified. Further change manifested itself during the 1864–1940 period. Justices of that era expanded the universe of cases in which dissent was appropriate, paid more attention to the thinking of individual Justices, and began to view separate opinions as a legitimate part of the American legal system. All of these shifts in attitude were an important precursor to the post–1941 explosion in nonunanimity rates. They are also the intellectual source of today's view that dissent is appropriate in any kind of case at all.

II. HISTORY

. . .

While the pre-Marshall Court used the per curiam and seriatim styles most frequently, it experimented with other styles as well. Two of its innovations were later adopted by the Court. The first innovative opinion-delivery style was the practice of having the Chief Justice deliver an opinion "for the Court." On at least three occasions, the Reporter identified the opinion of the Court not as being given by the Court itself, but rather as having been delivered by the Chief Justice. This minor semantic shift became important for two reasons—one short-term and one long-term.

The short-term significance is that John Marshall was to seize upon this method of opinion delivery and use it almost exclusively during the early years of his tenure as Chief Justice. The long-term effect is that this new practice dramatically increased the importance of a particular Justice's thinking. This method focused attention not on what the Court did, but on what an individual Justice thought. This enshrinement of a particular Justice's opinion as the operative opinion of the Court raised the stakes in opinion writing. Opinions were no longer delivered by either unanimous Courts or for Justices writing only for themselves. Now, what individual Justices thought was of serious consequence. The increased concern with what each Justice said naturally led to an increased concern with each Justice's doctrinal consistency. Concern over doctrinal consistency became, by the end of the Taney period, an important reason for Justices to write separately. It is ironic, then, that Marshall adopted the innovation of having one Justice speak for the Court as a means of unifying the Court. This same innovation also introduced heightened concepts of judicial consistency that later became an excuse for many Justices to write separately.

· · ·

B. *Marshall Period* . . .

John Marshall came onto a Supreme Court that had no set procedure for the delivery of opinions. During his tenure three important developments took place. First, nearly all opinions came to be delivered by one Justice speaking for the Court. Second, by the end of his tenure, Justices were free to file concurring and dissenting opinions when they disagreed with the majority. Third, Justices who filed separate opinions felt compelled to explain why they did so. This subsection describes and analyzes these developments.

· · ·

By 1814, . . . after twenty-four years of experimentation, the Court had developed a practice whereby nearly all of its opinions were delivered by an individual Justice speaking for the entire Court. The seriatim opinion had all but disappeared, and the Court had drastically reduced the number of opinions it issued per curiam.

John Marshall had succeeded, but his new practice was soon criticized. The most vocal critic was Thomas Jefferson. Jefferson argued that the practice of having one Justice speak for the entire Court limited the accountability of the individual Justices. In a letter to Justice William Johnson, Jefferson urged a return to the use of seriatim opinions:

> The Judges holding their offices for life are under two responsibilities only. 1. Impeachment. 2. Individual reputation. But this practice compleatly withdraws them from both. For nobody knows what opinion any individual member gave in any case, nor even that he who delivers the opinion, concurred in it himself. Be the opinion therefore ever so impeachable, having been done in the dark it can be proved on no one. As to the 2d guarantee, personal reputation, it is shielded compleatly. The practice is certainly convenient for the lazy, the modest, & the incompetent. It saves them the trouble of developing their opinion methodically and even of making up an opinion at all. That of seriatim argument shews whether every judge has taken the trouble of understanding the case, of investigating it minutely, and of forming an opinion for himself, instead of pinning it on another's sleeve. It would certainly be right to abandon this practice in order to give to our citizens one and all, that confidence

in their judges which must be so desirable to the judges themselves, and so important to the cement of the union.

.   .   .

Marshall himself had made his preference for unanimity public in an 1819 article he published in a Philadelphia newspaper:

> The course of every tribunal must necessarily be, that the opinion which is to be delivered as the opinion of the court, is previously submitted to the consideration of all the judges; and, if any part of the reasoning be disapproved, it must be so modified as to receive the approbation of all, before it can be delivered as the opinion of all.

Marshall was also known to acquiesce silently when his own opinion did not command a majority and even on occasion write opinions with which he did not agree.

[Justice] Johnson, however, was resistant to the pressures of his colleagues and persisted in the issuance of separate opinions. He eventually settled on a compromise. He wrote to Jefferson in 1823: "On the subject of seriatim opinions in the Supreme Court I have thought much, and have come to the resolution to adopt your suggestion on all subjects of general interest; particularly constitutional questions. On minor subjects it is of little public importance."

Eventually, it seems, Johnson won out. By 1827 opinion-delivery practices began to change. Johnson was no longer the only Justice willing to write separately. In Ogden v. Saunders,[31] the four Justices in the majority delivered their opinions seriatim and [Chief] Justice Marshall dissented. . . .

.   .   .

Rationales

Not only had Johnson's habit of writing separately survived, so too had his categorization of which cases justified the public expression of dissent. As noted above, Johnson wrote to Jefferson that he would write separately "on all subjects of general interest; particularly constitutional questions." . . .

.   .   .

At one point or another, nearly all of the other Justices expressed Johnson's idea that dissenting was acceptable in important cases, importance being measured by public interest or presence of a constitutional issue. Statistics show they practiced what they preached. Nonunanimity rates were considerably higher in constitutional cases throughout the Marshall era. In the seventy-four cases that Professor Currie cites as presenting a constitutional issue, Justices filed separate opinions in twenty-six—a rate of 35%. This is nearly four times higher than the 9%

31. [Footnote 73 in original] 25 U.S. (12 Wheat.) 213 (1827).

nonunanimity rate that prevailed in the 917 Marshall-era cases that Currie does not cite.

. . .

C. *The Taney Court*

Overview

. . .

Nonunanimity rates stayed more or less the same, and the form of the opinion did not change, but Justices began to offer different reasons for writing separately. Justices began to say that they were compelled to write separately to maintain personal consistency. The separate opinion was a means by which the individual Justices accomplished the newly-important goal of defending their own judicial records. This new attitude toward dissent was part of a larger shift in the Justices' conception of the Court. Justices for the first time began to think of the Court less as a cohesive whole and more as a collection of individuals.

. . .

As was true of the Marshall period, statistics from the Taney Court show that dissent was more prevalent in constitutional cases than in other areas. Professor Currie identifies 103 cases that presented a constitutional question to the Taney Court. Justices registered at least one separate opinion in forty-five of these cases—approximately 44%. In the 1337 cases that Currie does not cite, the Taney Court Justices registered at least one separate writing in 242—approximately 18%. Nonunanimity rates were almost two and one-half times higher in constitutional cases than they were in all other cases. The idea that dissent was appropriate in constitutional cases and cases in which the public had an interest was expressed throughout the Taney era. As time went on, however, Justices began to mention it less frequently. Although Justice Taney in particular continued to emphasize that dissent was acceptable in important cases, by the Civil War these refrains were less commonly heard. The still-low nonunanimity rates suggest that the Court had institutionalized a belief that dissent was generally to be avoided, but Justices less frequently gave voice to that belief.

There began, however, to develop another trend that was to have significant consequences for the Court's opinion-delivery practices. Justices began to state that dissent was acceptable in order to protect or maintain their own records or reputations. Justices began to defend dissent less by reference to the issues involved and more by reference to themselves.

Concern with Consistency—A New Reason To Dissent

Up until approximately 1839, Justices who explained why they chose to write separately nearly always placed their emphasis on the issue involved. Beginning in approximately 1841, however, Justices started to express another set of rationales for choosing to write separately. Justices frequently noted that they wrote separately because they did not wish to be individually associated with the majority's opinion.

Two early examples of this appeared in the slavery case Groves v. Slaughter.[32] It is no surprise that the earliest expressions of concern for consistency would arise in a case concerning slavery, the most contentious issue of the day. In *Groves* Justice McLean raised in a concurrence a question the majority had avoided: whether Congress had the power to regulate traffic in slaves between the different states. Justice Taney stated in his concurrence that he had not originally intended to write separately, but now that Justice McLean had stated his opinion on this question, Taney was "not willing, by remaining silent, to leave any doubt as to [his own beliefs]." Justice Baldwin also expressed regret that Justice McLean had raised the unnecessary question. He explained, however, that now that one of the Justices had raised the question, he was "not willing to remain silent; lest it may be inferred that my opinion coincides with that of the judges who have now expressed theirs."

As the Taney years went on, this rationale began to appear more frequently. Many different Justices explained their decision to dissent in terms that echoed those of Taney and Baldwin in *Groves*. In an 1853 case, Justice Catron explained his decision to write separately: "My object here is not to express an opinion in this case further than to guard myself against being committed in any degree to the [following] doctrine...."[33] The next year Justice Daniel dissented briefly in a case involving admiralty jurisdiction. Daniel declined to elaborate on his legal reasons for dissenting—saying that he had made them clear in earlier cases. He closed his dissent by writing: "My purpose is simply to maintain my own consistency in adhering to convictions which are in nowise weakened."[34] ...

... These explanations for dissent suggest that Taney-era Justices began to conceive of their role more as an individual effort and less as a part of a cohesive unit.

Two other pieces of evidence from the opinion-delivery practices of the Taney Court support this contention. First, the Taney period saw a dramatic increase in the use of dissents and concurrences without opinion....

Second, the late Taney Court saw an increased incidence of hostility in individual opinions. Marshall Court Justices had gone out of their way to express their respect for the opinions of their brethren. During the

---

32. [Footnote 122 in original] 40 U.S. (15 Pet.) 449 (1841) It is perhaps significant that this early expression of concern for individual consistency arose in a slavery case. Slavery cases were both constitutional in nature and of great interest to the public—so it would have been appropriate anyway for Justices to write separately....

33. [Footnote 126 in original] Ohio Life Ins. & Trust Co. v. Debolt, 57 U.S. (16 How.) 416, 442 (1853) (Catron, J., concurring).

34. [Footnote 127 in original] The Propeller Monticello v. Mollison, 58 U.S. (17 How.) 152, 156 (1854) (Daniel, J., dissenting). Daniel, the Taney era's most frequent dissenter, made this same assertion on numerous occasions.

Taney Court, cordiality was still the norm, but during the Court's later years Justices occasionally began their separate opinions with expressions of scorn or disdain. Separate opinions began to lack the civility that had marked the Marshall and early Taney Courts. Justice Grier began an 1860 dissent:

> I wholly dissent from the opinion of the majority of the court in this case, both as to the law and the facts. But I do not think it necessary to vindicate my opinion by again presenting to the public view a history of the scandalous gossip which has been buried under the dust of half a century, and which a proper feeling of delicacy should have suffered to remain so . . . [35]

. . .

These expressions of disdain, which are also found in the opinions of other Justices, are further evidence that the Taney-era Justices began to conceive of the Court less as a unified whole and more as a collection of individuals.

. . .

D.   1864–1940

Overview

At first glance, it appears the Court's opinion-delivery practices changed little in the period between Chief Justice Taney's death in 1864 and Harlan Fiske Stone's elevation to Chief Justice in 1941. The Court continued to present its opinions in the format it had settled on during the Marshall period. The average nonunanimity rate per term was 18%, very comparable to the Taney Court's 20%. Justices of the period frequently echoed their Taney-era predecessors in expressing their reluctance to dissent.

Despite these superficial similarities, this period saw a significant change in the attitude Justices took toward writing separately. First, the Justices expanded the universe of cases where dissent was appropriate. While the Justices still said that dissent was acceptable in "important" cases, they also said that writing separately was justified when a case had significant practical consequences, or when the majority ignored stare decisis, or when they just plain disagreed. Second, Justices between 1864 and 1940 continued the trend towards viewing the Court more as atomized and less as unified. Citation to the views of individual Justices became more and more frequent and the Court developed distinct ideological blocs. Third, there was an increased sense that dissents were a legitimate and important source of law. Justices began to distinguish between unanimous and nonunanimous cases, citations to dissents for propositions of law became more frequent, and several dissents were

---

35. [Footnote 134 in original] Gaines v. Hennen, 65 U.S. (24 How.) 553, 631 (1860)   (Grier, J., dissenting).

written into law. All of these changes laid the groundwork for the post–1941 explosion in nonunanimity rates.

. . .

Rationales

    1.   Case–Specific Rationales

. . .

The Justices of the 1864–1940 era inherited most of the case-specific rationales that Justices had expressed during the Taney era. As was the case during that period, the most frequent rationale for writing separately was that the case before the Court was "important." . . .

Justices of this era also followed the Taney Court in explaining that dissent was appropriate in constitutional cases. This rationale was not expressed frequently, but it never completely disappeared. . . .

. . .

Post–Taney Justices did not, however, limit themselves to the categories of cases that Taney-era Justices believed warranted dissent. As the years went by, they developed three other rationales for writing separately. These new rationales existed side by side with the rationales they inherited from the Taney Court. The effect was to expand greatly the universe of cases for which dissent was considered appropriate.

The first new rationale was that the "consequences" of a particular case justified writing separately. Justices frequently opened separate opinions with references to the "far-reaching," "grave," "injurious," "serious," or "alarming" consequences of the Court's opinion. Consequences such as these, the Justices often argued, justified the delivery of a separate opinion . . .

A second major new rationale that the Justices developed during this period was that it was appropriate to register dissent when the majority departed from principles established by earlier cases. Justices announced in several cases that they had a "duty" to call attention to the Court's disregard of its own precedents.

A corollary to this idea that dissent was acceptable to protect *stare decisis* was the principle that dissent was appropriate when the dissenter believed the majority's errant opinion had the potential to affect many other cases. . . . Justice Brandeis stated it clearly in 1927:

> Mere difference of opinion in the construction of intricate statutes can rarely justify expression of dissent. This is especially true where the two views lead, in the particular case, to the same result. But, in this instance, the construction adopted by the Court may have in other cases . . . regrettable results.[36]

36. [Footnote 168 in original] Maul v.   (Brandeis, J., concurring).
United States, 274 U.S. 501, 512 (1927)

The third and final new justification for writing separately was the least restrictive of the three. In a number of cases, Justices announced that they were going to state their views separately for no reason other than that they disagreed with the majority of the Court. This rationale, which is really no rationale at all, was a particular favorite of Justice Harlan's. He concluded an 1892 dissent by stating: "Believing the doctrine announced by the court to be unsound, upon principle and authority, [I] do not feel at liberty to withhold an expression of [my] dissent from the opinion."[37]

The development of these new rationales for expressing dissent significantly enlarged the universe of cases in which dissent was considered appropriate. . . . The new categories were significantly broader than the old ones had been. . . . The subject matter of a case no longer needed to be referenced in deciding whether to write separately.

. . .

One would . . . expect that this significant broadening of the categories of cases for which dissent was acceptable would lead to a great increase in the nonunanimity rate. To some extent this happened, in that the nonunanimity rate jumped between 1930–40. A far more substantial rise, however, was to occur in the years following 1941, long after these new post-Taney rationales had become established. The explanation for this anomaly is that these new rationales for which types of cases warranted dissent coexisted with the general belief that dissent was to be avoided. The tension between these two ideas kept the nonunanimity rate from rising too high.

2.   Justice–Oriented Rationales—"Consistency"

. . .

Justices throughout the 1864–1940 period echoed their Taney-era predecessors in stating that dissent was appropriate to explain or protect one's record. Justices frequently stated that they were choosing to write separately to make it clear that they, as individuals, had no part in the majority's opinion. Justice Bradley opened an 1873 concurrence by saying:

> Whilst I concur in the conclusion to which the court has arrived in this case, I think it proper to state briefly and explicitly the grounds on which I distinguish it from the *Slaughter–House Cases* . . . I prefer to do this in order that there may be no misapprehension of the views which I entertain in regard to the application of the fourteenth amendment to the Constitution.[38] . . .

---

37. [Footnote 169 in original] Brenham v. German Am. Bank, 144 U.S. 173, 197 (1892) (Harlan, J., dissenting).

38. [Footnote 179 in original] Bartemeyer v. Iowa, 85 U.S. (18 Wall.) 129, 135 (1873) (Bradley, J., concurring). The Justices who dissented in the *Slaughter–House*

Cases seem to have been particularly worried that their views were being misrepresented. Concurring in this same case, Justice Field wrote, "[A]s there has been some apparent misapprehension of the views of the dissenting judges in the Slaughter–

The Justices also followed the example of the Taney Court in writing that the majority's opinion was so repulsive to them that they had no choice but to dissent. . . .

It was noted above that this pattern of using separate opinions to clarify a Justice's own record was part of a shift during the Taney period toward conceiving of the Court less as a cohesive unit and more as a collection of nine individuals. Other evidence from separate opinions between 1864–1940 suggests that this trend accelerated during this era.

First, Justices often used the separate opinion as a forum to discuss their own views on a particular area of law. For example, Chief Justice Chase spent several pages in his *Legal Tender Cases* dissent explaining why his position in that case was not inconsistent with the position he had taken as Secretary of the Treasury.[39] Justice Brewer wrote in a 1904 dissent, "I have heretofore dissented in several cases involving the exclusion or expulsion of the Chinese . . . my views on the questions are unchanged."[40] . . .

Second, just as individual Justices began to pay more attention to their own records, so too did they begin to pay more attention to the records and analyses of other Justices. Justices began with greater frequency to link propositions of law with the Justice who spoke for the Court, rather than saying simply that the proposition had come from the Court itself. Sometimes reference to a specific Justice was made to bolster the legal point being made. Justice Nelson argued for his view of an issue by noting: "We have, therefore, the deliberate opinions of Marshall, and Taney, and Story concurring in this construction. . . ."[41] Other times, the views of a particular Justice were explored to see which way the Court would have gone on a specific issue. Whatever the purpose, during this period more and more emphasis was placed on what individual Justices thought.

The third piece of evidence . . . that the Court was becoming more atomized was the development of ideological blocs. For most of the Court's history, a great majority of the separate writings had been penned by a handful of Justices, who nearly always wrote only for themselves. Justices Johnson, Daniel, Clifford, and Harlan were each the dominant dissenter of their times, and they usually operated alone. By the twentieth century, however, subgroups of Justices developed. These tandems, first Holmes and Brandeis, later Holmes, Stone, and Brandeis, and later still the Four Horsemen, seemed to set themselves off from the

House Cases, I feel called upon to restate the grounds of their dissent." *Id.* at 141.

39. [Footnote 186 in original] *Legal Tender Cases*, 79 U.S. (12 Wall.) 457, 575–77 (1871) (Chase, C.J., dissenting).

40. [Footnote 187 in original] United States v. Sing Tuck, 194 U.S. 161, 171 (1904) (Brewer, J., dissenting). The *Chinese Exclusion Cases*, which sprang up around the end of the nineteenth century, sparked

some of the most passionate dissents of the entire era. See, e.g., Sing Tuck, 194 U.S. at 170; Fong Yue Ting v. United States, 149 U.S. 698, 732, 744, 761 (1893).

41. [Footnote 190 in original] Woodruff v. Parham, 75 U.S. (8 Wall.) 123, 147 (1868) (Nelson, J., dissenting); see also Educational Films Corp. v. Ward, 282 U.S. 379, 398 (1931) (Sutherland, J., dissenting) (noting in detail the views of then Judge Cardozo).

rest of the Court. These blocs had a particular point to make, and they used separate opinions to repeat that point over and over. Dissents by Holmes very frequently emphasized that the Court was not authorized to act as a superlegislature. The Four Horsemen repeatedly emphasized the limited regulatory powers of state governments. The development of these blocs, which is seen most clearly in the pattern of the separate opinions, made the Court appear less as a unified whole searching for truth and more as a collection of factions, each struggling for votes.

The cumulative effect of all of these developments was to make the Court much more focused on the views of the individual Justice than it had ever been. The Legal Realist perspective, which had come to dominate the academy from which so many of these Justices had been drawn, now dominated the Court as well. Law was no longer considered to be found, rather it was made. Given this shift in conception of law, an increased focus on individual Justices was inevitable. By the end of this period, the Court had moved even further from Marshall's conception of a unified Court and closer to what Justice Holmes purportedly referred to as "nine scorpions trapped in a bottle." . . .

Acceptance of Dissent

There was a final important development in the history of the Court's opinion-delivery practices that took place during this period. To an extent never before seen, during the 1864–1940 period separate opinions became a widely-accepted part of the legal culture. Justices began to view separate opinions as having an important and legitimate role in the process of deciding cases. Four pieces of evidence demonstrate this point.

The first is the frequent reference by Justices to whether or not a relied-upon case had been decided unanimously. . . . The point of these references, presumably, was that unanimous precedents were stronger than disputed precedents. Separate opinions thus played an important and legitimate role in distinguishing between strong and weak precedents.

The second piece of evidence that separate opinions had come to be regarded as an accepted and legitimate part of the legal culture was the increased frequency with which Justices began citing them. Justices started citing both their own separate opinions and those of other Justices. . . .

·   ·   ·

The third indication that the separate opinion had become more widely accepted was the relative infrequency with which Justices offered explanations for their decisions to dissent. By the 1930s the familiar judicial language of regret, reluctance, and diffidence had all but disappeared. The absence of such explanations suggests that Justices had fully accepted the view that separate opinions had a legitimate role in the American legal system.

The fourth ... sign that separate opinions were now viewed as playing an important role was that during this period, several separate opinions were written into law, either by statute or by subsequent overruling of the opinion for the Court. A number of these elevations of dissent occurred on issues of great public concern....

. . .

E.   The Stone Court

In 1941 Harlan Fiske Stone assumed leadership of a Court whose opinion-delivery practices had been stable for well over a century. There had been no significant change in the form in which opinions were delivered since the Marshall period. The rate at which these opinions were presented unanimously had also been remarkably constant.

The Stone Court, however, saw the beginnings of a significant change. While the form used to present opinions stayed the same, the rate at which dissent was expressed increased dramatically. Two statistics capture the significance of the Stone Court shift. The first is the nonunanimity rate, which is shown in Chart A. As the Chart reveals, the nonunanimity rate was relatively constant between the beginning of the Marshall Court and the early 1930s. From the early 1930s through 1940 the rate rose slowly but steadily. Beginning in 1941, however, the rate exploded. It peaked at 86% in 1947. It has hovered around 75% ever since.

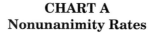

CHART A
Nonunanimity Rates

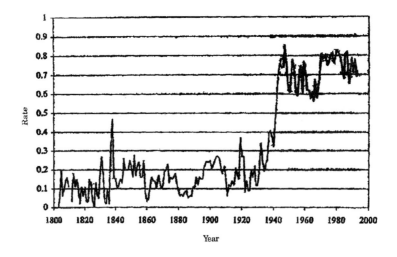

The second statistic that shows this dramatic change is the ratio of separate opinions to opinions of the Court. This statistic, which has not yet been discussed, is shown in Chart B. As was the case with the nonunanimity rate, this number was remarkably stable between 1800 and 1940.

CHART B
Total Separate Opinions Divided by Opinions
for the Court—1801–1989

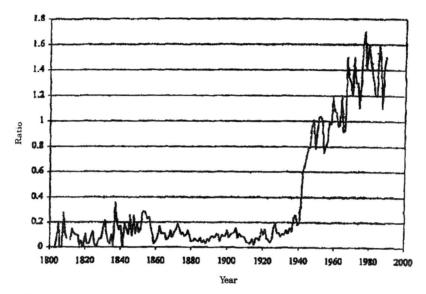

The following table gives the ratio of separate opinions to majority opinions during each of the following Chief Justice's tenure:

John Marshall	.07
Roger B. Taney	.18
Salmon P. Chase	.12
Morrison R. Waite	.08
Melville W. Fuller	.12
Edward D. White	.07
William H. Taft	.10
Charles E. Hughes	.17

As was the case with the nonunanimity rate, however, the 1941 Term was the beginning of a dramatic change. In 1941 the separate opinion to majority opinion ratio jumped from .19 to .34. The ratio continued to climb until 1948, when it topped 1.0 for the first time, meaning that the total number of dissents and concurrences in 1948 was higher than the total number of opinions for the Court. As Chart B indicates, the ratio hovered around 1.0 between 1948 and 1966 and has not dropped below that mark in any subsequent term.

This increase in the frequency of the issuance of separate opinions is a central event in the history of the Court's opinion-delivery practices. Before the shift, unanimity was the norm; afterwards, fragmentation was expected. This sharp rise has generated much commentary, some by Supreme Court Justices themselves. Most of this commentary has been abstractly normative, asking whether the increased number of separate opinions was good or bad.

At least two groups of scholars, however, have attempted to explain why the rate rose at the time it did. The first scholars to do so were Stephen Halpern and Kenneth Vines.[42] Halpern and Vines argue that the passage of the Judiciary Act of 1925, popularly known as the Judges' Bill, was the primary cause of the Stone-era increase in the nonunanimity rate. The Judges' Bill gave the Justices increased control over their docket. Halpern and Vines note a slight increase in the non-unanimity rate for the years following the passage of the Bill. They tie this increase to the greater freedom the 1925 Bill gave to the Justices, writing: "developing and articulating a coherent judicial philosophy perhaps took on a greater significance for individual Justices after the Act."

The second group of scholars to consider the question, Thomas Walker, Lee Epstein, and William Dixon, conclude that the Judges' Bill is not the primary reason for the Court's increased issuance of separate opinions.[43] This group notes that the rate at which separate opinions were issued did not begin to increase significantly until 1941, fifteen years after the Judges' Bill had taken effect. They ... argue that it was the leadership of Harlan Fiske Stone that was responsible for the increase in the dissent rate. Not only was Stone ineffective as a leader, he also was the first Chief Justice to believe that "imposed unanimity was no virtue in developing the law." Earlier Chief Justices had created a "no dissent unless absolutely necessary" tradition. Stone rejected this tradition and urged his colleagues to do the same. The Associate Justices, many of whom were new on the bench, readily agreed, and the tradition favoring unanimity was snuffed out forever.

Both the Halpern and Vines and the Walker, Epstein, and Dixon studies are helpful as short-term explanations of what happened in 1941. It is undoubtedly true that the increased control over the docket led to a proliferation of harder cases that carried with them greater opportunities for dissent. It is also true that the sharp increase would not have occurred had Chief Justice Stone not broken with his predecessors' attitude regarding the propriety of dissent.

Both of these explanations, however, are limited by a narrow temporal focus. The passage of the Judges' Bill and the elevation of Stone were important, but only as immediate causes. The Stone-era changes can be understood in another way.

Rather than being viewed as the result of specific changes made in 1925 or 1941, the Stone-era rise can also be explained by reference to the

42. [Footnote 245 in original] See Stephen Halpern & Kenneth Vines, *Institutional Disunity, The Judges' Bill and the Role of the Supreme Court*, 30 W. Pol. Q. 471 (1977).

43. [Footnote 248 in original] Thomas G. Walker et al., *On the Mysterious Demise of Consensual Norms in the United States Supreme Court*, 50 J. Pol. 361, 364–66 (1988).

historical trends discussed above. By 1941 attitudes toward separate opinions had changed dramatically. Justices no longer needed to justify a decision to write separately. The universe of cases for which dissent was appropriate had expanded dramatically. Much more attention was paid to the thinking of individual Justices, and Justices frequently used separate opinions to explain themselves. Separate opinions were cited for propositions of law and several had ultimately triumphed and become law.

Had these changes not occurred, the passage of the Judges' Bill and the elevation of Stone to Chief Justice would have had little effect on the rate at which Justices expressed dissent. These changes conditioned the attitude of the Justices, so that by the time Stone announced his attitude shift, they were more than willing to follow. Unlike previous generations of Justices, these Justices had inherited a tradition in which separate opinions were seen as having many uses.

The changes identified by Halpern and Vines and Walker, Epstein, and Dixon are therefore best understood as catalysts for change. Such changes would not have had the effect they did had the underlying attitude toward separate opinions not undergone the historical shift outlined above.

. . .

———

Robert Post,[44] *The Supreme Court Opinion as Institutional Practice: Dissent, Legal Scholarship, and Decisionmaking in the Taft Court*, 85 Minn. L. Rev. 1267 (2001)

. . .

... [T]he character of Supreme Court opinions has changed over time, and these changes track shifting notions of the role of the Supreme Court in the American legal system. In shape and configuration, opinions of the contemporary Court are demonstrably different from those of the Taft Court, in part because opinions suitable for a "court of last resort" differ from those appropriate for a "ministry of justice." But this transformation has been accompanied by a deeper shift in the implicit norms of Supreme Court decisionmaking. Justices of the Taft Court felt presumptively obligated to join Court opinions, even if they disagreed with their content, so as to preserve the influence and prestige of the Court. No such norm is apparent among modern Justices. This revolution in the practice of dissent in part reflects a shift in the Court's jurisprudential understanding of the nature of law, from a grid of fixed and certain principles designed for the settlement of disputes, to the site of ongoing processes of adjustment and statesmanship designed to

44. Alexander F. and May T. Morrison Professor of Law, School of Law (Boalt Hall), University of California, Berkeley at time of this article; currently David Boies Professor of Law at Yale University.

achieve social purposes. In part it also expresses an evolving conception of the distinction between law and politics. Norms concerning the citation of authority within Supreme Court opinions have also altered radically since the days of the Taft Court. Opinions of the modern Court routinely refer to law review articles, whereas such citations were quite rare during the 1920s. . . . [T]his shift signals an implicit alteration of the Court's understanding of its own institutional authority.

Because opinions are the primary means by which the Court intervenes to shape and affect its legal environment, opinion writing practices not only reflect the intellectual perspectives of the Justices, but also are themselves an important dimension of American law. The position of the Supreme Court is differently constituted because Court opinions are now written and designed "for the public at large, as distinguished from the particular litigants before it." Our law is actually less fixed and certain, in part because unanimous Supreme Court opinions, routine during the Taft Court, are now so unusual. We inhabit a different tension between law and politics than did contemporaries of the Taft Court, in part because in our time the very concept of a Supreme Court opinion has begun to splinter. The authority of our Supreme Court is different from that of the Taft Court because modern opinions now routinely engage in an ongoing dialogue with American legal academia. Supreme Court opinions both reflect and constitute the role of the Supreme Court itself.

. . .

I.

To appreciate the historically changing nature of Supreme Court opinions, we must first understand the institutional environment in which such opinions are produced. The Court publishes a full opinion for only a small fraction of the cases on its docket. So, for example, during the 1921 Term, which was Taft's first complete Term as Chief Justice, there were 669 new cases filed on the Court's appellate docket. Together with 343 cases that had been carried over from the 1920 Term, the Court faced an appellate docket of some 1,012 cases. Of these the Court disposed of 595 cases, in the process publishing 173 full opinions. The Court aspired to publish full opinions in about 29% of all the appellate cases of which it disposed. The remainder of [the] docket was decided primarily through short, unsigned "memorandum opinions" (almost all issued per curiam) or orders denying certiorari.

In 1921, a large proportion of the cases on the Court's appellate docket had come to the Court by way of appeal, writ of error, or certification. These comprised the Court's so-called "mandatory" jurisdiction, because the Court was obligated to decide such cases, either by full or memorandum opinion. At the beginning of the 1920s, the strain of keeping up with its mandatory jurisdiction was causing the Court to fall increasingly behind in its docket. The Court's clogged docket was in fact a major argument advanced by Taft to lobby Congress to enact the Judiciary Act of 1925, which essentially shifted the bulk of the Court's appellate jurisdiction to the discretionary writ of certiorari. The effect of the Act was "marvelous," enabling the Court sharply to diminish its backlog. Within a very few years the Court reduced the delay between the filing of a case and its argument from about a year and a half to less than six months. Indeed, in a speech before the American Law Institute, Taft joked that the 1925 Act had allowed the Court to make "such progress . . . that I think members of the bar are beginning to be a little embarrassed by the proximity of the Court to them. We are stepping on their heels."

The shift of the Court's appellate jurisdiction toward the discretionary writ of certiorari, however, produced additional and more subtle effects, including a change in the underlying significance of full court opinions. In 1912 the Court decided about 47% of its appellate cases with a full Court opinion. In 1916, partly in response to a sharp increase in the number of docketed cases and partly in response to the expansion of certiorari jurisdiction authorized by the Act of September 6, 1916, this percentage shrank to 33%, where it remained more or less constantly until the 1925 Act. The Act's reduction of the Court's mandatory jurisdiction appears to have precipitated a sharp drop in the percentage of the appellate docket that the Court decided by full opinion. The historical average of disposing of about 30% of its appellate docket by full opinion, which had persisted from 1916, shrank by almost 50% in three years. In the 1928 Term the Court wrote opinions in only 16% of its appellate cases.

The ultimate outcome of this trend is well known. In the 1998 Term, for example, the Court wrote full opinions in only 1% of the 7,043 appellate cases on its docket. It is clear, then, that the Supreme Court during the 1920s was in the process of transition from an institution that used full opinions to dispose of a significant portion of its appellate docket, to an institution that used full opinions to decide only an infinitesimal proportion of that docket. This process was sharply accelerated by the Act of 1925, which reduced the number of appellate cases that the Court was obliged to decide.

Not only does the contemporary Court compose full opinions in a smaller percentage of its total cases, but in absolute terms it writes far fewer opinions than did the Court in the 1920s. In 1924, for example, the Court handed down 231 full opinions, whereas seventy years later, in 1994, the Court handed down only 89 full opinions. This contrast reflects a relatively stable distinction between the eras. . . .

Comparisons of contemporary Supreme Court opinions with those of the past typically stress the current bureaucratization of the Court. Supreme Court Justices now can draw on the assistance of four law clerks, selected from among the very best recently graduated law students, so that, as Justice Lewis Powell has remarked, "We function as nine small, independent law firms." The resources of the Court were in fact quite different in the 1920s, when each Justice had only one law clerk, and clerks tended to be mature, professional lawyers who provided largely technical forms of assistance. What is striking about this difference, however, is that it might lead one to expect that the Taft Court would produce fewer rather than more opinions. But the contemporary Supreme Court actually publishes a far smaller number of opinions than did the Taft Court, in both absolute and proportional terms.

It is true, however, that opinions of the contemporary Court are longer and more substantial than Taft Court opinions. The average length of a full Court opinion during the 1921–1928 Terms 51 was 6.7 pages, whereas the average length of a Court opinion during the 1993–1998 Terms was 16.0 pages, more than twice as long. . . .

It is also worth observing that during the 1993–98 Terms the contemporary Court waited an average of 91.1 days after an argument before delivering a full opinion, whereas the Taft Court took one third less time, averaging only 60 days between argument and delivery of a full opinion. . . .

By far the most noteworthy distinction between full opinions of the Taft Court and those of the contemporary Court, however, concerns the relative rates of unanimity. Of the 1,554 full opinions announced by the Taft Court during the 1921–1928 Terms, 84% were unanimous; of the 507 full opinions announced by the Court during the 1993–1998 Terms, only 27% were unanimous. This remarkable contrast is illustrated in Figure 5.

FIGURE 5
Percentage of Full Opinions That Are Unanimous

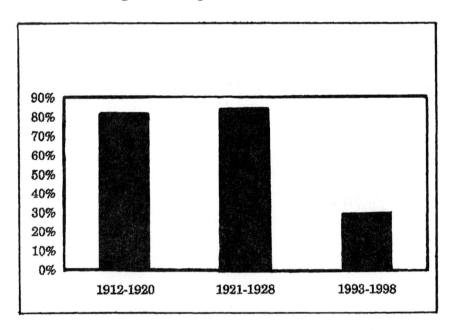

These distinctions between the Taft Court and its contemporary counterpart were sustained by complex webs of normative expectations. Norms against dissent, for example, were so prominent in the 1920s that they were explicitly embraced in Canon 19 of the American Bar Association's 1924 edition of the Canons of Judicial Ethics: "It is of high importance that judges constituting a court of last resort should use effort and self-restraint to promote solidarity of conclusion and the consequent influence of judicial decision."

There were also norms concerning the prompt dispatch of judicial business. When Justice Sanford, who joined the Court in February of 1923, began to find it increasingly hard to compose his opinions in a timely way, as measured by the Court's pace of production, he experienced his difficulty as a personal failure to meet legitimate expectations. . . .

In the 1924 Term the Court as a whole averaged 70 days from the argument of a case to the announcement of a full opinion; but in that same Term it took Sanford 121 days to produce his opinions. At the beginning of the 1925 Term, Sanford wrote Taft expressing his chagrin:

> [I] hope I can do my full share of the labor. I believe I have gotten into better methods of work, and can successfully lay aside some of my besetting meticulosity—But verily the writing of an opinion worthy of perpetual type is a task of the highest difficulty that takes every ounce of the best that one may have.

Even the length of opinions was governed by tacit norms. When Harlan Stone joined the Taft Court in March 1925, for example, he drew on his background in legal academia to draft long and intricate opinions. These were sharply criticized by the other Justices. McReynolds wrote to Stone about the latter's draft opinion in North Laramie Land Co. v. Hoffman:[45] "I agree. But I think your opinion would be much better if only half as long. There is really nothing new in the cause and simple statement of the issues with short reply to the points I think would better serve posterity. Think of the 12,000 who should read what you say here."

In response to Stone's draft opinion in Second Russian Insurance Co. v. Miller,[46] McReynolds commented,

> I think your conclusions are good. But I think you confuse the opinion by too much detail. It would be easier to understand and to me more satisfactory if you stated the substantive finding of fact below and approved this. Then discuss the essential law point and no others. My observation has been that unnecessary discussion returns to plague.

"Out of deference to the views of some of my associates," Stone was forced to revise and drastically to shorten his first attempt at an opinion

---

45. [Footnote 57 in original] 268 U.S. 276 (1925).

46. [Footnote 59 in original] 268 U.S. 552 (1925).

in May v. Henderson.[47] This discipline altered the way that Stone wrote opinions, ... Stone's opinions shrank 44% from an average of 10.8 pages during the 1924 Term to 6.1 pages in the 1926 Term....

These simple anecdotes indicate that we must view a Supreme Court opinion as a form of writing that in part takes its significance from institutional conventions and contexts that change over time. During the Taft Court, a full Supreme Court opinion was a routine method of deciding a large proportion of the Court's appellate docket. It was expeditiously produced, predominantly unanimous, and relatively short and succinct. This is one version of what one might expect from a "court of last resort" whose function was to vindicate "the specific rights of particular parties." By the 1990s, however, a full Supreme Court opinion had become the Court's way of addressing the very few cases on its docket of exceptional importance. Each opinion accordingly received fuller and more extensive attention, manifested both by its relative length and by the full complement of concurring and dissenting opinions that was likely to accompany it. Surely the influence of the Judiciary Act of 1925, which envisioned the Supreme Court as something akin to a "ministry of justice," is visible in this transformation.

To understand opinions of the Taft Court era, therefore, we must put ourselves in the frame of mind described by Justice John Hessin Clarke in his letter to Woodrow Wilson explaining his own resignation from the Court in September 1922:

> Unless you have much more intimate knowledge of the character of work which a Supreme Court judge must do than I had before going to Washington you little realize the amount of grinding, uninteresting, bone labor there is in writing more than half the cases decided by the Supreme Court. Much more than ½ the cases are of no considerable importance whether considered from the point of view of the principles or of the property involved in them, but, nevertheless, a conscientious judge writing them must master their details with the utmost care. My theory of writing opinions has always been that if clearly stated 9 cases out of 10 will decide themselves,—what the decision should be will emerge from the statement of the facts as certainly as the issues will. In this spirit I wrote always.... I protested often, but in vain, that too many trifling cases were being written, that our strength should be conserved for better things....

No one today would think to characterize "more than ½" of the Supreme Court's cases as "of no considerable importance." No one today would think to assert that "9 cases out of 10" on the Court's docket "will decide themselves." ... [T]he norms which define and sustain institutional practices of decisionmaking will likely be different in a Court whose docket contains a large proportion of "trifling cases" than in a Court like our own, where almost every opinion is momentous. And these practices of decisionmaking in turn shape the environment in

---

47. [Footnote 62 in original] 268 U.S. 111 (1925).

which all opinions are formed and written, even those that decide unambiguously important cases.

II.

A Supreme Court opinion is not merely a statement of the law. It is a written intervention, addressed to particular audiences, and designed to accomplish particular ends. The response of Justices to a changing institutional environment, or to evolving notions of law or of judicial authority, will be mediated by their conception of the nature and functions of Supreme Court opinions. . . .

At one end of the spectrum was Oliver Wendell Holmes, the oldest man on the Court and the Justice most influenced by English conceptions of the nature of opinion-writing. . . .

During the 1921–1928 Terms, Oliver Wendell Holmes announced his opinions an average of only 26.8 days after they were argued, and they were an average of only 3.4 pages long. . . . He once even complained to Stone about *McCulloch v. Maryland* that "I should not like to take so many pages to establish the obvious." Holmes knew that his aesthetic troubled his colleagues; he confessed to being "apprehensive . . . that my opinions were shorter than Brandeis inwardly approved . . . but if, as I meant to, I hit the nail on the head I am content."

Holmes's distinctive practice reflected his idiosyncratic understanding of the function and purpose of Supreme Court opinions. To Holmes an opinion expressed the "exuberance" of "personality," so that, for example, he could write of an opinion that "as originally written it had a tiny pair of testicles—but the scruples of my brethren have caused their removal and it sings in a very soft voice now." Holmes characteristically referred to opinions in such metaphors of personal artistic expression. He believed that "an opinion should" not "be like an essay with footnotes, but rather should be quasi an oral utterance." Holmes commented to his colleague Sanford that *"[n]on obstat* the effective and powerful example of Brandeis to the contrary, I don't think opinions should be written in the form of essays with notes. They are theoretically spoken." For Holmes the point of an opinion was to solve the legal puzzle, the "speculative twister," of a case by application of "the fundamentals of legal theory."

For Holmes's colleagues on the Court, however, opinions were conceived very differently. Willis Van Devanter, for example, did not conceptualize court opinions as the personal expression of a Justice, but instead as the institutional response of a Court whose obligation it was clearly and decisively to provide guidance to parties and to the legal system. He thus criticized Holmes's opinions because they "do not give an adequate portrayal of the case in hand or of the grounds of the decision," and he pointed with pride at the ability of his own opinions to provide convincing and practical guidance to the parties and to the public about disputed issues of law:

There are some who merely count the number of opinions regardless of their substance or the direction in which they go. When one does work on that line he can do what superficially seems a volume, and then the other federal courts and the state courts may grope as best they can in an effort to find out what was intended. My ideas and inclinations are not in that direction. It leads to uncertainty and confusion, makes for instability and in the long run results in tremendous waste. The number of petitions for rehearing during the term has been unusually large, but in my cases only one was presented.

The concision and oral quality of Holmes's opinions were inconsistent with these objectives. So, for example, ... Taft ... believed that despite Holmes's "genius for giving a certain degree of piquancy and character to his opinions by sententious phrases," his opinions lose "strength and value by his disposition to cut down."

> The chief duty in a court of last resort is not to dispose of the case, but it is sufficiently to elaborate the principles, the importance of which justify the bringing of the case here at all, to make the discussion of those principles and the conclusion reached useful to the country and to the Bar in clarifying doubtful questions of constitutional and fundamental law. In the old days, this Court, especially in the days of Harlan, Peckham and others, wrote too long opinions, so that the Bar grew tired. On the other hand, I think the Bar is not particularly well pleased with too short opinions, for the good reason that I have referred to above.

. . .

If we carefully attend to discussion among the Taft Court Justices, we can discern (at least) three distinct functions for Supreme Court opinions to which they implicitly appeal. First, the function of an opinion was to reflect the collective judgment of the Justices who joined it. To fulfill this function, an opinion had to satisfy an internal audience; it had to fulfill the expectations of as many Justices as were necessary to acquire the status of an institutional judgment of the Court....

Fidelity to the collective views of the Justices who joined an opinion meant not merely getting those views right, it also meant not materially exceeding them. Stone seems to have been a particular offender in this regard. Taft remarked that

> [Stone] has great difficulty in getting his opinions through, because he is quite disposed to be discursive and to write opinions as if he were writing an editorial or a comment for a legal law journal, covering as much as he can upon a general subject and thus expressing opinions that have not been thought out by the whole Court.... I am afraid he is disposed to interject a general disquisition looking toward an embarrassing recurrence on his part to some other principle that has been questioned or denied by the Court when that principle was plainly before us. Without impeaching at all

his good faith in matters of that sort, we find we have to watch closely the language he uses.

Taft's observation is amply confirmed by the correspondence accompanying Stone's draft opinions.... In response to Stone's opinion in Van Oster v. Kansas,[48] Van Devanter commented, "You have written discursively and in a vein much like that of a student writing for a law journal." Pierce Butler would agree to join Stone's *Van Oster* opinion only if Stone eliminated a paragraph containing a general statement of the law.

The extant records of the Taft Court reveal a surprisingly healthy dialogue and exchange as authors struggled to craft their opinions to express the specific views of the Justices who joined them. So, for example, when in the draft of his opinion in Risty v. Chicago, Rock Island & Pacific Railway Co.[49] Stone observed that federal courts "will ordinarily follow the decisions of state courts as to the interpretation of a state statute," Holmes immediately wrote back that "I think they ought always to follow state decisions on interpretation of state statutes. I should pay no attention to wobbly phrases in that matter." Stone omitted the adverb.

· · ·

If the Justices could sometimes be demanding in their expectations of an opinion, an opinion writer could sometimes alter the views of his colleagues. In McCarthy v. Arndstein,[50] for example, an important decision involving the question of whether Fifth Amendment protections against self-incrimination extended to the financial papers of a petitioner in bankruptcy, the vote of the Conference was to reverse and the case was assigned to Brandeis. After study, Brandeis "concluded that the entry should be judgment reaffirmed," and he accordingly circulated an opinion reaching a conclusion contrary to the conference. His proposed opinion carried a unanimous Court....

A second function served by Supreme Court opinions was justly to decide a particular case in a manner that satisfied litigants that the Court had fairly and rationally "considered arguments of counsel" and had adjudicated among them. The parties to a case thus constituted a relevant audience for an opinion. There was relatively little exchange among the Taft Court Justices with regard to this function, in part because its significance was simply taken for granted. From time immemorial an essential judicial function had been to offer judgment between contestants so as to preserve the peace.

Occasionally, however, the Justices would refer to their obligations to the parties. Thus Taft once suggested changes to a draft Holmes opinion (which the latter accepted) on the grounds that the draft "leaves

48. [Footnote 99 in original] 272 U.S. 465 (1926).

49. [Footnote 104 in original] 270 U.S. 378 (1926).

50. [Footnote 110 in original] 266 U.S. 34 (1924).

our decision less positive than it should be and is. You'll have a petition for rehearing and create an impression of doubt on our part which does not conduce to a 'once for all' decision." When Taft sought to praise Brandeis's opinion in United States ex rel. Bilokumsky v. Tod,[51] which upheld the deportation of an alien because of his possession of seditious literature, he wrote that "certainly [Walter] Nelles [the alien's lawyer] ought to be satisfied that his shadowy contentions have had close consideration and have been fully and overwhelmingly answered."

A third function of a Supreme Court opinion was "sufficiently to elaborate the principles, the importance of which justify the bringing of the case here at all, to make the discussion of those principles and the conclusion reached useful to the country and to the Bar in clarifying doubtful questions of constitutional and fundamental law." From the perspective of this function, the audience for a Supreme Court opinion was the general legal public, which included state courts and lower federal courts, the legal profession, Congress and state legislators. The purpose of an opinion was to clarify standards of federal law so as to provide guidance for those who needed to know the law.

... Taft ... for example, ... praised Brandeis's opinion in Great Northern Railway Co. v. Merchants' Elevator Co.[52] because "it will inform the courts and the profession and your ignorant colleagues. It will be a leading case showing what this Court is for." ...

The Judiciary Act of 1925, of course, emphasized this function of Supreme Court opinions. As Taft said in promoting the Act, "The real work of the Supreme Court has to do is for the public at large, as distinguished from the particular litigants before it." By empowering the Court to choose its own jurisdiction, the Act shifted the Court's emphasis away from opinions addressed to private litigants, and toward opinions addressed to those concerned with the development of American law. Justices like Taft and Van Devanter, however, seldom perceived a conflict between these two audiences. They believed that the Court could best offer guidance to the legal public by enunciating the same kind of stable and definite legal principles as it would announce to litigants in the resolution of a case. In their view, the 1925 Act merely affected the Court's control over its own docket; it did not alter the terms on which the Court would construct its opinions.

But in fact they were wrong. Fashioning an opinion justly to resolve a dispute between parties is closely related to conceiving an opinion as a routine method of disposing of a large mandatory docket. It is rooted in the conception of the Supreme Court as a tribunal of last resort that predominated during the first 150 years of the Court's existence. Crafting an opinion in order to influence the administration and development of the law, by contrast, requires reaching out beyond particular parties and addressing the entire community of legal actors. This alters the stakes of an opinion. It also transforms the position of the Court. If the

---

51. [Footnote 118 in original] 263 U.S. 149 (1923).

52. [Footnote 122 in original] 259 U.S. 285 (1922).

function of an opinion is to resolve disputes between parties, the Court can rest on its traditional authority as a tribunal deemed necessary to terminate strife and avoid violence. But to the extent that an opinion is addressed to the general legal public, this institutional function competes with the Court's character as a lawgiver, as an originator of law, somewhat in the fashion of a "ministry of justice." And this change may oblige an opinion to justify the authority of the Court in a manner that is different from what would be necessary were an opinion simply the means of resolving disputes between private parties.

The sharp contrast between the opinion writing practices of the Taft Court and those of the modern Court no doubt reflects these more subtle transformations. Of course such profound changes are driven by many different causes, not merely (or even especially) by the Judiciary Act of 1925. The Act, however, permanently and pervasively altered the institutional ecology of Supreme Court opinions, and this changed organizational environment in turn shaped the impact of the many influences that caused the decisionmaking practices of the Taft Court to evolve into those of the contemporary Court. . . .

III.

[Consider] how sharply unanimity rates have fallen between the Taft Court and the 1990s. In the 1921–1928 Terms, 84% of the Court's opinions were unanimous; by contrast, only 27% of the Court's opinions were unanimous during the 1993–1998 Terms. It has justly been observed that this "increase in the frequency of the issuance of separate opinions is a central event in the history of the Court's opinion-delivery practices."

. . .

. . . [Taft] wrote to Clarke,

I don't approve of dissents generally, for I think that in many cases, where I differ from the majority, it is more important to stand by the Court and give its judgment weight than merely to record my individual dissent where it is better to have the law certain than to have it settled either way.

He believed that "most dissents elaborated, are a form of egotism. They don't do any good, and only weaken the prestige of the Court. It is much more important what the Court thinks than what any one thinks." Taft strongly counseled Harding against nominating New York Court of Appeals Judge Cuthbert Pound to replace Mahlon Pitney on the Court, because

[Pound] has a marked trait as a Judge that would make him of very doubtful use on our Bench. He is a great dissenter. He was a professor of Law in Cornell for five or ten years, and he evidently thinks it is more important that he should ventilate his individual views than that the Court should be consistent and by team work should give solidarity and punch to what it decides. We have one dissenter on the Bench, and often two. It would not be well, it seems to me, to introduce a third.

... [Taft] work[ed] hard to build consensus and avoid dissents. He believed that an important task of the Chief Justice was "to promote teamwork by the Court so as to give weight and solidarity to its opinions." He successfully diminished dissension in such cases in United Mine Workers v. Coronado,[53] Hill v. Wallace,[54] Railroad Commission of California v. Southern Pacific Co.,[55] Opelika v. Opelika Sewer,[56] and FTC v. Claire Furnace Co.[57] He was willing to go to extraordinary lengths to modify his own opinions to reach out to others.... [writing to his colleagues in respect of one case:]

> I worked all summer on the constitutional part of the opinion, ... and satisfied myself completely by an examination of the briefs and the authorities on the subject, and I parted with it as a child that I was glad to father, if it needed any fathering, and it is a real sacrifice of my personal preference. But it is the duty of us all to control our personal preferences to the main object of the Court.

... Taft's interventions were responsible for marginal changes along the edges of a practice of unanimity that existed before Taft and that would persist after him....

. . .

There is some internal evidence ... that during the first half of the 1920s dissent was suppressed within the Court because of the need to fend off external attacks.... In 1922 Robert La Follette advocated that Congress be able to overturn Supreme Court decisions declaring Acts of Congress unconstitutional. In 1923 Senator William E. Borah proposed legislation that would require the concurrence of at least seven members of the Court in any decision invalidating an act of Congress. Matters came to a head when La Follette included his amendment as a plank in his Progressive Party platform during the 1924 presidential campaign. Contemporary antagonists of the Court, like Jackson Harvey Ralston, the General Counsel of the AFL, seized upon dissents as evidence of the Court's illegitimate usurpation of power:

> To show ... even more clearly the doubtful exercise of power by the Supreme Court ... we need but point to the repeated dissents on the part of a minority continually made against the assumption that the court knew more of the necessities of the times than the legislature. Surely if the majority had based their action upon definitely understood constitutional principles, no differences of moment need have arisen.

53. [Footnote 143 in original] 259 U.S. 344 (1922)....

54. [Footnote 144 in original] 258 U.S. 44 (1922)....

55. [Footnote 145 in original] 264 U.S. 331 (1924)....

56. [Footnote 146 in original]265 U.S. 215 (1924)....

57. [Footnote 147 in original] 274 U.S. 160 (1927)....

The point was not lost in the Court. Taft wrote a friend that La Follette "is probably framing an attack upon the Supreme Court's infamous nullification of valuable laws demanded by the people. He could find a good deal of material in Brandeis's dissenting opinions." By July of 1924 Brandeis could remark to Frankfurter that "the drive against the Court has tended" to reduce dissents.

> The whole policy is to suppress dissents, that is the one positive result of Borah 7 to 2 business, to suppress dissent so as not to make it 7 to 2. Holmes, for instance, is always in doubt whether to express his dissent, once he's "had his say" on a given subject & he's had his say on almost everything. You may look for fewer dissents. That's Van Devanter's particularly strong lobbying with the members individually, to have them suppress their dissents. He is perhaps closest with Butler, whom he treats as an elder brother, & while Butler is not easy to move, the prudential arguments of Van D. as to what is "good—or bad—for the Court" are weighty with him & with all of them.

> ... After La Follette's defeat, however, the Court could breathe a sigh of relief, because "the controversy over judicial review subsided for several years after the 1924 election." With external pressure diminished, unanimity rates were free to drop during the second half of the decade.

· · ·

The slide in unanimity rates was also encouraged by Taft's own failing health. In February 1924 Taft suffered severe palpitations of the heart that prevented him from attending Woodrow Wilson's funeral as an honorary pallbearer. He resolved "to try to do less work," ... In June 1926 Taft suffered yet another and far more disabling heart attack .... He began the 1926 Term hesitantly, and he never again was able to assume command of the Court with the same vigorous assurance as previously....

It seems likely that the Court's declining unanimity rates at the end of the 1920s in part reflects Taft's failing ability energetically and proactively to intervene into the Court's deliberations so as to achieve consensus.... By the end of his Chief Justiceship, Taft was merely hanging on. "I am older and slower and less acute and more confused. However, as long as things continue as they are, and I am able to answer in my place, I must stay on the Court in order to prevent the Bolsheviki from getting control."

In this vacuum of leadership, the Court slid toward factionalism. A month before his disabling stroke, Taft wrote his brother that "of course we have a dissenting minority of three in the Court. I think we can hold our six to steady the Court. Brandeis is of course hopeless, as Holmes is, and as Stone is." ...

· · ·

... [Y]et, ... 74% of the Court's opinions in the 1929 Term were unanimous. Although division and tension within the Court was high, it nevertheless decided cases with a degree of unanimity that would be quite unimaginable today. It is clear, therefore, that fluctuations in the dissent rate during the 1920s, although responsive to many factors, including changes in external circumstances, Court personnel, and Taft's own leadership, nevertheless occurred within boundaries that mark the Taft Court as genuinely different from the contemporary Court. The question is why this might be so.

One possibility is that the Court's docket during the 1920s was simply less divisive than today. Although this explanation threatens to collapse into tautology, since the question of what counts as divisiveness is what we are seeking to illuminate, there is nevertheless some plausibility in contrasting the contemporary Court, which publishes a relatively small number of opinions in highly-selected, controversial, and significant cases, with the Taft Court, which published many more opinions in routine and "trifling" cases. This hypothesis is sometimes phrased in terms of the Judiciary Act of 1925, which shifted the Court's docket away from trivial cases forced on the Court by its mandatory jurisdiction and toward the more important but controversial cases that could be chosen through certiorari.

· · ·

... In the 1921 Term, 19% of the Court's opinions were issued in cases that came to the Court through the discretionary writ of certiorari. By the 1928 Term this proportion had almost tripled, so that 55% of the Court's opinions were issued in such cases. Yet if unanimity rates are disaggregated by jurisdiction, the results do not show any apparent connection between the Court's jurisdiction and unanimous opinions.

In fact ... during the 1921–1928 Terms, 83% of the opinions written in cases reaching the Court through its mandatory jurisdiction were decided unanimously, whereas 87% of the opinions written in cases that reached the Court through the discretionary writ of certiorari were unanimous.

· · ·

This does not suggest that the Court's ability to achieve unanimity was substantially undermined by its capacity to select for more "controversial" cases through the exercise of certiorari jurisdiction.... [T]he Court's rates of unanimity did not begin their free-fall until the mid–1930s. Thus "changes in the Court's ratio of obligatory to discretionary cases do not coincide with the Justices' patterns of increasing dissent activity." ...

· · ·

[Post examined differences "between unanimity in published opinions and unanimity in conference voting."] Of the 1028 conference cases that were ultimately decided unanimously by a published opinion of the

Court, 58% were also unanimous in conference, 30% required a switch in vote in order to obtain ultimate unanimity, and a further 12% required Justices to overcome uncertainty in order to achieve unanimity. Within the complete set of 1200 conference cases the unanimity rate, as measured by a unanimous vote at conference, was only 50%. The unanimity rate for the published opinions of the conference cases was by contrast 86%. This establishes that it was common practice during the Taft Court for Justices to change their votes between conference and the publication of an opinion. In the complete set of 1200 published conference opinions, a Justice changed his vote to join the Court opinion 680 times. Like Taft, they were willing to "make the sign of the scissors" in private, but reluctant to do so "to the public."

. . .

. . . [T]he rate of unanimity in conference during the Taft Court (50%) was almost double that achieved now by the Court in its published opinions (27%). This suggests that the Court's spontaneous view of the substantive issues raised by its docket was in fact more cohesive in the 1920s than at present. If the Court's voting at conference is disaggregated by jurisdiction, however, it is clear that this cohesiveness was strained by the Judiciary Act of 1925. . . . [A]lthough there is virtually no difference in the rate of unanimity for the published opinions of the conference set when cases reaching the Court through its mandatory and discretionary jurisdictions are compared—84% and 87%, respectively—at conference the unanimity rate for the former was 55%, while it was only 41% for the latter.

. . .

This difference suggests that spontaneous unanimity was indeed harder to achieve in the more controversial cases selected through certiorari than in the more routine, "trifling" cases that the Court had been obliged to hear prior to 1925 because of its mandatory jurisdiction. But the fact that at conference the Court was able reach unanimity on 41% of even these controversial cases suggests that the Court's ideological cohesion was greater in the 1920s than today. There are no doubt many factors that could contribute to this. We might consider, for example, the massive increase of the reach and significance of federal law, which both augments the occasions for dissensus and magnifies the stakes in particular cases. Or we might ponder the assault on the cohesiveness of legal reasoning created by "American Legal Realism" that David M. O'Brien has suggested "made consensus more difficult." . . . [F]or our purposes it is sufficient to note that, at least when measured by conference voting in the more difficult cases arising from discretionary certiorari jurisdiction, members of the Taft Court seem to have had spontaneous reservoirs of ideological coherence apparently unavailable to their modern counterparts.

. . . [T]he huge discrepancy between the level of unanimity in conference and the level of unanimity in published opinions . . . clearly reflects an institutional aversion to dissent.... This norm of agreement is expressed in case after case in the extant record of circulated opinions. Justice Butler, for example, responded to a Stone opinion with a short disquisition on the subject:

> I voted to reverse. While this sustains your conclusion to affirm, I still think a reversal would be better. But I shall in silence acquiesce. Dissents seldom aid us in the right development or statement of the law. They often do harm. For myself I say: "Lead us not unto Temptation."

To Holmes, Butler announced, "I voted the other way & remain unconvinced, but dissenting clamor does not often appeal to me as useful. I shall acquiesce." ...

Brandeis concurred in an opinion of Stone, noting that "I think this is woefully wrong, but do not expect to dissent." In response to the draft of a Holmes opinion, Brandeis remarked, "I think the question was one for a jury—but the case is of a class in which one may properly 'shut up.'" To the draft of another unanimous Stone opinion, Holmes commented, "I incline the other way. If Brandeis who I believe voted as I did writes, ... probably I shall concur with him. If he is silent, I probably shall ... shut up." Sutherland wrote to Brandeis, "I thought otherwise, but shall probably acquiesce." To the draft of a unanimous Stone opinion, Sutherland replied, "I had a different view, and shall withhold final determination in order to see what the other stubborn members have to say." ...

Sanford replied to the draft of a unanimous Holmes opinion with the comment, "I regret that I cannot see my way clear to agree.... I shall probably not dissent, unless some one else does so." To the draft of another opinion, he answered, "I regret that I cannot concur but shall not dissent." ... McKenna, who ... was the most inclined of any Justice to alter his conference vote, turned concession into a virtual art form:

> "I voted the other way but my effort is to please so I will accede."

> "Plausible if not sound. And being alone there seems no reason for making a fuss." ...

What is fascinating about these various communications is that they do not so much express a "norm of consensus," as a norm of acquiescence. The Justices preserve their differences, but they each assume that in the absence of strong reasons, these differences should be put aside so that the Court can present a united front to the public, an image of unity expected to produce "the impact of monolithic solidarity on which the authority of a bench of judges so largely depends." ... [T]he Court may actually have striven harder to preserve unanimity as internal rates of dissensus at Conference increased. It is clear that this norm of acquiescence is responsible for sustaining the extraordinarily high rates of unanimity that characterize the published opinions of the Taft Court, rates that were 20 to 40 percentage points higher than unanimity in conference voting.

It is useful to begin our analysis of this phenomenon by considering the significance of the norm of acquiescence for the three distinct functions of Supreme Court opinions that we identified in Part II. With respect to the function of representing the institutional judgment of the Court, the norm of acquiescence facilitated the achievement of institutional unity. Justices must have believed that, in the absence of what Van Devanter called "strong conviction," it was their institutional responsibility to join an opinion for the Court. The norm of acquiescence also established among the Justices expectations of reciprocity, or, in McKenna's words, of "amiability." There was thus a price to be paid for failing to fulfill the responsibility of joining Court opinions.

Brandeis thus remarked to Frankfurter that "there is a limit to the frequency with which you can [dissent], without exasperating men; . . . You may have a very important case of your own as to which you do not want to antagonize on a less important case etc. etc." He noted that the "great difficulty of all group action . . . is when & what concessions to make. Can't always dissent—may have dissented much just then." He once responded to Taft's invitation to join a separate opinion, "I agree with your criticism of the . . . opinion. You will recall that I voted the other way; and the opinion has not removed my difficulties. . . . But I have differed from the Court recently in three expressed dissents and concluded that, in this case, I had better 'shut up,' as in Junior days."

It is not necessary to establish a norm of acquiescence in order to sustain amicable working relationships among members of the Court. The norm instead offers a way for individual Justices to negotiate potential conflicts between their own intellectual perspectives and their perceived obligation to contribute to "solidarity of conclusion and the consequent influence of judicial decision." The norm acquires its significance from the strength of this obligation. But the nature and force of this obligation depends upon the importance of the impact of Supreme Court opinions on persons outside the Court. To historically situate the norm of acquiescence, therefore, we must analyze it in connection to the outward-looking functions of Supreme Court opinions. We must focus on the relationship between the norm and the ability of Supreme Court opinions to resolve disputes between parties or to affect the future growth and administration of the law.

These two functions stand in very different relation to the norm of acquiescence. Although dissent can influence the attitude of litigants to the resolution of their case, it cannot modify the binding and dispositive force of the Court's judgment on the parties before it. That judgment, however, has no such dispositive force on the general legal public, which is therefore much more likely to be affected by a strong dissent. In addition, the trade-off between institutional solidarity and individual belief is quite different if all that is at stake in a Supreme Court opinion is the proper adjudication of a dispute between particular parties, than if the future development of the legal system also hangs in the balance.

These considerations suggest that the concept of the Supreme Court opinion at the core of the Judiciary Act of 1925 was singularly calculated to exert pressure on the norm of acquiescence. As the Court's opinions began to modulate from the relatively routinized decisions of a court of last resort to interventions designed to shape the progress of American law, it is no wonder that a norm which developed and flourished in the first context began to falter in the second. The collapse of unanimity and the changing nature of Supreme Court opinions are thus intimately connected.

The point requires careful formulation, however, because courts resolve disputes between parties by articulating legal principles, and these principles both decide specific cases and also become precedents for the resolution of future cases. The audience for all court opinions, therefore, hovers ambiguously between particular parties and the general legal public. The relationship between these two audiences very much depends upon a jurisprudential account of how law works to accomplish its ends. If judicial opinions are understood to influence the legal system through the enunciation of definite and stable principles, upon which legal actors can rely, there is essentially no distinction between opinions addressed to the general legal public and opinions addressed to the parties to a particular case. The purpose of an opinion is to announce certain and fixed legal standards that will simultaneously discharge the Court's obligation to both audiences.

This jurisprudential understanding of law casts potential dissenters into an exceedingly awkward position. Whether a potential dissenter looks to the effect of his dissent on the parties to the case, or to its effect on the future evolution of the law, dissent potentially undermines the certainty and confidence which is a principal virtue of judicial decision-making. And if *stare decisis* functions, as it should, to fix and establish a Court's opinion as regnant law, dissent seems merely ineffectual. As Edward White put it, "The only purpose which an elaborate dissent can accomplish, if any, is to weaken the effect of the opinion of the majority, and thus engender want of confidence in the conclusions of courts of last resort." A potential dissenter is thus relegated to registering his conscientious personal difference from the judgment of an opinion. That is why, in its effort to discourage dissent on courts "of last resort," Canon 19 of the ABA's 1924 Canons of Judicial Ethics focused primarily on the exhortation that a judge not "yield to pride of opinion or value more highly his individual reputation than that of the court to which he should be loyal. Except in cases of conscientious difference of opinion on fundamental principle, dissenting opinions should be discouraged in courts of last resort."

The norm of acquiescence that is visible in the Taft Court fits comfortably with this jurisprudential perspective. If the institutional justification for dissent is unclear; if dissent carries potentially large deleterious effects for the establishment of law, both with respect to the parties and to the legal public; if the benefits to a dissenter are chiefly personal; then a norm of acquiescence offers a face-saving way for a dissenter to mediate between private intellectual disagreement and participation in the common goal of creating effective law.

It should come as no surprise, therefore, that those who opposed judicial dissent at the turn of the century typically appealed to a jurisprudential account of law that stressed fixity and finality.

. . .

... Brandeis struggled to articulate a conception of dissent that undercut the jurisprudential foundations of the norm. Brandeis sought to distinguish circumstances in which judicial finality was a significant jurisprudential virtue from those in which it was not. "In ordinary cases," he said to Frankfurter in 1923, "there is a good deal to be said for not having dissents."

> You want certainty & definiteness & it doesn't matter terribly how you decide, so long as it is settled. But in these constitutional cases, since what is done is what you call statesmanship, nothing is ever settled—unless statesmanship is settled & at an end.

This is an unusually suggestive passage, because it explicitly ties the norm of acquiescence to an account of how law achieves its purposes, and it offers a discriminating explanation of the difference between ordinary law, where the value of finality is highly consequential, and constitutional law, where it is not. Brandeis's explanation of the diminished importance of finality in constitutional law does not turn on the primacy of constitutional justice, but rather on the fact that constitutional law is a form of "statesmanship," and statesmanship requires continuous flexibility and growth. It is no act of statesmanship to announce a rule and expect it, in the words of the Albany Law Journal, to "remain settled forever."

Brandeis advanced an image of constitutional law as requiring the continuous "capacity of adaptation to a changing world." In a draft dissent he made this point explicitly: "Our Constitution is not a straitjacket. It is a living organism. As such it is capable of growth.... Because our Constitution possesses the capacity of adaptation, it has endured as the fundamental law of an ever developing people." Fittingly enough, Taft, whose view of dissent was very different from that of Brandeis, insisted that this passage be omitted before he would join Brandeis's dissent. Taft believed that the "Constitution was intended, its very purpose was, to prevent experimentation with the fundamental rights of the individual." For Taft the fundamental point of constitutional law was precisely to fix these rights and to render them "settled."

The jurisprudential difference between Brandeis and Taft has important consequences for the norm of acquiescence. If the law is regarded as continuously and properly evolving, the costs of acquiescence increase, because assent to a mistaken opinion affects the future development of the law. So far from merely expressing conscientious personal disagreement, dissent constitutes, in the famous words of Charles Evans Hughes, "an appeal to the brooding spirit of the law, to the intelligence of a future day, when a later decision may possibly correct the error into which the dissenting judge believes the court to have been betrayed."

If the virtue of law is conceived to lie in its flexibility and adaptability, rather than in its stability and firmness, a potential dissenter must weigh the "dissatisfaction" that a dissent may engender against his obligation to future generations wisely to shape the development of the law. Once the institutional structure of the Court decisively oriented its opinions toward the development of the law and its reception by the general legal public, and once members of the Court began to regard "growth" as "the life of the law," the norm of acquiescence was undermined from within. By the end of the 1940s, ... the norm of acquiescence had utterly collapsed[;] a Justice like William O. Douglas, perhaps the most consummate dissenter in the history of the Court, could affirm that "philosophers of the democratic faith will rejoice in the uncertainty of the law and find strength and glory in it." And it is undoubtedly the case that the virtual disappearance of unanimous Court opinions, which is in part a consequence of this very jurisprudential view of the law, helped in turn to produce a law that was in fact more uncertain and labile.

IV.

A major justification for the norm of acquiescence was the need to preserve the authority of the Court. When progressives in the 1920s attacked judicial review, they pointed to dissent as evidence that the Court's decisions were not compelled by legal necessity and that they therefore represented a form of political judgment best left to "the legislature." At issue in this form of attack, as Taft rightly understood, was "the prestige of the Court," which derived from its prerogative to pronounce law. Unanimity preserved the appearance of legal compulsion, which is why Canon 19 recited that "solidarity of conclusion" was prerequisite to preserve the "influence of judicial decision." It was precisely this sense of "influence" that Chief Justice Warren sought to summon thirty years later when he struggled to make *Brown v. Board of Education* into a unanimous decision.

The norm of acquiescence aspired to achieve the "influence" of unanimity for as many of the Court's decisions as was possible. The norm was thus justified not only by a particular account of law, but also by the effort to maintain the institutional authority of the Court. That is why figures like Taft, who fervently believed in the institutional primacy of the Court, were so infuriated by dissent. . . .

. . .

By the 1940s, after the constitutional crises of the New Deal focused national attention on democratic control of the Court, there were Justices who were prepared to argue that democracy itself justified the practice of addressing dissents to the general public. William O. Douglas explicitly conceptualized dissent as a form of political speech, so that a judge's right and obligation to dissent was like the freedom of speech exercised by any citizen:

> Disagreement among judges is as true to the character of democracy as freedom of speech itself. . . .

.   .   .

> The truth is that the law is the highest form of compromise between competing interests; it is a substitute for force and violence. . . . It is the product of attempted reconciliation between the many diverse groups in a society. The reconciliation is not entirely a legislative function. The judiciary is also inescapably involved. When judges do not agree, it is a sign that they are dealing with problems on which society itself is divided. It is the democratic way to express dissident views. Judges are to be honored rather than criticized for following that tradition, for proclaiming their articles of faith so that all may read.

Because "no . . . group of men has a monopoly on truth," Douglas conceives Justices of the Court as "proclaiming their articles of faith," rather than as participating in the institutional and authoritative pronouncement of the law. The distinction between law and politics is effaced, as is any account of the distinct institutional authority of the Court. From this perspective it is only a short step to conceive dissent as, in the words of Justice Brennan, a contribution "to the marketplace of competing ideas." There is no doubt that some such transformation has contributed to the transformation of the Taft Court's norm of acquiescence into an ethic "of individual expression." To the extent that the norm of acquiescence was understood to uphold the Court's prestige as the unique voice of the law, the collapse of the norm can illuminate the shifting boundary between law and politics.

.   .   .

Although LaFollette's frontal assault on judicial review might be understood as a claim that constitutional meanings were to be democratically determined, his efforts did not strike a responsive chord within the Taft Court. What may be described as the Court's liberal wing was not tempted to deny the distinction between law and politics. The problem from their perspective was not that there was no law for the Court to apply, but that the Court was applying the law incorrectly. The audience for their dissent was thus typically those who were able expertly and accurately to comprehend the requirements of the law. At least that is how Stone framed the question in 1942, when he observed that the appeal of "a considered and well stated dissent . . . can properly be only to scholarship, history and reason, and if the business of judging is an intellectual process, as we are entitled to believe that it is, it must be capable of withstanding and surviving these critical tests."

Unlike Douglas, who postulated the general public as the audience for dissent, Stone imagined dissent as addressed to those in a position to evaluate the technical, "critical" work of judging, which is not reducible to mere political will. . . . Stone looked . . . toward the institution of legal "scholarship."

The Court's struggle to establish a relationship with legal scholarship during the 1920s nicely illuminates the tensions underlying the Court's claim of authority to define federal law. If a dissent addressed over the head of the Court to the general public called into question the Court's institutional prerogatives by blurring the boundary between law and politics, a dissent addressed over the head of the Court to the legal academy called into question the Court's unique competence to articulate law. Struggle over this issue is apparent not only in the willingness of dissenters to appeal to the scholarly literature of the legal academy, but in the Court's intolerance of such citations in its own majority opinions. . . .

We can interpret the contemporary Court's routine citation to law review articles as both expressing and sustaining the view that judicial decisions have the responsibility of arranging human affairs in a manner designed to fulfill the purposes of the law. To the extent that these purposes have become self-conscious, the authority of the courts has in part come to depend upon their competence in achieving legal objectives, and not merely upon judicial fidelity to the internal demands of a self-enclosed system of legal precedents. The struggle in the Taft Court over the citation of legal scholarship illuminates the beginnings of this profound shift.

V.

The decisionmaking practices of the Court can thus tell us a good deal about how the Court regards important but otherwise implicit tensions within the law. The nature of these practices sheds light, for example, on the question of whether the virtue of law is conceived to lie in its finality or in its capacity to serve social purposes, or whether law is seen as distinct from politics or as a product of popular will, or whether the authority of the Supreme Court is understood as lying in its raw power to declare law or in its capacity competently to achieve legal objectives.

Of course these tensions are ultimately irresolvable. No sane view of law could entirely abandon either the value of certainty or that of adaptability; the question is instead how a court will mediate the perennial tension between these two equally indispensable ideals. The same can be said of the boundary between law and politics. It is as implausible to draw an impermeable barrier between law and popular will, as it is to collapse law entirely into the domain of popular contestation. Similarly, the authority of the Court can wholly subsist neither in its control over the disposition of state legal power nor in its competence to serve legal purposes. The Court's actual legitimacy must always rest somewhere between these two extreme versions of its institutional position.

The demonstrable differences between the decisionmaking practices of the Taft Court and those of the contemporary Court indicate that the Court has substantially altered its approach to these questions from that which it pursued in the 1920s. The direction of the change roughly corresponds to the transition from what Philippe Nonet and Philip Selznick have called "autonomous" law to what they have termed "responsive law." In a system of "autonomous law," the "consolidation and defense of institutional autonomy are the central preoccupation of legal officials," who accordingly take pains to draw "a sharp line between legislative and judicial functions." The task of the judiciary is to maintain fidelity to a system of certain and definite rules, even at the cost of "the adaptation of law to social facts."By emphasizing procedural regularity above all else, autonomous law stresses "authority and obedience" to the positive institutional authority of courts.

"Responsive law," by contrast, conceives the authority of legal institutions to lie in their ability competently to achieve the law's purposes. This requires the law to assume an "openness and flexibility" that is incompatible with strict rule-bound decisionmaking. "Legal advocacy takes on a political dimension," and it accordingly becomes "more difficult to distinguish legal analysis from policy analysis, legal rationality from other forms of systematic decisionmaking." Rulemaking recedes in importance, as judicial legitimacy comes to depend upon "a union of legal authority and political will."

The norm of acquiescence reflected and sustained a world in which the authority of the Court depended upon its capacity to maintain a domain of fixed and certain rules, a domain rigorously separated from the legislative realm of political will. The Court's refusal to cite law review articles reflected and sustained a world in which the authority of the Court depended upon its fidelity to a self-referential system of precedent. But as American law increasingly began to submit to what Nonet and Selznick call "the sovereignty of purpose," which is to say that as the legitimacy of our legal system came increasingly to be measured by its ability to achieve social ends, neither the norm of acquiescence nor the isolation of legal authority from policy expertise could be maintained. The collapse of the norm of acquiescence both expresses and facilitates an emphasis on the law's role as a flexible instrument for the accomplishment of political purposes. Similarly, the contemporary Court's frequent citation to law review articles positions the Court as an institution whose authority derives in considerable measure from its capacity competently to fulfill the policies of the law.

These are subtle and largely silent changes. They reside in the interstices of consciousness. They are pervasive, but rarely explicit; fundamental, but rarely deliberate. They implicitly shape the way the Court perceives and engages its mission. They are readily compatible with, although not logically entailed by, the shift in the Court's role promoted by the Judiciary Act of 1925....

———

Questions and Comments

1. Recall Justice Ginsburg's reference to the surprise of French judges at the dissent practice in the United States. Having read these two historical treatments do you believe that the current approach to separate opinions was inevitable in the United States? Do you think it should change? Do you think it could change?

One scholar argues that the Justices are unlikely to "return to a consensual model of decision making. First, the Justices no longer live together, and the boardinghouse mentality that resulted from these arrangements has been irretrievably lost. Second, there is no longer any sense among the Justices that their authority is threatened by dissent. Third, the Court has grown more diverse in terms of class, gender, ethnicity, race, education, and geography, and these differences tend to foster greater disagreement. Fourth, the Court's heavy caseload means that there is little time to work out a consensus in difficult cases.... Finally, new technologies allow—even encourage—the Justices to work alone in chambers." Dickson, *The Supreme Court in Conference, supra* at 881–82. Yet Dickson also notes that if dissents continue to increase, "the Court's authority might eventually suffer," and suggests that there remains some "group identity" and "a tendency to keep any personal antagonisms private, by not speaking ill of other Justices in public." *Id.* at 881–82.

2. Could the changing understanding in the nature of law that Professor Post described be accommodated in a system that prohibited public judicial dissents? Note that such a rule exists in the European Court of Justice, see http://curia.europa.eu/en/instit/presentationfr/index_cje.htm. Such a rule also existed in the early years of the German Constitutional Court, but in 1970 the law was changed: As part of a compromise on a number of issues, the terms of the judges were changed, essentially from 8 year renewable terms to 12 year nonrenewable terms, and, in a move the majority of the judges favored, the bar on published dissents was dropped. See Donald Kommers, *The Constitutional Jurisprudence of the Federal Republic of Germany* 20–21 (2d ed. 1997).

3. Compare the examples given in Professor Post's articles with the descriptions of more contemporary intra-court deliberation found in the next section of this chapter: Do you think the shift in separate opinion writing practice has affected internal deliberations? For the better or for the worse?

4. In the period before World War II, the Justices each had one law clerk position authorized. A second clerk was authorized by legislation in 1941, and a third clerk by legislation in 1970. Since 1974, four law clerk positions per Justice have been authorized. See Artemus Ward & David L. Weiden, *Sorcerers' Apprentices: 100 Years of Law Clerks at the United States Supreme Court* 36, 45 (2006). Consider whether and how the numbers of law clerks might affect the propensity to write, or to publish, separate opinions–both in terms of ease of production, and the possibility for a Justice to want to avoid disappointing a clerk by not publishing a draft opinion on which the clerk may have worked hard. For further discussion of law clerks, see Chapter Five, Section B, below.

5. Recall that Chief Justice Roberts called for greater unanimity in Court opinions. Having read these two articles, do you think it is possible for the Court to return to the opinion writing style of the Taft Court? Recall the data provided earlier in this chapter about the percentage of 5–4 opinions in the first two Terms of the Roberts Court. But note that some observers have identified, in those Terms, a "potentially enduring effect"—some decrease in the number of separate dissenting and concurring opinions.[58]

6. Professor Geoffrey Stone has criticized Chief Justice Roberts' preference for " 'one clear and focused opinion of the Court.' " Geoffrey R. Stone, *A Narrow View of the Law,* Chicago Tribune, Feb. 6, 2007, at A17. Although Roberts has argued in favor of more unanimity in decision making on the ground that it tends to produce narrow decisions, see *Note on Chief Justice Roberts' Views and the Roberts Court,* above, Stone argues that narrow decisions of the Supreme Court leave citizens and government officials alike "in the dark." Especially for civil liberties like freedom of speech or religion, or freedom from unreasonable searches, Stone argues, uncertainty and ambiguity in legal rules should be avoided. He challenges Roberts' view that judicial legitimacy rests on unanimity or strong consensus; instead, Stone suggests, judges have a responsibility to state their own views. By provoking debate about different positions, he argues, separate opinions contribute to the development of the law, as evidenced by such influential dissents as Justice Harlan's in *Plessy* and the Holmes and Brandeis dissents in free speech cases after World War I. In short, "free and open judicial debate historically has led the Court to better results over time." While Stone acknowledges that too many cases with nine separate opinions might be inconsistent with the needs for a "coherent rule of law," and that on occasion the Court may need to decide a case on narrow grounds, he urges that the Court's most important responsibility of protecting individual liberties and minority rights can best be vindicated by the Court's willingness to "act boldly." *Id.*

In light of these competing views, how should a Justice decide whether or not to write a separate opinion? How does one decide when unanimity is more important than contributing to a robust debate?

C. CASE STUDIES: INSIDE THE COURT

In this section we present "inside the Court" stories in two major areas of controversy in recent decades: abortion and reproductive rights, and presidential power to withhold court-subpoenaed documents. Consider how these narratives reflect on the roles of the outside participants in Supreme Court adjudication, and the role of the Justices themselves, in crafting American constitutional law. Bear in mind that these cases might be considered "extraordinary," in their degree of societal controversy or in their relation to a constitutional crisis, so as you read, keep in

---

58. Georgetown University Law Center, Supreme Court Institute, *Supreme Court of the United States, October Term 2006 Overview* (June 29, 2007), at 5. For other discussion of the impact of a Chief Justice on norms of separate writing, see Frank B. Cross & Stephanie Lindquist, *Doctrinal and Strategic Influences of the Chief Justice: The Decisional Significance of the Chief Justice,* 154 U. Pa. L. Rev. 1665, 1681 (2006).

mind Professor O'Brien's descriptions earlier in this chapter of the give and take of members of the Court in a wider run of cases.

1.   Abortion and Reproductive Freedom: From *Roe* to *Casey*

Bernard Schwartz,[59] *The Ascent of Pragmatism: The Burger Court in Action* 297–307 (1990)

ROE V. WADE: CONFERENCE AND ASSIGNMENT

. . .

Roe v. Wade came before the Court with a companion case, *Doe v. Bolton.* In both cases, pregnant women sought relief against state abortion laws, contending that they were unconstitutional. At issue in *Roe* was a Texas statute that prohibited abortions except to save the mother's life. The statute in *Doe* was a Georgia law that proscribed an abortion except as performed by a physician who felt, in "his best clinical judgment," that continued pregnancy would endanger a woman's life or injure her health; the fetus would likely be born with a serious defect; or the pregnancy resulted from rape. In addition, the Georgia statutory scheme posed three procedural conditions: (1) that the abortion be performed in an accredited hospital; (2) that the procedure be approved by the hospital staff abortion committee; and (3) that the performing physician's judgment be confirmed by independent examinations by two other physicians.

. . .

Roe v. Wade and *Doe v. Bolton* were both discussed at the same postargument conference in December 1971. [At the time of this conference, the Court was composed of only seven Justices. Harlan and Black had died recently and neither Powell nor Rehnquist had yet been confirmed.] The Chief Justice devoted much of his *Roe v. Wade* discussion to the question of standing. On the merits, Burger said, "The balance here is between the state's interest in protecting fetal life and the woman's interest in not having children." In weighing these interests, the Chief Justice concluded, "I can't find the Texas statute unconstitutional, although it's certainly archaic and obsolete."

Douglas, who spoke next, declared categorically, "The abortion statute is unconstitutional. This is basically a medical and psychiatric problem"—and not [one] to be dealt with by prohibitory legislation. Douglas also criticized the statute's failure to give "a licensed physician an immunity for good faith abortions." Brennan, who followed, stressed even more strongly the right to an abortion, which should be given a constitutional basis by the Court's decision.

---

59. Webb Professor of Law at New York University Law School.

Stewart, next in order of seniority, stated, "I agree with Bill Douglas." He did, however, indicate that there might be some state power. "The state can legislate, to the extent of requiring a doctor and that, after a certain period of pregnancy, [she] can't have an abortion."

White said, "On the merits I am on the other side. They want us to say that women have a choice under the Ninth Amendment." White said that he refused to accept this "privacy argument." Marshall, on the other hand, declared, "I go with Bill Douglas, but the time problem concerns me." He thought that the state could not prevent abortions "in the early stage [of pregnancy]. But why can't the state prohibit after a certain stage?" In addition, Marshall said that he would use "liberty" under the Fourteenth Amendment as the constitutional base.

Blackmun, then the junior Justice, spoke last. Blackmun displayed an ambivalence that was to be reflected in his draft *Roe v. Wade* opinion. "Can a state properly outlaw all abortions? If we accept fetal life, there's a strong argument that it can. But there are opposing interests: the right of the mother to life and mental and physical health, the right of parents in case of rape, the right of the state in case of incest. I don't think there's an absolute right to do what you will with [your] body." Blackmun did, however, say flatly, "This statute is a poor statute that . . . impinges too far on her."

The conference outcome was not entirely clear; the tally sheets of different Justices do not coincide. What was clear, however, was that a majority were in favor of invalidating the laws: in *Roe v. Wade,* it was five (Douglas, Brennan, Stewart, Marshall, and Blackmun) to two (the Chief Justice and Justice White) according to one tally sheet, and four to three (with Blackmun added to the dissenters) according to a December 18, 1971, Douglas letter to the Chief Justice. Despite the fact that he was not part of the majority, Chief Justice Burger assigned the opinions to Blackmun.

Though the majority may have disapproved of the Burger assignment, only Douglas (whose tally sheet showed four votes for invalidating the laws, with himself as senior Justice in the majority) protested, in his December 18 "Dear Chief" letter: "As respects your assignment in this case, my notes show there were four votes to hold parts of the . . . Act unconstitutional. . . . There were three to sustain the law as written. I would think, therefore, that to save future time and trouble, one of the four, rather than one of the three, should write the opinion."

The Chief Justice replied with a December 20 "Dear Bill" letter. "At the close of the discussion of this case I remarked to the Conference that there were, literally, not enough columns to mark up an accurate reflection of the voting in either the Georgia or the Texas cases. I therefore marked down no votes and said this was a case that would have to stand or fall on the writing, when it was done. That is still my view of how to handle these two . . . sensitive cases, which, I might add, are quite probably candidates for reargument."

... Douglas and Brennan, who had led the proabortion bloc at the conference, decided to wait to see the Blackmun drafts before doing anything further. Though Douglas had tallied Blackmun with the minority, others had noted his vote with the majority. This might well mean Blackmun opinions agreeable to Douglas and Brennan, and make either a confrontation with the Chief Justice or a separate majority draft unnecessary.

ROE V. WADE: BLACKMUN DRAFT

Justice Blackmun has termed *Roe v. Wade* "a landmark in the progress of the emancipation of women." That could hardly have been said had his original draft become the final opinion of the Court. The draft did strike down the abortion statute, but it did so on the ground of vagueness—not because it restricted a woman's right to have an abortion. The draft expressly avoided the issue of the state's substantive right to prohibit abortions or "imply that a State has no legitimate interest in the subject of abortions or that abortion procedures may not be subject to control by the State." [sic]

The abortion opinion had been assigned in December 1971. Blackmun was the slowest worker on the Court, and the abortion cases were his first major assignment. He worked at them mostly alone.

Finally, on May 18, 1972, Blackmun sent around his draft *Roe v. Wade* opinion. "Herewith," began the covering memo, "is a first and tentative draft for this case.... [I]t may be somewhat difficult to obtain a consensus on all aspects. My notes indicate, however, that we were generally in agreement to affirm on the merits. That is where I come out on the theory that the Texas statute, despite its narrowness, is unconstitutionally vague."

"I think that this would be all that is necessary for disposition of the case, and that we need not get into the more complex Ninth Amendment issue. This may or may not appeal to you.... I am still flexible as to results, and I shall do my best to arrive at something which would command a court."

In *United States v. Vuitch*, decided the year before, the Court had upheld a similar District of Columbia abortion law against a vagueness attack. The Blackmun draft distinguished *Vuitch* on the ground that the statute there prohibited abortion unless "necessary for the preservation of the mother's life or health," while the Texas statute only permitted abortions "for the purpose of saving the life of the mother." Thus *Vuitch* "provides no answer to the constitutional challenge to the Texas statute."

In the Texas statute, "Saving the mother's life is the sole standard." This standard is too vague to guide physicians' conduct in abortion cases. "Does it mean that he may procure an abortion only when, without it, the patient will surely die? Or only when the odds are greater than even that she will die? Or when there is a mere possibility that she will not survive?"

"We conclude that Art. 1196, with its sole criterion for exemption as 'saving the life of the mother,' is insufficiently informative to the physician to whom it purports to afford a measure of professional protection but who must measure its indefinite meaning at the risk of his liberty, and that the statute cannot withstand constitutional challenge on vagueness grounds."

Blackmun's vagueness analysis was extremely weak. If anything, the "life saving" standard in the *Roe v. Wade* statute was more definite than the "health" standard upheld in *Vuitch*. But the draft's disposition of the case on vagueness enabled it to avoid the basic constitutional question. As the Blackmun draft stated, "There is no need in Roe's case to pass upon her contention that under the Ninth Amendment a pregnant woman has an absolute right to an abortion, or even to consider the opposing rights of the embryo or fetus during the respective prenatal trimesters."

Indeed, so far as the draft contained intimations on the matter, they tended to support state substantive power over abortions. "Our holding today does not imply that a State has no legitimate interest in the subject of abortions or that abortion procedures may not be subjected to control by the State.... We do not accept the argument of the appellants and of some of the amici that a pregnant woman has an unlimited right to do with her body as she pleases. The long acceptance of statutes regulating the possession of certain drugs and other harmful substances, and making criminal indecent exposure in public, or an attempt at suicide, clearly indicate the contrary." This was, of course, completely different from the approach ultimately followed in the *Roe v. Wade* opinion of the Court.

The *Roe v. Wade* draft did not deal at all with the right of privacy. It was, however, discussed in Blackmun's *Doe v. Bolton* draft, which he circulated on May 25, 1972. As summarized in the covering memo, his draft "would accomplish ... the striking of the Georgia statutory requirements as to (1) residence, (2) confirmation by two physicians, (3) advance approval by the hospital abortion committee, and (4) performance of the procedure only in [an] accredited hospital."

Blackmun's *Doe* draft dealt specifically with the claim that the law was an "invalid restriction of an absolute fundamental right to personal and marital privacy.... The Court, in varying contexts, has recognized a right of personal privacy and has rooted it in the Fourteenth Amendment, or in the Bill of Rights, or in the latter's penumbras." The draft flatly rejected the assertion "that the scope of this right of personal privacy includes, for a woman, the right to decide unilaterally to terminate an existing but *unwanted* pregnancy without any state interference or control whatsoever." As the draft put it, "Appellants' contention, however, that the woman's right to make the decision is absolute—that Georgia has either no valid interest in regulating it, or no interest strong enough to support any limitation upon the woman's sole determination—is unpersuasive."

The draft rejected as "unfair and illogical" the argument that "the State's present professed interest in the protection of embryonic and fetal 'life' is somehow to be downgraded. That argument condemns the State for past 'wrongs' and also denies it the right to readjust its views and emphases in the light of the more advanced knowledge and techniques of today."

The *Doe* draft, utterly unlike the final Blackmun opinions, stressed the countervailing interest in fetal life. "The heart of the matter is that somewhere, either forthwith at conception, or at 'quickening,' or at birth, or at some other point in between, another being becomes involved and the privacy the woman possessed has become dual rather than sole. The woman's right of privacy must be measured accordingly." That being the case, "The woman's personal right ..., is not unlimited. It must be balanced against the State's interest." Hence, "we cannot automatically strike down the remaining features of the Georgia statute simply because they restrict any right on the part of the woman to have an abortion at will."

The implication here was that substantial state power over abortion existed. Under the *Doe* draft, as the Blackmun covering memo pointed out, the state may provide "that an abortion may be performed only if the attending physician deems it necessary 'based upon his best clinical judgment,' if his judgment is reduced to writing, and if the abortion is performed in a hospital licensed by the State through its Board of Health." This was, of course, wholly inconsistent with the Court's final decision in *Roe v. Wade.*

Roe v. Wade: Reargument and Second Conference

It soon became apparent that the Blackmun drafts were not going to receive the five-Justice imprimatur needed to transform them into Court opinions. On May 18 and 19, 1972, Brennan and Douglas sent "Dear Harry" letters urging, in Brennan's words, "a disposition of the core constitutional question. Your circulation, however, invalidates the Texas statute only on the vagueness ground.... I think we should dispose of both cases on the ground supported by the majority." Douglas agreed. "That was the clear view of a majority of the seven who heard the argument.... So I think we should meet what Bill Brennan calls the 'core issue.' " Douglas also referred to the fact that, at the conference, "the Chief had the opposed view, which made it puzzling as to why he made the assignment at all."

The conference minority now sought to delay—and perhaps reverse—the abortion decisions. *Roe* and *Doe* had come before a seven-Justice Court. The two vacancies were not filled until Powell and Rehnquist took their seats in January, 1972. After the Blackmun drafts were circulated in May, the Chief Justice directed his efforts to securing a reargument in the cases, arguing that the decisions in such important cases should be made by a full Court.

At this point White sent around a brief draft dissent. Circulated May 29, it effectively demonstrated the weakness of the Blackmun vagueness approach in striking down the Texas law. Referring to the *Vuitch* decision that a statute that permitted abortion on "health" grounds was not unconstitutionally vague, the White draft declared, "If a standard which refers to the 'health' of the mother, a referent which necessarily entails the resolution of perplexing questions about the interrelationship of physical, emotional, and mental well-being, is not impermissibly vague, a statutory standard which focuses only on 'saving the life' of the mother would appear to be a fortiori acceptable.... [T]he relevant factors in the latter situation are less numerous and are primarily physiological."

On May 31, Chief Justice Burger circulated a Memorandum to the Conference favoring reargument—"[T]hese cases ... are not as simple for me as they appear to be for others. The states have, I should think, as much concern in this area as in any within their province; federal power has only that which can be traced to a specific provision of the Constitution.... I want to hear more and think more when I am not trying to sort out several dozen other difficult cases.... I vote to reargue early in the next Term."

The Burger move to secure reargument was opposed by the Justices who favored striking down the abortion laws. They feared that the two new Justices would vote for the laws. In addition, the White draft dissent might lead another Justice to withdraw his support from the Blackmun *Roe* draft—maybe even Blackmun himself whose position had been none too firm. Indeed, he had become convinced that the cases should be reargued and circulated a May 31 Memorandum to the Conference to that effect. "Although it would prove costly to me personally, in the light of energy and hours expended, I have now concluded, somewhat reluctantly, that reargument in *both* cases at an early date in the next term, would perhaps be advisable.... I believe, on an issue so sensitive and so emotional as this one, the country deserves the conclusion of a nine-man, not a seven-man court, whatever the ultimate decision may be."

Douglas replied to Justice Blackmun the same day, "I feel quite strongly that they should not be reargued." The next day, June 1, an angry Douglas wrote to the Chief Justice, "If the vote of the Conference is to reargue, then I will file a statement telling what is happening to us and the tragedy it entails."

The Douglas statement was never issued even though the Justices did vote to set the abortion cases for reargument. Only Douglas was listed as dissenting.

· · ·

The abortion cases were reargued on October 11, 1972. At the conference, the Justices who had participated in the earlier conference took the same positions as before. The two new Justices took opposing positions. Powell said that he was "basically in accord with Harry's position," while Justice Rehnquist stated, "I agree with Byron" White—who had declared, "I'm not going to second guess state legislatures in striking the balance in favor of abortion laws."

Several Justices agreed with Justice Stewart when he stated, "I can't join in holding that the Texas statute is vague." Stewart was for striking that law, but urged a different approach. He said that he would "follow John Harlan's reasoning in the Connecticut case and can't rest there on the Ninth Amendment. It's a Fourteenth Amendment right, as John Harlan said in *Griswold*."

ROE v. WADE: SECOND DRAFT AND FINAL OPINION

The most important part of Blackmun's postreargument conference presentation was his announcement, "I am where I was last Spring." However, he made a much firmer statement this time in favor of invalidating the abortion laws. He also said, "I'd make Georgia the lead case." But he was opposed on this by several others, particularly Powell, who felt that "Texas should be the lead case."

Most important of all, during the summer, Blackmun had completely rewritten the abortion opinions. On November 21, he circulated the revised draft of his *Roe v. Wade* opinion. "Herewith," began the covering memo, "is a memorandum (1972 fall edition) on the Texas abortion cases."

He expressly abandoned the vagueness holding. The holding on the constitutional merits "makes it unnecessary for us to consider the attack made on the Texas statute on grounds of vagueness."

The new Blackmun draft contained the essentials of the final *Roe v. Wade* opinion, including its lengthy historical analysis. In particular, Blackmun now grounded his decision upon *Griswold v. Connecticut*. According to Blackmun, "the right of privacy, however based, is broad enough to cover the abortion decision." In addition since the right at issue was a "fundamental" one, the law at issue was subject to strict-scrutiny review: the state regulation of the fundamental right of privacy "may be justified only by a 'compelling state interest.' "

The Blackmun privacy-strict scrutiny approach was substantially influenced by a Douglas draft opinion in *Doe v. Bolton,* which had been prepared in January, 1972. The Douglas draft had expressly invalidated the abortion law as violative of the right of privacy and adopted the strict-scrutiny review standard. There is a note in Douglas's hand, dated March 6, 1972, indicating that a copy of his draft had been "sent ... to HB several weeks ago."

At the postargument conference, the Chief Justice had asked, "Is there a fetal life that's entitled to protection?" Justice Stewart said that the Court should deal specifically with this issue, saying, "it seems essential that we deal with the claim that the fetus is not a person under the Fourteenth Amendment." The *Roe v. Wade* opinion met this Stewart demand with a statement that the word "person" in the Fourteenth

Amendment does not include a fetus—a point that is said to have been added at Justice Stewart's insistence.

The second draft also adopted the time approach followed in the final opinion. However, it used the first trimester of pregnancy alone as the line between invalid and valid state power. "You will observe," Justice Blackmun explained in his covering memo, "that I have concluded that the end of the first trimester is critical. This is arbitrary, but perhaps any other selected point, such as quickening or viability, is equally arbitrary."

The draft stated that, before the end of the first trimester, the state "must do no more than to leave the abortion decision to the best medical judgment of the pregnant woman's attending physician." However, "For the stage subsequent to the first trimester, the State may, if it chooses, determine a point beyond which it restricts legal abortions to stated reasonable therapeutic categories."

Later drafts refined this two-pronged time test to the tri-partite approach followed in the final *Roe* opinion. In large part, this was in response to the suggestion in a December 12 letter from Justice Marshall: "I am inclined to agree that drawing the line at viability accommodates the interests at stake better than drawing it at the end of the first trimester. Given the difficulties which many women may have in believing that they are pregnant and in deciding to seek an abortion, I fear that the earlier date may not in practice serve the interests of those women, which your opinion does seek to serve."

The Marshall letter stated that his concern would be met "If the opinion stated explicitly that, between the end of the first trimester and viability, state regulations directed at health and safety alone were permissible."

Marshall recognized "that at some point the State's interest in preserving the potential life of the unborn child overrides any individual interests of the women." However, he concluded, "I would be disturbed if that point were set before viability, and I am afraid that the opinion's present focus on the end of the first trimester would lead states to prohibit abortions completely at any later date."

Blackmun adopted the Marshall suggestion, even though Douglas and Brennan wrote expressing their doubts about the "viability" approach.

In a December 14, 1972, letter, Stewart delivered a more fundamental criticism of the Blackmun approach: "One of my concerns with your opinion as presently written is the specificity of its dictum—particularly in its fixing of the end of the first trimester as the critical point for valid state action. I appreciate the inevitability and indeed wisdom of dicta in the Court's opinion, but I wonder about the desirability of the dicta being quite so inflexibly 'legislative.'" This is, of course, the common criticism that has since been directed at *Roe v. Wade*. The high bench was acting like a legislature; its drawing of lines at trimesters and viability was, in the Stewart letter's phrase "to make policy judgments" that were more "legislative" than "judicial." Stewart worked on a lengthy opinion giving voice to this criticism, but in a December 27 letter he informed Blackmun that he had decided to discard it and "to file instead a brief monograph on substantive due process, joining your opinions."

————

Questions and Comments

1. Should the Justices have given more consideration to Justice Stewart's December 14 views? Why might Stewart have withdrawn that objection? Justice Blackmun's own notes reflect that he understood that "a majority of state statutes go down the drain" under his approach and that he had considered having the Court withhold its mandate, an unusual procedure to allow time for legislative revisions before the rule announced in the opinion would issue as a judgment. See Linda Greenhouse, *Becoming Justice Blackmun* 93 (2005). Is there a tension between the Court's felt obligation to articulate clear doctrinal rules for the lower courts and its role as a court, not a legislative body?

2. What would have been the likely impact—on the course of subsequent cases, on the politics of abortion, and on the availability of legal abortions—had Justice Blackmun's initial draft following re-argument become the opinion of the Court?

Note on Webster v. Reproductive Health Services, 492 U.S. 490 (1989)

In *Webster*, Chief Justice Rehnquist initially believed he might have a majority to revisit *Roe* and revise the doctrine to permit state regulations that "reasonably further the state interest in protecting human life" throughout pregnancy. Justice O'Connor, however, was not prepared to join this approach. *See* Greenhouse, *Becoming Justice Blackmun*, *supra*, at 191–93. According to Mark Tushnet's account, during the Court's conference following oral argument,

> ... Rehnquist said that he "disagrees with *Roe v. Wade*." Five justices, including Kennedy and O'Connor, took the same position, but O'Connor seemed to prefer a decision limiting rather than overruling *Roe*. Rehnquist took the case for himself and within a month circulated a draft saying that the case did not require the Court to overrule *Roe*. Instead, he proposed to change the constitutional standard. The right to choose an abortion was indeed a liberty interest protected by the due process clause, but states could regulate abortions without violating the Constitution—or impairing the woman's liberty—if a regulation "reasonably furthers the state interest in protecting potential human life."

> Stevens immediately responded with a letter pointing out that Rehnquist's approach gave "no weight at all" to "the woman's interest in making the abortion decision...."

White, Scalia and Kennedy promptly joined Rehnquist's draft, and then things hung fire. O'Connor apparently had misgivings about the draft. Three weeks later Blackmun circulated a draft dissent. Then came O'Connor's bombshell: She couldn't agree with the way Rehnquist discussed the testing requirement. Instead she proposed to uphold the requirement [for medical testing to determine fetal viability if more than 20 weeks had passed since conception, that is, within the second trimester under the *Roe* framework], on a new theory. Noting that determinations of fetal age were always somewhat inaccurate, she said that doctors thought there was roughly a four-week margin of error when they estimated fetal age. So the testing requirement was actually a third-trimester regulation and, because it was aimed at determining fetal viability, was indeed within the scope of third-trimester regulations under *Roe* itself. Drawing on a suggestion made in the solicitor general's amicus brief, O'Connor did propose a new constitutional standard—a regulation would be unconstitutional if it imposed an "undue burden" on the woman's right to choose—but that standard would pretty clearly produce greater restrictions on the ability of states to regulate abortions than Rehnquist's state interest test would.

O'Connor's position deprived Rehnquist of a majority for a substantial reworking of the constitutional standard.... Worse, from Scalia's point of view, he knew that O'Connor's late defection meant that Rehnquist wouldn't publish a strong opinion saying that *Roe* should be overruled. Once Rehnquist had a draft, that basically was it. He might tinker with it to get votes, but he wouldn't scrap it and start over. Things might have been different if O'Connor had let Rehnquist know her thinking earlier.... Instead, as Scalia saw it, O'Connor had led Rehnquist down the garden path, where he ended up with a plurality opinion anyway.

Scalia took it upon himself to attack *Roe*—and O'Connor.... His most pointed attack on her went to his understanding of *her* self-understanding as the Court's moderate and stateswoman: "The outcome of today's case will doubtless be heralded as a triumph of judicial statesmanship. It is not that, unless it is statesmanlike needlessly to prolong this Court's self-awarded sovereignty over a field where it has little proper business since the answers to most of the crucial questions posed are political and not juridical." As Supreme Court opinions go, this was venomous.

Mark Tushnet, *A Court Divided: The Rehnquist Court and the Future of Constitutional Law* 206–08 (2005).

Many scholars agree with Professor Tushnet's conclusion that Justice Scalia's attack on Justice O'Connor in the 1989 *Webster* decision may have "solidified her drift away from a strong anti-*Roe* position." Tushnet, at 208. The following year, he notes, she voted for the first time to invalidate a state abortion regulation (the requirement of two-parent notification for a minor's abortion). Yet, he argues, Justice Scalia believed it would be possible to overrule *Roe* once Justice Thomas joined the Court.

In October, 1991, the Third Circuit, reviewing Pennsylvania statutes imposing new restrictions on abortions, concluded, after extensive analysis of the different opinions in recent Supreme Court cases (including *Webster*), that *Roe*'s "strict scrutiny" standard was no longer applicable to review of all abortion regulations, and that the "undue burden" standard articulated by Justice O'Connor in *Webster* was now controlling. See Planned Parenthood v. Casey, 947 F.2d 682, 697–98 (3d Cir. 1991), aff'd in part, rev'd in part, 505 U.S. 833 (1992).[60] Below are brief excerpts from Professor Tushnet's description of the *Casey* litigation in the Supreme Court.

Mark Tushnet,[61] *A Court Divided: The Rehnquist Court and the Future of Constitutional Law* 209–19 (2005)

Pro-choice advocates decided to go for broke. They filed their petition for review two months before they had to and presented only the single question they wanted the Court to consider: "Has the Supreme Court overruled *Roe v. Wade*, holding that a woman's right to choose abortion is a fundamental right protected by the United States Constitution?" The lawyers described their decision as a "high stakes game of chicken" with the Court: Either overrule *Roe* or reaffirm it, and do so before the 1992 elections. The case was argued on the last possible day to get an opinion out before the elections. . . .

When the justices voted, only Blackmun and Stevens stuck with *Roe*. The seven others wanted to change the law of abortion, and it appeared as if five, including Kennedy, were willing to adopt the position Rehnquist set out in the Missouri case: The right to choose abortion was a liberty interest, but not a fundamental one, and therefore could be limited by reasonable regulations (just as the right to work as a barber was a liberty interest that could be limited by reasonable regulations). Rehnquist took the opinion for himself and drafted one along the lines of his Missouri opinion.

David Souter hadn't dealt with abortion before. He was acutely uncomfortable with the prospect of a decision overruling *Roe*, which he believed would be taken by the public to demonstrate that the Court's decisions were affected by politics acting through the appointment process and not by law. O'Connor continued to prefer her undue burden approach to Rehnquist's. Souter and O'Connor got together and then approached Kennedy with the idea of collaborating on an opinion that would preserve what they called the "core holding" of *Roe*—that states couldn't make abortion a criminal offense—but also allow for a wider range of regulations than *Roe* did. Kennedy was sympathetic to the idea, resolving the conflict between his Roman Catholic religious beliefs and

---

60. For excerpts of the Supreme Court's opinion in Planned Parenthood v. Casey, 505 U.S. 833 (1992), see Chapter One, above.

61. Carmack Waterhouse Professor of Constitutional Law at Georgetown University Law Center at time of book; now the William Nelson Cromwell Professor of Law at Harvard University Law School.

his mildly libertarian political and constitutional views in favor of the latter.

The three justices divided work on what ended up as a joint opinion. (Although it's sometimes described as a plurality opinion, technically it wasn't. To be a plurality opinion, an opinion has to have more votes than any other, and in the Pennsylvania case Rehnquist's opinion got four votes to the joint opinion's three. The joint opinion's undue burden rule is what matters today, though, because Blackmun and Stevens, who dissented, clearly agreed more with the joint opinion than with Rehnquist's.)

O'Connor drafted a section that modified *Roe* in two ways, both foreshadowed by her opinion in the Missouri case [*Webster*]. It abandoned the trimester framework and substituted a line drawn at viability. Doing so, the opinion said, respected the government's "profound interest in potential life." That interest existed throughout pregnancy and hadn't been given enough weight in *Roe*'s rules about the first trimester.

The viability line, it turned out, didn't matter that much. *Roe* barred essentially all first-trimester regulations, but O'Connor didn't mean to carry *that* rule over to stop states from regulating before viability. Here her second innovation came in, the undue burden standard. Now states could adopt regulations applicable before viability, if the regulations didn't impose an undue burden on the choice of abortion. And undue burdens were those that placed "a substantial obstacle in the path of a woman seeking an abortion of a nonviable [that is, not yet viable] fetus." The opinion then said that the rule *Roe* developed for the third trimester—that abortions could be regulated and even prohibited unless the procedure was necessary to preserve the woman's life or health—would now apply to all post-viability abortions.

. . .

Souter drafted the joint opinion's discussion of why the Court shouldn't overrule *Roe*. He carefully mentioned that "some of us" might have "personal reluctance" for "affirming *Roe*'s central holding." But, he said, the demands of adhering to precedent in constitutional law overrode any such reluctance. He made some standard points about overruling: It was easier to do when the earlier decision turned out to be "unworkable," but that wasn't true of *Roe*. Lots of people didn't like the decision, but courts had no real problems figuring out what its core holding was. Nor had later cases cast doubt on that core holding. These were straightforward commonplaces.

Other parts of Souter's discussion of overruling were more unusual. . . .

Kennedy took on the task of defending *Roe*'s "core holding." He noted, "Some of us as individuals find abortion offensive to our most basic principles of morality, but that cannot control our decision." After recounting the Court's efforts in a number of areas to define the liberties the Constitution protected, Kennedy concluded that the Constitution defined "a realm of personal liberty which the government may not enter." How to identify that realm? By using the "same capacity which by tradition courts always have exercised: reasoned judgment." This was not a mechanical task, of course. According to Kennedy, the Court's cases recognized an important sphere of personal autonomy. Decisions about "the most intimate and personal choices a person may make in a lifetime" were "central to personal dignity and autonomy" and equally "central to the liberty protected by the Fourteenth Amendment." In a passage that his critics derided, Kennedy concluded, "At the heart of liberty is the right to define one's own concept of existence, of meaning, of the universe, and of the mystery of human life."

. . .

He also wrote the joint opinion's sonorous—and almost meaning-less—opening and closing sentences. The opinion began: "Liberty finds no refuge in a jurisprudence of doubt." Justice Oliver Wendell Holmes might have responded that liberty finds refuge *only* in a jurisprudence of doubt. In a famous free speech dissent, Holmes wrote, "If you have no doubt of your premises or your power and want a certain result with all your heart you naturally express your wishes in law and sweep away all opposition." The joint opinion ended by describing the Constitution as "a covenant" running from the founding to the indefinite future . . . [quotation of last sentence of plurality opinion omitted] That might work as the conclusion of a president's State of the Union address, where we don't expect anything but platitudes. But exactly what it means remains entirely unclear.

Kennedy was nervous about his participation in the joint opinion. As he became committed to the joint opinion's approach, he went to Rehnquist and apologized for depriving him of a majority yet again. The affable Rehnquist reportedly told Kennedy that he "had to do what he thought was right." The same reports indicate that Scalia was so upset at Kennedy's defection that he "walked over to Kennedy's nearby house . . . to upbraid him." On the day the decision was released, Kennedy allowed a journalist into his office and enhanced the self-dramatization of the event by telling his guest, "Sometimes you don't know if you're Caesar about to cross the Rubicon, or Captain Queeg cutting your own tow line," and then excused himself, saying, "I need to brood" for the ten minutes before the Court convened.

At the end of the Court's Term, the law clerks staged a skit and used the theme from the television program *Flipper* as Kennedy's signature song. Why had Kennedy jumped ship? Conservatives had a conspiracy theory. Michael Dorf, one of Kennedy's law clerks that year, had worked closely with the pro-choice constitutional scholar Laurence Tribe. Conservatives suggested that Tribe had successfully used his protégé—and another, Peter Rubin, who was clerking for Souter—to lobby Kennedy. Others referred to the Greenhouse Effect. Yet another story was that Kennedy, who had initially been taken under Scalia's wing to the point that the law clerks referred to Kennedy as Nini, or little Nino, gradually was "put off by Scalia's fanged personal attacks on O'Connor" and found "Souter's low-key manner . . . a welcome contrast to Scalia's intensity."

Conservatives certainly overstated the influence of Rubin and Dorf, and Tribe even more; law clerks don't have much impact on the important decisions made by justices with strong self-images, like Kennedy. As Peter Keisler, a reliable Federalist Society lawyer who clerked for Kennedy, said, "No justice is going to abdicate" to a law clerk on an issue like abortion. The other things they identified may have played some role. In the end it's almost certain that Kennedy joined the joint opinion because he thought it offered a better interpretation of the Constitution—his interpretation and, to some degree, O'Connor's—than Rehnquist's.

· · ·

The *Casey* decision succeeded in taking the abortion issue largely off the Supreme Court's agenda. The authors of the joint opinion were right about that, and Scalia was wrong. Having lost the battle to overrule *Roe*, antiabortion activists turned to new tactics, including demonstrations at facilities where abortions were performed. In legislatures they began to develop an essentially cultural strategy to discredit the theories they believed underpinned public acceptance of abortion, the idea that abortion was an ordinary medical procedure and the belief that fetuses weren't really human beings. They initially focused on a couple of extremely gruesome procedures for aborting a fetus, which doctors sometimes called intact dilation and evacuation and dilation and extraction. Doctors performed these procedures relatively late in pregnancy and usually because they were at that point the only techniques that didn't threaten a woman's life. The techniques involved dismemberment of the fetus, sometimes after it had begun to emerge from the womb. Antiabortion activists called these techniques partial birth abortions. That label served important public relations purposes and stuck in the public's mind in a way that the more desiccated medical terminology did not.

· · ·

Questions and Comments

1. In Stenberg v. Carhart, 530 U.S. 914 (2000), the Court upheld a challenge to a state's ban on "partial birth abortions," invalidating the statute in part because it provided no exception for use of the prohibited procedure where necessary to protect the mother's health, and the courts had not been convinced by the state of Nebraska's arguments that there was never a need to use the procedure to protect the mother's health. Seven years later, the Roberts Court upheld a fairly similar federal statute banning the procedure. *See* Gonzales v. Carhart, 127 S.Ct. 1610 (2007). Although the

Court, in an opinion by Justice Kennedy, purported not to overrule *Stenberg*, Justice Ruth Ginsburg's unusually strongly worded dissent commented that it was the first time since *Roe* was decided that the Court upheld a ban on abortions that did not have an exception for protection of the pregnant woman's health.

2.   Recall the discussion in Chapter One about *stare decisis*. The issue arose in the context of an explicit discussion whether to overrule *Roe v. Wade* in *Casey*. Should the Court have explicitly overruled *Stenberg v. Carhart* in *Gonzales v. Carhart*? Why or why not? Should the Court have hesitated to overrule overtly because of the recent change in the Court's membership? Or should the demands of judicial candor have required either overruling or a more direct acknowledgment of the tensions between the two decisions?

3.   The distinction between overturning a precedent and distinguishing it can be a fine one, and controversial, even among Justices who agree on the outcome of a case. As Linda Greenhouse observed at the end of the 2006 Term, Justice Scalia was critical of Chief Justice Roberts' and Justice Alito's preference to distinguish prior cases and not overrule them; Scalia preferred explicitly to overrule them. See Greenhouse, *Even in Agreement, Scalia Puts Roberts to Lash,* N.Y. Times, June 28, 2007, at A1; see also, e.g. FEC v. Wisconsin Right to Life, 127 S. Ct. 2652 (2007) (upholding an as-applied challenge to provision of the McCain-Feingold law that had been upheld on a facial challenge in an earlier decision, which was distinguished); *id.* at 2683 n.7 (Scalia, J., concurring in the judgment) ("This faux judicial restraint is judicial obfuscation."); Hein v. Freedom from Religion Foundation, 127 S. Ct. 2553 (2007) (Alito, J., announcing the judgment of the Court) (distinguishing *Flast v. Cohen*, 392 U.S. 83 (1968), on the grounds that it involved a taxpayer challenge to a statute asserted to violate the Establishment Clause, to hold that petitioners lacked standing to challenge on Establishment Clause grounds the discretionary expenditures of a White House office); *id.* at 2582 (Scalia, J., concurring in the judgment) (arguing that "[m]inimalism is an admirable judicial trait, but not when it comes at the cost of meaningless and disingenuous distinctions that hold the sure promise of engendering further meaningless and disingenuous distinctions in the future").[62] Should such efforts be condemned as misleading the lower courts and as intellectually disingenuous or praised as incrementalist and leaving room for further "percolation" in the lower courts? Are there risks to making distinctions that might be difficult for lawyers and lower court judges to understand?

4.   The sequence of events from *Casey* through *Gonzales v. Carhart* is a vivid reminder that the Court is only one actor in developing the meaning of the Constitution's broad provisions. The Congress and the President of the United States, in enacting the federal Partial–Birth Abortion Ban Act of 2003, virtually guaranteed that the issue would be litigated again before the Court. Many observers believe that timing and changes in the Court's membership played a significant role: Justice O'Connor had joined in invali-

---

62.   For a leading scholarly discussion of minimalism, see Cass R. Sunstein, *The Supreme Court, 1995 Term: Foreword: Leav-* *ing Things Undecided*, 110 Harv. L. Rev. 6 (1996).

dating the Nebraska statute at issue in *Stenberg*, but by the time *Gonzales v. Carhart* was decided, she had resigned, and both Justice Alito and Chief Justice Roberts joined Justice Kennedy's opinion upholding the federal statute.

5. To review the Rehnquist draft, Stevens' memo, and other draft opinions in *Webster*, see Bernard Schwartz, *The Unpublished Opinions of the Rehnquist Court* 266–332 (1996).

---

2. The Nixon Tapes Case

The next excerpt is a journalistic description of the fairly unusual process by which the Court's opinion in the famous Nixon Tapes case was put together. To give readers an understanding of why the members of the Court believed it was urgent that they try to reach a unanimous and "tight" opinion, some historical background may be helpful on the serious constitutional crisis the nation was approaching.

On June 17, 1972, employees of the Committee to Re–Elect President Richard Nixon broke into the headquarters of the Democratic National Committee in the Watergate Hotel in Washington D.C., and attempted to install eavesdropping equipment. Although by October some newspapers were reporting that the FBI had discovered a large amount of "political spying and sabotage" on behalf of the Nixon campaign against the Democrats, the break-in and news reports had no discernible adverse effect on the President's re-election campaign, which Nixon won in a landslide with over 60% of the vote. In January, 1973, the first indictments of the Watergate burglars came down, and by February, 1973, newspaper disclosures about the break-in led the Senate unanimously to vote to create the Senate Select Committee on Watergate, to examine whether there was presidential involvement in the break-in.

In May, 1973, public pressure led the Attorney General (Elliot Richardson) to appoint Archibald Cox, a highly respected professor at Harvard Law School and a former Solicitor General of the United States, as a special prosecutor to investigate these matters. By July, 1973, public testimony by former White House aide John Dean before the Senate Select Committee had implicated the President himself; the existence of secret tape recordings of White House meetings had been disclosed; and the first impeachment resolution against President Nixon was introduced in the House of Representatives. Both the Senate Select Committee and the Special Prosecutor sought the tapes; the White House refused.

In October, 1973, Cox was fired on orders of the White House, in what came to be called the "Saturday Night Massacre." Attorney General Richardson had resigned, rather than carry out the order to fire Cox; then the Deputy Attorney General also resigned, rather than carry out the order. Robert Bork, then the Solicitor General and third in line at the Department of Justice, issued the order terminating Cox's position. But this only led to more public pressure for investigation, resulting eventually in the appointment of a new special prosecutor (Leon Jaworski) and adding to the pressure for impeachment. In February, 1974, the House of Representatives authorized its Judiciary Committee to hold hearings to consider whether to impeach the President. These hearings were actively underway at the time the Court issued its decision in this case.[63]

The following description of parallel criminal proceedings in the federal district is excerpted from the opinion of the Court in the case:

> On March 1, 1974, a grand jury of the United States District Court for the District of Columbia returned an indictment charging seven named individuals [including John Mitchell, formerly the Attorney General of the United States for Nixon, and high ranking White House officials] with various offenses, including conspiracy to defraud the United States and to obstruct justice. Although he was not designated as such in the indictment, the grand jury named the President, among others, as an unindicted coconspirator. On April 18, 1974, upon motion of the Special Prosecutor, a subpoena *duces tecum* was issued pursuant to Rule 17(c) to the President by the United States District Court and made returnable on May 2, 1974. This subpoena required the production, in advance of the September 9 trial date, of certain tapes, memoranda, papers, transcripts, or other writings relating to certain precisely identified meetings between the President and others. The Special Prosecutor was able to fix the time, place, and persons present at these discussions because the White House daily logs and appointment records had been delivered to him. On April 30, the President publicly released edited transcripts of 43 conversations; portions of 20 conversations subject to subpoena in the present case were included. On May 1, 1974, the President's counsel filed a "special appearance" and a motion to quash the subpoena under Rule 17(c). This motion was accompanied by a formal claim of privilege. . . .

> On May 20, 1974, the District Court denied the motion to quash and the motions to expunge and for protective orders. It further ordered "the President or any subordinate officer, official, or employee with custody or control of the documents or objects subpoenaed," to deliver to the District Court, on or before May 31, 1974, the originals of all subpoenaed items, as well as an index and analysis of those items, together with tape copies of those portions of the subpoenaed recordings for which transcripts had been released to

---

63. The description in this introduction is largely drawn from Geoffrey R. Stone et al., *Constitutional Law*, 396–97 (2d ed. 1991), and from the *Washington Post's* "The Watergate Story," available at http://www.washingtonpost.com/wp-srv/politics/ special/watergate/index.html#chapters. The quoted phrase in text above is from Carl Bernstein & Bob Woodward, *FBI Finds Nixon Aides Sabotaged Democrats*, The Washington Post, Oct. 10, 1972, at A01.

the public by the President on April 30. The District Court rejected jurisdictional challenges based on a contention that the dispute was nonjusticiable because it was between the Special Prosecutor and the Chief Executive and hence "intra-executive" in character; it also rejected the contention that the Judiciary was without authority to review an assertion of executive privilege by the President. The court's rejection of the first challenge was based on the authority and powers vested in the Special Prosecutor by the regulation promulgated by the Attorney General; the court concluded that a justiciable controversy was presented....

The District Court held that the judiciary, not the President, was the final arbiter of a claim of executive privilege. The court concluded that, under the circumstances of this case, the presumptive privilege was overcome by the Special Prosecutor's prima facie "demonstration of need sufficiently compelling to warrant judicial examination in chambers...." The court held, finally, that the Special Prosecutor had satisfied the requirements of Rule 17 (c). The District Court stayed its order pending appellate review on condition that review was sought before 4 p. m., May 24. The court further provided that matters filed under seal remain under seal when transmitted as part of the record.

On May 24, 1974, the President filed a timely notice of appeal from the District Court order ... On the same day, the President also filed a petition for writ of mandamus in the Court of Appeals seeking review of the District Court order.

Later on May 24, the Special Prosecutor also filed, in this Court, a petition for a writ of certiorari before judgment. On May 31, the petition was granted with an expedited briefing schedule. On June 6, the President filed, under seal, a cross-petition for writ of certiorari before judgment. This cross-petition was granted June 15, 1974, and the case was set for argument on July 8, 1974.

United States v. Nixon, 418 U.S. 683, 687–90 (1974). As you will see in the excerpt that follows, after granting the requests for certiorari before judgment, the Court released its decision in this case on July 24—just 16 days after it was argued.

Bob Woodward & Scott Armstrong,[64] *The Brethren*: *Inside the Supreme Court* 308–47 (1979)

[On July 9, 1974, the day following the July 8 oral argument in *United States v. Nixon*] the eight Justices met in conference to vote on the case. [Justice Rehnquist had recused himself.] Everyone was well

64. Woodward and Armstrong were reporters for the *Washington Post* at the time   of this book.

prepared. The memos [dealing with many of the legal questions and circulated before oral argument] from the chambers of Douglas, Powell, Brennan and Stewart had defined the scope of the case. Dealing first with the technical questions, they all agreed that the ruling [by federal District Court Judge Sirica] on the subpoena was of sufficient constitutional significance to be appealed to the Supreme Court. It was properly before them.

The first disagreement arose when Powell held firm to the position he had expressed in his memo on Rule 17(c), [which sets the standards for issuing subpoenas in federal cases,] that there was a need for a higher standard of evidence for presidents than for other people.

White disagreed completely. The Court should ensure that the President was treated like any citizen, no more, no less.... Thus, White said, he would be forced to dissent on that point if the others supported Powell's position.

The discussion was sharp and heated. The question of the standard was only one possible sticking point. The difficult questions revolving around the grand jury's naming of the President as an unindicted coconspirator should be sidestepped, they all agreed.

On the central question of executive privilege, the Justices agreed that the judiciary's specific need for sixty-four particular tapes for a criminal trial outweighed the President's generalized claim of confidentiality. At the same time, they all acknowledged that some form of executive privilege existed, at least implicitly.

Brennan saw the consensus immediately. The President did not have a single vote. Even more encouraging, there was reason to believe that the gaps among the Justices could be bridged. A single opinion seemed within reach. That would be the greatest deterrent to a defiant President....

... Brennan spoke up. The Nixon challenge had to be met in the strongest way possible. An eight-signature opinion would do it.... Brennan reminded them of the impact of nine signatures on the Little Rock school opinion [Cooper v. Aaron, 358 U.S. 1 (1958)]. It had been one of the Court's finest moments. The country would benefit from such a show of strength now.

... Brennan sat back, anticipating quick seconds. Instead there was an uneasy silence, not a word of support from anyone ...

The Chief broke the silence. He would take the opinion. The decision was similar to the Court's famous *Brown* school desegregation opinion; it required the Chief Justice....

Marshall was afraid a single opinion would never attract all eight votes. The Justices were agreed on the result, but not on the reasoning. The discussion in conference had been odd. Conversation at conference normally focused on a case in light of the Constitution. This discussion had centered more on the Court's role and power than on the case.

The Chief got right to work with two of his clerks. This would be his most historic opinion, perhaps the Court's most momentous opinion. This was an opinion that would establish the Chief's independence from Richard Nixon. And, like Earl Warren before him, he would pull together and hold a unanimous Court on an extraordinarily divisive issue.

. . .

This would be the opinion that would give the Chief a chance to draw on his legal knowledge about the separation of powers, an expertise he had refined in the Adam Clayton Powell case, when he was on the Court of Appeals, and which had been reversed by the Warren Court.

. . .

. . . Seated at the ceremonial desk in the conference room, the Chief told his clerks to pull up the two black leather chairs. They would work right there. He jotted down an outline in large block letters. Each of them would take one section and begin drafting. Then they would reconvene, read through the work line by line, and correct as they went. It was a tedious approach, but it was the Chief's style. He worked best talking out the question, with someone to keep him company. . . .

. . . The three men worked late into the night.

. . .

The Chief felt pressured. He had spent hours at his desk with his two clerks. The work was going smoothly. . . . [H]e decided that the first two sections of the draft were ready to circulate. One dealt with the facts, the other with the technical, though uncontroversial, question of appealability. Just over a week had passed since conference. Perhaps now he would convince the skeptics of his ability to turn out an opinion in timely fashion. Burger read the material over and decided to add a brief cover memo.

Memorandum to the Conference

The enclosed material is not intended to be final, and I will welcome—indeed I invite—your suggestions. Regards, WEB.

Though the job had eluded him, or he it, Potter Stewart knew what it meant to be a Chief Justice. A Chief must be a statesman, a master of the Court's internal protocols, able to inspire, cajole and compromise, a man of integrity, who commanded the respect of his colleagues. But, most of all, a Chief Justice had to be a student of the nation's capital, able to see the politically inevitable, willing to weigh the Court's destiny against other Washington institutions. A Chief Justice, Stewart believed, should be a man not unlike himself.

Warren Burger was none of these things. He was a product of Richard Nixon's tasteless White House, distinguished in appearance and bearing, but without substance or integrity. Burger was abrasive to his colleagues, persistent in ignorance, and, worst of all, intellectually dishonest. "On ocean liners," Stewart told his clerks, "they used to have two captains. One for show, to take the women to dinner. The other to pilot the ship safely. The Chief is the show captain. All we need now is a real captain." Stewart was convinced that the Chief could never lead them to a safe, dignified opinion befitting one of the most important cases in the Court's history.

When the Chief's first two sections came in, Stewart read them carefully. The facts section was poorly written, dashed off with little care. There was not enough attention to the sequence of events or to the key issues.

The section on appealability was not much better. It offered no cogent response to St. Clair's argument that Sirica should first have held Nixon in contempt before the case could be brought to the Court. This should not have become a complicated section to draft. Douglas's draft had already included two simple reasons why the Court could and had to intervene: the risk of a constitutional confrontation between the two branches of government; and the protracted litigation that might result if normal contempt procedures were followed.

The next afternoon, July 11, Stewart and Powell talked about what should be done with the Chief's sections. The two men agreed that they were awful. If they were not vastly improved, the sections would be an embarrassment to the Court. Even worse, if they foreshadowed the quality of what was to come, the opinion not only would hurt the Court's reputation, but could damage its future relations with the other branches of the government. This opinion would be analyzed and dissected for years to come.

All of the eight Justices seemed to be in general agreement on the basic outline. It would be a shame not to produce the best possible piece of legal work, which the Chief could not conceivably do alone. Despite what he said about welcoming comments from the rest, they knew Burger rarely incorporated individual suggestions unless he saw a risk of losing his majority.

Stewart and Powell talked strategy. Brennan's suggestion of a joint opinion could be implemented, but they would have to work behind the Chief's back. Each of the other Justices would systematically propose alternative drafts to various of the Chief's sections. They all could then express their preference for the substitute sections. Seeing that he was outnumbered, the Chief would be forced to capitulate. They would have to gauge White's thinking and see if he could be brought along. Blackmun would have to be won over at once. Although he had broken with Burger in the past and was disgusted by Watergate, Blackmun might support Burger here. They would have to enlist him quickly, tactfully, somewhat indirectly. They knew that Blackmun enjoyed preparing the detailed facts sections in cases. If he could be persuaded to redo the facts section, the others could praise it, suggest it be incorporated, in reality substituted. That would cement an alliance with Blackmun. In turn, he would support the alternative drafts on the other sections. Once committed, Blackmun could oppose the Chief as forcefully as any of them. Stewart left the discussion convinced that the center could once again control the outcome, though it would not be easy.

. . .

Later that afternoon, Powell and Stewart approached Blackmun. The Chief's facts were inadequate. Only Blackmun could repair the damage, they said. Blackmun readily agreed. He would do his best with the facts. He certainly could do better than the Chief had done. He gathered all the relevant material and headed for the Justices' library.

When Brennan heard of the Stewart–Powell plan, he thought it was magnificent. He was also delighted to learn that Blackmun had so enthusiastically expressed his independence. Brennan agreed that Blackmun should handle the facts. He thought the rest of the lineup equally obvious. Douglas should take on appealability; he himself standing; White the 17(c) rule on admissibility and relevance; and Powell and Stewart, together, the extremely sensitive executive privilege section. Marshall, the Court's least productive worker, could be mollified without giving him a section.

Stewart took the first step. "Dear Chief," he wrote, "Responding to your circulation of yesterday, I think, with all due respect, that Bill Douglas's draft on appealability is entirely adequate...."

Brennan quickly followed with a similar memo to the Chief praising Douglas's section.

Powell dictated a single cautious sentence: "Dear Chief: Potter's suggestion as to Bill Douglas's draft on appealability is entirely acceptable to me. Sincerely, Lewis."

Douglas sent his own "Dear Chief" memo saying Brennan had shown him a proposal on the standing section: " . . . It seems to me to be adequate and might put us quickly another rung up the ladder if the other Brethren agree."

When a copy of Douglas's memo arrived in his chambers, Brennan was afraid that it might appear that he was circulating sections privately. He immediately sent his standing section, previously given only to the Chief and Douglas, to all the others.

The four memos from Stewart, Powell, Brennan and Douglas were greeted by the Chief with some consternation. He had hardly begun and four of his colleagues were already criticizing his work. Everyone seemed to be in such a hurry. Deciding to meet what he thought they saw as the major problem—a possible delay of the opinion—Burger gathered together his drafts of the standing and 17(c) sections for circulation. In a cover memo, he said: "I believe we have encountered no insoluble problems to this point."

The Chief then decided to confront the others' concern about delay in a second memo:

Memorandum to the Conference

I have received various memos in response to preliminary and partial sections circulated.

With the sad intervention of Chief Justice Warren's death [shortly after oral argument in the case], the schedules of all of us have been altered. I intend to work without interruption (except for some sleep) until I have the "privilege" section complete and the final honing complete on all parts.

I think it is unrealistic to consider a Monday, July 15, announcement. This case is too important to "rush" unduly although it is in fact receiving priority treatment.

I would hope we could meet an end-of-the-week announcement, i.e., July 19 or thereabouts.

Brennan was extremely frustrated by the Chief's memo. Certainly there was agreement that July 15 was not a realistic announcement date, but not for the reasons Burger gave. The Chief simply did not perceive the problem: all of his sections needed major rewriting.

The next morning, Friday, July 12, Douglas was appalled at the Chief's standing section which dealt with the question of whether [Special Prosecutor Leon] Jaworski could sue the President. It borrowed from the Brennan draft, but contained neither a satisfactory explanation of the regulations governing the prosecutor's office nor the fact that those regulations had the force of law. In Douglas's view, the Chief had failed to fully and conclusively establish that the courts often resolved disputes within other branches of government. Obviously the Chief didn't really believe the courts should get involved in such disputes. Burger still believed he was right and Warren wrong in the Adam Clayton Powell case.

The day before, Douglas had told the Chief that Brennan's standing section was "adequate." Now Douglas decided to be more explicit. Putting his felt-tip pen to paper again, he wrote to Burger that he had just reread Brennan's suggestions and "would, with all respect, prefer it over the version which you circulated this morning."

· · ·

For three days, White had said little, lying in wait. He saw the Rule 17(c) section as the key. That was what the case was about. Would the existing rules and law be applied to the President in the same manner as they would be to any other citizen? The Chief's answer was ambiguous. He had tilted toward raising the standard. So White rewrote the section to enhance the importance of Rule 17(c) as a simple application of *existing law*.

· · ·

White had his suggestions retyped and took them to Stewart, who liked the approach. It answered questions that the White House could raise in order to keep the tapes from being used at trial.

With that, White decided to circulate his proposal. "DEAR CHIEF," he wrote, "The attached is the bare bones of an alternative treatment which I am now embellishing to some extent. Sincerely, BYRON."

Douglas got his copy and pounced at once. He agreed with White's proposed 17(c) section, he declared in a memo to the Chief. Brennan was also pleased with White's proposal. It seemed wholly in line with his own suggestions on Rule 17(c) that had circulated the day of orals. In order to preserve his position with Powell, he decided not to endorse White's memo formally.

Powell was distressed at White's memo; the President was getting nothing, no extra consideration. Even Brennan had said the courts should be "particularly meticulous" to insure that Rule 17(c) had been correctly applied. Desiring to reach a middle ground, Powell circulated his own revised memo. He dropped his "necessity" standard and substituted a requirement that a "special showing" be made to establish that the material was essential. At the bottom of Brennan's copy, Powell wrote in his own hand, "I have tried to move fairly close to your original memo on this point, as I understand it, and what you said at conference. LEWIS."

Brennan was confused by the personal note. In his own memo, Brennan had purposely steered clear of endorsing a higher standard, particularly a "special showing"—whatever that might be.

The Chief, who had at first been mildly bewildered by the sudden activity, was now angry. Brennan, Douglas, Powell, Stewart and now White—of all people—were sabotaging his work. Marshall had been silent, but he would certainly follow Brennan. Burger had an insurrection on his hands. He decided to waste no time in getting to Blackmun, his one remaining ally.

Blackmun had just finished his crash project of revising the statement of facts in the case when the Chief appeared at the door to his chambers. It was an awkward moment. Burger had no idea what Blackmun was preparing.

The Chief entered Blackmun's office and began complaining bitterly about the criticism he was getting on nearly all fronts. Ten critical memos had flown back and forth in the past two days. He could barely get a rough draft out of his typewriter before someone was circulating a counterdraft, suggestions or alternatives. It was amazing, he said. He could not get the counterdraft read before a barrage of memos arrived approving everyone's work but his own.

Blackmun listened.

Didn't the other Justices realize that he had been busy with the Warren funeral, the Chief said? He had his always-growing administrative duties, managing the building, the 600 federal judges. "It's my opinion," he finally asserted, "they are trying to take it away from me."

Blackmun hated scenes, and he disliked crossing the Chief. But it was time to tell the Chief where he stood.

"Before you go on, I think you should see this," Blackmun said, handing the Chief his revision of the facts section.

"What's this, Harry, a few suggested changes you'd like?"

"No," Blackmun said. "It's an entirely new section which I think you should substitute for your initial draft."

"Well," said the Chief, flustered, "it's too late now for such major revisions."

"Would you at least please read the new draft?" Blackmun asked.

Burger's eyes flashed. He turned and stormed out the door without a word.

Blackmun wanted to calm the Chief. He picked up one of the perfectly sharpened pencils on his desk and wrote a cover memo for his facts section.

"DEAR CHIEF, With your letter of July 10 you recommended and invited suggestions. Accordingly, I take the liberty of suggesting herewith a revised statement of facts and submit it for your consideration."

He continued in a more personal vein. "Please believe me when I say that I do this in a spirit of cooperation and not of criticism. I am fully aware of the pressures that presently beset all of us." The draft was circulated. The tone of the cover memo signaled several of the Justices that something had happened. Blackmun told them about his encounter with the Chief. The incident became known as the "Et Tu Harry" story.

When the clerk network passed word that Blackmun had agreed to draft a counterstatement of the facts, several clerks joked that Blackmun would write it like his *Flood v. Kuhn* baseball antitrust opinion. He would begin the facts, "There have been many great Presidents," and then list thirty-six Presidents, leaving out the thirty-seventh, Richard Nixon.

Brennan was elated both by the revised Facts section and by word that Blackmun had stood up to the Chief. He wrote a memo that rubbed salt in the wound. "DEAR CHIEF: I think that Harry's suggested revision of the Statement of Facts is excellent and I hope you could incorporate it in the opinion."

Stewart, too, was quite happy to see the Blackmun section. To one degree or another, all seven Justices were now confronting the Chief. But Burger's position could harden in the face of such pressure. Stewart had three minor points he wanted to add to Blackmun's section, to show that he was not just criticizing the Chief's work. He wrote Burger: "I think Harry Blackmun's revision of the statement of facts is a fine job, and I would join it as part of the Court opinion, with a couple of minor additions."

. . .

[A few days later, after a further discussion between Brennan, White and Stewart on a Saturday when they were all at the Court about the possibility of independent drafting of sections to replace those in the Chief's draft,] Stewart saw that White had dug in on 17(c). White could be as inflexible as the Chief. In addition to his original reservations about the other Justices developing substitute opinions and trying to force them on the Chief, White now had second thoughts about substituting sections one at a time. . . . The Chief would see Brennan's hand in this if he hadn't seen it already. White was loath to have it appear that he had drifted under Brennan's influence. He had to prove his independence both to the Chief and to Brennan.

White swiveled to the right for his typewriter.

DEAR CHIEF: Your statement of the facts and your drafts on appealability and (standing) are satisfactory to me, although I could subscribe to most of what is said in other versions that have been submitted to you.

My views on the Rule 17(c) issue you already have.

With respect to the existence and extent of executive privilege . . . I cannot fathom why the President should be permitted to withhold the out-of-court statements of a defendant in a criminal case. . . . For me, the interest in sustaining confidentiality disappears when it is shown that the President is in possession of out-of-court declarations of those, such as [Charles W.] Colson and Dean, who have been sufficiently shown to be co-conspirators. . . . Shielding such a conspiracy in the making or in the process of execution carries the privilege too far.

White had the memo retyped and sent simultaneously to the Chief and to all the other Justices. . . .

Brennan had to get White back in the fold. He jotted out a memo: "DEAR BYRON: I fully agree with your expanded Sec. 17(c) treatment, recirculated July 13, 1974, and hope it can serve to cover that issue in the Court's opinion." He specified that copies be sent to all the others, including the Chief. Maybe that would appease White.

Stewart followed with a similar memo to the Chief.

"I agree with Byron's revision of the discussion of the Rule 17(c) issues," Stewart said.

. . .

Brennan . . . undertook in some detail to bring Marshall up to date. His support was crucial, particularly given the widening difficulties with White and Powell. Douglas had deserted to Goose Prairie. And you could never tell when Blackmun would bolt to the Chief. Perhaps White had already done so.

Marshall said that he would go along. His clerks drafted a short memo for him to sign. It was the coldest prose they could fashion.

DEAR CHIEF:

1. I agree with Byron's recirculation . . . of the section on 17(c).

2. I agree with Harry's Statement of Facts.

3. I agree with Bill Brennan's treatment of the section on [Standing].

4. I agree with Potter's memorandum on the question of appealability.

Sincerely,
T.M.

Brennan was relieved. The memo was more direct than he expected. TM was back on the team.

Marshall's memo went off like a grenade in the Chief's chambers. Of all the memos this was the most combative. It obviously reflected the sentiments of Marshall's clerks, and the fact that Marshall was giving them free rein. It would be hard to budge that chambers.

It wasn't only Marshall's chambers. The Chief's clerks could see the hands of their fellow clerks in other chambers in all the various alternative drafts and supporting memos. They realized that because the seven other Justices had no other cases to work on, their clerks had little to do. So the Justices and the clerks spent their time cutting the Chief's rough, preliminary drafts to ribbons.

. . .

But the Chief decided to fight back with a memo to the conference on the nature of his prerogatives as the designated author.

My effort to accommodate everyone by sending out "first drafts" is not working out.

I do not contemplate sending out any more material until it is *ready*. This will take longer than I had anticipated and you should each make plans on an assumption that no more material will be circulated for at least one week.

. . .

At [the Saturday lunch meeting with Brennan and White,] Stewart had offered to redraft Powell's section on executive privilege, and now he got down to work. Altering Powell's deferential language, Stewart wrote that confidentiality in government was important, but he stated firmly that in every case, the Courts, never the executive, would make a final determination. Stewart chose a simpler argument than Powell. He adapted and enlarged upon the argument already made by Douglas, that due process would be denied everyone—prosecutors, defendants, witnesses, the public at large—if all the evidence was not turned over.

More importantly, on the sticky issue of the Rule 17(c) standard, Stewart lowered Powell's standard from "compelling justification" to a milder "sufficient justification." That might safely allow him to walk the line between Powell and White.

On Tuesday, July 16, Stewart privately sent his redraft to Powell, and Powell said it was acceptable. Stewart concluded that Powell had given up on the higher standard. Buttressed by Powell's support, Stewart sent copies to White, Brennan and Marshall. Those three then met to review Stewart's section and passed word to Stewart that it was acceptable. White and Powell had finally found a point of agreement, Stewart hoped.

As best he could tell, Stewart now had five votes for the section. Rather than further aggravate the Chief, Stewart decided not to send his own substitute draft to the Chief but to wait for the Chief's circulation on the privilege section.

Of all the Justices, Stewart was at once the most desirous of confrontation and the most committed to compromise. The tension between the two impulses at times seemed to exhilarate him.

The Chief spent the day grinding out his privilege section. The work went faster than he had expected. He tried to borrow generously from some of the ideas provided by Powell, Douglas, and even Brennan, and the pieces fell together nicely.... Brennan's "national defense, foreign affairs and internal security" exception to what would be initially submitted to Sirica's court was extraordinarily broad....

Since the White House had not claimed any such exemptions, the Chief did not want to invite them. "Absent a claim of a need to protect military, diplomatic or sensitive national-security interests," the Chief wrote, "the White House's invocation of executive privilege hardly suffers in this case from an in camera inspection of the subpoenaed tapes."[65]

By early evening, the Chief had what he felt was a satisfactory draft. He resolved to make an appeal to perhaps the most obviously conspiratorial of the Justices. He reached Brennan by phone at home.

Burger told Brennan he had finished a draft of the privilege section and would like him to have a copy before Brennan left for Nantucket for the weekend.

Brennan said he would be delighted to see it.

65. [Editors' Note: In the opinion as published, the Court writes: "Absent a claim of need to protect military, diplomatic, or sensitive national security secrets, we find it difficult to accept the argument that even the very important interest in confidentiality of Presidential communications is significantly diminished by production of such material for *in camera* inspection with all the protection that a district court will be obliged to provide." 418 U.S. at 706.]

Telling him that things were moving faster than he had indicated the day before, the Chief hinted that the opinion could come down shortly after the weekend—perhaps on Monday, July 22.

That indeed would be good, Brennan said. The Chief was obviously in an excellent mood. They fell into an animated discussion of non-Watergate matters.

Early the next morning, Wednesday, July 17, Brennan received his copy of the executive-privilege section. On initial reading, Brennan thought it was in better shape than the Chief's other sections. There were, however, some problems. First, the Chief was not emphatic in meeting the White House challenge by restating the ultimate responsibility of the courts to decide all such constitutional disputes. Second, the Chief talked of the "competing demands" of the executive and judicial branches, which had to be weighed in order to determine which would prevail. That determination turned on the extent to which each branch's "core functions" were involved. Such functions for the executive included war powers, the conduct of foreign relations, and the veto power. On the other hand, one of the "core functions" of the judiciary was ensuring that all evidence was available for a criminal trial.

The Chief then reasoned that in the tapes case a "core function" of the judiciary was clearly involved, whereas none was for the President. Under that reasoning the President lost. The Chief had also sidestepped Powell's demand for a higher standard by simply saying that the special prosecutor had shown "a sufficiently compelling need" for the material to be inspected by Judge Sirica.

Brennan assumed that the core functions formulation—a potentially vague and expandable creation—could probably be rendered harmless by limiting its meaning to foreign affairs, military or state secrets. It was doubtful, he felt, that the Chief would balk at that.

Though it was rough, Brennan felt that the draft was adequate and immediately told the Chief so. He recommended that Burger circulate it.

Encouraged by this response, Burger sent the section around. A full opinion draft, he told the others, would be ready by the end of the week.

The other Justices were not happy with the Chief's privilege section. Stewart didn't trust it. He particularly did not like the core functions analysis. Even if more narrowly defined than in the Chief's draft, the term implied that a President had an absolute constitutional prerogative over his core functions. These "core" functions were very loosely outlined as the Chief named them—war, foreign relations, the veto power or, as the Chief had written, whatever was implied when the President was "performing duties at the very core of his constitutional role."

. . .

Powell agreed with Stewart. When they met with Brennan and Marshall, Stewart made his case, and Powell supported him. Marshall agreed.

Brennan, however, disagreed. The term could be rendered harmless by narrowing the definition. It was more important to keep the Chief on track.

No, Stewart argued. The Chief had moved into dangerous territory.

Brennan saw the others were flatly opposed and was embarrassed by his initial enthusiasm. They might well be right about core functions. Brennan, holding out for a compromise, said he was sure the Chief was not wedded to the term or the analysis.

The four decided to nibble at the Chief's privilege section a subsection at a time. Stewart should circulate only the portions of his substitute section that might be added to the Chief's, particularly the *Marbury v. Madison* restatement—the portion that forthrightly and definitively ruled that the courts had absolute authority to resolve the dispute. They would wait until the Chief circulated his full opinion, all sections from facts to privilege, to attack the concept of *core functions.*

Before leaving for Nantucket on Thursday, July 18, Brennan dictated a memo to Burger.

DEAR CHIEF,

This will formally confirm that your "working draft" circulated July 17, of "The Claim of Executive Privilege" reflects for me a generally satisfactory approach.... I do however agree with Potter, that St. Clair's argument, that the President alone has the power to decide the question of privilege, must be dealt with. Potter's suggested way is satisfactory to me.

Brennan closed by saying that he expected to have some more suggestions and would pass them on.

Marshall's memo to the Chief was even fainter in its praise of Burger's draft. "I agree with its basic structure, and believe that it provides a good starting point with which we can work." But, he added, he agreed with Stewart that the White House position that the President should ultimately decide what is privileged should be "firmly and unequivocally" rejected.

. . .

White did not like what he had seen. The Chief was creating too much law to dispose of the case. He sat down at his typewriter and composed another message.

DEAR CHIEF:

I am in the process of considering your draft on executive privilege.

I am reluctant to complicate a difficult task or to increase your labors, of which I am highly appreciative, but I submit the following comments for your consideration.

First, he said, "I do not object to Potter's suggestion...." Then came the real message. There was too much discussion of executive privilege and a construction of newly defined power for the courts to decide these issues. Too little was being made of Rule 17(c). All citizens, Presidents among them, were obligated equally to cooperate in criminal trials. That was the heart of the case. In this case,

> The courts are playing their neutral role of enforcing the law already provided them, either by rule, statute, or Constitution.... I doubt, therefore, that we need discover or fashion any inherent powers in the judiciary to overcome an executive privilege which is not expressly provided for but which we also fashion today.

. . .

As the latest wave of memos arrived at his desk, Burger saw that large accommodations would be necessary. He decided first to add four long paragraphs at the front end of the privilege section, incorporating Stewart's suggestion. *Marbury v. Madison* ... was cited at the beginning and the end—"It is emphatically the province and duty of the judicial department to say what the law is." It was rather obvious, but if Stewart, Brennan and Marshall thought it was important, so be it.

Now for White. White's multiple memos on one subject were clear. Rule 17(c) was what concerned him. The Chief took his own 17(c) section, cast it aside, rearranged some of the paragraphs in White's 17(c) proposal, and incorporated it almost verbatim. Keeping only three of his own sentences on the admissibility of recorded conversations and one of his own footnotes, the Chief dropped only one of White's sentences, one that he deemed redundant, given what would follow in the executive privilege section. Several of White's footnotes were dropped as unnecessary. The Chief was now certain that each of White's major points was included in some form. White would have to join. And with White neutralized, and the others accommodated on the *Marbury v. Madison* issue, the Chief decided to phone Nantucket and talk to Brennan.

Brennan was surprised to get the call.

Burger said the entire opinion would be circulated in draft form by the weekend; sufficient revisions had been made to meet White's objections. He was hopeful that the opinion might come down by the next Wednesday. It would be helpful if Brennan could return to Washington by Monday to help finish work.

Brennan agreed and hung up. He was both pleased and disappointed. At last there would be a complete draft from which to work. But Brennan did not see how White could have been so easily accommodated. He also thought the Chief did not yet understand how profound were the disagreements. White's draft represented a full-fledged renewal of his debate with Powell over the standards applicable to a presidential subpoena. Skeptical, Brennan made arrangements to return to Washington.

. . .

The Chief spent the next day, Friday, July 19, in his chambers, working with his clerks to pull the opinion together for the first time. Though he tried to incorporate any reasonable suggestion from the memos of the other Justices, the Chief still had to modify the language in several of the memos. Powell's proposal that the courts show "solicitous concern" was changed to "great deference."

Brennan's repeated invitation to the White House to withhold national security material as privileged was also altered.

In the last ten days the Chief had tried to accommodate nearly all the others. He used some of Powell's language on the importance of confidentiality, and the need for deference and restraint by the courts. He simply incorporated Stewart's *Marbury v. Madison* section. He inserted almost verbatim White's section on Rule 17(c). He picked up some ideas from Douglas, particularly his appealability section. He used some of Brennan's standing section. And he tried to accommodate Marshall's objection to two footnotes: one was deleted completely, the other was modified.

That left Blackmun. The Chief used large parts of his statement of the facts. What difference did it make anyway? . . .

．　．　．

The Chief was in his chambers early Saturday. He was in an excellent mood. He read over the draft one last time and was proud of the work. Though the others had tried to pick the opinion to death, it was solid, complete, straightforward and well reasoned. The rest of them had gone over every word he had written, demanding changes. But they had essentially acceded to what he felt sure would be the most important part of the case—the part with the most far-reaching implications. The key sentence was still there. "The protection of the confidentiality of presidential communications has . . . constitutional underpinnings." Nixon was going to lose the case, but the larger principle he claimed to be fighting to protect would be upheld.

The Chief finally sent the draft down to the printer. With nothing more to do, he proposed that his clerks join him for lunch. . . .

．　．　．

Stewart had arrived at the Court that Saturday morning thinking that the first official full draft would come around. When it was brought to him, he read the twenty-nine pages slowly. As he had expected, the core functions analysis was there, the central part of the section on executive privilege that the Chief had labeled Part C. Stewart was uneasy. As inelegant as the writing was, something else worried him. The tone was odd, the references somehow stilted, the citations of cases slightly off the mark. Could there be some subtle meaning beneath the words that he was missing? Could the Chief be slipping something in to sabotage the opinion? Could he be omitting something to create a loophole?

Nixon was desperate. Surely he would look for any ambiguity or favorable point on which to base a last-ditch defense. He might accept the Court's judgment on the law but reinterpret some obscure reference in the opinion. Could there be a bubble of imprecision that would give the President the "air" he needed?

Stewart realized he might be getting too suspicious or paranoid, but the simple fact was that he just didn't trust the Chief, particularly on this case. . . . Stewart's instinct was to drop as much as possible from the Chief's draft and substitute his own analysis and language. If Stewart could not locate the loopholes, at least he might remove some of them, if only accidentally, by putting the argument in his own words. The best way to get the Chief to adopt changes was to go slowly, item by item. Once the Chief accepted a change, he generally forgot where it had come from and became certain it had been his idea.

But now there was not much time. The Chief was talking about an announcement in four days, and Stewart had not even told Burger his major complaint about the core function analysis. An early announcement looked impossible. However awkward, there was no choice but to move a step at a time even if the deadline had to be pushed back. Stewart could at least count on support from the others who had approved his version; at a minimum that included Powell, Brennan, and Marshall.

Then there was the matter of control. Since Burger had come to the Court, the major opinions had been the achievement of the center coalition. There was no reason that this opinion should be any different. To a great degree it was rightfully theirs. The Chief had to be reminded of this fact of life. It was not the Chief's Court, or a Nixon Court.

. . . After the Chief's draft had circulated, [White and Marshall] stopped by Stewart's chambers. Stewart was sitting at his desk in a polo shirt. White was still pleased that the Chief had adopted his 17(c) section. He and Marshall sat at the left end of the desk, and a small group of clerks hovered at the front and right side.

They went through the draft line by line. Stewart made his case against the core functions analysis, restating every argument. White and Marshall agreed that it would be better to substitute Stewart's simpler alternative. Powell and Brennan also agreed, Stewart reminded them, so they had five votes. There were other minor problems. *President* should be capitalized. Then they decided to list their nonnegotiable demands.

The door to Stewart's inner office was open, and they heard someone come into the outer office. There was a second of silence, and Marshall turned toward the door. "Hi, Chief," he boomed.

Burger hesitated in the doorway. He just wanted to make sure that everyone had received a copy of the full draft, he said. The printers, he said apologetically, had forgotten to heat the lead to set type that morning so the draft had been delayed until midday.

It was obvious what Stewart, White and Marshall were doing.

It looks good, Stewart said. His hands working furiously, he picked up a rubber band, put it in his mouth and began to chew it—an old nervous habit.

White was more direct. He said there were still some problems and they were trying to isolate the main ones.

Yeah, the Chief responded. He appeared tense, but he was gracious. Well, he said, he was still shooting for a Wednesday announcement. He said goodbye and left.

The group waited in silence as Burger closed the outer door behind him.

"Jesus," Marshall said, "it's like getting caught with the goods by the cops."

Stewart was visibly distressed. This could make the Chief more intractable.

In any event, they told each other, the Chief's little visit had changed things. Their small intrigue, or what remained of it, was no more. Before the Chief put a more sinister interpretation on the meeting than was warranted, they had to do something, and at once. They had to lay out their demands clearly.

Stewart said maybe they could turn the incident to their advantage. The Chief's discovery had given their convocation legitimacy. Burger would be expecting them to come to him with suggestions. It was important to find a way to present their demands with the force but not the appearance of an ultimatum.

With Stewart orchestrating, they singled out the necessary modifications. It boiled down to some changes in wording and the core functions problem.

"Well, Potter," White remarked, "I'm going home. You go tell him." Everyone laughed.

"I'm not going by myself," Stewart said to more laughter.

"Oh yes," White replied. Stewart was definitely the man for the job. Given his close relationship with the Chief, he would be most effective.

After some more moments of teasing, White agreed to go with Stewart and Marshall. They walked down the hall to Burger's office.

The Chief greeted them. They outlined their suggestions.

It all sounds fine with me, the Chief responded, except the elimination of the core functions analysis.

But that was the biggest problem they had, Stewart said.

Well, the Chief replied, he preferred his core functions section, and he was going to keep it. In fact, this was the part of the opinion that offered the most explicit reason for why the President had to lose—an essential core function of the judiciary was pitted against a general need for confidentiality.

Stewart could see that the Chief was growing increasingly adamant. Instead of debating it right now, Stewart suggested that perhaps he should go back to his office and draft an alternative subsection C along the lines that he and the others had been talking about. He would have it ready for the Chief's consideration by Monday.

The Chief had little choice but to agree. He would look over Stewart's proposal.

After the three Justices left, the Chief vowed to his clerks that he would hold his ground. He could see that Stewart was the leader. His suggestions were the most sweeping and unacceptable; Stewart was not going to carry it off. No way, the Chief said.

Back in his chambers, Stewart got out his uncirculated version of the privilege section. Brennan, Marshall and Powell had already approved it.

The fault in the Chief's reasoning lay in his effort to balance the President's interests against those of the courts. On one side, the Chief put the Article II powers of the President, which he said contained executive privilege. On the other side of the scale, the Chief put the Article III power of the courts. Since there was a specific demonstrated need for evidence in a criminal trial, the weight was on the Judiciary's side of the scale. Burger's conclusion in this case was that there was an imbalance. Little or nothing of weight on Nixon's side, and great weight on the Court's.

Stewart was opposed to creating new constitutional concepts such as core functions, but he had other important problems with this section as well. The definition of executive core functions was too broad and too vague. The term was an open door for a defiant reinterpretation by the President. And the definition of judicial core functions was apologetic. The judicial interest seemed manufactured. The Chief's opinion smacked of judicial legislation, as if the Court were conjuring new constitutional grounds for compelling the production of evidence as a special indulgence for fellow judges. Burger had dismissed Stewart's constitutional due process basis for the need for evidence in a footnote rather than in the text.

Also, Burger's effort to balance the needs of one branch of the federal government against the interests of another, raised the separation-of-powers question. Since such questions were generally left to the head of the affected branch rather than the courts, the Chief was simply asking for trouble.

Perhaps there was an easy way of handling this, Stewart thought. The Chief had balanced the needs of the President against those of the Court. Why not balance them against the Constitution? The Fifth and Sixth Amendments guaranteed due process and a fair trial with all the evidence. Taking some language from the memos of Douglas and White to develop a constitutional foundation for a subpoena, Stewart wrote that "the needs of due process of law in the fair administration of criminal justice" required the evidence. This line of argument would force Nixon to pit his claims against the Bill of Rights, the commitment to the rule of law, and the concept of due process.

. . .

Now that he had his foundation, Stewart began tinkering with both drafts, trying to develop an alternative that would change the thrust of the opinion but least challenge the Chief. He kept the Chief's first two paragraphs, and the next long paragraph except for the last sentence, which said the courts must have standards and procedures to ensure that the "legitimate confidentiality" of the executive is preserved. That sentence had originally come from Powell's pre-argument memo. Stewart then substituted a new line of reasoning for the Chief's core functions analysis. He wrote seven paragraphs in place of the Chief's final four, keeping only Burger's last sentence, which summarized the decision. Stewart had his clerks come in on Sunday, July 21, to type the new version, twelve pages, triple-spaced.

Early Monday morning, July 22, Stewart went over the draft. He was satisfied that it gave the tapes subpoena a firm constitutional basis while giving executive privilege a very limited constitutional status. He then went to White and Marshall and went over it with them in detail. They agreed that they would join the Chief only if he accepted Stewart's substitute. Afterward, Stewart sent a copy to the Chief. That still left four Justices out of the picture—Douglas, Brennan, Blackmun and Powell.

Stewart decided to make sure that everyone understood they were on a one-way street; there was no turning around. He wrote:

Re: Nixon cases

Memorandum to: Mr. Justice Douglas
                   Mr. Justice Brennan
                   Mr. Justice Blackmun
                   Mr. Justice Powell

Byron, Thurgood, and I were here in the building on Saturday afternoon when the printed draft of the tentative proposed opinion was circulated. After individually going over the circulation, we collected our joint and several specific suggestions and met with the Chief Justice in order to convey these suggestions to him.

. . . our joint suggestions were too extensive to be drafted on Saturday afternoon, and I was accordingly delegated to try my hand at a draft over the weekend. The enclosed draft embodies the views of Byron, Thurgood, and me, and we have submitted it to the Chief Justice this morning.

As of now, Byron, Thurgood, and I are prepared to join the proposed opinion, if the recasting of [the section] is acceptable to the Chief Justice. . . .

At this late stage it seems essential to me that there be full intramural communication in the interest of a cooperative effort, and it is for this reason that I send you this memorandum bringing you up to date so far as I am concerned.

P.S.

Copies to: The Chief Justice
               Mr. Justice White
               Mr. Justice Marshall

P.S. As you will observe, the enclosed draft borrows generously from the draft of the Chief Justice as well as Lewis Powell's earlier memorandum.

Blackmun was pleased to see someone stand up to the Chief. Stewart's proposal was far superior, if for no other reason than the weight and authority of the language. Blackmun made it known that he was now prepared to join if the substitution were made.

Powell also found Stewart's version preferable and gave his tentative approval. But he was not deluded. Very little had been taken from his early memo.

Brennan flew in from Nantucket later that afternoon and read the proposal. Though he thought it overly generous in its use of the Chief's language, there were no apparent major changes from the first version he had approved. He quickly called Stewart to say that he agreed strongly that the substitution was essential.

Douglas was scheduled to return from Goose Prairie that afternoon. The Chief sent a messenger to the airport to give Douglas a copy of the full draft he had circulated two days earlier. If Douglas ratified his version, it could puncture the counterdraft movement. Brennan, however, made sure that a copy of Stewart's proposal was also at the airport. He also took the precaution of sounding out Douglas before the Chief could get to him. Douglas agreed that the substitution should be made. That was seven votes, according to Brennan's count. The Chief was the only holdout to his own opinion.

Burger was exhausted. In addition to closing a Court term and attending his official functions, he had worked for more than two straight weeks without a day off. Burger felt the others had been merciless. And Stewart's memo calling for future "full intramural communication" was a joke, after the way he had operated behind his back for weeks. This was all particularly ironic given the Saturday meeting. The Chief didn't think the little gathering in Stewart's chambers he had wandered into on Saturday was in the spirit of "full intramural communication." Each of them had taken a section of his draft and chewed it to bits. If he had written only an eighth of the opinion, he too could have fussed over every word and each comma.

But what would the others do? The Chief had talked to some of them. All, to one degree or another, seemed sympathetic to Stewart's proposal. Burger felt he had been sandbagged; he needed time to consider his options. He dashed off a quick "Personal" memo to the conference.

> Potter's memo of July 22, 1974, enclosing a revision of Part "C" prompts me to assure you that I will work on it promptly with the hope to accommodate those who wish to get away this week.

> The two versions can be accommodated and harmonized and, indeed, I do not assume it was intended that I cast aside several weeks work and take this circulation as a total substitute.

> I will have a new draft of Part "C" along as soon as possible. I take it for granted voting will be deferred until the revised opinion is recirculated.

Once again, Brennan saw, Burger had not even understood the vast difference between the two approaches. The two simply could not be "accommodated and harmonized" as the Chief had proposed. Any attempt by the Chief to accomplish that would inevitably result in another half-baked, paste-up job.

At least the Chief finally perceived that he was up against the wall. For Burger to plead that any vote be deferred meant that they were gaining some ground.

Burger knew that he faced a tough choice. There was no "give" in Stewart's posture, and Stewart seemed to have lined up all the others. Burger read through the alternative drafts. They were really two different ways of saying the same thing; the approaches were different but the bottom line was the same. The President would have to turn over his tapes. Whichever version they used would not make any difference to history or constitutional law. Burger was sure his version was better, but the others thought differently. What was the big deal? It came down to three pages out of a thirty-page opinion. All of them, living day and night with the case for weeks, had become wrapped up in each word and phrase. Did the difference have any substance? Burger could find none. It would all seem silly in a few weeks. But the Chief knew that making concessions was part of holding the Court together. The main thing was to get the opinion delivered. He wanted it unanimous. They were on the final leg. The only thing holding them up seemed to be this section. Stewart had left the first two paragraphs the same. That was settled. The Chief then took Stewart's next two paragraphs about the rule of law and compressed them, shifting some of the sentences around, dropping others.

. . .

... He then switched around and condensed some of the next four Stewart paragraphs—the central basis of Stewart's argument that due process and the fair administration of justice required the President's relevant evidence.

Burger did not find it particularly painful to make the alterations. Stewart's draft didn't really say anything he would not have written himself. The core functions approach was just one of several possible lines of reasoning. Also, he had improved on Stewart's prose.

Late in the day, Burger had a rough draft of this amalgamation typed, and took it to Douglas, who now seemed the most reasonable of his colleagues. Douglas was happy with the new section and told the Chief it would win quick approval from the others.

Meanwhile Brennan had gone to dinner and returned to the Court. Having initially expressed fairly strong support for the Chief's privilege section, including the analysis of core functions, he felt guilty now. Perhaps the Chief didn't understand that Stewart's version was a necessary improvement. With his clerk, Brennan had begun writing a detailed letter to the Chief spelling out why Stewart's constitutionally based approach was better.

Fortified by Douglas's support, the Chief walked over to Brennan's chambers about 9 P.M. Burger was in an effusive mood. The last problem surely was solved. He told Brennan he had revised the "C" section and had just shown it to Douglas, who liked it.

Brennan was alarmed. The first vote for a draft was often the most important psychologically. Douglas's vote could make the other six appear to be the holdouts.

The effort of harmonizing the two versions, the Chief said, had been very difficult. Stewart's draft proposal could not be accepted as a substitute because it was so poorly written.

This remark struck Brennan as almost comic, but he decided that the time was ripe to step forward. He preferred Stewart's version, he said, and had just drafted a note explaining why. The core functions argument would not do.

Burger was surprised. *That* has been dropped in the new harmonized version, he said.

What was *that?* Brennan asked incredulously.

Core functions was dumped, Burger replied.

But of course, Brennan said, *that* was the dispute.

That, Burger said, was nothing more than "the little word discrepancies" between the two versions.

Brennan was skeptical. He asked to see the latest revision.

Sure, Burger said. They returned to Burger's chambers to get a copy.

Brennan read it quickly. Though still in rough form, the new version made no mention whatsoever of core functions. The whole notion had been jettisoned. Even more intriguing, Brennan thought he recognized whole sections, apparently verbatim, from Stewart's draft.

Though Burger's new version was not perfect, Brennan thought it was acceptable.

Brennan told the Chief he was delighted. If *this* is it, he would go along.

That is my compromise, the Chief said.

Brennan bid him a very pleasant goodnight and walked out. He reread the draft to make sure there were no hidden meanings, and he compared it carefully with Stewart's. He did not want to rush to accept something the others would oppose; it had been, after all, his initial encouragement of the Chief on the core functions argument that had slowed down the efforts to win concessions from Burger.

Brennan went to see Douglas. Was he right? It seemed like a capitulation by the Chief.

Douglas agreed.

Brennan was amazed. There were nine paragraphs in the section, some of them long. Only two, the introductory and least important paragraphs, were from the original. The other seven were from Stewart's draft. More than three quarters of the language was Stewart's. Most importantly, the basis was due process and not core functions. And all four footnotes in the section were Stewart's.

Brennan and Douglas decided that Brennan should phone the others that night. Brennan called Stewart first to tell him of the victory.

Stewart was dubious.

Brennan read every word of that section of the modified draft to Stewart.

If *that* was it, Stewart agreed, the Chief had caved in. Of course, he would join.

Unable to contain his enthusiasm, Brennan phoned White, then Marshall and finally Blackmun. It was a victory both in principle and for their strategy. They all three agreed that they could join if it turned out to be final.

Brennan could not reach Powell by telephone, but he conveyed the outcome of the calls to Douglas, who phoned the Chief to suggest a conference the next day in order to ensure that they were all on track.

The Chief agreed. His coalition was building.

By 10 A.M. the next morning, Tuesday, July 23, the Chief had formally circulated his revised section C as seven double-spaced pages.

Brennan read over Burger's cover memo. "As I view this revised Section 'C,' it does not differ in substance from the original circulation." Incredible, Brennan thought. Was it a face-saving rationalization, or did the Chief not comprehend what had been forced on him?

. . .

The Chief followed with a memo saying there would be a conference at 1:30. At 1:25, the conference bell rang. The tension was more pronounced than ever. Various pieces of the opinion draft had been okayed, but this was really their first look at the whole. It was now virtually impossible to trace the turns and twists the opinion had taken: ideas articulated by Douglas and Powell, modified by Brennan, quickly sketched by the Chief; a section substituted by White; a footnote dropped for Marshall; Blackmun's facts embroidered over the Chief's; Stewart's constant tinkering and his ultimatum. Still hanging over them all was the possibility that the President of the United States might ignore them.

Since the printed draft was not yet ready, they sat down and made sure that each had a complete typed draft. They discussed a few minor changes. All seemed to agree that they could join the Chief's opinion.

The eight Justices were exhausted. Summer was slipping away. As they proceeded, the tensions were replaced by a slightly self-conscious notetaking, as if they were preparing for some further drafts.

Douglas, just back from Goose Prairie, suddenly spoke up from his end of the table. There were too many changes that he had not seen or approved. The opinion had drifted in too many directions. Many elements were not derived from their original conference discussion, or from the Chief's initial work. If all these changes were left in, Douglas said, he would file a separate opinion, a concurrence.

Brennan felt helpless. It had been settled, but now, as in hundreds of cases over the years, Douglas was going to do his own thing. Before Brennan could say anything, Powell said that he too was considering a separate opinion. Through many small subtle changes, the Chief's opinion had shifted from the middle course he thought they had agreed upon. The notion of deference to presidential confidentiality, and the need for a higher standard to be applied for subpoenas to an incumbent President, had not been given real consideration in the opinion. They were ruling that any grand jury could subpoena material from the President in a criminal investigation. That was too sweeping. They could, and they should, rule more narrowly, fitting the circumstances to this unique case. Their job was, in part, to ensure that the presidency and the chief executive's decision making were protected from unwarranted intrusions. This opinion failed to do so.

The room erupted. The tentative unanimity that had prevailed only a few minutes before had evaporated.

White was sitting quietly for the moment, but Brennan thought he would probably be next. A separate opinion by Powell would likely touch him off and compel him to respond.

Brennan made an impassioned plea for unanimity. Everyone had problems with the opinion, he said. He too had problems. But it was a compromise document and it was essential both to the Court and to the nation. They might not be able to imagine what was at stake in this case, nor could they predict the consequences of their action. The Court must speak with one voice. He turned to Powell and Douglas. The opinion is fine, he pleaded. Please let it go, he beseeched them.

. . .

As Powell listened to Brennan's appeal, he could see that, like the others, Brennan was overwrought and frantic. Brennan spoke with a tremor in his voice. He was not expressing an ordinary argument, but a conviction. Powell had a nearly inflexible rule: If at all possible, never let a separate opinion or concurrence jeopardize personal relations. Brennan might be right. The need for one voice possibly outweighed the need to precisely state and limit the opinion. Certainly it was not an outrageous opinion. The corporate product was bland enough; and it would not be an embarrassment. Powell might have fought Brennan alone, but Brennan had support. Most significantly he had the Chief's.

Okay, Powell said, he would go along. He withdrew his threat graciously. He would accede to the majority.

Douglas also backed off, and the room itself seemed to cool.

. . .

The next morning, July 24, the Court convened at 11 A.M. Rehnquist was not present. Once on the bench, the Chief took a few moments to pay tribute to Earl Warren, since there had been no meeting of the Court since his death two weeks before. Then Burger announced the case and began reading a summary of its major points in his best, most forceful voice. A silent, unanimous Court sat on either side of him.

. . .

In San Clemente, California, President Nixon picked up his bedside phone. His Chief of Staff, Alexander M. Haig, told him that the Supreme Court decision had just come down. Nixon had seriously contemplated not complying if he lost, or merely turning over excerpts of the tapes or edited transcripts. He had counted on there being some exception for national-security matters, and at least one dissent. He had hoped there would be some "air" in the opinion.

"Unanimous?" Nixon guessed.

"Unanimous," Haig said. "There is no air in it at all."

"None at all?" Nixon asked.

"It's tight as a drum."[66]

After a few hours spent complaining to his aides about the Court and the Justices, Nixon decided that he had no choice but to comply.

Seventeen days later, he resigned.

———

66. [Footnote * in original] See *RN: The Memoirs of Richard Nixon,* pp. 1051–52.

Questions and Comments

1. The Court's decision played a very substantial role in the resignation of the President. But other constitutional processes were also in play. Two days after the Court's decision came down, the Judiciary Committee adopted its first article of impeachment, which charged the President with obstructing justice in connection with the Watergate break-in. Over the next three days, the Committee adopted two additional articles of impeachment, charging the President with abuse of executive power to violate constitutional rights and with wilful disobedience to Judiciary Committee subpoenas. Less than a week later, President Nixon made transcripts of the tapes available to the public; the uproar over their contents was so great that he resigned three days later, on August 9. See Geoffrey R. Stone et al., *Constitutional Law* 413 (5th ed. 2005), from which source this description is adopted.

2. In light of the ongoing proceedings in Congress, should the Court have agreed to so expedited a schedule? Or did the proceedings in Congress, as well as the criminal proceedings from which the case before them arose, provide compelling reason to act with greater urgency?

3. To what extent did subsequent events vindicate the concerns of the different Justices on the Court about the nature of the opinion? Recall the difference of opinion between Chief Justice Roberts' views on the value of unanimity and Professor Stone's critique of unanimity as a goal. How does the story of the *Nixon Tapes Case* affect your evaluation of their arguments? Or is the case too *sui generis* to shed light on this question?

4. The *Nixon Tapes Case* recognized an executive privilege, a constitutional doctrine that has had considerable important in recent history. According to the account excerpted above, to what extent were the Justices concerned with the longer range implications of the opinion? To what extent were they most focused on the case before them? Did they strike the right balance?

5. Given the secrecy of the Court's internal deliberations, how did Woodward and Armstrong obtain access to so much information about these deliberations so soon after its decision? They indicate that they are relying on confidential interviews. See Bob Woodward & Scott Armstrong, *The Brethren: Inside the Supreme Court* 3 (1979). Thus, sources for the specific account given in *The Brethren* are not identified. Their book generated considerable controversy when it was published, as well as concern by the Justices over possible breaches of confidentiality by members of the Court or by law clerks. (For further discussion of secrecy and confidentiality, see below, Chapters Five and Six.) Subsequent scholarly work has made more readily available some of the primary documents in this case, including some of the Conference Notes. Compare Del Dickson, *The Supreme Court in Conference* (1940–85), *supra*, at 185 (reporting Brennan's Conference notes as showing the eight participating Justices as unanimous on virtually all of the issues), with Linda Greenhouse, *Becoming Justice Blackmun* 254 (2005) (noting controversy over *The Brethren*'s account); *id.* at 124 (reproducing, from the Blackmun papers on the *Nixon Tapes Case*, Blackmun's letter to

Chief Justice Burger of July 12, which reads identically to that reproduced above from *The Brethren*). For drafts of what emerged as the Opinion of the Court, see Bernard Schwartz, *The Unpublished Opinions of the Burger Court* 276–82 (1988). You may find it interesting to compare these sources with the Woodward and Armstrong account.

Note on "Swing" Justices

In the later years of the Rehnquist Court, considerable attention focused on so-called "swing voters," Justices Kennedy and O'Connor. Consider these comments by Dalia Lithwick, *A High Court of One: The Role of the "Swing Voter" in the 2002 Term*, in *A Year at the Supreme Court* 13–31 (Neal Devins & Davison M. Douglas eds., 2004):

. . .

> During its 2002–03 term, the high court decided fourteen of its seventy-one published decisions by a 5–4 margin. This means almost one case in five was decided by a single justice. And in twelve of those fourteen cases, O'Connor was that justice. No other justice was in the majority as frequently, as evidenced by her having dissented in only five cases in 2002. Kennedy dissented in just nine. . . .

> This pattern is not unique to the 2002 term. Scholars have been noting the disproportionate influence of the two centrist justices for several years now. . . . Yet it is worth noting . . . that this dominance of a "swing voter" on the Court is not new. There have been moderate or centrist justices since the Supreme Court came into being. . . .

> Especially after the dramatic decisions in the affirmative action and Texas sodomy cases, however, court commentators from across the political spectrum began to suggest that the influence of the swing voter had got out of hand. . . . Increasingly O'Connor is cast as the constitutional equivalent of a careening drunken uncle at Thanksgiving dinner, and Kennedy as a dithering Hamlet. The consensus from the right is that they are not to be trusted, and from the left that they cannot be relied upon. . . .

> Some political scientists . . . caution that it is dangerous to try to make too much of the power of judicial moderates. Although centrist judges make it harder to predict the outcomes of cases, it is not empirically clear that they wield more influence than their brethren . . . [S]wing voters . . . are not necessarily ambivalent. They are simply not predictable, or more precisely, not predictable by any obvious metric.

> If, on the other hand, a defining feature of these moderate voters is that they are routinely undecided on close cases, then their choices become interesting. Why? Because their indecision opens up the possibility that some external force can inform their vote. . . .

> The notion that O'Connor and Kennedy are less firm in their legal convictions is manifest in the ways Supreme Court briefs are written (deliberately citing to and appealing to these two justices). . . . There can be no doubt that in close cases, advocates frame their arguments to appeal to the moderates. . . . One of the liabilities of being considered a

swing voter is that it brings with it the public certainty that one may be lobbied and swayed. But it does not follow that the perception is accurate.

. . . [N]o one who argues that O'Connor is dangerously powerful has been able to show that she is in fact being unduly influenced by extrajudicial forces. Her votes may not be ideologically consistent. But . . . [it] may only mean that context plays a greater role in her thinking. . . .

. . . Influence takes many forms. . . . Justice William Brennan . . . managed to become one of the most influential justices in history. Indeed, just as the Rehnquist Court is sneeringly dismissed as the "O'Connor Court," critics at the time derided the Warren Court as the "Brennan Court". Why did Brennan have such a huge impact . . . ? He was never an equivocal swing voter, but his vision and preferences shaped the Court for many years. Brennan was a politician, and he worked hard to influence his colleagues, lobbied aggressively, and thought constantly about the bigger picture, all the while managing to ensure that his colleagues all liked and admired him. . . . To place too much emphasis on the power of a swing justice is to overlook the fundamental changes effected by more ideological justices, who nevertheless shape the law through powerful personalities, vigorous opinions or broader vision. . . .

. . . There is one important way in which the modern swing justices differ from their predecessors: the role of the individual justice on the Supreme Court has expanded in recent decades, which makes the centrist appear more important. . . . Whereas the Court once placed a premium on speaking in one voice, . . . we live in an era in which it is deemed more important for each justice to express his or her distinct legal views . . . .

. . . In their book, *The Choices Justices Make*, Lee Epstein and Jack Knight . . . [argue that the Justices] rarely attempt to apply the law or do justice, and are far more engaged in strategic behaviors to promote individual preferences . . . Their discussion of the unique powers of the swing voter is illuminating: Employing the strategic model of decision making, they contend, means that "the fifth Justice clearly carries most of the power within the Court. . . ."

. . . While all this scholarship is fascinating, it assumes that there is some empirical means of testing whether judges are voting their policy preferences or just adhering to some conception of the law that may not seek consistency as much as some other value, such as the legitimacy of the courts, or doing equity in individual cases. It does not allow for justices, like Justice Harry A Blackmun, whose views evolved dramatically over his time on the bench. By setting up a binary metric according to which valid votes are never strategic and strategic votes are never valid, these scholars may be telling us more about their own anxieties than the making of justice. Since it is impossible to know whether Justice Kennedy decided the gay sodomy case based on his personal moral code, the amicus briefs, a gay friend, or what he ate for breakfast, we are left with fascinating theories which remain, in the end, untestable.

... [I]t is impossible to argue that justices who are more consistent—who vote according to their notion of some objective, existing law—are not also simply voting their policy preferences. They may just be hiding them better. In short, it is more instructive to look at the term's swing voters themselves, for insight into why their legal constellations are less fixed, or at least less predictable, than those of their colleagues. Game theory may tell us less than O'Connor's own temperament about why she votes as she does.

... That Justice O'Connor has held both appointed and elected political office is often invoked as a key to understanding her willingness to think institutionally and worry about the perceived legitimacy of the court, and her tendency to rule from the middle.... O'Connor is known as a pragmatist and realist before she is an ideologue. Once during a case conference, she listened quietly while Scalia gave a fifteen-minute lecture on the evils of affirmative action, and how particularly pernicious it was with regard to women. When he was done, O'Connor smiled, then offered, "Why Nino, how do you think I got my job?" ... Her need to temper legal abstraction with real-world understanding means that she is open, in ways her colleagues are often not, to arguments about slippery slopes, discussions about the actual parties, and arguments about the basic appearance of fairness. In some ways, she was born to be a moderate because she is as uncomfortable in an ivory tower as some of her colleagues are in the real world....

... In a profound way, the Court's moderates ... illustrate the reality[] that these issues which divide us are difficult, and complicated, and even possibly insoluble. How lucky to have a Court that mirrors that reality! To have a Court that keeps us guessing, that gets it wrong, then gets it right, that hikes one way and tacks another ... that may not, in the end, be a dangerous thing at all.

With Justice O'Connor now off the Court, and Chief Justice Roberts and Justice Alito having replaced Chief Justice Rehnquist and Justice O'Connor, news reports focus heavily on Justice Kennedy as the "swing" voter in the early Terms of the Roberts Court. Do Lithwick's observations apply to Justice Kennedy's position in the Roberts Court?

Note on Bush v. Gore

There is as yet little authoritative scholarly writing on the "inside story" of *Bush v. Gore*, another Supreme Court case that was, even more than the *Nixon Tapes Case*, decisive in who served as President. For a detailed account of the legal proceedings leading up to and including the Court's decisions, see Howard Gillman, *The Votes That Counted: How the Court Decided the 2000 Presidential Election* 17–171 (2001). For a somewhat controversial "insider" account based on law clerk impressions, see David Margolick, Evgenia Peretz & Michael Shnayerson, *The Path to Florida*, Vanity Fair (Oct. 2004). By at least one account, the case provided an occasion for Justice Breyer "self-consciously ... to separate himself from the other liberals in order to build bridges with" what Professor Tushnet calls "the Court's traditional republicans." Mark Tushnet, *Understanding the Rehnquist Court*, 31 Ohio N. U. L. Rev. 197, 202 (2005). According to Professor Tushnet, "Justice Breyer made overtures to Justice Kennedy in *Bush v. Gore*, offering to agree with the holding that Florida's recount procedures violated the Equal Protection Clause if Justice Kennedy would agree to give the Florida court more time to conduct a recount pursuant to constitutionally acceptable procedures.... Justice Breyer's ... efforts did not succeed.... [I]n the end Justice Kennedy decided not to give Florida more time for a recount." Nonetheless, in the end Justice Breyer agreed that there was an equal protection violation.

For discussion of the extraordinary time pressure under which this case was decided, see Chapter One, above. Should it be regarded as representative of the Court's deliberative process? What about *Roe*? The *Nixon Tapes Case*? Students should bear in mind that each of these cases was, in some respects, extraordinary: *Roe* was argued twice; the *Nixon Tapes Case* arose at a time of constitutional crisis, with impeachment proceedings pending; and *Bush v. Gore* was, well, *Bush v. Gore*.

Questions and Comments

1. As has been noted earlier, there is considerable academic debate over the role of ideological predispositions or attitudes, strategic voting, and legal analysis in the decisionmaking of multimember courts, including the U.S. Supreme Court. See, e.g., Lee Epstein & Jack Knight, *The Choices Justices Make* xiii (1998) ("[L]aw, as it is generated by the Supreme Court, is the long-term product of short-term strategic decision making."); Jeffrey A. Segal & Harold J. Spaeth, *The Supreme Court and the Attitudinal Model* 208–98 (1993) (discussing the role of "facts," which they find "strongly influence" decisions in the search and seizure cases they examined, "attitudinal" factors (based on past voting patterns), which they found predictive in some issue areas of civil liberties and criminal procedure but not in other areas of law, and such other (non-attitudinal factors) as the Justices' internal sense of judicial role and external influences on the Justices such as the position of the Solicitor General's office); Jeffrey A. Segal & Harold J. Spaeth, *The Supreme Court and the Attitudinal Model Revisited* 86 (2002) (arguing that the "attitudinal model," which posits that "the Supreme Court decides disputes in light of the facts of the case vis-a-vis the ideological attitudes of the justices," best accounts for how Justices decide cases); Paul H. Edelman & Jim Chen, *The Most Dangerous Justice Rides Again: Revisiting the Power Pageant of the Justices*, 86 Minn. L. Rev. 131 (2001) (developing and applying game theory models of "voting power" among Supreme Court Justices); Frank B. Cross, *Political Science and the New Legal Realism: A Case of Unfortunate Interdisciplinary Ignorance*, 92 Nw. U. L. Rev. 251, 265–311 (1997) (sketching and examining the attitudinal model). Debates over the relative significance of the "attitudinal model," perhaps supplemented by an understanding of strategic influences within such a model, or an "interest group" model, or a "legal model" (including attention to internalization of substantive and process constraints on a judge), or "institutional factors" (including concerns for compliance with judgments

and public acceptance of the Court) have generated a fascinating literature in both law and political science. For a helpful introduction and overview, see Barry Friedman, *The Politics of Judicial Review,* 84 Tex. L. Rev. 257 (2005) (describing and analyzing the "normative" and "positive" approaches to Supreme Court decisionmaking in the legal and political science communities).

2. Is there a role for strategic behavior by Justices acting within a predominantly "legal" model? For an interesting perspective, see Evan Caminker, *Sincere and Strategic Voting Norms in Multi–Member Courts,* 97 Mich. L. Rev. 2297 (1999). Professor Caminker (now Dean of the University of Michigan Law School) identifies his

> central premise concerning judicial motivation: subject to resource constraints, judges endeavor to discern and render their best judgment as to the proper resolution of cases according to their best conception of the law. By this assumption I intend to distinguish my analytical approach from that employed by much recent literature concerning judicial behavior, which posits that judges employ instrumental rationality to advance one or more personal agendas (such as a desire to imbue the substantive content of the law with their personal policy preferences, to enhance their professional reputation and personal prestige, and to enhance leisure).

Id. at 2303. Sometimes, he explains, members of multimember courts do not vote "sincerely"—that is, to express their own best view of the law, but "strategically"—to improve majority outcomes, to create super-majority opinions which have increased "durability," and/or to improve the content of legal rules. He develops as an example Justice Brennan's move from arguing for strict scrutiny of gender classifications in Frontiero v. Richardson, 411 U.S. 677 (1973) to accepting intermediate scrutiny in Craig v. Boren, 429 U.S. 190 (1976). "Brennan apparently concluded that it was preferable to vote strategically to establish a durable precedent now for [intermediate scrutiny], rather than to vote sincerely for [strict scrutiny]." Caminker offers possible explanations for this scenario, including this one:

> ... Brennan might have assumed that the Court would remain fractured across the three tests [strict scrutiny, intermediate scrutiny and rational basis scrutiny], and that Powell and his faction would join the Brennan faction in invalidating the sex-based classification. If so, Powell's [intermediate scrutiny] test would have established a precedent of sorts under the narrowest-grounds rule. But Brennan might plausibly have feared that an increasingly conservative Court would embrace [rational basis scrutiny] in [the future], brushing the weak *Craig* precedent for [intermediate scrutiny] aside. Brennan could then try to pretermit this most disfavored possibility by strengthening the *Craig* precedent, through joining Powell's position to forge a majority-opinion coalition invalidating the statute under intermediate scrutiny. This ... scenario illustrates Brennan's ability to forestall a highly disfavored outcome ... [in a future case] by influencing the precedential significance of the [case at hand].

Id. at 2325–26. Is this a normatively legitimate basis on which Justices should act? Are such reasons distinguishable from those assumed by those who believe that judges vote their nonlegal "preferences"? How do these questions relate to the earlier discussion about unanimity and separate opinions? See also Chapter Five, below, discussing strategic opinion assignment.

3.   Bernard Schwartz, after reviewing the unpublished opinions of the Rehnquist Court, writes: "My discussion and the draft opinions reproduced will show what too few realize: that the decisions of the highest Court are basically collaborative efforts in which nine supreme individualists must cooperate to bring about the desired result." *The Unpublished Opinions of the Rehnquist Court* 6 (1996). Moreover, Schwartz says, "all the 'lobbying' and efforts at persuasion that go on—the infighting, the drafts and memoranda back and forth among the Justices, the changes made in opinions as part of the bargaining process—all this is done for the purpose of reaching what the individual Justice considers the best result . . . all for the purpose of advancing not the Justices themselves but the judicial doctrines in which they believe." *Id.* at 26. Isn't the real question what "best result" means? or what "judicial doctrines they believe in" means? Does his statement suggest the difficulty of distinguishing between a "legal" model of decisionmaking and an "attitudinal" one? the possible importance of distinguishing between the internal, legal perspective experienced by a Justice as a decisionmaker and the other factors that may influence that internal perspective?

4.   One recent study sought to compare the relative predictive capacities of legal experts, presumably attuned to distinctively legal factors, with statistical models, embodying in part some assumptions of the attitudinal model. See Theodore W. Ruger, Pauline T. Kim, Andrew D. Martin & Kevin M. Quinn, *The Supreme Court Forecasting Project: Legal and Political Science Approaches to Predicting Supreme Court Decisionmaking*, 104 Colum. L. Rev. 1150 (2004). As explained in their summary:

> For every argued case during the 2002 Term, we obtained predictions of the outcome prior to oral argument using two methods—one a statistical model that relies on general case characteristics, and the other a set of independent predictions by legal specialists. The basic result is that the statistical model did better than the legal experts in forecasting the outcomes of the Term's cases: The model predicted 75% of the Court's affirm/reverse results correctly, while the experts collectively got 59.1% right. These results are notable, given that the statistical model disregards information about the specific law or facts of the cases. . . .

The model was built on six variables, described in the footnote below.[67] The experts were chosen by the researchers, and were heavily weighted with law school professors.[68] While the statistical model outperformed the entire

---

67. The six variables were: "(1) circuit of origin; (2) issue area of the case; (3) type of petitioner (e.g., the United States, an employer, etc.); (4) type of respondent; (5) ideological direction (liberal or conservative) of the lower court ruling; and (6) whether the petitioner argued that a law or practice is unconstitutional." *Id.* at 1163. The statistical model assumed that the Jus-

tices' voting patterns of the past would continue in the future.

68. "We researched their writings, checked their training and experience, and relied on our own personal knowledge and referrals from knowledgeable colleagues in their fields. The eighty-three individuals who participated comfortably qualify as 'experts,' having written and taught about, practiced before, and/or clerked at the

group, dominated by academics (71 out of 83), the predictions of the small group of lawyers who specialized in practicing before the Court (12 of the 83) outperformed the statistical model. The small group of specialists were correct 92% of the time, compared to 75% correct by the statistical model. *Id.* at 1171. Query whether these data should be read to suggest that detailed legal analysis of the facts and the law are less relevant to predicting votes than the factors in the model, or whether it might instead raise questions about the nature of the differing expertise of law professors and practicing lawyers.

5. Is it too much of an oversimplification to suggest that political scientists tend to assume that outcomes of cases can be largely predicted by the Justices' "predispositions" about issues of preference or policy, while lawyers tend to see the outcomes of cases as resulting from Justices' views of the law? To suggest that political scientists focus on results, and lawyers focus on both results and reasons? Note the methodological problems in distinguishing a Justice's "predispositions" from her best views of the law. Note, too, as sophisticated social scientists have, the difficulty of testing hypotheses if a Justice's views on the law, as evidenced by his or her past decisions, are treated as a "predisposition"—how, then can one distinguish (if it is worthwhile to attempt to do so) "predispositions" from "consistency" of legal judgment? The problem becomes even more complex if one posits that Justices have multiple views about the law—views about interpretation, views about process, views about substantive meanings of legal texts—and that different legal views may dominate in different settings. If that is true, can the approach of political science help shed light on why different aspects of their views may dominate in different settings?

6. Think about the deliberative processes as you have now read about them in this chapter: what framework(s) do you find most helpful in understanding how the Court arrives at its decisions and opinions?

7. This Chapter has focused on the Justices and their interactions in deciding cases. As the opening excerpt from Chief Justice Rehnquist indicated, and as you will see in the next Chapter, law clerks also play a role in the drafting of opinions, a role whose significance has been the subject of considerable discussion.

Court, and having developed significant expertise in one or more substantive fields of law. Collectively, they form an accomplished group of seventy-one academics and twelve appellate attorneys, comprised of thirty-eight former Supreme Court law clerks, thirty-three chaired professors, and five current or former law school deans." *Id.* at 1168.

Chapter Five

THE ROLES OF THE PARTICIPANTS

The Supreme Court is more than a collection of nine Justices. It is an institution, a bureaucracy. The Court has an extensive support staff, its own cafeteria and police force, a printing shop and a basketball court (which is located directly above the courtroom where the Justices hear oral arguments and, hence, is the "highest court" in the land).

In this chapter we consider the roles of certain people or offices that are closely connected to the Court's substantive decisional processes.[1] Section A reviews the office of the Chief Justice, focusing principally on what sets the Chief Justice apart from the eight others, formally termed the "Associate Justices." Section B presents materials on the Justices' law clerks, explaining who they are and what they do. Section C describes the advocates before the Court. We break these readings into three topics: (1) the general quality of advocacy before the Court; (2) the special roles played by the Solicitor General, the federal government's advocate before the Court; and (3) the use of the amicus curiae (literally translated as "friend of the court") brief to influence the Court's rulings in particular areas.

---

1. Although we focus on the Chief Justice and the advocates in this chapter, the Court has a number of "official Court officers" who today include the Administrative Assistant to the Chief Justice, the Clerk, the Librarian, the Marshall, the Reporter of Decisions, the Court Counsel, the Curator, the Director of Data Systems, and the Public Information Officer. See the Supreme Court's Website, at http://www.supremecourtus.gov/about/briefoverview.pdf Of these, the Clerk's Office is probably of most importance to litigants and their lawyers, providing as it does informal guidance on the Court's many rules and requirements.

The Legal Office, headed by the Court Counsel, was created in the 1970s to provide "more permanent and specialized" internal advice than law clerks could offer on procedural and jurisdictional issues (including, for example, recommended responses to special motions, such as requests for expedition, or on original jurisdiction cases or applications to the Supreme Court's Bar). David O'Brien, *Storm Center: The Supreme Court in American Politics* 143–45 (6th ed. 2003) (explaining, *inter alia*, that it was this office that advised the Court to expedite hearing the *Nixon Tapes Case*, discussed in Chapter Four, Section C, above).

A. THE CHIEF JUSTICE: ADJUDICATORY ROLES AND ADMINISTRATOR IN CHIEF

1. Overview

Historians have adopted the convention of designating periods of the Supreme Court's history by the name of the person who served as Chief Justice at the time. (For a list of the Chief Justices and their Terms, see Appendix A.) Thus, we have witnessed the "Warren Court," the "Burger Court" and the "Rehnquist Court." Is this manner of reference simply convenient, or does it reflect an important insight? What, other than the title, is special about being Chief Justice?

The initial excerpts in this section from works by Alpheus Mason and David O'Brien do two things. First, they acquaint us with the character and methods of our more recent Chief Justices, from Taft through Rehnquist. (Given that Chief Justice Roberts was appointed as the seventeenth Chief Justice only in 2005, analysis of his tenure must await future historians.) Second, the readings review and explain what we know about the two unique features of the Chief Justice's office that clearly affect the decisional process. These are the Chief Justice's responsibilities to preside at conferences and to determine who will write the Court's opinion in cases in which the Chief Justice is in the majority. After the introductory articles, we include readings that focus specifically on three Chief Justices: G. Edward White's discussion of Chief Justice Earl Warren and the *Brown* case; Bernard Schwartz's discussion of Chief Justice Warren E. Burger as adjudicator and administrator; and Sue Davis' examination of Chief Justice William H. Rehnquist's opinion-assignment practices.

As these readings suggest, the opinion assignment role, in particular, may be quite powerful. Can the Chief Justice influence colleagues' votes by rewarding them with plum assignments? What assignments might constitute such plums? What factors have Chief Justices usually employed in assigning opinions? How might research to date on these questions be improved?

After a short Note on Professor Mark Tushnet's 2005 views anticipating what to expect after the end of the Rehnquist Court, the final articles in this section (one by Alan Morrison and Scott Stenhouse, the other by Judith Resnik and Lane Dilg), examine Congress' recent tendency to assign administrative duties to the Chief Justice, especially in the appointment of judges to special courts and committees,[2] along with other expansions of the Chief Justice's non-adjudicatory roles. Does the federal judiciary need a new leadership position, a "legal chancellor," to

---

2. These assignments may be part of a wider trend in which Congress has been giving more administrative or other responsibilities, not involving the decision of individual cases, to the federal judiciary. See, *e.g.*, Morrison v. Olson, 487 U.S. 654 (1988) (judicial appointment of certain federal prosecutors); Mistretta v. United States, 488 U.S. 361 (1989) (U.S. Sentencing Commission located in judicial branch, although composed of both judges and non-judicial personnel).

take on some of the administrative and ceremonial tasks that now burden the Chief Justice?

Putting all these materials together, return to the question of what makes the position of Chief Justice distinctive. Should a President, in nominating someone to serve as Chief Justice, use criteria different from those employed in selecting an Associate Justice? How should the President decide whether to choose a new Chief Justice from among the sitting Associate Justices or from outside the Court? As noted above in Chapter Two, five of the 17 Chief Justices had previously served as Associate Justices, though only three of these were elevated directly from Associate Justice to Chief Justice. For discussion of the possible risks of appointment from within, and of some historical norm against doing so, see Edward Swaine, *Hail, No: Changing the Chief Justice*, 154 U. Pa. L. Rev. 1709 (2006).

In considering the selection process for Chief Justice, one could also ask, why does the President designate who shall serve as Chief Justice? Could the Justices take on this task themselves? Why does the position not go by seniority or rotate among the entire Court for specified terms? Could Congress limit the number of years any Justice may serve as Chief Justice? Should it?[3] If an Associate Justice is selected to be Chief Justice, why is confirmation required—does the Constitution treat the position as a separate office requiring the "advice and consent" of the Senate? How much constraint is imposed by the Constitution, and how much by historical practices?[4]

Alpheus T. Mason,[5] *The Chief Justice of the United States: Primus Inter Pares*, 17 J. Pub. L. 20 (1968)

President Washington offered John Jay whatever place in the new government he might prefer. Jay's choice of the Chief Justiceship apparently confirmed the President's belief that the judiciary would be "the keystone of our political fabric." In the long view, Washington's expectations have not been disappointed.

3. These questions, some of them raised in the first edition of this casebook, have been recently discussed in the political arena, see *Hearing on the Nomination of John G. Roberts, Jr. to Be Chief Justice of the United States, Before the S. Comm. on the Judiciary*, 109th Cong. 516–18 (2005) (statement of Judith Resnik) (suggesting limit on term of Chief Justiceship and discussing its legality), as well as in the scholarly literature, some of it excerpted below.

4. See Natalie Wexler, *In the Beginning: The First Three Chief Justices*, 154 U. Pa. L. Rev. 1373 (2006) (noting that Article III says nothing about a Chief Justice, and that the office is referred to only in Article I, in providing that the Chief Justice presides when the President is tried on impeachment in the Senate, and providing historical treatment of the early nature of the office and early appointments to it). Wexler's helpful article appears in an excellent symposium issue, *Symposium: The Chief Justice and the Institutional Judiciary*, 154 U. Pa. L. Rev. 1323 (June 2006).

5. McCormick Professor of Jurisprudence, Princeton University.

Popular interest in the Supreme Court centers around its titular head, the Chief Justice of the United States. The Court is often referred to by the name of the man who occupies the center chair, implying that he puts his peculiar stamp on the Court's work. The custom continues, although Chief Justice Marshall's regime is the only one that clearly sustains it. Chief Justices Waite, Fuller, White and Vinson were overshadowed by one or more eminent colleagues.

Reference is sometimes made to the "Stone" and "Vinson" Courts, but the identification suggests weakness, rather than persuasive command. Though a gifted administrator, Fred Vinson left no distinctive mark on American jurisprudence, while Harlan Fiske Stone suffered from administrative ineptitude. Certain Courts have been called by the name of a President. Chief Justice Chase's tenure was designated "Lincoln's Court"; the court during the years 1941–1946, covering Stone's Chief Justiceship, has been labeled the "Roosevelt Court." But, the label was affixed only to indicate that the President had appointed a majority of the Court's Members. All such labels are of limited usefulness and are often misleading. The times in our history when the Chief Justice epitomized the entire Court, especially at the high level of constitutional doctrine, are the exception rather than the rule.

"[T]here have been great leaders on the bench," Charles Evans Hughes wrote in 1928, "who were not Chief Justices." The center position has been occupied occasionally by jurists of high distinction, but "they gained nothing by virtue of their headship of the Court." Justice Holmes, who served under four Chief Justices, declared that "the position of Chief Justice differs from that of the other Judges only on the administrative side." "[B]eing Chief Justice of the Supreme Court," Chief Justice Stone remarked, "is a good deal like being Dean of the law school—he has to do the things that the janitor will not do." The Supreme Court, Justice Frankfurter has written, is "an institution in which every man is his own sovereign." During most of our history, the Chief Justice has been *primus inter pares,* the first among equals.

Though James Wilson and John Rutledge unblushingly appealed to President Washington for appointment to the position, the Chief Justiceship had relatively little prestige before John Marshall. Such distinction as it first enjoyed was diluted by the attitude of early incumbents toward it. John Jay resigned the Chief Justiceship for the governorship of New York; Associate Justice William Cushing, suffering from "impaired mental faculties," refused President Washington's offer of promotion to it. Jay was adamant in 1800 when President Adams begged him to return to his old station and thus save the country from President-elect Jefferson's "visionary schemes and fluctuating theories." "I left the Bench," Jay wrote Adams, "perfectly convinced that under a system so defective it would not obtain the energy, weight, and dignity which was essential to its affording due support to the national government; nor acquire the public confidence and respect which, as the last resort of the justice of the nation, it should possess."

Even after Marshall and Taney had raised the office to the most distinguished judicial position in the world, Chief Justice Chase declared:

> The extent of the power of the Chief Justice is vastly misconceived. In the Supreme Court he is but one of eight judges, each of whom has the same powers as himself. His judgment has no more weight, and his vote no more importance, than those of any of his brethren. He presides, and a good deal of extra labor is thrown upon him. That's all.

. . .

By the end of the [nineteenth] century, despite the blemish Chief Justice Taney's *Dred Scott* ruling inflicted, the office still enjoyed prestige considered worth preserving. Chief Justice Fuller declined to accept President Cleveland's offer of Secretary of State. The Chief Justice told the President, that "surrender of the highest judicial office in the world for a political position, even though so eminent, would tend to detract from the dignity and weight of the tribunal. We cannot afford this." Like his father Alphonso Taft, William Howard Taft prized the office even beyond that of President. "To be Chief Justice," Alphonso Taft wrote in 1864, "is more than to be President." On two occasions prior to his election to the Presidency in 1908, William Howard Taft refused to accept offers of a place on the Court as Associate Justice. After four years in the White House he still wanted to be Chief Justice of the United States. When, in 1921, his life-long ambition was finally realized, he considered it a step up, not only because the Court is "the most powerful instrumentality in carrying into execution the written will of the sovereign people," but also because he had been "less than four per cent of the Presidents" and "more than eleven per cent of the Chief Justices."

. . .

Taft made clear to President-elect Harding "that now under the circumstances of having been President and having appointed three of the present bench and three others and having protested against Brandeis, I could not accept any place but the Chief Justiceship."

Charles Evans Hughes, at 68, accepted President Hoover's offer of the Chief Justiceship, though this meant ending the career of his son as Solicitor General.

Ambitious for the Chief Justiceship, Robert H. Jackson was twice almost in possession of it. When one or more of his colleagues intervened to prevent it, Associate Justice Jackson, then Chief Prosecutor at the Nuremberg Trials, precipitated one of the ugliest feuds in judicial history. "It is," Jackson commented, "the most sought after, the longest living office." "[S]ince Marshall's time," Justice Frankfurter observed, "only a madman, a certified madman, would resign the Chief Justiceship to become governor [as John Jay did]...."

The Chief Justice has only one power comparable in explicitness to certain of those of the President. Article I, section 3, declares that "[w]hen the President of the United States is impeached the Chief Justice shall preside." Exercised only once in nearly two centuries,[6] this special function has proved to be of relatively small importance. In playing roles, large and small, not formally designated by the Constitution, the Chief Justice exerts influence unmatched by that of any of his colleagues.... Certain of the functions he discharges as head of his Court and of the federal judicial system belong to him alone. He is the Court's chief administrative officer; he presides over the secret conferences of the Justices and in open Court. He is Chairman of the Judicial Conference of the United States. He administers the oath of office to the President and speaks in the Court's behalf to other organs of government. He announces its orders.... As sole spokesman for the federal judiciary, his opportunities for influencing Congress, the President, and the public are incalculable, limited only by his desire and capacity to avail himself of them.

The opinion assigning function offers almost boundless possibilities for the Chief Justice to exert his influence. He can use it to advance his own prestige, taking the plums for himself, leaving the dry, inconsequential cases to his colleagues. The Chief Justice may exercise it so as to exploit the special talents of his Associate Justices, or use it in such a way as to develop specialties they do not already possess. He can use the opinion assigning function to give added weight to a particular decision, or to enhance his own public image. In a controversial case, he can use the assignment power to promote harmony by selecting a writer other than the obvious spokesman of the Court's divergent wings, or add to judicial asperities by singling out the previously vehement dissenter to voice the view now held by a majority. He may pick the man "who will write in the narrowest possible way ... [or] ... take the chance of putting a few seeds in the earth for future flowering." Responsibility for these choices rests solely with the Chief Justice. The use he makes of them will not only affect the dispatch of judicial business but may vitally influence the course of law and history.

Without thought of possible consequences, Chief Justice Stone selected Justice Frankfurter as the Court's spokesman in Smith v. Allwright, [321 U.S. 649 (1944)], the decision which outlawed the white primary in the face of a comparatively recent precedent. Certain Justices had misgivings, and Justice Jackson spelled these out to the Chief Justice in persuasive detail.

> I hope you will forgive me for intruding into the matter of assignments, the difficulties of which I feel you generally resolve with wisdom and always with fairness, but I wonder if you have not overlooked some of the ugly factors in our national life which go to the wisdom of having Mr. Justice Frankfurter act as the voice of this

6. [Editors' Note: After this article was written, Chief Justice William Rehnquist presided over the impeachment trial of President Clinton in early 1999.]

Court in the matter of *Smith v. Allwright*. It is a delicate matter. We must reverse a recent, well-considered, and unanimous decision. We deny the entire South the right to a white primary, which is one of its most cherished rights. It seems to me very important that the strength which an all but unanimous decision would have may be greatly weakened if the voice that utters it is one that may grate on Southern sensibilities. Mr. Justice Frankfurter unites in a rare degree factors which unhappily excite prejudice. In the first place, he is a Jew. In the second place, he is from New England, the seat of the abolition movement. In the third place, he has not been thought of as a person particularly sympathetic with the Democratic party in the past. I know that every one of these things is a consideration that to you is distasteful and they are things which I mention only with the greatest reluctance and frank fear of being misunderstood. I have told Mr. Justice Frankfurter that in my opinion it is best for this Court and for him that he should not be its spokesman in this matter and that I intend to bring my view of it to your attention. With all humility I suggest that the Court's decision, bound to arouse bitter resentment, will be much less apt to stir ugly reactions if the news that the white primary is dead, is broken to it, if possible, by a Southerner who has been a Democrat and is not a member of one of the minorities which stir prejudices kindred to those against the Negro.

I have talked with some of them [the other Justices] who are still in the building, and they feel as I do.

I rely on the good understanding which I have always felt existed between us and upon our mutual anxiety for the welfare and prestige of the Court to excuse my intrusion in a matter which, having spoken my piece, is solely for your judgment.

Stone retreated at once, withdrawing the case from Frankfurter and reassigning it to Reed.

Even before the assignment stage of a case is reached, the Chief Justice has opportunities to make his influence felt. He presents the case in conference and selects the lines along which it may be argued. "You can see," Frankfurter writes,

the important function that rests with the Chief Justice in determining who should be spokesman of the Court in expressing the decision reached, because the manner in which a case is stated, the grounds on which a decision is rested—one ground rather than another, or on one ground rather than two grounds—how much is said and how it is said, what kind of phrasing will give least trouble in the future in a system of law in which as far as possible you are to decide the concrete issue and not embarrass the future too much—all these things matter a great deal. The deployment of his judicial force by the Chief Justice is his single most influential function.

The way in which the Court does its work, the customary reliance on precedent, the large part that may be played by discussion, debate and compromise at every stage of the judicial process, impose on the Chief Justice responsibilities and opportunities not shared by his colleagues. Of the Chief Justice's strategic position, Justice Frankfurter has written:

> An important thing in the work of a Chief Justice which distinguishes his from other members of the Court, is that he is the presiding officer, and has guidance of the business of the Court in his hands. It isn't what he says in his opinions that is more important than what his brethren say, but what he advises on the mechanics of doing the job—should we give a lawyer extra time, should we hear this case now or later, should we grant a rehearing if the Court is divided; things that pertain to the way that the business should be done, things that cannot properly be managed without knowledge of the nature of the business, or, since you deal with eight other human beings, without knowledge of the ways of the other eight Justices. . . .

Essential to the Chief Justice's leadership, along with command of administrative detail, is familiarity with technical matters of procedure and jurisdiction. On this score, Hughes stands pre-eminent. Taft, on the other hand, confessed his inadequacy, and relied on Justice Van Devanter's knowledge of the authorities, procedure and practice, all necessary for keeping the Court consistent with itself.

A task no Chief Justice can delegate is the role of moderator, the job of guiding and directing. By smoothing troubled waters, the Chief Justice may prevent the Conference from degenerating into a row. Fuller did this with marked success. So did Taft. So does the present Chief Justice [Warren]. "His friendliness, obvious decency, and personality," a former Warren law clerk writes, "brought a coherence heretofore lacking in the Court." Stone, on the other hand, suffered not only from an inability to master the routine details of life and work, but also as a moderator. Outspoken himself, he would "descend to theatre, fight with the gladiators, needle one phalanx or the other. . . ."

Justice Frankfurter vividly described Hughes at Conference, surrounded by a mound of thick volumes, all flagged at points likely to arouse controversy. When a colleague raised a question, the Chief Justice's confident reach for the volume containing the answer was calculated to discourage interruption. By employing the methods of a military commander, Hughes made the Chief Justiceship a symbol of efficiency—"the very model of the master of his craft and office." In Conference, as in open Court, discussion was rationed, "lasting six hours," Justice Brandeis recalled, "and the Chief Justice did all the speaking." John W. Davis reports that "[A]t the close of the hour allotted for oral argument he would cut off counsel in the middle of the word 'if'. . . ."

Hughes succeeded in getting the jump on the brethren by his quickness in selecting the issue. Rarely did anyone speak out of turn. For him, Frankfurter recalled, "the Conference was not a debating society but a place where nine men do solos." If difference of opinion disclosed itself between two liberal members of the Court, the Chief Justice would put "his big toe in and widen the cleavage." When differences threatened to produce dissents or concurrences, the Chief Justice would blow his whiskers straight out and say, "Brethren, the only way to settle this is to vote."

Once, at a Saturday Conference, Stone asked permission to read an opinion he had not had time to print and circulate, expecting full discussion, followed by the Chief Justice's recommendation that the case go over a week. Not so; when Stone finished reading, Hughes commented: "Very powerful memorandum. Case goes down on Monday."

Stone's Chief Justiceship furnishes sharp contrasts to that of Hughes. After the first Conference, Justice Frankfurter mixed feelings of relief with words of caution: "I should like to say to you how much I enjoyed the relaxed atmosphere and your evident desire to have our Conference an exchange of responsible views of nine men, led by a considerate moderator, and so I am full of happy days ahead." "Of course I understand," Frankfurter went on, "that you did not want to pull at the reins with our brethren their first day in harness. But the deviations from the tradition of speaking out of turn only prove to me overwhelmingly how important that tradition is for the wise and effective conduct of the Court's business."

Believing profoundly in freedom of expression for others no less than for himself, Stone would not budge. The Saturday Conferences usually dragged on into the middle of the following week. Efficiency, in the narrow sense, suffered. But there were compensations. "Long before I came down here," Frankfurter observed, "I thought that Chief Justice Hughes was unduly emphasizing keeping the dockets clear as against the quality of the clearing." "Any Justice who kicks about the amount of time given to conference," Justice Jackson commented, "ought to resign." "Whatever the ultimate verdict," Justice Douglas wrote, "those who stand at close range know that the Court as an institution grew in stature under the influence of Harlan Fiske Stone."

After exploring the differing methods of Hughes and Stone, Professor Walter Gellhorn is not convinced of the superiority sometimes accorded the former.

> . . . I am shocked by the decisional process in the Supreme Court of the United States as it proceeded under Hughes. The judges heard arguments throughout the week on cases that had been for the most part carefully selected as the sort of cases that required the judgment of our highest Court. Few of the judges made any extensive notes about the cases they had heard; few of them made any careful study of the records or briefs of the cited authorities before they went to conference. Then in the space of four hours the Court decided not only the cases that it had heard, but also voted on the pending petitions for certiorari, jurisdictional statements, and other materials on the docket. This meant that the discussion in confer-

ence was perforce a statement of conclusions more than an exchange of mutually stimulating ideas. Some of the apparent unanimity in the Hughes Court derived, in my estimation, from the superficiality of the discussion which glossed over rather than illuminated difficulties in the path. If judging is as important a governmental task as we lawyers assert it to be, I am not at all inclined to say that extended conferences about the matters being judged should be viewed as a deficiency in a Court.... Hughes used to believe in the appearance of unanimity regardless of the reality. As a consequence of his policy, opinions were often published without the actual but with the apparent concurrence of the brethren. Hughes himself often switched his own vote in order to give a larger measure of apparent support to an opinion with which he did not in fact agree. I am dubious that this sort of intellectual flexibility is a sign of better judging than would be a more candid reflection of division when division exists.

The use a Chief Justice makes of his office depends in part on his concept of it, and on his determination to use it to accomplish results he considers desirable. William Howard Taft entertained a truly magisterial conception of the Chief Justiceship. Under him the Chief Justice was more than *primus inter pares*. ... Enamored of "the executive principle" and the need for "teamwork," and frowning on dissent unless "absolutely necessary," he set out to maximize the limited powers of the Chief Justice in a way that contrasts sharply with his failure to exercise the actual powers of the Presidency....

Taft brought to the Court a clear image of the Chief Justiceship— the office and its powers. Motivating his tenure was a passion for "teamwork"; it alone would give "weight and solidarity" to judicial decisions. "Massing the Court" was a consuming ambition. To this end, he persuaded by example, discouraged dissents, exploited personal courtesy and charm, maximized the assignment and reassignment powers and relied on the expertise of his Associate Justices.

Under Chief Justice Taft's leadership, a firmly united judicial majority envisioned itself in the van of national progress. The laissez-faire dogma, glorified in the writings of Herbert Spencer and William Graham Sumner, was the principal avenue to wealth and social happiness. Taft believed that courts were society's assurance that the sober second thought of the community would prevail. Viewing the Supreme Court as the last bastion against "Bolsheviks," "Socialists" and "progressives," he was determined to head it. Thanks to the judiciary, "[t]he leviathan, the people," he declared, "cannot ... be given a momentum that will carry them in their earnestness and just indignation beyond the median and wise line." "The Constitution was intended, [and] its very purpose was to prevent experimentation with the fundamental rights of the individual."

Soon after his appointment, the Chief Justice announced at Conference that he had "been appointed to reverse a few decisions," and with

his famous chuckle, "I looked right at old man Holmes when I said it."
To this end, Taft exerted influence on the White House to win appointment of those he favored, and to discourage selection of any "off-horse" whose mind might not go along with his own.

During the early years of his regime, Taft's success was remarkable. Wielding power far beyond that represented by his vote, Taft appears to have taken even Brandeis into his camp. Disappointing former President Wilson's hopes that Justices Clark and Brandeis would "restrain the Court in some measure from the extreme reactionary course," Clark resigned, explaining that "Justice Brandeis and I were agreeing less and less frequently in the decision of cases involving what we call . . . liberal principles."

As a judicial architect, Taft is without a peer. . . . On his own initiative, the tenth Chief Justice pressed for revisions in the judicial organization and administration. To his credit is the Act of September 14, 1922, establishing the judicial conference, the Judges Bill of 1925, giving the Justices considerable control over their docket, and the palatial Supreme Court Building. It may be that only one man, Senator Thomas J. Walsh, aided by sympathetic colleagues, kept Taft from winning the revised federal rules of procedure.

Taft's successor, former Associate Justice Charles Evans Hughes, singled out and deplored trends Chief Justice Taft had long combatted. . . . Hughes furnishes us this clue in his book on the Supreme Court, published two years before his appointment to the Chief Justiceship:

> The existence of the function of the Supreme Court is a constant monition to Congress. A judicial, as distinguished from a mere political, solution of the questions arising from time to time has its advantages in a more philosophical and uniform exposition of constitutional principles than would otherwise be probable. Moreover, the expansion of the country has vastly increased the volume of legislative measures and there is severe pressure toward an undue centralization. In Congress, theories of State autonomy, strongly held so far as profession goes, may easily yield to the demands of interests seeking Federal support. Many of our citizens in their zeal for particular measures have little regard for any of the limitations of Federal authority. We have entered upon an era of regulation with a great variety of legislative proposals, constantly multiplying governmental contacts with the activities of industry and trade. These proposals raise more frequently than in the past questions of National, as opposed to State, power. If our dual system with its recognition of local authority in local concerns is worth maintaining, judicial review is likely to be of increasing value.

Anticipated was the impasse between Court and Congress in the crucial term, 1935–1936, when the New Deal floundered on the shoals of constitutionality.

· · ·

Some of the fiercest battles in American constitutional history feature the President and the Chief Justice as antagonists—Jefferson and Marshall, Lincoln and Taney, Roosevelt and Hughes. But none is so dramatic or revealing as the drawn-out contest between the New Deal President and Charles Evans Hughes. . . .

The major antagonists during the first quarter of the nineteenth century, as in the nineteen thirties, were the Chief Justice and the President. The burden of Jefferson's complaint was national supremacy; of Roosevelt's judicial supremacy. Marshall used the judicial forum to enlarge national power. Hughes joined in judicial decisions that defeated the power to govern. . . .

Both Marshall and Hughes proved more than a match for their politically resourceful antagonists. The contemporary significance of *Marbury v. Madison,* declaring for the first time an Act of Congress unconstitutional, is the stern lecture Chief Justice Marshall gave President Jefferson and Secretary of State Madison concerning the proper discharge of official duties. Similarly, in the Gold Clause cases, Chief Justice Hughes lectured President Roosevelt, expressing shock at the Government's repudiation of its promise to liquidate Liberty Bonds in gold. Though knowing, as did Marshall in *Marbury,* that the moral imperatives he espoused were unenforceable, Hughes solemnly declared that "The United States are as much bound by their contracts as are individuals." In the eyes of their critics, both Marshall and Hughes were addicted to the habit, as Jefferson said, "of going out of the question before them, to throw an anchor ahead and grapple further hold for future advances of power." . . .

As judicial strategists, Marshall and Hughes were astute. Just as Federalist Chief Justice Marshall scored in his encounters with Democratic–Republican President Jefferson, so Republican Chief Justice Hughes was more than a match for Democratic President Roosevelt, the most astute politician of modern times. Certain observers thought the outcome in the Court-packing struggle was due, not to the merits of the issue, but to Chief Justice Hughes' superior skill as a political strategist. "Chief Justice Hughes," Harold Ickes recorded, "played a bad hand perfectly while we [the President and his advisers] have played a good hand badly." To defeat the President's plan, the Justices retreated. Roosevelt never doubted that his own "clear-cut victory on the bench" did more than anything else to bring about defeat of the plan in the halls of Congress.

Hughes' political victory in 1937 is comparable to that Marshall scored over Jefferson in 1803. Marshall's triumph was recognized by his contemporaries and credited in the perspective of history. No such accolade has yet been accorded Hughes. It seems odd that Hughes' admirers and apologists should be at great pains to note other similarities between the two Chief Justices, yet reluctant to portray their hero in the role that most closely resembles Marshall—that of political strategist. After the dust of battle had settled, Professor Frankfurter made this appraisal: "I learnt from Holmes that White C.J., had his ear to the ground, and Marshall was not without guile, nor was Taney naive—but no doubt the present Chief will be accorded the highest rank for cunning."

. . .

The qualities that make for greatness in a judge are no sure index of success as Chief Justice. Only two Associate Justices in our history, Edward Douglass White and Harlan Fiske Stone, have been promoted.[7] In neither case did elevation add cubits to their respective statures as jurists. Stone appears to have lost, rather than gained. President Lincoln, believing that appointment of the Chief Justice from within the Court would stir political rivalries, had refused to follow this course. President Grant accepted Lincoln's reasoning. In 1910, President Taft, breaching a century-old tradition, elevated Associate Justice White, a Democrat. President Roosevelt promoted Justice Stone, a Republican. In 1949 retired Justice Roberts, with fresh examples in mind of bitter rivalry among the Justices for promotion to the center chair, said, "as a matter of personal belief, I do not think an associate justice ought to be eligible to be Chief Justice. . . ."

. . . A Chief Justice with little or no claim to distinction as a jurist, who brings to his task no judicial experience, may make his mark. . . . Morrison R. Waite came to the Chief Justiceship a relatively obscure lawyer, without judicial or other public experience, except a short stint as presiding officer in the Ohio State Constitutional Convention. Wanting to be helpful, Justice Clifford suggested that he preside until the new Chief Justice caught on to the ropes. Profoundly aware of his own shortcomings, Waite though troubled, was not offended. "Those fellows up there," he told Benjamin Rush Cowen, "want to treat me as an interloper." Waite solicited Cowen's advice. "I would go up there tomorrow," Cowen declared firmly, "get on the box, gather up the reins and drive; and give them to understand that I was Chief Justice." Waite listened without comment. The next day he returned to Cowen's office in very good humor. The advice had been carried out; it worked "splendidly, splendidly! . . . [I] am going to drive and those gentlemen know it."

Chief Justice Fuller, a man of diminutive stature, faced a Court made of intellectual and physical giants, two of them—Harlan and Matthews—were over six feet tall; two others—Gray and Bradley—were intellectuals; all were confident, self-assured personalities. Fuller, who came to the Court without public experience of any sort, was so short, five and one-half feet, that while sitting on the bench he had to use a hassock to keep his feet from dangling. At first his towering colleagues regarded him with doubt and suspicion. However, self-effacing courtesy,

7. [Editors' Note: Professor Mason was writing as of 1968. Chief Justice William H. Rehnquist was the third Chief Justice nominated to that position from a position as Associate Justice. Two others, John Rutledge and Charles Evans Hughes, served as Associate Justices, then left the Court, and were later appointed as Chief Justice. *See* The Supreme Court's Website, at http://www.supremecourtus.gov/about/members.pdf.]

unimpeachable integrity, a strong sense of fairness and disarming humor made Melville W. Fuller one of the most successful presiding officers in the Court's history. Justice Holmes accorded him high praise. Fuller "had the business of the Court at his finger ends"; he was perfectly courageous, prompt, decided and able to turn off "matters that daily called for action easily, swiftly, with the least possible friction, with inestimable good humor and with a humor that relieved tension."

In the end, a Chief Justice's "actual influence will depend upon the strength of his character and the demonstration of his ability in the intimate relations of Judges." It will also depend on his conception of the office, and on the role he thinks the Court should occupy in the American structure of government. John Marshall, a robust nationalist, pursued a systematic course, using every opportunity to anchor national power in authoritative judicial decisions. . . .

Roger Brooke Taney had at least one thing in common with his distinguished predecessor. Like Marshall, he moved against the dominant political trend. Confronted with the abolitionist movement and national action designed to destroy slavery, Taney interposed constitutional roadblocks and finally brought down on his head a storm of protest. The Court became the focus of fierce controversy, the Chief Justice being featured as the villain in the plot.

. . .

Marshall and Taney demonstrated that, in the hands of one having the will and the capacity to exercise it, the office of Chief Justice affords opportunity to determine the course of history unequaled by that of any other, save the Presidency. John Quincy Adams credited John Marshall with giving "a permanent and systematic character to decisions of the Court," cementing "the Union which the crafty and quixotic democracy of Jefferson had a perpetual tendency to dissolve." The office of Chief Justice, Adams explained, is more important than that of the President

> because the power of constructing the law is almost equivalent to the power of enacting it. The office of Chief Justice of the Supreme Court is held for life, that of the President of the United States only for four, or at most for eight, years. The office of Chief Justice requires a mind of energy sufficient to influence generally the minds of a majority of his associates; to accommodate his judgment to theirs, or theirs to his own; a judgment also capable of abiding the test of time and of giving satisfaction to the public.

. . . Of all major governmental officials, none can compare in length of service with our Chief Justices. "Presidents come and go," Taft remarked in 1916, "but the Court goes on forever." It may be significant that two of our greatest judicial heads served a total of sixty-three years, Marshall from 1801 to 1834, Taney, from 1835 to 1864. . . . The Chief Justice's tenure being for life, it is not surprising that none of our Presidents, not even Franklin D. Roosevelt, matched the service records of Marshall, Taney, Waite and Fuller. Four Chief Justices—Chase,

White, Taft and Hughes—exceeded or equaled the usual Presidential term of eight years. . . .

We have had fourteen Chief Justices [as of the Warren Court] and thirty-six Presidents. Aside from President Washington, who appointed three (Jay, Rutledge and Ellsworth), no President has named more than one Chief Justice. John Adams appointed John Marshall to combat Democratic–Republicanism. Andrew Jackson selected his former Attorney General and close adviser, Roger Brooke Taney. With full knowledge of Salmon P. Chase's deep conviction that "rebellion could not be crushed with one hand while slavery was protected with the other," Lincoln appointed his political opponent Chief Justice. Grant, after two attempts to fill the office, turned to obscure Morrison R. Waite. Those close to the administration accepted him "with a sense of relief but no enthusiasm." Cleveland surprised the legal profession and the country by choosing his unknown and untried friend, Melville W. Fuller. Taft, looking ahead, perhaps, to possible fulfillment of his own ambition, passed over Charles Evans Hughes, age 48, and, for the first time in history, promoted an Associate Justice, sixty-five-year-old Edward Douglass White. President Hoover, conscious of the Republican party's debt to Charles Evans Hughes, and apparently wary of Justice Stone's "liberal tendencies," called the former Associate Justice from a lucrative Wall Street law practice to head the Court. Franklin D. Roosevelt, convinced that his action would contribute to national unity in the trying war years ahead, promoted Associate Justice Harlan Fiske Stone, a Republican. Truman, desirous of quelling unseemly bickerings within the Court, called on easy-going Fred Vinson to serve as peacemaker. President Truman tells an incredible story concerning the considerations that moved him to appoint Fred Vinson Chief Justice of the United States. The President did it on the advice of former Chief Justice Hughes and Justice Roberts. Both told him: "You don't need to look any further. The Chief Justice is administrator. He's administrator of the courts; he's got to be a man who can make the Court get along together, and everybody likes. You've got the man in your cabinet"—Fred Vinson. Eisenhower, breaking what became his unbroken policy of appointing to the Supreme bench only those having previous judicial experience, honored Thomas E. Dewey's 1948 running mate, Earl Warren.

. . .

No one function, nor all combined suffice to explain the office and power of the Chief Justice. Besides the functions themselves, the incumbent's influence depends on the use he makes of them and the manner in which they are discharged. Beyond all this is the human factor, the intangibles, the personality—the moral energy the man at the center releases. One may say of the office of Chief Justice of the United States what Woodrow Wilson said of the Presidency: his office "is anything he has the sagacity and force to make it." The Chief Justice, like the President, "is entitled to be as big a man as he can."

David M. O'Brien,[8] *Storm Center: The Supreme Court in American Politics* 269–77 (6th ed. 2003)

OPINION ASSIGNMENT

The power of opinion assignment is perhaps a chief justice's "single most influential function" and, as Tom Clark has emphasized, an exercise in "judicial-political discretion." By tradition, when the chief justice is in the majority, he assigns the Court's opinion. If the chief justice did not vote with the majority, then the senior associate justice who was in the majority either writes the opinion or assigns it to another.

. . . In unanimous decisions and landmark cases, the chief justice often self-assigns the Court's opinion. "The great cases are written," Justice John Clarke observed, "as they should be, by the Chief Justice." But chief justices differ. Fuller, even against the advice of other justices, frequently "gave away" important cases; Taft, by contrast, retained 34 percent, Hughes 28 percent, and Stone 11 percent of "the important cases." Various considerations may lie behind a chief justice's self-assignment, such as how much time he has already invested in a case and how he finally decides to vote.

Chief justices approach opinion assignment differently. Hughes tended to write most of the Court's opinions and was "notoriously inclined to keep the 'plums' for himself." Between 1930 and 1938, Hughes wrote an average of twenty-one opinions for the Court, while other justices averaged only sixteen each term. . . . Like Hughes, . . . Stone tended to take more of the opinions for himself. He averaged about nineteen, whereas other justices each wrote only about fifteen opinions for the Court every term.

The inequities in opinion assignments by Hughes and Stone angered some justices. When Vinson became chief justice, he strove to distribute opinions more equitably. The increase in the business of the Court also led Vinson to safeguard against justices' piling up of too many opinions and forcing the Court to sit for extra weeks while they were completed at the end of the term. On a large chart, he kept track of the opinions assigned, when they were completed, and which remained outstanding. Vinson was remarkably successful in achieving parity in opinion assignments. All justices on the Vinson Court averaged about ten opinions for the Court every term. Warren followed that practice and achieved the same result. Warren "was the Super Chief," in Brennan's view, and "bent over backwards in assigning opinions to assure that each Justice, including himself, wrote approximately the same number of Court opinions and received a fair share of the more desirable opinions." Burger likewise paid attention to equity in opinion writing, but tended to write slightly more opinions for the Court each term than the other justices. During his years as chief justice (1969–1986), Burger averaged 15.3 opinions for the Court each term, whereas the other justices averaged

8. Leone Reaves and George W. Spicer Professor in the Woodrow Wilson Depart- ment of Politics at the University of Virginia.

13.9 opinions. By comparison, Chief Justice Rehnquist strives for more equal distribution of the workload. In a 1989 memorandum Rehnquist said that "the principal rule" he followed in opinion assignments was "to give everyone approximately the same number of assignments of opinions for the Court during any one term." However, this policy did not take into account the difficulty of a case or the work backed up in different chambers, and Rehnquist explained that he therefore would henceforth give additional weight to whether "(1) A chambers has one or more uncirculated majority opinions that were assigned more than four weeks previously; (2) A chambers has one or more uncirculated dissenting opinions in which the majority opinion has circulated more than four weeks previously; and (3) A chambers has not voted in a case in which majority and dissenting opinions have circulated." In these ways, Chief Justice Rehnquist has achieved both equity in and expeditious processing of opinions for the Court.

Parity in opinion assignment now generally prevails. But the practice of immediately assigning opinions after conference, as Hughes did, or within a day or two, as Stone did, was gradually abandoned by the end of Vinson's tenure as chief justice. Following Warren and Burger, Rehnquist assigns opinions after each two-week session of oral arguments and conferences. With more assignments to make at any given time, they thus acquired greater flexibility in distributing the workload. Chief justices also enhanced their own opportunities for influencing the final outcome of cases through their assignment of opinions.

Assignment of opinions is complicated in controversial cases. Occasionally, a justice assigned to write an opinion discovers that it "just won't write," and it must then be reassigned. Chief Justice Taft once assigned himself an opinion, but wrote it reversing the vote taken at conference. He explained to his colleagues, "I think we made a mistake in this case and have written the opinion the other way. Hope you will agree."

Sometimes other justices switch votes after an opinion has been assigned, and thus necessitate reassignment. Rather dramatically in the course of writing an opinion for a bare majority in *Garcia v. San Antonio Metropolitan Transit Authority* (1985), Justice Blackmun changed his mind and wrote the opinion so as to reach the opposite result. Instead of extending an earlier controversial five-to-four ruling handed down by Rehnquist in *National League of Cities v. Usery* (1976), Blackmun wrote his *Garcia* opinion the other way and expressly overturned *Usery*. Rehnquist's opinion in *Usery* was divisive because the Court had not limited Congress's power under the commerce clause since striking down much of the early New Deal legislation, which precipitated the "constitutional crisis" of 1937. Yet Rehnquist had managed to persuade Blackmun, along with three others, to strike down Congress's setting of minimum wage and maximum hour standards for all state, county, and municipal employees under the Fair Labor Standards Act. He did so on a novel reading of the Tenth Amendment guarantee that powers not delegated to the federal government "are reserved to the States" and by claiming that the Court should defend states' sovereignty against federal intrusions on their "traditional" and "integral" state activities. The justices remained sharply divided on Rehnquist's position in *Usery.* Finally, when assigned *Garcia,* Blackmun was to write an opinion striking down the extension of federal wage and overtime standards to municipal transit workers. But he changed his mind about the wisdom of Rehnquist's earlier opinion and attempt to draw a line between "traditional" and "nontraditional" state activities in limiting congressional power. So he wrote his *Garcia* opinion in line with the views of the four dissenters in *Usery,* upholding Congress's power and overturning Rehnquist's earlier ruling.[9]

Dramatic instances of vote switching and opinion reassignment, however, are rare. Changes in voting alignments usually only increase the size of the majority. . . .

Since justices may switch their votes and since opinions for the Court require compromise, chief justices may assign opinions on the basis of a "voting paradox" or, as David Danelski has explained, "assign the case to the justice whose views are closest to the dissenters on the ground that his opinion would take a middle approach upon which both majority and minority could agree."

Some chief justices employ the strategy of assigning opinions to pivotal justices more than others do. Hughes, Vinson, and Warren tended to favor justices likely to hold on to a majority, and perhaps even win over some of the dissenters. Taft and Stone were not so inclined. Assigning opinions to pivotal justices presents a chief justice with additional opportunities for influencing the Court's final ruling. Because votes are always tentative, a chief justice may vote with a majority and assign the case to a marginal justice, but later switch his vote or even write a dissenting opinion.

---

9. [Footnote * in original] Notably, seven years later, after four appointees of Reagan and Bush joined the Court and only three justices who made up the majority in *Garcia* remained on the bench, the Court again reconsidered *Usery* and *Garcia.* At issue in *New York v. United States* (1992) was the constitutionality of Congress's imposing in 1985 a deadline for each state to provide disposal sites for all low-level radioactive waste generated within its borders by 1996. New York authorities contended that Congress had infringed on states' rights under the Tenth Amendment, but an appellate court rejected that argument on the basis of the ruling in *Garcia.* On appeal, moreover, the Rehnquist Court declined to reconsider and overrule *Garcia.* While strongly defending federalism in her opinion for the Court, Justice O'Connor tried to set that controversy aside. In a narrowly drawn opinion, O'Connor upheld all of the requirements imposed on the states by Congress except for a provision requiring states that failed to provide for radioactive waste disposal sites by 1996 to take title of and assume all liability for wastes generated and not disposed within their jurisdictions. That requirement intruded on states' sovereignty, O'Connor claimed, though dissenting Justices Blackmun, Stevens, and White sharply disagreed. In another bare majority ruling the Rehnquist Court further limited Congress's power under the Commerce Clause but again declined to overrule *Garcia* [in *United States v. Lopez* (1995) striking down the Gun Free School Zones Act of 1990, penalizing possession of a firearm within 1,000 feet of a school]. Subsequently, in *Printz v. United States* and *Mack v. United States* (1997), the same bare majority struck down the Brady Handgun Violence Prevention Act of 1993, but still declined to reverse *Garcia.* . . .

Chief justices may take other factors into account in assigning opinions. What kind of reaction a case is likely to engender may be important. Hughes apparently took this into account when giving Frankfurter the first flag-salute case, *Minersville School District v. Gobitis* (1940) because he was a Jewish immigrant. There the Court, with only Stone dissenting, denied the Jehovah's Witnesses' claim that requiring schoolchildren to salute the American flag at the start of classes violates the First Amendment. But three years later, in a second case, the Court reversed itself. In *West Virginia Board of Education v. Barnette* (1943), the Court held that the First Amendment guarantee of freedom of religion prohibits states from compelling schoolchildren to recite the pledge of allegiance to the flag.

Hughes was also inclined to give "liberal" opinions to "conservative" justices in order to defuse opposition to rulings striking down early New Deal legislation. . . .

A number of other cases [apart from the reassignment, away from Frankfurter, of the opinion in the Texas white primary case described in the prior reading] illustrate that public relations may enter into a chief justice's calculations. The leading civil libertarian on the Court, Hugo Black, wrote the opinion in *Korematsu v. United States* (1944), upholding the constitutionality of the relocation of Japanese–Americans during World War II. A former attorney general experienced in law enforcement, Tom Clark, wrote the opinion in the landmark exclusionary rule case, *Mapp v. Ohio* (1961), holding that evidence obtained in violation of the Fourth Amendment's requirements for a reasonable search and seizure may not be used against criminal suspects at trial. And a former counsel for the Mayo Clinic, experienced in the law of medicine, Harry Blackmun, was assigned the abortion case *Roe v. Wade* (1973).

These examples also suggest that chief justices may look for expertise in particular areas of law. Taney gave Peter Daniel a large number of land, title, and equity cases, but few involving constitutional matters. Taft was especially apt to assign opinions on the basis of expertise: John Clarke and Joseph McKenna wrote patent cases; Louis Brandeis, tax and rate opinions; and James McReynolds was "the boss on Admiralty," while Willis Van Devanter and George Sutherland, both from "out West," were given land and Indian disputes. Burger tended to give First Amendment cases to White and Stewart and those involving federalism to Powell or Rehnquist, depending on the size of the conference vote. By contrast, Warren expressly disapproved of specialization. He thought that it both discouraged collective decision making and might make a "specialist" defensive when challenged. Yet Brennan wrote the watershed opinions on the First Amendment and became a kind of custodian of obscenity cases during the Warren Court.

Some political scientists have argued that in their first couple of years on the bench "freshman" justices are assigned to write fewer opinions for the Court. Junior justices may be given fewer opinions due to the complexity of the case granted review, the Court's workload, and because they still may not have well-developed ideological opinions on the issues coming before the Court. By tradition, new justices are usually given a unanimous decision to write as their first opinion for the Court. And some justices (Frank Murphy, Sandra O'Connor, and David Souter, for instances) did write significantly fewer opinions on their first year on the bench. However, in a major study of opinion assignment ratios (OAR) of senior and junior justices, political scientists Terry Bowen and John Scheb, found no confirmation for the theory that junior justices are necessarily less likely to write opinions for the Court or are less likely to be assigned difficult opinions.[10] Moreover, recent appointees with extensive prior experience on the appellate bench, Justices Ginsburg and Breyer, gave no indication of a "freshman effect" in their first years on the Court.

The power of opinion assignment invites resentment and lobbying by the other members of the Court. Justice Frank Murphy, for instance, was known within the Court to delegate his opinion writing largely to his clerks. Neither Stone nor Vinson had much confidence in his work. Accordingly, he received few opinions in important cases from either chief justice. Murphy once complained to Vinson, when tendering back his "sole assignment to date": "I have done my best to write an opinion acceptable to the majority who voted as I did at the conference. I have failed in this task and a majority has now voted the other way." Only when Murphy's ideological ally, Hugo Black, as the senior associate, assigned opinions did he receive major cases.

"During all the years," Warren claimed, "I never had any of the Justices urge me to give them opinions to write, nor did I have anyone object to any opinion that I assigned to him or anyone else." Warren's experience was exceptional, but he also often conferred with other justices before making his assignments. Black and Douglas, for instance, urged Warren to assign Brennan the landmark case on reapportionment, *Baker v. Carr* (1962). They did so because Brennan's views were closest to those of Stewart, the crucial fifth vote, and his draft would be most likely to command a majority. Most chief justices find themselves lobbied, to a greater or lesser degree, when they assign opinions.

---

2. Some Recent Chief Justices

The practice of using the Chief Justice's name to refer to a particular period in the Court's history, noted above, need not imply that Chief Justices are the dominant figures of their Courts. Some scholars, for example, have argued that Associate Justice William Brennan was the most influential figure (at least for a time) on the Warren Court, and the

---

10. [Footnote 105 in original] See T. Bowen and J. Scheb, "Freshman Opinion Writing on the U.S. Supreme Court, 1921–91," 76 *Judicature* 239 (1993); and E. Slotnick, "Who Speaks for the Court? Majority Opinion Assignments from Taft to Burger," 23 *American Journal of Political Science* 60 (1979).

periodization of a particular Chief Justice's Term may not correspond with more substantive aspects of the Court's work.[11] Nonetheless, the Chief Justice has at least symbolic and formal importance, as the leader of the Court. The next three readings focus on distinctive aspects of three recent Chief Justiceships. Earl Warren's role as Chief Justice in the decision of *Brown v. Board of Education* is discussed by G. Edward White; Warren Burger's leadership style and contributions to the administration of the Court are discussed by Bernard Schwartz; and in the third reading, political scientist Sue Davis analyzes the opinion assignment practices of the Rehnquist Court.

a.   Earl Warren as Chief Justice: Brown v. Board of Education

G. Edward White,[12] *Earl Warren: A Public Life* 159–171, 188–190 (1982)

THE CRUCIBLE OF BROWN V. BOARD OF EDUCATION

Of all the journeys made by Earl Warren during his public career, that from the governorship of California to the Supreme Court of the United States was the most wrenching. There was, first of all, Warren's realization that he was about to occupy a position that must have seemed, for most of his working life, unfathomably remote and munificent. A Bakersfield iceman's delivery boy, Ezra Decoto's assistant, Culbert Olson's frustrated attorney general, and Thomas Dewey's spear carrier was becoming Chief Justice of the United States.

There was, in addition, the stark contrast between the office Warren was relinquishing and the office he was about to occupy. The Supreme Court sat in Washington, a city with which he was not familiar; its members engaged in tasks that he had apparently not performed before; the Court personified a professional world in which he had not immersed himself for ten years and with whose uppermost echelons he was barely familiar. On becoming attorney general and governor he had brought along his own staff to smooth the transition: In October, 1953 he was alone, not even, after his induction, accompanied by [his wife] Nina, who returned to California to supervise the move east.

.   .   .

The characteristic caution with which Warren approached new experiences surfaced as he assumed the office of Chief Justice. He asked Hugo Black, the senior associate justice, to "manage a few of the conferences until I could familiarize myself with proceedings." He observed as the rest of the Court disposed of certiorari petitions that had

---

11. For a sampling of the literature on how to periodize the work of the Warren Court (and whether to regard it as the Warren Court or the Brennan Court), see, for example, Lucas A. Powe, Jr., *The Warren Court and American Politics* 497–99 (2000); Morton J. Horowitz, *The Warren*

Court and the Pursuit of Justice 4, 37, 59 (1998).

12. David and Mary Harrison Distinguished Professor of Law at the University of Virginia Law School.

been filed over the summer, taking no part in the deliberations. He assigned himself a case "of no notoriety" for his first opinion, interpreting the Federal Longshoremen's and Harbor Workers' Compensation Act for the benefit of workers whose job-incurred injuries had not been adequately reported. . . .

Within a few months, however, Warren's presence as Chief Justice emerged rapidly and decisively. This development was striking, because Warren was not able, as Chief Justice, to make the typical changes in an office he had made as a California public official. While he retained a keen interest in such administrative matters as the Court's docket, the schedule of arguments and conferences, and the internal workings of the Court's permanent staff, he could not replace older, incompatible justices with new ones more aware of his executive style, as he had done with personnel in California. He could not cultivate the press; judges did not hold press conferences. He had no powers of the purse, being beholden to Congress for appropriations, no ability to expand his personal staff, few perquisites of office.

Warren's position as Chief Justice gave him no formal powers that his associates lacked, only informal opportunities to exercise leadership. He had no experience in being a judge; he had given little attention to the principal work of the Court, deciding complicated issues of constitutional law. He had no reputation as a legal scholar; he was expected to be a conciliatory, "middle-of-the-road" chief, overshadowed by such influential associates as Hugo Black, William O. Douglas, Felix Frankfurter, and Robert Jackson.

Despite these obstacles, and the relatively low expectations of performance that accompanied Warren's appointment, he soon became a formidable presence on the Court. The most important feature of Earl Warren's chief justiceship, in fact, was his presence. By the time of his retirement Warren was ranked with John Marshall, Roger Taney, and Charles Evans Hughes as the most influential Chief Justices in the history of the Supreme Court. This ranking was all the more surprising because, unlike those other occupants of the chief justiceship, Warren was not regarded as a judge possessing considerable intellectual talents or conspicuous analytical abilities. He was regarded as one of the great Chief Justices in American history because of the intangible but undeniable impact of his presence on the Court.

The episode that enabled Warren to establish his presence on the Supreme Court was the decision in the five segregation cases, which were handed down under the name of the Kansas case, *Brown v. Board of Education,* on May 17, 1954. The segregation cases, which had been set down for reargument in June, 1953, were reargued in December of that year, after Warren had become Chief Justice, and voted upon in March, 1954. Warren's opinion for the Court was approved by all the justices on May 15. The story of Warren's role in the *Brown* case is now a familiar one; my interest here is in examining *Brown* as a means by which Warren established his personal imprint on his new office and as a formative experience in his career as a judge.

Warren had been neither an outspoken supporter nor a vocal opponent of segregation during his California career.... At the time he came to consider the *Brown* decision in 1953, Warren's views on race relations seem to have been relatively undeveloped, as were his views on many other issues he would be facing as a judge.

The Court, meanwhile, was deeply split on the *Brown* case, as revealed by its inner history in the 1952 term. Four justices—Black, Harold Burton, Douglas, and Sherman Minton—had in that term declared themselves personally opposed to racial segregation and in favor of overruling *Plessy v. Ferguson,* the Court's 1896 precedent maintaining that "separate but equal" racially segregated public facilities did not violate the Fourteenth Amendment's Equal Protection Clause. Three justices—Tom Clark, Stanley Reed, and Chief Justice Fred Vinson—favored retaining *Plessy,* with varying degrees of enthusiasm, and two justices—Frankfurter and Jackson—were hard-pressed to find an adequate rationale for overruling *Plessy,* although personally unsympathetic to enforced racial segregation.

In response to repeated prodding by Frankfurter, the Court finally resolved to put the *Brown* case over for rehearing in the 1953 term.... The major purpose of the reargument was to give the justices more time to congeal their positions on the segregation cases. Frankfurter and Jackson, especially, were fearful that an opinion that invalidated segregation but did so in a strident or unreasoned fashion would do greater harm than the continuance of the practice.

Those supporting reargument had not anticipated, of course, that Chief Justice Vinson would die of a heart attack in September, and that the man who replaced him would take a different position toward the segregation cases. From the beginning Warren saw *Brown* as a comparatively simple case. He felt that Stone and Vinson Court precedents had crippled the separate but equal doctrine. He believed that "separate but equal" systems rarely resulted in comparable educational facilities for whites and blacks and thought that such a showing would be comparatively easy to make. He also believed, despite his ambivalent experience with racism in California, that the injustice of an enforced separation of human beings based on their color was apparent. Unlike Vinson, who worried about Congress's reluctance to change segregated practices, the entrenched practices of segregation in the South, and the longstanding existence of the *Plessy* principle, Warren was mainly concerned with the problem of how a decision to eradicate segregation in the public schools could be effectively implemented.

Warren's forging of a unanimous majority for the *Brown* decision established his presence on the Court. The task was one especially suited to his skills: It involved convincing others of the necessity for an arm of government to act decisively and affirmatively where a moral issue was at stake. The eradication of segregation, in his mind, was comparable to the establishment of compulsory health insurance [which he had promoted as governor]. Both were responses to an injustice; both sought to prevent humans from being disadvantaged through no fault of their own. A difference between the two responses was that Warren the judge did not need to rely upon another branch of government to make the response for him, as Warren the governor had had to rely upon the California legislature. But Warren the judge faced two problems of comparable difficulty. He needed to convince persons affected by the Court's response that they should accept it, and he needed to enlist support for his position on the segregation cases within the Court itself.

In the *Brown* case the fortuity of Warren's being appointed to the chief justiceship rather than to an associate justiceship first assumed significance. The protocol of the Court is based on seniority: The Court's most junior member states his views last in conference debate and has no power to assign opinions for authorship. But the Chief Justice is treated differently: He is ranked first in protocol and in formal privileges notwithstanding his seniority. Thus, new associate justices tend to receive insignificant opinions their first term, but not necessarily new Chief Justices, since the Chief Justice assigns opinions when he is in the majority. It would have been inconceivable for Warren to have written the opinion in *Brown v. Board of Education* if he had been an associate justice. Moreover, associate justices have no control over the internal management of cases: when they are argued, discussed in conference, and so on. That administrative task is reserved for the chief. Warren could not have carried out his strategy for bringing about a unanimous decision on the *Brown* case had he been an associate justice.

In addition, despite the convention that the Chief Justice has only one vote among nine justices and thus has no more power than any other justice, a Chief Justice has opportunities to exercise leadership not possessed by associate justices. . . . A person, such as Warren, who was accustomed to chairing meetings, managing agendas, and assigning office tasks, might find that the chief justiceship gave him ample opportunities to exercise power and to make his presence felt. If some of the tasks of a Chief Justice can be likened to those of a chairman of a small group called on regularly to make decisions, those were tasks that Warren had performed for much of his public life.

During the oral reargument of *Brown*, . . . Warren remained largely silent, in keeping with the low profile of his first months as chief. . . . [B]y December 12, 1953, when the first Court conference on *Brown* was held, he was ready to declare his views. He began by stating that in his judgment one could not sustain *Plessy* unless one granted the premise that blacks were inferior to whites. He did not grant that premise, and consequently he was prepared to invalidate segregation and to insure equal treatment of all children in the public schools. But while he had no doubts about the principle of *Brown*, he had not resolved how it was to be implemented, and he suggested that the Court take some time and care in the framing of a decree, being sensitive, especially, to conditions in the Deep South. He suggested that no vote on the segregation cases be taken that day, but that the case be "talk[ed] over, from week to week . . . in groups, over lunches, in conferences."

With this statement Warren communicated three messages to his colleagues. The first was that if there had been any doubt as to whether the Court would invalidate *Plessy,* that doubt was foreclosed. At least five justices would so vote, Warren being the fifth. The second was that Warren viewed the segregation cases as separable into two components: the framing of an opinion overruling or emasculating *Plessy* and the framing of a decree implementing the Court's decision. Warren's preliminary strategy on the segregation cases was, according to Justice Burton, to "direct discussion towards the decree—as probably the best chance of unanimity." In this strategy he had the enthusiastic support of Felix Frankfurter, who had resolved to work behind the scenes for a decision invalidating segregation and may have suggested the strategy to Warren.

Warren's remarks communicated one other message. The message was that those on the Court who remained prepared to defend the "separate but equal" doctrine would have to confront Warren's assertion that segregation and the idea that blacks were inferior to whites were intimately linked. Without labeling defenders of the *Plessy* decision white supremacists, he conveyed that association. This was a familiar Warren technique, the argument to induce shame. Opponents of Warren in California had repeatedly had their positions labeled immoral, unethical, or unjust by Warren, and found that they were forced to defend themselves against such alleged polarizations of their views. Warren continued this practice in his oral questioning of counsel in arguments before the Supreme Court. In cases, for example, where the police from a given state had allegedly intimidated a person suspected of committing a crime, Warren would occasionally ask the lawyer arguing the case for the state why he "had treated [the suspect] this way." The lawyer, of course, had not participated in the alleged intimidation and perhaps had not even met the state law enforcement officers whose conduct was being scrutinized. Warren, however, identified him with the practices and asked him to justify them.

Within a short time after Warren's remarks in conference, two additional justices on the Court revealed themselves as now prepared to support a majority opinion invalidating segregation. Clark, whom others in the 1952 term had thought to oppose a reversal of *Plessy,* identified himself in the December conference as prepared to declare segregation unconstitutional, although he remained concerned about the mechanics of implementation. Frankfurter, who a year earlier had suggested that nothing in the Fourteenth Amendment prevented racial segregation in the states, now made an ambiguous statement in conference that stopped short of committing himself to any majority opinion but indicated that he favored overruling *Plessy,* and followed his remarks with a memorandum to the justices supporting Warren's position.

. . .

Warren next let the segregation cases simmer among his colleagues. On January 15, 1954, the day that Frankfurter circulated his memorandum on the cases, Warren scheduled a luncheon at which the cases were discussed. Throughout January and February the justices continued to discuss the case informally, all save Frankfurter and Jackson meeting regularly for lunch. In late February or March a formal vote was taken. Eight justices voted to invalidate segregation; Reed voted to uphold it. Of the eight, Jackson had indicated that he would probably write a concurrence and had, as early as February 15, drafted a memorandum that was to be its basis. Warren assigned the majority opinion to himself and began to work on it in early April.

The Court had by now agreed on the strategy of separating its response to the cases into an opinion, which would invalidate segregation on principle, and a decree, which would implement the decision. The justices had also agreed to delay formulation of the decree another year, so that affected states could be invited to participate in its framing the following term. The hand of Frankfurter was visible here: His January memorandum had contained the phrase "all deliberate speed," which was later to be pivotal in the decree, and the Court had endorsed his and Warren's belief that implementation should be gradual and mindful of local conditions. Warren had only two hurdles left—the achievement of unanimity, including the suppression of concurrences, and the production of an opinion that was, as he put it, "non-rhetorical, unemotional, and, above all, non-accusatory."

In securing the first of these goals Warren was aided, it appears, by Jackson's heart attack on March 30, which left Jackson hospitalized and was to lead to his death. Warren produced an opinion on May 7, which shortly secured the consent of all the justices except Jackson and Reed. On May 10 Warren visited Jackson in the hospital and delivered his draft opinion. Jackson, whose condition had prevented him from working on any cases and who was therefore disinclined to develop his February memorandum into a concurrence, resolved to join the majority, making only minor suggestions. While Warren's opinion satisfied Jackson in its moderate tone and its absence of pretense, Jackson might well have written separately had he been in full health.

Meanwhile, Warren had a conversation with Reed between the seventh and the twelfth of May. One of Reed's law clerks, who was present at the conversation, reported that Warren said, "Stan, you're all by yourself in this now. You've got to decide whether it's really the best thing for the country." The issues for Reed, Warren suggested, were issues of conscience and of the effect of a southern justice's dissent on a matter so pivotal to the South. Reed eventually capitulated. Formal unanimity was secured on May 15, with Warren making another visit to Jackson on that day. The decision in the segregation cases was announced on May 17, with Jackson leaving the hospital to appear in the courtroom with the rest of the justices.

. . .

The plan of separating the opinion from the decree may have been Frankfurter's; the decision to reargue the case and avoid the deadlock forming on the Vinson Court was prompted by Frankfurter.

But the step-by-step process of converting recalcitrant justices to the majority position was formulated and carried out by Warren. Warren made the decision not to take a formal vote but to meet in informal lunches and conversations; Warren produced a draft opinion that won the consent of his colleagues without major alterations; Warren convinced Jackson and Reed of the importance of a unanimous opinion; Warren took special pains to conceal the decision from all but the participating justices until the moment it was announced. No justice on the Warren Court that had witnessed the new Chief Justice's handling of the segregation cases could fail to sense his presence. James Reston, in a March, 1954 column, reported that other justices had found in the new chief "a sensible, friendly manner," a "self-command and natural dignity," a "capacity to do his homework," and "an ability to concentrate on the concrete."

The *Brown* case, however, was more than an episode that conveyed to other justices the fact that Earl Warren was a person to be reckoned with. It was also a catalyst in helping Warren crystallize his thinking about the new office he held. There were two dimensions to *Brown,* and the case was susceptible to two different jurisprudential interpretations. One dimension of *Brown* was its short-range politics. Viewed from this perspective, it was a moderate, compromising decision, delaying action on its implementation, confining its impact to the public schools, avoiding emotional language or the stigmatization of segregationists, inviting representatives of the states to participate in the formulation of a forthcoming decree. . . .

Another dimension of *Brown,* however, was its meaning as a philosophical statement. This dimension became apparent in the Court's treatment of racial segregation cases after *Brown,* in which segregation in other public facilities was summarily declared unconstitutional by unanimous per curiam opinions that cited *Brown.* As a philosophical statement—that racial segregation in public facilities was inherently unfair and unjust, whatever the context—*Brown* became an example of the use of the Constitution by the Supreme Court to compel action by other branches of government. The states and Congress (which had permitted segregation in the District of Columbia) were told by the Warren Court in *Brown* and its progeny that many of their existing practices were illegal, that they had to change those practices, and that if they did not, the Court would support those persons—whom everyone understood to be hitherto disadvantaged blacks—who pressed for change. Seen from this perspective, *Brown* ushered in a new role for the Supreme Court in the twentieth century, that of an active enforcer of fairness and justice as embodied in the Constitution.

The feature of *Brown* that most clearly identified the emergence of the Court in this new role was the absence of conventional constitutional analysis in the *Brown* opinion. Warren's opinion for the Court invalidated segregation as a violation of the Equal Protection Clause not through any analysis of the historical meaning of that clause (the history was dismissed as inconclusive) or through a close analysis of precedents in the race relations area (they were treated summarily). Warren's opinion invalidated segregation on the basis of two findings. First, he found that "today" education was "perhaps the most important function of state and local governments," and that the Equal Protection Clause consequently required that "the opportunity of an education ... be made available to all on equal terms."

Second, he found that "[racially] separate educational facilities [were] inherently unequal," because "segregation of white and colored children in public schools has a detrimental effect on the colored children," being "interpreted as denoting the inferiority of the negro group." The basis for Warren's first finding was his own conviction of the importance of education; the basis for his second finding was social science literature of the 1940s and fifties on racial prejudice and its effects. The opinion in *Brown,* in short, declared racial segregation unconstitutional through appeal to contemporary social perceptions rather than to constitutional doctrine.

The ideal behind *Brown*—the intuitive justice of equality of opportunity—was an ideal not explicitly codified in the Constitution. The force of the case was in the decisive, almost summary fashion with which Warren's opinion announced the Court's dedication to that ideal in the race relations area. When coupled with the per curiams after *Brown,* the decision conveyed a jurisprudential message: The Warren Court, at least in race relations cases, was going to fuse constitutional interpretation with a search for justice, reading constitutional language in a way that could make the Constitution harmonize with current perceptions of what justice required. And if the Court's readings compelled a change in the practices of other branches of government, the Court was not going to avoid insisting on that change merely because those branches were purportedly more democratic in composition than it.

In *Brown,* then, can be seen the seeds of an activist support for "liberal" policies, such as equality of opportunity, that was to constitute an important theme of the Warren Court. The *Brown* decision was a classic manifestation of mid-twentieth-century liberal theory in its effort, through the affirmation of principles such as equality of opportunity, to fuse the idea of affirmative, paternalistic governmental action with the idea of protection for civil rights and civil liberties....

The two dimensions of *Brown* had suggested two possible roles for Warren the Chief Justice. One was as temporizer and compromiser, avoiding open confrontations on politically sensitive issues, burying internal differences beneath a hard-won statement of unanimity. Another was as activist promoter of the cause of justice, particularly justice for those who had been denied equal opportunities in American life. Both roles were consistent with Warren's California experience. He had been measured in his rhetoric and careful in the timing of his actions as a California public official; he had chosen, for the most part, not to polarize issues and to justify his decisions on the basis of propositions that had widespread public support. On the other hand he had been continually interested in having his offices take decisive action on issues, and he had not been deterred by the reluctance of other governmental institutions to be comparably activist. Warren had functioned, in California, as both the artfully "moderate" politician and the determinedly activist officeholder.

As Chief Justice of the United States, Warren was eventually to discard the role of temporizing politician for the role of activist judge. The subsequent course of his tenure revealed *Brown* to have been the seedbed of his activism. The momentum of the Court's mission in *Brown,* which came to be seen by Warren as a mission to vindicate ethical principles that were embodied in the Constitution, even if this meant dramatically expanding the Court's jurisdictional reach and power, eventually grew to the point where *Brown* now appears as the case where the Warren Court's ultimate character was first revealed.

. . .

As Warren began to move away from the cautious posture of his first years on the Court he became inclined to trust his instincts, to emphasize the significance of getting "good" results as a judge. He came to see Frankfurter's purported subordination of personal preferences to a theory of judicial restraint as regularly resulting in decisions that were obfuscated by a flood of academic language, or unnecessarily self-conscious, or sometimes simply misguided. . . .

Underneath Warren's hearty, pleasant persona, then, his peers on the Court confronted a Chief Justice who had confidence in his intuitive reactions, who had formed his own judgments about his peers, separating those he saw as potential supporters from those who appeared to be antagonists, who was used to getting his own way, and who was not afraid to speak his mind. They also confronted a Chief Justice willing to compromise on matters he regarded as relatively insignificant—technical language in a given opinion—to prevail on matters he thought important, such as decent and just results. This was the same Earl Warren contemporaries had confronted as governor, attorney general, and district attorney. If there was a continual discrepancy between Warren's persona and his composite personality, the discrepancy remained constant over time.

. . .

This posture—impatience with obstructionist doctrine when justice called out to be done—was to become identified with Earl Warren's chief justiceship; it was to serve as a powerful alternative jurisprudence to that of Frankfurter. Most of Warren's energy on the Court was directed toward achieving the "right" results. He did not often agonize, as did Frankfurter, over an outcome in a case, nor did he despair of finding an adequate constitutional basis for justifying his intuitions, nor did he worry about being overly activist. He spent his time on discerning results that seemed just and on marshaling support for those results by attempting to convince others of their inherent justice.

---

b. Warren Burger as Chief Justice: Adjudicatory Failure and Administrative Success?

In addition to the description excerpted below, readers may wish to review Chapter Four, Section C, above, for a description of Chief Justice Burger's role in the *United States v. Nixon* case.

Bernard Schwartz,[13] *The Ascent of Pragmatism: The Burger Court in Action* 1–15 (1990)

CHIEF JUSTICE BURGER AND HIS COURT

"Don't let them push you around." Chief Justice Burger once told me this was the principal advice given him by his predecessor, Earl Warren. But the leadership role of a Chief Justice depends more on his abilities than his position, and in the Supreme Court it is difficult for a Chief Justice to assert a *formal* leadership role. Aside from his designation as Chief of the Court and his slightly higher salary, the Chief Justice is not superior to his colleagues—and certainly is not legally superior.

The Justices themselves have always been sensitive to claims of Chief Justice superiority. As Justice Tom C. Clark said, "The Chief Justice has no more authority than other members of the court." And Justice Felix Frankfurter wrote "that any encouragement in a Chief Justice that he is the boss ... must be rigorously resisted.... I, for my part, will discharge what I regard as a post of trusteeship, not least in keeping the Chief Justice in his place...."

The Chief Justiceship should not, however, be approached only in a formalistic sense. The greatest Chief Justices have known how to make the most of the extralegal potential inherent in their position. The Chief Justice may be only *primus inter pares;* but he is *primus.* Somebody has to preside, both in open court and in the even more important work of deciding cases in the conference chamber. The Chief Justice controls the discussion in conference; his is the prerogative to call and discuss cases before the other Justices speak. A great Chief Justice leads the Court with all the authority, all the *bravura,* of a great maestro.

Yet even a strong Chief Justice is limited. The Supreme Court is a collegiate institution, which is underscored by the custom of the Justices calling each other "Brethren." The Justices can only be guided, not directed. As Frankfurter stated, "Good feeling in the Court, as in a

---

13. Chapman Distinguished Professor of Law at the University of Tulsa.

family, is produced by accommodation, not by authority—whether the authority of a parent or a vote."

. . .

In many ways, the individual Justices operate like "nine separate law firms." Justice Stewart told me that even Chief Justice Warren "came to realize very early ... that this group of nine rather prima donnaish people could not be led, could not be told, in the way the Governor of California can tell a subordinate, do this or do that."

. . .

BURGER ON OLYMPUS

Earl Warren brought more authority to the position of Chief Justice than had been the case for years, and the Warren Court bore his image as unmistakably as the earlier Courts of John Marshall and Roger B. Taney. The high bench was emphatically the *Warren* Court, and he and the country knew it.

This was plainly not as true under Warren E. Burger. The Burger tenure was not marked by strong leadership in molding Supreme Court jurisprudence.

Burger himself was cast from a different mold than Warren. Although, as a reporter pointed out, his "white maned, broad-shouldered presence on the bench is very reminiscent of his predecessor's," the men beneath the dignified exteriors were completely dissimilar. Burger's background was mostly in a law firm in St. Paul. He had nothing like the spectacular career and broad experience in politics of Warren, although he had been active in the Republican party. He worked in Harold E. Stassen's successful campaign for governor, and in 1952 he was Stassen's floor manager at the Republican convention when Minnesota's switch supplied the necessary votes for Eisenhower's nomination.

After the election, Burger was appointed assistant attorney general in charge of the Claims Division of the Department of Justice....

In 1956, Burger was named to the U.S. Court of Appeals in Washington, D.C., where he developed a reputation as a conservative, particularly in criminal cases. He was sworn in as Chief Justice in June 1969 and headed the Court until 1986.

Burger's critics contend that he stood too much on the dignity of his office and was aloof and unfeeling. Intimates stress his courtesy and kindness and assert that the office, not the man, may have made for a different impression. "The Chief," says Justice Blackmun, who grew up with him, "has a great heart in him, and he's a very fine human being when you get to know him, when the tensions are off. One has to remember, too, that he's under strain almost constantly."

Burger, not a person to develop intimate relations with colleagues, was as close to his law clerks as to anyone. And law clerks, in particular, speak of him with affection. One of them worked all day doing research for a conference that evening. She brought her work to the Chief Justice's home after 6:00 P.M. He asked her if she had eaten. "That's not important," she replied. "The main thing is to finish before the conference." At this Burger said, "You can't work if you don't eat." He brought in tomatoes from his garden and made her a sandwich. Later, just before the conference, Burger said, "You see, we finished on time."

Every Saturday at noon, Burger made soup in his tiny office kitchen for his clerks. Then Burger would sit and talk with them informally for hours, usually with colorful reminiscences about his career. The one rule was that no one could talk about the cases currently before the Court.

Another clerk recalls how one day Burger decided to eat in the Court cafeteria and after a few moments found himself posing for pictures with tourists and their children. "He seemed entirely comfortable, just like a politician, even though he never got his lunch."

Others picture the Chief Justice as a petty pedant, not up to the demands of his position and most concerned with minor details and the formal dignity of his office. Burger himself undertook the redecoration of the Supreme Court cafeteria and personally helped choose the glassware and china. He also redesigned the Court bench, changing it from a traditional straight bench to a "winged," or half-hexagon shape.

Burger was dismayed to find that his Supreme Court office was smaller than the one he had had at the court of appeals. Next door was the elegant conference room, which could serve admirably as a ceremonial office for the Court head. Burger did not go so far as to take over the conference room; instead, he placed an old desk in the room and moved the conference table to one side. Thus the conference room also became the Chief Justice's reception room.

Burger's use of the conference room irritated the others. Justice Hugo L. Black's wife noted in her diary that she was told "that C.J. Burger had decided to take the *Conference* Room for *his office!* Funny thing. Isn't that a kick! Hugo says he will not quarrel with him about such an insignificant matter but John Harlan called from Connecticut and was red-hot about it."

Burger was also criticized for his treatment of those who disagreed with him. Lewis Powell at one time cast a critical fifth vote in an emotional criminal case. Burger tried hard to get Powell to change his vote, and, after resisting weeks of pressure, Powell told another Justice: "I'm resigned to writing nothing but Indian affairs cases for the rest of my life." Or as Justice Blackmun said, "If one's in the doghouse with the Chief, he gets the crud."

Yet Burger himself could wryly refer to his reputation in this respect. During one term, the Chief Justice had had a number of disagreements with John Paul Stevens. One of the Court secretaries was taking a course in cake decorating, and each week she brought in the fancy cake she had baked. At the end of the course, she made a cake in the shape of a bench, with realistic figures of the Justices. There was a chocolate Thurgood Marshall and a Stevens with bow tie and glasses. It was decided that the cake should be sent up to the Justices, but the clerks had eaten the Stevens figure. When the cake was brought in, the Chief Justice turned to Stevens and declared with mock solemnity, "You see what happens when you disagree with me!"

. . .

Burger was always sensitive to what he perceived to be slights to his office and to himself; throughout his tenure he had an almost adversarial relationship with the press. According to one reporter, "He fostered an atmosphere of secrecy around the court that left some employees terrified of being caught chatting with us." When a network asked permission to carry live radio coverage of the arguments in what promised to be a landmark case, the Chief Justice replied with a one-sentence letter: "It is not possible to arrange for any broadcast of any Supreme Court proceeding." Handwritten at the bottom was a postscript: "When you get the Cabinet meetings on the air, call me!"

Burger was particularly concerned about leaks to the press. He once circulated a memorandum to the conference headed *"CONFIDENTIAL"* because a reporter had attempted to interview law clerks. "I have categorically directed," Burger declared, "that none of my staff have any conversation on any subject with any reporter. This directive was really not necessary since this is a condition of employment. I know of no one who is skilled enough to expose himself to any conversation with a reporter without getting into 'forbidden territory.' The reporter will inevitably extract information on the internal mechanisms of the Court, one way or another, to our embarrassment."

The Chief Justice was deeply hurt by derogatory accounts about his performance, particularly in the best seller *The Brethren,* and was gleeful when he told me that copies of the book were remaindered at ninety-eight cents in a Washington bookstore. . . .

Burger's critics often singled out his concern with food and attire. Author Lincoln Caplan quotes Burger as saying "that he himself should be in a wig and gown, and had been cheated out of it by Thomas Jefferson." Early Supreme Court Justices did wear wigs and gowns, but the practice was soon abandoned, in part at least because of Jefferson's opposition. Caplan does state that he "wasn't sure whether [Burger] was being humorous or not."

It cannot be denied that, from his "Middle Temple" cheddar, made according to his own recipe, to the finest clarets, Burger is somewhat of an epicure. One of the social high points of a 1969 British–American conference at Ditchley, Oxfordshire, was the learned discussion about vintage Bordeaux between Burger and Sir George Coldstream, head of the Lord Chancellor's office and overseer of the wine cellar at his Inn of Court. The Chief Justice was particularly proud of his coup in snaring some cases of a rare Lafite in an obscure Washington wine shop.

The effectiveness of a Chief Justice is, of course, not shown by his epicurean tastes. Indeed, the one Justice who was willing to talk to me frankly about Burger's professional performance was most uncomplimentary.

Burger, according to this Justice, "will assign to someone without letting the rest know, and he has five [votes] before the rest of us see it." The Justice also complained about the Burger conduct of conferences in criminal law cases. "If it's a case in which a warden is the petitioner, the Chief Justice goes on and on until the rest are driven to distraction."

The Chief Justice's votes were based upon his own scale of values, which were different from those that had motivated members of the Warren Court. When he considered a fundamental value to be at stake, Burger could be as stubborn as his predecessor. "Someone," he insisted to a law clerk, "must draw the line in favor of basic values and, even if the vote is eight-to-one, I will do it." ...

Among the things the Chief Justice felt strongly about was the dignity of the legal profession.... In one case, he wrote to the others, "The petitioner's counsel was somewhat above mediocre but the State's case was *miserably* presented." Because of this, the Court should "at least appoint amicus curiae for California and begin our drive to force the States to abandon their on-the-job training of their lawyers in this Court." In a case involving a doctor, he urged that the opinion should contain "a few well chosen (?) comments about the gross fraud perpetrated by this 'quack.'"

. . .

Burger was greatly offended when the Court reversed the conviction of a young man for wearing a jacket emblazoned with the words "Fuck the Draft" in a courthouse. The Chief Justice was particularly upset by the opinion's quoting the offensive four-letter word. He prepared a two-paragraph dissent, ultimately withdrawn, which, according to the covering memo, "is the most restrained utterance I can manage." In the draft dissent, Burger wrote, "I, too, join a word of protest that this Court's limited resources of time should be devoted to such a case as this. It is a measure of a lack of a sense of priorities and with all deference I submit that Mr. Justice Harlan's 'first blush' was the correct reaction. It is nothing short of absurd nonsense that juvenile delinquents and their emotionally unstable outbursts should command the attention of this Court."

Even though the Chief Justice may have felt strongly about them, these were relatively minor matters. On more important concerns Burger came to the Court with an agenda that included a massive dismantling of the jurisprudential edifice erected by the Warren Court, particularly in the field of criminal justice. In large part, Burger owed his elevation to the highest judicial office to his reputation as a tough "law and order" judge. He had commented disparagingly on the Warren Court decisions on the rights of criminal defendants. As Chief Justice, he believed that he now had the opportunity to transform his more restrictive views into positive public law.

Burger expressed opposition during most of his tenure to *Mapp* and *Miranda*—the two landmark criminal procedure decisions of the Warren Court—but he was never able to persuade a majority to cast those cases into constitutional limbo. The same was true of other aspects of Burger's anti-Warren agenda. No important Warren Court decision was overturned by the Burger Court. If Burger hoped that he would be able to undo much of the Warren "constitutional revolution," he was clearly to be disappointed.

Burger was more effective as a court administrator and as a representative of the federal courts before Congress than as a leader and molder of Supreme Court jurisprudence. Looking back at the Warren years, Byron White told me that, as far as relations with Congress were concerned, "Things have changed ... for the better as far as I can see.... Chief Justice Warren did have such a problem with the civil rights thing, and with prayers and reapportionment. Congress was in such a terrible stew that his name was mud [there], which rubbed off on all of us." Under Burger the situation was different. Few Chief Justices have had better relations with Capitol Hill.

As for court administration, Burger played a more active role than any Court head since Chief Justice Taft. His administrative efforts ranged from efforts at fundamental changes, such as his active support of the creation of a new court of appeals to screen cases that the Supreme Court would consider, to attention to such petty details as the shape of the bench.

One must conclude that Burger was miscast in the role of leader of the Court—a harsh but fair description of a man who devoted so much of his life to the bench and worked as hard as he could to improve the judicial system and one who also could be warm and charming in his personal relationships. Yet his personality was, in many ways, contradictory—"at once gracious and petty, unselfish and self-serving, arrogant and insecure, politically shrewd yet stupid and heavy-handed at dealing with people."[14]

Of course it was more than these personality contradictions that damaged Burger's effectiveness as a leader of the Court. A major part of his failure may be attributed to the manner in which he presided at conferences and assigned opinions. But an important factor was his inadequacy as a judge. One who examines the decision process in important cases must reluctantly conclude that Burger was out of his depth. Although the picture in some accounts of his intellectual inadequacy is certainly overdrawn, most of his colleagues could run intellectual rings around the Chief Justice.

14. [Editors' Note: The author's footnote 30 at this point refers to "Washington Post, July 7, 1986 (national weekly edition), p. 8;" a close to identical quotation can be found in Nina Totenberg & Fred Barbash, *Burger Loved the Law But Not the Hassle,* The Washington Post, June 22, 1986, at C1.]

Burger's ineffectiveness as a judge was particularly striking in the *Nixon* case. The Chief Justice's draft opinion was so inept that it had to be completely rewritten by the other Justices. The final opinion was described by a Justice as an "opinion by committee," instead of one written by its nominal author.

There was a comparable situation in the last important case decided by the Burger Court—*Bowsher v. Synar.* The Burger draft opinion contained a far more expansive view of presidential power than the other Justices were willing to accept. It was only after the Chief Justice revised his draft in accordance with the Justices' suggestions that the draft could come down as the *Bowsher* opinion.

Similarly, in the *Swann* school-busing case, the Chief Justice's opinion had to be substantially revised before it could come down as the opinion of the Court. His draft was not supported by the law or the rationale behind the decision itself. . . .

. . .

Conferences and Assigning Opinions

Traditionally the most important work of the Supreme Court has been done in private, particularly in the conference sessions that take place after cases have been argued. It is in the conference that the Court decides, and the primary role at the conference is exercised by the Chief Justice, who leads the discussion. He starts the conference by discussing the facts and issues involved. He then tells how he would vote. Only after his presentation do the other Justices state their views, in order of descending seniority.

The manner in which he leads the conference is the key to much of a Chief Justice's effectiveness. His presentation fixes the theme for the discussion that follows and, if skillfully done, is a major force in leading to the decision he favors.

The two strongest leaders of the conference during this century were Charles Evans Hughes and Earl Warren. Most students of the Court rank Hughes as the most efficient conference manager in the Court's history. He imposed a tight schedule on case discussions. . . .

If Hughes was the most efficient, Warren may have been the most effective in presiding over the sessions—the "ideal" conference head, Justice Stewart said to me. His forte was his ability to present cases in a manner that set the right tone for discussion. He would state the issues in a deceptively simple way, one stripped of legal technicalities, and, where possible, relate the issues to the ultimate values that concerned him. Opposition based upon traditional legal-type arguments seemed inappropriate, almost pettifoggery. As Justice Fortas once told me, "Opposition based on the hemstitching and embroidery of the law appeared petty in terms of Warren's basic-value approach."

Conference notes show that when Warren sought to lead the Court in a particular direction, he was usually able to do so. Conference notes taken during the Burger tenure do not give the same impression. Burger did not have anything like the Warren ability to state cases succinctly, to lead the discussion along desired lines. Burger was too often turgid and unfocused, with emphasis upon irrelevancies rather than central points. It was said that Burger's discussion of cases at conference left the Justices with the feeling that he was "the least prepared member of the Court." In a comment on Chief Justice William H. Rehnquist, Thurgood Marshall said, "He has no problems, wishy-washy, back and forth. He knows exactly what he wants to do, and that's very important as a chief justice." There is little doubt that Marshall was contrasting the Rehnquist conference approach with Burger's.

More important was Burger's lack of leadership. The conference notes in hundreds of cases reveal how frequently the lead was taken by the Associate Justices—particularly so in the major cases. It was not the Chief Justice who usually played the crucial role in the decision process.

One must also fault him for his use of the power to assign the writing of opinions—aside from managing the conference, the most important function of the Chief Justice. In discharging it, a Chief Justice determines what use will be made of the Court's personnel; the particular decisions he assigns to each Justice in distributing the work load will influence both the growth of the law and his own relations with his colleagues.

The power of the Chief Justice to assign the opinions probably goes back to John Marshall's day. During Marshall's early years, it is probable that he delivered the opinion of the Court even in cases where he dissented. Apparently the practice then was to reserve delivery of the opinion of the Court to the Chief Justice or the senior Associate Justice present on the bench and participating in the decision. But as time went on, other Justices also began to deliver opinions. By Chief Justice Taney's day, the Chief Justice assigned each opinion.

In the early years of opinion assignment by the Chief Justice, he may well have assigned all opinions. It was not very long, however, before the Chief Justice's assigning power was limited to cases where he had voted with the majority....

. . .

Chief Justice Burger did not always follow the established practice. According to an English comment, "Chief Justice Burger would sometimes vote against his instincts in order to preserve his prerogative of assigning the majority opinion." In other words, Burger would vote with the majority in order to control the assignment of opinions.

The one Justice who was willing to talk to me frankly about Burger's assignment practice spoke of it in a most denigratory fashion. "The great thing about Earl Warren was that he was so considerate of all his colleagues. He was so meticulous on assignments." Now, the

Justice went on, "all too damned often the Chief Justice will vote with the majority so as to assign the opinion, and then he ends up in dissent."

. . .

Of course, Chief Justice Burger also made use of more traditional assignment techniques. He took many of the most important cases, such as the *Nixon* case, since the Court in such cases should speak through its head; he assigned the more significant cases to his allies, such as Blackmun in his earlier years and Rehnquist more recently; and left lesser cases to his opponents on the Court, notably Brennan.

The Chief Justice also employed the technique of assigning a case to the most lukewarm member of the majority. An illustration can be found in a November 14, 1978, Burger letter to Justice Brennan: "Apropos your opinion (I believe at lunch Monday) whether Bill Rehnquist was an appropriate assignee of the above case, I had discussed this with Bill. He prefers his first choice disposition, i.e., no judicial review, but he was willing to write the holding to reflect the majority view otherwise. There were 8 to affirm and he fits the old English rule-of-thumb as the 'least persuaded,' hence likely to write narrowly."

---

c.　William H. Rehnquist as Chief Justice: Opinion Assignment

Sue Davis,[15] *Power on the Court: Chief Justice Rehnquist's Opinion Assignments*, 74 Judicature 66 (1990)

By the spring of 1989 it was clear that the Supreme Court had shifted to the right.[16] As observers proclaimed the arrival of a genuine Rehnquist Court, they seemed to take as a matter of faith that the leadership of the Chief Justice was instrumental in cementing the conservative majority. Although his clearly established record for four-teen-and-a-half years as the Burger Court's most conservative member made William H. Rehnquist seem to be the ideal choice to carry out the legacy of Ronald Reagan's presidency, a Chief Justice's ability to shape the Court's decisions is always constrained by the other members of the

---

15. Associate Professor of Political Science, University of Delaware, at the time of the article, now a Professor of Political Science at Delaware.

16. [Footnote 1 in original] *See for example,* Patterson v. McLean, 109 S.Ct. 2363 (1989) (narrowing the application of civil rights laws that prohibit discrimination in employment); Wards Cove Packing Co. v. Atonio, 109 S.Ct. 2115 (1989); Richmond v. Croson, 109 S.Ct. 706 (1989); Martin v. Wilks, 109 S.Ct. 2180 (1989) (curtailing af-

firmative action); ... Florida v. Riley, 109 S.Ct. 693 (1989) (making further exceptions to the rules established by the Warren Court that protect the rights of the accused); ... Stanford v. Kentucky, 109 S.Ct. 2969 (1989) (upholding the death penalty for convicted murderers who committed the crime at the age of sixteen and convicted murderers who are mentally retarded); Webster v. Reproductive Health Services, 109 S.Ct. 3040 (1989) (approving state restrictions on abortion).

Court. By 1988, the replacement of Lewis Powell by Anthony Kennedy and the presence of two other justices appointed by Ronald Reagan, combined with Justice White, made the emergence of a cohesive conservative majority quite likely. Indeed, the dynamic of the eight associate justices could have been as crucial to building a conservative majority to fulfill the goals of the Reagan Administration as the chief justiceship of William Rehnquist. This article examines the role that Rehnquist, in his capacity as Chief Justice, has played in the Supreme Court's turn to the right.

... Although he has one vote as do each of the eight associate justices, the Chief Justice who wishes to maximize his position as a policy leader has a number of devices. He has the opportunity to influence the outcome of cases in the leadership roles and strategies he adopts in conference, the strategy he uses in opinion assignments, in circulating the "discuss list" for petitions for certiorari, in the crafting of his own opinions, in the image he presents to the public, and in his personal interaction among the other justices.

In this article I examine one instrument of the Chief Justice's power—the assignment of majority opinions—in order to begin to assess the extent to which Rehnquist is acting as a policy leader. In cases in which the Chief Justice votes with the majority, the rules of the Court provide that he assign the writing of the opinion either to himself or to one of the other justices who voted with him. David J. Danelski explained that the selection of the author of the majority opinion is important because the opinion determines not only the value of a decision as a precedent, but also how acceptable it will be to the public.[17] The author of the opinion, moreover, may be responsible for holding the majority together in a close case, and may persuade would-be dissenters to join the majority.

David W. Rohde underlined the importance of the assignment of majority opinions by identifying two sets of concerns: intra-Court and extra-Court factors.[18] The first set of concerns includes holding together a tenuous majority, increasing the size of a solid majority, and promoting harmony among the justices. Walter F. Murphy pointed to an intra-Court factor when he reflected that a Chief Justice might reward his coalition within the Court by assigning the interesting and important cases to those "who tend to vote with him, leaving the dregs for those who vote against him on issues he thinks important."

Extra–Court factors include those that involve the relationship between the Court and the rest of the political system. The Chief should be sensitive to "public relations" in assigning opinions, particularly those that will be unpopular to a large segment of the public. Further, as

17. [Footnote 8 in original] [David] Danelski, [*The Influence of the Chief Justice in the Decisional Process of the Supreme Court,* in Goldman and Sarat, American Court Systems: Reading in Judicial Process And Behavior 506–19 (1978)].

18. [Footnote 9 in original] [David W.] Rohde, *Policy Goals, Strategic Choice and Majority Opinion Assignments in the U.S. Supreme Court,* 16 Midwest J. of Pol. Sci. 652–682, 679 (1972).

Elliot Slotnick noted, the Chief Justice may be the most appropriate member of the Court to author the majority opinion in critical cases because of his symbolic status.[19] Rohde also pointed to a third factor that "has to do with the personal policy preference of the assigner." The Chief Justice can make assignments strategically to members of the Court whose views are most similar to his own in order to maximize the likelihood that the majority opinion will further his objectives.

ASSIGNMENT STRATEGIES

Seeking to further an understanding of the Supreme Court as a collegial decisionmaking body, scholars have formulated and tested a number of hypotheses concerned with the strategies used by the assigners of majority opinions. Danelski formulated two assignment rules that a Chief Justice might use to influence others to join the majority. First, he might assign the opinion to the justice whose views are the closest to the dissenters in the belief that the justice would take an approach upon which both majority and minority could agree. Second, where there are blocs on the Court and a bloc splits, the Chief Justice might assign the case to a majority member of the dissenters' bloc. Danelski found that of the three Chief Justices he studied only Hughes appeared to follow such rules. A number of scholars, attempting to determine whether assigners followed Danelski's first rule, have found a pattern of overassignment to the justice closest to the dissenters in cases in which a change in one vote would have altered the outcome. Saul Brenner and Harold J. Spaeth found that assigning the majority opinion to the marginal justice ... did not actually help to maintain an original minimum winning coalition.[20] Thus, it is not clear what an assigner accomplishes by favoring the justice closest to the dissenters over the other members of the majority.

Rohde hypothesized that the justice who assigns the majority opinion will either write the opinion himself or assign it to the justice whose position is closest to his own on the issue in question. Analyzing civil liberties cases decided during the Warren era, he found that the pattern of opinion assignments supported his hypothesis. Moreover, the assigner's tendency to give opinions to the justice closest to him increased in important cases, and as the size of the majority increased.

When Gregory Rathjen replicated Rohde's study using economics rather than civil liberties cases he found that the pattern of assigning opinions to the closest justice disappeared.[21] While Rathjen endorsed the theory that justices assign opinions on the basis of policy preferences, he suggested that Rohde's hypothesis was most viable in cases that involved

19. [Footnote 11 in original] [Elliot E.] Slotnick, *Who Speaks for the Court? Majority Opinion Assignment from Taft to Burger,* 23 Am. J. of Pol. Sci. 60–77, at 75 (1979).

20. [Footnote 15 in original] [Saul] Brenner & [Harold J.] Spaeth, *Majority Opinion Assignments and the Maintenance of the Original Coalition on the Warren Court,* 32 Am. J. of Pol. Sci. 72–81, 77–78 (1988)....

21. [Footnote 17 in original] [Gregory James Rathjen,] *Policy Goals, Strategic Choices, and Majority Opinion Assignments in the U.S. Supreme Court: A Replication,* 18 Am. J. of Pol. Sci. 713–724 (1974).

issues of primary concern to the Chief. He surmised that the issues presented in economics cases were less salient to Warren than those of individual rights, so that the Chief Justice may have placed policy concerns aside in those cases in order to assign in a manner that would help to equalize the workload.

Slotnick explored an alternative to ideological concerns in assigning opinions: equality of workload. Examining two models of opinion assignment—the opinion assignment ratio (OAR), which is conditioned on the frequency with which each justice is a member of the majority, and the model of absolute equality of caseloads, whereby all justices would have substantially the same number of majority opinions regardless of how often they agreed with the majority—he found that the six chief justices from Taft through Burger followed a norm of absolute equality rather than the OAR model. Moreover, it was Chief Justice Burger's behavior that most closely approximated the model of absolute equality. Likewise, Spaeth found that Burger practiced equal distribution to an extent that was unmatched by any of his five predecessors.[22]

Slotnick discovered that chief justices departed from the norm of equality in important cases, assigning opinions to themselves at a substantially higher rate than they did for the universe of cases. That pattern of self-assignment in important cases was most pronounced in highly cohesive cases—in cases where the Court was divided the Chief tended to avoid writing the opinion. Slotnick found those who most often voted with the Chief Justice were favored in the assignment of opinions in important cases. Spaeth's analysis of Burger's assignments revealed the same pattern.

HYPOTHESIS

The theory and methods developed in previous judicial research provided the basis for the four hypotheses tested here. The hypotheses reflect the two expectations that Rehnquist has assigned opinions with a goal of equal distribution of workload and that he has also attempted to assign opinions so as to further his policy preferences.

Rehnquist can be expected to continue the tradition of distributing opinions on the basis of absolute equality that Slotnick found to be the norm for Chief Justices from Taft through Burger. By the Chief Justice's own account:

> [Assigning opinions] is an important responsibility, and it is desirable that it be discharged carefully and fairly.... At the start of the October 1986 term I tried to be as evenhanded as possible as far as numbers of cases assigned to each justice, but as the term goes on I take into consideration the extent to which the various justices are current in writing and circulating opinions that have previously been assigned.

22. [Footnote 19 in original] Spaeth, *Distributive Justice: Majority Opinion As-* *signments in the Burger Court,* 67 Judicature 299–304 (1984).

The Chief Justice's comments suggest that "evenhandedness" rather than ideology would be the dominant factor in his assignments. Accordingly, Hypothesis 1 states that the opinions have been evenly distributed among the nine justices.

Studies of opinion assignment decisionmaking by previous Chief Justices have revealed a departure from the norm of equality in important cases. Thus, Hypothesis 2 posits that in important cases the Chief Justice has overassigned opinions to himself but that evenhandedness has prevailed to the extent that he has not kept the important cases for himself at a significantly higher rate than his predecessors.

Rohde's theory, based on the assumption that "justices are rational and that their primary motivation in making decisions is their own personal preferences about what is good public policy," is considered in Hypothesis 3. If the Chief's goal is to keep the majority and to have the opinion written in a way that is compatible with his preferences, he should assign opinions to the justice whose views most resemble his own. Thus, according to Hypothesis 3, Rehnquist has overassigned opinions to himself or to the justice whose position is closest to his on the issue in question.

Finally, I address the question of whether the Chief Justice uses his authority to assign opinions to hold a minimum winning coalition together by assigning the majority opinion to the justice closest to the dissenters. Specifically, Hypothesis 4 states that in cases decided by a minimum majority coalition Rehnquist has overassigned to the justice closest to the dissenters.

ANALYSIS AND RESULTS

The data used here are comprised of all cases decided with full opinion during the term 1986 through 1988—a total of 445 cases.[23] To test Hypothesis 1, the total number of opinions assigned to each justice were determined and OAR's [opinion assignment ratios] for each justice for each of the three terms were calculated.[24]

The results suggest that Rehnquist has taken the assignments made by others into account in order to achieve an equal distribution of opinions.... Rehnquist has continued the tradition of absolute equality in opinion assignments.... When the three years are considered together each justice wrote an average of 15.35 opinions per term with a standard deviation of only 1.57.

23. [Footnote 24 in original] I used Harold Spaeth's United States Supreme Court Judicial Data Base, Phase I.

24. [Footnote 25 in original] A justice's OAR is calculated by dividing the number of majority opinions by the number of his or her votes with the majority and multiplying the result by 100 to obtain a percentage. Slotnick, who devised the OAR, pointed out that it is a measure that is sensitive to a justice's availability for assignment of majority opinions. A justice who was in the majority infrequently would not be likely to write as many majority opinions as a justice who voted with the Chief a great deal of the time....

... Rehnquist appears to be adhering to the norm of equality of workload in assigning opinions. The tests of the remaining three hypotheses should shed light on the extent to which he also uses policy considerations as a basis for allocating opinion assignments.

"Important cases"

Hypothesis 2 requires a definition of "important cases." Several methods of identifying such cases have been utilized in judicial research. For example, important cases may be identified as those that were cited most often by the Court in subsequent decisions, or those included in the leading constitutional law texts. All the methods share an element of arbitrariness and none of them take into account the importance of the cases to the Chief Justice at the time they were decided. I have chosen to utilize the method devised by Spaeth whereby the cases headlined in the *Lawyer's Edition* of the *United States Reports* are classified as "important cases." Spaeth's method has the advantage that it eliminates bias in favor of constitutional cases and makes it possible to classify cases that have been decided so recently that they have not been included in any of the casebooks.

... The *Lawyer's Edition* identified 48 [important] cases for the terms 1986 through 1988. Rehnquist assigned opinions in 36 of those cases, nine of which he assigned to himself (25 per cent). Both Spaeth and Slotnick found that Chief Justice Burger assigned about 25 per cent of the important cases to himself. Slotnick found the average self-assignment ratio for Chief Justices from Taft through the first five years of the Burger Court to be 24.8.... The data support Hypothesis 2 insofar as Rehnquist clearly overassigned opinions to himself....

The most interesting finding with regard to important cases was that Rehnquist assigned more opinions to Justice White than he did to himself. The Chief Justice's apparent preference for White may be a result of the latter's increasing alignment with Rehnquist. During the last five terms of the Burger Court White and Rehnquist voted together in 65.6 percent of the cases in which they both participated. During the first three years of the Rehnquist Court, however, their percentage of interagreement rose to 74.6 per cent. It is possible, therefore, that Rehnquist assigned opinions to White with the goal of maximizing the prospects of cementing the alliance between them and, thus, of drawing White close to the conservatives.

Agreement

Tests of Hypotheses 3 and 4 mandate a technique to measure agreement between the Chief Justice and the other members of the majority. Following the example of previous studies, I used cumulative scaling to identify the "closest" justice to the opinion assigner.... I constructed separate scales for the three issues of criminal procedure, civil rights, and the First Amendment and used the scale scores of the justices to determine their "closeness" to the Chief Justice. That is, in a given case the justice in the majority with the scale score nearest to

Rehnquist's was considered to be the justice in the position closest to that of the Chief Justice.

For Hypothesis 3 to be supported, Rehnquist's assignment of opinions should reveal a pattern of overassignment to himself (position 1) and to the justice in the majority with the scale score closest to his own (position 2). The distribution of opinions for the 1986 term, as well as previous research, suggests the existence of a "freshman effect" in opinion assignments. Accordingly, I excluded justices serving a first term on the Court from the analysis. . . .

In order to measure "overassignment" I began with the assumption that in any case each justice in the majority has an equal probability of being assigned the opinion. That made it possible to compare the actual proportion of majority opinions Rehnquist assigned to a position to the proportion that could be expected if he were assigning randomly. Thus, for the hypothesis to be supported, the comparisons would have to reveal a substantially greater proportion of opinions Rehnquist assigned to Positions 1 and 2.

The [results show that the] difference between the actual and expected proportion of opinions assigned is in the predicted direction but the difference is not great enough to be statistically significant. Thus, the hypothesis that Rehnquist has assigned opinions to the justices whose views are most compatible with his own failed to be supported.

The Chief Justice's goal of maintaining an equal workload may have acted as a constraint on his ability to assign opinions ideologically. Additionally, as Rathjen suggested, an opinion assigner may utilize his discretion to assign opinions to the justices most likely to further his policy goals in areas that are most salient to him and in the other areas concentrate on equality of workload, thereby conserving his resources. If one of the three issues is more important to the Chief Justice than the others, he might assign opinions accordingly. But the pattern of Rehnquist's assignments in each of the three areas does not suggest that to be the case.

· · ·

Rathjen's assertion concerning the importance of the issue to the assigner, Rehnquist's own statements regarding the importance of federalism, along with the lack of support for Hypothesis 3 lend credibility to the possibility that neither criminal procedure, civil rights, nor the First Amendment are particularly salient to Rehnquist. If federalism and/or economic issues are more important to Rehnquist than any sub-category of civil liberties, analysis may reveal a pattern of overassignment to the justice in the position closest to his in those areas. Unfortunately, attempts to scale both economics and federalism cases proved unsuccessful, rendering any identification of the closest justice to Rehnquist unreliable.

Hypothesis 4 predicts that in cases decided by a margin of one vote Rehnquist will assign the opinion to the justice in the majority whose scale score places him/her closest to the dissenters (the marginal position) in order to maintain the majority coalition. Thus, the data will support Hypothesis 4 if the results show that Position 5 received the assignment in a substantially greater proportion of cases than would have been expected by chance. It should be emphasized that the justice who occupies Position 5 varies according to the composition of the majority coalition—that is, Position 5 is not an individual justice. [The data show that] Position 5 received a greater proportion of assignments than the other positions and at a greater rate than was expected. Still, the difference between the actual and expected proportion was not statistically significant. Thus, Hypothesis 4 failed to be supported.

The lack of support for Hypotheses 3 and 4 indicates that Rehnquist did not favor the justice whom he believed would write an opinion that would further the Chief Justice's own policy goals, nor did he show a preference for the marginal justice in close cases. The failure of the analysis to reveal either that Rehnquist overassigned majority opinions to the justice closest to him or to the justice closest to the dissenters in close cases suggests that the Chief Justice has not used his discretion to assign opinions in order to advance his policy goals.

CONCLUSION

The results of the analysis of opinion assignments during the first three terms of the Rehnquist Court show that if the Chief Justice's goal has been to distribute the workload evenly he has been successful except with respect to the important cases. His assignments in important cases suggest that he combined a goal of equal workload with one of advancing his policy preferences by keeping opinions for himself and by assigning to White, thereby courting an increasingly close ally. But the assertion that he assigned opinions with an eye to advancing his policy preferences is not otherwise supported by the data. In short, the results suggest that Rehnquist has not fully utilized his opinion assigning prerogative as an instrument to shape the decisions of the Court.

This article, because it examines only one aspect of the Chief Justice's leadership, reveals nothing about Rehnquist's use of other resources that a Chief Justice may use to maximize his power. Moreover, it is important for the reader to be aware that the analysis, by necessity, is based only on the final vote of the Court, as conference votes are not available. Thus, it is impossible to take into account that in any given case Rehnquist may have voted with the minority in conference and then switched or that the members of a winning coalition in the final vote may not be the same as the original majority.

Still, the results are consistent with the assertion that Rehnquist's leadership has not been crucial to the emergence of a solid conservative majority. It is possible that the Chief Justice has not exercised the prerogatives of his office to their full extent simply because he has not needed to do so. The membership of the Court is such that opinion assignments may rarely make any difference to the outcome of the cases.

If so, the Chief Justice has no need to act as a strong leader. The dynamic of a Court whose members consist of four conservatives in addition to the Chief Justice may have rendered it unnecessary for Rehnquist to draw on all the resources of his power.

Questions and Comments

1. Although the readings suggest that important questions of strategy may sometimes influence the use of the opinion assignment power, the Davis study is consistent with several others in finding strategic uses of the assignment power to be constrained by institutional and organizational requirements, including rough equality in assignments. See, e.g., Sara G. Benesh, Reginald S. Sheehan & Harold J. Spaeth, *Equity in Supreme Court Opinion Assignment*, 39 Jurimetrics J. 377 (1999) (studying opinion assignments from the Vinson Court in 1950 through the fourth year of the Rehnquist Court in 1990 and finding that "overall distribution of assignments among the Justices ... does not vary much;" that within the norm of equality opportunities for strategic assignment exist; and that Chief Justice Rehnquist "overassigned" to Justices White, O'Connor and Stevens); Forrest Maltzman & Paul J. Wahlbeck, *May It Please the Chief? Opinion Assignments in the Rehnquist Court*, 40 Am. J. Pol. Sci. 421 (1996) (concluding that factors associated with the "organizational model" of opinion assignment—equity, efficiency and expertise—were the most important explanations of opinion assignments and that hypotheses associated with the attitudinal model were not borne out, except in assigning cases with a fragile majority, where assignments to more moderate members of the majority rather than to ideological allies of the Chief Justice were likely); Paul J. Wahlbeck, *Strategy and Constraints on Supreme Court Opinion Assignments*, 154 U. Pa. L. Rev. 1729, 1738–39, 1750–53 (2006) (noting one instance of apparently insincere voting by Chief Justice Burger in order to allow himself to control assignment of opinion, but concluding from analysis of assignments in cases between 1986 and 1993 that Chief Justice Rehnquist generally "did not assign opinions to shape the development of the law in line with his preferences" and that assignments, with some possible exception in "politically salient cases," were constrained by concerns for equitable assignments and efficiency).

2. The initial selection of the author of the majority opinion has effects in two arenas: first, in the collegial process within the Court and second, at least if the writer attracts sufficient votes, in the kind of majority opinion that is crafted and issued. Which arena would be most important to the Chief Justice (or to a senior Associate Justice making the assignment)? On what would your answer depend?

3. The Chief Justice's personality and priorities influence the kind of leadership the Chief can provide, and may create or diminish opportunities for leadership by other members of the Court. For a thoughtful perspective on the Rehnquist Court in its closing years, read the next selection.

Note on the Politics of Appointments and Predictions for the Future

Mark Tushnet,[25] *Understanding the Rehnquist Court*, 31 Ohio N.U. L. Rev. 197 (2005)

How can we best understand the Rehnquist Court, that is, the Supreme Court from the mid–1980s to the present? Conventionally commentators depict a struggle between "liberals" and "conservatives." That, I will argue, is a misleading picture of what happened on the Rehnquist Court. Rather, the Court's decisions were driven primarily by a division among those usually described as conservatives, although I prefer to describe the division as one between two types of Republicans. True, part of the story did involve the Court's liberals, because they were able to maintain a kind of unity that the Court's conservatives were not. Focusing for expository purposes on individual justices, I will begin by describing the division between the Court's Republicans, then turn to the liberals. After speculating about why the conservatives were unable to maintain the kind of unity the liberals were, I will conclude by discussing the implications of my analysis for the Supreme Court over the next few years.

Two kinds of Republicans populate the Rehnquist Supreme Court. First, there are the modern Republicans, members of the party shaped by Barry Goldwater and Ronald Reagan. Then, there are more traditional Republicans, of a sort that used to be called Rockefeller Republicans or northeastern Republicans or country-club Republicans. This distinction has been overlooked in analyses of the Rehnquist Court for two reasons. Today there are almost no traditional Republicans left in the congressional or presidential Republican parties, so it is easy to assume that there are no traditional Republicans anywhere in the national government. In addition, Ronald Reagan appointed four justices, and one would assume that his appointees would all be modern Republicans. But, as I will argue, they are not; Justices Sandra Day O'Connor and, somewhat less so, Anthony Kennedy are traditional rather than modern Republicans.

What is the difference between modern and traditional Republicans? Both are skeptical about expansive exercises of national power, and are particularly sensitive to claims that the regulatory bureaucracies of modern governments, on the state as well as the national level, have overreached and imposed unjustifiable burdens on business activity. The two types of Republicans divide, though, on what have come to be called the nation's "social issues," such as abortion, gay rights, and the place of religion in the public schools. Modern Republicans are strong social conservatives on these issues; traditional Republicans are sympathetic to claims about reproductive and gay rights, and are opposed to what they see as the intrusion of religion into the public schools.

25. William Nelson Cromwell Professor of Law, Harvard University Law School.

... Justice O'Connor has the biography of a classic suburban woman active in the Republican party, with one exception. After graduating from law school, she relocated several times to accommodate her husband's career. They settled in Arizona and Justice O'Connor practiced law in a small law office located, we would now say, in a mini-mall. She suspended her law practice for a while, to raise her young children. But, like many suburban women of her class and time, she became active in a number of civic associations. Her ambition led her to resume her law practice relatively quickly, and to invest some of her activist energy in a Republican party that had been revitalized by Arizona Senator Barry Goldwater. Still, though Justice O'Connor was an activist in the Arizona—and therefore in the Goldwater—Republican party, she was not attracted to the party because of its ideology. Rather, the Republican party was the place for politically active women of her class, no matter what their ideological views. Justice O'Connor's political moderation was also influenced by her service, including service as majority leader, in a closely divided legislature, where she had to accommodate not only members of her own party but those of the Democratic party if the legislature was to function effectively. These experiences reinforced Justice O'Connor's natural tendencies toward finding attractive the values associated with traditional Republicanism, such as civility, politeness, and moderation.

Justice Kennedy is something of a puzzle, because, unlike Justice O'Connor, his political experience and contacts were with the modern Republican party. He was a lobbyist in California who came to the attention of Ronald Reagan and Edwin Meese when he worked effectively on drafting tax-limitation legislation. Justice Kennedy's work as a lobbyist may have pushed him in the direction of accommodation rather than confrontation, but I believe that other factors have been more important in shaping Justice Kennedy's self-understanding. It is clear, for example, that Justice Kennedy has an instinctive attraction to libertarian positions on a wide range of issues. Libertarianism is obviously compatible with the deregulatory impulses shared by modern and traditional Republicans. But, modern Republicans are strongly regulatory on the social issues, whereas Justice Kennedy's libertarian inclinations lead him to be skeptical about efforts to regulate abortion and sexual conduct, as well as speech of all sorts, including commercial speech (again, an issue on which all Republicans can agree) and speech with sexual content, where he once again sets himself apart from modern Republicans.

At the same time, and perhaps again a result of his experience as a lobbyist, Justice Kennedy has a genial confidence in the good sense of the American people. Integrating that confidence and libertarianism into a coherent jurisprudence is difficult, perhaps impossible, because libertarianism kicks in precisely at the point where the sensible American people have nonetheless adopted some regulatory program. Justice Kennedy is not a systematic constitutional theorist, though, and as a practical matter one can combine the impulses he has by finding constitutional balancing attractive. Yet, balancing is almost inevitably incompletely ideological, which means that a balancer will not fit easily into the constitutional framework modern Republicans have created. . . .

I turn now to the Court's liberals. As I have indicated, the story here is one of unity. The Court's liberals could not take the initiative on any important issues. And, when the Court's Republicans were unified, as they were on issues of federalism and on some aspects of economic regulation, the liberals were relegated to sitting on the sidelines, able only to fulminate against the grave errors the Court's majority was committing. While on the sidelines, though, the liberals were waiting for the opportunities provided by divisions among the Court's Republicans. They could take advantage of those opportunities if they remained united.

Yet, the divisions among the Court's "conservatives," and of the history of divisions on the Court among ideologically compatible justices, demonstrate that unity is something that needs to be explained rather than taken for granted. My explanation is that the liberals have hung together because of the leadership provided by Justice John Paul Stevens, whose role is, in my view, one of the major untold stories of the Rehnquist Court. For many years the leadership role was played by Justice William J. Brennan, whose combination of personal charm and intellectual integrity gave him a central role on the Court for nearly two decades. As Justice Brennan's health failed and after he left the Court, Justice Stevens took his place.

How Justice Stevens has led the liberals is a bit of a puzzle. That is so in part because his views on constitutional doctrine are often rather idiosyncratic. So, for example, he rejects the now conventional analysis of equal protection law as entailing an examination of one, two, or three tiers of scrutiny in favor of the proposition that there is but one Equal Protection Clause. Justice Stevens's intellectual fire-power may matter some. For example, he circulated a letter to his colleagues in the *Webster* abortion case of 1989 astutely pointing out defects in Chief Justice Rehnquist's doctrinal formulation that may have helped convince Justice O'Connor to refrain from joining the opinion.

Like Justice Brennan, Justice Stevens combines charm and integrity. In addition, Justice Stevens has been extremely skilled in his use of his power to assign majority opinions when one of the Court's traditional Republicans joined the liberals to make up a majority. As would any sensible strategist, Justice Stevens assigns opinions to Justices O'Connor or Kennedy when he can. This usually locks them in to the position they took in the initial vote. Oddly, Justice Stevens has been abetted in his opinion assignments by the Chief Justice, who tried to enforce a rather rigid rule that by the end of each Term every justice should have written the same number of majority opinions. Justice Stevens's opinion assignments "used up" some of the quota the Chief Justice allotted to the traditional Republicans. The effect was to leave the Chief Justice with fewer opinions to assign to them. And the effect of that was to give assignments to the modern Republicans, running the risk that the modern Republican's draft opinion would be too hard-edged, too conservative, for one or another of the traditional Republicans. Justice Stevens's opinion-assignment policies thus increased the chance that the modern Republicans would lose the Court—shift from the conservative outcome to a more moderate one—or at least would end up with a plurality rather than a majority opinion.

So far I have emphasized the unity found among the Court's liberals. I need to qualify that, though, with reference to Justice Stephen Breyer. He is not as reliably liberal as the others on his side.... He is basically a statist and a technocrat, which sometimes—particularly in cases involving the regulation of expression by means of new technologies—puts him at odds with the Court's other liberals.

In addition, Justice Breyer has more or less self-consciously tried to separate himself from the other liberals in order to build bridges with the Court's traditional Republicans. In doing so, he is in essence making a bid to become a leader inside the Court by implicitly trading his vote on some issues for the traditional Republicans' votes on others. For example, in Hamdi v. Rumsfeld [542 U.S. 507 (2004)], Justice Breyer joined Justice O'Connor's plurality opinion, endorsing the President's power to detain U.S. citizens pursuant to congressional authorization found in the resolution authorizing the use of military force in Afghanistan, rather than Justice Souter's opinion, which found the resolution insufficient to authorize such detentions.... Justice Breyer made overtures to Justice Kennedy in Bush v. Gore [531 U.S. 98 (2000)], offering to agree with the holding that Florida's recount procedures violated the Equal Protection Clause if Justice Kennedy would agree to give the Florida court more time to conduct a recount pursuant to constitutionally acceptable procedures.[26] ... Justice Breyer's bid for leadership should be understood as a long term strategy, because his efforts did not succeed ... [since] in the end Justice Kennedy decided not to give Florida more time for a recount.

With a number of qualifications and limitations, I have so far told a story of division among the Court's Republicans and unity among the Court's liberals. This should provoke an obvious question: Why haven't the Court's conservatives or Republicans been able to come up with a leader who could keep the troops together?

Each of the three candidates for leadership chose not to seek to become a leader of that sort. The Chief Justice was a leader of the Court as a whole, but not of the Court's conservatives. His experience as an associate justice when Warren Burger was Chief Justice left Rehnquist with an abiding sense that the job of the Chief Justice was to administer the Court effectively—something that Burger had never been able to do. And administer the Court effectively Chief Justice Rehnquist did. He ran

26. [Footnote 12 in original] *See* David Margolick et al., *The Path to Florida*, Vani- ty Fair, Oct. 2004, at 310....

the Court's conferences with an iron hand, letting each justice do no more than state his or her position on each case without allowing back-and-forth arguments among the justices. He was almost as effective in keeping oral arguments flowing, intervening to chastise Justice Antonin Scalia for taking over an argument or failing to let an advocate answer another justice's question. The Chief Justice's effectiveness as an administrator led William Brennan to call Rehnquist the best chief under whom Brennan served—a class that included Earl Warren—and Thurgood Marshall to praise Rehnquist equally effusively.

Yet, Rehnquist's interest in getting the Court's work done efficiently impaired his ability to act as a leader of one of the Court's factions. He had to be seen as an honest broker by both sides. Had he become a leader of the conservatives, the liberals would have had to worry at every moment whether what the Chief Justice was doing was aimed at getting the Court to work effectively, or instead at giving his "side" some advantage that the liberals might not immediately discern. As the end of the Chief Justice's tenure neared, he was simply old and tired, not interested in devoting much effort to anything other than getting the work done and getting out of the building.

Justice Antonin Scalia too chose a path other than leadership, preferring acclaim outside the Court to leadership inside it. [T]he division between the Court's modern Republicans and its traditional ones was exacerbated by personal issues.... Justice Scalia's acerbic comments on his colleagues' work ... led Justice O'Connor to say that Justice Scalia was "not a very polite man." That statement obviously expressed Justice O'Connor's positive valuation of politeness, and, to the extent that the statement itself might be seen as a bit impolite, demonstrated how strongly she felt about Justice Scalia.

The tensions between Justices O'Connor and Scalia came to a breaking point in Webster v. Reproductive Health Services [492 U.S. 490], decided in 1989. [See excerpt in Chapter Four, above from Professor Tushnet's book, describing the internal process on *Webster*] ... Justice Scalia's ire was directed more at Justice O'Connor than at *Roe*, though, and she seems to have taken his opinion as reason for moving even further from the positions attractive to modern Republicans.

... [T]here seems little doubt that [Justice Scalia's] style has gradually eroded the respect other justices have for him. In a revealing televised interview, Justice O'Connor said, "When you work in a small group of that size, you have to get along, and so you're not going to let some harsh language, some dissenting opinion affect a personal relationship." What is most notable about this is not its express content, but that Justice O'Connor did not mention—because she did not have to— the only person to whom she could have been referring....

The interaction between Justices Scalia and O'Connor brings out another point about personal relations on the Court. For years Justice Scalia has presented himself—and has been supported by his admirers in the media and the legal academy—as the smartest person on the Supreme Court. . . .

. . . Perhaps in his first few years on the Court Justice Scalia could reasonably have thought of himself as the smartest kid on the block. By the mid–1990s that was clearly no longer true. . . . By the mid–1990s Justice Scalia was clearly out-shined, in purely academic terms, by the "smarts" of Justices Souter and Breyer, to the point where Justice O'Connor was able to see in Justice Breyer a clear counter-weight to Justice Scalia's intellectual bullying. And . . . [in] their own ways, the Chief Justice and Justice Stevens were as smart as, if not smarter than, Justice Scalia—and I think a case can even be made that Justice O'Connor's exercise of judgment demonstrates a dimension of intelligence on which she ranks higher than Justice Scalia, and that Justice Clarence Thomas's willingness to think things through from ground up gives him a certain intellectual advantage over Justice Scalia. In short, Justice Scalia's position on the Court has become increasingly marginal as his so-called advantages in "smarts" have been reduced or even eliminated.

Justice Scalia's marginalization can be traced in the trajectory of the doctrinal campaigns with which he has been most associated: against the use of legislative history, for a restrictive doctrine of standing, against substantive due process. In each area Justice Scalia appeared to achieve some initial successes, but ultimately the Court rejected his positions. Consider the question of legislative history. Early on Justice Scalia got the Court to abjure use of legislative history. Then the Court began to refer to legislative history as supporting the outcome indicated by the more text-focused methods of interpretation, setting their discussion of legislative history apart, sometimes in subsections, sometimes in footnotes, thereby giving Justice Scalia the opportunity to concur in the opinion except for the subsection or footnote discussing legislative history. When Justice Scalia disagreed with the result, the discussion of legislative history could be integrated smoothly into the opinion, and his dissenting opinion could chastise the majority for its use of legislative history. The final stage was reached when the Court reached a result with which Justice Scalia agreed, and the opinion's author did not separate the discussion of legislative history out from the rest, forcing Justice Scalia to concur only in the judgment.[27] . . .

In sum, the Rehnquist Court had a coherent body of liberals who stuck together, and divisions among the Court's Republicans that allowed liberals to win enough victories, particularly on the so-called social issues, to sustain the image of the Court as neither entirely conservative nor consistently liberal. What will happen on the Chief Justice's departure?

27. [Footnote 21 in original] *See* Intel Corp. v. Advanced Micro Devices, Inc., 124 S. Ct. 2466 (2004). *See also*, Koons Buick Pontiac GMC v. Nigh, 125 S. Ct. 460 (2004) (describing statutory interpretation as a "holistic" enterprise).

The first, and probably most important, point is that the Court over the next few years will be operating in a novel context. For much of the Chief Justice's tenure in that position the national government was divided. Sometimes Democrats, sometimes Republicans, controlled the presidency but not Congress. The Court's role when government is divided could be to take the initiative. But, the divisions within the Court's Republicans made that impossible, and instead the Rehnquist Court engaged in small steps toward a more conservative constitutional vision.

Now the Court is operating within a unified government, with conservative Republicans controlling both Houses of Congress, the Presidency, and—more or less—the Supreme Court. The Court's task when government is unified is simple: collaborate with the governing majority. Sometimes that will mean wiping off the statute books laws that are the legacies of divided government or, even older, of the Great Society and the New Deal. Sometimes it will mean pushing a bit ahead of where the political branches are, in the expectation that the Court's initiatives will stimulate the political branches to move farther than they have in the conservative direction all agree is the correct one. These latter decisions might get described in the popular press and academic commentary as a conservative judicial revolution. And so they might be, if the base line of comparison is the doctrine in place in the 1990s. Yet, these decisions will not be revolutionary relative to the array of political power at the time they are handed down.

With one exception. A Supreme Court remade with two or three appointments drawn, as they are highly likely to be, from the modern Republican Party, will be a consistently conservative Court. It will be able to collaborate with a government unified under modern Republican control. The prospect of such control is good, but it is not guaranteed. A return to divided government is entirely possible. A divided Court—the Rehnquist Court—could get along with a divided government. A unified Court facing divided government might not. Suppose, for example, that a Democrat becomes president while Congress remains under control by modern Republicans. A unified modern Republican Court would find that its principled decisions played out in the public arena as merely partisan support for the modern Republicans in Congress. A Democratic president facing opposition from both Congress and the Supreme Court might take that opposition as the occasion for provoking a deep rethinking of the relationship between the Court and the political branches. The situation would (misleadingly) be described as a constitutional crisis. And, of course, the outcomes of crises are never known in advance.

After the Rehnquist Court, then, we are likely to see a modern Republican Court—a consistently conservative one—collaborating for a few years with modern Republicans controlling the other agencies of the national government. After that, who knows?

Questions and Comments

1.   As Professor Tushnet's article suggests, a Chief Justice who focuses on his role as Chief may give less emphasis to efforts to influence substantive direction in order to enhance other aspects of his role. During the Warren Court, there was some debate whether the dominant figure was Earl Warren as Chief Justice, or William J. Brennan, whose skills in building majorities have been earlier noted. To what extent does the position of Chief Justice add to the negotiating power of the person who holds that office?

2.   Chief Justices who have previously served as Associate Justices have models of being Chief Justice to emulate or react against. For example, Linda Greenhouse, long-time Supreme Court reporter for the *New York Times*, argues "that Rehnquist took Burger as a negative model, and that his apprenticeship ... helped him learn how not to be Chief Justice.... [H]e ... observ[ed] specific problems with Burger's leadership that he then determined to avoid when his own time came." Linda Greenhouse, *How Not To Be Chief Justice: The Apprenticeship of William H. Rehnquist*, 154 U. Pa. L. Rev. 1365, 1366 (2006). She contrasted Chief Justice Rehnquist's speedy and equitable opinion assignment practice with Chief Justice Burger's, noting that INS v. Chadha[28] had to be re-argued because Chief Justice Burger never made an assignment of the opinion, being torn between his view that the legislative veto was unconstitutional and his concern for the effects such a ruling would have on invalidating a large number of existing federal statutes. *Id.*; *see also* Linda Greenhouse, *Becoming Justice Blackmun* 154–60 (2005). By contrast, "Rehnquist's fairness in assigning opinions was commonly cited as a contrast to Burger." Greenhouse, *The Apprenticeship*, *supra*, at 1369. She raises the question what we might expect from Chief Justice Roberts, who clerked for then-Justice Rehnquist on the Burger Court.

3.   While it is too early to assess Roberts' performance as Chief Justice, it is not too early to note his own aspirations to influence his judicial colleagues to produce more unanimous and fewer splintered opinions. In addition to Roberts' Georgetown Law Commencement Address of May, 2006, noted in Chapter Four, Section B, above, see his interview with Jeffrey Rosen in February, 2007. Jeffrey Rosen, *Roberts' Rules*, The Atlantic Online, January/February 2007. Reiterating themes sounded earlier, Roberts indicated that the most successful Chief Justices are those who are able to achieve greater unanimity. Rosen describes Roberts' view that decisions which are unanimous (or close thereto) contribute both to the stability of the law and to public respect for the Court "as an impartial institution that transcends partisan politics." Holding up John Marshall as his role model in the interview, Roberts expressed concern that over the prior three decades the Court had " 'erod[]ed ... the capital that Marshall built up ...' " and suggested that multiple separate opinions, and cases decided by 5–4 votes, have adverse effects on the Court as an institution. Evidently seeking to fight the historical trend described by the Post and Kelsh readings in Chapter Four above, Roberts argued that the Justices should focus more on

28.   462 U.S. 919 (1983).

" 'the Court . . . acting as a Court, rather than being more concerned about the consistency and coherency of an individual judicial record.' " To achieve more unanimity, Roberts indicated that he allowed conference discussion of cases to run longer than the "briskly efficient conference" that Rehnquist was known for. *Id.*

From what you have learned, how much influence do you think the Chief Justice can exercise on the other Justices' votes, or tendency to file separate opinions?

3. Non-adjudicatory Roles of the Chief—and Proposals for Reform

The next readings and the notes that follow focus more on the Chief Justice's non-adjudicatory roles. Written more than two decades apart, they raise questions about the compatibility of the Chief's non-adjudicatory responsibilities with the Chief's more judicial duties and about whether the position of Chief Justice of the Supreme Court should, like that of chief judges in the lower federal courts, be rotated on a regular basis among the Justices.

Alan B. Morrison & D. Scott Stenhouse,[29] *The Chief Justice of the United States: More than Just the Highest Ranking Judge,* 1 Const. Comment. 57 (1984)

The Chief Justice has always been more than first among equals. His position as chair of the Supreme Court's weekly conferences, at which tentative votes are taken on cases that have been argued, and decisions made on which cases will have full briefing and argument, is more than titular. His power to choose who will write the majority opinion, if he is on that side, can influence the course of the law, which depends at least as much on the rationale as on the result. And his symbolic function as the leader of our entire judicial system has always been important.

Such differences between his role and that of the other Justices are traditional and probably necessary. This article is about a more recent and more disturbing phenomenon: the plethora of nonjudicial responsibilities that modern Chief Justices have assumed or, more often, been assigned by Congress. Every Justice, and indeed every federal judge, has some administrative duties. But the Chief Justice has more of them, and on the whole his are more significant. Cumulatively, his responsibilities raise several serious questions.

29. [Footnote * in original] Mr. Morrison, a Washington attorney, [at the time of this article directed] the Public Citizen Litigation Group, which he founded with Ralph Nader in 1972. The basic research for this article was done by Mr. Stenhouse, who now practices law in Atlanta, while he was a student and Mr. Morrison was a Visiting Professor at Harvard Law School.

The first is time. With increasing outside duties and an increasing caseload, is it possible for one person to continue to handle all of these tasks effectively? Or will nonjudicial activities detract from the Court's primary function?

As a result of these activities, there has also been a significant increase in the power of the Chief Justice.... [T]he power to appoint important committees and to act as spokesman for the federal judiciary, entail significant policy-making functions. Should we be concerned about such concentrations of power in one individual? No Chief Justice has been accused of any scandalous improprieties. But scandal is not the only danger inherent in extra-judicial endeavors. The administrative work of every Chief Justice inevitably brings him or her into situations that could tarnish the image of the Court, to the point where it is seen as simply another participant in political disputes. If that were to occur, it might do serious damage to the confidence most Americans have in the fundamental fairness of our court of last resort.

A final reason for studying the Chief Justice's duties is to broaden our conception of the qualities that should be sought in those who are considered for the office. What does the job involve?

I. TIME COMMITMENTS

"If the burdens of the office continue to increase as they have in the past years, it may be impossible for the occupant to perform all of the duties well and survive very long." Those words were spoken by Chief Justice Burger in December, 1978. Nearly ten years earlier, however, he endorsed the idea of judges serving on the boards of nonprofit groups "so long as the demands on their time and energy do not violate the absolute priority of their court duties."

Are those statements consistent, and if so, where is the problem? To begin, most of the Chief Justice's nonjudicial duties have been imposed by Congress. Has this occurred too often? One standard by which to answer that question was supplied by Senator Ervin, who declared that a judge's first responsibility is to "be a full-time judge in his own court." The most time-consuming obligation of the Chief Justice, apart from judging, is his role as head of the Judicial Conference of the United States, which is, in essence, the policy-making body of the federal judiciary. It is comprised of the chief judges of all federal courts of appeals and a district judge from each of the circuits (other than the new Federal Circuit). The Conference is charged with supervision of the federal court system—trying to assure that cases are promptly decided, recommending rules changes, initiating or responding to legislation relating to virtually every aspect of what transpires in the federal courts, and the like. When it was created by Congress in 1922, the Conference met for one day each year. Now it has two two-day meetings, and according to the Chief Justice each of these requires an additional two or three days for preparation.

Besides serving as presiding officer, the Chief Justice appoints the chairmen of over twenty committees, dealing with subjects like court administration, the jury system, probation, and federal magistrates. Among the most important are those which consider possible changes in procedural rules. The Conference's committees on judicial conduct advise judges about the propriety of various activities, review their reports of extra-judicial income, and assist them with their financial disclosure forms required by the Ethics in Government Act. The Chief Justice also appoints the principal staff on several of these committees. Because of the key role played by the committees, he keeps in close touch with their chairs. In 1972, Congress authorized the appointment of an Administrative Assistant to the Chief Justice, in part to relieve him of some of the liaison functions with groups such as the Judicial Conference. But as Chief Justice Burger himself recognized, "there is a limit to the delegation of functions and a limit in delegating decisionmaking."

A second major responsibility is his position as chair of the Board of the Federal Judicial Center. Congress has directed that he, the six sitting federal judges, and the Director of the Administrative Office of the United States Courts, who comprise the Center's Board, meet quarterly to oversee its work. The Center, whose primary function is to engage in research, training, and education for the judicial branch, has a budget which has increased from $500,000 at its inception in 1967 to almost $8,600,000 today [1984]. It engages in a wide range of research projects, offers training sessions for judges and nonjudicial personnel in the system, and has committees on such topics as prisoners' civil rights suits, revising jury instructions, and conducting conferences for appellate judges. Like the committees of the Judicial Conference, those working under the Federal Judicial Center also require the time and attention of the Chief Justice.

A third duty concerns the Administrative Office of the United States Courts. This Office works closely with the Federal Judicial Center and the Judicial Conference in the broad area of judicial administration. It is almost impossible to assign many of the Chief Justice's duties to any one of the three because there is so much overlap. His specific responsibilities for the Administrative Office arise because its director and deputy are appointed by the Supreme Court and their work is under the direction of the Judicial Conference. Since courts or conferences cannot, as a practical matter, supervise individuals, much of the responsibility falls on the Chief Justice.

A great deal of what the Administrative Office does, such as handling pay and purchasing books and other supplies, is generally no burden to the Chief Justice. But the Office is also the major source of data for the Judicial Conference and the Congress about the use of the federal courts. These, in turn, are vital to the Chief because of his concerns about the increasing case load, the adequacy of judicial salaries, and the number of judges. For these reasons he has become involved, although probably to a lesser degree than in other areas of court administration, in the work of the Administrative Office.

Another major responsibility is what he has referred to somewhat facetiously as his "role of building manager of the Supreme Court building." Of course, the day to day operations are handled by the marshall, clerk, librarian, reporter of decisions, and the Chief's administrative assistant. They in turn are subject to the supervision of the whole Court. In some cases this is done by Court committees; in others the job has fallen to individual Justices, particularly the Chief Justice.

Chief Justice Burger [for example, spent time] making decisions relating to the modernization of the Court's equipment [and was involved] in such details as ordering paint, planting flowers, having the reflecting pools painted blue, and installing exhibits for tourists. He ... also changed the lighting of the courtroom, altered the shape of the Justices' bench, moved the journalists' location, and improved the cafeteria. . . .

Congress has also required the Chief Justice to make various kinds of appointments. Many involve temporary or special purpose courts such as the Temporary Emergency Court of Appeals, which in recent years has concentrated on energy price litigation, and the Judicial Panel on Multi-district Litigation, which coordinates complex cases arising in various locations around the country. He is also empowered to assign judges within the federal system to fill temporary needs—with their consent and that of their chief judge—including trips to such places as the Northern Mariana Islands, Guam, and the Virgin Islands. These assignments do not comprise a significant portion of his work load, but they are one more straw on the camel's back. Equally important, they may permit the Chief to exercise extraordinary influence in certain areas of the law.

Congress has assigned to the Chief Justice many activities which are remote from judicial administration. In 1846 it made him a Regent of the Smithsonian and more recently a trustee of the National Gallery of Art and the Joseph M. Hirshhorn Museum and Sculpture Garden. Other outside positions, not congressionally imposed, include: Honorary Chairman of the Board of Trustees of the Supreme Court Historical Society (a group formed at [Chief Justice Burger's] urging); Honorary Trustee of the National Geographic Society; and Honorary Chairman of the Institute on Judicial Administration and the National Judicial College. Some of these are pleasant diversions, yet they can become demanding. It is worth recalling that Chief Justice William Howard Taft resigned from the Board of Yale University because he felt the ten meetings a year did not permit him to maintain his work load on the Court.

There is a great deal that the Chief Justice has to do simply because he is the Chief Justice—the inevitable swearings-in, receptions, and attendance at joint sessions of Congress addressed by the president. While every other Justice is assigned to one federal judicial circuit for administrative and other duties, the Chief and two other Justices are assigned an additional circuit. Each year the circuit holds a conference which its Justice usually attends and often addresses. The Chief Justice also makes an annual address on the state of the judiciary to the American Bar Association, and frequently speaks before the American Law Institute, law schools, and other gatherings.

How much time does all this take? By one report, the Chief Justice has timed his own work week at seventy-seven hours, with about one-third devoted to non-case activities. He has also stated that no member of the Court works less than sixty hours a week. Surely, by any measure, his work load is considerable, and the burdens from his non-case activities are significant.

. . .

Have outside activities prevented the Chief Justice from writing a reasonable share of the Court's opinions? During the five terms ending in June, 1982, he averaged the same number of majority opinions as his colleagues. Yet he wrote far fewer concurrences and dissents than any other Justice, perhaps partly because he cast relatively few dissenting votes. This may reflect a conviction that, as Chief Justice, he should try to harmonize the Court's work and that therefore concurrences and dissents should be used sparingly. But there is at least some evidence that in a few cases each year there is not enough time for the Chief to add his concurring or dissenting views, and so he joins others rather than separately stating his own position.

Can a Chief Justice, despite considerable nonjudicial work, devote adequate thought to judging? Charles Evans Hughes and Joseph R. Lamar, who served on presidential commissions while they were Associate Justices, were reportedly unable to maintain their full judicial work loads. Indeed, Hughes acknowledged that he was so worn out by the added burdens that his work was impaired for several months even after the commission was concluded. This was during an era when the Court's case load was relatively light. Chief Justice Burger says that the Court should give full treatment to no more than 100 cases each year if it is to maintain adequate quality. The current level, including full per curiam opinions, is more than fifty percent beyond this figure.[30]

. . . As Chief Justice Burger put it, just "because the Chief Justices, up to now, have somehow managed to cope, we should not assume that these glacial pressures can always be kept under control."

II. Political Power

. . . Congress has assigned [the Chief Justice] a major role in three significant policymaking fields: creating rules for the federal courts, participating in the legislative process, and appointing judges to certain special courts.

The role of judges—and particular Supreme Court Justices—in fashioning or approving procedures derives from the common-sense

---

30. [Editors Note: Readers will note that in recent years, the number of argued cases is closer to 80 and has been below 100 for several years. See Chapter Three, above.]

notion that they are uniquely qualified for this task. In 1934 Congress gave the Court the job of writing federal rules of civil procedure, subject only to the right of Congress to override them by statute. Since then Congress has also given the Court responsibility for the criminal, appellate, and bankruptcy rules, and—subject to a veto by either house of Congress—the rules of evidence (except those relating to the law of privilege).

As every attorney knows, procedural rules sometimes determine cases. Indeed, when the Court sent over its Rules of Evidence in 1972, they created such a controversy that Congress substantially rewrote them.

· · ·

In theory, the power of the Chief Justice, as one of nine Justices who vote on all rule changes, is no greater than that of his colleagues. In fact, that is not the way the system works. Of necessity, the Justices give proposed rules only a cursory glance. This reality elevates the importance of the drafters. Rules proposals come from the Judicial Conference, headed by the Chief Justice, after passing through the Standing Committee on Rules of Practice and Procedure and the appropriate advisory committee, whose members are his appointees. In addition, the staff person who does the basic research for the advisory committee (known as the reporter) is selected by the Chief Justice. Since most potential reporters are academics, their views are often readily ascertainable, making it possible to ensure that appointees concentrate on areas of importance to the Chief and rarely suggest rule changes that are inconsistent with his philosophy. While the committee system is not simply an extension of the Chief Justice's personal staff, there is a close connection between them not readily apparent from the formal structure established by Congress. At the very least it provides a substantial protection against unfriendly rule changes reaching the Supreme Court where they would have to be formally voted down to be defeated.

One recent addition to the Chief Justice's powers in the rule-making process deserves special mention. In the Classified Information Procedures Act of 1980 Congress sought a solution to the problem of what to do with classified materials that become part of court proceedings, as well as the problem of "graymail"—the threat by a defendant in a criminal case to use classified information to defend himself. The job of writing the security procedures was given jointly to the Chief Justice, the Attorney General, the Director of the CIA, and the Secretary of Defense. Aside from any problems that may arise if the Supreme Court ever has to decide the validity of those rules, the notion that the Chief Justice and members of the Executive Branch should jointly issue regulations of this kind contradicts the basic tenets of separation of powers....

Another major source of the Chief's political power is his ability to influence legislation. The formal power to propose or evaluate bills resides in the Judicial Conference, not the Court or the Chief Justice. The Federal Judicial Center and the Administrative Office of the United

States Courts also play a role through their research and the statistics they provide, which are often used by the Chief Justice in his speeches to support or oppose a given recommendation. Their evidence is especially influential in congressional decisions about the number of federal judges and support personnel and, less directly, on whether new kinds of cases should be allowed in the federal courts in light of the current case load. In addition, the Judicial Center's research "often involves matters that are subjects of legislative consideration—for example, criminal code revision, the Speedy Trial Act, or proposals to restructure judges' sentencing discretion...."

. . .

The influence of the Chief Justice himself on legislation may in some senses be more powerful than in rule making, even though the Conference can only make recommendations. Unlike rule making, in which every Justice has a vote, none of the remaining eight has a legislative role since the views are expressed by the Judicial Conference, not the Court. Some of the Conference's legislative recommendations come from standing committees over which the Chief Justice has the considerable powers described above; in other cases special committees are formed, where the Chief's decision to create a new group may be the single most important aspect of the process.

It is impossible to assess fully the Chief Justice's impact on legislation because his influence is often subtle.... [M]eetings of the committees, as well as of the Judicial Conference itself, are conducted behind closed doors—a prerogative the Conference fought hard to maintain in 1980 when Senator Dennis DeConcini proposed to open virtually all of them to the public.

Appointments are the third major source of the Chief Justice's political power. In addition to appointing committees and top staff for the Judicial Conference and the Judicial Center, he is authorized to select, from the federal judiciary, the chief judge and the members of several special courts. One of these courts—the Temporary Emergency Court of Appeals—is now responsible for appeals in all oil and gas pricing and allocation cases. Obviously, his choice of these judges can have a major impact on the development of the law. While no one has suggested that the Chief Justice has unfairly balanced TECA, the possibility nonetheless exists and warrants serious thought.

Another extremely important power that Congress has given the Chief Justice is the right to name the members of the trial and appellate benches of the Foreign Intelligence Surveillance Court, created by Congress to oversee the use of wiretaps by the executive branch in the foreign intelligence area. Most of the original appointees were judges with reputations for upholding the government's position in criminal cases; in 1981 they lived up to their reputations by approving all 431 Justice Department requests to start or continue electronic surveillance. Unlike the President's judicial appointments, these designations by the Chief Justice are not subject to Senate confirmation.... [I]t surely would be more consistent with stated congressional intentions to ensure better balance, perhaps by requiring that the assignments be approved by the Supreme Court as a whole.

In suggesting that the Chief Justice has political power, it is important not to overstate the case. He obviously does not possess non-judicial power comparable to that of, say, a leader of Congress. But he has enough influence to justify a reevaluation of this aspect of the office.

III.   MAINTAINING THE APPEARANCE OF IMPARTIALITY

The Supreme Cour[t's] ... power ultimately rests on public support. That in turn requires a popular belief that it is an impartial tribunal.

At least some of the Chief Justice's activities are potentially damaging to this aura of impartiality. One of the themes echoed by almost every witness at the 1969 Senate hearings on non-judicial activities of federal judges was that judges ought to stay out of controversial matters. As Senator Ervin said, "There seems to be widespread agreement with Chief Justices Hughes' statement that the business of judges is 'to hear appeals and not to make them.' "

The witnesses were aware of the contrary history, beginning with John Jay, who served as secretary of state, ambassador to Great Britain, and candidate for governor of New York, all while he was sitting as our first Chief Justice. A number of other Justices also served on non-judicial bodies, such as the postal investigation commission (Chief Justice Hughes) and the group, headed by Justice Lamar, that attempted to mediate the boundary dispute between Venezuela and British Guiana. In the period around World War II Justice Reed became chairman of the Committee to Improve the Civil Service, Justice Roberts investigated Pearl Harbor, and Justice Jackson took a year's leave to serve as the American prosecutor at Nuremburg. The most famous recent example of extra-judicial service was when Chief Justice Warren chaired the committee investigating the assassination of President Kennedy.

. . .

Whatever short-term benefit may have accrued as a result of Chief Justice Warren's service in the investigation of the Kennedy assassination seems to be outweighed by the doubts that have arisen about that investigation. In his memoirs Warren recalled his initial reservations about serving: it would be inconsistent with the principle of separation of powers; it would take time away from his work on the Court; it might cause him to disqualify himself from litigation arising out of the investigation. Yet he took the job, and his memoirs reflect no sense that this was an unwise decision. Justice Roberts, in contrast, confessed that he had made a mistake in accepting outside appointments while on the Court....

Today no active Justice sits on an investigative commission. However, the Chief Justice has become involved in several other endeavors that raise similar questions. For example, in Congress, the Judicial Conference and hence the Chief Justice speak for the federal judiciary. There are three dangers whenever a judge takes a legislative position on a controversial question: it may detract from his or her real or apparent impartiality in a subsequent case; the judge may be unable to limit himself to technical advice and thus become a special interest pleader like every other lobbyist; and, finally, it is hard to say what kinds of legislation are proper subjects of comment by the Justices.

. . .

Chief Justice Burger has twice been the center of the kind of controversy that is likely to recur when judges engage in lobbying. In one incident, he was reported to have sent Roland Kirks, then director of the Administrative Office, in the company of an influential Washington lawyer-lobbyist, to visit House Speaker Albert to campaign against some aspects of pending consumer legislation. Kirks subsequently denied that the Chief Justice even knew about the lobbying trip until after it occurred.... What is significant is that the Chief Justice was so personally involved in the lobbying process that he had to defend his actions in the public press.

He also became very much involved with the Bankruptcy Reform Act of 1978, making extensive eleventh hour efforts to delay the bill, including telephone calls to its sponsors and to highly placed persons on the Senate Judiciary Committee. One of the bill's Senate supporters received a call from the Chief Justice in which Burger reportedly "not only lobbied, but pressured and attempted to be intimidating," calling the Senator "irresponsible" for approving the bill and threatening to get the President to veto it. Appeals Court Judge Ruggero Aldisert, Chairman of the Bankruptcy Committee of the Judicial Conference, defended the Chief Justice, arguing that he was merely fulfilling his statutory duty to report the adverse recommendations of the Judicial Conference. Even assuming that the Chief Justice was carrying out the will of the Judicial Conference, its position could readily have been communicated with far less direct personal involvement of the Chief Justice and consequent loss of prestige to the Court.

Such activities have led a popular network television news program to air a report about the Chief Justice, investigating his off-the-bench activities. In October 1980 *Congressional Quarterly* ran an article debating the wisdom of lobbying by federal judges and especially Chief Justice Burger. And the *New York Times* admonished that the duties of Chief Justice and lobbyist "sit uneasily in the same chair ... ; the need for prudence should be evident." ... [W]hen a Supreme Court Justice engages in lobbying ... [the] resultant media coverage is potentially damaging to the perceived neutrality of the Court.

Which legislative topics are out of bounds for judges? Chief Justice Burger has stated that he would not comment on any subject other than those relating to his "responsibilities for the administration of justice." Professor Bickel said that he would like the Court to comment only on jurisdictional statutes, because they are "highly technical" and, without judicial advice about them, legislatures would operate nearly blindly.

Limiting comments to legislation affecting the administration of justice has a neutral and self-defining ring, but its parameters are quite amorphous. The Chief Justice has regularly expressed his dislike of proposals which would have created additional work for the federal courts. Yet in a recent interview, when asked about a bill to prevent federal courts from proceeding in controversial areas such as busing and school prayer, he declined to offer an opinion, replying "[t]hat is a subject I will have to leave to others." ... [These] two examples demonstrate that in some sense all these bills relate to "the administration of justice." Because the term is so potentially broad, it is an uncertain standard by which to decide which legislation is appropriate for judicial comment.... [W]here should the line be drawn and who should draw it? One answer ... is to stay out of the legislative arena entirely. At most, the judiciary should answer legislative requests for its views, keeping replies as technical and objective as possible.

Whenever the Chief Justice ventures beyond his judicial role, the possibility of creating an appearance of impropriety exists. One such opportunity is provided in the numerous appointments that he makes to committees of the Judicial Conference. Students of the Conference have recognized that these committee assignments, though often arduous and always unremunerated, are coveted by judges because they are one of the few means of status differentiation within the judiciary. The assignment power enables a Chief Justice to reward friends and allies. Consider this letter from Chief Justice Taft to a retired district judge, discussing legislation that would give the Chief more power regarding the assignment of judges to other locations: "[I]t may be that you and I can agree occasionally on your hearing cases in one of the Southern Districts in the winter time when the beauties of living in Maine are a matter of retrospect or prospect." Such a tiny reward is unlikely to destroy the judiciary's moral fiber, but one wonders whether the Chief Justice should be a part of this sort of petty patronage system.

Consider also the role of Chief Justice Burger in the formation of the Supreme Court Historical Society, whose purpose is to promote the presentation of the history of the Court. Unlike the National Geographic Society, on whose board he also serves, the Chief Justice has not had to disqualify himself from any cases involving the Historical Society. Still, his participation has raised questions about his role in the Society's fund raising, which involves soliciting money from lawyers who appear before the Court and from litigants whose cases may be there. Some observers believe that he unnecessarily damages the prestige of the Court by serving on the Society's board with, for example, Robert Stevens, the retired head of a textile firm that is frequently involved in extremely bitter litigation, some of which reaches the Court. The situation is further clouded by Stevens's additional gift of $8,500 ... which was used to commission a portrait of the Chief Justice for the National Portrait Gallery. Although these kinds of activities may produce only a faint whiff of impropriety, even that minimal damage is an excessive price to pay for the Chief's participation.

Even the Chief Justice's role as chancellor of the Smithsonian Institution causes problems that may reflect on the Court.... A recent newspaper story reported that the Internal Revenue Service has cracked down on what the Service alleges are "sham" valuations of gifts to the Smithsonian for which the donors deducted five times the amount they paid for them. The Chief Justice ... and the Smithsonian's Secretary hosted a black tie dinner honoring two of the four donors, a fact that appeared in the third paragraph of the article. Although there is not even a hint of wrongdoing on the part of Chief Justice Burger, the incident cannot have helped his image or the Court's and, if the tax case goes to the Supreme Court, it will at least cause some concern over whether the Chief Justice can hear it.

Even as seemingly innocuous a task as "building manager," has produced unwanted litigation and publicity. Two individuals carrying signs (one of which merely recited the first amendment) on a sidewalk outside the Court were threatened with arrest because a federal statute made such conduct on the Court's grounds illegal. They brought suit under the first amendment against the Supreme Court marshal, who is responsible for supervising the building under the direction of the entire Court, and Chief Justice Burger, who has the statutory duty of approving regulations governing the security and decorum of the Court's property. Eventually, the case went to the Court, but despite his status as a named defendant the Chief Justice did not recuse himself. The fact that eventually the Court unanimously upheld the challenge did not prevent a columnist from highlighting the arguable conflict of interest in banner headlines in Sunday papers around the country: "Suing Burger in the Burger Court." ... [T]he problem would surely have been diminished if Congress had not made the Chief Justice responsible for the regulations, but instead had assigned the job to the General Services Administration, which manages most federal property, so that it rather than he had been named as a defendant.

A recent series of events offers further evidence that the problems created by the multiple roles of the Chief Justice are not merely theoretical. On June 28, 1982, the Supreme Court declared that the provisions of the bankruptcy law which allowed bankruptcy judges, who were not appointed for life, to decide certain kinds of cases, were unconstitutional. The Chief Justice cast one of three dissenting votes. Recognizing that the entire bankruptcy system could be seriously disrupted, the Justices agreed to suspend the effect of their ruling until October 4, 1982, to enable Congress to remedy the matter.

At that point, exit the Chief Justice as adjudicator, and enter the Chief Justice as lobbyist and administrator. One solution to this problem would be to make all bankruptcy judges lifetime federal judges. The Judicial Conference apparently saw the addition of 227 bankruptcy judges as a diminution of the prestige of the current district judges and spoke out against it. At one point the Chief Justice even considered appearing on television to express his opposition to the proposal.

Meanwhile, as the October 4 deadline approached, it became apparent that Congress was unlikely to act. In early September the Conference, charged by Congress with overall responsibility for the smooth operation of the federal courts, decided to do something if Congress did not act. With no opportunity for public comment, it issued rules, which it recommended to all federal courts, on how to handle the problem if Congress continued to procrastinate.

Whether because of doubts about the rules' legality or for some other reason, the Justice Department asked the Court to give Congress more time—until December 24, 1982, when the lame-duck session was expected to be over. The Court agreed, and the problem was avoided for another two and a half months. But once again Congress could not agree on a solution, once again the Conference's interim solution was sent out, and once again the Department of Justice asked for more time. This time the Court, with the concurrence of the Chief Justice, said no. That left the federal courts with only the interim rules suggested by the Conference, with the Chief Justice's blessing.

It is unclear whether the interim rules are valid. Even if Congress eventually acts, the saga is not likely to end since some of those who lost cases under the interim rules will seek reversals on the ground that the Conference had no authority to issue them.

If such a case goes to the Court, the Chief Justice will be hard put to maintain a semblance of judicial detachment. Indeed, he is not likely to be the only one with a predilection on the issue. He may well have talked to his colleagues when the second request for more time was denied in December and told them that doom would not truly result from the denial of the stay because the Judicial Conference rules would prevent chaos. Hence anyone challenging the rules could hardly be accused of being cynical if he felt that the judicial deck was stacked against him.

The point is not that anyone did anything wrong or assumed roles not specifically authorized by Congress in trying to cope with this genuine problem. The difficulty arose because Congress had assigned nonjudicial functions to the Chief Justice which are plainly inconsistent with his judicial role.

IV. WHAT CAN BE DONE?

... The first remedy should be a moratorium on new duties for the Court or the Chief Justice....

Developing an earlier suggestion of Chief Justice Burger, Professor Daniel Meador urged that the administrative functions of overseeing the work of the committees of the Judicial Conference, supervising the Administrative Office, and heading the Federal Judicial Center be assigned to a newly created post called "Chancellor of the United States Courts." Creating that job, which might well be filled by a sitting federal judge who would assume the duties on a full-time, but temporary basis, would relieve the Chief Justice of most of his administrative duties pertaining to the federal judicial system. . . . [T]he concept deserves further study.

If one of our concerns is the amount of power possessed by Chief Justices, then one way to attack the problem would be to limit the time that any person may serve as Chief Justice. The Constitution gives all federal judges life tenure; it does not require that the Justice who is also designated as Chief must remain in that position as long as he or she remains on the Court. Since 1958, the chief judges of the district and circuit courts have been required to step down at the age of seventy, although they may remain active judges. In 1982 Congress further reduced the period that any person may serve as chief judge to seven years or the age of seventy, whichever comes first. The same approach makes even more sense for the Chief Justice of the United States. Not only does he have more nonjudicial duties than do most lower court judges, but his influence is far greater than the leader of any circuit or district court. A fixed term, whether determined by age or years of service in the job, would militate against the possibility that any Chief Justice would wield too much power or become out of touch with the political mood of the country. And to the extent that nonjudicial obligations drain the Chief's energy, relieving him of his special duties as Chief will help in the later years when even the most vigorous tend to slow down.

In the meantime, we need to acknowledge that the job of being Chief Justice is not simply that of the highest judge in the land. It seems unlikely that any Chief Justice could greatly reduce his nonjudicial activities merely by eliminating the relatively few tasks that Congress has not imposed. It should be apparent that the position calls not only for a superior lawyer, but also an able administrator, an extraordinarily energetic individual with a broad view of our system of justice and a commitment to exercise the powers of the office in an even-handed manner.[31] . . .

Judith Resnik & Lane Dilg,* *Responding to a Democratic Deficit: Limiting the Powers and the Term of the Chief Justice of the United States*, 154 U. Pa. L. Rev. 1575 (2006)

. . .

31. [Editors' Note: For a more recent comment, see Alan B. Morrison, *Opting for Change in Supreme Court Selection, and for the Chief Justice, Too?*, in *Reforming the Court: Term Limits for Supreme Court Justices* 203 (Roger C. Cramton & Paul D. Carrington eds., 2006).]

* Resnik is Arthur Limon Professor of Law, Yale Law School; Dilg is Yale J.D. 2004.

... However much their styles varied, the agendas of Chief Justice Rehnquist forwarded much of what Chief Justice Burger had begun. To augment the judiciary's institutional resources devoted to planning, an "Office of Judicial Impact Assessment" came into being in 1991 inside the [Administrative Office (AO)] to focus on anticipating the effects of proposed legislation. That process proved complex and controversial. One issue was how to count the costs and the benefits of proposed new causes of action, new federal crimes, or of different remedies. Another was the challenge of estimating the number of claims that would be brought if a new law were to be enacted. In general, the focus has been on predicting whether and how much federal court dockets would change; projections of additional filings have generally been assumed to have negative consequences.

In the early 1990s, under Chief Justice Rehnquist, the Judicial Conference created a Committee on Long Range Planning; in 1995, it put forth the judiciary's first (and currently only) Long Range Plan, making ninety-three recommendations. Included was a request that Congress have a presumption against enacting any new rights for civil litigants, if those actions were to be enforced in federal court, as well as a presumption against prosecuting more crimes in federal courts. The Judicial Conference formally adopted that position as its policy, and the Conference also endorsed many other recommendations related to the allocation of power among state, federal, and administrative adjudicators and to the structure of decisionmaking and administration within the federal courts.

[U]nder the leadership of the last three Chief Justices and with the support of the AO and the FJC, the Judicial Conference has enlarged its own purview in a variety of directions, and the Chief Justice's job has changed. In many respects, the judiciary's growth resembles that of other administrative agencies seeking to equip themselves to discharge assigned tasks. As concerns grew that demands of the cases filed exceeded the resources provided by Congress to decide them, the Federal Judicial Center developed and the Judicial Conference approved a "weighted case" system for the district courts to document why more slots were needed in particular courts. Further, when seeking resources for building courthouses or for staffing the Probation Department, paying public defenders, and keeping abreast of the workload, the judiciary has learned that it needs to provide data to a sometimes uninterested, unreceptive, or critical Congress....

But the parameters of the lobbying efforts on behalf of the judiciary and its leadership require further examination. While proposals for better facilities or more staff fall under the rubric of requests that would be made by any organization hoping to protect or to improve its own situation, other recommendations—such as taking stances against increasing the ranks of life-tenured judges, against more avenues to the federal courts through congressional enactment of specific new civil causes of action and federal crimes, or for transferring more responsibility from federal courts to administrative adjudicators—embody serious questions of constitutional law and of policy. While the Judicial Conference once categorized a range of matters as issues of "legislative policy" about which it should not comment, the Conference now regularly lets Congress know its views on an array of pending bills. The Chief Justice and the Conference have become important presences in the legislative process.

Furthermore, the retrenchment in federal rights enforcement that marked the jurisprudence of both the Burger and Rehnquist chief justiceships can also be seen in the administrative agendas that they personally championed and that the Judicial Conference, under their leadership, often endorsed. Through a host of discretionary judgments, these Chief Justices have used their status as presiding officers to shape institutional decisions about what jurisdictional and remedial powers ought to reside in courts and agencies, both state and federal.

. . .

In addition to guiding the Judicial Conference as it adopts formal policy through voting and influencing the work of the AO and FJC, the Chief Justice has an independent platform from which to speak. Chief Justice Taft and his successors went regularly to the American Bar Association and to the American Law Institute to give major addresses on their views of the judiciary's needs and priorities. [I]n the 1980s, Chief Justice Burger initiated another practice: providing annual "state of the judiciary" reports. While not quite the dramatic presentation to joint houses of Congress that some had suggested, the Chief Justice's annual statements, now customarily released on January 1, gain some attention in the national news as they recap one year and set out concerns for the next.

Reading the statements of the different Chief Justices serving between the 1920s and today, certain issues—the size of dockets, the needs for regularization and rulemaking, and support of and funding for the judiciary—are regularly addressed. But under Warren Burger and William Rehnquist, another theme—curtailing the jurisdiction of the federal district courts—came into sharp relief. On several occasions, Burger opined against enlarging federal jurisdiction: "The federal court system is for a limited purpose.... People speak glibly of putting all the problems of pollution, of crowded cities, of consumer class actions and others in the federal courts." Chief Justice Burger objected to liberal standing doctrine, too "expansive" interpretations of federal statutes, too many prisoner petitions, and too narrow understandings of the immunity of government officials.

While changing the format somewhat in terms of the style and timing of the yearly reports, William Rehnquist also used that medium to insist that too many issues were before the federal courts. For example, in one address, he cited as problematic new civil causes of action, such as the Child Support Recovery Act of 1992 (nicknamed the "Deadbeat Dad Act" and aimed at using federal courts to enforce support obligations of out-of-state parents).[32] In another year-end report, he opposed the creation of new federal crimes, "such as those involving juveniles and handgun murders."[33] Chief Justice Rehnquist also identified whole sets of cases, such as those filed under the Federal Employee Liability Act (FELA) and the Jones Act, as candidates for Congress to remove from the federal docket.

. . .

In the literature on judicial lobbying, Burger is infamous—with many commentators citing in particular his impact on the design of the bankruptcy system. . . .

Chief Justice Rehnquist pursued a similarly focused campaign, when he opposed aspects of the Violence Against Women Act (VAWA), legislation that was first introduced in 1990 and enacted in 1994. This multifaceted statute had provisions for new federal criminal jurisdiction, funding for programs to protect victims of violence (with special attention paid to college campuses), enforcement of interstate protection orders, and a new civil rights damage remedy in federal court for victims of violence motivated by gender.[34] It was the proposed new cause of action—permitting private damage actions in federal district court—that drew the Chief Justice's ire. After an initial draft was introduced in the early 1990s, the Judicial Conference chartered an Ad Hoc Committee on Gender–Based Violence, appointed by Chief Justice Rehnquist, to review the pending statute.

The Ad Hoc Committee's recommendation of opposition became official federal judicial policy.[35] The Chief Justice explained that position in his 1991 year-end report, stating that the "broad definition of criminal conduct is so open-ended, and the new private right of action so sweeping, that the legislation would involve the federal courts in a whole host of domestic relations disputes." Relying on claims that a flood of lawsuits (tens of thousands, with costs estimated to range from "$44 million dollars and 450 work years" to "$81 million dollars and 922 work years") would follow if women had federal remedies for gender-based violence, the Judicial Conference reported to Congress that it did not support enactment of the new civil rights remedy of VAWA.

32. [Footnote 134 in original] *See* William H. Rehnquist, Address to the American Law Institute, 75 A.L.I. Proc. 55, 58 (1998) (stating that "one senses [about this and other bills] from the context in which they were enacted that the question of whether the states are doing an adequate job in this particular area was never seriously asked"); Child Support Recovery Act of 1992, Pub. L. No. 102–521, 106 Stat. 3403 (Oct. 25, 1992) (codified as amended at 18 U.S.C. § 228).

33. [Footnote 135 in original] William H. Rehnquist, 1993 Year–End Report on the Federal Judiciary 5 (1993). . . .

34. [Footnote 156 in original] *See* Violence Against Women Act of 1994, Pub. L. No. 103–322, §§ 40001–40304, 108 Stat. 1796, 1902–42 (codified in scattered sections of 8, 18, and 42 U.S.C.) [hereinafter VAWA].

35. [Footnote 158 in original] *See* Chief Justice William H. Rehnquist, Chief Justice's 1991 Year–End Report on the Federal Judiciary, Third Branch, Jan. 1991, at 1 (objecting that the proposed private right of action was too "sweeping").

After the draft legislation was modified in response to the concerns raised by both state and federal judges and its scope narrowed, the Judicial Conference took no position on the propriety of enacting the civil rights remedy and supported aspects of the legislation related to education on fair treatment in courts. In 1994, with the support of attorneys general from some forty jurisdictions and many others, VAWA came into being. That version of the legislation included the provision of new federal jurisdiction (supplemental to that available in state courts) giving civil remedies to victims of gender-motivated violence.

Thereafter, the Chief Justice continued his criticism of VAWA. In 1998, in a speech before the American Law Institute, Chief Justice Rehnquist cited the civil rights remedy of VAWA (as well as other statutes) as an inappropriate expansion of federal jurisdiction. In his view, "traditional principles of federalism that have guided this country throughout its existence" should have relegated these issues to state courts. In 2000, in United States v. Morrison, the Chief Justice wrote the majority opinion that ruled, five to four, that Congress lacked the power under either the Commerce Clause or the Fourteenth Amendment to create the civil rights remedy of VAWA.[36] . . .

. . .

Yet another aspect of the powers held by the Chief Justice is important: the authority to select sitting jurists to serve on specialized courts and on committees. In the federal system, Congress has created a series of courts staffed by life-tenured judges already commissioned and temporarily assigned an extra obligation. Rather than using a system that mixes elements of randomness with purposive sampling (for example, drawing one name by lot from judges grouped by circuits), Congress has endowed the Chief Justice with the power to pick individual judges to sit on particular tribunals.

Specifically, the Chief Justice appoints the seven judges on the Judicial Panel on Multidistrict Litigation, the body created in the 1960s at the behest of the Judicial Conference to decide whether to consolidate cases pending around the country and to centralize pretrial decisionmaking in a judge designated by that panel. The Chief Justice also chooses the eleven judges who sit for seven-year terms on the Foreign Intelligence Surveillance Act (FISA) court (now frequently in the news), which, since 1979, is reported to have approved more than 18,000 government requests for surveillance warrants. Furthermore, the Chief Justice selects the three judges comprising the appellate body empowered to review FISA Court denials of government requests—an activity that reportedly rarely occurs. The Chief Justice holds the power to select the five judges who constitute the Alien Terrorist Removal Court, chartered in 1996 to respond if and when the Department of Justice files cases seeking to deport legal aliens suspected of aiding terrorists.... As a

36. [Footnote 164 in original] United States v. Morrison, 529 U.S. 598, 627 (2000).

result of these various statutes, according to Professor Theodore Ruger, Chief Justice Rehnquist made "over fifty such special court appointments," a total that Ruger noted was greater than the number of judicial appointments made during the first several decades of the United States.[37]

That this appointment authority is an important power can be seen from opposition to the idea of the Chief Justice wielding it. In the first decades of the twentieth century, Taft (both before and after he became Chief Justice) sought to detach the appointment of judges from a position on a particular court.... Taft wanted Congress to commission eighteen "judges-at-large" to be dispatched at the discretion of the Chief Justice. Given that the lower federal courts had, in 1914, about 126 judges, the Taft proposal would have both increased the ranks of the judiciary by fourteen percent and helped to produce a cohort more affiliated with the national system than a particular locality....

... [Taft's] concept was rebuffed, in part because opponents were concerned that the Chief Justice would dispatch judges supportive of the national edict on Prohibition to recalcitrant jurisdictions and in part because it undercut local politicians' patronage possibilities. Understood then was the potential that the power to select appointees and to make assignments could affect the outcomes of cases.

Although Taft formally lost that fight, he won a congressional license for the Chief Justice to reassign judges (upon request of the borrowing court) temporarily from one court to serve on another. Several statutes now authorize "lending" practices within circuits, but only the Chief Justice can designate district and circuit court judges to serve on courts outside the circuits to which they are appointed. While the Chief Justice no longer does that work personally but relies instead on the Judicial Conference Committee on Intercircuit Assignments to approve requests, the Chief Justice appoints that committee and retains the power to allocate judges.

More generally, and in conjunction with the Director of the AO, the Chief Justice appoints many committees, some of which are standing committees of the Judicial Conference and others of which are groups convened ... to review a particular issue [such as gender violence]. As decades of scholarship about federal court rulemaking activities have made clear, a line between "practice and procedure" and "substantive rights" is hard to draw. As Judicial Conference committees craft rules that create or narrow opportunities for access to courts (through pleading and class action requirements, for example) or for information disclosure (through discovery and disclosure obligations), the range of opportunities for plaintiffs and defendants change. The appointment power gives the Chief Justice the ability to select particular people who

---

37. [Footnote 172 in original] [Theodore W.] Ruger, *The Judicial Appointment Power* *er of the Chief Justice* [7 U. Pa. J. Const. L. 341, 343 (2004)].

shape these decisions. . . . [and] to endow some [lower court] jurists with significant social (or juridical) capital—and to marginalize others.

. . .

A review of yet other statutory powers of the Chief Justice reveals an odd assortment of assignments running with the position. . . . For example, Congress has authorized the Chief Justice to promulgate regulations on garnishment of the wages of members of the judicial branch. The Chief also has rule-making power to prevent disclosure of classified information by the federal courts. Moving outside the federal courts (and potentially raising an important question of the power of Congress to do so), the Chief Justice approves selections of persons to sit on special North American Free Trade Agreement (NAFTA) dispute resolution panels. . . .

Congress has also authorized the Chief Justice to assist the Library of Congress in purchasing books for the law library and to recommend individuals to serve on the Board of Trustees of the James Madison Memorial Fellowship Foundation. In addition, the Chief Justice serves on various boards . . . [A]ccording to those who have served within the judiciary, the work—for example, chairing the Smithsonian Board— involves real contributions of time and energy.

Further, as is familiar, Presidents have sometimes turned to Chief Justices to take on other tasks. Twentieth-century examples include chairing investigations such as the 1960s Warren Commission inquiry into the assassination of President Kennedy and arbitrating border disputes in the 1930s between Guatemala and Honduras. In short, just as the Chief Justice is both a "boss" and a symbol of the Supreme Court, the Chief Justice is also a practical as well as an iconic leader of the federal judiciary. Time and again, individual Chief Justices have proven to be the judiciary's most effective lobbyists, the judiciary's most visible spokespersons, and the nation's most important judicial leaders.

. . . [The authors argue that this "life-tenured multi-tasking" is anomalous.]

The concentration of the powers of adjudication and administration in the chief justiceship prompts questions about how one role affects the other. Through the obligation to multi-task, the Chief Justice is distracted from being either a full-time adjudicator or administrator. When the two roles are combined, a well-intentioned and astute Chief Justice, aiming to forward only legally appropriate policy proposals, has to think simultaneously about the administratively desirable, the politically feasible, and the constitutionally plausible.

But none of those categories exists ex ante. Adjudication can reframe administrative possibilities, just as administration can make clear why constitutional parameters ought to be reexamined. . . . [T]he amalgam both amplifies the power of the individual serving as the Chief at a potential cost to the collective power of the Court and puts at risk the disinterested quality required of adjudication.

One worry is distraction: in principle, being a Justice is a full-time position. . . .

. . . The Chief Justice's current tasks—ceremonial head, diplomat, manager, speaker, planner, career-enhancer, policymaker, adjudicator, intellectual leader, CEO, trustee, rulemaker, museum trustee—are implausible from a bureaucratic perspective. In personal terms, the challenge of endurance has been noted repeatedly by those close to the process. Warren Burger himself described how he spent "four to six hours a day on administrative matters apart from my judicial work" and that such a schedule was "not possible—not physically possible—to continue" for too long.

Of course, in practice, the Chief Justice delegates to others, but unlike dozens of comparable federal positions regulated by statutes requiring senatorial confirmation, the three high-level officials in the judiciary's bureaucracy [the Director of the Administrative Office, the Administrative Assistant to the Chief Justice, and the Director of the Federal Judicial Center] obtain their jobs through the Chief Justice.

The Chief Justice has . . . been in the position to mediate the tensions that have arisen between the authority of the AO and the FJC. . . . [When the AO Director reportedly called for the abolition of the FJC,] Chief Justice Rehnquist reportedly supported the FJC, and an ad hoc Judicial Conference committee, appointed by the Chief Justice, thereafter rejected the suggestion to fold the FJC into the AO. In short, the federal judiciary has attributes familiar to many bureaucracies, complete with internal disputes and power struggles whose outcomes are affected by the Chief Justice, who as the CEO, can choose how involved to be in the policymaking of these subdivisions of the judiciary.

. . .

[A] Chief Justice can shape the Court's doctrine to make feasible certain kinds of administrative innovations that once seemed legally troubling. Examples include Chief Justice Burger's insistence on delegation of authority to judges without life tenure, and Chief Justice Rehnquist's efforts to restrict habeas corpus through rulemaking. Although initially faced with what commentators have styled a "revolt" or "rebuff" in the Judicial Conference, Rehnquist was able—by staying focused over many years—to limit habeas petitions through Court-made doctrine and interpretations of congressional legislation.

Yet, as the Chief Justice gains power, erosion of certain other forms of authority is also a risk. Chief Justice Hughes (whose term, from 1930 to 1941, spanned a period before and after the 1939 creation of the Administrative Office) is identified with raising the concern that administration and lobbying involve judges in political conflicts that could potentially undermine the understanding that the Court's decisions are legally, rather than politically, motivated. [For example, the authors note, he resisted calls for the judges to protest bills to divest the federal courts of diversity jurisdiction.] . . .

Yet ... the approach of Chief Justice Hughes has been replaced by a very different stance. The Conference now regularly records its views. Moreover, rather than protest against divesting the federal courts of jurisdiction, the Judicial Conference, with Chief Justices Burger and Rehnquist at its helm, has supported divestiture of many forms of federal jurisdiction, diversity included. Further ..., we [can] compare administrative stances and adjudicative outcomes. We can review, for example, Chief Justice Rehnquist's comments in speeches, the Judicial Conference's calls under his leadership for retrenchment in federal jurisdiction, both civil and criminal, and the constitutional decisions in cases such as United States v. Lopez [514 U.S. 549 (1995)], and *United States v. Morrison*. In both of those decisions, the Chief Justice was part of a bare majority concluding that Congress lacked the constitutional power to confer jurisdiction on the federal courts over the kind of claims the "administrative" judiciary had advocated be curtailed.

[The authors raise concern over "the well-intended but inappropriate conflation of the administratively desirable with the legally permissible...."]

... While one might balk at the [Judicial] Conference offering its opinion on the constitutionality of a law, that seems the most appropriate ... tack to take, for the added value provided by judges comes from their expertise on the law rather than from a subset of judges assessing a proposed law's potential trade-offs or utilities—tasks which are within the bailiwick of the legislative branch. Yet the Judicial Conference and the Chief Justice do not discuss directly the constitutionality of proposed bills but often comment instead on the bills' wisdom and the possible effects such enactments could have on their workload.

The two roles (advisor ex ante and adjudicator ex post) cannot help but bleed into one another. Many important legal questions are indeterminate, with answers changing over time. One such example is the issue on which Chief Justice Burger spent much of his personal capital–life tenure for bankruptcy judges. The question was (and remains) how much of the power of judgment should and can constitutionally be devolved to federal adjudicators who lack the Article III attributes of life tenure and protected salaries. As an administrator, Chief Justice Burger did not want bankruptcy judges to have life tenure. Of the various reasons that he and others proffered, one major argument was (and is) that qualified individuals would not be interested in Article III judgeships if too many slots were open. As an adjudicator, Burger believed— unlike other members of the Court who found the 1978 bankruptcy reforms gave too much power to non-tenured judges—that the broad grant of jurisdictional authority was constitutional.[38] His views as the chief administrator, appropriately attuned to the needs of the federal courts, may well have affected his understanding of the constitutionality of outsourcing adjudication to non-Article III actors. Indeed, he should

---

38. [Footnote 239 in original] *See* N. Pipeline Constr. Co. v. Marathon Pipe Line Co., 458 U.S. 50, 92 (1982) (Burger, C.J., dissenting).

not have supported any administrative innovation that he thought was not constitutionally viable.

. . . [M]ulti-tasking is often celebrated but here has a negative effect. . . . [A]djudication is purposefully unlike other forms of decision-making. Judging is a role that . . . situates the person so endowed both with unusual power over other persons' lives and property and with unusual constraints, in terms of the kind and nature of information received and the kinds of discourse permitted. Ethics rules and customs seek to extract judges from other activities in order to enshrine role delineations that are much harsher than those of many other government posts.[39] Yet the Chief Justice, the most visible icon of adjudication in the country, is now the least protected from having to function in realms appropriately labeled political.

. . .

[The authors emphasize concern over undue accumulation of power and possible failures of democracy:]

The packet of powers now possessed by the Chief Justice is thus unduly enabling and also disabling, with one set of tasks either constraining or invading the work to be done under the other rubric. In addition, the concentration of power undermines democratic governance that is committed to distributing and accounting for power.

. . . Many other democracies shape the mandate of their high court jurists by requiring either retirement at a fixed age or a term of office limited to a specified number of years. For example, both Australia and Israel set the age of retirement at seventy, and India requires its Supreme Court judges to step down at sixty-five. In Canada, mandatory retirement comes at seventy-five. The constitutional courts of Germany and France rely on another system: fixed terms. The new International Criminal Court has adopted that model, providing for a nine-year non-renewable term. Within the United States, Massachusetts, Vermont, New Jersey, and New Hampshire authorize lifetime judgeships, yet also require retirement at age seventy.

Moreover, the chief justiceship's mixture of an unending term and so much unfettered and relatively invisible discretion is not readily assimilated into either the model of adjudication or administration. Jurists on appellate courts work collectively; they must persuade others

---

39. [Footnote 240 in original] *See* Model Code of Judicial Conduct (2004), available at http://www.abanet.org/cpr/mcjc/mcjc home.html (last visited Mar. 30, 2006); Code of Conduct for United States Judges, available at http://www.uscourts.gov/guide/vol2/ch1.html (last visited Mar. 30, 2006). The Code of Conduct for United States Judges, adopted by the Judicial Conference, requires, for example, that judges refrain from engaging in political activities and ad-

monishes judges against commenting on the merits of pending actions or participating in extrajudicial activities that might create an actual conflict in a current or future proceeding or even an appearance of impropriety. *See id.* The Code allows judges to engage in extrajudicial activities to "improve the law, the legal system, and the administration of justice" so long as doing so "does not cast reasonable doubt on the capacity to decide impartially any issue that may come before the judge." *Id.* at Canon 4.

of the correctness of their views in order to prevail. And because both constitutional and common law traditions mandate openness in courts, most decisions are explained by reasons that are available to public scrutiny and then revisited as new cases arise. In contrast, the administrative powers of the Chief Justice are neither officially shared nor constrained by obligations of accounting other than very general reports to Congress.

The many grants of power to the Chief Justice contrast sharply with the shape of authority of other executive officials. Even . . . a President who asserts extraordinary powers, . . . still cannot continue in office beyond the end of his second term. Heads of independent agencies generally also have limited terms, and cabinet members serve at the pleasure of the President. But currently, the Chief Justice has lifetime consolidated authority over the administration of both the Supreme Court and the lower federal courts, and does not have legal obligations to share that power with other jurists or administrators, nor to explain decisions made.

Further, in contrast to increased insistence on accountability for, and transparency in, governance, the chief justiceship has accumulated, during the twentieth century, power that is neither easily seen nor required to be explained. . . .

. . . The judiciary has a statutory exemption from both FOIA and Title VII. Additionally, . . . while Congress has mandated openness in rulemaking for the lower courts, the Supreme Court has authority to make its rules without any such obligation.

. . .

A different kind of democratic failure comes to light when one considers the platform that Chief Justices have erected. Both Chief Justices Burger and Rehnquist often suggested that their various comments represented positions of "the federal judiciary." As a procedural matter, the official mechanism from which positions emerge and become "policy" is the Judicial Conference, which takes formal votes on specific questions.

But how does this group of under thirty know how to vote and speak on behalf of the twelve-hundred-plus Article III judges and the eight-hundred-or-so non-life-tenured judges? . . .

[T]he elaboration of principles through adjudication assumes that judges differ. In dialogic exchanges over time, questions are played out through the prism of the facts and relevant law of particular cases; judgments made by small cohorts of judges attentive to nuances shape the law. Dissent has become an important part of these exchanges, yet norms of administration—expressed recently in the context of the conflict between the FJC and the AO—now seek to damp down difference in order to forward judicial "policy" with a single voice.

. . . [T]he Article III judiciary [was] created not to "represent" anything or anyone, but to exercise "the judicial Power of the United

States." Judges are not supposed to have an "interest" as an institutional matter in a particular interpretation of a legal rule, nor are individual judges—whether or not affiliated in the past with political parties—supposed to bring a "party position" to bear. Further, while pressures to democratize the judiciary are sometimes couched in the language of representation, once selected and confirmed, judges are not charged with pressing any point of view. And the better argument for a diverse judiciary is not an essentialist one that all women or men of a particular color or class hold a certain view but rather that, as a matter of equality, the distribution of judgeships ought not to track exclusively one set of demographic characteristics. When the Chief Justice and the Judicial Conference, however, put forth positions on federalism and the allocation of power to non-life-tenured judges and use their powers to shape programmatic agendas for the federal judiciary, they undermine the signature of adjudication as the activity of the disengaged, rendering judgments with no individual and no collective interest to be furthered. . . .

[The authors propose time limits on the position of Chief Justice and evaluate the constitutionality of this approach.]

. . . [L]acking much by way of text, consensus at the framing, or implicit structure, . . . one could turn to another constitutional interpretative technique—developing premises from an amalgam of text and practice. Article III provides that the "judicial Power of the United States" shall vest in courts with judges holding "their Offices during good Behavior." The Constitution does not define either the words "hold" or "Offices" or the phrase "during good Behaviour."

Since the country's founding, however, Article III judges have not had either a defined term of office or an age at which retirement is mandatory. Further, since the founding, the practice has been for the President to nominate a Chief Justice and for the Senate to hold a separate confirmation hearing even when an individual (such as Chief Justice Rehnquist) has already been confirmed for an associate justiceship. If one reads the prescription that judges hold their offices "during good Behaviour" to require an unfettered run, adds the fact that the nomination of a Chief Justice has been treated as a separate commission, and then invokes concerns that congressional intervention could violate separation-of-powers principles, one could mount an argument that the system currently in place—of an unending term of office for anyone taking the commission of the Chief Justice—is a constitutional requirement.

But competing interpretations are also possible. First, one can argue that the lack of mention of the chief justiceship in the part of the Constitution specifically devoted to the courts gives Congress a range of permissible constitutional choices for restructuring—so long as the chosen congressional intervention meets the Article III requirements that jurists "hold their Offices during good Behaviour" and does not undermine the capacity of the Court or its Chief Justice to perform essential functions. Second, one can bracket the administrative portfolio of the Chief Justice and argue that it does not merit Article III protection. Doctrinal support for that analysis comes from the law of judicial immunity, in which the Supreme Court has held that when judges are sued for actions taken as they administer or promulgate rules, they cannot assert the defense of judicial immunity but can only rely on the kind of immunity accorded to officials from other branches discharging analogous functions.[40]

Third, ... to claim that Article III commissions run exclusively to one particular office ... would render constitutionally suspect congressional statutes, extant since 1922, authorizing the Chief Justice to license judges to "sit by designation" in districts and circuits other than those to which they had been appointed.... Further put into question would be [congressionally] set term limits for the chief judgeships of the lower courts. In short, a good deal of practical evidence supports an understanding that Congress can define different charters for sitting jurists without undermining the constitutional guarantees of Article III.

. . .

[A] better reading of the Article III requirements is that, so long as a person retains the office of a federal judge with salary protected, both reassignment from one particular post to another and divestiture of administrative responsibilities are permissible. Moreover, given the absence of a mention of the chief justiceship in Article III, no special rule about "holding office" attaches to that post. Therefore, the Constitution would permit a rotating chief justiceship similar to that of some state courts and of the lower federal courts, with the position of chief justice moving by seniority or some other system.

Two constitutional caveats are required. Article I requires the Chief Justice to preside at impeachment trials of the President. A statute fixing term limits for the chief justiceship would have to provide for that unlikely contingency by including automatic extensions of a Chief Justice's term if an impeachment trial were underway. Further, ... currently, the Chief Justice receives a small increment in compensation over that paid to Associate Justices. To avoid violating the non-diminution mandate [of Article III], the salaries of all Justices could be equalized or the person who serves as Chief could continue to receive that modest premium after ceasing to hold that special post.

Another constitutional question would then need to be addressed—how to select successor Chief Justices. Could Associate Justices select the Chief Justice (as in some state systems), or does that proposition violate the Appointments Clause, with its mandate to the President to appoint "Judges of the supreme Court?" Once again, constitutional silence (no

40. [Footnote 275 in original] *See* Supreme Court of Va. v. Consumers Union of the U.S., 446 U.S. 719, 731–34 (1980) (holding that, when the Virginia Supreme Court promulgated and administered disciplinary rules, that Court was not entitled to "judicial" immunity but rather, under a functional analysis, the forms of immunity accorded to either legislators or executive branch members).

mention of a special appointment or designation process for the Chief Justice) makes difficult the claim of a constitutional breach, so long as the President has nominated the person to the Supreme Court. Further, given the tradition of inherent judicial powers and statutes that authorize self-governance of the judiciary, selection from within by other jurists could be seen as supportive of the independence of the Supreme Court.

That Congress could constitutionally alter the term of the Chief Justice does not mean that either the President or the Congress could shape the job in a way that undercuts the Court's capacity to work. The more general rubric of separation of powers requires the preservation of the Supreme Court specifically (and of the federal courts more generally) as a coordinate branch of government, not to be micromanaged by Congress, which could, through thousands of small cuts, immobilize the federal judicial system. Were Congress, for example, to require that the chief justiceship change for each case or each month, such a statute would be unconstitutional. Similarly, if either the President or the Congress were to reappoint Chief Justices at brief intervals, ... the ability of the Court to function would be disrupted.

In contrast, if the person who served in the position of the Chief Justice did so for seven years (to parallel the length of service described in the statutes addressing the chief judges of the district and appellate courts), and afterwards retained the status of a federal judge or Justice, that person's tenure would be protected but that person's power cabined. Such a rule would also enable an orderly succession of service ....

Questions and Comments

1. Both articles raise questions about conflicts between the Chief Justice's adjudicatory and non-adjudicatory roles. How serious a concern do you think this is? Is it of greater concern for the Chief Justice's adjudicatory or non-adjudicatory duties? Or is it of concern for the legitimacy and stature of the Court? If so, which way do the Chief Justice's many duties cut? What, if anything, should be changed? By whom?

2. How would you evaluate, from both a policy perspective and a constitutional perspective, a bill specifying that the Chief Justiceship should rotate every seven years based on seniority? Or should be chosen by the other Justices?[41] Should Congress consider creating a "Chancellor" of the U.S. courts to assume some of the administrative and ceremonial duties currently performed by the Chief Justice? What duties would you recommend assigning to such a position?

3. Resnik and Dilg raise important questions about the unlimited tenure and power of the Chief Justice from the perspective of democratic accountability and ask why a single person should have so broad a range of

---

41. For additional discussion of the constitutionality of such proposals, see also Swaine, *Hail, No, supra*, 154 U. Pa. L. Rev. at 1720–24.

powers for so long a time; Morrison emphasizes the possible compromise of
the Chief Justice's appearance of impartiality. For another useful treatment
of the Chief Justice's powers, focusing on the fact that the Chief's powers are
not "limited by the collective structures of the federal judiciary," that is, are
not exercised jointly with other judges, nor constrained "by the normative
expectation that judges give express reasons for their decisions," see Theodore W. Ruger, *The Chief Justice's Special Authority and the Norms of
Judicial Power*, 154 U. Pa. L. Rev. 1551 (2006). Ruger raises the question
whether Chief Justices should "seek assent from Supreme Court colleagues
even where not statutorily required ... [and] ... make a practice of publicly
expressing the general criteria that would guide various features of [his or]
her authority...."

Would Resnik and Dilg favor or oppose a more collective judicial approach to the range of decisions and activities the Chief Justice performs?
Why? What about requirements for transparent criteria and reason giving
for exercises of the Chief's discretionary, administrative authority? What do
you think—is there a problem? If so, what is it, exactly, and which solutions
make most sense?

B. THE LAW CLERKS

Our experience has been that law clerks, in describing themselves,
often inflate their importance and power. But there can be no doubt that
these young lawyers do have some influence. Typically, law clerks are
the only people trained in law (other than the Justices) to whom Justices
can and do talk candidly and conveniently about pending cases.

The readings that follow describe the origins and evolution of the
role of the law clerk. Do the clerks have too much power? Are they
necessary to the Justices' ability to manage the workload? Why do the
Justices typically choose as clerks people who are only a year or two out
of law school and hire them for only one or two years? Is too much
experience after law school a disqualification for the job? If you were a
Supreme Court Justice, what tasks do you think you would assign to
your clerks?

In Chapter Three above we discussed the law clerks' role in the
certiorari process. (Chapter Four also included some discussions of the
law clerks' role in drafting opinions in the excerpt by Chief Justice
Rehnquist.) In the readings and comments in this section, we focus on
other issues: the relationships between Justices and their law clerks; the
law clerks' influence *vel non* on the Court's work; the connection
between service as a law clerk and service as a Justice; the diversity and
backgrounds of clerks; and the confidentiality which former law clerks
do or should maintain in describing their experiences.

David M. O'Brien,[42] *Storm Center: The Supreme Court in American Politics* 131–43 (6th ed. 2003)

JUSTICE AND COMPANY—NINE LITTLE LAW FIRMS

When Potter Stewart joined the Court in 1958, he expected to find "one law firm with nine partners, if you will, the law clerks being the associates." But Justice Harlan told him, "No, you will find here it is like nine firms, sometimes practicing law against one another." Each justice and his staff work in rather secluded chambers with virtually none of the direct daily interaction that occurs in lower federal appellate courts. No one today follows Frankfurter's practice of sending clerks— "Felix's happy hotdogs"—scurrying around the building. "As much as 90 percent of our total time," Powell underscored, "we function as nine small, independent law firms."

> I emphasize the words *small* and *independent*. There is the equivalent of one partner in each chamber, three or four law clerks ..., two secretaries, and a messenger.[43] The informal interchange between chambers is minimal, with most exchanges of views being by correspondence or memoranda. Indeed, a justice may go through an entire term without being once in the chambers of all of the other eight members of the Court.

A number of factors isolate the justices. The Court's members decide together, but each justice deliberates alone. Their interaction and decision making depend on how each and all of the nine justices view their roles and common institutional goals. According to [Justice] John Harlan, "decisions of the Court are not the product of an institutional approach, as with a professional decision of a law firm or policy determination of a business enterprise. They are the result merely of a tally of individual votes cast after the illuminating influences of collective debate." Intellectual and personal compatibility and leadership may determine whether justices embrace an institutional, consensual approach to their work or stress their own policy preferences. Chief Justice Rehnquist has said, "When one puts on the robe, one enters a world ... which sets great store by individual performance, and much less store upon the virtue of being a 'team player.'" At worst, as Harry Blackmun observed, the justices are "all prima donnas."

The growing caseload has affected the contemporary Court in several ways. By Chief Justice Stone's time, it was well established for each justice to have one law clerk and for the chief justice to have one additional clerk. During Fred Vinson's chief justiceship, the number increased to two and more or less remained the same through the years

42. Leone Reaves and George W. Spicer Professor in the Woodrow Wilson Department of Politics at the University of Virginia.

43. [Editors' Note: Professor O'Brien noted that, at the time of his writing, seven Justices used four law clerks, but that Chief Justice Rehnquist and Justice Stevens used only three. All of the Justices, including Chief Justice Roberts and Justices Alito and Stevens, now employ four law clerks. See, e.g., 2007 *Summer Judicial Staff Directory* 5–6 (30th ed. 2007).]

of the Warren Court. Beginning in 1970, the number gradually grew to three and to four, with Burger having a fifth senior clerk.... The number of secretaries likewise increased, at first in place of additional clerks and later to help the growing number of clerks. The Legal Office was created in 1975 to assist the justices; subsequently, the staff of research librarians was increased and the secretarial pool was enlarged.

Computer technology also affects the operation of the chambers. In the late 1970s, each chamber acquired a photocopying machine and five or more terminals for word processing and computerized legal research in the library.... Each chamber [now] has a fax machine and also communicates by e-mail.

The justices' chambers tend to resemble, in Chief Justice Rehnquist's words, "opinion writing bureaus." ...

LAW CLERKS IN THE CHAMBERS

Law clerks have been in the Court just over a century. As the Court's caseload increased, the justices acquired more clerks and delegated more of their work. But in addition to relieving some of the justices' workload pressures, clerks bring fresh perspectives to the Court. For young lawyers one or two years out of law school, the opportunity of clerking is invaluable for their later careers. After their year at the Court, clerks have gone on to teach at leading law schools or to work for prestigious law firms.

On his appointment in 1882, Horace Gray initiated (at first at his own expense) the practice of hiring each year a graduate of Harvard Law School as "secretary" or law clerk. When Oliver Wendell Holmes succeeded Gray, he continued the practice, and other justices gradually followed him. Most justices have had clerks serve for only one year. There are some notable exceptions: one clerk for Pierce Butler served sixteen years; McKenna's first clerk worked for twelve; Frank Murphy kept Eugene Gressman for six; and Owen Roberts had a husband-and-wife team as his permanent clerk and secretary.... Burger had his special legal assistant sign on for three to four years.

The selection of clerks is entirely a personal matter and may be one of the most important decisions that a justice makes in any given year. The selection process varies with each justice. But four considerations appear to enter into everyone's selection process: the justice's preference for (1) certain law schools, (2) special geographic regions, (3) prior clerking experience on certain courts or with particular judges, and (4) personal compatibility.

Following Gray and Holmes, Brandeis, Frankfurter, and Brennan chose graduates of Harvard Law School. Some other justices also tended to choose graduates of their alma maters, while several others tended to favor particular geographical regions when selecting clerks. Most of the justices now rely on former clerks to screen candidates, though Justice O'Connor wades through the some 500 applications that annually arrive in her chamber.

As the Court's caseload and the number of law clerks grew, the justices started drawing clerks from lower federal or state courts. Consequently, clerking for a respected judge or on a leading court in the country is now just as important as attending a top law school. The typical clerk is twenty-five years old, white, male and a year out of Harvard or Yale law school. During the last thirty years, less than 5 percent were Asian Americans, less than 2 percent African Americans, and only 1 percent Hispanic. Nearly 40 percent attended Harvard or Yale. More than two thirds of them were graduates of six law schools: Harvard, Yale, Chicago, Stanford, Columbia and Virginia....

The position and duties of clerks naturally vary with the justice and with the historical development of the institution. Oliver Wendell Holmes initially had little casual contact with his clerks, but when his eyesight began to fade in his later years, they served as companions and often read aloud to him. According to Walter Gellhorn, Stone "made one feel a co-worker—a very junior and subordinate co-worker, to be sure, but nevertheless one whose opinions counted and whose assistance was valued." Likewise, Harold Burton told his law clerks that he wanted each "to feel a keen personal interest in our joint product," and he encouraged "the most complete possible exchange of views and the utmost freedom of expression of opinion on all matters to the end that the best possible product may result." Earl Warren's law clerks communicated with him almost always by memorandum. By contrast, Rehnquist, Scalia, Souter, and Stevens set up rather warm working relationships with their clerks.

The level of work and responsibility depends on the capabilities and the number of the clerks and varies from justice to justice and over the course of the clerkship year. At one extreme, perhaps, is Dean Acheson, who said of his working with Brandeis in the 1930s, "He wrote the opinion; I wrote the footnotes." At the other are clerks like Butler's, Byrnes's, and Murphy's, who in the 1940s and 1950s drafted almost all of a justice's written work. Indeed, within the Court, Murphy's law clerks were snidely referred to as "Mr. Justice Huddleson" and "Mr. Justice Gressman." In one instance, Wiley Rutledge wrote to the chief justice, "After discussion with Justices Black and Douglas and Justice Murphy's clerk, Mr. Gressman, it has been agreed that I should inform you that the four of us" agree that the petition should be granted review and that "the case should be set for argument forthwith." On another occasion, Gressman wrote Rutledge, "I have tried in vain to reach Justice Murphy. But I know that he would want to join Black's statement if he files it. It certainly expresses his sentiments. I feel it perfectly O.K. to put his name on it—he would want it that way, especially since you are putting your name on it."

In historical perspective, most clerks' roles fall somewhere between these two extremes. Stone let his clerks craft footnotes that often announced novel principles of law.... Frankfurter had his clerks prepare lengthy memoranda, such as the ninety-one-page examination of segregation prepared by Alexander Bickel in 1954, as well as some of his better-known opinions, such as his dissent in the landmark reapportionment case, *Baker v. Carr* (1962).

From the perspective of other justices, Frankfurter "used his law clerks as flying squadrons against the law clerks of other Justices and even against the Justices themselves. Frankfurter, a proselytizer, never missed a chance to line up a vote." ... Unlike Frankfurter, ... Brennan rarely tried to directly lobby his colleagues. Instead, as one of his law clerks recalled, Brennan used his clerks "to talk to other clerks and find out what their Justices [were] thinking." Brennan then would pitch his points at conference or in draft opinions at particular justices in order to mass and hold onto a majority.

. . .

By all accounts, most justices now delegate the preliminary writing of opinions to their clerks. Chief Justice Rehnquist, for instance, usually has one of his clerks do a first draft, without bothering about style, and gives him about ten days to prepare it. Before having a clerk begin work on an opinion, Rehnquist goes over the conference discussion with the clerk and explains how he thinks "an opinion can be written supporting the result reached by the majority." It is not "a very sweeping original type of assignment," he emphasizes. "It is not telling the clerk just figure out how you'd like to decide this case and write something about [it]. It's not that at all." Once a clerk has finished a preliminary draft, Rehnquist reworks the opinion—using some, none, or all of the draft—to get his own style down. The draft opinion then typically circulates three or four times among the clerks in his chambers before Rehnquist sends it to the other justices for their comments. As a result, Chief Justice Rehnquist concedes that his "original contributions to [some opinions] are definitely a minor part of them; other opinions, my original contributions are a major part of them."

Even though they delegate the preliminary opinion writing, justices differ in their approach when revising first drafts. If a clerk's draft is "in the ball park," they often edit rather than rewrite. But some, like Burton, virtually rewrite their clerks' drafts, while others, like Reed, tend to insert paragraphs in the draft opinions prepared by their clerks. As one former clerk recalled, Reed simply "didn't like to start from the beginning and go to the ending." Consequently, his opinions tend to read like a dialogue with "a change of voice from paragraph to paragraph."
. . .

Though there are differences in the duties and manner in which clerks function, certain responsibilities are now commonly assigned in all chambers. Clerks play an indispensable role in the justices' deciding what to decide. As the number of filings each year rose, justices delegated the responsibility of initially reading all filings: appeals, which required mandatory review, and petitions for *certiorari*—"pets for *cert.*," as Justice Holmes referred to them—which seek review but may be denied or granted at the Court's own discretion. Clerks then [used to write] a one-to two-page summary of the facts, the questions presented, and the recommended course of action—that is, whether the case should be denied, dismissed, or granted full briefing and plenary consideration.

This practice originated with the handling of indigents' petitions—*in forma pauperis* petitions, or "Ifps"—by Chief Justice Hughes and his clerks. Unlike paid petitions and appeals, which are filed in multiple copies, petitions of indigents are typically filed without the assistance of an attorney in a single, handwritten copy. From the time of Hughes through that of Warren, these petitions were solely the responsibility of the chief justice and his law clerks (and this also explains why the chief justice had one more law clerk than the other justices). Except when an Ifp raised important legal issues or involved a capital case, Chief Justice Hughes as a matter of course neither circulated the petition to the other justices nor placed it on the conference list for discussion. Stone, Vinson, and Warren had their law clerks' *certiorari* memos routinely circulated to the other chambers. Chief justices, of course, differ in how carefully they study Ifps. Hughes and Warren were especially conscientious and scrupulous about Ifps; the latter told his clerks, "[I]t is necessary for you to be their counsel, in a sense." As the number of Ifps and other filings grew, they became too much for the chief's chambers to handle alone. They were thus distributed along with other paid petitions and jurisdictional statements to all chambers for each justice's consideration. Accordingly, almost all filings, with the exception of those handled by the Legal Office, are now circulated to the chambers, where clerks draft short memos on most.

With the mounting workload in the 1970s and 1980s, the role of law clerks in the screening process changed again. In 1972 [as discussed in Chapter Three above], at the suggestion of Lewis Powell, a majority of the Court's members began to pool their clerks, dividing up all filings and having a single clerk's *certiorari* memo then circulate to all those participating in the "*cert.* pool." . . .

. . .

After the justices vote in conference to hear a case, each usually assigns that case to a clerk. The clerk then researches the background and prepares a "bench memo." Bench memos outline pertinent facts and issues, propose possible questions to be put to participating attorneys during oral arguments, and address the merits of the cases. The clerk stays with the case as long as the justice does, helping with research and draft opinions. The nature of the work at this stage varies with the justice and the case, but it includes research, a hand in drafting the opinion and in commenting on other justices' responses to it, and the subsequent checking of citations and proofreading of the final version. Justices may also tell their clerks to draft concurring or dissenting opinions, while they themselves concentrate on the opinions they are assigned to write for the Court. As each term draws to a close and the justices feel the pressure of completing their opinions by the end of June, clerks perhaps inevitably assume an even greater role in the opinion-writing process.

Has too much responsibility been delegated to law clerks? Do they substantively influence the justices' voting and the final disposition of cases? After thirty-six years on the bench, Douglas claimed that circumstances were such that "many law clerks did much of the work of the justices." Rehnquist has provided one perspective on the function of law clerks: "I don't think people are shocked any longer to learn that an appellate judge receives a draft of a proposed opinion from a law clerk." He added, however:

> I think they would be shocked, and properly shocked, to learn that an appellate judge simply "signed off" on such a draft without fully understanding its import and in all probability making some changes in it. The line between having law clerks help one with one's work, and supervising subordinates in the performance of *their* work, may be a hazy one, but it is at the heart ... [of] the fundamental concept of "judging."

Fifty years ago, Rehnquist, who clerked for one-and-a-half years with Robert Jackson, had charged that law clerks—who he also claimed tended to be more "liberal" than the justices for whom they worked—had a substantive influence on the justices when preparing both *certiorari* memos and first drafts of opinions. The degree to which law clerks substantively influence justices' voting and opinion writing is difficult to gauge, and it certainly varies from justice to justice. With the increasing caseload, justices have perhaps inevitably come to rely more heavily on their law clerks' recommendations when voting in conference. Yet even when Rehnquist served as a clerk and the caseload was less than a third of its present size, justices no doubt voted overwhelmingly along the lines recommended by their law clerks. Vinson, for one, tallied the number of times he differed with his clerks. There were differences in less than 5 percent of the cases.

Clerks would look very powerful indeed if they were not transients in the Court. Clerks, as Alexander Bickel once noted, "are in no respect any kind of a powerful kitchen cabinet." ...

As part of the institutionalization of the Court, law clerks have assumed a greater role in conducting the business of the Court.... Their role in the justices' screening process is now considerably greater than it was in the past. At the stage of opinion writing, the substantive influence of law clerks varies from justice to justice, and from time to time in each chamber, as well as from case to case. No less important, the greater numbers of law clerks and of delegated responsibilities contribute to the steady increase in the volume of concurring and dissenting opinions written each year and to the justices' production of longer and more heavily footnoted opinions.

———

Questions and Comments

1. *Too much influence?* A controversial book—*Closed Chambers* (1998), by Edward Lazarus—paints a picture of undue influence by a "cabal" of clerks, a portrait that elicited considerable controversy. But not everyone agrees. Additional assessments are offered in two very recent books, noted below.

Describing a change in the role of law clerk from "stenographer" in the first decades, to "legal assistant" in the period of the 1930s to 1950s, to the last several decades in which law clerks function as "law firm associates," Todd C. Peppers concluded that "there is no evidence that any justices have abdicated their authority to make decisions regarding the winners and losers of a case. Justices, not law clerks, vote," though "[s]ome justices ... have vested their law clerks with substantial authority to decide how to reach" the outcome; nonetheless, "law clerks do not wield an inordinate amount of influence." Todd C. Peppers, *Courtiers of the Marble Palace: The Rise and Influence of the Supreme Court Law Clerk* 207–11 (2006). Drawing an interesting link between law clerk hiring and the possibilities for undue influence by clerks, he argues that "[w]hile the substantive job duties delegated to law clerks have expanded, the ideological distance between clerks and their justices has diminished—thus minimizing the likelihood that divergent goals of the clerk and justice would result in law clerk shirking or defection. Moreover, traditional monitoring devices—the weekly conferences and circulation of opinions—have been supplemented by intrachamber review of work product by multiple law clerks."[44] *Id.* at 211. A particularly interesting suggestion in this work is that the cert pool might be a "monitoring device" by which the justices, as "principals," seek to assure that their "agents" (the law clerks) do not distort or fail to present a complete account of each petition. See *id.* at 210.

Intra-chambers review processes are also emphasized by Artemus Ward & David L. Weiden, *Sorcerers' Apprentices: 100 Years of Law Clerks at the United States Supreme Court* (2006), although they express more concern about law clerks acting as "Junior Justices," or even as "Sorcerers' Apprentices," to whom the actual Justices have "ceded greater responsibility ... in recent years." *Id.* at 23, 201. They conclude that "most of the time, clerks are not able to change their Justices' minds about cases or issues," but sometimes do, and that law clerks have gained in influence over time. *Id.* at 198–99. They express particular concern that "drafts written entirely by clerks have been released as opinions with little or no changes made by Justices," *id.*, though they also report that 70% of the clerks surveyed reported that their Justices made revisions in drafts in "all cases." *Id.* at 225 (Table 5.2); *see also id.* at 217 (stating that once a law clerk completes a draft, "the Justice usually revises it"). They also note that drafting practices vary among chambers, with Justice Stevens still generally doing the initial

---

44. Each of the three coauthors of this book, who clerked for Justice Thurgood Marshall (O.T. 1976, O.T. 1977) and Justice John Marshall Harlan II (O.T. 1970), participated in "intrachamber review" of drafts, that is, the practice of different law clerks within a chamber reading and editing drafts other law clerks were working on, so this practice is of relatively long standing.

drafts of his own opinions and with much editing and revising back and forth in other chambers. *Id.* at 200–01, 222–23. This work also provides support for the view that having more law clerks may have contributed to the growth in separate opinions on the Court. *See id. at* 231.

2. *Declining quality of opinions?* Bernard Schwartz, in *The Ascent of Pragmatism: The Burger Court in Action* 35–39 (1990), discussed law clerks:

> The growing number of law clerks has naturally led to an increase in the length, though plainly not the quality, of opinions. What Douglas once wrote about Court opinions has become increasingly true: "We have tended more and more to write a law-review-type of opinion. They plague the Bar and the Bench. They are so long they are meaningless. They are filled with trivia and nonessentials."
>
> ... Law clerks have a similar academic background and little other experience. For three years they have had drummed into them that the acme of literary style is the law review article. It is scarcely surprising that the standard opinion style has become that of the student-run reviews: colorless, prolix, platitudinous, always erring on the side of inclusion, full of lengthy citations and footnotes—and above all dull.

See also Richard A. Posner, *The Federal Courts: Crisis and Reform* 115 (1985) (arguing that the increased number of law clerks is "the proximate cause of the enormous increase in the federal judicial output of separate opinions, footnotes, citations, and above all words").[45] (Might law clerks, on occasion, improve opinion-drafting? Cf. William N. Eskridge, Jr., *The Crime Against Nature on Trial*, Bowers v. Hardwick, *1986*, in *Civil Rights Stories* 151,167 (Gilles & Goluboff, eds. 2008)(reporting that Justice White himself drafted the much-criticized and since overruled opinion in *Bowers* because his law clerk was taking too long).) To assess Schwartz' views, try to compare opinions with those from the 1950s and earlier.

3. *Testing for influence?* In the readings in this and in earlier Chapters, you have seen a number of approaches to "testing" for law clerk influence. See, e.g., David Stras, *Book Review Essay: The Supreme Court's Gatekeepers: The Role of Law Clerks in the Certiorari Process*, 85 Tex. L. Rev. 947 (2007) (excerpted in Chapter Three, above) (suggesting that expansion of the cert pool helps explain decline in numbers of cases granted because law clerks have incentives to recommend denial, rather than grant, in close cases); Posner, *supra*, at 114–15; see also Paul J. Wahlbeck, James F. Spriggs II & Lee Sigelman, *Ghostwriters on the Court? A Stylistic Analysis of U.S. Supreme Court Opinion Drafts*, 30 Am. Pol. Res. 166 (2002) (analyzing law clerk's stylistic "fingerprints" in draft opinions by Thurgood Marshall

45. See also *id.* at 112–14 (including Table 4.3, showing a substantial increase in words per Justice published per Term between 1969 and 1972, from 42,000 to 116,-000, following addition of a third law clerk). It is interesting to note, however, that the Table shows no similar magnitude increase in the mid–1970s when a fourth clerk was added in most chambers, raising at least a question about the causal relationship between more words published and more law clerks. Posner presents other data suggesting that the numbers of footnotes and citations per opinion may also be related to the addition of law clerks. See e.g., *id.* at 112 (Table 4.2). In thinking about the causes of increased opinion length, consider, as well, the introduction of word processing technology to the Court in the late 1970s.

and Lewis Powell, suggesting that they relied on their clerks to a different degree, with Marshall delegating more writing to the clerks). Yet on many issues—including the numbers of cert grants, the length of opinions and the number of separate of opinions—there are other factors to be considered, which may include changes in the Justices on the Court, changes in the technology of producing written materials, or a changing private Bar that participates in advocacy in the cert process. Perhaps most controversial is the question whether law clerks influence outcomes. Justices might be thought to have self-interested reasons to deny such influence; clerks might likewise have self-interested reasons to claim influence. (See the discussion, below, of Edward Lazarus' book, *Closed Chambers*). For a recent attempt by political scientists to test for law clerk influence on outcome, by analyzing individual Justice's voting patterns under different sets of clerks, see Todd C. Peppers & Christopher Zorn, Law Clerk Influence on Supreme Court Decision Making, Version 5.2, June 14 (2007), available at http://ssrn.com/abstract=925705. Lawyers are typically not trained in the tools of regression analyses on which social scientists rely to analyze complex correlations; political scientists may not be attuned to the impact of doctrinal influence; does this suggest the benefit of inter-disciplinary study of the Court?

4. *Who are the clerks?* According to a recent study, until after World War II, clerks were—with the exception of one woman and one African–American man—entirely white men. See Peppers, *Courtiers of the Marble Palace, supra,* at 20–21 (first female clerk, Lucile Lomen, hired in 1944; second female clerk, Margaret Corcoran, hired in 1966); *id.* at 22 (first African–American clerk, William Coleman, hired in 1948, the second, Tyrone Brown, hired in 1967). As Peppers describes, concerns about the low levels of minority law clerks surfaced in 1998, when Tony Mauro reported that "Chief Justice Rehnquist and Associate Justices Scalia, Kennedy and Souter had never hired an African–American law clerk," and that most of the other Justices had rarely hired African–American clerks. Over the next five years, the number of minority clerks increased somewhat. See *id.* at 22–23; see also *id.* at 24 (Table 2.1) (minority hiring on Rehnquist Court). As for where the Court's law clerks are educated, most Justices hire most of their law clerks from a small group of selective law schools. According to one study, between 1882 and 2002, 45% of the clerks hired attended either Harvard or Yale. Ward & Weiden, *supra,* at 72. Ninety percent of the clerks, in another study of the period 1986–2004, came from Harvard, Yale, University of Chicago, N.Y.U., Stanford, University of Michigan, University of Virginia, University of Pennsylvania, Georgetown, University of Texas, Northwestern, and U.C.-Berkeley. Peppers, *supra,* at 25–27.[46]

5. *How are they hired?* Although law clerks are relatively junior lawyers, they are likely to have more experience now than in the period before World War II, when they were often hired right out of law school. As the readings indicate, excellent academic credentials and law review experi-

46. Over a longer period—from 1882–2004, in Peppers' study, at p. 24—the largest contributors of law clerks to the Court, listed in order, were Harvard (29%), Yale (16%), University of Chicago (8%), Columbia (7%), Stanford (6%) and, with under 5% each, the Universities of Michigan, Virginia, and Pennsylvania, Georgetown Law Center and New York University. See also Ward & Weiden, *Sorcerers' Apprentices,* at 72 (Chart of Law Schools Attended By Supreme Court Law Clerks: 1882–2002).

ence are generally important criteria. A prior clerkship on a lower court is almost always required; indeed, some young lawyers clerk and then spend a year or so in the practice of law before being accepted as a Supreme Court clerk. Some Justices have used committees of trusted advisers (often former clerks) to pre-screen or even interview applicants; some rely on particular "feeder" judges in the lower courts and some Justices give weight to geographic as well as demographic diversity in their choices. Justice Harry A. Blackmun apparently relied on a one-page list of topics (some typed, some handwritten) during his interviews of prospective clerks; the list included, *inter alia*, "Attitudes towards the lower courts," "Military service," "Hours. long," "No memo or other item leaving the building," "Where else applied," "Favorite branch of law," "No comment about the Justices or their division," "Parking ...," "Room tidiness," "Health," "No interviews." Law Clerk Applicant Interviews, undated document in The Blackmun Papers, Box 1568, Library of Congress (underlining in original). A complete version of this document is reproduced in Ward & Weiden, *supra*, at 267 (App. D).

6. *Former law clerks as Justices?* The late Chief Justice Rehnquist, the current Chief Justice John G. Roberts, Jr., and Justices Stevens and Breyer were themselves law clerks on the Supreme Court: Rehnquist for Justice Robert Jackson, Roberts for Justice Rehnquist, Stevens for Justice Wiley Rutledge and Breyer for Justice Arthur Goldberg. For Rehnquist, his service as Robert Jackson's law clerk led to controversy—both at the time of his nomination as an Associate Justice and again when he was nominated as Chief Justice—over whether a memo he wrote Jackson as his clerk, arguing that *Plessy v. Ferguson* should not be overruled, represented his views, or those of Justice Jackson or those of a "devil's advocate." For Stevens, his service as a clerk to Justice Rutledge during the 1947 Term may have influenced his decisions in recent cases involving the "war on terror," including Rasul v. Bush, 542 U.S. 466 (2004) and Hamdan v. Rumsfeld, 126 S. Ct. 2749 (2006). For discussion, see Joseph T. Thai, *The Law Clerk Who Wrote* Rasul v. Bush: *John Paul Stevens's Influence from World War II to the War on Terror*, 92 Va. L. Rev. 501 (2006); Craig Green, *Wiley Rutledge, Executive Detention, and Judicial Conscience at War*, 84 Wash. U. L. Rev. 99 (2006). (For a helpful treatment of Justice Rutledge, see John M. Ferren, *Salt of the Earth, Conscience of the Court: The Story of Justice Wiley Rutledge* (2004).) For other discussions of law clerks who became Justices, see, e.g., Linda Greenhouse, *How Not to Be Chief Justice: The Appenticeship of William H. Rehnquist*, 154 U. Pa. L. Rev. 1365 (2006); Louis Henkin, *Byron White: Early Colleague, Old Friend*, 116 Harv. L. Rev. 5 (2002) (discussing White's clerkship with Chief Justice Vinson).

7. *Law clerks and confidentiality*: At least two controversial publications in recent years have raised issues about the scope of any duty of confidentiality Supreme Court law clerks owe. An article on the 2000 *Bush v. Gore* case reported on law clerks' unhappiness about the nature of the decision process. See David Margolick, Evgenia Peretz & Michael Shnayerson, *The Path to Florida*, Vanity Fair, Oct. 2004 (reporting, for example, that "an O'Connor clerk said that O'Connor was determined to overturn the Florida decision and was merely looking for grounds.... [because, according to the clerk] 'she thought the Florida court was trying to steal the election and they had to stop it' "). This report, in turn, occasioned comment and

threats of investigation. Charles Lane, *In Court Clerks' Breach, A Provocative Precedent*, The Washington Post, Oct. 17, 2004 at D01 (reporting concern about the willingness of "former clerks to liberal justices who opposed the ruling" to provide information to the *Vanity Fair* reporters; noting letter "from 96 mostly conservative former law clerks and lawyers" calling it "conduct unbecoming any attorney or legal adviser working in a position of trust;"; and reporting that three senators had called for hearings on whether there had been misconduct by the clerks). Far more controversy was raised by the publication of a book by a former law clerk to Harry Blackmun, Edward Lazarus' *Closed Chambers*, discussed in the next two readings.

Sally J. Kenney,[47] *Puppeteers or Agents? What Lazarus's Closed Chambers Adds to Our Understanding of Law Clerks at the U.S. Supreme Court*, 25 Law & Soc. Inquiry 185 (2000)

Written by a former law clerk to Justice Harry Blackmun, *Closed Chambers: The First Eyewitness Account of the Epic Struggles Inside the Supreme Court* is a lively and well-written clerk's-eye view of the U.S. Supreme Court during a pivotal and contentious term, 1988–89. Lazarus vividly evokes what it feels like to participate in the day-to-day business of the Court. That powerful first-person narrative is reminiscent of William H. Rehnquist's account of his days clerking for Justice Jackson in 1952 (1987)....

... Lazarus, unlike Rehnquist, has sharply critical things to say about the way the Court does its work, individual justices, and outcomes in particular cases, and he intersperses these criticisms with deeply unflattering gossip. The mere fact of publishing his account, his telling the tale, the arguments criticizing the Court, and the gossip have all generated a furor in the legal community over the book, a firestorm stoked by dust-jacket copy and press release.

Lazarus makes three principal arguments. First, he claims that both liberals and conservatives on the Court abandoned their obligations as judges to offer principled legal reasons for decisions. Instead, he maintains that they now merely generate ex post facto rationalizations for preferred policy outcomes that show no respect for precedent or even consistency with their own previous writings. Second, justices have failed to fulfill their obligation as judges to deliberate with open minds and work collegially. He claims that they currently labor in isolation, divide into rigid factions, and harbor petty bitter resentments. Since all pretense at collegiality has broken down, and justices have failed to both reason and deliberate, we can no longer justify transferring political

47. Professor of Women's Studies, Political Science and Law and Director, Center on Women and Public Policy at the Humphrey Institute of Public Affairs at the University of Minnesota.

decision making from democratically elected majorities to an unelected body of nine. Third, Lazarus argues that law clerks such as himself have far too much power. The excessive power of law clerks is both a cause and an effect of the breakdown of reason and deliberation.

Rather than covering all the important cases of the 1988–89 term, Lazarus gives a detailed account of three important issues: abortion (Webster v. Reproductive Health Services, 492 U.S. 490 [1989]), race discrimination (Patterson v. McClean Credit Union, 491 U.S. 164 [1989]), and the death penalty (Tompkins v. Texas, 490 U.S. 754 [1989]), and precedes the contemporary behind-the-scenes story by a succinct and well-written history of the law and politics of these three issues. He freely shares his opinions on nearly every case discussed, often attributing the outcome of any case "wrongly" decided to one of three causes: lack of intellect (usually of the swing members Justices O'Connor and Kennedy), deliberate dishonesty and hypocrisy (he directs this charge at both liberals and conservatives), or undue clerk influence, rather than attributing the outcome to principled disagreement on important fundamental legal and political issues about which reasonable people disagree. . . .

. . . While I am primarily interested in the question of what Lazarus adds to our knowledge of law clerks at the U.S. Supreme Court, I also consider whether he should have published his account and assess the merits of his criticisms of particular justices and the Court in general. Last, I make some observations on epistemology and method.

.   .   .

. . . *Closed Chambers* can be read as a text of our time, or at least a text of our time 10 years ago. Lazarus contends that the failure to confirm Bork poisoned the atmosphere on the Court, particularly among the clerks his year. He reports to being "haunted" by his experience on the Court and, when he concluded after the Clarence Thomas hearings that the bitter divisions on the Court were likely to continue, he wanted to know how the Court came to be so bitterly divided. The description of the "Cabal," the self-ascribed label for a group of conservative clerks who dined together weekly and maintained a separate email network, will be familiar to every feminist and progressive at a major law school or university department in the 1990s, familiar with "the swagger of ascendent conservatism"—another good example of Lazarus's ability to turn a phrase. The gloves have come off in the dialogue about race and federalism and choice, among other issues. Lazarus's diagnosis of the malaise as specific to an institution he loves, and attributable to the failure of individuals (clerks and justices who lack integrity), is one of the shortcomings of the book—not seeing the Court as embedded in the larger political and social context.

Although Lazarus does not shy away from attributing motive to others, it is hard to clearly identify his motive in writing the book, a book that has made him a pariah among the legal community. He argues that writing the book is an act of "devotion not disloyalty" by holding the justices accountable to high ideals. What is his real objective? To recount his experience? To expose wrong? To criticize the Court? To call for change? Are we convinced that his stated motive is genuine? And more important, do we agree with his position that the public interest justifies his revelations?

I. THE ROLES AND POWERS OF CLERKS

. . .

What do we know about the work that law clerks do? How justices use their clerks has varied over time and between justices. Clerks perform research functions, summarize the contents of briefs, make recommendations on cases, edit, check cites, or even draft preliminary opinions. They discuss cases with their justice, argue about them with other law clerks, attend conferences, run errands, file documents, and perform library maintenance....

1. They Discuss Cases with Their Justices

From the beginning, the justices themselves praised the use of recent law graduates as a way of bringing the latest legal thinking to sitting judges. Their recent exposure to elite law professors provides the judge with a continuing seminar. Justice Douglas opposed Chief Justice Burger's innovation of having one permanent clerk:

> Under [a more permanent clerk] system the law clerks would acquire more and more power, with no fresh minds coming in annually to ventilate the old stuffy chambers; under such a system the ideas of the "boss," usually stuffy and stereotyped, would never be challenged. That movement would mean the end of the seasoning of the pudding—it would eliminate the spice that fresh young minds [bring] to the job.

Law clerks are the sounding boards for judges.... Since clerks are among the few people the judge can openly discuss cases with ..., and since they share in and mitigate the crushing workload, the relationship between judges and clerks can be intense. Judge Patricia Wald calls the relationship "the most intense and mutually dependent one ... outside of marriage, parenthood, or a love affair". It is precisely because justices view their clerks as their inner circle, a place to vent and try out ideas, a place where they may rail against colleagues or opinions without self-consciousness, that Lazarus's book must feel to them like such a betrayal.

Lazarus claims that clerks hold too much influence over their justices—they succeed in persuading the justice to accept the clerk's view.... [T]he argument about undue clerk influence is at odds with the argument about justices failing to deliberate. Setting aside for the moment whether the justices should be deliberating with each other rather than with clerks, I think clerks do have a positive influence on the justices and the Court by bringing fresh ideas and providing a close-knit group wherein justices can reconsider their positions if they choose to do so. Being persuaded by clerks to reconsider a position or accept an argument is very different from being manipulated by them. Justices are influenced by what they read, discussions at the law schools they visit, views pressed on them by family and friends, and films, television, and so on. I think this is a good thing. I think it is also unlikely that neophyte law school graduates will, through force of reason and intellect, persuade justices to reject a long-held position or approach to constitutional interpretation. But in the application to a new question, or technical matters, whether it is telecommunications or consideration of the privacy rights of gays and lesbians, justices may be attentive to what appear to be generational shifts in attitudes. Lazarus wants justices to keep their minds open to new arguments, but then seems to condemn them for being persuaded by others, particularly clerks, and especially, clerks from the Cabal (the clique of conservatives). The extended case that Lazarus does consider, McClesky v. Kemp, 481 U.S. 282 (1987), is actually evidence against his assertion of undue clerk influence. Lazarus argues that the clerks, even those strongly in favor of the constitutionality of the death penalty and its desirability or at least necessity as a public policy, were troubled by the Baldus evidence showing that those who killed whites were more likely than those (black or white) who killed blacks to receive a capital sentence. Lazarus reports, however, that even conservative clerks made no headway in altering the positions of the justices, who seemed to have a shockingly poor grasp of elementary statistics. Nor could the Cabal persuade Justices O'Connor or Kennedy to overrule *Roe* in *Webster*.

2. THEY SCREEN PETITIONS FOR CERTIORARI

. . .

What does Lazarus's evidence contribute to the debate over whether clerks wield too much power in sifting through petitions for certiorari, and thus, in setting the Court's agenda? As noted above, justices rely extensively on clerks to sift the meritorious from the nonmeritorious petitions—they do not review the individual papers but rely, at least for the first cut, on the cert pool memoranda. Yet, in the end, Lazarus moves away from the claim of undue clerk influence:

> What effect our cert. process machinations really had is difficult to gauge. In the first place, each side checked the other's work and, where necessary, called slanted or inaccurate cert. pool memos to the attention of their respective Justices. More important, each of the Justices usually had a good idea of what issues in what kinds of cases they wanted the Court to hear, especially in contentious areas of law. With the possible exception of one or two on each side, I doubt the Court granted any cert. petitions because of something clerks did and, if some clerks did manage to bury a few cases along the way, the same issues, assuming they were worth the Court's time, were sure to resurface.

Although clerks do have the potential to slant or frame a question in certain ways in order to enhance or reduce the likelihood that a petition will be granted, two factors mitigate against them doing so. First, as Coenen argues, "producing written work that brings disrepute on themselves and their chambers is little less than a heart-stopping prospect"; clerks are terrified that their work might bring embarrassment to themselves or their justices. Second, Lazarus argues that given the poisonous atmosphere of Libs against Cabalists, each was vigilantly checking each other's work and quick to cry foul if any deviation from objectivity occurred. What Lazarus identifies as a concern occurs after he left the Court: with more justices in the cert pool (all but Justice Stevens), clerks have no one with whom to check their work.... Justices Blackmun and Kennedy have both expressed concern for a checking function. Justices Scalia and Kennedy have proposed reforming the system for precisely those reasons.

3. They Talk with Each Other

Lazarus's argument about certiorari is less that clerks wielded too much influence but rather that the skirmishes over certiorari between the "dreaded Libs" and the "Cabal" further contributed to the poisonous atmosphere at the Court.... [T]his is one of Lazarus's most important assertions: that law clerks, particularly a group that was as polarized as was his class, seriously impeded collegial relations between the justices and therefore undermined the deliberative process that is the essence of judging in a collegiate court. Law clerks may tell their justices unflattering things that other justices and clerks are saying about them. They may also provide a buffer and a community that may prevent justices from talking to other justices. Lazarus reports that clerks often communicate with their justices by writing. Anyone who has ever been a member of a faculty who fought by memos (and now email) knows how quickly differences can escalate, and how easy it is to be inflammatory in writing while face-to-face interactions may lead to greater civility. Lazarus shows how the clerk back channel that justices used in the past as a way of gathering intelligence, a way of feeling out another justice's intensity of feeling or willingness to compromise, facilitated consensus building. During 1988–89, that channel had the opposite effect.

One thing that is not well addressed in the literature is the role that clerks may play in sharing information and even negotiating between chambers.... Lazarus argues that clerks acted collectively to persuade (manipulate? trick?) the justices into taking a position consistent with their views. Although Lazarus inadvertently acknowledges that liberal clerks formed a social group ("the dreaded Libs") and discussed cases and, presumably, strategy together, it is the conservative clerks whose communications rise to the level of sinister collusion and conspiracy. Lazarus charged the Cabal with policing its members in a form of groupthink and in reaching out to influence other chambers, specifically through the "infiltration" of Justice Kennedy's chambers by ... a former Scalia clerk.

... I interpret the evidence differently from Lazarus. Celebrating executions (with or without champagne) IS unseemly, particularly to those of us who oppose the death penalty (although surely the Libs would have celebrated a decision to declare the death penalty unconstitutional). It does not, however, support the proposition of undue clerk influence, but rather evidences a realignment of the Court against reviewing capital cases—a realignment of the justices that results in the presence of strongly pro-death penalty clerks. Clearly, for 12 years, presidential staff screened prospective nominees to the Court to be closer to Chief Justice Rehnquist than Justice Marshall on this issue. And finally, just before Lazarus arrived, the pendulum swung the other way. Chief Justice Rehnquist's position, which Lazarus carefully describes—a position he had consistently taken at least since he joined the Court—at last became ascendant. The bitterness between clerks mirrored rather than caused the bitterness between justices, and all concerned were stressed by the volatility of this emotional constitutional issue.

4. They Research, Edit, and Draft Opinions

Perhaps the most controversial task clerks perform is drafting opinions. According to one former clerk, Williston, the practice of having clerks draft opinions was as old as Justice Gray, the first to use clerks, although Williston notes that most drafts did not withstand Justice Gray's scrutiny and ended in the wastebasket. Williston clearly viewed the final opinions as the work product of the justices themselves. As clerical and stenographical clerks (who also cut hair, delivered messages, and performed other personal services) evolved into legal clerks, Justice Hughes worried that others would believe the clerks had written the opinions. As clerk to Justice Brandeis, Dean Acheson claimed credit for writing the footnotes of opinions, as did Louis Lusky, a former law clerk of Justice Stone, who claimed credit for footnote four of United States v. Carolene Products Company [304 U.S. 144, 153 n. 4 (1938)]. Justice Douglas charged that under the Burger Court, clerks did much of the work of the justices and "that was not right".

Controversy about all-powerful clerks who write opinions seems to appear almost cyclically. [The author describes the 1957 *U.S. News and World Report* article and Rehnquist and Bickel responses]

. . .

The publication of Woodward and Armstrong's *The Brethren* in 1979 revived the charges that clerks write opinions. In my view, neither *Closed Chambers* nor *The Brethren* succeeds in demonstrating that law clerks write decisions or unduly sway their bosses. What both do, however, is pull back the curtain and report gossip and conjecture about the behavior of the justices and the purity of their decision-making processes. They also raise the question of whether clerks should speak to journalists and whether what the journalists report is indeed true.... [T]he most damning revelation of *The Brethren* was not that the justices were demonstrated to be the puppets of the clerks—but that the justices were portrayed as human, with human shortcomings, and as people who are motivated in their decision making by considerations other than legal principle.

The anecdotal evidence does tend to suggest that the institutional culture is more tolerant than previously of greater delegation to clerks in the writing of opinions and that the practice was more widespread by 1988 than in the 1950s, 60s, and even 70s. Although in 1987 Chief Justice Rehnquist quoted Justice Brandeis as attributing the high prestige of the U.S. Supreme Court compared with the other branches of government to the fact that justices do their own work (Rehnquist 1987, 261), Chief Justice Rehnquist seemed to rely more on his clerks for writing than Justice Jackson relied upon him. Wade McCree, former judge and solicitor general, argues that the problem is not the use of clerks per se, but their increasing number combined with the dramatic growth in workload. He argues that judges cannot meaningfully supervise more than two clerks without crossing the line into excessive delegation.

Lazarus argues that the justices delegate too much responsibility to their clerks to write opinions:

> As extreme as this might seem, the broadest exercise of what has become known politely as clerk influence occurs not on the death watch but in the Court's written rulings. For while it is, of course, true that only the Justices cast votes at the Court and that no Justice would ever circulate or publish an opinion that he or she has not approved, during October Term '88 the vast majority of opinions the Court issued were drafted exclusively by clerks. Indeed, only Justices Stevens and Scalia made it a regular practice to participate in first drafts. The other Justices consigned themselves to a more or less demanding editor's role.

Lazarus briefly summarizes a handful of commentaries that criticize the increasing length of opinions, the law-review style of lengthy footnotes and jargon, the proliferation of concurrences and dissents, and the increased emphasis on balancing tests and that also lament the absence of the great opinions of the legendary legal minds of old, blaming law clerks for these problems. But once again, Lazarus fails to either give us detailed evidence for his bold declarations or explains how he knows about the practices of the chambers he most criticizes.

The charge of undue clerk influence ultimately dissolves into the recurring claim that the justices are failing to reason and deliberate. Lazarus argues that a chasm separates writing and editing and that unless justices are writing first drafts, they are not really grappling with the great legal questions. Only through writing first drafts can one encounter an opinion that "won't write," the experience of which causes a justice to interrogate her position and contemplate change. In Lazarus's view that is vastly different from an opinion that "won't read." Furthermore, stating that the "devil is in the details," he asserts that the construction of the argument—how the author frames it and summarizes precedent—is vital and does not get the scrutiny of justices too focused on bottom-line results. For the most part, law clerks are well-intentioned yet overexuberant novices who lack the depth of understanding of the case law and desperately want to make their mark on the law, perhaps at the expense of faithfully executing their justice's will. Lazarus also argues, however, that some clerks are not well-meaning and have overstepped the bounds ("many infractions have been egregious"). They miscite cases, mischaracterize facts, stir up bad feelings between the justices, and insert wild theories in the hope that some will survive the editing process. . . . I agree with Lazarus that more of that work should be done by the justices. I am not convinced, however, that justices are duped or that the reasoning in important cases reflects the views of the clerks and not the justices. I think his account does lend support to the argument that clerks are preparing more first drafts than they did in the past, and that the justice's role may have shifted more from writer to editor. . . .

In the section discussing opinion writing, Lazarus targets Justices O'Connor and Kennedy as especially vulnerable to clerk influence (although he also criticizes Justice Marshall later). What is the evidence that Justices O'Connor and Kennedy delegate too much power to clerks and fail to even perform the task of opinion editing properly? The evidence seems to be that they are centrists, not captured reliably by either faction, and select law clerks who are liberals and conservatives, making the clerk infighting in their chambers especially intense. . . . But even though I do not agree with Justice O'Connor's undue-burden test for fundamental rights, I am loathe to attribute it to a clerk without strong evidence. Lazarus makes bold, damning declarations, but he does not give us details of either where justices failed to edit conscientiously or where clerks deliberately misled them. All supervisory situations contain the possibility of excessive delegations to underlings; however, this does not mean that it routinely occurs.

For evidence that clerks write opinions with only the most minimal checks by their bosses, Lazarus appears to rely on an article by Eastland in *National Review* that criticizes Justice Marshall for watching too much television and calls on the "over the hill justices" (all conveniently liberals) to resign (Eastland 1989 . . .). Eastland's article, however, goes on to note how carefully Justices Marshall and Brennan chose clerks whose views coincided with their own and how diligently the clerks sought to represent the views of their justices . . . .

5. THEY PROCESS, SCREEN, AND SUMMARIZE PETITIONS FOR STAYS OF EXECUTION

The role of clerks has changed dramatically in death penalty cases since *The Brethren* and other examinations of law clerks. Only 94 people had been executed in the 12 years since the reauthorization of the death penalty in Gregg v. Georgia, 428 U.S. 153 (1976) . . . . When the Supreme Court ruled against the equal protection argument in *McClesky v. Kemp* just before Lazarus came to work for Justice Blackmun, more than 2,000 people awaited execution on death row. In that pivotal term then, recent appointments precluded any possibility that the death penalty would be declared unconstitutional in any general sense, and lawyers for the condemned had to make arguments more particular to their individual cases.

Lazarus's chapter entitled "The Death Watch" is a gripping account of the role clerks play as lawyers for those facing a death sentence file their last appeals. The final hours before executions, almost always scheduled between midnight and dawn, found the clerks assigned to the case alone in chambers as others left for the day. These clerks would consider any last minute appeals and face the agony of trying to persuade other clerks to wake up their justices and issue a stay if they believed the appeals had merit. Those advocating a stay waited alone for the votes from other chambers in the form of written memoranda that came in under the door with a whoosh—an awesome responsibility for anyone, let alone someone so young.

Lazarus argues each case turned on four justices in the middle, the other five having made up their mind already to vote for every stay or no stays. And Lazarus clerked for one of those justices, Harry Blackmun (although Justice Blackmun eventually took the position in 1994 that the death penalty could not be fairly administered and that he would no longer "tinker with the machinery of death," Callins v. Collins, 510 U.S. 1141, 1145 [1994]).

> Certainly, the ultimate power to grant or deny a stay rested with the Justices. Still, when the final arguments reached the Court, the Justices were almost always long since home for the night.... The Justices counted on their clerks to distill for them the essence of the case, the facts, the issues, and the precedents that should inform their vote. They relied on us for advice.... Those of us who worked for Justices Blackmun, Stevens, O'Connor, and Kennedy ... shared a middle ground where, in many cases, no fixed rule or policy dictated our Justice's vote.... How we described a given case, which facts we put in and which we left out, how we characterized the competing arguments, and how insistently we put forward our own points of view—these things mattered deeply and, at least in a few instances, undeniably made the difference between life and death.

But the power of clerks was not to decide who lived and died but which cases, based on instructions from their justices, merited Supreme Court review.... [M]ore important, the clerks of the four middle justices possessed this power because their bosses delegated it to them—that is, their justices decided matters on a case-by-case basis.... A pro-death penalty clerk would have no influence in the Brennan or Marshall chambers, nor would an abolitionist clerk wield power in the chambers of Rehnquist, or Scalia, and now Thomas.

The strongest evidence of clerk influence on the death penalty is Lazarus's deeply unflattering portrait of Justice Kennedy—and to a lesser extent, Justice O'Connor—as a ditherer.... Lazarus alleges that

Justice Kennedy especially hated to be the deciding vote in these cases (who wouldn't?), and so his clerk would try to get him to commit to a position early in the process before all the votes had been decided. And the clerk, a member of the conservative Cabal, allegedly tried to get him to commit early to the position of allowing an execution to go forward. Like most of the important information in the book, Lazarus does not tell us how he comes to know this "fact" or how often this scenario occurred. The claim in its strongest form is that Cabal members, some of whom had "infiltrated" the O'Connor and Kennedy chambers, so relished executions that if they drew the case, no arguments no matter how sound would ever persuade them to issue a stay.

The death penalty cases may be a good example of how direct personal experience can sometimes skew one's overall judgment. I have no doubt that what happened on the night of executions was as Lazarus describes it: that Libs were literally screaming at recalcitrant Cabalists in the wee hours, frustrated at failing to get the much-needed last vote for a stay, and feeling that it was capricious—that because of the luck of the draw, a man would be executed. But the clerks possessed this power only because Justices O'Connor and Kennedy did not share Justices Brennan, Marshall, and ultimately Blackmun's abhorrence of executions and suspicion of justice meted out by state courts and reviewed by federal courts. . . .

6.   CONCLUSIONS: NEW EVIDENCE OF CLERKS' POWERS?

. . .

While I do not share Lazarus's conclusion that clerks wield too much power at the U.S. Supreme Court . . . , I do agree that clerks affect how the institution operates. And in fact, one of my complaints about Lazarus is that by focusing the debate on whether clerks do or do not write opinions and manipulate justices, he deflects our attention from the significant impact clerks do have on how the Court does its work and how it organizes itself to respond to its growing workload. O'Brien, and others, have warned of the dangers if justices function as opinion-writing bureaus rather than as one deliberative body. Without question, the presence of and increase in number of clerks allows justices to write more separate concurring and dissenting opinions than they could otherwise and to spend more time supervising staff than writing themselves or interacting with colleagues. . . . The opinions have lengthened (the U.S. Supreme Court Reports went from 2,133 pages in 1960 to 4,269 pages in 1983) and became more fragmented into concurring and dissenting opinions. "Between 1969 and 1972—the period during which the justices each became entitled to a third law clerk . . . the number of opinions increased by about 50 percent and the number of words tripled." . . .

. . . Although I believe that using law clerks for many tasks is a natural response of an organization trying to manage its workload, as that workload increases, the dangers of bureaucratic justice are real.

Most evidence confirms that several factors limit the power of clerks on the Supreme Court. First is the clerks' youth and inexperience. Law clerks are often law students or recent law school graduates rather than skilled litigators, legal scholars, or political negotiators. Second, justices need to gain a consensus, and consequently, they do the bargaining. Third is their short term—almost always only one year. Fourth, evidence suggests that both justices and law clerks see the job as one of mirroring the views of the justice rather than putting forth a personal viewpoint. Lazarus's term was a particularly polarized one, even if it was not as historically significant as he might claim. The Court changed and overturned important doctrines and precedents, and the justices differed profoundly in their views on particular significant legal issues and approaches to constitutional interpretation. The clerks, I believe, reflected those profound differences rather than caused them, although they may have reinforced and exacerbated the alienation between the justices.

II. THE ETHICS OF THE EXPOSÉ

. . . After the publication of *The Brethren*, when it became clear that many clerks had spoken with Woodward and Armstrong (if only to confirm or deny what another source had told them), . . . the Court issued guidelines, a *Law Clerk Code of Conduct*, making it explicit that clerks were to keep the confidences of their justices and the institution in perpetuity. Although commentators at the time criticized the clerks for talking to journalists (and for journalists in taking at face value the clerks' inflated claims of importance), fewer argued that the Court should be somehow immune among governmental institutions from the scrutiny of journalists or that the journalists had acted unethically. Although Lazarus at times tries to straddle the categories of participant observer, journalist, and historian, his ethical and legal obligations to the Court as a former clerk differ from those of journalists like Woodward and Armstrong. Legal commentators discussed whether Lazarus violated his obligations under legal professional ethics. Judge Kozinski, for example, compares Lazarus's ethical misconduct to violating a lawyer's duty of confidentiality to a client. In his defense, Lazarus asserted that his obligation of confidentiality only applied while he was working at the Court, or at best, some time after leaving, and second, that he is not alone in talking about the internal dynamics of the Court.

A third argument Lazarus offers in his defense is more interesting. He argues that he has not violated his duty of confidentiality to Justice Blackmun and the Court because he has not relied on his experiences as a clerk as an independent source of information. Instead, his experience merely provided the necessary interpretative framework for information he gleaned from interviews and public sources such as the Marshall papers. He discloses very little of what occurred within the Blackmun chambers. He does not identify which opinions he drafted that Justice Blackmun excessively deferred to, which cert petitions he managed to get accepted or rejected because of his personal interventions, or which men's executions were stayed because he persuaded a Kennedy or O'Connor clerk. He levels few criticisms at Justice Blackmun, though he does criticize the reasoning in *Roe*.

Finally, Lazarus argues that airing his criticisms of the Court serves the public interest—that he answers "a call of history". In my view, only this defense has any merit. Clearly, the clerk's duty of confidentiality, while perhaps not legally enforceable, is an institutional expectation with no statute of limitations. Lazarus has clearly violated both the shared norm and the specific Court guidelines. 1 am not persuaded, however, that it is as legitimate for clerks as it is for justices to talk to journalists and members of the legal profession; subordinates have a very different institutional role. Many reminiscences of clerks reveal little about the justices' decision making, or are about former rather than sitting justices. Lazarus's book, however, differs only in quantity and accessibility from self-aggrandizing or titillating asides of clerks to friends, students, or colleagues about the internal workings of the Court. In my mind, the transgression is somewhat less than the CIA agent who writes a book about covert operations (and who may violate specific statutes in so doing) and somewhat more than memoirs of presidential aides or legislative staffers (at one point, Lazarus compares himself to Richard Holbrooke, a fellow whistle-blower). The claim that he does not rely on his own personal experience is harder to evaluate, since he tells us so little about the sources for his claims, a shortcoming I discuss below.

... For me, the ethical issue is less whether Lazarus betrayed his obligations to an institution than whether he betrayed his friends and former boss.... I have not systematically interviewed former U.S. Supreme Court law clerks, but I have encountered several over the past year and asked them about Lazarus. He has clearly violated a strongly held norm—particularly by identifying clerks by name.... Lazarus tells us he obtained information talking to clerks after he left the Court ... yet he does not tell us what he told those clerks. Did he phone and say, "I'm writing a book. What happened in Justice O'Connor's chambers when she was drafting her concurring opinion in *Casey*?" I fear the more likely sequence of events was that clerks and former clerks confided in him as a friend and coworker, one of the few people, by virtue of being members of the same club, with whom they felt they could talk freely....

Clearly, many human relationships require trust. And justice-law clerk, clerk-clerk friendships are two of them. Most of us operate on the assumption that our close personal employees, although not legally required to do so, will keep our confidences—will not publish accounts of our personal foibles. And we conduct our business accordingly.... Thus, each reader must ask, "is what Lazarus has to say so important (as he argues) that institutional norms and trust should be sacrificed to serve the public's need to know?" Must he reveal this information in order to make his argument persuasive? Or does he include the sensational material merely to sell more books? . . .

III. EPISTEMOLOGICAL ISSUES

I have questions about the information that Lazarus reports as fact. . . . Some of his claims can be checked against public documents, and his errors on these points lead me to be skeptical about his assertion that he relied on public documents or interviews rather than secondhand accounts and firsthand personal experience. For example, Chief Justice Rehnquist did not hold over *Webster* for more than one conference. Justice O'Connor did not refuse to join any of Justice Brennan's opinions because he had double-crossed her in the past (in fact the record shows she joined several). Justice O'Connor does not have daughters, only sons. . . .

What professional standards of truth does Lazarus abide by? How do we assess his knowledge claims? Despite the promotional material trumpeting "the eyewitness account," Lazarus has witnessed firsthand few of the events described in *Closed Chambers*. In fact, Lazarus would be much more convincing if he wrote about what happened in Justice Blackmun's chambers and made more tentative claims about what he knew secondhand from other clerks. Instead, Justice Blackmun for the most part gets a bye . . . .

Although Lazarus claims to be a historian, much of the account clearly does rely on his personal experience; for example, he tells us about his interview with Justice Blackmun when he was being considered for a clerkship. Lazarus, however, never interrogates his own subject position, so to speak—he does not question whether his interpretation of the Court as a neophyte, a clerk, or a liberal is partial or distorted. . . .

. . .

One can imagine (since Lazarus does not identify sources) that one of Lazarus's principal sources of information and guide to interpretation is Justice Blackmun himself. Lazarus did not attend conferences. But he reports Justice Blackmun returning from conference to give his clerks a "blow by blow" account of events, complete with quite impressive impersonations of the other justices. . . . Lazarus never offers the slightest glimmer of awareness that his sense of events may be filtered through Justice Blackmun's eyes and reflect Blackmun's opinion of events and personalities.

. . . We have all experienced getting the "low down" when we join a new organization only to learn that our informer is inaccurate, a bad judge of character, dishonest, or has an axe to grind. The reflective person, when pressed about how she knows things, will recognize the tenuous basis of this knowledge. . . . If Lazarus questioned what he knows, he does not reveal so in the text. . . . How do we "know" that Justice Kennedy was overly concerned with "the Greenhouse effect"—

whether Linda Greenhouse will criticize his opinions in her columns in the *New York Times*? Since Lazarus is ... using ... unflattering information to make serious charges—that justices on the left and right are unprincipled and care only about outcomes, not reasons—we need to know more about the evidence. . . .

Interpretations of conflicts and causes are highly contested terrain, and I am not persuaded that Lazarus has wisely captured what is "really going on." ... To his credit, Lazarus devotes considerable attention to the history (political and doctrinal) of the three issues, but in the end, I believe he gives too much weight to personal rather than principled differences between the justices. To ultimately be persuasive in the interpretive contest over the meaning of events internal to the U.S. Supreme Court, Lazarus ... must tell us how the specific evidence supports his position. And, for us to weigh the evidence, he must tell us how he knows what he knows. And that he does not do. For the scholar, then, let alone one who is not already favorably disposed to his argument, the compression of those last two stages into the first will render the overall argument unconvincing, however riveting and illuminating the story may be.

IV. NATURE OF JUDGING AND HUMAN INSTITUTIONS

At bottom, Lazarus's criticisms of individual justices and the Court as a whole stem from an unarticulated position on the nature of judging and his idealistic views on how human institutions should work. Justice Blackmun comes closest to his judicial ideal, Justice Powell a close second. Justices Brennan, Marshall, Scalia, and Chief Justice Rehnquist deviate from the ideal by having made up their minds already on all the key issues. . . . Justices O'Connor and Kennedy deviate from the ideal in the opposite respect, not knowing their own minds, ... being susceptible to pressure from clerks, other justices, or public opinion. . . . Lazarus's condemnation of Justices O'Connor and Kennedy is inconsistent with his deification of Justice Blackmun for being open-minded, especially since he reports that other justices criticized Justice Blackmun for being an "agonizer"—one whose positions on cases do not come easily. . . .

... Lazarus is appalled at how little the justices interact with one another. He holds Chief Justice Rehnquist responsible for failing to bring the Court together in general and to command a principled majority in *Casey* in particular. Yet, setting aside for a moment Justice Blackmun, the consensus seekers on the Court get very harsh treatment by Lazarus. Justices Kennedy, O'Connor, and Souter, in seeking to find a middle ground in *Casey*, are criticized as sneaky and unprincipled. Justice Brennan is characterized as a manipulator rather than a charismatic person who could lead other justices toward a shared position. On the one hand, Lazarus demands that the Court deliberate until it find a singular consensus position that would be good law. On the other, he savages those members of the Court who alter their principled position in order to command a greater following on the Court, thereby perhaps taking a position inconsistent with a previous opinion.

. . . If Lazarus had more experience in collective workplaces, . . . he might be more hesitant in demanding that the justices continue to debate the same fundamental issues. While perhaps the Court should try to emulate a utopia of continuous open discussion, it is an unrealistic expectation of small human institutions, whether they be courts, families, or academic departments. Is it reasonable to expect real debate to occur at conference rather than one-to-one, or not at all once justices have staked out their positions? And it is just as unrealistic to expect the Court as a whole to find a peaceful consensus on these issues (anymore than Chief Justice Taney could manufacture it in *Dred Scott*, despite his best intentions) when the country is so severely divided.

. . .

VI. CONCLUSIONS

. . .

In the end, . . . Lazarus does not support his three principal arguments, and furthermore, I have serious questions about the ethics of how he obtained his information as well as doubts about its accuracy. Many Supreme Court opinions merit criticism, but they do not necessarily arise from evil motives. Contrary to Lazarus, I would argue that the justices are not, on the whole, unprincipled actors who have failed in their responsibility as judges. They are, instead, rather deeply divided. Frequent changes in the doctrine of the Court and the fragmentation of the reasoning are problems, but they are predictable ones given divisions within the country and the changes in the presidency. Most important, law clerks are agents, not puppeteers, even if everything Lazarus says about them is true. Because, in the end, Lazarus's arguments are not persuasive, and he does not sufficiently serve the public interest to justify his cheap personal attacks on the members of the Supreme Court community . . . however much I experience what Kathleen Sullivan aptly calls "the prurient thrill of insiderdom".

In the same year that Edward Lazarus' *Closed Chambers* appeared, Professor Dennis Hutchinson, a former law clerk to Justice Byron White, published *The Man Who Once Was Whizzer White: A Portrait of Justice Byron R. White* (1998). David Garrow, a legal historian, reviews both books in the following excerpt, offering a somewhat different perspective, more sympathetic than Professor Kenney's, to law clerk disclosures of internal court matters.

David J. Garrow,[48] *Book Review, "The Lowest Form of Animal Life?" Supreme Court Clerks and Supreme Court History,* **84 Cornell L. Rev. 855 (1999)**

Early in 1980 . . . John P. Frank, a former October Term 1942 clerk to Justice Hugo L. Black, decried the extent to which former Supreme Court law clerks had supplied so much of the behind-the-scenes fodder for Bob Woodward and Scott Armstrong's book *The Brethren.* Prior to *The Brethren,* Frank asserted:

> There have been no significant breaches of confidences by the young persons employed in that capacity for the 90 or so years since the custom originated. There have been anecdotes—I have published some myself and so have others—but none of these has gone to details of particular cases or to work habits and attitudes of justices as they relate to other justices.

Eighteen years later similar complaints greeted the publication of *Closed Chambers: The First Eyewitness Account of the Epic Struggles Inside the Supreme Court,* a book by Edward P. Lazarus, a former October Term 1988 clerk to Justice Harry A. Blackmun. The well-known Supreme Court journalist Tony Mauro announced that "Lazarus' book may be even more damaging than *The Brethren,*" and *Closed Chambers* immediately generated a host of denunciations . . . that Lazarus had violated a sacred personal duty to the Court.

. . . Columbia Law Professor Gerard E. Lynch, a former October Term 1976 clerk to Justice William J. Brennan, Jr., equated Lazarus's "personal loyalty" to that of former Monica Lewinsky friend Linda Tripp, and Judge Alex Kozinski of the U.S. Court of Appeals for the Ninth Circuit [and former October Term 1976 clerk to Chief Justice Burger] declared that Lazarus . . . "betrayed his trust to make a quick buck, to make fame and fortune at the expense of the Supreme Court."

. . .

In perhaps the most prominent condemnation of *Closed Chambers,* Gretchen Craft Rubin, a former October Term 1995 clerk to Justice Sandra Day O'Connor, lambasted Lazarus on the op-ed page of the *Washington Post.* Rubin cited specifics from the Supreme Court's Code of Conduct for law clerks—"A law clerk should never disclose to any person any confidential information received in the course of the law clerk's duties, nor should the law clerk employ such information for personal gain"—that she believed "clearly bar the writing of his book." . . . In reply, Lazarus repeatedly asserted that the "Code of Conduct, including its confidentiality provision, applies only to clerks during their time at the court (to protect deliberation on pending and impending cases) and has no bearing on the propriety of a former clerk writing a book." . . .

---

48. Presidential Distinguished Professor, Emory University School of Law (at the time this article was published).

James N. Gardner, a former October Term 1975 clerk to Justice Potter Stewart, succinctly summarized the widespread conventional wisdom when he spoke of "the lifelong obligation of confidentiality to which Supreme Court law clerks have historically adhered with remarkable consistency." But Gardner's perception of "remarkable consistency," just like John P. Frank's 1980 declaration that prior to *The Brethren*, no former clerk's public recollections had ever "gone to details of particular cases or to work habits and attitudes of justices as they relate to other justices," is seriously in error. A careful review of former clerks' published writings and "on the record" interview comments readily and repeatedly reveals that various "little beasts" have been telling "inside" stories "out of school" since long before Edward Lazarus even was born.

I. THE HISTORICAL RECORD

The Supreme Court's tradition of utilizing young law clerks began in 1882. . . .

The only untoward notoriety occasioned by the Justices' employment of law clerks came in late 1919, when one Ashton F. Embry, who had served for nine years as clerk to Senior Associate Justice Joseph McKenna, was discovered to have leaked advance word of at least one forthcoming case decision, United States v. Southern Pacific Co. [251 U.S. 1 (1919)], to three co-conspirators who utilized the information to garner stock market profits of $1,412.50. Word of the scheme reached the Court, which in turn notified the Department of Justice. Embry resigned his clerkship on December 16, 1919, and four months later he was criminally indicted for "conspiracy to defraud the Government of its right of secrecy concerning the opinions." He and his three fellow defendants unsuccessfully challenged the indictment, contending that they had violated no actual law. The District of Columbia trial court sustained the charges and both the D.C. Court of Appeals and the Supreme Court refused review.

. . . [H]istorical forerunners to Edward Lazarus have been both far more numerous and decidedly more illustrious than the long-forgotten Ashton Embry. Indeed, perhaps the first true precursor to Lazarus among former clerks was one of Justice Gray's own early appointees, Samuel Williston, who later served for many decades as one of the most distinguished members of the Harvard Law School faculty. Writing in a 1940 memoir, Williston explicitly and revealingly recalled how during his October Term 1888 clerkship, "I would also frequently be asked to write an opinion on the cases that had been assigned to [Justice Gray]." Williston quickly added that Justice Gray nonetheless "wrote his own opinions" and that Williston's drafts "served only as . . . suggestions." Yet Williston underscored his belief that he was not obliged forever to remain publicly silent about private exchanges to which he had been privy as a clerk when he forthrightly volunteered that "[Justice] Gray's comments on his colleagues were often free, and after the lapse of many years it may no longer be indiscreet to mingle some of them with my own impressions of those who were the members of the Court." For instance, Williston recounted how, in private, Gray would call Justice Samuel F. Miller, who sometimes committed "gross blunders on elementary questions of private law," the "little tycoon."

. . . Future Secretary of State Dean Acheson, who had clerked for Justice Louis D. Brandeis during both October Term 1919 and October Term 1920, volunteered that he had prepared the first drafts of some Brandeis opinions. In the fall of 1919 Acheson began keeping a detailed notebook recounting his conversations both with Brandeis and with other Justices. In his autobiography Acheson reprinted verbatim both his notes of a November 29, 1919 conversation with Justice Oliver Wendell Holmes at Holmes's home and selected excerpts of his regular discussions with Justice Brandeis. . . . Acheson explained that "for years I was convinced, and often said, that I had burned it [the notebook] when my wife pointed out the dubious propriety of making notes of confidential conversations," but he later discovered that he had not. Acheson had no hesitancy about including his notes of Brandeis's comments in his autobiography, explaining that "giving [Brandeis's] views now after forty-five years involves no impropriety." One brief excerpt reported Brandeis's private comments about the purpose and importance of his (and Justice Holmes's) dissenting views in the Espionage Act cases. Another segment offered a brief inside account of how Justice Holmes managed to retain his five-to-four majority in the 1919 Arizona Employers' Liability Cases [250 U.S. 400] only because of Justice Pitney's persuasiveness with Justice Day. Perhaps most memorably of all, Acheson quoted Justice Holmes's private, disparaging characterization of the intellect of former Justice John Marshall Harlan: "Harlan's mind was like a vise, the jaws of which did not meet. It only held the larger objects."

. . . One October Term 1924 clerk to Chief Justice William Howard Taft, C. Dickerson Williams, disclosed years later that the initial December 1924 conference vote on the landmark legislative investigatory power case of McGrain v. Daugherty [273 U.S. 135 (1927)] had been contrary to how the Court eventually (and unanimously) decided the case twenty-five months later. The initial vote would have affirmed the district court's ruling that the Senate lacked investigatory power. In the end, however, the McGrain Court reversed the district court's holding and recognized that the power to investigate was an "essential and appropriate" part of Congress's legislative powers. Williams wrote in 1989 that

> So far as I am aware, it has never previously been revealed that the original vote of the Court had been to affirm. I never mentioned the subject because I thought it confidential. As over sixty years have passed and all the parties (except perhaps some law clerks of that day) are dead, I think it now a matter of history. . . .

The following October Term 1925 produced two law clerks who, in subsequent years, publicly recounted significant behind-the-scenes stories from their year of service. In 1946 Alfred McCormack, a former clerk to Justice Harlan Fiske Stone, provided a detailed rendition of how

Stone successfully rewrote the entire opinion that Chief Justice Taft subsequently handed down on behalf of a six-to-three Court majority in the famous executive power case of Myers v. United States [272 U.S. 52 (1926)]. According to McCormack, after reading Taft's initial draft Stone said, " 'There is nothing left to do with this opinion . . . except to rewrite it.' Accordingly he directed his clerk [McCormack] to go through the opinion and outline the points. . . ." Once Stone completed his rewrite, the Chief Justice accepted the revision as a replacement for his earlier draft.

McCormack also described how Justice George Sutherland in the still well-known case of Village of Euclid v. Ambler Realty Co. [272 U.S. 365 (1926)] "was writing an opinion for the majority . . ., holding the zoning ordinance unconstitutional, when talks with his dissenting brethren (principally Stone, . . .) shook his convictions and led him to request a reargument, after which he changed his mind and the ordinance was upheld." . . .

. . . James M. Landis, who had clerked for Justice Brandeis [in October Term 1925] prior to serving as dean of Harvard Law School from 1937 to 1946, [recalled] in a 1957 public talk . . . how he once had asked Brandeis why seven of Brandeis's eight colleagues—all except Holmes—were refusing to acknowledge dispositive evidence in a maritime case[.] Landis quoted Brandeis's reply: " 'Sonny, when I first came to this Court I thought I would be associated with men who really cared whether they were right or wrong. But sometimes, Sonny, it just ain't so.' "

· · ·

Those October Term 1925 law clerk stories are hardly exceptional. Professor Newland, in his landmark 1961 article on law clerks, recounted how "one of Justice Butler's clerks, . . . who remained with the justice for sixteen years[, an occasional practice during the pre-World War II era], wrote first drafts of many opinions, expressing the justice's views so accurately that the drafts often required few changes." [brackets in original] Even one of the most proper and discreet of former Brandeis clerks, Harvard Law Professor Paul A. Freund, who worked for the Justice during October Term 1932, publicly revealed how "on occasion some sentences in the law clerk's memoranda would find their way into the opinion [Brandeis issued]."

· · ·

Justice Stone's October Term 1937 clerk, Louis Lusky, confessed his authorship of the famous "footnote four" in United States v. Carolene Products Co. [304 U.S. 144, 152 n. 4 (1938)], which "Stone adopted . . . almost as drafted," in a 1952 letter to Stone biographer Alpheus T. Mason. That same year, one of by then Chief Justice Stone's two October Term 1945 clerks, Herbert Prashker, gave Mason an even more detailed account of the preparation of Stone's 1946 dissent in Girouard v. United States [328 U.S. 61 (1946)]:

> On at least two occasions during the two-week period while the opinion was in preparation ... the Chief made the long stomp from his office to our office on the other side of the conference room to talk about *Girouard*. [Fellow clerk Eugene] Nickerson and I thought he was wrong, and I think Nickerson (who was helping on the dissent and who wrote parts of it) made an [unsuccessful] effort to get him to change his mind.

Former clerks' willingness to acknowledge publicly that they had performed much of the Court's opinion-drafting in the post-war years was far from exceptional. William T. Coleman, Jr., a subsequent Secretary of Transportation and prominent Washington attorney who had clerked for Justice Felix Frankfurter in October Term 1948, told an early 1970s interviewer,

> After a conference, Frankfurter would ask my co-clerk, Elliot Richardson, or me to draft an opinion. While we worked on it, he would come in with suggestions or ask us if we had looked up a certain case. Then we would come in with a draft and discuss it. I could not say that there was any opinion that was my own. They all expressed his views.

Only eight years after his clerkship with Justice Frankfurter during October Term 1945, prominent University of Chicago Law Professor Philip B. Kurland publicly revealed that one of Frankfurter's fellow Justices during Kurland's term, Frank Murphy, as well as Stone's successor as Chief Justice, Fred M. Vinson, had both been "absolutely dependent upon their law clerks for the production of their opinions."

Like former clerks from the 1920s and 1930s, clerks from the late 1940s and early 1950s also subsequently felt free to quote publicly once-private remarks that their Justices had made about the Court's deliberations on particular cases. One October Terms 1951 and 1952 clerk to Justice Robert H. Jackson, who later became perhaps the best-known former clerk in Supreme Court history, future Chief Justice William H. Rehnquist, publicly recounted in a 1987 book how, in May of 1952, Jackson had returned from the Justices' private conference on the famous executive power steel seizure case of Youngstown Sheet & Tube Co. v. Sawyer [343 U.S. 579 (1952)] to tell Rehnquist and his co-clerk, " 'Well, boys, the President got licked.' "

October Term 1952 and October Term 1953 clerks have offered far more substantive private revelations concerning the Court's two-year consideration of Brown v. Board of Education [347 US. 483 (1954)]. William K. Bachelder, who had clerked for Justice Sherman Minton during October Term 1952, told author Richard Kluger in 1974 of private Court accounts of how several of Chief Justice Vinson's judicial colleagues "would discuss in his presence the view that the Chief's job should rotate annually and ... made no bones about regarding him—correctly—as their intellectual inferior." Regarding details of the case itself, Alexander M. Bickel, who had clerked for Justice Frankfurter during October Term 1952 and later served as Sterling Professor at Yale

Law School, recounted to Kluger how Frankfurter's "main concern during the '52 Term ... was to prevent the Court from taking a premature vote" on the substantive constitutional merits of *Brown*'s challenge to the "separate but equal" doctrine of Plessy v. Ferguson [163 U.S. 537 (1896)]. Bickel related how Frankfurter, after returning from a late May 1953 conference of the Justices, had said,

> It looked as if we could hold off a decision that term, that no one on the Court was pushing it, that no vote had actually been taken throughout the term—and that if we could get together some questions for discussion at a reargument, the case would be held over until the new term.

Similarly forthcoming with Kluger was John D. Fassett, who had clerked for Justice Stanley F. Reed during October Term 1953. Fassett told Kluger that shortly before Chief Justice Vinson's sudden death on September 8, 1953, he had asked Justice Reed whether the Court would reach the *Plessy* question. "[Reed] replied in the affirmative ... and added, 'They know they have the votes and they are determined to resolve the issue.' " Reed also said that he expected both Chief Justice Vinson and one other Justice, perhaps Minton, to join him in dissent in *Brown*.

Fassett also recounted to Kluger how, after the arrival of Vinson's successor as Chief Justice, Earl Warren, Reed had told him that Warren would be with the *Brown* majority and that Reed probably would be alone in dissent. Fassett's co-clerk for Reed that term, George V. Mickum III, surpassed even Fassett's firsthand frankness, telling Kluger how he had witnessed perhaps *the* crucial face-to-face interchange between Warren and Reed regarding *Brown*. The Chief Justice, Mickum related, had said, " 'Stan, you're all by yourself in this now ... You've got to decide whether it's really the best thing for the country' " if Reed went ahead with a solo dissent, thereby depriving the *Brown* Court of unanimity. Mickum told Kluger that Warren's demeanor during the conversation with Reed "was quite low-key and very sensitive to the problems that the decision would present to the South," but that the Chief Justice nonetheless "was quite firm on the Court's need for unanimity."

. . .

But the unique historical status of *Brown* did not cause Reed and Frankfurter clerks, such as Fassett and Bickel, to become dramatically more forthcoming than were Reed and Frankfurter clerks from subsequent, less exalted terms of the Court. Roderick M. Hills, a prominent attorney who clerked for Justice Reed during October Terms 1955 and 1956, readily told the Los Angeles Times fifteen years after his clerkship how "he wrote an opinion [in a 1957 case] by himself" that, according to Hills, " 'was probably the least significant case decided that term.' " More notably, Richard N. Goodwin, a subsequently well-known presidential speech writer who clerked for Justice Frankfurter during October Term 1958, graphically recounted in a memoir thirty years later the evaluation that Frankfurter had offered him of Justice William O. Douglas. According to Goodwin, after Douglas failed to attend the August 1958 Special Term argument of the Little Rock school desegregation case, Cooper v. Aaron [358 U.S. 1 (1958)], Frankfurter told Goodwin, " 'That man [Douglas] is an opportunist and a malingerer. He's more concerned about his public personality than the work of the Court. In fact, he doesn't do his work. He just decides who he wants to win and then votes—a lazy, contemptible mind.' "

. . . In mid–1957 both *U.S. News & World Report*, in an article entitled *The Bright Young Men Behind the Bench*, and the *New York Times*, in a story whose second headline announced *Recent Law Graduates Aid Justices with Their Facts but Not Their Decisions*, drew prominent attention to the Court's clerks. The *New York Times* piece betrayed its purpose all too visibly, for the unnamed reporter declared, "It has been suggested that the clerks have an important influence on the court, but former clerks say in persuasive language, that nothing could be further from the truth."

One former clerk, however, publicly dissented from the *New York Times*'s claim by writing a two-page essay in *U.S. News & World Report* provocatively headlined, *Who Writes Decisions of the Supreme Court?* William H. Rehnquist, who had clerked for the now-deceased Justice Jackson during October Terms 1951 and 1952, and who in 1957 was practicing law in Phoenix, readily volunteered that "[o]n a couple of occasions each term, Justice Jackson would ask each clerk to draft an opinion for him . . . [and i]f the clerk were reasonably faithful to his instructions and reasonably diligent in his work, the Justice could be quite charitable with his black pencil and paste pot."

However, Rehnquist's most controversial assertion was not his disclosure of opinion-drafting practices within Justice Jackson's chambers, but his characterization of his fellow clerks. Rehnquist claimed that "the political cast of the clerks as a group was to the 'left' of either the nation or the Court," and that "a majority of the clerks I knew [exhibited] extreme solicitude for the claims of Communists and other criminal defendants." Rehnquist conceded that he knew of no "conscious" effort on the part of his fellow October Terms 1951 and 1952 clerks to employ their own ideological biases in their winnowing of the thousands of petitions for certiorari that they reviewed, but because he felt that "unconscious bias did creep" into his own certiorari petition work, Rehnquist contended that the same must have been true for "many of my fellow clerks."

Both the Associated Press ("AP") and the *New York Times* found Rehnquist's essay newsworthy, and the *New York Times* published the AP's dispatch under the headline *'Sway' of Clerks on Court Cited*. The essay quickly generated a rejoinder from William D. Rogers, who had clerked for Justice Reed during October Term 1952. Characterizing Rehnquist's contention that "politically biased" clerks had "an impact on the work of the Court" as "a grave and a serious charge," Rogers deftly contended that "it would be possible to view all the law clerks who worked during the 1952 term of Court as 'left' only from a 'far right' position." . . . Three months later Democratic Senator John C. Stennis of Mississippi went public with a speech on the Senate floor. Quoting at length from Rehnquist's essay on law clerks, Stennis advocated both a shift to more experienced, longer-term appointees and suggested that Congress "determine whether or not Senate confirmation should be required for these positions of ever-increasing importance and influence."

. . .

The public controversy of 1957–1958 had seemingly little effect, if any, on the willingness of subsequent clerks to enrich the historical record with regard to inside-the-Court developments. . . .

. . . Laurence H. Tribe, one of Justice Potter Stewart's clerks in October Term 1967, later offered an unusually frank and unforgettable account of the origins of one of Justice Stewart's most memorable and oft-quoted statements:

> One of the exciting things about the clerkship was that he [Justice Stewart] would let his law clerks, if he liked their style, write drafts and very often the drafts would become the opinion. A number of opinions I worked on that term are really almost exactly as I drafted them; cases like Katz v. United States [389 U.S. 347 (1967)] dealing with the fact that electronic eavesdropping is a form of search even though there's no physical trespass. I wrote some of the key phrases thinking that this is what Stewart would want to say, and it turned out to be exactly what he wanted. 'The Fourth Amendment protects people, not places' [389 U.S. at 351] is a line from my draft in *Katz*.

Kenneth Bass, an October Term 1969 clerk to Justice Hugo L. Black, offered a more general acknowledgment similar to that of Tribe in an interview that took place less than two years after his own clerkship:

> With the possible exception of one case, what my co-clerk and I did had no *substantive* effect on what the justices did. The real influence of law clerks was not on the result, but on the decision used to explain the result. A lot of the wording in the opinions comes from the clerks.

Despite these statements, Thomas Krattenmaker, an October Term 1970 clerk to Justice John M. Harlan, has asserted to Harlan biographer Tinsley Yarbrough that the clerks did have a decisive "substantive effect" in one notable case. Boddie v. Connecticut [401 U.S. 371 (1971)] first had been argued in December 1969, and the Court held it for reargument in November 1970. Chief Justice Burger assigned the majority opinion to Justice Harlan, and according to Krattenmaker, "a clerk in Justice Marshall's chambers, at the urging of Thomas Krattenmaker, the Harlan clerk responsible for *Boddie* in the 1970 term, persuaded Marshall to agree to a due process holding, giving Harlan a majority for his rationale as well as the Court's decision."

. . .

. . . [T]he book that drew the most attention to the experiences of Supreme Court law clerks was . . . Bob Woodward and Scott Armstrong's *The Brethren*. Published in late 1979, The Brethren offered an "inside the Court" account of Justices' deliberations from October Term 1969 through October Term 1975. Yet because *The Brethren* never identifies by name a single former clerk "source," critics such as *New York Times* columnist Anthony Lewis were able to mount blistering critiques of the underlying factual accuracy of several clerk-based stories. *The Brethren* did allow academic commentators such as Professor Philip B. Kurland to renew and expand their complaints about how "more and more of the [Court's] opinions are written by the law clerks rather than their Justices." . . . Former Justice Arthur J. Goldberg, however, warned that one ought to discount *The Brethren*'s clerk-based description of the Court, because law clerks "lack the maturity, experience and perspective to evaluate what they are told and what really takes place."

II. Edward Lazarus and *Closed Chambers*

Reviewers . . . examining Edward Lazarus's *Closed Chambers* ought to have cited repeatedly Justice Goldberg's warning about Woodward and Armstrong's *The Brethren*. . . . Far too much attention and energy has focused on Lazarus's supposed ethical shortcomings, and far too little has addressed the way in which *Closed Chambers*'s overheated and melodramatic denunciations of the Justices mortally detract from Lazarus's credibility as an analyst and critic of the Court.

The historical record of the past six decades demonstrates that a host of professionally respected and academically celebrated former clerks have recounted, by name and "on the record," stories of (1) case-specific intra-Court incidents, (2) private remarks of one Justice about another, and (3) their influence in the drafting and construction of important, well-known opinions. In *Closed Chambers*, Edward Lazarus recounts only a modest amount of the first, little if any of the second, and absolutely none of the third. Indeed, Lazarus's refusal to offer any substantive details of his own interactions with Justice Blackmun, aside from the most predictable and mundane, deprives *Closed Chambers* of its *potentially* richest and most memorable material.

. . .

One topic, however, where Lazarus's comments *are* right on target concerns the authorship of the Court's opinions. Lazarus's use of the phrase "editorial Justices" already has drawn attention, and the way in which Lazarus challenges the Court's opinion-writing process hits the mark. While Lazarus reveals nothing explicit in *Closed Chambers* about opinion-drafting procedures within Justice Blackmun's Chambers, he does stress that during October Term 1988, "the vast majority of opinions the Court issued were drafted exclusively by clerks." "Drafted" is, of course, the crucial word. Lazarus accurately asserts that it is "in wielding the enormous power of the first draft and, specifically, in the selection of words, structure, and materials, that clerks may exercise their greatest influence ... Rarely do the Justices disassemble the drafts they've been given to examine the crucial choices that went into their design."

. . .

Hard as it may be for some of Lazarus's most vituperative critics to accept, a careful comparison of *Closed Chambers*'s mundane "revelations" with history's extensive track record of clerk-told tales and self-aggrandizing assertions shows that Lazarus accurately and convincingly defends himself on this score. *Closed Chambers* is repeatedly guilty of name-calling, gratuitous insults, and inane exaggerations, but measured against the historical record of what former clerks have and have not subsequently disclosed about case deliberations, Justices' private remarks, and opinion-drafting practices during their clerkships, Lazarus has violated no norm or standard....

If *Closed Chambers* contains any detectable violations of behavioral norms or standards for former clerks, it is the former clerks of Justices O'Connor and Kennedy, and perhaps of Justice Souter, who have committed them, not Edward Lazarus. Lazarus has disclosed absolutely nothing of any substantive import that ever occurred in the Blackmun Chambers, or between Justice Blackmun and any of his colleagues, during his clerkship. Lazarus could not have written certain segments of *Closed Chambers* without (1) access to copies of October Term 1988 documents from the O'Connor Chambers that one or more former clerks retained after the conclusion of their clerkship, and (2) detailed renditions of conversations within the Kennedy Chambers recalled by another former clerk.... Perhaps some might want to charge Lazarus with enticing other former clerks to violate an obligation of confidentiality to their Justices, but if that is the charge, the number of former clerks and the number of eagerly complicit historians who will be standing alongside Lazarus—as the long historical record of talkative "little beasts" shows—will be very large indeed.

III. Dennis Hutchinson and "Whizzer White"

Nothing more starkly illuminates how both Edward Lazarus *and* those other former clerks who actively aided him in the preparation of *Closed Chambers* fully and accurately emulated the historical norms for former clerk behavior than Dennis J. Hutchinson's even more recent book, *The Man Who Once Was Whizzer White*—a biography of Justice Bryon R. White. Hutchinson clerked for Justice White during October Term 1975, but he makes no visible use of any confidential information obtained during his clerkship. He also does not hesitate to critique White's judicial service. Hutchinson received no active cooperation from Justice White, nor did Hutchinson have any access to what remains of

White's Court papers and case files. In fact, less than thirty percent of Hutchinson's biography deals with Byron R. White's thirty-one years as an Associate Justice (1962–1993). Hutchinson occasionally offers some implicitly inside information. However, the primary sources for two of Hutchinson's three principal chapters on White's judicial service—profiles of White and the Court during October Terms 1971 and 1981—come from the document holdings of the William O. Douglas, Thurgood Marshall, and William J. Brennan Papers.

Far and away the most remarkable chapter in Hutchinson's well-written and thoroughly researched biography is his twenty-five page account of October Term 1991.... No publicly available sources have documented their "internal" stories, as the active service—and ergo the case files—of Justices Brennan and Marshall end with October Terms 1989 and 1990 respectively.

But Hutchinson has succeeded in acquiring "inside" information on the events of October Term 1991—presumably from two or more of the four clerks who worked for Justice White that year—that puts Edward Lazarus to shame. For example, Hutchinson reports that early in the term, newly confirmed Justice Clarence Thomas sent White a note changing his vote in one of the first three cases in which Thomas had heard argument, Foucha v. Louisiana [504 U.S. 71 (1992)]. It was "the first time in thirty years that White could recall losing a vote from his proposed opinion for the Court before the draft circulated."

One month later, the Court heard argument in Franklin v. Gwinnett County Public Schools, [503 U.S. 60 (1992)] and Hutchinson not only describes the Justices' votes at conference and how White assigned the majority opinion to himself, but also details how "[w]hen White sat down with his law clerk to outline the structure of the opinion, it was apparent that precedent controlled his view of the case." Furthermore, Hutchinson reports that White added "somewhat laconically that he did not care if he obtained only four votes for the view, because it was correct."

.   .   .

Hutchinson provides an even more notable inside-the-Court account when he describes the handling of Jacobson v. United States, [503 U.S. 540 (1992)], a well-known case in which a five-to-four majority reversed a child pornography conviction that had resulted from a federal "sting" operation. "White successfully pushed for the Court to grant Jacobson's petition for certiorari," Hutchinson explains, but after argument the "vote at conference was 7–2 to affirm Jacobson's conviction, with White and Stevens dissenting." Justice O'Connor received the majority opinion assignment, but "White produced a powerful dissent that picked up Justices Blackmun and Thomas rather readily. Then two months went by before Justice Souter switched his vote and provided White with a majority."

Even more intriguing is Hutchinson's account of the Court's internal deliberations in United States v. Fordice [505 U.S. 717 (1992)], an important case concerning the desegregation of Mississippi's public colleges and universities. Hutchinson describes the Justices' private deliberations:

> When the justices met in conference to vote on whether to sustain the Fifth Circuit, there was no consensus on the appropriate outcome or analysis—"nine different takes," according to one clerk in another chamber. The chief justice assigned the case to White and told him lightly to "figure it out."

Hutchinson then describes how White's colleagues reacted to his *Fordice* draft:

> White did not circulate a draft in *Fordice* until February 17 ... Justice Stevens notified White three days later that he would join the opinion, then a long silence set in. Justice Blackmun provided a third vote for the opinion a month after it circulated. Justice O'Connor had reservations about White's formulation of the standard of liability, wrote a letter detailing her concerns in early March, and then visited White to discuss her concerns but did not commit herself pro or con on his opinion.

Resolution of the case remained unsettled for over two more months, with only Chief Justice Rehnquist joining White's initial threesome. Then White's opinion found more support:

> Justice Thomas visited White on June 5 to discuss, for the first time, his views of the case, and he left White's chambers with a promise to join the proposed opinion for the Court as long as one sentence—referring to the historical context of racially segregated colleges—was omitted from the circulating draft.

Matters finally jelled when both Justices O'Connor and Kennedy formally joined White's opinion on June 16, with Justices Thomas and Souter following thereafter.

Lastly, Hutchinson offers some novel inside details concerning the Court's consideration of *Planned Parenthood v. Casey*. The respondent, the State of Pennsylvania, had petitioned the Court to address whether the Court should overrule *Roe v. Wade*, "but Justice Souter convinced his colleagues to rephrase the questions [presented] solely in terms of the specific provisions of the statute reviewed below. Only four—the bare minimum—voted to hear the case: White, Stevens, Scalia, and Souter." After oral argument, at conference on April 24, five Justices—Rehnquist, White, Scalia, Kennedy, and Thomas—voted to "uphold all of the challenged aspects of the Pennsylvania law." But, as is now well known, in early June three Justices—O'Connor, Kennedy, and Souter—circulated a joint draft of an opinion that left the Chief Justice with only a four-vote minority. Hutchinson declares that "[t]he key man was Kennedy, who changed his vote. . . . Kennedy's decision triggered hard feelings between some chambers; Justice Scalia's staff canceled a group outing with the

Kennedy staff to see the [Baltimore] Orioles play at Camden Yards when Scalia suddenly refused to go." The final five-to-four resolution of *Casey*—with Justices Blackmun and Stevens joining the O'Connor–Kennedy–Souter trio to preserve *Roe v. Wade*—came on June 29.

Even though Dennis Hutchinson barely devotes fifteen pages to inside events at the Supreme Court during October Term 1991, he provides more descriptive and revealing details about previously unpublicized Supreme Court case deliberations and opinion drafting than Edward Lazarus does in the entire 518 pages of *Closed Chambers*. Furthermore, Hutchinson has done so thanks to the age-old practice of "little beasts" offering their recollections (and perhaps copies of documents that they retained). Such a tradition, for decade after decade, greatly has enriched public historiography concerning the United States Supreme Court.

. . .

Unlike Edward Lazarus, ... Dennis Hutchinson is no one's potential renegade. Hutchinson is a law professor at the University of Chicago and an editor of the *Supreme Court Review*. Moreover, his book has received the public endorsement of perhaps the best known, and certainly the most prolific, member of the federal circuit bench—Judge Richard A. Posner. It is difficult to imagine that any of the critics who so energetically have denounced Edward Lazarus for telling inside stories will mount a similar onslaught against Professor Hutchinson.

CONCLUSION

A careful and impartial comparison of *Closed Chambers* and *The Man Who Once Was Whizzer White* that focuses on what each book discloses about previously nonpublic details of internal Supreme Court deliberations reveals two similarities: (1) both Lazarus and Hutchinson have used exactly the same methods to make almost exactly the same sorts of novel disclosures, and (2) both authors' successes in persuading former clerks to disclose details about once-private events are simply the most recent manifestations of the long-standing historical tradition that has developed over the past sixty years.

Anything new and revelatory in *Closed Chambers* about internal Supreme Court decision making and opinion drafting comes not from any confidences that Edward Lazarus violated, but solely from Lazarus's success in persuading other former clerks to relate and document private developments that occurred in their chambers, primarily during October Term 1989. Similarly, Dennis Hutchinson has not violated any confidences stemming from his own October Term 1975 clerkship with Justice White. His most notable chapter in *The Man Who Once Was Whizzer White* stems from his ability to induce several former clerks from the relatively recent October Term 1991 to provide strikingly detailed descriptions of the Court's consideration of many significant cases and the Justices' personal interactions concerning them. As to which book and author have more extensively recounted previously undisclosed internal Supreme Court deliberations, Dennis Hutchinson's *The Man Who Once Was Whizzer White* decisively trumps Edward Lazarus's *Closed Chambers.*

But even more important than the as yet publicly-unappreciated historiographical (and ethical or professional) parallels between Edward Lazarus's and Dennis Hutchinson's books, one must recognize that both authors' use of former clerks' recollections concerning case-specific details and Justice-to-Justice interchanges stand firmly within a long and rich historical tradition. This tradition reaches back to Samuel Williston and Dean Acheson, and likewise includes such major portraits of internal Court decision making as Richard Kluger's *Simple Justice*. The conventional wisdom, at least that propounded by John P. Frank in 1980 and James N. Gardner in 1998, is utterly and demonstrably wrong.... Everyone with a scholarly and historical interest in the United States Supreme Court, including Edward Lazarus and Dennis Hutchinson, has benefitted from this under-appreciated tradition....

Questions and Comments

1. Does Professor Garrow's account of prior disclosures by clerks reveal a pattern of disclosure as detailed, as critical, as public and as close-in-time to the Term discussed as those in *Closed Chambers*? (Note the very different reactions among lawyers, journalists, social scientists and historians. Kenney is a social scientist, Garrow a legal historian.)

2. On Professor Garrow's account, Lazarus' use of clerk disclosures is comparable to and more minor than Hutchinson's. Would Kenney agree? (Recall her emphasis on Lazarus' possible betrayals of the trust of his former colleagues.)

3. If disclosure of internal deliberations within a decade of their occurring were to become a norm—as it plainly has not—how would this affect the quality of deliberation? the role of the clerks? the candor of Justices' conversations with their clerks? For further consideration of issues of confidentiality relating to the internal deliberations of the Court, see Chapter VI, below.

4. For a more appreciative view of Lazarus' book, see Erwin Chemerinsky, *Book Review: Opening Closed Chambers*, 108 Yale L.J. 1087 (1999). Professor Chemerinsky considers in detail charges that Lazarus was unethical, immoral or unlawful and concludes that "Lazarus did nothing wrong." *Id.* at 1089. He also argues that the Lazarus book provides quite useful accounts of important cases. For example, Chemerinsky writes:

> Lazarus devotes two full chapters and part of another (over sixty pages) to the Supreme Court's handling of Warren McCleskey's case. This litigation produced two landmark Supreme Court rulings. In McCleskey v. Kemp [481 U.S. 279 (1987)], the Supreme Court ruled, 5–4, that statistics proving racial disparity in the imposition of the death penalty were not sufficient to demonstrate an equal protection violation.

In McCleskey v. Zant, [499 U.S. 467 (1991)], the Court held, 6–3, that individuals may present only one habeas corpus petition and that successive petitions are permissible only if (a) there is proof of good cause and prejudice would result from not being heard; or (b) there is a showing that actual innocence is likely.

Lazarus provides a more detailed account of the factual background of the case than I have seen anywhere else, and he also gives us an insightful account of the Court's internal discussions concerning it. Most striking is a memorandum Lazarus found in the Marshall papers that Justice Scalia wrote to the other Justices. While Justice Powell's majority opinion points to the inadequacy of the proof of discrimination, Justice Scalia wrote: "Since it is my view ... that the unconscious operation of irrational sympathies and antipathies, including racial, upon jury decisions and (hence) prosecutorial decisions is real, acknowledged in the decisions of this court, and ineradicable, I cannot honestly say that all I need is more proof." In other words, Justice Scalia says that he was convinced that the death penalty is administered in a racially discriminatory fashion, but he still voted to affirm McCleskey's death sentence. Even more troubling, Justice Scalia says that additional persuasive proof of systemic discrimination would make no difference for him.

Lazarus marshals the evidence to show that there was substantial doubt as to McCleskey's guilt and that serious legal errors were subsequently discovered in the handling of the case. When these were presented to the Court, it announced a new rule that habeas petitioners were barred from subsequent petitions, except in extraordinary circumstances, and denied McCleskey relief. He was then executed by the State of Georgia.

Lazarus devotes over ten percent of his book to the *McCleskey* saga. Although I have taught the *McCleskey* decisions countless times in my Constitutional Law and Federal Courts classes and have also written about them, I learned a great deal of new information from Lazarus's account. This information, presented clearly and forcefully, suggests that McCleskey may have been innocent of the crime for which he was executed and that his execution was founded on serious violations of the law by police and prosecutors.

... *Webster* was an important abortion case decided in 1989, in which Justice Scalia expressly urged the overruling of *Roe v. Wade* and three other Justices implicitly called for its overruling by advocating rational basis review for the evaluation of government abortion regulations.

Lazarus provides much new information about the Court's internal handling of the case. For example, Lazarus describes the Justices' discussion at conference and recounts that Chief Justice Rehnquist, who had dissented in *Roe*, recanted that position and "stated that he now thought *Roe v. Wade* had reached the right result given the specific facts of that case. Texas had banned all abortions except in the narrow circumstance where the life of the mother was at stake. In Chief Justice

Rehnquist's revised view, that was too restrictive." According to Lazarus, the vote at conference was 5–4 to uphold all aspects of the Missouri law that was being challenged, and the disagreements among the five in the majority over how to handle *Roe* were to be " 'worked out in the writing.' "

Lazarus reveals a secret memorandum that Chief Justice Rehnquist circulated exclusively to his conservative colleagues, Justices White, O'Connor, Scalia, and Kennedy. In it, the Chief Justice urges them to stick together: " 'Because of the "media hype" that this case has received . . . and because we are cutting back on previous doctrine in this area, I think it more than usually desirable to have an opinion of the Court if we possibly can.' " Lazarus describes the draft opinion Chief Justice Rehnquist circulated to these Justices and how it would have instituted rational basis as the standard for judicial scrutiny of abortion regulations and at the same time proclaimed that the government has a compelling interest in protecting fetal life from the moment of conception. Although the Chief Justice disavowed overruling *Roe*, that result would obviously have followed from such an opinion.

Lazarus then describes how Justice O'Connor refused to join Chief Justice Rehnquist's opinion, favoring a narrower approach that would leave the future of *Roe* for later cases to decide. Lazarus also recounts the reactions from other Justices, including Justice Kennedy's request for a relatively minor change and Justice Scalia's "barbed" reply to Justice O'Connor. After describing in detail the Court's internal debate and the various drafts and memoranda circulated, Lazarus reveals—and this, too, I have never seen before—that Justice Stevens drafted a strongly worded response to Justice Scalia's harsh attack on Justice O'Connor, though he later omitted this rebuke from his dissent.

Although the Court's subsequent decision in *Planned Parenthood v. Casey* has lessened *Webster*'s significance, I still teach *Webster* to my students. From now on, I will use Lazarus's account to describe how the opinions emerged from the Court. At the very least, his account offers a fascinating glimpse of how the Court handles controversial cases.

Chemerinsky, *supra*, at 1111–1114. Does Professor Chemerinsky's perspective change your evaluation of the potential benefits of law clerk disclosures about the Court? about the balance between the benefits and any costs to the deliberative process of decreased confidentiality?

C. THE ADVOCATES

1. The General Quality of Lawyering before the Supreme Court

Lawyers before the Supreme Court bar have included such important national figures as Daniel Webster, Luther Martin, and William Pinckney, each of whom also served in important elected or appointive public offices—Webster as both a Representative and Senator from states in New England, Martin as Attorney General of Maryland, and Pinckney as a Senator from Maryland. In the earliest days, the lawyers' most important opportunity to influence the Court was in oral argument, as, following the practice of the King's Bench in England, briefs were not filed and arguments were supposed to be presented orally.[49] And, in the beginning, advocates could argue for as long as they wanted. The argument in *Gibbons v. Ogden,* for example, went on for five days;[50] the advocates in *Trustees of Dartmouth College v. Woodward* argued for three days.[51] But, as the Court's calendar became more crowded and concern for efficiency increased, the Court began to consider limiting the time allotted for oral argument. In 1849, the Court imposed time-limits, allocating two hours to each side.[52] These limits were subsequently reduced so that by 1970, the norm had become one-half hour per side.[53]

Today the limit remains at thirty minutes per side, with exceptions made for extraordinary cases. Although the lawyer for each side usually uses his or her full thirty minutes, occasionally the Solicitor General or other amicus curiae is given a slice, usually ten or fifteen minutes, of the allotted thirty minutes. See, e.g., Barefoot v. Estelle, 460 U.S. 1067 (1983) in which the NAACP was given a portion of the petitioner's time. In special cases, the Court may give both sides additional time. In United States v. Nixon, 417 U.S. 927 (1974), for example, substantial extra time was allocated to each side for argument.[54] Similarly, in Bowsher v. Synar, 475 U.S. 1009 (1986), each side was permitted one hour for oral argument. Occasionally, one or both sides allocate some of the additional time to an amicus. In Wheeler v. Barrera, 414 U.S. 1140 (1974), for example, each side was given an extra fifteen minutes and the respondent gave the United States its extra fifteen minutes.

In the first reading that follows, Chief Justice Rehnquist describes a variety of types of oral advocates, including the "lector," the "debating champion," the "Casey Jones," the "spellbinder," and finally the "all American oral advocate." While he notes that almost all oral arguments are useful, he urges lawyers to emulate the "all American oral advocate."

49. See David C. Frederick, *Supreme Court Advocacy in the Early Nineteenth Century*, 30 J. Sup. Ct. Hist. 1, 8–12 (2005); see also G. Edward White, vols. 3–4 (combined) *Oliver Wendell Holmes Devise History of the Supreme Court of the United States, The Marshall Court and Cultural Change 1815–35*, 203 (1988).

50. George Dangerfield, *The Steamboat Case*, in *Quarrels That Have Shaped the Constitution* 67 (John A. Garraty, ed. 1987). The opinion in Gibbons v. Ogden may be found at 22 U.S. (9 Wheat.) 1 (1824).

51. Maurice G. Baxter, *Daniel Webster and the Supreme Court* 80–88 (1966). The opinion in The Trustees of Dartmouth College v. Woodward may be found at 17 U.S. (4 Wheat.) 518 (1819).

52. See 48 U.S. (7 How.) v (1849); Frederick, *supra*, at 13.

53. Bennett Boskey & Eugene Gressman, *The 1970 Changes in Supreme Court Rules*, 49 F.R.D. 679, 689–90 (1970). In the 1950s, the Court had two different dockets: the "regular" and the "summary" docket. The more difficult cases were assigned to the regular docket and were given one hour per side; the cases thought to be more simple were allotted only one-half hour per side. See William H. Rehnquist, *The Supreme Court: How It Was, How It Is* 274 (1987).

54. See also Rehnquist (1987), *supra*, at 274 (stating that three hours were given for this oral argument).

In the second reading, then Judge John G. Roberts argues that in the close to two decades since Rehnquist's book first appeared, a specialized Supreme Court bar has developed. As elaborated by Professor Richard Lazarus, this development has important consequences not only on the mix of cases that the Court hears full argument on but on the quality of briefing and advocacy before the Court. Consider whether this development of a specialized Supreme Court bar is, on balance, a good thing, and by what criteria this question should be analyzed.

William H. Rehnquist, *The Supreme Court: How It Was, How It Is* 271–283 (1987)

How the Court Does Its Work: Oral Argument

The time that elapses between the grant of certiorari in a case and its oral argument depends upon the time of year at which certiorari is granted and the state of the Court's calendar. Usually a case granted review in September will be argued in January or February, but a case granted review in June will not be argued until December. Several weeks before the oral argument is scheduled, the briefs filed by the parties are available to the justices to read. . . .

Each justice prepares for oral argument and conference in his own way. Several of my colleagues get what are called bench memos from their law clerks on the cases—bench memos being digests of the arguments contained in the briefs and the law clerk's analysis of the various arguments pro and con. I do not do this, simply because it does not suit my own style of working. When I start to prepare for a case that will be orally argued, I begin by reading the opinion of the lower court which is to be reviewed. . . . I then read the petitioner's brief, and then the respondent's brief. Meanwhile, I have asked one of my law clerks to do the same thing, with a view to our discussing the case.

I let my law clerks divide up the cases among themselves according to their own formula. Since there are usually twenty-four cases for each two-week session of oral argument, this means that each law clerk will end up with eight cases for which that clerk is responsible. I think that most years my clerks have divided up the cases with a system something like the National Football League draft, in which those morsels viewed as more choice are taken first in rotation, with the cases viewed as the dregs left until the end.

When the law clerk and I are both ready to talk about the case, we do just that; . . . I tell the law clerk some of my reactions to the arguments of the parties, and am interested in getting the clerk's reactions to these same arguments. If there is some point of law involved in the case that doesn't appear to be adequately covered by the briefs, I may ask the law clerk to write me a memorandum on that particular point. Either before or after I talk about the case with the law clerk, I also go back and read several of our previous opinions that are relied upon by one side or the other. If it is a recent opinion, it is quite easy to imagine that you remember what was said without having to look at it again, but this often turns out to be exactly that: imagination, rather than reality.

I have used this process pretty much since the time I first came to the Court, but when the process I have just described came to an end, I used to wonder what I should do next. If it was an important constitutional question, it obviously deserved extended and deliberate consideration, and I felt there was obviously more that I should do. I would then begin reading decisions from other courts, and cases from our Court that were only tangentially related to the one to be argued; I even set aside a particular time at which I would simply sit down and "think" about the case. None of these backup procedures seemed to advance me much toward my goal; it is much easier to read what someone else has said about a particular legal problem than to try to figure out what *you* think about it. Then I began to realize that some of my best insights came not during my enforced thinking periods in my chambers, but while I was shaving in the morning, driving to work, or just walking from one place to another. This phenomenon led me to revise my approach to preparation for argued cases by sharply cutting down on collateral reading in most of them, and simply allowing some time for the case to "percolate" in my mind.

After I finished reading the lower-court opinion and briefs, reading the controlling precedents, and talking to the law clerks, I would simply go on to the next item of business. I did that not because I had finally reached a conclusion about the case, but with the idea that I now knew enough that thoughts about it would probably occur between then and the time for conference discussion and voting. They might come in a chance bit of conversation with a colleague; they might come some night while I was lying awake in bed; they might come during oral argument. But once I had made myself sufficiently familiar with the case, come they inevitably did. Probably the most important catalyst for generating further thought was the oral argument of that *case.*

The only publicly visible part of the Supreme Court's decision process is the oral argument. It is the time allotted to lawyers for both sides to argue their positions to the judges who will decide their *case.* In our Court, it takes place in the courtroom of the Supreme Court building fourteen weeks out of each year; two weeks each in the months of October through April.... Oral arguments are open to the public, and one can generally find in the newspaper what cases are going to be argued on a particular day.

In the fifteen years that I have been on the Court, the presentation of each side of a case has been limited to one half hour except in cases of extraordinary public importance and difficulty.... My experience ... as a justice convinces me that by and large our present rules for oral argument are about right. There may be an extremely rare case which because of both its importance and its complexity requires more than an hour for oral argument, but in such cases the Court is generally willing to grant additional time. The Supreme Court of the United States does not generally review evidentiary matters, and so the only questions before us in a given case are pure questions of law. Even these are sometimes limited to one or two in number by the order granting certiorari. A good lawyer should be able to make his necessary points in such a case in one half hour.

. . .

Lawyers often ask me whether oral argument "really makes a difference." Often the question is asked with an undertone of skepticism, if not cynicism, intimating that the judges have really made up their minds before they ever come on the bench and oral argument is pretty much of a formality. My answer is that, speaking for myself, it does make a difference: . . . [I]n a significant minority of the cases in which I have heard oral argument, I have left the bench feeling different about the case than I did when I came on the bench. The change is seldom a full one-hundred-and-eighty-degree swing, and I find that it is most likely to occur in cases involving areas of law with which I am least familiar.

There is more to oral argument than meets the eye—or the ear. Nominally, it is the hour allotted to opposing counsel to argue their respective positions to the judges who are to decide the case. Even if it were in fact largely a formality, I think it would still have the value that many public ceremonies have: It forces the judges who are going to decide the case and the lawyers who represent the clients whose fates will be affected by the outcome of the decision to look at one another for an hour, and talk back and forth about how the case should be decided.

But if an oral advocate is effective, how he presents his position during oral argument *will* have something to do with how the case comes out. Most judges have tentative views of the case when they come on the bench, and it would be strange if they did not. . . .

But a second important function of oral argument can be gleaned from the fact that it is the only time before conference discussion of the case later in the week when all of the judges are expected to sit on the bench and concentrate on one particular case. The judges' questions, although nominally directed to the attorney arguing the case, may in fact be for the benefit of their colleagues. A good oral advocate will recognize this fact, and make use of it during his presentation. Questions may reveal that a particular judge has a misunderstanding as to an important fact in the case, or perhaps reads a given precedent differently from the way in which the attorney thinks it should be read. If the judge simply sat silent during the oral argument, there would be no opportunity for the lawyer to correct the factual misimpression or to state his reasons for interpreting the particular case the way he does. Each attorney arguing a case ought to be much, much more familiar with the facts and the law governing it than the judges who are to decide it. Each of the nine members of our Court must prepare for argument in four cases a day, on three successive days of each week.* One can do his level best to digest from the briefs and other reading what he believes necessary to decide the case, and still find himself falling short in one aspect or another of either the law or the facts. Oral argument can cure these shortcomings.

On occasion of course we get lawyers who do not come up to even the minimum level of competence in representing their client before our Court, either from lack of training and ability or, even worse, lack of preparation. But the great majority of advocates who appear before us exceed the minimum level of competence one might expect, and most of them are far above average in the profession. In my day as a law clerk, it seemed to me that criminal defendants were not as capably represented as they might have been, because at that time the so-called "criminal lawyer" was often possessed of a second-rate education and second-rate abilities. But that is no longer true today with the proliferation of public defender and similar offices which attract bright and able younger lawyers. The truly outstanding advocate before our Court is still a great rarity ...: the lawyer who knows the law, knows the facts, can speak articulately, but who knows that at bottom first-rate oral advocacy is something more than stringing together as many well-constructed relevant sentences as is possible in one half hour.

We who sit on the bench day after day to hear lawyers practice this art are bound to become, whether we like it or not, connoisseurs of its practitioners. Rather than try to draw up a long list of do's and don'ts for the oral advocate, I have tried in the following paragraphs to catalog some of the species of practitioners who have argued before the Court in my time.

The first is the lector, and he does just what his name implies: He reads his argument. The worst case of the lector is the lawyer who actually reads the brief itself; this behavior is so egregious that it is rarely seen. But milder cases read paraphrases of the brief, although they train themselves to look up from their script occasionally to meet the judges' eyes. Questions from the judges, instead of being used as an opportunity to advance one's own arguments by response, are looked upon as an interruption in the advocate's delivery of his "speech," and the lawyer after answering the question returns to the printed page at exactly where he left off; returns, one often feels, with the phrase "as I was saying" implied if not expressed. One feels on occasion that at the conclusion of his argument the lector will say, "Thus endeth the lesson for today."

The lector is very seldom a good oral advocate. It would be foolish for a lawyer to stand before an appellate court with *nothing* written out to guide his presentation, but the use of notes for reference conveys a far

* [Editors' Note: With its reduced docket,   cases a day.]
the Court today generally hears only two

different effect from the reading of a series of typed pages. The ultimate purpose of oral argument, from the point of view of the advocate, is to work his way into the judge's consciousness and make the judge think about the things that the advocate wishes him to think about. One of the best ways to begin this process is to establish eye contact with as many of the judges as possible, and this simply can't be done while you are reading your presentation.

An oral advocate should welcome questions from the bench, because a question shows that at least one judge is inviting him to say what he thinks about a particular aspect of the case. A question also has the valuable psychological effect of bringing a second voice into the performance, so that the minds of judges, which may have momentarily strayed from the lawyer's presentation, are brought back simply by this different sound. But the lector is apt to receive fewer questions than a better advocate just because he seems less willing than other lawyers to take the trouble to carefully answer the questions. When he has finished reading a presentation to the Court, all he has done is to state a logical and reasoned basis for the position he has taken on behalf of his client before the Court; but this much should have been accomplished in his briefs. If oral argument provides nothing more than a summary of the brief in monologue, it is of very little value to the Court.

The second species of oral advocate who comes to my mind is what I shall call the debating champion. He has an excellent grasp of his theory of the case and the arguments supporting it, and with the aid of a few notes and memorization can depart from the printed page at will. But he is so full of his subject, and so desirous of demonstrating this to others, that he doesn't listen carefully to questions. He is the authority, and every question from the bench is presumed to call for one of several stock answers, none of which may be particularly helpful to the inquiring judge. He pulls out all the stops, welcomes questions, and exudes confidence; when he has finished and sat down, one judge may turn to another and say, "Boy, he certainly knows his subject." But simply showing how well you know your subject is not the same as convincing doubters by first carefully listening to their questions and then carefully answering them.

The third species of oral advocate I shall simply call "Casey Jones." This lawyer has a complete grasp of his subject matter, *does* listen to questions, tries to answer them carefully, and does not read from any prepared text. He is a good oral advocate, but falls short of being a top-notch oral advocate because he forgets about the limitations of those he is trying to convince. The reason I call him Casey Jones is because he is like an engineer on a nonstop train—he will not stop to pick up passengers along the way.

He knows the complexities of his subject, and knows that if he were permitted to do so he could easily spend an hour and a half arguing this particular case without ever repeating himself. He is probably right. For this reason, in order to get as much as possible of his argument into half an hour, he speaks very rapidly, without realizing that when he is arguing before a bench of nine people, each of them will require a little time to assimilate what he is saying. If the lawyer goes nonstop throughout the thirty minutes without even a pause, except for questions, even able and well-prepared judges are going to be left behind. To become a truly first-rate oral advocate, this lawyer must simply learn to leave the secondary points to the brief, to slow down his pace of speaking, and to remember that the lawyer who makes six points, of which three are remembered by the judges, is a better lawyer than a lawyer who makes twelve points, of which only one is remembered by the judges.

Next we come to the spellbinder, who is fortunately today much more of a rara avis than even in the days when I was a law clerk. The spellbinder has a good voice, and a good deal of that undefinable something called "presence" which enables him to talk *with* the Court rather than talk *to* the Court. This species of oral advocate has much going for him, but he tends to let his natural assets be a substitute for any careful analysis of the legal issues in the case. He is the other side of the coin from Casey Jones, who won't let up on legal analysis long enough to give the judges even a mental breathing spell. The spellbinder's magniloquent presentation of the big picture could be copied in part with profit by Casey Jones, but the thorough attention to the subject of the latter could be copied by the spellbinder. The spellbinder's ultimate weapon is his peroration, or at least so he thinks. A florid peroration, exhorting the Court either to save the Bill of Rights from the government or to save the government from the Bill of Rights, simply does not work very well in our Court.

These are but a few of the varied species of oral advocates that have come before our Court in my time. If we were to combine the best in all of them, we would of course have the All American oral advocate. If the essential element of the case turns on how the statute is worded, she will pause and slowly read the crucial sentence or paragraph. She will realize that there is an element of drama in an oral argument, a drama in which for half an hour she is the protagonist. But she also realizes that her spoken lines must have substantive legal meaning, and does not waste her relatively short time with observations that do not advance the interest of her client. She has a theme and a plan for her argument, but is quite willing to pause and listen carefully to questions. The questions may reveal that the judge is ignorant, stupid, or both, but even such questions should have the best possible answer. She avoids table pounding and other hortatory mannerisms, but she realizes equally well that an oral argument on behalf of one's client requires controlled enthusiasm and not an impression of *fin de siècle* ennui.

One of the common misapprehensions about practice before the Supreme Court, which I heard often during my days in private practice in Phoenix and still hear since I have been on the Court, is that if one has business before the Supreme Court of the United States it is best to retain a "Washington lawyer" or a "Supreme Court specialist." The first of these statements is simply not true, and the second is true only in a very limited sense.

During particular times in the history of the Supreme Court, there has been a very definite "Supreme Court bar," consisting of lawyers who follow the work of the Court closely, and appear before the Court regularly year in and year out. Daniel Webster and his colleagues at the bar did this in the days of John Marshall and Roger Taney; Reverdy Johnson, William Evarts, and Matthew Carpenter did it in the days of Salmon P. Chase and Morrison Waite; and Charles Evans Hughes and John W. Davis did it in the days of William Howard Taft. Whether any of these lawyers had any special influence upon the Court I do not know, but apparently a number of clients thought so or they would not have been retained in so many cases.

Based on personal observation during my sixteen years of service on the Court, I am quite firmly of the belief that there is no such Supreme Court bar at the present time. With the exception of the attorneys in the office of the solicitor general of the United States, who of course are not available to represent private clients, it is quite remarkable if a single lawyer argues more than one or two cases a year before us. . . .

. . .

. . . I do *not* mean to say that it makes no difference whom a client retains to represent him before our Court. It makes a great deal of difference, but that difference lies not in the geographic location of the lawyer, or his reputation, but in the kind of performance he puts on in any particular client's behalf. A lawyer in Prescott, Arizona, who knows very little about Supreme Court cases and makes equally little effort to find out about them in the process of preparing a brief in the Supreme Court will be of little use to the client. But a Washington lawyer of similar ignorance and laziness will be of equally little use to the client. Every lawyer who stands up and begins to argue orally before our Court is presumed by us to be capable of doing full justice to the client's cause. That presumption may be rebutted, but if so it will be only as a result of the lawyer's performance, and not because of any lack of reputation or experience as a Supreme Court advocate.

Writing almost twenty years after Chief Justice Rehnquist, John G. Roberts, then a relatively new Court of Appeals judge (and now, in 2007, the Chief Justice), addressed the "Reemergence of a Supreme Court Bar." Excerpts follow.

John G. Roberts, Jr., *Oral Advocacy and the Reemergence of a Supreme Court Bar*, 30 J. Sup. Ct. Hist. 68 (2005)[55]

Over the past generation, roughly the period since 1980, there has been a discernible professionalization among the advocates before the Supreme Court, to the extent that one can speak of the emergence of a real Supreme Court bar. Before defending that proposition, it is probably worth considering whether advocacy makes a difference—whether oral argument matters. My view after one year on the opposite side of the bench is the same as that expressed by no less a figure than Justice John Marshall Harlan—the second one—forty-nine years ago, after he completed his year on the Court of Appeals for the Second Circuit. Justice Harlan lamented what he saw as a growing tendency among the bar "to regard the oral argument as little more than a traditionally tolerated part of the appellate process," a chore "of little importance in the decision of appeals." This view, he said, was "greatly mistaken." As Justice Harlan told the bar, "[Y]our oral argument on appeal is perhaps the most effective weapon you have got."

. . .

My main conclusion after a year of being on the other side of the bench is that oral argument is terribly, terribly important. I feel more confident about that now than I ever did as an advocate—now, when the question "does oral argument ever matter?" does not carry the same existential angst it did when it was what I did for a living. Oral argument matters, but not just because of what the lawyers have to say. It is the organizing point for the entire judicial process. The judges read the briefs, do the research, and talk to their law clerks to prepare for the argument. The voting conference is held right after the oral argument—immediately after it in the court of appeals, shortly after it in the Supreme Court. And without disputing in any way the dominance of the briefing in the decisional process, it is natural, with the voting coming so closely on the heels of oral argument, that the discussion at conference is going to focus on what took place at argument.

Oral argument is also a time—at least for me—when ideas that have been percolating for some time begin to crystallize. I—and I think many judges—are aggressively skeptical when they prepare to confront a case. Upon reading a brief, my reaction is not typically "Well, that's a good argument," or "That's persuasive," but instead "Says you. Let's see what the other side has to say." In researching the cases, my reaction is, "I bet there's some authority on the other side that balances it out." But however open you try to keep yourself to particular positions, those doors begin to close at oral argument. After all, the voting is going to take place very soon thereafter, and the luxury of skepticism will have to yield to the necessity of a decision. Those closing doors often get a push from what happens at argument, whether it be the questions from the other judges or the responses by the attorneys. And the former can be

55. [Editors' Note: This article is from a speech given in 2004.]

just as important as the latter, because it is the protocol on the inferior court on which I sit—and, I believe, the general practice on the Supreme Court as well—that the judges do not discuss the cases before oral argument except in unusual situations. Thus, oral argument is the first time you begin to get a sense of what your colleagues think of the case through their questions.

. . .

Over the last generation of advocacy before the Supreme Court, one thing that has remained fairly constant has been the level of questioning. I took the first and last cases of each of the seven argument sessions in the 1980 Term and the first and last cases in each of the seven argument sessions in the 2003 Term and added up the questions, and the statistics confirm that impression. There was an average of eighty-seven questions per argument in 1980 and ninety-one per argument in 2003. In both the 1980 and 2003 Terms, there were significantly more questions, on average, for the respondent than for the petitioner.

Davis famously said that an advocate should "[r]ejoice when the Court asks questions." "[A]gain I say unto you," he wrote, "rejoice." But apparently too much rejoicing can be a bad thing. Recent studies have begun to suggest that you can tell how a case is going to come out simply by seeing which side was asked the most questions: the side with the most questions is going to lose. In the twenty-eight cases I looked at, fourteen from the 1980 Term and fourteen from 2003, the most-questions-asked "rule" predicted the winner—or more accurately, the loser—in twenty-four of those twenty-eight cases, an 86 percent prediction rate. So the secret for successful advocacy . . . is simply to get the Court to ask your opponent more questions.

. . .

. . . [T]he sharp decline in the number of opportunities for lawyers to argue before the Court has been accompanied, perhaps paradoxically or perhaps not, by an even more dramatic rise in the number of experienced Supreme Court advocates appearing before the Court, both in absolute terms and proportionately. That, in any event, was my impression, and I decided to test it by comparing the lawyers who argued in the 1980 Term and those who argued in the 2002 Term. In 1980, looking at oral arguments by non-federal government attorneys—that is, basically excluding the Solicitor General's Office—fewer than 20 percent of the advocates had ever appeared before the Supreme Court before. In 2002, that number had more than doubled, to over 44 percent.

The change is even more dramatic if you look at what I will call experienced advocates, or recidivists—those with at least three previous arguments before the Court. In 1980, only 10 percent of non-Solicitor General arguments were presented by experienced counsel. In 2002, that number had more than tripled, to 33 percent. In 1980, only three lawyers outside the Solicitor General's Office argued twice before the Court, out of some 240 argument slots for non-Solicitor General lawyers, accounting for 2.5 percent of the arguments. (For two of those three, it was their first and second arguments ever.) But in 2002, there were fourteen different non-Solicitor General repeat performers who argued at least twice—many more than twice—accounting for fully 24 percent of the non-Solicitor General argument slots, a tenfold increase.

I should be quick to point out that an experienced advocate does not necessarily make for a better argument. Several of the Justices have gone out of their way to emphasize that many first-timers—many only-timers—have presented wonderful arguments. I observed first arguments in the Supreme Court by Michael Dreeben, Walter Dellinger, and Seth Waxman from the very uncomfortable position of the opposing counsel's chair. On each of those occasions, I would have gladly traded for a grizzled veteran as an opponent. But is it reasonable to suppose that arguing before the Court is, like most things (including judging), something that you hope to get better at as you go along.

This rise in the number of experienced practitioners before the Supreme Court is reflected in, and abetted by, another development over the past generation: the rise of Supreme Court and appellate practice departments in major law firms. This is largely a phenomenon of the past twenty-five years, not limited to Washington, D.C., but certainly very evident there. In establishing Supreme Court and appellate practice as a recognized specialty, these private law offices, of course, have a very successful model on which to draw. Since 1870, the federal government has had such a specialized office—the Solicitor General's Office. This type of development in the profession has had something of a snowball effect. If one side hires a Supreme Court specialist to present a case, it may cause the client on the other side to think that they ought to consider doing that as well. This is just a variant on the old adage that one lawyer in a town will starve, but two will prosper.

There has been a corresponding development on the state and local government side. More and more states are copying the federal model and establishing state solicitor general's offices. These offices certainly are devoted to and focused on litigation before their state supreme court and their state courts of appeals. But they also appear far more frequently before the Supreme Court of the United States now than they did in 1980. In the 2003 Term, for example, a solicitor general or someone from that office appeared for the states of Alabama, Illinois, Michigan, Ohio, Tennessee, Texas, and Washington. I do not want to put too much weight on the label, but in fact if you do have an office of appellate specialist at the state level, I think it is natural to hope and assume that lawyers from that office will bring more experience and expertise to their cases before the Supreme Court.

Along with the rise of specialists in the private bar and the rise of specialists representing state and local government, the United States Office of the Solicitor General is appearing in proportionately more cases before the Supreme Court than it did before. That office has gone from appearing as a party or an amicus in just over 60 percent of the cases in

1980 to appearing at argument in over 80 percent of the cases in the last three Terms. Interestingly, the office's absolute numbers have remained about the same as the Court's docket has contracted. In 1980 the Solicitor General appeared in some sixty-six cases; in the last three Terms, he was in sixty-five, sixty-two, and sixty-two. I do not think the Supreme Court's docket has contracted simply by eliminating cases in which there was no interest on the part of the federal government. Instead, over the past several years the Solicitor General has filed and argued in cases that that office would have let pass twenty-five years ago.

There is a certain institutional dynamic at work here: the Solicitor General must sign off on every appeal by the federal government throughout the federal judiciary, from any level to any other level. If the federal government loses in a district court and wants to appeal to the court of appeals, that has to be approved by the Solicitor General. That role is much appreciated by those of us on the inferior courts, because it helps ensure (at least in theory) that the United States is maintaining a consistent litigation position throughout the country. But it is an enormously heavy burden on the very limited resources of the Solicitor General's Office to review, in every case, whether the government should appeal and what position it should take. The lawyers who do that work end up working extremely hard, often on very mundane issues. The reward, of course, is that those same lawyers have the opportunity to appear for their country before the Supreme Court. So however much the Supreme Court's docket may contract, there is pressure to have someone from the Solicitor General's Office appear in more and more of those cases.

The net result is that the experienced lawyers of the Solicitor General's Office, on a relative basis, are appearing far more frequently before the Supreme Court than they did a generation ago. This, too, contributes to the snowball effect. A client may not think that it needs a Supreme Court specialist until it finds out that the federal government's Supreme Court specialist is joining what, up to then, had been a purely private dispute.

Now, when you step back from all these developments and look at the net consequence, it is eye-catching. In 1980, the odds that the advocate making his way to the lectern for an oral argument before the Supreme Court had ever been there before were about one in three, including representatives of the Solicitor General's Office. By 2002, those odds were over 50 percent. It is interesting to note that a generation ago, a number of the Justices commented quite critically on the quality of oral argument before the Court. Justice Lewis F. Powell said that he had high expectations of the bar when he joined the Court, but that the bar's performance "has not measured up to my expectations." From Justice Powell, those are very harsh words. Chief Justice Warren Burger made the need for improved advocacy a recurring theme of his speeches, focusing on the poor quality of advocacy by those representing the states and local governments. Around 1980, retired Justice Douglas said that

40 percent of the oral advocates before the Court were "incompetent." And in a 1983 lecture, the current Chief Justice attributed the disrepute into which oral argument was falling to the prevailing poor quality of oral advocacy, noting that for many advocates before the Supreme Court, oral argument seemed to be an opportunity to present their brief "with gestures."

My bold claim today, looking back at the last twenty-four years, is that things have changed, and for the better. First, there have been some very specific institutional changes. The establishment of an advocacy program at the Academy of State and Local Governments and similar programs at the National Association of Attorneys General were a direct response to Chief Justice Burger's critique. These organizations provide not only amicus help, but also moot court training and other assistance to the representatives of state and local government. There has been a recent rise of similar programs available to all advocates before the Court. The Georgetown University Supreme Court Institute provided rigorous moot court preparation for advocates in two-thirds of the cases argued before the Supreme Court during the 2003 Term. The Institute's moot court program is highly valued by novice and experienced advocates alike because of the high quality and skill of the judges that Institute director Professor Richard Lazarus is able to attract to do the moot courts. These programs have made it easier for both first-timers and experienced advocates to do a more professional job before the Court.

There have even been changes along these same lines in the Solicitor General's Office. Everyone who has served in the Solicitor General's Office shares a belief that that office enjoyed a golden age roughly corresponding to the time that they served there. Suggesting that something has improved in the Office of the Solicitor General will to many seem like heresy, because it implies that there was at one time a need for improvement. All I will note is that a generation ago it was not the rule—certainly a practice, maybe even a common practice, but not the rule—that Solicitor General's Office lawyers went through moot courts before their arguments. That requirement was instituted by Judge Kenneth Starr, and I believe it has stuck, which I think has allowed some lawyers from the Office of the Solicitor General to become even better advocates.

I would not go so far as to say that the re-emergence that I have identified of a Supreme Court bar was a response to the judicial criticism prevalent a generation ago. But perhaps to the extent that the Justices at that time identified an opportunity for improved quality and professionalism, the bar identified the same opportunity and responded. The Supreme Court bar that I have been discussing is, of course, nothing like the Supreme Court bar of the John Marshall era. No one today is going to argue in half of the Court's cases, as William Pinkney did one year. But more and more, there are familiar faces appearing at the lectern— not just the curiously attired lawyers from the Solicitor General's Office, but faces from the private bar and from the states as well. If I am right about this, I think it raises a number of interesting questions. If there has been a re-emergence of the Supreme Court bar, when did the old one die, and what killed it? What is the relationship between the Court's shrinking docket and the rise of the Supreme Court bar? More generally, is a specialized bar a good thing or a bad thing for the Court?

Obviously better advocacy—if in fact that is what comes with more experienced advocates—is a good thing. A well-argued case will not necessarily be well decided; sometimes the judges get in the way. But there is a significant risk that a poorly argued case will be poorly decided. That is a risk of our adversary system. More experienced, better advocates should be a good thing.

But the developments I have noted do raise some concerns. Take the presence of someone from the Office of the Solicitor General in more than 80 percent of the Court's argued cases. If you asked me as an abstract proposition whether I would be troubled by the idea that the executive branch was going to file something in every case before the Supreme Court explaining its views, as a sort of super law clerk, my answer would be yes, I would find that very troubling. Eighty percent is pretty close to every case, and as the discernible federal interest in a matter before the Court wanes, concern about the role being played by the government increases.

On the private side, I would suppose that the Justices are pleased to see good and experienced advocates present a case. But there is no denying that something is lost as the bar becomes more specialized. The Chief Justice has referred to the "intangible value of oral argument," the point at which counsel and Court look each other in the eye and have a public "interchange" about the case. If you have a case arising in Iowa that works its way through the Iowa courts, goes to the Iowa Supreme Court, and works its way to Washington, I think there is something beneficial both for the U.S. Supreme Court and certainly for the Iowa bar to have Iowa attorneys present that case. That is true, of course, only to the extent that those attorneys are able and willing to learn what practice before the Supreme Court is like and what it demands of them. That may turn out to be a very big challenge. It may be that not many lawyers with different practices to maintain can set aside the months necessary effectively to brief and to prepare for argument in a case before the Supreme Court. There is a corresponding challenge on the part of the specialist as well: to become intimately steeped in the local character and details of any particular case, so that they are able to convey that to the Justices.

Whether an advocate is a recidivist or presenting his first and only argument before the Court, he needs to have something of the medieval stonemason about him. Those masons—the ones who built the great cathedrals—would spend months meticulously carving the gargoyles high up in the cathedral, gargoyles that when the cathedral was completed could not even be seen from the ground below. The advocate here must meticulously prepare, analyze, and rehearse answers to hundreds of questions, questions that in all likelihood will actually never be asked by the Court. The medieval stonemasons did what they did because, it was said, they were carving for the eye of God. A higher purpose informed their craft. The advocate who stands before the Supreme Court, whether a veteran or novice, also needs to infuse his craft with a higher purpose. He must appreciate that what happens here, in mundane case after mundane case, is extraordinary—the vindication of the rule of law—and that he as the advocate plays a critical role in the process. The advocate who appreciates that does infuse his work with a higher purpose, and that higher purpose will steel him for the long and lonely work of preparation, will bring the proper passion to his cause, will assuage the bitterness of defeat and moderate the elation of victory, and will, more and more, forge a special bond with his colleagues at the Supreme Court bar.

Questions and Comments

1.   Soon-to-be Chief Justice John Roberts' observations about the reemergence of a specialized Supreme Court bar has received thorough scholarly treatment in Richard J. Lazarus,[56] *Advocacy Matters Before and Within the Supreme Court: Transforming the Court by Transforming the Bar*, 96 Geo. L. J. ___ (forthcoming 2008) (manuscript of Aug. 5, 2007) (hereafter Lazarus, *Advocacy Matters*). Professor Lazarus recounts the development, beginning in the 1980s, of specialized Supreme Court practices in private law firms (often employing attorneys with prior experience in the Solicitor General's office), whose success in obtaining cert grants, he shows, is far greater than the norm. His article offers a persuasive, and complex, account of how a specialized Supreme Court bar has grown at the same time that the Court has drastically reduced its docket of argued cases. Lazarus also raises fascinating questions about the relationship between the specialized bar and the shrinking docket of fully argued cases, suggesting that (1) having experienced lawyers acting as counsel to respondents may have contributed to the decline because they can do a better job explaining why certiorari should not be granted; (2) having high quality certiorari petitions written by expert specialists may have "raised the bar" for others, so that by comparison, a smaller number of cert petitions are found worthy and (3) members of the private, specialized bar may—in order to maintain their credibility with the Court as reliable repeat players—now play something akin to the screening role that the SG's office plays for government appeals, in discouraging private clients from pursuing those cert petitions less likely to be granted. (See Chapter Three, above.)

2.   More provocatively, Professor Lazarus suggests that the private bar is having a significant impact on the mix of cases selected for review and even on the merits decision of the Court. "The expert Supreme Court

---

56.   This is Professor Richard J. Lazarus, who is different from and unrelated to Edward Lazarus, the author of *Closed Chambers*, discussed earlier in this Chapter.

Richard J. Lazarus is a Professor of Law at Georgetown University Law Center and a Director of the Georgetown Supreme Court Institute.

advocates do not merely discern the existing priorities of the Justices. They deliberately and systematically educate the Justices concerning what the priorities should be. Through repeated filings of cases and amicus support from weighty authorities and interest groups, the advocates identify for the Court what legal issues are sufficiently important for the Court to resolve." Lazarus, *Advocacy Matters, supra,* at 52. He notes that the lawyers influencing the Court's priorities are no longer from the public interest organizations, like the ACLU or NAACP, which may have done so in the past, but rather represent primarily business-oriented clients. He has identified their influence on (1) issues relating to punitive damages, (2) anti-trust questions, and (3) issues affecting the Norfolk & Southern Railroad (represented by Sidley Austin, a firm that includes Carter Phillips, a leading advocate in the private Supreme Court bar). *Id.,* at 52–60.

3.　Lazarus' conclusion is that the re-emergence of a specialized Supreme Court bar is both significant, because advocacy matters, and on the whole, a "positive development." Yet he noted some concerns:

> . . . Better decisions require better advocacy on all sides, not just on behalf of some sides. And . . . there is reason for concern that some business interests before the Court are receiving a disproportionate amount of the talent available in the modern day Supreme Court Bar and yielding the related benefits of the resulting advocacy advantage: a Supreme Court docket and rulings on the merits more responsive to their economic concerns.

> · · ·

> Fortunately, to some extent, market forces, the significant professional prestige closely associated with Supreme Court advocacy, and the personal commitment of some attorneys to provide able representation to under-represented interests afford some of the incentive necessary to close the advocacy gap. . . .

Id. at 79–82. However, Lazarus concludes that these forces are not sufficient to "close the gap" between the quality of advocacy available to some but not others:

> There is no systematic effort to ensure adequate representation to under-represented interests and those interest groups that are best able to secure such outstanding pro bono counsel tend, naturally, to be those that are already well connected within the legal profession. . . . There are also areas of law [representing plaintiffs in employment discrimination, tort and environmental pollution control cases] in which the vast majority of the private Supreme Court Bar regularly declines to serve as pro bono counsel because of their concern that doing so will upset some of their most financially important business clients. . . .

Id. at 86. The criminal defense bar, he notes, is averse to seeking or accepting help from more experienced Supreme Court counsel. And pro bono assistance is almost never available at the certiorari stage—where, he argues, "expert advocacy tends to be the most influential." *Id.*

4.　Professor Lazarus suggests a number of reforms to ensure a more "fair distribution of advocacy expertise," at both the jurisdictional (certiorari) and the merits stages. He argues that "the Bar needs to be more willing to overcome 'conflicts' that have no true legal ethical dimension but merely reflect a desire to avoid advancing legal arguments that might upset business clients." He also would encourage the Court to reduce the advocacy gap by, *inter alia*, appointing expert Supreme Court advocates in criminal defense cases and more readily allowing organizations with experienced Supreme Court advocates as counsel to present oral argument as amicus curiae. *Id.* at 87–88. Are there other approaches? Could the Court require counsel who has not previously argued before the Court to certify that she or he had been "mooted" by experts in Supreme Court advocacy?[57]

5. Between OT 1980 and OT 2006, Lazarus found, the percentage of lawyers (from outside the Solicitor General's office) giving their first Supreme Court argument fell from 76% to 52%, while the percentage of those with ten or more prior Supreme Court arguments rose from 3% to 25.5%. *Id.* at 41–42 (Table). In addition to the effects on the Court's decisions, what other impacts does the emergence of so specialized a bar have? This specialized bar includes only a very small number of women, and even fewer persons of color. *See id.* at 79 n. 237 (reporting that former Solicitor General Drew Days is apparently the only African American active in the Supreme Court Bar with a large number of arguments (29)). For discussion of the history of women as advocates before the Supreme Court, see Mary L. Clark, *Women as Supreme Court Advocates, 1879–1979*, 30 J. Sup. Ct. Hist. 47 (2005). Consider whether the increased specialization of the Supreme Court bar may have disadvantages for traditionally disadvantaged groups within the legal profession. How much concern, if any, should this possibility raise?

2. The Solicitor General

In 1870, Congress decided that the Attorney General needed more permanent assistance and therefore created both the Office of Solicitor General and the Department of Justice.[58] The statute provides that the responsibility of the Solicitor General, or "SG" as the position has come to be called, is "to assist the Attorney General in the performance of his duties."[59] As the readings in this section show, the SG's responsibilities are extensive.

The SG is a political appointee who serves at the pleasure of the President. At the same time, he or she has a special relationship to the Court. The Office of Solicitor General is the only litigant with a permanent office in the Supreme Court building and it is allowed to file a brief as a friend of the Court (that is, as amicus curiae) without the permis-

57. The Georgetown University Law Center Supreme Court Institute provides on a pro bono, nonpartisan basis moot courts for counsel in Supreme Court arguments. In October Term 2006, counsel in more than 90 percent of the cases argued before the Court were mooted by the Institute. Two of this book's co-authors, Bloch and Jackson, serve on the Institute's Faculty Advisory Committee.

58. Act of June 22, 1870, ch. 150, 16 Stat. 162 (1870), codified in relevant part at 28 U.S.C. §§ 501, 505. Prior to the 1870 legislation, the Attorney General operated without any official department and often relied on ad hoc appointments to argue cases on behalf of the United States. See Susan Low Bloch, *The Early Role of the Attorney General in Our Constitutional Scheme: In the Beginning There Was Pragmatism*, 1989 Duke L.J. 561.

59. 28 U.S.C. § 505.

sion of the parties to the suit.[60] And, unlike other litigants who must color code their briefs according to the document's role in the case—e.g., petitions for cert must be white, responses orange, petitioners' briefs on the merits light blue, respondents' merits briefs light red—the SG's briefs are always grey, making them readily identifiable.[61] As the readings below will also suggest, the SG's special relationship to the Court may present conflicts with the SG's relationship to the President.

The first three readings in Part (a) below, by Lincoln Caplan, Rebecca Salokar, and Cornelia Pillard, provide historical background and contemporary description of the various functions of the SG. As these readings show, the Solicitor General is responsible for all government litigation before the Supreme Court. Because the United States is the most frequent litigant to appear before the Court, this responsibility is considerable. The SG decides whether a case in which the United States has lost should be appealed to the Supreme Court. Occasionally, the SG will even "confess error," when he or she believes a government victory in the lower court was erroneous. If and when the Supreme Court grants review in a case in which the government is a party, it is the SG's responsibility to decide what position the United States will take, to write the brief, and ultimately to argue the case.

Moreover, as the United States' "gate-keeper" to the Court (and in most cases to the courts of appeals in cases in which the government has lost in the federal district courts), the SG is also called upon to resolve conflicts among various governmental agencies. The excerpt by Professor Salokar and the reading from the Rex E. Lee Conference on the SG's office, published in the *Brigham Young University Law Review* (2003), explore the significance of this gate-keeper function.

The SG also frequently participates as amicus curiae ("friend of the court"), at both the certiorari stage and the merits phase. Often that participation comes at the invitation of the Court. The Court may invite the SG to give its opinion on the "certworthiness" of a petition being considered by the Court or to file an amicus brief in a case in which cert has already been granted, invitations the SG finds difficult to refuse. As numerous studies have found, a petitioner's chances of persuading the Court to grant cert rise substantially when the SG files in support of a petition, whether the SG's opinion comes by invitation or on its own initiative.

To what extent is the SG's success rate at the certiorari stage due to the fact that the SG is a "repeat player" who knows what factors the Court considers important and may be acting essentially as a super law clerk in advising the Court? To what extent is the SG's success rate due to the fact that the Court is likely to ask the SG for its opinion only in cases that have a good chance of being heard? Whatever the reasons for

60. Supreme Court Rule 37.4. States and local governments are also permitted to file through their attorneys general or authorized law officers, respectively, without seeking consent or making a motion before the Court.

61. Supreme Court Rule 33.1 (e); see also *id.*, 33.1(g).

the SG's rate of success, advocates believe they are well-advised to try to get the Solicitor General on their side. Yet, as suggested by readings in Part (c) below, the capacity of the Solicitor General to influence the merits' decisions of the Court may be greater in some areas than in others.

Caplan's book argues that the SG is not merely an advocate but, as the title "Tenth Justice" suggests, must act with independence from political pressures in order to fulfill its obligations to the Court, a claim which has generated much thoughtful discussion and disagreement. Several additional readings in Part (b) below—articles by former SGs or their deputies, including Richard Wilkins, Michael McConnell, and Drew Days; the formal opinion issued by the Office of Legal Counsel under Attorney General Griffin Bell; and comments by former members of the SG's Office in the BYU Conference—explore the controversial question of the degree to which the Solicitor General is and/or should be directed by the political preferences of the Attorney General and President, as well as providing further insight on how the SG's office works.

In Part (c), we excerpt from two articles by Seth Waxman, Solicitor General in the second Clinton Administration, who explores some of the limitations on the ability of SGs to influence the Court. And in Part (d), we invite readers to think about connections between constitutional theory—in particular, the role of courts in interpreting the Constitution—and the institutional realities of how the SG's office works, in an excerpt from a law review article by Professor Nina Pillard, who served in the Office of the Solicitor General.

A good way to deepen one's understanding of the role of the Solicitor General is to examine current cases in which the United States is a party as well as cases in which it is amicus curiae. We therefore urge the reader to find such cases, study the SG's briefs, and assess their influence.

a. The History and Functions of the Office of Solicitor General

Lincoln Caplan,[62] *The Tenth Justice: The Solicitor General and the Rule of Law*, 3–13, 134 (1987)

THE TENTH JUSTICE

The United States takes pride in its commitment to the rule of law, and during this century the individual who has best represented this dedication may be a little-known figure called the Solicitor General. The nation's constitutional government is distinguished by its need for the consent of the governed, and the law is the compact between the people and their representatives. Of all the nation's public officials, including the Attorney General and the Justices of the Supreme Court, the Solicitor General is the only one required by statute to be "learned in

---

62. Lincoln Caplan was at the time a staff writer for The New Yorker magazine; he later was editor and president of Legal Affairs.

the law." Although he serves in the Department of Justice, and his title, like the Attorney General's, is displayed in large bronze letters on the facade of the Department's building, he also has permanent chambers in the Supreme Court. The fact that he keeps offices at these two distinct institutions underscores his special role. The Solicitor General's principal task is to represent the Executive Branch of the government in the Supreme Court, and when he takes the lectern before the Justices, his status is clear. With his assistants and other lawyers for the government, the Solicitor General is among the last attorneys to carry on the custom of arguing at the Court in formal garb of striped pants, dark vest, and tails. The Justices expect the substance of his remarks to be distinguished as well. They count on him to look beyond the government's narrow interests. They rely on him to help guide them to the right result in the case at hand, and to pay close attention to the case's impact on the law.

Because of what Justice Lewis Powell has described as the Solicitor's "dual responsibility" to both the Judicial and the Executive Branch, he is sometimes called the Tenth Justice. Although he operates in a sphere of government that is invisible to almost all citizens, his influence is undeniable. Some parts of it are not hard to measure. During the 1983 Term of the Supreme Court, of the 3,878 petitions for writs of certiorari (the form in which most parties ask the Court to review a case) submitted by lawyers across the country, the Justices granted only 3 percent. Of petitions from the Solicitor General, they approved 79 percent, or almost four out of five. Whenever the government supported a petition as amicus curiae, or friend of the Court, in a case where it was not directly involved, the chances that the Court would approve the petition rose from 2 percent to 78 percent—up thirty-nine times. The Solicitor General, unlike the ordinary legal counsel, appeared to have almost a standing invitation to come to the Court, and was able to bring along most advocates he sponsored. Once he arrived before the Court, he was even more effective. Of the 262 cases the Justices considered that Term, the government took part in 150. The Solicitor General (or SG, as he is called) won 83 percent of his cases outright and partial victories in another 2 percent, for an exceptional overall success rate of 85 percent.

While the SG's performance has only rarely reached this level, it has been remarkably better than the record of nongovernmental attorneys in almost every year since the SG became the government's chief lawyer and began to do what most people assume falls naturally to the Attorney General. Until 1853, the Attorney General's was a part-time job....

In the mid-nineteenth century, as the country grew, the volume of official legal work expanded and became more than the government could handle. Private attorneys then took on the public's cases. But their judgments about the law were sometimes at odds with the government's, and their fees were high. As dissatisfaction with this arrangement spread, a congressional panel known as the Joint Committee on Retrenchment recommended that a Ministry of Justice be established to save money and consolidate the government's legal work under one master. The legislators also realized that the Attorney General was increasingly preoccupied with management and politics, and had little time for the intricacies of courtroom law.

In 1870, when Congress created the Justice Department, it drew on the model of Treasury's Solicitor and directed that "there shall be ... an officer learned in the law, to assist the Attorney–General in the performance of his duties, to be called the solicitor-general...." Congressman Thomas Jenckes, a Republican from Rhode Island who sponsored the bill establishing the office, explained: "We propose to have a man of sufficient learning, ability, and experience that he can be sent to New Orleans or to New York, or into any court wherever the government has any interest in litigation, and there present the case of the United States as it should be presented." Though early SGs tried occasional cases before juries (the first Solicitor was Benjamin Bristow, who had made his reputation prosecuting the Ku Klux Klan), the people in the office have for many years concentrated on the government's appeals, especially to the Supreme Court.

In 1986, the Justice Department had 5,107 attorneys. The SG's office had only twenty-three, the size of a small law firm. The Solicitor's team has always been relatively tiny, but within the Executive Branch the SG has played a powerful and almost judicial role consistent with his standing as the Tenth Justice. For every petition the SG sends to the Supreme Court, he rejects five from federal agencies with grievances they want the Justices to settle. Often he spurns an agency's request because he thinks it is wrong about the law. (A Solicitor General once wrote, "Government lawyers, like those in general practice, may experience that marvelous adjustment of perspective which often comes to the most ardent advocate when he loses—that is, the realization that he really should have lost.") Even if he thinks the agency is right, the SG is not easily persuaded to allow an appeal. As the then Associate Justice William Rehnquist noted with approval in a 1984 opinion, "The Solicitor General considers a variety of factors, such as the limited resources of the government and the crowded dockets of the courts, before authorizing an appeal." If the facts of a case that the government has lost are so unusual as to give it little weight as a precedent, or if there is general agreement among the dozen regional U.S. Courts of Appeals about the law under scrutiny, the SG will usually accept the defeat.

Lawyers on the Solicitor's team prefer to talk about the cases they present to the Supreme Court, but they spend half their time sifting through proposed appeals from trial-court rulings against the government. In a speech at the University of Oklahoma, one Solicitor General bragged, "If the district court in Oklahoma City makes a decision which the United States Attorney doesn't like, he may well tell the press, 'I am going to appeal.' When I see those statements in the press, I say to myself, 'Yes, he is going to appeal if I say he can.' But sometimes I don't." The SG and his staff have a reputation for stinginess, and the trait matters because they are in effect a court of last resort. By screening cases that they believe are not ready for hearing by the Courts of Appeals or the Supreme Court, the Solicitor General and his aides help assure that judges rule on those the SG does consider ripe for appeal.

. . .

The influence of the Solicitor at the Court goes beyond helping the Justices set their docket. The Justices also turn to the SG for help on legal problems that appear especially vexing, and two or three dozen times a year they invite him and his office to submit briefs in cases where the government is not a party. In these cases especially, the Justices regard him as a counselor to the Court. But in every case in which he participates, the Justices expect him to take a long view. The Solicitor General advises the Court about the meaning of federal statutes as well as about the Constitution, so his judgments regularly affect the work of the Legislature as much as the Executive and the Judiciary. Lawyers who have worked in the SG's office like to say that the Solicitor General avoids a conflict between his duty to the Executive Branch, on the one hand, and his respect for the Congress or his deference to the Judiciary, on the other, through a higher loyalty to the law.

. . .

LORE

In a corridor on the fifth floor of the Justice Department, where the lawyers in the SG's office work, photographs of thirty-six of the thirty-eight men who have served as Solicitor General hang in a kind of gallery. Aside from one in color and a sepia-toned print whose border seems tinged with gold, the photos are black-and-white. Like the reputation of the archetypical SG, the subjects of the pictures appear direct, upright, and somehow eccentric. Almost half wear mustaches. None is a woman, and two—Supreme Court Justice Thurgood Marshall and former appeals court judge Wade McCree—are black. Their average tenure has been three years.

... The history of the Solicitor General is passed on among the small circle of lawyers who know about it—usually by moving down the line of men pictured in the gallery and telling stories of what they and their teams contributed to the office. The stories are then retold to a new SG or lawyer in the office so he will know the tradition he's expected to uphold.

By most accounts, John W. Davis, who was SG from 1913 through 1918, was one of the truly distinguished Solicitors. He was then appointed Ambassador to Great Britain (in 1918), and ran for President (in 1924), but while he was SG he made the job more prestigious than the Attorney General's. As soon as Davis began his first argument before the Supreme Court as Solicitor General, Chief Justice Edward White sighed in relief: the government's brief was in good hands. As SG, Davis often took long walks with the Chief Justice, who used the chance to remind Davis about the Court's reliance on him. White generally did not say much about himself, but one day he stopped, planted his feet, and said, "You know, Mr. Davis, I'm not an educated man. Everything I get I've got to get through my ears. If you say that something happened in 1898, and the next time you say it happened in 1888, why Sir, it's just as if you'd stuck a knife in me!"

Thomas Thacher, SG from 1930 through 1933, perfected a technique that became an insider's signal of the Solicitor's views. Thacher had given up one judgeship to take the job, and subsequently filled another judgeship, and, perhaps because of his judicial temperament, he was reluctant to sign briefs whose legal validity he doubted; but he was also unwilling, on the other hand, to withhold from the Supreme Court arguments he could not fully discredit. In close cases, he decided, he would sign the government's brief, but tag on a disclaimer that became known among the SG's lawyers as "tying a tin can." "The foregoing is presented as the position of the Internal Revenue Service," the brief would clatter, letting the Justices know it was not the Solicitor General's view. Since the Court rarely subscribes to the arguments of a brief from any part of the government without the SG's sponsorship, the judgment that Thacher (and, later, others) expressed by tying a tin can was usually decisive.

One of the SG's more distinctive practices is known as "confessing error." If a private attorney wins a case he thinks he should have lost in a lower federal court, he is likely to accept his victory in diplomatic silence. But when the government wins on grounds that strike the Solicitor General as unjust, he may "confess error" and recommend that the Supreme Court overturn the flawed decision. Most confessions of error involve criminal convictions, and happen for a range of reasons: a jury was selected unfairly; a judge gave faulty instructions to the jury before asking its members to reach a verdict; there was scant evidence supporting the verdict.

Confessions of error please almost no one but the SG and the defendant, who goes free. The government lawyers who have tried the case feel betrayed. The judge whose decision the SG wants overturned thinks the rug has been pulled out from under him by a double-dealing government. Judge Learned Hand sometimes complained, "It's bad enough to have the Supreme Court reverse you, but I will be damned if I will be reversed by some Solicitor General." Some current members of the Supreme Court—Chief Justice Rehnquist and Justice Byron White, in particular—clearly dislike the practice, and browbeat the SG when he steps up to confess. Rehnquist has urged his colleagues that they should not "respond in Pavlovian fashion" when the SG confesses error, but should instead make their own ruling on the case.

But Archibald Cox, who was SG from 1961 to 1965 and who ranks with Davis and former Supreme Court Justice Robert Jackson as one of the three most respected Solicitors, has expressed a stalwart's faith in the practice of confessing error. "It tests the strength of our belief that the office has a peculiar responsibility to the Court," he told the Chicago

Bar Association in 1962, during his tenure as Solicitor. "It affects the way all our other cases are presented. If we are willing to take a somewhat disinterested and wholly candid position even when it means surrendering a victory, then all our other cases will be presented with a greater degree of restraint, with a greater degree of candor, and with a longer view, perhaps, than otherwise." The view expressed by Cox was originally endorsed in 1942 by the Supreme Court, in an opinion that declared, "The public trust reposed in the law enforcement officers of the Government requires that they be quick to confess error when, in their opinion, a miscarriage of justice may result from their remaining silent."

The best-known instance of a Solicitor General acting with candor and disinterest, to use Cox's terms, occurred in 1955, when Senator Joseph McCarthy was just past his heyday and the influence of McCarthyism was still heavy. Someone accused John Peters, a physician, of disloyalty to the United States and membership in the Communist Party. Peters was a senior professor of medicine at Yale University, and had advised the Surgeon General for years as a consultant. The government found Peters innocent of the charges in eight separate hearings held over four years, but he was eventually judged unfit for government service by an agency known as the Loyalty Review Board. The board relied on confidential informers and would not let Peters know the identities of, or cross-examine, these witnesses. He claimed he had a constitutional right to confront them and to rebut the charges they made against him. At every stage of the board's hearings against him, the only evidence publicly introduced was favorable testimony from an ex-president of Yale, a distinguished federal judge, and others in the doctor's corner. The case against him was based on secret testimony—as the chairman of the review board put it, on "evidence given by confidential informants not disclosed" to Peters.

The Solicitor General was Simon Sobeloff, who held the post from 1954 to 1956. When Peters appealed, Sobeloff concluded that it would do no one any good for the Justice Department to oppose him in the Supreme Court. With the encouragement of Attorney General Herbert Brownell, Jr., the SG set out narrow grounds for siding with the doctor. As Sobeloff indicated, the case had "far-reaching importance." It was bad for Peters to be kept in the dark about his accusers, but it was worse that the members of the Loyalty Review Board, acting as judges, were also ignorant about the identities and, therefore, the reliability of some of the informants. The SG called this "well-nigh indefensible," and concluded. "The President recently said in his State of the Union Message: 'We shall continue to ferret out and to destroy communist subversion. We shall, in the process, carefully preserve our traditions and the basic rights of every American citizen.' Now is the time, and this case the appropriate occasion, I believe, for showing the country that the Administration is as firmly pledged to the second sentence as the first."

Brownell asked other senior officials at the Justice Department to consider Sobeloff's argument. FBI Director J. Edgar Hoover strongly disapproved, and Brownell rejected the Solicitor General's proposal. Sobeloff decided his only option was to withhold the SG's backing from the government's case. He refused to sign the government's brief or to argue its merits before the Supreme Court, and another Justice Department official took over the case. The Court ruled against the government and for Peters, though the Justices did not address the major constitutional question.

Outside the Court's rarefied circle, the idea of refusing to represent the government may sound like the gesture of a prima donna. If you do not like what the government stands for, why not quit? The answer lies in the SG's responsibility to the Court as well as the Executive, and, because of that, Sobeloff's decision set a standard of integrity for SGs to come. It also cost him considerably. Prior to Sobeloff's taking his stand, he had been promised a seat on the Court of Appeals for the District of Columbia, perhaps as a step to the Supreme Court. ("Every time Sobeloff comes to see me," said Justice Felix Frankfurter, "I feel as if he's taking my temperature.") Not long afterward, a seat on the appeals court came open, but Sobeloff was passed over in favor of the man who had taken on the Peters case for the government—Warren Burger. Burger made his name as a conservative foil to the liberal majority of the D.C. Circuit, and later was appointed Chief Justice of the United States. Sobeloff eventually filled a seat on the federal Court of Appeals in Maryland.

Had Sobeloff gone on to the Supreme Court, he would have been one of a handful of SGs who have subsequently won such appointment. They include William Howard Taft, Stanley Reed, Robert Jackson, and Thurgood Marshall. . . . With such other distinguished figures as Archibald Cox, the first Watergate Special Prosecutor, the SGs-turned-Justices lead a pantheon of highly respected lawyers who have served in the SG's office and gone on to positions of wide esteem in the law. Many of the more prominent former SGs may have become judges in part because the SG's office itself has a judicial cast. A young law professor who hopes to work there said, "It's the only spot, besides a judgeship, where your job is to figure out what you think is the right answer for the law and then to present your argument to the highest court in the land."

The post itself gets a lot of deference from members of the bar, whatever their station. In 1940, Frank Murphy, an experienced and vain politician then freshly appointed to the Supreme Court, asked a clerk if any member of that bench had ever held as many important public offices as Murphy himself. "Well, there was Taft," the clerk answered. "He was Solicitor General, he was a Circuit Court judge, he was president of the Philippines Commission, he was Secretary of War, he was President of the United States, and, of course, he was Chief Justice." Crestfallen, the new Justice asked, "He was Solicitor General, too?"

· · ·

[In a later chapter, called "Meese's Law," Caplan criticizes the view of Attorney General Meese in the Reagan Administration that "the

Executive Branch's judgments about the law [were] equal" to those of the Court, and links this view to what he regards as departures by the Solicitor General's office, especially under Charles Fried, from the "tenth Justice" model:]

... There was no need for the Solicitor to defer to the Court if the Court's rulings did not establish what the law was anymore than did the judgment of the Executive Branch, and the SG might then just as well carry to the Justices the politics of the Administration even where they conflicted with the law as previously expounded by the Court. In the abortion case, Acting Solicitor General Charles Fried served notice that this was what he intended to do [by urging the Court to overrule *Roe* and other abortion related decisions].

Cornelia T.L. Pillard,[63] *The Unfulfilled Promise of the Constitution in Executive Hands*, 103 Mich. L. Rev. 676 (2005)

... Although Supreme Court litigation is his most visible task, the Solicitor General also has responsibility for supervision of all federal government litigation in lower appellate courts as well. The SG is appointed by the president with the advice and consent of the Senate, and is subject to removal by the president. The SG is the only federal official who is required to be "learned in the law"; when the SG job was established, the prior statutory requirement that the Attorney General have that qualification was dropped. That change captures a distinction still operative today between the legal role of the SG and the political, policymaking, and managerial role of the Attorney General.

1. DUTIES

The SG's office conducts all Supreme Court litigation on the federal government's behalf. The SG's Supreme Court work breaks down into several categories: The merits work includes deciding which cases are worthy of a government petition for certiorari, preparing the petitions, and, once the Court grants the petitions, briefing and arguing the cases on the merits. In addition, the SG's office prepares hundreds of briefs in opposition to petitions for certiorari filed against the government. The SG also selects those Supreme Court cases in which federal amicus participation is warranted, frames the government's positions, prepares the amicus briefs, and often participates as amicus in oral arguments in the Court. Finally, he responds to what are referred to within the Office

---

63. In the biographical footnote to this article, Pillard was described as "Associate Professor of Law, Georgetown University Law Center; Assistant to the United States Solicitor General, 1994–97; Deputy Assistant Attorney General for the Office of Legal Counsel, U.S. Department of Justice, 1998–2000." She is now a Professor of Law at Georgetown University Law Center.

as "invitations," or CVSGs (Calls for the Views of the Solicitor General), whereby the Court, usually at the petition stage, asks the SG for his views on whether it should grant a writ of certiorari. The SG typically appears in approximately two-thirds of the cases the Supreme Court decides on the merits.

The SG oversees lower-court cases as well. He has responsibility for authorizing all appeals or suggestions for rehearing en banc to intermediate appellate courts that any part of the federal government might want to take from an adverse decision. One recent SG reported that he acted on an average of approximately three such requests per day, year-round. The SG also decides whether the government should intervene in an existing litigation in which a federal statute has been challenged. In any pending case in which the United States is not already a party, the federal courts are obligated to inform the Attorney General whenever a question is raised as to the constitutionality of any federal statute. The United States then has a statutory right, exercisable by the SG, to intervene as a party to participate in the resolution of the question.

2. Role Separation

The SG and his office operate with something of the isolation, formality, and regularity of judicial chambers, keeping a distance from the president and Attorney General, agency clients and counsel, and even other lawyers within the Justice Department. In its insulation, and in its emphasis on legal analysis as distinct from policy or politics, the SG's Office somewhat mimics within the executive branch certain attributes of the Article III courts.

As a formal matter, the SG is "subject to the general supervision and direction" of the Attorney General. In practice, however, the SG formulates legal positions on his own, without input from the Attorney General or the president, and with rare exceptions, his superiors do not second-guess the SG's decisions. The Attorney General customarily argues a Supreme Court case during his or her tenure, but that tradition is designed not to exert supervisory authority over the SG, but to give the Attorney General the opportunity of a Supreme Court appearance.

The SG is assisted by a small legal and administrative staff operating within a relatively flat office hierarchy. Only two of the office's lawyers—the SG and one of his four Deputies—are political appointees; all of the others, including the three other Deputies and all of the Assistants to the SG, who research and draft the office's briefs, are "career" employees with civil-service protection. The office's functional separation from policymaking is further shown by the pattern of hiring lawyers for their general skill at legal analysis and appellate advocacy, rather than for any particular area of substantive expertise. Consistent with that pattern, SGs routinely hire lawyers from the Justice Department's appellate divisions, but rarely hire from client agencies.

The work flow in the SG's Office typically follows a bottom-up path that reflects an assumption that skilled, dispassionate legal analysis by career lawyers will unearth constitutional issues relevant to the litigating position proposed by an agency or a component of the Justice Department. The SG and his Deputies assign each matter to an Assistant who completes the research and drafting. Sometimes the assigning Deputy will discuss the merits of a new assignment briefly with the Assistant, but more often the Deputy has no advance conversation with the Assistant. The Assistant typically learns of the assignment once it is deposited in his or her in-box by an office courier, and the Assistant independently develops a draft. Thus, the SG's Office's work is not a collaborative political-legal enterprise, promoting "all-things-considered" judgments, but is quite formally doctrinal. Only occasionally do executive agency officials—i.e. those who are responsible for executive branch policy decisions—even meet with the Solicitor General or his staff. Those patterns reflect the office's focus on legal, rather than policy-oriented or political, analysis.

3. CLIENT-CHECKING

The SG is not merely a mouthpiece for his federal clients. Although he seeks to advocate (or authorize other government lawyers to advocate) the positions and interests of the client entities, lawyers in the SG's Office critically evaluate the input they get from the government's policymaking agencies. Departments and agencies seek the SG's approval for hundreds of petitions each year, but he typically authorizes less than ten to twenty percent of them. He also turns down a sizeable fraction of requests for authorization to appeal, and the overwhelming majority of requests for authorization to seek rehearing en banc.

The SG often declines to make particular arguments in briefing and may even confess error, abandoning the government's victory in a lower court. If the SG's own analysis disagrees with the judgment of the lower court that sustained the government's position, he can choose not to defend the favorable decision against the opposing party's appeal or effort to obtain Supreme Court review. Giving up a victory already in hand is virtually unheard of in the private bar, but it is an established practice by the SG, occurring on average two to three times per year.

Each of these ways through which the SG checks client initiatives—rejecting requests to appeal or petition, declining to make certain proposed arguments in briefs to the courts, and even confessing error—might be thought to illustrate the law's capacity to constrain politics within the executive branch. . . .

Rebecca Mae Salokar, *The Solicitor General: The Politics of Law* (1992)[64]

. . . [The SG's] responsibilities are accomplished not only by drawing on the expertise of the staff within the solicitor general's office but

---

64. Associate Professor of Political Science, Florida International University.

through close cooperation with the various staff attorneys assigned to the other divisions of the Department of Justice (for instance, Civil, Civil Rights or Antitrust Divisions), the senior counsels of governmental departments (Labor, Transportation, et cetera) and with the lawyers for independent agencies (such as the National Labor Relations Board, Interstate Commerce Commission, or Federal Trade Commission). Because these other agencies have been working on the cases since the trial stage, they often provide the solicitor general with a thorough history of the cases, as well as insight on the contested legal issues. As Solicitor General Charles Fried noted in an oversight hearing before the House of Representatives, "We do not sit on the fifth floor of the Department of Justice, scan the legal universe, and then decide what will happen. Rather, they, divisions and departments of Government with programmatic responsibilities come to us with recommendations, which we approve, and then proceed, in the Supreme Court, to brief and argue for them." In essence, the Office of the Solicitor General is not insulated from other areas of government in accomplishing its work. Rather, it is subject to a range of influences from the executive branch, Congress, and even the Supreme Court, itself.

. . .

Agenda Success [On Certiorari] . . .

The most frequent form of government participation in certiorari cases was as respondent, responding to a suit brought by an aggrieved private litigant or state against the United States. The solicitor general responded to 38,412 certiorari cases during the 1959 to 1989 terms. . . .

. . .

As petitioner, . . . the solicitor general has a significant advantage over private litigants. As the attorney for the United States, the solicitor general has available a large pool of possible certiorari requests and selects only a small number of cases that will most likely meet the standards of the Court in granting review and, subsequently, result in a decision favoring the government. And even if the government is denied review, it is likely that cases raising similar issues will flow into the office at a later time providing other opportunities for Supreme Court review. Private litigants, on the other hand, are usually involved in only one case and do not enjoy the same selection of opportunities. A denial of certiorari by the Court generally means the end of the litigation for the private petitioner.

The advantage that the solicitor general enjoys in his capacity as a petitioner is clear. The solicitor general sought certiorari in 1,294 cases between 1959 and 1989, and was successful in obtaining the Court's review 69.78 percent of the time. Certiorari requests were granted in only 4.9 percent of the private litigation. Given such poor odds, it is no wonder that private litigants seek the government's support through an amicus brief.

The amicus curiae or "friend of the court" brief permits the government (and other litigants) to participate in a case in which the United States is not formally named as a party.... By filing an amicus brief, the solicitor general has the opportunity to present the government's views on a range of issues.... [T]he solicitor general is likely to address the potential impact a decision will have on federal law and federal agency operations and programs or simply provide additional information and legal considerations not contained in the litigants' documentation. Finally, the amicus brief has served as a vehicle to express the administration's policy positions and goals on issues that have historically been considered outside the scope of federal law.

· · ·

... When the government filed an amicus brief on behalf of the appellant or petitioner, the Court granted review in 87.6 percent of the cases....

... [However, of] the 484 cases in which the United States sided with the respondent or appellee, the private litigant had only a 60 percent chance of getting the most favorable outcome, a denial of review. [65] ...

· · ·

Success in Merit Decisions

... [T]he grant of a writ of certiorari by the Supreme Court to the request of the United States, is only a partial victory. The agreement by the Court to review a lower-court decision against the government is not a guarantee that the final outcome of the case will reverse the lower-court's decision....

· · ·

During the 1959 to 1989 terms, the Court decided 8,926 cases on the merits. The government participated either as a party to the suit or as an amicus in 4,329 (47.5 percent) of these cases....

The success that the solicitor general enjoys at the early stages of the Court's decision making continues in decisions on the merits. The government's position prevailed in 2,961 (67.6 percent) of the cases in which it participated....

· · ·

65. [Editors' note: The author suggests that government filing as amicus in opposing certiorari may be "bad" for respondents; she also notes that the government is sometimes asked by the Court to file as amicus, noting an earlier study (Steven Puro, "The Role of the Amicus Curiae in the United States Supreme Court: 1920–1966" (Ph.D. Dissertation, State University of New York at Buffalo, 1971)), which found that nearly half of the solicitor general's amicus filings resulted from a request from the Court. Consider the possibility that the government is likely to file an amicus in support of a respondent only in cases that are by their nature controversial and more likely to be granted, whether the government participates or not.]

THE DEFINITIVE "REPEAT PLAYER"

In a study of why certain litigants prevail in the courtroom over others, Marc Galanter recognized a distinction between "Repeat Players" and "One–Shotters." The Repeat Player enjoys a substantial measure of success over the less frequent litigant. He defines a Repeat Player as "a unit which has had and anticipates repeated litigation, which has low stakes in the outcome of any one case, and which has the resources to pursue its long-run interests."

Solicitors general are the definitive Repeat Players. They enjoy the numerous advantages of the Repeat Player including advance intelligence, access to specialists, a wide range of resources, expertise, opportunities to build informal relations with the Supreme Court, and a high degree of credibility before the Court. In addition, the government is more interested in the long-term development of the law and rules than in the immediate success of a particular case.

Institutional overload also favors the Repeat Player. According to Galanter, "Typically there are far more claims than there are institutional resources for full dress adjudication of each." The sheer number of cases on the Court's docket favors the solicitor general over the One–Shotter, the infrequent litigant who attempts to take her case before the Supreme Court. Lastly, Galanter has pointed out that the rules, "a body of authoritative normative learning," also favor Repeat Players since these litigants have "successfully articulated their operations to pre-existing rules."

· · ·

[On the SG's role in mediating between positions of different parts of the government:]

Rex Lee [SG from 1981–85] felt that he was more than a mediator; he felt he was acting as a judge in determining which position would be presented to the Court.

> When there was a conflict within government, as not infrequently happened, I would hold a hearing and hear the opposing points of view. And when I made the decision, that was the position that was taken by the federal government. And it usually meant that the opposite point of view simply would not be represented. It always sobered me because I realized that the decision I was making, unlike the circumstance in private practice, precluded one of my clients from presenting that client's point of view to the Supreme Court. It not only meant that I would not present it, it meant that no one would.

Lee hesitated to resolve these conflicts by allowing both points of view to be presented to the Court, a practice that has occurred in the past. But he did recognize that occasionally he would act as a mediator, attempting to resolve the issue so that all sides were content. One such case involved the three bank regulatory agencies and the Securities and Exchange

Commission (SEC). The compromise position presented by the government was ultimately accepted by the Court. Lee's successor, Charles Fried, also viewed his role in this light, serving as a broker between the agencies and divisions to negotiate a resolution to the impasse.

Cox [SG from 1961–65] was more adamant about his part in dispute resolution. "My view was that I would try to knock heads together and impose a unified position. I think there was only one instance in which I simply couldn't do it." That case was *St. Regis Paper Co. v. United States* [368 U.S. 208 (1961)]. The issue involved a conflict over an attempt by the Federal Trade Commission (FTC) to force a manufacturer to submit file copies of census reports as part of an antitrust investigation, reports that the government had promised would be kept confidential. With the Census Bureau, the Department of Commerce, and the Bureau of the Budget on one side of the case and the FTC and Antitrust Division on the opposite side, Cox prepared a brief that addressed both positions. In an effort to dissuade the Court from reaching a decision on the merits, Cox also argued that the matter was rendered moot by the submission of the requested reports in conjunction with the judicial investigation. He wanted, if possible, to avoid a decision against either side. At oral argument, he presented the standing issue and argued both sides. The Court was not convinced by Cox's effort to avoid the merits and acknowledged the dispute within the executive branch in its decision for the FTC and Antitrust Division.

. . .

Griswold's perspective [Griswold was SG 1967–73] on resolving agency conflicts suggests that he would attempt to get a consensus, but that, in the end, he would make his own decision. In one particular case that involved the rebroadcasting of television programs to remote locations, the Copyright Office of the Library of Congress, the Federal Communications Commission and the Antitrust Division of the Department of Justice each had their own position. "I found the problem far from easy to solve. I had a meeting with all of them together. Couldn't get any kind of agreement or hearing from any of them and finally decided to make my own decision. And my staff and I prepared a brief. . . . I've forgotten just how they [the Court] did decide it. But the Congress came along about four years later and passed a statute exactly that way."

. . .

The work with other areas of the executive branch becomes even more complicated when an independent regulatory agency seeks access to the Supreme Court. In the legislation establishing several of the regulatory agencies (particularly, the National Labor Relations Board [NLRB], the Securities and Exchange Commission [SEC], the Federal Trade Commission [FTC], Tennessee Valley Authority [TVA], and others), Congress specifically granted them the authority to litigate their own cases. Although the degree of this authority varies by agency and by the level of adjudication, Olson found that thirty-five agencies had been given this power by 1982. The question that has come up several times, but has generally been avoided, is whether or not the independent regulatory agencies have the right to take their own cases to the Supreme Court without the approval of the solicitor general.

Rather than address this potential conflict, the solicitor general traditionally has authorized the counsel of an independent agency to proceed with its own arguments. But this approval is only given when the agency counsel threatens to broach the controversy. "There was an occasion when a question came up with the SEC and where the SEC had been refused a number of times for filing petitions and decided at one point that they would then represent themselves and ask for authority from the solicitor general to do so. I don't know whether they needed it or not. In any event, they went ahead and they lost, huge losses, 9–0, 9–0, and I think that at some point along the line, they decided they better come back into the fold."

One former staff attorney suggested that the Court would probably refuse to hear a case that the solicitor general had not authorized. "At a minimum, if the petition were filed on behalf of a government agency without the solicitor general's name on it or authorization, it would immediately draw the conclusion that the solicitor general doesn't think much of this case."

. . .

In working with the agencies, the solicitor general also ensures that the legal positions the government takes are consistent over time. This is particularly difficult when there have been changes in administrations and in policies. Lee was confronted with such a case in 1982, *Utah Power and Light Company v. Federal Energy Regulatory Commission*. In the Federal Power Act of 1918, the Federal Energy Regulatory Commission (FERC) was permitted to favor publicly owned utilities over investor-owned companies when granting ownership licenses for hydroelectric dams. This policy had been followed through the Carter administration. With license renewals pending, private companies filed suit to block this preferential treatment. While the case was being litigated, however, the Reagan administration came into office. With new appointees to the FERC, the agency shifted its position on municipal preference and asked Lee to urge the Supreme Court to vacate the lower-court's decision. This lack of consistency was exactly what the solicitor general tried to avoid. Rather than filing a motion to vacate, Lee recommended that the Supreme Court remand the case to the court of appeals for further consideration. The Court denied certiorari, [463 U.S. 1230 (1983),] however, leaving the lower-court's decision intact.

In a second example of the solicitor general's efforts to maintain the consistency of the government's positions, the Court had invited the solicitor general to submit an amicus curiae brief. Solicitor General Bork and his staff took the issue to the State Department for their views: "When it [the State Department] finally did submit its views, they were contrary to statements that we had made on behalf of the State Department eight years earlier or some similar period of time. And we concluded, having advised the State Department eight years ago that the law should be 'x,' we couldn't turn around now just because there was a different legal advisor at the State Department who said that the law really should be 'y.' But that meant we had a tremendous conflict with the State Department which the solicitor general had to resolve and he resolved it in favor of what had been before." The case was *Alfred Dunhill of London, Inc. v. Republic of Cuba* [425 U.S. 682 (1976)]. The position taken by the government as amicus urged reversal and was argued by Antonin Scalia. The Court ruled in favor of the petitioner and the United States.

The relationship of the agencies, divisions, and departments with the Office of the Solicitor General is an important one. The examples provided give credence to the argument that the solicitor general is a critical actor in the policy decisions of the executive branch. . . .

. . .

TRANSITION CASES: A PROBLEM OF UNFINISHED BUSINESS?

. . . [A]dministrations differ on policy issues, priorities, and their ideological beliefs about the role of government; cases [pending before the Court when a new Administration takes office] can pose a dilemma for the newly elected president and appointed solicitor general.

. . .

. . . In my interviews and research, I came across only one instance in which an administration was so disgruntled by a position taken before the Court by the previous administration that it tried to force the solicitor general to reverse the government's position. Transitional cases are simply not a problem.

The pressures to resist changing the position of the United States and to argue the case as it was filed are directly tied to the belief that the solicitor general must maintain his reputation before the Court. A blatant reversal of position "would not but undermine the respect traditionally accorded the Department of Justice and the Office of the Solicitor General by the justices on the Court." As a former staff member explained,

> It is very, very difficult once a case has been filed in the Supreme Court involving the government, for the government to shift position because it kind of destroys its credibility with the Court. In other words, the factors that led the government to ask the Supreme Court to hear a case have not changed. If it turns out that there is a change in the administration and suddenly the new administration says, "Well, we don't think you should hear this case," you begin to wonder how correct the first one was. And then two years later when the new solicitor general says something, how accurate is that?

In short, any evidence of being a "wishy-washy" litigant can damage the reputation of the solicitor general and irritate the Court.

There are other reasons the government does not change its position when a new administration takes office. One has to do with timing. Because cases in which the government has filed a petition have usually been docketed, a new solicitor general would have to ask the Court to delay the oral arguments or even defer their decision and set the case for reargument in order to permit the new administration to file its views. "Such a move, however, would require lightning-fast coordination by the new and yet-to-be-coordinated team."

A second reason that transitional cases are not treated any different-ly than other cases is that, "Cases have a life of their own. There are too many people interested in succeeding." Deputy Solicitor General Law-rence Wallace explained that the solicitor general's office works closely with the career staff in the various divisions of the Department of Justice and the independent regulatory agencies. By the time the case gets to the solicitor general, the attorneys in these divisions and agencies as well as their "publics" have become careful watchdogs of the proceed-ings.

In my analysis of the Supreme Court decisions of cases in which the government was a participant, I isolated those cases that would have been filed by one administration and argued by another. I detected no differences in the success rates of the government in these transitional cases. In testing the hypothesis that an incoming administration might subtly try to "throw" the cases as a result of a disagreement with the former administration's positions, I found absolutely no evidence of such behavior. The cases that are inherited by an incoming administration are argued and briefed as diligently as the cases that are filed by the new administration.

There have been occasions in the past in which the government did switch sides during the judicial proceedings. However, this usually occurs during the trial stage or between the trial stage and the first appeal. . . .

· · ·

FRIEND OF THE COURT: THE GOVERNMENT AS AMICUS

Amicus participation is another facet of the solicitor general's work before the Supreme Court. . . . The Court's practice of inviting the government to express its views is of particular interest since the "invitation" limits the discretionary nature of the solicitor general's decisions.

. . . Unlike cases in which the government is a party, the outcome of an amicus case is less likely to have a direct impact on the executive branch. In some respects, amicus participation is a low-risk venture for the government. But more important, it allows the executive branch to further its political agenda before the Court.

· · ·

The solicitor general can also request argument time from the Court in order to present the government's views. In practice, the solicitor general makes this request only when his arguments are substantially different from those of the litigants or when his participation is specifically requested by a litigant who is willing to forego a portion of its assigned time. In the mid–1980s, the solicitor general was denied permission by the Court to argue in several cases. Rumors around the Court were that the denials were the justices' way of telling the solicitor general that he had become "too political." "There was a time when there were rumors from the Court, from the clerks, that the Court had much less confidence in whatever the solicitor general might have to say about the agenda cases than everybody had thought was the case in prior years." There is no way to substantiate the story. However, it had an impact on the staff of the Solicitor General's Office. The message that was received was, "You can file a brief because the rules say that you don't need anybody's permission, so we've got your brief, but we really don't need to hear from you."

. . .

Since the outcomes of cases in which the government files an amicus brief may have little effect on the overall operation of government, the solicitor general feels more comfortable in advancing positions that are not likely to prevail on the merits. In *Hobbie v. Unemployment Appeals Commission of Florida,* [480 U.S. 136 (1987),] then-Solicitor General Fried explained that he knew it was unlikely that the government's position would be accepted. "But it was a position which deserved to be put in front of the Court, deserved to be attended to and responded to, and there it was. Sometimes, even though you didn't think you were going to win, nevertheless, you did want to have a particular position put before the Court." . . . Fried further explained that even though the government loses some of these cases, the arguments of the solicitor general can still be useful to the Court.

. . .

Amicus cases provide an opportunity to study solicitors general in cases where their decisions to participate are, perhaps, the least constrained. . . .

[The author explains that research by Puro in 1968 identified three considerations influencing SG amicus filings: whether the issue was of significant concern to the federal government or the public, whether the case was a good one to present the issue, and whether the SG's participation would be helpful to the Court.] Although these criteria are still used, they have been expanded to encompass the more "politicized" use of the amicus brief. As Philip Kurland noted . . . the intervention by a third party is no longer for the purposes of enlightening the Court on issues of the law, but to show support in a very public way for a specific litigant. This change is not limited to the government's use of the tactic but can be seen in virtually all amicus submissions.

. . .

Solicitors general consider the fact situation of a case when deciding whether or not to submit an amicus brief. During Fried's tenure, a minority set-aside suit from Dade County, Florida reached the Supreme Court, and the justices asked for the solicitor general's input on the case. In his brief, Fried pointed out that a better case, *City of Richmond v. J.A. Croson Co.*, [488 U.S. 469 (1989),][66] was on its way to the Court. The *Croson* suit dealt with less complicated issues and would provide the justices with a more direct fact situation than the case from Dade County.

. . . [On] whether or not the government would make any contribution to the case by filing an amicus brief[,] . . . former staff members . . . recalled instances in which the decision not to file was based on the fact that there were a large number of amicus briefs submitted from other organizations and interest groups. . . .

In discussing amicus participation, Lee suggests that there are two categories of cases eligible for briefs. The first category includes the cases that involve the federal interest. The second category are those cases, "which fall right at the core of the current administration's broader agenda. For me [Lee] these included cases involving obscenity, the religion clauses, and abortion." These latter cases have been dubbed the "agenda" cases and are evidence for those who point to the "politicization" of the office.

Lee pulled no punches in explaining his amicus participation in these types of cases. "One of the purposes of the solicitor general is to represent his client, the president of the United States. One of the ways to implement the president's policies is through positions taken in court. When I have that opportunity, I'm going to take it." Lee's desire to carry out the president's agenda was tempered, however, by his belief that "it is a mistake to file in too many. . . . while I think it is proper to use the office for the purpose of making my contribution to the President's broader agenda, a wholesale departure from the role whose performance has led to the special status that the solicitor general enjoys would unduly impair that status itself. In the process, the ability of the solicitor general to serve any of the President's objectives would suffer."

Former assistant Kathryn Oberly also noted the problem of agenda cases. "The question is whether you lose some of that credibility by filing briefs in cases where it is clear to everybody, including the Court, that the only interest is political, political in the sense that this is this administration's philosophy." . . .

66. [Editors' Note: The issue was the constitutionality of affirmative action plans in government contracting. In *Croson*, the Court struck down the City of Richmond's affirmative action plan for government contracting.]

The term, "agenda" case, was coined during the Reagan administration to refer to the cases in which Lee and Fried filed amicus briefs for the purpose of advancing the president's policies through the Court. Prior to the Reagan administration, the government had remained out of abortion cases.... But abortion was a key issue for the administration and both Lee and Fried argued to weaken and, ultimately, to reverse the standards established in *Roe v. Wade.*

. . .

... For Cox [SG during the 1960s], agenda cases involved civil rights and reapportionment. He did not attract as much attention as Reagan's solicitors general since Cox's positions were a logical progression of the Warren Court's development of the law. Lee and Fried, however, brought a new agenda to the Court that urged wholesale reversal in established areas of the law, a request that was granted with increased frequency as Reagan exercised his opportunities to change the Court's membership. Not so long ago, two other solicitors general, Stanley Reed (1935–1938) and Robert H. Jackson (1938–1940), found themselves trying to "unsettle" the law in their pursuit of the New Deal agenda before the Supreme Court. In sum, agenda cases have always been a part of the solicitor general's work since he is responsible for defending the client's legal interests before the Court.

... Lee's concern as solicitor general was that he not become involved in so many cases that the Court should begin to expect the government's views and, as a result, give them less weight. "It is almost as though I had a certain number of chips that I could play. Where was the best place to play them?" Lee also believed that the Court's tolerance of these agenda cases may be limited. "There's an inverse relationship between the effectiveness of that kind of advocacy and the frequency with which you use it." The decision to file an amicus brief in an agenda case was carefully considered in light of the credibility of the office and the potential gains that may result from the case.

. . .

The Order to Befriend

The discretion that the solicitor general enjoys in selecting the cases for amicus participation is greatly reduced when the Supreme Court invites the government to present its views in a case that the solicitor general had no intention of entering. This invitation, as it is called, is viewed by the office as an order, and it is an order that all solicitors general have tacitly acknowledged....

. . .

In my discussions with former staff members and solicitors general, I sensed that there were mixed feelings about the amicus invitations. On the one hand, the staff view the Court's request as an acknowledgment of their expertise. However, others suggested that the Court would often turn to the government "to act as extra law clerks for the Court, because we couldn't figure out what they thought our interest, meaning the federal interest, was [in the case]..."

. . .

Fried acknowledged that the amicus invitations can make for a very awkward situation: "They are often cases in which you would really rather not say what you think. The best example of all is the *Beck* case, *Communications Workers of America v. Beck,* [487 U.S. 735 (1988)]. That was a Court request where the position we had to take, which supported the union, was a position that the administration was very uncomfortable with as a matter of policy. I didn't like it and I didn't feel very enthusiastic about helping it out. Had it not been for a Court request, we would have stayed out of it."

. . .

In my study of the 1959 to 1986 Court terms, the government was invited to participate as an amicus in 440 cases. The trend toward increased use of the amicus brief is reflected in the number of invitations issued to the solicitor general.... In short, the Court has quadrupled its reliance on the solicitor general's expertise.

. . .

... My research, which incorporates all amicus activity on the merits, confirms that the government does win nearly 60 percent of the time when it has been invited.

. . .

―――――――――

Questions and Comments

1. Note two different models of the Solicitor General that have emerged from the readings thus far: the SG as a "tenth justice," with special obligations of impartial argument about the law, and the SG as an advocate for the current Administration's constitutional agenda. Yet note, too, the idea that restraint in "agenda" advancement is informed by a perception that too frequent resort to agenda advancement would deprive the office of the credibility on the law that it has with the Court. Does this suggest that both models co-exist?

2. Recall that in *Casey,* the plurality opinion began by stating:

Liberty finds no refuge in a jurisprudence of doubt. Yet 19 years after our holding that the Constitution protects a woman's right to terminate her pregnancy in its early stages, Roe v. Wade, 410 U.S. 113 (1973), that definition of liberty is still questioned. Joining the respondents as *amicus curiae*, the United States, as it has done in five other cases in the last decade, again asks us to overrule *Roe*. See Brief for Respondents 104–117; Brief for United States as *Amicus Curiae* 8.

Planned Parenthood of Southeastern Pennsylvania v. Casey, 505 U.S 833, 843 (1992). Recall former Solicitor General Rex Lee's comments that it is a mistake to file in too many "agenda" cases. Does this passage suggest that the three Justices in the plurality were out of patience with the SG?

3. As Professor Salokar's book makes clear, the duties of the SG are wide-ranging. The SG's gate-keeping function—selecting which of the many appeals to the Supreme Court federal departments and agencies want to take—is a powerful one. See 28 U.S.C. §§ 518(a), 519. Even among the independent agencies, only a few are authorized to represent themselves in the Supreme Court, though on infrequent occasions multiple views from parts of the U.S. government may be presented to the Court. See Neal Devins, *Unitariness and Independence: Solicitor General Control over Independent Agency Litigation*, 82 Calif. L. Rev. 255 (1994); cf. FEC v. NRA Political Victory Fund, 513 U.S. 88 (1994) (construing independent litigating authority of the FEC not to extend to authority independently to seek review in Supreme Court in certain civil enforcement actions). Does the SG's ability to pick and choose which cases to seek review of improve the office's capacity to advocate effectively before the Court? If so, how?

b. Solicitors Generals and Their Presidents

The relationships between Solicitors General, Attorneys General and their Presidents are complex, notwithstanding that both Attorneys General and Solicitors General are appointed by the President (subject to Senate confirmation) and serve at the pleasure of the President.[67] Some of these complexities are explored below.

Note on Bakke and the Office of Legal Counsel Memorandum Opinion on the Role of the Solicitor General:

In 1977, during the administration of President Carter, the issue of the constitutionality of affirmative action in higher education was before the Supreme Court in Regents of the University of California v. Bakke, 438 U.S. 265 (1978). The process of deciding on the position to be taken by the Solicitor General on behalf of the United States as amicus curiae was hotly contested within the executive branch, with some career lawyers arguing that the United States should support Bakke's challenge to the state's affirmative action plan while others in the administration, including Joseph Califano, then Secretary of the Department of Health, Education and Welfare,[68] argued in favor of the constitutionality of such plans. Cabinet level officers, as well as the Attorney General and the President of the United States, were involved in reviewing drafts.

As Lincoln Caplan describes it, the case "came to stand in some lawyers' minds for the proposition that, in the final analysis, it is proper for the

---

67. See 28 U.S.C. §§ 503, 505. For discussion of the "Saturday Night Massacre," in which the Attorney General and the Deputy Attorney General resigned rather than carry out a presidential order to dismiss a Special Prosecutor investigating White House wrongdoing, an order then carried

out by Solicitor General Robert Bork, see Chapter Four, Section C(2), above.

68. This department was later split into two: the Department of Education and the Department of Health and Human Services.

President and his aides to intervene at will in the affairs of the SG and to dictate the government's legal positions in the Supreme Court. In fact, the case helped persuade Griffin Bell, who was the first Attorney General of the Carter administration, of the opposite." Caplan, *The Tenth Justice, supra,* at 40. Following the filing of the government's amicus brief (but before the case was decided), the following opinion was issued in what some saw as an attempt to reclaim the independence of the Solicitor General's office from the kinds of interventions that occurred during the government-wide process of deciding the position to be taken in the *Bakke* amicus brief.

Memorandum Opinion for the Attorney General, Role of the Solicitor General, 1 Op. Off. Leg. Counsel 228 (1977)*

The purpose of this memorandum opinion is to discuss (1) the institutional relationship between the Attorney General and the Solicitor General, and (2) the role that each should play in formulating and presenting the Government's position in litigation before the Supreme Court.

I.

The Judiciary Act of 1789 created the Office of the Attorney General and provided that the Attorney General would prosecute and conduct all suits in the Supreme Court in which the United States was "concerned." Act of September 24, 1789, ch. XX, § 35, 1 Stat. 73. The Office of the Solicitor General was created in 1870. Act of June 22, 1870, ch. CL, § 2, 16 Stat. 162. The statute provided that there should be in the Department of Justice "an officer learned in the law, to assist the Attorney General in the performance of his duties, to be called the Solicitor General ...."; and it provided further that the Attorney General could direct the Solicitor General to argue any case in which the Government had an interest. *See* Fahy, "The Office of the Solicitor General," 28 A.B.A.J. 20 (1942).

The statute was enacted at the behest of Attorney General Henry Stanbery. Mr. Stanbery had argued that his work load was great and that he needed assistance in preparing opinions and arguing cases before the Supreme Court. He suggested that a new office be created for the purpose of discharging these functions. Congress, perceiving that the measure would make it possible to discontinue the expensive practice of retaining special counsel to represent the Government in cases argued before the Supreme Court, acceded to his request. *Id.*

In 1878 the language of the statute was partially revised. The language of the revision has survived to the present day. The modern statute, codified at 28 U.S.C. § 518, provides in pertinent part:

* [Editors' Note: The Office of Legal Counsel, in the U.S. Department of Justice, gives legal advice to executive branch offices.]

(a) Except when the Attorney General in a particular case directs otherwise, the Attorney General and the Solicitor General shall conduct and argue suits and appeals in the Supreme Court and suits in the Court of Claims in which the United States is interested.

(b) When the Attorney General considers it in the interests of the United States, he may personally conduct and argue any case in a court of the United States in which the United States is interested, or he may direct the Solicitor General or any officer of the Department of Justice to do so.

The Department's own regulations provide that the Solicitor General performs his duties "subject to the general supervision and direction" of the Attorney General. 28 CFR § 0.20. The same language is used to describe the relationship between the Attorney General and the offices that report directly to him, such as the Office of Legal Counsel. The Assistant Attorneys General in charge of the various divisions perform their duties subject to the Attorney General's supervision, but under the direction of the Associate or Deputy Attorney General. From a legal standpoint, the relationship between the Attorney General and the Solicitor General would thus appear to be substantially the same as that existing between the Attorney General and the Assistant Attorneys General.

II

We think it plain from the language and history of the relevant statutes that the Office of the Solicitor General was not created for the purpose of relieving the Attorney General of the responsibility for formulating or presenting the Government's case in litigation before the Supreme Court. Congress simply intended to provide the Attorney General with a learned helper who would perform these functions at the Attorney General's direction. We note in passing that at least one Solicitor General has adopted this view publicly. *See, Fahy, supra,* at 21. We know of no public utterance by a Solicitor General to the contrary. *See, generally,* Cox, "The Government in the Supreme Court," 44 Chi.B.Record 221 (1963); Sobeloff, "The Law Business of the United States," 34 Ore. L. Rev. 145 (1955); Stern, "Inconsistency in Government Litigation," 64 Harv. L. Rev. 759 (1951). The short of the matter is that under law the Attorney General has the power and the right to "conduct and argue" the Government's case in any court of the United States. 28 U.S.C. § 518(b).

III

Traditionally, however, the Attorney General has given the Solicitor General the primary responsibility for presenting the Government's views to the Supreme Court, and in the discharge of that function the Solicitor General has enjoyed a marked degree of independence. Indeed, his independence has been so great that one Solicitor General, Francis Biddle, was led to remark:

He [the Solicitor General] determines what cases to appeal, and the client has no say in the matter, he does what his lawyer tells him, the lawyer stands in his client's shoes, for the client is but an abstraction. He is responsible neither to the man who appointed him nor to his immediate superior in the hierarchy of administration. The total responsibility is his, and his guide is only the ethic of his law profession framed in the ambience of his experience and judgment. (F. Biddle, In Brief Authority 97 (1962).)

Because the question of the "independence" of the Solicitor General has a direct and important bearing upon the general question to which this memorandum is addressed, we shall consider it in some detail.

Mr. Biddle's statement suggests that the Solicitor General has enjoyed two kinds of independence. First, he has enjoyed independence within the Department of Justice. It is he, of all the officers in the Department, who has been given the task of deciding what the Government's position should be in cases presented to the Supreme Court. The views of subordinate officers within the divisions of the Department are not binding upon him, and the Attorney General has made it a practice not to interfere. With respect to his relation to the Attorney General, we feel constrained to add, however, at the risk of repetition, that the Solicitor General's independent role has resulted from a convenient and necessary division of labor, not from a separation of powers required by law. Moreover, Francis Biddle may have overstated the case to some degree. Under the relevant statutes, as noted, the Attorney General retains the right to assume the Solicitor General's function himself, if he conceives it to be in the public interest to do so.

Secondly, the Solicitor General has enjoyed independence within the executive branch as a whole. He is not bound by the views of his "clients." He may confess error when he believes they are in error. He may rewrite their briefs. He may refuse to approve their requests to petition the Court for writs of *certiorari*. He may oppose (in whole or in part) the arguments that they may present to the Court in those instances where they have independent litigating authority.

The reasons for this independence are, for the most part, familiar:

First, it has been thought to be desirable, generally, for the Government to adopt a single, coherent position with respect to legal questions that are presented to the Supreme Court. Because it is not uncommon for there to be conflicting views among the various offices and agencies within the executive branch, the Solicitor General, having the responsibility for presenting the views of the Government to the Court, must have power to reconcile differences among his clients, to accept the views of some and to reject others, and, in proper cases, to formulate views of his own.

Second, as an officer of the Court and as an officer of Government, the Solicitor General has a special duty to protect the Court in the discharge of its constitutional function. He protects the Court's docket by screening the Government's cases and relieving the Court of the burden of reviewing unmeritorious claims. He prepares accurate and balanced summaries of the records in the cases that are presented for review; and within the limits of proper advocacy, he provides the Court with an accurate and expert statement of the legal principles that bear upon the questions to be decided.

Third, as an officer who plays an important role in the development of the law, he has a duty to protect the law from disorderly growth. He is called upon to decide questions of "ripeness" in the most general sense: on a case-by-case basis he must determine whether *this* is the appropriate time for presenting *this* issue to the Supreme Court on *this* record. *See* Cox, *supra,* at 226. In order to discharge that function, he must have, among other things, the power to refuse requests for petitions for *certiorari* and the power to decline to present the Government's views, as *amicus,* in cases in which the Government might otherwise have an interest.

Finally, and most importantly, the Solicitor General has assumed an independent status because of the prevalent belief that such independence is necessary to prevent narrow or improper considerations (political or otherwise) from intruding upon the presentation of the Government's case in the Nation's highest Court. It was a Solicitor General, Frederick W. Lehmann, who wrote that "the United States wins its point whenever justice is done its citizens in the courts"; and the burden of history is that justice is done most often when the law is administered with an independent and impartial hand. The Nation values the Solicitor General's independence for the same reason that it values an independent judiciary. The Solicitor General has been permitted his independence largely because of the belief, as Mr. Biddle put it, that "the ethic of his law profession framed in the ambience of his judgment and experience" should be his only guide.

IV

In what circumstances should the Attorney General exercise his right to "conduct" litigation before the Supreme Court? To the extent that the Solicitor General's traditional role reflects a simple division of labor within the Department, it is plain that the Attorney General may exercise his prerogative whenever it is administratively convenient for him to do so. The real question is to what extent he can intervene, in individual cases, without doing violence to the important principles or functions that have justified the Solicitor General's independence within the Government at large.

We have identified four such principles or functions: the Solicitor General must coordinate conflicting views within the executive branch; he must protect the Court by presenting meritorious claims in a straightforward and professional manner and by screening out unmeritorious ones; he must assist in the orderly development of decisional law; and he must "do justice"—that is, he must discharge his office in accordance with law and ensure that improper concerns do not influence the presentation of the Government's case in the Supreme Court.

In our opinion, there is no institutional reason why the Attorney General could not, in individual cases, discharge all four of these functions as well as the Solicitor General. However, in practice the Attorney General could never be sure that he was exercising the independent judgment essential to the proper performance of those functions if he acted alone without the advice of an independent legal adviser, *i.e.,* the Solicitor General.

The Attorney General is responsible for the objective and evenhanded administration of justice independent of political considerations or pressures. However, he is also a member of the President's Cabinet and responsible for advising the President on many of the most important policy decisions that are made in the executive branch. He is necessarily exposed repeatedly to nonlegal arguments and opinions from other Cabinet members. His is the difficult task of separating the different factors that might properly be considered in his role as a policy adviser from those relevant to his duties as the chief legal officer of the Government.

The Constitution requires the President, and thus the Attorney General, to execute the laws faithfully. It requires them to follow the law, even if that course conflicts with policy. For this reason alone, in our view, the tradition of the "independent" Solicitor General is a wise tradition. It has arisen because it serves a useful constitutional purpose. Very simply, an independent Solicitor General assists the President and the Attorney General in the discharge of their constitutional duty: concerned as they are with matters of policy, they are well served by a subordinate officer who is permitted to exercise independent and expert legal judgment essentially free from extensive involvement in policy matters that might, on occasion, cloud a clear vision of what the law requires. While it is doubtful whether either the President or the Attorney General could "delegate" to the Solicitor General the ultimate responsibility for determining the Government's position on questions of law presented to the Supreme Court, as a matter of practice, in the discharge of their offices, they can allow themselves the benefit of his independent judgment, and they can permit his judgment to be dispositive in the normal course.

The dual nature of the Attorney General's role as a policy and legal adviser to the President strengthens, in our view, the necessity for an independent Solicitor General. To the extent the Solicitor General can be shielded from political and policy pressures—without being unaware of their existence—his ability to serve the Attorney General, and the President, as "an officer learned in the law" is accordingly enhanced. For this reason we believe the Solicitor General should not be subjected to undue influence from executive branch officials outside the Department of Justice. The Solicitor General should not be viewed as having final, essentially unreviewable authority in controversial cases, because such a role would inevitably subject him to those policy pressures that can obscure legal insights. The Attorney General, we believe, reinforces the independence of the Solicitor General by allowing himself to act as the final legal authority in those small number of cases with highly controversial policy ramifications. As such, the Attorney General and not the Solicitor General will be the focus of policy pressures from both within and outside the executive branch.

We do not believe that the Attorney General's power to direct the prosecution of cases in the Supreme Court should never be exercised, but we do believe that the tradition of the independent Solicitor General is one that should be preserved. We think that the Attorney General can participate in the formulation of the Government's position before the Court in certain circumstances without doing violence to that tradition; but, because of the value of the Solicitor General's independence, there are procedural and substantive considerations that should guide and temper the exercise of that power.

V

Procedural Considerations. Undoubtedly, the working relationship between the Attorney General and the Solicitor General is one that will vary from Administration to Administration in accordance with the personalities of the individuals who hold these offices; but as we have said, the traditional pattern is one of noninterference. From this tradition we derive a rule of procedure: in our opinion, with respect to any pending case, the Solicitor General should be given the opportunity to consider the questions involved and to formulate his own initial views with respect to them without interference from the Attorney General or any other officer in the Administration.

There are at least two reasons for following a procedure of this kind. First, the procedure ensures that the Attorney General (and the President) will enjoy the benefit of the Solicitor General's independent judgment in every case. That independence would be compromised if the Solicitor General were subjected to frequent advice or suggestions from the President or the Attorney General before he is allowed to formulate his own position. Second, this procedure helps to ensure that the Attorney General will not exercise his supervisory powers gratuitously. No one can say what the Solicitor General's position will be before he has taken it.

This brings us to a related point. The Solicitor General should be allowed to formulate a position with respect to pending cases, and he should be allowed to act independently in the discharge of that function, but he should not be required to make his decision in an informational vacuum. He is not omniscient, and he should be free to consult the various offices and agencies in the executive branch that may have views on the questions presented by the case at hand. In fact, this is the traditional practice. The Solicitor General does consult and is consulted by other officers of Government. Far from detracting from his independent function, this practice enhances its value. It ensures that the Solicitor General's judgment will be informed judgment.

Substantive Considerations. Once the Solicitor General has taken a position with respect to a pending case, that position will, in most cases, become the Government's position as a matter of course. However, in some cases the Attorney General may need to determine whether or not the Government should adopt that position. Plainly, the Attorney General, as well as the President, have the power to decline to adopt it, but to exercise that power is to reject the Solicitor General's independent and expert legal counsel in favor of other legal advice or policy considerations.

We should make one observation at this point. We have said that an independent Solicitor General assists the Attorney General and the President in the discharge of their constitutional duty to put law before policy. It is our opinion that if the Solicitor General is to be of real value in that regard, his judgment must be permitted to be dispositive in the ordinary course. The Government's position should be changed by the Attorney General only in rare instances.

How does one identify the "rare instances" in which intervention by the Attorney General may be justifiable? We can offer no litmus test, but we wish to make several observations that bear upon the question.

First, in our opinion, the mere fact that the Attorney General may disagree with the Solicitor General over a question of law is not ordinarily a sufficient reason for intervention in a given case. If the Solicitor General has fallen into error, the Supreme Court will have an opportunity to correct the error, and the Government's ultimate interest in a just result will be vindicated. If the Court upholds his position, then all the better, for his legal judgment and not that of his superiors, was correct. In either case, for all of the reasons given above, the potential benefit of intervention is usually outweighed, in our view, by the mischief inherent in it.

There may be a case in which the Attorney General is convinced that the Solicitor General has erred so far in the legal analysis that intervention is required. We believe such cases will be quite rare, but when they arise the Attorney General must follow the rule of law himself and be guided by his own experience and judgment.

There is another category of questions that may be involved in cases presented to the Supreme Court with respect to which the Attorney General's or the President's judgment may be essential. Our analysis turns upon the uncertain but traditional distinction between questions of law and questions of policy.

All of the cases that are decided by the appellate courts can be said to involve "questions of law" in a technical sense. The outcome in each case must be justified by reference to rules or principles that are prescribed in the Constitution, statutes, regulations, ordinances, or in the previous decisions of the courts. In some cases, however, questions of "policy" are integrally intertwined with questions of law. In other cases the major decision may be a discretionary one such as filing of an *amicus* brief when there has been no request from the Court for the views of the Government.

The Solicitor General can and should enjoy independence in matters of legal judgment. He should be free to decide what the law is and what it requires. But if "law" does not provide a clear answer to the question presented by the case before him, we think there is no reason to suppose that he, of all the officers in the executive branch, should have the final responsibility for deciding what, as a matter of policy, the interests of the Government, the parties, or the Nation may require. To our knowledge, no Solicitor General has adopted a contrary view.

The short of the matter is that cases may arise in which questions of policy are so important to the correct resolution of the case that the principles that normally justify the Solicitor General's independent and dispositive function may give way to the greater need for the Solicitor General to seek guidance on the policy question. Questions of policy are questions that can be effectively addressed by the Attorney General, a Cabinet officer who participates directly in policy formation and who can go to the President for policy guidance when the case demands.

But the Attorney General and the President should trust the judgment of the Solicitor General not only in determining questions of law but also in distinguishing between questions of law and questions of policy. If the independent legal advice of the Solicitor General is to be preserved, it should normally be the Solicitor General who decides when to seek the advice of the Attorney General or the President in a given case.

JOHN M. HARMON
Assistant Attorney General
Office of Legal Counsel
Dated: September 29, 1977

———

Richard G. Wilkins,[69] *An Officer and an Advocate: The Role of the Solicitor General,* 21 Loy. L.A. L. Rev. 1167, 1167–1177 (1988)

... For the most part, the Solicitor General and his staff have performed their duties in distinguished obscurity, receiving generally high praise for professional comportment and rarely prompting public comment or attention. All that has changed. In 1982, the editorial staff of the *New York Times* blasted Solicitor General Rex E. Lee for presenting the Supreme Court with "political tract[s]" rather than "principled counsel." More recently, Lincoln Caplan, author of *The Tenth Justice,*

---

69. The author is identified in the article as having served as an Assistant to Solicitor General Rex E. Lee from July 1981 to May 1984.

has charged that "the Reagan Administration has stripped the office of its traditional autonomy, debased its credibility and turned it into an ideological mouthpiece."

. . .

Although Caplan's critique of the Solicitor General's office "is largely a polemic against the Reagan Administration," it raises serious questions. Has the Office of the Solicitor General been subjected to unusual political pressure? A review of the available literature, including articles by past Solicitors General and a comparative statistical study, suggests that the office has always responded to the political inclinations of then-current administrations. Thus, the assertion that the Solicitor General has lost his "independence" is something of an overstatement; he has never been completely autonomous. Nevertheless, the recently perceived political sensitivity of the Solicitor General prompts a more difficult inquiry: How should the Solicitor General respond to ideological demands? Here, no ready solution exists. Those who see the Solicitor General primarily as an advocate of the administration that appointed him will give one answer. Those—like Caplan—who see the Solicitor General primarily as an officer of the Court and an independent moderating force within the administration will give another.

I believe that the Solicitor General's proper role lies between that of unquestioning advocate and independent officer of the Court. While the Solicitor General appropriately serves as an advocate, his advocacy must be tempered by the realization that he occupies a unique position of influence with the Supreme Court of the United States. Thus, Mr. Caplan notwithstanding, the Solicitor General should support the administration's views on sensitive legal issues. However, in the course of that advocacy, the Solicitor General must never sacrifice his credibility and reliability as a trusted officer of the Court. Maintaining a balance between the sometimes conflicting duties of advocate and officer of the Court is a difficult and often thankless task. The recent experience of Rex E. Lee suggests that a person who accomplishes the feat may have few friends in any quarter—the administration may find the Solicitor General's reasoned advocacy too tame, while political opponents may find any such advocacy outrageous. Achieving and maintaining that balance, however, is the fundamental mission of the Solicitor General.

I. PRESSURE AND POLITICS: THE INDEPENDENCE OF THE SOLICITOR GENERAL

. . . The "most visible responsibility of the office [of Solicitor General]" is the actual conduct of the government's appellate practice before the Supreme Court. That responsibility embraces several discrete steps, beginning with the decision "whether the government should petition the Supreme Court for certiorari, or acquiesce in or oppose the petitions filed by others," and concluding with the actual preparation and presentation of the government's cases before the Court. The confluence of these duties imposes a ponderous decision-making burden upon the Solicitor General.

In performing these day-to-day tasks, the Solicitor General and his staff have achieved "an exceptional degree of autonomy." Much of this autonomy derives from the simple fact that the bulk of the Solicitor General's staff consists of civil service employees who are not subject to removal for political or ideological reasons. Moreover, the workload within the office is assigned without regard to the ideological leaning of particular attorneys. Additionally, in the vast majority of cases, questions regarding "politics" never arise—the majority of the litigation passing through the office involves matters that simply do not attract political attention. Indeed, freedom from constant political scrutiny is essential to both the efficient functioning of the office and the broader litigation strategy of the government as a whole. The government loses "literally thousands" of cases in the lower courts each year, and the attorneys and officials involved often have strong opinions regarding the future course of those cases. Without a significant degree of independence from disappointed government officials, the Solicitor General would quickly lose the important ability to say "No."

. . .

The general independence so critical to the ongoing successful management of the government's Supreme Court litigation has always had limits, however. . . .

Any assertion that the Solicitor General should be free of political suasion ignores the reality that he is an official within the executive branch who serves at the pleasure of the President who appointed him. . . . As Justice Sutherland once noted, "[i]t is quite evident that one who holds his office only during the pleasure of another, cannot be depended upon to maintain an attitude of independence against the latter's will."

Of course, the foregoing is only a partial answer to recent claims that the Reagan Administration has "turned the post of Solicitor General from a position of independence into the job of a good-natured mouthpiece." It establishes that the Solicitor General cannot legitimately claim true independence from the President, but it does not refute the submission that the Reagan Administration has been unusually heavy handed in its dealings with its Solicitor Generals. The available evidence, however, suggests that recent events at the Office of the Solicitor General do not represent a radical departure from past practice. On the contrary, past Solicitor Generals have consistently reflected the position of the presiding administration in their presentations to the Court.

Erwin Griswold, who served as Solicitor General under Presidents Lyndon Johnson and Richard Nixon, and who is generally highly regarded even by recent critics, "tried to keep the Republicans as happy with his advocacy as he had the Democrats." Indeed, one scholar has noted that Griswold took explicit cues from the Nixon Administration regarding what the Solicitor's position should be in politically sensitive cases. Even Caplan, who tries mightily to downplay any political influence upon Griswold's decisions while Solicitor General, reports that Griswold filed a brief in the *Pentagon Papers* case[70] that was contrary to his own "judgments behind closed doors." Despite Griswold's own conclusion that "the government should stop objecting to publication of the history, because the only harm that would come of it was political embarrassment," he nevertheless filed a brief asserting that publication of the Pentagon Papers could cause "immediate and irreparable harm to the security of the United States." Moreover, while Griswold had consistently taken a strong pro-civil rights stand under President Johnson, he modified his views regarding appropriate civil rights remedies after President Nixon "publicly announced that his administration would no longer support forced busing to achieve integration."

Robert Bork, who was appointed by Nixon to succeed Griswold, and who served under Nixon and Gerald Ford, was likewise willing to tune his advocacy to reflect administration views.... Caplan summarized Bork's service as Solicitor as follows:

> Bork regularly found means to carry the Administration's message to the Court. He was a more enthusiastic advocate of Nixon's legal notions than Griswold had been (and, in the process, drove away one assistant who believed that the former Yale professor had compromised the integrity of the Solicitor General's judgment about the law), and he was equally forthright about making arguments favored by Ford.

Any given Solicitor General's enthusiastic sponsorship of administration goals, of course, may stem more from personal commitment to those goals than explicit pressure from the Oval Office. The President's careful selection of a person committed to the administration's agenda is, nevertheless, a plain example of political influence on the Office of the Solicitor General.

Jimmy Carter appointed Wade McCree as Solicitor General. McCree, like his predecessors, gave distinguished service during his four years in office. He also glanced toward Pennsylvania Avenue when preparing briefs in politically sensitive matters. When a draft of the government's brief in Regents of the University of California v. Bakke,[71] which supported Bakke and argued against affirmative action, was leaked to the press, substantial pressure to reverse that position—from the White House on down—was brought to bear upon the Department of Justice and McCree in particular. The brief ultimately filed with the Supreme Court did not support Bakke, but instead urged the Court to remand the matter to the California Supreme Court for further proceedings. Caplan asserts that the change in position did not result from political pressure, but rather occurred because "the Solicitor General knew about and shared the President's belief in affirmative action." The fact that McCree "shared" the President's beliefs, however, cannot avoid the pragmatic reality that he "knew about" them, too.

70. [Footnote 51 in original] New York Times v. United States, 403 U.S. 713 (1971).

71. [Footnote 58 in original] 438 U.S. 265 (1978).

In any event, the *Bakke* matter is not the only known instance during the Carter Presidency when administration policy exerted substantial influence over the Solicitor's affairs. After heated public opposition greeted the government's presentation in Personnel Administrator of Massachusetts v. Feeney,[72] Attorney General Griffin Bell "institute[d] a policy requiring the solicitor to give notice to Bell of all cases involving policy issues. This policy permitted Bell to examine the matter, and if necessary, consult with the President *before* the solicitor's brief was written."

In addition to the preceding anecdotal evidence, a statistical study of the amicus curiae presentations of Solicitors Griswold, Bork and McCree confirms that they were sensitive to the ideological viewpoints of their respective administrations.[73] The study examined each case in which one of the three Solicitor Generals had participated as amicus curiae during the 1967 to 1979 Terms of the Court. The briefs were classified as "pro" or "anti" in each of three areas: personal liberties, civil equality and criminal rights. The study found that Griswold, under President Johnson, and McCree, under President Carter, "took decidedly more pronounced 'pro-rights' positions than did Bork" under Presidents Nixon and Ford. Moreover, during their tenure under President Nixon, both Griswold and Bork "adopted 'anti-rights' positions more frequently than McCree." McCree "advanced a pro-civil equalities claim in a slightly higher percentage of his amicus briefs than either solicitors Griswold or Bork." These results were explained, at least in part, by reference to the political agendas of the Johnson, Nixon, Ford and Carter presidencies. McCree's record on civil liberties, for example, "meshes with his philosophy as a jurist, as well as those of the Carter administration generally." The study also concluded that "Griswold and Bork's 'anti-rights' position was probably rooted in the Nixon administration's strong law and order stance."

The records of Griswold, Bork and McCree are hardly ones of staid independence from presidential politics. And, while nothing in the foregoing details detracts from the professional integrity of any former Solicitor General, their records demonstrate that they consistently advocated views in sensitive cases that were consistent with those of their particular administrations. Thus, nothing terribly surprising—or new— arises from the fact that the Solicitors General in the current administration have similarly advocated President Reagan's views. The charge that President Reagan has "turned [the Solicitor] into an ideological mouthpiece" is decidedly overblown; the Solicitor General has always been a mouthpiece. The real question raised by the recent criticisms of the Office of the Solicitor General is not whether the Solicitor General should listen to the President or not. The evidence shows that he always

---

72. [Footnote 63 in original] 442 U.S. 256 (1979). The case involved a challenge to a statutory veteran's preference scheme. The government's stance angered many women's rights groups....

73. [Footnote 65 in original] O'Connor, [*The Amicus Curiae Role of the U.S. Solicitor General in Supreme Court Litigation*, 66 Judicature 256, 260–64 (1983).]

has. The current debate, therefore, boils down to basic disagreement with the positions the Solicitor is advocating. Critics, such as Caplan, may couch their arguments in terms of "misuse" or "abuse" of the Solicitor General's office, but they are essentially champing at the fact that the Court is being presented with substantive legal arguments they strongly dislike.

. . .

Michael W. McConnell,[74] *The Rule of Law and the Role of the Solicitor General*, 21 Loy. L.A. L. Rev. 1105, 1105–1112 (1988)

I. THREE APPROACHES TO THE SOLICITOR GENERAL'S FUNCTION

Let us grant the attractive premise that the Solicitor General, more than the ordinary advocate, must comply with and promote the rule of law in his representation of the United States in the Supreme Court. The President is charged to "take Care that the Laws be faithfully executed";[75] the Solicitor General, as the executive officer entrusted with Supreme Court litigating authority, exercises the "take Care" responsibility in that sphere. But what does the rule of law mean in this context?

There are three prominent approaches to the Solicitor General's responsibility: (1) he must make only those arguments to the Court that he believes to be substantively valid, even if the interests of his client would be better served by other plausible legal arguments; (2) he must make only those arguments to the Court that are consistent with the Court's interpretation of legal requirements; and (3) he must make the arguments with the best prospect of serving his clients' interests, that is, upholding government action.

Generally, the first approach—the "independence" approach—is invoked to criticize the Solicitor General when he allows the interests of the client agencies, the views of the President, or the opinions of other lawyers in and out of the Department of Justice to influence what arguments he will make to the Court. Generally, the second approach—the "precedent" approach—is invoked to criticize the Solicitor General for asking the Court to modify its precedents or for making an argument that the present nine Justices are unlikely to adopt. Generally, the third approach—the "government interests" approach—is invoked to criticize the Solicitor General for failing to defend federal statutes or government action, or for filing briefs not directly related to that end.

The "independence" and "precedent" approaches emphasize the distinction between the role of the Solicitor General and that of other

----

74. The author is identified as "Formerly Assistant to the Solicitor General (1983–85)." He is now a Judge on the U.S. Court of Appeals for the Tenth Circuit.

75. [Footnote 1 in original] U.S. Const. art. II, § 3.

advocates. They seem, at first blush, to have more to do with the rule of law than the "government interests" approach. The Solicitor General, it is said, has responsibilities to the rule of law that so far exceed the ordinary advocate that he can almost be called a "Tenth Justice." This title captures the view that the Solicitor General properly exercises a judicial-type function, accepting and rejecting legal arguments on the basis of his best understanding of what the Constitution and laws require rather than the interests of the client agencies. As expressed in an official memorandum on the role of the Solicitor General issued under Attorney General Griffin Bell [in 1977 and reprinted above], "the Solicitor General ... must protect the Court by presenting meritorious claims in a straightforward and professional manner and by screening out unmeritorious ones[.]" The same memorandum states that "[t]he Nation values the Solicitor General's independence for the same reason that it values an independent judiciary," and endorses former Solicitor General Francis Biddle's formulation that the Solicitor General's "only guide" should be " 'the ethic of his law profession framed in the ambience of his judgment and experience.' "

Alternatively, the Solicitor General is said to be like a "Tenth Justice" because his arguments are designed principally to be of service to the Court rather than to advance the interests of the executive or legislative branches. His name appears below those of the Justices in the front of each issue of U.S. Reports. He is not an outsider or a critic of the Court, but their partner in a common effort to uphold the Constitution and laws. To be useful, his arguments ought to proceed from the Court's recent precedents and help the Court to fit the current case into a settled framework of existing decisions. Just as continuity and stability are desirable features of the law, they are desirable features of the Solicitor General's argumentation.

The "government interests" approach to the Solicitor General's role is more modest. It treats the Solicitor General less like a "Tenth Justice" and more like an ordinary lawyer—more skilled, more distinguished, more responsible, perhaps, but still a lawyer for a client. Under this approach, it is the function of the adversary process, and ultimately of the Court, to uphold the rule of law. The Solicitor General best serves by making the best arguments he can for upholding government action, rather than by exercising independent opinions or by trying to "protect" the Court from arguments. Indeed, by failing to make the best possible case for the government's position—assuming the position is at least tenable—the Solicitor General makes the Court's job harder and vindication of the rule of law that much more difficult.

The "government interests" approach, like the others, recognizes the Solicitor General's responsibility to present the facts and legal background of a case with scrupulous accuracy and fairness. No responsible theory of the Solicitor General's function would tolerate shading or hiding the truth. Indeed, as the most common repeat player in the Supreme Court, the Solicitor General should feel these constraints more keenly than other lawyers, since his credibility in other cases will suffer if a brief is less than fully accurate. But this responsibility of full and fair appellate advocacy is shared, even if to a lesser degree, by all Supreme Court advocates.

The three approaches to the Solicitor General's function each contain a valuable insight. Unfortunately, they are in obvious conflict with one another. The first approach establishes the independent professional judgment of the Solicitor General as the criterion for fealty to the rule of law; the second establishes either judicial precedent or predictions about how the current nine Justices will decide a case as the criterion; the third leaves the rule of law to be achieved through the adversary process. Except in the happy event that the Solicitor General's own professional judgment on legal issues coincides perfectly with both the interests of the government and with precedent—or with his predictions about how the current Court would decide the question—he will be faced with a choice. Should he present the view he believes to be correct? Should he present the view that best accords with the Court's interpretations? Or should he present the view that most advances government authority?

Perhaps the three approaches should be viewed as tactical or strategic considerations—as part of a lawyerly prudence directed to winning cases. A Solicitor General is unlikely to win by tilting at precedents that command the support of a majority of the Justices. To put his argument in terms consistent with the Court's other recent decisions, rather than openly confronting the Court's recent errors, is plain good sense and good strategy. Similarly, for the Solicitor General to establish a reputation for presenting only "meritorious" arguments will increase his rhetorical effectiveness. If he can establish that he is more than a "hired gun," his arguments will carry greater weight and conviction. And finally, when the Solicitor General confines his arguments to the specific practical needs of the client agencies, rather than wasting precious time and resources on mere matters of constitutional principle, he will be less likely to ruffle feathers and more likely to win cases of immediate interest to his "clients."

Perhaps the entire professional tradition of the Solicitor General's office can be explained in terms of these prudential considerations, without reference to controversial propositions like the "rule of law." One could predict that the Solicitor General, as the only lawyer who frequently appears before the Court, would develop a strong tradition of following precedent, would exercise strong independent judgment, and would emphasize the interests of the government agencies. Seen as prudential considerations, there is little or no contradiction between the three approaches. Each is subsumed in the lawyer's creed: win as many cases as you can.

And yet, the dictates of prudence do not seem to exhaust the responsibilities of the Solicitor General. Prudence is an instrumental virtue, just as winning cases is instrumental. Great Solicitors General have not hesitated, in appropriate cases, to criticize precedent—even recent precedent; to offer arguments that are likely to be rejected; to spurn arguments that would foster greater governmental power and discretion; even to take positions that they would not agree with in their individual capacities. Following the dictates of prudence will help the Solicitor General and his Office to accumulate reputational capital with the Court; but cases will arise when the Solicitor General will, and should, choose to spend that capital.

The three commonly offered approaches to the Solicitor General's role thus do not offer a clear-cut basis for evaluating a particular decision, or even a particular Solicitor General. A Solicitor General's performance cannot be judged according to tidy criteria, for the available criteria are conflicting and require a different balance in different cases. One must understand the Solicitor General's function in light of his own assessment of what the times require. Substantive disagreement over the desirable direction of constitutional law should not be confused with transgression of the rule of law.

II. Illustrations of the Conflict

Any lawyer who has served in the Office of the Solicitor General could offer illustrations of cases in which these approaches conflict. I will describe three such cases during my tenure as Assistant to the Solicitor General. . . .

In the October 1984 Term, the Supreme Court granted certiorari in Tony and Susan Alamo Foundation v. Donovan [471 U.S. 290 (1985)]. The case concerned application of federal minimum wage laws to a religious community in which all the members worked for the community and in return received housing, food, clothing, medical care, and other necessities of life. The members believed they were working for God and that acceptance of a wage would be an affront to God. They therefore sought an exemption under the free exercise clause. The Department of Labor defended the constitutionality of applying the minimum wage laws to the Alamo Foundation, and prevailed in the district court and the court of appeals.

My own assessment of the case was that the Alamo believers were right: they had an unquestionably strong and sincere belief that was frustrated by the government action, and the government's interest in forcing them to accept a wage was, in my judgment, far from compelling. Under the "independence" approach—assuming that the Solicitor General agreed with my assessment—the government should confess error. On the other hand, the Supreme Court had rejected every free exercise challenge to a neutral government action in the preceding fifteen years, except in the narrow context of unemployment compensation. If the question were how the Supreme Court would decide the case—the "precedent" approach—I thought that it was likely that the Court would uphold the government's action. Finally, the "government interest" was clear: Congress had passed the statute with no exceptions for religious accommodation, and the agency had enforced it.

After some agonizing, we filed a brief in defense of the Labor Department. So far as I can evaluate my own work, the brief was accurate and fair, and there was ample precedent for our position. I also continue to believe the brief was wrong on the merits. The Supreme Court decided the case unanimously in favor of the government.... I took no pleasure in the victory; rather the opposite. The notion, fostered by the 1977 Memorandum to Griffin Bell, that when the Supreme Court accepts the Solicitor General's argument it proves "his legal judgment ... was correct," obviously confuses winning with being right. The development of constitutional law would have been better served if the Alamo Foundation's legal position had been more forcefully presented. Yet it did not seem then, nor does it seem now, that that was *our* responsibility.

Estate of Thornton v. Caldor, Inc. [472 U.S. 703 (1985),] presented a different twist. In *Thornton,* a state supreme court had struck down under the establishment clause a state statute allowing workers who observe a sabbath day to designate that day as their day off. In *Thornton,* unlike *Alamo Foundation,* the real question was whether to file a brief, rather than what position the brief should take, since the United States was not a party. In my independent judgment, the state law fully comported with the first amendment. The federal government interest was that the reasoning of the lower court decision, if not reversed, could call into doubt the religious accommodation requirements of Title VII of the Civil Rights Act of 1964. Perhaps more important in our thinking, however, was that the case presented an attractive context for the "accommodation" theory the Department of Justice was urging in a variety of establishment clause cases.

The problem was that the lower court opinion was a straightforward application of the Supreme Court's usual test for establishment clause violations.... [O]n the basis of precedent, it was likely that the Supreme Court would agree with the lower court. Should that factor be viewed, as it usually would, as a strong argument against participating in the case? Or should this be viewed as an opportunity to demonstrate to the Court, in an attractive context, why it should modify its approach to establishment clause cases?

Solicitor General Lee decided to file amicus curiae briefs urging the Court to grant certiorari in the case and reverse the lower court. We concluded that the important legal principle presented in *Thornton,* coupled with the substantial—even if not compelling—client interest, justified this course of action even though federal government programs were not directly involved. The brief on the merits devoted most of its attention to showing why a rigid application of the usual establishment clause test would be inconsistent with the overall purposes of the religion clauses. While it was respectful in tone, the brief forthrightly urged a significant reformulation of constitutional doctrine.

In *Thornton* and several other decisions handed down at about the same time, the Court reaffirmed its establishment clause precedents and affirmed the lower court. Rather than advancing the "accommodation" theory, it was a setback. . . . [But] I continue to believe that the government was right in the case, and the Court wrong. The only way for the Court to profit by attorneys' arguments is for attorneys to offer theories that may depart from current precedent. . . . A harder question is whether the *Thornton* brief, and others filed on related issues at about the same time, were strategic errors. In the fall of 1984, when these briefs were written, the time had seemed ripe for reconsideration of first amendment doctrine. By late spring, 1985, the Court's temper had shifted. Some have suggested that our briefs "scared" moderates on the Court, notably Justice Powell, and thus were counterproductive. My guess is that the real stimulus for the Court's shift was the divisive religious squabbling in the 1984 Presidential election; the Court may have judged it an unpropitious time to reconsider its separationist approach to church-state relations. Since that time, the Court's decisions have moved somewhat closer to the position we urged in *Thornton*.[76] Without access to the Court's inner councils we will never know.

A final case from my years at the Solicitor General's Office, one in which I did not participate directly, rounds out the discussion. In Garcia v. San Antonio Metropolitan Transit Authority, [469 U.S. 528 (1985),] the question was whether application of federal wage and hour laws to a municipal transit authority was an unconstitutional infringement on state sovereignty under the doctrine of National League of Cities v. Usery [426 U.S. 833 (1976)]. Here the government interest was clear: to defend the statute. But the independent constitutional judgment of the Solicitor General was more sympathetic to state sovereignty. One of the central elements of the constitutional philosophy of the President and his chief lawyers was a return to more generous notions of federalism. Moreover, the precedents were equivocal: *Usery* stood for the principle of state sovereignty but subsequent decisions had eroded *Usery* in various contexts. The Court ordered reargument in the case on whether *Usery* should be overruled, which removed much of the usual prudential constraint against attacking precedents. Not surprisingly, the case generated strenuous debate and disagreement among lawyers in and out of the department.

The Solicitor General decided to file a brief defending the federal statute, but to do so on the basis of a strict reading of *Usery*. Other parties to the case urged that *Usery* be overruled—a position at once more radical and more consonant with the government's client interests. The brief made a persuasive case both that *Usery* was good law and that the San Antonio transit system could be subjected to federal regulation. The Court, however, overruled *Usery* in a sweeping five-four decision,

---

76. [Footnote 10 in original] *See* Witters v. Washington Dep't of Servs. for the Blind, 474 U.S. 481 (1986) (establishment clause does not preclude state from paying tuition for ministry training under vocational education program for the blind); Corporation of Presiding Bishop of Church of Jesus Christ of Latter Day Saints v. Amos, 107 S.Ct. 2862 (1987) (establishment clause does not preclude Congress from carving out exception from religious antidiscrimination laws for protection of religious organizations).

with no Justice adopting the Solicitor General's approach to the case. Should this be seen as a rebuff? It seems to me the brief made a significant contribution: it provided the vehicle, had the Court wished it, to uphold the government's interests in the case without shutting off further doctrinal development of the *Usery* principle. It presented a plausible intermediate position. That the Justices did not adopt it does not mean that it was not the right position for the government to take.

The foregoing illustrations cast doubt on the notion that any single criterion can be substituted for the Solicitor General's admittedly subjective judgment of the needs and potentialities of a case. In *Alamo Foundation* the Solicitor General took the "government interest" approach where it conflicted with "independent" constitutional judgment; in *Thornton* he took the "independence" approach where it conflicted with precedent; and in *Garcia* he took the "precedent" approach where the other approaches tugged in opposite directions. In each of these cases the Solicitor General might be criticized, and probably has been. I suspect, however, that few fair observers—whatever their ideological persuasion—would consistently espouse any one of the three approaches across the full range of cases. Does this mean that the rule of law is an empty concept as applied to the role of the Solicitor General?

. . .

Drew S. Days, III,[77] *When the President Says "No": A Few Thoughts on Executive Power and the Tradition of Solicitor General Independence,* 3 J. App. Prac. & Process 509 (2001)

. . .

Although the Solicitor General is appointed by the President and serves under the Attorney General, he has gradually come to enjoy a tradition of independence in carrying out his official responsibilities. He is only rarely subject to direction by either the President or the Attorney General, and as a practical matter, he is in most cases the final decisionmaker with respect to both designing a strategy for government litigation in the Supreme Court and deciding whether to appeal trial court decisions adverse to the government.

On occasion, however, a President will put deference aside and involve himself directly in determining what the government's legal positions are going to be. Documented instances of such presidential involvement are rare, since most occur in the course of rather low-profile discussions within the administration that never become known to the public. Nevertheless, a few examples have received significant attention,

---

77. Alfred M. Rankin Professor of Law, Yale Law School and Solicitor General of   the United States (1993–96).

either contemporaneously or some years afterwards, often as the result of revealing memoir accounts.

In the Truman Administration, for example, the President was reportedly involved in the groundbreaking decision to authorize the government's amicus brief in Shelley v. Kraemer,[78] its first in a civil rights case. For his part, President Eisenhower added several sentences to the government's brief in *Brown v. Board of Education*, which were then edited by an assistant in Solicitor General Simon Sobeloff's office. And President Nixon once ordered Acting Attorney General Kleindienst to drop the government's pursuit of an important antitrust suit, although Solicitor General Erwin Griswold had already approved an appeal to the Supreme Court. But Griswold bided his time and sought several extensions while waiting for final instructions, and eventually received clearance to file the government's brief.

A comprehensive history of the Solicitor General's office would probably include other examples, but I discuss in this essay only some recent cases in which Presidents intervened, most of which are familiar to me from firsthand experience. . . .

THE PRESIDENTS AND THE CASES

CARTER

I have yet to write a memoir of my tenure as Assistant Attorney General for Civil Rights in the Carter Administration. I can, however, offer this personal account of events leading up to the government's filing of its amicus brief in Regents of the University of California v. Bakke.[79] Under my leadership, the Civil Rights Division of the Department of Justice recommended amicus participation in support of the University of California and its affirmative action program, while the Assistant and Deputy in Solicitor General Wade McCree's office recommended amicus participation in favor of Bakke. Before McCree himself became fully involved, President Carter gave a press conference at which he pledged to support affirmative action. The Solicitor General's office nonetheless drafted a brief supporting Bakke, which, unsurprisingly, met with resistance at the White House. Following contentious meetings at various levels, Attorney General Griffin Bell attempted to shield McCree from the pressure emanating from the White House and the Department of Health, Education and Welfare, and McCree indicated later that he never received any direct orders from the White House. He was, however, aware of the pressure being put on Bell.

In the end, McCree did not follow the advice of his career staff, and he eventually decided to recommend that the Court remand the case to the California courts for decision. He and I then spent several days working with his top staff in a nearly nonstop session that produced a brief supporting the principle of affirmative action. That brief appears to have influenced Justice Powell, for he opined—as we had argued—that

78. [Footnote 1 in original] 334 U.S. 1 (1948).

79. [Editors' Note: See Note on *Bakke*, above.]

race may, under some circumstances, be used as one factor in a system that includes a whole range of admissions criteria, so long as no quotas result.

Reagan

The Bob Jones Case

During the Reagan Administration, a major controversy arose over Bob Jones University v. United States,[80] which involved the question of a tax exemption for a religious, but racially segregated, institution. Solicitor General Rex Lee decided to recuse himself from the case, because he had before becoming Solicitor General been involved in the debate over tax exemptions for religious institutions. As a result of Lee's decision, Lawrence Wallace, the Senior Deputy Solicitor General, became Acting Solicitor General. But as a career member of the Solicitor General's staff, Wallace too had a history. He had signed a Supreme Court brief during the Carter Administration supporting the Internal Revenue Service's revocation of the university's tax-exempt status, which made him understandably uncomfortable about supporting the successor administration's contrary position. The Reagan administration nonetheless pushed for an argument in support of the university.

After what must have been several highly charged discussions, the government's brief ultimately argued the administration's line, but Wallace was authorized to include a footnote pointing out that he personally did not subscribe to the government's position on the first and central question presented. The Court eventually ruled eight to one in favor of the Internal Revenue Service, demonstrating among other things that the President's success in prevailing upon the Solicitor General's office to espouse his position is no guarantee of his administration's success before the Supreme Court.

The Beck Case

Charles Fried, who followed Rex Lee as President Reagan's Solicitor General, recounts only one incident of White House interference with his work. The case, Communications Workers of America v. Beck,[81] involved the use of union dues and fees to support pro-union candidates and parties. Fried believed that no state action was involved in the practice, and that the Taft–Hartley Act could not plausibly be read to forbid the compulsory use of union dues in support of union-approved candidates. When proofs of Fried's brief were circulated to the White House, however, someone there contacted Attorney General Edwin Meese to express displeasure with Fried's analysis of the law. This objection prompted Meese to call a high-level meeting at which various members of the administration expressed dissatisfaction with the brief, but it was ultimately filed as written. In the end, the White House position—that the Taft–Hartley Act could be construed to prohibit the compulsory use

80. [Footnote 11 in original] 461 U.S. 574 (1983).

81. [Footnote 14 in original] 487 U.S. 735 (1988).

of union dues—prevailed five to three in the Court. Discussing the incident later, Fried emphasized that "in *Beck* [he] received no direct order [but] was made aware that 'the White House' did not like the position [he] was about to take."

BUSH

In the first Bush Administration, my predecessor as Solicitor General, Kenneth Starr, argued for the government in United States v. Mabus[82] that the state of Mississippi should not be responsible for providing additional funding for traditionally black colleges. After meeting with a group of black college presidents, however, President Bush ordered Starr to reverse the government's position in the case (eventually to be known as United States v. Fordice[83]), and to argue instead that increased state aid to black public colleges was necessary in order to remedy past discrimination. Deferring to the President, Starr filed a reply brief that urged the Court to require the state to supply additional funding to traditionally black colleges in order to overcome the effects of its segregated system of higher education.

CLINTON

No doubt it is obvious by now that "into every Solicitor General's life a little rain must fall!" And so it was with me. I remember two occasions on which President Clinton either in effect, or explicitly, directed me to reverse legal positions that I had taken after consulting with the Attorney General.

The Knox Case

The first was in Knox v. United States,[84] which involved the child-pornography conviction of a Penn State graduate student who had a previous conviction for receiving child pornography through the mails. Using information that came to their attention some time after his earlier conviction, law enforcement agents obtained and executed a search warrant at Knox's residence, turning up several videocassettes that contained vignettes of barely dressed teenage and pre-teen girls. The legal issue before the district court was whether any of the tapes depicted a minor engaging in "sexually explicit conduct," which was defined in the statute as "lascivious exhibition of the genitals or pubic area." The court concluded that the tapes fit that definition, finding that although none of the girls were nude, the videos' focus on areas in close proximity to the genitals, specifically "the uppermost portion of the inner thigh," was included within the statute's prohibition against displays of the pubic area.

Knox took an appeal. Although it first went out of its way to reject the district court's definition of pubic area, the Third Circuit affirmed,

---

82. [Footnote 20 in original] 499 U.S. 958 (1991).

83. [Footnote 22 in original] 505 U.S. 717 (1992).

84. [Footnote 24 in original] 510 U.S. 939 (1993).

holding that "nude exposure of the genitals or pubic area [was] not necessary for an exhibition to take place." Knox then filed a petition for certiorari that was granted over the government's opposition. And that is where I came in. My job was to prepare the brief on the merits.

I reviewed the case, and concluded that the Third Circuit's decision represented an extremely strained and incorrect construction of the statute. I was concerned, therefore, that the grant of certiorari did not bode well for the government's defense of that interpretation. I was also concerned about the possibility of the Court's issuing a broad adverse ruling likely to jeopardize later child-pornography prosecutions that presented no novel questions like those raised in *Knox*.

My consideration of the facts surrounding Knox's prosecution made me even more uneasy. First, no other such prosecution had ever been brought by the Justice Department. Second, the United States Attorney who brought the *Knox* prosecution did so without prior approval from the Department of Justice, which was a violation of department regulations. Third, the prosecutor had intentionally left out evidence of Knox's collection of hard-core child pornography because, as he told me, he wanted it to be a test case.

Given the legal and factual circumstances, I believed that it was important to get the *Knox* case out of the Supreme Court as quickly as possible. I did so by filing a brief confessing error and urging the Court to vacate and remand the case to the Third Circuit for further consideration in light of an alternative reading of the statute, one that inferred a test requiring the genitals or pubic area to be discernible in order for a particular pose to constitute an illegal exhibition.

The Supreme Court did as I requested, and "all hell broke loose." Now, I was prepared for *some* criticism of my decision. A distinguished career lawyer in my office had in fact advised me simply to advance the arguments already made by the office, which would have allowed the Supreme Court to rule against the position so unwisely taken by the federal prosecutors who had initiated the case. I knew, then, that there were those who disagreed with my strategy, but I had no idea that my decision would produce a torrent of criticism from Congress, child protection groups, and fundamentalist religious organizations. . . .

The Senate responded to the Supreme Court's ruling by passing a unanimous resolution that indicated its rejection of my analysis. Shortly thereafter, the President publicly released a letter to Attorney General Janet Reno in which he fully agreed "with the Senate about what the proper scope of the child pornography law should be," and directed her to work with Congress to develop "the broadest possible protections against child pornography and exploitation." . . . The House ultimately joined the Senate in criticizing my position, and it too passed a resolution that rejected my reading of the statute, albeit by a smaller margin.

I was happy to escape the storm by getting back to the work of briefing the case, and on remand, the Third Circuit affirmed in a way that I found promising. In essence, it concluded that Knox's conviction should be affirmed irrespective of whether its reading of the statute or mine controlled. Knox sought certiorari once again. I thought that the prudent approach at this juncture was for the government to file an opposition to certiorari on the grounds that any ruling from the Court would be unlikely to affect Knox's conviction. Under such circumstances, I believed that the Court would not be predisposed to accept the case for review a second time. But the Attorney General concluded that we should express our wholehearted agreement with the Third Circuit's test. She and I attempted in earnest to reach a compromise but failed, because I told her that I could not sign briefs taking diametrically opposing positions at different stages of a single case. She respected that decision, and filed a brief bearing her signature and those of certain other Department of Justice officials, but no signature from anyone in my office. And there it all ended, for certiorari was denied.

The Christians Case

The second occasion on which the power of the Presidency had a direct impact on my work in the Clinton administration occurred about a year later in a case with the incredibly ironic title of Christians v. Crystal Evangelical Free Church.[85] There, a trustee in bankruptcy brought an adversary proceeding against Crystal Evangelical to recover about $13,500.00 in pre-petition contributions. The bankruptcy court granted the trustee's motion, the district court affirmed, and the church then appealed to the Eighth Circuit.

By the time the case reached the circuit court, Congress had passed and the President had signed as one of his first pieces of legislation, the Religious Freedom Restoration Act (RFRA). That act provided that the government was permitted to substantially burden a person's exercise of religion only if it demonstrated that the burden met a compelling governmental interest and was the least restrictive means of achieving that important end. The Eighth Circuit notified the Attorney General of the case and invited her views on the apparent conflict between the Bankruptcy Code and RFRA.

After a long and spirited debate in the Justice Department, I decided, with the Attorney General's approval, to file a brief supporting the trustee. In short, our position was that the Code did not in this case substantially burden free exercise, since the money given to the church actually belonged to the bankruptcy estate when the debtors made their tithes, and the debtors were not entitled to treat the estate's money as their own. Moreover, even if there was a substantial burden, the bankruptcy law's treatment of pre-petition transfers like these met a compelling need—preventing tax evasion by those inclined to hide their assets by pretending to have donated them to churches—that could not be achieved in a less restrictive manner. Satisfied with our analysis, we filed our brief and waited for the case to be set for oral argument.

85. [Footnote 38 in original] 148 B.R. 886 (Bankr. D. Minn. 1992)

Several months passed. And then, about ten days before the Eighth Circuit was to hear the case, I began to get a sense that some members of the White House staff and, more important, the President himself, were having second thoughts about our brief. In an effort to satisfy those questioning the Justice Department's position, the Attorney General held a mock oral argument at which I presented our position, and a top official in the Department who disagreed with me argued for the church. Afterwards, the Attorney General expressed her continuing approval of the brief we had filed. I was heartened and relieved.

On the White House front, though, the press reported that a group critical of the Department's position had managed to schedule a meeting with the President at which to express its members' concerns. On the afternoon before oral argument, I was advised to stay close to my telephone because the *Christians* case was being actively discussed at the White House. Late that night, I learned that the President had decided that we should withdraw our brief and decline to participate in the oral argument. I immediately called the Civil Division lawyer who was to argue the case, advised him of the President's decision, and got his agreement to sign the withdrawal letter that I was about to fax to his hotel in St. Louis. He filed the letter the next morning, and the Eighth Circuit went on without us, eventually holding for the church by a two-to-one vote. I learned later that one of the judges on the panel remarked during the argument that the government was absent because "[s]ome-one spoke to them from on high." And so the President's view prevailed.

CONCLUSION

Those who view the Solicitor General's independence as sacrosanct might find the tale I have just told somewhat shocking. Indeed, Francis Biddle, who served as Solicitor General and Attorney General in turn, would almost certainly have found it alarming, for he described the Solicitor General's role as follows:

> He determines what cases to appeal and the client has no say in the matter, he does what his lawyer tells him, the lawyer stands in his client's shoes, for the client is but an abstraction. . . . [H]is guide is only the ethic of his profession framed in the ambience of his experience and judgment.

But although I am admiring of Biddle, the matter is not so simple for me. After all, the executive power of the United States is vested in the President. He is ultimately responsible, in both legal and political terms, for the positions his administration takes in court. That important reality was never far from my mind when I served as Solicitor General. And perhaps it led me to be a little too candid with President Clinton during what turned out to be my job interview.

Partway through a rather wide-ranging discussion between us in the Oval Office, the President said to me, "What is the relationship between the Solicitor General and the President?" I responded, "Mr. President, it is very simple. You are in the Constitution and the Solicitor General is not." That statement certainly let the President know that I would defer to his authority. And of course I also happened to draw a President who was a lawyer, a former law professor and, I was informed, a faithful reader of my briefs. He was without a doubt sincerely interested in the Solicitor General's work. Whatever the background of a particular President, however, I remain persuaded that the question of the President's involvement in the work of the Solicitor General is not one of whether so much as it is one of when and how.

During my tenure, the President second-guessed my decisions only in cases that raised difficult legal issues about which reasonable people could disagree, so it was no surprise to find that the President and I might see them differently. In the *Christians* case, in particular, the President felt a special responsibility for seeing to it that RFRA was aggressively supported by his Administration, and I respected his position. Appearances matter, however. In neither *Knox*, where the President sent an open letter to the Attorney General, nor *Christians*, where he granted a special audience to critics of the Justice Department's position, did the President's handling of the situation seem to me sufficiently sensitive in this regard. . . . [T]he President should think about the ways in which his intervention will be perceived by those outside the Oval Office, and how it may affect the Solicitor General's continuing ability to serve as a credible advocate for the government, particularly in his appearances before the Supreme Court. I do not think that either *Knox* or *Christians* impaired my later effectiveness, but denied as I am the perspective of history, I will never know for sure. . . .

Having described several instances in which my predecessors and I experienced the intervention of Presidents in our work, I conclude with the observation that these occurrences are so notable because they have been so few. The history I have related here indicates more that the tradition of an independent Solicitor General retains real vigor 131 years into its history than that it is in any danger of being overwhelmed by undue interference from the President. And that, I think, is as it should be.

Questions and Comments

1. Does the SG have a client? Who is it? Is the SG an advocate or a quasi-adjudicator? How does the SG's role in mediating among federal agencies affect his role as an advocate for the United States?

2. Should the Solicitor General be more fully independent of the President? Should Congress revise the position so as to make it more independent of the President, by, for example, giving the position a fixed term of years? Can Congress do so consistently with the Constitution? Consider both of these questions in the next set of readings.

3. As Lincoln Caplan's book indicates, the "lore" of an office may play an important role in constructing the norms that govern its work. We hope

readers will find in the next reading examples that support—and challenge—the various theoretical accounts offered of the SG's role.

---

c. A Conversation Among Members of the Solicitor General's Office

In an unusual set of public discussions, current and former members of the Solicitor General's office across many administrations discussed the functioning of the office at a conference held at Brigham Young University in 2002. We excerpt from these discussions in the next reading, using the headings given in the transcript printed in the *Brigham Young University Law Review,* and providing in brackets identifying information about the different speakers.

Transcript, Rex E. Lee Conference on the Office of the Solicitor General of the United States, In Memory of Rex E. Lee (1937–1996), 2003 BYU L. Rev. 1

Advocate as Friend: The Solicitor General's Stewardship Through the Example of Rex E. Lee

Theodore B. Olsen:[86]

. . .

... [I]n Garcia v. San Antonio Metropolitan Transit Authority,[87] Rex argued on behalf of the Department of Labor that San Antonio's Transit Authority was not immune from the minimum-wage and over-time provisions of the Fair Labor Standards Act under *National League of Cities*. The Court agreed, overruling *National League of Cities*. Rex had not asked the Court to overrule *National League of Cities*, which he had hoped the Court would leave in place, but the Court did so anyway.

(I have a keen memory with respect to *Garcia* because Rex permitted me to argue that case when it first came before the Court. When the Court set it for reargument with specific instructions to address whether *National League of Cities* should be reversed, I tried to no avail to convince Rex to let me argue the case again. He knew then, as I did not appreciate then, but do now, that when the Supreme Court is considering overruling itself on an important constitutional issue, it expects to see before it the solicitor general, not the assistant attorney general for the Office of Legal Counsel.) . . .

---

86. [Footnote * in original] Solicitor General of the United States. This article was the Keynote Address given at the Rex E. Lee Conference on the Office of the Solicitor General at Brigham Young University, in Provo, Utah on September 12, 2002.

87. [Footnote 12 in original] 469 U.S. 528 (1985).

In *Garcia*, Rex thus defended the validity of agency action implementing a congressional enactment against the states under the Commerce Clause, despite his deeply held Madisonian concern that the regulations might pose a serious threat, as he would later express, to the "double security [which protects] the rights of the people" under a federalist structure of government. Rex felt that the *Garcia* Court "abdicat[ed] its duty to interpret the Constitution" and transferred some of its interpretative powers to Congress, thereby "radically alter[ing] the state of separation of powers and federalism in America." As solicitor general, however, he understood his role, and he faithfully exercised the responsibilities of his office. Sometimes the solicitor general is obligated by his office to defend causes to which he does not personally subscribe. Some people regard that as remarkable, but as Rex well understood, the solicitor general's client is the government, and it matters considerably less what the individual solicitor general believes than what the interests of his clients require.

But Rex also argued a case that stands as a classic example of one of those relatively rare instances in which it is appropriate for the solicitor general to challenge rather than defend the constitutionality of an act of Congress—Immigration and Naturalization Service v. Chadha.[88]

In the Immigration and Nationality Act, Congress delegated to the attorney general the authority to suspend the deportation of aliens in certain situations. But in order to retain control over the exercise of that power, Congress reserved to itself a one-house legislative veto over each decision by the attorney general to suspend deportation, so that the vote of one house of Congress could reverse the attorney general's decision. Chadha, the plaintiff, was one of several aliens with respect to whom the House of Representatives had exercised that veto.

Chadha came along in an interesting context. Presidents going back as far as Franklin Roosevelt had acquiesced in various manifestations of the legislative veto device. In fact, President Carter and his attorney general had supported their constitutionality and had even proposed a legislative veto as a part of a bill authorizing a presidential reorganization of government. Later in the Carter administration, however, he and his Department of Justice had perceived how invasive of presidential authority legislative vetoes had become and had changed their position to one challenging their constitutionality. But Rex found himself serving a president who had supported legislative vetoes during his campaign, and powerful Republican senators strongly supported them. But after much internal debate and strife, and considerable pressure to reverse course, the Reagan administration endorsed the Carter administration's legal position that legislative vetoes were unconstitutional. Faced with the serious encroachment on the authority of the executive branch that legislative vetoes represented, Rex argued in the Supreme Court that the legislative veto violated the Presentment Clause of Article I, Section 7, Clause 2, which requires that every bill be presented to the president for

88. [Footnote 15 in original] 462 U.S. 919 (1983).

his signature so that he may decide whether to veto it. Further, because the particular veto provision at issue could be exercised by one house, Rex contended that it contravened the bicameralism requirement of Article I, Sections 1 and 7, according to which both houses of Congress must pass a bill before it can become law, or, at least, that is how the story goes in that famous Schoolhouse Rock cartoon about how a bill becomes a law.

The Supreme Court agreed that the House had exercised legislative power in exercising the veto and thus had violated the Constitution's presentment and bicameralism requirements. Its decision was sweeping in its effects, essentially striking down virtually every type of more than 200 legislative veto provisions Congress had enacted over a fifty-year period, many, as I said, with the approval and occasional outright complicity of past presidents. The Court thus effectively invalidated more federal statutory provisions in that one decision than it had over its entire previous history since first declaring an act of Congress unconstitutional in *Marbury v. Madison.*

> Looking back more than a decade later, Rex considered *Chadha*

> one of the dozen most important cases ever decided by the Supreme Court. It would be difficult to imagine a more important issue than the one decided by *Chadha*: how legislation is to be enacted in this country, and particularly, whether the constitutionally authorized presidential veto—which effectively gives the President one-sixth of the votes in each house of Congress—can be taken away by majority vote of both houses of Congress.

Rex's experience with *Chadha* teaches us that, as an executive officer, the solicitor general's constitutional duty to the president is paramount to his duty to Congress where core executive power is threatened.

. . .

There is a widely held, and I believe substantially accurate, impression that the Solicitor General's Office provides the Court from one administration to another—and largely without regard to either the political party or the personality of the particular Solicitor General—with advocacy which is more objective, more dispassionate, more competent, and more respectful of the Court as an institution than it gets from any other lawyer or group of lawyers.

Rex identified "[t]he advantage to the Court" that such advocacy confers. "[I]n more than half of its cases," he wrote, "it has a highly-skilled lawyer on whom it can count consistently for dependable analysis rendered against the background of an unusual understanding and respect for the Court as an institution."

The government now participates in a greater percentage of cases than it did when Rex was solicitor general. As I mentioned earlier, the Justices heard argument seventy-eight times in eighty-eight cases last term ... and the United States participated as a party or amicus in eighty-three percent of the docket. In the 1983 term, by contrast, the

Court heard argument in 184 cases, and the government participated in 118 of them, or sixty-four percent of the docket. That was the term in which Rex guided the government to a remarkable eighty-three percent winning percentage. By comparison, the average winning percentage from 1943 through 1983 was sixty-nine. (I am proud to say that last term the government matched Rex's outstanding October 1983 term, prevailing in fifty-four of sixty-five arguments or 83.3%.) That is a tribute to the skilled career lawyers who work in the Office of the Solicitor General. Imagine, 65 arguments, 130 moot courts, scores of briefs, several hundred op certs, 2000 or so appeals, interventions, other decisions, and other cases occasionally assigned to the solicitor general by the attorney general, all handled by about twenty lawyers, virtually all career professionals, dedicated lawyers who must be protected from political pressures. Rex was extremely proud of his career staff and invariably demonstrated a willingness to take the heat for tough decisions.

In that regard, the government's increased rate of participation makes it all the more important that the solicitor general make responsible use of his role as the government's litigation gatekeeper. He must reconcile the positions of the components within the Department of Justice, the U.S. attorneys, the other executive departments, and the administrative agencies, and he must exercise restraint in seeking to invoke the Court's jurisdiction to ensure that only the most important cases in which the government has an interest will receive the Court's close scrutiny. He thus conveys important information to the Court that would be obscured if he were too aggressive in seeking Supreme Court review. He also helps them to maintain control over a caseload that remains daunting.

· · ·

[Rex Lee] understood that success in realizing the president's overall litigation objectives ultimately depended on his preserving the solicitor general's special relationship with the Court. As Rex put it, "[A] wholesale departure from the role whose performance has led to the special status that the Solicitor General enjoys would unduly impair that status itself. In the process, the ability of the Solicitor General to serve any of the President's objectives would suffer."

For example, Rex recounts in Wallace v. Jaffree,[89] "It was seriously urged that [the government] advance—as one argument in support of the constitutionality of Alabama's moment of silence statute—that the first amendment generally and the establishment clause in particular were not binding on the states." Rex declined to do so, and he later explained why:

> If, as the Solicitor General of the United States, I had advocated that the first amendment was not binding on Alabama, I would have destroyed—with one single filing—the special status that I enjoyed

89. [Footnote 29 in original] 472 U.S. 38 (1985).

by virtue of my office. I would have also acquired a new status, equally special. The Court would have written me off as someone not to be taken seriously.

As Professor Wilkins later explained, Rex appreciated, as some others did not, that "the law moves in careful modulations rather than great leaps."

In cases such as *Wallace*, Rex was effective in serving not only the Supreme Court, but also his president over the long run by exercising lawyerly restraint in a given case. He would later reveal the historical perspective that informed his judgment:

> There has been built up, over 115 years since this office was first created in 1870, a reservoir of credibility on which the incumbent Solicitor General may draw to his immediate adversarial advantage. But if he draws too deeply, too greedily, or too indiscriminately, then he jeopardizes not only that advantage in that particular case, but also an important institution of government. The preservation of both—and striking just the right balance between their sometimes competing demands—lies at the heart of the Solicitor General's stewardship.

. . .

Pre-Reagan Panel

Judge Frank H. Easterbrook [Deputy Solicitor General, 1978–79; Assistant to the Solicitor General, 1974–77]: . . .

. . . The office long has valued its independence and its ability to make a reasoned decision, but yet as in cases like Buckley v. Valeo,[90] dealing with the Federal Election Campaign Act, the political forces are very strong on all possible sides of the question. As the name suggests, *Buckley v. Valeo* involved two politicians. The plaintiff was Senator James Buckley; Valeo was the clerk of the House of Representatives. So there was no way to avoid a very heavy dose of politics.

If you go back in history, it turns out the very first time a solicitor general refused to defend the constitutionality of an act of Congress was in 1926. The case was Myers v. United States,[91] involving principles behind the Tenure of Office Act. Ever since *Myers*, solicitors general have felt themselves to have an independent power, but one to be exercised only sparingly in three categories of cases, two of them less controversial than the third. One category is abandoning statutes that are incompatible with recent decisions of the Supreme Court. That has been very important in civil rights cases. After the Supreme Court decided *Brown*, the solicitor general could have gone statute by statute trying to defend every law but did not.

In the 1970s, during the Ford and Carter administrations, there were a long series of cases involving sex discrimination and illegitimacy

90. [Footnote 44 in original, relocated] 424 U.S. 1 (1976).

91. [Footnote 47 in original] 272 U.S. 52 (1926).

discrimination in the social welfare programs like social security. Many of them were defended with some tenacity.... They were not defended to the very last. There were hundreds of these provisions, and by the time Solicitor General McCree came to office, it was common not to defend one or another of these ... provisions essentially identical to something that had been held unconstitutional. The Congress required a report to the Secretary of the House and Senate ... when the solicitor general was willing to leave a statute in the lurch. So even though I had characterized this as a noncontroversial use of their power, it has political consequences.

[Another] category is clashes between Congress and the executive. A good example of that is the history of the one-house veto litigation, which finally came before the Supreme Court when Rex Lee was solicitor general but had been kicking around ever since FDR's time in the White House, when he concluded that statutes of this kind were unconstitutional. When Bob Bork was solicitor general, there were several occasions in which one-house veto provisions were challenged in the Supreme Court. It turned out *Buckley v. Valeo* was one of them. There was a one-house veto provision in the Federal Election Campaign Act. The solicitor general, as I will tell you shortly, filed three briefs in *Buckley v. Valeo*. These three briefs covered every conceivable position and its opposite. There is a footnote in one of those saying, "Well, this is a one-house veto provision. This is plainly unconstitutional." Stop. No elaboration. It turned out it did not have to be reached in *Valeo*.

· · ·

... I am going to give you the third and most difficult category, both for the solicitor general trying to figure out what best to do and for those who must ask what is politically astute. These entail statutes that do not involve recent Supreme Court decisions, do not directly involve the powers of the executive branch, and yet the solicitor general is in grave doubt that the laws should be viewed as constitutional. One stream of argument some solicitors general have accepted is that statutes should be defended if you can make an argument in their favor without breaking out laughing. It is the risibility test for a constitutional defense. If trying to state the defense of the statute does not have you rolling in the aisles, you should defend the statute. That has been the position of some solicitors general.

I do not think it is the correct decision because it turns the solicitor general into a parrot. Whatever strands of argument the solicitor general can get from the Supreme Court's opinions, he is supposed to parrot back to the Supreme Court. But the solicitor general is in fact the spokesman for the executive branch of government. Just as the judicial branch and legislative branch can have a view about the constitutionality of statutes, so can the executive branch. Now having teased you, I arrive at *Buckley* where this question comes up front and center.

Congress passed the Federal Election Campaign Act. It has in it several things: it has a one-house veto clause that managed not to get reviewed; it has a clause providing that the appointment of members of the Federal Election Commission bypasses the president—two members are to be appointed by the president; two members are to be appointed by the Senate directly; two members are to be appointed by the House directly. That falls within the clash of branches the president and the SG believe violates Article II. And it was uncontroversial to file a brief saying that in the president's view vesting appointment in the Congress is unconstitutional. The other things in this law regulated campaign finance, both contributions and expenditures. It also created the federal system underwriting presidential campaigns.

Senator Buckley, who attacked it, and Ralph Winter, then on the Yale faculty, who was Senator Buckley's lawyer, did not have any difficulty persuading Solicitor General Bork that that statute was unconstitutional root and branch. In fact, Bob Bork kept referring to the issue involved in this case, the constitutionality of the FECA, as the "fecal matter." He was not in favor of this statute. Defenders insisted that the law represented a "narrow" regulation of politics. And his reaction was, "Yeah, it has been narrowed right to the core of the First Amendment." What to do? Well, in the end he authorized the filing of three briefs; he came to the bold conclusion to do everything.

One brief was titled "Brief for the Attorney General as a Party and the United States as Amicus Curiae." This brief attacked, on Article II grounds, the appointment the FEC by Congress and then offered the Supreme Court a lot of gratuitous advice about the rest of the law— suggesting things to think about. The solicitor general concluded that it would not be acceptable directly to challenge the Act's constitutionality. But this brief did imply that independent thought might raise a lot of deep questions, and by defending some parts of the Act, the brief conveyed a signal about the rest. That is brief number one, signed by—to give you an indicator of the importance of the case—Attorney General Levi, Solicitor General Bork, Deputy Solicitor General Randolph, and an insignificant assistant to the solicitor general, me.

Brief number two is styled "Brief for the Federal Election Commission as a Party and the United States as Appellee" (implying: Except to the Extent that the United States Has Already Filed the Other Brief). It vigorously defended the constitutionality of the Federal Election Campaign Act except with respect to the Article II issue. It was signed by Attorney General Levi, Solicitor General Bork, Deputy Solicitor General Friedman, and Louis Clayborn who was a once and future deputy solicitor general. Last, Solicitor General Bork authorized the FEC to file its own brief on behalf of itself defending the constitutionality of the appointments matter.

This was all quite extraordinary. Three briefs in one case is well beyond stating two sides in a single brief or filing a brief urging an outcome (with an appendix). Both the attorney general and the solicitor general signed separate briefs on (effectively) different sides of the same proposition.

Why did this occur? It is a shame that Bob Bork is not here to tell you himself. I was not privy to that final decision. It obviously entailed an assessment of what the Ford administration, given the politics of the time, thought was tolerable. It shows that if the political heat is high enough, then even if the solicitor general is very much convinced that an important act of Congress is unconstitutional, that argument still cannot be made....

. . .

Andrew L. Frey [Deputy Solicitor General, 1973–86]: ... By and large the solicitor general's development of legal positions that he, or maybe someday she, will adopt asks the question, "What are the institutional interests of the United States?" The United States as an institution is only temporarily in the custody of any given political party, any given administration. It has certain institutional interests. And I am going to pause here for a minute to say that I think probably the person here who is the strongest proponent of a different view was probably Charles Fried. I know he and I have had many discussions about this question of "who the client is." I have come to think of Charles's view— and something Dan said about the way that Solicitor General Cox handled problems, who was also a Harvard law professor confirms this metaphor—as the Harvard law professor model of the solicitor general. And that model is that naturally Harvard law professors know what is right and what is wrong in the law. Their role is to help guide the Supreme Court to reach a correct decision. And then there is the humble lawyer model where you have this client that may have institutional interests, and you ask yourself, "Well, what are their interests?"—not what do I personally think....

. . .

Judge Daniel M. Friedman [Deputy Solicitor General, 1969– 78; Acting Solicitor General, January–March, 1977]: Well, part of it, I think, depends basically on the concept of the individual who holds the solicitor generalship. That is, does he think his job is to try to take positions that he believes are right or is his job somewhat other than that? Let me give an example under Solicitor General Bork. One of my jobs as a deputy was to be in charge of the antitrust cases. Practically every antitrust case that came through the office from the Antitrust Division took what Bob Bork believed to be an absolutely ridiculous position and quite wrong. But, he told me on several times that his job as solicitor general was not to make antitrust policy. That was the job of the assistant attorney general in charge of the Antitrust Division. He said, "As solicitor general, as long as you can write a brief that seems within its own terms reasonably convincing, I have no basis to refuse to sign it." But he said, "I am not going to get up in the Supreme Court on my two hind legs and try to defend that position." From my point of view it was splendid because it gave me a chance to argue a large number of antitrust cases that I probably would not have gotten to argue under some other solicitors general. ...

Judge Frank Easterbrook: If I could throw in a few words on this client question. I think Andy and I may have a disagreement. It may go to the same issue that Andy raised with Charles Fried. My inclination is to say that the client of the solicitor general is the executive branch of the United States government. Not to say that the solicitor general is an independent agent, but he is litigating on behalf of the executive branch. The president's job is to take care that the laws be faithfully executed, and he is representing that part of the government that takes care that the laws be faithfully executed. I think Bob Bork had that same sense. That was why he took the position in the antitrust cases and civil rights cases that have been mentioned. The executive branch of the United States government, acting through the people appointed for that purpose, had settled on a particular antitrust policy and civil rights policy. Given that the executive branch had taken that view, his job was to defend it.

Many of the great difficulties for a solicitor general arise when you have that conception of who the client is and the executive branch will not take a position or cannot take a position or is internally conflicted. One of the cases that arose while I was deputy solicitor general had to do with OSHA's regulation of benzene.[92] The OSHA adopted a regulation that most people thought would save on average one to two lives a year and cost three or four billion dollars a year to implement. Alfred Khan, the president's chief regulation officer at the White House, thought that was terrible. The EPA, it turns out, also thought that it was terrible. They were not against saving lives, but their fear was that the OSHA benzene regulation would divert so much money into reducing the amount of benzene that industry would not have the resources left to implement other regulations that EPA thought would be more productive. But F. Ray Marshall, the Secretary of Labor, refused to recede from OSHA's view about the significance of benzene. That led to a series of impassioned pleas by these different actors within the executive branch, each asking the solicitor general to represent his side. The solicitor general very much wanted the president to resolve that problem—to resolve this fight among his advisors. President Carter refused. What does the solicitor general do in that case?

What Solicitor General McCree did was to say, "Okay, the designated decision maker for OSHA regulations is the Secretary of Labor. The Secretary of Labor refuses to recede. We will defend the benzene regulations as best we can (and the next year the cotton dust regulations, posing some of the same problems)." But this was still a very hard decision for Wade McCree. It was hard for Griffin Bell to fend off the political pressure from the EPA who wanted Wade McCree to sandbag the Department of Labor. It seems to me very difficult for a solicitor

---

92. [Footnote 58 in original] See Am. Petroleum Inst. v. Occupational Safety & Health Admin., 581 F. 2d 493 (5th Cir. 1978), aff'd sub. nom., Indus. Union Dept v. Am. Petroleum Inst., 448 U.S. 607 (1980).

general to operate if you think you know who your client is, but your client will not make the hard decision. . . .

. . .

Reagan I Panel . . .

Richard G. Wilkins [Assistant to the Solicitor General, 1981–84]: . . . [Y]ou have to balance the fact that as solicitor general, you do have a unique role in that you are speaking for the executive branch. There are conflicts that have been noted within the political branches of the executive branch. Not everyone within the executive branch has the same view. Also, as the chief advocate for the United States of America you have to be very careful and present reasoned arguments. You cannot just dash off on a horse because you want to reverse case X . . .

So, . . . I was involved in one of the busing cases, and I will just mention it briefly without naming any names. One of the briefs came up and it had a sentence that said, "This court has never ordered busing as a remedy for racial discrimination." I knew that was not right. Swann v. Charlotte–Mecklenburg [Bd of Educ.][93] said that busing was a remedy, and I knew I could not put that in the brief. Rex knew that it could not go in the brief. So, the brief was rewritten. It still argued against the extension of busing, but it did not make arguments that simply flew in the face of legal reality at the time. Now when you did that, you made people who were, you know, really true believers very, very mad. . . .

. . .

Kenneth S. Geller [Deputy Solicitor General, 1976–86]: . . .

. . . [T]here are really two types of cases that the Solicitor General's Office handles. The overwhelming majority of the cases involve purely legal issues in which there is very little doubt about what the government's position is, there is a long-held institutional interest. On the other hand, there is a small segment of cases that really does not involve so much law as policy. I think that many of the civil rights cases fall into that category as do some other cases involving antitrust policy. It is clearly the case that the government's position in those cases varies from administration to administration. I think that the Supreme Court appreciates that when it gets a brief in one of those cases, it's getting the position of the current administration rather than the institutional interest of the United States. That, as Richard said, has been the history of the Solicitor General's Office for a very long time. . . . I don't think there is anything wrong with presenting the president's position on those issues. If the president can give a speech on busing or abortion or some other issue of great public concern, it is not clear to me why his solicitor general cannot present views to the Supreme Court on those issues when a case arises.

I do think, though, that when those cases arise the Court appreciates, as I said, that it is hearing from the administration rather than the

93. [Footnote 65 in original] . . . 402 U.S. 1 (1971).

institutional interests of the United States. It is incumbent on the solicitor general to present those positions in a way that is faithful to precedent and completely professional. . . .

. . . [A]s to the first category of cases . . . there were many cases that arose during those four years, and I worked on several of them, where it was clear to me that the government had a consistent, long-held, and important position to present to the Supreme Court but it was clearly inconsistent, I think, with Rex's personal views. I never saw in my time that there was any wavering on his part in terms of what his role should be in those types of cases. One case [in] which certiorari was never granted, so it never became a published decision but took up a lot of time when I was there, was a case involving right-to-work laws.[94] The issue arose of whether state right-to-work laws applied on federal enclaves within a state where the state has ceded its legislative jurisdiction to the federal government. One circuit had held that state right-to-work laws did not apply, and the employee sought Supreme Court review, and the Court asked for our views.

I know that this was an issue close to Rex's heart and he got lobbied very, very strongly and over a long period of time by people who wanted him to take the position that state right-to-work laws applied in those federal enclaves. It was clear, though, that there was a consistent federal government position to the contrary. The NLRB felt strongly about the issue. Rex not only filed briefs saying that certiorari should be denied because state right-to-work laws did not apply there, but also he wrote a letter, which I still have a copy of, to some people on the other side explaining what the proper role of the solicitor general should be.

. . .

Richard Wilkins: I would just add that I agree with everything that Ken said. My remarks were aimed more at . . . what he calls, the category-two cases. I know for a fact that it was anguish for Rex to argue *Garcia* because he taught me constitutional law. I remember him enthusing about *National League of Cities v. Usery* in class—about how this was the best decision of the Supreme Court in fifty years. And then as solicitor general he was faced with the task of arguing to reverse *National League of Cities v. Usery*, and he did. He did so very, very well. And I remember being in his office late at night one night just talking about that case and he said, "You know, it's kind of ironic, isn't it, Richard?"

Michael W. McConnell [Assistant to the Solicitor General, 1983–85]: Am I misremembering? I could have sworn that the resolution of this—one of the biggest federalism controversies of our time—is that the position that Rex argued was that the federal government should prevail but should prevail under the rule of *National League of Cities v. Usery*, rather than by overruling that decision. It was a position,

---

94. [Footnote 67 in original] Lord v. Local Union No. 2088, Int'l Bhd of Elec. Workers, 646 F. 2d 1057 (5th Cir. 1981), cert. denied, 458 U.S. 1106 (1982).

by the way, which no member of the Supreme Court—not one justice—bought. They split five to four, with five of them overruling *National League of Cities v. Usery* and the other four dissenting and saying that the federal government should have lost. It was, I think, a very interesting case to think about in terms of both jurisprudence and lawyerly strategy because it presented such an array of possible positions. The heart of the problem, and I had not known what an enthusiast Rex may have been for *National League of Cities*, but the heart of the problem was that *National League of Cities* was itself a very ill-thought-through opinion. Even if you agree, as I do, with the fundamental federalism thrust of it, the actual doctrinal superstructure of the opinion made very little sense. It was indeed paradoxical. I do not mean from a left-right or federalism or anti-federalism point of view. I just mean it was not a very well constructed opinion. Nonetheless, *National League of Cities* was an icon, in a sense, of federalism, so you could not quite attack it. So, Rex was in a doubly difficult position.

The ideal thing would have been to be able to file a brief that would help the Court to reformulate the *National League of Cities* doctrine in a way which would have retained its solid core. Unfortunately, the facts of that particular case did not lend themselves very well to an intelligent reformulation, because if there was a case where the federal government should lose under *National League of Cities*, it was probably that case.

Kenneth Geller: I can remember a lot of meetings. . . . I know Ted Olson was involved in some of them as head of the OLC [Office of Legal Counsel], involving what position we should take. There seemed to be unanimity that we should not ask that *National League of Cities* be overruled. It was not so clear what position we should take that would defend the statute in the context of this transit authority. Rex had to decide between making an argument that Congress could not regulate core governmental functions, as I recall, or another argument that was being put forward, which went off on a government/proprietary distinction, which some people found much too slippery. But you are right. Ultimately, the Court concluded that it could not work its way out of that box without overruling *National League of Cities*. Rex, I think, to a large extent, submerged his personal views because he understood what the government's interest was there.

· · ·

John H. Garvey [Assistant to the Solicitor General, 1981–84]: Let me try to shift the focus but not the question. . . . There are a few cases that are politically sensitive, and the government might want to shift positions from one administration to the next. The place where you see this a lot is in the filing of amicus briefs . . . .

In the great majority of these cases, as Ken says, we either were parties taking the government's side or filed an amicus brief asserting a government position of long standing. But there were a few where this was not true. One was Lynch v. Donnelly,[95] the first crèche case. School prayer was a big issue in the first Reagan administration. I want you to think about *Lynch* for a minute. When the government files an amicus brief, the earliest section in the brief is entitled "The Interest of the United States." It is a paragraph in which the Solicitor General's Office is obliged to state why the government is filing—what is our interest? This was a ticklish thing in the crèche case. What business does the government of the United States have filing about crèches or school prayer? This is an issue that Andy and I are divided on.

I am going to sound like an academic, but let me ask you to think about four different kinds of reasons. I think they sum up the positions people have taken. First, you might say, the solicitor general ought to stay out because there is not a federal statute and this is the business of the states. This is a federalism argument for the SG's Office staying out. I think this is a mistake. The reason the question comes up is that the Constitution of the United States has been interpreted by the Supreme Court of the United States and other branches of the federal government to apply to school prayer in 1962. The federal government is *already* regulating the states in this regard. If there is a problem, it is not that intervention by the United States upsets the balance of federalism.

There is a second possible reason. Maybe ... this is a separation of powers problem. Maybe the SG's Office ought to stay out because this is the business of another branch of the federal government, in this case the judicial branch (though sometimes it might be Congress that we are deferring to). I feel about that pretty much the way Judge Easterbrook does. I think it might actually be good for the Solicitor General's Office to get in. If the Court is already involved, as it is in interpreting the First Amendment, maybe they could use a little help. Maybe it would bring a little balance or separation to the various branches of the federal government. It might be good for the Solicitor General's Office to think of itself as an agent of the executive branch (It is a part of the attorney general's department, after all). But there are a couple of reasons why the office holds back. You have heard them from most of the lawyers who have been talking.

A third reason for holding back on amicus filings is that the office has some fidelity, not to the United States as its client (Andy's view), but to the Constitution and statutes of the United States. If you are not a devotee of critical legal studies, you will think that the Constitution and laws have a lot of meaning, and one of the things that ought to constrain the SG's Office from swerving from one position to the next, from one administration to the next, is that it is bound within certain limits by the law. This is the sort of thing that good lawyers do. Rex sometimes felt that he had to hold back in a particular case because there was a long-standing interpretation of the law. The office has an obligation of fidelity to what the Constitution or the statute is saying. You can only do

95. [Footnote 71 in original] 465 U.S. 668 (1984). These cases deal with the con- stitutionality of displaying crèches (a Nativ- ity scene) in public Christmas displays.

so much within those limits. I do not want to overstate this. A lot of the positions we took on religion cases in 1985 that were slapped down by the Court, have changed now. The court now takes the position that the Solicitor General's Office took in the 1984 term. So I do not want to overstate this argument. But that is one thing that constrains you.

The fourth, and last, constraint is that it may be tactically stupid. The Roosevelt administration did better when it started listening to its lawyers. You do not want to spend the office's capital by taking extreme positions that the Court is going to be angry with you because they are so dumb. You do not want to jeopardize the next brief you file because the Court will think you said something stupid the last time. I do think that there are reasons for restraint. But I am not above seeing the office take political positions from one administration to the next.

Andrew Frey: My views may be in the minority in this, but the question that I ask is, what is the legitimacy of government involvement when the question involves an issue like school prayer? I do not believe the fact that the First Amendment bears on that question means that it is the federal government's business. It seems to me whether or not there may permissibly be school prayer is between the students, the schools, and the Supreme Court. . . .

. . .

Bush I Panel . . .

Maureen Mahoney [Deputy Solicitor General, 1991–93]: . . . [Mahoney describes how a coup in Haiti in 1991 and the ensuing flood of refugees led to an Administration decision, after more than 12,000 refugees were at Guantanamo for processing, to begin interdicting ships on the high seas and directing them back to Haiti. Legal challenges to this policy followed, on the grounds that either the Immigration and Nationality Act or the U.N. Treaty on Refugees required asylum processing before someone claiming asylum could be turned away, and Ken Starr, the SG, assumed responsibility for the litigation in the lower courts, to defend the policy.]

As we were preparing our briefs for the Supreme Court, Bill Clinton was campaigning for president, and one of the things that he campaigned on was that this policy was illegal, a view that was shared by an editorial in the *New York Times*. So, this was very much an election issue. As you all know, President Bush lost his job and so Ken Starr did too. And that left me in the office to begin preparation for an oral argument to defend a policy that had been condemned by the new president while he was campaigning. So, we were sitting there in the office and there was not a successor at the time. Drew Days did not arrive until, I think, May, after the argument in the case had occurred. And so there was a bit of a vacuum of leadership, and we were kind of waiting for instructions but nevertheless continued on. And the White House ultimately decided to simply go forward not to make any changes in the policy. There was nothing announced. It was all just—we waited.

Nothing happened. I went into Court, argued the issue as if there had never been a change of administration, and the Court upheld the legality of the policy in an eight to one decision.[96] As it turned out, the only real implications of the election was that there was this tremendous uncertainty during this period of time. But I also want to tell one other anecdote about this case because it is really a testimonial to just the tremendous talent that is in the Solicitor General's Office, and I am going to name Ed Kneedler by name because when I was preparing for the argument in this case, Ed, [who] was the deputy there now and has been there for many, many years, said to me, "Well, Maureen, do you think you should go to Haiti because Justice Blackmun is going to ask you if you have ever been there?" And I said, "Oh, Ed, I do not need to go to Haiti. I can handle the argument without going to Haiti." But sure enough, just as Ed predicted, Justice Blackmun asked me if I had ever been to Haiti....

John G. Roberts [Deputy Solicitor General, 1989–93; Chief Justice, 2005–]: ...

In 1994, I argued a case in the Supreme Court against General Lee, as I always called him and as he liked to be called. With the foresight that I might someday be speaking at a symposium in honor of Rex Lee, I had the graciousness to lose nine to nothing. But the argument was revealing. I was the petitioner. I got up first. It was immediately apparent from the questioning that there were three independent grounds on which the Court was going to rule against me unanimously, and they proceeded to beat me over the head for a half hour. I staggered to my seat and then Rex got up. And early on into his argument, Justice O'Connor—in a very uncharacteristic burst of cruelty—asked Rex Lee why he had neglected to raise a fourth argument which would also be a winning argument. Rex turned and looked down at me, literally and figuratively, and, with a wink that I am sure was perceptible only to me, said something to the effect that he did not want to be accused of piling on. So Rex, among other things, was a very gracious winner. I would like to be able to tell a story about him being a gracious loser, but unfortunately I never did beat him in a case.

One thing you can perhaps discern from some of the presentations is that everyone who has served in the Office of the Solicitor General agrees that the office enjoyed a golden age roughly corresponding to the time that they were in the Office of the Solicitor General....

. . .

On the issue of the controversial cases that create some division in the office, what impressed me the most coming into the office was how controversial the "non-hot button" cases could be within the government, and how almost every one of the cases generated some degree of

---

96. [Footnote 92 in original] See Sale v.   (1993).
Haitian Ctrs Council Inc., 509 U.S. 155, 188

controversy. I was surprised about the degree of disagreement through-out the executive branch in a wide variety of cases. I remember a case coming across my desk that I recall as Commodities Futures Trading Commission v. Securities and Exchange Commission.[97] I am looking at that and said, "Well, how can that be? They are on the same team. They cannot be against each other." And, of course, both of them were knocking on our door and saying, "You are our lawyer now in the Supreme Court." One is saying file a certiorari petition and the other is saying oppose a certiorari petition. That was resolved by holding, and this was typical, a series of interminable meetings with all interested parties that looked like nothing so much as Thanksgiving dinner at a dysfunctional family because—as you rapidly find out—these agencies have a long history of sort of squabbling with each other and now they are—it is wrong to view it this way, but—before their parents and the parents are going to decide which one gets punished and which one gets rewarded. I have always been a little surprised at the prominence of the office in resolving those types of decisions.

The president is the chief executive, but so many intra-executive branch disputes end up in the Solicitor General's Office and were resolved by the solicitor general saying, "Well, this is the position we are going to take before the Supreme Court" and that became the executive branch position. And again, I think it is a surprising development that the office has that authority. I remember in particular . . . there was a dispute that was captioned Resolution Trust Corporation v. Internal Revenue Service—again two players I thought were on the same team.[98] It involved a very complicated thing called a mortgage swap deal that the regulatory agency had set up to allow failing S & Ls to take huge tax deductions without recognizing any loss on their books and thereby allow them to continue to exist. And the IRS was not buying it. They thought this was ridiculous. . . . And this was a novel situation for me for a number of reasons. One, Ken [Starr] was recused. He had adopted a very aggressive recusal policy for cases coming out of the D.C. Circuit. Ken had been a judge on the court, of course, and remarkably to me after having reached that pinnacle of the legal profession had decided to resign to become solicitor general. He was recused from this case, so I was the acting solicitor general. And I basically got to decide which side of this case I wanted to be on. The people from the regulatory agency said, "You should take our side." The people from the IRS came in and said, "You should take our side." I sided with the IRS and lost ignomini-ously. So, it is one of those rare cases when you get to choose your side, and I still made the wrong decision. But I did what I had occasion to do on a couple of other occasions, which is I filed a brief for the Internal

---

97. [Footnote 101 in original] The case was actually captioned Chicago Mercantile Exchange v. SEC, 883 F. 2d. 537 (7th Cir. 1989), cert. denied, 496 U.S. 936 (1990), but the CFTC and SEC had filed dueling briefs, taking opposing positions in the Court of Appeals.

98. [Footnote 102 in original] *See* United States v. Centennial Savs. Bank. (Resolution Trust Co., Receiver), 499 U.S. 573 (1991); Cottage Sav. Ass'n v. Comm'r, 499 U.S. 544 (1991).

Revenue Service and then authorized the opposing regulatory agency to participate in the Supreme Court through their own attorneys, which they did.... I did not feel that the exercise of an authority to say to the regulatory agency that you may not take your case to the Supreme Court was appropriate in this situation largely because, as you might imagine, on both sides of the case there were private interests involved and I thought it was best for that agency to present its view when I had decided to side with the other agency....

... I did the argument in the case of Hudson v. McMillian,[99] which established that certain brutality by prison guards violated the Eighth Amendment. I went back just yesterday and read our "statement of interest." It is remarkable. The first sentence says, "The United States is interested because it prosecutes cases of brutality in which the civil rights of the prisoner are violated." The second sentence says, "The United States is interested because it defends federal officials who are sued for violating civil rights of prisoners." There is a delicate dance that went on throughout. The writing of the brief in that case was an extraordinarily delicate dance because this is not a situation—and this, I think, is one of the key differences between the private sector and the Solicitor General's Office—in the private sector, you want to win or lose and, yes, you know, your client is a little bit interested in what the reason is. The reasoning might affect him, but they want to win or lose. In the Solicitor General's Office, you have got to call your shot. It is not enough to win. The Civil Division that defends federal prison officials would want to hear a lot more when you came from this case other than that we won because they are going to have to follow the rule of law on the other side in future cases. So you have to get the rationale right. I know that results in instructions to the oral advocates that make the job much more difficult than in the typical private case. Quite often, the instruction is: "Okay. You can take this position on what the brief says, but whatever you do, do not get into this area because that is going to cause problems. You cannot take a position on that question, or if you get into that, you have got to take a position that undermines the result you are trying to reach in the particular case." The care that goes into the crafting of a balanced brief that is acceptable to prosecutors bringing cases against prison guards and to government lawyers defending prison guards has to carry through to the oral argument as well, which is an extraordinary challenge for any advocate.

... Those who have worked in the office know that, I do not want to say that the bulk of the office's work, but a big chunk of it does not involve the Supreme Court at all. It involves authorizing appeals to a higher court by government agencies and government officials who have lost in the lower courts. Ken, when he was solicitor general, adopted an initiative that I thought was very valuable, which was he went to a number of the courts of appeal to argue cases there. The purpose of that, as I understood it, was to symbolically remind the court of appeals'

99. [Footnote 103 in original] 503 U.S. 1 (1992).

judges that every time they are seeing an appeal from a United States agency it is not just the losing lawyer in the U.S. Attorney's Office who says, "I am going to get a second opinion." It has been carefully vetted by lawyers in the office and signed off on by the solicitor general. I was surprised as this initiative unfolded to learn how many of the sitting judges were unaware of that. I think it was very valuable for Ken to do that. . . .

Kenneth W. Starr [Solicitor General, 1989–93]: . . .

. . . [On] the Nancy Beth Cruzan so-called right-to-die case.[100] And I had not thought about these end of life issues seriously at all. Happily, my family had not been confronted at that time with any such issues. And so enjoying that blissful ignorance, I simply was not steeped in the area when it came up through the state system and the Court granted certiorari without CVSG-ing—"calling for the views of the solicitor general"—we were confronted with what do we do. Do we participate . . . ? The process, which perhaps has already been described, is when the Court grants certiorari there is a fanning out very professionally of the papers throughout the far-flung reaches of the executive branch. And I was quite astonished to get the feedback of how many agencies of government, departments and agencies of government, were very keenly interested in the issue of right to die. I thought HHS might be interested but there were a legion. I am not going to burden the discussion with it. So it became quite obvious quite apart from what the right to life community might be urging upon us at a political level that there was this programmatic interest that was very, very deep and very keen.

It became a very delicate process that John has so ably and brilliantly described of sorting out what the position would be. The brief writing itself was very delicate, as you can imagine, given the subject matter, given the novelty of the issue, the lack of case law. But our basic urging was, "Please, do not do what you did in *Roe v. Wade*," which is constitutionalize this area of social policy. Happily, the Court has seen fit—that in the main—to say [that in] these burgeoning areas of morality ethics and the like of social policy we are going to allow the democratic process to work. But while that could be criticized as an agenda-type thing of "Why are you involved?" it just was quite striking to me throughout my tenure how programmatically interested the government is in so many different issues.

· · ·

Reagan II Panel . . .

Charles Fried [Solicitor General, 1985–89]: . . .

Well, talking about the duties of the solicitor general and the standards by which he acts, what was said yesterday was very interesting but struck me—when I think back to my own experience—as a little

---

100. [Footnote 116 in original] See Cruzan v. Mo. Dept. of Health, 497 U.S. 261 (1990).

bit over abstract and overly rigorous as if there is some kind of checklist: Was this in the government's interest? If not, was it in the interest of the executive branch? . . . I had a much . . . looser notion. My notion was that the president had chosen me to do a particular kind of job because there was a particular sense of how things had developed and how they ought to develop. It is not as if I had been chosen to run the Bureau of Weights and Measures.

I was not at all shy about stating my conception of the job and had the advantage of having acted as deputy solicitor general, so the people who chose me knew exactly what I thought. They paid their money, and they took their choice. And what I thought was that on the whole, the legal system had gone a little bit off the rails. I would say in the direction of what one might call the Skelly Wright–William Brennan direction and that one of the things that it was important to do was to try to haul it back a little bit. If you can explain that in terms of the government's interests or the interests of the executive, okay, that is fine, but that is not exactly how I viewed it.

I had another sense and that is because I was hearing quite a lot about the solicitor general as the tenth justice. That kind of thought had two aspects to it. It denigrated the integrity of other government officials throughout the government. For instance, the head of the Commerce Department when he announces the consumer price index must do so with perfect accuracy. And if somebody asks him to fiddle with figures for political reasons, he has to say, "No. If you want somebody to do that, fire me and get somebody else to do it." The secretary of labor, the Bureau of Labor Statistics, and the unemployment figures, similarly. And the secretary of state has to be able to keep the word that he gives to foreign countries. So, I think there is a morality to doing these jobs throughout the government and that it is not particularly to the solicitor general.

Similarly, I think it denigrates a little bit the ideal of a lawyer altogether. I think of Tony Kronman's picture of the Lost Lawyer. I do not think that that Lawyer is all that lost and I think the solicitor general is Kronman's kind of lawyer. He is a person who believes that his duty to the courts and the system and his client generally is to speak the truth—to do so as accurately as possible, not to misstate the record, not to misstate the precedents, and not to do silly things. That is the duty of lots of lawyers. . . .

Well, let me tell you a story and then I will subside. Then you can help me figure out whether I followed the canons of being a solicitor general . . . .

. . . [The] Landrum–Griffin Act . . . was passed in 1959 as part of the redressing of the balance in our labor laws. But, those who have the feeling that it is the natural condition of man to belong to a union objected to a profession called "labor persuaders." Labor persuaders are people who are hired by a company during a representational election to help the company make the case to the workers that maybe it is not the best idea to unionize. Well, this is thought to be a little bit like cigarette advertising.

In order to express this, the Congress and the Department of Labor ["department" or "DOL"] could not quite say, "You cannot do this" because that would violate the First Amendment. They said that anybody who is in this profession of labor persuader must register all his labor persuader clients and how much they pay them, and disclose that regularly with the department. With this exception: if what you do is you give legal advice to a company in a representational fight, then you do not need to disclose that. . . .

Well, this is the problem: there are some law firms that do both. Way back, I think in 1959, the Department of Labor adopted the position that if you are a law firm also doing persuader work, you must disclose not only your persuader clients but also your legal clients. . . . It was a position that had been challenged but prevailed in many circuits until the Eighth Circuit got hold of it—Dick Arnold actually. He said, "This is crazy. That cannot be right. You must disclose your persuader clients, but not your legal clients. The DOL's interpretation is a terrible stretch, and I do not care how many circuits went the other way. It is not right." And that was his decision.

The solicitor of labor came to me and said, "Would you authorize rehearing en banc?" I said, "I am very uncomfortable about this because you are wrong. Dick Arnold is dead right. This is a terrible stretch. It is a distortion of the law. You know, you were named by Ronald Reagan just like me. And one of the things that he named us for was that the bureaucracy should stop stretching its authority well past any intended legislative purpose to try and cover the world. You should not be doing this." He said, "Hey, thanks for the lecture. Can I go for en banc?" I said, "All right. I will let you go en banc because I do not have to sign that, but you are not going to go any further." He lost en banc, and needless to say, he was back asking to go for certiorari. I said, "No. I am not going to sign my name to a piece of paper which defends an outrageous bureaucratic overstretch like that. And I do not care how many circuits have gone along with it. I am not going to do it."

Well, the Secretary of Labor got very upset about it, and he called for a meeting with the attorney general. He wanted to meet with the attorney general. This, by the way, is very typical of a much underappreciated attorney general. So, he called for a meeting with Ed Meese. And Ed Meese said, "Fine. I would love to meet with you about it." He asked for a memo from me beforehand, which I prepared, and he had the meeting.

Well, the meeting was a very large meeting. It is what we used to call a "monster rally." Many people were present: the Secretary of Labor, and so was the attorney general, and so was I. He presented his position; I presented mine. And then the attorney general sat there taking notes, which he often did—copious notes. As I remember, the Secretary of Labor was talking all about politics and how the Senate "this" and how this committee "that," and one thing or another. And then the attorney general afterwards said to me, "You do what you want." And what I wanted to do was not to authorize that certiorari, which, by the way, put the DOL in an embarrassing position because it meant that Eighth Circuit labor persuaders had a different policy, and in the end the DOL changed the policy for the whole country. The Secretary of Labor did not take it to the president, which we did not expect he would, and there it rested.

Well, what model of the solicitor general's role did that exemplify? I am not at all sure. . . .

Thomas W. Merrill [Deputy Solicitor General, 1987–90]: . . .

. . . The appeal authorization function of the solicitor general has been mentioned a couple of times, but it has not been given a lot of attention. This was a very unusual appeal recommendation because, as best I know, it is the only one that ever was resolved in the Oval Office of the White House. The president of the United States, in effect, was the person who finally decided whether or not we were going to appeal the case from the district court to the court of appeals.

The issue involved a statute that Congress had passed which required the Justice Department to seek to close the PLO observer mission of the United Nations in New York City. The statute and the issue, needless to say, were very political. The statute had been lobbied for vigorously by AIPAC, the American Israeli Political Action Committee. There was a lot of opposition to this in the State Department and also in the international community, but Congress had passed the statute and the Civil Division had gone into court in New York and sought an order closing the PLO observer mission.

The district judge, whose name I do not recall, had issued an opinion saying, and here I am paraphrasing, "I am not going to grant relief because even though the statute seems plain, the PLO mission enjoys a status under customary international law." There was no argument that the mission was protected by a treaty. But he said, "Protected by customary international law, and I think that Congress must specifically say that it intends to abrogate customary international law before it can do so by statute." Now, as the appeal recommendation came up to us from the Civil Division, two things were obvious. One was this was a political hot potato, and two, the legal reasoning was weak. Ordinarily you would think that this would lead to a rather routine "yes" authorization of appeal. But one thing bothered me, in particular, about the papers that came up to our office: there was no mention in the Civil Division's memo whatsoever of the president's prerogative in the field of foreign affairs, and in particular there was no mention of the fact that, in Article II of the Constitution, one of the relatively few enumerated powers given to the president is the right to receive ambassadors and other foreign ministers. And one can readily see how deciding whether or not there should be a PLO observer mission in the United States would be within the scope of receiving or not receiving ambassadors or public ministers. And so I was concerned that if we aggressively appealed this decision and sought vindication of the statute, we would create a precedent that says that Congress has the power to legislatively control the president's constitutional authority to receive or not receive public ministers.

Well, in what Charles [Fried] would probably characterize as a standard mid-level bureaucratic response, I decided what was needed was more memos. I recommended to Charles that we deny an appeal until the Civil Division came up with a more complete analysis of how this recommendation was consistent with Article II and separation of powers.

Charles, being more imaginative and direct, instead issued what I think is the most unusual appeal authorization I ever saw, which was "Appeal—*comma*—Subject to the Condition that the President States Publicly that This Is Consistent with the Foreign Policy Interests of the United States." And this was very ingenious. I think what Charles was saying here, and he can speak to this himself if there is any time left, is that we were not getting involved in politics—the solicitor general has nothing to do with that. We were perfectly satisfied with the legal case for an appeal—there was no question about that, but we were deeply concerned that the separation of powers concern had to be addressed. If the president wanted this mission closed, then there was nothing inconsistent between his constitutional power and enforcement of the statute. But if he did not want the mission closed, then this was inconsistent with his constitutional prerogatives, and that needed to be faced head on. Well, needless to say, the Civil Division was unhappy with this resolution. They sought—what was the phrase—"monster meeting?"

Charles Fried: "Monster rally."

Thomas Merrill: ... "Monster rally" in the Attorney General's Office. Abe Sofaer came over from the State Department. He was the legal advisor at that time. He made the argument in favor of not appealing. For Civil Division, John Bolton said, "Let's appeal." The attorney general, I believe it was Richard [Thornburgh] at that time, agreed with the appeal recommendation. I think he stripped away, although the details escape me now, the Charles Fried qualification. That was the last I heard of it until I read the newspapers for the next several days to see what happened to my little appeal recommendation.

The first article in the *Washington Post* said that a meeting had been scheduled in the White House in which Secretary of State George Schultz was going to appeal directly to the president from Attorney General Richard [Thornburgh's] appeal authorization. And then the next day there was an article reporting that the president of the United States had decided not to authorize an appeal; that the State Department won and the Justice Department lost.

Now, what did this say about the Solicitor General's Office? I am not really sure. I have no idea what was said in the Oval Office. Ronald Reagan probably did not read my memo or any of the other legal papers that were generated. I have often fantasized, however, that maybe, just maybe, because of what we did in the Solicitor General's Office, somebody in the White House mentioned Article II in the course of these discussions and thought about the constitutional implications rather than just thinking about the political and foreign policy implications. If in fact that did happen, then I think here is another illustration of how the Solicitor General's Office, by consistently attending to these issues, consistently can have the impact and protect the separation of powers.

. . .

Clinton I Panel . . .

Michael R. Dreeben [Assistant to the Solicitor General 1988–94; Deputy Solicitor General, 1994–]: . . .

There have been several competing accounts of what the role of the solicitor general should be, or is. . . .

One is that the solicitor general represents the United States, or sometimes, "the people of the United States." This is a great phrase and it is certainly true, but it is so vague as to be of absolutely no help in resolving any particular controversy. And usually when someone says that they want to advocate a position that is in the interest of the people of the United States, you can be fairly confident that you are going to get their view of what is in the interest of the people of the United States. You are going to have to go further if you want to get significant guidance as to what to do.

Another theory is that the solicitor general is the lawyer for the executive branch. That is undoubtedly correct in a purely formal sense. The solicitor general works for an administration. He is appointed by a president. The executive power is lodged in that president. The solicitor general is not a free agent that can impose his own policy decisions on the rest of the government without accountability. But it still is not particularly helpful to make that observation because when the executive branch interests collide with acts of Congress that may be more or less clear, a parochial view that says, "Well, we just represent the president and the executive branch," is a lot easier to put forward by those people who do not actually have to go before the Justices and argue a case. The Justices are going to expect lawyers from our office to be able to respond to problems in their [legal] positions by reasoning from precedent and along the lines that the Court is accustomed to hearing, and you have to be able to function in that kind of environment in order to represent the United States as a lawyer in court.

A third view is that the office really represents the institutional interest of the government, which is, I think as Andy Frey put it, distinct from whoever happens to be occupying the particular office at any one moment. It is undoubtedly true that that is a very valid consideration that often has a great bearing on what position the solicitor general will decide to take in a particular case. But even describing the office's mission as representing institutional interests does not help you all that much when those institutional interests conflict. This can occur over very important matters, but as John Roberts indicated, it can also be over seemingly technical or unimportant matters. A lawyer who has recently announced that he is leaving our office and going back to private practice wrote an email that reported some of his strong memories of being in the office, and one of them was being in a meeting in which there was a shouting and screaming match between the Labor Department and the Federal Maritime Commission over the definition of a Jones Act seaman. I mean, you are working with people who can get excited enough to scream at each other over those things, and the solicitor general is going to have to make judgments about which institutional interests of the government he is going to represent.

. . .

A fourth model, which I do not think has been discussed, is one that comes from the Supreme Court itself in a case called *Providence Journal*,[101] which involved whether judges could petition for certiorari to obtain review of decisions that had rejected contempt findings that judges had imposed. The Court held that the judges could not file their own petition for certiorari. The solicitor general was the only officer in the government who had that power because the solicitor general represents the United States, and the Court concluded that "the United States," within the meaning of the statute, encompasses all three branches of government: the Congress, the executive, and the judicial branch. As a result of that interpretation, I think it is fair to say that we really have as clients the United States in all branches of government, and it would be difficult to say that we can exclude any one of them and single-mindedly pursue one particular branch's interest. Ted Olson last night, I think, put that point in a somewhat different way, but it reflects what we actually do in the office, and that is that we have responsibilities to all three branches of government.

. . .

The SG's credibility in the interpretation of the law and in knowing what can be sold or what cannot be sold to the Supreme Court gives him a measure of independence as against institutional interests of the government and against political pressures that are put on him. At the same time, the institutional interests can sometimes be played off against each other or against political objectives to put the SG in a position to frame a brief which is characteristically, in my experience, more nuanced, less hard-edged than any of the more bright-line proponents of a particular theory are urging him to do. I wanted to talk about a couple of cases that illustrate that very briefly.

But before I go to the cases, it is important to say that part of how the SG is able to achieve some measure of independence by playing off

101. [Footnote 185 in original] United   693 (1988).
States v. Providence Journal Co., 485 U.S.

his interpretations of the law with other policy objectives and institutional objectives is through the creation of very powerful traditions in the office that are passed down to new lawyers who join the office, usually in the form of stories about what happened. These stories may not always be accurate. Some of them may be wholly apocryphal. Some of them may be shaded. If you hear Larry Wallace's account of *Bob Jones*,[102] for example, you get a very different picture than I suppose you would get from Don Ayer or Tom Merrill. But the important thing is that these stories tend to reinforce a culture within the office that emphasizes technically excellent legal work, a real sense of obligation, and devotion to present to the Supreme Court an honest product. [That does not mean] a product that is not an advocate's brief; believe me, we are advocates, and as the alums who are in the audience know from opposing us, we play hard when we have decided what we want to do. We will definitely argue hard for our positions, but always with the sense that you just do not want to be standing up in front of the Supreme Court arguing a position that is untenable for any reason—because it is obviously political, because it is contrary to established doctrine that the Court is not going to overrule, or because it is contrary to the record.

. . .

I'll just talk briefly about a couple of cases that illustrate on a more mundane level, but I think perhaps a more characteristic level, how the SG moderates positions by virtue of being between the Court, the institutions of government that have their own agendas, and political actors.

One of them is Wilson v. Arkansas,[103] which was a case that came to the Supreme Court at least twenty years after anyone in the country really cared about the issue. It involved no-knock entries by police to execute a search warrant. This was a very hot issue during the Nixon administration when President Nixon secured legislation that authorized no-knock entries. And I can remember as a high school student reading editorials denouncing this. But as a legal matter it just simmered and went below the surface. Nothing ever happened about it until the early 1990s, when the Supreme Court of Arkansas decided to issue an opinion that held that there is no requirement that police knock and announce before entering to execute a search warrant. The Fourth Amendment prohibition against unreasonable searches and seizures does not incorporate that common law principle. The defendant, Wilson, then sought certiorari and obtained it, and we were looking at filing an amicus brief.

Normally the government does file amicus briefs in criminal cases if there is any possible way to support the state. We very rarely file amicus briefs in criminal cases that do not support the state. That is the dominant institutional pattern though, I think it is safe to say, all solicitors general that I am aware of. In *Wilson*, however, we had a little

---

102. [Footnote 187 in original] Bob Jones Univ. v. United States, 461 U.S. 574 (1983).

103. [Footnote 188 in original] 514 U.S. 927 (1995).

bit of a problem. After thorough research by an assistant in our office, it became clear that the Arkansas Supreme Court's position was entirely untenable. There was an incredible wealth of common law history that supported the notion that the knock-and-announce rule was embedded in the fabric of how searches and seizures were done. There was a lot of movement on the Supreme Court, at least among some Justices, toward adopting a view that referred back to the common law to determine what protections were incorporated into the Fourth Amendment, although not consistently.

So, we were facing the problem of having great difficulty seeing how we could support the state in the face of this case law. We ultimately determined that we could file a brief that supported the state, but it would not be a brief that said there is no knock-and-announce rule. It would be a brief that says there is one, but it is subject to exceptions, as for instance, when the police think that the suspect is about to destroy the evidence to be seized, like drugs, or the suspect will escape, or the suspect will resist violently. These were all common law exceptions that we wanted to get foursquare before the Court and, therefore, filed a brief that argued those.

This could be said to be somewhat contrary to the narrowly conceived institutional interest of the United States because certainly law enforcement would be better off if they did not have to justify knock-and-announce under any standard. They could just go in; the evidence would not be suppressed. And yet, we determined that this was an untenable position, and the solicitor general authorized the kind of brief that I described.

When we got to argument, the attorney general of Arkansas, General Bryant, was defending his position of the firm line in the sand—there is no knock-and-announce principle. He got a lot of rough sledding from Justices who were saying, "You mean, you can take a bulldozer and just knock somebody's door down? Would that be okay?" He was nodding his head, and we were sort of shaking our heads. Finally, the Court had enough and Justice O'Connor asked a question, and this is a quote: "Well, what's the matter with the proposal of the solicitor general? That would certainly take into account the long common law tradition. I, for one, can't buy your proposal at all. You have no comment on what the solicitor general proposes?" She went on in that vein for a while and finally the attorney general of Arkansas conceded and said, "Well, you have described the U.S. government's position, and that is the state's fallback position," at which point Justice Scalia leaned forward and said, "Time to fall back, General."

. . .

d. The Solicitor General and the Court: A Limited Influence?

While the SG has undoubted influence in the Court's decisions about which cases to hear, and files briefs—either as amicus or as a party—in an increasing percentage of the cases heard, the next set of readings by former SG Seth Waxman suggests that there are real limits on the SG's ability to influence the Court's decisions, at least in some areas.

————————

Seth Waxman, *Twins at Birth: Civil Rights and the Role of the Solicitor General*, 75 Indiana L. J. 1297 (2000)

. . .

The position of Solicitor General was created by Congress in 1870, shortly after ratification of the Fifteenth Amendment. . . .

. . . What almost no one appreciates is the extent to which the position of Solicitor General has been linked with the national imperative to foster equal rights. . . .

. . .

. . . By my reckoning, civil rights law in this country has largely developed in two distinct epochs: the first began with the Civil War and ended with Plessy v. Ferguson;[104] the second was launched by the Second World War. I plan to examine the relationship between the development of civil rights doctrine and the work of the Solicitor General by looking at two Solicitors General from each period: for the first epoch, Benjamin Bristow and Samuel Phillips, the country's first two Solicitors General; for the second, Philip Perlman, who served from 1947 through 1952, and Archibald Cox, who was Solicitor General from 1961 through 1965.

. . .

By the advent of the Civil War, litigation on behalf of the United States was hopelessly confused. Much of it was conducted, even in the Supreme Court, by private attorneys retained for individual cases. These attorneys—many of whom were simply political favorites—made ill-considered and inconsistent representations about the position of the United States with respect to interpretations of law. And when the Civil War created an avalanche of litigation, the system simply collapsed. . . .

. . . . As the report accompanying the 1870 Act stated:

We propose to create . . . a new officer, to be called the solicitor general of the United States, part of whose duty it shall be to try . . . cases [on behalf of the United States] in whatever courts they may arise. We propose to have a man of sufficient learning, ability, and experience that he can be sent to New Orleans or to New York, or into any court wherever the Government has any interest in litigation, and there present the case of the United States as it should be presented.

104. [Footnote 5 in original] 163 U.S. 537 (1896).

Now obviously no individual, no matter how "learned," could represent the United States in the Supreme Court, deliver legal opinions for the President, serve as a second-in-command to the Attorney General, and travel around the country trying important cases. Any Solicitor General would need to prioritize. And Congress and President Grant had in mind what that priority should be. It was reflected unambiguously in the selection of the first two Solicitors General, men who occupied the position for its first fourteen years.

* * * * * * * *

Benjamin Helm Bristow, the first Solicitor General, was a renowned lawyer, a loyal Republican, and an ardent defender of black civil rights. For the four years immediately preceding his appointment as Solicitor General, he served as United States Attorney in Kentucky, and during that tenure he distinguished himself as one of the most aggressive and successful prosecutors of Ku Klux Klan cases in the country. When Bristow resigned his position as U.S. Attorney, newspapers as far away as New York hailed him as a "civil rights champion."

That is precisely what Congress and the President wanted. They wanted the Civil War Amendments and the legislation implementing those Amendments enforced, particularly in the South; and they wanted an expansive interpretation of these laws defended in the courts, particularly in the Supreme Court. That, as I see it, is how the civil rights mandate of the Solicitor General was set in train.

No one thought this mandate would be easy, and it was not. Violence against southern blacks, frequently perpetrated by members of the Ku Klux Klan, was on the rise. In some southern states, egregious attacks were going unremedied by local law enforcement. And several southern states had passed so-called "Black Codes," which, in the very face of the Thirteenth Amendment, reinstated a race-based caste system, keeping blacks as an inferior and dependent class by disabling them from owning, renting, or transferring property, pursuing skilled callings, or seeking access to courts. This great State of Indiana had in its constitution—and enforced through legislation—an article providing that "[n]o Negro or Mulatto shall come into or settle in the State" and further providing that "[a]ll contracts made with any Negro or Mulatto coming into the State ... shall be void; and any person who shall employ such Negro or Mulatto, or otherwise encourage him to remain in the State shall be fined."

Congress responded by enacting the Civil Rights Act of 1866, the Enforcement Act of 1870, the Ku Klux Klan Act of 1871, and the Civil Rights Act of 1875. When Congress passed the 1866 Act, the Fourteenth Amendment—which is the focus of most contemporary discussions regarding Congress's power to legislate over civil rights—had not yet been ratified. Thus, Congress asserted power under the Enforcement Clause of the Thirteenth Amendment, which grants Congress the power to enforce the prohibition on slavery by appropriate legislation. The 1866 Act granted all citizens "the same right ... to make and enforce contracts, to sue, be parties, and give evidence, to inherit, purchase, lease, sell, hold, and convey real and personal property ... as is enjoyed by white citizens." It declared the infringement of those rights under color of law to be a federal crime; it created a federal civil right of action to vindicate those rights; and it permitted the removal of state actions where a party claimed that the vindication of those rights was not possible in state court. [The 1870, 1871 and 1875 Acts] built on the 1866 Act, and invoked the by-then-ratified Fourteenth Amendment as authority for expanding federal criminal jurisdiction to cover racially motivated violence and general interference with national civil rights, like the right to vote.

But enforcing those statutes and convincing federal courts to sustain their constitutionality was a tall order, and it required a Janus-like posture for the Solicitor General—looking in one direction to the district courts for enforcement, and in the other to the Supreme Court for validation. On the enforcement side, the prospects of obtaining civil rights jury verdicts in the Old Confederacy seemed remote. And with respect to challenges in the Supreme Court, the Solicitor General would be required to persuade an institution that by its very nature tends to be conservative and inclined toward incrementalism, to uphold a legislative program that was, by its very nature, far-reaching, indeed revolutionary.

Overall, the Solicitors General fared much better with enforcement in the district courts than they did with defense in the Supreme Court. Let me give you a few examples. In United States v. Rhodes,[105] Bristow, while U.S. Attorney, prosecuted three white defendants under the 1866 Act for robbing a black family in Louisville. Bristow premised federal jurisdiction on the theory that state authorities could not prosecute the case since state law precluded blacks from testifying in cases in which whites were parties. The defendants challenged the Civil Rights Act as an unconstitutionally broad grant of federal jurisdiction over matters properly left to state criminal law. Supreme Court Justice Swayne, sitting as a Circuit Justice, held that the Act permissibly granted federal jurisdiction in the case (citing as authority an opinion of the Supreme Court of Indiana that had invalidated an article of the Indiana Constitution under the Thirteenth Amendment and the 1866 Civil Rights Act). In November 1869 Bristow was able to report to the Attorney General that as a result of the *Rhodes* decision, he had been able to " 'proceed[] with the trials of a large number of parties ... under the Civil Rights Act and a number of those tried have been sentenced and are now serving their respective terms.' "

But in the Supreme Court Bristow could not sustain his legal theory ..... By a vote of 7–2 the Supreme Court held that the 1866 Act did not permit federal courts to assert jurisdiction over a criminal case, even where a state prosecution could not proceed because all of the witnesses

---

105. [Footnote 23 in original] 27 F. Cas.   785 (C.C.D. Ky. 1866) (No. 16,151).

were black and therefore unable to testify against a white defendant under state evidentiary rules. [106]

The phenomenon of success in enforcing the civil rights acts in the district courts, followed by frustration in the Supreme Court, became a pattern. . . .

[V]igorous prosecution [under the Enforcement Act] reduced the incidence of racially motivated violence. But in 1876 the Court struck down portions of the Enforcement Act in United States v. Reese[107] and narrowly construed the constitutional guarantees protected by another provision in United States v. Cruikshank[108]—effectively gutting prosecution efforts under the Act. Both cases were argued for the government by Samuel Phillips, who succeeded Bristow as Solicitor General in November 1872.

Like Bristow, Phillips came with a civil rights pedigree. As a federal prosecutor in North Carolina, he had conducted and overseen several important Klan prosecutions. But Phillips' remarkable tenure as Solicitor General—he served for twelve years under six Attorneys General—was marked by bitter defeats in the Supreme Court in a host of civil rights cases.

Most notable were the Civil Rights Cases[109] and United States v. Harris,[110] both decided in 1883. In the former, the Court struck down the provision in the Civil Rights Act of 1875 that prohibited racial discrimination in public accommodations, conveyances, and places of public entertainment. Observing that the provision in question did "not profess to be corrective of any constitutional wrong committed by the States," the Court held, 8–1, that it exceeded Congress's power to enforce any substantive provision of the Fourteenth Amendment. Similarly in *Harris*, the Court struck down § 2 of the Ku Klux Klan Act of 1871, which outlawed conspiracies to deprive citizens of the equal protection of the laws. The Fourteenth Amendment, the Court held, could not be violated by the conduct of private parties, no matter how invidious their purpose or how egregious their acts. The Court allowed that racially motivated murder by a private party might violate the Thirteenth Amendment, but § 2 of the Ku Klux Klan Act was not limited only to race and thus could not be upheld on that theory either.

One explanation for the civil rights defeats that Phillips—and, before him, Bristow—suffered at the Court may be that by the time cases implicating Reconstruction civil rights laws began reaching the Court with regularity in 1875 and later, much of the political ardor of Reconstruction had subsided. . . .

106. [Footnote 27 in original, citing Blyew & Kennard v. United States, 80 U.S. 581 (1875).]

107. [Footnote 34 in original] 92 U.S. 214 (1876).

108. [Footnote 35 in original] 92 U.S. 542 (1876).

109. [Footnote 37 in original] 109 U.S. 3 (1883).

110. [Footnote 38 in original] 106 U.S. 629 (1883).

Samuel Phillips's best-known civil rights argument is one he made long after his twelve-year tenure as Solicitor General. In 1896, representing a black railroad passenger named Homer Plessy in the infamous case of *Plessy v. Ferguson*, Phillips argued that a Louisiana statute requiring railroad companies to provide "equal but separate accommodations for the white and colored races" violated the Equal Protection Clause. The Court, we all know, held otherwise. The sole dissenter in both the *Civil Rights Cases* and *Plessy v. Ferguson* was Benjamin Bristow's former law partner, Justice John Marshall Harlan.

The Court's ruling in *Plessy* brought to an unmistakable end the country's first civil rights era. Following the string of earlier losses in defense of many of Congress's civil rights statutes, *Plessy*'s overwhelming rejection of what today seems like a bedrock principle of equal protection left few options, and little enthusiasm for further legal challenges. For fifty years little happened.

* * * * * * * *

And then another great war ended. Black soldiers returned home in 1945 with a new perspective on their abilities and their treatment. President Truman appointed a Committee on Civil Rights, which urged the federal government to become active in seeking an end to racial discrimination in all its forms. Truman publicly committed that the federal government would be a "friendly vigilant defender of the rights and equalities of all Americans. . . . Our National Government," he said, "must show the way."

But who was to lead? The Department of Justice had no Civil Rights Division, and generations of federal prosecutors had come and gone with no experience whatsoever in civil rights prosecution. . . .

The mission fell to Solicitor General Philip Perlman and his staff to devise a strategy. In this new phase, the posture of the United States was quite different. Litigation now came to the Supreme Court not in enforcement suits brought by the United States, but in private litigation brought by the likes of Charles Hamilton Houston, Thurgood Marshall, and the attorneys of the NAACP. . . in an incremental progression, generating momentum one small step at a time.

The United States was not a party in these cases. But there can be little doubt, in this period of utmost fragility in civil rights litigation, that the cautious Supreme Court would attach great significance to the position—if any—the Tenth Justice might choose to take. And in a series of filings, the Solicitor General lent unqualified support to the plaintiffs.

Shelley v. Kraemer[111] was one of several cases involving constitutional challenges by private parties to racially restrictive covenants on real property. Perlman filed a brief amicus curiae, urging the Supreme Court to declare that the Fourteenth Amendment prohibits judicial enforcement of racially restrictive covenants. The brief reminded the Court that, although formal, de jure residential segregation no longer

---

111. [Footnote 51 in original] 334 U.S. 1 (1948).

existed, "[a]ctual segregation, rooted in ignorance, bigotry and prejudice, and nurtured by the opportunities it affords for monetary gains from the supposed beneficiaries and real victims alike, does exist because private racial restrictions are enforced by courts." In bold language asserting a broad right to be free from race-based discrimination, the Solicitor General urged the Court to prohibit judicial enforcement of restrictive covenants. And the Court did. [112]

Shelley was the first time the United States had gone on record in the Supreme Court broadly condemning all manifestations of racial discrimination. Two years later, a civil rights case came to the Court in which the United States was a party—a party defendant. In an unusual and bold filing, the Solicitor General announced that he would not defend the judgment in favor of the United States, but instead would argue in support of the civil rights plaintiff. The case was Henderson v. United States,[113] and here is what happened.

Elmer Henderson, a black passenger on a train, was declined service in the train's dining car because the tables conditionally reserved for blacks were partially occupied by whites when he arrived in the dining car. The dining car steward refused to seat Henderson at those tables, even though they had empty seats. Henderson filed a complaint with the Interstate Commerce Commission ("ICC"). During the litigation, the railroad changed its rules so that a separate table surrounded by a partition would always be reserved for black passengers. But that still left the question of whether such segregation was itself permissible. Henderson maintained that it was not, and contended specifically that it violated the Interstate Commerce Act. The ICC rejected his claim on the ground that the provision of separate but equal facilities was not discrimination. Henderson appealed to a three-judge district court, naming both the United States and the ICC as defendants. The Justice Department defended the ICC's decision, the district court agreed, and Henderson appealed directly to the Supreme Court.

Consistent with his now-public stand against racial discrimination, Perlman refused to defend the district court's judgment and switched sides in the case. The brief filed on behalf of the United States contended that segregation on trains violated the Interstate Commerce Act. But Perlman did not stop there. He also argued that the doctrine of "separate but equal" was itself unconstitutional, and that *Plessy* should be

---

112. [Footnote 53 in original] There is an ironic footnote to this proud moment. The brief for the United States in *Shelley* was written by four Jewish lawyers named Philip Elman, Oscar Davis, Hilbert Zarky, and Stanley Silverberg. Their names, however, were deliberately omitted from the filed brief. According to a subsequent account by Mr. Elman, Arnold Raum, the Solicitor General's principal assistant (and himself a Jew) told the others that it was "bad enough that Perlman's name has to be there, to have one Jew's name on it, but you have also put four more Jewish names on. That makes it look as if a bunch of Jewish lawyers in the Department of Justice put this out." Philip Elman & Norman Silber, *The Solicitor General's Office, Justice Frankfurter, and Civil Rights Litigation, 1946–1960: An Oral History,* 100 Harv. L. Rev. 817, 819 (1987).

113. [Footnote 55 in original] Henderson v. United States, 339 U.S. 816 (1950).

overruled. Never before had the United States called for the overruling of *Plessy*, and to fully appreciate the significance of this step it is necessary to understand how very rarely the Solicitor General ever asks the Supreme Court to overrule one of its precedents. But in Henderson, the Solicitor General left no room for doubt. As Philip Elman, then an attorney in the Solicitor General's Office, later described the brief, it "took a flat, all-out position that segregation and equality were mutually inconsistent, that separate but equal was a contradiction in terms."

The Supreme Court was not prepared to take such a bold step. It found for Henderson without reaching the constitutional question. But even though the Court did not reach *Plessy* in *Henderson*, it seems reasonable to surmise that the Solicitor General's willingness to do so made an impression with the Court.

That impression was of the utmost importance in the succession of all-important school desegregation cases Thurgood Marshall had lined up for the Court. On the same day the Court announced its decision in Henderson, it decided two cases—Sweatt v. Painter[114] and McLaurin v. Oklahoma[115]—involving racial segregation in universities. Again, the Solicitor General filed amicus briefs in both cases urging the Court to overrule *Plessy* and declare that state-sponsored racial segregation is unconstitutional in all cases.

Again the Court ruled on narrow grounds. This time, it did reach the Constitution: it found equal protection violations in both *Sweatt* and *McLaurin,* but it did so by focusing on the inferiority of the education black students had received in both cases, not on the fact of segregation itself. Because blacks' educational opportunities were not equal to those of whites, the Court emphasized that the cases did not require any reconsideration of whether "separate but equal" was itself a valid doctrine.

But the Court could not avoid *Plessy* forever. In its landmark 1954 decision in *Brown v. Board of Education*,[116] a unanimous Court held that state-mandated segregation in public education is unconstitutional, without regard to the relative quality of the educational opportunities available to either race.

. . .

The actual parties in the *Brown* litigation presented the Court with a stark choice: either uphold "separate but equal" or end school segregation virtually immediately. Were those truly the Court's only options, there is reason to doubt whether *Brown* would have come out quite as it did. An order compelling immediate desegregation almost certainly could not have commanded unanimous support on the Court, and many on the

114. [Footnote 60 in original] 339 U.S. 629 (1950).

115. [Footnote 61 in original] 339 U.S. 637 (1950).

116. [Footnote 65 in original] 347 U.S. 483 (1954).

Court may well have worried that attempts at executing such an order might have been met with widespread civil disobedience and violence.

Speaking as an amicus curiae supporting the plaintiffs, the Solicitor General proposed a third option: hold segregation to be unconstitutional, but allow school districts some leeway in the implementation of desegregation.[117] As Philip Elman described it, this option "offered the Court a way out of its dilemma, a way to end racial segregation without inviting massive disobedience, a way to decide the constitutional issue unanimously without tearing the Court apart." By balancing its principled opposition to segregation with a pragmatic view of what sorts of arguments were actually viable to the Justices, the Solicitor General helped the Court to arrive at a decision that was both forceful in principle and workable, even if neither side was fully satisfied.

The United States's position in *Brown* reflected an important aspect of the Solicitor General's unique role with respect to the Supreme Court. In our constitutional system, respect for precedent and the rule of law are of surpassing importance, and adherence to those principles makes the Supreme Court an inherently cautious institution. The United States as a litigant benefits from, and shares, the Court's institutional adherence to doctrines of stability in the law. And for that reason, the Court has come to rely on the Solicitor General to present briefs of the most scrupulous fidelity, and to combine statements of principle with strategies by which the Court may rule in a manner most consistent with principles of stability. Thus, the Solicitor General's position in *Brown* combined an unambiguous, principled insistence on an end to "separate but equal" with a suggestion for a mechanism by which the Court could abandon *stare decisis* in a matter of critical societal importance with a minimum of upheaval and risk to the Court's institutional authority.

The suggestion of "all deliberate speed" has been criticized as both without legal foundation and responsible for a great deal of foot-dragging in the post-*Brown* era. There is some force to both of those points. But it also seems clear that the Court could not have resolved *Brown* as it did—and certainly could not have done so unanimously—without the cushion of "all deliberate speed." Although both sides in the case opposed it, "all deliberate speed" proved to be the ground on which all members of the Court felt they could stand together.

* * * * * * * *

117. [Footnote 66 in original] The actual phrase "deliberate speed" did not appear in the United States's initial brief. According to Elman, that phrase "made its first appearance in *Brown* in [Assistant Attorney General J. Lee] Rankin's oral argument in 1953." [Philip Elman & Norman Silber, *The Solicitor General's Office, Justice Frankfurter, and Civil Rights Litigation, 1946–1960: An Oral History*, 100 Harv. L. Rev. 817, 830 (1987)]; see 49A *Landmark Briefs and Arguments of the Supreme* *Court: Constitutional Law* 538 (Philip B. Kurland & Gerhard Casper eds., 1975); Mark V. Tushnet, *Making Civil Rights Law* 208 (1994). [Editors' Note: The United States' initial brief had argued that the Court should allow district courts a "reasonable period of time" to plan for and implement decrees; the phrase "all deliberate speed" had been used previously by the Court and on several occasions by Justice Frankfurter. See Jim Chen, *Poetic Justice*, 28 Cardozo L. Rev. 581, 586–88 (2006).]

The approach manifested in *Brown*—tempering principle with pragmatism and a respect for precedent—was the very hallmark of the government's strategy in the next phase of civil rights litigation. Archibald Cox was John F. Kennedy's Solicitor General. A Harvard law professor with expertise in labor law and government experience during the Truman administration, Cox enjoyed a storied tenure as Solicitor General. Many of his important victories came in civil rights cases.

. . .

Archibald Cox was a cautious litigator by nature, and his views about the appropriate posture for the Solicitor General with respect to positions taken before the Court was similarly conservative. As a result, in several civil rights cases, he found himself in tactical disagreement with Attorney General Robert F. Kennedy. Kennedy envisioned the Department of Justice championing a broad vision of the Reconstruction Amendments as prohibiting all forms of race-based discrimination and as authorizing Congress to pass legislation concerning even purely private conduct. Cox was more circumspect. He was mindful of the Supreme Court's opinion in the *Civil Rights Cases* and skeptical that the Court would agree that the Fourteenth Amendment authorized Congress to reach purely private conduct, however discriminatory.

Moreover, Cox thought it inappropriate for the Solicitor General to be pressing expansive and doctrinally tenuous arguments before the Court. He knew that the views of the Solicitor General carried considerable weight with the Court, and he felt he had a duty (as Robert Kennedy once described Cox's view) " 'to protect the Court from itself' " when it came to delicate questions of constitutional rights.

Bouie v. City of Columbia[118] is a prime example of Cox's approach. *Bouie* was one of a series of cases arising out of the convictions of black protestors for violating state trespass laws by staging sit-ins at whites-only lunch counters. In the Supreme Court, the protestors argued that the States had enforced their trespass statutes in a racially discriminatory manner, and they urged the Court to find that such discrimination violated the Equal Protection Clause.

Many in the Department of Justice wanted the United States, as amicus curiae, to take a similar position.... But Cox chose a much more narrow ground ... focus[ing] the Court's attention on statutory interpretation. Cox contended that the South Carolina trespass statute could not fairly be read to proscribe the conduct of the protestors. And even if the statute was susceptible of such a reading, he argued, the defendants in *Bouie* certainly did not have fair warning that the statute would be so construed.

To me, that position seems rather far-fetched, since an obvious objective of the plaintiffs' demonstration had been to get arrested. But the Supreme Court accepted Cox's invitation to rule narrowly. The South Carolina courts were free to construe the trespass statute to cover

---

118. [Footnote 72 in original] 378 U.S. 347 (1964).

a protestor's refusal to leave a lunch counter, it held, but because such a reading was an unforeseeable expansion of the previous meaning of the statute, it could not be applied against the defendants in *Bouie.*

The next Term, Cox again adopted a cautious approach, this time in two landmark cases involving challenges to the Civil Rights Act of 1964—the first significant civil rights legislation since the Civil Rights Act of 1875 was struck down in the Civil Rights Cases. The cases were Heart of Atlanta Motel v. United States[119] and Katzenbach v. McClung.[120]

At issue was the 1964 Act's "public accommodations" section, which prohibited discrimination in restaurants, motels, movie theaters, and the like. For the United States, the question was whether to defend the provision under the Fourteenth Amendment, or under the Commerce Clause, or under both. The Attorney General, many leading civil rights lawyers and constitutional scholars, and even reportedly the President, preferred the Fourteenth Amendment. The underlying aims of the Civil Rights Act, after all, sound more in equal protection than interstate commerce, and so the Fourteenth Amendment seemed a more appropriate choice.

Cox disagreed. In his view, the Court could accept the Fourteenth Amendment argument only if it were prepared to overrule its decision in the *Civil Rights Cases.* The "public accommodations" section of the Act was directed specifically at private action, and the Court had held in the *Civil Rights Cases* that Congress could not reach purely private discrimination under Section 5 of the Fourteenth Amendment. Not only did a decision overruling the *Civil Rights Cases* seem unlikely to Cox, but his regard for *stare decisis* made him uncomfortable at the prospect of mounting an argument that conflicted directly with an eighty-year-old precedent.

In contrast, Cox considered the Commerce Clause argument to be "as easy as rolling off a log." A former labor law professor, Cox knew that during the New Deal Solicitor General Stanley Reed had used a succession of NLRB cases to coax the Supreme Court into a remarkable expansion of Congress's Commerce Clause authority. And since in passing the Civil Rights Act Congress had determined that motels, restaurants, and other public accommodation establishments "affected" interstate commerce, Cox believed the Court would have to accept that determination unless it could conclude that Congress had acted irrationally.

He was, of course, right. Relying on the Commerce Clause, the Court unanimously upheld the 1964 Civil Rights Act in both cases. Two members of the Court—Justices Douglas and Goldberg—wrote separately to indicate that they would also uphold the Act under Section 5 of the Fourteenth Amendment. But with respect to the Court as a whole, just as in the sit-in cases, Cox's strategy was effective in achieving the

119. [Footnote 80 in original] 379 U.S. 241 (1964).

120. [Footnote 81 in original] 379 U.S. 294 (1964).

desired result without requiring the Court to revisit entrenched precedent or create wholly new areas of jurisprudence. Cox was, in that sense,
a successful civil rights advocate during a period in which the Court
might not have been as willing as many in the Department of Justice
and elsewhere to redefine the foundations of civil rights law.

. . .

. . . I do not mean to leave the impression either that promotion of
civil rights doctrine was the principal reason the position of Solicitor
General was created, or that Solicitors General have pursued civil rights
objectives at the expense of other responsibilities. The overarching
imperative for creating the office, and the mandate under which Solicitors General have acted ever since, focused on the need to vest in one
position the responsibility for ascertaining, and promoting, the interests
of the United States with respect to all litigation, regardless of subject
matter. At the same time, though, it would be a mistake to overlook the
undeniable civil rights subtext for creation of the office, the consequent
special responsibility many Solicitors General have felt for civil rights
litigation, and the contribution they have made to the development of
this unique area of law.

. . . The role played by Bristow and Phillips was unique to the
period. Their impact in quelling persistent violence by vigorous enforcement was significant, but riding circuit and overseeing criminal prosecutions in the district courts has long since passed from the Solicitors'
General repertoire. Also entirely unique was the opportunity Bristow
and Phillips had to write on a truly clean slate. The Civil War Amendments and the Reconstruction civil rights legislation were all new. They
fundamentally altered the relationship between the national government
and the states. Then—unlike now—*stare decisis* was simply not a major
consideration.

Why Bristow and Phillips were so notably unsuccessful in the
Supreme Court is a question that calls out for research. An advocate
with the orientation of Archibald Cox might question whether the
approach his early progenitors took—using creative arguments in support of broad readings—presented a bridge that was simply too long and
uncertain for cautious jurists to cross. And yet Bristow and Phillips did
not have the luxury Cox enjoyed—surveying 100 years of precedent to
determine what might and might not work.

Philip Perlman did have the benefit of hindsight; and yet he pursued
a litigation strategy quite reminiscent of the one Bristow and Phillips
had followed—this time with great success. The position staked out by
the United States in *Shelley, Henderson*, and the early school desegregation cases was broad and uncompromising. The Court did not go as far,
as fast, as the Solicitor General advocated, but it seems reasonable to
conclude that the arguments of the United States—particularly the
unequivocal embrace of a broad theory of equal protection and the
outright call for the overruling of *Plessy*—had considerable influence,

coming as they did from an office that is itself institutionally committed to the principle of stare decisis.

Archibald Cox was quite different, and caution in his case was rewarded with an enviable record of success. Cox's approach was grounded in pragmatism, but it also reflected something more. Like many other Solicitors General, Cox had a strong reverence for *stare decisis* and the Solicitor General's special obligation to safeguard the institutional integrity of the Court. And Cox's approach in civil rights litigation was a lineal continuation of the posture adopted by the United States in *Brown*—pointing the Court at a momentous juncture toward an approach that would permit all members of the Court to articulate with one voice a result the nation would respect.

. . .

Seth Waxman, *Does the Solicitor General Matter?*, 53 Stan. L. Rev. 1115 (2001)

. . .

[A]t the losing end of every federalism decision in the past nine years has been a Solicitor General. Kenneth Starr started us off in 1992 with New York v. United States.[121] Drew Days doubled that, with watershed losses in *Lopez*[122] and *Seminole Tribe*.[123] Not to be outdone, in a single year as Acting Solicitor General, Walter Dellinger matched that number with *Printz*[124] and *Boerne*.[125] But I have left my predecessors far, far behind. *College Savings*,[126] *Florida Prepaid*,[127] *Alden*,[128] *Kimel*,[129] *Morrison*,[130] *Garrett*[131]—I have lost them all, five to four. I may be the only Solicitor General to have actually *won* a federalism case in the last decade—Reno v. Condon.[132] . . .

. . . We all know that the Solicitor General is popularly termed the "Tenth Justice." We know that many legendary figures have held the position. And we know that for most of its venerable history the office has earned and enjoyed a unique respect in the Supreme Court. But does

121. [Footnote 2 in original] 505 U.S. 144 (1992).

122. [Footnote 3 in original] United States v. Lopez, 514 U.S. 549 (1995).

123. [Footnote 4 in original] Seminole Tribe of Florida v. Florida, 517 U.S, 44 (1996).

124. [Footnote 5 in original] Printz v. United States, 521 U.S. 898 (1997).

125. [Footnote 6 in original] City of Boerne v. Flores, 521 U.S. 507 (1997).

126. [Footnote 7 in original] College Sav. Bank v. Florida Prepaid Postsecondary Educ. Expense Bd., 527 U.S. 666 (1999).

127. [Footnote 8 in original] Florida Prepaid Postsecondary Educ. Expense Bd. v. College Sav. Bank, 527 U.S. 627 (1999).

128. [Footnote 9 in original] Alden v. Maine, 527 U.S. 706 (1999).

129. [Footnote 10 in original] Kimel v. Florida Bd. of Regents, 528 U.S. 62 (2000).

130. [Footnote 11 in original] United States v. Morrison, 529 U.S. 598 (2000).

131. [Footnote 12 in original] Board of Trustees of the Univ. of Ala. v. Garrett, 121 S. Ct. 955 (2001).

132. [Footnote 13 in original] 528 U.S. 141 (2000). . . .

that matter? Does the Solicitor General have any special ability to influence the development of Supreme Court doctrine?

Sometimes—and sometimes often—the answer is yes [both substantively and procedurally]....

... When the Solicitor General speaks about the needs of the national economy, when he warns of the real-world consequences of interpreting statutes or structuring remedies in a particular way, when he explains the context in which laws are executed, the Court properly takes heed. Not because Solicitors General are uniquely persuasive, or because they wear a funny costume. But rather because the views they express constitute a distillation—a reconciliation—of the often-disparate long-term interests of a national, representative government.

When I speak of *procedural influence*, I am referring in part to the ability of the Solicitor General—on occasion—to affect which cases come to the Court on a particular issue, and in what order. Why should this matter? Well, for one thing, because judges are human beings: Facts and context influence not just the outcome, but sometimes also the reasoning of a decision. For another thing, judges in the common law tradition are incrementalists. They are generally more comfortable moving the law in small steps rather than in a gigantic leap. Considering cases in incremental fashion permits the Court, over time, both to address the content of constitutional doctrine and to explore in step-by-step fashion its logical limits. And it permits developments in constitutional doctrine to develop momentum. It's important that each journey start out on the right foot. And sometimes the Solicitor General can help.

One way is through the unique tradition whereby the Court "invites" the Solicitor General to express the views of the United States with respect to petitions pending in nongovernment cases. When so invited, the Solicitor General advises the Court of the United States' views both on the merits of the issues presented and on whether the case presents an appropriate vehicle for resolving those issues.

The Solicitor General may also influence the progression of cases by exercising strategic judgment about which to bring before the Court, and in what order. When Franklin Roosevelt ushered in the New Deal, the political branches confronted a conservative Court whose constitutional doctrines stood squarely in the path of their programs. Much has been written about how the Court's doctrine came to accommodate the New Deal. But in several critical respects careful litigation strategy played an indispensable role—for example, in the deliberate ordering of the Gold Clause cases, and especially the Commerce Clause cases culminating in *Jones & Laughlin Steel*.[133]

* * * * * * * *

133. [Footnote 20 in original] NLRB v.   (1937)....
Jones & Laughlin Steel Corp., 301 U.S. 1

My aim here is to explore—tentatively and sketchily—the extent to which in the modern federalism cases the Solicitor General retains any unique ability to assist in the development of the law. If Stanley Reed and Robert Jackson could claim some credit for assisting the Hughes Court in moving Commerce Clause doctrine from "direct effects" to Wickard v. Filburn,[134] should their remote successors get correlative blame for the reversal of that trend? Does the Court, in other words, particularly care what the views of the United States are in federalism cases? Does the Solicitor General retain any influence over the sequence in which cases and issues reach the Court? . . .

I'll speak first about substantive views. I think it's pellucidly clear that the bottom-line views of the United States as to the appropriate balance between national and state power are uniquely unimportant to the Court. . . .

. . .

In the sovereign immunity cases the majority does seem unconcerned even with the United States' arguments about consequences. . . . Thus, the point emphasized by the United States in *Alden*—that the Labor Department's handful of inspectors cannot possibly investigate all state violations of the minimum wage laws—was not even addressed in the Court's opinion. Generally . . . it is both simplistic and wrong to conclude that in federalism cases what the United States says doesn't matter. It does—and it matters a great deal that the Solicitor General is there to say it.

But whatever influence the Solicitor General's substantive views may retain, the office's ability to influence the order in which cases reach the Court is severely diminished in the federalism area. There are several reasons why this is so.

First of all, we live in an era in which private rights of action are the norm; litigation under laws protecting civil rights, working conditions, and the environment, for example, is now largely out of the hands of the federal government. And the availability of attorneys fees makes it more likely that counsel will press even weak cases to the next highest court.

Second, the advent of well-funded public-interest litigation groups of all stripes has eroded the ubiquity of the Solicitor General's ability, and incentive, to present cases designed to promote long-term strategic goals, rather than simply the interests of a particular case. Beginning in the late 1940s, Thurgood Marshall broke the Solicitor General's monopoly in this area, and with style: his careful staging of education cases culminating in *Brown v. Board of Education* was historic and overwhelmingly successful. It is now a model for advocacy groups of every political persuasion.

Third, not only does the United States no longer monopolize the ability to influence the order in which cases percolate up to the Court,

---

134. [Footnote 21 in original] 317 U.S. 111 (1942).

but in truth the Solicitor General is now uniquely impaired in this respect. That is so because modern federalism doctrine is being developed at the expense of a series of enactments that Congress passed at a time when another paradigm—a paradigm of greater national power—prevailed. Many of the statutes now subject to constitutional challenge . . . were drafted on the now unjustified, and then perhaps too-cavalier assumption that Congress had virtually unfettered power under the Commerce Clause and the Fourteenth Amendment, so long as it did not intrude on individual liberties. Traditionally, and except in very unusual circumstances, Solicitors General have considered it extremely important to defend the constitutionality of Acts of Congress whenever they are seriously challenged—even in the weakest of cases. . . . [But] adherence to this practice may turn out to have accelerated the decline of national authority. In the dozen or so federalism cases considered by the Court on my watch, only two were cases in which the United States was an original party. One of those, *Condon*, we won; and in the other one . . . the Court avoided the constitutional question. In all of the cases we lost, the United States was an intervenor in someone else's lawsuit.

Finally, and perhaps most basically, in federalism cases, from the Solicitor General's perspective the very premise of ordering cases is gone. The ability to move the law incrementally is just that—the ability to *move* the law. But on questions of federalism, the position of the United States in recent years has been to preserve the constitutional status quo. With the significant exception of *Garcia*, in the area of federalism it has been the States, and the Court itself, that have been trying to move the law. The Solicitor General has been playing defense for over twenty years.

* * * * * * * *

Let me come then to the more fundamental question: Does the sequence in which these federalism cases arise even matter? If it doesn't, no one need worry or gloat about the diminished capacity of the Solicitor General to "help" the Court in the orderly development of the law.

Here I think it makes sense to distinguish among the various federalism doctrines. In the Eleventh Amendment cases it seems clear, in hindsight at least, that order never mattered. The issue of state sovereign immunity is really one of theology, with little room for shades of grey. When Justice Scalia chose sides in *Union Gas*[135] and Clarence Thomas replaced Thurgood Marshall on the Court, there were five votes for every case in which what the majority has termed a "fundamental postulate" could be called into play. I think the Court's decision in *Seminole Tribe*—in which a majority interested in incrementalism could easily have avoided the Eleventh Amendment—proves the point. In this area, the Court is simply uninterested in baby steps. This is in-for-a-penny, in-for-a-pound—on both sides.

135. [Footnote 28 in original] Pennsylvania v. Union Gas Co., 491 U.S. 1 (1989).

. . .

The Fourteenth Amendment cases present a closer question. At least before *Garrett* was decided, it was not at all clear that the Court had a distinct or cohesive vision of how far to scale back Congress's power. In that environment—where a majority believes things have gone too far but is not committed to a shared conception of a stable end state—the characteristics and sequence of the cases presented may well play some role.

If it does, then the order in which recent Section Five cases have arisen has been strikingly unkind to the defenders of Congress's power. There is, in fact, no better example of the Solicitor General's inability to prevent a march of exceptionally weak cases.

Let's start with *Boerne*. The law at issue in that case, the Religious Freedom Restoration Act (RFRA), was nothing less than a sharp stick in the eye of the Supreme Court. RFRA was an avowed legislative nullification of Employment Division v. Smith,[136] and in the absence of any legislative record that state or local governments were in fact purposefully disadvantaging religious practice, the case put an impossible strain on Katzenbach v. Morgan.[137] The United States as intervenor opposed certiorari, but the respondent Church acquiesced and the Court obliged. The irritant in *Boerne*, of course, was the perceived separation of powers affront. But since everything relating to the Fourteenth Amendment is a federalism issue, it was the power of the national government to protect civil rights that took the brunt. The anomaly of *Boerne* gave birth to a newly minted judicial limitation—"congruence and proportionality." Would the next case in line, *Florida Prepaid*, have provoked that doctrine if it had come first? I doubt it.

And things did not get better. The next case was *Kimel*, challenging Congress's abrogation of Eleventh Amendment immunity for suits brought under the Age Discrimination in Employment Act (ADEA). Of all forms of discrimination, without a doubt the weakest vehicle in which to test drive the new "congruence and proportionality" doctrine was age discrimination. The Supreme Court had thrice examined constitutional challenges to personnel practices based on age, and in all three cases it had emphatically rejected the challenges. Indeed, in contrast to other forms of discrimination, the Supreme Court had never met an age discrimination claim it liked. And the legislative record in *Kimel* was underwhelming. . . .

Morrison . . . completed the trifecta of weaklings. The Violence Against Women Act (VAWA) addressed a serious historic problem in a careful way. There is much to criticize in the Court's opinion. But as a vehicle with which to slow or reverse the Court's development of "congruence and proportionality," *Morrison* was a most unlikely candidate.

---

136. [Footnote 32 in original] Employment Div. Dept. of Human Res. of Or. v. Smith, 494 U.S. 872 (1990).

137. [Footnote 33 in original] 384 U.S. 641 (1966).

For one thing, Virginia law included remedial provisions the petitioner in that case, a victim of campus rape, could have invoked. But she elected not to pursue them. Moreover, VAWA provided a damages remedy even if a victim never notified a state official—and conversely even if a state justice system had acted exemplarily. In addition, the law had been invoked only in a handful of reported cases, and rarely successfully. And finally, *Morrison* was not only unlikely to reverse the Court's momentum; in the context of such an otherwise weak case, it also presented the Court an opportunity to extend restrictive 19th Century precedents in the *Civil Rights Cases* and *United States v. Harris*, by means of the "congruence and proportionality" doctrine.

. . .

Let me say a few words about the Commerce Clause cases. Here, even more clearly than with respect to the Fourteenth Amendment and unlike the Eleventh, the majority appears motivated not by a shared vision of an ideal end state, but rather by a consensus only that the doctrine had previously settled in the wrong place. Congress has substantially provoked that sense of dissatisfaction by enacting ever more laws extending federal jurisdiction—especially criminal jurisdiction—into areas with which the national government had never previously been concerned—often with little evidence of deliberative reflection. The Driver's Privacy Protection Act at issue in *Condon* and the Gun–Free School Zones Act struck down in *Lopez* are paradigmatic examples.

The point about a shared dissatisfaction with the status quo ante— unlike a shared vision of the ideal end state—is, again, that how far and in what direction doctrine moves may well depend upon context. And with respect to the commerce power, the Court seems even less sure of where it wants to go than under the Fourteenth Amendment.... With respect to the commerce power, the guiding principle remains quite unformed; indeed, it has progressed little beyond the admonition in *Jones & Laughlin* itself that limits must be found so that Congress does not "obliterate the distinction between what is national and what is local." Given the realities of our interdependent world, crafting a stable doctrine from that broad principle will be extremely difficult.

Does that mean that case selection and sequence matter? I think they may well. The New Deal Commerce Clause cases are, as noted, a textbook example of this principle.... *Lopez*, of course, was a shock.... But it was a shock in the way that any sudden reverse in a long, steady march must be. And as the majority (and particularly the concurring Justices) chose to present the case, *Lopez* could have been understood to be little more than a shot across Congress's bow. Look, for example, at how Congress reacted: It amended the statute simply to require that the gun have "moved in or otherwise affected interstate commerce"—hardly a significant challenge in any prosecution.

The next Commerce Clause case, *Morrison*, was, as I have noted, a challenging case in which to assert uniform national authority before the current Court. *Morrison*'s resolution of the commerce issue can readily be criticized in part because Congress's obvious purpose to remedy the substantial economic effects of historic and entrenched gender bias could have provided the Court an important foothold on the slippery "truly-national/truly-local" slope. But the obvious specter of federalizing all of domestic relations law—in the majority's view the paradigmatic "truly local" subject—made it impossible for the Court to accept that point.

What we are seeing, I suggest, is a non-teleological step-by-step retreat along the line of march that began [in the New Deal and led through the 1960s.] It is almost as if a winter hiker, trudging with small steps through deep snow for a long time, has now begun to retrace the same footsteps—for how far no one knows. The very tentativeness of the Court's incipient journey is well-demonstrated, I think, by its recent decisions . . . in which it went to considerable lengths to construe both the federal arson statute and the Clean Water Act so as *not* to have to resolve the Commerce Clause challenges. We are at a delicate point in the Commerce Clause journey—one in which context and advocacy may make all the difference. . . .

Questions and Comments

1. On what factors might the influence of the Solicitor General depend? The office's expertise? Its reputation for independence? What factors may limit the SG's influence? In addition to the Waxman articles (exploring the SG's inability to influence the post-Reconstruction Court, or the Court in the 1990s on federalism issues), see also Helen J. Knowles, *May It Please the Court? The Solicitor General's Not-so-"Special" Relationship: Archibald Cox and the 1963–64 Reapportionment Cases*, 31 J. Sup. Ct. Hist. 279 (2006) (arguing that SG Cox's position had virtually no influence on an important reapportionment case). For a study raising questions whether, as the Solicitor General participates as amicus in a higher percentage of cases, the influence of the office may be declining, see Rebecca E. Deen, Joseph Ignagi & James Meernik, *The Solicitor General as Amicus 1953–2000: How Influential?*, 87 Judicature 60 (2003) (noting substantial variability in the success of SGs across different issues and different Administrations, and identifying a downward trend in success rates of amicus briefs filed by the SG (with the exception of during the Bush Administration, 1989–93)).

2. Interestingly, Professor Salokar, examining "those cases that would have been filed by one [presidential] administration and argued by another," found "no differences in the success rates" of the SG's office in those cases. See Salokar, *The Solicitor General, supra* at 132. She also found, during her period of study (1959–86), that whether Republicans or Democrats controlled the White House "was not significantly related" to the government's success in filing as amicus curiae. *Id.* at 147. But cf. Deen, Ignani & Meernik, *supra* (finding in study of SG's amicus filings between 1953 and 2000 some differences in success rates of SG amicus briefs in different Administrations and notable differences with respect to amicus success on particular issues, for example, civil rights, in different administrations). Would it be surprising

that on controversial issues, different SGs would take positions that would be more, or less, persuasive to a Court whose composition changes more gradually than the leadership of the SG's Office?

3. On the relevance of political alignments to the nature of the SG's influence on particular justices, see Michael A. Bailey, Brian Kamoie & Forrest Maltzman, *Signals from the Tenth Justice: The Political Role of the Solicitor General in Supreme Court Decision Making*, 49 Am. J. Pol. Sci. 72 (2005) (exploring variation of the SG effect among the justices).

4. For an important study finding that even as the SG has come to participate in an increasing percentage of the Court's merits cases, the office's relative influence has declined because of the growth of a private bar of Supreme Court specialists, see Lazarus, *Advocacy Matters, supra*, at 68–69 ("[T]he emergence of a private Supreme Court Bar capable of matching and sometimes even bettering the Solicitor General in Supreme Court advocacy experience is particularly significant because it is reducing the Solicitor General's disproportionate influence on substantive outcome.")

e. Confession of Error and Refusals to Defend a Statute on Grounds of Its Unconstitutionality

The tensions between the SG's roles as advocate and impartial officer of the Court, or between the SG's duty to the Administration in which he or she serves and the duty to the Constitution, or between the short-term and long-term interests of the United States, are apparent in two relatively rare, but interesting and controversial practices.

Refusing to Defend the Constitutionality of a Statute: First, what should the SG do when a statute is challenged as unconstitutional and the President, or the SG, is inclined to believe that the statute is of doubtful constitutionality? Must the SG nonetheless defend it? What if the alleged unconstitutionality is that the statute infringes on the constitutional prerogatives of the executive branch? What if the alleged unconstitutionality is something other than an intrusion on the executive branch? See Seth Waxman, *Defending Congress,* 79 N.C. L. Rev. 1073 (2001) (arguing that the principal exceptions to the Solicitor General's duty to defend acts of Congress involve separation of powers issues concerning legislative intrusions on executive power, as in INS v. Chadha, 462 U.S. 919 (1983), and concerns for *stare decisis*). As to the latter, Waxman argued that the SG should only rarely ask the Court to reconsider constitutional precedents. On this basis he defended his own refusal, as SG, to defend the constitutionality of a 1968 federal statute explicitly designed to overrule Miranda v. Arizona, 384 U.S. 436 (1966). In Dickerson v. United States, 530 U.S. 428 (2000), the Court agreed with the views of the SG, reaffirmed *Miranda* and struck down the federal statute, by a vote of seven to two. For a different perspective, see Neal Devins, *Politics and Principle: An Alternative Take on Seth P. Waxman's Defending Congress*, 81 N.C. L. Rev. 2061 (2003) (arguing that the decision not to defend the federal statute in *Dickerson* was political, not principled).

Does the possibility—rare as it may be—that the SG will *not* defend the constitutionality of an Act of Congress suggest that Congress needs its own counsel to defend its legislation before the Court? In 1978 the Senate created the Office of Senate Legal Counsel for exactly this purpose.[138] The Senate had preferred to establish a joint House–Senate Office of Congressional Legal Counsel, but the House of Representatives disagreed. Rather than setting up a joint office or a special office for itself, the House chose to have the Clerk of the House handle litigation that involves its members, officers, and staff.[139] Should Congress revisit this issue? Is there any constitutional objection to Congress establishing its own office to defend legislation, separate from the Executive Branch?

Confessions of Error: For a very helpful survey and discussion of the controversial, and unusual, practice of "confessions of error" by the United States before the Supreme Court, see David M. Rosenzweig, Note, *Confessions of Error in the Supreme Court by the Solicitor General*, 82 Geo. L.J. 2079 (1994). A brief excerpt follows:

> [There are] four categories of cases in which Solicitors General confess error. The first category includes confessions of errors of law, fact, or procedure in lower court rulings in favor of the Government. The second category involves violations of discretionary Justice Department prosecutorial policies that would have precluded prosecution if properly applied. In this second group of cases, the Solicitor General asks the Court to reverse in order to help the Justice Department enforce its policy.

> The two remaining categories of cases involve behavior or motives by which the Solicitor General or the Court may abuse the practice of confessing error. While the actual errors confessed are the same as in the first two categories, the potentially improper behavior exhibited in such cases renders them problematic. In the third category, the Solicitor General confesses error for "strategic" reasons, such as avoiding Supreme Court review of an issue that the Solicitor General fears might be decided against the Government on the merits.[140] In cases falling in the fourth category, the Solicitor General confesses error but defends the judgment in favor of the

---

138. Title VII of the Ethics in Government Act of 1978, Pub. L. No. 95–521, § 701, 92 Stat. 1824 (codified at 2 U.S.C. §§ 288–288n).

139. H.R. Rep. No. 95–1756, at 14 (Conf. Rep.), *reprinted in* 1978 U.S.C.C.A.N. 4381, 4396. For discussion of the House's decision not to agree to establish an Office of Congressional Legal Counsel to represent both houses, see Susan Low Bloch, *The Early Role of the Attorney General in Our Constitutional Scheme: In the Beginning There Was Pragmatism,* 1989 Duke L.J. 561, 624 n. 200. Cf. INS v. Chadha, 462 U.S. 919, 922, 929 n.4 (1982) (noting that "certain members of the House of Repre-

sentatives" were represented by counsel and also noting that 9 members of the House filed a separate amicus brief disagreeing with the views expressed by the House and the Senate).

140. [Footnote 20 in original] See, e.g., Rogers v. United States, 422 U.S. 35, 42–43 (1975) (Marshall, J., concurring) (complaining that "the Solicitor General confessed error, but on a point that had not been raised either here, in the Court of Appeals or at trial. The Court today seizes on that point to reverse the conviction, leaving unresolved the issue that we granted certiorari to consider.") . . .

Government on other grounds. The Court, however, summarily reverses without affording the Solicitor General the opportunity to support her contention that the judgment should stand. This category implicates the Court's potential to exploit the Solicitor General's traditional candor in her briefs and arguments.

. . .

The first of the four categories into which this note classifies confessions of error includes a diverse array of cases involving confessions of errors of law, fact, and procedure. On occasion, the Solicitor General confesses that a judgment in favor of the Government should be reversed in light of a decision rendered by the Supreme Court after the lower court's ruling. In two cases which reached the Court shortly after it decided *Jencks v. United States*,[141] for example, the Solicitor General confessed error because the courts of appeals had affirmed convictions based on procedures he admitted were improper in light of *Jencks*.

In most such cases, the Court reverses and remands for reconsideration in light of the intervening precedent. . . . Where the new precedent renders remand futile, the Court reverses and directs that the action be dismissed entirely.

Another set of cases in the first category involves confessions of clear legal errors that were not perceived or corrected by the lower courts. Such cases, for example, may involve jury instructions that misstate the applicable law or improper interpretations of statutes, regulations, or Court decisions. In a few instances, the Solicitor General has confessed error as to the sufficiency of the evidence to support a judgment or finding by a lower court, and some cases involve purely factual errors by lower courts.

Finally, Solicitors General have confessed to a variety of errors that loosely can be termed procedural. For example, the Court reversed a conviction under the Selective Service Rules in light of the Solicitor General's concession that the Department of Justice had not reviewed an appeal board's denial of a conscientious objector exemption, as required by law. Other cases have involved improprieties in the selection or conduct of the jury or judge. Others have concerned procedural issues of access to the courts and the distribution of functions among the lower courts.

. . .

[With respect to strategic confessions of error:] No Solicitor General has ever admitted to . . . "strategic" motives directly; instead, these cases have been identified through observations made by Justices in their opinions and by observers of the Court.

141. [Footnote 85 in the original] 353 U.S. 657 (1957). . . .

The common denominator in cases involving strategic behavior is the Government's willingness to sacrifice victory in the immediate case to avoid a ruling on the merits of some issue....

... For example, the Solicitor General may have confessed error in *Knox* for strategic reasons. The Solicitor General's office maintained that the broad standard applied by the court of appeals was not supported by the language or legislative history of the statute. It seems unlikely, of course, that Days's motive was to assist the defendant or intentionally to weaken child pornography laws. One commentator suggested, however, that the Solicitor General confessed error in *Knox* because the Court seemed likely to rule against the Government on the merits. Under the interpretation suggested by Days, the Government could still try to sustain the conviction on remand. In any event, the Solicitor General avoided an immediate ruling by the Court that the statute was unconstitutionally vague or overbroad, thus preserving executive discretion to develop prosecutorial policies and bring similar charges in the future....

Questions and Comments

1. Consider Rosenzweig's argument, made in 1994, that *Knox* may have involved a "strategic" confession of error. Re-evaluate this claim in light of Solicitor General Drew Days' 2001 account, excerpted above, of what happened in that case.

2. Rosenzweig argues that the Court should not feel bound to simply accept confessions of error, particularly where it may involve "manipulative behavior." How should the Court determine whether a confession of error is strategic or sincere?

3. Assuming that the Solicitor General's relatively rare confessions of error are sincere, what weight should the Court give to them? The Court's practice is often to vacate and remand a case to the lower court to consider the SG's confession of error. See, e.g., Mariscal v. United States, 449 U.S. 405 (1981). Justice Rehnquist argued against this practice:

One may freely concede that with 93 United States Attorneys and 11 Courts of Appeals, there will be differing views as between prosecutors, as well as between prosecutors and courts, as to legal issues presented in criminal cases. But the Executive *is* one branch of the Government, and the Judiciary another. The Office of the Solicitor General, while having earned over the years a reputation for ability and expertise in presenting the Government's claims to this Court, is nonetheless a part of the Executive Branch of the Federal Government, not of the Judicial Branch. I think it ill behooves this Court to defer to the Solicitor General's suggestion that a Court of Appeals may have been in error after another representative of the Executive Branch and the Justice Department has persuaded the Court of Appeals to reach the result which it did.

The Office of the Solicitor General may be quite faithfully performing its obligations under our system by calling our attention to what it perceives to be errors in the decisions of the courts of appeals. But I harbor serious doubt that our adversary system of justice is well served by this Court's practice of routinely vacating judgments which the Solicitor General questions without any independent examination of the merits on our own. With the increasing caseloads of all federal courts, there is a natural temptation to "pass the buck" to some other court if that is possible. Congress has given us discretionary jurisdiction to deny certiorari if we do not wish to grant plenary consideration to a particular case, a benefit that other federal courts do not share, but it has not to my knowledge moved the Office of the Solicitor General from the Executive Branch of the Federal Government to the Judicial Branch. Until it does, I think we are bound by our oaths either to examine independently the merits of a question presented for review on certiorari, or in the exercise of our discretion to deny certiorari. . . .

Id. at 406–07. Does Rehnquist's argument against the Court's deferring to the SG's confessions of error give too little weight to the incentives that the SG's office has not to confess error lightly?

4. Rosenzweig also criticizes the Court for its own strategic reliance on confessions of error about the reasoning below to reverse judgments even when the SG defends them on other grounds. In what ways is such reliance "strategic"—in avoiding addressing the merits of the SG's defense? Is the Court always obligated to give all its reasons for decision, or to address all the arguments made by the parties?

f. The Solicitor General and Constitutional Theory

In the final reading, Professor Pillard considers the implications of how the SG operates for constitutional theories opposed to "judicial supremacy" in constitutional interpretation. Professor Pillard's article refers to constitutional scholars, such as Mark Tushnet, who have argued for "taking the Constitution away from the Courts"[142] by placing "greater reliance on the political branches to supplement or even supplant judicial enforcement of the Constitution." Cornelia T.L. Pillard, *The Unfulfilled Promise of the Constitution in Executive Hands*, 103 Mich. L. Rev. 676 (2005). Her article is motivated by the view that "[a]nyone contemplating taking the Constitution away from the courts, or claiming that the executive has power to act on a different view of the Constitution from the Court's, or even those who merely recognize a role for judicial deference to the political branches, must closely consider the political branches' actual practices." *Id.* Pillard focuses on both the SG's office and the Office of Legal Counsel, an office that gives advice to executive branch agencies (generally in nonlitigation contexts); we excerpt from the article so as to focus on the SG's office.

Cornelia T.L. Pillard, *The Unfulfilled Promise of the Constitution in Executive Hands*, 103 Mich. L. Rev. 676 (2005)

.   .   .

142. See Mark Tushnet, *Taking the Constitution Away From the Courts (1999).*

[T]heorists who praise the more democratic or politically responsive character of political-branch constitutionalism do not explain in any detail how the executive might police the boundary between constitutional principle and political opportunism. . . .

. . .

. . . The SG's . . . formal doctrinalism and . . . courtlike insulation from the day-to-day functioning of government mean that [the SG lacks] the insight into executive practical experience and varied institutional capabilities or limitations that distinguish the executive from the courts. To the extent that the [SG's office] . . . [is] effectively shielded from politics or policy preferences in order to foster dispassionate analysis, [it is] unlikely to speak with the "populist" voice that many commentators claim for political-branch constitutionalism. When the lawyers are responsive to political or institutional exigencies, on the other hand, their decisions can seem opportunistic and unprincipled.

I conclude that our current executive constitutionalism is underdeveloped even for the modest role that judicial supremacy leaves it. It is unrealistic under current circumstances to expect that the executive will play a significant generative role in elaborating a distinctive executive vision of constitutional obligation that could supplement, let alone supplant, the Court's. Existing approaches leave a systemic shortfall in fulfillment of the Constitution's promise of principled constraint, and muffle a potentially distinctive executive . . . approach to such constraint. Those shortcomings should give us pause in embracing the more ambitious claims of extrajudicial constitutionalists.

. . . One model characterizes executive-branch lawyering as closely analogous to private legal representation of institutional clients, both in the context of litigation and counseling. The SG . . . under this model, uses lawyers' judgment and craft to implement the interests of the executive, as expressed by the president and his programmatic subordinates. As applied to executive decisions not subject to judicial review and often beyond public scrutiny, the client-driven approach generates a rights-minimizing bias, because the government officials will not want to tie their own hands or pull punches in court in the name of individual rights if a different course of action would better enhance executive power, serve the public, or even merely advance their own political careers. Under the client-driven model, nonjusticiability is thus less likely to be construed as an invitation to employ the executive's institutional competencies in the service of a . . . distinctive executive-branch vision of individual rights than as a constitutional blank check for executive preferences.

The other principal model of SG . . . lawyering found in the institutional literature maintains that we can trust the foxes to guard the henhouse because the foxes have consciences. Without disputing the president's ultimate constitutional authority over the SG . . ., this second model holds that the lawyers act, not as mere advocates for executive power, but as proponents of the best view of the law. They . . . can be counted on to be the executive's "constitutional conscience," insisting on respect for constitutional constraint even when politics, institutional self-interest, or the misguided or underdeveloped views of others might threaten them. Their arms-length client relations, and the many instances in which the SG ... [has], in practice, questioned or rejected proposals of client agencies, support the appearance of such independence.

... [But] what is cast as independence actually relies overwhelmingly on a court-centered view of constitutional law. It is largely because the SG can backstop his judgments in judicial doctrine—and because his judgments are often subject to Supreme Court evaluation—that he speaks with a level of authority that his clients overwhelmingly respect.... [The SG's] ability to act as [a] meaningful constitutional check[] on executive prerogative in the many areas in which the Court has not drawn limits is considerably more precarious, often depending on the ways in which they themselves very loosely and imperfectly mimic the courts: specializing in legal interpretation, remaining somewhat institutionally insulated from clients, passively waiting for matters to come to them, and generating and relying on a body of precedent. Thus, to the extent that the SG ... play[s] an "independent" role in enforcing the Constitution against the executive branch, that role rests largely on both the substance and methods of judicial constitutionalism.

... Given the paucity of non-court-centered executive constitutionalism, current practices hardly warrant abandoning judicial supremacy.

. . .

1. CLIENT-DRIVEN ADVICE AND ADVOCACY: FACILITATING EXECUTIVE INTERESTS

The first model is perhaps most dramatically illustrated by a question posed by Chief Justice Rehnquist during a 1995 oral argument. The case, Board of County Commissioners v. Umbehr,[143] presented a relatively straightforward application of First Amendment principles to the context of government contracting. The United States appeared as amicus curiae and argued that the First Amendment prohibited cancellation of a public contract with a trash hauler for making political comments on his own time with which government officials disagreed. The Court ultimately decided by a clear majority that such a cancellation was indeed unconstitutional. The government's position nonetheless attracted special notice: during oral argument, Chief Justice Rehnquist leaned forward, glared at the Assistant to the Solicitor General before him, and boomed, "Well, that's an extraordinary argument for the government to be making." The Chief Justice ... apparently thought that the SG had stepped out of his proper role by advocating constitutional constraints on governmental action. Even though the governmental entity in that case was local rather than federal, the approach the SG proposed would equally apply to any level of government, state or federal, so the SG was, at least indirectly, inviting the Court to identify constitutional limits applicable to his own client.

143. [Footnote 127 in original] 518 U.S. 668 (1996).

The view implicit in the Chief Justice's criticism from the bench in *Umbehr* is that the executive branch, at least when acting in an advocacy role, should not pull its punches by declining to make available, nonfrivolous arguments to support broad governmental prerogatives. Instead, the Chief Justice implied, the SG should consistently argue against constitutional constraints on government where reasonable arguments are available. In that view, elaborated in the institutional literature on the SG's Office, the Solicitor General's role is to advocate for government prerogative; advocacy of constitutional constraint should be left to the individuals challenging the law, with courts playing the role of arbiter.

a. *In favor of the client-driven approach.* There are simple, traditional, and appealing arguments in favor of the client-driven model: The SG is the government's Supreme Court advocate, and should present only the government's interests, not those of third parties. The Solicitor General's job is not to act like a court, but to advocate in court for the government as an institutional client.... The premise of the adversary system is that each side musters its strongest arguments and presents them to courts, which then neutrally evaluate the arguments and reach decisions that reflect the best view of the law. If one side fails to present its strongest arguments, the court gets a distorted picture, potentially skewing the outcome. The Chief Justice, no doubt, thought that it was the role of Mr. Umbehr and his counsel, not the Solicitor General of the United States, to highlight the constitutional constraints against speech-based retaliation in government contracting.

... Where there is room for reasonable argument, let the judges do the judging....

b. *Against the client-driven model.* The client-driven model of constitutional rights protection falls short.... The public's attention for, and will to protect, individual constitutional rights is limited, ... so public pressure only operates on that small set of issues that have become central enough and sufficiently established to be in the public mind. Where even those rights are threatened in contexts difficult for the public to perceive (e.g. reproductive rights or religious free exercise on the part of persons in prison or detention), they are unlikely to be the subject of either public pressure or corresponding presidential mandate. Similarly, the public is unlikely to be engaged effectively when questions of the particular contours of rights arise at levels of specificity too detailed for general political mobilization (e.g.... roving wiretaps on cell phones ...). But such relatively arcane questions matter a great deal in terms of the quality of rights we enjoy, and they are the daily fare of the executive branch.

... There are substantial reasons to question whether the routine constitutional instincts of executive-branch clients will give due weight to constitutional obligations.... [T]he executive branch has many programmatic responsibilities. That mixture of roles, as both interpreter and executor of laws, creates tremendous incentives for the executive to view the Constitution in self-serving ways. Under the client-driven model, then, the countermajoritarian provisions of the Constitution seem inadequately shielded from popular will, likely to be "enforced" extrajudicially only when it is politically popular to do so—that is, where constitutional constraints are least necessary.

2. NEUTRAL EXPOSITORS OF THE CONSTITUTION: CONSTITUTIONAL CONSCIENCES FOR THE EXECUTIVE BRANCH?

Those who find the client-driven model wanting typically advocate a more dispassionate role for the SG.... [The SG's] independence, such as it is, results largely from institutional design, custom, and tradition.... Nonetheless, the SG ... stand[s] apart from executive politics and policy, and carr[ies] a level of authority within the executive that potentially enables [the office] to insist on executive branch respect for constitutional rights even when courts might not.

a. *The apparent independence of the Solicitor General.* Many SGs describe their role as serving not only an institutional client, but also the United States, the people, and the interests of justice. As former Solicitor General Frederick W. Lehmann famously wrote, in words engraved on the facade of the main Justice Department building in Washington, "The United States wins its point whenever justice is done its citizens in the courts." Former Solicitor General Francis Biddle declared that "the Solicitor General has no master to serve except his country."

Biddle described the SG as an independent justice-seeker and expressly rejected the client-driven model....

The official executive branch view of the SG similarly highlights his independence. An OLC opinion [the 1977 opinion excerpted above] on the role of the SG notes that, despite his formal subordinacy, the SG "has enjoyed a marked degree of independence." ...

The key reason for supporting this independence, according to the OLC opinion, is that it "is necessary to prevent narrow or improper considerations (political or otherwise) from intruding upon the presentation of the Government's case in the Nation's highest Court.... The Nation values the Solicitor General's independence for the same reason that it values an independent judiciary." The opinion notes that, in contrast to the SG, the Attorney General is consistently exposed to the president's and the cabinet's political and policy views, making it difficult for him to separate those considerations from legal ones. As a result, the Attorney General implements the president's constitutional duty to "take care that the laws are faithfully executed" by delegating to the SG the framing of legal positions and, "in the ordinary course," permitting the SG's views to be dispositive.

· · ·

Lincoln Caplan's book, *The Tenth Justice*, popularized the notion of the independent SG. The book is an extended critique of the approach of President Reagan's second SG, Charles Fried, whom Caplan argues tarnished the SG's independence by acting as an aggressive proxy in the courts for Reagan's right-wing political agenda. The backdrop for Caplan's critique is an image of the SG as a highly principled and independent legal official, insulated from political and institutional pressures from without and within the administration, seeking only to advance the best view of the law. . . . Caplan's view is frequently invoked in confirmation hearings.

Scholars, too, stress the SG's independence. In a 1987 congressional oversight hearing during Solicitor General Fried's tenure, Burt Neuborne testified that . . . :

> [T]he Solicitor General's role as a reliable, non-ideological and, essentially, non-political source of technically excellent advice to the Supreme Court and the President about what the law is (as opposed to what it ought to be), is much more important than the Solicitor General's potential role as a President's mouthpiece engaged in a campaign to push the law in an ideologically-tinged direction.

Sanford Levinson expresses confidence that we can "expect a greater independence of judgment from the Solicitor General than we do from other presidential appointees." . . .

In sum, the SG is often characterized not as a client-driven lawyer, but rather as a highly independent, principled official. Indeed, if independence is measured in terms of the freedom to make important decisions without presidential consultation or approval, the SG is arguably functionally more independent than the Attorney General. Traditionally, the SG makes judgments about which cases to pursue and the positions to take in appellate and Supreme Court litigation without much, if any, substantive supervision by the Attorney General or the president, even when agency heads or other high-ranking officials might disagree with him.

. . .

. . . [But] what is commonly called independence is revealed to be highly derivative of judicial doctrine. The SG . . . [lawyers gain the] ability to say "no" to their own client typically by reference to the Court's precedents. To the extent that they shape or alter client proposals, these lawyers' "independent" positions are, in fact, married to the Supreme Court's doctrine and the Court's role as expositor of law. [But they are] likely to fail to supplement existing doctrine where the Court's underenforcement leaves gaps. Their court-centrism also means that they are not likely to tap into what the theoretical literature on extrajudicial constitutionalism celebrates as the executive's potentially distinctive institutional or populist sources of constitutional inspiration, and therefore do not offer additional or different ways of effectuating constitutional rights beyond what the Court's constitutional doctrine supplies.

A. THE SG'S STRATEGIC CLIENT–CHECKING AND COURT–RELIANT INDEPENDENCE

A closer look at the writing of observers who highlight the SG's independence reveals that what they champion as independence from the government's institutional or political agenda is really either adherence to Supreme Court precedent, or is not independence from those client interests at all. What passes as SG independence usually amounts to the SG telling his client that the law, as the Supreme Court has developed it, would not permit the course of action the client prefers. In that sense, the SG does have significant authority to act as a constitutional brake within the executive branch. But that brake is largely either strategic or court-based.

. . .

... Rather than manifesting independent constitutional judgment when he curtails an agency's more ambitious position, the SG is often merely acting strategically in order to increase his credibility, reduce risks of damaging losses, and thereby better serve the government's interests over the long term.

The SG also refuses requests when he finds an inconsistency in the proposed position, viewed on behalf of the government as a whole rather than simply from the client entity's particular vantage point. The need to reconcile the legal positions of the numerous and varied parts of the executive branch and to evaluate each agency's expressed interest through a government-wide lens may lead the SG to reject the more narrowly opportunistic constitutional analysis of a particular client entity. The SG may look independent in those instances, but SG coordination of the government's diverse interests simply serves the executive's institutional interests from a broader perspective, and does not necessarily reflect an SG's independent view of constitutional constraints....

The SG also moderates client positions in light of the government's long-term interests as a "repeat player" before the Supreme Court. The SG's effectiveness in the Court depends on his gaining and maintaining the Court's trust over time. The SG cannot afford to press every case to the hilt the way a lawyer for a private client might, because his effectiveness in future government cases would suffer. Indeed, that was precisely Lincoln Caplan's criticism of Solicitor General Fried.... But, again, acting as a brake on client interests for intertemporal strategic purposes is not the same thing as independence.

. . .

The SG is, however, more than a skilled strategic advocate; he also plays a role in assuring the executive's respect for the law. His is a decisive voice of executive constitutionalism. Yet, the SG's approach is fundamentally court-centered, and therefore, does little to fulfill the promise of a distinctively executive constitutional vision that supplements or conceivably supplants the Court's.

... One of the SG's key roles is to "provide the Court with an accurate and expert statement of the legal principles that bear upon the questions to be decided." In that account, "the law" is the law as delineated by the Supreme Court. As such, the SG's "independence" is unlikely to provide any systematic corrective to the Court's jurisprudence, nor ... to yield a version of constitutionalism free from the institutional limitations that constrain the Court but need not similarly constrain the executive.

... Caplan's critique of Fried as failing to perform his function as the "Tenth Justice" rests on an assumption that the best, most accurate view of the Constitution was the then-existing Supreme Court doctrine, and that therefore Fried's attempt to challenge the status quo was deeply problematic. Neuborne's vision of an independent SG is similarly one who gives advice "about the state of the law," i.e. advice "about what *the law is (as opposed to what it ought to be)*." These views are plainly opposed to distinctly executive constitutionalism.

Even the standard the SG uses to decide whether to confess error—a practice so often cited to distinguish the SG's independence from a private lawyer's service to client self-interest—is really only a concrete example of court-centered doctrinalism. In practice, the SG confesses error when the victory in the lower court appears unsustainable in light of the Supreme Court's own precedents ... that is, when he is almost certain to lose upon Supreme Court review. The SG's apparent independence is in this way, too, derivative of the Court's doctrine and driven by judicial precedent.

. . .

... [T]he SG's practice remains court-centric ..., tending to accept the Court as both the supreme and exhaustive interpreter of constitutional rights.

. . .

... Lawyers in the SG's Office ... are unlikely to insist that government conduct be curtailed in the name of the Constitution unless they can ground their position on judicial doctrine.... [R]eliance on the Court's doctrine as describing the high water mark of the executive's constitutional duties means that their work is destined to recapitulate the shortfalls of the courts, unnecessarily truncating executive constitutionalism. The gaps in judicial doctrine that call for constitutional interpretation within the executive branch are not bridged, but replicated, by the executive's own court-centered analysis.

. . .

... [T]he centralization of executive branch constitutional deliberation in the elite OLC and SG's Office suggests to other government officials that constitutional concerns are taken care of elsewhere, effectively lulling them into thinking they need not examine their own spheres through a constitutional lens....

That is especially problematic under the client-driven approach, insofar as ... the SG take[s] ... cues from clients who themselves lack habits of constitutional vigilance. Agency personnel, who often are the only ones with the practical experience "on the ground" to perceive constitutional problems and appreciate ways they could be ameliorated, do not ordinarily view doing so as part of their jobs. At the same time, the separation of ... the SG from the day-to-day operations of government, ... mean that [it is] in no position to assure that constitutional rights are fully effectuated.

... If the courts are institutionally ill-equipped to impose constraints on prosecutorial discretion, for example, or to second-guess assertions of national security interests, so, too [is] the SG ... [whose] lawyers ... are, like judges, neither schooled nor steeped in the norms and practicalities of getting the work of government done. They operate in a kind of naive isolation from the institutional capabilities of their client agencies, largely missing the added insight that the executive's concrete experience, distinct institutional expertise, and vantage point could afford.

The SG ... thus lack[s] thick experience with the kinds of matters that are at the heart of the executive branch's potentially distinct contributions to constitutional analysis. Much of constitutional law pits public needs for efficiency, security, administrability, and the like, asserted by the government, against individual claims of right. The precise lines drawn depend in part on contextual assessments of the importance of government interests, and the feasibility of serving them well in alternative ways ... : if a client agency asserts that it simply lacks the capability to accommodate HIV-positive or openly gay service members on warships, to set up procedures or criteria to eliminate apparent racial bias in prosecutorial decisions, or to expedite the clearance and release of persons mistakenly detained in investigation of terrorism, the executive's own top constitutional lawyers ordinarily would not be in a position to evaluate those contentions critically....

[C]onstitutionalism by the political branches is frequently hailed as more populist or democratic than the judicial brand. Insofar as the executive branch is concerned, however, hopes for a democratic, populist constitutionalism have largely foundered on the institutional separation of the SG ... from policy and politics. Neither the insight of the public, nor the initiative-taking character of the executive branch, nor the democratic political legitimacy available to the representative branches, applies much, if at all, to the work of the SG.... Constitutional interpretation in the hands of the executive's constitutional lawyers relies overwhelmingly on the traditional constitutional sources used by courts, such as text, history, and judicial precedent.... [T]he potentially distinctive democratic voice of the executive branch is muted, and both the populist vitality and legitimacy attributed to extrajudicial constitutionalism are largely unfulfilled.

Questions and Comments

1. Professor Pillard critiques an important line of theoretical literature which assumes that the distinctive contribution of executive branch constitutional interpretation lies in its capacity to capture populist, democratic views or insights. Consider, however, whether the distinctive contribution of executive branch constitutionalism comes from the need to reconcile varying governmental interests, across a wide range of programs and postures, as described, for example, in John Roberts' description of *Hudson v. McMillan*, found in the *Rex Lee Conference Transcript* excerpted above.

2. Reconsider the various relationships among and between the SG, the Court and the President. How would you describe those relationships? How *should* the SG relate to the Court and the President?

3. Should the SG have greater forms of statutorily secured independence? Professor Pillard concludes that doing so would be quite difficult and would not necessarily increase Executive Branch rights-consciousness. Instead, she argues for "[s]upplying the 'missing-plaintiff perspective' within the executive branch [to] counteract the executive tendency to reflexively overprotect its own prerogatives," by, for example, involving the Civil Rights Division in decisionmaking by the SG's office, or enhancing executive branch fact gathering capacity to build on its comparative institutional advantage over courts. Pillard, *supra*, at 747–52. How practical or effective are these approaches likely to be? How desirable?

3. Amicus Curiae

Rule 37 of the Supreme Court's rules governs the filing of amicus curiae briefs.[144] Translated literally, "amicus curiae" means "friend of the court."[145] When not formally a party to a case, but concerned with its outcome or the kind of doctrine the opinion may embrace, a special interest group or a government office can use the vehicle of an amicus brief to inform the Court of its concerns.[146]

Amicus briefs vary widely in their content, principally because the motives for filing them vary widely. At one extreme is the brief, filed solely to let the Court know that an organized group hopes for a particular outcome,[147] that contains no legal analysis and a scanty, one-

---

144. Supreme Court Rule 37 provides that amicus briefs may be filed supporting or opposing a petition for a writ of certiorari or in cases in which cert has already been granted. Generally, to file an amicus brief, one must seek consent from the parties to the case. If all parties consent, the brief may be filed, but if any party objects, the amicus may move the Court for permission to file. An important exception to these requirements is that consent is not required for an amicus brief submitted on behalf of the United States, an agency of the United States, a state or a subdivision of a state. In practice, in the large majority of cases, the parties routinely consent to requests to permit amicus briefs to be filed.

145. The plural is "amici curiae" or "friends of the court."

146. Occasionally, amici are permitted to join in oral argument as well. This happens very infrequently, however, and in the few cases in which it occurs, it is usually the U.S. Solicitor General who is allowed to participate.

147. Such briefs may also be motivated by the desire to strengthen support for the organization among its members or to increase its membership.

sided policy argument. At the other extreme is the brief, filed by an expert, that is far superior to anything filed by either of the parties.[148]

Today, highly visible Supreme Court cases very often attract two or more amicus briefs of each type. Indeed, the rate of increase in total amicus filings and filings per case has been so substantial that by the 2005 Term, 96% of the cases heard on the merits had at least one amicus brief filed. Lazarus, *Advocacy Matters, supra*, at 35. Professor Lazarus reports that in the first post World War II decade (1946–55), there were an average of 53 amicus briefs filed each term, with an average of .5 per case, with only 23% of the cases having amicus briefs. By 1986–95—the latest period included in the data base constructed and analyzed by Professors Kearney and Merrill, below—Lazarus found an average of 490 amicus briefs filed per term; he reported an average of 4.3 amicus briefs filed per case, with 85% of the cases having amicus briefs. Lazarus, *Advocacy Matters, supra*, at 34. If the 2005 data also reported by Lazarus are representative, the increase in amici filings has continued.

The materials that follow describe in more detail how large a role amicus briefs now play in the strategy of an advocate presenting a major case to the Court.

The materials consist of five readings. The Ennis article, though written in the 1980s, sets the stage by describing the vast and varied volume of amicus activity in the Supreme Court and summarizes three principal strategic purposes amicus briefs can serve.

Following Ennis, we excerpt substantial parts of an important study of amicus curiae practice by Professors Kearney and Merrill. This study summarizes prior research, and analyzes data on amicus filings and influence through the lens of three different theories of judicial decision-making: attitudinal or strategic models of judging, "interest" based models of judicial politics, and legal models of judicial decisionmaking. Although the authors find support for each of the models in aspects of their data, they argue that the data provide greatest support for the view that the Court makes decisions based on legal, rather than attitudinal, strategic, or interest group factors.

We follow this with three shorter excerpts. In the first, on states as amici, Professor Morris describes increasing amicus activity by states and steps taken to increase coordination among states in filing amicus briefs. He details the factors that go into a state attorney general's decision whether or not to file (or join in another state's brief) in particular cases and suggests that increased coordination among states has raised their success rates. (Since this article was published, increasing numbers of states have developed specialized offices for appellate litigation. *See* Lazarus, *Advocacy Matters, supra.*)

---

148. For thoughtful analyses of the differing approaches of medical, scientific and technical groups as experts filing amici curiae briefs, and an argument for increased participation by the latter, see Stephanie Tai, *Friendly Science: Medical, Scientific and Technical Amici Before the Supreme Court*, 78 Wash. U. L. Q. 789 (2000).

Finally, we excerpt two studies of interest group amicus participation in highly visible law reform efforts. Professor Schubert, drawing heavily on the work of Professor Vose, details the NAACP's coordination of amicus briefs in Shelley v. Kraemer, 334 U.S. 1 (1948). *Shelley* held unconstitutional the use of judicial enforcement of racially restrictive covenants to invalidate real property transfers. (Recall the discussion of *Shelley* above in the section on the Solicitor General.) The NAACP's extensive effort to sponsor and control amicus activity in *Shelley* is commonly regarded as the starting point of the modern trend toward massive amicus participation in highly visible and controversial cases. Professor Behuniak–Long shows how this form of advocacy has evolved as she reviews the 78 amicus briefs filed in Webster v. Reproductive Health Services, 492 U.S. 490 (1989), a controversial abortion case predating *Casey* in which the Court upheld several restrictions imposed by Missouri on the availability of abortions.[149] (*Webster* was also discussed above in the section on law clerks.) In the questions and comments that follow, we note or excerpt more briefly other studies dealing with private amici in employment discrimination cases, states in dormant commerce clause cases, and the range of amici in the 2003 affirmative action cases.

The careful reader will note that the materials as a whole reveal that a particular amicus brief may be filed for any of several reasons. Although it is extremely difficult to gauge the impact amicus briefs have on the Court's decisions, it is nevertheless clear that many people think they can make a difference. Surely, the central fact that emerges from all these readings is that coordination of amicus activity is now a part of the established and accepted role of counsel for the parties in most major cases before the Court. A good way to review these materials is to read and analyze several amicus briefs filed in a pending Supreme Court case.

Bruce J. Ennis,[150] *Effective Amicus Briefs*, 33 Cath. U. L. Rev. 603, 603–608 (1984)

I. THREE MISCONCEPTIONS ABOUT AMICUS BRIEFS

Let's begin by dispelling three common misconceptions about amicus briefs. The first is that amicus briefs are not very important; ... Amicus briefs have shaped judicial decisions in many more cases than is commonly realized. Occasionally, a case will be decided on a ground suggested only by an amicus, not by the parties. Frequently, judicial rulings, and thus their precedential value, will be narrower or broader than the parties had urged, because of a persuasive amicus brief. Courts

---

149. Note a contrast between the two case studies: Writing in 1960, Schubert seems to regard the amicus brief as exceptional and questionable. For Behuniak–Long, it is an established practice. Un-

doubtedly, this reflects a shift in prevailing attitudes between the times the two pieces were written.

150. Mr. Ennis was at this time a partner of Ennis, Friedman, Bersoff & Ewing.

often rely on factual information, cases or analytical approaches provided only by an amicus. . . .

The second misconception is that amicus briefs are not filed very often, and then only in great constitutional cases. That was not true twenty years ago, and is even less true today. . . .

. . .

. . . [I]f you have a case in the Supreme Court there is a good chance your opponent will be supported by an amicus brief. So it is no longer enough for you to write a first rate brief. In today's world, effective representation of your client requires that you at least seriously explore the possibility of enlisting persuasive amicus support on your client's behalf.

The third misconception is that amicus briefs are filed primarily by politically "liberal" public interest groups. . . . [Today, there] are . . . almost as many "conservative" public interest groups as liberal ones. Groups such as the Mountain States Legal Foundation, the Capital Legal Foundation, the Pacific Legal Foundation, and the New England Legal Foundation appear alongside the ACLU, the NAACP Legal Defense Fund, and the Natural Resources Defense Council in the lists of amici.

In addition, the United States frequently files amicus briefs. . . .

Moreover, the amicus brief is not limited to public interest groups or the United States. Professional associations such as the American Bar Association and the American Psychological Association, other governmental entities, corporations, unions, and banks now appear regularly as amici.

II. EFFECTIVE COOPERATION BETWEEN PARTY AND AMICUS

Of course, there does not have to be any cooperation. Amici frequently file briefs supporting neither side, but advancing their own positions and interests. The Court will occasionally request the participation of an amicus when it suspects collusion between the parties, or when the parties do not have an adversary posture with respect to certain issues in the case.[151] Let's assume, however, as is more common (and as the Supreme Court's rules contemplate) that the amicus will support one of the parties. In that case, there is a great deal of support that can be provided in addition to filing an amicus brief. The amicus

---

151. [Footnote 4 in original] Perhaps the first amicus to appear in the United States Supreme Court was Henry Clay, who was allowed to appear as amicus because the Court suspected collusion between the parties. See Green v. Biddle, 21 U.S. (8 Wheat.) 1 (1823). . . . Another example is Bob Jones Univ. v. United States, 103 S.Ct. 2017 (1983), in which both the United States and Bob Jones University, the nomi- nal parties, took the position that the Internal Revenue Service lacked authority to issue a regulation which effectively denied tax exemptions for religious private schools which discriminated on the basis of race. . . . The Supreme Court appointed a distinguished private attorney, William T. Coleman, Jr., [who argued successfully, as an amicus, in favor of the validity of the regulation].

and its counsel can help the party plan the *party's* strategy, and can provide research, drafting, and editorial assistance to the party. The amicus can organize one or more moot courts, etc. This assistance is a much neglected resource that can be extremely useful.

In the amicus brief itself, support for a party will usually take one of three forms:

A. Helping the Party Flesh Out Arguments the Party is Forced to Make in Summary Form

Because of page limits, or considerations of tone and emphasis, parties are frequently forced to make some of the points they wish to make in rather abbreviated form. A supportive amicus can flesh out those points with additional discussion and citation of authority. Or the amicus can support points the party is making by providing a detailed legislative or constitutional history, a scholarly exposition of the common law, or a nationwide analysis of relevant state laws.

For example, in ... Toll v. Moreno,[152] the World Bank submitted an amicus brief urging the Supreme Court to rule, on Supremacy Clause grounds, that certain state statutes which disadvantaged alien college students were unconstitutional. The alien students touched briefly on the Supremacy Clause, but the thrust and greater portion of their brief was necessarily concerned with their equal protection and due process arguments. The Court ruled for the students, but it chose to decide the case on the basis of the Supremacy Clause theory that had been advocated primarily by the amicus.

Similarly, in the Supreme Court's latest round of abortion decisions, the plaintiffs devoted only one paragraph in their brief to the argument that nonphysicians should be allowed to engage in abortion counseling because they thought they would probably lose that issue. Instead, the plaintiffs chose to stress other important issues they thought they had a better chance to win. But the American Psychological Association, as amicus, marshaled empirical studies to show why counseling by nonphysicians would help to promote truly informed consent, and the Court agreed.

B. Making Arguments the Party Wants to Make But Cannot Make Itself

It frequently happens that a party wants a particular argument to be made but is not in a position to make that argument itself. The party may simply lack credibility on that issue, or it may be unable to make the argument for political or tactical reasons. For example, governmental entities often feel compelled, for political reasons, to argue for very broad rulings: eliminate the exclusionary rule entirely, absolute immunity for

---

152. [Footnote 6 in original] 458 U.S. 1 (1982).

all governmental employees, etc. But courts, including the Supreme Court, are institutionally conservative and usually prefer to decide cases on narrower grounds if possible. An amicus can suggest those narrower grounds: qualify the exclusionary rule rather than eliminate it, distinguish a prior case rather than overrule it, or dismiss certiorari as improvidently granted, among others.

A good example of this type of cooperation is Metromedia, Inc. v. San Diego[153] in which San Diego sought to exclude most billboards from designated sections of the city, on grounds of traffic safety and aesthetics. The billboards carried primarily commercial messages, but they occasionally carried political messages as well. The billboard owners were represented by an experienced and extremely sophisticated Supreme Court advocate. He knew the Court would be closely divided, and would be more troubled by the regulation's prohibition of political speech than by its prohibition of commercial speech. The billboard owners, however, were not in a position to argue credibly on behalf of political speech because ... they simply leased billboard space, primarily to commercial speakers. Their lawyer decided it would be important to demonstrate to the Court that organizations traditionally concerned with the protection of political speech were opposed to the San Diego ordinance, so he asked the ACLU if it would file an amicus brief emphasizing the political speech aspects of the case, and the ACLU agreed.

The Court, as expected, was closely divided. Although a majority of the Court agreed to a judgment striking down the San Diego ordinance, only three other Justices joined in Justice White's plurality opinion. Those four thought the ordinance was constitutional insofar as it regulated only commercial speech, but they struck down the entire ordinance because it unconstitutionally regulated political speech, and the commercial and political regulations were not severable. Given the closeness of this decision, it seems clear that the billboard owners advanced their interests by enlisting amicus support.

C. Informing the Court of the Broader Public Interests Involved, or of the Broader Implications of a Ruling

One of the most common forms of amicus support is to inform the court of interests other than those represented by the parties, and to focus the court's attention on the broader implications of various possible rulings. Governmental entities are uniquely situated to define and assert the "public interest," and their views as amicus will, therefore, carry substantial weight. If a governmental entity is already a party, amicus support from other governmental entities will enhance the credibility of the party's arguments. . . .

---

153. [Footnote 8 in original] 453 U.S. 490 (1981).

Joseph D. Kearny & Thomas W. Merrill,[154] *The Influence of Amicus Curiae Briefs on the Supreme Court,* 148 U. Pa. L. Rev. 743 (2000)

INTRODUCTION AND OVERVIEW

The last century has seen little change in the conduct of litigation before the United States Supreme Court. The Court's familiar procedures—the October Term, the opening-answering-reply brief format for the parties, oral argument before a nine-member Court—remain essentially as before. The few changes that have occurred, such as shortening the time for oral argument, have not been dramatic.

In one respect, however, there has been a major transformation in Supreme Court practice: the extent to which non-parties participate in the Court's decision-making process through the submission of amicus curiae, or friend-of-the-court, briefs. Throughout the first century of the Court's existence, amicus briefs were rare. Even during the initial decades of this century, such briefs were filed in only about 10% of the Court's cases. This pattern has now completely reversed itself. In recent years, one or more amicus briefs have been filed in 85% of the Court's argued cases. Thus, at the close of the twentieth century, cases without amicus briefs have become nearly as rare as cases with amicus briefs were at the beginning of the century.

Attitudes within the legal community about the utility and impact of amicus briefs vary widely. Perhaps the most common reaction among lawyers and judges is moderately supportive. Amicus briefs, it is said, can provide valuable assistance to the Court in its deliberations. For example, they can present an argument or cite authorities not found in the briefs of the parties, and these materials can occasionally play a critical role in the Court's rationale for a decision.[155] Alternatively, these briefs can provide important technical or background information which the parties have not supplied. Those sharing this perspective can point to the frequent citation of amicus briefs in the Justices' opinions in support of the supposition that the Court often finds such briefs helpful.

Other members of the legal community, however, offer a much more negative assessment of amicus briefs. For example, Chief Judge Richard Posner of the Seventh Circuit has written that the amicus briefs filed in his court provide little or no assistance to judges because they largely

---

154. Kearney at this time was Assistant Professor of Law, Marquette University; Merrill at this time was John Paul Stevens Professor of Law, Northwestern University.

155. [Footnote 5 in original] The Court will on occasion base its decision on a point or argument raised only in an amicus brief. *See, e.g.,* Teague v. Lane, 489 U.S. 288, 300 (1989) (plurality opinion of O'Connor, J.) (ruling against petitioner on question of retroactivity even though the issue "has been raised only in an amicus brief"); Oregon ex. rel. State Land Bd. v. Corvallis Sand & Gravel Co., 429 U.S. 363, 368 n.3, 382 (1977) (overruling an earlier case even though this action was urged only by amici); Mapp v. Ohio, 367 U.S. 643, 646 n.3 (1961) (overruling Wolf v. Colorado, 338 U.S. 25 (1949), and adopting exclusionary rule in cases of Fourth Amendment violations by state officials, even though that course of action had been urged only by amicus ACLU). As a general rule, however, the Court will not address issues raised only by an amicus . . . .

duplicate the positions and arguments advanced by the parties. Those who share this assessment regard such filings as largely a nuisance— imposing unwarranted burdens on judges and their staffs with few, if any, mitigating benefits. According to those who harbor this negative assessment, the judicial system would be improved if amicus filings were prohibited or at least sharply curtailed.

Justice Scalia recently offered a third perspective on the widespread filing of amicus briefs. The occasion was Jaffee v. Redmond [518 U.S. 1 (1996)], where the Supreme Court recognized a "psychotherapist's privilege" under Rule 501 of the Federal Rules of Evidence. In a dissenting opinion joined in part by Chief Justice Rehnquist, Justice Scalia offered the following observation:

> In its consideration of this case, the Court was the beneficiary of no fewer than 14 amicus briefs supporting respondents, most of which came from such organizations as the American Psychiatric Association, the American Psychoanalytic Association, the American Association of State Social Work Boards, the Employee Assistance Professionals Association, Inc., the American Counseling Association, and the National Association of Social Workers. Not a single amicus brief was filed in support of petitioner. That is no surprise. There is no self-interested organization out there devoted to pursuit of the truth in the federal courts. The expectation is, however, that this Court will have that interest prominently—indeed, primarily—in mind. Today we have failed that expectation, and that responsibility.

Justice Scalia's reference to "self-interested organizations" and his lack of surprise in finding no amicus arguing against creation of an evidentiary privilege suggest that amicus briefs reflect a form of interest group lobbying directed at the Court. His remarks further suggest, in keeping with the interest group theory of politics, that well-organized interest groups will be more likely to file amicus briefs than will diffuse and poorly organized interests. Most significantly, Justice Scalia intimates that the over-representation of well-organized interest groups through amicus filings may have an influence on the outcomes reached by the Court. He at least suggests that this is what happened in *Jaffee*, in which the highly disproportionate amicus support for the respondent may have sent a clear signal to the Court that a decision recognizing a psychotherapist's privilege would more likely receive acclaim from organized groups than one rejecting such a privilege.

The critical but unstated variable that divides these different perspectives is the model of judicial decision making adopted by each commentator. Each of the three positions corresponds to a different model of judging, which in turn suggests a different pathway of influence that amicus briefs may have on the outcomes reached by courts.

The first or moderately supportive view of amicus briefs implicitly adopts the conventional legal model of judicial decision making. Under this model, judges are regarded as seeking to resolve cases in accordance with the requirements of law, as understood by professional actors in the legal community. Amicus briefs are assumed to have an impact on this process insofar as they contain new information—legal arguments and background factual material—that would be relevant to persons seeking the correct result in light of established legal norms.

The second or sharply negative view is often associated with what political scientists call the "attitudinal model" of judicial behavior. This model posits that judges have fixed ideological preferences, and that case outcomes are a product of the summing of the preferences of the participating judges, with legal norms serving only to rationalize outcomes after the fact. Under this view, amicus briefs should have little or no impact on the outcomes reached by a court, because each judge's vote in a case is assumed to be the product of his or her preestablished ideological preferences with respect to the issue presented. A judge can obtain all the information needed to determine his or her vote, the attitudinal model would suggest, by reading the "Question Presented" and the statement of facts contained in the parties' briefs.... [A]micus briefs [that] provide additional legal arguments and factual background, under this model ... offer information of no relevance to judges.

The third view, which we have extrapolated from Justice Scalia's comments in *Jaffee*, implicitly adopts an interest group theory of the judicial process. In contrast to the attitudinal model, the assumption here is that judges do not have strong ideological preferences about most issues. Rather, they are empty vessels who seek to decide cases so as to reach those results supported by the most influential groups in society that have an interest in the question at hand. Amicus briefs on this view should be important to the judicial process because of the signals that they convey about how interested groups want particular cases decided. If, as in *Jaffee*, the groups filing amicus briefs all want a case to come out a certain way, this tells the judges how to rule if they want to secure the approval of organized groups.

... Unfortunately, when courts devise policies regarding the filing of amicus briefs, and when lawyers advise clients about filing such briefs, they almost always proceed on the basis of anecdotal information or recent episodes that may be unrepresentative of the larger universe of amicus curiae participation.... [T]his highly fragmentary information may be processed through a perceptual lens based on a particular implicit model of judging, which model, again, is untested and may or may not be a reliable guide to underlying realities.

In this Article, we present empirical evidence designed to enhance our understanding about the impact of amicus curiae briefs on the Supreme Court and therefore also about the validity of different models of judging. To this end, we have assembled a large database consisting of fifty years of Supreme Court merits decisions—every argued case from the 1946 Term through the 1995 Term. For each decision, we recorded, among other things, the outcome of the case, the number of amicus briefs supporting the petitioner, the number supporting the respondent, and whether certain key institutional litigants filed amicus briefs in the case. We then analyzed these data using standard statistical techniques to try to differentiate between different hypotheses about the influence of amicus briefs on judicial behavior.

Briefly, our principal findings are as follows. First, our study shows conclusively that the incidence of amicus curiae participation in the Supreme Court has increased dramatically over the last fifty years. While the number of cases that the Court has disposed of on the merits has not appreciably increased during this time (indeed it has fallen in recent years), the number of amicus filings has increased by more than 800%.

In terms of the influence of amicus briefs on outcomes, our study uncovers a number of interesting patterns. We find that amicus briefs supporting respondents enjoy higher success rates than do amicus briefs supporting petitioners; that small disparities of one or two briefs for one side with no briefs on the other side may translate into higher success rates but larger disparities do not; that amicus briefs cited by the Court appear to be no more likely to be associated with the winning side than briefs not cited by the Court; and that amicus briefs filed by more experienced lawyers may be more successful than briefs filed by less experienced lawyers.... [W]e confirm the finding of other researchers that the Solicitor General ... enjoys great success as an amicus filer.... We also ... find that [the American Civil Liberties Union (ACLU) and the American Federation of Labor–Congress of Industrial Organizations (AFL–CIO)] enjoy some success as amicus filers, although less than the Solicitor General.

We cautiously interpret these results as providing more support for the legal model than for either the attitudinal or interest group models. Contrary to what the attitudinal model would predict, amicus briefs do appear to affect success rates in a variety of contexts. And contrary to what the interest group model would predict, we find no evidence to support the proposition that large disparities of amicus support for one side relative to the other result in a greater likelihood of success for the supported party. In fact, it appears that amicus briefs filed by institutional litigants and by experienced lawyers—filers that have a better idea of what kind of information is useful to the Court—are generally more successful than are briefs filed by irregular litigants and less experienced lawyers. This is consistent with the legal model's prediction that amicus briefs have an influence to the extent they import valuable new information. Moreover, the greater success associated with amicus briefs supporting respondents can be explained by the supposition that respondents are more likely than petitioners to be represented by inexperienced lawyers in the Supreme Court and hence are more likely to benefit from supporting amici, which can supply the Court with additional legal arguments and facts overlooked by the respondents' lawyers.

· · ·

I. The Rising Tide of Amicus Curiae Briefs

Amici curiae today play an integral role in Supreme Court litigation. In this Part, we offer a statistical overview of how the frequency of amicus participation has changed in the last fifty years to the point where amicus briefs have become an everyday occurrence in Supreme Court practice....

A. *The Level of Amicus Curiae Activity, 1946–1995*

The phenomenon of increasing amicus participation in the Supreme Court was not evident to all while it was taking shape. Writing in the 1960s, Nathan Hakman was able to argue that amicus curiae influence on the Supreme Court was exaggerated—an example of "Political Science Folklore," as he put it.... By 1982, it was apparent that a major shift was underway. Karen O'Connor and Lee Epstein reported that for the period from 1970 to 1980, amicus participation had risen to three times the level of the World War II era. Most recently, Andrew Koshner has documented a continuing and steady increase in the overall percentage of cases with at least one amicus brief from 1950 to 1994.

Our study ... shows conclusively that a major reorientation in practice has taken place. Amicus participation has risen dramatically over the last fifty years. The point can be conveyed, as in Figure 1, by a simple examination of the number of amicus briefs filed in each of the five decades of our study. The Court received some 4907 amicus briefs in the last decade (1986–1995), as opposed to 531 briefs in the first decade (1946–1955)—an increase of more than 800%.

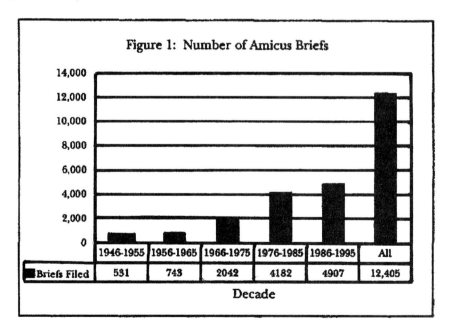

Figure 1: Number of Amicus Briefs

	1946-1955	1956-1965	1966-1975	1976-1985	1986-1995	All
Briefs Filed	531	743	2042	4182	4907	12,405

Decade

The increase in amicus briefs is equally impressive when expressed in terms of the percentage of total argued cases. Although the number of cases set by the Court for oral argument increased during the first four decades, in the most recent decade it has fallen back to a level closer to that of the 1946–1955 period. The percentage of argued cases with one or more amicus briefs, however, has marched ever higher throughout our study period. . . . Whereas one or more amicus curiae briefs were filed in 23% of argued cases in the decade from 1946 to 1955, this figure rose steadily and steeply to 85% of argued cases in the most recent decade, 1986 to 1995. . . .

Another measure of the intensity of amicus participation is the number of amicus briefs per argued case. The mean (average) number of briefs per case has also shot up in the last fifty years. Expressed in terms of total cases, the mean has increased from about 0.50 per case to 4.23 per case over the course of the five decades. Perhaps more instructively, when expressed in terms of the cases in which one or more amicus briefs were filed, the mean number of amicus briefs per case has also multiplied, going from 2.12 in the first post-War decade to 5.00 in the most recent period.

. . . [L]ooking at the cases where there is some amicus activity, the median number of briefs jumps from one to three over the period of our study. Thus, . . . it is clear that the intensity of participation—whether measured in terms of the mean or median numbers of briefs per case—is also rising.

The phenomenon of certain cases attracting extraordinarily large numbers of amicus briefs warrants special comment. The phenomenon is not entirely new; earlier landmark decisions such as *Brown v. Board of Education*, *Baker v. Carr*, and *Furman v. Georgia* also drew above-average numbers of amicus filings. As with other aspects of Supreme Court amicus curiae practice, however, the most recent decades have seen a qualitative change in the number of cases attracting extraordinarily large numbers of amicus filings. All of the cases that have attracted twenty or more briefs have come since the twenty-fifth year of our fifty-year study (i.e., since 1970). Indeed, no argued case elicited more than thirty amicus briefs until the last twenty years of our study.

Most but not all of the thirty-four cases that have triggered twenty or more amicus briefs during the fifty-year period of our study involve controversial social and political issues such as abortion, affirmative action, free speech, church-state relations, and takings of property. The all-time record-setter in terms of amicus participation is Webster v. Reproductive Health Services,[156] an abortion case which drew seventy-eight briefs—forty-six supporting the petitioner (the Attorney General of Missouri, who asked the Supreme Court to overrule its decision in *Roe v. Wade*) and thirty-two supporting the respondents (who asked that *Roe* be reaffirmed). Other notable cases with large numbers of briefs include

156. [Footnote 31 in original] 492 U.S. 490 (1989).

Regents of the University of California v. Bakke,[157] the 1978 affirmative action case, whose fifty-four briefs stood as a record until *Webster*, and Cruzan v. Director, Missouri Department of Health,[158] where the right-to-die issue attracted thirty-nine briefs. Although falling outside the period of our study, the Court's 1997 assisted-suicide decisions continued this trend, each eliciting more than forty amicus briefs.

The very large numbers of amicus briefs filed in a small number of controversial cases have probably done more than anything else to raise public consciousness about amicus briefs.... [A] number of commentators have associated the outpouring of amicus filings in abortion cases with the public protests and letter-writing campaigns that have been directed at the Court and others over this issue. As our study reveals, however, the phenomenon is by no means limited to such high-profile cases. Large numbers of amicus briefs have also been filed in cases involving copyright protection, punitive damages, and the apportionment of state taxes.... [A]micus participation is now well-established in all areas of Supreme Court litigation.

B.   Citation and Quotation of Amicus Briefs, 1946–1995

Clearly, amici curiae are playing an increasingly active role in supplying input to the Court's decision-making process. What can be said about the impact of these briefs on the Court's output? The only publicly visible manifestation of the impact of amici is the frequency with which their briefs are cited or quoted in the opinions of the Justices....

... [W]e examined every reference by the Court [between 1946 and 1995] to an amicus in the case before the Court, whether the reference was in a majority, plurality, concurring, or dissenting opinion.

... [T]he likelihood of a Supreme Court decision's referring to an amicus in the case increases over the five decades of our study, beginning with close to 18% of the cases with amicus filers decided between 1946 and 1955 and ending with just under 37% of the cases with amicus filers between 1986 and 1995....

We also catalogued the extent to which the Court over the past fifty years has actually quoted the arguments of amici.... Particularly noteworthy is the fact that the rate of such cases with quoted amici jumps in the most recent decade to over 15%, which is more than double the rate of the first three decades and almost double the rate of the fourth.

. . .

... [B]ecause there is also relatively little ambiguity about when the Court refers to an amicus brief of a specific institutional litigant, we can compute the trend line with respect to the rate of references per amicus brief for three of the institutional litigants tracked in our study—the Solicitor General, the ACLU, and the AFL–CIO. The king of the citation-frequency hill is the Solicitor General, and this is increasingly true. The

157. [Footnote 33 in original] 438 U.S. 265 (1978).

158. [Footnote 34 in original] 497 U.S. 261 (1990).

Court referred to the Solicitor General as amicus in 402 cases [out of a total of 936 in which there were references to any amicus] during the fifty years of our study, which works out to just over 40% of the cases where the Solicitor General filed a brief. Significantly, the frequency of the Court's citation of the Solicitor General as amicus rises each decade.... This strongly suggests that the Court has come to rely more heavily on the Solicitor General's amicus filings in the last fifty years, at least in the writing of opinions.

In contrast, when we look to the two other institutional litigants, we find no such pattern of increased incidence of citation.... The AFL CIO fared slightly better [than the ACLU], being cited twenty-eight times, or in 10.45% of the 268 cases where it appeared as amicus. After a sharp increase during the Warren Court decade of 1956–1965, this rate also has remained more or less steady over the last thirty years.

... [T]he rate of citations and quotations per brief is more or less keeping pace with the increase in filings. The one notable exception to the pattern is the Solicitor General, whose office has seen its amicus briefs cited with significantly increased frequency during the period of our study, suggesting ... that the Solicitor General's office is in a class by itself in terms of its influence as an amicus filer.

II. THE OPEN DOOR POLICY TOWARD AMICUS BRIEFS

. . .

The biggest change in the last fifty years has occurred not in the Court's formal rules, but in the manner in which they are implemented. The Court's current practice in argued cases is to grant nearly all motions for leave to file as amicus curiae when consent is denied by a party. Because the Court in recent years has routinely granted such motions, parties that are represented by experienced lawyers will in most cases consent to such filings, if only to avoid burdening the Court with the need to rule on the motion. The effect of the Court's liberality in ruling on motions for leave to file, therefore, is to permit essentially unlimited filings of amicus briefs in argued cases.

The Court has not always followed this "open door" policy. In the late 1940s and early 1950s, large numbers of amicus briefs were submitted in several controversial cases involving government investigation of Communist Party activities, including the prosecution of the "Hollywood Ten" for failing to testify before the House Un–American Activities Committee and the espionage convictions of Ethyl and Julius Rosenberg. Some Justices were reportedly put off by the "propagandistic" tone of these filings, and the Court sought to curtail the filing of amicus curiae briefs. In terms of formal action, the Court amended its rules to emphasize that the consent of all parties was required for a nongovernmental entity to file an amicus brief, and spelled out in detail the procedure for filing a motion with the Court for leave to file if consent was denied. More importantly, the Court adopted the unwritten policy of denying virtually all motions for leave to file as amicus curiae when consent was denied. The Solicitor General viewed this policy as a signal from the Court that it wanted the government to refuse to consent to amicus filings in cases in which the United States was a party, and the Solicitor General obliged. The net effect of these coordinated efforts was that the number of amicus filings in argued cases declined around 1949 and remained at a relatively depressed level throughout the 1950s.

Several years after this clamp-down on amicus filings, some of the Justices began to have a change of heart. In published opinions, Justices Frankfurter and Black each indicated unhappiness with the Solicitor General's restrictive policy of denying consent in virtually all cases. In 1957, the Solicitor General responded by issuing a "policy statement" softening the government's attitude toward consent to amicus participation. By 1959, it was clear that when consent to file was refused, the Court was granting far more motions for leave to file than it was denying ... [and] the number of amicus briefs soon started to increase. After the early 1960s, the attitude of the Court toward amicus filings in argued cases gradually became one of laissez-faire.... Today, it can truly be said, the Supreme Court's policy "is to allow essentially unlimited amicus participation."

The Court's open door policy toward amicus briefs undoubtedly provides a part of the explanation for the rising tide of such briefs in the last half-century. Whatever the benefits of filing an amicus brief may be—whether they consist of influencing the Court's decisions, being cited by the Court, or just assuring the members of an organization that its leaders are on the watch—those benefits are more readily obtained in a regime where every brief is automatically accepted. Under a regime with a significant risk of rejection, in contrast, the benefits would have to be discounted by the probability of rejection and the costs of litigating to obtain permission to file. The open door policy inaugurated after around 1960 thus had the effect of increasing the benefits of seeking to file amicus briefs relative to the costs—which one would expect to lead to an increase in filing activity.

The open door policy, however, cannot supply the whole explanation for the rising tide of amicus activity. This is because the Court's policies remained essentially unchanged over the next thirty-five years. If the open door policy initiated in the early 1960s were the only factor at work, one would expect to see an increase in filing in the 1960s followed by a levelling off thereafter. Yet ... when we plot the expected number of amicus briefs after 1970 based on the rate of filings from 1960 through 1969, we see a much lower projected number of briefs than were actually filed during the latter half of our study. Some of the later increase may be due to perceptual lag among practicing lawyers, as the Court's open door policy gradually became more ... more visible to lawyers. Yet it seems obvious that some additional factor or factors must also be influencing groups to intensify their efforts in filing amicus briefs....

More recently, there has been a modification in the Court's rules regarding amicus curiae participation that may betoken a further change in the Court's attitude toward amicus briefs. The Court in 1997 adopted what is probably the most important amendment to its formal rules regarding amicus participation since they were first promulgated in 1939.[159] The new Rule 37.6 requires the disclosure of certain relationships between the parties to the case and any person or entity that files an amicus brief. Specifically, the amended rule now requires that each amicus brief disclose in the first footnote on the first page of text "whether counsel for a party authored the brief in whole or in part," as well as the identity of "every person or entity, other than the *amicus curiae*, its members or its counsel, who made a monetary contribution to the preparation or submission of the brief."

The Court provided no rationale for these new disclosure requirements. The changes could mean simply that the Justices want to know if an amicus brief is written or financed by one of the parties so that they can more appropriately evaluate the contents of the brief for possible bias. Alternatively, the changes could reflect a perception by the Justices that some parties are funding or ghost-writing amicus briefs to get around the page limits that apply to the parties' briefs on the merits. Or, the amendments could reflect a growing concern on the part of the Justices that amicus filings are being manipulated in order to create an impression of widespread political support for a particular position....

The long term implications of the Court's new disclosure rules are unclear. Whatever concerns underlie the requirement of a disclosure of interest or participation on the part of the parties with respect to the filing of amicus briefs, the Court has not yet changed its basic open door policy towards amicus filings.

III. PREVIOUS STUDIES OF THE INFLUENCE OF AMICUS BRIEFS ON SUPREME COURT OUTCOMES

By far the most important question about amicus briefs is not whether they are easy to file, or whether, if filed, they are likely to be cited or quoted. Rather, it is whether such briefs have any influence on the decisions reached by the Court.... [I]f amicus briefs have no impact on the Court's decision-making process, then the tidal wave of amicus briefs becomes harder to explain....

[The authors here provide an excellent review of all prior empirical studies, which we omit for reasons of space.]

159. [Editors' Note: Readers should note that on July 17, 2007, further amendments to Rule 37 were announced. The revisions, *inter alia*, require electronic transmission (in addition to paper filing) in cases scheduled for oral argument; provide new requirements for amici wishing to file at the jurisdictional stage; and allow amicus briefs on the merits to be filed within seven days after the due date of the side they are supporting (rather than simultaneously). See Revised Supreme Court Rule 37.2(a), 37.3(a), available on the Supreme Court's website, http://www.supremecourtus.gov/ctrules/2007revisedrules.pdf.]

... [T]he existing empirical literature on the relationship between amicus briefs and Supreme Court outcomes provides confusing and contradictory results. Some studies ... suggest that amicus support is associated with enhanced chances of success. Other studies ... show no relationship between amicus support and outcomes. The only finding that has been consistently replicated is that the Solicitor General enjoys a unique degree of success as an amicus filer.

IV. THREE MODELS OF JUDGING AND THEIR
IMPLICATIONS FOR AMICUS BRIEFS

... Perhaps further progress can be made in understanding the impact of amicus briefs by delineating more precisely how different models of judicial behavior generate different hypotheses about how amicus briefs influence (or fail to influence) the Court.... [W]e discuss three models of judicial behavior and specify the implications of each model in terms of the pathway of influence of amicus briefs. This in turn suggests, in a general way, the type of empirical results that would tend to corroborate or disprove the model.

A. *The Legal Model*

The first model, and the one with which lawyers will be most familiar, we call the legal model.... [It] posits that Justices resolve cases in accordance with their understanding of the requirements of the authoritative sources of law relevant to the question presented. These include the text of the applicable constitutional and statutory provisions, the structure and history of these provisions, precedents of the Court, and arguments about the policy consequences of different outcomes.

The legal model is without doubt the "official" conception of how information, including that provided by amicus briefs, influences judges. Since 1990, the Court's rules governing the filing of amicus briefs have begun with this admonition:

> An *amicus curiae* brief that brings to the attention of the Court relevant matter not already brought to its attention by the parties may be of considerable help to the Court. An *amicus curiae* brief that does not serve this purpose burdens the Court, and its filing is not favored.

In other words, the Court's rules suggest that amicus briefs can influence the Court ("may be of considerable help to the Court") insofar as those briefs have value, both in the sense that they speak to the merits of the legal issue before the Court (supply "relevant matter") and provide new information ("matter not already brought to its attention by the parties").

The legal model is also the conception of the judicial role implicit in the procedures that the Court follows in deciding argued cases. Those procedures are designed to facilitate a careful sifting of arguments and authorities. They include the dialogic pattern reflected in the filing of opening briefs, followed by responsive briefs, followed by reply briefs; the close questioning of counsel at oral argument; the exchange of views and preliminary votes at the conference of the Justices; and the circulation of draft opinions among the Justices for comment and revision before a final decision is reached. This sifting process can be seen as a collective weighing by the Justices of the strength of different legal perspectives with respect to the controversy at hand.

Notwithstanding the legal model's preferred status as reflected in the Court's rules and procedures, political scientists have long been intensely skeptical about whether the legal model has any explanatory power in predicting the outcomes reached by the Court. They note that the legal factors the Court considers are complex and have no fixed ordinal ranking. Thus, they contend, the legal model is open to manipulation and simply serves as a post hoc rationalization for results reached on political grounds.

A proponent of the legal model might respond that it is unrealistic to demand that the law produce highly predictable outcomes, at least at the highest level of appellate litigation. The fact that the cases reaching the Supreme Court are those that produce disagreement among lawyers does not mean that law is irrelevant to the resolution of these disputes. The lawyers appearing before the Court debate these issues in terms of legal doctrine, and they frequently reach a consensus about which outcomes are most appropriate. Indeed, the fact that the Court rules unanimously in nearly 40% of its argued cases suggests either that there is a strong core of agreement among the Justices about the law's requirements in a significant percentage of cases, or at least that their disagreements are not sharp enough to provoke a dissent.

Given the assumption of the legal model that Justices are anxious to resolve the cases before them correctly, in light of the complex norms of the legal profession, they should be eager to explore different legal perspectives on the issue, including different legal theories concerning how the issue should be resolved. These norms include, for many Justices, the social consequences of adopting different legal rules. Thus, these Justices should be receptive to "Brandeis Brief"-type information that sheds light on the wider social implications of the decision.

The legal model therefore generates a clear prediction about what results we should expect from an empirical study of amicus briefs. Amicus briefs should affect the likelihood of a party's success in the Supreme Court, but only insofar as they are of high quality, i.e., they provide new, legally relevant information to the Court beyond that supplied by the parties. The sheer quantity of amicus submissions, on the other hand, should have little impact. Indeed, low-quality briefs that are merely repetitious should have no impact, or perhaps even a negative impact insofar as they "burden the Court," to use the Court's own phrase. Measuring "high quality" in a study that relies on counting large numbers of briefs in large numbers of cases is inherently problematic. Nevertheless, as reported in Part V we have attempted in our empirical study to devise various proxies for high-quality briefs in an effort to test this prediction.

B. *The Attitudinal Model*

The second model of judicial behavior is the attitudinal model, which is today the dominant model used by political scientists studying the Supreme Court. The attitudinal model posits that the Justices decide cases in accordance with their political beliefs. These beliefs are assumed to be fixed by the time a Justice is appointed to the Court; the Justices do not change their ideological predispositions by interacting with their colleagues or by reflecting on the cases they hear or other information they acquire during their years on the Court.

Under the attitudinal model, individual Justices are viewed as each having a package of political "attitudes" that can be ranked along ordinal scales. These are usually scaled from "liberal" to "conservative," but are sometimes expressed more specifically, such as pro-to anti-death penalty or pro-to anti-labor union. The model assumes that as cases presenting facts that implicate these attitudes arise, the outcomes are determined in accordance with the preferences of the majority of the voting Justices. Thus, if the issue involves a conflict between management and labor, and a majority of judges fall on the pro-labor end of the pro-to anti-labor scale, the party representing labor wins.

Lawyers and law professors usually react to the attitudinal model with hostility, regarding it as at best a caricature of the legal process. The proponents of the model acknowledge that it is highly reductionistic, but counter that any model of judicial behavior, if it is to be useful, must be "simpl[e] and parsimoniou[s]." They maintain that the attitudinal model, for all of its oversimplification, does a better job of predicting the outcomes of Supreme Court cases than any other model. It is this claim to predictive superiority, rather than any subtlety or verisimilitude, that has caused the attitudinal model to become the dominant approach to study of the Court among political scientists.

The important point for present purposes is the implications of the attitudinal model for how Justices react to information beyond that supplied by the parties .... Under the attitudinal model, judges need very little information to decide cases. Ordinarily, the list of "Questions Presented" in the petitioner's brief and the bare outlines of the underlying controversy should do. The assumption that Justices decide cases based on only a few key bits of information in turn suggests that it will be an extremely rare case in which amicus briefs will supply critical information that invokes a different preference and changes the outcome. In short, the attitudinal model generates what statisticians would call the null hypothesis: amicus briefs will have no discernible impact on outcomes.

Recently, some political scientists have begun to question the assumption of the attitudinal model that the Justices do not modify their positions in light of information about how other institutional actors are likely to respond to their decisions. Instead, they have sought to explain judicial behavior in accordance with a "strategic actor" model.[160] This is essentially the attitudinal model with the added assumption that the Justices are rational actors who modify their voting behavior in order to maximize the chances of their ideological preferences actually being adopted as policy. Thus, the Justices do not vote in accordance with their "knee jerk" reaction to the facts of a case, but instead consider how other institutional actors are likely to respond to their decisions. In particular, the Justices will consider whether a given interpretation of a statute is likely to be overruled by Congress, or whether the recognition of a particular constitutional right is likely to be nullified by lackluster executive enforcement.

Although it is difficult to derive testable hypotheses about the influence of amicus briefs from the strategic actor version of the attitudinal model, at least two predictions would seem to flow from this perspective. First, since the interests of the executive branch and of Congress are nearly always represented in the Supreme Court by the Solicitor General, one would expect a strategic Justice to pay very close attention to the amicus briefs filed by the Solicitor General. This might translate into higher success rates for the Solicitor General's amicus briefs relative to those of other filers. Similarly, though less dramatically, one would expect a strategic Justice to pay more than ordinary attention to the amicus briefs filed by the States since the States are often called upon to implement judicial decisions. This might translate into a somewhat higher success rate for the States as amicus filers relative to others.

C. The Interest Group Model

The third model of judging posits that Justices will seek to resolve cases in accordance with the desires of the organized groups that have an interest in the controversy. We call this the interest group model. Political scientists have long perceived an analogy between interest groups lobbying legislatures and interest groups seeking to influence judicial decisions through the filing of amicus briefs. More recently, some legal scholars influenced by public choice theory have begun to model the judiciary in accordance with the rational-maximizer assumptions of the interest group theory of politics. Indeed, the interest group model may be the dominant conception that amicus filers have today regarding their own efforts.

What has not been perceived is that the interest group model of the judicial process, although it shares with the attitudinal model the basic hypothesis that judicial behavior is political, in fact adopts a very

160. [Footnote 130 in original] *See, e.g.,* [Lawrence] Baum, [*The Puzzle of Judicial Behavior* (1997)], at 89–124 (concluding that Justices routinely vote strategically, rather than always following their own optimal policy preferences, in order to advance broader policy goals); Lee Epstein & Jack Knight, *The Choices Justices Make* 10 (1998) ("[J]ustices are strategic actors who realize that their ability to achieve their goals depends on a consideration of the preferences of other actors, the choices they expect others to make, and the institutional context in which they act.") . . .

different assumption as to why judges behave politically. In contrast to the attitudinal model, which views judges as having fixed political beliefs and as seeking to advance those beliefs through judicial decisions, the interest group model depicts judges as having no fixed beliefs, but rather as seeking to satisfy the political demands of the best-organized groups appearing before them. The distinction between the attitudinal model and the interest group model of judging thus exactly parallels the distinction in political science between the "ideological" and the "interest group" model of legislative behavior.... [T]he former model depicts government actors as utilizing their office in order to advance their view of the public good, while the latter model depicts government actors as utilizing their office in order to maximize their own private good.

The immediate question raised by the interest group model is why Supreme Court Justices, who have lifetime tenure and guaranteed compensation, should care about the political demands of organized groups. Two possible reasons have been offered.

The first suggests that Justices have the same self-regarding tendencies that economists impute to other individuals to explain both market and non-market behavior. Thus, just as firms are assumed to maximize profits, and politicians are assumed (by analogy) to maximize their chances of reelection, so judges can be assumed (by further analogy) to maximize some private good they value. It is possible to imagine various private goods that lower court judges might seek to maximize, such as the chances of promotion to a higher judicial or executive office.... But at least at the Supreme Court level, the reputation of the judge (as measured by laudatory articles, honorific awards, invitations to make appearances at elite law schools and to conduct seminars at exclusive resorts, and the like) seems like the most plausible maximand. This concern with enhancing their reputation, the self-interest argument suggests, drives the Justices to adopt the preferred positions of the most influential interest groups....

An alternative explanation would focus not on each Justice's concern about personal reputation, but rather on the Justices' collective concern about the prestige and power of the Court as an institution. Scholars who study the relationship between public opinion and the Court have long hypothesized that the Justices recognize that "the Court is a political institution whose authority depends on public deference and respect." Consequently, at least some Justices will modify their decisions "in response to what they individually perceive as long-term and fundamental changes in public opinion." Justice Roberts's famous "switch in time" to preserve New Deal programs from invalidation and Justice Kennedy's apparent reversal of position on whether to overrule *Roe v. Wade* are familiar examples.

Whatever the assumed source of the Justices' sensitivity to organized public opinion, the implications of the interest group theory for amicus activity are reasonably clear. In order to maximize their own public reputations or the reputation of the Court, the Justices need information about public opinion.... On some issues that reach the Court, such as whether abortions should be constitutionally protected or compulsory busing used to achieve integration in public schools, public opinion polling data is available. However, with respect to most issues the Court must decide—such as whether to recognize a psychotherapist's privilege (the issue in *Jaffee v. Redmond*)—there is no public opinion, or at least no polling data about public opinion. This does not mean, however, that specific interest groups do not have strong views about such issues. Those groups most affected by a decision are likely to have very pronounced views about how these issues should be resolved as a policy matter. Thus, in the vast run of cases that the Court decides, "public opinion" translates into "interest group opinion."

The interest group model therefore generates a third hypothesis about the role of amicus briefs in transmitting information to the Court. Insofar as the Justices are assumed to try to resolve cases in accordance with the weight of public opinion, they should look to amicus briefs as a barometer of opinion on both sides of the issue. Moreover, the information that amicus briefs convey about organized opinion is such that it can largely be assimilated simply by looking at the cover of the brief. The Justices can scan the covers of the briefs to see which organizations care strongly about the issue on either side. The fact that the organization saw fit to file the brief is the important datum, not the legal arguments or the background information set forth between the covers of the brief.

The understanding that amicus briefs transmit the views of interest groups appears to be the animating idea of Justice Scalia's dissenting opinion in *Jaffee*. In *Jaffee*, Justice Scalia noted that fourteen groups, most of them representing different types of psychotherapists, filed amicus briefs in support of creating a "psychotherapist's privilege" in federal court. Such a privilege, by shielding psychotherapists from having to testify about information disclosed to them by patients while undergoing therapy, would enhance the value of therapeutic services and would elevate the prestige of therapists by associating their services with those provided by more traditional professionals such as lawyers. The filing of the fourteen briefs could be viewed as sending a clear message to the Court that the weight of organized public opinion strongly supported the recognition of such a psychotherapist's privilege. Thus, if the Justices are assumed to be concerned primarily with public opinion, amicus briefs offer a road map about how to rule.

The interest group model generates a clear prediction about what results we should expect from an empirical analysis of amicus briefs. We should expect to find that disparities in amicus support for one side over another would translate into a greater probability of success for the side with the greater support. Such disparities would signal to the Court that organized interest groups, and through them public opinion, are aligned with one side of the controversy rather than another. The greater the disparity of amicus support for one side, the more likely the Court will rule for that side. The quality of the legal analysis contained in amicus briefs, however, would make little difference to the outcome.

V.　An Empirical Study of the Influence of Amicus Briefs

In an effort to test these rival conceptions about the influence of amicus briefs, we undertook to conduct an empirical study....

Our database consists of all Supreme Court decisions from the beginning of October Term 1946 to the end of October Term 1995 in which the Court heard oral arguments and rendered a decision on the merits or by dismissing declined to do so. For each of 6141 cases, we classified the outcome as falling into one of three categories: *p-win* (short for petitioner win), meaning that the judgment below was set aside; *p-loss* (short for petitioner loss), meaning basically that the judgment below was sustained or at a minimum not set aside; and mixed result, meaning that the judgment was partially sustained and partially set aside. Using the tabulation of amicus briefs at the beginning of each decision in the official *United States Reports* by the Reporter of Decisions, we also recorded for each case the number of amicus briefs supporting the petitioner, the number of amicus briefs supporting the respondent, and the number of amicus briefs not classified as supporting either party (we term this last category "other" briefs).

In addition, we tracked the amicus curiae briefs of four institutional litigants—the Solicitor General, the American Civil Liberties Union, the AFL–CIO, and the States. Each of these four institutional actors frequently appears as amicus before the Supreme Court and has done so throughout the fifty years of our study. Moreover, each of these institutional litigants has been identified in the previous literature as being especially successful in influencing the Court through amicus curiae submissions. We wanted to test these assertions and also to be able to control for the impact of these litigants in assessing the effectiveness of other amicus filers.

We used our large database of decisions to try to answer three questions, corresponding to our three models of judging and their associated hypotheses. The first, which was suggested by the attitudinal model, is whether amicus briefs in general have any measurable impact on the outcomes reached by the Supreme Court. The second, which was stimulated by Justice Scalia's dissenting opinion in *Jaffee v. Redmond* and the interest group model, is whether disparities in amicus support for one side or another have an impact on the outcomes reached by the Supreme Court. The third, which is responsive to the legal model, is whether high-quality amicus briefs have an impact on outcomes reached by the Court.

A.　*The Overall Success Rates of Amicus Filers*

.　.　.

In assessing the impact of amicus filers in general, the point of departure is to determine the benchmark rate of success for petitioners and respondents without regard to amicus support. We computed the benchmark rate by determining the mean *p-win* and *p-loss* rate for petitioners and respondents in cases in which no amicus briefs were filed. Rounding to whole numbers, we found that in such cases petitioners are successful 60% of the time, respondents are successful 37% of the time, and mixed results are obtained 3% of the time....

... Previous studies have found that the Supreme Court is more likely to rule in favor of petitioners than respondents. Analysts have suggested that this reflects the fact that one factor that presumably motivates the Court to grant review is the perception of at least four Justices that the case below was wrongly decided. Our large database ... confirms that petitioners fare better than respondents....

Given that the benchmark rates of success vary slightly by decade, we have used decade-specific success rates in reporting data.... [explanation of certain simplifications in data presentation is omitted]

. . .

... [T]he success rate of amicus filers supporting petitioners over the entire fifty-year span differs very little from the benchmark rates of success. Amicus filers supporting petitioners obtained a *p-win* rate less than 1% higher than the benchmark rate of success. When we break the results down by decade, we see some intriguing variations. Filers supporting petitioners exceeded the benchmark in the second (Warren Court) decade of 1956–1965 by nearly 9%, and beat the benchmark success rate in the third (Warren Court/Burger Court) decade of 1966–1975 by slightly less than 4%. In the last two decades, however, filers supporting petitioners were much more numerous and achieved success at rates that hover just under the benchmark rates of success, bringing the overall result closely in line with the benchmark rate. It is possible, therefore, that amicus filers supporting petitioners had some effect on outcomes from 1956 to 1975, but then lost this advantage as the numbers of amicus briefs surged in the last two decades.

When we turn to filers supporting respondents, we see a different picture. Filers supporting respondents have experienced a consistent degree of success relative to the benchmark rates of success throughout the period of our study. Overall, ... amicus filers supporting respondents obtained a *p-win* rate of less than 53%, which, for a filer supporting respondents, is substantially better than the benchmark rate of 60%. When we break down the results by decade, we see that filers supporting respondents have consistently outperformed the benchmarks. Moreover, filers supporting respondents, unlike filers supporting petitioners, have continued to do better than the benchmark rates in the last two decades. ...[O]ur data show in a variety of contexts that amicus briefs supporting respondents have greater success than amicus briefs supporting petitioners.

. . .

B. Disparities in Amicus Support

One of the primary reasons we developed our large database of decisions is that we wanted to gather as many cases like *Jaffee v.*

Redmond as possible in order to test the interest group theory. That is, we wanted to uncover a subset of cases involving extreme disparities of amicus support of a magnitude similar to *Jaffee*, where the petitioner had no amicus support and the respondent was supported by fourteen briefs. Somewhat to our surprise, we discovered that no such subset of cases exists. *Jaffee* is in a league by itself.... [N]o other case in our database of 6141 decisions had a disparity of at least fourteen briefs on one side and zero on the other.

We were therefore forced to examine the effect of much smaller disparities in amicus support in order to consider the interest group model. "Disparities" in this context could be measured in different ways.... [We decided to use as a measure of disparity] multiples of briefs supporting one side with no briefs supporting the other side. Each measurement presents its own problems, especially in terms of handling the briefs in the "other" column. We settled on th[is] measure because it struck us (as it apparently did Justice Scalia in *Jaffee*) as the type of disparity most likely to suggest to the Court that organized groups are aligned in favor of one side of a case rather than the other. In other words, we studied cases in which there were one, two, or three or more briefs supporting petitioner, none supporting respondent, and none in the "other" column (x–0–0 cases), and then studied cases in which there were one, two, or three or more briefs supporting respondent, none supporting petitioner, and none in the "other" column (0–x–0 cases).

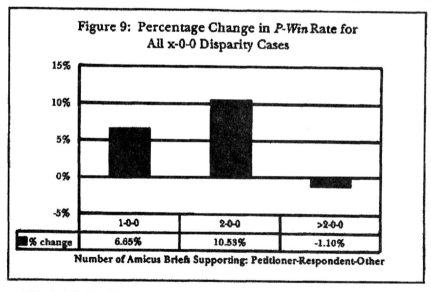

Figure 9: Percentage Change in *P-Win* Rate for All x-0-0 Disparity Cases

	1-0-0	2-0-0	>2-0-0
% change	6.65%	10.53%	-1.10%

Number of Amicus Briefs Supporting: Petitioner-Respondent-Other

Data Underlying Figure 9	1-0-0	2-0-0	>2-0-0
Number of Cases	545	165	121

Our first step was to compare the rates of success over all the cases in our database that fit this definition of disparity against the benchmark rate of success (p-win = 60%). Figure 9 depicts the increase in *p-*

win rates that we found with different degrees of disparity favoring the petitioner. The interest group model predicts that higher levels of disparity for petitioner should increase the success rate of petitioners above 60%. What we see tends to support this hypothesis, at least for disparities of one and two amicus briefs. When one amicus brief is filed in support of petitioner and none for respondent, the *p-win* rate rises by nearly 7%. When two amicus briefs are filed in support of petitioner and none for respondent, the *p-win* rate rises by more than 10%. When we reach a disparity of three or more briefs, however, the results no longer correspond to the prediction of the interest group hypothesis. Indeed, the success rate of petitioners drops slightly *below* the benchmark rate of success, a puzzling result.

Figure 10 shows the parallel findings with respect to disparities of amicus support for the respondent. Here, the hypothesis we are testing predicts that increasing levels of disparity should push the *p-win* rates below the benchmark level of 60%. The pattern we uncover resembles that seen with respect to disparities of support for petitioners. The success rate follows the predicted pattern with respect to disparities of one brief and two briefs, with respondents supported by one amicus brief reducing the *p-win* rate by slightly over 4% and those supported by two amicus briefs reducing the *p-win* rate by somewhat more than 10%. When we reach the third column, for disparities of three or more, the differential shrinks back toward the benchmark, as it did with three or more briefs on the petitioner side, although this time the change in the success rate is still in the predicted direction (a greater than 3% reduction in *p-win* rate).

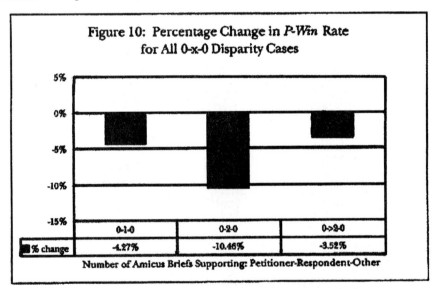

Figure 10: Percentage Change in *P-Win* Rate for All 0-x-0 Disparity Cases

	0-1-0	0-2-0	0->2-0
% change	-4.27%	-10.46%	-3.52%

Number of Amicus Briefs Supporting: Petitioner-Respondent-Other

Data Underlying Figure 10	0-1-0	0-2-0	0->2-0
Number of Cases	400	146	112

These results ... appear to provide some support for the hypothesis that disparities of amicus support affect success rates, at least for small disparities of one or two briefs on one side and none on the other. As our survey of the prior literature suggests, however, it is important to control for the influence of institutional litigants, especially the Solicitor General.... When we analyzed the cases in which the Solicitor General was not an amicus filer, we discovered that the success rates with different degrees of disparity were close to the benchmark success rate in almost all instances. Only with a disparity of three or more on the petitioner's side and of two on the respondent's side did we find substantial effects. This suggests that the influence on success rates shown in the aggregate data may largely be a product of the influence of the Solicitor General as an amicus filer....

On further consideration, however, we realized that removing the Solicitor General as an amicus filer did not fully neutralize the Solicitor General's influence. Prior studies suggest that the Solicitor General enjoys extraordinary success not only as an amicus filer, but also as a party. Accordingly, we re-ran the disparity analysis looking only at cases in which the Solicitor General did not participate in any capacity, either as an amicus or as a party.... We found, somewhat to our surprise, that when the Solicitor General is completely eliminated from the picture, disparities of amicus support appear once again to be associated with greater success; indeed, small disparities have a greater impact on this subset of the database than they do with respect to disparities over all the cases in the database.... [W]ith the first brief supporting petitioners, the success rate of petitioners rises by almost 7%; with the second brief, it rises a remarkable 19%. The success rate with three or more briefs again falls back toward the benchmark rate, but still remains over 8%. The number of cases each column represents is not large, but in no case does it fall below forty....

On the respondent's side, ... the impact of disparities once the Solicitor General is altogether removed from the picture is even more dramatic. With the first amicus brief supporting respondents, the *p-win* rate falls by more than 14%; with the second brief, it falls a striking 24%. Little effect is shown at three briefs and higher, but the number of those cases here is relatively small. It may be, therefore, that disparities of amicus support have an impact on outcomes, at least for small disparities of one or two briefs to none, but that this effect is masked by the considerable success of the Solicitor General as a Supreme Court litigant and thus clearly appears only in cases where the Solicitor General is not involved.

. . .

Of particular interest to us is the robustness of the different case variables in altering the odds of a *p-win* outcome, controlling for other variables. To facilitate this assessment, we included odds ratios for a *p-win* outcome. These ratios show that if the Solicitor General is present as petitioner, all other factors being equal, the odds of a *p-win* are effectively doubled. If the Solicitor General is present as respondent, all other factors being equal, the odds of a *p-win* are effectively reduced by roughly half. We found less robust effects for the disparity figures: 1–0–0 and 2–0–0 cases with the Solicitor General filtered out as amicus increase the odds of a *p-win* by roughly 27% and 50%, respectively; 0–1–0 cases and 0–2–0 cases decrease the odds of a *p-win* outcome by roughly 20% and 45%.

. . .

. . . [B]y focusing on different subsets of our database in our analysis, we uncovered some evidence that disparities of amicus support may have an impact on the outcomes reached by the Supreme Court. The effect of disparities of one or two amicus briefs on success rates for petitioner is not strong enough to overcome the heightened probability of success enjoyed by the Solicitor General as amicus and as a party. Consequently, the effect can only be seen by comparing means across subsets of data that exclude the Solicitor General. Moreover, this effect appears only when there are either one or two briefs in support of one party and no briefs in support of the other. For some reason, the effect largely disappears when there are three or more briefs in support of one party and no briefs in support of the other. Finally, even the small effect of disparities of one or two briefs loses statistical significance when we analyze these disparities as independent variables in a regression model that includes all four institutional litigants.

C. The Impact of Amicus Brief Quality

By far the most difficult model to test quantitatively is the legal model, which predicts that the Court is influenced by briefs that present especially valued information but not by briefs that are merely repetitive of the parties' briefs. Because reading and assessing the quality of more than 12,000 individual amicus briefs was a task far beyond our endurance, we had to come up with a proxy for briefs that contain information valued highly by the Court. We adopted three approaches. First, we inquired whether cases with an amicus brief from one of our institutional litigants had different success rates from those supported by "ordinary" amicus briefs. Second, we examined the success rates of amici whose briefs the Court or an individual Justice explicitly relied upon through citation. Third, we considered whether briefs filed by more experienced Supreme Court litigators enjoy greater success than briefs filed by less experienced litigators.

1. Success Rates of Institutional Litigants

We examined the success rates of the Solicitor General, the ACLU, the AFL–CIO, and the States over each of the five decades. We reasoned that the first three of these entities are good proxies for high-quality amicus briefs, i.e., those containing valued information. Not only has each of these entities filed numerous amicus briefs in all five decades, but each employs or retains counsel with substantial Supreme Court litigation experience.... Only the States as institutional litigants represent a problematic proxy for quality. The offices of state attorneys general vary widely in terms of the skill of the lawyers they employ and the degree of experience they bring to the task of filing Supreme Court briefs. On balance, therefore, the overall quality of the States' filings should be closer to "average"....

Among the three institutional litigants with experienced Supreme Court lawyers, the largest deviation from the benchmark success rates occurred in cases where the Solicitor General appeared as amicus. As shown in Figure 13, the *p-win* rate in cases in which the Solicitor General appears as an amicus for the petitioner increases substantially beyond the mean rates in each decade. Indeed, the average differential between *p-win* rates in cases where the Solicitor General appears as amicus and the benchmark rate is just under 17%, and in no decade is the Solicitor General's presence as amicus supporting petitioner marked by less than a 12% increase in the *p-win* rate.

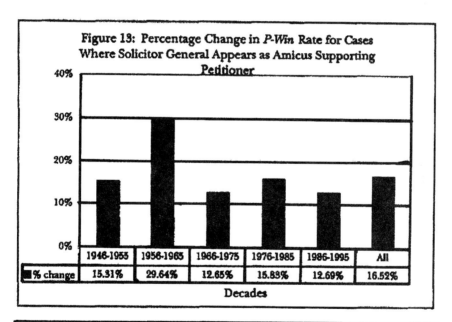

Figure 13: Percentage Change in *P-Win* Rate for Cases Where Solicitor General Appears as Amicus Supporting Petitioner

% change	1946-1955	1956-1965	1966-1975	1976-1985	1986-1995	All
% change	15.31%	29.64%	12.65%	15.83%	12.69%	16.52%

Decades

Data Underlying Figure 13	1946-1955	1956-1965	1966-1975	1976-1985	1986-1995	All
Number of Cases	47	80	92	167	192	578

As shown in Figure 14, there is a corresponding decrease in *p-win* rates in cases in which the Solicitor General appears as an amicus supporting the respondent. The first two decades of our study may be disregarded for these purposes because of the low numbers of cases (although their percentages are nonetheless not outliers). In each subsequent decade, however, the *p-win* rate decreases by at least 21% where the Solicitor General took the respondent's side as amicus. Indeed, the average decrease in the *p-win* rate was almost 26% over all cases. This is the single most pronounced deviation from benchmark success rates we uncovered in our study.

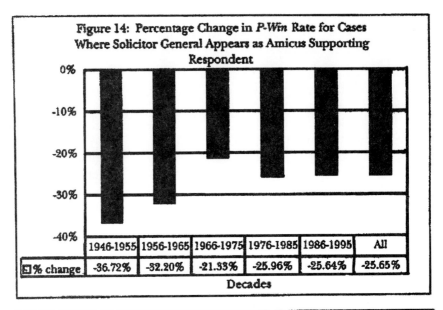

Figure 14: Percentage Change in *P-Win* Rate for Cases Where Solicitor General Appears as Amicus Supporting Respondent

	1946-1955	1956-1965	1966-1975	1976-1985	1986-1995	All
% change	-36.72%	-32.20%	-21.33%	-25.96%	-25.64%	-25.65%

Decades

Data Underlying Figure 14	*1946-1955*	*1956-1965*	*1966-1975*	*1976-1985*	*1986-1995*	*All*
Number of Cases	11	17	38	110	120	296

The changes from benchmark *p-win* rates are substantially less pronounced when we look at cases in which the ACLU or AFL–CIO appeared as an amicus. Indeed, the changes in some instances are not in the direction of the side supported by the institutional litigant.... [T]he ACLU has achieved fluctuating, but usually favorable, rates of success relative to the benchmark when it files briefs supporting the petitioner. In two of the decades, the *p-win* rate when the ACLU filed is higher than the benchmark rate by more than 10%. For the 1966–1975 decade, however, the *p-win* rate when the petitioner was supported by the ACLU as amicus is actually *lower* than the benchmark by nearly 8%. For the entire fifty-year period, the ACLU achieved a positive differential of just under 6% in cases supporting petitioner....

Contrary to the usual pattern in which petitioner success rates decline with amicus support for respondent, the results where the ACLU appears as an amicus for the respondent are much less impressive.... [I]n the three decades where there are reasonable numbers of cases, the ACLU achieved at best only modest differential rates of success, and, in one decade (1986–1995), it underperformed the benchmark rate of success for respondents.

. . .

The cases in which the AFL–CIO participated as an amicus provide yet a third pattern.... [T]he AFL–CIO's support of petitioner produces inconsistent results. After achieving less success than the benchmark rate in the first decade, the AFL–CIO achieves an increase in *p-win* rates relative to the benchmark in the second and third decades, but then falls back into negative territory in the last two decades. Overall, the AFL–CIO shows a modest positive differential of less than 3%. The underlying pool of cases is small in each instance (only 1976–1985 has more than thirty cases). . . .

When the AFL–CIO appears as an amicus supporting the respondent, however, we see our usual pattern of higher success rates again. . . . [D]ifferential success is obtained in the last two decades. No clear pattern can be discerned in the first three decades, where the numbers of briefs are small. Overall, the AFL–CIO exhibits a substantial differential some 14% better than the benchmark rate. . . .

Finally, to provide a source of comparison, it is instructive to consider the success of the States as amicus filers. When the States file amicus briefs supporting the petitioner, and no State appears as a different kind of amicus, they show modest success overall, securing a *p-win* rate about 5% higher than the benchmark rate. When we break the results down by decade, [analysis] reveals that during the last three decades, when the States were filing significant numbers of briefs supporting petitioners, they achieved small and declining success.

.   .   .

The States have been moderately more active, and successful, on the respondent's side. . . . Measured over all five decades the respondents supported by States have bettered the benchmark rate by nearly 9%. This robust number is driven by the large numbers of cases in the last two decades. . . .

In order to gain a clearer sense of the relative power of the different institutional litigants, we ran a multivariate regression incorporating variables for all four institutional litigants as well as variables similar to those used in our disparity studies. We also included new variables for amicus briefs cited by the Court and those filed by experienced lawyers. The results of this regression . . . largely confirm what our figures based on compared means suggest. The Solicitor General's amicus briefs have a statistically significant impact on outcomes (all other variables held constant) for both the petitioner's and respondent's side. The ACLU's briefs have a statistically significant impact on the petitioner's side but not on the respondent's side. Conversely, the AFL–CIO's briefs have a statistically significant impact on the respondent's side but not the petitioner's. The States have a statistically significant impact only on the respondent's side as well.

.   .   .

2.   Success Rates of Cited Briefs

We also decided to use as a proxy for quality the amicus briefs that members of the Court cited in their opinions. We reasoned that a cited brief is one that provided at least some valued information to the Court beyond that supplied by the briefs of the parties. Thus, briefs that are cited may be regarded as "high quality" in the relevant sense of supplying valued and nonrepetitive information. Of course, one must exercise caution here. It is possible that cited amicus briefs play no role in the decision-making process, and are mined by the Justices (or their clerks) only at the opinion-writing stage. Nevertheless, it is plausible to think that cited briefs are more valuable briefs, and if the legal model is correct, we should find that more valuable briefs will, over large numbers of cases, prove to be more successful.

The characteristics of our database made it possible to identify cited briefs that supported the decision of the Court only in those cases that contained only one cited amicus brief. Of the 758 majority or plurality opinions citing amicus briefs, 548 cited only one amicus brief. Of these 548 opinions, we excluded 121 of them because it was not clear whether the Court ruled in favor of the party that filed the amicus brief the Court cited. Of the remaining 427 cases, in 240 the cited brief was filed on the petitioner's side, and in 187 the cited brief was filed on the respondent's side. With this information, . . . we were able to determine success rates for cited briefs supporting petitioners and for cited briefs supporting respondents.

Our results . . . provide no support for the proposition that cited briefs enjoy greater success than noncited amicus briefs. The cases including a cited brief supporting petitioner have a *p-win* rate less than 2% above the benchmark. The cases including a cited brief supporting respondent have a *p-win* rate about 7% below the benchmark. These success rates are very close to those of the "average" amicus filer over our entire set of cases, which show an increase in the *p-win* rate of less than 1% for briefs supporting petitioner and a decrease in the *p-win* rate of about 7% for briefs supporting respondent. Thus, the success rates of the cited amicus filers appear to parallel the success rates of amicus filers overall. In any event, our regression model indicates that these results are not statistically significant predictors of petitioner success. . . .

3. *Success Rates of Briefs Filed By More Experienced Lawyers*

In a final effort to measure the effect of high-quality amicus briefs, we undertook to differentiate among amicus briefs based on the degree of Supreme Court experience of the lawyers who wrote the briefs. Kevin McGuire, a political scientist, has authored several studies examining whether more experienced lawyers enjoy greater success in the Supreme Court than less experienced lawyers. McGuire reasons that experienced lawyers are more likely to frame issues and arguments in a way that is persuasive to the Court, and are likely to have greater credibility with the Court. Hence, he predicts, their submissions should have a greater impact on the decisional process, which should be reflected in greater success before the Court.

McGuire's studies generally measure advocate experience by counting the number of times a lawyer is recorded as having entered an appearance at either oral argument or on the briefs of the parties in cases in the Supreme Court. He then determines which side's advocate is more experienced. Using this method, McGuire shows that more experienced lawyers are more successful at getting certiorari petitions granted, and are more likely to prevail on the merits. Most recently, he has argued that the success rate of the Solicitor General is almost entirely attributable to the greater experience of the lawyers in the Solicitor General's office relative to their opponents in most cases.[161]

We sought to replicate McGuire's method in the context of assessing the influence of amicus briefs.... [W]e limited our consideration to those cases in which one amicus brief was filed in support of petitioner and one in support of respondent (1–1–0 cases). In addition, we excluded cases with amicus briefs filed by the Solicitor General and cases with amicus briefs filed by a State. Within the remaining set of cases, we ... determine[d] how many times each member of the Supreme Court bar who appeared on each amicus brief had previously appeared on behalf of a party or amicus before the Supreme Court. Following McGuire's method, the lawyer with the highest number of appearances in each case was deemed the more experienced. We then computed the change in p-win rates where the petitioner's amicus was more experienced than the respondent's, and where the respondent's amicus was more experienced than petitioner's. As a benchmark, we used the *p-win* rate in all 1–1–0 cases excluding the Solicitor General and the States as amici.

The results are ...[that] amicus briefs filed by more experienced lawyers supporting petitioners experienced a *p-win* rate about 8% higher than the benchmark rate, and amicus briefs filed by more experienced lawyers supporting respondents experienced a *p-win* rate nearly 10% lower than the benchmark rate. However, the numbers of cases in both of these categories are fairly small (56 cases and 64 cases, respectively), and these results were not statistically significant in our regression model. Thus, although our results are suggestive and are generally consistent with McGuire's findings about the impact of experienced lawyers, they must be used with caution....

D. Interpretation of Results

Overall, our results arguably provide some support for each of the models of judging set forth in Part IV. A proponent of the attitudinal model can point to the lack of impact from amicus filers in general (at least on the petitioner's side), the failure to find that the ACLU and the AFL–CIO enjoy consistent success even though they file high-quality briefs, and the failure to find that cited amicus briefs are any more likely to support prevailing parties than those that are not cited. The pronounced influence of the Solicitor General and the milder influence of

---

161. [Footnote 181 in the original cites Kevin T. McGuire, *Explaining Executive* *Success in the U.S. Supreme Court*, 51 Pol. Res. Q. 505, 513–14 (1998)].

the States might be explained away by the attitudinalist as ad hoc exceptions to the model.

A proponent of the strategic actor variation on the attitudinal model would stress the consistent findings suggesting the high success rate of the Solicitor General. Since the executive branch is critical to the implementation of the Court's policy preferences, it is not surprising to find that the Court apparently pays careful attention to the positions of the Solicitor General. Likewise, the States are important political actors and play a role in implementing the Court's decisions, so it is consistent with the strategic actor model that they too should achieve a measure of success as amici.

The interest group theory also finds something to point to in support of its contentions that the Justices decide cases so as to maximize their own reputations or the public standing of the Court as an institution. Disparities of support by amicus filers appear to matter, in that parties supported by one or two amicus briefs when there is no brief filed on the opposing side experience greater rates of success, at least once we control for the influence of the Solicitor General. The interest group theorist might even offer an explanation of the success of the Solicitor General, to the effect that the executive branch pays close attention to the views of the public, and hence its legal representative before the Court is likely to take positions that are popular with the general public. The Court, the interest group theorist might argue, is aware of the executive's desire to track public opinion, and so the Court follows the lead of the Solicitor General in order to assure that it does not run afoul of public opinion.

Notwithstanding these arguments in support of other theories, on the whole we interpret our results as providing the most support for the legal model. We reach this conclusion for four reasons.

First, throughout all our results we find a fairly consistent pattern in which amicus briefs supporting respondents show more success relative to the benchmarks than do amicus briefs supporting petitioners. . . .

Why might amicus filers supporting respondents achieve more success than filers supporting petitioners? The explanation may be that petitioners typically must be represented by able counsel in order to convince the Court to grant review. The Court grants certiorari in only about 4% of all cases in which it is sought. Thus, there is a strong presumption against review, and a petitioner's counsel must carry a heavy burden in persuading the Court to hear her case in preference to thousands of others. The lawyer who can carry this burden must typically be highly skilled. In contrast, respondents obviously do not have to be represented by able counsel in order to have the Court grant review; indeed, the Court is more likely to grant review if the respondent is not represented by able counsel who can distinguish circuit conflicts and offer prudential reasons why review should be denied.

If it is true that petitioners are, on average, represented by more able counsel than respondents, then respondents may obtain a greater boost from the assistance of an amicus brief. In effect, an amicus brief may function in significant numbers of cases as a "stand in" for a high-quality brief on the merits, and respondents may benefit more than petitioners from such briefs. This explanation, if valid, would tend to support the legal model because it suggests that amicus briefs have an impact insofar as they provide relevant legal and background information missing from the party's brief on the merits.

Second, there is the intriguing feature of the disparity studies that shows that success rates exceed the benchmark with one or two briefs filed in support of a party and no amicus briefs on the other side, but fall back toward the benchmark with three or more briefs filed in support of a party and no briefs on the other side. This result is rather puzzling and, given that it is not significant under our regression models, may reflect other factors which we were not able to test. Nonetheless, there are two possible explanations, both somewhat supportive of the legal model.

One possible explanation is that the pool of cases with only one or two amicus briefs and the pool of cases with larger numbers of amicus briefs reflect different sorts of controversies. The pool with small numbers of briefs may consist largely of "low profile" controversies that turn on questions of statutory interpretation or procedure. Legal doctrine may play a relatively large role in the resolution of these sorts of controversies, with the result that one or two amicus briefs filed on one side and none on the other will have a demonstrable effect on outcomes—especially if the Solicitor General is out of the picture. In contrast, the pool of cases that contains three or more amicus briefs may include a much higher percentage of "high profile" cases. In these sorts of cases, legal doctrine may play a less significant role, and judicial behavior may more closely approximate what the attitudinal model depicts. If so, this would account for the puzzle that amicus briefs evidently have much less impact on outcomes in these cases. All this is quite speculative ... and ... additional research is warranted ... to determine whether amicus briefs play a different role in low-profile as opposed to high-profile cases.

An alternative explanation is that it very rarely takes more than two amicus briefs to supply whatever additional information is valued to the Court under the legal model. The Court may view three or more amicus briefs as repetitious or as an annoying effort to "lobby" the Court, producing counterproductive results. We regard this explanation as less plausible than the first explanation. The Court's most likely response to repetitive amicus briefs is to ignore them, not to punish the party they support.

Third, there is the dramatic success of the Solicitor General as an amicus filer. As we have seen, there are a variety of explanations for the Solicitor General's success with amicus briefs, including the possibility that the Justices defer to the views of the Solicitor General for strategic reasons and the possibility that the Justices defer because they assume that the executive branch will tend to endorse politically popular positions. But these explanations are weak. Often the Solicitor General files amicus briefs at the invitation of the Court, or on issues as to which the executive branch previously has had no views or only mild preferences. In addition, most of the cases in which the Solicitor General files amicus briefs involve issues as to which it is unclear what the public's preferences might be. Both the Justices themselves and close observers of the Solicitor General's office attribute the high rate of success to the Solicitor General's reputation for objectivity in accurately stating the law. It is reasonable to assume that this is at least part of the explanation for the Solicitor General's remarkable success as an amicus filer, and this too tends to support the legal model.

Fourth, our other attempts to measure the impact of high-quality amicus briefs, while admittedly not always supportive of the legal model and often not producing statistically significant results, provide modest support for the legal model. Although the ACLU and the AFL–CIO, two other filers of high-quality briefs, do not consistently beat benchmark rates of success, they have been successful more than the average amicus filer. Our study of the impact of amicus briefs filed by experienced lawyers also provides suggestive support for the legal model.

In arguing that the legal model is best supported by our findings, we do not suggest that the legal model provides the sole explanation for Supreme Court decisions, or that our data do not also provide some support for the rival models. . . . [H]owever, . . . our study provides evidence that amicus briefs that speak to the requirements of the law exert some influence on the outcomes reached by the Court. In other words, law matters, and because law matters, amicus briefs that speak to the requirements of the law matter.

VI. RECONSIDERING THE RISING TIDE OF AMICUS BRIEFS

. . .

As noted in Part II, the Court's adoption of an open door policy toward the filing of amicus briefs provides one part of the explanation for the surge in amicus filings in the last three decades. . . . Still . . . , the continued proliferation of amicus briefs into the 1980s and 1990s is difficult to attribute to the open door policy alone, which has now been firmly in place for several decades.

An awareness that amicus briefs can influence outcomes, even if that understanding is only intuitive among Supreme Court litigators, may also account in part for the increase in filings. To be sure, our study reveals no evidence that would suggest that amicus briefs in general have had an increasing impact on outcomes over the fifty years of our study. The various measures we have developed of success rates over time suggest at most a constant or perhaps downward trend in terms of success rates over the period of our study. Nevertheless, it may be that perceptions of impact have grown as anecdotal examples of influence have multiplied. With respect to the amicus filings of the Solicitor

General, for example, our study shows that such briefs are associated on average with a 17% increase in petitioner success and a 26% increase in respondent success. If the Justice Department has become aware of this remarkable record, even if only impressionistically, it would stand to reason that the Department would make increasing use of Solicitor General amicus briefs in order to influence Supreme Court decision making. In fact, we find that the Solicitor General's office has dramatically increased its amicus filings during the period of our study. Similar points could be made, albeit with more qualifications, about the States, the ACLU, and the AFL–CIO.

With respect to other filers, however, it is far from clear that impact on outcomes provides much, if any, explanation for the popularity of amicus participation. The average filer supporting petitioners, in particular, cannot be shown to have any impact on outcomes. We need some other explanation to account for the behavior of these filers.

One possible explanation is that amicus filings have proliferated in accordance with a kind of "arms race" phenomenon. The theory would be that interest groups file amicus briefs out of fear that rival groups will file for the other side.... [T]he general counsel of an organization considering whether to file an amicus brief may harbor few illusions that such a brief will have any impact on the outcome of the case. But other officers or the membership of the organization may not be so sophisticated. The great fear of the general counsel may be that the Court will rule adversely to the organization's interest, and in so ruling, may even cite an amicus brief filed in support of the other side. Should this happen, the other officers or members of the organization may demand an explanation for why the group did not file its own brief to protect its interest.... [I]f enough general counsel engage in this kind of worrying, amicus briefs might begin to proliferate, even without any solid evidence that such briefs have much effect on outcomes.

If the arms race conception of amicus participation has any validity, then the number of amicus briefs should tend to be about the same on both sides of a case.... [The authors confirmed this prediction by] plo[tting] the dispersion of the difference in number of briefs supporting petitioner and respondent in cases in which two or more amicus briefs were filed.... [T]he dispersion ... spike[s] at zero, it is highly symmetrical, and the numbers of cases showing differences greater than three fall off very rapidly....

. . .

The tendency of amicus briefs to be evenly distributed on both sides not only helps explain the proliferation of amicus briefs, but may also account in part for why a study such as ours has difficulty detecting the substantive impact of amicus briefs. Consider in this regard the interest group theory. Even if the interest group theory of amicus briefs were valid, the arms race phenomenon would make this difficult to detect. This is because one side would rarely succeed in filing large numbers of briefs signalling strong political support to the exclusion of similar filings on the other side. Each side's enlistment of multiple supporting briefs would in most cases cancel out the signalling effects of the other side's efforts. It is theoretically possible, therefore, that the interest group model—or simply a widespread acceptance of the validity of the interest group model among organizations interested in Supreme Court litigation—could explain both the rising incidence of amicus participation and the lack of evidence of impact on outcomes, at least as a general matter, from the filing of amicus briefs.

The phenomenon of cases with unusually high numbers of briefs ... seems consistent with this explanation. For example, in the most extreme case, *Webster v. Reproductive Health Services*, pro-life forces generated forty-six briefs and pro-choice forces mustered thirty-two. At least on the pro-life side, it appears that there was a deliberate strategy among pro-life groups to try to create the impression, by filing as many briefs as possible, of widespread and intense opposition to *Roe v. Wade*. The pro-choice forces made greater efforts to coordinate their filings so as to avoid repetitive argument. Still, it is hard to imagine that thirty-two briefs were needed in order to lay out all the considerations relevant to a reaffirmation of *Roe v. Wade*. At some level, the pro-choice forces appear also to have sought to generate the impression of powerful interest group support for the outcome desired. The net effect was that the two sides largely neutralized each other, at least in terms of trying to demonstrate greater public support for their respective positions.

The relatively even distribution of amicus filings between sides may also explain why we do not see stronger evidence of any effect on outcomes from high-quality briefs, as predicted by the legal model. Insofar as the legal model accurately portrays the judicial process as being concerned with deciding cases correctly—or insofar as organizations interested in Supreme Court cases believe that this is a fair characterization of the judicial process—these organizations will have an incentive to try to commission amicus briefs that provide additional legal arguments and factual data that are of value to the Court in reaching decisions consistent with jurisprudential norms. If both sides share this belief, then we should see some increase in amicus filings—although presumably not as extreme an increase in numbers as the interest group theory would predict.

Again, however, the net effect of this increase in amicus activity might not be noticeable in terms of overall outcomes. This is because each side's attempt to file amicus briefs with additional arguments and information would to some extent cancel out the other side's effort to come up with new arguments and information. Clearly, there are inherent limits to how many new ideas and background studies can be submitted to the Court. Further, in many cases, by the very nature of things, better arguments and empirical support will favor one side over the other. So the potential for cancelling out the effect of a brief on the other side will not be as dramatic under the legal model as under the interest group model. Still, a combination of the legal model and the arms race hypothesis can also explain how the incidence of amicus participation might rise even though it is not evident from the aggregate data that there are notable benefits from the filing of amicus briefs.

The abortion controversy again illustrates how under the legal model one might see an increase in amicus filings on both sides of an issue. Suppose it is known that pro-choice forces plan to file an amicus brief by a group of legal historians arguing that there was no tradition of regulating abortion at the time of the enactment of the Fourteenth Amendment. Pro-life forces are likely to regard such a brief as supporting the case for a constitutional right to abortion, and hence would feel compelled to sponsor amicus briefs seeking to show the opposite. The net effect would be that the Court would receive additional and perhaps valuable information to assist its deliberations. It is unlikely, however, that the new information would tip the outcome in one direction or another (although it might have such an impact if only one side submitted . . .).

In addition to the open door policy, the impact on outcomes, and the arms race possibility, it is also important to consider the internal benefits to groups of filing amicus briefs. Political scientists have long been sensitive to the possibility that the real audience for amicus briefs is not the Court but the membership of the group sponsoring the brief. The Court's increasing proclivity to cite and quote from amicus briefs . . . is particularly relevant here. Citation or quotation of a brief in the official Reports of the United States Supreme Court can lend legitimacy to a group, and may be used by the group in its publicity efforts to create the impression that it has "access" to or "influence" with the Court. Interest groups can use this impression to obtain new members and contributions. Even if the group's briefs are never cited, the brief can be distributed to members and others as evidence that the group's leadership is diligently pursuing its members' interests in high places. . . . [And if] one group starts filing amicus briefs and touting this to its members and others, other groups may be more likely to start filing as well.

Finally, there may be structural explanations for the increase in amicus brief activity. Andrew Koshner, in a recent study, has outlined a number of possible structural causes.[162] Included in his list are increased activism on the part of the Court, increased legislative activity by Congress, and increased numbers of organized interest groups with permanent offices in Washington, D.C. Specifically, Koshner argues that the Court became more activist in the 1960s and 1970s, which increased the possibility of securing legal change through litigation. This of course is when the tide of amicus filings started to rise. He also points out that the volume of new legislation from Congress increased substantially about the same time. New legislation increases the number of unresolved legal questions that have an impact on interest groups, and may stimulate more amicus filings. The growth of interest groups in Washington

162. [Footnote 205 in the original, citing Andrew Jay Koshner, *Solving the Puz-* *zle of Interest Group Litigation* (1998)].

also parallels the proliferation of amicus briefs, plausibly suggesting that the permanent institutional presence of these groups in the capital has brought the activity of filing amicus briefs within the reach of many more organizations than was the case before the 1960s.

We would add two other factors to Koshner's list. The first is the growth in the caseloads in the lower courts. The Supreme Court is extremely constrained in the number of argued cases it can hear and resolve in any given year. At its peak, the Court heard around 150 cases; today, due to the abolition of mandatory appeals and the Court's own restrictive policies in granting certiorari, the total is closer to half that. Meanwhile, the number of cases decided in the lower courts has continued to grow. Thus, most litigants in the lower courts ... will never be able to secure a direct ruling on their issue from the Supreme Court. This situation may create great pressure for litigants and groups to try to influence the way the Court writes opinions in the cases it does decide, in order to secure broad rulings or dicta that may influence the disposition of other matters in the lower courts in a favorable manner. One obvious way to do this would be to file amicus briefs in the most directly relevant cases.

The second factor we would add to Koshner's list is the growth in the number of lawyers. One possible explanation for the surge in amicus filings is that it is lawyer-driven, at least in part, rather than client-driven. For example, it could be argued that participation in Supreme Court litigation is a highly prestigious activity for law firms, useful in recruiting new associates, retaining talented lawyers in the firm, and securing clients. Given both the severe constraint on the number of cases argued before the Supreme Court and the increased numbers of lawyers competing for opportunities to appear in such cases, however, the chances of any law firm's having many cases before the Supreme Court are small. Preparing and filing amicus briefs in this context becomes a kind of surrogate activity for real Supreme Court litigation. Law firms may have some control over the volume of this surrogate litigation, insofar as they can either try to persuade their clients that filing amicus briefs is a good idea or offer to file briefs at a reduced rate or even on a pro bono basis.

Figure 24 shows, for purposes of comparison, the rates of change in the number of amicus briefs, the number of cases in the federal courts of appeals, and the number of practicing lawyers in the United States from 1951 (the first date for which common comparative data were readily available) through 1994. As can be seen, all three lines increase substantially from 1951 to 1994. Interestingly, however, the rate of change of cases in the courts of appeals tracks the rate of change in amicus briefs more closely than does the rate of change in the number of lawyers....

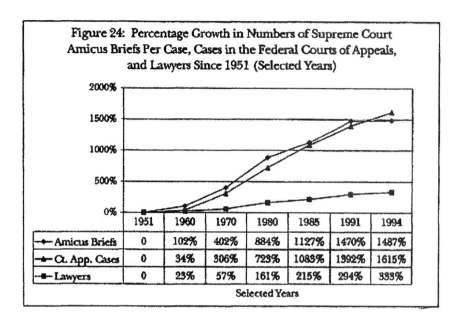

Figure 24: Percentage Growth in Numbers of Supreme Court Amicus Briefs Per Case, Cases in the Federal Courts of Appeals, and Lawyers Since 1951 (Selected Years)

	1951	1960	1970	1980	1985	1991	1994
Amicus Briefs	0	102%	402%	884%	1127%	1470%	1487%
Ct. App. Cases	0	34%	306%	723%	1083%	1392%	1615%
Lawyers	0	23%	57%	161%	215%	294%	333%

Selected Years

... [W]e are not in any position to offer any definitive judgment about why the amount of amicus curiae activity has risen so much in the Supreme Court during the last fifty years. Further research will be needed....

CONCLUSION

. . .

The obvious question is whether, or to what extent, these submissions influence the decisions rendered by the Court. Although political scientists and, to a lesser degree, law professors have turned increasingly to empirical analysis in recent years, no one has undertaken to try to answer this question by analyzing the patterns of amicus participation and associated outcomes in a large number of cases decided over a significant span of time. One reason such a study has not been done is that the political scientists who study the Supreme Court overwhelmingly start from the attitudinal model, which explains outcomes in terms of the preexisting political beliefs of the Justices. Such a model suggests that amicus briefs should have little or no impact on outcomes. Perhaps not surprisingly, therefore, the database political scientists use to study the Court (which was developed by attitudinal scholars) does not include information on the number of amicus briefs filed in each case in support of each side or by key institutional litigants. The lack of readily accessible data has undoubtedly discouraged empirical research.

In this Article, we report our efforts to fill this gap in our knowledge by developing and analyzing a database consisting of over 6000 Supreme Court decisions over fifty years. Some of our results confirm the findings of previous, more limited studies. Most prominently, our survey shows that the Solicitor General enjoys a unique degree of success as an amicus filer. . . .

In two respects, however, our study generates results wholly unanticipated by the prior literature. First, we show that amicus filers supporting respondents consistently enjoy more success than do amicus filers supporting petitioners. For example, amicus filers who support respondents are in general 7% more successful than those who support petitioners, and the Solicitor General is 9% more successful when supporting respondents than when supporting petitioners.

Second, we find that although small disparities of amicus support (one or two briefs to none) may be associated with increased success for the supported party, larger disparities (three briefs or more to none) show little sign of increased success and may possibly even be counterproductive. Undoubtedly one reason we find little support for higher success rates with larger disparities of filings is that there are very few cases that have such disparities. In most cases the amicus briefs are symmetrically distributed between the parties; patterns like that encountered in *Jaffee v. Redmond*, where fourteen briefs supported respondent and none supported petitioner, are extremely rare.

Regarding the implications our results have in terms of identifying the factors that motivate Supreme Court Justices, we must speak much more tentatively. The attitudinal model, at least in its undiluted form, seems to find the least support in our findings. . . . The strategic actor variation on the attitudinal model fares better, since the Court appears to be more attentive to information supplied by the Solicitor General (representing the executive branch). . . . The interest group model, which predicts that the Justices will respond to signals suggesting that organized interest groups disproportionately favor one side over the other, finds only equivocal support. Small disparities of support for one side may matter, although only weakly. Large disparities, however, perhaps because they occur so rarely, cannot be shown to have any impact; indeed, they appear often to work against the interests of the supported party.

We think the explanatory model that fares the best overall is the traditional legal model reflected in the rules and procedures of the Court. Amicus briefs matter insofar as they provide legally relevant information not supplied by the parties to the case—information that assists the Court in reaching the correct decision as defined by the complex norms of our legal culture. . . . This does not mean that the legal model explains all the Court's decisions. Nevertheless, we think our findings support the conclusion that legal doctrine matters in at least a significant portion of the Court's business.

Questions and Comments

1. In describing the "interest group" model, the authors include the interest in the status of the Court as an institution, along with the Justices' concern for their personal reputations, as factors that might motivate attention to interest groups. Are they equivalent motivations?

2. The authors assess whether "law matters" primarily through various measurements of whether lawyers of a certain quality—associated with repeat player organizations, or with experience before the Court—have success. Is this a test of whether "law" matters (in the sense the authors define it), or of whether, in Professor Richard Lazarus' words, "advocacy matters"? Does answering this question require a theory of what "law" is?

3. The Kearney–Merrill Study was based on data that ended in 1995. Professor Richard Lazarus presents some more recent data, focusing on the efficacy of those members of the private bar who are experienced Supreme Court counsel. See Lazarus, *Advocacy Matters, supra.* What would you hypothesize will happen in the future to the Solicitor General's advantage? Is the Solicitor General likely to continue to enjoy some advantage, by virtue of institutional characteristics of the office?

Thomas R. Morris,[163] *States before the U.S. Supreme Court: State Attorneys General as Amicus Curiae,* **70 Judicature 298 (1987)**

. . . [A]ny evaluation of governmental representation before the U.S. Supreme Court is incomplete without consideration of the litigation activities of state attorneys general and their staff attorneys. As a group, their rate of participation both as direct parties and *amici curiae* in Supreme Court cases is second only to the Solicitor General's Office. The reappearance of federalism as a dominant constitutional value makes the period of the Burger Court an appropriate one for examining representation of state interests.

. . .

The Solicitor General's Office submitted *amicus* briefs in 20 per cent of the cases argued before the Supreme Court during the 1974 through 1983 terms of the Court; state attorneys general, by comparison, participated as *amici curiae* in 13 per cent of the cases during that time period. . . .

This article examines the *amicus* participation of the states before the nation's highest court for a ten-year period of the Burger Court era. . . .

THE ROLE OF STATE ATTORNEYS GENERAL

The position of state attorneys general is unique in American government. It operates in the interstices of law and politics, on the

---

163. Associate Professor of Political Science, University of Richmond.

front line of federal-state relations, and at the conjunction of the executive, legislative, and judicial processes. Prior to the 1970s, state attorneys general tended to look upon their role as being merely ministerial functionaries of the state administration; they were in office to do the bidding of other political executives and defend the state establishment from legal attacks. The size and responsibilities of state attorneys general's offices expanded in the 1970s to include public advocacy roles in such areas as consumer protection, antitrust enforcement, utility rate intervention, and environmental protection. Largely passive attorneys general's offices were transformed into activist ones. A new breed of state attorneys general, younger and better educated than their predecessors, increasingly exploited the political advantages of their offices. Popularly elected in 43 states, state attorneys general supplemented the traditional legal defense roles of the office with public advocacy activities that contributed to the growing perception of the office as a political stepping stone to higher elective office.

Initially appointed to the Minnesota attorney generalship in 1961 at the age of 32, Walter Mondale was one of the earliest of the new breed of state attorneys general. Declaring himself an "activist," Mondale sought "ways of using the office not in the old traditional passive way, but in an affirmative public protection role." Confronted with complaints of a furnace-repair hoax and initially stymied by the absence of a consumer fraud statute, Mondale's consumer protection unit took action against the company based on a public nuisance law originally written to protect citizens from barking dogs.

Mondale's service as attorney general is also remembered for his involvement in the landmark decision of the U.S. Supreme Court in *Gideon v. Wainwright* (1963). In the early summer of 1962, Florida Attorney General Richard W. Ervin mailed a letter to his counterparts in the other states inviting them to submit *amicus* briefs supporting the 1942 precedent of *Betts v. Brady* on which Florida's restrictive right-to-counsel policy for indigents was based. His letter carried the familiar appeal to states as states by invoking "the right of states to determine their own rules of criminal procedure."[164]

Mondale's surprising response detailed his support of the policy followed by Minnesota and 34 other states to provide for the appointment of counsel for indigents in all felony cases. He sent a copy of his letter to Massachusetts Attorney General Edward J. McCormick, Jr., whose office took on the responsibility of drafting an *amicus* brief arguing for a change of the *Betts* precedent. Mondale and McCormick enlisted 21 other attorneys general, including three from states which had no such requirement for counsel, to join them in filing a brief with the Court opposing the existing policy in Florida. Only two states—North Carolina and Alabama—supported Florida's position. In his opin-

164. [Footnote 6 in original] Lewis, Books. 1964).
Gideon's Trumpet 142 (New York: Vintage

ion for the Court, Justice Black took notice of the unexpected position of the states: "Twenty-two states as friends of the Court argue that *Betts* was an anachronism when handed down and that it should be overruled. We agree."

. . .

Unanimity of state legal positions, of course, does not assure supportive decisions by the Supreme Court. When the Court was faced with the extension of *Gideon* in *Argersinger v. Hamlin* (1972) nine years later, for example, all state participation supported the position taken by Florida, but the outcome was the same as before—the court ruled against Florida's policy. The attorneys general of ten states joined the respondent state of Florida and separate *amicus* briefs were filed by three states supporting Florida's practice of restricting right to counsel to offenses punishable by more than six months imprisonment.

COMPARISONS WITH SOLICITOR GENERAL

. . .

For complex political reasons, state attorneys general have not generally enjoyed the same degree of independence as the Solicitor General in deciding which cases to take to the Supreme Court. They interact with a wide array of officials at both the state and local levels of government, and most of them participate in campaigns for re-election or election to other offices in which litigation records (especially the failure to appeal cases) can become an issue. In 1984, for example, Dennis Roberts, Attorney General of Rhode Island, was locked in a close re-election contest with Arlene Violet, who had challenged him two years earlier. His decision to petition the U.S. Supreme Court for review of his state supreme court's decision to grant Claus von Bulow a new trial was dismissed by the accused's attorney as "political" and by Justice Stevens as "frivolous." Roberts ultimately lost both the appeal and the election. A 1985 *National Law Journal* article also reported a sudden upsurge in petitions to the Supreme Court from Missouri during the period when the state's attorney general, John Ashcroft, was running for governor.

In the 1970s, the states were generally criticized by scholars and justices alike as poor litigators in the Supreme Court. In a 1975 address to the Fifth Circuit Judicial Conference, Justice Powell noted that "some of the weakest briefs and arguments came from . . ." assistant state attorneys general, especially when compared with the lawyers representing the advocacy groups most likely to oppose state governments.[165] The National Association of Attorneys General (NAAG) responded to the criticisms of state performance in the nation's highest court by designating a lawyer to work full-time as the Supreme Court counsel to the attorneys general. . . . [whose] counsel now arranges moot courts several days prior to scheduled arguments for attorneys general and their staff

---

165. [Footnote 12 in original] Quoted in Baker and Asperger. *Foreword: Toward A*   *Center for State and Local Advocacy,* 31 Cath. U. L. Rev. 368 (1982).

attorneys before the Court. The counsel also orchestrates a communications network among the state offices that informs them about pending litigation and *amicus* activity in other states. The network has been credited with more "effective coordination" of *amicus curiae* briefs filed by the states in some 100 cases.

The effort to provide more centralized coordination of state litigation since 1982 is an important development, but it cannot expect to match the tight control of the Solicitor General's Office.... Despite the modern trend encouraged by NAAG toward consolidation of all state legal authority in a centralized attorney general's office, some states permit local government attorneys and state agencies to initiate and appeal cases impacting on statewide interests without the approval, or even over the objection, of the state's chief legal officer.

In Texas, the attorney general decided it was in the best interests of the state not to appeal a federal trial court's decision invalidating a state sodomy statute. After unsuccessfully trying to have the state supreme court order the attorney general to pursue an appeal, a local prosecutor succeeded in his effort to have the U.S. Court of Appeals for the Fifth Circuit permit him to intervene and appeal the case over the objections of the attorney general. Texas' petition for *certiorari* to the Supreme Court was supported by the Attorney General of Oregon, who filed an *amicus* brief joined by 25 other states requesting reversal of the Fifth Circuit's inappropriate and potentially disastrous signal to lower echelon and nonlegal state policymakers: If you disagree with the Attorney General's legal advice and litigation strategy, you may be treated as a spokesperson for the state in the federal courts.[166]

The high court denied *certiorari* on July 2, 1986, but an earlier case provided some support for the position of the *amici* states. When a New York district attorney appealed a decision by the state high court invalidating a state statute regulating deviant sexual behavior, the Supreme Court indicated that the determination of what state officials should represent the state is "wholly a matter of state concern." The New York Attorney General submitted an *amicus* brief in the case arguing that the statute as applied in the case violated free speech and privacy rights, but that it should not have been struck down on its face. The conflict in the positions taken by the attorney general and the district attorney was cited as one reason for dismissing the writ of *certiorari* as improvidently granted. In the process of explaining its decision, however, the Court did concede that "in addressing the constitutionality of a statute with statewide application we consider highly relevant the views of the State's chief law enforcement official."[167]

. . .

166. [Footnote 14 in original] Brief Amici Curiae for the States, Texas v. Hill (No. 85–1251), Oct. Term. 1985, p. 2. On the issue of whether state attorneys general may appeal cases against the wishes of their state clients, state court precedents are divided....

167. [Footnote 15 in original] New York v. Uplinger, 467 U.S. 246, 247, n. 1 (1984).

THE STATUS OF *AMICUS* BRIEFS

Rule [37.4] of the Supreme Court facilitates the filing of "friend of the court" briefs. States represented by their attorneys general, as well as any other public agency at any level of government represented by its appropriate legal representative, are exempt from the requirement imposed on private groups to secure the consent of other parties to the litigation or the approval of the Court before filing *amicus* briefs. In most instances, state officials merely file briefs with the Court, although on rare occasions they argue as *amici curiae*. For the ten terms of the Court examined in this study, state attorneys general or their staff attorneys argued as *amicus curiae* in only 14 cases, and five of those were the death penalty cases heard on March 30 and 31, 1976.

... The availability of attorneys otherwise committed to representing traditional clients in state legal offices becomes an important factor in *amicus* activity. Attorney General Dave Frohnmayer of Oregon estimated that five hours per case are necessary for the approximately eight requests each month for his office to write or join in an *amicus curiae* brief. Even though the briefs usually address the most important issues of the day, he notes that there is no way to charge the cost of the screening time to any particular client-agency. Finally, assuming the office files two major *amicus* briefs in the U.S. Supreme Court at 150 hours per case, 780 attorney hours would be necessary each year for *amicus* activity.

While it is difficult to determine how much effect *amicus* briefs have on Supreme Court decisions, the large number of *amicus* briefs submitted to the Court by government officials and private groups provides some indication of the importance attributed to them. Developments during the oral arguments in the short-lived precedent of *National League of Cities v. Usery* (1976) are instructive in this regard. Four states—Alabama, Colorado, Michigan and Minnesota—filed *amicus* briefs in opposition to the state position taken by California and 19 other states. The position of the four states was cited by the Solicitor General during oral argument as an indication that state sovereignty was not threatened, as the majority maintained, by the extension of the Fair Labor Standards Act to all state and local employees. The attorney for the majority state position replied that he had a letter from the Governor of Colorado instructing the attorney general of his state to withdraw his name from the brief referred to by the Solicitor General. Upon hearing about the Solicitor General's comment, Governor George Wallace of Alabama responded by immediately sending a telegram to the Supreme Court indicating his state supported the position taken by the majority of states participating in the case.

Opposing positions by the states before the Court was a rarity during the period of this study. . . .

Commerce clause cases were most frequently the source of divisions among the states. In *Commonwealth Edison Co. v. Montana* (1981), Montana's 30 per cent severance tax on coal precipitated seven *amicus* briefs addressing the question of whether the tax constituted an unconstitutional burden on interstate commerce. Support for the tax came from states rich in energy resources—New Mexico, North Dakota, West Virginia, Wyoming, Colorado, Nevada, Idaho, Washington and Oregon. Meanwhile, the existence of half of the nation's low-sulphur coal reserves within Montana's borders prompted energy-consuming states to complain that the state was unfairly exploiting its strategic advantage over the other states; *amicus* briefs opposing the tax were filed by Kansas, New Jersey, Michigan, Minnesota, Iowa and Wisconsin....

· · ·

NATURE AND EXTENT OF PARTICIPATION

State *amicus* activity has steadily increased over the past 25 years....

One measure of the importance attached to *amicus* activity is the number of states joining such briefs. Twenty-four cases in this study attracted more than half of the states as *amici*. The states won all five of the criminal cases falling into that category; three of those cases were decided in the 1983 term when the states enjoyed the *amicus* support of the Solicitor General's Office. In one-third of the non-criminal cases, the states joined together as *amici* in important antitrust cases before the Court.

· · ·

The states suffered three major setbacks in antitrust enforcement despite the *amicus* support of the Solicitor General.[168] *Illinois Brick Co. v. Illinois* (1977) restricted antitrust actions to direct purchasers, thereby limiting the effectiveness of state attorneys general acting as *parens patriae* on behalf of state consumers because most such suits are indirect purchaser actions. In *Illinois v. Abbott and Associates* (1983), the states also failed in their effort to convince the Court that federal law should be interpreted to permit state attorneys general access to grand jury files pertaining to federal antitrust violations without having to demonstrate a "particularized need." Finally, in a 1984 decision, the Court rejected the states' argument on the standard of proof to find a vertical price-fixing conspiracy.

Unanimous state support was forthcoming for Maryland's position of categorically denying in-state status to domiciled non-immigrant aliens holding G–4 visas. Nevertheless, the state policy was held invalid under the Supremacy Clause of the United States Constitution.[169] Other cases attracting large numbers of state *amici* dealt with the award of attorney's fees for plaintiffs prevailing in civil rights actions (three

168. [Footnote 25 in original] Illinois Brick Co. v. Ill., 431 U.S. 720 (1977); Ill. v. Abbott and Associates, 460 U.S. 557 (1983); Monsanto Co., v. Spray–Rite Service Corp., 465 U.S. 752 (1984).

169. [Footnote 26 in original] Toll v. Moreno, 458 U.S. 1 (1982).

cases), Indian ownership of land, and the preemption of California's food labeling statute by federal laws.[170]

Noticeably missing from the category of large-scale state *amici* participation were the major decisions of the Burger Court during the period of this study in such controversial areas as race and sex discrimination, abortion, freedom of speech and press, and church-state relations. Only two cases of those involving half the states could be classified as civil liberty cases.[171] Thirty-three states filed two *amicus* briefs supporting Florida's challenge to an interpretation of the Rehabilitation Act of 1973 requiring "affirmative conduct" by states in the admission of handicapped persons to clinical training programs. The Court agreed with the states' position even though opposing *amicus* briefs were filed by the Solicitor General and the attorney general of California. Similarly, in 1982, 31 states joined in a brief *amicus curiae* where the petitioner alleged that her state employer had denied her employment opportunities solely on the basis of her race and sex. The Court rejected the states' argument that state administrative remedies must be exhausted as a prerequisite to the petitioner's action under federal law.

Whereas the Solicitor General has generally been active in civil liberty and civil rights cases, states seldom choose in either large or small groups to participate as *amici* in cases litigating First and Fourteenth Amendment issues. . . .

Not surprisingly, the cases most likely to attract significant state *amici* are those dealing with federalism issues. Twenty-six (38 per cent) of the non-criminal cases involving more than ten states fell into this category. . . . The Solicitor General's Office participated in opposition to the state position in all but three of the cases. The states, not surprisingly, were only half as likely to be in agreement with the Court as was the Solicitor General. In the Section 1983 cases, only one of which attracted federal participation, the states fared better, agreeing with the Court three out of five times. . . .

· · ·

PATTERNS AND SUCCESS

The California attorney general's office participated in one-third of the cases attracting state *amicus* briefs. It earned the top ranking for the states by filing more separate briefs than any other state and by participating in well over half of the criminal cases in this study. The New York office was also a leader in drafting briefs and was involved in 28 per cent of the state *amicus* cases. After the top two states, the rate of participation did not vary dramatically; three-fourths of the states were

170. [Footnote 27 in original] Hensley v. Eckerhart, 461 U.S. 424 (1983); Patsy v. Board of Regents, 457 U.S. 496 (1982); Blum v. Stenson, 465 U.S. 886 (1984); Wilson v. Omaha Indian Tribe, 442 U.S. 653 (1979); and Jones v. Rath Packing Co., 430 U.S. 519 (1977).

171. [Footnote 28 in original] Southeastern Community College v. Davis, 442 U.S. 397 (1979): Patsy v. Board of Regents, 457 U.S. 496 (1982).

involved in from 15 to 25 per cent of the cases, and no state participated in fewer than 10 per cent of the state *amicus* cases. . . .

The dominant role played by the California and New York offices is not surprising when you consider that each employs more than 450 attorneys while more than half the state legal offices have fewer than 100 lawyers on their staffs. California and New York also lead the states as direct parties in Supreme Court litigation. States with few cases before the high court and small legal staffs can, nevertheless, magnify their impact by choosing to participate as a friend of the court. Interviews by this author with selected attorneys general revealed that they take seriously the decision as to whether to join *amicus* briefs submitted to their offices. They recognize that whether they like it or not, a U.S. Supreme Court decision adverse to the interests of another state may very well apply to their state. . . .

. . .

If anything, movement toward greater cooperation among the states has reduced the number of cases in which more than two state briefs are filed. What has changed, in addition to the greater number of cases in which states are participating, is the number of states involved in each case. There are almost as many instances, for example, when more than ten states participated as *amici* during the 1981, 1982, and 1983 terms of the Court as there were in the preceding seven terms. . . .

CONCLUSION

. . .

. . . Increased coordination of state *amicus* activity as part of an overall effort to improve state advocacy has apparently been successful in increasing state participation. Not all state cases are "winnable," of course, but *amicus* briefs can contribute to narrowing the legal or constitutional basis for a decision in hopes of avoiding a sweeping ruling that might adversely affect all states. After all, an *amicus* brief joined by a good number of states provides the Court with an excellent impact analysis in state litigation.

———————

Questions and Comments

1. The Morris piece was written in 1987, based on cases decided in the 1970s and early 1980s. According to a recent scholarly paper, the capacity of state and local governments for effective advocacy in the Supreme Court has improved:

> Nor has [the] resurgence of a highly active, successful, specialized Supreme Court Bar been confined to the private law firms. In recent years, the States have responded in kind. Several states have created or rejuvenated the position of State Solicitors General modeled after the

U.S. Solicitor General. In addition to having primary responsibility for arguing cases before their own state supreme courts, these State Solicitor Generals have increasingly focused their attention on the need to possess expertise in advocacy before the U.S. Supreme Court. Accordingly, Ohio, New York, Illinois, Texas, Alabama, and others recruited to their Solicitor General Offices highly credentialed attorneys, often former clerks to U.S. Supreme Court Justices, to work within or run those Offices. These State Solicitors General now routinely appear before the Court and are quickly developing their own expertise in High Court advocacy. Both the National Association of Attorneys General and the State and Local Legal Center also now commit considerable resources to assisting state and local governmental lawyers with cases before the Court.

Lazarus, *Advocacy Matters, supra,* at 17–18. It was not until 1983 that the State and Local Legal Center, referred to by Professor Lazarus, was founded to provide assistance to state and local governments with cases in the Court.[172] Query whether a repeat study would find improvement in the performance of the states as parties or amici?

Glendon Schubert,[173] *Constitutional Politics* 69–70, 78–82 (1960)

LOBBYISTS BEFORE THE SUPREME COURT

The lobbying of interest groups with Congress and state legislatures is accepted today as a fundamental and desirable political process in a democratic polity.... When it comes to the judiciary, however, the norms of our society engender an attitude of open hostility toward lobbying tactics.... Thus, group behaviors that are considered to be the very essence of the politics of democracy, when focused upon the Congress, are castigated as the antithesis of "a government of laws, not men" when the object of group pressures is the Supreme Court.

Nevertheless, lobbying with the Supreme Court has been going on for a long time. As Twiss has shown, the now staid American Bar Association was originally formed, in 1878, as a national organization stemming from the Association of the Bar of the City of New York, which began in 1870. The latter association was organized "chiefly to combat the corruption of the judiciary by the Tweed Ring. At least in its early years it was a good example of how a bar association can be an important political pressure group." During the first three decades of the present century, the National Consumers' League was particularly active in defending labor legislation from attack in the courts. The League enlisted the services of such distinguished counsel as Louis Brandeis and

---

172. See Linda Greenhouse, *Supreme Court: A Savvy New Friend for Local Governments*, The New York Times, July 29, 1983, at A10; Al Kamen & Ed Bruske, *Law-* yers, The Washington Post, Aug. 1, 1983, at B2.

173. Professor of Political Science, Michigan State University.

Felix Frankfurter; and although its efforts met with greater success in the state courts than in the Supreme Court, a major change in the technique of persuasion before the Supreme Court resulted from the League's sponsorship of advocacy by means of the sociological or Brandeis brief. The purpose of such briefs, which were in essence compendious compilations of economic and social facts, with a minimum of emphasis upon the citation of legal precedents and doctrines which (then as now) made up the substance of conventional legal briefs, was to educate Supreme Court justices concerning the facts of industrial life in a changing world. Half a century ago, the novel sociological briefs met with just as severe criticism and resistance as has the Court's own reliance, in a more recent period, upon generalizations regarding human behavior based upon the research of social psychologists.

Three Tactics for Lobbying with the Supreme Court

The conventions surrounding judicial decision-making, at least as a formal process, stigmatize as illegal or unethical certain kinds of group-pressure activity. Thus, for instance, the picketing of federal courthouses is defined as a criminal act by congressional legislation; and the sending of mass petitions to the Supreme Court on behalf of condemned criminals has been condemned by the justices. There are, however, a number of pressure tactics which have become increasingly common, including (1) the use of test cases; (2) building up a favorable professional climate of opinion in the law reviews; and (3) presenting the Court with a show of strength, by the temporary alliance of groups to support a formal party to a case through the *amicus curiae* device. . . .

Is the *amicus curiae* brief incompatible with the dispensation of "dispassionate justice" in the Supreme Court? Or is it a desirable device for extending the vision of the justices beyond the blinders imposed by the record of and the immediate interests of the direct parties to a case? The answers to these questions hinge, no doubt, upon the assumption that most appropriately defines the modern role of the Court. If the justices sit as a "Supreme Tribunal of Errors and Appeals" to right every wrong in the lower courts, then the rights of the immediate parties are most important. But if the justices sit as major formulators of national policy, then it would seem desirable to encourage a broad proliferation of interest representation before the Court.

The NAACP as a Supreme Court Lobby

During the modern period, organizations prominent for their attempts to mold policy-making by the Supreme Court have included the American Liberty League of anti-New Deal fame; the Watch Tower Bible and Tract Society (Jehovah's Witnesses), which built up the imposing record of forty-four wins out of fifty-five cases in the Supreme Court, for a batting average of .800; and the National Association for the Advancement of Colored People, which won more than fifty Supreme Court cases in the half-century following its establishment. The victories of the NAACP in the Supreme Court have had a tremendous impact upon our national policy, our political system, and our very way of life, so we shall use the lobbying activities of this group as a concrete example of the three lobbying tactics described above.

NAACP Strategy in the Restrictive Covenant Cases[174]

. . .

Scrutiny of the NAACP's part in the successful litigation which ended the court enforcement of racial restrictive covenants will indicate how the organization went about urging constitutional change. This was a long campaign from 1918, speeded up after 1945 and climaxed in 1948. Then, in *Shelley v. Kraemer,* the Supreme Court ruled that when a state court enjoins Negroes from taking restricted property it is state action in violation of the equal protection guarantee of the Fourteenth Amendment. In two cases from Washington, D.C., it was held contrary to the Civil Rights Act of 1866 and the nation's public policy for federal courts to use their equity powers to enforce racial restrictive covenants. [In 1953], in *Barrows v. Jackson,* the Supreme Court extended the doctrine by holding that a state court could not sanction a racial covenant by awarding damages in a suit at law.

. . .

. . . It takes time for a group to persuade the Court to accept a case as a test. Through the years after 1926 when the judicial enforcement of a covenant was sanctioned by the Supreme Court, the NAACP made five applications for writs of certiorari. In 1929 and 1937 these applications were denied outright. In 1940 the Court heard a case from Chicago and held the covenant unenforceable because of fraud so did not reach the constitutional issue. In 1945 the NAACP gained encouragement despite another denial of certiorari. Since only four votes are needed for certiorari to be issued, the dissents of Justices Rutledge and Murphy in 1945 told the Association that its chances were improving.

. . .

By 1945 potential test cases had begun in the trial courts of Los Angeles, Chicago, St. Louis, Columbus, Detroit, New York and Washington, D.C. The controversies grew out of Negro-white rivalry for homes with suits for injunction originating from the white side. Negroes in jeopardy turned naturally to the leading NAACP attorneys in their own city. As the cases progressed these lawyers shared notes at four conferences on racial covenants called by the national leaders of the Association. Careful work was done to establish a sound trial record in order to have the best possible vehicle available for the constitutional test be-

174. [Footnote 19 in original] This selection is taken from "The Impact of Pressure Groups on Constitutional Interpretation," a paper read by Professor Vose at the Annual Convention of the American Political Science Association (Chicago, Illinois: September 8, 1954), pp. 1–4. For an extend-ed development and documentation of these same points, see Vose, *Caucasians Only: The Supreme Court, the NAACP, and the Restrictive Covenant Cases* (Berkeley and Los Angeles: University of California Press, 1959).

cause there was no way of knowing which cases would be accepted for review by the Court. In 1947 new writs of certiorari were applied for and granted in cases from St. Louis, Detroit and Washington, D.C.

Planning test cases is a necessity for any pressure group desiring a hearing before the Supreme Court for it is their primary means of access. The test case represents others which never advance to appellate courts. Quite clearly, the pressure group with continuity, central control and a far-flung network of alert attorneys is well-equipped to produce the necessary number of cases from which the Supreme Court may select a test.

... In addition [to] presenting a "case or controversy" to the Supreme Court—the one essential that any person or group must do to test a constitutional rule—other things will be attempted by a resourceful organization like the NAACP. Thus the campaign against racial covenants included an effort to influence legal opinion by publicizing a favorable innovation in constitutional theory. Scholars like Professor Robert Hale of Columbia had long stood for a broad view of state action when, in 1945, in the *California Law Review,* Professor D.O. McGovney offered a carefully prepared argument that the concept of state action should encompass the enforcement of racial restrictive covenants by state courts. This filled a serious gap in Negro legal theory. McGovney's argument was taken up in other law review articles and soon found its way into NAACP briefs.

The accumulated losses of thirty years standing as precedents against the NAACP led to reliance on sociological argument. In order to quote authority, leaders of the Association arranged for publication of social and economic criticism of racial restrictive covenants. A coordinated effort was made to place articles in the law reviews. Spontaneity doubtless played its part to produce an impressive list of publications supporting the Negro position with only a single article in opposition.

Briefs filed with the Supreme Court relied heavily on the law review articles and thereby brought these constitutional and sociological points to the attention of the justices. In this way the NAACP sought again to bring a change in constitutional doctrine. If the bar and the law schools are regarded as part of the justices' professional constituency, then it may not be the election returns but the law reviews that the Supreme Court follows.

... In the *Shelley* case nineteen briefs were filed by friends of the NAACP while five amici curiae briefs were entered by opposing groups. Since the parties permitted all interested groups to present briefs, a record number in a single Supreme Court case was established.

The NAACP had an impossible task of controlling the substance of these briefs as each organization had its own ideas of the best content. Some groups repeated the points of the main briefs without a line of novelty while others wrote briefs to distribute to its membership for propaganda purposes. Of course, each group opposed racial discrimination for its own private reasons. Jews, Indians and Japanese–Americans feared discrimination against themselves. Congregationalists and Unitarians preached the brotherhood of man while briefs of the A.F. of L. and C.I.O. protested that housing discrimination against Negroes nullified their economic gains as trade unionists. Civil liberties groups like the A.C.L.U. contended that restrictive covenants prevent the achievement of constitutional rights. The American Association for the United Nations pointed to the injury of United States prestige abroad. At times the NAACP feared that its friends would bore the Court with duplication of these and other arguments but no serious effort was made to eliminate briefs or fashion their content.

The reading of these briefs, and those filed in opposition by various neighborhood protection associations and the National Association of Real Estate Boards, shows the successful adjustment of numerous pressure groups to the judicial process. These amici curiae briefs provide a fascinating display of the accommodation of constitutional values to self-interest.

An amicus curiae brief by the Department of Justice in the *Shelley* case was another expression of interest group effort to influence the Court. Solicitor General Perlman has explained that he and the Attorney General, Tom Clark, were urged by organized groups to enter the case as a friend of the Negroes. The Department's action thus reflected pressures and added an official group to the Negro alliance[, one that supplies] matchless prestige and expertness in preparing cases to the groups it favors. . . .

Susan Behuniak–Long,[175] *Friendly Fire: Amici Curiae and Webster v. Reproductive Health Services*, 74 Judicature 261 (1991)

The unprecedented number of amicus curiae briefs filed in *Webster v. Reproductive Health Services* [492 U.S. 490 (1989),] signaled not only the intensity of the abortion battle, but also the extent of interest group politics before the United States Supreme Court. If the response of 57 amicus briefs to *Regents of the University of California v. Bakke* was unusual, the response to *Webster* was extraordinary. A total of 78 amicus briefs were filed; 46 on behalf of the appellants and 32 on behalf of the appellees. With over 400 organizations signing on as cosponsors, and thousands of individuals joining as signatories, *Webster,* though not a typical case, demonstrates the importance of interest group politics before the Court.

With the 1988 appointment of Justice Anthony Kennedy to fill the vacancy left by Justice Lewis Powell, a reversal of *Roe v. Wade* was

---

175. Associate Professor of Political Science at Le Moyne College in Syracuse, New York.

possible. Court watchers tallied a 4–1–4 line-up. Expected to support *Roe* were Justices Harry Blackmun, William Brennan, Thurgood Marshall and John Paul Stevens. The original dissenters in *Roe,* Justices William Rehnquist and Byron White were expected to be joined by Justices Antonin Scalia and Kennedy. With Justice Sandra Day O'Connor viewed as the swing vote, *Roe* was now subject to a 5–4 reversal. When the Court agreed to hear *Webster* during its 1988 term, the time was ripe for a major abortion decision. Such anticipation led to the unprecedented number of amicus briefs.

At issue in *Webster* was a Missouri statute which contained: (1) a preamble stating that "the life of each human being begins at conception," (2) sections restricting public facilities and employees from performing or assisting in an abortion (except to save the mother's life), (3) sections prohibiting the use of public funds, employees or hospitals from encouraging or counseling a woman to have an abortion (again, with the maternal life preservation exception), and (4) sections requiring that when a physician believes a woman to be 20 or more weeks pregnant, viability will be tested by performance of "such medical examinations and tests as are necessary to make a finding of the gestational age, weight, and lung maturity of the unborn child."

... [S]everal questions will frame the study: who submitted the briefs, what was argued in the briefs, and what impact did the briefs have on the outcome of the case? These questions are asked with two goals in mind. First, what do the amicus briefs demonstrate regarding this type of interest group activity? Second, what do the amicus briefs reveal concerning the nature of the two movements involved in the struggle over abortion rights?

WHO FILED?

. . .

Eighty-five organizations filed on behalf of appellants, while 335 filed on behalf of appellees. The percentage of briefs with a single sponsor was 76 per cent for the appellants and 44 per cent for the appellees. The number of appellants' sponsors per brief ranged from 1 to 19 (the high being the 19 branches of the Rutherford Institute), while the number of the appellees' filers per brief ranged from 1 to 115 (the high being the brief submitted by the National Council of Negro Women and 114 others). Using rough averages, appellants had 2 sponsors per brief, while appellees had 10 sponsors per brief. What these numbers suggest is that the two sides differed concerning the value of coalition building.

Clearly, the appellees acted as if the number of sponsors was more important than the number of briefs filed, while the appellants favored the strategy of filing the most briefs (46 to 32). This raises the question of which is a more effective strategy, to file as many individual briefs as possible or to gather a larger total number of cosponsoring organizations? Caldeira and Wright have observed that there "is [a] general absence of large coalitions of groups on individual briefs," and that this implies that those who make the decision about filing the amicus believe "it is the number of briefs, not the number of organizations listed on each brief, that impresses the justices."[176]

So why did the appellees appear to reject this general belief? There are several possible explanations: . . .

First, while the amicus brief offers groups that are limited in time and resources the access to influence litigation without assuming the financial and time burdens required of a full-fledged party, there is no question that even the filing of an amicus makes demands upon the organization. In Caldeira and Wright's study of the amicus briefs filed during the Court's 1982 term, the cost of preparing and filing a brief ranged from $500 to $50,000 with a mean slightly above $8,000. For some groups, the cost of filing an amicus is prohibitive. Caldeira and Wright note, "The litigation budgets of most organizations are quite modest, and most do not have sufficient in-house manpower and legal expertise to prepare briefs on their own." Many of the appellees' cosponsoring groups would appear to fit this profile. For them, cosponsorship allowed participation in the *Webster* case without the financial hardship involved in preparing an individual brief.

Second, the appellees seemed to act on the democratic belief that the justices would be swayed by the numbers associated with the abortion rights position. Indeed, several of their briefs resembled petitions as they included lists of individuals as signatories.[177] Collectively, the appellees' briefs signaled to the Court that their position has the support of the majority of the population and that a reversal of *Roe* would place the Court in the uncomfortable position of fighting against the mainstream. However, reliance on the democratic argument also poses risks. Justices may take offense at being pressured to defer to majority rule.[178] Another risk of assembling petition briefs is that coalition building may work to limit the number of arguments presented to the Court by decreasing the number of amicus briefs.

The appellees, however, seemed to minimize both risks. While the democratic argument was implicit in the number of sponsors and signatories, this claim was not explicitly made by the appellees. Instead, appellees let the numbers speak for themselves, thereby avoiding reliance on the democratic argument while at the same time signaling to the Court in a not-so-subtle way where the majority of the population stood

176. [Footnote 8 in original] Caldeira and Wright, *Amici Curiae Before the Supreme Court: Who Participates, When and How Much?,* Forthcoming 18 J.Pol. (1990).

177. [Footnote 12 in original] *See,* Brief for Women Who Have Had Abortions (2887 signatures and 627 signatures of friends); Brief for 608 State Legislators from 32 States; Brief for Group of American Law Professors (885 signatures); 281 American Historians; Brief for 167 Distinguished Sci-

entists and Physicians; Brief for Certain Members of the Congress of the United States; Brief for Catholics for a Free Choice; Brief for Bioethicists for Privacy.

178. [Footnote 13 in original] In fact, Justice Scalia's *Webster* opinion did object to the belief of interest groups that unelected and life-tenured justices should weigh popular opinion. *See,* Scalia's dissent at 3065–66.

on the issue. The second risk was overcome by the filing of a significant number of briefs. While 14 less than the number submitted by the appellants, 32 briefs is by any measure a considerable number. Therefore, the appellees' coalitions did not come at the price of sacrificing the number of arguments presented. In sum, the appellees' strategy of garnering the support of several hundred cosponsors was intended to add weight to the already numerous briefs.

A third explanation of the appellees' coalition building is that since there is a finite number of legal arguments to be made on any issue, too many briefs lead to repetition and perhaps even work to irritate the justices. In light of charges that amicus briefs are a waste of time, "repetitious at best and emotional explosions at worst," and that a large number would increase the already heavy burden on the justices, the appellees may have opted to limit the number of briefs even though they knew that the appellants would file more.

Fourth, an examination of multi-issue interest groups versus single-issue interest groups may explain the different values appellants and appellees attributed to coalition building. Appellees' base of support was largely multi-issue interest groups while single-issue interest groups were more prevalent among the amici of the appellants. [This fact will be discussed in greater detail below.] Multi-issue interest groups enjoy more of a choice in determining whether or not to file an amicus brief than do single-issue interest groups. "The broader a group's political interests, the less intense its attachment to a particular interest.... Focus is crucial to intensity." Single-issue interest groups must react when there is a direct threat to their membership's interests. Within this context, the appellants' pro-life organizations were compelled to file independent briefs. In contrast, the multi-issue interest groups of the appellees could meet internal demands through coalitional activity rather than as independent sponsors.

Finally, the appellees' amici were organized according to a strategy that favored impact over the number of briefs. Kathryn Kolbert, who worked on behalf of the American Civil Liberties Union and Planned Parenthood Federation to coordinate all of the amicus briefs, attempted to discourage duplication among the briefs and to encourage coalition building among amici with similar interests. It was believed that overlapping arguments would work to "dilute the overall impact of the collection," so groups who shared interests were encouraged to form a coalition. Coalitions were organized so that each argued points most appropriate to their interests and expertise. This contrasted with appellants who appeared to strive for a large number of briefs at the expense of repetition. For example, attorney Robert L. Sassone filed six separate briefs on behalf of clients with very similar interests rather than one brief with six sponsors.

... An attempt was also made to look closer at the groups who filed in order to determine the level of diversity among the first sponsors of the 78 briefs. Seven of the 14 membership categories developed by

Caldeira and Wright were used to distinguish the groups: individuals, citizen-based interest groups, professional organizations (where members share the same occupation), public interest law firms or research groups, government sponsors, peak organizations (an organization consisting of groups), and other. . . .

[B]oth appellants and appellees drew the most support from briefs filed by citizen-based groups, 45.7 per cent and 46.8 per cent, respectively. Of all seven categories employed, the citizen-based groups category contains the most diversity in ideology, membership numbers, prestige, goals, and resources. For instance, The American Civil Liberties Union, Population–Environmental Balance, American Life League, and Agudeth Israel of America are all classified as citizen-based groups.

Next in order of frequency for the appellants were briefs filed by: public interest law firms (15.2 per cent), government sponsors (13 per cent), professional groups and individuals (both with 10.9 per cent), then peak organizations, and other (both with 2.2 per cent). Appellees had no briefs filed by individuals, public interest law firms or other. After the citizen-based groups, the order of frequency were briefs filed by: professional groups (31.3 per cent), peak organizations (12.5 per cent), and government sponsors (9.4 per cent).

One drawback of the seven divisions is that they hide three types of groups relevant to the abortion controversy—the religious groups associated with the pro-life position, the feminist groups aligned with the pro-choice cause, and the single-issue interest groups present in both movements. . . . The appellants drew great support from religiously oriented groups (16 sponsors), but also drew support from one feminist sponsor (Feminists for Life). There were nine feminist sponsors for the appellee side, but also two from religious groups. Altogether, these 28 religious and feminist sponsors account for only about 36 per cent of the amicus briefs filed. Clearly, the abortion issue was of great concern to organizations whose memberships did not fit either description.

Indeed, . . . single-issue interest groups played an important role in this case. In order to study the abortion issue here, a single-issue interest group is defined as an organization that is formed to advocate a position on the abortion rights question. While it is admittedly arguable whether a pro-life group has an agenda that is broader than the abortion issue, or whether NOW is more a single-issue than a multi-issue interest group, an initial appraisal of the groups indicates that about 70 per cent of the first sponsors on behalf of the appellants were single-issue interest groups, while about 40 per cent of the appellees' first sponsors were single-issue interest groups. When these single-issue interest groups are compared, it becomes evident that there was a difference in the nature of the permanency of the groups. Appellants drew support from permanent single-issue organizations, while appellees' single-issue organizations tended to be ad hoc groups of professional individuals or peak organizations.

Some tentative conclusions can be drawn from this information concerning the nature of the two movements. Overall, the appellants' amici appear to be more singular in purpose. The public interest law firms, the individuals, the governmental coalitions, and even the professional groups were united in that most were specifically formed either to oppose abortion rights or already had religious tenets supportive of such a political posture. With the exception of the government coalitions, these were permanent groups. In contrast, the appellees relied heavily on the support of professional groups with multiple interests, five of which were ad hoc organizations formed in order to file a brief. These observations suggest that the appellants had a more single-mindedly committed and more permanent group of amici, while the appellees relied on the support of amici who joined together temporarily and who distributed their resources over a range of issues. . . .

In sum, the question of who filed these 78 briefs has revealed differences in coalition building and a diversity of interests among the sponsoring groups. It is expected that these organizations employed an assortment of strategies as well as provided the Court with a variety of information. The next question to be examined, therefore, is what was argued in the briefs. Did the diversity among the sponsors translate into a richness of resources for the Court?

WHAT WAS ARGUED?

Both Webster and the Reproductive Health Services had to launch an offensive campaign while maintaining a defensive posture. The appellants had to defend the Missouri statute while attacking the legal doctrines set down in *Roe.* The appellees guarded *Roe* as precedent while they took aim at the restrictive law. The strategies of the sides and the roles left to the amicus briefs are best informed by an examination of the party briefs. . . .

The appellants' brief first summarized the case and then opened its argument by attacking *Roe,* criticizing the "viability" dividing point as arbitrary and calling for the Court to overrule *Roe.* This offensive took only four pages. The rest of the party brief, approximately 28 pages, was a point-by-point defense of the Missouri law. In contrast, the appellees' brief, which omitted a reconstruction of the case, began by defending *Roe* as a fundamental constitutional right and supporting the viability concept as both legally and medically sound. This defense occupied 17 pages. The next 32 pages challenged the Missouri law section by section. For both sides, then, *Roe* was of primary concern. It was only once this precedent was either challenged or defended that a discussion of the state law could begin.

Arguments. Turning to the amicus briefs . . . a point and counterpoint pattern emerges. There were six main points of contention concerning *Roe:* (1) fetal vs. women's rights, (2) if a constitutional basis for a right to abortion exists, (3) whether the trimester scheme is of utility, (4) how abortion fits within the context of American history and tradition, (5) the applicability of the doctrine of *stare decisis,* and (6) the consequences of overturning or following *Roe* as precedent. There were also six main disputes regarding the Missouri statute: (1) whether the state had the power to restrict abortion through its democratic process, or whether the Court must act to prevent the violation of constitutional rights, (2) the rational basis test vs. strict scrutiny as the appropriate standard of review, (3) if the statute's preamble was prefatory or of substance, (4) the constitutionality (or mootness) of the ban on funding abortion counseling, (5) the constitutionality of the ban on abortions in public facilities, and (6) the constitutionality of the viability tests requirement.

Amid the noise of these debated issues, silence is also instructive. Some of the arguments presented by the amici were not present in the party briefs.... [A]bsent from the appellants' party brief were arguments that: fetuses are constitutionally protected persons; abortion has harmful effects on women and on society; the law would not involve criminal prosecutions; and the states are better suited than the courts to decide such a politically charged issue. On the appellee side, there was a greater overlap between the party and amicus briefs. Only two major points made by amici were not present in the party brief: the freedom of religion argument and an examination of the consequences of a *Roe* reversal. The latter, nonlegal point constituted an important focus for many of the appellee amicus briefs.

Strategies. The differences between party and amicus argumentation suggest that appellants and appellees adopted different strategies. Once again the 4–1–4 Court configuration must be appreciated. Litigants had to hold together their four-person coalition while vying for O'Connor's vote....

The appellants' party brief is striking in its avoidance of any "prolife" rhetoric or argumentation. It carefully sidesteps any discussion of the rights of the "pre-born," the sacredness of human life, or the uncertain basis for the right to privacy (discussing it in terms of a liberty interest instead). The party brief challenges *Roe* in terms that would most appeal to O'Connor. It questions the textual, historical, and doctrinal basis of *Roe* and challenges the trimester approach by citing O'Connor's dissent in Akron v. Akron Center for Reproductive Health.[179] The brief also argues that should the Court uphold *Roe,* then it should apply the "undue burden" test (favored by O'Connor) to uphold the Missouri regulations. This moderate approach, then, appears to be crafted for O'Connor. However, this strategy was not universally applied as some of the amici did include language and claims from the pro-life movement. The more controversial arguments on behalf of fetal rights and a ban on abortion were voiced not by the parties but by the amici. It was the amici who urged Rehnquist, White, Scalia, and Kennedy to go further than the party brief suggested and to make abortions illegal by recognizing constitutionally protected fetal rights.

179. [Footnote 21 in original] 462 U.S. 416, 452 (1988).

In contrast, the appellees appeared to assign the amici the task of capturing O'Connor's vote. There were at least two routes to her. One was to challenge O'Connor to use her test of whether the abortion restrictions in question posed an "undue burden" on women exercising their constitutional right. The amicus briefs presented her with technical information regarding the dire impact of a *Roe* reversal. In fact, the brief from the National Council of Negro Women, citing the disproportionate impact on women of color, the poor, and the young, was crafted especially for O'Connor and her test. A second strategy was to challenge her statement in *Akron* that *Roe* is "on a collision course with itself." O'Connor had used scientific sources to conclude that the point of "viability" would shift forward as medical technology improved. The Brief by 167 Scientists and Physicians not only refuted her argument, but included the signatures of some of the authors on whom she had relied in *Akron*.

What may seem surprising is that the more diverse appellee side produced the more internally consistent argument. This can be explained in two ways. First, the parties and all the amici were aware of how the Court had already chipped away at the right to abortion. All understood that there was no room for concessions without jeopardizing the right itself. Second, this consistency was yet another payoff of organization and coalition building. Kathryn Kolbert, the coordinator of the briefs, helped groups identify what was at issue in *Webster* and how they could best contribute to the case. What emerged was a collection of evidence startling in its singularity of purpose.

Roles. While it is difficult to accurately assess the roles adopted by each interest group, the amici do appear to serve three general purposes. First, there are the endorsement briefs that either repeat the party's position or offer a variation. These briefs may recount all the party's arguments or may center and expand on one point alone. Second are the technical briefs which offer the Court specialized knowledge which is predominantly nonlegalistic in nature. Third are the risk takers. These briefs range from those who undertake an unconventional legal argument to those who shun the legal elements of the case in favor of an emotional appeal. Among the *Webster* briefs, all three types of briefs were present on each side. Some examples illustrate the different roles and strategies that amici can assume.

The endorsement briefs allow interest groups to throw their prestige behind a party. While these briefs are often repetitive, Barker argues that "this very repetition reflects the 'group combat' flavor of the briefs."[180] This was true with the briefs on behalf of appellants filed by the United States, National Right to Life Association, and the Center for Judicial Studies and on behalf of appellees filed by Members of Congress, NOW, and 77 Organizations Committed to Women's Equality. These

180. [Footnote 29 in original] Barker, *Third Parties in Litigation: A Systemic* *View of the Judicial Function*, 29 J. Pol. 62, (1967).

briefs presented legal arguments already present in the party briefs, although they usually focused on one element and expanded on it.

The technical briefs concentrated on providing information concerning history and medical science. Many focused on the questions of whether abortion is a part of the American social tradition, how the medical and social sciences contribute to our understanding of fetal life, and what impact legal versus illegal abortion has on women. For the appellants, the Association for Public Justice and Certain American State Legislators argued against abortion being an acceptable part of American society. Briefs filed by the American Association of Pro-life Obstetricians and Gynecologists, Doctors for Life, Paul Marx, and Bernard Nathanson argued that the "preborn" are persons. For the appellees, refutations of these arguments were offered by 281 American Historians, the American Medical Association, 167 Distinguished Scientists, and the Association of Reproductive Health Professionals. The National Council of Negro Women (with 114 other groups) offered both statistical and anecdotal information illustrating the disproportionately severe impact that a reversal of *Roe* would have on poor women and women of color.

The risk takers offered the most unusual arguments. On the appellants' side, the Free Speech Advocates took a confrontational approach, arguing that the abortion cases were "shams" and that the Court "has grown to accept fawning over all its errors." James Joseph Lynch, Jr. contradicted the party brief's assurance that preambles are without legal effect by asserting that the fetus is protected by the reference to "posterity" made in the United States Constitution's preamble. Agudeth Israel also challenged the party line by insisting that the Missouri preamble be struck down as a violation of religious freedom. American Collegians adopted an argument sometimes used by abortion rights advocates that the Ninth and Tenth Amendments are substantive in that they reserve rights that are not listed in the Constitution's text to the states and citizens. Birthright admitted that its brief contained "very little legal precedent," and instead relied on "logic, common sense, reasoning, intelligence, and conclusions in accord with what is best for all the people of this nation."

The risk takers on behalf of the appellees argued that there was a right to be free from government imposed harm to health (American Public Health Association), that a denial of abortion rights would violate the equal protection clause (National Coalition against Domestic Violence), and that religious freedom demanded that women be free to choose (Catholics for a Free Choice). An emotional appeal made by Women Who Have Had Abortions took the form of a petition-like brief containing letters of testimony.

This survey of the three types of amici suggests that certain types of groups tend to gravitate to a specific amicus role. The most obvious connection is that between professional organizations and technical briefs. A professional organization has the knowledge and expertise necessary to provide the Court with information outside of the legal realm. There also seems to be a relationship between single-issue interest groups and the role of risk taker. Since these groups enjoy a unified constituency that is devoted to promoting a particular issue, these groups may have more freedom in speaking from a perspective outside the mainstream. They can assume a challenging voice without losing their constituents. The endorsement briefs are sponsored by a variety of groups, but tend to gain the support of multi-issue interest groups. These groups tend to have less of a stake in the interest at issue, and they have to hold together a diversified constituency. Multi-issue interest groups can satisfy organizational demands by merely endorsing the party brief.

This analysis would explain why the appellants had more amici act as risk takers while the appellees had more amici submit technical briefs. Since single-issue interest groups were more prevalent among appellants' amici, it could be expected that appellants would have more amici who assumed the role of risk taker. In contrast, since professional organizations were three-to-one behind the appellees, it was predictable that this side would submit more technical briefs.

Together these three types of briefs offered the Court not only an abundance of information concerning abortion, but a sense of the urgency and complexity of this political issue as well. The Court saw briefs which towed the party line, others which offered specialized information, and still others that challenged the Court to break new legal ground. While many perspectives were present, the next question is how many were heard?

What Impact?

While the main purpose of an amicus brief is to persuade the Court to rule on behalf of a particular litigant, ... [i]nterest groups may also claim success if the Court adopts the language or perspective of the brief, or if the litigant's argument is strengthened by the endorsement of the amicus. In filing an amicus, an interest group may gain publicity, an opportunity to refine and articulate its position, and experience in the judicial system. Such third-party involvement also allows groups to feel as though they have participated in the decisional process. Some of the impact of amici may not be apparent until future cases emerge which reflect the information, argument, or concerns of the earlier amici.

Impact is of course most readily identifiable in terms of the winners and losers of a case. However, such an approach is obviously limited for a case like *Webster* where the Court lineup was 4–1–4 from the start.[181] With this in mind, the discussion here will also include a content analysis of which briefs were cited by the justices in the decision, and a

---

181. [Editors' Note: Earlier in this article Behuniak–Long attributed to "Court watchers" the assumption that the Court was "4–1–4" in the period leading up to *Webster*, with Justice Kennedy assumed to be against *Roe*. How does that assumption fit with his later vote in *Casey*? In *Gonzalez v. Carhart*? See Chapter One above.]

study of how some of the arguments made by the amici seemed to sway certain justices.

In a 5–4 vote with two concurrences and two dissenting opinions, the *Webster* decision upheld the sections restricting public employees and facilities from performing or assisting in abortions, and the sections requiring viability testing. While the Court did not rule on the constitutionality of the statute's preamble, it declared the counseling section moot. In the course of deciding these issues, the Court also began to dismantle the principles of *Roe,* the trimester scheme in particular. Chief Justice William Rehnquist, with Justices Byron White and Anthony Kennedy, attacked the "rigid trimester analysis" as inconsistent with the Constitution. He argued, "We do not see why the State's interest in protecting human life should come into existence only at the point of viability...." Justice Antonin Scalia concurred stating that Rehnquist's argument would effectively overrule *Roe,* but that he would do so more explicitly. Justice Sandra Day O'Connor agreed with the constitutionality of the Missouri statute, but not with the need to unravel *Roe.* She relied instead on *Roe* and its progeny to uphold the Missouri law. The four dissenting justices, Harry Blackmun, William Brennan, Thurgood Marshall, and John Paul Stevens, would have used *Roe* to void the Missouri statute.

Therefore, when speaking strictly in terms of win versus lose, the appellants emerged as the victors in this case. The Missouri law was upheld, the Court signaled its willingness to uphold restrictive state abortion policies, and four justices indicated a willingness to overturn *Roe.* Within these terms, appellees could claim only that *Roe* survived—for now. Yet, measuring impact in this way assumes that the win is due to arguments set forth by amici. It also ignores the fact that amici on the losing side have impact as well. Therefore, it is important to consider as well two other indicators: the amici cited by the Court, and evidence that the Court accepted arguments advanced only by the amici.

... References to the appellants' party briefs totaled six while the appellees' party briefs were cited eight times. Excluding party briefs, amicus briefs were cited 29 times. Twelve different amicus briefs, six from each side, were cited at least once. Appellants' amici were cited 12 times while appellees' amici were cited 17 times. The amicus briefs cited tended to be those that contained either religious arguments or which provided technical information on medicine or on the law. Besides the direct references to the amicus briefs, Justices Blackmun and Stevens together cited seven different published articles: three which were largely scientific, two commenting on religious issues, one on the impact of illegal abortions, and one on the law.

Rehnquist, writing for the majority, cited the appellants' brief four times and the appellees' brief five times. The only amicus to which he referred was that of the United States. In O'Connor's concurring opinion, she cited the appellees' brief three times, and referred to the four amicus briefs containing medical and scientific information, again indicating her struggle with the viability issue. Scalia's concurrence made no direct references to briefs or outside sources. The dissents of Justices Blackmun and Stevens did not cite the party briefs of either side. These justices referred instead to the amicus briefs for a total of 29 citations. As with O'Connor, most of Blackmun's references came from the technical medical briefs. In contrast, Stevens cited mostly the religiously oriented briefs.

Yet, briefs can be cited and then rejected. Did the briefs have any real influence on the justices in constructing their decision? It is suggested that the answer is yes. Consider again the role of the amici. The appellants' amici seemed to urge their coalition of four justices to overturn *Roe*. The appellees' amici appeared to focus on convincing O'Connor to cast the fifth vote to protect *Roe*. The amici on both sides enjoyed some success.

The victory enjoyed by the appellants was not of the parties' making alone. The Court went further than the parties had urged, surging ahead on the path marked by the appellants' amici. When the Court accepts an argument that was advanced only by an amicus brief, it is an indication of influence. Again, the party brief had devoted only four pages to challenging *Roe* and the viability point. It was instead the amici who supplied both the technical and legal information which subverted the *Roe* trimester scheme.

There are signs that the appellees' amici had influence as well. Again, their target was O'Connor and the two routes to her were to have her apply her "undue burden" test to strike down the Missouri statute, and to have her retreat from her criticism of *Roe*'s trimester scheme. While the amici were unsuccessful concerning the first point, there are signs that they made some progress concerning the second.

It is not what O'Connor's *Webster* opinion says but what it does not say that is important. Considering her *Akron* dissent in which she argued that the trimester approach was "completely unworkable" and on a "collision course with itself," and that she adhered to this position three years later in Thornburgh v. American College of Obstetricians and Gynecologists,[182] it is curious that in *Webster*—a case that brings the viability issue to the forefront and causes four other justices to voice concerns that the trimester framework is indeed unworkable—O'Connor remarks only that she continues to regard the trimester approach as "problematic." She cites her *Akron* dissent not to repudiate the trimester scheme, but to illustrate how to apply the "undue burden" test. If indeed O'Connor is retreating from her *Akron* critique, the appellees' amici may be responsible for planting the seed of doubt in her mind.

Conclusion

The 78 *Webster* amici produced an incomparable collection of information on the abortion rights issue. While *Webster* is certainly not a typical case, nor was the response of interest groups usual, it does serve

---

182. [Footnote 45 in original] 476 U.S. 747, at 814 (1986).

to magnify the amicus curiae role. Interest groups can lobby the Court concerning an issue even as politicized as abortion if they enter the Court through the open door extended to amici. In working to present their arguments before the Court, the pro-life and pro-choice movements also revealed something about themselves. The briefs reflected the composition of their constituencies, their legal strategies, and their core values. The study of amici, then, is not only instructive for court watching but for monitoring interest group politics as well.

The writing and organization of 78 briefs was a monumental undertaking, but it was not a wasted effort. It appears that the amici on both sides made in-roads with the Court. The briefs were not only read; they also had impact. Their arguments and information helped to shape the terms of the Court debate. Whether the justices refuted the briefs, modified an argument because of them, or accepted and integrated their points, the amici mattered. Through the presentation of the briefs, the battle over abortion rights was waged before the Court. It is no surprise, then, that in the midst of this friendly fire, some of the justices were struck.

Questions and Comments

1. Amicus filings have risen at both the certiorari and the merits stages. At which stage would one predict the presence of an amicus brief would have more impact? Cf. Gregory A. Caldeira & John R. Wright, *Organized Interests and Agenda Setting in the U.S. Supreme Court*, 82 Am. Pol. Sci. Rev. 1109, 1119 (1988) (finding that "justices pay close attention to the demands of outside parties when making certiorari decisions").

2. Re-evaluate the argument about the impact of amicus curiae briefs in *Webster* in light of (1) the Kearney–Merrill analysis of the more limited impact of amicus briefs in high filing cases and (2) the narrative provided by Professor Tushnet in Chapter IV, Section C, of the internal dynamics on the Court in *Webster* and *Casey*. Does "quotation" or citation translate into "influence"?

3. Kearney and Merrill report "success" rates for institutional amici, including the SG, the ACLU and the AFL–CIO. Does correlation here necessarily imply influence—that is, that the Court decided some particular cases differently than it would have without the amicus filing? Or is it possible that, given their expertise, these groups are particularly good at picking cases where the Court is more likely to rule their way than the "benchmark" would predict? What would you need to know to answer this question?

4. Recall Behuniak–Long's statement that O'Connor's *Webster* opinion is notable for "what it does not say." She suggests that appellee's amici may have had success in preventing adverse development of doctrine, notwithstanding their "loss" in the case. Does this complicate the question of how to measure influence, especially within the Kearney–Merrill "legal model"? (For

example, Kearney and Merrill describe the ACLU's relative lack of success: a qualitative analysis might explore whether in some of these case the Court avoided doctrinal moves that an ACLU brief cautioned against.) Do these questions suggest the importance of multiple modalities of empirical research?

5. Consider whether, in order to assess the influence of amici, it may be necessary to focus on very particular contexts, involving specific litigants and issues. Compare, e.g., Christopher R. Drahozal, *Preserving the American Common Market: State and Local Governments in the United States Supreme Court*, 7 Sup. Ct. Econ. Rev. 233 (1999) (analyzing relationship between state government participation in challenges to the constitutionality of another state's law as in violation of the dormant commerce clause; finding that such participation acted as a "fire alarm" to call the Court's attention to dangers to the American common market) with Andrew P. Morris, *Private Amici Curiae and the Supreme Court's 1997–98 Term Employment Law Jurisprudence*, 7 Wm. & Mary Bill Rts. J. 823 (1999) (concluding that amici on both employer and employee sides made virtually no contribution to the Court's analysis or decision of three major Title VII cases).

A more general question is whether the parties' resources make a difference in Supreme Court decisions. In "a time series analysis of the success of different categories of litigants over a 36 year period," from 1953 to 1988, the authors conclude that the factor of litigant resources (measured by party status) may play a *less* important role in how the Supreme Court decides cases than it does in the lower appellate courts. Reginald S. Sheehan et al., *Ideology, Status and the Differential Success of Direct Parties Before the Supreme Court*, 86 Am. Pol. Sci. Rev. 464, 469 (1992). These authors suggest that the ideological views of the Justices are a more significant factor than party resources, and that the Court's control of its docket reinforces the significance of the Justices' own views in merits decision-making. *Id.* at 468, 465. This study focused only on merits decisions: consider possible differences at the certiorari and merits stages in the impact of party status and resources on Supreme Court decision-making.

6. Many observers believe that amici filings—especially an amicus brief filed by former military officials, concerning the benefits of affirmative action and diversity in the nation's military academies—were significant to the Court's 2003 decision upholding the University of Michigan Law School's use of race in the admissions process. See Grutter v. Bollinger, 539 U.S. 306 (2003). A companion case, Gratz v. Bollinger, 539 U.S. 244 (2003), held unconstitutional the use of race in admissions to the undergraduate program at the University of Michigan because it, unlike the law school, relied on a fixed (and substantial) assignment of points based on race, rather than a wholistic evaluation of each applicant. According to Neal Devins, who pursues an "interest group" analysis, the amici filings and the Court's decision in *Grutter* "highlighted the pivotal role that elite opinion plays in shaping the Court rulings." Neal Devins, *Explaining* Grutter v. Bollinger, 152 U. Pa. L. Rev. 347 (2003). According to Professor Devins,

> One hundred two amicus briefs were filed in *Grutter* and *Gratz*—eighty-three supporting the University of Michigan and nineteen supporting the petitioners. The gap between supporters and opponents of

affirmative action, however, was far more lopsided than this four-to-one ratio. Consider the following: no member of Congress opposed the University. Indeed, one hundred twenty-four members of the House and thirteen Senators joined four briefs supporting the university, which emphasized that the federal government had repeatedly endorsed race-conscious decision making as constitutional, and argued that the Court should give deference to the constitutionally significant opinions of the other branches. Though all brief signers were Democrats, four moderate Republicans made public their support of the university. In a letter to President Bush, Senators Lincoln Chafee, Olympia Snowe, Susan Collins, and Arlen Specter urged the administration to "support the position that diversity is a compelling government interest."

States also rallied behind the University. Unlike earlier challenges to the constitutionality of state-sponsored affirmative action (where states typically did not file briefs), twenty-three states and the Virgin Islands joined one of three briefs supporting the university.... Only one state, Florida, filed a brief supporting the petitioner....

Big-business, labor, education, and civil-rights interests also backed the university. While these interests had all embraced the constitutionality of racial preferences prior to the Michigan cases, support for the Michigan plans was more emphatic than it had been in earlier affirmative action cases. Ninety-one colleges and universities, as well as every major educational association, filed briefs in support of the university. Not one college or university filed a brief opposing affirmative action.... [B]riefs filed by Fortune 500 companies and other business interests claim that business needs a diverse pool of potential employees in order to compete effectively in the global marketplace. To achieve this diversity objective, schools must be able to consider race.

This emphatic, near-unanimous reaffirmation of affirmative action helped propel the University of Michigan affirmative action programs. Perhaps more significantly, a coalition of former high-ranking officers and civilian leaders of the military (including William Crowe, Bud McFarlane, Norman Schwarzkopf, and Anthony Zinni) joined forces with longstanding supporters of affirmative action. In a brief that figured prominently in both oral arguments and the Court's decision, the "military brief" linked "the military's ability to fulfill its principal mission to provide national security" with existing preferential treatment programs at the nation's military academies and its ROTC programs. Noting the problems of low morale and heightened racial tension in Vietnam, the brief argued that "a highly qualified, racially diverse officer corps educated and trained to command our nation's racially diverse enlisted ranks is essential to the military."

The amicus curiae filings in *Grutter* and *Gratz* are a testament to the breadth and intensity of support for affirmative action. By detailing the perceived benefits of affirmative action, they provided the Court with information it could use to explain why racial diversity is a compelling government interest. In sharp contrast, opponents of affirmative action remained politically isolated. The only notable brief that supported this position was an ambiguous filing by the Bush administration. But ... that brief probably did more harm to their cause than good. Indeed, when compared to other controversial social issues (abortion or religion in the schools), the absence of important, powerful voices on one side of the issue seems especially stark.

. . .

The biggest boost for affirmative action may have come from an unlikely source: George W. Bush. On January 15, 2003, the President announced that he "strongly supports diversity ... including racial diversity in higher education," but that he considered the University of Michigan's affirmative action plans to be "at their core" an unconstitutional "quota system." The very next day, the George W. Bush Justice Department submitted a brief that, "far from insisting that any consideration of race was impermissible," did not even ask the justices to overturn the *Bakke* decision, ... [instead] allowing race to be used as a "plus factor." The brief argued that government "may not employ race-based means without considering race-neutral alternatives and employing them if they would prove efficacious." In other words, unlike the absolutist filings of the Reagan and first Bush administrations, the Bush Justice Department sought to steer a middle path on racial preferences. Indeed, following the Court's decisions in *Grutter* and *Gratz*, the President declared victory, "applaud[ing] the Supreme Court for recognizing the value of diversity on our Nation's campuses."

The President's decision is readily understandable. On the one hand, he could not embrace the University of Michigan's programs without alienating his conservative base, represented by Attorney General John Ashcroft and Solicitor General Ted Olson. On the other hand, he could not risk rejecting affirmative action because his political advisors told him that he must do better with minority voters to win reelection. . . .

If amicus briefs in cases like *Grutter* correspond to elite opinion, which should be treated as the influence—the briefs or the elite opinion? And how precise are the tools by which to distinguish between the information about elite opinion that the amici briefs provided and the substantive arguments they made?

7. Moving now from the positive to the normative (that is, putting to one side whether or not amici are "successful" in influencing the Court), are there normative arguments for and against certain kinds of amici practice? Is amici practice a form of "lobbying," incompatible with legalized under-

standings of the Court? See Morris, *supra* (arguing that amici participation as "lobbyists," that is, advancing arguments based on policy grounds or on nonlegal authority of "questionable" reliability, was incompatible with an understanding of the Court making decisions based on the law). Or is it a helpful way of informing the Court of a broader array of views and information relevant to the Court's role in deciding not only concrete cases but on rules of law that will apply to many others?

Chapter Six

THE COURT AND JUDICIAL INDEPENDENCE: CHALLENGES FOR THE FUTURE

In the first edition of this book, much of the focus of this final chapter was on proposals to create a national court of appeals to ease the burden the Supreme Court was facing at the time, when it was hearing about 150 merits cases per Term. With the Court now hearing roughly half that number (about 80 merits cases per Term), the issues on the agenda for reform have changed. Proposals for a national court of appeals, described as "[p]erhaps the most recurring suggestion" for reform,[1] have fallen from the current agenda and recently have been pronounced close to dead.[2] Indeed, in recent years some scholars have proposed that the Court should *increase* its workload by choosing to hear more cases on the merits, or that Congress should increase the Court's workload by limiting the Court's discretion to refuse to hear cases or even by requiring that the Justices take up circuit riding again. The materials in the prior chapters, especially in Chapter Three, address some of these proposals and hopefully provide sufficient background for you to begin forming your own judgments.

In this final chapter we introduce other areas of recent controversy and proposals for reform of the Court. The history of the federal

---

1. Richard H. Fallon, Jr., et al., *Hart & Wechsler's The Federal Courts and the Federal System* 54 (5th ed. 2003).

2. See, e.g., Arthur D. Hellman, *The View from the Trenches: A Report on the Breakout Sessions at the 2005 National Conference on Appellate Justice*, 8 J. App. Prac. & Process 141 (2006). In light of the enormously increased caseload of the courts of appeals, this may be a surprising development. See Richard J. Lazarus, *Advocacy Matters Before and Within the Supreme Court: Transforming the Court by Trans-* *forming the Bar*, 96 Geo. L. J. ___ (forthcoming 2008) (manuscript of Aug. 5, 2007, at 33–34) [hereafter Lazarus, *Advocacy Matters*] (noting that the number of "paid" cert petitions being filed in the mid–2000s was less than the number of paid petitions being filed in the 1980s, even though the number of cases in the federal courts of appeals had doubled in that time). Lazarus attributes the absence of a corresponding increase in cert petitions filed to the Supreme Court to many factors, possibly including the work of the private bar in filtering or screening would be petitions.

judiciary in the United States reveals cycles of public support and attack. In the last few years, courts in general and the Supreme Court in particular have once again become focal points of political attack. Obviously the importance of judicial independence and impartiality of judges is not new. But the discussion of those issues has recently become more heated and contested.

The U.S. Constitution creates strong structural supports for the independence of federal Article III judges, providing that they serve "during good behavior," and that their salary cannot be diminished while in office.[3] Unlike most of their counterparts in western, democratic nations, which employ either a mandatory retirement age or a term limit or both, the members of the U.S. Supreme Court essentially serve for life or until they choose to retire. At the same time, the U.S. Constitution contemplates a political appointment process by the President and Senate, not a process of judicial self-selection, nor a "merit system" of selection by nominating commission. It thereby provides some means of public control over its membership. Finding the right balance between independence and accountability defines a wide range of issues that affect the Court.

Some contentious issues, including those relating to the secrecy versus transparency of the Court's processes, are enduring ones that have been controversial for decades. In Section A, we first discuss persistent calls for more access to the Court's public proceedings, the Court's responses by making transcripts and audiotapes of oral arguments more readily available, and continued calls for the Court to permit cameras in the courtroom. The role of the press, and the challenges of providing intelligible and accurate public information, are then considered. Next, we turn to a different set of questions about the confidentiality of the Court's internal deliberations. While Chapter Five addressed the law clerks' public discussions of the Court's private deliberations, here we address the appropriate disposition of the Justices' papers: when, if ever, should their internal deliberations be made public and what, if any, control should the public have over the Justices' papers?

In Section B, we touch briefly on a range of controversies that have in recent years evoked media and political attention. These include (1) jurisdiction-stripping efforts, in connection both with the Guantanamo detainees and with controversies concerning, for example, the public role of religion; (2) recusals or failures to recuse by Supreme Court Justices (an issue that has arisen episodically since John Marshall sat on *Marbury v. Madison*); and (3) interpretive control and threats of impeachment directed at some Justices' references to foreign or international law in the decision of constitutional cases. Plenary treatment of these and

---

3. These constitutional provisions have co-existed with important strands in the popular culture of respect for judicial independence. See e.g., Barry Friedman, *The History of the Countermajoritarian Difficulty, Part Four: Law's Politics*, 148 U. Pa. L. Rev. 971, 1028–46 (2000) (describing how public commitment to judicial independence and concern over Franklin Roosevelt's Court-packing plan contributed to its defeat).

other issues will be found in other courses; here we provide only a brief overview, in order to expand readers' sense of the political and constitutional context in which today's Court operates.

Finally, in Section C, we consider proposals to modify the current life tenure rules for Supreme Court Justices. Although proposals for fixed retirement ages or fixed terms are not entirely novel, these recent proposals received considerable attention in light of the unusually long, eleven year period of continuity on the Court with no new members, a period that ran roughly from the year in which the first edition of this book was published until 2005. Should we see these proposals as a positive step toward maintaining the appropriate balance between democratic accountability and judicial independence in a high court which decides such important issues in our society? Or should we see them as a threat to judicial independence? Consider also the related question about the use (or nonuse) of impeachment as a mechanism of accountability, an issue addressed in our closing excerpt from the late Chief Justice, William H. Rehnquist.

A. PUBLIC ACCESS TO THE COURT'S PROCEEDINGS

Debates over access and transparency revolve around two quite different sets of issues: those relating to public access to the Court's public proceedings, and those relating to its internal deliberations. The parties' briefs are accessible to everyone, but oral arguments are open only to the 300 or so people who can squeeze into the courtroom. The Court's conferences are open to no one except the Justices. Only final opinions, not the exchanges that generate them, are published.

To some extent, the Court's veil of secrecy lifts as time goes by. The Justices often choose to leave their papers to libraries, usually providing for their availability to researchers or the public sometime after the donor's death. These papers can provide rich insights into the Court's otherwise hidden deliberative processes, if and when the Justices make them available.[4] Law clerk disclosures may also provide insights, as the materials found in Chapter Five, Section B above, indicate.

In the materials that follow, we discuss first, public access to already public proceedings and second, the tensions between the role of secrecy in the internal deliberative process and the benefits of historic knowledge of those internal decision process.

1. Expanding Public Access to and Awareness of Public Proceedings?

Supreme Court arguments have long been "open" to the public in a literal sense. The Court allows spectators who can afford the time, and

---

4. Many of the scholarly analyses of the Court's internal decisionmaking, excerpted in Chapters Three and Four, above, are based on internal memoranda concerning particular cases made public in the papers of former Justices.

are early enough to get on line to gain entry to the limited public seating available to witness the arguments. However, most Americans will not be able to view oral arguments. The technology exists to increase that capacity, but the Court has been reluctant to allow its use.[5]

Although the Supreme Court has taped oral arguments since 1955, the Court only began making the tapes publicly accessible in 1969. In that year, the Court adopted the practice of depositing the tapes of each Term's oral arguments in the National Archives, but only after the Term was over. While the media had access to these tapes, their usefulness to journalists was diminished by the fact that cases of public interest had already been reported on before the tapes were available. Furthermore, unclear rules governing the reproduction of oral argument recordings dissuaded television and radio stations from replaying them.

Following a 1981 CBS broadcast of the oral argument in the *Pentagon Papers Case* (in a program by journalist Fred Graham on the tenth anniversary of that decision), Chief Justice Warren Burger stopped providing the National Archives with tapes for several years. Transcripts provided the public's only available means of reviewing Supreme Court oral arguments during this period. However, transcripts were not easily accessible, and they identified members of the Court only as "Associate Justice" or "Chief Justice," leaving the reader to guess which of the eight Associate Justices was posing a question. Chief Justice Burger began providing tapes to the National Archives again only after requiring those seeking to copy the tapes to sign a form promising not to distribute copies for commercial purposes.[6]

In 1993, Professor Peter Irons published *May It Please the Court*, a collection of audiotapes of what he regarded as the fifty most important oral arguments since 1955, with commentary. Publication of the tapes violated the agreement, prohibiting reproduction of oral argument tapes for commercial purposes, that Irons, like all other users, was obliged to sign when he duplicated the tapes at the National Archives.[7] Although the Court evidently considered suing Irons, it instead changed its entire policy regarding the oral arguments tapes.[8] From 1993 on, the tapes deposited at the National Archives were available for reproduction without limitation. The tapes are now the subject of several CD–ROM compilations and are often broadcast on stations such as NPR, or PBS.

5. The authors acknowledge the helpful memo by Professor Bloch's Research Assistant, Glenn Laken, GULC Class of 2009, which contributed to this introduction.

6. For accounts from which this paragraph is drawn, see Thomas E. Baker, *Book Review: May It Please the Court: The Most Significant Oral Arguments Made Before the Supreme Court Since 1955*, 69 Tul. L. Rev. 319, 324–325 (1994) and Tony Mauro, *Supreme Court to Legal Scholar: Keep Oral Arguments to Yourself,* Legal Times, Aug. 16, 1993, at 1.

7. *See* Mauro, *supra* (reporting that after the CBS broadcast, the Court required that all persons seeking to copy a tape of a Supreme Court oral argument sign an agreement pledging to " 'use such audiotape for private research and teaching purposes only' " and " 'not to reproduce or allow to be reproduced for any purposes any portion of such audiotape' ").

8. Baker, *supra*, at 326.

The next major development in making the Court more accessible to the general public came in 2000. In the days preceding oral arguments in *Bush v. Gore*, the president of C–SPAN and Senators Arlen Specter (R–PA) and Joseph Biden (D–DE) wrote the Court requesting that it permit television coverage of the oral arguments. While Chief Justice Rehnquist refused to allow video recording or live broadcast of the arguments, he took the unprecedented step of providing an audiotape of the oral arguments for immediate release following their completion.[9] Since then, the Court has agreed to allow the immediate release of the audiotape of oral arguments in more than a dozen cases, while rejecting requests in several others.[10] While news outlets consider this to be a great improvement over previous conditions, considerable mystery shrouds what criteria are employed in deciding whether to provide an immediate release of taped coverage upon media request.

Despite repeated requests over the last several decades, the Court has declined to allow video broadcasts of the Court's oral arguments or public proceedings.[11] However, in 2000, the Court began offering the quick release on its internet website of written transcripts of oral argument for all cases, within a week or two of their completion. In the October 2006 Term, the Court began posting oral argument transcripts the same day.[12] The transcripts themselves have also been improved by identifying which justice is speaking.

If the Court began releasing tapes and transcripts as a means to satisfy public pressure for greater access to the Court, its efforts have not been entirely successful. Senator Arlen Specter has introduced legislation to require the Court to televise all of its oral arguments

9. Glen Elsasser, *Advocates of TV Coverage Object to Justices' Ruling Against Cameras,* Chicago Tribune, Nov. 30, 2000, at N13.

10. According to C–SPAN, in the following 16 cases requesting early release of audiotapes the requests were granted: *Bush v. Gore* (2000), *Grutter v. Bollinger* (2003), *Gratz v. Bollinger* (2003), *McConnell v. FEC* (2003), *Rasul v. Bush* (2004), *Al Odah v. United States* (2004), *Cheney v. US District Court* (2004), *Hamdi v. Rumsfeld* (2004), *Rumsfeld v. Padilla* (2004), *Ayotte v. Planned Parenthood* (2005), *Rumsfeld v. Forum for Academic and Institutional Rights* (2005), *Hamdan v. Rumsfeld* (2006), *Parents Involved v. Seattle School District No. 1* (2006), *Meredith v. Jefferson County* (2006), *Gonzalez v. Planned Parenthood* (2006), *Gonzales v. Carhart* (2006). In 13 other cases, C–Span reports, the requests were denied: *Roper v. Simmons* (2004), *Van Orden v. Perry* (2005), *McCreary County v. ACLU* (2005), *League of United Latin v. Perry* (2006), *Travis County v. Perry* (2006), *Jackson v. Perry* (2006), *GI Forum v. Perry* (2006), *Davenport v. Washington Education Association* (2007), *Washington v. Washington Education Association* (2007), *Rita v. United States* (2007), *Claiborne v. United States* (2007), *FEC v. Wisconsin Right to Life* (2007), *McCain v. Wisconsin Right to Life* (2007). *See* C–Span Website, at http://www.cspan.org/camerasinthecourt/timeline.asp.

11. See Todd Piccus, *Demystifying the Lease Understood Branch: Opening the Supreme Court to Broadcast Media,* 71 Tex. L. Rev. 1053, 1056–57 (1993) (describing 1982 request of national broadcaster's association to set up a demonstration of broadcast equipment and a 1988 request made by Washington lawyer Timothy Dyk on behalf of 13 broadcast organizations, again to set up a demonstration). There was a demonstration in 1988, but in early 1989, Chief Justice Rehnquist informed Mr. Dyk that the Court had decided not to permit televising of the proceedings. *Id.*

12. Editorial, *Timely Transcripts at Last; The Supreme Court Becomes a Bit Less Bashful,* Washington Post, Sept. 17, 2006, at B06.

unless a majority of the Court votes to disallow cameras for a particular case on the grounds that it would violate a party's due process rights.[13] Current Supreme Court Justices have a range of opinions on the advisability of televising Court proceedings, but a decided majority of the Justices do not want the Court to be subject to live visual coverage.

In the readings that follow, three short excerpts from a recent symposium—by U.S. Court of Appeals Judge Boyce Martin, by law professor (and former Supreme Court law clerk) Christina B. Whitman, and by journalist Tony Mauro—give you a sense of the issues in the present debate, framed by Senator Specter's introduction in January 2007 of legislation to mandate television coverage in most cases. These are followed by comments from political scientist Elliot Slotnick and journalist Linda Greenhouse on the relationships between journalists and the Court and how they affect public understanding of the Court's work. How would you evaluate the merits of the arguments over broadcasting the Court's oral arguments and opinion delivery? And how much will expanding the public's ability to view oral arguments contribute to public understanding of the Court's work?

Boyce F. Martin, Jr.[14], *Gee Whiz, The Sky is Falling!*, 106 Mich L. Rev. First Impressions 1 (2007)[15]

... [S]ome comments, most notably Justice Souter's famous exclamation in a 1996 House subcommittee hearing that "the day you see a camera come into our courtroom, it's going to roll over my dead body," make it sound as if the Justices have forgotten that our nation's court system belongs to the public, not merely the nine Justices who sit atop it. I write this essay in order to give my own perspective. Having served as a judge on the Sixth Circuit Court of Appeals for nearly twenty-eight years, I believe that I am in a unique position to understand the concerns raised by televising oral arguments. I can make this guarantee—televising the Supreme Court's oral arguments will not produce the disastrous results predicted by some frightened Justices; rather, it will yield positive results. Most notably, it will increase the public's knowledge of the appellate process.

· · ·

One of [Justice Kennedy's] concerns ... is the "soundbite" problem. He believes that televising oral arguments will give the Justices the "insidious temptation" to speak in short, catchy soundbites that can be easily relayed to a general audience.... While Justice Kennedy's fear of

---

13. See S. 344, 110th Congress. The bill was referred to the Senate Judiciary Committee, which held hearings on February 14, 2007; no further congressional action is reported as of June 2007.

14. Circuit Judge, U.S. Court of Appeals for the Sixth Circuit

15. This essay may be found online at http://www.michiganlawreview.org/first impressions/vol106/martin.pdf.

grandstanding is understandable, I believe it is exaggerated. Although the production of soundbites might be an adverse consequence of televising arguments, this problem is not terribly different than the problems that exist under our current practices. Reporters already attend oral arguments, so any Justice who truly wants to create a stir with a catchy soundbite already has the means by which to do so. And can't it be said that appellate judges' written opinions yield a soundbite problem of equal magnitude? ... [T]he press focuses on the most controversial or entertaining parts of my opinions, even if those parts are relatively unimportant to the legal issues in dispute. The advent of blogs has dramatically increased the quantity of these—shall we call them—"wordbites" dispensed to the public. It is true that video broadcasts of Supreme Court oral arguments will make it easier for the media to deliver the most interesting tidbits of legal proceedings to the public, as written opinions and audio recordings clearly have their limitations. However, the remote chance that a Supreme Court Justice will become the appellate version of Judge Judy is significantly outweighed by the very real possibility that even snippets of the Justices in action will help improve public awareness of how the Court operates.

. . .

I trust that even with cameras aimed at them, the Justices will maintain the same degree of decorum and decency. I do not deny there is a risk that some lawyers arguing before the Court will use their time to pander to public opinion, perhaps jeopardizing their clients' interests or making a mockery of the Court. But this is quite unlikely to become a big problem. In the Sixth Circuit, without a television camera in sight, my colleagues and I have our fair share of grandstanding lawyers. When lawyers' arguments exceed the bounds of propriety, we simply rein them in. Likewise, the Justices of the Supreme Court (as I am sure they have done many times before) can do the same. Even if cameras do encourage some lawyers to showboat, other lawyers will surely take advantage of the opportunity to study oral arguments in order to improve their own appellate advocacy, which will in turn serve the interests of their clients.

One upshot of allowing cameras in the Supreme Court, which will perhaps allay some of Justice Kennedy's fears, is the fact that the Internet—not television—will likely be the primary medium over which Supreme Court oral arguments will be broadcast. Unlike television, the Internet will allow viewers to watch entire oral arguments anytime and anywhere, thus minimizing the number of people who receive their "Supreme Court TV" solely in soundbite format.

The most serious concern posed by placing cameras in the Supreme Court is the danger that the due process rights of the parties—particularly criminal defendants—could be undermined. This is easily preventable. In fact, the legislation introduced in January by Senator Arlen Specter contains an explicit exception to televising oral arguments where a majority of the Justices finds that "allowing such coverage in a particular case would constitute a violation of the due process rights of 1 or more of the parties before the Court." Such a provision creates a win-win situation: the public has access to proceedings before the Supreme Court, but consideration of the parties' interests remains paramount.

Christina B. Whitman,[16] *Televising the Court: A Category Mistake*, 106 Mich L. Rev. First Impressions 5 (2007)[17]

. . . Whatever the Justices' motives, televising the Court's arguments is a terrible idea. It is both misleading and unnecessary. Misleading because it would only randomly tell us something useful about the Court, and unnecessary because the Court is already more open than the other branches.

Oral arguments and announcements of decisions are the only moments of public performance in the work of the Court, but they are more performance than work. Arguments come in the middle of the Justices' consideration of a case—after considerable reading, discussion, and thought, but before more of the same. Individual Justices use arguments differently. Some Justices simply do not work out their thoughts orally. The Justice with whom I am most familiar, Justice Lewis F. Powell, Jr., preferred to communicate through memoranda—even with his clerks. He was an extremely successful litigator, but also a Southern gentleman. Showing off his intelligence, much less asking a snide question or making a cutting remark, was just not his style. Conversely, other Justices enjoy the give-and-take with each other and with the advocates for the sake of the encounter alone. Their dialogue may or may not focus on what really matters to their decision in a case. They might just be pouncing on a weak argument for the pure pleasure of the kill. Either way, every comment is already overanalyzed for a hint as to what is on the Justices' minds.

Oral arguments already receive too much of the wrong kind of attention because Court watchers enjoy the game of predicting outcomes, and arguments provide an occasion to justify a story or a comment on a blog. But this attention gives arguments a misleading importance. It is common to say that a lawyer cannot win a case by her oral argument, but that she can lose her case that way. This is as it should be. Ideally, we want effective advocates for both sides, but we should hope that the Justices can rise above a poor argument and reach a result that reflects judgment and justice despite the shortcomings of its advocate. Most arguments are lost not by embarrassing advocacy, but rather because a lawyer is not always able to avoid admitting under direct questioning to a weakness in his case that was concealed in his brief.

16. Former law clerk to Lewis Powell and the Francis A. Allen Collegiate Professor of Law at the University of Michigan.

17. This essay may be found online at http://www.michiganlawreview.org/first impressions/vol106/whitman.pdf.

I enjoy reading the argument transcripts, which are now available almost immediately, and I use them in my classes. But they are a treat rather than a meal. On television and radio, the availability of transcripts already promotes emphasis on the kinds of insights and ripostes that can be conveyed in soundbites. There are Justices whose performances lend themselves to soundbites, who have a quick and provocative wit, and these Justices inevitably attract the most attention. Although these qualities are not inconsistent with greatness, they are not the qualities that make a Justice great. Despite the fun, focusing on these qualities distracts us from less flashy indications of excellence. So, the televising of oral arguments is misleading. It is also unnecessary.

... The Court has always been an open institution on the matters that count. The judiciary, at least at the appellate level, has always been required to expose the reasons underlying its actions more than either of the other branches of government—through the discipline of writing published opinions. That is the process through which judges are publicly accountable, and it has no counterpart in the political branches. It is not easy to spot dishonest reasoning or evaluate quality of judgment as captured in opinions, but it is possible. It requires effort, and it is admittedly undemocratic in that it also requires expertise. But it is exactly the process of struggling with writing that gives the judiciary its unique character and disciplines the tendency to rely on first impressions or subjective reactions. The voices of individual Justices can be traced through their separate opinions and even found in their collegial opinions for a group. But the individual is not obscured just to create an insiders' guessing game. The collegial process is the whole point. A Justice who speaks for the greatest number of her colleagues speaks with the most authority.

. . .

The standard arguments against televising the Court are true, too. Media attention might already be encouraging individual Justices to play to an audience. It would be unfortunate and inappropriate if the most attractive, or even the fastest wit, were to become the public face of the Court.

Politicians are accustomed to performing in the spotlight. They may not appreciate how invasive the camera can seem to people who have not lived their lives this way. Justice Powell took media access seriously, but he saw it as a duty rather than a pleasure. Even more exposure to public scrutiny might have made his years on the Court deeply uncomfortable. For people like Powell, for whom public service is an obligation and public performance a necessary evil, becoming a media celebrity might be too costly. Yet we need people like Justice Powell in part because they understand the costs of public scrutiny and the value of privacy.

A narrow view of accountability, one that reduces it to public observation, has already turned too much governmental decision-making away from substance. Media attention already focuses on the sharpest tongue on the bench. Let us not give verbal skill more importance than it deserves, lest it change the character of our least democratic but most open branch.

Tony Mauro,[18] *The Right Legislation for the Wrong Reasons,* 106 Mich. L. Rev. First Impressions 8 (2007)[19]

Senator Arlen Specter took a bold and long-overdue step on January 22, 2007, when he introduced legislation that would require the Supreme Court to allow television coverage of its proceedings. But instead of making his case with a straightforward appeal to the public's right to know, Specter has introduced arguments in favor of his bill that seem destined to antagonize the Court, drive it into the shadows, or both. Chances of passage might improve if Specter adjusts his tactics.

Both the Congress and the Supreme Court have tiptoed around the issue of cameras in the Supreme Court for decades. Even after the Court in 1981 ruled in *Chandler v. Florida* that, in light of improved technology, there is no general constitutional bar to the televising of criminal trials, the Justices have clung to a NIMBY (Not in my Back Yard) position when it comes to televising their own proceedings. They have kept cameras out in part because they still can. . . . In unguarded moments, Justices . . . acknowledge that personal privacy—the ability to tramp around Washington, D.C. unrecognized—is a major reason for their stance. . . .

More recently, security concerns have bolstered the Justices' self-interested arguments. After Justice David Souter was mugged one evening in 2004 as he jogged near his D.C. dwelling, many expressed surprise that Justices are not guarded around the clock. Several Court police officers told me they try to press more security on the Justices, but the Justices don't want it. Their anonymity, they say, is their first line of defense.

Justices also articulate loftier reasons for keeping cameras out. Justice Antonin Scalia has said common law judges are supposed to stay out of the limelight, and besides, the public would not understand much of what the Court does. "That is why the University of Chicago Law Review is not sold at the 7–Eleven," Scalia said famously in a 1989 speech.

· · ·

Justice Anthony Kennedy recently added a new . . . argument to the debate. . . . The Court doesn't tell Congress how to conduct its business, Kennedy argues (though some in Congress would disagree with that

---

18. Supreme Court Correspondent, Legal Times, American Lawyer Media, and law.com; member of the steering committee of the Reporters Committee for Freedom of the Press.

19. This essay may be found online at http://www.michiganlawreview.org/first impressions/vol106/mauro.pdf.

statement). In return, Kennedy continues, Congress should not tell the Court how to operate. "[M]andat[ing] direct television in our court in every proceeding is inconsistent with that deference, that etiquette, that should apply between the branches," Kennedy said before a House subcommittee in April 2006. "[W]e feel very strongly that this matter should be left to the courts."

Kennedy's comments serve as a backdrop to Senator Specter's introduction of S. 344 on January 22, 2007... [which is receiving more attention than earlier efforts.] One reason may be the inexorable momentum of the information age, which with every passing month and year makes the Supreme Court appear, because of its no-cameras policy, more and more like a relic of some bygone era.

Another reason is the recent flood of attention given to the Court in light of two vacancies—prompted by Justice Sandra Day O'Connor's retirement and Chief Justice William Rehnquist's death—as well as President George W. Bush's three nominations to fill them: John Roberts, Jr., Harriet Miers, and, finally, Samuel Alito, Jr. (The nomination of Miers, of course, was withdrawn.). The nominees' confirmation hearings were extensively televised, providing the general public an education about the Court that the public had not received since Bush v. Gore in 2000, if then.

The Roberts and Alito nominations were followed by a bout of openness on the part of several Justices.... Roberts himself made several televised appearances, Justice Ruth Bader Ginsburg turned up on the CBS Sunday Morning show, Justice John Paul Stevens spoke on ABC News about the death of President Gerald Ford, and Breyer gamely appeared on an NPR quiz show (failing, ultimately, to give any correct answers).

Senator Specter alluded to the increased visibility of individual Justices in his floor speech in support of S. 344. But his tone was not celebratory ... By stepping out in front of the public more than before, Specter was suggesting, the Justices are already making themselves more recognizable; therefore, a little more television face time from the bench won't make them any more vulnerable to attack.

... Justices should be applauded, not criticized, for increasing their engagement with the public. Hearing Specter's comment, the Justices might be forgiven for shaking their heads and repeating the axiom, "No good deed goes unpunished."

But that was not the only point in Specter's floor speech when he seemed to be arguing for cameras in the Supreme Court as a way of punishing the Justices. As he has before, Senator Specter complained about several recent Supreme Court decisions that, he said, have shown less than proper respect for the role of Congress in the constitutional scheme.

One of Senator Specter's targets is *United States v. Morrison*, a 2000 decision that struck down parts of the federal Violence Against Women

Act. The Court invalidated provisions affording victims of domestic violence the right to sue in federal court on the ground that the Commerce Clause did not justify their enactment. But what sticks in Specter's craw is that the Court questioned Congress's "method of reasoning." In his sometimes quaint way of speaking, Specter went on to say in his floor speech that the *Morrison* decision raises "a fundamental question as to where is the superiority of the Court's method of reasoning over that of the Congress. But that kind of decision, simply stated, is not understood." Later in the speech, Specter went back to *Morrison* and elaborated: "I wondered what kind of a transformation there was . . . with method of reasoning that there is such superior status when going to the Court." Plain English translation: What makes the Supreme Court think it is smarter than the Congress?

The senator from Pennsylvania also took aim at two Supreme Court decisions that interpreted parts of the Americans with Disabilities Act: *Tennessee v. Lane* and *Board of Trustees of the University of Alabama v. Garrett*. Both, he said, employed the reasoning from *City of Boerne v. Flores* that there must be "congruence and proportionality" between the problem Congress is trying to solve and the method it uses to solve it. "I defy anyone to say what those words mean in a standard which can be applied in a way which can be predicted by lawyers and understood by state legislators and understood by clients," Specter said on the floor of the Senate.

Specter seems to raise these same issues whenever the subject of the Supreme Court comes up. He even asked about these cases during the confirmation hearings of Roberts and Alito. Senators often treat Supreme Court confirmation hearings as an occasion for sending a message to the Court. Specter's message during those hearings, as in his speech on S. 344, was that Congress deserves more respect from the Supreme Court.

But what does this significant complaint from one branch to the other have to do with television access? Specter makes the connection this way: cameras, he hopes, will make it clear to the public the extent to which the Supreme Court is dissing Congress. In his floor speech he said that if cameras are allowed and C–SPAN regularly broadcasts oral arguments at the Court, this new level of exposure will "inform the American people about what is going on so that the American people can participate in a meaningful way as to whether the Court is functioning as a super-legislature—which it ought not to do, that being entrusted to the Congress and state legislatures, with the Court's responsibility being to interpret the law."

When he speaks this way, it is hard not to conclude Specter's objective is not merely to let the sun shine in, but also to train an accusatory spotlight on the Justices. . . .

[B]y framing the case for camera access in terms of a complaint about past decisions he does not like, Specter is bound to raise the hackles of Supreme Court Justices and other federal judges who are smarting already from threats to their judicial independence.... Justice Kennedy's reference to the "etiquette" between branches, quoted *supra*, illuminates a powerful if intangible force that usually makes Congress think twice before passing laws affecting the Supreme Court.

Sure enough, when Specter raised his objections to the *Morrison* decision at a Senate Judiciary Committee hearing attended by Justice Kennedy on February 14, 2007, it became clear that Specter's arguments already had rankled the Court. "I think it's a non sequitur to use that so that you can have cameras in the courtroom," Kennedy told Specter. "We didn't tell Congress how to conduct its proceedings. We said that, in a given statute, we could not find in the evidence that Congress had shown us that interstate commerce was involved.... I think that that just doesn't follow [that] therefore we should have cameras in the courtroom. I don't understand that."

Traditionally, the federal judiciary exerts influence over pending legislation in more behind-the-scene ways. But Kennedy's comments, aired by C–SPAN, amounted to an extraordinary public repudiation of a key senator's views. Kennedy was signaling—if such a signal was needed—that Specter's rationale was wanting, and that the judiciary was unpersuaded, to say the least.... [I]f Senator Specter wants his worthy bill to pass, it seems evident that he should take Kennedy's hint and argue for cameras in the Court as a public good, not as punishment.

Note on the Dynamics of Court–Media Relations

The debate over cameras in the courtroom is only one aspect of the broader set of questions concerning the relationships between the Court and the media, and the media's role in publicizing and interpreting the Court's decisions, some of which are noted below. "One of the major problems confronting the Supreme Court reporter is the great tension that often exists between making a story both understandable to a lay audience as well as accurate. There is an ever-present risk of oversimplifying things to the point where important nuances of a critical ruling are lost in translation.... Perhaps the most common inaccuracy to appear in print or over the airwaves is the assertion that the Court 'affirmed,' 'upheld,' or 'let stand' a lower court ruling when, in fact, its only 'decision' may have been an allegedly neutral denial of certiorari." Elliot E. Slotnick, *Media Coverage of Supreme Court Decision-making: Problems and Prospects*, 75 Judicature 128, 136 (1991). Behind these and other difficulties lie important role differences in the work of the Court and the work of journalists who report on the Court, as both Linda Greenhouse and Elliot Slotnick discuss below. And there is the challenge, as Greenhouse discusses, of trying to identify what is the most accurate characterization of the Court's work, especially in cases with subtle, and multiple, opinions. Consider: why does it matter whether and how the press reports on the Court?

Elliot E. Slotnick,[20] *Media Coverage of Supreme Court Decision Making: Problems and Prospects,* **75 Judicature 128, 128–136 (1991)**

The importance of journalistic coverage of governmental activities in the policy-making arena is difficult to overestimate since the media serve as the primary link between the government and the governed. The multifaceted nature of the media's role in American politics is well tapped by Paletz and Entman:

> Much of what most adults learn about government—its institutions and members, their activities, decisions, defects, strengths, capabilities—stems from the mass media. . . . By dint of the subjects they cover (and do not cover) and the ways they structure them, the mass media tell Americans what to think about, how to think about it, sometimes even what to think.

. . . [F]or most Americans, the press may be the sole source of information about the Supreme Court. As noted by Caldeira, "Research on the attitudes of adults reveals that there is only a relatively shallow reservoir of knowledge about . . . the Court in the mass public. . . . Few . . . fulfill the most minimal prerequisites of the role of a knowledgeable and competent citizen vis-a-vis the Court." It is in this context of the importance of media coverage for public information and opinion about the Court that this essay focuses on the inherent problems in and future prospects for media coverage of Supreme Court decision making.

The reasons for the Court's relative invisibility . . . lay partly at the doorstep of the institution itself and its members. As noted by Duke, "The justices themselves are among the most anonymous public figures, preferring to stay out of the spotlight. . . . In the face of trends toward more openness in government, the Court still clings to its Delphic ways, perpetuating the remoteness that is part of its character."[21] Indeed, as Justice Antonin Scalia concluded in a recent speech that explored the relationship between the judge's decision-making obligations and press coverage of the Court, "I hope to have explained . . . the wisdom of [the] judge's ancient belief that no news, by and large, is good news."

The Court's shunning of the public eye, low general levels of knowledge about the Court and its work, and the primacy of media coverage for whatever understanding of the Court that does exist all serve to strengthen the media's role in determining the public consequences of judicial decisions. . . .

. . .

Justice William Brennan has characterized the press as "the medium of circulation" in American society, "the currency through which the knowledge of recent events is exchanged, the coin by which public

---

20. Associate Dean and Professor of Political Science, Ohio State University.

21. [Footnote 6 in original] Duke, *The U.S. Supreme Court: A Journalist's View,* 28 Washburn L. J. 343–56 (1989).

discussion may be purchased." This has particular relevance for the Court according to Brennan, "because through the press the Court receives the tacit and accumulated experience of the Nation, and because the judgments of the Court ought also to instruct and to inspire—the Court needs the medium of the press to fulfill this task."

For his part, Justice Scalia has demeaned the press' instructional and inspirational roles as portrayed by Justice Brennan. According to Justice Scalia, the unique nature of the judicial process and the real world operation of the journalistic calling render it impossible for the press to well serve the Court vis-a-vis the public.

> My intent ... is not to disparage ... reporting and commentary. It is what it is for very understandable reasons.... But I do hope to induce some of you to read that reporting and commentary with an appreciation that things are not always as they seem.... I am about to appeal to the principle that law is a specialized field, fully comprehensible only to the expert. That is not, I confess, an attractive proposition.... The "this is too complicated for you to understand" argument is trotted out to cloak incompetence in many fields. Let me try to explain why it has unique validity in the field of judging. In most areas of human endeavor, no matter how technical or abstruse the process may be, the product can be fairly evaluated by the layman: the bridge does or does not sustain the loads for which it was designed; the weather forecast is or is not usually accurate; the medical treatment does or does not improve the patient's condition. I maintain that judging, or at least judging in a democratic society, is different. There, it is frequently the case that the operation is a success, even though the patient dies. For in judging, process is a value unto itself and not—except in a very remote sense—merely a means to achieving a desirable end. The result is validated by the process, not the process by the result.

Thus, for Justice Scalia, "Like moral rectitude, judicial rectitude is ultimately determined not by result but by reason. Judges must of course give reasons, unlike umpires who can simply call the runners safe without specifying whether that is because the throw arrived too late or because the first baseman's foot was off the bag." In such a setting, being right for wrong reasons "is a disaster." Yet the media focus on results, not reasons, which "is to miss the principal point.... [H]ow easy it is for the casual observer to make that mistake."

· · ·

For Justices Brennan and Scalia the media-Court link appears to offer uniquely different possibilities and prospects. For Brennan, the media can be the vehicle through which a democratic polity is informed and energized and through which the Court learns about the public it serves. For Scalia, the media cannot fulfill effectively an informative function. Consequently, its task need not be facilitated by judges, and media (and public) criticism are treated as generally irrelevant to the pursuit of the judicial function.

. . .

[T]he media help to shape the judiciary's views of the public its decisions affect. Perhaps more importantly the centrality of television news in the public's information network suggests that much of what we know and our attitudes about our perceptions are derived from the media's message. As noted by Judge Irving Kaufman, "The force of judicial decisions . . . depends on a fragile constitutional chemistry, and it flows directly from popular knowledge and acceptance of their decisions. Courts cannot publicize; they cannot broadcast. They must set forth their reasoning in accessible language and logic, and then look to the press to spread the word." If the press "gets it wrong," . . . public misperception of a ruling can have a direct effect on compliance with the ruling as well as on its broader impact. . . .

. . .

. . . From the press' perspective, its difficulties are not simply or solely explained by accusations that reporters are "untrained" although, as developed below, this has been a historically significant problem. Clearly, however, journalistic needs for speed in reporting and brevity in reports are coupled with the demands of pressured editing to exacerbate the troubled relationship of the fourth estate with the least dangerous branch.

. . .

Supreme Court decisional processes are not open to the reporter's view as they are, at least in part, in other governmental settings. Yet, as Anthony Lewis has noted, "The process of decision is often more newsworthy than the end result. And it can certainly be more instructive in the ways of our government. . . . Judges make accommodations just as their political brothers do, but we can only guess at what they were." While critical judicial decisions are made in private, "What reporters see inside the Courtroom—all they see—is designed more to elevate than to display the judicial process."

. . .

Any consideration of the problems that exist in media coverage of the Court must take full account of the inherent difficulties associated with understanding complex litigation and technical legal arguments and then filing stories on them within a few minutes or a few hours. Case decisions often include numerous concurring and dissenting opinions that may obfuscate the issues even further and, as Dennis has noted, "The opinions of the Court as a source of news are only as informative as the reporter's lay comprehension of them." . . .

Supreme Court opinions are not written for a lay or journalistic audience and justices rarely do anything to make them more accessible to such publics.... [A] lack of concern for the general audience is perhaps the greatest weakness in Supreme Court messages. It places the responsibility of interpreting decisions squarely on the press ... and other encoders. As Wasby has observed, when this situation occurs, " 'the chances for misinterpretation ... increase radically.' "

Other facets of media coverage of the Court are dictated by the operating regimens of both institutions and the difficulties of effectuating change, even where such change seems possible. From the media's perspective, the idiosyncrasies of the newsday have much to say about whether and how well a Supreme Court decision is covered. In addition to competing with other news beats, Supreme Court cases are often in competition with each other as the media follow "the practice of highlighting what is felt to be the major decision of the day at the expense of the other decisions that day." This problem would not be a major one if Supreme Court rulings were announced randomly during the news year or, indeed, during the Court's less lengthy nine-month term. Such randomness is, however, patently not the case. Historically, all Supreme Court decisions were announced during a series of "decision-Mondays" ... In 1965, the exclusivity of Mondays for the announcing of decisions was abandoned, making newsworthy rulings less likely to pile up on a given newsday. Chief Justice Warren, it appears, initiated such reforms in an explicit effort to facilitate media coverage.

Such reforms have been beneficial but in no way have they sufficiently alleviated the problems they address. For one, decisions are not spread equally across the newsweek despite the formal demise of "decision Monday." More importantly, over a third of the Court's rulings (and the preponderance of its important ones) are generally announced in June reflecting the difficulties of reaching decision closure as well as the demands of opinion writing. As Graham notes, "On Monday, June 12, 1967, the Warren Court handed down enough decisions and new Court rules to fill an entire 991 page volume of the Supreme Court's official case reports. There was no way for us even to read so many pages, much less write coherent stories about them." ... Mackenzie adds, "Many of these decisions have remained under advisement until the end of the term precisely because of their difficulty and complexity, elements that frequently correlate with newsworthiness." ...

In some instances over 40 per cent of the Court's opinions were released during the last three weeks of the term, while nearly one-fifth were released during the final week of the term.

·   ·   ·

... Supreme Court reporters find themselves more isolated than journalists acting in other governmental arenas. Interviews with justices remain rare, despite their relative increase during the past decade, and they remain inadequate and inappropriate mechanisms for in-depth coverage of actual cases and controversies. Press briefings and press conferences are not held by justices or other Court personnel. In short, "The newsman has only his background knowledge, notes, typewriter, desk and phone—and whatever resources or contacts they can provide as he hastens ... to get down ... what the Court has decided." ... [And, in] "... contrast to other areas of newswork, the Supreme Court reporter operates with few special advantages or facilities, few special means of access to personal sources, and few special materials or documents."

As already noted, most judges simply do not see a great deal to be gained in an exchange relationship where the reporter's work is facilitated. The numerous contrasts between the two functionaries begins with their very work ethic. According to Knoche, "The fora for judge and reporters are quite different. A judge may take three pages to discuss a minute point of law, while a reporter may have three sentences to explain the meaning and impact of the entire decision." The judiciary is distinct from the other branches in the "sober second look" that lies behind its formulations, the attempt to develop reasoned, logical arguments. The media and, most particularly, television bow to brevity and simplicity....

This is not to suggest that press relations with the Court have been completely static and that no changes have occurred in them. For one, as we have seen, some reforms have been made with regard to decision Mondays and the Court's traditional starting time. Over time, many other alterations have transpired in the judge/journalist interface. Indeed, until the late 1920s reporters did not have access to copies of opinions at the time that they were announced and they were forced to rely on their understanding of what they had heard. At that time proofs of decisional texts became available, but only after rulings were completely read or announced in the courtroom. In the mid–1930s press aides began to distribute proofs at the start of a decision's announcement rather than at its conclusion. Today, concurrences and dissents are available concurrently with the announcement of the Court's decision, which is accompanied by a summary headnote. Formerly, the headnote was only available with the opinion's eventual publication.... [R]eporters no longer have to wait to have opinions dispatched to them by the press officer through antiquated (and now closed) pneumatic tubes.

Curiously, many of these recent reforms transpired during the watch of staunch media critic Warren Burger as Chief Justice. According to Graham,

> Burger never conceded that there was a legitimate public interest in such matters as the justices' health, their finances, their reasons for disqualifying themselves from cases, their votes on deadlocked appeals and their off-the-bench activities. To him, the news media's role was to convey to the public the official actions of the justices, no more. Thus, Burger became an enthusiastic reformer of the mechanics of covering the Supreme Court, perhaps in hopes that by facilitating our efforts to cover the formalities we would be less likely to fritter away our energies on personalities and gossip.

In this sense, the chief justice sought to bring added efficiency to dissemination of the information already distributed by the press officer. In no sense was the scope of distributed information altered. . . .

Reforms

Proposals for more radical reforms to facilitate the media's job in covering the Court have met with little success. Clearly, the most-often-mentioned desire, at least among the broadcast media's functionaries, is the allowance of cameras in the courtroom. More generally, reporters have sought advance notification that a decision was to be announced and/or advance access to opinions. . . . [I]n an interview with Stephen Wasby, Chief Justice Earl Warren noted that the television network heads had met with him and "suggested giving reporters the opinion earlier in the day, keeping them under lock and key until the opinion was announced in Court. Warren said that the Court 'would be laughed out of town' for doing that, and rejected the idea."

. . . Regarding the suggestion that reporters receive advance word that a specific decision was about to come down, [Tim] O'Brien adds,

> Reporters regularly assigned to the Court really don't need advance word on what decision is going to be announced. By the time a major ruling is released by the Justices, the regular correspondents . . . have had three prior opportunities to examine the case and the issues it raised: when certiorari was sought, when certiorari was granted and when the case was argued. Advance word to reporters would only help those poor chaps assigned to the Court on an infrequent or irregular basis.

. . .

Linda Greenhouse,[22] *Telling the Court's Story: Justice and Journalism at the Supreme Court*, 105 Yale L.J. 1537 (1996)

. . .

This Essay starts from the premise that press coverage of the courts is a subject at least as worthy of public concern and scholarly attention as press coverage of politics, perhaps even more so. Political candidates who believe that their messages are not being conveyed accurately or fairly by the press have a range of options available for disseminating those messages. . . . But judges, for the most part, speak only through their opinions, which are difficult for the ordinary citizen to obtain or to understand. Especially in an era when the political system has ceded to the courts many of society's most difficult questions, it is sobering to acknowledge the extent to which the courts and the country depend on

---

22. [Footnote* in original] Supreme Court correspondent, the New York Times.   B.A., Radcliffe College, 1968; M.S.L., Yale Law School, 1978. . . .

the press for the public understanding that is necessary for the health and, ultimately, the legitimacy of any institution in a democratic society.

My focus in this Essay is journalism about the Supreme Court of the United States, which I have covered since 1978 as a correspondent in the Washington Bureau of the New York Times....

... To the public at large, the Supreme Court is a remote and mysterious oracle that makes occasional pronouncements on major issues of the day and then disappears from view for months at a time. The nine individuals who exercise power in its name are unaccountable and essentially faceless. The Court looms so large in the consciousness of readers of this journal that it may be helpful to note, as the Washington Post did last fall, that while fifty-nine percent of the public, in a sample of 1200 randomly selected adults, could name the Three Stooges, fifty-five percent could not name a single Supreme Court Justice. Given such widespread ignorance, and in light of the Court's role as an important participant in the ongoing dialogue among American citizens and the various branches and levels of government, journalistic miscues about what the Court is saying and where it is going can have a distorting effect on the entire enterprise.

. . .

My thesis is that there exist conventions and habits both within the press and within the Supreme Court itself that create obstacles to producing the best possible journalism about the Court, journalism that would provide the timely, sophisticated, and contextual information necessary for public understanding of the Court. Some of the habits and traditions I identify as obstacles are unlikely ever to change, and I do not necessarily think that they should; I do not expect to see Justices holding news conferences to explain and elaborate on their written opinions, however appealing or even titillating that prospect might be to journalists. Nor do I expect newspapers to call up reserve troops and open up page after page of shrinking news holes to accommodate the flood of late-June opinions. I also recognize that the interests of these two vital and powerful institutions, the Court and the press, can never be entirely congruent; the press is always going to want more information than the Court is ever going to want to share. But I hope that the process of identifying where the obstacles lie may nonetheless foster some fruitful discussion ... of those problems that can be solved and of those mutual concerns that can be addressed without threatening the identity or integrity of either institution.

I.   GETTING THE STORY

Covering the Supreme Court is such an unusual form of journalism that it may help to describe the process itself. Sources, leaks, casual contact with newsmakers—none of these hallmarks of Washington journalism exists on the Court beat, leaving even experienced reporters baffled and disoriented, as I was when I began my job there.

Before I began covering the Court, I was a member and eventually chief of the New York Times bureau in Albany that was responsible for covering the New York State government. The mid–1970s in Albany was a chaotic and cacophonous period of fiscal crisis and public policy innovation. The press room in the state capitol was located on the third floor, fittingly between the Assembly and Senate chambers. The two houses of the State legislature were controlled by different parties, and, in the process of shuttling back and forth in search of the latest developments, reporters inevitably became messengers between the leadership of the two houses and between the legislature and the office of the Governor on the floor below. The press, in other words, was very much part of the process in Albany . . .

. . .

When I arrived in Washington, D.C., to take up my new assignment at the Supreme Court, I was met by silence. The contrast with my past life could scarcely have been greater. The press room at the Court is far from the action, in a ground-floor location that is actually a kind of half-basement, with small windows high up on a few walls. The Court's newsmakers, the Justices, are rarely seen on that floor, except for the few who eat an occasional meal in the public cafeteria down the hall. The Justices are visible, of course, on the bench whenever the Court is in session, but opportunities for casual or unscheduled contact are almost nonexistent. The journalist's job is almost entirely paper-dependent. . . . While most politicians will cheerfully or angrily critique any story in which their name has appeared, Justices rarely respond to public comment, or even to rank error.

The press corps at the Court is a small one, with about three dozen accredited correspondents representing organizations ranging from the Wall Street Journal to the Cable News Network to USA Today. Many additional reporters show up and receive one-day press passes to the courtroom on the days of major arguments and toward the end of the Term, when important decisions are expected. But on a typical day during the Term, when the Court is not on the bench and when the business at hand consists of reading certiorari petitions and briefs on the merits in granted cases, the numbers are much smaller. It would be unusual to find more than a half-dozen reporters at work at their desks on such a day, fewer now than when I began reporting on the Court.

The reason is that the commitment of the media to full-time coverage of the Court is shrinking, and most of the reporters assigned to the Court are also responsible for covering the Department of Justice, other courts, perhaps the Judiciary Committees in Congress, or, often, legal developments in the country at large. The television networks have cut back sharply on the attention they pay to the Court, a very unfortunate development considering the number of people who rely on television as their primary news source. . . .

Developments like these represent a major failure of journalistic responsibility and pose a significant obstacle to achieving excellence in writing about the Court. Major decisions will be covered, one way or another. What is lost to the reader or viewer is the texture and flavor of the Court's day-to-day work, particularly its performance in its case-selection function—the circuit conflicts left unresolved, the open questions left unanswered for another Term. . . .

II. TELLING THE STORY: WHAT HAPPENED? . . .

A. *"The Supreme Court ruled today . . ."*

. . . Which, if any, of fifty or more denials of certiorari are worth reporting in a limited space—perhaps 1200 words for a round-up Court story in the New York Times, significantly less for most of my colleagues on the Court beat. Which of several decisions should be the focus of the story? Is a second, or even a third story warranted? What about the oral arguments that morning? More than in many other beats, the reporters tend to make these calls because editors have no independent means for evaluating the importance of the dozens of discrete events that may constitute the Supreme Court's activities on a given day. While this circumstance offers an unusual amount of freedom to the reporter, it also means there is unlikely to be much informed discussion with colleagues and editors back at the office.

The most consequential judgment call of all is probably that of evaluating the meaning and importance of a Supreme Court decision on the merits. A few examples from the 1994 Term may suffice to illustrate what may be involved in completing the sentence: "The Supreme Court ruled today that. . . ." I offer these examples to illustrate the process, not because I am sure that I was right; the articles that resulted simply represented my best judgment by deadline time.

First, was affirmative action dead in the wake of Adarand Constructors v. Pena?[23] It was obvious both to me and to my editors that this was the question I needed to answer. On the face of the decision, it appeared so, because the Court for the first time held that federal affirmative action programs must be narrowly tailored to achieve a compelling state interest—in the equal protection context, the constitutional standard of strict scrutiny, which sets a hurdle nearly impossible to overcome. But what did it mean when the author of the *Adarand* opinion, Justice Sandra Day O'Connor, wrote for the five-to-four majority that "we wish to dispel the notion that strict scrutiny is 'strict in theory, but fatal in fact' "? What kind of strict scrutiny was this?

So my lead the next day did not declare federal affirmative action to be dead: If the Court blinked at the last minute, so did I. The first paragraph of my story, which led the paper under a three-column headline, read as follows: "In a decision likely to fuel rather than resolve the debate over affirmative action, the Supreme Court today cast doubt on the constitutionality of Federal programs that award benefits on the basis of race."

23. [Footnote 5 in original] 115 S. Ct. 2097 (1995).

That was an easy call compared to the decision two weeks later in Miller v. Johnson,[24] striking down a majority-black Georgia congressional district as a racial gerrymander. What was the story there? Were dozens of majority-black legislative districts around the country now presumptively unconstitutional? Had the Court dropped the other shoe it had been holding over the new majority-black districts since its decision in *Shaw v. Reno* two years earlier? It looked that way to me, and I was in the middle of crafting just such a lead in mid-afternoon on the final day of the Court's Term when I got a call informing me that the Court had just announced that it would hear two new redistricting cases in the coming Term. This announcement, which was completely unexpected—ordinarily, the Court would have remanded those cases back to the lower courts for disposition in light of the newly announced standard in the Georgia case—suddenly made sense of the unusual and cryptic comment that Justice Ruth Bader Ginsburg, one of the dissenters in the Georgia case, had made from the bench that morning to the effect that the Court had not yet spoken its "final word" on the role of race in redistricting. Suddenly, things did not appear to be quite so conclusively decided. I pushed the delete button on my computer and erased the sweeping implications I was in the process of drawing, substituting instead a more conditional verb tense and tone. My lead paragraph read: "In a bitterly contested decision that could erase some of the recent electoral gains made by blacks in Congress and state legislatures, the Supreme Court ruled today that the use of race as a 'predominant factor' in drawing district lines should be presumed to be unconstitutional."

So what's the story? These examples demonstrate a singular feature of journalism about the Court: the impossibility of using one obvious journalistic technique for fathoming the Court's actions, that of interviewing the newsmakers to ask them what they meant. . . .

As Justice Ginsburg pointed out in a recent talk at Georgetown Law School on how the Court communicates, not only does the Court speak to the public solely through its opinions, but the case law process itself precludes the Court from including, even if Justices were so inclined, a " 'practical effects' section in which [the Justices] spell out the real world impact of the opinion" because a Supreme Court decision is usually only one segment of a continuing public dialogue with or among "other branches of government, the States, or the private sector."

We are all so accustomed to these journalistic facts of life that we rarely think about them. Yet they underscore the importance of the role of the press in conveying the meaning of the Court's work. Other courts, of course, are similarly reticent about speaking directly to the public, but judges of lower federal courts and state courts are at times willing to help reporters understand opinions. Informal arrangements under which these judges make themselves available, on background, for this purpose are not uncommon. I recall one decision by the New York Court of Appeals that I covered during my tenure in Albany. The court rejected a

24. [Footnote 8 in original] 115 S. Ct. 2475 (1995).

constitutional challenge to a piece of the solution to New York City's fiscal crisis, and the judges were highly aware of the importance to the financial markets of accurate reporting about the ruling. The court invited reporters to participate in a "lock-up," an arrangement under which those willing to take part could come to the court early in the morning, perhaps an hour before the decision was to be publicly announced, to read the opinion at leisure. Once in the room, no one was permitted to leave until the time of announcement. One of the judges then made himself available by telephone for the rest of the day as a resource, not to be quoted, that reporters could contact to verify their understanding of the decision and its implications. I availed myself of this offer. To my knowledge, none of the reporters who took part in this episode broke the rules or betrayed the court's confidence. If it did nothing else, the exercise underscored, for each reporter who took part, the need for care and accuracy, forcefully reminding us that we were doing the public's business . . . . .

It is obvious from the earlier examples that a useful story about a Supreme Court decision, in my view, is necessarily interpretive. . . . Readers . . . need to know the context of the decision, what the decision means, how the case got to the Court in the first place, what arguments were put to the Justices, what the decision tells us about the Court, and what happens next. Not all of these elements are necessary in each story, and not all of the questions can be answered in every case. There are ways—conditional verb tenses or outright confessions of ignorance— . . . of preventing the story from pretending to be more definitive than it could possibly be under the circumstances.

B. *What Did Not Happen*

. . . The story sometimes lies in what the Court, or a particular Justice, did not do, and that has its own journalistic perils. Exaggerating the meaning of a denial of certiorari is a common journalistic error. While denials of certiorari can certainly be important and newsworthy in their own right, the reader should be reminded in each such story that the denial does not represent a judgment by the Court on the merits of the case. The Court's recent denial of certiorari in a case challenging the constitutionality of the new federal law to protect abortion clinics against violent protest was widely reported as an "upholding" of that law or, somewhat more subtly but no less incorrectly, as a survival of the law in a major Supreme Court test. Much of the public is now substantially misinformed about the legal status of the law, which continues to be challenged . . . [and] may yet be reviewed on the merits by the Supreme Court, where the outcome is by no means preordained.

. . .

Justice John Paul Stevens has adopted the commendable practice—I can only assume in reaction to incidents such as this—of occasionally writing opinions "respecting the denial of certiorari" that serve as explicit reminders that "an order denying a petition for certiorari expresses no opinion on the merits of the case." Most recently, he wrote such a memorandum when the Court denied certiorari in a highly visible California death penalty case. He explained that, while the case raised "a novel and important constitutional question," it arguably did not present a final judgment for the Court to review.

If it is important not to exaggerate the meaning of a Court action, it is also important to resist oversimplifying. When a decision turns on a concept like state action or standing or some other threshold jurisdictional issue, this can be explained to the reader quite explicitly, so that the disposition makes sense, and not simply swept under the label of "for technical reasons."

. . .

C. *Choices and Values ...*

Those who cover the Court, to be sure, have views and find themselves more sympathetic to some results and to some Justices than to others. The question is, how germane are those views to the work we do? I have found that years of reading conflicting lower court opinions and hearing arguments on both sides of every question have made me much less certain of the right answers than I was in the simple days when I covered real politics.... [T]he nuances and complexities of the issues before the Court are my constant companions when I sit down to write. What I want from the Court on a day-to-day basis, as I sit down to face my deadline, is clarity, coherence, and reliability. And compared with covering politics, although it would certainly be rewarding to have behind-the-scenes discussions with the Justices about the Court's work, there is a certain liberation in not having the kind of personal, mutually beneficial relationships that many political journalists have with the people they cover. I don't have to worry about losing access.

Of course, deciding what is important among the thousands of individual Court actions, which will be reported, and what pattern will be discerned from them can never be value-free.... I am still chagrined that it took me until the late 1980s to understand and write about the revolution in habeas corpus jurisprudence that had been taking place in the Court right under my nose. I simply had not understood either the subject or its importance. I failed a few years ago to appreciate the import of a Tenth Amendment decision that anticipated the regrouping and rebirth of a majority on the Court concerned with state sovereignty in the federal system. In retrospect, I think I was so mesmerized by the school prayer and abortion decisions that came down during the same Term that I was unable to take account of a major opinion....

Inattentiveness or lack of sophistication on the part of those who cover the Court, myself included, is surely an obstacle to good journalism about the Court. In her speech at Georgetown, Justice Ginsburg recounted the classic story that when the Court handed down *Erie Railroad v. Tompkins*, the 1938 landmark decision that created a revolution in federal jurisdiction by ruling that there is no universal common law and that federal courts must apply state law in diversity cases, every newspaper in New York failed not only to understand but even to report the case. Not until Justice Stone complained a week later to Arthur Krock, the chief of the New York Times Washington Bureau, and prodded him to write about what Krock was finally persuaded to call a "transcendentally significant opinion," did the lay public know anything about this development. . . .

A variety of journalistic needs and practices also pose obstacles to good journalism about the Court. Newsprint is expensive, and space is tight in newspapers and getting tighter all the time. On a busy decision day in June, when the Court issues four, five, or six major decisions, the news hole does not expand correspondingly. Nor do presses start later. Deadlines remain deadlines, no matter how much news there is to process. On the final day of the 1988 Term, the Court not only decided an important abortion case, *Webster v. Reproductive Health Services*, but also granted certiorari in *Cruzan v. Director, Missouri Department of Health*, portending a major ruling on the right to die. Although I had prepared the *Cruzan* case on the basis of the certiorari petition, . . . I ran out of time and the paper ran out of space. The Times used a wire-service story for the grant in *Cruzan*.

I am always a little uncomfortable with the convention that calls for wrapping up the Term with a sweeping analysis that discerns and proclaims a theme, a movement from some point to another. Is this really accurate? Suppose the Justices just think they are deciding cases, one at a time. What's the story, after all? . . .

· · ·

III. TELLING THE STORY: WHO WON?

In addition to whatever oversimplification is involved in adhering to the journalistic convention of finding a yearly theme of the Court's calendar cycle, the convention also inherently requires the designation of a winner. . . . I am often uneasy about the binary won-lost approach to reporting on the Court. To what extent do stories like these, even the most nuanced and sophisticated, mislead readers and risk overly politicizing discourse about the Court and its work?

A. *Wrapping It Up*

One point the sweeping end-of-Term wrap-up usually overlooks is that every Term is more a work-in-progress than a finished story. And while it may be dramatically inviting to portray the Court as the venue for an ongoing Manichean battle, the reality is, of course, quite different. Of the eighty-two signed opinions last Term, thirty-five, or forty-three percent, resolved cases by nine-to-zero votes. Yet, because the Term's most consequential decisions tended to be the closely divided ones, the overwhelming impression that journalism about the Court—including my own—probably conveyed to the casual reader was of an institution locked in mortal combat, where sheer numbers rather than force of argument or legal reasoning determined the result....

. . .

... The week before the current Term opened, I was a guest on a National Public Radio talk show. One caller asked for comment on the numerous five-to-four decisions from the Supreme Court. He said it was distressing that such important issues were decided by such narrow margins. I answered that question as I usually do, by saying that I find it neither surprising nor particularly distressing that issues that have divided the country, and in most cases have also split the lower courts, should prove divisive on the Supreme Court. The next caller found this answer inadequate. Why don't we just cut out the pretense that these people are anything more than politicians, he said, placed on the Court by other politicians to carry out a political agenda? According to this caller, it was simply naive to talk about the Court in any other way.

Even if I believed that to be the case, and I do not, I would find that view disquieting for the long-term health of our democracy. In fact, I told my caller that I disagreed with him. While the Justices naturally draw on their own values and perspectives in approaching cases, most of them, most of the time, act not as politicians but as judges, working within the constraints of precedent and of the judicial enterprise to give judicial answers to the problems that people bring to the Court.

The answer is not, of course, quite that easy. While I do not think that "low" politics plays a major role at the Court, "high" politics certainly does ... [T]here is no denying that fault lines exist on the Court these days over the most profound questions about the structure of our political system and the relationship of the individual to the state. Nearly forty years ago, during another tumultuous time in the Court's relationship with the political system, political scientist Robert Dahl wrote that "Americans are not quite willing to accept the fact that [the Court] is a political institution and not quite capable of denying it; so that frequently we take both positions at once."....

Furthermore, with gridlock elsewhere in the political system, the Court happens to be the battleground on which some of the major political wars of our time are being fought. I remember the day in 1992 when the Court decided *Planned Parenthood v. Casey*.... By the time I got back to my office, there were two huge stacks of faxes on the floor by my desk, one pile generated by the right-to-life side and the other by the pro-choice side. Both sides were claiming defeat, surely an interesting variant on the usual Washington spin control. The right-to-life reaction was understandable.... The pro-choice reaction had more to do with institutional politics: The pro-choice groups, anticipating a loss of *Roe v. Wade* in its entirety, had planned a major political campaign on that premise and were simply unable to switch gears as quickly as the Court had appeared to. I remember one of the lawyers on that side calling me with her statement. I became exasperated. "You're telling me you lost this case, and I'm telling you that you won it and I'm going to tell my readers that you won it," I remember saying to the startled lawyer. That was an unusual day and an unusual case, but efforts to influence public perceptions of important cases are quite common, and at times like these I have found that there are relatively few honest brokers.... For political purposes, ... what the Court is perceived to have done is often as important as what the Court actually did.

B.   The Struggle for History's Verdict

Because the Court is so important and is being asked to carry so much weight, a fierce battle is being fought across the political spectrum over the Court's story—over which ideas will prevail and how history will judge this period. It is a battle of public perception as well as reality, and journalism about the Court matters a great deal to the combatants.... Aiming his sarcasm at the three authors of the [*Casey*] plurality opinion, Justices Kennedy, O'Connor, and Souter, [Robert Bork, in an op-ed one week after the decision came down] said that the opinion was "intensely popular with just about everybody Justices care about: *The New York Times*, *The Washington Post*, the three network news programs, law school faculties and at least 90 percent of the people Justices may meet at Washington dinner parties."

. . .

For the past decade, conservatives rather than liberals have expressed the most concern about journalistic judgments about the Court, a fact that I interpret as reflecting frustration with the fitful nature of the vaunted conservative revolution at the Court and a search for an explanation as to why it has not proceeded more smoothly. Judge Bork's 1992 op-ed article, cited above, is one example....

Any discussion of factors bearing on the judgment of history and on public perceptions of the Court's legitimacy cannot ignore recent confirmation battles like the struggle over Judge Bork's nomination. There is a direct trajectory between my cynical caller on the public radio program and some of the political battles over nominations to the Court....

[There was] a recent discussion at my newspaper over whether to require identification, in all articles that name federal judges in the course of describing court decisions, of the President who appointed those judges. For a time ... such a rule was ... in force. Several of my colleagues and I objected that the rule placed the *Times* in the position of insinuating that all federal judges are simply carrying out the agendas of their political sponsors; in other words, that they are acting as politicians and not as judges. After further consideration, the rule was dropped. Federal judges will be identified by the Presidents who named them only if such identification makes sense as a news judgment in the context of the specific story. The fact that the rule existed even for a short time at the *Times* tells us something disquieting about the legacy of the confirmation battles of the Reagan and Bush years. I do not mean to single out the *Times*. I have a pile of commentary on the Court from a range of publications, much of it making the unstated or explicit assumption that some of the Justices are just politicians in robes. Anyone who has evidence that such is the case should of course document it and write it. But to incorporate the untested assumption into journalism about the Court disserves the goal of increasing public understanding.

IV. TELLING THE STORY: DOES THE ORACLE SPEAK?

There is also the question of the Court's own responsibility for telling its story. The Court's habits present substantial obstacles to conveying the work of the Court accurately to the public. To cite one example, on June 29, 1995, the final day of the Court's last Term, the Court handed down opinions in two voting rights cases, two important religious speech cases, and a major statutory case construing the Endangered Species Act. Together, these decisions take up nearly eighty pages in the tiny type of *United States Law Week*. Even for a paper like the *Times*, with a commitment to opening up some extra space and giving me help on excerpting text, and even with a colleague on the environmental beat to whom I could farm out the Endangered Species Act case, this was pressing the limits of the possible. The Court had issued no opinions at all on the preceding two days, a Tuesday and Wednesday. Perhaps none of these decisions was ready for release until Thursday morning. Perhaps, as I suspect, there was a lack of desire on the Justices' part to interrupt their mornings earlier in the week by going on the bench to announce those opinions that were ready.

That closing day was relatively easy compared with some others. The last day of the 1987–1988 Term was a journalistic nightmare that has attained the status of legend. The Court issued nine decisions that filled 446 pages in the United States Reports, including a number of important cases and one, the decision that upheld the independent counsel statute, of landmark significance.

I once mentioned this problem to Chief Justice Rehnquist, suggesting the Court make a greater effort to spread out the decision announcements in the last weeks of the Term. He received my suggestion cordially and made a counterproposal of his own. "Just because we announce them all on one day doesn't mean you have to write about them all on one day," he said. "Why don't you save some for the next day?" On one level, this was harmless, and cost-free, banter. On another, it offered a dramatic illustration of the gulf between us. It appeared to me that the Chief Justice understood my comment to be a form of journalist's special interest pleading. My point, rather, was that the decisions would all be reported on the day they were released in any event, and that a slight change in the Court's management of its calendar could substantially increase the odds that the decisions would be reported well, or at least better—an improvement the Court might see as serving its own interest as well as the interest of the press.

. . .

CONCLUSION

One recent book about Supreme Court journalism ... concluded that the Court has developed an elaborate apparatus to keep itself mysterious and remote, thus maintaining "public deference and compliance." In the view of the author, political scientist Richard Davis, "the press is a public relations tool for the Court specifically for the task of reinforcing deference toward its decisions." That is not the Court and not the press corps I have observed for these last eighteen years. Rather, I see a Court that is quite blithely oblivious to the needs of those who convey its work to the outside world, and a press corps that is often groping along in the dark, trying to make sense out of the shadows on the cave wall. . . .

Is there a model for press-Court interaction that would serve the needs of both and, ultimately, lead to greater public understanding of the Court? A story from long ago offers a starting point for looking ahead. In 1932, following his retirement, Justice Oliver Wendell Holmes received a letter of congratulations and gratitude from a journalist to whom, sixteen years earlier, he had extended a hand in an hour of great journalistic need. As the letter writer, George Garner of the *Manufacturers Record* in Baltimore, recounted the incident to Justice Holmes, Mr. Garner had been a young Washington reporter for the *Louisville Courier–Journal* when he found himself suddenly assigned to report on an opinion by the Justice. Not knowing where else to turn, he presented himself late in the afternoon at the Justice's home. Mr. Garner's letter (referring to both himself and his addressee in the third person) described their meeting:

> Called to the door, Justice Holmes explained to the correspondent that he was entertaining guests at tea and might not very well desert them; but, if the scribe would drop around later, he would be glad to help. Then, spontaneously: "No; come upstairs with me now, and we'll go over it." For an hour, this Justice of the Supreme Court of the United States patiently and clearly spelled out the story to the scribe, literally dictating much of the article in newspaper language. It ran, as one recalls, a couple of columns in the *Courier–Journal* and was esteemed as a clear and intelligible newspaper story. Never has the correspondent forgotten that great kindness and courtesy by Justice Holmes. Often he has related it to friends.

I obviously could not offer this charming and quaint episode as a model for today; for one thing, Mr. Garner's need for emergency assistance reflected an ignorance of the Court's docket and a lack of preparation that I certainly do not advocate on the part of the Supreme Court press corps. Nor should busy Justices be expected to interrupt tea parties or other endeavors to give a helping hand to what would soon become an endless stream of deadline-panicked journalists.

But neither is this incident completely irrelevant. It reflects, on the part of Justice Holmes, an openness and a willingness to step out of the institutional role that would be quite unthinkable under similar circumstances today. There is a loss there, surely.

It is clear that the interests of the press and the Court can never be consonant. To cite just one example, it would greatly simplify my life if, in addition to receiving the weekly conference list of new petitions for certiorari that are ready for the Justices' action, I could also see the "discuss list" of those cases ... that are the only actual candidates for a grant of cert. Yet I cannot imagine the Court permitting press access to the discuss list, for the reason that all of the cases not on the discuss list would thereby be publicly identified, in advance, as "cert. denied" in all but name.

Yet despite our divergent interests—the press corp's interest in accessibility and information, the Court's in protecting the integrity of its decisional process—I ... think of these two institutions as, to some degree, partners in a mutual democratic enterprise to which both must acknowledge responsibility. The responsibility of the press is to commit the resources necessary to give the public the most accurate and contextual reporting possible about the Court, its work, its members, and its relationship with other branches of government. The Court's responsibility is to remove unnecessary obstacles to accomplishing that task.

I recognize that the word "unnecessary" assumes shared premises that may simply not exist. Nevertheless, it should be easy to define some practices, such as ... the refusal to space opinions during a given week, as unnecessary.... I do not expect the impossible. I simply propose a mutual journey of self-examination from which the press, the Court, and, ultimately, the public can only benefit.

Questions and Comments

1. Given how much is publicly known and available about oral argument—including what are now daily transcripts, and occasional permission to audiotape particular cases—how much more information would allowing cameras in the courtroom provide to the public about oral argument? about the Court?

2. Should Congress act to require cameras in the courtroom? Would such a statute raise separation of powers problems?

3. In Chandler v. Florida, 449 U.S. 560 (1981), the Court clarified that its earlier decision in Estes v. Texas, 381 U.S. 532 (1965), did not necessarily preclude television broadcasts of trial court proceedings.[25] A student note,

25. In *Estes*, the Court reversed a conviction, following a state court trial in which broadcast media had been obtrusively present in the courtroom, as a violation of due process rights to a fair trial. In *Chandler*, however, the Court rejected any per se rule concerning the constitutionality of broadcast media in the courtroom. It noted that due to technological changes, "many of the negative factors found in *Estes*—cumbersome equipment, cables, distracting lighting, numerous camera technicians—are less substantial factors today than they were at that time." 449 U.S. at

relying on *Chandler* and on the Court's acknowledgment in other cases of the electronic media's valuable role in providing public information about law and the justice system,[26] accuses the Court of inconsistency in not allowing cameras in its own public courtroom. See Todd Piccus, *Demystifying the Least Understood Branch: Opening the Supreme Court to Broadcast Media*, 71 Tex. L. Rev. 1053, 1068 (1993) ("If [in *Chandler*], the Supreme Court can permit vulnerable lay persons—including jurors, witnesses, victims, and defendants—to be placed in front of an unblinking and unforgiving camera lens, then how can the Justices, who 'are supposed to be men [and women] of fortitude, able to thrive in a hearty climate,' rationalize maintaining the broadcast ban in their own courtroom?"). Are there any differences between the Supreme Court, its role or its members, and the state and federal trial court benches, that justify the absence of cameras from the Supreme Court? Or would you agree with the student note that the absence of jurors, laypersons, and witnesses shows that the Court is unjustified in continuing to ban broadcast media in its courtroom?

4. Based on your readings, do you agree with Professor Whitman's assessment about the relatively small role of oral argument? About the possibility of misleading the public by televising oral argument? Or with Justice Scalia's view that the public lacks capacity to understand and evaluate the Court's work?

5. After reading Greenhouse's description of the relations between the Court and the press, were you inclined to credit or reject the position she attributes to Professor Davis, that " 'the press is a public relations tool for the Court specifically for the task of reinforcing deference towards its decisions.' "?

6. To what extent, if any, does the Court's judicial independence and impartiality depend on its members not being seen, and not seeing themselves, as public celebrities? On whether the media identifies judges or justices primarily by the political party of the President who appoints them?

7. Are there other approaches the Court should consider to improve public knowledge and awareness of the Court? Off the record press briefings after opinions issues? Spacing out the issuance of opinions at the end of the term? Can any of those approaches constitutionally be required by legislation enacted by the Congress?

576. Rather than a per se rule banning broadcast of trials, a case-by-case inquiry was required, in which "a defendant has the right on review to show that the media's coverage of his case—printed or broadcast—compromised the ability of the jury to judge him fairly [or, alternatively, to] show that broadcast coverage of his particular case had an adverse impact on the trial participants sufficient to constitute a denial of due process." *Id*. at 581. The Court found neither showing had been made in *Chandler* and upheld the conviction.

26. See, e.g., Richmond Newspapers v. Virginia, 448 U.S. 555, 572–73 (1980) ("Instead of acquiring information about trials by firsthand observation or by word of mouth from those who attended, people now acquire it chiefly through the print and electronic media. In a sense, this validates the media claim of functioning as surrogates for the public. While media representatives enjoy the same right of access as the public, they often are provided special seating and priority of entry so that they may report what people in attendance have seen and heard. This 'contribute[s] to public understanding of the rule of law and to comprehension of the functioning of the entire criminal justice system. . . .' [citation omitted]").

2.   Secrecy and Internal Deliberations

In Chapter Five, above, we introduced the debate over the ethical propriety of law clerk revelations about internal decision-making processes. As this section discusses, controversy has also arisen about the Justices' dispositions of their private papers.

In the first reading, Alexandra Wigdor provides a historical overview both of secrecy in deliberation, which she links to John Marshall's efforts to issue a single opinion for the Court, and of the treatment of the Justices' working papers. As she describes, until the mid-twentieth century there was some tradition that the papers should be destroyed, a tradition that has been changing. The debate about the appropriate disposition of the Justices' papers, she suggests, involves conflicts between different views of the need for judicial independence and public accountability, and even different jurisprudential understandings of the process of constitutional adjudication.

In 1993, provoked by the outcry over what many believed to be a premature release by the Library of Congress of Justice Thurgood Marshall's papers,[27] the Senate Subcommittee on Regulation and Government Information held hearings addressed to three issues—first, whether Justices' papers should ever be made public; second, if their papers are to be made public, when this should occur; and third, who should make these decisions. This was not the first time these issues had been considered. Chief Justice Warren Burger had appointed a committee to review these issues twenty years earlier.[28] The issues were explored in 1977 by the National Study Commission on Records and Documents of Federal Officials, a commission established by Congress and chaired by former Attorney General Brownell. The Commission— whose report formed the basis for the Presidential Records Act of 1978[29] —recommended that a Justice's working papers be made public property, and that public access be allowed fifteen years after the Justice leaves

---

27.   Compare Louis Michael Seidman, *A Modest Proposal for Solving the Marshall Mystery,* Legal Times, June 7, 1993, at 28, with Susan Low Bloch & Vicki Jackson, *The Marshall Papers: The Library (and Our Colleague) Got It Wrong,* Legal Times, June 14, 1993. According to the *New York Times,* Chief Justice Rehnquist also criticized the Library of Congress for the early release of the papers. Editorial, *Thurgood Marshall is Heard Again,* N.Y. Times, May 28, 1993, at A28 ("The Chief Justice—speaking, he said, for a majority of the nine active justices— berated the library for alleged bad judgment in using the broad discretion given by Justice Marshall to grant unusually generous and early public access.").

28.   See E. Barrett Prettyman, Jr. & Allen R. Snyder, *Breaching Secrecy at the Supreme Court—An Institutional or Individual Decision,* Legal Times, June 12,

1978, at 6 (describing Chief Justice Burger's appointing a committee soon after he became Chief Justice, noting its recommendation to adopt restrictions on the release of Court-related files, and lamenting the ultimate failure of the Court ever to act on the recommendation). Evidently, the Chief Justice had hoped (but was to be disappointed) that the committee would recommend a Court rule to require the Justices to destroy their conference notes upon their deaths. Del Dickson, ed., *The Supreme Court in Conference (1940–1985): The Private Discussions Behind Nearly 300 Supreme Court Decisions* 16–17 (2001).

29.   Presidential Records Act of 1978, 44 U.S.C. §§ 2201–2207 (1978). The Court rejected constitutional challenges to this Act in Nixon v. Administrator of General Services, 433 U.S. 425 (1977).

the Court.[30] Notwithstanding Congress' adoption of the Commission's proposals with respect to presidential papers, nothing was done to implement the recommendations concerning Supreme Court documents.

One of the key witnesses before the Senate Subcommittee hearings in 1993 was E. Barrett Prettyman, Jr., a private practitioner who clerked for the Court and has been concerned with this issue for years. In testimony excerpted below, he suggested that Justices' papers should be made public but only twenty-five years after the death of the particular Justice. As to what institution should make this decision, Prettyman prefers that the judiciary make it but believes, based on past experience, that no such consensus exists on the Court and therefore suggests that Congress can, and should, mandate such a rule. After Mr. Prettyman's testimony, note the letter by Chief Justice Rehnquist in which he, speaking on behalf of the Court, both declines the Senate's invitation to testify at the hearing and then warns the Senators not to consider legislation in this area. Note also that he does not promise any action by the Court itself. And, to date no formal action has been taken by either the Court or the Congress.

After reading all this, consider what should happen in this area. Who should act and how? Should the Court be able to control access to its proceedings and papers in any manner it chooses? Should the individual Justices be free to decide what to do with their papers? Or should Congress make these decisions? To what extent will new technology, including the Internet and e-mail, make these problems easier or harder to solve?

Alexandra K. Wigdor,[31] *The Personal Papers of Supreme Court Justices: A Descriptive Guide* **3–19 (1986)**

Past Practice and Current Attitudes Toward the Preservation of Judicial Collections

Justices of the Supreme Court and judges of the lower federal courts have traditionally treated the papers they create for their own use as a species of personal property, protected by and alienable according to the laws of private property. Insofar as the chambers files of judges are preserved in research institutions—and the trend for Supreme Court collections is certainly in that direction—they reside there as the gift or loan of judges, their heirs or executors, or by purchase.

A judge's chambers files often contain two kinds of materials: 1) working papers, by which is meant all the papers generated in the course of rendering decisions, including conference notes, notes exchanged

30. Final Report of the National Study Commission on Records and Documents of Federal Officials, (March 31, 1977).

31. Wigdor was at the time of this book with the National Research Council. She received her BA and MA from the University of Missouri.

between judges or justices, bench notes, draft opinions, research notes, law clerks' memoranda, docket books, notes of conversations, and certiorari memoranda; and 2) private papers, including correspondence with family, friends, and professional colleagues, . . . private financial papers, and personal diaries.

The history of the preservation and disposition of the papers of Justices of the Supreme Court and of lower court judges has been governed by the preferences of individual members of the bench and their families and by the availability of repositories to receive collections. Until the emergence of manuscript repositories in the twentieth century, the principal custodians of such papers were families and private collectors, which made for a high probability of irretrievable dispersal and chance destruction.

. . .

Two factors unique to the judiciary have affected the content and survival of the chambers files of Supreme Court Justices. The first of these is the fact that the Supreme Court is a court of record. According to the practice of common-law courts, certain kinds of materials were retained as the record of the official acts of the Court. . . . [T]he existence of a clearly defined official record seems to have discouraged the preservation of the preliminary working materials. Until recent decades, most Supreme Court Justices have not placed any great value upon such materials. The William Howard Taft Papers, for example, one of the largest and most valuable collections among the holdings of the Library of Congress, contain very little in the way of judicial working papers, but virtually everything concerning the presidency. The great value of the Taft papers for the Court years lies in the voluminous correspondence files, for Taft frequently discussed important cases, his fellow Justices, and the decision-making process with numerous correspondents.

The responses to a questionnaire sent by the Public Documents Commission in August 1976 to all members of the federal judiciary except Justices of the Supreme Court indicate that this attitude is still very prevalent among lower court judges. Almost 80 percent of the 369 respondents reported that they had made no plans to place their personal papers in a research institution. . . .

The second factor affecting the content of judicial collections is the tradition of judicial secrecy, which was firmly established by the Marshall Court. The felt necessity to protect the confidentiality of the Court has been so pervasive that, until recently, judges have tended to destroy their working papers. Herbert A. Johnson, editor of the Papers of John Marshall, reports that no substantial amount of material concerning Marshall's actual work on the bench exists, and has offered the opinion that the habit of destroying working papers and conference notes was established early in the Court's history.

Attitudes toward the Supreme Court and toward the appropriate means of ensuring the confidentiality of judicial proceedings have changed dramatically in recent decades, as the existence of the Murphy, Burton, Frankfurter, Brennan, and other collections of working papers and judicial correspondence indicates.[32] Yet the tradition of secrecy with its attendant assumptions has had such an impact on the content and survival of judicial papers as to merit some discussion.

JUDICIAL SECRECY IN HISTORICAL PERSPECTIVE

The tradition of judicial secrecy is rooted in the procedures and conventions of the Marshall Court and may, in large part, be attributed to the personal influence and particular political vision of its Chief. . . .

Marshall, it will be remembered, was appointed Chief Justice late in the administration of the Federalist President, John Adams, and remained to carry into the decades of Republican ascendancy the nationalist principles of that otherwise shattered party. Marshall was motivated by three major concerns: the prestige of the Supreme Court; the supremacy of the national government; and the authority of law. These concerns are reflected not only in the famous opinions that went far to establish the bases of our constitutional system, but in the procedure for judicial decision-making that he established immediately upon assuming leadership of the Court.

Marshall convinced his brethren on the bench of the novel proposition that the Court should speak with a single voice. . . .

. . .

The Justices of the early Supreme Court lived together in a boarding house during the term and shared meals in a common dining room. They discussed current cases not only in conference, but also in the informal atmosphere of the parlor. Marshall's ability to encourage uniformity of opinion and to ensure for the most part that that opinion would be in the direction of a nationalist explication of the Constitution was greatly enhanced by the physical closeness of the Justices during term. He was very upset at Justice Johnson's decision to live apart from the group in 1831, fearing that separate living quarters would lead to seriatim opinions.

Chief Justice Marshall's system ultimately triumphed so completely that his predilections came to be viewed as the necessities of our constitutional system. . . . [Yet] Thomas Jefferson, whose political adherents and descendants controlled the popular branches of government during the period of Marshall's tenure on the Court, was violently opposed to judicial secrecy. It reflected, he complained, an elitist political

---

32. [Editors' Note: Hugo Black, however, reportedly directed the destruction of his extensive conference notes. He did so in part because of his unhappiness over Alpheus Mason's biography of Harlan Fiske Stone, which was written from internal papers and portrayed Stone as disliking Black, and second, over the mis-reading of Justice Burtons' conference notes by a political scientist who incorrectly asserted that Black had initially proposed to reaffirm *Plessy* in *Brown*. Del Dickson, *The Supreme Court in Conference (1940–1985)*, supra, at 17. It is also reported that Justice White had a similar reaction to the release of Thurgood Marshall's papers within a few months of his death, destroying his own conference notes in response. *Id.* at 18.]

theory. Marshall and his Federalist colleagues wanted to keep government and law remote from the people, inaccessible to the popular will.

. . .

In 1822, disturbed by a series of Supreme Court decisions that both expanded federal powers and asserted federal judicial review of state laws and judicial decisions (*McCulloch v. Maryland*, the *Dartmouth College Case*, and *Cohens v. Virginia*, among others), the aged Jefferson struck up a correspondence with Justice William Johnson, whom he had appointed to the Supreme Court in 1804. In this correspondence Jefferson attacked not only the constitutional interpretation of the Marshall Court but its instrumentation through the novel procedures that Marshall had brought to the Court. Jefferson reminded Johnson that, with the exception of Mansfield's Court, English judges had always rendered their opinions seriatim. He suspected that Mansfield's novel practice "... of making up opinions in secret and delivering them as the Oracles of the Court, in mass," had been introduced into America after the Revolution by Mansfield's great admirer, Edmund Pendleton, of the Court of Appeals in Virginia. Whether inspired by Mansfield, Pendleton, or some other source, Marshall had introduced the single opinion, contrary to the main body of English and American tradition, into the practice of the Supreme Court.

Jefferson opposed judicial secrecy and the single opinion on two grounds: it contradicted the fundamental republican principle of responsible government; and it implied a false simplicity in judicial decision-making.

Since Justices are appointed for life and not subject to popular control through the ballot, Jefferson explained, their sole constraints are the threat of impeachment and concern for their reputation. Secret opinions destroy both constraints, for no one could know who had written an opinion that constituted an impeachable offense, or indeed whether "the lazy or incompetent justice" had bothered to make up an opinion at all.

Jefferson applauded the system of seriatim opinion-giving because it threw greater light on difficult subjects, it was more educative, and it showed whether the judges were unanimous or divided, thus giving more or less weight to the decision as a precedent. In Jefferson's view, the Marshall Court, although it had decided cases of tremendous gravity and difficulty, rendering decisions that were offensive to large sectors of the community, deprived the citizenry of the chance to consider other opinions. The authority of law so produced, Jefferson felt, was hollow.

In a later letter to Johnson, Jefferson warned:

> The very idea of cooking up opinions in conclave, begets suspicions that something passes which fears the public ear, and this, spreading by degrees, must produce at some time abridgement of tenure, facility of removal, or some other modification which may promise a remedy.

Justice Johnson responded favorably to Jefferson's plea for a return to seriatim opinions. He wrote to Jefferson that he had decided to register his opinion in all big cases, and he did so .... [But, when] he dared to deliver a dissenting opinion, he

> ... heard nothing but Lectures on the Indecency of Judges cutting at each other, and the Loss of Reputation which the Virginia appellate Court had sustained by pursuing such a Course.

The seriatim mode was not reestablished, although the judges on two occasions, in 1805 and 1806, took advantage of Marshall's absence to deliver their opinions seriatim. But Justice Johnson did, during his early years on the Court, break the Chief Justice's monopoly on delivering the opinion of the Court, and managed through the years to win grudging acceptance of the practice of dissent.

Johnson, however, did not agree with Jefferson that the whole process of reaching a decision should be open to public scrutiny. The confidentiality of the conference must be maintained, he felt,

> ... for I do verily believe that there is no Body of Men, legislative, judicial or executive, who could preserve the public Respect for a single year, if the public Eye were permitted always to look behind the Curtain.... I never met with but one Man who could absolutely leave his Vanity and Weakness at home!

. . .

Jefferson called a judiciary independent of the will of the people in a republic a "solecism." He voiced the traditional republican suspicion of unrestrained power and called for specific measures to make judicial power responsive to the people. Jefferson understood judicial accountability to extend to the substance of a judge's opinions as well as a judge's behavior, for he considered the people themselves to be the ultimate interpreters of the Constitution. He sought to reestablish judicial accountability by suggesting at various times the legislative instrument of impeachment; removal by the President on the request of both houses of Congress; institution of a six-year term with the possibility of reappointment by the President with the approval of both houses of Congress; joint remonstrances in Congress against unconstitutional decisions, which would lead the states to block execution within their borders of those decisions; and of course, a return to seriatim argument.

Jefferson and those of a similar persuasion ... were the partisans of a lost and now largely forgotten cause.... By the end of the nineteenth century, the Supreme Court had attained the pinnacle of prestige and power, far removed from popular control, and, some felt, from popular concerns. Marshall's reputation was virtually unassailable.

. . .

Since the 1920s, however, there has been significant questioning of robism and the traditions of judicial secrecy, first on a jurisprudential and later on a functional level.

Mechanical jurisprudence, as the dominant nineteenth-century legal philosophy came to be called by its detractors, posited law as a closed system containing fixed principles of certain application. Legal precepts were considered to be the reasoned extrapolation of the accumulated experience of humankind. In effect, the mechanical jurist reduced all legal problems to a series of assumptions and applied those assumptions in accordance with their internal logic. The premise contained the conclusion within itself. As Roscoe Pound, a major early twentieth-century critic defined it, mechanical jurisprudence was "the rigorous logical deduction from predetermined conceptions in disregard of and often in the teeth of the actual facts."

Mechanical jurisprudence was complemented by assumptions about the role and the status of judges that critics have since labeled the "Cult of the Robe." If the law was seen as a set of universals floating far above the mundane battle of competing interests, so the judge was understood to be a disinterested law finder, the living symbol of an abstract impersonal justice. Judicial secrecy was an essential element in sustaining the assumptions of judicial neutrality, decisional certainty, and the rule of law.

In the 1920s and 1930s, the legal realists, drawing upon the insights of pragmatism, sociological jurisprudence, the ideas of Oliver Wendell Holmes, and the example of Louis D. Brandeis, launched a many-sided attack upon mechanical jurisprudence and its attendant assumptions about the status and function of judges. Skepticism lay at the core of legal realism. The realists were suspicious of all quests for first principles. The most commonly shared suspicion among the realists was "rule-skepticism," which Karl Llewellyn defined as the "distrust of the theory that traditional prescriptive rule-formulations are the heavily operative factor in producing court decisions." The rules of law, said the realists, are inadequate descriptions of the realities of law, and their prominence in published judicial opinions often obscures more basic determinants of judicial decision-making.

The emerging discipline of sociology led the realists to study law in terms of its environment. Psychology encouraged the reevaluation of legal decision-making. Realists argued that traditional legal thinking began with conclusions rather than premises, and that lawyers undertook the search for relevant principles only as a final ritualistic gesture.

The legal realists wanted to clear away the layers of secrecy and myth surrounding law and lawmakers. They called for functional analysis rather than speculative thinking, and talked much of facts and consequences and the difference between "paper rules" and "real rules." Their examination of the judicial process replaced the analysis of rules with the study of behavior. The realists looked at judges—and asked judges to look at themselves—not as impersonal and impartial vehicles of judgment, but as people like all others with class affiliations, economic interests, and social assumptions. The realists called for judicial introspection and the analysis of unspoken assumptions as a first step in bringing the law and its administrators into tune with the needs of modern society....

... The legal realists focused scholarly attention on the judicial process. Realism, as two recent commentators put it, "is an effort to find out how the law in operation, as contrasted to the law on the books, is working." This impulse can be seen along the whole spectrum of current research on the American judiciary, for example: behavioralist studies, with their emphasis on the prediction of decisions; projects like the University of Chicago studies of the operation of the jury system; and the new style of judicial biography ushered in by A.T. Mason's Harlan Fiske Stone: Pillar of Law (1956).

It is within this larger framework that the heightened interest in the working papers and correspondence of members of the judiciary must be viewed.

While "piercing the curtain" of judicial secrecy has by no means lost its controversial aspects, the interest of scholars in understanding the process of judicial decision-making has been complemented by the willingness of many Supreme Court Justices and a number of prominent federal judges to make available for research the manuscript evidence of their labors. Justice Frankfurter was very much concerned that the public understand the Supreme Court if it were to retain its respect for law. To understand the Court, he wrote, it is necessary to understand both what manner of men make it up, and to know about the "private rehearsals ... behind the impenetrable draperies of judicial secrecy," which tell much more about the individual and the group than the public performance remotely reveals. Although Frankfurter objected to certain features of Mason's biography of Stone, his objections did not prevent him from donating his extensive collections of personal and Court papers to the Library of Congress and the Harvard Law School.

Despite ambivalence, and in some cases outright rejection, the trend in recent decades has been for Supreme Court Justices to create, preserve, and ultimately donate to a manuscript library large collections of papers including both correspondence and case files.

CURRENT VIEWS ON BALANCING THE NEEDS OF
THE COURT AND THE PUBLIC INTEREST

In the course of its study, the Public Documents Commission communicated with a large number of scholars who have used collections of personal papers to supplement the official record of the Court. These scholars were unanimously of the opinion that such collections are of immense value in understanding the judiciary and the law.... Several made the point that more than the written opinion is required if one is interested in the judicial process or in the behavioral aspects of judicial decision-making.

There is, however, a certain amount of ambivalence as to the propriety of using these materials and producing the kinds of studies they make possible. If the myths and symbols surrounding the Supreme

Court are now recognized as such, still they are justified in some quarters on the grounds of functional legitimacy.

A number of arguments have been advanced for maintaining a cloak of secrecy around the judicial process. These include the need to uphold the authority of law, the need to protect the interplay of ideas preceding collective judgment, and the need to secure judicial independence within the tripartite structure of government and, given the distinctive political tasks of the Supreme Court, in the face of popular pressure.

While readily admitting that the Blackstonian concept has many shortcomings as a description of reality, Paul Mishkin, a well-known legal scholar, defends the "declaratory theory" precisely because it expresses a symbolic concept of the judicial process upon which, he feels, much of our courts' prestige and power, and, therefore, the authority of legal decisions depend. There is, Mishkin has written,

> ... a strongly held and deeply felt belief that judges are bound by a body of fixed, overriding law, that they apply that law impersonally as well as impartially, that they exercise no individual choice and have no program of their own to advance.

Mishkin emphasizes the central role of symbol and myth in cementing the social bonds. He argues that a tremendous loss would occur if judges could not appeal to "the law" or "the Constitution" to justify their decisions. He recognizes ... the political element in Supreme Court decision-making, but sees in the Court's political tasks a functional justification of secrecy. Because the Court must decide matters of major public concern, and because its decisions will often be very unpopular with certain sectors of the community, it needs the shield of secrecy and symbol to operate effectively.

Other commentators have stressed the damaging effects of breaching the tradition of confidentiality upon the collegial functioning of the Supreme Court and the United States Courts of Appeals. In his 1957 review of Alpheus T. Mason's biography of Harlan Fiske Stone—the first judicial study to be based primarily upon judicial working papers, correspondence, and intra-court communications—Edmond Cahn expressed a widely held feeling of concern about this "unprecedented" breach of confidentiality. "If the present trend continues," he wrote, "our lecherous curiosity may produce nine bitter adversaries instead of a Supreme Court." This reaction may now seem a bit overheated, but the publication of *The Brethren* a few years ago rekindled such anxieties.

One of the participants in the *Buffalo Symposium on Secrecy*[33] suggested another possible problem with the current interest in going beyond the printed opinion to study the inner workings of the judicial process. How can we be sure, he asks, without creating some sort of massive waste retrieval system, that the whole decisional picture has

---

33. [Editors' Note: The spring 1973 edition of the Buffalo Law Review presented a symposium addressed to "Piercing the Red Velour Curtain," and included articles by Eugene Gressman, Arthur S. Miller, D.S. Sastri, and J. Woodford Howard. See 22 Buffalo Law Review 799 (Spring 1973).]

been reconstructed. Even the complete decisional file of one judge will reflect but a partial understanding of how a particular decision was reached. And if the mass of material contained in a judge's working files is made available to outsiders, "who is to decide what is relevant . . . ?" A number of responses to the questionnaire the Public Documents Commission sent to federal judges echoed the latter concern.

What might be called the Jeffersonian position in the discussion of myths, symbols, and secrecy was advanced by Professors Arthur S. Miller and D.S. Sastri in the *Buffalo Symposium on Secrecy*. They argued that democratic theory requires that the citizenry know not only who governs, but how policy decisions are made. In order to effect such openness in the federal court system, the writers suggested a return to open deliberation of cases in court. They expressed the opinion that the secrecy of the Supreme Court's conference cannot be successfully defended on functional grounds. "It came into existence at a time when the Court was a weak, infant institution . . . ," which has long since ceased to be the case. Secrecy, Miller and Sastri conclude, is neither a universal nor a necessary practice. Public conference would make possible a fuller understanding of the Supreme Court, and thereby improve the process of judicial policy-making. It would, moreover, advance the ideal of the accountability of public officials in a democratic society.

Between the extremes of complete secrecy and immediate disclosure during the decisional process itself is the more frequently held position that the privilege of present confidentiality should be accompanied by the responsibility of eventual disclosure. Professor J. Woodford Howard contributed an articulate exposition of this position to the *Buffalo Symposium on Secrecy*. The robist contention that secrecy produces a mystique that is the basis of the Court's power, he acknowledged, was a Platonic lie, compatible with neither the republican nor the nationalist traditions of American jurisprudence; but Howard advanced some compelling arguments for the proposition that secret deliberations are functionally necessary both to the effective working of the judicial system and to the just adjudication of causes. "One need only," he wrote, "imagine the financial windfalls of leaks in the *Penn Central Merger*, not to mention the political uproar surrounding open deliberations in *Brown v. Board of Education*," to grasp the continuing importance of preventing premature disclosure and protecting the independence of judges. (The "Impeach Warren" campaigns of the 1950s might also be adduced in defense of using confidentiality to protect the independence of judges.)

Howard also discussed the importance of secret deliberations in permitting the ripening of judgment. If not forced to take a public stand on an issue under consideration, appellate judges can more readily avail themselves of the benefits of collegial discussion and thoughtful compromise. He pointed out that many of the recent judicial collections—those of Stone, Frankfurter, Murphy, and Burton—reveal vigorous discussions among Justices, the development of ideas, and, on occasion, complete changes of mind. There would, Howard feels, be small opportunity for this process to take place in a system that allowed immediate or premature disclosure.

Howard proposed one final reason for the efficacy of secret deliberations, this one based on the policy-making aspects of appellate judicial decision-making. Confidential deliberations allow judges to test out the implications of their ideas and thereby avoid "cutting too broad a legislative swath."

Against these positive values of judicial secrecy, Howard wrote, must be balanced the risks involved when power is exercised unseen—risks of corruption, impropriety, and irrationality. His opinion is that the balance will be well met if judges accept the responsibility of "ultimate exposure at the bar of history":

> ... the judicial papers of deceased Justices should be left to the public, preferably in public depositories like the Library of Congress, under reasonable restrictions as to laws of libel, state secrets, and passage of time to prevent intrusion in the Court's current functioning.

Whatever their views on judicial secrecy, many commentators are opposed to any abridgement of the property rights traditionally exercised by judges with respect to their working papers and court-related correspondence. Some of the scholars whose work depends upon such materials take this position and are concerned that any radical changes in the system will dry up what in recent decades have become tremendously valuable sources of information about judges and the judicial process. They stress instead the desirability of strengthening the present voluntaristic system through education and various incentives. At least one federal judge, however, would carry Howard's reasoning to its logical conclusion. The Hon. J. Skelly Wright, of the U.S. Court of Appeals for the District of Columbia, wrote to the Public Documents Commission in 1976:

> It would seem obvious that any papers and other materials which are generated by persons on the public payroll, working in government offices, doing the government's business, should belong to the government and should not be the private property of the head of the office or of the person or persons in the office who contributed to their preparation. It would seem further that any memoranda, tapes, and drafts generated in the production of such documents or other materials for the same reasons should also be the property of the United States. In short, if the government paid the cost of production of the papers or other materials they should belong to the government.

Public Papers of Supreme Court Justices: Assuring Preservation and Access, Hearing Before the Subcomm. on Regulation and Gov't Information, S. Comm. on Governmental Affairs, 103d Cong., 1st Sess., 18–19 (1993) (testimony of E. Barrett Prettyman, Jr.)

MR. PRETTYMAN....

Some 15 years ago, my partner, Allen Snyder and I wrote an article that dealt with this precise problem. . . .[34]

. . .

And in this article, we pointed out that it was Chief Justice Burger's view . . . that all conference notes and other personal papers ought to be destroyed. It was his experience, both on the Circuit Court and as Chief Justice, that these notes were very misleading in the sense that these notes often were in conflict with each other and did not often accurately reflect what had actually gone on at conference.

And it was our point that if one Justice's papers were to be preserved, all of them should receive the same treatment. An example we gave then . . . is equally applicable today[.] . . . Justice Black . . . had his conference notes destroyed, whereas Justice Burton kept very extensive notes, and his were made immediately open to the public upon his death, so that in researching a book like [Richard Kluger's] "Simple Justice," on the case of *Brown v. Board of Education*, the researcher would go when he or she wanted to find out what Justice Black thought not to Justice Black's notes, which were then non-existent, but rather to Justice Burton's notes to find out what Justice Black thought.

And it has since been revealed . . . that, in fact, Justice Black thought that Justice Burton's notes were not wholly reliable.

So what we suggested in the article was that preferably the Court, but if not that, then Congress should perhaps address this problem and try to get some system that was applicable to all. Unfortunately, that has not happened. The Court has, as I understand it, tried to address this problem, has not gotten agreement among the Justices, and consequently . . . while I have absolutely no inside information of any kind, it is my hunch that perhaps the Court would welcome a Congressional statute dealing with this problem, so long as—and this is extremely important— . . . the statute did not trench upon the inner workings of the Court[.] . . . By that I mean making papers available so early, either upon the death of the Justice or too soon thereafter, that, in fact, you learn what is going on right now in regard to cases that may have begun, had their progeny back some years before.

I use an example in my [written] testimony of a note which has been found in the Marshall papers, a memo by Justice Souter, in which he writes his views about the retroactivity of rulings on the constitutionality of State taxes.[35]

34. [Editors' Note: Mr. Prettyman, a former law clerk to Justices Jackson, Frankfurter and Harlan, and a well-known attorney in Washington D.C., was referring to an article in *The Legal Times of Washington* (June 12, 1978, p. 6), cited above in note 28].

35. [Editors' Note: Mr. Prettyman is here referring to a March 1991 memo by Justice Souter in which he writes to his colleagues, " 'I am disposed to preserve the judicial option to rule purely prospectively' if the alternative is a crushing financial blow to government." Paul M. Barrett, *Marshall's Files Offer Businesses Hint on Justices*, The Wall Street Journal, B1, B2, reproduced in the 1993 Hearing on Public Papers of Supreme Court Justices, cited above, at pp. 112–13.]

My own view is that this revelation is unfair to Justice Souter, whose views may be developing, and could be misleading to litigants who rely upon it, and that in any event, even if it accurately reflects the Justice's views, it provides an unfair advantage to those of us who live and work in Washington and have easy access to these papers, as opposed to someone in Montana or California who does not.

Consequently, I think that making papers immediately available works much mischief. I would suggest that if any attempt by Congress is made to deal with the problem, that it first of all deal with all papers in the same way, and secondly that if it Federalizes, if you will, the papers, that it makes them available to the public only after they have indeed become history.

And while I recognize that even historians would not agree perhaps as to when a piece of paper has become history, I think something on the order of 25 years. That may be a little long. But in my [written] testimony, I give examples of papers which, if they had been made available at the time that the Presidential Act applied some 12 years ago, would reveal papers that very much affected ongoing cases before the Court today.

So I would hope that the Court itself would act in the light of this most recent incident with Justice Marshall's papers. But if after a period goes by and the Court has once again failed to act, that the Congress at least look seriously toward a statute which would not intrude upon the ongoing deliberations of the Court, which would respect the fact that these papers do deal not only with the personal views of the Justices, but views that are extraordinarily important, the ongoing evolution of cases before the Court and that, as I say, then treat all of the papers in the same manner.

. . .

SENATOR LIEBERMAN. Thank you, Mr. Prettyman. Your statement is an excellent one.

. . . I would say for the record and for those who are in the room and may be watching across the country on television that you have an extraordinary record, having clerked for three Supreme Court Justices, written a book on the Court [and] brought almost 20 cases before the Court. . . . So you come to these questions with some experience, and we thank you for that. . . .

Letter of Chief Justice William Rehnquist to Senator Joseph Lieberman, June 7, 1993[36]

Supreme Court of the United States
Washington D.C. 20543

CHAMBERS OF THE CHIEF JUSTICE

June 7, 1993

The Honorable Joseph I. Lieberman
Chairman
Subcommittee on Regulation and Government Information
United States Senate
Washington, D.C. 20510–0703

Dear Mr. Chairman,

My colleagues and I have discussed at Conference your letter of June 1st which was sent to each of us. They have each requested that I respond on their behalf as well as my own. We recognize the importance of the issues into which your Subcommittee will be inquiring, and regret that we are unable to either appear personally on Friday, June 11th, or furnish any detailed response to your questions. We have our usual Friday Conference scheduled for June 11th, and the month of June is traditionally one of our busiest because it is then that we try to wind up the Court's business for the current term.

Even with the limited time available to us, however, we have no hesitancy in expressing the opinion that legislation addressed to the issues discussed in your letter is not necessary and that it could raise difficult concerns respecting the appropriate separation that must be maintained between the legislative branch and this Court.

We appreciate your having advised us of the hearings and of the questions that your Subcommittee wishes to explore.

Sincerely,
William H. Rehnquist/s/

Questions and Comments

1. Of the principal arguments Mr. Prettyman made—the risk of embarrassment to the Justices (and perhaps, related disruption to collegial deliberation), the risk of misleading the litigants, and the unfairness of advantaging Washington D.C. lawyers—which are most persuasive to you?

2. Also testifying before the same congressional hearing as Mr. Prettyman was Dennis Hutchinson, a former clerk to Justice Byron White and an

---

36. This letter is reprinted in Public Papers of Supreme Court Justices: Assuring Preservation and Access: Hearing Before the Subcomm. on Regulation and Gov't Info. of the Senate Comm. on Governmental Affairs, 103d Cong. 71 (1993).

Editor of the *Supreme Court Review*. Although Hutchinson favored earlier release than Prettyman, he pointed out that there were multiple models for how long a time should elapse from when "a Justice retires and his working papers [should] become open for research." *1993 Hearing on Public Papers of Supreme Court Justices, supra,* at 20. He noted that 30 years was the rule followed in "Britain ... with respect to official State papers," and that Felix Frankfurter had "suggested and used 16." A "more common practice," according to Professor Hutchinson, has been to make the papers available "either at the death of the donor or after the retirement of the last Justice with whom the donor served," the latter restriction being one that Justice O'Connor used in deeding papers to the Library of Congress and that Justice Stewart used in transmitting his papers to the Yale Library. Hutchinson suggested that a consensus could be obtained that "2 years is way too short; 15–25 may be unduly scrupulous." *Id.*

3. As noted above, Congress took no action concerning the Justices' papers following this hearing. Justice Blackmun, who retired from the court in 1994, left his papers, a large collection with more than half a million documents, to the Library of Congress with instructions not to disclose them until 5 years after his death. He died in 1999. Five years later, the papers were released initially only to two news reporters (Nina Totenberg of NPR (National Public Radio) and Linda Greenhouse of the *New York Times*), according to arrangements the Justice had discussed with his family and former law clerk Harold Koh (now Dean of Yale Law School and creator of an oral history of Justice Blackmun). The special, early release to these two reporters was to facilitate a better public understanding of the more important aspects of the papers when they were ultimately released to the public. See Harold Hongju Koh, *Unveiling Justice Blackmun*, 72 Brooklyn L. Rev. 9, 20–21 (2006). By mid–2004, the papers were open to the public. Reactions varied. See Tony Mauro, *Lifting the Veil: Justice Blackmun's Papers and the Public Perception of the Supreme Court*, 70 Mo. L. Rev. 1037, 1040 (2005) ("[W]hat is the story line of the Blackmun Papers thus far? As with the Marshall Papers, I think the Blackmun Papers reveal a Supreme Court that is extremely conscientious and dedicated to reaching the right answer. They discuss, they research, they agonize; they even change their minds...."); Linda Greenhouse, *Becoming Justice Blackmun* 221–22 (2005) (noting Justice Blackmun's distinctive views on criminal procedure and clerks' lack of influence); David J. Garrow, *The Brains Behind Blackmun*, Legal Affairs, May/June 2005, at 27, 28 (arguing that the papers reveal that the Blackmun clerks wrote politicized and disrespectful memos and were the "brains behind" Justice Blackmun); Koh, *supra*, at 18–19 (arguing that Garrow misread the record because he did not realize that "Justice Blackmun always communicated with his clerks orally, while the clerks always replied in writing.... [Garrow] never heard all of the instructions, all of the oral messages from Justice Blackmun, all of the ways in which he guided his law clerks and inspired their responses").

4. The organization of this part of the chapter suggests that issues of greater publicity for public proceedings are distinct from those concerning access to internal deliberations. Notwithstanding the Miller-Sastri suggestion noted above, most scholars agree that internal deliberations should remain secret (at least until the case is announced), both to facilitate

reasoned, collegial decisionmaking and to prevent potential disruptions of financial markets.[37] Debate has focused more on when, if ever, after the decision is announced, the internal deliberations should be revealed. Political scientist Del Dickson has argued that "[t]he need to protect the secrets of the conference is compelling only until the case is decided" and perhaps for a brief period while the case is concluded on remand; "[o]therwise, once a case has been decided the Justices' residual interest in secrecy should [give] way to the more compelling interests of open government, public accountability, and public understanding of government decision making." Del Dickson, ed., *The Supreme Court in Conference (1940–85)* 19–20 (2001). Dickson further argues that Supreme Court deliberations are "not like military or diplomatic secrets" where long term confidentiality may be warranted. The deliberative process does not need further protection, Dickson asserts, because "virtually all of the Justices are experienced lawyers and politicians . . . inured to the ways of public life . . . [and] unlikely to be intimidated or dissuaded from speaking their minds by the mere prospect that their remarks might some-day be made public." *Id.* at 16. Do you agree? If so, should the conference notes be posted at the end of each Term, as transcripts of oral argument are now routinely made available? Why or why not? Consider whether any harms to the decisionmaking process might result from such quick disclosures of individual Justices' notes. Does sound decisionmaking require some mix of private deliberation and public reason-giving? Do Justices in a long term relationship need to be able to count on the confidentiality of some part of their deliberative process, at least for some period of time? Why have Justices tended to prefer to wait until at least their own death, and often some years later, to allow their papers to become public?

5. "Federal courts do not consider the judiciary's internal records as interpretive sources bearing on the meaning of published opinions or judicially-promulgated rules. In accord with this entrenched practice, current scholarship assumes that internal judicial materials are useful only as historical documentation, rather than as legally admissible authority." Adrian Vermeule, *Judicial History*, 108 Yale L. J. 1311, 1313 (1999). Professor Vermeule's article concludes that this norm against using internal deliberative material to "interpret" the Court's opinions is justified: "[A]llowing litigants and officials to introduce judicial history to support their interpretations would predictably inflict serious harm on the judiciary's processes of deliberation and upon a complex of rule-of-law values associated with the publication of judicial texts. This conclusion follows despite the recent widespread use of judicial history for journalistic, historical, and predictive ends, because the interpretive use of judicial history would implicate judges' powerful incentives to influence the future content of the law." *Id.*, at 1348. How would judges' incentives to posture in internal deliberations be affected if, as some propose, the conference records became public quickly and automatically?

---

37. But cf. Louis Michael Seidman, *Eavesdropping on the Justices*, 5 Green Bag 2d. 117 (2001) (reviewing Del Dickson, *The Supreme Court in Conference (1940–85)* (Oxford, 2001)) (arguing that records of the conferences suggest a decline in the quality of interchange and deliberation among Justices over the time period of Dickson's book and suggesting that the conferences, as well as oral arguments, should be televised).

6. If there are functional values to secrecy in deliberation, is there a period of time after which disclosure of those deliberations would not harm the functioning of the Court? A fixed period of years? A time when none of the Justices whose views are reflected in confidential materials are still sitting?

7. Should there be a uniform statute dealing with the question of ownership of and access to the Justices' papers? Or is the present "voluntarist" system, which has not changed since Wigdor's essay and decentralizes the decision to each Justice, worth retaining?

8. Would there be constitutional authority to enact such a statute, or would it violate separation of powers—either as a matter of substance or of what Justice Kennedy called "etiquette"?[38] Compare Nixon v. Administrator of General Services, 433 U.S. 425 (1977) (upholding congressional statute concerning ownership and control of presidential papers). If Congress can control presidential papers, does it necessarily follow that it could constitutionally control the Justices' papers?

B. JUDICIAL INDEPENDENCE AND POLITICAL CONTROVERSY

Although the Court's legitimacy as an institution is widely accepted in the United States, the Court has also engendered controversy throughout American history. Much of the Court's work is of relatively low "political salience,"[39] but when its decisions do generate controversy, it is not unusual for the political process to respond in ways designed to limit the power or authority of the Court. Consider whether these responses should be seen as worrisome (even unconstitutional?) threats to desirable judicial independence, or as healthy (constitutionally authorized?) mechanisms for political accountability. We discuss three areas of recent controversy.

1. Constitutional Amendment, Court–Packing and Jurisdiction–Stripping

As is covered in courses on constitutional law and federal courts, the Constitution provides several mechanisms that have at times been used, or threatened, to control the work of the Court. First, constitutional

---

38. Cf. United States v. Lopez, 514 U.S. 549, 583 (1995) (Kennedy, J., concurring) (referring to the "etiquette of federalism").

39. See Frederick Schauer, *The Supreme Court, 2005 Term: Foreword: The Court's Agenda—and the Nation's,* 120 Harv. L. Rev. 4, 8–9 (2006). Thus, Schauer writes, "[I]n a year in which the war in Iraq, terrorism, escalating fuel prices, healthcare, immigration reform, Social Security, the nuclear capability of Iran and North Korea, Hurricane Katrina, the estate tax, corporate scandals, CEO salaries, bird flu, and the minimum wage appeared to dominate the nation's public agenda and the workload of the nation's policymakers, only with respect to terrorism and related issues of homeland security—and then only as to one aspect of those—was there much overlap between the agenda of the nation's governance and the agenda of the Supreme Court. And even more striking is that, with few exceptions—one of which is the New Deal era but ... not the era of Warren Court activism—things have rarely been otherwise." *Id.* at 8–9.

amendments may be and have been adopted to overcome the effect of Supreme Court decisions. See U.S. Const. amends. XI, XIII, XIV, XVI, XXVI. Many others have been proposed and not adopted. Second, as readers will recall from Chapter Two, the appointment of Justices by the political branches is an opportunity for the political branches to affect the direction of the Court. Moreover, the numbers of Justices is not set in the Constitution and has, on occasion, been changed in order to affect particular President's appointment powers. Thus, for example, during the Civil War period, Congress, in 1863, expanded the Court's number to ten to allow Lincoln to appoint Stephen J. Field as an Associate Justice; thereafter, Congress in 1865 reduced the authorized number of seats to six (to take effect prospectively, that is, upon the retirement of sitting Justices) in order to deny President Andrew Johnson any appointments; and then, in 1869, Congress returned the number to nine. As already noted, President Franklin D. Roosevelt's proposed court-packing plan in the 1930s, which would have added one Justice to the Court for each sitting Justice above the age of 70 (up to a total of 15 Justices), met considerable opposition, though it received extensive consideration in the Senate.[40] (Tenure and removal of Justices is discussed below in Section C).

Congress also has some power to control the jurisdiction of the federal courts, including the power to make "exceptions" to the appellate jurisdiction of the Court. According to a leading casebook, "congressional power over the appellate jurisdiction of the Supreme Court has occasionally assumed considerable importance, with proposals to prevent the Supreme Court from hearing cases involving (among other things) school prayer, reapportionment, school desegregation, and abortion." See Geoffrey R. Stone et al., *Constitutional Law* 85 (5th ed. 2005). None of these proposals has passed, nor (as of this writing) has more recent proposed legislation providing, *inter alia*, that "the Supreme Court shall have no appellate jurisdiction, to hear or decide any question pertaining to the interpretation of, or the validity under the Constitution of, the Pledge of Allegiance . . ." H.R. 2028, 108th Cong. (2004). This bill passed the House of Representatives on September 23, 2004, but did not move out of the Senate.[41]

40. For a provocative article suggesting that Congress does not have the power to decide the number of Justices and that instead, the President and Senate, through their respective powers to nominate and confirm—or not—can control the number of Justices serving on the Court at any time, see Peter Nicolas, *Nine, Of Course: A Dialogue on Congressional Power to Set by Statute the Number of Justices on the Supreme Court*, 2 N.Y.U. J. L. & Liberty 86 (2006).

41. For an effort to combine a jurisdiction-stripping statute over constitutional questions with a threat of impeachment to forestall review of the constitutionality of

the jurisdiction-strip, see Constitution Restoration Act of 2004, H.R. 3799, 108th Cong. §§ 101, 302 (2d Sess. 2004) (defining as an impeachable offense "any activity that exceeds the jurisdiction of the court" by reason of proposed limitations on jurisdiction to review challenges to public "acknowledgment of God as the sovereign source of law"); Constitution Restoration Act of 2004: Hearing Before the Subcomm. on Courts, The Internet, and Intellectual Property of the H. Comm. on the Judiciary, 108th Cong. 28 (2004) (statement of Michael J. Gerhardt, Professor of Law, William. & Mary Law School) (criticizing this provision, which appears to authorize im-

On one important occasion, however, Congress exercised its "exceptions" power successfully to remove a pending case from the Supreme Court's appellate jurisdiction. Ex parte McCardle, 74 U.S. 506 (1869), upheld the constitutionality of the repealing legislation, designed to prevent the Court from deciding the merits of a habeas corpus petition rejected by the lower court, challenging the use of military authority against civilians in the post Civil War Reconstruction regime. Yet the meaning of the case is uncertain: The *McCardle* Court observed, and in a later case the Court confirmed, that it retained appellate jurisdiction under a different statute to review the same kind of matters. Whether and how the "essential role of the Supreme Court in the constitutional plan"[42] operates as a limit on Congress' "exceptions power," or how that "exceptions" power is otherwise limited, has generated a large scholarly literature. See generally Richard H. Fallon Jr., et al., *Hart & Wechsler's The Federal Courts and the Federal System* 337–42 (5th ed. 2003). We do not propose to canvass that literature here, or discuss the difficult constitutional questions they raise, but simply want to remind readers of the possibility of jurisdiction-stripping responses to political controversies concerning the Court and its work.

More than a century after *McCardle*, the Court's decisions have again prompted legislative jurisdiction-stripping in habeas cases. In Rasul v. Bush, 542 U.S. 466 (2004), the Court held that the U.S. District Court for the District of Columbia could exercise habeas corpus jurisdiction over a challenge by foreign detainees, who had been captured abroad as part of the so-called "war on terror" and held for very long periods at the U.S. Naval Base at Guantanamo Bay, Cuba.[43] Congress responded to this decision by enacting the Detainee Treatment Act of 2005, Pub. L. No. 109–148, 119 Stat. 2739 (DTA), which repealed the federal courts' habeas corpus jurisdiction for all non-U.S. citizens held in military custody at Guantanamo. See DTA § 1005(e)(1) (providing that "no court . . . shall have jurisdiction to hear or consider . . . an application for . . . habeas corpus filed by . . . an alien detained . . . at Guantanamo Bay"). In an opinion again written by Justice Stevens, the Court

peachment of judges who find the limitation on jurisdiction unconstitutional, as inconsistent with constitutional traditions of judicial independence).

42. See Henry M. Hart, Jr., *The Power of Congress to Limit the Jurisdiction of the Federal Courts: An Exercise in Dialectic*, 66 Harv. L. Rev. 1362, 1365 (1953).

43. Justice Stevens wrote the Opinion of the Court, concluding that given the terms of the lease under which the U.S. controlled Guantanamo, the base was within the "territorial jurisdiction" of the court. In a separate opinion concurring only in the judgment, Justice Kennedy agreed that the district court had jurisdiction but did not agree with other discussion in the Court's opinion which implied that so long as the ultimate custodian of the prisoner was

within the jurisdiction of the district court, habeas jurisdiction could be exercised. Justice Scalia's dissent took pains to attack the language in the majority opinion as "extend[ing] the scope of the habeas statute to the four corners of the earth." *Id.* at 498 (Scalia, J., dissenting). The Court's judgment was 6–3, with Chief Justice Rehnquist and Justice Thomas joining in Justice Scalia's dissent. For discussion of the possible impact of Justice Stevens's having served as a law clerk to Justice Wiley Rutledge, see Joseph T. Thai, *The Law Clerk Who Wrote* Rasul v. Bush: *John Paul Stevens's Influence from World War II to the War on Terror,* 92 Va. L. Rev. 501 (2006) (discussing Stevens's work, as a law clerk, on Justice Rutledge's dissent in Ahrens v. Clark, 335 U.S. 188 (1942)).

in Hamdan v. Rumsfeld, 126 S. Ct. 2749 (2006) held that the DTA did not apply to pending habeas petitions by Guantanamo detainees. Addressing the merits, the Court also concluded that the military commissions established by the Executive Branch were not in conformity with applicable law. The Court's decision was 5–3, with Chief Justice Roberts not participating.[44]

In response to *Hamdan*, Congress within a few months enacted the Military Commissions Act of 2006, Pub L. No. 109–366, 120 Stat. 2600 (MCA). In this statute, Congress went further, apparently repealing habeas corpus jurisdiction for any non-U.S. citizen, held anywhere by the United States, who has "been determined by the United States to have been properly detained as an enemy combatant or is awaiting such determination."[45] The constitutionality of the MCA was promptly challenged in pending cases as an unconstitutional suspension of the writ of habeas corpus. As this book was going to press, the Court—in a highly unusual course of action—granted certiorari on a petition for rehearing, after having previously denied the petition for certiorari. See Boumediene v. Bush, 127 S. Ct. 3078 (June 29, 2007) (granting petitions for rehearing, vacating earlier denial of certiorari and granting certiorari); 127 S. Ct. 2930 (June 4, 2007) (inviting a response to the petition for rehearing); 127 S. Ct. 1725 (April 26, 2007) (denying application for extension of time in which to file petition for rehearing of denial of certiorari and denying request for suspension of order denying certiorari); 127 S. Ct. 1478 (April 2, 2007) (denying certiorari to review Boumediene v. Bush, 476 F. 3d 981 (D.C. Cir. 2007)).[46] Whether Congress will

44. Then–Judge Roberts had participated below in the U.S. Court of Appeals for the District of Columbia before he was appointed Chief Justice. Cf. 28 U.S.C § 47 (providing that no judge may sit to hear an appeal of a case he or she decided below). For a discussion of recusal, see Section B (2), below.

45. See 28 U.S.C. § 2241(e)(1) ("No court, justice, or judge shall have jurisdiction to hear or consider an application for a writ of habeas corpus filed by or on behalf of an alien detained by the United States who has been determined by the United States to have been properly detained as an enemy combatant or is awaiting such determination."). This is one part of a complex set of provisions, which authorize limited review in the U.S. Court of Appeals for the District of Columbia Circuit of (1) decisions by Combatant Status Review Tribunals concerning whether a detainee is an enemy combatant, and (2) decisions by military commissions on whether detainees have committed war crimes. See 10 U.S.C. § 801(e)(2). Both the adequacy of these pro-

visions as a substitute for habeas, and their constitutionality in other respects, are at issue in pending cases.

46. In the original order denying certiorari, Justices Stevens and Kennedy filed a joint "statement ... respecting denial of certiorari." See *id.* at 1479 (noting the "obvious importance of the issues," reiterating that denials of certiorari express no views on the merits, and stating: "If petitioners later seek to establish that the Government has unreasonably delayed proceedings under the Detainee Treatment Act of 2005, ... or some other and ongoing injury, alternative means exist for us to consider our jurisdiction over the allegations made by petitioners before the Court of Appeals. See 28 U.S.C. §§ 1651(a), 2241. Were the Government to take additional steps to prejudice the position of petitioners in seeking review in this Court, 'courts of competent jurisdiction,' including this Court, 'should act promptly to ensure that the office and purposes of the writ of habeas corpus are not compromised.' "). What, if any, light does this statement shed on the possible reasons for the Court's unusual change of position on whether to grant certiorari? See

prove successful in its efforts to cut off federal habeas review, or the Court will declare the MCA unconstitutional or interpret it so as to avoid the issue, remains to be seen.

Questions and Comments

1. There is considerable scholarly disagreement over whether legislation completely stripping the Court of jurisdiction over a constitutional issue is itself constitutional. If that question is answered affirmatively, is jurisdiction-stripping in constitutional cases an appropriate *political* response to substantive disagreement with the Court? How does it compare with other political approaches—court-packing, the regular nomination and replacement of Justices, or efforts to modify the governing law by constitutional amendment?

2. Is the possibility of a political response to a ruling—on statutory issues, by an overriding statute; on constitutional issues, by attempts at constitutional amendment or attacks on the Court's jurisdiction—a relevant factor for a Justice to consider in resolving a case? An illegitimate factor to consider? For a provocative effort to study whether anticipated congressional responses influence the Court's constitutional rulings, see Anna Harvey & Barry Friedman, *Pulling Punches: Congressional Constraints on the Supreme Court's Constitutional Rulings, 1987–2000*, available at http://ssrn. com/abstract=1002626. See also Barry Friedman, *The Politics of Judicial Review*, 84 Tex. L. Rev. 257 (2005). Note that Charles Black suggested that the legitimacy of the Court's exercise of its powers of judicial review depends, in part, on Congress' power to divest it of jurisdiction. See Charles L. Black, Jr., *Decision According to Law: The 1979 Holmes Lectures* 17–19, 37–39 (1981). Does this imply that concern for political reactions is a legitimate factor for the Court to consider?[47] Or does it imply that the Court is given jurisdiction to focus on law, not politics? Can the two be entirely separated in resolving constitutional questions?

2. Extrajudicial Speech or Conduct and Recusal

There are many statutes, rules, and conventions of behavior designed to sustain and protect the impartiality and appearance of impartiality of judges. Whole books on this topic have been written and it is not our desire or goal to reproduce or replace them. But one issue that is unique to the Supreme Court is the fact that if one of the nine Justices recuses him or herself, there will be only eight left; the case cannot be reassigned to another judge or panel. Thus, recusals on the Court not

---

also Chapter Three, Section C, above, at 449.

47. Cf. William H. Rehnquist, *The Supreme Court* 191–92 (2001) (arguing that public opinion influenced the Court's decision in the *Youngstown Steel Case;* expressing his view that Justices should read the papers and follow current events; and stating: "No honorable judge would ever cast his vote in a particular case simply because he thought the majority of the public wanted him to vote that way, but that is quite a different thing from saying that no judge is ever influenced by the great tides of public opinion that run in a country such as ours."). He also reported being recently questioned about whether the Justices could "isolate themselves from public opinion," and his own response: "we are not able to do so, and it would probably be unwise to try." *Id.* at 192.

only raise the possibility of an equally divided Court, a clearly undesirable event,[48] but more important, deprive the process of the deliberative capacities of the full Bench. While these factors might be thought to support a more relaxed standard of recusal for Supreme Court justices than for lower court judges, at the same time, as members of the final court exercising the most power—and most in the public eye—arguments could be made that it is particularly important that Supreme Court justices be held to the most rigorous standards of impartiality and the appearance of impartiality.

The question of whether Justices should participate in particular cases has arisen since the Court's earliest years. John Marshall sat on *Marbury v. Madison*, even though the case involved the legal consequences of a course of events in which he was intimately involved as the outgoing Secretary of State. See Susan Low Bloch, *The* Marbury *Mystery: Why Did William Marbury Sue in the Supreme Court?*, 18 Const. Comment. 607 (2001). By contrast, Marshall did not sit on Martin v. Hunter's Lessee, 14 U.S. 304 (1816), which involved a dispute over property in which Marshall had a financial interest. The distinction between issues of impartiality due to prior involvement in government action, and issues relating to financial interests, continues to play some role in more recent times in whether Supreme Court Justices recuse themselves, or are thought to be obligated to do so. Thus, the 1971 nomination of Court of Appeals Judge Clement Haynesworth to the Supreme Court was scuttled, in part, because he had sat on cases involving companies in which he held a small amount of stock. The federal disqualification statute today provides detailed rules about disqualification not only where a Justice holds stock but also where family members of the Justice have financial interests or are involved in the case. See 28 U.S.C. § 455(4), (5).

In 1972, newly appointed Justice William H. Rehnquist decided to participate in Laird v. Tatum, 408 U.S. 1 (1972), even though he had participated in some of the underlying events prior to his appointment to the Court. In that case, he made the fifth vote in a closely divided decision to refuse to review the constitutionality of surveillance activities, a program that Rehnquist had defended in congressional testimony when he served as head of the Office of Legal Counsel in the Department of Justice. In response to a request for rehearing by the losing plaintiffs, who argued that Rehnquist should have recused himself, Justice Rehnquist filed an unusual, and detailed, statement explaining why he disagreed. Laird v. Tatum, 409 U.S. 824 (1972). First, he explained, he had never acted as counsel nor been a material witness in the litigation, and thus the mandatory disqualification provisions of 28 U.S.C. § 455 as it then existed did not apply. As for the discretionary provision of this statute, "requiring disqualification where the judge 'is so related to or connected with any party or his attorney as to render it improper, in his

---

48. If those Justices able to participate are equally divided, the Court enters a judgment of affirmance, which has no prece-dential effect. See Robert L. Stern, et al., *Supreme Court Practice* 4 (2002).

opinion, for him to sit on the trial, appeal, or other proceeding therein,' "
Justice Rehnquist concluded that it was proper for him to sit. He argued
that his prior expression of views on the constitutional question was no
different from, for example, Justice Black—who voted for the Fair Labor
Standards Act as a Senator—sitting on a case challenging its constitutionality. 409 U.S. at 831. Although Justice Rehnquist indicated that
reasonable judges could decide the question differently, he concluded
that the possibility of a recusal resulting in affirmance by an equally
divided Court, "is a reason for not 'bending over backwards' in order to
deem oneself disqualified." *Id.* at 838. For a discussion of this issue, see
Jeffrey Stempel, *Rehnquist, Recusal, and Reform*, 53 Brook. L. Rev. 589
(1987).

Soon thereafter, the federal disqualification statute was amended to
provide that "[a]ny justice . . . shall disqualify himself in any proceeding
in which his impartiality might reasonably be questioned." 28 U.S.C.
§ 455(a). The language thereby moved from contemplating a determination by the individual Justice whether it would be "improper" for him to
sit, to a more objective standard mandating disqualification if impartiality "might reasonably be questioned." (As noted above in note 44, 28
U.S.C § 47 provides that no judge may sit to hear an appeal of a case he
or she decided below.)

Although it might have been thought that participation by a member of the Justice's family in a law firm that litigated a case before the
Court would meet this standard, several Justices have concluded otherwise. In 1993, Chief Justice Rehnquist and six of the Associate Justices
adopted the following Statement of Recusal Policy: " '[W]e do not think
it would serve the public interest to go beyond the requirements of the
statute, and to recuse ourselves, out of an excess of caution, whenever a
relative is a partner in the firm before us or acted as a lawyer at an
earlier stage. Even one unnecessary recusal impairs the functioning of
the Court,' " *quoted in* Cheney v. United States Dist. Court for the Dist.
of Columbia, 541 U.S. 913, 915–16 (2004) (Scalia, J., mem.).[49] Thus, they
concluded: " 'Absent some special factor, . . . we will not recuse ourselves
by reason of a relative's participation as a lawyer in earlier stages of the
case. . . . We shall recuse ourselves whenever, to our knowledge, a
relative has been lead counsel below. Another special factor, of course,
would be the fact that the amount of the relative's compensation could
be substantially affected by the outcome here. That would require our
recusal even if the relative had not worked on the case, but was merely a
partner in the firm that shared the profits. . . .' " Debra Lyn Bassett,
Recusal and the Supreme Court, 56 Hastings L.J. 657, 681 (2005). The
entire Recusal Policy is reprinted in Richard E. Flamm, *Judicial Dis-*

---

49. See Ross E. Davies, *The Reluctant
Recusants: Two Parables of Supreme Judicial Disqualification*, 10 Green Bag 2d 79,
91–92 & n.44 (2006) (explaining that Chief
Justice Rehnquist and Justices Stevens,
O'Connor, Scalia, Kennedy, Thomas, and
Ginsburg had issued this informal statement November 1, 1993); see also Microsoft
Corp. v. United States, 530 U.S. 1301,
1301–03 (2000) (statement of Rehnquist,
C.J.) (noting that his son is a partner in a
law firm that represents the petitioner and
explaining his conclusion that he ought not
disqualify himself under 28 U.S.C. § 455).

qualification: Recusal and Disqualification of Judges, Addendum to App. A, at 1068–70 (1996).

Recent controversies over recusals include Justice Scalia's denial of a motion to recuse in an important Freedom of Information Act case involving the Vice–President, and Justice Ruth Bader Ginsburg's refusal to recuse in cases involving groups in which she had been involved. In Cheney v. United States Dist. Court for the Dist. of Columbia, 541 U.S. 913 (2004) (Scalia, J., mem.), Justice Scalia explained why his social visits with then Vice–President Cheney on duck-hunting expeditions did not require his recusal in the FOIA case involving vice-presidential records. He explained that he had never discussed the case with Cheney, and had hardly been alone with him, usually being in a larger group. He argued:

> A rule that required Members of this Court to remove themselves from cases in which the official actions of friends were at issue would be utterly disabling. Many Justices have reached this Court precisely because they were friends of the incumbent President or other senior officials—and from the earliest days down to modern times Justices have had close personal relationships with the President and other officers of the Executive.

Id. at 916. He concluded that his impartiality "could not reasonably be questioned" based on his social mingling with the Vice President, who was named only in an official and not a personal capacity in the lawsuit. And he noted a number of precedents, including Justice Byron White sitting on cases in which Robert Kennedy was a named party as Attorney General during a term when White had vacationed with Kennedy, and Robert Jackson's sitting on cases involving the Roosevelt Administration even as he maintained a close social relationship with the President. *Id.* at 924–26.

Justice Scalia argued that in accepting a free flight on a government plane with Cheney, he had done nothing disqualifying because there was no cost to the government, he had to incur the cost of a roundtrip ticket to return home, and thus he received nothing of value, but only a more convenient mode of transport. *Id.* at 920–21. Justice Scalia expressed particular concern at the idea that public belief that he should recuse had any role to play, and raised the specter of the press, politicians and lawyers going after Justices' friendships and activities as a basis to stir up controversy and recusals. Is Justice Scalia's reasoning consistent with the disqualification statute's objective standard, that a judge or Justice should recuse if his impartiality could "reasonably be questioned"? For different perspectives on his opinion on recusal, compare Monroe H. Freedman, *Duck-Blind Justice: Justice Scalia's Memorandum in the* Cheney *Case,* 18 Geo. J. Legal Ethics 229 (2004) with Timothy J. Goodson, *Duck, Duck, Goose: Hunting for Better Recusal Practices in the United States Supreme Court in Light of* Cheney v. United States District Court, 84 N.C. L. Rev. 181 (2005) and R. Matthew Pearson,

Duck Duck Recuse? Foreign Common Law Guidance & Improving Recusal of Supreme Court Justices, 62 Wash. & Lee L. Rev. 1799 (2005).

Justice Ginsburg's failure to recuse in cases in which groups she had supported were parties or amici has also come under criticism. According to one article:

> When the Sierra Club filed its motion to have Justice Scalia recuse himself, conservative watch-dog groups engaged in tit-for-tat and demanded that Ruth Bader Ginsburg recuse herself from several cases involving abortion issues because of a lectureship called, oddly, the Justice Ruth Bader Ginsburg Distinguished Lecture Series on Women and the Law. The lecture series named in honor of the Justice is sponsored by NOW Legal Defense and Education Fund. The watch-dogs pointed out that Justice Ginsburg was prepared to vote on cases in which NOW had filed amicus curiae brief[s]. Indeed, just two weeks prior to a NOW Legal Defense Fund speech and appearance, Justice Ginsburg had cast a favorable vote for NOW's position as an amicus in a case. Twelve Republican members of Congress also wrote a joint letter to Justice Ginsburg demanding her recusal in all cases in which NOW has filed "friend of the court" briefs.

Marianne M. Jennings & Nim Razook, *Duck When a Conflict of Interest Blinds You: Judicial Conflicts of Interest in the Matters of Scalia and Ginsburg*, 39 U.S.F. L. Rev. 873, 888–89 (2005). Although Justice Ginsburg responded by noting that the lecture in her name was not a commercial venture and that she derived no financial benefit from it, some commenters noted that her involvement was used by NOW to raise money. See *id.* at 891 & n. 60 (noting a donation by Justice Ginsburg to a NOW auction); see also, *id.* at 891 n. 61. Like Justices Scalia and Rehnquist, Justice Ginsburg argued that Supreme Court Justices need to be careful not to recuse too readily. See David G. Savage & Richard A. Serrano, *Ginsburg Stands by Involvement with Group; The Supreme Court Justice Says She and Her Colleagues Should Avoid Recusing Themselves from Cases Because They Can't Be Replaced*, L.A. Times, Mar. 13, 2004, at A14.[50]

Questions and Comments

1.   How important are these questions of recusal to the Court's appearance of impartiality? to the actual independence with which the Justices work? to the respect for judicial autonomy which the other branches, and the public, have for the Court? Are the public's views irrelevant to the question

---

50. Thurgood Marshall generally recused himself from cases in which the NAACP was a party in his early years on the Court (he had led the NAACP Legal Defense Fund earlier in his career); however, in 1984, after consulting the other Justices, Marshall decided enough time had passed that he no longer needed to do so. See Mark V. Tushnet, *The Supreme Court and Race Discrimination, 1967–1991: The View from the Marshall Papers*, 36 Wm. & Mary L. Rev. 473, 509 n.206 (1995); see also Davies, *supra* note 49, at 84–85 (describing how, even prior to 1984, Marshall on occasion participated in cases where the NAACP appeared as a party or amicus).

of recusal? Or are they central to the determination of when a Justice's impartiality can reasonably be questioned?

2.   Given the strong structural guarantees of independence provided by Article III, should Supreme Court Justices feel "free to travel, write, and give lectures as a professional service even when the lectures include paid travel and involve exotic locations"?[51] Is doing so an important way for Justices to remain aware of developing ideas in law and the world that will better enable them to fulfill their judicial functions? An important way for them to develop their own views? Or do such patterns of traveling to lecture present temptations to align, consciously or not, with those who would sponsor such trips in ways that interfere with the independence that the structural guarantees are supposed to provide?

3.   Justice Scalia drew a contrast between his decision not to recuse in *Cheney* and his recusal in Elk Grove Unified School District v. Newdow, 542 U.S. 1 (2004). In his Statement in the *Cheney* case, Justice Scalia wrote: "[R]ecusal is the course I must take—and will take—when, on the basis of established principles and practices, I have said or done something which requires that course. I have recused for such a reason this very Term. See Elk Grove Unified School District v. Newdow, 540 U.S. 945 . . . (cert. granted, Oct. 14, 2003)." *Cheney v. United States District Court*, 541 U.S. at 916 (Scalia, J., Mem.). *Newdow* involved a constitutional challenge to the inclusion of the words "under God" in the Pledge of Allegiance that school children generally recited. Why did Justice Scalia recuse in that case? What had he "said or done . . . which requires that course"? Justice Scalia did not file a statement explaining his decision; however, commentators speculated that recusal was related to his having made widely reported remarks, in a public speech to the Knights of Columbus (an organization that had originally lobbied for inclusion of the words "under God" in the Pledge of Allegiance) commenting on or referring to the lower court decision in ways that arguably went to the merits. See Vikram David Amar, *Why Did Justice Scalia Decline to Participate in the "One Nation Under God" Case? Recusal Decisions and When They Should, and Should Not, Be Required*, Findlaw.com (Oct. 31, 2003), at http://writ.news.findlaw.com/amar/20031031. html. Professor Amar has argued that there was more ground for recusal in the *Cheney* case than in *Newdow*. See Vikram David Amar, *Lower Court Obedience & the Ninth Circuit*, 7 Green Bag 2d 315, 321 n.27 (2004).

4.   Compare Justice Rehnquist's decision not to recuse in *Laird* with Justice Scalia's decision to recuse himself in Public Citizen v. United States Department of Justice, 491 U.S. 440 (1989). Justice Scalia later explained his decision: "My opinion as Assistant Attorney General addressed the precise question presented in *Public Citizen:* whether the American Bar Association's Standing Committee on Federal Judiciary, which provided advice to the President concerning judicial nominees, could be regulated as an 'advisory committee' under FACA [Federal Advisory Committee Act]. I concluded that my withdrawal from the case was required by 28 U.S.C. § 455(b)(3), which mandates recusal where the judge 'has served in governmental

---

51.   Jennings & Razook, *supra*, at 892 (attributing these views to Justice Ginsburg).

employment and in such capacity … expressed an opinion concerning the merits of the particular case in controversy.' " *Cheney,* 541 U.S. at 922 n.3. Note that Congress had changed the statute after *Laird*. *See* discussion above at [p. 1056]

5. When the Court decided *Bush v. Gore* in 2000, a number of critics contended that several of the Justices should have recused themselves. The reasons varied: O'Connor because of comments she was reported to have made at a party on Election Night; Scalia because two of his sons' law firms were involved in representing Bush; Thomas because his wife was involved in the Heritage Foundation helping to plan proposals for nominations for the next Administration. See Richard K. Neumann, Jr., *Conflicts of Interest in Bush v. Gore: Did Some Justices Vote Illegally?*, 16 Geo. J. Legal Ethics 375, 375–79 (2003). If three Justices had recused themselves, how would this have affected the perceived legitimacy of the Court's ruling (assuming the Court would have gone on to decide the case with only six sitting Justices)?

6. Recusals have been the subject of occasionally tense inter-branch communications. See Letter from Senators Patrick Leahy & Joseph I. Lieberman to Chief Justice William H. Rehnquist, Jan. 22, 2004, reprinted in *Irrecusable & Unconfirmable*, 7 Green Bag 2d 277, 278–79 (2004) (expressing concern about Justice Scalia's non-recusal in *Cheney* and inquiring whether the Court had mechanisms available to disqualify a Justice who refused to recuse him or herself). Chief Justice Rehnquist responded, emphasizing that it was up to each Justice to determine individually whether, under the standards of the federal recusal statute (28 U.S.C. § 455), to recuse himself or herself. Letter from Chief Justice William H. Rehnquist to Senator Patrick Leahy, Jan. 26, 2004, reprinted in *Irrecusable and Unconfirmable, supra* at 280.[52]

Is the adoption of a policy on recusals a matter solely for the Court to decide? Is that too much an example of the fox guarding the hen-house? Could Congress constitutionally require other mechanisms—for example, a requirement of consultation with the other Justices, a requirement of published reasons for denying recusal, or a requirement that a denial of recusal be concurred in by a majority of the other Justices, or by a group of other Article III federal judges? Would these violate the separation of powers? Would it be consistent with the separation of powers—would such legislation be "necessary and appropriate" to reinforce the Court's appearance of impartiality? Should the Court voluntarily adopt such mechanisms? A journalist has taken it upon himself to try to monitor the Justices' recusal decisions. See Tony Mauro, *Recusal Report,* Legal Times, October 9, 2006, at 11.

52. See also Rehnquist, *The Supreme Court, supra,* at 145–47 (discussing intra-Court dispute over a petition for rehearing based on Justice Black's failure to recuse in the *Jewell Ridge* case); Jewell Ridge Coal Corp. v. Local No 6167, UMW, 325 U.S. 897 (1945) (Jackson J., concurring in denial of rehearing) (explaining that there were no "authoritative standards" for recusal and it has "always been considered the responsibility of each Justice to determine for himself the propriety of withdrawing in any particular circumstance"). Jackson also noted that there was understandable "confusion as to what the bar may expect and as to whether the action in any case is a matter of individual or collective responsibility," but said he was aware of no authority "under which a majority of this Court has power under any circumstances to exclude one of its duly commissioned Justices from sitting or voting in any case." *Id.*

7.   A number of proposals have been made for changes in the standards and procedure for recusals of Supreme Court Justices. Several writers have proposed that the full Court review questions of recusal whenever an individual Justice denies a motion to recuse himself or herself, with the Justice being recused unless a majority agree with the nonrecusal decision. See, e.g., Jeffrey W. Stempel, *Rehnquist, Recusal, and Reform,* 53 Brook. L. Rev. 589, 654–656 (1987); see also Goodson, *supra,* 84 N.C. L. Rev. at 217–20. Would this proposal essentially create a presumption of recusal? Would it create incentives for more recusal motions? Would this be a bad thing? For an affirmative answer, see Jennings & Razook, *supra,* at 923.[53]

Another approach is to require or encourage the individual Justices more regularly to explain their actions on motions to recuse, in order to create greater transparency. Can you think of any arguments *against* developing a practice of providing a brief statement of reasons for denials of motions to recuse? Would the same arguments apply with respect to *grants* of motions to recuse? What would you think of an asymmetric rule, not requiring explanations of decisions to recuse but requiring explanations of decisions to deny recusal motions?

3.   Citing Foreign Law: Congressional Efforts to Control the Sources Relied on For Decision by the Court

In 1997, a sedate dispute over the use of foreign law in constitutional adjudication occurred in a federalism case, Printz v. United States, 521 U.S. 898 (1997), between Justices Scalia and Breyer. Justice Breyer, dissenting from the Court's holding, would have upheld the federal statute requiring local law enforcement personnel to perform background checks on gun purchasers. In support, he noted that a number of vibrant federal systems in Europe permitted the central government to require member units to implement central government legislation. *Id.* at 976–78. Justice Scalia, writing for the majority, argued that while it was appropriate to consider comparative experience in drafting a constitution, it was not relevant to do so in interpreting one already adopted. *Id.* at 921 n.11.

Over the Court's history, foreign or international law has been episodically referred to in constitutional cases. In a tradition dating back to the earliest merits decisions of cases raising Eighth Amendment "cruel and unusual punishment" challenges, the Court considered international or foreign practice. See Vicki C. Jackson, *Comment, Constitutional Comparisons: Convergence, Resistance, Engagement,* 119 Harv. L. Rev. 109, 109–10 (2005). Justice Robert Jackson's justly famous concurrence in Youngstown Sheet & Tube Co. v. Sawyer, 343 U.S. 579, 651–52

---

53.   Other proposals to change recusal procedures have been made as well. See, e.g., Caprice L. Roberts, *The Fox Guarding the Henhouse? Recusal and the Procedural Void in the Court of Last Resort,* 57 Rutgers L. Rev. 107 (2004) (proposing legislation to permit convening a panel of judges, made up of the Chief Judges of all the circuit courts of appeals, who could substitute for a recused Justice). For a helpful historical account, and argument for a range of procedural reforms, see also Amanda Frost, *Keeping Up Appearances: A Process–Oriented Approach to Judicial Recusal,* 53 U. Kan. L. Rev. 531 (2005).

(1952), devoted considerable attention to analyzing different foreign approaches to executive power in emergencies. In a number of other important decisions, the Court referred to international or foreign practice, including Jacobson v. Massachusetts, 197 U.S. 11, 31–33 & n.1, 35 (1905) (upholding mandatory vaccination), Muller v. Oregon, 208 U.S. 412, 419 n.1 (1908) (upholding state limitations on working hours for women), Wickard v. Filburn, 317 U.S. 111, 125–26 & n.27 (1942) (upholding federal regulation of wheat grown on family farms), Trop v. Dulles, 356 U.S. 86, 102 (1958) (plurality opinion) (concluding that imposing loss of citizenship, or statelessness, as punishment was unconstitutional); Washington v. Glucksberg, 521 U.S. 702, 710 n.8, 718 n.16, 734 (1997) (rejecting challenge to state law prohibiting assisted suicide).

Yet by 2004, the Court's occasional references to foreign or international law—especially in Atkins v. Virginia, 536 U.S. 304 (2002) (holding that the death penalty could not constitutionally be imposed on a defendant who was mentally retarded) and Lawrence v. Texas, 539 U.S. 558 (2003) (holding that the states could not constitutionally prohibit consensual adult private homosexual conduct)—had created a significant controversy within the Court and something of a political firestorm outside the Court. By early 2004, the first of several proposals to prohibit the Court from referring to foreign law in resolving constitutional cases was introduced in Congress and hearings held.[54] Bills continued to be introduced, with evocative titles. See, e.g., Constitution Restoration Act of 2004, S. 2082, 108th Cong. § 201 (2004) (seeking to prohibit reliance on foreign law, except English constitutional and common law, in interpreting the Constitution); American Justice for American Citizens Act, H.R. 4118, 108th Cong. § 3 (2004) (indicating that federal judges should not resort to foreign law in constitutional interpretation, except English law as it influenced the Framers); The Reaffirmation of American Independence Resolution, H.R. Res. 568, 108th Cong. (2004) (seeking to restrict references to foreign law in interpreting federal law). The Court's decision in Roper v. Simmons, 543 U.S. 551 (2005), holding unconstitutional the imposition of the death penalty on a defendant who was under the age of 18 at the time of the offense fanned the flames further by devoting an entire, though short, section at the end of Justice Kennedy's opinion for the Court discussing international and foreign law.

Does Congress have the constitutional authority to dictate what sources the Court may rely on in constitutional interpretation? To threaten to impeach Justices who ignore such a directive? See, e.g., Tom Curry, *A Flap Over Foreign Matter at the Supreme Court: House Members Protest Use of Non–U.S. Rulings in Big Cases*, MSNBC, Mar. 11, 2004, http://www.msnbc.msn.com/id/4506232 (discussing Rep. Feeney's implicit threat of impeachment for judges who would ignore a proposed resolution forbidding the use of foreign law). Is this controversy just a

---

54. See Mark Rahdert, *Comparative Constitutional Advocacy*, 56 Am. U. L. Rev. 553, 555–56 & n.11 (2007) (listing nine bills and resolutions introduced between 2003 and 2005 on the subject).

passing "tempest in a teapot"? a sign of a significant level of mistrust between the Court and the political branches? a true threat to judicial independence?

C. RECONSIDERING LIFE TENURE?

As noted earlier, by 2005 the Court had undergone no change in membership for close to 11 years—one of the longest such stretches in its history. This long period prompted critics of the Court, on both the left and the right, to reconsider several of the Court's institutional structures, including life tenure. Scholars expressed concern over the possibility that some Presidents would have no opportunity to make appointments to the Court, diminishing the possibility of democratic accountability; about a Court becoming stagnant with no new members; about the possibilities of physical or mental decrepitude impairing Justices' performance on the Court; and over the possibility of Justices' timing their own resignations strategically to benefit or disadvantage particular Presidents. These concerns led to a number of proposals, including term limits and mandatory retirements. While these ideas are not new,[55] they were no doubt given added impetus by the unusually long period without new appointments.

In the first reading below, Professors Steven Calabresi and James Lindgren consider several different proposals and recommend a constitutional amendment to impose eighteen year terms. Professor Ward Farnsworth disagrees with these proposals and defends life tenure as producing a form of "slow law" that is a helpful counterbalance to the "fast law" enacted by legislatures. At the end of the chapter, we invite readers to reflect on "life tenure" and current understandings of the "during good behaviour" clause in securing the role and position of the Supreme Court as we have come to know it.

Steven G. Calabresi & James Lindgren,[56] *Term Limits for the Supreme Court: Life Tenure Reconsidered*, 29 Harv. J. L. & Pub. Pol'y 769 (2006)

INTRODUCTION

In June 2005, at the end of its October 2004 Term, the U.S. Supreme Court's nine members had served together for almost eleven years, longer than any other group of nine Justices in the nation's history. Although the average tenure of a Supreme Court Justice from 1789 through 1970 was 14.9 years, for those Justices who have retired since 1970, the average tenure has jumped to 26.1 years. Moreover,

---

55. Professor Henry Monaghan proposed consideration of both age and term limits in 1988, see Chapter Two (C) above.

56. Calabresi is the George C. Dix Professor of Constitutional Law and Lindgren is Professor of Law, both at Northwestern University.

before the death of Chief Justice William Rehnquist in September 2005 and Justice Sandra Day O'Connor's announcement in July 2005 of her retirement that eventually took effect on January 31, 2006, five of the nine Justices had served on the Court for more than seventeen years, and three of those had served for more than twenty-three years. The other four Justices had each already spent between ten and fourteen years on the Court. At the same time, four of these nine Justices were seventy years of age or older, and only one was under sixty-five—once the traditional retirement age in business. Because of the long tenure of these members of the Court, there were no vacancies on the high Court from 1994 to the middle of 2005.

We believe the American constitutional rule granting life tenure to Supreme Court Justices is fundamentally flawed, resulting now in Justices remaining on the Court for longer periods and to a later age than ever before in American history. This trend has led to significantly less frequent vacancies on the Court, which reduces the efficacy of the democratic check that the appointment process provides on the Court's membership. The increase in the longevity of Justices' tenure means that life tenure now guarantees a much longer tenure on the Court than was the case in 1789 or over most of our constitutional history. Moreover, the combination of less frequent vacancies and longer tenures of office means that when vacancies do arise, there is so much at stake that confirmation battles have become much more intense. Finally, as was detailed in a recent article by Professor David Garrow,[57] the advanced age of some Supreme Court Justices has at times led to a problem of ''mental decrepitude'' on the Court, whereby some Justices have become physically or mentally unable to fulfill their duties during the final stages of their careers. A regime that allows high government officials to exercise great power, totally unchecked, for periods of thirty to forty years, is essentially a relic of pre-democratic times. Although life tenure for Supreme Court Justices may have made sense in the eighteenth-century world of the Framers, it is particularly inappropriate now, given the enormous power that Supreme Court Justices have come to wield.

· · ·

To resolve the problems of life tenure, we propose . . . that lawmakers pass a constitutional amendment pursuant to Article V of the Constitution instituting a system of staggered, eighteen-year term limits for Supreme Court Justices. The Court's membership would be constitutionally fixed at nine Justices, whose terms would be staggered such that a vacancy would occur on the Court every two years at the end of the term in every odd-numbered calendar year. Every one-term President would thus get to appoint two Justices and every two-term President would get to appoint four. Our proposal would not apply to any of the

57. [Editors' Note: The authors refer here to David J. Garrow, *Mental Decrepitude on the U.S. Supreme Court: The Historical Case for a 28th Amendment*, 67 U. Chi. L. Rev. 995 (2000) (arguing that a number of Justices in the 20th century continued to serve past the point of competency and urging a constitutional amendment to provide for a mandatory retirement age of 75).]

nine sitting Justices or to any nominee of the President in office when the constitutional amendment is ratified. Supreme Court term limits ought to be phased in, as was done with the two-term limit for Presidents, which did not apply to the incumbent President when it was ratified.

. . .

Although many commentators have thus called for term limits on Supreme Court Justices, their proposals have received little attention, perhaps for two reasons. First, many Americans mistakenly believe that a system of life tenure is necessary to preserve an independent judiciary. Second, despite these scholars' various proposals, a comprehensive case has yet to be made in the literature for the need to reform life tenure. We seek to make that case by demonstrating that the real-world, practical meaning of life tenure has changed over time and is very different now from what it was in 1789 or even 1939. This significant change provides a strong, nonpartisan justification for reconsidering life tenure.

Our proposal is ultimately a Burkean reform intended to move the Justices back toward an average tenure that is similar to what the average tenure of Justices has been over the totality of American history. Just as the two-term limit on Presidents restored a tradition of Presidents stepping down after eight years in office, our eighteen-year term limit on Supreme Court Justices would push the average tenure of Justices back toward the 14.9–year average tenures that prevailed between 1789 and 1970 and away from the astonishing 26.1 year average tenure enjoyed by Justices who stepped down between 1970 and 2005. Our proposed amendment would thus merely restore the practice that prevailed between 1789 and 1970 and would guarantee that vacancies on the Court would open up on average every two years, with no eleven-year periods without a vacancy as has happened between 1994 and 2005. This then is a fundamentally conservative call for reform, all the more so because we resist the calls of many commentators for a very short tenure for Supreme Court Justices. The eighteen-year nonrenewable term we propose is more than long enough to guarantee judicial independence without producing the pathologies associated with the current system of life tenure.

Our proposal for imposing on Supreme Court Justices a staggered, eighteen-year term limit, with a salary for life and an automatic right to sit on the lower federal courts for life, could theoretically be established in a variety of ways, but the only way we approve of is through passage of a constitutional amendment pursuant to Article V. Accordingly, we outline in Part II below our proposal for a constitutional amendment instituting term limits. We then highlight the advantages of passing such an amendment and address potential counter-arguments. Short of amending the Constitution, Professors Paul Carrington and Roger Cramton have recently proposed a system of term limits for Supreme Court Justices instituted by statute. . . . [We conclude] that statutorily imposed term limits on Supreme Court Justices are unconstitutional.... [Such an approach poses a] grave danger ... that it would be manipulable by future Congresses. For these reasons, we believe that term limits ought to be established by a constitutional amendment and that the proposed statute is unconstitutional.

. . .

I. THE NEED FOR REFORM: THE EXPANSION OF LIFE TENURE

A. *The Expansion of Life Tenure Documented*

Life tenure for Supreme Court Justices has been a part of our Constitution since 1789, when the Framers created one Supreme Court and provided that its members "shall hold their Offices during good Behaviour." The Framers followed the eighteenth-century English practice, which developed in the wake of the Glorious Revolution of 1688, of securing judicial independence through life tenure in office for judges. But since 1789, Americans have experienced drastic changes in medicine, technology, politics, and social perceptions of judges and of the law that have changed the practical meaning of life tenure for Justices.

We analyzed this change by calculating the age and tenure in office for each Justice and by examining the number of years between vacancies on the Court. This empirical analysis revealed three critical and significant trends: the real-world, practical meaning of life tenure has expanded over time; Justices have been staying on the Court to more advanced ages than in the past; and, as a result, vacancies have been occurring less frequently than ever before.

Surprisingly, these trends have not been gradual.

... [T]he average tenure of a Supreme Court Justice has increased considerably since the Court's creation in 1789, with the most dramatic increase occurring between 1971 and the present. In the first thirty-two years of the Supreme Court's history, Justices spent an average of just 7.5 years on the Court, perhaps due in large part to the difficult conditions of circuit riding and a series of very short-lived initial appointments, including a short recess appointment for Chief Justice Rutledge. The average tenure of Justices then increased significantly between 1821 and 1850 to 20.8 years before declining over the next four thirty-year periods (spanning the period from 1851 through 1970) to an average tenure of only 12.2 years from 1941 through 1970. Then, from 1971 to 2000, Justices leaving office spent an average of 26.1 years on the Court, an astonishing fourteen-year increase over the prior period, 1941–1970. Justices leaving office between 1971 and 2006 thus spent more than double the amount of time in office, on average, than Justices leaving office between 1941 and 1970....

A cumulative average for the period of 1789–1970 puts this dramatic increase, reflected in the tenure of post–1970 retirees, in perspective. Compared to the average of 26.1 years in office for Justices retiring after 1970, the average Justice leaving office between 1789 and 1970 spent only 14.9 years on the bench. Thus, regardless of the basis for comparison—the average of 12.2 years for Justices leaving office during 1941 through 1970 or the average of 14.9 years for Justices leaving office from 1789 through 1970—the increase to an average tenure of 26.1 for Justices leaving office since 1970 is astounding. Indeed, four of the seven longest-serving Justices of all time are among the dozen Justices who have left the bench since 1970: Justices Douglas (36.6 years), Black (34.1 years), and Brennan (33.8 years), and Chief Justice Rehnquist (33.7 years).

. . .

In the five thirty-year intervals between 1789–1940, the average age of Justices upon leaving office rose from 58.3 to 72.2 years of age, but then dropped to about 67.6 years of age for the 1941–1970 period. Yet in the last period, 1971–2006, Justices left office at an average age of 78.7 years. Justices who have left office since 1970 have thus been, on average, eleven years older when leaving the Court than Justices who left office in the preceding thirty-year period, 1941–1970, and more than six years older than Justices in the next highest period, 1911–1940, one that famously included the era of the so-called nine old men. In addition, comparing the average retirement age since 1970 with a cumulative average age of all Justices retiring from 1789 through 1970 is equally revealing. The average Justice leaving office after 1970 (age 78.7) is ten years older than the average Justice leaving office prior to 1970 (age 68.3). Thus, the average age at which Justices have retired has increased markedly throughout history, and most sharply in the past thirty-five years.

. . .

Given that Justices have been staying on the Court for longer periods and retiring later in life than ever before, it is not surprising that vacancies on the Court have been opening up much less frequently than in the past. . . .

. . .

Moreover, the Court went for nearly eleven years—between 1994 and 2005—without a vacancy, the longest period between vacancies since the Court's membership settled at nine Justices. Eleven years is long enough in theory to deprive a successful, two-term President of the chance to appoint even a single Justice.

. . .

These historical trends represent a grand change in the practical meaning of the Constitution's grant of life tenure to Supreme Court Justices. The Founding Fathers were famously known for their disdain for "unaccountable autocrats out of touch with the typical citizen's concerns; who cling to power long after they have sufficient health to perform their duties; who cannot be removed from office by democratic agency." The Framers gave Supreme Court Justices life tenure in an era when the average American could expect to live only thirty-five years. Now, Justices are appointed at roughly the same average age as in the early years of our history, but they benefit from an average life expectancy of seventy-seven years. Of course, this statement alone significantly overstates the relevant difference because of higher rates of infant mortality two hundred years ago. Thus, a more relevant comparison might be that in 1850, white men who reached the age of forty could expect to live another 27.9 years, compared to such men in 2001, who could expect to live another 37.3 years. Largely as a result of this 9.4–year increase in life expectancy, today the average Justice who is appointed to the Court in his early fifties can expect to sit on the Court for nearly three decades, whereas the average Justice appointed to the Court in his early fifties in 1789 might have expected to sit on the Court for only two decades. Today's Justices enjoy a potential tenure that is fifty percent longer than that of their typical eighteenth- and nineteenth-century predecessors.

. . .

C. Explaining the Trends in Life Tenure

Identifying the trend toward longer tenures is much easier than explaining all of its causes. Nevertheless, one cause is the increased average lifespan of human beings who have lived to reach adulthood in recent times. Presidents have appointed Justices of substantially similar ages throughout American history: between fifty-two and fifty-seven years old since 1811. . . . [T]he average appointment age in the most recent period (1971–2006), 53.2 years, match[es] almost exactly the mean appointment age of 53.3 years throughout the Court's history (1789–2006). Yet Justices are retiring at much more advanced ages than ever before. Thus, the expansion of life tenure is caused not by Presidents' appointing younger Justices, but by the Justices' living longer and retiring later.

A second possible cause for longer tenures—the increased politicization of the Court over the last century—may have made political motives a more important factor in Justices' retirement decisions, which could have resulted in their deciding to stay on the Court longer for strategic reasons. While it has always been recognized that the Court has had some influence on politics, in the last fifty to eighty years the Court has come to be seen as a more important player than ever before in effectuating political and social change. As a result, the political views of individual Justices have become correspondingly more important. To sitting Justices contemplating retirement, the political views of a likely replacement (and hence those of the presiding President) may lead to their timing their resignations strategically. Such strategic resignations may have led more politically minded Justices to stay on the Court longer and later in age, which has expanded the real-world, practical meaning of life tenure.

Politics and strategic factors in Justices' retirement decisions may have been enhanced in recent years by frequent splits in party control of the Senate and the executive branch between 1968 and 2002. When one party controls both the Presidency and the Senate, that party should be more likely to name a Justice who reflects its views. For this reason, a Justice thinking about retirement might feel more comfortable resigning if her party controlled both the White House and the Senate. But when different parties are in control, the likelihood of controversial confirmation hearings for any replacement goes up. A Justice considering retirement in such a political environment will naturally want to avoid putting the country, and his party, through political controversy and will therefore wish to remain on the Court for longer periods of time, hoping that his party will attain control of both in the future. Thus, the political dynamic of the Presidency and the Senate being controlled by different parties could lead to longer tenures on the Court, older Justices, and less regular vacancies. And because such split-party control of the Senate and the Presidency has been a main-stay of the last thirty-seven years, it could easily have contributed to the trend of Justices staying longer on the Court during that period.

Indeed, strategic, political behavior by a series of Justices may help explain part of the increase in Justices' terms on the Supreme Court since 1970. Chief Justice Earl Warren, for example, purportedly (and unsuccessfully) tried to time his resignation in order to let a Democratic President name his successor, although in Warren's case this did not involve staying longer in office. Justices Black and Douglas, both very liberal in their jurisprudential outlook, allegedly stayed on the Court as long as possible, in futile attempts to avoid letting Presidents Nixon or Ford name their successors. Likewise, Justices Marshall and Brennan supposedly stayed on the Court for as long as possible in order to wait out the twelve years of Presidents Reagan and Bush; ultimately, though, they had to retire. Justice White, a Kennedy appointee, was alleged to have considered retirement in 1978 because of his concerns that President Carter would not be re-elected, and he ultimately remained in office long enough to allow fellow Democrat Bill Clinton to name his successor in 1993. And some have speculated that several current Justices have remained on the Court for as long as they have in order to avoid letting President Clinton (or President Bush, depending on the Justice) name a successor.

Anecdotal evidence aside, the historical data are mixed on whether there is statistically significant evidence that Justices engage in strategic decision making regarding their retirements. On the one hand, several studies suggest that Justices do not strategically retire during the terms of Presidents of the same party as the President who initially appointed the Justice. On the other hand, at least one study suggests that there is an effect. The data in yet another study suggests that there is a political effect, but this effect is not consistent. Without redoing the statistical analyses ourselves, we face several problems in trying to make sense of this conflicting research on the existence of strategic retirement.

. . .

[After describing their concerns with the various studies, the authors conclude:] In short, the statistical picture is inconclusive, awaiting a well designed study of the existence, size, and meaning of any strategic retirement by Supreme Court Justices. . . .

A third explanation for the trend toward lengthier tenure is drastic improvement in the social status associated with being a Justice and in the social perception of law and of judges more generally. For example, the life of a Justice in the Court's early days was marked by time-consuming and physically demanding circuit riding. Indeed, the arduous lifestyle of Justices riding circuit is widely thought to have caused a number of premature resignations. With the lack of a stable working environment and the other numerous difficulties involved in being a Supreme Court Justice in those days, it is not entirely surprising that many Justices retired relatively young after brief periods on the Court. Since the working conditions have improved dramatically with the elimination of circuit riding and the prestige of being a Supreme Court Justice has increased immensely, more recent Justices have understandably wanted to serve longer tenures and have been able to serve later in their lives.

Of course, the impact of circuit riding on the tenure and retirement age of Justices cannot begin to explain the most recent upward trends in tenure since the mid-Twentieth Century. Circuit riding was abolished early in the Twentieth Century, and longer life expectancies were already largely a reality by 1950. Interestingly, though, the longevity of Supreme Court Justices appears to have surged most dramatically only in the last thirty-five years. This appearance is somewhat misleading because some of the longest serving retirees of the 1971–2006 period were Justices Black and Douglas, both appointed in the late 1930s. The increase in Supreme Court tenure lengths was, for them at least, well underway during the 1960s. Yet this trend toward greater longevity may suggest that recent enhancements in the general social perception of law and of judges—of Supreme Court Justices, in particular—might have made serving longer on the Court more prestigious and more desirable.

A fourth factor that could explain this longer tenure is the increase in the size of the Justices' law clerk support staff since the late 1960s. Prior to 1970, each Justice had two law clerks each; that number increased to the present-day four-clerk staff in [the later 1970s]. This doubling in the size of the law clerk support staff makes the job of serving as a Justice on the Court much less demanding, and allows a Justice to delegate significant amounts of work to law clerks. It is striking that the increase in the number of law clerks post–1970 corresponds precisely with the period during which Justices have been staying longer on the Court.

Fifth, reductions in the workload of the Court—stemming both from Congress's near elimination of the Court's mandatory caseload and from the Court's drastic reduction in the number of certiorari petitions that it grants each year—have probably also made it possible for Justices to serve longer. Over the past fifteen years, the Court's annual caseload has fallen from about 150 to about 80. This, too, is a huge change: a staggering reduction of the Justices' workload by nearly half. The fact of the matter is that the job of being a Supreme Court Justice is much easier today with four law clerks, no mandatory appellate jurisdiction, fewer grants of certiorari, and three months of summer vacation, than was the case at other times in American history. These factors, coupled with lengthened life expectancies, less traveling, and the enhanced prestige of being a Supreme Court Justice, might help explain why Justices are staying on the Court for longer periods of time.

D. Consequences of the Expansion of Life Tenure

These historical trends—namely, later retirement and less frequent vacancies—have three primary consequences for the current state of the judiciary: the Court's resistance to democratic accountability, the increased politicization of the judicial confirmation process, and the potential for greater mental decrepitude of those remaining too long on the bench. Based on these consequences alone, a change in the current tenure system is desirable.

1. Reduced Democratic Accountability

The Supreme Court is, by design, independent of the political branches of government. Indeed, one of the most admired features of our judiciary is that Supreme Court Justices (and other federal judges) decide cases without the threat of political recourse or retaliation by other elected officials. The Constitution provides only two channels of democratic accountability for the Supreme Court. The first is the appointment process, and the second is impeachment. The only democratic control over the Supreme Court beyond the selection and removal of its members is the very remote possibility that its decisions will be overturned by constitutional amendment.

Supreme Court Justices are nominated by the popularly elected President, and are then confirmed by the people's representatives in the Senate. Conversely, the people, through their representatives in the House and the Senate, retain the power to remove Supreme Court Justices. Other than these explicit mechanisms for controlling Justices, the Court is subject to no other formal checks or balances.

Democratic checks on the Court via constitutional amendment are unlikely, and impeachment has been of no use whatsoever for controlling the behavior of Supreme Court Justices. In 217 years of American constitutional history, not a single Justice has ever been successfully impeached and removed from office by the Senate....

The appointment process is thus the most direct and important formal source of democratic control over the Supreme Court. Realistically, it is the only check that the other two branches have on the Court. Indeed, other countries that provide for political appointments to their respective constitutional courts do so precisely because "the democratic legitimacy of constitutional review rests upon the appointment of judges by elected authorities." . . .

For this process to work, turnover on the Court must be relatively frequent and regular. . . . [S]ince 1970 Justices have stayed on the Court for longer than ever before, and the democratic instillation of public values on the Court through the selection of new judges has been correspondingly infrequent and irregular. Moreover, . . . when vacancies do occur they are sometimes packed together in "hot spots," such that years will pass without any openings and, suddenly, two, three, or even four seats may open up within the space of a few years, followed by another long period without any vacancies. When this happens, the party in power at that particular time has a disproportionate impact on the Supreme Court, which can again prevent the American people from being able regularly to check the Court when it has strayed from following the Constitution's text and original meaning.

We think that the problem of hot spots is a serious one that can contribute to the Court's being out of step with the American people's understanding for long periods of time. For example, the Court of the "nine old men" was largely a function of the fact that Presidents Taft and Harding made six and four Supreme Court appointments, respectively, while Woodrow Wilson made only three appointments despite serving longer as President than both Taft and Harding combined. Other famous hot spots include Richard Nixon's appointment of four Justices in five years as President, followed by Jimmy Carter's inability to appoint even a single Justice in four years as President. It is hard to see why some four-year or eight-year Presidents should get so many more appointments than others . . .

Of course, Supreme Court Justices ought to be independent of at least some political pressures and, with fixed eighteen-year nonrenewable terms, they would still be quite independent. As Professor Martin Redish has noted, "Absent an independent judiciary free from basic political pressures and influences, individual rights intended to be insulated from majoritarian interference would be threatened, as would the supremacy of the countermajoritarian Constitution as a whole." The point, however, is that judicial independence is not the only value at stake here. If it were, then there would be no reason not to allow the Justices to elect their own successors—as happens in some countries— because such an appointment process would lead to a judiciary that is even more independent of the political process than is the system we have now. The reason we do not allow the Justices to pick their own successors is precisely because we believe that the judiciary, just like the legislature and the executive, needs to be subject to popular control and to the system of checks and balances. As a practical matter, the only check and balance on the Supreme Court is the appointment process. With Justices staying on the Court since 1970 for ten years longer than they have historically, and with vacancies on the Court opening up only half as often, this key check on the Court has been allowed to atrophy. It is time to go back to our practice from 1789 to 1970 of having independent Justices who stay on the Court for closer to fifteen years than to twenty-six years.

In sum, judicial independence is not an unqualified good. What we really need is a substantial measure of judicial independence, combined with some degree of a democratic check on the Court. To get back to the right balance, we need to amend the Constitution to provide for fixed, staggered eighteen-year terms for Supreme Court Justices. There should be no hot spots of vacancies and no eleven-year (or even four-year) droughts. There should also be no incentive to retire strategically and no ability of one political movement to lock up the Court for thirty years, as Republicans did at the start of the Twentieth Century and as Democrats did after the New Deal. A Supreme Court completely divorced from democratic accountability is an affront to the system of checks and balances. Accordingly, we should return to the practice that prevailed in this country from 1789 to 1970, when Supreme Court vacancies opened up on average once every two years and when justices stayed on the Court for closer to fifteen years than to twenty-six years.

2. Increased Politicization of the Confirmation Process

A second cost incurred by less frequent vacancies and by Justices serving for ever longer periods of time is that the process for confirming all federal judges can become so political and contentious as to grind to a halt. Under the current system, the irregular occurrence of vacancies on the Supreme Court means that when one does arise, the stakes are enormous, for neither the President nor the Senate can know when the next vacancy might arise. Moreover, a successful nominee has the potential to remain on the Court for a very long and uncertain period of time. So much is at stake in appointing a new Justice that the President and the Senate (especially when controlled by the party opposite the President) inevitably get drawn into a political fight that hurts the Court both directly and indirectly. The Court is affected directly, since it is deprived of one of its nine members, and indirectly, since rancorous confirmation battles lower the prestige of the Court.

Of course, a breakdown in the confirmation process is nothing new. Political battles between the President and the Senate over Supreme Court confirmations have occurred throughout history. However, in the last twenty years, with the lack of vacancies and the lengthening duration of the Justices' terms, the fighting between the political branches over the confirmation of Supreme Court Justices has reached new lows. The 1987 confirmation hearings of Judge Robert H. Bork and the 1991 confirmation hearings of Justice Clarence Thomas were among the most bitterly fought Supreme Court confirmations in all of American history. Moreover, the high profile confirmation fights over Bork and Thomas created a powerful (and undesirable) incentive for Presidents to find candidates without paper trails. Thus, the increased politicization of the confirmation process for Supreme Court Justices in recent years has undermined the ability of the President to fulfill his constitutional duty to appoint the best new Justices to the Court and even the ability of the Supreme Court itself to function effectively.

. . .

3. A Rise in "Mental Decrepitude" on the Court

. . .

Although mental decrepitude of Justices has been a problem on and off for 200 years, David Garrow reports that "a thorough survey of Supreme Court historiography reveals that mental decrepitude has been an even more frequent problem on the Twentieth–Century Court than it was during the nineteenth." Before the Twentieth Century, the Court was plagued by only five Justices whose mental abilities were diminished; in the Twentieth Century, at least twelve Justices served longer than they should have. . . .

For those commentators who pretend the current system does not need reform—"If it ain't broke, don't fix it"—it is time to recognize that the system is definitely broken. Whether one uses as the relevant rate of decrepitude 35% (of those leaving office after serving more than eighteen years since 1897), 45% (of the last eleven Justices leaving office), or 50% (of the last six Justices leaving the bench), the rate is unreasonably high. Mental decrepitude, a rare problem in the past, now strikes from a third to a half of Justices before they are willing to retire.[58]

The most common responses to the problem of mental decrepitude on the Court, as detailed by Professor Garrow, have been proposals for a constitutional amendment or a statute imposing a mandatory retirement age upon Supreme Court Justices. But a mandatory retirement age for Justices and judges would be unfair in that it would blindly discriminate against judicial service on the basis of age in a harsh way, one that does not take into account the actual mental condition of a given individual. A term limit on the tenure of Supreme Court Justices, such as that which we propose, would achieve nearly all the goals intended by a mandatory retirement age in a more uniform and respectful manner, without discriminating against a member of the Court based solely on age.

E. The Rarity of Life Tenure in the World's Constitutional Courts

The United States is alone "among the constitutional courts of western democracies . . . that [have] had judicial review since at least the early 1980s," and it is alone among all but one of its own states in providing its Justices with life tenure. The American system of life tenure for Supreme Court Justices has been rejected by all other major democratic nations in setting up their highest constitutional courts. . . . Every major democratic nation, without exception, instead provides for

58. [Editors' Note: The claims about the significance of decrepitude are controversial. See below at 1102–03.]

some sort of limited tenure of office for its constitutional court judges. Members of the constitutional courts of France, Italy, Spain, Portugal, Germany, and Russia serve fixed, limited terms of between six and twelve years. Moreover, judges on Germany's constitutional court also face a mandatory retirement age of sixty-eight, in addition to the twelve-year, nonrenewable term. Likewise, members of the Russian Constitutional Court face a mandatory retirement age of seventy, in addition to the fixed term of twelve years. Through term limits, many countries provide for regular, relatively frequent rotation in the membership of their constitutional courts.

Instead of fixed term limits, many other countries limit the tenure of their constitutional court justices and judges by imposing a mandatory retirement age. For example, the highest courts in such Western common-law democracies as Canada, Australia, and England enjoy tenures limited by a mandatory retirement age of [75, 70 and 70] respectively. In addition, other major countries, such as India and Japan, have instituted a mandatory retirement age in order to limit the tenure of members of their respective constitutional courts. Like Germany and Russia, South Africa has . . . a compulsory retirement age [as well as] a fixed term of office. . . .

Thus, every other major democratic nation that we know of—all of which drafted their respective constitutions or otherwise established their supreme constitutional courts after 1789—has chosen not to follow the American model of guaranteeing life tenure to justices equivalent to those on our highest court. In light of the strong worldwide trend against having lifetime tenure for members of the highest courts, the U.S. Supreme Court's system of life tenure is truly an anomaly.

Not only is lifetime tenure a rarity for judges worldwide, but, within the United States, nearly all states considering the question since 1789 have decided against giving life tenure to the members of their courts of last resort. Of the fifty U.S. states, only one—Rhode Island—provides for a system of life tenure for its Supreme Court justices. . . . Justices on the high courts in Massachusetts and New Hampshire face a mandatory retirement age of seventy. North Carolina's justices, who must be re-elected every eight years, must nonetheless retire at seventy-two. The other forty-six states all provide for limited terms of office for the justices of their highest courts, with the terms ranging from six to fourteen years. . . .

This comparative analysis—both outside the United States and within it—bolsters the case against life tenure and raises this question: Given the trend in all other jurisdictions as well as the pathologies associated with life tenure, if the Philadelphia Convention were reconvened today, would the Framers still opt for life tenure?

II. Term Limits for the Supreme Court

Historically, the most powerful case for life tenure for Supreme Court Justices was made by Alexander Hamilton in The Federalist No. 78. But Hamilton's argument has not stood the test of time. . . .

First, the Supreme Court is far more powerful today than Hamilton could ever have imagined in the 1780s, so it is far less in need of protection from the President and Congress than Hamilton expected. Second, life tenure is no longer justified, as Hamilton claimed in Federalist No. 78, by the need to encourage the best candidates to aspire to become Justices. Today, other incentives lure the best candidates to want to be Supreme Court Justices. Third, Hamilton's desire to insulate the Supreme Court from public opinion has been turned on its head; we believe the post–1970 Supreme Court has become, if anything, too insulated from public opinion, because Justices stay on the Court for an average of twenty-six years and because vacancies have opened up only once every three years or so. The Supreme Court should be made more responsive to the popular understanding of the Constitution's meaning, not less so. Fourth, contrary to Hamilton's argument that life tenure is necessary for us to attract Justices who will follow the Constitution, life tenure does not cause Justices to follow the text and original meaning of the Constitution. In fact, as Prakash argues, life-tenured Justices may be less likely to be textualists and originalists, not more so. Long tenures on the Supreme Court can, and do, seem to corrupt the Justices and to cause them to become policymakers, instead of followers of the law. Thus, Alexander Hamilton's defense of life tenure in Federalist No. 78 rings hollow today.

All these arguments against life tenure for Supreme Court Justices support our belief that the United States should adopt a system of term limits for its Justices. The next section lays out constitutional, statutory, and other informal ways of imposing an eighteen-year term limit on Supreme Court Justices.

A. Imposing Term Limits Through Constitutional Amendment

... It is well established that the Good Behavior Clause guarantees life tenure to all Article III judges. As a result, most of the advocates of Supreme Court term limits to date, except for Professors Carrington and Cramton, have conceded that life tenure can only be limited by means of a constitutional amendment. We agree with the majority view, and we take up the merits of such an amendment below.

B. The Term Limits Proposal

We propose that, in accordance with the Article V amendment process, Congress and the states should pass a constitutional amendment imposing an eighteen-year, staggered term limit on the tenure of Supreme Court Justices. Under our proposal, each Justice would serve for eighteen years, and the terms would be established so that a vacancy on the Court would occur every two years at the beginning of the summer recess in every odd-numbered year. These terms would be structured so the turnover of Justices would occur during the first and third year of a President's four-year term. This would diminish the possibility of a Supreme Court appointment's being held up by Senate confirmation so as to deprive the President of the ability to nominate either of his two appointees to the Supreme Court. The terms would also be set up so an outgoing Justice would complete his tenure on the last day of the Supreme Court's term and the new Justice could be confirmed in time to begin serving his term in October, before the beginning of the Supreme Court's next term. The Justices' terms would be nonrenewable: no Justice could be reappointed to a second term. This provision would help guarantee the independence of the Justices by removing any incentive for them to curry favor with politicians in order to win a second term on the high Court. Retired Justices would be permitted to sit, if they wanted to, on the lower federal courts for life.

. . .

[W]e propose that any term limit would be prospective only and that it would take effect only upon the election . . . of a new President. . . .

. . .

Instituting our proposal without immediately applying it to the current Justices or the sitting President would not be difficult. For example, suppose the amendment were ratified immediately. When the first new vacancy occurs after a new President takes office, the new Justice would be put into the eighteen-year slot that, if an odd year, started that year. If the vacancy arose in an even year, the Justice would be put into the slot that started the following year, and she would also serve the additional year until that slot began. So if the first vacancy occurred in 2009, the first transitional Justice would be appointed to an eighteen-year term starting in 2009. If the first vacancy arose in 2010, then the newly appointed Justice would be appointed to the slot beginning in 2011, plus the period between appointment in 2010 and 2011. If the next vacancy occurred in 2015, then the slot starting that year would be filled. If the next slot were already filled with a transitional Justice, then the new Justice would be appointed to the next open slot, plus the time until that slot began. Thus, during the phase-in period, some Justices would be appointed to the Court for eighteen years, while others would be appointed to somewhat longer terms. Of course, those who replaced these transitional Justices would serve only eighteen years. If an Associate Justice were elevated to be Chief Justice, she would remain in her eighteen-year slot, and leave the Court after serving a total of eighteen years.

Another special problem that might arise under our system of term limits is the early death or resignation of a Justice. . . . To handle this situation, we propose that if a Justice dies or resigns prior to the expiration of her term, an interim Justice would be appointed through the regular confirmation process (presidential nomination and Senate confirmation) to fill the remainder of the deceased or retired Justice's term. For example, if a Justice were to leave the Court following her tenth year of service, the sitting President at the time of death or resignation would be entitled to appoint a replacement Justice who, subject to confirmation by the Senate, would then serve only the remaining eight years of the departing Justice's eighteen-year term. She would then be constitutionally ineligible for reappointment to the Court. This method of naming successor Justices to complete only the original eighteen-year term of the predecessor Justice would enable mid-term turnover without sacrificing the benefits of staggered term limits—namely, the regularized updating of the membership of the Court. This would also eliminate the current incentive of Justices to time their retirements strategically, since retiring early would not result in one's successor being able to serve longer than the eighteen-year term to which one was appointed initially.

This proposed system of appointing an interim Justice to serve only a limited portion of the term finds support both in the high courts of other nations and in many other government positions in this country. For example, the judges of the French Constitutional Council serve a nonrenewable term of nine years. When a vacancy occurs prior to the expiration of a member's term, a new member is then nominated for the Council for the remainder of the deceased member's term. Likewise, Vice–Presidents of the United States, when acting for longer than two years as replacements for deceased Presidents, lose their eligibility to run as an elected President for one term. More generally, Vice–Presidents, senators, and representatives in this country who succeed a deceased or a resigned predecessor always fill out only the unfinished portion of their predecessor's term before they must be re-elected. Such a provisional replacement system is a sensible way of preserving the consistency of the staggered term limits proposal. . . .

Our term limits proposal resurrects the views of Thomas Jefferson and our American Brutus, Robert Yates. Both long ago advocated limits on the tenure of Supreme Court Justices and predicted calamity as a result of the life-tenured judges who, in Yates's words, "will generally soon feel themselves independent of heaven itself." Moreover, our specific proposal is a combination of the suggestions and plans advocated by Judge Laurence Silberman and Professor Oliver and draws heavily on the plans put forth by others like Gregg Easterbrook and Professors John McGinnis, Saikrishna Prakash, and Henry Monaghan.

The most persuasive of the many prior commentaries advocating Supreme Court term limits is the term limits proposal first made by Professor Oliver in 1986. Oliver begins by stating that "[t]he primary features of the proposal are that Justices should serve for staggered eighteen-year terms, and that if a Justice did not serve his full term, a successor would be appointed only to fill out the remainder of the term. Reappointment would be barred in all cases." . . .

C. Advantages of the Proposal

Our term limits proposal responds directly to the jump in the average tenure of Supreme Court Justices from an average of 12.2 years during 1941–1970, and 14.9 years during 1789–1970, to an average tenure of 26.1 years during 1971–2006. It also responds to the fact that, since 1970, Justices have retired or died at an average age of 78.7 years, while the average age for the prior 200–year period was 68.5 years. Finally, because of these other two trends, our proposal responds to the fact that vacancies on the Court have occurred with much less regularity since 1970 than over the whole of American history. Although between 1789 and 1970, a vacancy on the Court occurred, on average, every 1.9 years, in the last thirty-five years, a vacancy has occurred only every 3.1 years.

Our proposal should reverse all these trends. First, our term limits proposal would set eighteen years as the fixed term, in sharp contrast to the norm since 1970 of 26.1 years. Since the average tenure of all Justices throughout history is 16.2 years, our proposal would guarantee Justices a term longer than the historical average from 1789 to 2006, yet shorter than the current post–1970 trend of alarmingly long terms. . . .

Second, our proposed fixed term of only eighteen years would likely lead in practice to a younger average retirement age for Justices than the current age of 78.7 years. . . .

Third, and perhaps most important, our proposal would respond to the problem of hot spots and the increasingly irregular timing of vacancies by guaranteeing that a vacancy on the Court will occur like clockwork once every two years. . . . By fixing terms of eighteen years, and staggering them, a vacancy would occur at least once every two years. This would have two important effects. First, it would guarantee that every elected President would be able to appoint two individuals to the Court in a four-year presidential term. Second, it would reduce the stakes of the nomination process and eliminate the uncertainty that now exists regarding when vacancies will occur, which has had bad consequences for the confirmation process of Justices and for democracy itself.

Our proposal would not only correct all the current problems posed by life tenure for Justices, but it would make the Supreme Court more democratically accountable and legitimate by providing for regular updating of the Court's membership through the appointment process. Each time the public elects a President, that President will make at least two nominations to the Supreme Court, leading to a more direct link between the will of the people and the tenor of the Court. Our proposed term limit "would ensure that high courts that have become too conservative or too liberal can be turned over on a reasonable basis in keeping with the people's will (as reflected by the party they put in the White House)." While this would not make the Court accountable to popular sentiment in any direct sense, avoiding any threat to judicial independence, it would reinforce the one formal check on the Court's understanding of the Constitution that actually works.

At this point, it is logical to ask whether the popular understanding of the Constitution's meaning ought to guide the Supreme Court's understanding more directly. We believe that it should: the general public is more likely than are nine life-tenured lawyers to interpret the Constitution in a way that is faithful to its text and history, which is how constitutional decision making ought to proceed. The general public has a great reverence for the constitutional text and for our history, and much of the public intuitively understands that radical departures from text and history are illegitimate. The lawyer class in this country, on the other hand, is still imbued with a legal realist or post-modernist cynicism about the constraints imposed by the constitutional text. For this reason, we believe that enhancing popular control over the Court's constitutional interpretations will actually lead to better decisions than are produced under the current system.

Further, regularizing the occurrence of Supreme Court vacancies would equalize the impact of each President on the composition of the Court and would eliminate occasional hot spots of multiple vacancies.... And "[e]nsuring that every chief executive would have regular influence on the makeup of the Court ... would not only restore some of the check-and-balance pressure the Founders intended for all government branches but also inject more public interest into presidential campaigns."

Because of this democracy-enhancing goal of term limits for the Supreme Court, our proposal should not be viewed as merely another tired application of the once popular term limits movement. Term limits for elected officials ... restrict the ability of one candidate to seek office in a regularly scheduled election, which is arguably undemocratic because it limits the choices for the voting public. Term limits for unelected officials like Supreme Court Justices, on the other hand, provide for regular and more frequent appointments. Regularizing the timing of appointments to the Court thus has a dramatic democracy-enhancing effect, since it permits the people, through their elected representatives in the Senate and through the President, to update the membership of the Court more frequently and predictably to keep it in line with popular understandings of constitutional meaning. For this reason, a limit on the tenure of Supreme Court Justices, unlike other forms of term limits, would actually provide for a Supreme Court that is more, rather than less, democratically accountable.

By making vacancies a regular occurrence, and by limiting the stakes of each confirmation to an eighteen-year term ..., our proposal would greatly reduce the intensity of partisan warfare in the confirmation process....

Some may argue that our proposed amendment would actually increase the politics surrounding confirmations: because there is so much at stake in appointing Supreme Court Justices (or even lower federal appellate judges), our systematizing of the process would only make the already political event occur more often. This increased frequency, some might argue, would cumulatively increase the political nature of confirmations and, by letting parties plan on when the next vacancy might occur, our proposal would make the politics of confirmations begin even before the vacancy occurs. We disagree. The regularization of vacancies on the Court and the more frequent appointments to the Court would make each appointment less important politically and should have a net effect of reducing the politicization of the process.

From the current appointment battles we have direct evidence that the stakes do matter. President George W. Bush's federal district court nominees were seldom opposed, while many of his circuit court of appeals nominees were filibustered or not acted on. And when John Roberts was confirmed for the U.S. Court of Appeals, his confirmation on the Senate floor was by acclamation, whereas when he was nominated to be Chief Justice, many Senate Democrats opposed him. To those academics who would argue that lowering the stakes of a Supreme Court appointment would not lower the acrimony, we have ample evidence tending to support the opposite conclusion. By creating a predictable schedule of frequent appointments, our proposed amendment should reduce the intensity of the politics associated with confirmations at the Supreme Court level.

. . .

[O]ur proposal, though not directly responsive to the problem of mental decrepitude on the Court, would significantly further the goal of preventing mentally or physically decrepit Justices from serving on the Court. Limiting the length of service of any Justice to only eighteen years would reduce greatly the likelihood of a Justice continuing service on the Court despite incapacity. Of the eighteen instances of mental decrepitude on the Supreme Court discussed by Professor David Garrow, nine-fifty percent involved Justices who had been on the Court for more than eighteen years. . . .

Admittedly, even given an eighteen-year term, some Justices could still become mentally or physically decrepit during their tenure and continue to serve on the Court. Nonetheless, an eighteen-year term would still be an improvement over the status quo, for one thing because term limits would "end the psychological and political pressure on Justices to hang on long after their mental acuity falters." Whereas life tenure would allow, and perhaps even persuade, a disabled Justice to continue serving on the Court until his death, an eighteen-year tenure would affirmatively cap the Justice's career. This would ameliorate such situations "because forced retirement at the end of a stated term of office, rather than at death, would cause the situation to arise less often." . . .

Several scholars have instead proposed an alternate solution of mandatory retirement ages for the Justices as a way of reducing mental decrepitude on the Supreme Court. A mandatory retirement age is undesirable, however, either as a substitute or as a complement to an eighteen-year term. First, a mandatory retirement age is unfair, for it blindly discriminates against individuals based on age and cannot account for the capability of a seventy-year-old continuing in office, while a sixty-year-old might be best advised to retire due to differing individual capacities. A term limit, however, would more fairly permit individualized and informal determinations of capacity.

Second, it is a mistake in general to write numbers into the Constitution because they can become obsolete with the passage of time. The requirements that Presidents be at least thirty-five years old and that the right to jury trial be preserved in all suits at common law in which more than twenty dollars is at stake are classic examples of this. It seems quite possible that in fifty or one hundred years a mandatory retirement age of seventy or even seventy-five might seem absurdly young if people were routinely living to be over 100. It would be a bad idea to insert a mandatory retirement age for Justices into constitutional law, and it would not solve problems associated with life tenure on the Court.

An eighteen-year term offers several other benefits, including bringing the tenure of the members of our highest court into conformity with the practice of the rest of the world and of forty-nine of our fifty states. Assuming an eighteen-year term were coupled with permitting retired Justices to sit on the lower federal courts following their Supreme Court service, the lower federal courts would be enriched with the Justices' experiences and knowledge.

Finally and of critical importance, our proposal would eliminate the current practice of Justices strategically timing their resignations, a practice that embroils Justices in unseemly political calculations that undermine judicial independence and that cause the public to view the Court as a more nakedly political institution than it ought to be.... [T]here is mixed evidence that Justices throughout American history have timed their resignations for political reasons, including what is often a delay in retirement in order to avoid allowing a sitting President of the opposite party to name a successor. Our eighteen-year fixed term limit, however, would make it impossible for a Justice to time his resignation strategically. Of course, a Justice still could leave the Court prior to the completion of her term for political reasons, but under our proposal the retiring Justice's successor would be appointed only to complete the remainder of a fixed eighteen-year term. Therefore, an early strategic retirement decision would be of no avail, for it would not permit a President to lock up a Supreme Court seat for another eighteen years. As a result, under our proposal the Justices would lose the power they now have to keep a Supreme Court seat in the hands of their own political party by retiring strategically. This would promote the rule of law and the public's respect for the Court by precluding nakedly political decision making by Justices with respect to retirement.

D. Objections to the Proposal (and Responses Thereto)

Moving to a system of Supreme Court term limits would significantly enhance the overall legitimacy and functioning of the Court and our constitutional democracy. Yet our proposal is not uncontroversial. To date, by far the best case against Supreme Court term limits has been made by Professor Ward Farnsworth ... [see below].

First, some might argue that our proposed amendment would impair judicial independence, a value our Constitution was designed to protect through the Compensation Clause and the guarantee of life tenure. As Alexander Hamilton argued, life tenure secures the freedom of a judge from the political branches, as well as from public opinion, ensuring that judges can objectively interpret the law without risk of political reprisal. This benefit of life tenure is still recognized as critical. Professor Martin Redish argues, "Article III's provision of life tenure is quite obviously intended to insulate federal judges from undue external political pressures on their decisionmaking, which would undermine and possibly preclude effective performance of the federal judiciary's function in our system." Impinging upon life tenure, it is argued, would weaken this insulation, jeopardizing judicial independence.

We would not favor this proposed constitutional amendment if we thought it would undermine judicial independence in any serious way. As others have argued, moving from life tenure to a lengthy fixed term—a term longer than the average tenure of Justices who have served on the Court between 1789 and 2006—means that no independence will be lost relative to the other branches or to the public generally. Professor Monaghan states:

> But even assuming that such complete judicial independence is desirable, eliminating life tenure need not materially undermine it. Presumably, what relieves judges of the incentive to please is not the prospect of indefinite service, but the awareness that their continuation in office does not depend on securing the continuing approval of the political branches. Independence, therefore, could be achieved by mandating fixed, nonrenewable terms of service.

As Monaghan points out, the key to securing judicial independence is to guarantee that a Justice's tenure is not subject to the political decisions of the other branches or the public. Life tenure has made judges independent of the political branches, and we believe that this independence would be secured by our lengthy eighteen-year nonrenewable term limit with a salary set for life. Our eighteen-year term limit proposal would preserve judicial independence because it does not allow for reappointment, because it guarantees the Justices a longer tenure on average than they have historically had between 1789 and 2006, because it guarantees Justices their salary for life, and because the Justices would be secure from new means of removal by the political branches. As a result, except for the minimal and positive effect that more regular appointments would make the Supreme Court more responsive to the public and the political branches' understanding of the Constitution's meaning, there is no plausible argument that judicial independence would be endangered by our proposal.

Professor Ward Farnsworth offers a pragmatic defense of life tenure and suggests that an advantage of the current constitutional structure is that its resulting judicial independence contributes to a faster and a slower form of lawmaking: the first accomplished by Congress through the ordinary legislative process and the second accomplished by the Supreme Court. That the Supreme Court represents the political forces that prevailed ten or fifteen years ago and that it may take decades for a political movement to gain control over the Supreme Court's slower lawmaking process appeals to this scholar, whose argument is fundamentally conservative. In essence, Farnsworth thinks it is a good thing that progressives had to struggle from 1901 to 1937 to gain a majority on the Supreme Court and that conservatives had to struggle from 1968 to 1991 to get five solidly Republican Justices who even then refused to overrule *Roe v. Wade*. Farnsworth sees the Court as a major anchor to windward that slows down social movements for change, and he argues that to some extent judicial independence is desirable because a slowed-down lawmaking process is desirable as a matter of good public policy.

Farnsworth's argument is a powerful one, and we are sympathetic to his claim that it is desirable for the Court to slow down the forces of change in our democracy.... The question, however, is just how much conservatism one wants in one's lawmaking processes. Arguably, with separation of powers, checks and balances, federalism, and the Senate filibuster, we do not also need a Supreme Court whose fundamental direction can be reversed only by a sustained twenty-five or thirty year campaign. Different conservatives will answer this question in different ways, and those who are most averse to legal change may join Professor Farnsworth in praising life tenure. A Supreme Court with eighteen-year term limits will still be an anchor to windward in the American polity; it just will not be as much of an anchor to windward as has become the case in the last thirty-five years.

A second big objection that could be raised against our proposal is that it could lead to "Supreme Court capture." If a particular party were to prevail in five consecutive presidential elections, then, assuming that the President nominates and the Senate confirms individuals of the President's party, that party would have "captured" the entire Supreme Court for itself, a result that life tenure is designed to protect against. And, as Professor Farnsworth points out, even the appointment of four Justices by a two-term President could be enough to tip the ideological balance on the Court from Republicans to Democrats or vice versa. Accordingly, Professor Charles Fried has suggested to us that our proposal could cause the Supreme Court to become like the National Labor Relations Board, which is always captured by labor under Democratic administrations and by management under Republican rule. Farnsworth adds that because a "two-term President may reflect a single national mood ... there may be value in a court that cannot be remade by one such gust."

As a practical matter, however, Supreme Court capture would be extremely difficult to accomplish. First, members of either political party represent a diversity of viewpoints on judicial philosophy. For example, both Presidents and Justices range from extreme to moderate in their viewpoints, and sometimes moderates cannot be thought of as Democrats or Republicans as we label them. The six Republican appointees on the current Supreme Court certainly do not vote as a bloc any more than Democrat Byron White voted in lock-step with Democrat Thurgood Marshall. Indeed, the most left-wing and most right-wing members of the current Court (Justices Stevens and Thomas) were both appointed by Republicans. That some of our most liberal Justices were appointed by surprised Republican Presidents and some of our more conservative Justices were appointed by surprised Democrats makes Supreme Court capture an unlikely result, regardless of the tenure term.

Second, giving a two-term President four seats on the Court should not bother traditionalists like Farnsworth. From the time that the Court was fixed at nine Justices in 1869 until 1980, every President who served two full terms except Wilson was able to appoint at least four Justices: Presidents Grant (four), Cleveland (four), Franklin Roosevelt (eight, with five in his first two terms), and Eisenhower (five). Indeed, five Presidents who served less than two full terms got at least four appointments: Harrison (four), Taft (five), Harding (four), Truman (four), and Nixon (four). Wilson got three appointments, as did Hoover and Theodore Roosevelt (as well as Ronald Reagan after the temporal meaning of life tenure had changed). If our term limit proposal had been in force from 1869 through 1980, it would have enabled Wilson to get his fourth slot, but its primary effect on capture would have been to reduce the number of Presidents who got to choose four or five Justices though they served as President less than two full terms.

Third, with the gradual change that staggered terms would encourage, we should expect less violent lurches to the left or to the right of the kind that we have experienced since the 1930s. Any capture that did occur would tend to be mild and temporary. For example, the longest that one party has held the White House in the last sixty years is the twelve-year period from 1981 to 1993 when it was held by the Republicans. Some commentators worried about our proposal imagine a Court with four Reagan appointees and two by George H.W. Bush. But remember that such a Court should have had two Carter appointees as well, and if the elder President Bush's first appointment remained Justice Souter, he might well have replaced Justice Rehnquist when he would have stepped down in 1989. Thus, even at the height of Republican influence in the brief window between 1991 and 1993, the Court might plausibly have had Justices Stevens, Souter, and two Carter appointees on the left, Justices O'Connor and Kennedy in the middle, Justices Scalia and Thomas on the right, and another Reagan appointee in the middle or on the right. Instead of Justices Blackmun and White, we should have had two Carter appointees and instead of Rehnquist, we might have had a Reagan appointee like O'Connor, Kennedy, or Scalia. In short, at the height of possible Republican capture, the likeliest of many possible 1991 to 1993 Courts might well have been to the left of the one that we in fact had in 1993. . . . [Consider] the likely effect of adding four Clinton appointees starting in 1993. The Clinton Justices might not have shifted the Court much to the left because the first three should have been replacing Stevens and the two Carter appointees, and the last would have replaced O'Connor.... [Thus,] the sudden swings that can be imagined in capture scenarios would have been unlikely to have occurred in our last period of maximum capture by one party.

In addition to these practical difficulties of Supreme Court capture, the political check of Senate confirmation can, and often does, prevent a party from capturing the Court. While it is not uncommon for one of the two major political parties to prevail in consecutive presidential elections, since the election of President Nixon nearly forty years ago, it has been relatively rare for a President and the Senate to be controlled by the same party for more than two to four years. The Senate, when controlled by the party opposite the President, can use its constitutional role in confirming Justices to ensure that a President will appoint moderate individuals....

Moreover, even to the extent that our proposed system permits a party to "capture" the Supreme Court, the current system of life tenure permits precisely the same result. For example, during the twenty years of Democratic rule between 1933 and 1953, Presidents Franklin Roosevelt and Harry Truman were able to appoint a total of twelve Justices. This provided a perfect opportunity to capture the Court, a capture that was realized as to economic issues but not as to judicial protections of civil liberties. Additional examples abound ... Therefore, while our proposed term limit might make it slightly more likely that capture of the Court would arise, since our proposal leads to vacancies at reliable two-year intervals, the fact is that, even under the current system of life tenure, Supreme Court capture is always a real possibility. The primary effect of our proposal on capture should be to make it less intense and less persistent....

Nevertheless, one overriding goal of our proposal is to make the Supreme Court somewhat more reflective of the popular understanding of the Constitution than is presently the case. If a party manages to "capture" the popular will for consecutive elections with its vision of constitutional law, then that party will best represent the popular understanding of the Constitution's text and original meaning; it is only proper that the Supreme Court reflect that understanding. By tying the makeup of the Court more closely to presidential elections, we will allow the people to select (albeit indirectly) the kind of Justices they want on the Court, given the prevailing public understanding of the Constitution's text and original meaning. If the public becomes dissatisfied with the Court, then an eighteen-year term would permit the public to elect a new President who could initiate change on the Court with the next two appointments. Thus, our proposal causes the Supreme Court's judicial philosophy and understanding of constitutional meaning to reflect more truly that of the public's judicial philosophy and understanding of constitutional meaning than is currently the case. We emphatically believe this would be both a good thing and a return to the practice that prevailed for most of American history.

A third objection that might be raised against our proposed constitutional amendment is that imposing a limit on the tenure of Supreme Court Justices would force them to become too activist. Justice Kennedy, responding to a Judiciary Committee questionnaire during his confirmation process, wrote, "Life tenure is in part a constitutional mandate to the federal judiciary to proceed with caution, to avoid reaching issues not necessary to the resolution of the suit at hand, and to defer to the political process." Eliminating life tenure, one might argue, would endanger the virtue of patience that life tenure affords a Supreme Court Justice. Individuals with a limited opportunity period in which to affect the law might overreach in important cases and actively seek out opportunities to change doctrine. Alternatively, Justices serving their last years in office might face a final-period incentive to go out with a splash, knowing that in a short time they might no longer have to work and live with their current Supreme Court colleagues.

Any proposal leading to such judicial activism would undermine one of the chief advantages of an independent (and life-tenured) Supreme Court. Indeed, some of the more radical term limit proposals would more predictably lead to such problems. For example, under a term ranging from one to five years as proposed by Judge Silberman and Professors McGinnis and Prakash, Justices would likely feel pressure to accomplish a great deal in a very short amount of time. Under an eighteen-year term limit, however, no such activism should result, for such a period is sufficiently long that any individual Justice ought not to feel hurried in making his impact on the law. Under our proposed term, Justices would have the luxury, in Justice Kennedy's words, to "proceed with caution" and "defer to the political process."

Moreover, it is hard to believe that final-period problems would be more severe under our proposal than under the current system, in which old, life-tenured Justices know that retirement is just around the bend. Surely, on the current Court, Justice Stevens knows that he is in the final period of his tenure. Yet no one suggests his voting behavior has been influenced by a final-period problem. Nor did Chief Justice Rehnquist's and Justice O'Connor's behavior change during their last years on the Court, when they each knew they faced a final-period problem. We do not see why such a final-period problem would be any more likely under our system of fixed eighteen-year terms....

A fourth objection that could be made against our term limits proposal is its potential to erode the prestige of the Court by producing constant turnover. A system of staggered term limits, however, would in no way erode the prestige associated with the job of being a Supreme Court Justice. Significantly, each Justice's term would still be eighteen years long, which is ample time for Justices to become known individually and to acquire prestige. Nor would the Justices suffer a loss of prestige from performing a less weighty task: the immense powers and responsibilities of the Court's members would remain unchanged from what they are now. At most, the public's esteem and respect might be shifted from individual Justices and onto the Supreme Court as an institution—a very positive development in our view.

A fifth objection that might be raised against our proposal is that by making the Court more obviously responsive to public opinion, our amendment would cause the public to think of the Court as being even more of a policymaking body and even less a body restrained by law than is presently the case. Our proposal could thus be faulted on the ground that it would undermine the textual and historical constraints that ought to bind the Court by making everyone think of the Court more as being an indirectly elected, political body. As Professor Farnsworth puts it, our eighteen-year term proposal "may cause Justices to think of themselves as political officeholders in a more traditional way than they now do." This is a very substantial objection, and it is one that gives us pause. Happily, we think there are a number of responses that can be made to this point.

First, our amendment would end the current distasteful process whereby Justices strategically time their departures depending on which party controls the White House and the Senate when they retire. This process causes informed elites to view the Justices as being very political creatures, and it surely breeds cynicism about whether the Justices are currently applying the law or are simply making it up. . . .

Second, we think the American public is now more committed than are lawyerly elites to the notion that constitutional cases should be decided based on text and history. We thus think that augmenting public control over the Court will lead to more decisions grounded in text and history than are arrived at by life-tenured lawyers schooled in legal realism or post-modernism. The American public has a more old-fashioned belief in law as a constraining force than do lawyerly elites. It is for this very reason that we consider it so desirable to empower the American public relative to those lawyerly elites.

Professor Farnsworth challenges this idea and, citing Richard Posner, he argues that "the popular demand for originalism is weak." We disagree. We think the public has consistently voted since 1968 for presidential candidates who have promised to appoint Supreme Court Justices who would interpret the law rather than making it up. Even the Democrats who have won the Presidency since 1968 (Jimmy Carter and Bill Clinton) were from the moderate wings of the Democratic party, and the two Democrats appointed to the Court since 1968 are well to the right of Earl Warren or William Brennan. We think the public, while it is not very well informed about what outcomes originalism leads to, is still more originalist than are members of the elite lawyer class that under a system of life tenure dominates the Supreme Court, which is why Supreme Court opinions claim to follow text and precedent rather than claiming to follow Rawls, Nozick, Dworkin, Ackerman, or Tribe. The public may be induced, as it was in the Bork confirmation, into opposing an occasional originalist nominee. (Even so, it should be noted that in the Thomas, Roberts, and Alito confirmation fights, public opinion supported Thomas's, Roberts's, and Alito's appointments.) Overall, however, we think the public is more supportive of text and history in constitutional interpretation than are elite realist or post-modernist lawyers. We thus disagree with Farnsworth and Posner that popular support for originalism is weak.

Finally, we note again that the system our amendment would create of vacancies opening up on the Supreme Court once every two years is merely a return to the system that prevailed between 1789 and 1970. Ours, then, is a conservative reform—a restoration, if you will, of the traditional American status quo. . . .

· · ·

Undoubtedly, there are additional objections to our proposal that we have failed to address. But . . . until now, the system of life tenure has been retained mostly by inertia; the affirmative defenses of life tenure, and the objections to term limits for Supreme Court Justices, have not been thoroughly made. Our hope is that making a strong case for abolishing life tenure and replacing it with eighteen-year term limits will put the burden on the proponents of life tenure to make a reasoned case for preserving the current system.

III. ALTERNATIVE MEANS OF SOLVING THE TENURE PROBLEM AND THEIR DRAWBACKS

Other methods for solving the increasing tenure problem exist . . . that might be viewed as less drastic than the constitutional amendment we have proposed here. The first of these solutions is the imposition of term limits by statute. At first glance, this appears to be a viable option but upon further review, it must be seen as being unconstitutional and undesirable. The second type of solution would impose term limits through an informal process—by Senate-imposed limits through pledges obtained during confirmation hearings, by Court-imposed limits through the adoption of internal rules, or by Justice-imposed limits through tradition—all of which suffer from large drawbacks and lack enforceability. . . .

A. *Imposing Term Limits by Statute . . .*

1. *The Calabresi–Lindgren Proposal*[59]

The Calabresi–Lindgren statutory proposal . . . [is] that the President would appoint an individual to a vacancy on one of the lower federal courts, where, as Article III dictates, that person must enjoy life tenure. Then, by a separate act of presidential nomination and senatorial confirmation, that life-tenured lower federal court judge would be "designated" to serve on the Supreme Court for a term dictated by statute to last for eighteen years. At the end of the eighteen years, the statutory

---

59. [Editors' Note: The authors are here evaluating their own statutory proposal.]

designation of the lower federal court judge to sit on the Supreme Court would expire, ending the Justice's tenure on the Court, and returning him to the federal circuit court or district court bench for life. Thus, the individual would always enjoy life tenure (subject to impeachment) as a member of the federal judiciary, but he would serve on the Supreme Court for only eighteen years. . . .

. . .

Th[is] proposal for Supreme Court statutory term limits draws on . . . historical precedents [circuit-riding and sitting by designation] for authority. . . . If circuit riding was constitutional, as the first Congress thought, and as the Supreme Court held in Stuart v. Laird,[60] then Supreme Court riding for an eighteen-year period of designation ought to be constitutional as well.

2. The Carrington–Cramton Proposal

Under the statutory proposal put forward by Professors Paul Carrington and Roger Cramton, the Court's membership would be constitutionally fixed at nine Justices, and one new Justice would be appointed in each two-year session of Congress. At any given time, the Supreme Court would consist of the nine most junior commissioned Justices. Other, more senior Justices would be eligible to sit by designation on the lower federal courts. Those senior Justices could also be called back to the Court if one of the nine junior Justices were recused or during any period when the Senate failed to fill a vacancy on the Court during a session of Congress. . . .

. . . The main difference between the Carrington–Cramton proposal and circuit riding is that, under the former, Justices would spend their first eighteen years on the Supreme Court and any other time beyond that sitting by designation on the lower federal courts.

3. The Constitutionality of the Two Statutory Proposals

One major objection to both [proposals] is that the text of the Appointments Clause specifically contemplates a separate office of Supreme Court Justice. Thus the Clause provides that the President "shall nominate, and by and with the Advice and Consent of the Senate, shall appoint Ambassadors, other public ministers and Consuls, Judges of the supreme Court, and all other Officers of the United States, whose Appointments are not herein otherwise provided for, and which shall be established by Law." Neither [of the two statutory proposals] provides life tenure as an active duty Supreme Court Justice for those appointed to the Supreme Court. Given that the Appointments Clause plainly contemplates a separate office of judge of the Supreme Court, it is hard to see how that office could constitutionally be filled for only eighteen years and not for life. . . .

. . .

---

60. [Footnote 310 in original] 5 U.S. (1 Cranch) 299 (1803).

. . . Arguably, circuit riding, which involved appending some limited lower court duties to the job of being a Supreme Court Justice, still respected the mandate of the Appointments Clause that there be a separate office of Supreme Court Justice. Moreover, spending most of each year as a Supreme Court Justice and only a few months circuit riding arguably meant that some germane lower court duties had been attached to the job of being a Supreme Court Justice.[61] Under a system of lower court judges riding on the Supreme Court, there would be no separate office of Supreme Court Justice and the lower court judge would take an eighteen-year complete sabbatical from his lower federal court judgeship. This can hardly be described as the addition of a germane additional duty. We are thus in the end unpersuaded that the circuit-riding precedent permits a practice of lower court judges sitting by designation on the Supreme Court.

. . .

This reading of the Appointments Clause is in our view bolstered by the Clause in Article I that provides that there shall be a Chief Justice of the United States who shall preside over Senate impeachment trials of the President. That Clause clearly contemplates a separate office of Chief Justice, much as the Appointments Clause contemplates a separate office of Justices of the Supreme Court. Put together, we think the most plausible reading of these two clauses—and the reading most in accord with 217 years of actual practice—is that the office of Supreme Court Justice is a separately commissioned office.

Just as important, the two statutory proposals could be challenged under the provision granting life tenure to members of the federal judiciary. Article III, Section 1 of the Constitution provides that "[t]he Judges, both of the supreme and inferior Courts, shall hold their Offices during good Behaviour." There are two distinct readings of the language in this Clause. First, because of the phrase "both of" and because of the placement of "their," the provision might require that "Judges" of the Supreme Court must have life tenure, as must "Judges" of the inferior courts. This reading, probably the more natural one, would dictate that the Supreme Court and the inferior courts are distinct entities, and therefore life tenure must be guaranteed to members of both courts. It would follow that limiting the tenure of "Judges" of the "supreme Court," under both statutory proposals violates this provision even though it would grant life tenure to the former Justice as a judge of the "inferior" court.

A second plausible interpretation of the language would be that it simply requires that "Judges" at all levels ("both of the supreme and inferior Courts") must enjoy life tenure. . . . Under this interpretation, limiting an individual's tenure on the Supreme Court would pass consti-

61. [Editors' Note: The authors are referring here to cases under the Appointments Clause, including Weiss v. United States, 510 U.S. 163 (1994), which they describe as holding that "Congress [can] annex new duties to an existing office so long as those duties are germane to the duties of an existing office."]

tutional muster so long as that individual otherwise enjoyed life tenure on the federal bench (that is, on the "supreme and inferior Courts").....

. . .

The text of Article III, Section 1 (unlike that of the Appointments Clause) is ambiguous on whether it specifies a Supreme Court distinct from inferior courts....

Despite [this ambiguity] the Appointments Clause and the Clause providing for the Chief Justice to preside at Senate impeachment trials of the President seem to us most plausibly to suggest that the office of being a Supreme Court Justice is a separate and distinct office to which nongermane lower federal court duties cannot be attached. Admittedly, this is a somewhat formalistic reading of these two Clauses in conjunction with the Good Behavior Clause, but separation of powers rules often rely on such formalism....

Carrington and Cramton might nonetheless argue that their reading of the Good Behavior Clause is consistent with the purpose behind the life tenure provision—to preserve judicial independence—by ensuring judges do not depend on the political branches for their tenure of office. To achieve this purpose, it is not at all necessary that life tenure be guaranteed for any particular court. Rather, judges need only be guaranteed that they may stay on the federal bench for life and that they will not face retaliation for their decisions by Congress, the President, or the public. Both statutory proposals would satisfy this purpose and would guarantee that judges have life tenure and that their terms on the Supreme Court are fixed by time.

The Appointments Clause and the Chief Justice Presiding Clause, however, both seem to contemplate a separate office of Supreme Court Justice—a problem unaddressed by this functionalist argument. The Carrington–Cramton proposal runs afoul of these two clauses, no matter what functional justifications might underlie it....

. . .

4. *The Desirability of Imposing Term Limits by Statute*

Even if the two statutory proposals could pass constitutional muster, which we believe they cannot, the question remains whether it is desirable to institute a system of Supreme Court term limits by statute....

[A] key problem in the concept of establishing term limits through a statute ... is that term limits established by statute rather than by constitutional amendment are subject to greater manipulation by future Congresses[.]...

... [A]dopting a statutory term limits proposal runs the risk, as Professor Farnsworth points out, that interest groups, Congress, or the President might attempt to tamper with the statutory scheme of term limits in the future in order to achieve political gain. For example, if one party were to gain control over both the Presidency and Congress, they might manipulate the statute to permit their appointees to serve for longer than eighteen years or even for life, a result that would be particularly pernicious if the other party had abided by the statutory term limits during preceding years when they were in power. This risk of manipulation through the political process, which would not exist for a term limits constitutional amendment, greatly undermines the desirability of any effort to reform life tenure by statute. Of even greater concern is that, if Congress were to establish a precedent of being able to change the tenure of Justices and other federal judges by statute, Congress might become even more daring and later experiment with other independence-threatening forms of limits, perhaps even in substantive ways. For example, as Professor Redish suggests, interpreting the constitutional provision as Carrington and Cramton have suggested might permit Congress to pass a statute that allows it to demote a single Justice to the lower federal courts whenever it chooses. . . .

. . .

We think the manipulability of statutory term limits by future Congresses makes this a very dangerous constitutional road to go down. . . . The tenure of Justices of the Supreme Court is not a matter that should be settled by Congress as a matter of good public policy; it is something that ought to be constitutionally fixed. Thus, even if the statutory term limits proposals were constitutional, which they are not, we believe it would be a bad idea as a matter of policy for Congress to start tinkering by statute with the tenure of Supreme Court Justices for the first time in American history.

. . .

B. *Imposing Term Limits through Informal Practice* . . .

1. *Senate–Imposed Limits Through Term Limit Pledges*

The Senate could use its crucial constitutional role in the appointments process to push toward a system of term limits for the Supreme Court by "insist[ing] that all future court nominees publicly agree to term limits, or risk nonconfirmation. Though such agreements would be legally unenforceable, justices could feel honor-bound to keep their word."

. . . [S]enators could require each nominee to agree to retire after eighteen years or after some other suitable term. Of course, such an agreement would be unenforceable, and there is no guarantee that a Justice would feel compelled to follow the pledge. Indeed, having made a term limits pledge has not deterred some legislators from continuing to run for Congress beyond their self-imposed limits. . . .

This kind of term limits pledge "would not raise judicial independence or due process problems" that accompany the kinds of "promises" that nominated Justices are sometimes asked to make in Senate confirmations, like pledges to rule certain ways on particular issues. Unlike such substantive promises, term limits pledges are merely "a promise to resign on a fixed date, . . . comport[ing] with judicial integrity."

Notwithstanding these considerations, we do not favor term limit pledges. Any Justice who arrives on the Court having pledged to step down after a term of years will likely be viewed by the other members of the Supreme Court as having compromised a key bulwark of judicial independence. He would look so eager to serve on the Court that he was willing to undercut a standard practice of the Court, thereby increasing pressures on future nominees. If a Justice thinks it proper to step down after eighteen years, he may do so; what he . . . should not do is appear to offer a promise to step down to gain a place on the Court. . . .

2. *Limits Imposed Through Internal Court Rules*

The Supreme Court itself could play a role in deterring Justices from serving as long as possible on the Court and in moving us toward a system of de facto term limits . . . As Professors Akhil Amar and Calabresi observed, "perhaps the Justices themselves might collectively codify retirement guidelines in court rules modifying the seniority system or creating an ethical norm of retirement at certain milestones." The Court could thus adopt a retirement rule requiring Justices to step down after eighteen years of service on the Court. Though such internal rules would not be legally enforceable, the pressure on a Justice from his fellow Justices, as well as from the institution, could be a valuable method of limiting tenure. . . .

Another way for the Court itself to decrease the incentives for Justices to remain on the bench is to modify its seniority system. Currently, the most senior Justice in the majority decides which Justice will write the majority opinion. . . . Rewarding the most senior Justices with priority in assigning opinions creates an incentive for Justices to remain on the Court for long periods and to a later age. By eliminating this seniority system, or modifying it in some regard, the Court can eliminate these incentives.

To be sure, appointing more senior Justices to assign decisions is logical, and abolishing the seniority system might seem too drastic. Alternatively, through its various political checks on the Court, Congress could play a positive role in persuading the Court to develop a system of term limits through its internal court rules. For example, "Congress could . . . restructure judicial salaries, pensions, office space and other perks to give future justices incentives" to step down after a set number of years. Giving a huge pension to any Supreme Court Justice who retired after his eighteenth year of service might well accomplish a de facto term limit. Or Congress could reduce the number of law clerks allowed each Justice, which, by increasing the Justice's personal responsibilities, might reduce the ability or willingness of a Justice to continue serving as late in age as they currently do. Likewise, by statutorily increasing the mandatory jurisdiction of the Court or otherwise adding to the Court's workload, Congress can reduce the incentives for Justices to remain on the Court as long as they currently do.

Of course, a political war between Congress and the Court over these incentives is undesirable, and Congress must be cautious and deliberative in using these mechanisms as a way of encouraging the Court to move voluntarily toward a system of term limits. But these measures may be effective ways for Congress to encourage the Justices to move toward informal term limits. And, short of amending the Constitution, Court-imposed term limits on Justices, with or without congressional prodding, might be the most desirable method of reforming life tenure.

3. Justice–Imposed Limits Through Voluntary Retirement

In theory, at least, Supreme Court Justices themselves could individually lead the way toward a reform of life tenure, even without a formal Court-ordered arrangement. Conceivably, a group of Justices could try to start a tradition of retiring from the Court after a certain number of years, or at a set age, in the hopes that institutional pressure could develop that would bear on all future Justices. Some federal courts of appeals, like the Second Circuit, do have an established norm that all judges on the court take senior status on the first day they are legally eligible to do so. . . .

But this solution has its own difficulties. Is it realistic or even desirable for one or two Justices to try to start a tradition of retiring from the Supreme Court after a set number of years? Probably not. Such Justices would face a major collective-action problem in trying to persuade their long-serving colleagues to follow their good example. Given the level of partisan hostility on the Supreme Court, and given the extent to which most recent Justices seem to have tried to practice strategic retirement, we believe urging a Justice to retire after a set term without regard to strategic considerations would be like unilateral disarmament during the Cold War. . . .

CONCLUSION

. . . Although defenders of life tenure have long been able to say, "If it ain't broke, don't fix it," this Article has shown that the current system of life tenure for Justices is deeply flawed. The effects are subtle and not readily visible to the American public, but the dangers are real and the threat is severe. Life tenure deserves serious reconsideration; indeed, it should be abolished. Inertia should no longer justify its continuation.

. . .

Moving to a system of eighteen-year, staggered terms for Supreme Court Justices is fundamentally a conservative, Burkean idea that would restore the norms in this country that prevailed on the Court between 1789 and 1970. . . . The United States Supreme Court ought not to become a gerontocracy like the leadership cadre of the Chinese Communist Party. It is high time that we imposed a reasonable system of term limits on the Justices of the U.S. Supreme Court.

———————

Ward Farnsworth,[62] *The Case for Life Tenure,* in *Reforming the Court: Term Limits for Supreme Court Justices* 251 (Roger C. Cramton & Paul D. Carrington eds., 2006)

INTRODUCTION

My purpose in this essay is to offer a defense of life tenure for Supreme Court justices, and in the process to offer some new ways of thinking about the current function of life tenure and its implications. I argue that while there are some solid arguments for replacing life tenure with fixed terms, there likewise are strong arguments for leaving it in place; many of the benefits claimed for fixed terms are illusory or likely would be offset by new problems they would cause. I also discuss the case for age limits and find it somewhat stronger than the case for fixed terms.

FASTER AND SLOWER LAW: A PRAGMATIC ACCOUNT
OF THE FUNCTION OF LIFE TENURE

Americans live under two types of law, fast-moving and slow. The faster law is made by Congress, state legislators, and other actors subject to replacement every few years through normal political channels. The slower law mostly is made by a committee of officials called justices. (Subordinate officials known as judges make contributions as well, but my focus will be on the Supreme Court.) The fast and slow labels arise from several features of legislation and adjudication; a key feature of the Court that causes it to move slowly, and my focus here, involves turnover. Since the justices keep their jobs for a long time, it takes a long time to replace them if the public does not like what they do.

The special value of the Court as a slow lawmaker is based on distrust of short-term or even medium-term majoritarian judgments relative to long-term ones. Putting issues on a slower track helps protect them from swifter currents of opinion more likely to produce bad law, perhaps because the swift currents are more likely to have disproportionate force of the kind discussed by public choice theorists or because they represent views that seem appealing for a while but whose deficiencies become clear with time. A constitutional document may not serve much of a slowing function if the act of interpreting it is made too politically responsive. When people want things done they will find lawyers who think the Constitution allows their preferred results and fit them with robes. The slowing function arises when the authority to declare the trumping law is assigned to an institution whose members are replaced infrequently, and still more when the replacements are made through a

———————
62. Professor of Law and Nancy Barton Scholar, Boston University.

means that provides some insulation from the public will. Rare but steady turnover on a constitutional court thus may be a superior mechanism to constitution plus-amendment if the goal is to test the durability of an idea before adding it to a slow-moving corpus of law.

The question is whether these mechanisms of braking and entrenchment have value. Sometimes the difficulty of remaking the Court makes it harder to overthrow good and bad legal conventions alike. The attractiveness of the package depends on one's satisfaction with current legal conditions and fear of the alternatives. The Court is set up to reflect a strong sense of satisfaction with the outlines of the slower law and a corresponding interest in decelerating changes in them. Speeding up the rate of change would create winners and losers, but it is hard to be sure who they would be, and in the meantime most Americans enjoy a combination of expansive liberties and social stability that makes them understandably risk-averse. If they interested themselves in the debate over the Court's role they would find Robert Bork on the right and Mark Tushnet on the left, both dismayed by the Supreme Court's frustration of their projects; possibly our hypothetical onlookers would say that any institution capable of providing so much discouragement to both men must be doing something right.

These points can be made more concrete. A main consequence of the most common proposals for fixed terms—the proposals to have justices serve for eighteen years apiece—is that they would guarantee every two-term president at least four appointments to the Court: the ability to create a near-majority, which easily could become a majority with the addition of an interim appointment or the presence on the Court of a like-minded justice appointed some years before. This can happen already, but it usually does not. The question is whether we should ensure that it always does. A two-term president may reflect a single national mood, and I contend there is value in a Court that cannot be remade by one such gust. And as the lengths of the proposed terms get shorter, the risks become greater that a burst of political sentiment will take the slower law along with it as well as the faster—or rather that the slower law would not be much slower after all.

· · ·

SENSES OF ACCOUNTABILITY

Many critics of life tenure believe it has made the Supreme Court insufficiently accountable. But what do they mean? A first kind of accountability involves outcomes of specific cases. The Court might make decisions the public hates; the sooner the justices are forced to retire, the sooner they can be replaced with nominees the president thinks will reverse the disliked decisions. This often is what people have in mind when they speak of holding the Court accountable. They want *Roe v. Wade* reversed or want to prevent its reversal. But there are good reasons to avoid tampering with the Court's turnover mechanisms to make particular decisions easier to change. First, one of the valuable things courts do is make unpopular decisions that stick—decisions protecting the rights of minorities or preserving structural features of the Constitution that frustrate the majority's will but have long-run benefits. The public naturally may feel outrage when decisions of that sort are made, yet might rather endure the outrage than make it easier to convert it into reversal. At present we put a large share of trust in a body we know will let us down often instead of taking chances on a more responsive system that would allow good and bad outrage alike to carry the day and let us down in other ways. Forcing the reversal of a disliked decision by replacing the justices who made it is kept a possibility only in the very long run.

A different but related kind of accountability involves more amorphous preferences. Presidents, senators, and interested members of the public take an interest in what *sorts* of decisions the justice will make; they do not know quite what questions will arise but are anxious that they not be disappointed by the Court's answers to them. So they settle for (or object to) the appointment of types to the Court—a conservative or liberal type, a hawk or a dove. The types refer to clusters of values and preferences that a holder of them is expected to bring to bear when confronted with whatever problems arise later. Thus in the twelve years leading up to 1992 the country elected Republican presidents friendly toward notions of states' rights and skeptical of the value of a large federal government. Those presidents made five appointments to the Court. In 1995 their appointees began issuing decisions limiting congressional power and enhancing the power of the states in various ways. The decisions in these cases often owed nothing to conservative judicial philosophy, and in their details they probably were not foreseen by those involved in the appointment of the justices who made them. The decisions nevertheless were congenial to conservatives as matters of policy and can be heard as echoes of the elections that indirectly produced those justices' appointments. Those federalism cases illustrate how the Court often is responsive to the public will in a general and delayed fashion. One might object that the responsiveness should be greater, but it seems unlikely that a shortage of this type of accountability is what troubles the critics of life tenure, for many of them are originalists who decry the Court's tendency to reflect the recent political past.

Perhaps what critics of life tenure mean when they worry about accountability is that it should be easier for the public to rein in the Court when it makes bad decisions as matter of method rather than outcome. The trouble with trying to make the Court more accountable to the public as a matter of method, however, is that there is no evidence the public understands these issues or is interested in them. Nor is there much evidence that presidents are interested when they pick their nominees. There are no known cases where a president nominated a justice because he liked the nominee's theory of interpretation despite thinking he would produce disagreeable results. Meanwhile the opposite pattern is common: a president picks someone expected to produce pleasing results even though the nominee's views about interpretation, if any, are hard to discern. These practices sometimes create the illusion that theories of interpretation make an important difference: originalists fantasize that their theory is making headway on the Court when it is just the felt desirability of the outcomes produced by originalism that is making headway; when those outcomes lose their appeal, originalism loses appeal or adapts to produce other outcomes. There is no evidence to support the notion that anyone involved in the selection process is interested in interpretive theory *per se*.

Now of course one could argue that all this is unfortunate: we need a new commitment to appointing justices for their ideas about interpretation in some purer sense, not the results they would produce. The crucial point for our purposes, though, is that whether the current tendencies are good or bad, adjusting the length of the justices' terms would not be likely to change them. Indeed, life tenure and the long terms it creates is the regime most consistent with a vision of the justices as impersonal appliers of interpretive theories. Fixed terms would give us more often what we already get; they would cause the public's appetites to be satisfied more regularly, but there is no reason to think they would change the content of the appetites or the relationship between the appetites and judicial behavior.

POLITICIZATION

... It often is said that the process of confirming justices has become too politicized. The hard part is figuring out what this claim means. Sometimes nominations provoke bitter combat—but only sometimes: the two most recent ones, those of Ginsburg and Breyer, did not give rise to any savagery; nor did the recent hearings on the confirmation of John Roberts. It is true, of course, that some other recent nominations have been hotly contested and that fear of such contests helped produce the tamer nominations just mentioned. This is the heart of the matter: the proceedings turn ugly when presidents put forth nominees believed to have strong, evident ideologies. The most conspicuous example is Robert Bork. Bork's difficulty, however, was not that he would be serving for life rather than for eighteen years; he was sixty years old, so he probably would not have stayed on the Court for much more than eighteen years anyway. The trouble was that he held controversial views. . . . [I]t is hard to see why his defeat represents a failure of the nomination process if one believes (as opponents of life tenure generally do) that nominations provide an important chance for the public to have something to say about how the Court makes its decisions.

Let us look harder at why some nominations produce bitter debate. The stakes are high when a president puts forward a nominee likely to try to change the slower law in a way that much of the country does not want. It becomes worthwhile for those who do not like the nominee to inflict costs on him, on their opponents, and on themselves to prevent him from being confirmed. If one wants to lower the heat associated with nominations, one can pick nominees who seem moderate and will not provoke aggressive efforts to derail them. Or one can be more unyielding and stand the heat. As an example of the latter approach we cannot do better than the advice once offered by Steven Calabresi: "a conservative President must at all costs keep nominating one pro-Rule of Law Justice or judge after another." Very well, but no one who urges such a strategy should be heard to complain when its opponents resist with the same ferocity. The resulting process will be a negotiation, and negotiations of such a high-stakes character usually are not enjoyed by the participants and do not put them in an attractive light. Things are said that one regrets; relationships are injured and reputations soiled; the impression that the process has become undignified and unpleasant—politicized— naturally takes hold. The unpleasantness becomes especially likely when either or both sides are committed to playing hardball, as Calabresi evidently is—an insistence on having one's way, as he says it, "at all costs." Nor can it be surprising if the strategy is reciprocated by one's opponents in the bottom half of the inning.

Of course it is possible that this account complements rather than contradicts the case for limited terms; it may be that life tenure inflames the perceptions that lead to the hard results and that fixed terms would put both sides into a more giving humor. Yet it is hard to see why. There would be no evident reason for the advice we just saw Calabresi offer to change if the justices served for eighteen years, nor any reason to think the best reply to such tactics would be different. There has been no shortage of polarizing debate over controversial recent nominees to other positions where they are expected to serve for no more than a few years.

Meanwhile there is reason to worry that fixed terms would make the unappealing features of the confirmation process worse. By attaching nominating chances to presidencies they would create more natural cycles of revenge. The effect *could* work the other way: knowing that more nominations will be coming soon, everyone would show restraint; knowledge that the other player will have chances for revenge can help deter bad behavior. But games of this kind can go badly if distrust runs high and the best play for each side depends on error-prone judgments about the good faith of the other. Each comes to think the other misbehaved first and needs a lesson. We see this pattern now in nominations to the courts of appeals, and perhaps one reason we have not seen cycles quite like it in Supreme Court nominations, despite the occasional rancorous case, is that they do not arise frequently and predictably enough to provoke this structured sort of turn-taking.

A related objection to fixed terms is that they would facilitate the work of interest groups trying to influence the composition of the Court. If justices served terms of eighteen years, one no longer would speak of the *possibility* ... [of] appointments to the Court. Every winner would be guaranteed two of them. The stakes for the Court in every campaign thus would be higher than they currently are; interest groups would see larger expected returns from pressuring candidates to make promises about how they would use their two nominations if elected, from condemning candidates who fail to do so or who say the wrong things, from putting pressure on those who say the right things to keep their promises, and so forth. As the expected returns on political pressure rise, so will investments in creating it. Fixed terms also would make it easier to co-ordinate pressures farther in advance. Today vacancies on the Court arise unpredictably. Suddenly a retirement is announced; there is an outburst of political jostling; usually a nominee is named a few weeks later and confirmed within a month or two. But with fixed terms everyone would know far ahead of time when the next vacancy would arrive and what seat would be involved. Campaigns to have it filled would begin far in advance, just as a new political campaign begins as soon as the prior one ends. Of course many groups already try to build reserves of pressure in advance of retirements on the chance that they might pay off, but their labors often end up a waste of time when nobody retires. Fixed terms would eliminate that risk. Depriving pressure groups of a fixed target, as life tenure does, makes it a little harder for them to organize their efforts and concentrate their energies too pointedly.

A note on pressure to appoint the young. It sometimes has been suggested that life tenure creates too strong an incentive for presidents to choose young nominees.... [But the] average age of appointment over the past thirty years is the same as it had been during the previous one hundred eighty years: about fifty-three years old. The only recent justices who were younger than fifty when appointed were Rehnquist, who was forty-six, and Thomas, who was forty-three. Thomas's appointment might have been expected to provoke retaliatory nominations of young justices next time a Democrat got the chance. It did not happen. The next was made by President Clinton; it was Ruth Ginsburg, who was sixty. Clinton's next appointment was Stephen Breyer, who was almost fifty-six.

Why have we not had a race to the bottom? One reason is that presidents make decisions in the shadow of the confirmation process; repeated efforts to appoint forty-three-year-olds to the Supreme Court are likely to be met with public hostility because most people of that age have not accomplished enough to inspire confidence in their judgment. But probably the more important reason why presidents do not usually appoint the youngest plausible candidates they can find is that they lack incentives to do so. An actual goal of many presidents—perhaps most of them—is to maximize their political fortunes.... [T]he insights of public choice theory have their application to the selection of judges as well as to the creation of legislation. Both the president and the constituencies he worries about satisfying may have limited time horizons, applying a discount rate that makes the present value of possible changes on the Court twenty-five years away too small to matter.

· · ·

THE DISTRIBUTION OF APPOINTMENTS AMONG PRESIDENTS

... Probably the best argument for fixed terms is the one pressed hardest by Professor Oliver: they would spread nominations to the Court evenly among presidents. The argument is impressive but not, I think, as decisive as it might seem at first. First, there are countervailing influences that help smooth out misallocations of chances to the two parties. It usually is hard to predict how someone will behave on the Court; there is noise in the process that prevents appointments from being very accurate registers of political consensus. But the more important point is that the Senate helps compensate for the lumpy way in which nominations are distributed to presidents. The Republican presidents who appointed John Stevens and David Souter wanted to avoid trouble in the Senate and so deliberately chose nominees who carried more ideological risk than the alternatives. The risks paid out badly for conservatives; but another way to view the results is that pressure from the Senate helped prevent flukes in the timing of justices' retirements from causing a comparable shift in the balance of ideologies on the Court. Nobody in the Senate needed to have been thinking this way at the time. They served a useful purpose just by providing friction against the president's preferences; in this way the Senate works as a hedge against the vicissitudes of election cycles and retirements from the Court....

... Another question is how helpful fixed terms really would be in giving the Court a better political pedigree. This part of the argument for fixed terms supposes that the distribution of Supreme Court nominations ought to correspond in an intelligent way to the distribution of political will in the society at large. The premise makes enough sense, but promising two appointments to every president hardly would assure any such correspondence. Presidential elections are themselves lumpy, winner-take-all events. There is no guarantee that a political minority representing x percent of the population will carry x percent of elections. They may win none, and a large minority that repeatedly fails to win any presidential elections may not see its views represented at all on the Court. Meanwhile the narrow winner of a presidential election gets no fewer nominating chances than a winner by a landslide.

These sorts of anomalies are common features of our political system; there are various ways that fifty-one percent of some set of voters can wind up with one hundred percent of the power. But there also are mechanisms in place to check and dilute those effects. If one wants ideological control over the Court tied in a satisfying way to the ideological composition of the polity, using checks is a sounder strategy than trying to make sure every president gets the same number of appointments. The obvious check would be to shift more power in the nominating process to an institution that reflects a wider range of inputs: the Senate. We have seen that a strong role for the Senate helps mitigate the effects of the arbitrary assignment of nominations to presidents. Now we can also see that it helps tie the Court's membership to a source of political authority more satisfying than the presidency even if every president were to get two appointments. The Senate has great shortcomings as a representative institution, of course, but at least both parties always are represented there at the same time and so create possibilities for debate and compromise missing if the choice is given to the president alone. Giving two appointments to every president will make only a small contribution to political equity if the Senate has a weak role; and if the Senate's role is strong, the distribution of appointments to presidents becomes less important in any event.

If a strong role for the Senate is salutary in this way, notice that it is likely to be reduced by giving the justices fixed terms. The two appointments given to a president would likely be claimed by as his own to spend as he sees fit. He earned them. No doubt many in the Senate and elsewhere would resist this way of thinking, but the case for deference to the president's choices undoubtedly would be strengthened relative to where it currently stands; for at present the Senate justly can resist a president's aggressive nominations on the ground that the chance to make them was delivered to him by luck. By weakening this argument fixed terms would enlarge the president's powers and worsen the distortions created by putting nominations into a single person's hands.

. . . Another likely drawback of precisely allocating appointments to presidents would be the dynamic consequences: they might increase the justices' sense of obligation to carry out the wishes of whoever appointed them. We find a danger here parallel to the one concerning the Senate. If everyone knows that two seats on the Court are a spoil the president won fair and square, those seats may be regarded as his to fill in a stronger sense than we currently see; so his nominees may feel more pressure to carry out the president's agenda. They will know they owe their membership on the Court to a decision by the leader of a political party about how to spend his turn and that turns are given to the other party in regular fashion, not distributed by luck. They will be Republican appointees or Democratic appointees in a more explicit sense than they now are. Some may therefore view their own roles in a manner a little more political and a little less law-like.

There are other reasons to think fixed terms would increase the political character of the justices' work. Fixed terms resemble the arrangements in the legislative and executive branches of the government and so may cause justices to think of themselves as political office-holders in a more traditional way than they now do. Moreover, some of the proposals for fixed terms are pitched expressly as efforts to make the Court more responsive to popular will. New justices will be familiar with the rationale of such a plan if it is enacted; they will understand that they are serving fixed, limited terms precisely in order to keep the Court accountable to current political values. The implication is that the justices are supposed to give effect to those values and to popular sentiment when they make their decisions—but this is just how we do not want them thinking about their jobs. . . . In this sense switching to fixed terms is worse than would have been their adoption in the first instance.

Other Dynamic Effects: Limited Terms and Humility

Professors McGinnis and Prakash, along with Judge Silberman, want limited terms for the sake of other dynamic effects they hope they will produce. Their theory is that once judges become justices they gradually stop thinking of their job as being to decide cases; they style themselves more as statesmen and soon cannot resist declaring their policy preferences as constitutional law. The first point to grasp in reply is that most of the hubris in Supreme Court opinions probably is attributable mostly to sources other than life tenure. It may be true ... that leaving justices on the Court for a long time increases their incentive to make rulings that enlarge the Court's power because they know they will be around to enjoy it. Yet if this were quite how it worked one might expect young justices to be the most aggressive and older ones to become more deferential as they have less prospect of using any powers they accumulate for themselves. No such pattern appears to exist. A more plausible conjecture ... is that as some justices spend years at the Court they start to enjoy a sense that the world revolves around their decisions and then make rulings that perpetuate the feeling. A more generous reading of the emboldening phenomenon, if it exists, is that only after handling several years' worth of cases does a justice develop a strong sense of an area and feel comfortable suggesting something different; it takes a long time for justices to understand their role in the country's system of liberty. At any rate, an empirical case has yet to be made for the claim that the justices lose their humility as years go by.

Meanwhile there are reasons more conventional than life tenure why the Court's work differs from that produced by other courts. First, circuit judges write humbler opinions because they are bound by the Supreme Court's case law in a way that the justices are not. Second, the Supreme Court's docket does not resemble the docket of a court of appeals, which in most situations must decide every case brought to it. Many appellate cases are easy in the sense that judges with different ideologies quickly agree on how they should be resolved. The Supreme Court hears about one percent of the cases in which review is sought, and they tend to involve questions to which the legal materials furnish no conclusive answer (that is why they are taken for review; they provoked disagreement below). So it should not be surprising that Supreme Court opinions are less likely than ordinary appellate opinions to confine themselves humbly to the legal materials involved; and none of this would change if the justices served shorter terms.

The Question of Age Limits

... Life tenure creates a risk that justices will stay on the job after their powers of judgment have deserted them. Professor Garrow's fine study of decrepitude found eleven such cases during the twentieth century and five since 1970; he makes convincing claims that some justices have stayed on the Court despite slipping below any reasonable threshold of competence one might propose for them. Garrow makes a good prima facie case for age limits, but there are some arguments against them as well. The first is that the problem of decrepitude is less serious than it sounds. Garrow believes that justices have become mentally decrepit eleven times since 1900, and in no case did the problem last more than a year or two. Thus of the nine hundred man-years of service provided by Supreme Court justices since the start of the twentieth century, perhaps ten or twenty of those years—between one and two percent of them—were tainted by serious mental deterioration.

When decrepitude did occur it was mitigated in two ways. Its impact was diluted by the presence of the eight other justices; while a decrepit justice may serve as a swing vote, he generally cannot do anything significant unless four of his colleagues go along with him. Second, the onset of mental infirmity causes the justice's responsibilities to devolve to his law clerks, who generally can keep a chambers running without a drop-off in quality remotely commensurate with the justice's drop-off in functionality. This may sound appalling, and of course there are good reasons not to want it to occur. But as a practical matter the devolution can help control—it undoubtedly *has* helped control—the consequences of decrepitude until the justice leaves the Court. Thurgood Marshall may have stayed on the Court for a period of time when he was not fully engaged in the work of his chambers. Yet it is difficult to detect a difference between the opinions bearing his name from this period and the ones that issued from his chambers ten or twenty years earlier. The implications of this seamlessness may be troubling in their own right, but that is a question for another day. The point for now is that we should pause before trading away the advantages of life tenure to address a problem that sounds bad but seems to have been, as a practical matter, relatively minor.

Another difficulty in departing from life tenure involves the question of out-placement. Most members of the Supreme Court are content to make the job of justice the last one they hold—so long as they can hold it for as long as they like. But any regime other than life tenure will push some justices out of office while they still are lucid and thus create a risk that they will use their time at the Court to angle for attractive situations afterwards. It need not be a question of bad faith; the greater hazard is a subtle bias reminding its holder that letting down one's friends now can have disappointing professional consequences later. The problem is especially important for proposals to give the justices fixed terms (as opposed to an age limit), since the result often may be to produce ex-justices still in the prime of their careers.

Some critics of life tenure believe the out-placement problem can be solved by making service on the Supreme Court a temporary form of work followed by life service on a court of appeals. But the critics err in taking for granted that a justice would accept such a designation. Life tenure is an offer, not a sentence, and perhaps not all justices would want to become circuit judges afterwards. . . . Those who did become appellate judges would find that they were served a duller diet of cases than they were accustomed to seeing, that they were more constrained in what they could say about them, and that the world was less interested in their pronouncements. Some might be comfortable with this; others might seek more intriguing opportunities elsewhere. Apart from the remunerative lure of affiliation with firms, there would be the chance to pursue interesting positions in public service—cabinet posts, ambassadorships, and so on, the prospects for which would depend on the justice's ability to stay well-liked by the party in power. (The advocates of these proposals also overlook another nagging implication of them: a justice would be limited to eighteen years partly out of fear of mental decrepitude, but then would be assigned to a court of appeals—as if mental decrepitude there were not a concern.)

The average justice may be affected by none of these possibilities, succumbing neither to dementia nor to the temptations of career planning regardless of whether any new proposals were enacted. Both risks would exist at the margin, like most of the others discussed in this essay. Whatever the severity of the risks, however, there are stronger objections to limited terms than to age limits. A justice at the end of an eighteen-year term may still be in his sixties and thus have significant professional prospects—better prospects, at any rate, than would tempt a justice who knows he will be forced out at seventy-five. At the same time, another justice appointed later in life to an eighteen-year term may well serve past age seventy-five, making limited terms also less reliable than age limits as measures to reduce the risk of decrepitude.

Strategic retirement: A most bothersome feature of life tenure is that the justices—or at least those who retire before death, which includes most of them—decide for themselves when to leave the Court and thus determine who will choose their replacements. Everyone suspects that some justices have taken advantage of this by trying to retire when they can be replaced by a president of their preferred party. Most of the suspicions are founded in conjecture, but in some cases the worries seem supported by fairly reliable reporting, and Chief Justice Rehnquist said publicly that justices have a "slight preference" for leaving under a president of their own party. Here as in the case of mental decrepitude, however, it is not clear that the problem of strategic retirement is very serious in fact. There is convincing statistical evidence that it occurs, but how often is hard to say. The plausible window of retirement for a justice tends to be short enough to make such decisions hard to carry out. Some have supposed that William Douglas, Thurgood Marshall and William Brennan tried to hold out in hopes of being replaced by a Democrat; if so, they failed. Meanwhile other justices seem to enjoy their positions enough to make strategic retirement a low priority. They leave no sooner than they must. The net result during the twentieth century was that a seat on the Court rarely stayed in the hands of the same party more than twice in a row.

It seems likely in any event that most problems of strategic retirement can be met with age limits without need for fixed terms. Notice that there are two kinds of strategic retirement: justices who hang on longer than they otherwise would while waiting for a friendly president to take office, and justices who step down earlier than they otherwise would to make sure the current president names their replacements. But against the latter possibility there is a natural check. Justices do not want to leave their jobs too early; ... Thus the problem of strategic retirement more often appears to take the other form: justices waiting rather than rushing to retire. In the case of the justice who waits there is not much check on temptation; the costs to him are not very high if he decides to hang on in hopes that a like-minded president will arrive to rescue his seat. If an elderly justice goes this route he can delegate most of his work to his law clerks while continuing to enjoy the pleasures of his rank. This analysis suggests that an age limit of seventy-five probably would cure most justices of the temptation to retire strategically. It would force them out while the benefits they derive from their jobs are great enough to discourage them from leaving voluntarily any sooner.

An age limit would relieve the problem of strategic retirement in another way as well. There currently is no default assumption about when justices should leave the Court; they are expected to retire when they feel like retiring, which could be at sixty-five, seventy-five, or eighty-five. But of course the justices often may be unsure whether they quite feel like leaving. With the decision about when to leave unguided by any external criteria, it no doubt is hard for them *not* to think about who their replacement will be when considering whether to stay or go. Resistance would be easier if there were an objective benchmark suggesting the right time to leave. An age limit of seventy-five or eighty would provide such a marker—a focal point. The natural thing would be for justices to serve until seventy-five if they can; for a justice in good health to voluntarily step aside at seventy-three under a friendly president would look bad, and the fear of tainting one's legacy by that hint of corruption would discourage strategic behavior. The legal academy can help enforce the norm by heaping opprobrium on whoever defies it.

CONSTITUTIONAL VS. STATUTORY AVENUES OF REFORM

The idea that justices generally serve on the Court until they die, choose to retire, or are impeached has always been understood as a constitutional rule. Professors Carrington and Cramton want to change that. They hope to replace life tenure with fixed terms *by statute*; and one consequence of doing this would be to establish that Congress has a general ability to tinker with the lengths of the justices' terms so long as the justices continue to serve for life in some capacity on the federal courts. Calabresi and Lindgren, in their earlier analysis, have concluded on formalist grounds that this would be unconstitutional. I agree with them, but want to add a few more pragmatic notes about why.

Many of the consequences of life tenure are invisible; they are things we *have not* seen. Here is an example: even in moments of the Court's greatest unpopularity, nobody has called for Congress to jigger the justices' terms; nobody has called for this because everyone has thought that it obviously would be unconstitutional. A court-packing plan was discussed during the Roosevelt administration, but not a plan for reducing the justices' terms to, say, a few years apiece. . . . Nor have we had attempts by Congress to isolate individual justices and say that *this* one's service at the Court shall end, say, right now, with immediate reassignment to some other federal court.

It seems to me that all the moves just described become constitutional once one admits the logic of the Carrington–Cramton proposal. Life tenure is the only safeguard in Article III (besides the provision about pay) to prevent the kinds of retaliation I have described; if its meaning is diluted, there is no other provision to fall back on to avoid abuses. It is true that the scenarios I have sketched raise far deeper policy concerns than the eighteen-year terms now being proposed, but I do not see how one can map those different policy concerns onto any hook in the Constitution. The language to be interpreted here is quite brief: it is a reference to "good Behaviour." Once that term is defined as Carrington and Cramton suggest, then any subdistinctions, such as the idea that one can not single out individual justices, or can not make the terms as short as one or two years, have to be invented out of nowhere.

The saving distinction most often mentioned in reply to this argument is that perhaps changes to the meaning of life tenure are constitutional so long as they are prospective—so long, in other words, as they always apply only to justices still to come, and never to justices already sitting on the Court. I do not find the distinction . . . reassuring . . . , since it would imply that Congress could limit future justices' terms to very brief rotations on the Supreme Court (followed by a return to a lower federal court). But in any event there is a deeper problem with the distinction between prospective and retrospective efforts to redefine life tenure: it is, again, that the distinction is made up for the sake of convenience. There is no such distinction in Article III. It is offered by the proponents of fixed terms simply because it sounds sensible to them and they hope it will save their proposal from devastating objections. And yet it does not even do that; for as John Harrison suggests in his contribution to [Cramton & Carrington, eds., *Reforming the Court, supra* at 361.], even a limitation to prospective changes would allow abuses. A bad-humored Congress could define life tenure as meaning "tenure on the Supreme Court for life," then confirm its favorite nominees, and then rewrite the rule on a prospective basis so that future justices . . . serve shorter terms. Is all this *likely* to occur? Of course not; but rules about the separation of powers generally are not written, and should not be written, for times of ordinary temper. When it is time to decide whether those boundaries have been breached, public passions tend to be running high and the dangers of self-serving interpretation are high as well. We should want everything as clear, and as capable of objective determination, as it can be made.

Finally, one might suggest that tinkering with the lengths of the justices' terms is just one of many ways that Congress can tamper with the Supreme Court within the bounds of Article III. Congress can change the number of justices; it presumably could move the Court to some less attractive location; shortening the justices' terms is just another such mechanism, no more worrisome than the others. I have some sympathy with this argument, but would note the strong custom disfavoring the use of any of these tools. Assigning the justices eighteen-year terms by statute would be like moving the Supreme Court to New York City: it would be a relatively small change, but by setting a precedent it would open up the possibility of further changes of the same sort in the future—such as moving the Court to Buffalo or giving the justices much shorter terms. I consider it a good thing that Congress does not generally feel comfortable passing legislation to bring the Court more into line; I would not welcome inroads against that custom.

CONCLUSION

Most claims about the consequences of life tenure and fixed terms are speculative. Terms of eighteen years would cause more frequent turnover than we now see; this may or may not have perceptible effects on the Court's output. Fixed terms might decrease the intensity of the politics that characterize the confirmation process, or might make matters worse. They would even out the chances for presidents to make nominations, a good thing, but they might cause justices to feel more responsibility to the parties who chose them. They would reduce the risks of strategic retirement and mental decrepitude, but then so would age limits. And at the same time it is not clear that either problem is great as a practical matter. These all are empirical questions, and the discussion here has shown that there are two plausible sides to most of them. The resulting uncertainties make it hard to conclude that any of these approaches is likely to produce noticeably better results than the others. Talk of the urgency of fixed terms, or the urgency of avoiding them, probably is misplaced. . . .

Dramatic measures are worthwhile to address problems that are clear and serious. The benefits of an age limit are fairly clear and there are few costs on the other side. It is true that age limits would make it easy to predict the day of departure for most justices many years in advance, thus facilitating the co-ordination of political pressures on the process. And an age limit probably would increase the temptation to appoint young justices. But these costs maybe worth incurring to discourage the risks of strategic retirement and mental decrepitude. Age limits also preserve some flexibility in fashioning the expected lengths of the justices' terms while avoiding some of the drawbacks of fixed terms—the explicit assignment of appointments to presidents and other features that might increase the justices' sense that their duties are political. The case for age limits deserves serious consideration.

In closing, note that there are some arguments for life tenure I have not considered here—viz., that justices who serve for long periods of years come to be more protective of liberties over time, perhaps because they see at length how vulnerable the citizenry is to the legislative and executive branches. I regard those arguments as strong, but whether they appeal to the reader naturally will depend on whether the reader shares this preference for a protective Supreme Court—an ideological position. As this essay has shown, however, there are powerful arguments for retaining life tenure even if that position is not shared.

––––––––––

Ward Farnsworth,[63] *The Ideological Stakes of Eliminating Life Tenure,* **29 Harv. J.L. & Pub. Pol'y 879 (2006)**

Professors Calabresi and Lindgren have written the strongest attack yet on life tenure for Supreme Court Justices.... I wish to talk about some ideological implications and consequences of the authors' proposals that they do not emphasize. I also will offer a few words in reply to a point on which they take issue with my prior article [excerpted above].

I. IDEOLOGICAL CONSEQUENCES

First, the authors say that theirs is a "nonpartisan" proposal. That term, and its fit to their plan, calls for some reflection. Let us start by distinguishing between two sorts of stakes in efforts to get rid of life tenure: the ideological and the non-ideological. The non-ideological stakes are things that people with different political priors nevertheless can agree about. Everyone can agree that mental decrepitude on the Court is a bad thing; nobody is for it. The same goes, I think, for the uneven distribution of appointments to Presidents, or for possibilities of strategic retirement. Nobody praises these consequences of life tenure or would be sorry to see them go. They are costs of our current regime, and the question is simply whether one would rather bear them than switch to an alternative rule with other trade-offs.

The ideological arguments for abolishing life tenure are different; they involve the Court's role in public life. When someone says that the Court has become too unaccountable, or that life tenure makes the Justices arrogant, ... these are ideological claims: their appeal will depend on the listener's satisfaction with the Court's current performance and predictions about how the substance of its output would change under a new rule to govern turnover. These disputes generally have a zero-sum character. If some given reform makes one audience happy because it causes the Court to decide cases differently—especially those cases that cause the frequent concerns about the Court's "activism"—it is likely to make another audience comparably unhappy. The different reactions of the audiences are likely to track their political commitments.

The advocates of fixed terms differ in the emphasis they give to these two sorts of stakes. Professor Oliver makes his case only on non-ideological grounds. Others, such as Professor Prakash, seem mostly focused on the ideological side: he wants a more "populist" Supreme Court, and thinks that abolishing life tenure will help get us there. Still other commentators draw on both sorts of arguments; that is Calabresi and Lindgren's approach. They claim, for example, that fixed terms will

63. Professor of Law and Nancy Barton Scholar, Boston University.

help relieve the problem of mental decrepitude (a non-ideological point) and that they also will help promote originalism (an ideological or "partisan" point). I suppose one could try to avoid this conclusion by saying there is nothing partisan about originalism—that it's merely a preference for the rule of law—but that is the sort of argument which appeals only to those already converted to the cause.

I think the "nonpartisan" label is best reserved for proposals that will create no losers predictably identifiable by their politics. It strikes me as quite strained to declare a proposal "nonpartisan" just because it is supported by some academics whose politics vary. Life tenure is a complicated issue involving many different trade-offs, and people take positions on it for all sorts of reasons. Some academics might support its abolition despite the partisan consequences they think the proposal would have, concluding that fixed terms have other offsetting advantages. Nor does "nonpartisan" seem very interesting if it is merely a claim by the authors that their own interest in the proposal arises from its non-zero-sum features—the ones that everyone is likely to consider good. For why would anyone care what the authors' own motives are? Consequences are what count; whatever Calabresi and Lindgren's motives might be, they believe their proposal will have some consequences that would be certain to provoke very different reactions among different sorts of partisans.

.   .   .

What *are* the ideological effects of life tenure? Nobody knows for sure, and the empirical void is curious. When I have had the pleasure of debating Professor Calabresi on these issues in live settings, he has been more emphatic than he allows in his article that of course there is a trend of Justices becoming more liberal as they serve longer (and, perhaps, as they grow older). He hopes and expects fixed terms to help curb this tendency. Many other conservative theorists likewise feel sure that life tenure is at least partly to blame for decisions they dislike. Yet if it really were so clear that Justices drift to the left as time goes by, one would expect to see a rigorous empirical case to that effect. No such case has been made. The most careful study of the effect of aging on Supreme Court Justices found no general trend toward liberalism. The case instead depends on the casual observations of the Court's critics. They see Harry Blackmun and John Paul Stevens, both Republican appointees who seemed to move to the left during their careers, and they become convinced that there is a general and insidious dynamic at work. They may imagine that one reason for the dearth of empirical evidence on the dynamic is that it is too recent: it results from the modern conflation of elite liberal culture, pressure from the media, and a Court that has assumed a larger role in the country's life over the past forty years than it ever had before.

Perhaps they are right. In any event, though, the weakness of the empirical case for ideological drift raises a nice question about the role of impressionistic judgments in debates of this kind. The impressions of the critics might be an illusion—a story that the Court's critics repeat to each other and of which they become ever more convinced—when in reality Justices Blackmun and Stevens might be random and perhaps exaggerated cases. But it also is possible that there is wisdom embedded in their unrigorous impressions, especially given the absence of anyone making the contrary claim (there may be those who deny that Justices drift to the left, but I know of nobody who argues that they systematically drift to the right). An interesting literature considers the accuracy of judgments reached by pooling the unscientific estimates of onlookers to a situation and finds that the average guesses in such circumstances—say, the average estimate of the number of jelly beans in a jar—sometimes are remarkably accurate. Perhaps the accumulated impressions of the Court watchers, though of a different character than the impressions in the jelly bean case, are likewise accurate. Maybe we do owe partly to life tenure decisions like *Roe v. Wade, Planned Parenthood v. Casey, Romer v. Evans*, and *Lawrence v. Texas*—or for that matter *Brown v. Board of Education*. In the end it all is a question of odds. The conservative opponents of life tenure are prepared to gamble that its elimination would do no harm and might well do their interests a good turn. Those who prefer a liberal Court would be prudent to regard the movement for fixed terms with corresponding alarm. (I do not quite put myself in that category, but I do like a liberty-loving Supreme Court, so the alarm that I feel at the prospect of fixed terms is modest.) There certainly is no guarantee that the result would be a permanently more conservative Court, but when playing for stakes of this sort one need not wait for a guarantee before deciding to take precautions. The enthusiasm of one's opponents ought to be enough.

II.   The Effect of Life Tenure on the Selection of Justices

Professors Calabresi and Lindgren try to gain support for their proposal by pointing out the vicious recent struggles over appointments to the courts of appeals and, sometimes, the Supreme Court. Calabresi and Lindgren say that:

> So much is at stake in appointing a new Justice that the President and the Senate (especially when controlled by the party opposite the President) inevitably get drawn into a political fight that hurts the Court both directly and indirectly. The Court is affected directly, since it is deprived of one of its nine members, and indirectly, since rancorous confirmation battles lower the prestige of the Court.

The most natural reaction to this claim is a double-take; it just doesn't seem true. The last four nominations of Supreme Court Justices were not particularly rancorous. Perhaps the authors would reply that in all those cases the Senate was controlled by the President's party. But the Souter confirmation was not rancorous; nor, particularly, was the O'Connor confirmation or even the Scalia confirmation. So far as appears, the authors are fixated on the cases of Bork and Thomas. Those nominations do suggest that ideologically robust nominees will tend to produce ugly confirmation fights; they certainly do not suggest that life tenure makes ugliness inevitable.

The authors fortify their claim in an odd manner. They point out that confirmations of appellate judges are more acrimonious than confirmations of trial judges, and that Supreme Court confirmations are the hardest of all. They say this shows that acrimony in the confirmation process rises with the stakes; so reducing the stakes, by replacing life tenure for Supreme Court Justices with fixed terms, naturally will reduce the acrimony. The argument works fine until the last step, which doesn't follow at all. There is an obvious reason why acrimony increases as we move from nominations to trial courts to appellate courts to the Supreme Court. It is that each of those courts is far more powerful than the last; that is why the stakes rise from one case to the next, and this wouldn't be changed by the authors' proposal. I believe they are mistaken to think life tenure creates much higher stakes than terms of "only" eighteen years would; the stakes in either case are high enough to provoke plenty of passion. As I mentioned in my earlier paper, Robert Bork was sixty years old at the time of his nomination. Does anyone really think that the prospect of "only" eighteen years of Justice Bork would have provoked different reactions to his nomination?

Possibly it is true that, as Calabresi and Lindgren claim, eliminating life tenure would make Supreme Court nominations seem a bit less important and therefore reduce the heat brought to bear on them. Let me then note, however, a likely side effect: elimination of life tenure will produce more ideologically extreme Justices. If life tenure helps make a Supreme Court nomination a high-stakes affair, this has the nice consequence—appealing to me, anyway—of forcing Presidents to play toward the middle when they pick Justices. Relaxing the stakes at the margin will reduce that moderating effect at the margin. It will make it easier for the next Bork to be confirmed; that really is the practical point of this part of their argument, and one of its most important consequences if they are right.

In reply it might be said that abolishing life tenure would reduce the stakes on both sides—the stakes for the President as well as for the Senate—and therefore cause no net change in the politics of nominees. The Senate wouldn't resist as much, since the nominees would be serving for "only" eighteen years; but for the same reason, the President wouldn't push his nominees as hard, either. I think this vision of the likely outcome almost certainly is wrong. The reason has to do with asymmetries between the President's role and the Senate's role in the confirmation process. The President is one person. He is negotiating with a body consisting of a hundred people, and needs the votes of fifty of them. Imagine, to oversimplify a bit, that the members of the Senate are arrayed, from one to one hundred, in order of their preferences for Supreme Court Justices. Each senator has preferences that can be weighted by their intensity and each has a breaking point: a nominee objectionable enough to cause the senator to stand in opposition. The President's goal, whether he is making a nomination for life or for eighteen years, is to pick the nominee he likes best who also can secure fifty votes in the Senate. If abolishing life tenure causes some senators to care a little less who ends up on the Supreme Court, that makes the President's task a bit easier; it won't be quite as hard to find fifty votes. Again, this model is simplified at various junctures, but in its essentials I believe it is accurate. To put the point in more straightforward terms, fixed terms will give the proponents of an extreme nominee another tool they can use to try to beat any opponents into submission: the appointment isn't for *life*, after all, and there are certain to be other chances to make more nominations after the next election.

III.   The Demand for Originalism

In my earlier article I discussed the possibility that fixed terms would give the public more frequent chances to replace wayward Justices with others who will adhere to the original understanding of the Constitution. I found the claim unpersuasive because I don't think the voting public has much interest in originalism or any other theory of interpretation; they do care about the results the Court reaches, but interpretive theories are of interest only as means to those ends. Professors Calabresi and Lindgren dispute this claim; they say the public does have an appetite for originalists. . . .

The support the authors offer for this claim comes in two forms. First is the observation that "the public has consistently voted since 1968 for presidential candidates who have promised to appoint Supreme Court Justices who would interpret the law rather than making it up." I offer these points by way of refutation:

1.   A presidential candidate's likely choice of Supreme Court appointments tends to be low on the list of things that most voters use as a basis for decision, ranking far behind considerations of economic and foreign policy. . . .

2.   Saying that the public has shown it prefers "Justices who would interpret the law rather than making it up" seems to me a nearly comical straw man. I struggle to recall a presidential candidate saying he wanted Justices who would make up the law, or any Justices or nominees describing that as their activity. The more usual debate is between those who want the Constitution interpreted according to the original understanding of its text and those who want enforcement of what it might seem to mean to a modern reader. Well, there are much better ways than that to state the question, but this version has the advantage of being subject to an opinion poll. When the question was put that way, a 1987 poll showed a preference for "modern interpretation" over the "founding fathers' interpretation" by a margin of fifty-five to forty-two percent. Other polls produce different results; the outcomes seem to be highly sensitive to the way the questions are phrased.

3.   Meanwhile, however, public opinion polls consistently show that substantial majorities believe *Roe v. Wade* was rightly decided and that it should not be overruled. This suggests that a majority of voters either

don't want originalism or don't understand its implications. What most members of the public more probably want, as Judge Posner has suggested, is originalism and their preferred results. But they often can't have both, and I find it implausible to think that most people, if pressed to make a sacrifice, are more committed to ideas about legal theory (which they rarely understand; see the data in the previous paragraph) than to the results they like. Some evidence of a preference for results is supplied by the fate of Robert Bork, the last Supreme Court nominee to step forward as an open and vigorous defender of originalism. The authors suggest that the public was "induced" to oppose Bork. They can't bring themselves to credit the possibility that his nomination failed because large numbers of the public either didn't like his theory of interpretation or didn't like the results it would produce (and considered the results more important than the theory)....

The authors also point out that the public generally supported confirmation of Justices Thomas, Roberts, and Alito; they say this, too, shows that the public wants originalists on the Court. Again the argument is weak:

1. Justice Thomas did not present himself as an originalist. This is easy to forget now because of his work as a Justice, but in his confirmation hearings he was careful not to align himself with any particular interpretive approach. Public accounts, which are what matter for purposes of this inquiry, treated his position as ambiguous. It often was suggested that he had been advised to follow this path because more specificity might have doomed his chances for confirmation.

2. Chief Justice Roberts did not present himself as an originalist. He said at his hearings, "I do not have an overarching judicial philosophy that I bring to every case.... I tend to look at the cases from the bottom up rather than the top down." One astute observer of his confirmation hearings thus concluded that Roberts "is not in the mold of Scalia and Thomas.... They have more of a theory of how to decide cases, and they look to text and original meaning. Roberts will look at text and original meaning, but he will also look to precedent and the consequences of his decisions." The observer was Professor Calabresi.

3. Justice Alito came closer to presenting himself as an originalist, though it still wasn't considered clear. But against this data point there are others the authors do not mention. Ruth Bader Ginsburg's nomination met with similar public support, as did Stephen Breyer's. There is no evidence to support the authors' apparent view that originalist or even just conservative nominees are received more enthusiastically by the public than nominees of other sorts.

... The notion that more frequent nominating chances will be used to impose theoretical discipline on the Court seems to me a fantasy.

Questions and Comments

1. Calabresi and Lindgren argue that the appointment process is the only meaningful control the public, through their representatives, have over the Court's substantive output. Do you agree? Professor Farnsworth mentions other possibilities, such as altering the number of Justices or the location where the Court sits. Are there others? As in Congress' authority to enact new substantive legislation; to restrict the jurisdiction of the federal courts; to control the budgets of the federal courts (short of decreasing compensation for Article III judges)? What about constitutional amendment, or the informal influences of public opinion, or other actions by the political branches?

2. Other legal scholars have also found some increase in the tenure of Supreme Court Justices using slightly different time periods for comparison than Calabresi and Lindgren. See, e.g., Judith Resnik & Lane Dilg, *Responding to a Democratic Deficit: Limiting the Powers and the Term of the Chief Justice of the United States*, 154 U. Pa. L. Rev. 1575, 1595 (2006) (finding a twenty-year average tenure for Supreme Court Justices whose tenure terminated between 1833 and 1853 and a twenty-four-year average tenure for Justices whose service terminated between 1983 and 2003). However, at least one political scientist who has studied the Court concluded, looking at the same data, that the 1994–2004 period may have been an anomaly. See Kevin T. McGuire, *Are the Justices Serving Too Long? An Assessment of Tenure on the U.S. Supreme Court*, 89 Judicature 8, 9–12 (2005) (arguing that by several measures Justices "are spending no more time on the Court than their brethren who have served over the past 150 years," and concluding that the announced retirement of Justice O'Connor, together with one more vacancy (which soon thereafter arose with Chief Justice Rehnquist's death) "would return the Court to its historical norm" median years of service). See also David Stras & Ryan Scott, *An Empirical Analysis of Life Tenure: A Response to Professors Calabresi & Lindgren*, 30 Harv. J. L. & Pub. Pol'y 1, 41 (2007) (challenging Calabresi & Lindgren's claim that there has been a "dramatic and unprecedented increase in average tenure on the Supreme Court since 1971"). Contending that the Calabresi & Lindgren analysis had two flaws—a "period-selection" problem and a "date-of-observation" problem—Stras and Scott argue that the data actually show a "slow and steady growth in length of tenure over time." *Id.* at 41. At present (June 2007), the average years of service of those sitting on the Court is 15 years.

3. Calabresi and Lindgren disagree with Farnsworth about whether changes in the Justices' tenure would affect their interpretive approaches. They disagree in part over what the public values in the selection of Justices. On this point, see also Stephen Burbank, *Alternative Career Resolution II: Changing the Tenure of Supreme Court Justices*, 154 U. Pa. L. Rev. 1511, 1514, 1529 (2006) (finding "little basis to believe that the public at large has understandings of constitutional meaning, as opposed to results ..., let alone understandings of competing interpretive approaches" and reporting on studies that show such seemingly contradictory public views about interpretation as support for reliance (1) on the specific intent of the drafters of the Constitution, and (2) on "what the majority of the public favors," and

(3) on "the judges' views of what is good for the public" (internal quotations omitted)).

4. Professors Calabresi and Lindgren refer to the practices of other western democracies with high courts engaged in constitutional review. How relevant is this foreign practice to choices to be made in the United States? Consider this comment:

> Although many of the European courts rely on single nonrenewable terms, they do so for courts which, in the European tradition, are specialized constitutional courts that do not hear the range of cases the U.S. Court does. The supreme courts of Canada and Australia may be more comparable to the U.S. Court than the specialized constitutional courts of Europe; Canada and Australia, in the common law tradition, have "generalist" supreme courts with jurisdiction over constitutional and statutory matters, and their judges now serve until mandatory retirement ages.

Vicki C. Jackson, *Packages of Judicial Independence: The Selection and Tenure of Article III Judges*, 95 Geo. L.J. 965, 1005 (2007). The original Canadian constitutional instrument of 1867 was amended in 1961 to include a mandatory retirement age of 75 in addition to the "good behaviour" provisions.[64] Australia amended its 1901 Constitution in 1977 to provide for a mandatory retirement age of seventy for its High Court and other federal judges.[65] Australian and Canadian judges are removable only by the government's "address" to the legislature, [66] and in Australia only on a finding of "proved misbehaviour or incapacity."[67] In Britain, which has not fully embraced binding judicial review of the constitutionality of legislation, higher court judges generally hold office "during good behaviour" up to a mandatory retirement age of 70. *See* Judicial Pensions and Retirement Act 1993, c. 8, § 26 (Eng.) It thus appears that those high courts most comparable to the U.S. in jurisdictional structure and legal background have responded to changing conditions in the modern world by adopting retirement ages to limit the duration of a life tenure system, rather than single unrenewable terms.

5. Some critics believe that the reason Supreme Court Justices tend not to retire when many other professionals their age are retiring is that the job is too easy and "cushy." Stuart Taylor, Jr. & Benjamin Wittes, *Of Clerks and Perks: Why Supreme Court Justices Have More Free Time than Ever— and Why It Should Be Taken Away*, The Atlantic Monthly, July/August 2006, at 50. To deal with this "problem," critics have proposed a variety of "reforms." One proposal would, for example, reintroduce circuit riding for a four week session in July. Steven Calabresi & David Presser, *Reintroducing Circuit Riding: A Timely Proposal*, 90 Minn. L. Rev. 1386 (2006). The authors believe that circuit riding would "get the Justices in touch with popular opinion outside the Beltway," and help them to understand the "real-world impact" of some of their opinions. *Id.* at 1389. Others have

---

64. *See* Constitution Act, 1867, § 99 (Can.).

65. Constitution Alteration (Retirement of Judges) Act 1977 (No. 83 of 1977) (NAA: A1559/1, 83/1977).

66. *See* Constitution Act, 1867, § 99(1) (Can.) (judges to hold office "during good behaviour" and are "removable by the Governor General on Address")

67. *See* Const. of Austl., art. 72(ii).

suggested reducing the number of law clerks. See, e.g., Taylor & Wittes, *supra*, at 50 (suggesting that, in light of the reduced caseload, the Court should go back to one clerk per Justice, thereby "forc[ing] the justices to focus more on legal analysis and . . . less on their own policy agendas" and arguing that "best of all, it would effectively shorten their tenure by forcing them to do their own work, making their jobs harder and inducing them to retire before power corrupts absolutely or decrepitude sets in"). Still others have questioned the unlimited discretion the Justices have in selecting their docket, see Edward A. Hartnett, *Questioning Certiorari: Some Reflections Seventy–Five Years After the Judges' Bill*, 100 Colum. L. Rev. 1643, 1650 (2000), or have encouraged the Court to decide more merits cases. See Kenneth Starr, *The Supreme Court and Its Shrinking Docket: The Ghost of William Howard Taft*, 90 Minn. L. Rev. 1363 (2006).

6. Another proposal designed to encourage earlier retirements, alluded to by Calabresi and Lindgren, is to increase the financial incentives. Professor McGuire, for example, proposed a statutory financial incentive for Justices to retire by setting higher pensions for those who retire before a specific age. Kevin T. McGuire, *Are the Justices Serving Too Long? An Assessment of Tenure on the U.S. Supreme Court,* 89 Judicature 8, 15 (2005) (suggesting a statute providing for pensions of 200% of salary if Justices retire prior to a certain set age or term of years; Justices retiring after those points would receive only 100% of their salary.). See also David Stras, *The Incentives Approach to Judicial Retirement*, 90 Minn. L. Rev 1417 (2006) (arguing that simple initiatives, such as increasing retirement pensions and increasing the workload of active Justices, can change the incentive structure facing Justices contemplating retirement). The nature and availability of pensions has, historically, made a significant difference in the willingness of Justices to retire from rather than die in office. See generally David Stras & Ryan Scott, *Retaining Life Tenure: The Case for a "Golden Parachute,"* 83 Wash. U. L. Q. 1397 (2005); Artemus Ward, *Deciding to Leave: The Politics of Retirement from the United States Supreme Court* 16–19, 69–210 (2003).

7. Although Calabresi and Lindgren argue against adopting a mandatory retirement age, many other scholars over the years have proposed such a change. See, e.g., Henry Paul Monaghan, *The Confirmation Process: Law or Politics?*, 101 Harv. L. Rev. 1202, 1211 (1988), reprinted above at Chapter Two, Section C; David Garrow, *Mental Decrepitude on the U.S. Supreme Court: The Historical Case for a 28th Amendment*, 67 U. Chi. L. Rev. 995, 1085 (2000). See also *id.* at 997 (noting that Charles Evan Hughes, in 1928, had advocated mandatory retirement at age 75); *id.* at 1055 (describing how Justice Byron White—disagreeing with the constitutionality of his colleagues' internal decision in 1975 not to assign opinions to Justice Douglas nor to make any decision that would "hinge on" Douglas' vote in light of his condition—stated his view that a constitutional amendment providing some specific mandatory retirement age would be desirable). Those who favor a mandatory retirement age are motivated at least in important part by a concern that, with aging, there is a greater likelihood of "mental decrepitude;" indeed, Garrow argues that at least eleven Justices who served in the twentieth century suffered some degree of mental decrepitude while still on the bench. Garrow, *supra*, at 1085. In three cases—those of Justices McKenna, Holmes and Douglas—Garrow describes how other members of the Court

discussed the failing Justice's situation and in at least two instances spoke with their failing colleague to urge retirement, which quickly followed.[68] Does the fact that these interventions occurred illustrate the need for change? Or does it suggest that the current structures provide sufficient informal means to redress mental decrepitude should it occur? Professors Calabresi and Lindgren explain in the excerpt above what they see as the comparative disadvantages of a mandatory retirement age. Are there any advantages of a mandatory retirement age over a fixed term of years? Consider, *inter alia*, the possibility that an appropriate retirement age avoids Justices having to be concerned about employment after a fixed term of years.

8. In responding to proposals for term limits for Supreme Court justices, Professor Farnsworth suggests that there is a difference between designing a system *ab initio* and reforming an existing one. Consider this elaboration of a similar concern, over the effects of the direction of the change, by Professor Vicki Jackson:

> Most other western democracies, including those whose high courts are regarded as independent and of high quality, provide for single nonrenewable terms, mandatory retirement ages, or both. These approaches thus appear to be compatible with judicial independence. The "during good Behaviour" provisions of Article III were enacted in the late eighteenth century, when average life spans were far shorter than today. Some reasons given at the time for providing life tenure, including the need to avoid judges' worrying about earning a living after their service, have been basically mooted by the provision for pensions for Article III judges. And studies indicate some lengthening of the average term in fact served by Justices of the Supreme Court, though magnitudes depend somewhat on the precise periods selected for comparison.

> Thus, if we were starting from scratch in designing an independent judiciary, there would be a range of alternatives to life tenure, some perhaps superior, to consider. But we in the United States have an ongoing working system; we are not starting from scratch; making changes could have unforeseen effects, including a sense of diminished independence born from the direction of the proposed change. It is thus important carefully to consider the problems such a significant change would address.

Vicki C. Jackson, *Packages of Judicial Independence: The Selection and Tenure of Article III Judges*, 95 Geo. L.J. 965, 1002 (2007). Professor Jackson further argues that the role of the Supreme Court, in a federal system with elected state court judges, must be considered:

> The federal Article III courts function as part of a much larger set of connected systems of adjudicators, including the state courts and non-Article III federal courts. Many other courts, federal and state, whose

---

68. Recall that Garrow's characterization of the magnitude of the problem of decrepitude has been challenged. See, e.g., Farnsworth, excerpted above (arguing that even accepting Garrow's characterizations, the problem has been small and, to the extent it existed, mitigated by the presence of other justices and law clerks); cf. David Atkinson, *Leaving the Bench* 169 (1999) ("[T]he danger of extended service on the part of a decrepit justice is today less than in the earlier periods of Court history."). For additional discussion, see Ward, *Deciding to Leave, supra.*

judges lack Article III protections, make initial decisions on these important questions—and most of these decisions end up not being reviewed in an Article III court. Yet they are made in the shadow of the supremacy of federal law and the possibility of Article III review.

The United States is unusual, not only in providing for life-tenure for its Article III judiciary ..., but perhaps even more so in the degree to which it relies on popular elections for the selection or retention of the state court judges, some of whom serve fairly short terms before they must stand for re-election. The strong institutional independence of Article III judges anchors the legal infrastructure that accommodates elected judges in the state courts with the rule of law. This anchoring role of the Article III judiciary provides added reason why proposals to jettison central features of the traditional structure of federal judicial independence should be evaluated with great caution. For the federal courts do not function alone, but as part of a broader federal system.

Id. at 1006–1008. In that federal system, the Supreme Court sits at the apex. Evaluate these and other proposals for reform that you have read about— would you favor any of them?

Concluding Note on Impeachment, Life Tenure and An Independent Judiciary

One of the reasons that U.S. Supreme Court Justices enjoy relatively long tenures in office is because of the understanding that federal judges can be removed from office only by impeachment for and conviction of "Treason, Bribery or other high Crimes and Misdemeanors." U.S. Const., art. II, § 4. The Supreme Court itself has said, "the Clause securing federal judges appointments 'during good Behaviour,' [is] the practical equivalent of life tenure." United States v. Hatter, 532 U.S. 557, 567 (2001); see U.S. Const. art. III, § 1. Although periodically the question is raised whether the "during good Behaviour" clause would permit the removal of federal judges through means other than impeachment, including, for example, by disciplinary trials held before other Article III judges,[69] the weight of scholarly opinion thus far has been that while judicial discipline short of removal is constitutionally permissible through the Judicial Branch, the only constitutional mechanism to remove a federal judge from office is through impeachment proceedings in Congress.[70]

---

69. For arguments that the "good behavior" clause contemplates removal by means other than impeachment, see, for example, Raoul Berger, *Impeachment of Judges and "Good Behavior" Tenure*, 79 Yale L.J. 1475 (1970); Burke Shartel, *Federal Judges—Appointment, Supervision, and Removal: Some Possibilities Under the Constitution: Part III*, 28 Mich. L. Rev. 870 (1930). For a recent revival and elaboration of this view, see Saikrishna Prakash & Steven D. Smith, *How to Remove a Federal Judge*, 116 Yale L.J. 72, 129–30 (2006).

70. See, e.g., Michael J. Gerhardt, *The Federal Impeachment Process* 83–91 (1996);

Robert Kramer & Jerome A. Barron, *The Constitutionality of Removal and Mandatory Retirement Procedures for the Federal Judiciary: The Meaning of "During Good Behaviour,"* 35 Geo. Wash. L. Rev. 455, 466–67 (1967); James E. Pfander, *Removing Federal Judges*, 74 U. Chi. L. Rev. 1227 (2007); Peter M. Shane, *Who May Discipline or Remove Federal Judges? A Constitutional Analysis*, 142 U. Pa. L. Rev. 209, 239 (1993); Martha A. Ziskind, *Judicial Tenure in the American Constitution: English and American Precedents*, 1969 Sup. Ct. Rev. 135, 138.

In his 1992 book, *Grand Inquests*, the late Chief Justice William H. Rehnquist argued that two failed impeachment proceedings—one against Supreme Court Justice Samuel Chase, the other against President Andrew Johnson—were central to building key institutions in the American constitutional system.[71] Chief Justice Rehnquist wrote that the idea of an independent judiciary was one of the most "original contributions to the art of government" made by the Constitutional Convention that met in Philadelphia. William H. Rehnquist, *Grand Inquests: The Historic Impeachments of Justice Samuel Chase and President Andrew Johnson* 275 (1992). He recounts in some detail the events leading up to the House of Representatives' adoption of articles of impeachment against Supreme Court Justice Samuel Chase, largely based on Chase's conduct of criminal trials of political opponents of the Federalists.[72] Chase was a fervent Federalist, and engaged in some plainly questionable behavior in these criminal cases. Yet in Rehnquist's view, the Senate, by refusing to vote to convict Chase, rejected the proposition that federal judges could be removed from office based on political disagreement with a judge's decisions or views. This understanding, which crystallized over time, was, for Rehnquist, central to the success of the idea of the independent judiciary: Even though in times of intense conflict and polarization it would be natural for those "engaged in the struggle to see it as an apocalyptic confrontation between good and evil, when customary restraints must be cast off," enough Senators put devotion to the Constitution ahead of narrow partisan interest, and helped secure judicial independence through their vote to acquit. *Id.* at 275–78. The Senate's acquittal of Samuel Chase had, said Rehnquist, "a profound effect on the American judiciary:"

> First, it assured the independence of federal judges from congressional oversight of the decisions they made in the cases that came before them. Second, by assuring that impeachment would not be used in the future as a method to remove members of the Supreme Court for their judicial opinions, it helped to safeguard the independence of that body.

Id. at 114.

Reflect on the extent to which the independence of the Supreme Court is the product not only of the constitutional structure, but of how the Court, and the political branches, have interpreted and exercised their powers over time. Consider, if you were designing an institution like the Court from scratch, how you might do it differently. Now consider, in light of the ongoing institution you have learned about and the various critiques you have read, what if any changes you would recommend at this time—as a lawyer, as a citizen, and (perhaps) as a future member of the Court.

---

71. This paragraph is adapted in part from Vicki C. Jackson, *Packages of Judicial Independence: The Selection and Tenure of Article III Judges*, 95 Geo L.J. 965, 1006 (2007).

72. This was during the period in which Supreme Court Justices spent part of their time riding circuit, trying cases.

APPENDIX A
Chief Justices of the United States*

Chief Justice	Appointing President	Dates
John Jay	George Washington	1789–95
John Rutledge	George Washington	1795–95
Oliver Ellsworth	George Washington	1796–1800
John Marshall	John Adams	1801–35
Roger Brooke Taney	Andrew Jackson	1836–64
Salmon P. Chase	Abraham Lincoln	1864–73
Morrison R. Waite	Ulysses S. Grant	1874–88
Melville W. Fuller	Grover Cleveland	1888–1910
Edward D. White	William Howard Taft	1910–21
William Howard Taft	Warren G. Harding	1921–30
Charles Evans Hughes	Herbert Hoover	1930–41
Harlan Fiske Stone	Franklin D. Roosevelt	1941–46
Fred M. Vinson	Harry S. Truman	1946–53
Earl Warren	Dwight D. Eisenhower	1953–69
Warren Earl Burger	Richard M. Nixon	1969–86
William H. Rehnquist	Ronald Reagan	1986–2005
John G. Roberts, Jr.	George W. Bush	2005–

* Data are from the U.S. Supreme Court website, http://www.supremecourtus.gov/about/members.pdf.

1122

Index

†